Lecture Notes in Computer Science 527

J. C. M. Baeten J. F. Groote (Eds.)

CONCUR '91

2nd International Conference on Concurrency Theory
Amsterdam, The Netherlands, August 26-29, 1991
Proceedings

Springer-Verlag
Berlin Heidelberg New York
London Paris Tokyo
Hong Kong Barcelona
Budapest

Series Editors

Gerhard Goos
GMD Forschungsstelle
Universität Karlsruhe
Vincenz-Priessnitz-Straße 1
W-7500 Karlsruhe, FRG

Juris Hartmanis
Department of Computer Science
Cornell University
Upson Hall
Ithaca, NY 14853, USA

Volume Editors

Jos C. M. Baeten
Department of Software Technology, CWI
Kruislaan 413, 1098 SJ Amsterdam, The Netherlands
and
Programming Research Group, University of Amsterdam
Kruislaan 403, 1098 SJ Amsterdam, The Netherlands

Jan Frisco Groote
Department of Software Technology, CWI
Kruislaan 413, 1098 SJ Amsterdam, The Netherlands

CR Subject Classification (1991): F.1.2, D.1.3, D.3.1, D.3.3, F.3.1

ISBN 3-540-54430-5 Springer-Verlag Berlin Heidelberg New York
ISBN 0-387-54430-5 Springer-Verlag New York Berlin Heidelberg

Printed in Germany

Typesetting: Camera ready by author
Printing and binding: Druckhaus Beltz, Hemsbach/Bergstr.
2145/3140-543210 - Printed on acid-free paper

Preface

CONCUR'91 is the second international conference on concurrency theory, organised in association with the NFI project Transfer. It is a sequel of the CONCUR'90 conference. Its basic aim is to communicate ongoing work in concurrency theory.

This year 71 papers were submitted, 17 more than last year. From these, 30 papers were selected for presentation at the conference. The selected papers appear in these proceedings, together with four papers of invited speakers. Furthermore, abstracts of the other invited lectures are included.

CONCUR'91 received support from CWI, the University of Amsterdam, and ERCIM, the European Research Consortium for Informatics and Mathematics.

The editors want to thank the members of the program committee and the subreferees for their careful selection of the submitted papers. Thanks also go to CWI for hosting the conference, and to the organising committee for all their efforts.

Amsterdam, July 1991

The Editors

Program Committee

J.C.M. Baeten (*general chair*)

Section Process Algebras
R.J. van Glabbeek
K.G. Larsen (*chair*)
W.P. Weijland

Section Logics and Model Checking
H. Barringer
J.-J.Ch. Meijer
C.P. Stirling (*chair*)

Section Applications and Specification Languages
M. Broy (*chair*)
J. Sifakis
F.W. Vaandrager

Section Models and Net Theory
E. Best (*chair*)
R. De Nicola
L. Pomello

Section Design and Real-Time
C.A.R. Hoare (*chair*)
W.P. de Roever
C.A. Vissers

Section Tools and Probabilities
E. Madelaine
F. Moller
S.A. Smolka (*chair*)

Section Programming Languages
J.W. de Bakker (*chair*)
G.L. Burn
L. Monteiro

Organising Committee

J.A. Bergstra (*chair*)
M. Drolschbach
J.F. Groote
S. Mauw
A. Ollongren
F. Snijders

List of Referees

J.-M. Andreoli
A. Azcorra
J.C.M. Baeten
J.E. Barnes
H. Barringer
J.A. Bergstra
L. Bernardinello
A. Bertoni
E. Best
G. Boudol
J.P. Bowen
J.C. Bradfield
A. Brogi
M. Broy
G. Bruns
G.L. Burn
P. Caspi
F. de Cindio
K.L. Clark
W.R. Cleaveland
A. Corradini
G. Costa
M.F. Dam
Ph. Darondeau
J. Davies
F. Dedericks
G. De Michelis
C. Dendorfer
R. De Nicola
R. Deniot
J.-C. Fernandez
G. Ferrari
D. Frutos Escrig
M. Fuchs
H. Garavel
P.H.B. Gardiner
R. Gerth
S. Gilmore
R.J. van Glabbeek
R. Gorrieri
U. Goltz
G.D. Gough
T.F. Gritzner
J.F. Groote
W.H. Hesselink
C.A.R. Hoare
J.J.M. Hooman
M. van Hulst
A. Ingólfsdóttir
D.M. Jackson
M. Jantzen
L. Jategaonkar
He Jifeng
M.B. Josephs
Y.-J. Joung
W.T.M. Kars
A.S. Klusener
W.P. Koole
H.P. Korver
H.-J. Kreowski
A. Labella
C. Laneve
R. Langerak
K.G. Larsen
G. Linde
E. Madelaine
G. Mauri
J.-J.Ch. Meyer
C.A. Middelburg
F. Moller
B. Monahan
L. Monteiro
Y. Ortega-Mallen
C. Palamidessi
I.C.C. Phillips
A. Poigné
L. Pomello
A. Ponse
D.J. Pym
J. Quemada
G. Reggio
W. Reisig
A. Rensink
W.-P. de Roever
M. Ronsangue
J.J.M.M. Rutten
S.A. Schneider
K. Seidel
N. Sabadini
J. Sifakis
H. Simmons
A. Skou
S.A. Smolka
C.P. Stirling
C. Tofts
G.J. Tretmans
I. Ulidowski
F.W. Vaandrager
R. Valk
D. Vergamini
C.A. Vissers
K. Voss
R. Weber
W.P. Weijland
J. Winkowski
J. Zwiers

Table of Contents

Invited Lectures

Selected Presentations

Formal Techniques for Parallel Object-Oriented Languages

Pierre America
Philips Research
P.O. Box 80.000
5600 JA Eindhoven
The Netherlands

Abstract

This paper is intended to give an overview of the formal techniques that have been developed to deal with the parallel object-oriented language POOL and several related languages. We sketch a number of semantic descriptions, using several formalism: operational semantics, denotational semantics, and a new approach to semantics, which we call *layered semantics*. Then we summarize the progress that has been made in formal proof systems to verify the correctness of parallel object-oriented programs. Finally we survey the techniques that we are currently developing to describe the behaviour of objects independently of their implementation, leading to linguistic support for behavioural subtyping.

1 Introduction

Over the last few years, object-oriented programming has gained widespread use and considerable popularity. Until now, the use of object-oriented techniques for parallel programming is mainly restricted to research environments, but nevertheless it holds considerable promises to contribute to the solutions of many problems associated with the programming of parallel computers.

At the Philips Research Laboratories in Eindhoven, the Netherlands, several research projects in this area have been carried out. The DOOM project (Decentralized Object-Oriented Machine) was a subproject of ESPRIT project 415: 'Parallel Architectures and Languages for Advanced Information Processing — a VLSI-directed Approach' [AHO+90]. This ESPRIT project aimed at improving the performance of computers in the area of symbolic applications by the use of large-scale parallelism. Several approaches were explored in different subprojects, which were tied together at a disciplinary level by working groups [Bak89, Tre90]. The DOOM subproject had chosen an object-oriented approach [AH90]. This subproject developed a parallel object-oriented programming language POOL in which applications can be written, together with a parallel machine architecture suitable to execute programs in this language. A number of example applications have been developed as well.

Another project, PRISMA (PaRallel Inference and Storage MAchine), built on the same object-oriented principles as the DOOM project. It aimed at developing a system that is able to handle very large amounts of knowledge and data, again using parallelism to reach a high performance. One of the concrete results of this project is a prototype relational database machine which can automatically exploit parallelism in evaluating the users' queries [AHH+90]. Together with the DOOM project, a prototype computer, POOMA (Parallel Object-Oriented Machine Architecture), has been built, on which the software developed in these projects is running. It comprises 100 processor nodes, each with its own local memory, and connected by a high-speed packet switching network.

This paper was written in the context of ESPRIT Basic Research Action 3020: *Integration*.

The language POOL (Parallel Object-Oriented Language) used in these projects has been the subject of extensive theoretical studies. In the present paper, we give a survey of the results of these studies, and we shall try to assess their influence on the design and the use of the language. In fact, the name POOL stands for a family of languages, developed over a period of seven years. The most important one is POOL2 [Ame88], the language that was implemented on the POOMA machine. Whenever the exact member of the POOL family does not matter, we shall just use the name POOL.

Section 2 gives an introduction to the language POOL itself. Section 3 gives an overview of the techniques that have been used to describe the semantics of POOL in a formal way. Then section 4 sketches the research that has been done in the area of formal verification of POOL programs. Finally, in section 5 we describe the typically object-oriented phenomena of inheritance and subtyping, and show how formal techniques can help to clarify many of the issues involved.

2 An overview of the language POOL

This section gives a summary of the most important ingredients of the POOL language. For more details, we refer the reader to [Ame89b], or to the official language definition [Ame88].

In POOL, a system is described as a collection of *objects*. An object can be thought of as a kind of box, containing some data and having the ability to perform some actions on these data. An object uses *variables* to store its data. A variable contains a *reference* to another object (or, possibly, to the object containing the variable itself). The object's ability to perform operations on its internal data lies in two mechanisms: First, an object can have a set of *methods*, a kind of procedures, which can access and change the values of the variables. (Up to this point, the mechanisms that we have described are generally present in object-oriented languages.) Second, an object has a so-called *body*, a local process that can execute in parallel with the bodies of all the other objects in the system. This is specific for POOL; it constitutes the main source of parallelism in POOL programs.

A very important principle in object-oriented programming is *encapsulation:* The variables of one object are not directly accessible to other objects. In fact, the only way for objects to interact is by sending *messages*. A message is a request to the receiving object to execute one of its methods. The sending object explicitly mentions the receiver and the method name. It can also pass some parameters (again references to objects) to the method. The sender blocks until the receiver has answered its message. The receiver also explicitly states when it is prepared to answer a message. However, it does not specify the sender but only lists a set of possible method names. As soon as synchronization between sender and receiver takes place, the receiver executes the required method, using the parameters that the sender gave. The method returns a *result* (once again, a reference to an object), which is then passed back to the sender. After that, sender and receiver both continue their own processing in parallel.

Because of the above mechanisms, the only parallelism in the system is caused by the parallel execution of the bodies of the different objects. Inside each object everything happens sequentially and deterministically, so that the object is protected from the parallel and nondeterministic (and therefore 'dangerous') outside world. The interesting thing in POOL is that, like in other object-oriented languages, new objects can be *created dynamically* in arbitrary high numbers. In POOL, where as soon as an object is created, its body starts executing, this means that also the degree of parallelism can be increased dynamically. (Objects are never destroyed explicitly; rather, useless objects are removed by a garbage collector working behind the screens).

In order to describe these dynamically evolving systems of objects in a static program, the objects are grouped into *classes*. All the objects in one class (the *instances* of the class) have the same names and types for their variables (of course, each has its own private set of variables) and they execute the same methods and body. In a program, a *class definition* is used to describe this internal structure of the objects. Whenever a new object is to be created, a class is named which serves as a blueprint.

3 Semantics

A number of different techniques have been used to describe the semantics of POOL in a formal way. The following subsections sketch several of these approaches. In all of these descriptions, a syntactically simplified version of POOL is used. This is more convenient in the semantic definition but not very well readable in concrete programs. There is a straightforward translation from POOL2 or POOL-T (an older version) to this simplified notation.

3.1 Operational Semantics

The simplest semantic technique is the use of *transition systems* to define an *operational* semantics. This technique has been introduced by Hennessy and Plotkin [HP79, Plo81, Plo83]. It describes the behaviour of a system in terms of sequences of *transitions* between *configurations*. A configuration describes the system at one particular moment during the execution. Apart from a component describing the values of the variables, it typically contains as a component that part of the program that is still to be executed. The possible transitions are described by a *transition relation*, a binary relation between configurations (by having a relation instead of a function, it is possible to model nondeterminism). This transition relation is defined by a number of *axioms* and *rules*. Because of the presence of (the rest of) the program itself in the configurations, it is possible to describe the transition relation in a way that is closely related to the syntactic structure of the language.

The term 'operational' can now be understood as follows: The set of configurations defines a (very abstract) model of a machine, and the transition relation describes how this machine operates: each transition corresponds to an action that the machine can perform. The fact that the semantic description follows the syntactic structure of the language so closely (as we shall see below) is a definite advantage of the transition system approach to operational semantics.

In the operational semantics of POOL [ABKR86] uses configurations having four components:

$$Conf = \mathcal{P}_{fin}(LStat) \times \Sigma \times Type \times Unit$$

The first component is a finite set of *labelled statements*:

$$\{\langle\alpha_1, s_1\rangle, \ldots, \langle\alpha_n, s_n\rangle\}$$

Here each α_i is an object name and the corresponding s_i is the statement (or sequence of statements) that the object is about to execute. This models the fact that the objects $\alpha_1, \ldots, \alpha_n$ are executing in parallel. The second component is a *state* $\sigma \in \Sigma$, which records the values of the instance variables and temporary variables of all the objects in the system. The third component is a typing function $\tau \in Type$, assigning to each object name the class of which the object is an instance. Finally, the last component is the complete POOL program or *unit*, which is used for looking up the declarations of methods (whenever a message is sent) and bodies (when new objects are created).

The transition relation $\rightarrow$ between configurations is defined by axioms and rules. In general, an axiom describes the essential operation of a certain kind of statement or expression in the language. For example, the axiom describing the assignment statement looks as follows:

$$\left\langle X \cup \{\langle\alpha, x := \beta\rangle\}, \sigma, \tau, U\right\rangle \rightarrow \left\langle X \cup \{\langle\alpha, \beta\rangle\}, \sigma\{\beta/\alpha, x\}, \tau, U\right\rangle$$

Here, X is a set of labelled statements which are not active in this transition, β is another object name, a special case of the expression that can in general appear at the right-hand side of an assignment, and $\sigma\{\beta/\alpha, x\}$ denotes the state that results from changing in the state σ the value of the variable x of the object α into the object name β.

Rules are generally used to describe how to evaluate the components of a composite statement or expression. For example, the following rule describes how the (general) expression at the right-hand side of an assignment is to be evaluated:

$$\frac{\left\langle X \cup \{\langle\alpha, e\rangle\}, \sigma, \tau, U\right\rangle \rightarrow \left\langle X' \cup \{\langle\alpha, e'\rangle\}, \sigma', \tau', U\right\rangle}{\left\langle X \cup \{\langle\alpha, x := e\rangle\}, \sigma, \tau, U\right\rangle \rightarrow \left\langle X' \cup \{\langle\alpha, x := e'\rangle\}, \sigma', \tau', U\right\rangle}$$

According to this rule, *if* the transition above the line is a member of the transition relation, *then* so is the transition below the line. In this way the rule reduces the problem of evaluating the expression in an assignment to evaluating the expression on its own. The latter is described by specific axioms and rules dealing with the several kinds of expressions in the language. Note that as soon as the right-hand side expression has been evaluated completely, so that an concrete object name β results, the assignment axiom above applies and the assignment proper can be performed.

The semantics of a whole program can now be defined as the set of all maximal sequences of configurations $\langle c_1, c_2, c_3, \ldots \rangle$ that satisfy $c_i \rightarrow c_{i+1}$. Each of these sequences represents a possible execution of the program.

3.2 Denotational semantics

The second form of semantic description that has been used to describe POOL is *denotational* semantics. Whereas operational semantics uses an abstract machine that can perform certain actions, denotational semantics assigns a mathematical value, a 'meaning', to each individual language construct. Here, the most important issue is compositionality: the meaning of a composite construct can be described in terms of only the *meanings* of its syntactic constituents.

For sequential languages, it is very natural that the value associated with a statement is a function from states to states: when applied to the state before the execution of the statement, this function delivers the state after the execution. However, for parallel languages this is no longer appropriate: Not only does the presence of nondeterminism lead to a *set* of possible final states, in addition, information on the intermediate states is required to be able to compose a statement in parallel with other statements. This leads us to the concept of *resumptions* (introduced by Plotkin [Plo76]). Instead of delivering the final state after the execution of the statement has completed, we divide the execution of the statement into its atomic (indivisible) parts, and we deliver a pair $\langle \sigma', r \rangle$, where σ' is the state after the execution of the first atomic action and r is the resumption, which describes the execution from this point on. In this way, it is possible to put another statement in parallel with this one: the execution of the second statement can be interleaved with the original one in such a way that between each pair of subsequent atomic actions of the first statement an arbitrary number of atomic actions of the second one can be executed. Each atomic action can inspect the state at the beginning of its execution and possibly modify it.

For a very simple language (not yet having the power of POOL) we get the following equation for the set (the *domain*) in which the values reside that we want to assign to our statements:

$$P \cong \{p_0\} \cup \big(\Sigma \rightarrow \mathcal{P}(\Sigma \times P)\big). \tag{1}$$

The intended interpretation of this equation is the following: Let us call the elements of the set P *processes* and denote them with letters p, q, and r. Then a process p can either be the terminated process p_0, which cannot perform any action, or it is a function which, when provided with an input state σ, delivers a set X of possible actions. Each element of this set X is a pair $\langle \sigma', q \rangle$, where σ' is the state after this action, and q is a process that describes the rest of the execution.

It is clear that equation (1) cannot be solved in the framework of *sets*, because the cardinality of the right-hand side would always be larger than that of the left-hand side. In contrast to many other workers in the field of denotational semantics of parallelism, who use the framework of complete partial orders (cpo's) to solve this kind of equations (see, e.g., [Plo76]), we have chosen to use the framework of *complete metric spaces*. (Readers unfamiliar with this part of mathematics are referred to standard topology texts like [Dug66, Eng89] or to [BZ82].) The most important reason for this choice is the possibility to uses Banach's fixed point theorem:

> Let M be a complete metric space with distance function d and let $f : M \rightarrow M$ be a function that is *contracting*, i.e., there is a real number ϵ with $0 < \epsilon < 1$ such that for all $x, y \in M$ we have $d(f(x), f(y)) < \epsilon . d(x, y)$. Then f has a unique fixed point.

This ensures that whenever we can establish the contractivity of a function we have a *unique* fixed point, whereas in cpo theory mostly we can only guarantee the existence of a *least* fixed point.

Another reason for using complete metric spaces is the naturalness of the power domain construction. Whereas in cpo theory there are several competing definitions (see, e.g., [Plo76, Smy78]) all of which are somewhat hard to understand, in complete metric spaces there is a very natural definition:

> If M is a metric space with distance d, then we define $\mathcal{P}(M)$ to be the set of all *closed* subsets of M, provided with the so-called *Hausdorff distance* d_H, which is defined as follows:
> $$d_H(X,Y) = \max\Big\{\sup_{x\in X}\{d(x,Y)\}, \sup_{y\in Y}\{d(y,X)\}\Big\}$$
> where $d(x,Z) = \inf_{z\in Z}\{d(x,z)\}$ (with the convention that $\sup\emptyset = 0$ and $\inf\emptyset = 1$).

(Minor variations on this definition are sometimes useful, such as taking only the nonempty subsets of M or only the compact ones. The metric is the same in all cases.)

The domain equation that we use for the denotational semantics of POOL (see [ABKR89]) is somewhat more complicated than equation (1), because it also has to accommodate for communication among objects. For POOL, the domain P of processes is defined as follows:

$$P \cong \{p_0\} \cup \big(\Sigma \to \mathcal{P}(Step_P)\big)$$

where the set $Step_P$ of *steps* is given by

$$Step_P = (\Sigma \times P) \cup Send_P \cup Answer_P,$$

with

$$Send_P = Obj \times MName \times Obj^* \times (Obj \to P) \times P$$

and

$$Answer_P = Obj \times MName \times \big(Obj^* \to (Obj \to P) \to^1 P\big).$$

The interpretation of these equations (actually, they can be merged into one large equation) is as follows: As in the first example, a process can either terminate directly, or it can take one out of a set of steps, where this set depends on the state. But in addition to internal steps, which are represented by giving the new state plus a resumption, we now also have communication steps. A *send step* gives the destination object, the method name, a sequence of parameters, and *two* resumptions. The first one, the *dependent* resumption, is a function from object names to processes. It describes what should happen after the message has been answered and the result has been returned to the sender. To do that, this function should be applied to the name of the result object, so that it delivers a process that describes the processing of that result in the sending object. The other resumption, also called the *independent* resumption, describes the actions that can take place in parallel with the sending and the processing of the message. These actions do not have to wait until the message has been answered by the destination object. (Note that for a single object the independent resumption will always be p_0, because a sending object cannot do anything before the result has arrived. However, for the correct parallel composition of more objects, the independent resumption is necessary to describe the actions of the objects that are not sending messages.) Finally we have an *answer step*: This consists of the name of the destination object and the method name, plus an even more complicated resumption. This resumption takes as input the sequence of parameters in the message plus the dependent resumption of the sender. Then it returns a process describing the further execution of the receiver and the sender *together*.

Equations like (1) can be solved by a technique explained in [BZ82]: An increasing sequence of metric spaces is constructed, its union is taken and then the metric completion of the union space satisfies the equation. The equation for POOL processes cannot be solved in this way, because the domain variable P occurs at the left-hand side of the arrow in the definition of answer steps. A more general, category-theoretic technique for solving this kind of domain equations has been developed to solve this problem. It is described in [AR89]. Let us only remark here that it is necessary to restrict ourselves to the set of *non-distance-increasing* functions (satisfying $d(f(x), f(y)) \leq d(x,y)$), which is denoted by $\to^1$ in the above equation.

Let us now give more details about the semantics of statements and expressions. These are described by the following two functions:

$$[\![\ldots]\!]_S : Stat \to Env \to AObj \to Cont_S \to^1 P$$

$$[\![\ldots]\!]_E : Exp \to Env \to AObj \to Cont_E \to^1 P.$$

The first argument of each of these function is a statement (from the set *Stat*) or an expression (from *Exp*), respectively. The second argument is an *environment*, which contains the necessary semantic information about the declarations of methods and bodies in the program (for more details, see [ABKR89]). The third argument is the name of the (active) object executing the statement/ expression. The last argument is a *continuation*. This is explained in more detail below. Continuations are necessary to describe the sequential composition of statements that can create processes and for dealing with expressions that can have arbitrary side-effects (such as sending messages).

Continuations work as follows: The semantic function for statements is provided with a continuation, which is just a process ($Cont_S = P$), describing the execution of all the statements following the current one. The semantic function then delivers a process that describes the execution of the current statement plus the following ones. Analogously, the semantic function for expressions is fed with a continuation, which in this case is a function which maps object names to processes ($Cont_E = Obj \to P$). This function, when applied to the name of the object that is the result of the expression, gives a process describing everything that should happen in the current object after the expression evaluation. Again, the semantic function delivers a process describing the expression evaluation plus the following actions.

Let us illustrate this by giving some examples of clauses that appear in the definition of the semantic functions $[\![\ldots]\!]_S$ and $[\![\ldots]\!]_E$. Let us start with a relatively simple example, the assignment statement:

$$[\![x := e]\!]_S(\gamma)(\alpha)(p) = [\![e]\!]_E(\gamma)(\alpha)\big(\lambda\beta.\lambda\sigma\{\langle\sigma', p\rangle\}\big).$$

This equation says that if the statement $x := e$ is to be executed in an environment γ (recording the effect of the declarations), by the object α, and with continuation p (describing the actions to be performed after this assignment), then first the expression e is to be evaluated, with the same environment γ and by the same object α, but its resulting object is to be fed into an expression continuation $\lambda\beta.\lambda\sigma\{\langle\sigma', p\rangle\}$ that delivers a process of which the first action is an internal one leading to the new state σ' and having the original continuation p as its resumption. Here, of course, the new state σ' is equal to $\sigma\{\beta/\alpha, x\}$.

The semantic definition of sequential composition is easy with continuations:

$$[\![s_1; s_2]\!]_S(\gamma)(\alpha)(p) = [\![s_1]\!]_S(\gamma)(\alpha)\big([\![s_2]\!]_S(\gamma)(\alpha)(p)\big).$$

Here the process describing the execution of the second statement s_2 just serves as the continuation for the first statement s_1.

As a simple example of a semantic definition of an expression let us take an instance variable:

$$[\![x]\!]_E(\gamma)(\alpha)(f) = \lambda\sigma.\big\{\big\langle\sigma, f(\sigma(\alpha)(x))\big\rangle\big\}.$$

Evaluating the expression x takes a single step, in which the value $\sigma(\alpha)(x)$ of the variable is looked up in the state σ. The resumption of this first step is obtained by feeding this value into the expression continuation f (which is a function that maps object names into processes).

As a final example of a semantic definition, let us take object creation: The expression $\mathsf{new}(C)$ creates a new object of class C and its value is the name of this object. Its semantics is defined as follows:

$$[\![\mathsf{new}(C)]\!]_E(\gamma)(\alpha)(f) = \lambda\sigma.\big\{\big\langle\sigma', \gamma(C)(\beta) \parallel f(\beta)\big\rangle\big\}.$$

Here β is a fresh object name, determined from σ in a way that does not really interest us here, and σ' differs from σ only in that the variables of the new object β are properly initialized. We see that execution of this new-expression takes a single step, of which the resumption consists of the parallel composition of the body $\gamma(C)(\beta)$ of the new object with the execution of the creator, where the latter is obtained by applying the expression continuation f to the name of the new object β (which is, after all, the value of the new-expression). The parallel composition operator $\|$ is a function in $P \times P \to P$, which can be defined as the unique fixed point of a suitable contracting higher-order function $\Phi_{PC} : (P \times P \to P) \to (P \times P \to P)$ (an application of Banach's fixed point theorem).

From the above few equations it can already be seen how the use of continuations provides an elegant solution to the problems that we have mentioned.

There are a number of further steps necessary before we arrive at the semantics of a complete program. One interesting detail is that in the denotational semantics, sending messages to standard objects is treated in exactly the same way as sending messages to programmer-defined objects. The standard objects themselves (note that there are infinitely many of them!) are represented by a (huge) process p_{ST}, which is able to answer all the messages sent to standard objects and immediately return the correct results. This process p_{ST} is composed in parallel with the process p_U, which describes the execution of the user-defined objects in order to give the process describing the execution of the whole system.

Despite the fact that the two forms of semantics described above, the operational and the denotational one, are formulated in widely different frameworks, it turns out that it is possible to establish an important relationship between them:

$$\mathcal{O} = abstr \circ \mathcal{D},$$

which in some sense says that the different forms of semantics of POOL are *equivalent*. Here $\mathcal{D}$ is the function that assigns a process to a POOL program according to the denotational semantics and $\mathcal{O}$ assigns to each program a set of (finite or infinite) sequences of states, which can be extracted from the sequences of configurations obtained from the operational semantics. Finally, *abstr* is an abstraction operator that takes a process and maps it into the set of sequences of states to which the process gives rise. The complete equivalence proof can be found in [Rut90].

3.3 Layered semantics

The denotational semantics described above has one significant disadvantage: it does not describe the behaviour of a single *object*. In order to get a better grip on this fundamental concept of object-oriented programming, a layered form of denotational semantics for POOL has been developed [AR90]. In this formalism, there are different semantic domains (again complete metric spaces) for the meanings of statements, objects, and systems.

The semantic domain *SProc* of *statement processes* is used for the semantic descriptions of POOL statements and expressions. It reflects precisely the different ways in which statements and expressions can interact with their environment:

$$\begin{aligned} SProc \cong \{p_0\} & \cup (\Sigma \times SProc) \\ & \cup (CName \times (Obj \to SProc)) \\ & \cup (Obj \times MName \times Obj^* \times (Obj \to SProc)) \\ & \cup (MName \xrightarrow{fin} (Obj^* \to SProc)) \\ & \cup (MName \xrightarrow{fin} (Obj^* \to SProc)) \times SProc \\ & \cup (Obj \times SProc) \end{aligned}$$

(With $A \xrightarrow{fin} B$ we denote the set of finite partial maps from A to B.)

A statement (or expression) can do nothing, it can do an internal step, it can create a new object, it can send a message, it can answer a message, it can conditionally answer a message, or it can send the result of a message back to the original sender. In all these cases, the exact mechanism to perform the task (e.g., determining the name for a new object or synchronizing on communication) is not described here, but only the information necessary to perform it (e.g., the class of the new object). We should also note that a state $\sigma \in \Sigma$ only describes the variables of a single object. Semantic functions like the ones in section 3.2 deliver for each statement or expression the statement process that describes its meaning.

The domain *OProc* of ***object processes*** is very similar to *SProc*, but it does not include the internal steps:

$$\begin{aligned} OProc \cong \{q_0\} & \cup (CName \times (Obj \to OProc)) \\ & \cup (Obj \times MName \times Obj^* \times (Obj \to OProc)) \\ & \cup (MName \xrightarrow{fin} (Obj^* \to OProc)) \\ & \cup (MName \xrightarrow{fin} (Obj^* \to OProc)) \times OProc \\ & \cup (Obj \times OProc) \end{aligned}$$

The semantics of an object is obtained by applying an abstraction operator $abstr : SProc \to OProc$ to the meaning of the body of this object. This operator *abstr* removes all the internal steps. It turns out that this operator is not continuous (in the classical metric/topological meaning), since it has to transform an arbitrarily long sequences of internal steps followed by a non-internal step into this non-internal step, but an infinite sequence of internal steps by q_0. For the mathematical treatment, this non-continuity presents no problem.

Finally, the domain *GProc* of ***global processes*** is determined by the following domain equation:

$$\begin{aligned} GProc &= \{r_0\} \cup \mathcal{P}_{cl}(GStep) \\ GStep &= Obj \times MName \times Obj^* \times Obj \times GProc \\ &\cup\ Obj \times (Obj \to GProc) \\ &\cup\ MName \times Obj \times (Obj \to Obj^* \to GProc) \\ &\cup\ Obj \times Obj \times Obj \times GProc \\ &\cup\ Comm^+ \times GProc \end{aligned}$$

where

$$\begin{aligned} Comm^+ &= Comm \cup \{*\} \\ Comm &= Obj \times MName^+ \times Obj^* \times Obj \\ MName^+ &= MName \cup \{*\} \end{aligned}$$

The possible steps in a global process are either one-sided communication attempts (sending or receiving a message or result) or completed communications, reflected by a communication record $c \in Comm$.

An object process in *OProc* is 'globalized', i.e., transformed into a global process, by an operator ω. This operator ω also takes care of the naming of new objects and it remembers to which object the result of a method should be returned. There is a parallel composition operator $\|: GProc \times GProc \to GProc$, which takes care of synchronization between sender and receiver of a message or result. The global process describing the whole execution of a program can be obtained by applying ω to the object process that belongs to the root object (the first object in the system).

If desired, the set of traces of all successful communications in program executions can be obtained from this global process. However, it is much more interesting to determine the real observable input/output behaviour of a program. This is done by distinguishing a special object *world* to which input and output messages can be sent. By concentrating on the interactions of the rest of the system with this object, one can view a program as a nondeterministic transformation from an input stream of standard objects (integers, booleans) to an output stream of standard objects.

The advantage of this layered approach to POOL semantics is not only that it really gives a semantic interpretation of a single object, but also that it develops a framework in which issues about ***full abstractness*** can be studied (a denotational semantics is called fully abstract if it does not give more information than necessary to determine the observable behaviour of a program construct in context). These issues are present on two levels: the statement/expression level and the object level. They are subject of ongoing research.

In addition to the different forms of semantics described above, POOL has been the subject of a number of other semantic studies. In [Vaa86], the semantics of POOL is defined by means of *process algebra* [BK84, BK85]. In [ELR90], a simplified version of POOL is used as an example to illustrate POTs (Parallel Object-based Transition systems), an extended version of Petri nets. Finally, in [DD86, DDH87] a description is given of an abstract POOL machine. In contrast to the 'abstract machine' employed in the operational semantics described above, this abstract POOL machine is intended to be the first step in a sequence of refinements which ultimately lead to an efficient implementation on real parallel hardware. This abstract POOL machine is described formally in AADL, an Axiomatic Architecture Description Language.

4 Verification

Developing a formal proof system for verifying the correctness of POOL programs is an even harder task than giving a formal semantics for this language. Therefore this work has been done in several stages. A more detailed account of the research on verification of POOL programs is given in [Boe91].

4.1 A sequential version

First the proof theory of SPOOL, a sequential version of POOL, has been studied (see [Ame86]). This language is obtained by omitting the bodies (and the possibility to return a result before a method ends) from POOL, such that now at any moment there is only one active object and we have a sequential object-oriented language. For this language a Hoare-style [Apt81, Hoa69] proof system has been developed. The main contribution from the proof theory of SPOOL was a formalism to deal with dynamically evolving pointer structures. This reasoning should take place at an abstraction level that is at least as high as that of the programming language. More concretely, this means the following:

1. The only operations on 'pointers' (references to objects) are
   - testing for equality
   - dereferencing (determining the value of an instance variable of the referenced object)
2. In a given state of the system, it is only possible to reason about the objects that exist in that state, i.e., an object that does not exist (yet) cannot play a role.

Requirement 1 can be met by only admitting the indicated operations to the assertion language (however, this excludes the approach where pointers are explicitly modelled as indices in a large array that represents the 'heap'). In order to satisfy requirement 2, variables are forbidden to refer to nonexisting objects and the range of quantifiers is restricted to the existing objects. (The consequence is that the range of quantification depends on the state!)

In reasoning about pointer structures, first-order predicate logic is not enough to express interesting properties, and therefore several extensions have been explored. The first extension is the possibility to use recursively defined predicates. One variant of this formalism uses a so-called μ-notation to express these predicates. More precisely, the phrase

$$\mu X(z_1, \ldots, z_n)(P)$$

is used to denote the smallest predicate X satisfying

$$\forall z_1, \ldots, z_n \quad X(z_1, \ldots, z_n) \leftrightarrow P.$$

(In order to be sure that such a predicate exists, we require that X must not occur negatively in P.)

In this notation, the assertion

$$\mu X(y, z)\Big(y \doteq z \lor X(y \,.\, x, z)\Big)(v, w) \tag{2}$$

can be used to express the property that the object denoted by the variable w is a member of the linked list starting with v and linked by the variable x, or in other words, that starting from v one can get to w by following the reference stored in the variable x an arbitrary number of times.

Another notational variant for using recursively defined predicates is to name and declare them explicitly. The declaration

$$q(z_1, \ldots, z_n) \Leftarrow P$$

defines q to be the smallest predicate satisfying

$$\forall z_1, \ldots, z_n \quad q(z_1, \ldots, z_n) \leftrightarrow P.$$

The property expressed in equation (2) can now simply be written as $q(v, w)$, where the predicate q is declared by

$$q(y, z) \Leftarrow y \doteq z \vee q(y.x, z).$$

The μ-notation is easier to deal with in reasoning about the proof system, but the version with declared predicates is more convenient in actual proofs.

Since an assertion language with recursively defined predicates does not admit the standard techniques for establishing the completeness of the proof system, we have also explored a different extension to first-order logic: quantification over finite sequences of objects. In this formalism, the property in equation (2) can be expressed as follows:

$$\exists z \Big(z \cdot 1 \doteq v \wedge z \cdot |z| \doteq w \wedge \forall n \; (0 < n \wedge n < |z|) \rightarrow (z \cdot n).x \doteq z \cdot (n+1) \Big)$$

where z ranges over finite sequences of objects, $z \cdot n$ denotes the nth element of the sequence z, and $|z|$ denotes its length.

It is somewhat surprising that even with the restrictions on pointer operations, mentioned above as items 1 and 2, it is possible to describe, e.g., the creation of a new object. This is done by an axiom that is similar in form to the traditional axiom of assignment:

$$\Big\{P[\mathsf{new}/u]\Big\} \; u \leftarrow \mathsf{new} \; \Big\{P\Big\}.$$

The trick is in the definition of the substitution operation $[\mathsf{new}/u]$, which is not ordinary substitution, but fulfils the same goal: replacing any expression or assertion by another one that, when evaluated in the state before the assignment, has the same value as the original one in the state after the assignment. In the case of object creation, this is not possible for every expression, because the variable u will refer to the new object after the statement and this object cannot be denoted by any expression before the statement. However, this variable u can only in two contexts in an assertion: either it is compared for equality with another expression, or it is dereferenced. In both cases we know what the result will be. The precise definition of the substitution $[\mathsf{new}/u]$ is somewhat complicated, so here we just give a few examples (see [Ame86] for full details):

$$\begin{aligned} u \doteq y.x[\mathsf{new}/u] &= \mathsf{false} \\ u \doteq u[\mathsf{new}/u] &= \mathsf{true} \\ u.x \doteq z[\mathsf{new}/u] &= \mathsf{nil} \doteq z \\ u.x \doteq u[\mathsf{new}/u] &= \mathsf{false} \end{aligned}$$

In the case of quantification, the substituted assertion contains one component that ranges over the old objects and one component that talks about the new one, for example:

$$(\forall z \, P)[\mathsf{new}/u] = \forall z \, (P[\mathsf{new}/u]) \wedge P[u/z][\mathsf{new}/u].$$

In the presence of recursively defined predicates or quantification over finite sequences, similar measures are taken to ensure correct functioning of the substitution operation, so that the axiom for object creation can be shown to be sound, i.e., everything that can be proved is actually true.

If the left-hand side of the assignment is an instance variable instead of a temporary variable, then certain other modifications to the substitution used in the assignment axiom are necessary to deal with *aliasing*, i.e., the possibility that two different expressions denote the same variable. For example, applying the substitution $[1/x]$ to the assertion

$$\forall z\,(z \not\doteq \mathsf{self} \rightarrow z\,.\,x \doteq 0)$$

yields the assertion

$$\forall z\,(z \not\doteq \mathsf{self} \rightarrow \mathsf{if}\ z \doteq \mathsf{self}\ \mathsf{then}\ 1\ \mathsf{else}\ z\,.\,x\ \mathsf{fi} \doteq 0),$$

which can be simplified to $\forall z\,(z \not\doteq \mathsf{self} \rightarrow z\,.\,x \doteq 0)$.

Another contribution of the SPOOL proof system is a proof rule for message passing and method invocation (in a sequential setting). In this rule the context switching between sending and receiving object and the transmission of parameters and result are representing by appropriate substitution operations. For details, see [Ame86].

In the version with quantification over finite sequences, the SPOOL proof system has been proved to be not only sound but also complete [AB89], i.e., every correctness formula that is true can be proved in this system.

4.2 Dealing with parallelism

Along a different track a proof theory was developed to deal with parallelism, in particular with dynamic process creation. In [Boe86] a proof system was given for a language called P, which essentially only differs from POOL in that message passing only consists of transmitting a single value from the sender to the receiver (like in CSP [Hoa78]).

Whereas the proof system in [Boe86] uses an explicit coding of object references by numbers, an integration with the work on SPOOL has led to a more abstract proof system for the same language P [AB88, AB90].

To deal with parallelism, this proof system uses the concepts of *cooperation test*, *global invariant*, *bracketed section*, and *auxiliary variables*, which have been developed in the proof theory of CSP [AFR80]. Described very briefly, the proof system for the language P consists of the following elements:

- A *local* stage. This deals with all statements that do not involve communication or object creation. These statements are proved correct with respect to pre- and postconditions in the usual manner of sequential programs [Apt81, Hoa69]. At this stage, *assumptions* are used to describe the behaviour of the communication and creation statements. These will be verified in the next stage.

- An *intermediate* stage. In this stage the above assumptions about communication and creation statements are verified. For each creation statement and for each pair of possibly communicating send and receive statements it is verified that the specification used in the local proof system is consistent with the global behaviour.

- A *global* stage. Here some properties of the system as a whole can be derived from a kind of standard specification that arises from the intermediate stage.

In the local stage, a *local assertion language* is employed, which only talks about the current object in isolation. In this assertion language, the variables of the current object can be named directly, but the variables of other objects cannot be named at all. Likewise, quantification over integers (and booleans) is possible, but quantification over all (existing) objects is not available. In the intermediate and global stages, a *global assertion language* is used, which reasons about all the objects in the system. Here quantification over all existing objects and even over finite sequences of existing objects is possible. An assertion p in the local assertion language can be transformed to a global assertion $p \downarrow z$ by applying a syntactic substitution (denoted by $\downarrow z$, where z is a global expression that denotes the object that p should talk about). For example, if the local assertion p is

$$b \not\doteq \mathsf{nil} \rightarrow \forall i\,(i < m \rightarrow \exists j\; i \times j \doteq b)$$

then $p \downarrow z$ is

$$z\,.\,b \not\doteq \mathsf{nil} \rightarrow \forall i\,(i < z\,.\,m \rightarrow \exists j\; i \times j \doteq z\,.\,b).$$

Whereas in the local stage the axioms and rules are the same as in traditional Hoare logic, the axioms and rules of the intermediate stage make use of the same techniques as the ones developed for SPOOL to deal with object creation and aliasing.

The global proof system makes use of the fact that the initial state is precisely known: there is one single object and all its variables have the value nil. Therefore the precondition can have the form $(p \wedge x_1 \doteq \mathsf{nil} \wedge \cdots \wedge x_n \doteq \mathsf{nil}) \downarrow z$, where p is an assertion talking only about logical variables (variables that do not occur in the program).

Again this proof system has been proved to be sound and complete (for details see [AB88]). Moreover, using the same basic ingredients, but with the addition of an assumption/commitment mechanism, a sound and complete proof system has been developed for the full language POOL, with its rendezvous communication [Boe90, Boe91]. Nevertheless, this proof system also has its shortcomings. The most important problem is that it involves *global reasoning*: the invariant incorporates all the objects in the system. For even slightly complicated programs, this leads to an unmanageably complex proof. The only way out here seems to be the use of compositional proof techniques (see [HR87] for a survey). Unfortunately, since the configuration of objects in POOL is not static but dynamic, it is not so clear how the decomposition should work here.

5 Inheritance and subtyping

Inheritance is a mechanism that is tightly bound to the notion of object-oriented programming. Its basic idea is that in defining a new class it is often very convenient to start with all the ingredients (variables, methods) of an existing class and to add some more and possibly redefine some in order to get the desired new class. The new class is said to *inherit* the variables and methods of the old one. This can repeated several times and one can even allow a class to inherit from more than one class (multiple inheritance). In this way a complete *inheritance hierarchy* arises. By sharing code among classes in this way, the total amount of code in a system can sometimes be drastically reduced and its maintenance can be simplified.

This inheritance relationship between classes also suggests another relationship: If a class B inherits from a class A, each instance of B will have at least all the variables and methods that instances of A have.Therefore it seems that whenever we require an object of class A, an instance of class B would do equally well, or in other words, that we can regard the class B as a *specialized version* of A. Note, however, that inheritance is concerned with the *internal structure* of the objects (variables and methods), whereas this specialization phenomenon is about the possible use of the objects, characterized by their *externally observable behaviour*. For a long time the idea has prevailed in the object-oriented community that the inheritance hierarchy coincides completely with the specialization hierarchy. However, recently it is becoming clear that identifying these two hierarchies leads to several problems and that it is useful to separate them (see also [Ame87, Sny86]).

In order to get a clear conceptual view, we proposed the following definitions [Ame89a]: Whereas a class is a collection of objects that have (exactly) the same internal structure (variables, method code, body), a *type* is a collection of objects that share the same externally observable behaviour. In this context we can see that inheritance forms a relationship between classes, while subtyping is a relationship between types. A language called POOL-I has been designed that works according to these principles [AL90]. Now inheritance is adequately described by the syntax for writing code in the programming language under consideration (which does not mean that it is a simple task to design an inheritance mechanism that works well in practice), but in order to get a good formal grip on subtyping we need to do some more work.

Let us start with realizing that a type is in essence a specification of object behaviour. The important point here is that the specification should only consider those aspects of this behaviour that can be observed from outside the object, independently of its internal structure. Ideally, the specification should only talk about the messages that are received and sent by the object. Now specifying objects in terms of possible sequences of messages is certainly possible, but for most kinds of objects, this is not the best way to characterize them. For example, consider the following specification, which is written in English to avoid notational problems:

> The object will accept put and **get** messages, but it will accept a **get** message only if the number of put messages already received exceeds the number of **get** messages. A put message contains one integer as an argument and does not return a result. A **get** message contains no arguments and it returns as its result the integer that was the argument of the last put message that has preceded an equal number of put and **get** messages.

It is not immediately clear that this specification characterizes something as simple and well-known as a stack of integers. The most important reason for this difficulty is that the intuitive view most people have of such an object is that inside it stores a certain amount of information (a sequence of integers) and that the messages interact with this information. A more technical disadvantage is that reasoning in terms of sequences of message fails to make explicit that different sequences may lead to the same end result: a stack into which three elements have been inserted and subsequently removed is equivalent to an empty stack.

Therefore we propose to specify object behaviour in terms of an *abstract state*, which is an abstraction from the object's concrete internal state. For our stack, the abstract state would just be a sequence of integers. In a sequential setting, methods can now be described by pre- and postconditions formulated in terms of the abstract state. For example, the method **get** of the above stack is specified by

$$\left\{s \neq \langle\rangle\right\} \mathbf{get}() \left\{s_0 = s * \langle r\rangle\right\}.$$

Here s is the sequence representing the current state of the stack, s_0 in the postcondition stands for the value of s before the method execution, and r stands for the result of the **get** method. Furthermore, the operator $*$ denotes concatenation of sequences, $\langle\rangle$ is the empty sequence, and $\langle n\rangle$ is the sequence having n as its only element.

In general, a specification of a type σ consists of a domain Σ, representing the set of possible abstract states of objects of type σ, plus a set of method specifications of the form $\{P\}m(\bar{p})\{Q\}$, where the precondition $P = P(s, \bar{p})$ describes the state of affairs before the method execution and the postcondition $Q = Q(s, s_0, \bar{p}, r)$ describes the situation after its execution (s always stands for the current abstract state, s_0 for the abstract state before the method execution, $\bar{p}$ for the method parameters, and r for the result). The meaning of such a method specification is that each object of type σ should have a method with name m available such that if the method is executed in a state where the precondition P holds, then after the method execution Q holds.

The next important question is under what conditions the objects of a given class C are members of a type σ, in which case we say that the class C *implements* the type σ. We do this as follows: We require a *representation function* $f : \mathcal{C} \rightarrow \Sigma$, where $\mathcal{C}$ is the set of possible concrete states of objects of class C, i.e., the set of possible values of the variables $\bar{v}$ of such an object, and Σ is the set of abstract states associated with the type σ. The representation function f maps the values $\bar{v}$ of the variables of an object of class C to an element s of the mathematical domain Σ that is used in the specification of the type σ. We also need a *representation invariant* I, which is a logical formula involving the values of the variables of the class C. This invariant will describe the set of values of these variables that can actually occur (in general this is a proper subset of the set $\mathcal{C}$). The representation function f should at least be defined for all concrete states for which the invariant I holds.

For the class C to implement the type σ the following conditions are required to hold:

1. The invariant I holds initially, i.e., just after the creation and initialization of each new object.
2. Every method m of the class C (the ones that are mentioned in σ's specification as well as the ones that are not mentioned) should maintain the invariant.
3. For every method specification $\{P\}m(\bar{p})\{Q\}$ occurring in the specification of σ, the class C should also have a method m with parameters $\bar{p}$ of the right number and types. Furthermore this method should satisfy
$$\{P \circ f \wedge I\}\ m(\bar{p})\ \{Q \circ f \wedge I\}.$$
Here $P \circ f$ stands for the formula P where every occurrence of the abstract state s is replaced by the function f applied to the variables and analogously with s_0: $P \circ f = P[f(\bar{v})/s, f(\bar{v_0})/s_0]$.

Now we can say that a type σ is a subtype of a type τ if all objects belonging to σ also belong to τ (note that nontrivial subtyping relationships are indeed possible, because one can write specifications that leave some degree of freedom in behaviour so that other specifications can be more specific). Of course, we would like to be able to conclude such a subtyping relationship from the specifications of σ and τ. At a first glance, it seems sufficient to require that for every method specification $\{P\}m(\bar{p})\{Q\}$ occurring in τ's specification there should be a method specification $\{P'\}m(\bar{p})\{Q'\}$ in the specification of σ such that the latter implies the former, which can be expressed by $P \rightarrow P'$ and $Q' \rightarrow Q$. Under these circumstances we can indeed use any element of σ whenever an element of τ is expected: When we send such an object a message listing the method m, using it as an element of τ guarantees that initially the precondition P will hold. By the implication $P \rightarrow P'$ we can conclude that the precondition P' in σ's specification also holds. Then after the method execution the postcondition Q' from σ will hold and this again implies the postcondition Q that is required by τ.

However, in general we must assume that the type τ has been specified using a different mathematical domain T than the domain Σ used in σ's specification. Therefore in order to show that a type σ is a subtype of the type τ, we require the existence of a function $\phi : \Sigma \rightarrow T$, called *transfer function*, that maps the mathematical domain Σ associated with σ to T, the one associated with τ. This time we do not need an extra invariant, because we can assume that Σ has been chosen small enough to exclude all the values that cannot actually occur. We now require that for every method specification $\{P\}m(\bar{p})\{Q\}$ occurring in τ's specification there should be a method specification $\{P'\}m(\bar{p})\{Q'\}$ in the specification of σ such that

1. $P \circ \phi \rightarrow P'$.
2. $Q' \rightarrow Q \circ \phi$.

Again $P \circ \phi$ can be obtained from P by replacing the abstract state of τ by ϕ applied to the abstract state of σ and analogously for the old values of the abstract states.

On the basis of the above definitions one can easily prove the desirable property that whenever a class C implements a type σ and σ is a subtype of τ, then C implements τ.

In order to make these ideas more formal, a language, called SPOOL-S, has been defined that allow the formal expression of the abovementioned ingredients: classes and types, connected by representation and transfer functions [DK91]. The abstract domains, in which the abstract states reside, can be specified in any formalism in which mathematical entities can be specified (in [DK91] the Larch Shared Language [GHM90] was chosen as an example). Method specifications can be written using a formalism that is slightly different from the one above. In addition to a pre- and a postcondition, a method specification also contains a so-called *modifies-list*, in which all the objects are mentioned that could be modified by the method. This is necessary to be able to describe an object on its own, because ordinary Hoare logic does not provide a mechanism to state that 'all the rest stays the same'.

The language also allows for the situation where one abstract object is implemented by a collection of concrete objects. For example, a stack can be implemented by a linked list of objects that each store a single item. This can be expressed in the representation function, which maps the concrete state of an object into its abstract state, possibly using the abstract states of other objects as well. In our example, if the modifies-list allows a method to change a stack object, then all the concrete objects implementing this stack could possibly be modified.

Up to now, a formal proof system for verifying SPOOL-S programs has not yet been developed, but it seems certainly possible with the techniques that have been used for SPOOL (see section 4.1). It is a much greater challenge, however, to generalize them to deal with parallelism. Here the techniques described in section 4.2 definitely fall short, because they involve global reasoning on an abstraction level that is as high as that of the programming language, but not higher. Probably a viable approach to this problem will still include the use of abstract internal states, but in the presence of parallelism it will be hard to avoid reasoning about sequences of messages. Perhaps a judicious combination of compositional proof techniques and the techniques describe above will lead to a satisfactory solution.

References

[AB88] Pierre America and Frank de Boer. A proof system for a parallel language with dynamic process creation. ESPRIT Project 415 Document 445, Philips Research Laboratories, Eindhoven, the Netherlands, October 1988. Chapter 2 (pages 121–200) of [Boe91]. A slightly shortened version was published as [AB90].

[AB89] Pierre America and Frank de Boer. A sound and complete proof system for a sequential version of POOL. ESPRIT Project 415 Document 499, Philips Research Laboratories, Eindhoven, the Netherlands, 1989. Chapter 2 (pages 15–119) of [Boe91].

[AB90] Pierre America and Frank de Boer. A proof system for process creation. In *IFIP TC2 Working Conference on Programming Concepts and Methods*, Sea of Galilee, Israel, April 2–5, 1990, pages 303–332.

[ABKR86] Pierre America, Jaco de Bakker, Joost N. Kok, and Jan Rutten. Operational semantics of a parallel object-oriented language. In *Conference Record of the 13th Symposium on Principles of Programming Languages*, St. Petersburg, Florida, January 13–15, 1986, pages 194–208.

[ABKR89] Pierre America, Jaco de Bakker, Joost N. Kok, and Jan Rutten. Denotational semantics of a parallel object-oriented language. *Information and Computation*, 83(2):152–205, November 1989.

[AFR80] Krzysztof R. Apt, Nissim Francez, and Willem Paul de Roever. A proof system for Communicating Sequential Processes. *ACM Transactions on Programming Languages and Systems*, 2(3):359–385, July 1980.

[AH90] J. K. Annot and P. A. M. den Haan. POOL and DOOM: The object-oriented approach. In P. C. Treleaven, editor, *Parallel Computers: Object-Oriented, Functional, Logic*, Wiley, 1990, pages 47–79.

[AHH+90] Peter Apers, Bob Hertzberger, Ben Hulshof, Hans Oerlemans, and Martin Kersten. PRISMA, a platform for experiments with parallelism. In Pierre America, editor, *Parallel Database Systems: Proceedings of the PRISMA Workshop*, Noordwijk, The Netherlands, September 24–26, 1990, Springer Lecture Notes in Computer Science 503, pages 169–180.

[AHO+90] Pierre America, Ben Hulshof, Eddy Odijk, Frans Sijstermans, Rob van Twist, and Rogier Wester. Parallel computers for advanced information processing. *IEEE Micro*, 10(6):12–15, 61–75, December 1990.

[AL90] Pierre America and Frank van der Linden. A parallel object-oriented language with inheritance and subtyping. In *Proceedings of OOPSLA/ECOOP '90*, Ottawa, Canada, October 21–25, 1990, pages 161–168.

[Ame86] Pierre America. A proof theory for a sequential version of POOL. ESPRIT Project 415 Document 188, Philips Research Laboratories, Eindhoven, the Netherlands, October 1986.

[Ame87] Pierre America. Inheritance and subtyping in a parallel object-oriented language. In *ECOOP '87: European Conference on Object-Oriented Programming*, Paris, France, June 15–17, 1987, Springer Lecture Notes in Computer Science 276, pages 234–242.

[Ame88] Pierre America. Definition of POOL2, a parallel object-oriented language. ESPRIT Project 415 Document 364, Philips Research Laboratories, Eindhoven, the Netherlands, April 1988.

[Ame89a] Pierre America. A behavioural approach to subtyping in object-oriented programming languages. In M. Lenzerini, D. Nardi, and M. Simi, editors, *Workshop on Inheritance Hierarchies in Knowledge Representation and Programming Languages*, Viareggio, Italy, February 6–8, 1989, Wiley, 1991, pages 173–190. Also appeared in *Philips Journal of Research*, Vol. 44, No. 2/3, July 1989, pages 365–383.

[Ame89b] Pierre America. Issues in the design of a parallel object-oriented language. *Formal Aspects of Computing*, 1(4):366–411, 1989.

[Apt81] Krzysztof R. Apt. Ten years of Hoare logic: A survey — part I. *ACM Transactions on Programming Languages and Systems*, 3(4):431–483, October 1981.

[AR89] Pierre America and Jan Rutten. Solving reflexive domain equations in a category of complete metric spaces. *Journal of Computer and System Sciences*, 39(3):343–375, December 1989.

[AR90] Pierre America and Jan Rutten. A layered semantics for a parallel object-oriented language. In *Foundations of Object-Oriented Languages: Proceedings of the REX School/Workshop*, Noordwijkerhout, The Netherlands, May 28–June 1, 1990, Springer Lecture Notes in Computer Science 489, pages 91–123. To appear in *Formal Aspects of Computing*.

[Bak89] J. W. de Bakker, editor. *Languages for Parallel Architectures: Design, Semantics, Implementation Models*. John Wiley & Sons, 1989.

[BK84] J. A. Bergstra and J. W. Klop. Process algebra for synchronous communication. *Information and Control*, 60:109–137, 1984.

[BK85] J. A. Bergstra and J. W. Klop. Algebra of communicating processes with abstraction. *Theoretical Computer Science*, 37(1):77–121, May 1985.

[Boe86] Frank S. de Boer. A proof rule for process creation. In Martin Wirsing, editor, *Formal Description of Programming Concepts III — Proceedings of the Third IFIP WG 2.2 Working Conference*, Gl. Avernæs, Ebberup, Denmark, August 25–28, 1986, North-Holland, pages 23–50.

[Boe90] Frank S. de Boer. A proof system for the language POOL. In *Proceedings of the 17th International Colloquium on Automata, Languages, and Programming*, Warwick, England, July 16–20, 1990, Springer Lecture Notes in Computer Science 443.

[Boe91] Frank S. de Boer. *Reasoning about Dynamically Evolving Process Structures: A Proof Theory for the Parallel Object-Oriented Language POOL*. PhD thesis, Free University of Amsterdam, April 15, 1991.

[BZ82] J. W. de Bakker and J. I. Zucker. Processes and the denotational semantics of concurrency. *Information and Control*, 54:70–120, 1982.

[DD86] W. Damm and G. Döhmen. The POOL-machine: A top level specification for a distributed object-oriented machine. ESPRIT Project 415 Document 1, Lehrstuhl für Informatik, RWTH Aachen, West Germany, October 3, 1986.

[DDH87] W. Damm, G. Döhmen, and P. den Haan. Using AADL to specify distributed computer architectures: A case study. In J. W. de Bakker, editor, *Deliverable 3 of the Working Group on Semantics and Proof Techniques*, Chapter 1.4, ESPRIT Project 415, October 1987.

[DK91] Hans Demmers and Pieter Kleingeld. SPOOL-S: An object-oriented language with behavioural subtyping. Master's thesis, University of Utrecht, Department of Computer Science, Utrecht, the Netherlands, May 1991.

[Dug66] J. Dugundji. *Topology*. Allyn and Bacon, Boston, Massachusetts, 1966.

[ELR90] Joost Engelfriet, George Leih, and Grzegorz Rozenberg. Net-based description of parallel object-based systems, or POTs and POPs. In *Foundations of Object-Oriented Languages: Proceedings of the REX School/Workshop*, Noordwijkerhout, The Netherlands, May 28–June 1, 1990, Springer Lecture Notes in Computer Science 489, pages 229–273.

[Eng89] R. Engelking. *General Topology*, volume 6 of *Sigma Series in Pure Mathematics*. Heldermann, Berlin, 1989.

[GHM90] John V. Guttag, James J. Horning, and Andrés Modet. Report on the Larch shared language, version 2.3. Report 58, DEC Systems Research Center, Palo Alto California, April 1990.

[Hoa69] C. A. R. Hoare. An axiomatic basis for computer programming. *Communications of the ACM*, 12(10):576–580,583, October 1969.

[Hoa78] C. A. R. Hoare. Communicating sequential processes. *Communications of the ACM*, 21(8):666–677, August 1978.

[HP79] Matthew Hennessy and Gordon Plotkin. Full abstraction for a simple parallel programming language. In J. Bečvář, editor, *Proceedings of the 8th Symposium on Mathematical Foundations of Computer Science*, Springer Lecture Notes in Computer Science 74, 1979, pages 108–120.

[HR87] Jozef Hooman and Willem-P. de Roever. The quest goes on: A survey of proof systems for partial correctness of CSP. In J. W. de Bakker, W. P. de Roever, and G. Rozenberg, editors, *Current Trends in Concurrency*, Springer Lecture Notes in Computer Science 224, 1987, pages 343–395.

[Plo76] Gordon D. Plotkin. A powerdomain construction. *SIAM Journal on Computing*, 5(3):452–487, September 1976.

[Plo81] Gordon D. Plotkin. A structural approach to operational semantics. Report DAIMI FN-19, Aarhus University, Computer Science Department, Aarhus, Denmark, September 1981.

[Plo83] Gordon D. Plotkin. An operational semantics for CSP. In D. Bjørner, editor, *Formal Description of Programming Concepts II*, North-Holland, 1983, pages 199–223.

[Rut90] Jan Rutten. Semantic correctness for a parallel object-oriented language. *SIAM Journal on Computing*, 19(3):341–383, 1990.

[Smy78] Michael B. Smyth. Power domains. *Journal of Computer and System Sciences*, 16:23–36, 1978.

[Sny86] Alan Snyder. Encapsulation and inheritance in object-oriented programming languages. In *Proceedings of the ACM Conference on Object-Oriented Programming, Systems, Languages and Applications*, Portland, Oregon, September 1986, pages 38–45.

[Tre90] P. C. Treleaven, editor. *Parallel Computers: Object-Oriented, Functional, Logic*. Wiley, 1990.

[Vaa86] Frits W. Vaandrager. Process algebra semantics for POOL. Report CS-R8629, Centre for Mathematics and Computer Science, Amsterdam, the Netherlands, August 1986.

Causal Models for Rational Algebraic Processes

Amar Bouali
ENSMP-CMA Sophia-Antipolis
FRANCE
amar@cma.cma.fr

Robert de Simone
I.N.R.I.A. Sophia-Antipolis
FRANCE
rs@cma.cma.fr

Abstract

We shall call "rational" a process algebra term (in CCS, Meije, TCSP, ACP, Lotos, etc...) when it is composed in a two-layered fashion, with a lower level at which "dynamic operators" construct individual sequential components, and an upper level at which "static" operators provide a network topology setting the components in parallel and figuring proper connections for communication. It is well-known that this class of processes correspond to finite automata in the classical interleaving semantics, and therefore lend themselves to automatic verification. A number of tools have been implemented to this end.

Recently questions have been asked -and hopes have been raised- about the possibility of performing *some* verification activities without explicitly build the underlying automaton. Indeed several intermediate description formalisms exist, which are now well studied on the theoretical side, and through which the translation can be divided into progressive steps. These are:

Synchronised Vectors of Automata introduced by Arnold and Nivat (a special case is Zielonka's Asynchronous Automata). At this stage the sequential automata components are provided in a given order, and (labelled) *global actions* are provided in terms of combinations of local actions (or inactions) at the respective local components. These global actions are the *Synchronisation Vectors*, deduced from the algebraic syntax of the algebraic network level, altogether with the interface action sorts of the local automata.

1-safe Petri Nets in which *global events* are derived as these combinations of local transitions that meet the requirements of synchronisation vectors. Places are the disjoint union of the components local states, and pre- or post-conditions gather the outgoing or incoming states of all transitions sharing in such an event respectively. Of course a global event comprises exactly one transition for each local automaton whose activity is required by the corresponding synchronisation vector, and this transition label has to agree with the proper row in the vector.

Causal Automata introduced by Gunawardena as an extension of Events Structures, and in particular Winskel's **Stable Event Structures** provide a direct causality enabling relation in between such global events, and therefore lay a bit on the side of this trajectory, as long as automata are aimed at.

Unfortunately, a closer analysis allows to realize that surprisingly little can be said in general in verification at any of these levels. In particular we faced the (early) problem of deciding, out of these possible global events, which could be really performed. Apart from somehow trivial cases, notably the non-recursive case of finite tree components, this problem can only easily be solved by computing the underlying *state space*. Many other subsequent problems actually also seemed to include computation of this state space (or *reachability graph*) as a preliminary.

These considerations triggered us to try and adapt procedures for computing symbolically the state space (which is still less space-consuming as the full automaton, with the transitions). This is done through the techniques of *Binary Decision Diagrams*, which have been recently introduced to cover at a low cost such constructions of parallel synchronised systems. The construction is largely based on a state transition relation drawned exactly from the global events described above. The talk shall expand on the key points of interest in this realisation.

Another interest of the symbolic description is that it allows to compute the classical bisimulations (strong, weak or branching) and provide elegant representation of equivalence classes of local states vectors. These types of data are of value in "practical" verification, as they are typical information needed to allow bridges in between various tools, so that different analysis techniques could be performed on the same algebraic term specification.

Last part of the talk is devoted to a second problem, refining this of finding out which events are performable. We now try to derive **under which causes** (sets of events) a given event may **actually** be performed. So we are striving towards a more faithful causality relation as the one syntactically deduced from the term shape, without concern for accessibility of the proper circumstances. This second problem reflects closely the first, uplifting the computations from state vector sets to transition vector sets (or more accurately: events local projection sets).

Action and State-based Logics for Process Algebras

Rocco De Nicola
Scienze dell'Informazione
Università "La Sapienza", Roma
Via Salaria 113, 00198 Roma -- ITALY

ABSTRACT

Process algebras are generally recognized as a convenient tool for describing concurrent systems at different levels of abstraction. They rely on a small set of basic operators which correspond to primitive notions on concurrent systems and on one or more notions of behavioural equivalence or preorder. The operators are used to build complex systems from more elementary ones. The behavioural equivalences are used to study the relationships between different descriptions of the same system at different levels of abstractions and thus to perform part of the analysis.

Specifications by means of process algebras have a major disadvantage: they tend, even at the most abstract level, to be too concrete; they are, anyway, descriptions of system behaviours even when it is assumed that some of the actual actions are invisible. Logic is a good candidate to provide more abstract specifications because it permits describing systems properties rather than systems behaviours. Indeed, different types of temporal and modal logics have been proposed for the abstract specification of concurrent systems; in particular, modal and temporal logics have been recognized as suitable for specifying system properties due to their ability to deal with the notions of *necessity, possibility, eventuality*, etc.. Logics are often equipped with model checkers to prove satisfiability of formulae and thus system properties: a system, usually a finite state system, is considered as a potential model for the formula expressing the desired property.

Thus, the behavioural and logical approaches to system specification and verification can be seen as complementary; the first is more fruitfully used to specify abstract properties while the second permits describing more naturally behavioural and structural properties of systems. It would be of great importance to have a uniform setting for reasoning with the tools made available by both methods. Unfortunately, up to now the most successful representatives of the two approaches have been based on different semantic

Note: The research has been partially supported by Esprit Basic Research Action Program, Project 3011 CEDISYS and by CNR Progetto Finalizzato Sistemi Informatici e Calcolo Parallelo, project LAMBRUSCO.

models which take a different standpoint for looking at specifications. State changes and state properties are the base for interpreting logical specifications. Actions causing state changes are the key for interpreting systems behaviours described via process algebras. The semantic model used in the two cases are Kripke Structures and Labelled Transition Systems, respectively. In the first kind of structures, states are labelled to describe how they are modified by the transitions, while in the second, transitions are labelled to describe the actions which cause state changes.

In spite of their similarity, Kripke Structures and Labelled Transition Systems have mostly been considered as alternative to each other and there are strong advocates standing on each side. Recently with Vaandrager, we have shown that one of the behavioural equivalence for Transition Systems, namely branching bisimulation, coincides with the equivalence induced by a well known logic interpreted over Kripke Structures, namely CTL* (to say the full story CTL* without the next operator) [1]. This result throws some light on the relationships between the world of modal logic and that process algebras and permits further development. For example, we defined a new logic for process algebras which is very similar to the state based logics CTL* but is based on actions and interpreted over Labelled Transition Systems [2]. We called it ACTL* since we see it as the natural analogue of CTL* in a setting where transitions are labelled. The new logics contains relativized modalities (e.g. $X_a\varphi$ - to be read "the next transition is labelled with an action a and the subsequent path satisfies φ"-) as demanded by the interpretation model. Together with the new logic, two transformation functions from KS's to LTS's and viceversa were introduced which preserve essential properties of systems. In correspondence of the two transformation functions, there are two mappings between the logics, one from CTL* to ACTL* and the other in the opposite direction, which, in combination with two transformation functions on the models, preserve truth. More specifically, we have that, if $\mathcal{A}$ is an LTS, $\mathcal{K}$ is a KS , $\mathfrak{ks}$ and $\mathfrak{lts}$ are the transformation functions, and the two $\models$'s are the satisfaction relations, then:

- $\mathcal{A}, \rho \models \varphi$ iff $\mathfrak{ks}(\mathcal{A}), \mathfrak{ks}(\rho) \models \mathfrak{ks}(\varphi)$

and

- $\mathcal{K}, \rho \models \varphi$ iff $\mathfrak{lts}(\mathcal{K}), \mathfrak{lts}(\rho) \models \mathfrak{lts}(\varphi)$.

Like for CTL*, a branching time subset of ACTL* has been introduced and called ACTL. It is more expressive than Hennessy Milner Logic and is sufficiently expressive to describe safety and liveness properties. An adaptation of the translation functions permits introducing a linear translation function from ACTL to CTL and thus using existing model checkers for CTL also to check validity of ACTL formulae. Indeed, the translations functions from ACTL to CTL formulae and from Labelled Transition Systems to Kripke Structures are also proved to preserve the truth of the formulae, thus the verification of an ACTL formula on a given system is correctly reduced to the corresponding verification of a CTL formula on a Kripke Structure. Both the translation functions needed to perfom model checking for ACTL via CTL are linear; this, coupled with the linear algorithm used by the EMC tool, guarantees linear model checking.

The possibility of moving from one basic model to the other permits easily building a verification environment that permits both to verify equivalences of systems described by means of a process algebra and to verify properties of such systems expressed in ACTL [3]. The environment consists of two existing tools, AUTO and EMC model checker, and of two modules performing the necessary translations. AUTO builds the labelled transition systems corresponding to process algebra terms and permits minimizing and checking equivalences of transition systems. The model translator transforms the transition systems built by AUTO into Kripke structures. The latter are used as models to verify, via EMC model checker, satisfiability of ACTL formulae which have been translated into CTL by the logic translator.

The architecture of our environment is summarized by the picture below:

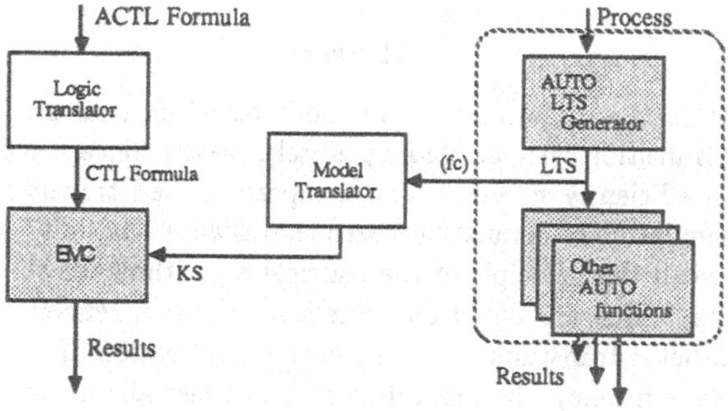

During the talk both the action based version of CTL and the verification environment will be discussed. The presentation, like this extended abstract, will be essentially based on [2] and on [3].

Acknowledgements

I would like to thank Frits Vaandrager, Sandro Fantechi, Stefania Gnesi and Gioia Ristori for joint work and discussions on the topics of the paper.

References

[1] De Nicola,R. and Vaandrager,F.W.: Three Logics for Branching Bisimulations (Extended Abstract) in *LICS '90*, Philadelphia, USA, June 1990, IEEE Computer Society Press, Los Alamitos, CA, 1990, pp. 118-129. Full paper appeared as CWI Report CS-R9012, 1990.

[2] De Nicola,R. and Vaandrager,F.W.: Action versus State based Logics for Transition Systems. *In Proceedings Ecole de Printemps on Semantics of Concurrency*, April 1990, (I. Guessarian ed.), Lecture Notes in Computer Science 469, 1990, pp. 407-419.

[3] De Nicola,R., Fantechi,A., Gnesi,S. and Ristori,G.: An action-based framework for verifying logical and behavioural properties of concurrent systems. In Proc. of 3rd Workshop on *Computer Aided Verification*, Lecture Notes in Computer Science, Springer Verlag, 1991, to appear.

A Tool Set for deciding Behavioral Equivalences *

Jean-Claude Fernandez †

Laurent Mounier†

Abstract

This paper deals with verification methods based on equivalence relations between labeled transition systems. More precisely, we are concerned by two practical needs: how to efficiently minimize and compare labeled transition systems with respect to bisimulation or simulation-based equivalence relations.

First, we recall the principle of the classical algorithms for the existing equivalence relations, which are based on successive partition refinements of the state space of the labeled transition systems under consideration. However, in spite of their theoretical efficiency, the main drawback of these algorithms is that they require to generate and to store in memory the whole labeled transition systems to be compared or minimized. Therefore, the size of the systems which can be handled in practice remains limited. We propose here another approach, allowing to combine the generation and the verification phases, which is based on two algorithms respectively devoted to the comparison (*"on the fly" comparison*) and the minimization (*minimal model generation*) of labeled transition systems. Then, we present the results obtained when implementing some of these algorithms within the tool ALDÉBARAN.

1 Introduction

This paper deals with some methodological considerations on tools associated with verification methods of distributed systems. More precisely, we aim to relate our experiments with the implementation within the tool ALDÉBARAN of various decision procedures for behavioral equivalence relations.

By *verification*, we mean the comparison of a *system description*, i.e., a program, noted $\mathcal{D}$, with its *specifications*, noted $\mathcal{S}$, namely the description of its expected properties. A program semantics is defined by a congruence on a class of program models. Examples of classes of program models are Labeled Transition Systems (LTS for short), event structures, Petri nets, etc ... In this paper, we are concerned by LTS and equivalence or preorder relations between LTS. According to the formalism used for the specifications, two main verification approaches can be distinguished:

*This work was partially supported by ESPRIT Basic Research Action "SPEC" and french project research C^3

†LGI-IMAG, IMAG Campus, BP 53X, 38041 GRENOBLE cedex, FRANCE; e-mail: {fernand, mounier}@imag.imag.fr

Behavioral specifications : they characterize the behavior of the system, observed from a certain abstraction level. Such specifications can be also expressed in terms of LTS. In this case, the verification consists in comparing the two LTS $\mathcal{D}$ and $\mathcal{S}$ with respect to a given equivalence or preorder relation. Thus, any decision procedure for these relations defines a verification method.

Logical specifications : they characterize the *global properties* of the system, such as deadlock freedom, mutual exclusion, or fairness. *Temporal logics* are suitable formalisms, since they allow to describe the whole system evolution. In this case, a formula of $\mathcal{S}$ is interpreted as a set of *computations* on $\mathcal{D}$. For example, in linear time semantics a computation is a maximal sequence, whereas in branching times semantics a computation is a tree. Then, verification consists in checking that all the computations of $\mathcal{D}$ belong to $\mathcal{S}$.

These approaches are complementary: it turns out in practice that some of the expected properties of a distributed system are easier to express using a logical formalism, and the others by giving an abstraction of the expected behavior. Moreover, a logic can *characterize* a behavioral relation: two systems are related if and only if they satisfy the same set of logical formulas. As a consequence, a practical verification method associated with such a logic consists in minimizing first the LTS $\mathcal{D}$ with respect to the corresponding behavioral relation, and then checking that all the computations of this reduced LTS belong to $\mathcal{S}$. For example, branching bisimulation is characterized by a fragment of CTL^* [NV90], and safety equivalence is characterized by a fragment of the μ-calculus [BFG*91].

The principle of the usual LTS-based verification methods is the following: first generate a LTS from the program description, and then apply the decision procedure associated with the considered specification formalism. Many automated verification tools, [dSV89, GV90, CPS90, Fer90] for behavioral specifications and [RRSV87, CES86] for logical specifications, are based on this design. However, the main drawback of this method is that the whole LTS have to be stored in memory, and therefore the size of the graphs which can be compared or minimized is limited. For ALDÉBARAN, running on a workstation, the maximal size of LTS which can be treated is of the order of one million of states. Consequently, an attractive solution would be to combine the generation and verification phases: the verification is performed during the generation, without keeping in memory the sets of states and transitions of the whole LTS ("on the fly" verification). Several algorithms have been proposed to implement such a verification method for temporal logics [JJ89, BFH90a, CVWY90].

Applying the "on the fly" approach to the verification of behavioral specification seems promising. For this purpose, we study currently the implementation of suitable algorithms for bisimulation-based equivalence and preorder relations within ALDÉBARAN, in association with the LOTOS compiler CÆSAR [GS90]. More precisely, given a LOTOS program we consider its abstract representation, which can be either a Petri net or a set of communicating automata. ¿From this representation, we intend to cover the two practical needs:

"on the fly" LTS comparison: the algorithm consists in performing the comparison during a depth-first traversal of a product of the two transitions functions (the one of the abstract model and the one of the specification LTS). The definition of this product is parametrized by the behavioral relation under consideration. This method has been successfully applyed for several relations, like strong bisimulation, strong simulation, delay bisimulation, branching bisimulation (when the specification is τ-free, i.e., without τ-action), safety equivalence and safety preorder.

minimal LTS generation: the principle is to refine a partition of the reachable state space of the abstract representation of the program, and to compute its transition relation at the same time. This method is based on symbolic computations, which impose some restrictions on the types of the values used in the LOTOS program in order to obtain an efficient implementation.

This paper is organized as follows: first we give the definitions used in the following sections. In section 3, we recall some definitions of equivalence and preorder relations. In section 4, we survey the usual methods for the minimization and comparison of LTS. In section 5, we present the principle of the "on the fly" verification methods, and we give in section 6 the state of the experiments currently realized in ALDÉBARAN.

2 Equivalences Relations

Equivalence relations for distributed systems can be defined in several ways, according to their semantics and the description formalism upon which they are based. For example, trace equivalence has been defined for automata, readiness and failures semantics for CSP [BHR84], observation bisimulation [Mil80], branching bisimulation [GW89] and strong bisimulation [Par81] for process algebra such as CCS or ACP. However, as these description formalisms can be translated in terms of LTS, all these relations can also be expressed as equivalence relations between LTS.

We will focus here on some bisimulation or simulation based equivalences defined on LTS which, when ordered by the relation "finer than", are positioned between *bisimulation equivalence* and *trace equivalence*. We first give some notations, and then we recall the definitions of the relations that we will consider in the following. Finally, we propose a practical characterization of the "non-bisimilarity" between two LTS.

2.1 Labeled Transition Systems

Let *States* be a set of states, A a set of names (of actions), τ a particular name not in A, which represents an internal or hidden action and $A_\tau = A \cup \{\tau\}$. For a set X, X^* will represent the set of finite sequences on X.

In the following, we consider a LTS $S = (Q, A_\tau, \{\xrightarrow{a}\}_{a \in A_\tau}, q_{\text{init}})$ where: Q is the subset of *States*, $\longrightarrow \subseteq Q \times A_\tau \times Q$ is a labeled transition relation, and q_{init} is the initial state.

We will also consider the usual pre- and post-conditions functions from 2^Q to 2^Q, where X (resp. B) is a subset of Q (resp A_τ):

$$\begin{aligned} pre_a(X) &= \{q \in Q \mid \exists q' . \, q \xrightarrow{a} q' \wedge q' \in X\} \\ post_a(X) &= \{q \in Q \mid \exists q' . \, q' \xrightarrow{a} q \wedge q' \in X\} \end{aligned}$$

$$pre_B(X) = \bigcup_{a \in B} pre_a(X)$$
$$post_B(X) = \bigcup_{a \in B} post_a(X)$$

$Act(q)$ will denote the set of the actions which can be performed in a state q:

$$Act(q) = \{a \in A \mid \exists q' \in Q \,.\, q \xrightarrow{a} q'\}.$$

Let $\lambda \subseteq A^*$, and let $p, q \in Q$. We write $p \xrightarrow{\lambda} q$ if and only if:

$$\exists u_1 \cdots u_n \in \lambda \wedge \exists q_1, \cdots, q_{n-1} \in Q \wedge p \xrightarrow{u_1} q_1 \xrightarrow{u_2} q_2 \cdots q_i \xrightarrow{u_{i+1}} q_{i+1} \cdots q_{n-1} \xrightarrow{u_n} q.$$

Let Λ be a family of disjoint languages on A_τ.

$$Act_\Lambda(q) = \{\lambda \in \Lambda \mid \exists q' \,.\, q \xrightarrow{\lambda} q'\}.$$

The set of the finite execution sequences from a state q of Q (noted $Ex(q)$) is defined as follows:

$$Ex(q) = \{\sigma \in Q^* \,.\, \sigma(0) = q \wedge \forall i \,.\, 0 \leq i < |\sigma| - 1,\ \exists a_i \in A \,.\, \sigma(i) \xrightarrow{a_i} \sigma(i+1)\}.$$

In the following, for a LTS S, the term *execution sequences* of S represents the set $Ex(q_{\text{init}})$. Furthermore, an execution sequence is said *elementary* if and only if all its states are distinct. The subset of $Ex(q)$ containing the elementary execution sequences of a state q will be noted $Ex_e(q)$.

2.2 Bisimulations and Simulations

We recall the definition of the simulation and the bisimulation relations.

Definition 2.1 *(simulation) For each $R \in Q \times Q$, we define:*

$$\mathcal{I}_\Lambda(R) = \{(p_1, p_2) \mid \forall \lambda \in \Lambda \,.\, \forall q_1 \,.\, (p_1 \xrightarrow{\lambda} q_1 \Rightarrow \exists q_2 \,.\, (p_2 \xrightarrow{\lambda} q_2 \wedge (q_1, q_2) \in R))\}$$

The simulation preorder $\sqsubseteq^\Lambda$ for the language Λ is defined as the greatest fixed-point of $\mathcal{I}^\Lambda$ and the simulation equivalence is $\approx^\Lambda = \sqsubseteq^\Lambda \cap (\sqsubseteq^\Lambda)^{-1}$.

Definition 2.2 *(bisimulation) For each $R \in Q \times Q$, we define:*

$$\begin{aligned} \mathcal{B}_\Lambda(R) = \{(p_1, p_2) \mid \forall \lambda \in \Lambda \,.\, & \forall q_1 \,.\, (p_1 \xrightarrow{\lambda} q_1 \Rightarrow \exists q_2 \,.\, (p_2 \xrightarrow{\lambda} q_2 \wedge (q_1, q_2) \in R)) \\ & \forall q_2 \,.\, (p_2 \xrightarrow{\lambda} q_2 \Rightarrow \exists q_1 \,.\, (p_1 \xrightarrow{\lambda} q_1 \wedge (q_1, q_2) \in R))\} \end{aligned}$$

The bisimulation equivalence $\sim^\Lambda$ for the language Λ is defined as the greatest fixed-point of $\mathcal{B}^\Lambda$.

Definition 2.3 *(branching bisimulation) For each $R \in Q \times Q$, we define:*

$$\begin{aligned} \mathcal{B}^{br}_\Lambda = \{(p_1, p_2) \mid \forall \lambda \in \Lambda \,.\, & \\ & \forall q_1 \,.\, (p_1 \xrightarrow{\lambda} q_1 \Rightarrow (\lambda = \tau \wedge (q_1, p_2) \in R) \vee \\ & \quad (\exists q_2 q_2' \,.\, (p_2 \xrightarrow{\tau^*} q_2' \wedge q_2' \xrightarrow{\lambda} q_2 \wedge (p_1, q_2') \in R \wedge (q_1, q_2) \in R))) \\ & \forall q_2 \,.\, (p_2 \xrightarrow{\lambda} q_2 \Rightarrow (\lambda = \tau \wedge (p_1, q_2) \in R) \vee \\ & \quad (\exists q_1 q_1' \,.\, (p_1 \xrightarrow{\tau^*} q_1' \wedge q_1' \xrightarrow{\lambda} q_1 \wedge (q_1', p_2) \in R \wedge (q_1, q_2) \in R)))\} \end{aligned}$$

The branching bisimulation equivalence $\sim_{br}^{\Lambda}$ for the language Λ is defined as the greatest fixed-point of $\mathcal{B}^{\Lambda}$.

¿From these general definitions, several simulation and bisimulation relations can be defined. The choice of a class Λ corresponds to the choice of an *abstraction criterion* on the actions. The *strong simulation* and the *strong bisimulation* [Par81] are defined by $\Lambda = \{\{a\} \mid a \in A\}$, the *w bisimulation* [FM91] is the bisimulation equivalence defined by $\Lambda = \{\tau^*a \mid a \in A\}$, the *safety preorder* [BFG*91] is the simulation preorder defined by $\Lambda = \{\tau^*a \mid a \in A\}$ and the *safety equivalence* is the simulation equivalence where $\Lambda = \{\tau^*a \mid a \in A\}$. Observation equivalence [Mil80] is the bisimulation equivalence defined by $\Lambda = \tau^* \cup \{\tau^*a\tau^* \mid a \in A\}$. Delay bisimulation [NMV90] is the bisimulation equivalence defined by $\Lambda = \tau^* \cup \{\tau^*a \mid a \in A\}$. Branching bisimulation [GW89] is the branching bisimulation where $\Lambda = \{\{a\} \mid a \in A\}$.

Remark Note that when we consider the languages $\Lambda_1 = \{\tau^*a \mid a \in A\}$ or $\Lambda_2 = \{\tau^*a\tau^*a \mid a \in A\}$ or $\Lambda_3 = \Lambda_1 \cup \tau^*$ or $\Lambda_4 = \Lambda_2 \cup \tau^*$, we obtain the same preorder against bisimulations. □

Each equivalence relation R^{Λ} defined on states can be extended to an equivalence relation comparing LTS in the following manner: let $S_i = (Q_i, A_\tau, \{\xrightarrow{a}\}_{a\in A_\tau}, q^i_{\text{init}})$, for $i = 1,2$ be two LTS such that $Q_1 \cap Q_2 = \emptyset$ (if it is not the case, this condition can be easily obtained by renaming). Then we define $S_1\ R^{\Lambda}\ S_2$ if and only if $(q^1_{\text{init}}, q^2_{\text{init}}) \in R^{\Lambda}$ and $S_1\ \not R^{\Lambda}\ S_2$ if and only if $(q^1_{\text{init}}, q^2_{\text{init}}) \notin R^{\Lambda}$.

2.3 Other Equivalences

In this section, we consider readiness semantics, failure semantics and other semantics of CSP. We do not present these equivalences in detail.

Definition 2.4 Failure semantics:
*$(\sigma, X) \in A^* \times 2^{A_\tau}$ is a failure pair for a LTS $(Q, A_\tau, \{\xrightarrow{a}\}_{a\in A_\tau}, q_{\text{init}})$ if there is $q \in Q$ such that $q_{\text{init}} \xrightarrow{\sigma} q$ and $X \cap Act(q) = \emptyset$. Let $F(q)$ denote the set of failure pairs of q.
Two LTS $S_i = (Q_i, A_\tau, \{\xrightarrow{a}\}_{a\in A_\tau}, q^i_{\text{init}})$, for $i = 1,2$ are failure equivalent if $F(q^1_{\text{init}}) = F(q^2_{\text{init}})$.*

Definition 2.5 Readiness semantics:
*$(\sigma, X) \in A^* \times 2^{A_\tau}$ is a ready pair for a LTS $(Q, A_\tau, \{\xrightarrow{a}\}_{a\in A_\tau}, q_{\text{init}})$ if there is $q \in Q$ such that $q_{\text{init}} \xrightarrow{\sigma} q$ and $X = Act(q)$. Let $R(q)$ denote the set of ready pairs of q.
Two LTS $S_i = (Q_i, A_\tau, \{\xrightarrow{a}\}_{a\in A_\tau}, q^i_{\text{init}})$, for $i = 1,2$ are ready equivalent if $F(q^1_{\text{init}}) = F(q^2_{\text{init}})$.*

Other variants of these equivalences can be found in [Gla90], in which states of transitions systems can be labeled by subset of actions.

2.4 Expressing non bisimilarity

Several formalisms have been proposed in order to express the "non bisimilarity" of two labeled transition systems (for example Hennessy-Milner Logic in [Cle90]). We present here a more intuitive solution, suitable either for bisimulation or simulation relations (both denoted by R^{Π}).

Let $S_i = (Q_i, A_\tau, \{\xrightarrow{\alpha}\}_{\alpha \in A_\tau}, q^i_{\text{init}})$, for $i = 1, 2$, be two LTS. Whenever the two labeled transition systems S_1 and S_2 are not related, we define an *explanation sequence* as an execution sequence σ of a *synchronous product* $S = S_1 \times_{R^{\Pi}} S_2$ (see section 4 for a precise definition of this product) such that:

- All the states (p_i, q_i) belonging to σ (where p_i is a state of S_1 and q_i is a state of S_2) are not comparable against R^{Π}.
- σ is terminated by a state which is not in R^{Π}_1 (i.e, from which it clearly appears that S_1 and S_2 are not related)

Definition 2.6 *An explanation sequence of $S_1 \not R^{\Pi} S_2$ is an execution sequence σ such that:*

- $\sigma = \{(q_{01}, q_{02}) = (p_1, q_1), (p_2, q_2), \ldots, (p_k, q_k)\}$
- $\forall i \,.\, 0 \leq i \leq k,\ (p_i, q_i) \notin R^{\Pi}_{k-i+1}$.
- $(p_k, q_k) \notin R^{\Pi}_1$

This definition is motivated by the following propositions, which allow to express that S_1 and S_2 are not comparable against R^{Π} in terms of the execution sequences of $S_1 \times_{R^{\Pi}} S_2$.

Proposition 2.1 $(q^1_{\text{init}}, q^2_{\text{init}}) \notin R^{\Pi}$ *if and only if it exists an elementary execution sequence σ of S ($\sigma \in Ex_e(q_{01}, q_{02})$) such that:*

- $\sigma = \{(q^1_{\text{init}}, q^2_{\text{init}}) = (p_0, q_0), (p_1, q_1), \ldots (p_k, q_k)\}$.
- $\forall i \,.\, 0 \leq i \leq k,\ (p_i, q_i) \notin R^{\Pi}_{k-i+1}$.

The proof of this proposition is based on the following lemma:

Lemma 2.1 *Let $S = (Q, A, T, q_0)$ be a labeled transition system. Then we have,*
$\forall k \geq 1, \forall p, q \in Q,\ \ (p, q) \notin R^{\Pi}_{k+1} \wedge (p, q) \in R^{\Pi}_k \Rightarrow$

$$\exists \lambda \in \Pi \,.\, \exists p' \,.\, \exists q' \,.\, p \xrightarrow{\lambda}_T p' \wedge q \xrightarrow{\lambda}_T q' \wedge (p', q') \notin R^{\Pi}_k \wedge (p', q') \in R^{\Pi}_{k-1}.$$

If one of the two labeled transition systems is deterministic, proposition 2.1 can be improved. In this case, the converse of lemma 2.1 holds: $(q_1, q_2) \in R^{\Pi}_k$ if and only if all the successors (q'_1, q'_2) of (q_1, q_2) verify $(q_1, q_2) \in R^{\Pi}_{k-1}$ and $(q_1, q_2) \in R^{\Pi}_1$.

Lemma 2.2 *Let us suppose that S_1 or S_2 is deterministic (S_1 if the $(R^{\Pi}_k)_{k \geq 0}$ are simulations).*
$\forall k \geq 1, \forall p, q \in Q,$

$$\exists \lambda \in \Pi \,.\, \exists p' \,.\, \exists q' \,.\, p \xrightarrow{\lambda}_T p' \wedge q \xrightarrow{\lambda}_T q' \wedge (p', q') \notin R^{\Pi}_k \Rightarrow (p, q) \notin R^{\Pi}_{k+1}$$

¿From this lemma, we can deduce proposition 2.2:

Proposition 2.2 *Let us suppose that S_1 or S_2 is deterministic (S_1 if the $(R^{\Pi}_k)_{k \geq 0}$ are simulations). Then:*
$S_1 \not R^{\Pi} S_2 \Leftrightarrow \exists \sigma \,.\, \sigma = \{(q^1_{\text{init}}, q^2_{\text{init}}) = (p_0, q_0), (p_1, q_1), \ldots (p_k, q_k)\} \wedge (p_k, q_k) \notin R^{\Pi}_1$.

All the proof can be found in [FM91].

3 Classical Verification Methods

The usual comparison and minimization methods of LTS with respect to an equivalence relation are based on the structure of the LTS and are independent from the generation techniques.

minimization: For a given bisimulation-based equivalence relation, a *normal-form* of a LTS S (i.e, the smallest LTS in number of states and transitions equivalent to S) can be obtained by applying the two following steps:

1. Compute a pre-normal form S' of S by transforming the transition relation of S. This step depends on the equivalence relation under consideration. Examples of transformations are various transitive closure computations of the τ-transition relation (τ*-saturation phase*), or determinization .
2. Compute the normal-form of S' with respect to strong bisimulation. This is obtained by solving the *RCP* problem (see 3.2) on the states of S' using a partition refinement algorithm. The obtained LTS is then the normal-form of S.

For the particular case of branching bisimulation, the first step can be avoided since a normal-form can be straightly obtained by solving the *GRCP* problem (see 3.3) on S.

comparison: Two LTS can be compared either by checking if their normal-form are identical or by computing the normal-form or their union and checking if the initial states of the original LTS belong or not to the same equivalence class.

In this section, we describe the classical algorithms for the computation of normal-forms with respect to the different equivalence relations presented in the previous section.

3.1 Partitions

Let $S = (Q, A_\tau, \{\xrightarrow{a}\}_{a \in A_\tau}, q_{init})$. We consider partitions of Q instead of equivalence relations on Q: let ρ be a partition (a set of pairwise disjoint non-empty subsets X_i such that $\bigcup_i X_i = Q$), then the induced equivalence is $p \sim_\rho q$ if and only if $\exists X_i \in \rho$ such that $p \in X_i \wedge q \in X_i$.

Lattices Let $\mathcal{P}$ be the set of partitions of Q. We consider the refinement relation, noted $\sqsubseteq$ over $\mathcal{P}$:

$$\rho \sqsubseteq \rho' \text{ if and only if } \forall X \in \rho \,.\, \exists X' \in \rho' \,.\, X \subseteq X'.$$

With this order, $\mathcal{P}$ is a complete lattice, with the greatest lower bound operator $\sqcap$ defined by:

$$\bigsqcap_i \rho_i = \{T \neq \emptyset \mid T = \bigcap_i X_i \text{ and } X_i \in \rho_i\}$$

with least upper bound,

$$\bigsqcup_i \rho_i = \bigsqcap_{\forall i, \rho_i \sqsubseteq \rho} \rho$$

and with the infimum $\{\{q\} \mid q \in Q\}$ and the supremum $\{Q\}$. We denote by $[q]_\rho$ the class of the partition ρ containing the state q. Let $pre_{a,\rho}$ and $post_{a,\rho}$ denote the pre and post-conditions functions corresponding to a partition ρ:

$$\begin{aligned} pre_{a,\rho}(X) &= \{[q]_\rho \mid q \in pre_a(X)\} \\ post_{a,\rho}(X) &= \{[q]_\rho \mid q \in post_a(X)\} \end{aligned}$$

We also consider the lattices 2^Q or 2^{2^Q}.

Fixed-points Let F be an increasing total function, either from 2^Q to 2^Q or from 2^{2^Q} to 2^{2^Q} and let G be an increasing total function from $\mathcal{P}$ to $\mathcal{P}$. We denote by

- $\mu\pi.F(\pi)$ the least fixed-point of F with respect to the ordering $\subseteq$
- $\nu\pi.G(\pi)$ the greatest fixed-point of G with respect to the ordering $\sqsubseteq$

3.2 Strong Bisimulation

The computation of the normal-form of a LTS with respect to strong bisimulation can be expressed in terms of a partition refinement problem, known as the *Relational Coarsest Partition (RCP) problem*:

The *RCP* problem: it consists in *finding the coarsest stable refinement of an initial partition* ρ_{init} *of* Q. (A partition is stable if and only if it is an equivalence relation which is a bisimulation). The solution of this problem corresponds to the equivalence classes of Q for the strong bisimulation relation.

Kanellakis and Smolka studied first the connection between the *RCP* problem and the minimization of LTS up to strong bisimulation [KS83]. Then, an efficient algorithm was proposed by Paige and Tarjan [PT87] and implemented within the tool ALDÉBARAN [Fer90]. Its time and space complexities are respectively $O(m \log(n))$ and $O(m+n)$, where n and m are the number of states and transitions of S.

Starting with an initial partition of the state space, this algorithm proceeds by refining the current partition ρ until it becomes stable, according to the following definitions:

Splitting and refining: These functions are defined as follows:

$$\begin{aligned} split(X,Y) &= \bigsqcap_{a \in A_\tau} \{X \cap pre_a(Y), X \setminus pre_a(Y)\} \\ Ref(\rho,Y) &= \bigsqcap_{X \in \rho} split(X,Y) \\ Ref(\rho,\rho') &= \bigcup_{Y \in \rho'} Ref(\rho,Y) \end{aligned}$$

Stability: An subset X of Q is said to be stable with respect to ρ if and only if $X = Ref(\rho, X)$. A partition is stable if it is stable with respect to its elements.

The solution of the *RCP* problem consists in computing the greatest fixed-point

$$\nu\rho \,.\, \rho_{\text{init}} \sqcap Ref(\rho,\rho).$$

An algorithm in $O(mn)$ time can easily be derived. To improve this complexity, the Paige and Tarjan's idea is to keep track how blocks of the current partition are split into subblocks at each refinement step, in order to always process the "smaller half" subblock.

3.3 Branching Bisimulation

In [GV90], Groote and Vaandrager present a variant of the *RCP* problem: the *Generalized Relational Coarsest Partition with Stuttering (GRCP) problem*, which allow to compute the normal of a LTS with respect to branching bisimulation and stuttering equivalence. They also give an efficient algorithm, in $O(n(n+m))$ time and $O(m+n)$ space.

The *GRCP* problem: The *GRCP* problem can be stated in the same terms than the *RCP* problem. The difference lies in the notion of splitting.

As the Paige and Tarjan's one, the principle of the algorithm given in [GV90] is to refine a partition of the state space of the LTS until it becomes stable, according to the following splitting functions:

$$\begin{aligned}
\mathcal{F}_a(X,Y) &= \mu Z.(X \cap pre_\tau(Z) \cup X \cap pre_a(Y)) \\
split(X,Y) &= \bigsqcap_{a \in A_\tau} \{\mathcal{F}_a(X,Y), X \setminus \mathcal{F}_a(X,Y)\} \text{ if } X \neq Y \\
split(X,X) &= \bigsqcap_{a \in A} \{\mathcal{F}_a(X,X), X \setminus \mathcal{F}_a(X,X)\}
\end{aligned}$$

As for the *RCP* problem, the solution of the *GRCP* problem consists in computing the greatest fixed-point

$$\nu\rho \,.\, \rho_{\text{init}} \sqcap Ref(\rho,\rho).$$

Remark The algorithm described in [GV90] requires to suppress first the τ-cycles by finding the strongly connected components of the τ-relation. □

3.4 Observation Equivalence

The algorithm for computing the normal-form of a LTS S with respect to observation equivalence is the following:

1. First, compute the transitive closure of the τ-relation of S:
   let S' be the LTS $(Q, A_\tau, \{\xrightarrow{a}'\}_{a\in A_\tau}, q_{init})$ where $q \xrightarrow{a}' q'$ if and only if $q \xrightarrow{\tau^* a \tau^*} q'$.
2. Then solve the *RCP* problem for S' with initial partition $\rho_{\text{init}} = \{Q\}$.

This algorithm can be implemented in $O(n^3)$ time and $O(m+n^2)$ space.

3.5 Safety equivalence

Safety equivalence is a simulation-based equivalence which preserves *Safety properties* [BFG*91]. Each equivalence class may be characterized by a formula of a fragment of a μ-calculus and conversely. The algorithm for computing the normal-form of a LTS S with respect to safety equivalences is the following:

1. Compute the pre-normal form $S' = (Q', A_\tau, \{\xrightarrow{a}\}'_{a\in A_\tau}, q_{\text{init}})$ where:

- $Q' = \{c(q) \mid q \in Q \,.\, c(q) = \{q' \mid q \xrightarrow{\tau^*} q'\}\}$,

- $c(p) \xrightarrow{a}' c(q)$ if and only if $p \xrightarrow{\tau^* a} q \wedge \forall q' p \xrightarrow{\tau^* a} q' \Rightarrow q \not\sqsubseteq q'$.

2. Solve the *RCP* problem for S' with initial partition $\rho_{\text{init}} = \{Q'\}$.

In practice, the sets $c(q)$ are computed by performing a depth-first search on the LTS S. Then the greatest simulation is computed on Q' and the *redundant transitions* $c(p) \xrightarrow{a}' c(q')$ such that $c(p) \xrightarrow{a}' c(q)$ and $c(q') \sqsubseteq c(q)$ are removed.

3.6 w bisimulation

This bisimulation-based relation is stronger than safety equivalence. The normal-form of a LTS with respect to this relation can be obtained in the two following way:

- either, compute the states $c(q)$, as in the safety equivalence, and the relation $c(p) \xrightarrow{a}' c(q)$ if $p \xrightarrow{\tau^* a} q$, and then solve the *RCP* problem with initial partition $\rho_{\text{init}} = \{Q\}$,

- or solve the *RCP* problem for the language $\Lambda = \{\tau^* a \mid a \in A\}$ with initial partition $\rho_{\text{init}} = \{Q\}$. The function *split* is then:

$$split(X, Y) = \bigsqcap_{a \in A_\tau} \{X \cap pre_{\tau^* a}(Y), X \setminus pre_{\tau^* a}(Y)\}.$$

The difference between Safety equivalence and w bisimulation only lies in the removal of redundant transitions.

3.7 Readiness and Failure Semantics

The algorithm for computing the normal-form of a LTS with respect to these equivalence proceeds as follows:

- determinization of the LTS and labeling each state by a powerset. Let $S' = (Q', A_\tau, \{\xrightarrow{a}\}'_{a \in A_\tau}, q_{\text{init}})$ the LTS obtained in this way:

  - $\{q_{\text{init}}\} \in Q'$,
  - if $X \in Q'$ then $post_a(X) \in Q'$.
  - $X \xrightarrow{a}' Y$ if and only if $Y = post_a(X)$.

  Let $\mathcal{L} : Q \longrightarrow 2^A$ the labeling function depending of the chosen equivalence relation (Ready, or Failure). Then, the labeling function $\mathcal{L}' : Q' \longrightarrow 2^{2^A}$ for S' is:

$$\mathcal{L}'(X) = \{\mathcal{L}(q) \mid q \in X\}.$$

- Then solve the *RCP* problem for S' with initial partition

$$\rho_{\text{init}} = \{C \mid X, Y \in Q' \,.\, X, Y \in C \text{ if and only if } \mathcal{L}'(X) = \mathcal{L}'(Y)\}.$$

4 The "on the fly" approach

In spite of their theoretical efficiency, the classical verification methods described in the previous section suffers from a practical limitation: they require to generate and to store in main memory the whole LTS of the program to be verified (i.e, its sets of states and transitions). Moreover, apart from branching and strong bisimulation, another serious drawback of these methods is the need for a "preprocessing phase" of the LTS (i.e, the computation of a pre-normal form) which turns out to be very time expensive and to increase the size of the original LTS.

However, most of the equivalence relations presented in section 2 can be dealt with using another approach. In this section, starting from an *abstract representation* of the program to be verified (i.e., a Petri net, a term of a process algebra, or a net of communicating LTS) we describe two aspects of an "on the fly" verification method:

On the fly comparison: We compare the *abstract representation* of the program and its behavioral specification (i.e, a LTS which characterize its expected behavior). Rather than translating the abstract representation into a LTS and comparing it to the specification, we construct a synchronous product between this partially translated LTS and the specification LTS. The comparison is performed during this construction, and we only need to store the states of this product.

minimal LTS generation We consider partitions of the whole state space of the abstract representation of the program (the reachable and unreachable states). For example, if $\mathcal{P}$ is a program with two variables $x_1, x_2 \in \mathbb{N}$, we will consider partitions of $\mathbb{N} \times \mathbb{N}$. Then, starting from the universal partition, we progressively refine the reachable classes of the current partition until stability.

4.1 "On the fly" comparison

In this section, we describe the principle of a decision procedure which allows to check if two LTS S_1 and S_2 are similar or bisimilar without explicitly constructing the two graphs.

In the following, we consider two LTS $S_i = (Q_i, A_\tau, \{\xrightarrow{a}\}_{a \in A_\tau}, q^i_{\text{init}})$, for $i = 1, 2$. We use p_i, q_i, p'_i, q'_i to range over Q_i. R^Π and R^Π_k will denote either simulations or bisimulations ($R^\Pi = \bigcap_{k=0}^{\infty} R^\Pi_k$).

A synchronous product

We define the synchronous product $S_1 \times_{R^\Pi} S_2$ between the two LTS S_1 and S_2 in the following manner:

- a state (q_1, q_2) of $S_1 \times_{R^\Pi} S_2$ can perform a transition labeled by an action λ if and only if the state q_1 (belonging to S_1) and the state q_2 (belonging to S_2) can perform a transition labeled by λ.
- in the case of a simulation, if only the state q_1 can perform a transition labeled by λ, then the product has a transition from (q_1, q_2) to the sink state noted *fail*.

- in the case of a bisimulation, if only one of the two states (q_1 or q_2) can perform a transition labeled by λ, then the product has a transition from (q_1, q_2) to the sink state *fail*.

Definition 4.1 *We define the labeled transition system $S = S_1 \times_{R^{\Pi}} S_2$ by:*
$S = (Q, A, T, (q^1_{\text{init}}, q^2_{\text{init}}))$, with $Q \subseteq (Q_1 \times Q_2) \cup \{fail\}$, $A = (A_1 \cap A_2) \cup \{\phi\}$, and $T \subseteq Q \times A \times Q$, where $\phi \notin (A_1 \cup A_2)$ and $fail \notin (Q_1 \cup Q_2)$.
T and Q are defined as the smallest sets obtained by the applications of the following rules: R0, R1 and R2 in the case of a simulation, R0, R1, R2 and R3 in the case of a bisimulation.

$$(q^1_{\text{init}}, q^2_{\text{init}}) \in Q \qquad [R0]$$

$$\frac{(q_1, q_2) \in Q,\ \mathit{Act}_{\Pi}(q_1) = \mathit{Act}_{\Pi}(q_2),\ q_1 \xrightarrow{\lambda}_{T_1} q_1',\ q_2 \xrightarrow{\lambda}_{T_2} q_2'}{\{(q_1', q_2')\} \in Q, \{(q_1, q_2) \xrightarrow{\lambda}_{T} (q_1', q_2')\} \in T} \qquad [R1]$$

$$\frac{(q_1, q_2) \in Q,\ q_1 \xrightarrow{\lambda}_{T_1} q_1',\ T^2_{\lambda}[q] = \emptyset}{\{fail\} \in Q, \{(q_1, q_2) \xrightarrow{\phi}_{T} fail\} \in T} \qquad [R2]$$

$$\frac{(q_1, q_2) \in Q,\ q_2 \xrightarrow{\lambda}_{T_2} q_2',\ T^1_{\lambda}[q] = \emptyset}{\{fail\} \in Q, \{(q_1, q_2) \xrightarrow{\phi}_{T} fail\} \in T} \qquad [R3\ \text{bisimulation}]$$

Let's notice that $(p_1, p_2) \xrightarrow{\phi}_{T} fail$ if and only if $(p_1, p_2) \notin R_1^{\Pi}$. According to the propositions given in section 2.4, the S_1 and S_2 are not bisimilar if and only if it exists an explanation sequence on $S_1 \times_{R^{\Pi}} S_2$. Similar propositions hold in case of non-similarity (see [FM91]).

Algorithms

We have expressed the bisimulation and the simulation between two labeled transition systems S_1 and S_2 in terms of the existence of a particular execution sequence of their product $S_1 \times_{R^{\Pi}} S_2$. We show that this verification can be realized by performing depth-first searches (DFS for short) on the labeled transition system $S_1 \times_{R^{\Pi}} S_2$. Consequently, the algorithm does not require to previously construct the two LTS: the states of $S_1 \times_{R^{\Pi}} S_2$ are generated during the DFS ("on the fly" verification), but not necessarily all stored. And the most important is that transitions do not have to be stored. Moreover, in the case where S_1 and S_2 are not related, explanation sequences are straightly obtained.

We note n_1 (resp. n_2) the number of states of S_1 (resp. S_2), and n the number of states of $S_1 \times_{R^{\Pi}} S_2$ ($n \leq n_1 \times n_2$). We describe the algorithm considering the two following cases:

Deterministic case: if R^{Π} represents a simulation (resp. a bisimulation) and if S_2 (resp. either S_1 or S_2) is deterministic, then, according to proposition 2.2, it is sufficient to check whether or not the state *fail* belongs to $S_1 \times_{R^{\Pi}} S_2$, which can be easily done by performing a usual DFS of $S_1 \times_{R^{\Pi}} S_2$. The verification is then reduced to a simple reachability problem in this graph. Consequently, if we store all the visited states during the DFS, the time and memory complexities of this decision procedure are $O(n)$. Several memory efficient solutions exist to manage such a DFS ([JJ91]).

General case: in the general case, according to the proposition 2.1, we have to check for the existence of an execution sequence σ of $S_1 \times_{R^\Pi} S_2$ which contains the state *fail* and which is such that for all states (q_1, q_2) of σ, $(q_1, q_2) \notin R_k^\Pi$ for a certain k. According to the definition of R_k^Π, this verification can be done during a DFS as well if:

- the relation R_1^Π can be checked.
- for each visited state (q_1, q_2), the result $(q_1, q_2) \in R_k^\Pi$ is synthesized for its predecessors in the current sequence (the states are then analyzed during the back tracking phase).

More precisely, the principle of the general case algorithm is the following: if R^Π is a simulation (resp. a bisimulation) we associate with each state (q_1, q_2) a bit_array M of size $|T_1[q_1]|$ (resp. $|T_1[q_1]| + |T_2[q_2]|$). During the analysis of each successor (q_1', q_2') of (q_1, q_2), whenever it happens that $(q_1', q_2') \in R^\Pi$ then $M[q_1']$ (resp. $M[q_1']$ and $M[q_2']$) is set to 1. Thus, when all the successors of (q_1, q_2) have been analyzed, $(q_1, q_2) \in R^\Pi$ if and only if all the elements of M have been set to 1.

As in the deterministic case algorithm, to reduce the exponential time complexity of the DFS the usual method would consist in storing all the visited states (including those which do not belong to the current sequence) together with the result of their analysis (i.e, if they belong or not to R^Π). Unfortunately, this solution cannot be straightly applied:

During the DFS, the states are analyzed in a postfixed order. Consequently, it is possible to reach a state which has already been visited, but not yet analyzed (since the visits are performed in a prefixed order). Therefore, the result of the analysis of such a state is unknown (it is not available yet). We propose the following solution for this problem: we call the *status* of a state the result of the analysis of this state by the algorithm. The status of (q_1, q_2) is "$\sim$" if $(q_1, q_2) \in R^\Pi$, and is "$\not\sim$" otherwise. Whenever a state already visited but not yet analyzed (i.e, which belongs to the stack) is reached, then we assume its status to be "$\sim$". If, when the analysis of this state completes (i.e, when it is popped), the obtained status is "$\not\sim$", then a TRUE answer from the algorithm is not reliable (a wrong assumption was used), and another DFS has to be performed. On the other hand, a FALSE answer is always reliable.

The detailed algorithm can be found in [FM91].

4.2 Minimal LTS Generation

This approach [BFH90b] combines the construction of the graph of accessibles states with its reduction by bisimulation equivalence. The termination of the algorithm imposes that the quotient of the whole space of accessible and unaccessible states by bisimulation is finite. The algorithm combines a least fixed-point (accessibility on the classes) and a greatest fixed-point (greatest bisimulation). In the classical method, the set of accessible states is computed and then, given an initial partition ρ_{init}, the current partition is refined until all the classes are stable. Another algorithm may be given, refining first the initial partition and computing the accessible classes (which are stable). In the intermediate method presented here, the set of accessible classes is computed and then refined until all the accessible classes are stable.

Let $S = (Q, A_\tau, \{\xrightarrow{\alpha}\}_{\alpha \in A_\tau}, q_{init})$ be a LTS.

Splitting We modify the definition of the section 3.2. A class is split by all its successors.

$$split(X,\rho) = \bigsqcap_{Y\in\rho} \bigsqcap_{a\in A_\tau} \{X \cap pre_a(Y), X \setminus pre_a(Y)\}$$

Stability X is said to be stable with respect to ρ if and only if $\{X\} = split(X,\rho)$. ρ is stable if and only if it is stable with respect to itself.

Let $Stable(\rho) = \{X \in \rho \mid split(X,\rho) = \{X\}\}$.

Accessibility Let ρ be a partition of Q. We define the function Acc_ρ:

$$Acc_\rho(X) = [q_{\text{init}}] \cup \bigcup_{a\in A_\tau} post_{a,\rho}(X).$$

Given a partition ρ, the set of accessible states is the least fixed-point of Acc_ρ in the lattice 2^{2^Q}. However, the fact that a class belong to Acc_ρ does not imply that it contains an accessible state. This property becomes true when all the accessible classes are stable.

In [BFH90b], we propose an algorithm which compute the greatest fixed-point

$$\nu\rho \,.\, \rho_{\text{init}} \sqcap Ref(\mu\pi \,.\, Acc_\rho(\pi \cap Stable(\rho)), \rho)$$

by taking into account the stability on accessible classes. A step of the algorithm consists of choosing and refining a class, accessible from the stable classes.

4.2.1 Discussion

We can easily extend this algorithm to w-bisimulation and branching bisimulation, by modifying the definition of the function *split*:

w bisimulation

$$split(X,\rho) = \bigsqcap_{Y\in\rho} \bigsqcap_{a\in A_\tau} \{X \cap pre_{\tau^*a}(Y), X \setminus pre_{\tau^*a}(Y)\}.$$

Branching bisimulation

$$split(X,\rho) = \bigsqcap_{\substack{Y\in\rho \\ X\neq Y}} \bigsqcap_{a\in A_\tau} \{\mathcal{F}_a(X,Y), X \setminus \mathcal{F}_a(X,Y)\} \sqcap \bigsqcap_{a\in A} \{\mathcal{F}_a(X,X), X \setminus \mathcal{F}_a(X,X)\}$$

5 Experiments using the tool ALDÉBARAN

We summarize some of the results obtained when using the verification methods presented in this paper within the tool ALDÉBARAN. In particular, we compare the two distinct approaches (i.e, classical versus "on the fly") as well as the practical behavior of the algorithms associated to different relations. We first briefly present the tool ALDÉBARAN and give its current state.

5.1 ALDÉBARAN

ALDÉBARAN is a tool performing the minimization and comparison of labeled transition system with respect to several simulation and bisimulation-based equivalence relations. It is either used as a verification tool (in association with a LTS generator) or "internally" (for example inside another tool, as a graph minimizer). The two approaches mentioned above have been implemented within ALDÉBARAN, with respect to various relations:

classical approach: minimization and comparison algorithms have been implemented for strong bisimulation, observational equivalence, w bisimulation, safety equivalence and acceptance model equivalence, which is a variant of readiness semantics.

"on the fly approach": comparison algorithms have been implemented for strong and safety preorder, strong bisimulation, w-bisimulation, safety equivalence, delay bisimulation, and branching bisimulation when one of the LTS is τ-free (i.e, without τ actions). Theoretically branching bisimulation could also have been implemented in the general case but to obtain an efficient algorithm it was better considering this restricted case. In fact, it does not seem unrealistic in practice to consider that a specification is τ-free, and it has been shown that in this case branching bisimulation and observation equivalence coincides.

Remark

- The comparison algorithm which is currently implemented does not process yet the LOTOS program description "on the fly": as in the classical method, the two LTS are previously generated and the comparison phase consists in simultaneously building the LTS product and checking for the existence of an explanation sequence as described in section 4.
- The minimal model generation algorithm is still under implementation.

□

In addition, in both approaches *diagnostic features* are computed by ALDÉBARAN when the two LTS under comparison are not related: in the classical approach the set of all the explanation sequences is given, whereas in the "on the fly" approach one explanation sequence is exhibited.

5.2 Experiments

Two examples are discussed here: the first one is the well known scheduler described by Milner in [Mil80], and the second one is an alternating bit protocol called Datalink protocol [QPF88]. For each example, we proceed as follows:

- generating the labeled transition system S_1 from a LOTOS description, using CÆSAR.
- building the labeled transition system S_2, representing the expected behavior of the system.
- comparing S_1 and S_2 with respect to w-bisimulation, branching bisimulation and safety preorder using the "on the fly" algorithm.

- minimizing S_1 with respect to observational equivalence and w-bisimulation using the classical algorithm.

The times have been obtained on a SUN 4 SparcStation using the *times*() UNIX standard function. Only the verification phase is taken into account. In each table, the first value represents the *system* time, whereas the second one represents the *user* time.

Milner's Scheduler

The problem consists in designing a scheduler which ensures that N communicating processes start a given task in a cyclic way. The LOTOS specification considered has been straightly obtained from Milner's CCS solution which can be found in [Mil80]. The results are given for different values of N.

The first table contains the sizes of the LTS obtained from the LOTOS program:

N	number of states	number of transitions
8	3073	13825
9	6913	34561
10	15361	84481
11	33793	202753
12	73729	479233

Sizes of the LTS obtained from the LOTOS programs

Using the classical minimization algorithm, due to memory shortage the LTS cannot be processed when $N > 8$ for observation equivalence, and when $N > 11$ for w bisimulation. For smaller LTS, the system and user times obtained are the following:

N	Paige Tarjan		Transitive Closure	
8	0.017	4.417	1.533	134.200
9	0.250	15.333	8.417	918.917

Minimization with respect to Observation Equivalence

N	Paige Tarjan		Transitive Closure	
8	0.000	0.533	0.067	4.367
9	0.000	1.650	0.250	20.350
10	0.050	5.333	0.617	111.517
11	0.433	7.600	2.633	581.017

Minimization with respect to w Bisimulation

Using the "on the fly" algorithm, the comparison can be carried out up to 12 cyclers:

N	Branching Bisimulation		w Bisimulation		Safety Preorder	
8	0.150	0.950	0.050	1.650	0.133	0.483
9	0.300	2.850	0.217	5.900	0.317	1.233
10	1.033	7.300	0.633	21.800	1.217	2.933
11	2.783	15.333	1.767	83.950	2.117	6.883
12	7.283	39.300	6.750	341.283	9.150	16.383

Comparison using the "on the fly" approach

Datalink Protocol

The Datalink protocol is an example of an alternating bit protocol. The LOTOS specification provided to CÆSAR is described in [QPF88]. By varying the number of the different messages (noted N), labeled transition systems of different sizes can be obtained. The sizes of the LTS are the following:

N	number of states	number of transitions
40	27281	40320
50	42101	62400
70	81341	120960
80	105761	157440
90	133380	198719
100	167459	249672

Sizes of the LTS obtained from the LOTOS programs

Again, for memory shortage reasons, the LTS cannot be minimized when $N > 50$ with respect to observation equivalence and w bisimulation using the classical approach. For smaller LTS, the times obtained are the following:

N	Paige Tarjan		Transitive Closure	
40	0.150	7.417	0.080	3.317
50	2.133	13.650	1.000	2.650

Minimization with respect to Observation Equivalence

N	Paige Tarjan		Transitive Closure	
40	0.033	4.050	0.017	1.950
50	0.117	7.667	0.033	2.983

Minimization with respect to w Bisimulation

Using the "on the fly" approach, the comparison can be carried out up to 100 messages and more:

N	Branching Bisimulation		w Bisimulation		Safety Preorder	
40	0.717	3.350	0.117	0.250	0.600	2.000
50	1.017	5.250	0.200	2.033	1.000	3.083
70	2.233	9.950	0.483	3.850	1.817	6.050
80	4.033	5.600	0.450	6.117	2.750	9.583
90	4.933	6.600	0.633	6.700	3.433	9.817
100	5.783	28.250	0.850	8.500	1.217	2.933

Comparison using the "on the fly" approach

6 Conclusion

In this paper, we have presented an overview of the methods implemented in ALDÉBARAN. ALDÉBARAN is a part of a tool set including CÆSAR and CLÉOPÂTRE [Ras91]. CÆSAR is a

LOTOS compiler translating a LOTOS description in LTS. CLÉOPÂTRE is a verification tool for branching-time logic specifications, including a verification module and a diagnostic module.

Initially, we have dealt with classical method in ALDÉBARAN: computation of a normal form for LTS with respect to a given equivalence, followed by a minimization or a comparison up to strong bisimulation. The limitation of this method is now well known.

¿From this limitation, we experiment now algorithms presented in 4. However, we do not yet combine generation algorithm and verification algorithm in the current implementation, since the method is applied to LTS already constructed. We want to combine the generation phase, (i.e., from Petri Nets to LTS), of the LOTOS compiler CÆSAR with verification algorithms of ALDÉBARAN.

For this purpose, a depth first search generation algorithm can be combined with the algorithm constructing the partial product. Thus, larger LOTOS programs could be carried out. In particular, there is no restriction on the data types.

Minimal LTS generation can also be implemented. This method may require symbolic computations in order to determine the *pre* and *post* functions, inclusion and intersection of classes. Such symbolic computations are reasonably achievable in the boolean case, (i.e., LOTOS description with boolean value). We think that this method is also suitable for other simple data types.

References

[BFG*91] A. Bouajjani, J.C. Fernandez, S. Graf, C. Rodriguez, and J. Sifakis. Safety for branching time semantics. In *18th ICALP*, july 1991.

[BFH90a] A. Bouajjani, J. C. Fernandez, and N. Halbwachs. *On the verification of safety properties.* Tech. report, Spectre L 12, IMAG, Grenoble, march 1990.

[BFH90b] A. Bouajjani, J.C. Fernandez, and N. Halbwachs. Minimal model generation. In *Workshop on Computer-aided Verification*, to appear in LNCS, Springer Verlag, june 1990.

[BHR84] S. D. Brookes, C.A.R Hoare, and A.W. Roscoe. Theory of communicating sequential processes. *JACM*, 31(3), 1984.

[CES86] E. M. Clarke, E. A. Emerson, and A. P. Sistla. Automatic verification of finite-state concurrent systems using temporal logic spec ifications. *TOPLAS*, 8(2), 1986.

[Cle90] R. Cleaveland. On automatically distinguishing inequivalent processes. In *Workshop on Computer-Aided Verification*, june 1990.

[CPS90] R. Cleaveland, J. Parrow, and B. Steffen. The concurrency workbench. In *Workshop on Computer-Aided Verification*, june 1990.

[CVWY90] C. Courcoubetis, M. Vardi, P. Wolper, and M. Yannakakis. Memory efficient algorithms for the verification of temporal properties. In *Workshop on Computer-Aided Verification*, june 1990.

[dSV89] R. de Simone and D. Vergamini. *Aboard Auto.* Rapport Technique 111, INRIA, Sophia Antipolis, 1989.

[Fer90] J. C. Fernandez. An implementation of an efficient algorithm for bisimulation equivalence. *Science of Computer Programming*, 13(2-3), May 1990.

[FM91] J.-C. Fernandez and L. Mounier. "on the fly" verification of behavioural equivalences and preorders. In *Workshop on Computer-aided Verification*, To appear, july 1–4 1991.

[Gla90] R.J. van Glabbeek. *The Linear Time - Branching Time Spectrum.* Technical Report CS-R9029, Centre for Mathematics and Computer Science, 1990.

[GS90] Hubert Garavel and Joseph Sifakis. Compilation and verification of lotos specifications. In L. Logrippo, R. L. Probert, and H. Ural, editors, *Proceedings of the 10th International Symposium on Protocol Specification, Testing and Verification (Ottawa)*, IFIP, North-Holland, Amsterdam, June 1990.

[GV90] Jan Friso Groote and Frits Vaandrager. *An Efficient Algorithm for Branching Bisimulation and Stuttering Equivalence.* CS-R 9001, Centrum voor Wiskunde en Informatica, Amsterdam, January 1990.

[GW89] R.J. van Glabbeek and W.P. Weijland. *Branching time and abstraction in bisimulation semantics (extended abstract).* CS-R 8911, Centrum voor Wiskunde en Informatica, Amsterdam, 1989.

[JJ89] Claude Jard and Thierry Jeron. On-line model-checking for finite linear temporal logic specifications. In *International Workshop on Automatic Verification Methods for Finite State Systems, LNCS 407*, Springer Verlag, 1989.

[JJ91] Claude Jard and Thierry Jéron. Bounded-memory algorithms for verification on-the-fly. In K. G. Larsen, editor, *Proceedings of the 3rd Workshop on Computer-Aided Verification (Aalborg, Denmark)*, July 1991. to appear.

[KS83] P. Kanellakis and S. Smolka. Ccs expressions, finite state processes and three problems of equivalence. In *Proceedings ACM Symp. on Principles of Distribued Computing*, 1983.

[Mil80] R. Milner. A calculus of communication systems. In *LNCS 92*, Springer Verlag, 1980.

[NMV90] R. De Nicola, U. Montanari, and F.W. Vaandrager. *Back and Forth Bisimulations.* CS-R 9021, Centrum voor Wiskunde en Informatica, Amsterdam, 1990.

[NV90] R. De Nicola and F. Vaandrager. Three logics for branching bisimulation. In *Proc. of Fifth Symp. on Logic in Computer Science*, Computer Society Press, 1990.

[Par81] D. Park. Concurrency and automata on infinite sequences. In *5th GI-Conference on Theorical Computer Science*, Springer Verlag, 1981. LNCS 104.

[PT87] R. Paige and R. Tarjan. Three partition refinement algorithms. *SIAM J. Comput., No. 6*, 16, 1987.

[QPF88] Juan Quemada, Santiago Pavón, and Angel Fernández. Transforming lotos specifications with lola: the parametrized expansion. In Kenneth J. Turner, editor, *Proceedings of the 1st International Conference on Formal Description Techniques FORTE'88 (Stirling, Scotland)*, pages 45–54, North-Holland, Amsterdam, September 1988.

[Ras91] A. Rasse. Error diagnosis in finite communicating systems. In *Workshop on Computer-aided Verification*, To appear, july 1–4 1991.

[RRSV87] J.L. Richier, C. Rodriguez, J. Sifakis, and J. Voiron. *Xesar: A Tool for Protocol Validation. User's Guide.* LGI-Imag, 1987.

Causality Based Models for the Design of Concurrent Systems

Ursula Goltz*
Gesellschaft für Mathematik und Datenverarbeitung
Postfach 1240
D-5205 St. Augustin

Abstract

A design calculus for concurrent systems or, more specifically, for *reactive systems*, will need the following components:

- A (logical) language for the property oriented specification of systems.
- A system description language to represent abstract and more concrete design specifications.
- Models for concurrent systems which are used as semantic domains for both the logical language and the system description language.

In such a framework, proof methods for showing the correctness of a design with respect to a property oriented specification may be investigated.

We are concerned here with the features of semantic models, suited for this purpose. We discuss these features by choosing a particular system description language and considering semantic models for it. The language allows the construction of systems by means of composition operators like parallel composition, sequential composition and choice. Additionally, it allows for a hierarchical approach to system design by providing a refinement operation.

The horizontal composition operations of the language are taken from CCS, CSP and ACP. For changing the level of abstraction, actions may be interpreted as processes (*action refinement*); we will discuss the power and limitations of this approach.

*The work presented here has been partially supported by the Esprit Basic Research Action

We assume a fixed set *Act* of *action names*. We do not consider hiding of actions here, so we do not distinguish internal and visible actions. The set of terms (or programs) of our language is given by

$$\begin{aligned}\mathcal{P} \;=\; & skip \;\mid\; a \quad (a \in Act) \;\mid\; \mathcal{P};\mathcal{Q} \;\mid\; \mathcal{P}+\mathcal{Q} \;\mid \\ & \mathcal{P}\|_A\mathcal{Q} \quad (A \subseteq Act) \;\mid\; \mathcal{P}[a \rightsquigarrow \mathcal{Q}] \quad (a \in Act, \mathcal{Q} \neq skip).\end{aligned}$$

skip denotes the empty process which is able to terminate successfully without performing any action. In the process a just the action a occurs. $P;Q$ denotes the sequential composition of P and Q. $P + Q$ behaves either like P or like Q, the decision is taken as soon as either P or Q performs any action. In $P\|_A Q$, P and Q run independently in parallel as long as they execute actions not in A, actions in A may only be performed as a joint action by both partners together. In $P[a \rightsquigarrow Q]$, each occurrence of a is refined into Q (however the interplay between refinement and communication needs to be treated carefully). Additionally, we will consider recursion or iteration for modelling infinite processes.

Usually, process algebras are based on interleaving models for concurrent systems. Alternatively, *causality based models* have been suggested where concurrency and nondeterminism may be clearly distinguished. The relative merits of these approaches are being discussed. In particular, it has been pointed out that interleaving semantics are based on the assumption that actions are atomic entities. This may cause problems, for instance when changing the level of abstraction by interpreting actions as processes, as in our approach. It has been shown that this problem does not occur for causality based semantics.

The most well known model for causality based semantics are Petri nets. *Event structures* have been derived as a more basic model, tailored to the action-oriented view in process algebras. We suggest several semantics for our language, using Petri nets and different representations of event structures. All these semantics are *compositional* in the following sense. Assuming that we already have denotations $[P]$ and $[Q]$ of the behaviour of P and Q, respectively, we infer the behaviour of a composed process $P\ op\ Q$ by applying a semantical operator op' to $[P]$ and $[Q]$: $[P\ op\ Q] = [P]\ op'\ [Q]$.

We compare these semantics; in particular, we discuss the following points:

- the complexity of the model versus the difficulty in defining the semantic operators,
- the treatment of successful termination, deadlock, and the empty process *skip*,
- the modelling of infinite processes.

We discuss the power and the limitations of the approach, using a simple example from the area of communication protocols.

Modal Logics for Mobile Processes

Robin Milner*, Joachim Parrow† and David Walker‡

Abstract

In process algebras, bisimulation equivalence is typically defined directly in terms of the operational rules of action; it also has an alternative characterisation in terms of a simple modal logic (sometimes called *Hennessy-Milner logic*. This paper first defines two forms of bisimulation equivalence for the *π-calculus*, a process algebra which allows dynamic reconfiguration among processes; it then explores a family of possible logics, with different modal operators. It is proven that two of these logics characterise the two bisimulation equivalences. Also, the relative expressive power of all the logics is exhibited as a lattice.

1 Introduction

This paper presents a logical characterisation of process equivalences in the *π-calculus* [6], a process algebra in which processes may change their configuration dynamically. In this introduction we place the results in context. First we review the corresponding results for process calculi which do not allow this dynamic re-configuration. Then we give plausible reasons for introducing modalities and an equality predicate into the logic, in order to extend these results to the π-calculus. In the later sections, we prove that these new connectives do indeed provide the characterisation.

For a typical process algebra without mobility, the equivalence relation of strong bisimilarity [8] can be characterised by a modal process logic, sometimes called Hennessy-Milner logic [2]. To be specific, let $\mathcal{P}$ consist simply of the processes P given by

$$P \ ::= \ \alpha.P \ \mid \ \mathbf{0} \ \mid \ P+P \ \mid \ C$$

where α ranges over *actions*, and C over *process constants*. We assume that for each C there is a *defining equation* $C \stackrel{\mathrm{def}}{=} P_C$. (Usually there will also be parallel composition and other operators, but we do not need them for this discussion.) We also assume that a labelled transition relation $\xrightarrow{\alpha}$ is defined over $\mathcal{P}$ in the usual way. Then *strong bisimilarity* is the largest symmetric relation $\sim$ over $\mathcal{P}$ for which, whenever $P \sim Q$ and $P \xrightarrow{\alpha} P'$, there exists Q' such that $Q \xrightarrow{\alpha} Q'$ and $P' \sim Q'$.

The process logic $\mathcal{PL}$ has formulae A given by

$$A \ ::= \ \langle\alpha\rangle A \ \mid \ \bigwedge_{i \in I} A_i \ \mid \ \neg A$$

where I stands for any denumerable set. (The smallest formula is the empty conjunction, written **true**.) $\mathcal{PL}$ is given meaning by defining the *satisfaction relation* $\models$ between processes and formulae; in particular, one defines

$$P \models \langle\alpha\rangle A \ \text{ if, for some } P',\ P \xrightarrow{\alpha} P' \text{ and } P' \models A$$

*University of Edinburgh, Scotland. Supported by a Senior Research Fellowship awarded by the British Science and Engineering Research Council.

†Swedish Institute of Computer Science, Sweden. Supported by the Swedish Board of Technical Development under project 89-01218P CONCUR and by Swedish Telecom under project PROCOM.

‡University of Technology, Sydney, Australia.

It may be shown that two processes are strongly bisimilar iff they satisfy the same formulae of $\mathcal{PL}$; this is the sense in which $\mathcal{PL}$ characterises $\sim$. Under mild restrictions, such as when every P_C in a defining equation is *guarded* (i.e. contains no process constant except within a term of the form $\alpha.P$), only finite conjunctions in $\mathcal{PL}$ are needed.

Before considering what should be included in a logic to characterise equivalences over the π-calculus, we must discuss an issue about equivalence which arises in any *value-passing* calculus, of which the π-calculus is a rather special case. In general, in any value-passing calculus, an action α may "carry a value". By this, we mean that there are *input actions* $a(x)$, where a is a link-name and x a value variable, and x is bound in $a(x).P$; there are also *output actions* $\bar{a}e$, where e is an expression denoting a value. Such calculi have been studied in depth [3, 1], and many different equivalences have been defined over them. The choice of equivalence is complicated by the passing of values. Consider the following two processes:

$$\begin{aligned} R &= a(x).(\textbf{if } x = 3 \textbf{ then } P \textbf{ else } Q) + a(x).\mathbf{0} \\ S &= a(x).(\textbf{if } x = 3 \textbf{ then } P) + a(x).(\textbf{if } x \neq 3 \textbf{ then } Q) \end{aligned} \tag{1}$$

We understand the one-armed conditional process "**if** b **then** P" to be equivalent to $\mathbf{0}$ if b is false. (The full conditional "**if** b **then** P **else** Q" can be expressed as the sum of two one-armed conditionals with conditions b and $\neg b$.) Now, is R equivalent to S? Both answers are possible.

They are strongly bisimilar in Milner [5], where the calculus with value-passing is reduced by translation to a value-free calculus – but with infinite sums. In fact R reduces to

$$\sum_{n\in\omega} a_n.R_n + \sum_{n\in\omega} a_n.\mathbf{0} \tag{2}$$

where $R_3 = P$, and $R_n = Q$ for $n \neq 3$. (We assume for simplicity that P and Q do not involve value-passing, so do not contain the variable x.) Correspondingly, S reduces to

$$\sum_{n\in\omega} a_n.P_n + \sum_{n\in\omega} a_n.Q_n \tag{3}$$

where $P_3 = P$ and $Q_3 = \mathbf{0}$, while $P_n = \mathbf{0}$ and $Q_n = Q$ for $n \neq 3$; this sum is equivalent to (2).

But there is a different view, according to which R and S are not equivalent. [1] In this view we do not consider R capable of an infinity of actions a_n, one for each natural number, but essentially only two actions, one of which is

$$R \xrightarrow{a(x)} \textbf{if } x = 3 \textbf{ then } P \textbf{ else } Q \tag{4}$$

yielding a family of processes indexed by the variable x. For another process to be equivalent to R, it must yield under $\xrightarrow{a(x)}$ an indexed family which is element-wise equivalent to the above family – i.e. equivalent for each value of x. But S does not have this property; it yields two indexed families, both different, namely:

$$\begin{aligned} S &\xrightarrow{a(x)} \textbf{if } x = 3 \textbf{ then } P \\ S &\xrightarrow{a(x)} \textbf{if } x \neq 3 \textbf{ then } Q \end{aligned} \tag{5}$$

These two equivalences can both be expressed as forms of bisimilarity. For the π-calculus we concentrated on the second – finer – equivalence in our original paper [7], but also commented on the coarser equivalence. Both seem reasonable. In this paper we shall show that both bisimilarities can be elegantly characterised by appropriate process logics. Actually, we shall examine a family of 2^5 logics, defined by including any combination of five logical connectives – mostly modalities –

[1] This view amounts to equating processes iff they denote identical *communication trees*, as defined in Milner[4], Chapter 6. The view was not pursued thoroughly there.

over and above a fixed set of connectives. It turns out that these yield eleven equivalences (several logics being equipotent), including our two bisimilarities. We are not yet interested in most of these equivalences per se; but the lattice which they form gives insight into the power of the various logical connectives.

Now, what logical connectives should we expect in a logic for the π-calculus? Here, value expressions and value variables are themselves nothing but link-names. All computation is done with names $x, y, \ldots$; thus, input and output actions take the form $x(y)$ and $\bar{x}y$. It is natural to include some modality for each form of action; in particular, a modal formula

$$\langle x(y)\rangle A$$

for input actions where y is bound. In fact, to characterise the finer of our two bisimilarities, we shall define a modality $\langle x(y)\rangle^{\mathrm{L}}$ such that

$$P \models \langle x(y)\rangle^{\mathrm{L}} A \quad \text{iff} \quad \text{for some } P',\ P \xrightarrow{x(y)} P' \text{ and for all } z,\ P'\{z/y\} \models A\{z/y\}$$

The superscript L here stands for "late". It refers to the lateness of instantiation of the variable y; P' is chosen *first*, and then for all instances of y it must satisfy the corresponding instantiation of A. The coarser equivalence will be reflected by a modality with superscript E for "early"; this refers to the fact that the instance z of y is chosen *first*, and then a different P' may be chosen for each z.

It may be expected that, once we have included in our logic a suitable modality for each form of action, our characterisation will be achieved. But this is not so, due to the special rôle of names in the π-calculus.

At first sight the π-calculus may appear to be just a degenerate form of value-passing calculus, which can then be translated (as above) to a value-free calculus, and hence characterised essentially by the logic $\mathcal{PL}$, for suitable actions α. But this neglects a crucial ingredient of π-calculus, namely the process form $(x)P$, known as *restriction*. This combinator gives *scope* to names – in other words, it allows the creation of *private* names; it is responsible for much of the power of the π-calculus, and prevents us from treating names as values in the normal way.

Thus the algebra of names cannot be "translated away" from the π-calculus, in the same way that the algebra of (say) integers can be translated away from CCS. But what is this algebra of names? It is almost empty! There are no *constant* names, and no *operators* over names; this explains why the only value expressions are names themselves (as variables). But what of boolean expressions, and the conditional form "**if** b **then** P"? Well, names have no properties except identity; thus the only *predicate* over names is equality – and indeed the π-calculus contains the *match expression*[2]

$$[x = y]P$$

which is another way of writing "**if** $x = y$ **then** P". It is therefore reasonable to expect that, by including an equality predicate in the form of a *match formula*

$$[x = y]A$$

in our logics, we succeed in characterising the bisimilarities. This indeed turns out to be the case. Moreover, the match formula is strictly necessary; furthermore – which is not obvious – it is needed in the logic even if the match expression is omitted from the calculus.

In the next section we present the π-calculus and its operational semantics; the reader therefore need not refer to previous papers, although familiarity with the π-calculus will certainly help; we also define the two bisimilarities. In the third section we define all the logical connectives we wish to consider, and derive a complete picture for the relative power of their different combinations.

[2]Hitherto we have not given much consideration to the negative form $[x \neq y]P$; it requires further investigation.

2 Mobile Processes

In this section we will recapitulate the syntax of agents from [7] and give agents two kinds of transitional semantics, corresponding to late and early instantiation of input parameters. Based on these we will define late and early bisimulation equivalences.

2.1 Syntax

Assume an infinite set $\mathcal{N}$ of *names* and let x, y, z, w, v, u range over names. We also assume a set of *agent identifiers* ranged over by C, where each agent identifier C has a nonnegative *arity* $r(C)$.

Definition 1 The set of *agents* is defined as follows (we use P, Q, R to range over agents):

$$
\begin{array}{rcll}
P & ::= & 0 & \text{(inaction)} \\
 & \mid & \bar{x}y.\,P & \text{(output prefix)} \\
 & \mid & x(y).\,P & \text{(input prefix)} \\
 & \mid & \tau.\,P & \text{(silent prefix)} \\
 & \mid & (y)P & \text{(restriction)} \\
 & \mid & [x{=}y]P & \text{(match)} \\
 & \mid & P \mid Q & \text{(composition)} \\
 & \mid & P + Q & \text{(summation)} \\
 & \mid & C(y_1, \ldots, y_{r(C)}) & \text{(defined agent)}
\end{array}
$$

In each of $x(y).\,P$ and $(y)P$ the occurrence of y in parentheses is a *binding* occurrence whose scope is P. We write $\mathrm{fn}(P)$ for the set of names occurring free in P. If $\tilde{x} = x_1, \ldots, x_n$ are distinct and $\tilde{y} = y_1, \ldots, y_n$ then $P\{\tilde{y}/\tilde{x}\}$ is the result of simultaneously substituting y_i for all free occurrences of x_i $(i = 1, \ldots, n)$ with change of bound names if necessary. Each agent constant C has a unique *defining equation* of the form

$$C(x_1, \ldots, x_{r(C)}) \stackrel{\mathrm{def}}{=} P$$

where the x_i are distinct and $\mathrm{fn}(P) \subseteq \{x_1, \ldots, x_{r(C)}\}$. □

The order of precedence among the operators is the order listed in Definition 1. For a description of the intended interpretation of agents see [6]. In examples we will frequently omit a trailing $.0$; for example $\tau.\,0 + \bar{x}y.\,0$ will be abbreviated $\tau + \bar{x}y$. Also we sometimes write $\mathrm{fn}(P, Q, \ldots, x, y, \ldots)$ as an abbreviation for $\mathrm{fn}(P) \cup \mathrm{fn}(Q) \cup \ldots \cup \{x, y, \ldots\}$.

2.2 Transitions

A *transition* is of the form

$$P \xrightarrow{\alpha} Q$$

Intuitively, this transition means that P can evolve into Q, and in doing so perform the *action* α. In our calculus there will be five kinds of action α as follows. The *silent* action τ corresponds to an internal computation, and the *free output* action $\bar{x}y$ and *free input* action xy correspond to the transmission and reception of the free name y along x. The *bound input* action $x(y)$ means that any name can be received along x, and (y) designates the places where the received name will go. The *bound output* $\bar{x}(y)$ means that a local name designated by y is exported along x. A summary of the actions, their *free names* $\mathrm{fn}(\alpha)$ and *bound names* $\mathrm{bn}(\alpha)$ can be found in Table 1. We write $\mathrm{n}(\alpha)$ for $\mathrm{fn}(\alpha) \cup \mathrm{bn}(\alpha)$.

The silent and free actions are familiar from CCS. In particular a free input action corresponds to an early instantiation of an input parameter, since it carries both the port name and received value. In contrast a bound input action carries only a port name, implying that the bound parameter will be instantiated at a later stage. The bound output actions are used to infer so called scope extrusions; their parameters will never be instantiated to free names so the issue of "late vs. early" does not arise.

α	Kind	fn(α)	bn(α)
τ	Silent	$\emptyset$	$\emptyset$
$\bar{x}y$	Free Output	$\{x, y\}$	$\emptyset$
$\bar{x}(y)$	Bound Output	$\{x\}$	$\{y\}$
xy	Free Input	$\{x, y\}$	$\emptyset$
$x(y)$	Bound Input	$\{x\}$	$\{y\}$

Table 1: The actions.

Definition 2 The *structural congruence* $\equiv$ on agents is the least congruence satisfying the following clauses:

1. If P and Q differ only in the choice of bound names, i.e. they are alpha-equivalent in the standard sense, then $P \equiv Q$,
2. $P|Q \equiv Q|P$,
3. $P + Q \equiv Q + P$,
4. $[x = x]P \equiv P$,
5. If $C(\tilde{x}) \overset{\text{def}}{=} P$ then $C(\tilde{y}) \equiv P\{\tilde{y}/\tilde{x}\}$.

A *variant* of the transition $P \xrightarrow{\alpha} Q$ is a transition which only differs in that P and Q have been replaced by structurally congruent agents, and α has been alpha-converted, where a name bound in α includes Q in its scope. □

As an example the following transitions are variants of each other:

$$x(y).\,\bar{y}z \xrightarrow{x(y)} \bar{y}z$$
$$x(y).\,\bar{y}z \xrightarrow{x(u)} \bar{u}z$$
$$[x = x]x(y).\,\bar{y}z \xrightarrow{x(y)} \bar{y}z$$

Below we will give two sets of rules for inferring transitions, one set corresponding to early and one corresponding to late instantiation. In each rule, the transition in the conclusion stands for all variants of the transition. The use of variants and structural congruence makes it possible to formulate the rules more concisely than would otherwise be possible. We begin with the set of rules in [7] which can now be rendered as follows:

Definition 3 The set of rules LATE consists of the following:

ACT : $\dfrac{-}{\alpha.\,P \xrightarrow{\alpha} P}$ SUM : $\dfrac{P \xrightarrow{\alpha} P'}{P + Q \xrightarrow{\alpha} P'}$

PAR : $\dfrac{P \xrightarrow{\alpha} P'}{P|Q \xrightarrow{\alpha} P'|Q}$ $\mathrm{bn}(\alpha) \cap \mathrm{fn}(Q) = \emptyset$

L-COM: $\dfrac{P \xrightarrow{\bar{x}y} P' \quad Q \xrightarrow{x(z)} Q'}{P|Q \xrightarrow{\tau} P'|Q'\{y/z\}}$ CLOSE : $\dfrac{P \xrightarrow{\bar{x}(y)} P' \quad Q \xrightarrow{x(y)} Q'}{P|Q \xrightarrow{\tau} (y)(P'|Q')}$

RES : $\dfrac{P \xrightarrow{\alpha} P'}{(y)P \xrightarrow{\alpha} (y)P'}$ $y \notin \mathrm{n}(\alpha)$ OPEN : $\dfrac{P \xrightarrow{\bar{x}y} P'}{(y)P \xrightarrow{\bar{x}(y)} P'}$ $y \neq x$

We write $P \xrightarrow{\alpha}_{\mathrm{L}} Q$ to mean that the transition $P \xrightarrow{\alpha} Q$ can be inferred from LATE. □

As elaborated in [7], the name bound by an input prefix form $x(y).P$ becomes instantiated in L-COM when a communication between two agents is inferred. Note that no rule in LATE generates a free input action. Also, note that special rules for identifiers and matching are unnecessary because of Clauses 4 and 5 in Definition 2.

In contrast, with an *early instantiation* scheme the bound name y is instantiated when inferring an input transition from $x(y).P$:

Definition 4 The set of rules EARLY is obtained from LATE by replacing the rule L-COM with the following two rules:

$$\text{E-INPUT: } \frac{-}{x(y).P \xrightarrow{xw} P\{w/y\}} \qquad \text{E-COM: } \frac{P \xrightarrow{\bar{x}y} P' \quad Q \xrightarrow{xy} Q'}{P|Q \xrightarrow{\tau} P'|Q'}$$

We write $P \xrightarrow{\alpha}_{\mathrm{E}} Q$ to mean that the transition $P \xrightarrow{\alpha} Q$ can be inferred from EARLY. □

The new rule E-INPUT admits an instantiation to any name w, so there will always be a suitable free input action available as a premise in E-COM. Note that the rule ACT remains in EARLY, so an input prefix may still generate bound input actions — these are needed with the rules OPEN and CLOSE to achieve scope extrusions such as

$$x(y).P \,|\, (y)\bar{x}y.Q \xrightarrow{\tau}_{\mathrm{E}} (y)(P|Q)$$

The following example highlights the difference between LATE and EARLY. Assume that we want to infer a communication in the agent

$$x(y).P(y) \,|\, Q(y,u) \,|\, \bar{x}u.R$$

(We write "$P(y)$" to signify that P depends on y, and similarly for Q.) Using LATE we need a new name z in the PAR rule to avoid conflicts with the free names in $Q(y,u)$:

$$\frac{\dfrac{\dfrac{-}{x(y).P(y) \xrightarrow{x(z)}_{\mathrm{L}} P(z)}}{x(y).P(y) \,|\, Q(y,u) \xrightarrow{x(z)}_{\mathrm{L}} P(z) \,|\, Q(y,u)} \qquad \dfrac{-}{\bar{x}u.R \xrightarrow{\bar{x}u}_{\mathrm{L}} R}}{x(y).P(y) \,|\, Q(y,u) \,|\, \bar{x}u.R \xrightarrow{\tau}_{\mathrm{L}} P(u) \,|\, Q(y,u) \,|\, R}$$

Using EARLY the same communication can be inferred:

$$\frac{\dfrac{\dfrac{-}{x(y).P(y) \xrightarrow{xu}_{\mathrm{E}} P(u)}}{x(y).P(y) \,|\, Q(y,u) \xrightarrow{xu}_{\mathrm{E}} P(u) \,|\, Q(y,u)} \qquad \dfrac{-}{\bar{x}u.R \xrightarrow{\bar{x}u}_{\mathrm{E}} R}}{x(y).P(y) \,|\, Q(y,u) \,|\, \bar{x}u.R \xrightarrow{\tau}_{\mathrm{E}} P(u) \,|\, Q(y,u) \,|\, R}$$

The following lemma shows how $\xrightarrow{\alpha}_{\mathrm{E}}$ and $\xrightarrow{\alpha}_{\mathrm{L}}$ are related.

Lemma 1

1. $P \xrightarrow{\bar{x}y}_{\mathrm{E}} P'$ iff $P \xrightarrow{\bar{x}y}_{\mathrm{L}} P'$
2. $P \xrightarrow{\bar{x}(y)}_{\mathrm{E}} P'$ iff $P \xrightarrow{\bar{x}(y)}_{\mathrm{L}} P'$
3. $P \xrightarrow{x(y)}_{\mathrm{E}} P'$ iff $P \xrightarrow{x(y)}_{\mathrm{L}} P'$
4. $P \xrightarrow{xy}_{\mathrm{E}} P'$ iff $\exists P'', w : P \xrightarrow{x(w)}_{\mathrm{L}} P''$ with $P' \equiv P''\{y/w\}$
5. $P \xrightarrow{\tau}_{\mathrm{E}} P'$ iff $P \xrightarrow{\tau}_{\mathrm{L}} P'$

Proof: A standard induction over LATE and EARLY. The proof of 2 uses 1, and the proof of 5 uses all of 1–4. □

In view of this lemma we can drop the subscripts L and E of $\xrightarrow{\alpha}$ from now on.

2.3 Late and Early Bisimulations

We first recall the definition of bisimulation in [7]:

Definition 5 A binary relation $\mathcal{S}$ on agents is a *late simulation* if $P\mathcal{S}Q$ implies that

1. If $P \xrightarrow{\alpha} P'$ and α is τ, $\bar{x}z$ or $\bar{x}(y)$ with $y \notin \mathrm{fn}(P,Q)$,
   then for some Q', $\quad Q \xrightarrow{\alpha} Q'$ and $P'\mathcal{S}Q'$
2. If $P \xrightarrow{x(y)} P'$ and $y \notin \mathrm{fn}(P,Q)$,
   then for some Q', $\quad Q \xrightarrow{x(y)} Q'$ and for all w, $P'\{w/y\}\mathcal{S}Q'\{w/y\}$

The relation $\mathcal{S}$ is a *late bisimulation* if both $\mathcal{S}$ and $\mathcal{S}^{-1}$ are late simulations. We define *late bisimilarity* $P \dot{\sim}_{\mathrm{L}} Q$ to mean that $P\mathcal{S}Q$ for some late bisimulation $\mathcal{S}$. □

Note that late simulations do not require anything of free input actions. Instead, there is a strong requirement on bound input actions: the resulting agents P' and Q' must continue to simulate for all instances of the bound name. The theory of $\dot{\sim}_{\mathrm{L}}$ is explored in [7], where we also observed that an alternative equivalence can be obtained by commuting the quantifiers in clause 2:

Definition 6 A binary relation $\mathcal{S}$ on agents is an *alternative simulation* if $P\mathcal{S}Q$ implies that

1. If $P \xrightarrow{\alpha} P'$ and α is τ, $\bar{x}z$ or $\bar{x}(y)$ with $y \notin \mathrm{fn}(P,Q)$,
   then for some Q', $\quad Q \xrightarrow{\alpha} Q'$ and $P'\mathcal{S}Q'$
2. If $P \xrightarrow{x(y)} P'$ and $y \notin \mathrm{fn}(P,Q)$,
   then for all w, there is Q' such that $\quad Q \xrightarrow{x(y)} Q'$ and $P'\{w/y\}\mathcal{S}Q'\{w/y\}$

The relation $\mathcal{S}$ is an *alternative bisimulation* if both $\mathcal{S}$ and $\mathcal{S}^{-1}$ are alternative simulations. We define $P \dot{\sim}' Q$ to mean that $P\mathcal{S}Q$ for some alternative bisimulation $\mathcal{S}$. □

It is obvious that every late simulation is also an alternative simulation, so $\dot{\sim}_{\mathrm{L}} \subseteq \dot{\sim}'$. To see that this inclusion is strict, consider the following example:

$$\begin{aligned} P &= x(u).\tau + x(u) \\ Q &= P + x(u).[u\!=\!z]\tau \end{aligned}$$

Then $P \dot{\sim}' Q$, but $P \not\dot{\sim}_{\mathrm{L}} Q$. To see this consider the transition

$$Q \xrightarrow{x(u)} [u\!=\!z]\tau \tag{6}$$

P has no transition which simulates (6) for all instantiations of u. However, for each instantiation of u there is a simulating transition: for z it is

$$P \xrightarrow{x(u)} \tau$$

(since $([u\!=\!z]\tau)\{z/u\} \equiv \tau$) and for all other names it is

$$P \xrightarrow{x(u)} \mathbf{0}$$

(since $([u\!=\!z]\tau)\{z'/u\} \dot{\sim}' \mathbf{0} \equiv \mathbf{0}\{z'/u\}$ for all $z' \neq z$).

We will now support our claim from [7] that $\dot{\sim}'$ corresponds to bisimilarity in the early scheme.

Definition 7 A binary relation $\mathcal{S}$ on agents is an *early simulation* if $P\mathcal{S}Q$ implies that

If $P \xrightarrow{\alpha} P'$ and α is any action with $\mathrm{bn}(\alpha) \cap \mathrm{fn}(P,Q) = \emptyset$,
then for some Q', $\quad Q \xrightarrow{\alpha} Q'$ and $P'\mathcal{S}Q'$

The relation S is an *early bisimulation* if both S and S^{-1} are early simulations. We define *early bisimilarity* $P \stackrel{\cdot}{\sim}_{\mathrm{E}} Q$ to mean that PSQ for some early bisimulation S. □

Note that the extra requirement on bound input actions has disappeared; instead we include input actions, both free and bound, in the first requirement.

Lemma 2 $\stackrel{\cdot}{\sim}' \;=\; \stackrel{\cdot}{\sim}_{\mathrm{E}}$

Proof: From Lemma 1.4 it follows that the following two requirements on any relation S are equivalent:

$$\forall P, Q, x, y, P' : \text{If } P \xrightarrow{xy} P' \text{ then } \exists Q' : Q \xrightarrow{xy} Q' \text{ and } P'SQ'$$

$$\forall P, Q, x, w, P'' : \text{If } P \xrightarrow{x(w)} P'' \text{ then } \forall y \exists Q'' : Q \xrightarrow{x(w)} Q'' \text{ and } P''\{y/w\}SQ''\{y/w\}$$

Hence, S is an alternative simulation iff it is an early simulation. □

We will not explore the theory of $\stackrel{\cdot}{\sim}_{\mathrm{E}}$ here. Just like $\stackrel{\cdot}{\sim}_{\mathrm{L}}$ it is an equivalence relation and is preserved by all operators except input prefix, and if $P\{w/y\} \stackrel{\cdot}{\sim}_{\mathrm{E}} Q\{w/y\}$ for all w then $x(y).\,P \stackrel{\cdot}{\sim}_{\mathrm{E}} x(y).\,Q$.

3 Modal Logics

In this section we establish characterizations of late and early bisimilarity in terms of properties expressible in various modal logics. In addition we compare in detail the distinguishing power of a number of logics. We begin by introducing a logic encompassing all those we consider and establishing some properties of its satisfaction relation.

3.1 Connectives

Definition 8 The logic $\mathcal{A}$ is a subset, specified below, of the set of formulae given by:

$$\begin{array}{lcll} A & ::= & \bigwedge_{i \in I} A_i & (I \text{ a denumerable set}) \\ & | & \neg A & \\ & | & [x=y]A & \\ & | & \langle \alpha \rangle A & (\alpha = \tau, \bar{x}y, xy, \bar{x}(y), x(y)) \\ & | & \langle x(y) \rangle^{\mathrm{L}} A & \\ & | & \langle x(y) \rangle^{\mathrm{E}} A & \end{array}$$

In each of $\langle \bar{x}(y) \rangle A$, $\langle x(y) \rangle A$, $\langle x(y) \rangle^{\mathrm{L}} A$ and $\langle x(y) \rangle^{\mathrm{E}} A$, the occurrence of y in parentheses is a binding occurrence whose scope is A. The set of names occurring free in A is written $\mathrm{fn}(A)$. The logic $\mathcal{A}$ consists of those formulae A with $\mathrm{fn}(A)$ finite. □

In Definition 9 below we shall introduce a satisfaction relation $\models$ between agents and formulae of $\mathcal{A}$. Although the definition will be a little more complex, the relation will have the following simple characterization:

Proposition 1 For all agents P,

$$\begin{array}{lll} P \models \bigwedge_{i \in I} A_i & \text{iff} & \text{for all } i \in I, P \models A_i \\ P \models \neg A & \text{iff} & \text{not } P \models A \\ P \models [x=y]A & \text{iff} & \text{if } x = y \text{ then } P \models A \\ P \models \langle \alpha \rangle A & \text{iff} & \text{for some } P', P \xrightarrow{\alpha} P' \text{ and } P' \models A, \text{ for } \alpha = \tau, \bar{x}y, xy \end{array}$$

and assuming that the name y is not free in P

$$
\begin{array}{lll}
P \models \langle \bar{x}(y)\rangle A & \text{iff} & \text{for some } P',\ P \xrightarrow{\bar{x}(y)} P' \text{ and } P' \models A \\
P \models \langle x(y)\rangle A & \text{iff} & \text{for some } P',\ P \xrightarrow{x(y)} P' \text{ and for some } z,\ P'\{z/y\} \models A\{z/y\} \\
P \models \langle x(y)\rangle^{\mathrm{L}} A & \text{iff} & \text{for some } P',\ P \xrightarrow{x(y)} P' \text{ and for all } z,\ P'\{z/y\} \models A\{z/y\} \\
P \models \langle x(y)\rangle^{\mathrm{E}} A & \text{iff} & \text{for all } z \text{ there is } P' \text{ such that } P \xrightarrow{x(y)} P' \text{ and } P'\{z/y\} \models A\{z/y\}
\end{array}
$$

□

The assumption on y is no constraint since Lemma 3(a) below asserts that alpha-convertible formulae are logically equivalent.

Before embarking on the formal definitions we will explain the intuition behind the connectives. Conjunction, negation, and the silent, output and free input modalities work as in the logic $\mathcal{PL}$ described in the introduction. We will write **true** for the empty conjunction and **false** for $\neg$**true**. The *matching* connective $[x=y]A$ gives us the power of an equality predicate over names: $[x=x]A$ holds of an agent iff A holds of it, and if x and y are distinct then $[x=y]A$ holds of any agent. Note that an atomic equality predicate on names can be defined in terms of matching; the formula

$$\neg[x=y]\textbf{false}$$

holds of P precisely when $x = y$, regardless of P.

The bound input modalities come in three kinds. They all require an agent to have a bound input transition of type $P \xrightarrow{x(y)} P'$ but they differ in the requirements on P'. The *basic* bound input modality $\langle x(y)\rangle A$ merely requires that P' satisfies A for *some* instantiation of the parameter y. The *late* modality $\langle x(y)\rangle^{\mathrm{L}}$ is stronger, it requires P' to satisfy A for *all* such instantiations. Finally the *early* modality $\langle x(y)\rangle^{\mathrm{E}}$ is weaker than the late modality; it admits *different* derivatives P' to satisfy A for the different instantiations of y. As an example let

$$
\begin{array}{rcl}
A & = & \langle x(y)\rangle\neg\langle\tau\rangle\textbf{true} \\
A_L & = & \langle x(y)\rangle^{\mathrm{L}}\neg\langle\tau\rangle\textbf{true} \\
A_E & = & \langle x(y)\rangle^{\mathrm{E}}\neg\langle\tau\rangle\textbf{true}
\end{array}
$$

First put

$$P_1 = x(y).\,[y=u]\tau$$

It then holds that

$$P_1 \models A$$

The derivative P' is here $[y=u]\tau$ and there are instantiations of y, namely all but u, where P' has no τ-transition and thus satisfies $\neg\langle\tau\rangle$**true**. But for $y = u$ there is such a transition, hence P_1 neither satisfies A_E nor A_L. Next assume $u \neq v$ and consider

$$P_2 = x(y).\,[y=u]\tau \;+\; x(y).\,[y=v]\tau$$

Here there are two possible derivatives under the bound input action $x(y)$. The derivative corresponding to the left branch lacks a τ transition for $y \neq u$, while the right branch lacks a τ transition for $y \neq v$. It follows that for any instantiation of y we can choose a derivative lacking a τ; thus

$$P_2 \models A_E$$

Of course P_2 also satisfies A, but it does not satisfy A_L since no single derivative lacks a τ for all instantiations of y. Finally consider

$$P_3 = x(y)$$

Then P_3 satisfies all of A, A_E and A_L.

The dual operators $[\alpha]$, $[x(y)]^{\mathrm{L}}$ and $[x(y)]^{\mathrm{E}}$ of $\langle\alpha\rangle$, $\langle x(y)\rangle^{\mathrm{L}}$ and $\langle x(y)\rangle^{\mathrm{E}}$ are defined in the standard way: $[\alpha]A = \neg\langle\alpha\rangle\neg A$ etc. We note in particular the following properties:

$$P \models [x(y)]A \quad \text{iff} \quad \text{for all } P', \text{ if } P \xrightarrow{x(y)} P' \text{ then for all } z,\ P'\{z/y\} \models A\{z/y\}$$
$$P \models [x(y)]^{\mathrm{L}}A \quad \text{iff} \quad \text{for all } P', \text{ if } P \xrightarrow{x(y)} P' \text{ then for some } z,\ P'\{z/y\} \models A\{z/y\}$$
$$P \models [x(y)]^{\mathrm{E}}A \quad \text{iff} \quad \text{there is } z \text{ such that for all } P', \text{ if } P \xrightarrow{x(y)} P' \text{ then } P'\{z/y\} \models A\{z/y\}$$

So $[\cdot]$ signifies universal quantification over derivatives, whereas $\langle\cdot\rangle$ implies existential quantification. It is interesting to note that with the three bound input modalities and their duals we cover all combinations of existential/universal quantifications of derivatives and parameter instantiation.

We now return to the formal definition of the satisfaction relation:

Definition 9 The *satisfaction relation* between agents and formulae of $\mathcal{A}$ is given by:

$$
\begin{array}{lll}
P \models \bigwedge_{i \in I} A_i & \text{if} & \text{for all } i \in I,\ P \models A_i \\
P \models \neg A & \text{if} & \text{not } P \models A \\
P \models [x = y]A & \text{if} & \text{if } x = y \text{ then } P \models A \\
P \models \langle \alpha \rangle A & \text{if} & \text{for some } P',\ P \xrightarrow{\alpha} P' \text{ and } P' \models A, \\
 & & \text{for } \alpha = \tau, \bar{x}y, xy \\
P \models \langle \bar{x}(y) \rangle A & \text{if} & \text{for some } P' \text{ and } w \notin \mathrm{fn}(A) - \{y\}, \\
 & & P \xrightarrow{\bar{x}(w)} P' \text{ and } P' \models A\{w/y\} \\
P \models \langle x(y) \rangle A & \text{if} & \text{for some } P' \text{ and } w,\ P \xrightarrow{x(w)} P' \\
 & & \text{and for some } z,\ P'\{z/w\} \models A\{z/y\} \\
P \models \langle x(y) \rangle^{\mathrm{L}} A & \text{if} & \text{for some } P' \text{ and } w,\ P \xrightarrow{x(w)} P' \\
 & & \text{and for all } z,\ P'\{z/w\} \models A\{z/y\} \\
P \models \langle x(y) \rangle^{\mathrm{E}} A & \text{if} & \text{for all } z \text{ there are } P' \text{ and } w \text{ such that} \\
 & & P \xrightarrow{x(w)} P' \text{ and } P'\{z/w\} \models A\{z/y\}
\end{array}
$$

□

Recall that by Lemma 1 we may combine the late and early schemes in giving and working with this definition. Before commenting on it in detail we note the following facts. We write $\equiv$ for alpha-equivalence of formulae.

Lemma 3 (a) If $P \models A$ and $A \equiv B$ then $P \models B$.
(b) If $P \models A$ and $u \notin \mathrm{fn}(P, A)$ then $P\{u/v\} \models A\{u/v\}$.

Proof: The two assertions are proved together by showing by induction on A that if $P \models A$, $A \equiv B$ and $u \notin \mathrm{fn}(P, A)$ then $P\{u/v\} \models B\{u/v\}$. The proof, though not unduly difficult, contains some points of technical interest and requires careful attention to detail. It is given in the appendix. □

The final four clauses in the definition of satisfaction are complicated by the inclusion of the name w. This is required to define $P \models A$ in the case that a name occurs bound in A and free in P. For suppose the clause for the bound output modality were simplified to that given in Proposition 1 above. If $P \equiv (w)\bar{x}w.\,y(z)$ and $A \equiv \langle \bar{x}(y) \rangle \mathbf{true}$ then according to Definition 9, $P \models A$; but under the simplified definition, $P \not\models A$. A similar difficulty arises with the other three clauses.

However by Lemma 3(a), when considering an assertion $P \models A$, given any name x bound in A, we may always assume that x is not free in P. This assumption, which we make from now on, leads to a simple proof of the more elegant characterization given above in Proposition 1. This characterization helps to make clear the significant points in the definition. Note in particular that the clause for $\langle \bar{x}(y) \rangle$ may be subsumed under that for $\langle \alpha \rangle$ for $\alpha = \tau, \bar{x}y, xy$.

The following useful lemma describes some relationships among the modalities.

Lemma 4 (a) Suppose $w \notin \mathrm{fn}(A, y)$. Then

$$P \models \langle xy \rangle A \text{ iff } P \models \langle x(w)\rangle^{\mathrm{L}}[w=y]A$$
$$\text{iff } P \models \langle x(w)\rangle^{\mathrm{E}}[w=y]A$$
$$\text{iff } P \models \langle x(w)\rangle \neg [w=y]\neg A$$

(b) $P \models \langle x(y)\rangle^{\mathrm{E}} A$ iff for all z, $P \models \langle xz \rangle A\{z/y\}$
(c) $P \models \langle x(y)\rangle A$ iff for some z, $P \models \langle xz \rangle A\{z/y\}$

Proof: Straightforward from the definitions. See the appendix. □

3.2 Characterizations of Equivalences

Suppose $\mathcal{K}$ is a sublogic of $\mathcal{A}$. Then $\mathcal{K}(P) = \{A \in \mathcal{K} \mid P \models A\}$. We write $=_{\mathcal{K}}$ for the equivalence relation determined by $\mathcal{K}$: $P =_{\mathcal{K}} Q$ iff $\mathcal{K}(P) = \mathcal{K}(Q)$. We say $\mathcal{K}$ *characterizes* a relation $\mathcal{R}$ if $=_{\mathcal{K}} = \mathcal{R}$.

A number of sublogics of $\mathcal{A}$ will be considered. They share a common basis $\mathcal{A}_0$ consisting of the formulae of $\mathcal{A}$ built from conjunction, negation and the modalities $\langle\tau\rangle$, $\langle\bar{x}y\rangle$ and $\langle\bar{x}(y)\rangle$. The sublogics of $\mathcal{A}$ extending $\mathcal{A}_0$ are named by indicating which of $\langle x(y)\rangle$, $\langle x(y)\rangle^{\mathrm{E}}$, $\langle xy\rangle$, $\langle x(y)\rangle^{\mathrm{L}}$ and $[x=y]$ are added to $\mathcal{A}_0$, using the letters $\mathcal{B}, \mathcal{E}, \mathcal{F}, \mathcal{L}$ and $\mathcal{M}$ respectively. For instance, $\mathcal{LM}$ is the extension of $\mathcal{A}_0$ obtained by adding the late bound input modality $\langle x(y)\rangle^{\mathrm{L}}$ and matching $[x=y]$, while $\mathcal{F}$ is obtained by adding the free input modality $\langle xy\rangle$ alone.

We now give the main characterizations of $\dot{\sim}_{\mathrm{L}}$ and $\dot{\sim}_{\mathrm{E}}$.

Theorem 1 $\mathcal{LM}$ characterizes $\dot{\sim}_{\mathrm{L}}$.

Proof: The proof follows a standard pattern but contains some novelty. First we show that $\dot{\sim}_{\mathrm{L}} \subseteq =_{\mathcal{LM}}$ by proving by induction on A in $\mathcal{LM}$ that if $P \dot{\sim}_{\mathrm{L}} Q$ then $P \models A$ iff $Q \models A$. The argument for the converse amounts to a proof that if $P \dot{\not\sim}_{\mathrm{L}} Q$ then there is $A \in \mathcal{LM}(P) - \mathcal{LM}(Q)$ with $\mathrm{fn}(A) \subseteq \mathrm{fn}(P,Q)$. The principal point of interest is the use of a combination of the late bound input modality $\langle x(y)\rangle^{\mathrm{L}}$ and matching. The proof is given in the appendix. □

We need infinite conjunction only if the transition system is not image-finite. In particular, if all recursive definitions are guarded then finite conjunction suffices. Recalling the quantifier switch in the semantic clauses for $\langle x(y)\rangle^{\mathrm{L}}$ and $\langle x(y)\rangle^{\mathrm{E}}$, in view of the preceding theorem it may be expected that $\mathcal{EM}$ characterizes $\dot{\sim}_{\mathrm{E}}$. In fact we have:

Theorem 2 Each of $\mathcal{EM}$, $\mathcal{F}$ and $\mathcal{BM}$ characterizes $\dot{\sim}_{\mathrm{E}}$.

Proof: By utilizing the characterization of $\dot{\sim}_{\mathrm{E}}$ in the early scheme, Lemma 2, a proof that $\mathcal{F}$ characterizes $\dot{\sim}_{\mathrm{E}}$ is easily obtained. That $\mathcal{EM}$ and $\mathcal{BM}$ also characterize $\dot{\sim}_{\mathrm{E}}$ then follows using Lemma 4. For details see the appendix. □

We have seen that $\mathcal{F}$ characterizes $\dot{\sim}_{\mathrm{E}}$ and that the free input modality corresponds to combinations of the bound input modalities and matching. A natural question concerns the power of the bound input modalities in the absence of matching. We give a sequence of examples which establish the relationships among the various logics. These are summarized in a picture below.

Lemma 5 $P =_{\mathcal{EL}} Q$ but $P \neq_{\mathcal{B}} Q$ where

$$P = x(y)$$
$$Q = x(y) + x(y).[y=z]\tau$$

Proof: Note that if $A \equiv [x(y)]\neg\langle\tau\rangle\mathbf{true}$ then $P \models A$ but $Q \not\models A$. To see that $P =_{\mathcal{EL}} Q$ we prove by induction on A in $\mathcal{EL}$ that $P \models A$ iff $Q \models A$. See the appendix. □

Lemma 6 $P \dot{\sim}_{\mathrm{E}} Q$ but $P \neq_{\mathcal{L}} Q$ where

$$P = x(y) + x(y).([y=z]\tau + [y=w]\tau)$$
$$Q = x(y).[y=z]\tau + x(y).[y=w]\tau$$

Proof: Clearly $P \dot{\sim}_{\mathrm{E}} Q$. To see that $P \neq_{\mathcal{L}} Q$ simply note that if $A \equiv \langle x(y)\rangle^{\mathrm{L}}\neg\langle\tau\rangle\mathbf{true}$ then $P \models A$ but $Q \not\models A$. □

Lemma 7 $P =_{\mathcal{BL}} Q$ but $P \neq_{\mathcal{E}} Q$ where

$$P = x(y).[y=z]\tau + x(y).([y=z]\tau + [y=w]\tau)$$
$$Q = x(y).[y=z]\tau + x(y).[y=w]\tau$$

Proof: To see that $P \neq_{\mathcal{E}} Q$ note that if $A \equiv \langle x(y)\rangle^{\mathrm{E}}\neg\langle\tau\rangle\mathbf{true}$ then $Q \models A$ but $P \not\models A$. To see that $P =_{\mathcal{BL}} Q$ we prove by induction on A in $\mathcal{BL}$ that $P \models A$ iff $Q \models A$. See the appendix. □

Lemma 8 $P =_{\mathcal{BEL}} Q$ but $P \dot{\not\sim}_{\mathrm{E}} Q$ where

$$P = x(y).[y=z]\tau$$
$$Q = x(y).[y=w]\tau$$

Proof: Clearly $P \dot{\not\sim}_{\mathrm{E}} Q$. To see that $P =_{\mathcal{BEL}} Q$ we prove by induction on A in $\mathcal{BEL}$ that $P \models A$ iff $Q \models A$. The proof is similar to that of Lemma 7. We omit the details. □

Lemma 9 $P =_{\mathcal{FL}} Q$ but $P \dot{\not\sim}_{\mathrm{L}} Q$ where

$$P = x(y) + x(y).\tau$$
$$Q = x(y) + x(y).\tau + x(y).[y=z]\tau$$

Proof: Clearly $P \dot{\not\sim}_{\mathrm{L}} Q$. To see that $P =_{\mathcal{FL}} Q$ we prove by induction on A in $\mathcal{FL}$ that $P \models A$ iff $Q \models A$. The proof is similar to that of Lemma 7. We omit the details. □

To complete the picture we note the following. Let us say that two logics $\mathcal{J}$ and $\mathcal{K}$ are *equipotent* if $=_{\mathcal{J}} \;=\; =_{\mathcal{K}}$.

Lemma 10 Let Z be any combination of $\mathcal{B}, \mathcal{E}, \mathcal{F}, \mathcal{L}, \mathcal{M}$. Then in an obvious notation

(a) $\mathcal{F} + Z$, $\mathcal{BF} + Z$ and $\mathcal{EF} + Z$ are equipotent.
(b) $\mathcal{BM} + Z$, $\mathcal{EM} + Z$ and $\mathcal{FM} + Z$ are equipotent.
(c) $\mathcal{LM} + Z$ and $\mathcal{FLM} + Z$ are equipotent.
(d) Finally, $\mathcal{M}$ and $\mathcal{A}_0$ are equipotent.

Proof: See the appendix. □

We summarize the relationships among the logics established by the preceding results in the following theorem.

Theorem 3 In the picture below, each point represents a distinct relation. A line between two relations signifies inclusion, while the absence of a line signifies that they are incomparable. By 'etc.' we mean any other combination equipotent by Lemma 10.

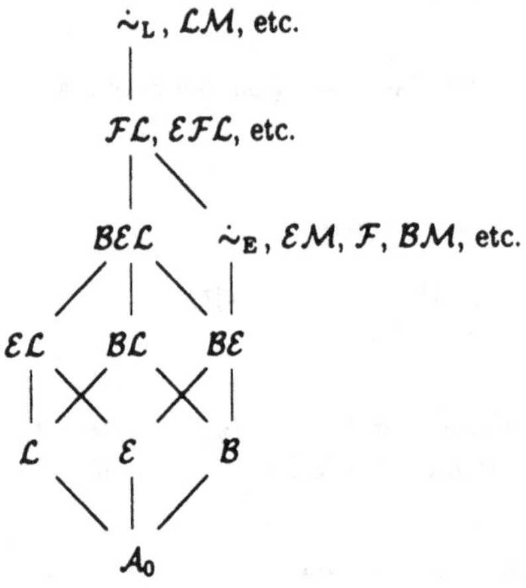

□

The examples in Lemmas 5–9 all involve the match expression of the calculus. However, its use is in each case inessential. For example, Lemma 5 asserts that $P =_{\mathcal{EL}} Q$ but $P \neq_{\mathrm{B}} Q$ where $P = x(y)$ and $Q = x(y) + x(y).[y{=}z]\tau$. Alternatively we can take:

$$P = x(y).(\bar{y}.z + z.\bar{y})$$
$$Q = x(y).(\bar{y}.z + z.\bar{y}) + x(y).(\bar{y} \mid z)$$

Similar modifications can be made to the other examples.

4 Future work

The logic we have introduced no doubt has interesting intrinsic properties, which we have not begun to study. Here, we only wish to mention two questions about its relationship with the π-calculus which appear to be of immediate interest.

First, what happens when we introduce the *mismatch* form

$$[x{\neq}y]P$$

into the calculus? Note that the corresponding mismatch connective

$$[x{\neq}y]A$$

does not add power to our logic since it already has matching and negation.

Second, considering the input modalities, can we factor out their quantificational content? It is attractive to factor $\langle x(y)\rangle^{\mathrm{L}}$ thus:

$$\langle x(y)\rangle^{\mathrm{L}} A \stackrel{\mathrm{def}}{=} \langle x\rangle(\forall y A)$$

Now, to express the satisfaction relation, we appear to need also to factor the input prefix $x(y)$ of the calculus thus:

$$x(y).P \stackrel{\mathrm{def}}{=} x.\lambda yP$$

– in other words, we need to give proper status to (λ-)*abstractions*, which abstract names from processes. This step has considerable interest, since there appear to be other independent advantages to be gained from it.

References

[1] Hennessy, M., **Algebraic Theory of Processes**, MIT Press, 1988.

[2] Hennessy, M. and Milner, R., *Algebraic Laws for Non-determinism and Concurrency*, Journal of ACM, Vol 32, pp137–161, 1985.

[3] Hoare, C.A.R., **Communicating Sequential Processes**, Prentice Hall, 1985.

[4] Milner, R., **A Calculus of Communicating Systems**, Lecture Notes in Computer Science, Volume 92, Springer-Verlag, 1980.

[5] Milner, R., **Communication and Concurrency**, Prentice Hall, 1989.

[6] Milner, R., Parrow, J. and Walker, D., *A Calculus of Mobile Processes, Part I*, Reports ECS-LFCS–89–85, Laboratory for Foundations of Computer Science, Computer Science Department, Edinburgh University, 1989. Also to appear in J. Information and Computation.

[7] Milner, R., Parrow, J. and Walker, D., *A Calculus of Mobile Processes, Part II*, Reports ECS-LFCS–89–86, Laboratory for Foundations of Computer Science, Computer Science Department, Edinburgh University, 1989. Also to appear in J. Information and Computation.

[8] Park, D.M.R., *Concurrency and Automata on Infinite Sequences*, Lecture Notes in Computer Science, Vol 104, Springer Verlag, 1980.

Appendix

This section contains the proofs omitted from the main text.

Proof of Lemma 3: We prove the two assertions by showing by induction on A that:

$$\text{if } P \models A,\ A \equiv B \text{ and } u \notin \mathrm{fn}(P, A),\text{ then } P\{u/v\} \models B\{u/v\}$$

Let $\sigma = \{u/v\}$.

The conjunction case is trivial.

Suppose $A \equiv \neg A'$ so $B \equiv \neg B'$ with $A' \equiv B'$. Since $P \not\models A'$, by induction hypothesis $P \not\models B'$ and so $P \models B$. Hence if $u = v$ the claim holds. Suppose $u \neq v$ so $v \notin \mathrm{fn}(P\sigma, B\sigma)$. If $P\sigma \not\models B\sigma$ then $P\sigma \models B'\sigma$ so by induction hypothesis $P\sigma\sigma^{-1} \models B'\sigma\sigma^{-1}$, so $P \models B'$. Then again by induction hypothesis $P \models A$. Contradiction. Hence $P\sigma \models B\sigma$.

Suppose $A \equiv [x = y]A'$ so $B \equiv [x = y]B'$ with $A' \equiv B'$. If $x \neq y$ then certainly $P\sigma \models B\sigma$ since $B\sigma \equiv [x\sigma = y\sigma]B'\sigma$ and $x\sigma \neq y\sigma$. If $x = y$ then $P \models A'$ and by induction hypothesis $P\sigma \models B'\sigma$ so again $P\sigma \models B\sigma$.

Suppose $A \equiv \langle\alpha\rangle A'$ where $\alpha = \tau, \bar{x}y, xy$, so $B \equiv \langle\alpha\rangle B'$ with $A' \equiv B'$. Since $P \models A$ there is P' such that $P \xrightarrow{\alpha} P'$ and $P' \models A'$. Then $P\sigma \xrightarrow{\alpha\sigma} P'\sigma$ and by induction hypothesis $P'\sigma \models B'\sigma$. Hence $P\sigma \models B\sigma$ since $B\sigma \equiv \langle\alpha\sigma\rangle B'\sigma$.

Suppose $A \equiv \langle\bar{x}(y)\rangle A'$ so $B\sigma \equiv \langle\bar{x}\bar{\sigma}(y')\rangle B'\sigma$ where $A'\{y'/y\} \equiv B'$ and y' is fresh. Since $P \models A$ there are P' and $w \notin \mathrm{fn}(A) - \{y\}$ such that $P \xrightarrow{\bar{x}(w)} P'$ and $P' \models A'\{w/y\}$. Choose $w' \notin \mathrm{fn}(P, A)$. Then $P \xrightarrow{\bar{x}(w')} P'' \equiv P'\{w'/w\}$ and by induction hypothesis $P'' \models B'\{w'/y'\}$. Also $P\sigma \xrightarrow{\bar{x}\bar{\sigma}(w')} P''\sigma$ and again by induction hypothesis $P''\sigma \models B'\{w'/y'\}\sigma$. Hence $P\sigma \models B\sigma$ since $B'\{w'/y'\}\sigma \equiv B'\sigma\{w'/y'\}$.

Suppose $A \equiv \langle x(y)\rangle^{\mathrm{L}} A'$ so $B\sigma \equiv \langle x\sigma(y')\rangle^{\mathrm{L}} B'\sigma$ where $A'\{y'/y\} \equiv B'$ and y' is fresh. Since $P \models A$ there are P' and w such that $P \xrightarrow{x(w)} P'$ and for all z, $P'\{z/w\} \models A'\{z/y\}$. Choose $w' \notin \mathrm{fn}(P, A)$. Then $P \xrightarrow{x(w')} P'' \equiv P'\{w'/w\}$ and by induction hypothesis for all z,

$$P''\{z/w'\} \models B'\{z/y'\} \qquad (*)$$

Now $P\sigma \xrightarrow{x\sigma(w')} P''\sigma$.

Claim For all z, $P''\sigma\{z/w'\} \models B'\sigma\{z/y'\}$.

Proof of Claim: If $u = v$ the claim is immediate from $(*)$, so suppose $u \neq v$.

Case 1: $z \neq u, v$. Then $P''\sigma\{z/w'\} \equiv P''\{z/w'\}\sigma$ and $B'\sigma\{z/y'\} \equiv B'\{z/y'\}\sigma$. By induction hypothesis and $(*)$, $P''\{z/w'\}\sigma \models B'\{z/y'\}\sigma$ since $u \notin \mathrm{fn}(P''\{z/w'\}, B'\{z/y'\})$. Hence again by induction hypothesis, $P''\{z/w'\}\sigma \models B'\sigma\{z/y'\}$.

Case 2: $z = u$. Now $P''\sigma\{u/w'\} \equiv P''\{v/w'\}\sigma$ and $B'\sigma\{u/y'\} \equiv B'\{v/y'\}\sigma$. By $(*)$, $P''\{v/w'\} \models B'\{v/y'\}$ so by induction hypothesis, $P''\{v/w'\}\sigma \models B'\{v/y'\}\sigma$ since $u \notin \mathrm{fn}(P''\{v/w'\}, B'\{v/y'\})$. Hence by induction hypothesis, $P''\{v/w'\}\sigma \models B'\sigma\{u/y'\}$.

Case 3: $z = v$. Then $P''\sigma \models B'\sigma$ by induction hypothesis since $u \notin \mathrm{fn}(P'', B')$. So again by induction hypothesis, $P''\sigma\{v/w'\} \models B'\sigma\{v/y'\}$ since $v \notin \mathrm{fn}(P''\sigma, B'\sigma)$.

This completes the proof of the Claim and hence of the case $\langle x(y)\rangle^{\mathrm{L}}$.

The cases $A \equiv \langle x(y)\rangle^{\mathrm{E}} A'$ and $A \equiv \langle x(y)\rangle A'$ involve similar arguments. □

Proof of Lemma 4: First note that if $w \neq y$ then

$$\begin{aligned} & P \models \langle x(w)\rangle^{\mathrm{L}}[w=y]A \\ \text{iff} \quad & P \models \langle x(w)\rangle^{\mathrm{E}}[w=y]A \\ \text{iff} \quad & P \models \langle x(y)\rangle\neg[w=y]\neg A \\ \text{iff} \quad & \text{for some } P',\ P \xrightarrow{x(w)} P' \text{ and } P'\{y/w\} \models A\{y/w\} \end{aligned}$$

Now suppose $w \notin \mathrm{fn}(A, y)$. If $P \models \langle xy\rangle A$ then for some P', $P \xrightarrow{xy} P'$ and $P' \models A$. Then $P \xrightarrow{x(w)} P''$ with $P''\{y/w\} \equiv P'$. Since $P''\{y/w\} \models A\{y/w\} \equiv A$ it follows by the above that $P \models \langle x(w)\rangle^{\mathrm{L}}[w=y]A$ etc. Conversely, if $P \xrightarrow{x(w)} P''$ and $P''\{y/w\} \models A\{y/w\}$ then $P \xrightarrow{xy} P' \equiv P''\{y/w\}$ and $P' \models A$, so $P \models \langle xy\rangle A$. □

Proof of Theorem 1: We first show by induction on structure that for all A in $\mathcal{LM}$, if $P \dot{\sim}_{\mathrm{L}} Q$ then $P \models A$ iff $Q \models A$. Suppose $P \models A$. The conjunction and negation cases are trivial.

Suppose $A \equiv [x = y]A'$. If $x \neq y$ then certainly $Q \models A$. Otherwise $P \models A'$ and by induction hypothesis $Q \models A'$ and so $Q \models A$.

Suppose $A \equiv \langle\alpha\rangle A'$ where $\alpha = \tau, \bar{x}y$ or $\bar{x}(z)$ where $z \notin \mathrm{fn}(P, Q)$. Then there is P' such that $P \xrightarrow{\alpha} P'$ and $P' \models A'$. Since $P \dot{\sim}_{\mathrm{L}} Q$ there is Q' such that $Q \xrightarrow{\alpha} Q'$ and $P' \dot{\sim}_{\mathrm{L}} Q'$. By induction hypothesis $Q' \models A'$, so $Q \models A$.

Suppose $A \equiv \langle x(y)\rangle^{\mathrm{L}} A'$ where $y \notin \mathrm{n}(P, Q)$. Then there is P' such that $P \xrightarrow{x(y)} P'$ and for all z, $P'\{z/y\} \models A'\{z/y\}$. Since $P \dot{\sim}_{\mathrm{L}} Q$ there is Q' such that $Q \xrightarrow{x(y)} Q'$ and for all z, $P'\{z/y\} \dot{\sim}_{\mathrm{L}} Q'\{z/y\}$. By induction hypothesis for all z, $Q'\{z/y\} \models A'\{z/y\}$, so $Q \models A$.

Hence $\dot{\sim}_L \subseteq =_{\mathcal{LM}}$.

For the converse it suffices to show that $\mathcal{S}$ is a late bisimulation where $P\mathcal{S}Q$ iff for all A in $\mathcal{LM}$ with $\mathrm{fn}(A) \subseteq \mathrm{fn}(P,Q)$, $P \models A$ iff $Q \models A$. Suppose $P\mathcal{S}Q$.

Suppose $P \xrightarrow{\alpha} P'$ where $\alpha = \tau, \bar{x}y$ or $\bar{x}(z)$ with $z \notin \mathrm{n}(P,Q)$, let $\langle Q_i \rangle_{i \in I}$ be an enumeration of $\{Q' \mid Q \xrightarrow{\alpha} Q'\}$, and suppose that for all i, not $P\mathcal{S}Q_i$. Choose $\langle A_i \rangle$ with for each i, $A_i \in \mathcal{LM}(P') - \mathcal{LM}(Q_i)$ and $\mathrm{fn}(A_i) \subseteq \mathrm{fn}(P', Q_i)$. Set $A \equiv \langle \alpha \rangle \bigwedge_{i \in I} A_i$. Then $A \in \mathcal{LM}(P) - \mathcal{LM}(Q)$ and $\mathrm{fn}(A) \subseteq \mathrm{fn}(P,Q)$, so not $P\mathcal{S}Q$. Contradiction.

Suppose $P \xrightarrow{x(y)} P'$ where $y \notin \mathrm{n}(P,Q)$, let $\langle Q_i \rangle$ be an enumeration of $\{Q' \mid Q \xrightarrow{x(y)} Q'\}$, and suppose that for each i there is z such that not $P'\{z/y\}\mathcal{S}Q_i\{z/y\}$. Set $N = \mathrm{fn}(P,Q,y)$ so that $\mathrm{fn}(P') \subseteq N$ and $\mathrm{fn}(Q_i) \subseteq N$ for each i. Note that by Lemma 3(b), if $P'\mathcal{S}Q_i$ then $P'\{z/y\}\mathcal{S}Q_i\{z/y\}$ for all $z \notin N$. So for each i there are $z_i \in N$ and B_i such that $B_i \in \mathcal{LM}(P'\{z_i/y\}) - \mathcal{LM}(Q_i\{z_i/y\})$ and $\mathrm{fn}(B_i) \subseteq \mathrm{fn}(P'\{z_i/y\}, Q_i\{z_i/y\})$. Set $A_i \equiv B_i\{y/z_i\}$ for each i, and $A \equiv \langle x(y) \rangle^{\mathrm{L}} \bigwedge_i [y = z_i] A_i$. Then $A \in \mathcal{LM}(P)$ since for all z, $P'\{z/y\} \models \bigwedge_i [z = z_i] A_i \{z/y\}$, but $A \notin \mathcal{LM}(Q)$ since $Q_i\{z_i/y\} \not\models [z_i = z_i] A_i \{z_i/y\}$. Moreover $\mathrm{fn}(A) \subseteq \mathrm{fn}(P,Q)$, so not $P\mathcal{S}Q$. Contradiction.

Hence $\mathcal{S}$ is a late bisimulation so $=_{\mathcal{LM}} \subseteq \mathcal{S} \subseteq \dot{\sim}_L$. □

Proof of Theorem 2: Recall the characterization of $\dot{\sim}_E$ in the early scheme, Lemma 2. Using this characterization, the proof is similar in structure and in much detail to that of Theorem 1, but is more straightforward due to the simpler clause for free input actions. These are treated exactly as bound output actions.

To show that $\dot{\sim}_E \subseteq \mathcal{EM}, \mathcal{BM}$ we show by an induction similar to that in the proof of Theorem 1 that for all A in $\mathcal{BEM}$, if $P \dot{\sim}_E Q$ then $P \models A$ iff $Q \models A$. For the converse we use the fact that $\mathcal{F}$ characterizes $\dot{\sim}_E$ and the relationships between the modalities and matching in Lemma 4. □

Proof of Lemma 5: To see that $P =_{\mathcal{EL}} Q$ we first note by induction on A in $\mathcal{BEL}$ that for all substitutions σ, $\mathbf{0} \models A$ iff $\mathbf{0} \models A\sigma$. Then we show, again by induction, that for A in $\mathcal{EL}$, $P \models A$ iff $Q \models A$. We consider only the case $A \equiv \langle x(y) \rangle^{\mathrm{L}} A'$. Clearly if $P \models A$ then $Q \models A$. If $Q \models A$ but $P \not\models A$ then, amongst other things, it must be the case that $[y = z]\tau \models A'$, so $\mathbf{0} \models A'$, but for some w, $\mathbf{0} \not\models A'\{w/y\}$, contradicting the above observation. The case $A \equiv \langle x(y) \rangle^{\mathrm{E}} A'$ uses a similar argument. □

Proof of Lemma 7: The argument is somewhat similar to that in the proof of Lemma 5. Recall that for all A in $\mathcal{BEL}$ and all substitutions σ, $\mathbf{0} \models A$ iff $\mathbf{0} \models A\sigma$. Similarly we show by induction on A in $\mathcal{BEL}$ that $\tau \models A$ iff $\tau \models A\sigma$. Then we prove by induction on A in $\mathcal{BL}$ that $P \models A$ iff $Q \models A$. Suppose $A \equiv \langle x(y) \rangle^{\mathrm{L}} A'$. Let $P' \equiv [y = z]\tau + [y = w]\tau$ and $Q' \equiv [y = z]\tau$. Using the properties of $\mathbf{0}$ and τ stated above, it suffices to show by case analyses that for all v, $P'\{v/y\} \models A'\{v/y\}$ iff for all v, $Q'\{v/y\} \models A'\{v/y\}$. The reader may care to check the details. The case $A \equiv \langle x(y) \rangle A'$ is similar. □

Proof of Lemma 10: (a) follows from Lemma 4(b),(c). (b) and (c) then follow from (a) and Lemma 4(a). Finally, (d) is proved by a trivial induction. □

Towards a Design Calculus for Communicating Programs

Ernst-Rüdiger Olderog

FB Informatik, Universität Oldenburg
Postfach 2503, 2900 Oldenburg, Germany

Abstract

This paper presents some rules of a design calculus for communicating programs. The rules can be used to transfrom specifications written in a specification language SL_0 stepwise into occam-like programs. Intermediate stages of such a design are expressed by using terms that mix programming and specification notation. Application of the rules guarantees the correctness of the resulting program with respect to the initial specification in a combined state-trace-readiness model of communicating systems. Correctness of the individual design rules can be conviently shown in a uniform predicative semantics for specifications, programs, and mixed terms expressing the observables of that model.

1 Introduction

This paper presents some rules of a design calculus for occam-like communicating programs. The rules enable a user to transform a given specification stepwise into a program satisfying that specification.

The details reported here are based on part of the work in the ESPRIT Basic Research Action "ProCoS" as done in Oldenburg by Stephan Rössig, Jens Sander, Michael Schenke and the author, in Lyngby by Kirsten Mark Hansen, Wiesław Pawłowski, Anders Ravn and Hans Rischel, and in Oxford by He Jifeng. "ProCoS" stands for "Provably Correct Systems" and is a wide-spectrum verification project where embedded communicating systems are studied at various levels of abstraction ranging from requirements' capture over specification language and programming language down to the machine language [Bjo89]. This paper is about the link between the ProCoS specification and programming language.

At this level of abstraction a communicating system is a pair consisting of an *interface* and a *behaviour*. The interface lists the communication channels of the system with their direction and value type plus the global variables with their access mode and value type. The behaviour describes how communications can take place on the interface channels and how such communication affects the values of the global variables. To specify such a system, we use a combination of language-theoretic and assertional techniques. To implement such a system, we have to decompose the given specification into the operators that are available in the considered occam-like programming language.

Here the design calculus comes into play. Each design rule explains how a given specification can be implemented by a so-called *mixed term* where occam programming operators are applied to derived specifications. The mixed term language contains the specification and the programming language as special cases; additionally it is suitable to describe all intermediate stages in the design of a communicating program from a given specification.

The purpose of a stepwise design of a communicating program with the calculus is to ensure its correctness with respect to the initial specification. The notion of correctness used here is based on a combined state-trace-readiness model of communicating systems. That each design rule of the calculus preserves the correctness, can be conviently shown by using uniform predicative semantics for specifications, programs, and mixed terms. This semantics identifies the behaviour of a communicating system with a predicate where the free variables correspond to the observables of the system in the state-trace-readiness model. Thus correctness proofs of the design rules boil down to reasoning in predicate logic.

2 Specification Language

In this section we describe a specification language SL_0 for communicating systems [JROR90]. The main idea of SL_0 is to split the description of the desired system behaviour in two parts:

- a trace specification part, and
- a state specification part.

The trace part specifies the sequencing constraints on the interface channels whereas the communicated values are ignored. This is done by stating one or more *trace assertions*, each one consisting of an alphabet, i.e. a subset of the interface channels, and a regular expression over these channels. The regular expression describes the sequencing constraints on the interface channels mentioned in the alphabet. By stating several such trace assertions, we can specify different aspects of the intended system behaviour in a modular fashion. The informal semantics of this part of an SL_0 specification is that the described behaviour must satisfy the sequencing constraints of all trace assertions simultaneously.

The state part of an SL_0 specification describes what the exact values are that can be exchanged over the interface channels. To this end, this part starts with the introduction of certain local state variables. These variables are used in *communication assertions* specifying the link between values and channels but need not appear in the implementation of the specification. A communication assertion for a given channel has two predicates, a first one describing when a communication may occur on the channel and a second one describing the effect of the occurrence of such a communication.

An example is the following specification of a simple autopilot for a ship:

```
autopilot = spec
              input s of -1..1
              output a of int

              trace {s,a} in pref (s.a)*

              var ps of int init 0
              var cs of int init 0

              com s write {ps, cs}
                  when true
                  then ps' = cs /\ cs' = @s

              com a read {ps, cs}
                  when true
                  then (ps =  0 => @a = 2 * cs) /\
                       (ps <> 0 => @a = cs)
            end
```

The idea is that the autopilot inputs values in the range $-1..1$ on a channnel s standing for "sensor" and – to maintain the correct course of the ship – outputs appropriate corrections in the form of integer values on a channel a standing for "actuator". The specification has only one trace assertion stating that communications on the channels s and a should occur in alternating order starting with s, or equivalently, that at each moment the global channel trace of the autopilot should be a prefix of some word in the regular language $(s.a)^*$.

To specify the allowed communication values on the channels s and a, two communication assertions are used referring to local variables ps and cs standing for "previous state" and "current state". The communication assertion for s states that a communication on channel s may write on both variables ps and cs, that due to the when-predicate it is always enabled, and that due to the then-predicate its effect is as follows: the termination value of ps is the initial value of cs and the termination value of cs is the communication value on the channel s. We use primed versions of variables to refer to their value at the moment of termination, and we use channel names prefixed by the symbol @ as variables referring to the communication values on these channels. The communication assertion for a states that a communication on channel a may only read the variables ps and cs. Thus their termination value is identical to their initial value, a fact that need not be stated any more in the then-predicate of this communication assertion.

Although the communication assertions state that communications on both s and a are always enabled, the meaning of the whole autopilot specification is that these communications can occur only if they are simultaneously possible according to the trace assertion. Thus the specified behaviour of the autopilot is that it should be ready for communications on the channels s and a in alternating order starting with s and that the values communicated on these channels should agree with the values specified in the communication assertions.

In general an SL_0 specification has the following structure:

specification ::= **spec** *basic_item** **end**

where

basic_item ::= *interface_component*
| *trace_assertion*
| *local_variable*
| *communication_assertion*

interface_component ::= *directed_channel* | *global_variable*

directed_channel ::= *direction name* **of** *type*

direction ::= **input** | **output**

global_variable ::= *access_mode name* **of** *type*

access_mode ::= **read** | **write**

trace_assertion ::= **trace** *alphabet* **in** *reg_expr*

local_variable ::= **var** *name* **of** *type* **init** *expr*

communication_assertion ::= **com** *name* **read** {*name**} **write** {*name**}
when *enable_predicate* **then** *effect_predicate*

The order of basic items in a specification will be irrelevant for its semantics. Therefore we shall analyse a specification S in the form

$$S = \textbf{spec}\ \Delta\ TA\ V\ CA\ \textbf{end}$$

where Δ, TA, V, CA are the sets of the directed channels, trace assertions, local variables, and communication assertions in S. We use the following abbreviations: $Chans(\Delta)$ denotes the set of channel names occurring in Δ; for a given trace assertion $ta \in TA$ we refer to its components by writing

$$ta = \texttt{trace}\ \alpha_{ta}\ \texttt{in}\ re_{ta}\ ;$$

for a given communication assertion $ca \in CA$ we refer to its components by writing

$$\begin{aligned} ca = \quad & \texttt{com}\ ch_{ca}\ \texttt{read}\ R_{ca}\ \texttt{write}\ W_{ca} \\ & \texttt{when}\ wh_{ca}\ \texttt{then}\ th_{ca}\ . \end{aligned}$$

Here R_{ca} and W_{ca} are the sets of variables listed after the keywords `read` and `write`. The enable-predicate wh_{ca} and the effect-predicate th_{ca} satisfy the following restrictions on their free variables:

$$\begin{aligned} free(wh_{ca}) & \subseteq R_{ca} \cup W_{ca}\ , \\ free(th_{ca}) & \subseteq R_{ca} \cup W_{ca} \cup W'_{ca} \cup \{@ch_{ca}\}. \end{aligned}$$

Note that there may be more than one communication assertion for a given channel name ch declared in Δ. It is therefore convenient to introduce the following abbreviations for $ch \in Chans(\Delta)$:

$$wh_{ch} =_{df} \bigwedge_{ca \in CA} (ch_{ca} = ch \Rightarrow wh_{ca})\ ,$$

$$th_{ch} =_{df} \bigwedge_{ca \in CA} (ch_{ca} = ch \Rightarrow th_{ca})\ ,$$

$$W_{ch} = \bigcup_{ca \in CA, ch_{ca} = ch} W_{ca}\ .$$

Note that in the special case where there is no communication assertion $ca \in CA$ with $ch_{ca} = ch$, we obtain $wh_{ca} = \texttt{true}$, $th_{ca} = \texttt{true}$, $W_{ch} = \emptyset$.

The motivation for organizing an SL_0 specification in two parts is to ease its stepwise transformation into occam-like programs. The trace part should yield a synchronisation skeleton and the state part should tell us how to complete this skeleton to a communicating program by adding purely sequential parts.

These pragmatic considerations resulted in the specification language SL_0 that combines known specification formats for concurrent systems. The trace part corresponds to path expressions in the sense of [CH74] or to a regular fragment of trace logic in the sense of [Zwi89] and [Old91]. The state part describing the effect of a communication in terms of variables appears in many approaches, e.g. in [Lam83]. New is the semantic treatment of the combined effect of trace part and state part: see Section 5.

3 Programming Language

We consider here an occam-like programming language PL [IN88]. Typical for such languages is the notion of a *process* which can engage in internal actions like the assignment of a value to a variable and external actions like the communication with its environment. Elementary processes in occam are `STOP`, `SKIP`, multiple assignments, inputs and outputs on channels. Complex processes are composed from simpler ones by the operators `SEQ`, `PAR`, `IF`, `ALT` and `WHILE`.

Except for `WHILE`, the operators are applied to a possibly empty list of arguments. As in occam the application of an operator to its arguments is written by using indentation as shown in the following program which implements the autopilot of the previous section:

```
pilotprog = system
            input s of -1..1
            output a of int
            var x of int -1..1 init 0
            var y of int init 0
            var ps of int init 0
            var cs of int init 0
            WHILE true
              SEQ
                s?x
                ps,cs :=cs,x
                IF
                  ps =  0 --> y := 2 * cs
                  ps <> 0 --> y := cs
                a!y
           end
```

The **system**-**end** brackets emphasise that programs represent implementations of communicating systems. Therefore the system interface, consisting here of the input channel s and the output channel a, is stated explicitly.

In general a PL program has the following structure:

program ::= **system** *interface process* **end**

where

interface ::= *interface_component**

and

process ::= *declaration** *process*
| STOP | SKIP | *assignment* | *input* | *output*
| SEQ [*process**]
| IF [(*bool_expr* → *process*)*]
| ALT [(*bool_expr* & *input* → *process*)*]
| WHILE (*bool_expr*, *process*)
| PAR [*program**]

declaration ::= *local_variable* | *local_channel*

local_channel ::= CHAN *name* of *type*

Note that we present here the arguments of the programming operators in a linear list notation instead in an indented form.

4 Mixed Terms

To express the intermediate stages in the stepwise design of programs from specifications we need terms that mix programming and specification notation. Therefore we introduce the following language MIX of *mixed terms* which contains SL_0 and PL as proper subsets:

system ::= *specification*
| *program*
| **system** *basic_item** **end**
| **system** *interface system* **end**
| SEQ [*system**]
| IF [(*bool_expr* → *system*)*]
| ALT [(*bool_expr* & *input* → *system*)*]
| WHILE (*bool_expr*, *system*)
| *name*
| REC *name* • *sequ_system*
| PAR [*system**]
| SYN [*system**]
| HIDE *name* in *system*
| REN *name* into *name* in *system*
| *declaration** *system*

where *sequ_system* is *system* without the operators SYN or PAR.

5 Predicative Semantics

Semantically, a communicating system is a pair $\Delta : P$ consisting of an interface Δ and a behaviour or process P. Interfaces are sets of directed channels and global variables. To describe the meaning of processes, we use a *predicative semantics* as advocated e.g. by Hehner [Heh84] and Hoare [Hoa85].

The basic idea of predicative semantics is simple. First one decides on the observables or relevant aspects of system behaviour and takes as semantic domain predicates with free variables ranging over these observables. We take here first-order predicates extended by the μ-operator for introducing recursive definitions [Par76]. Processes are then *identified* with predicates describing their observable values. Thus in predicative semantics the application of semantic functions that is typical for denotational semantics is suppressed. So predicative semantics aims at both a conceptual simplification ("processes are predicates") and a notational simplication.

Here we use the predicative semantics style to describe the observables of a combined state-trace-readiness model of communicating systems [OH86] [He90]. The purpose of this model is to describe the interaction of systems with their environments by synchronous communication via the interface channels. Mathematically, a *communication* is just a pair $< ch, m >$ consisting of a channel name ch and a value m. By $Comm(\Delta)$ we denote the set of all communications $< ch, m >$ where ch is a channel in Δ and where m is an element of $\mathcal{I}[\![ty_{ch}]\!]$, the set of values of the declared type ty_{ch} of ch.

The state component of the model refers to the initial values of the global variables of a system and to their final values when the system has terminated. The trace component describes the order in which the communications can occur by finite sequences of communications called *traces*. The readiness component describes the possible continuations of the system behaviour after a communication trace has occurred with the help of so-called *ready sets*. These are the sets of channels that are ready for the next communication when the system is stable. Since a system may behave nondeterministically, there may be more than one ready set associated with the same trace. In particular, the empty ready set represents system deadlock. If a system is neither stable nor terminated, it pursues some internal action. If it engages in an infinite sequence of internal actions, it is known as divergent. The state-trace-readiness model considers divergence as an undesirable system behaviour and treats it accordingly.

These intuitions are behind the following predicative semantics. For a given system interface Δ the system behaviour is therefore a predicate in the following free variables:

- a variable st standing for *status* and ranging over the set $\{stable, term, div\}$ where *term* stands for *terminated* and *div* for *divergent*,

- a variable tr standing for *trace* and ranging over $Comm(\Delta)^*$, the set of finite sequences of communications on the interface channnels,
- a variable Rdy standing for *ready set* and ranging over the subsets of $Chans(\Delta)$, the set of interface channels,
- all global read or write variables x of Δ, each one ranging over $\mathcal{I}[\![ty_x]\!]$, the set of values of the declared type ty_x of x,
- a primed version x' for each of the above global variables x ranging over $\mathcal{I}[\![ty_x]\!]$.

Intuitively, these primed versions represent the values of the global variables at termination, i.e. when the variable st holds the value *term*.

We summarise the above type conventions for the variables in a given interface Δ by the following *type condition predicate* $tcp(\Delta)$:

$$\begin{aligned} tcp(\Delta) \quad \Longleftrightarrow_{df} \quad & (st \in \{stable\,, term\,, div\} \\ & \wedge\; tr \in Comm(\Delta)^* \\ & \wedge\; Rdy \subseteq Chans(\Delta) \\ & \wedge \bigwedge_{x \in Vars(\Delta)} x \in \mathcal{I}[\![ty_x]\!] \wedge x' \in \mathcal{I}[\![ty_x]\!]). \end{aligned}$$

Since processes are predicates, we can introduce the following semantic relations between systems:

- system equivalence: $\Delta_1 : P_1 \equiv \Delta_2 : P_2$ if $\Delta_1 = \Delta_2$ and $\models P_1 \Leftrightarrow P_2$,
- system implication: $\Delta_1 : P_1 \equiv\!> \Delta_2 : P_2$ if $\Delta_1 = \Delta_2$ and $\models P_1 \Rightarrow P_2$,
- reverse system implication: $\Delta_1 : P_1 <\!\equiv \Delta_2 : P_2$ if $\Delta_1 = \Delta_2$ and $\models P_1 \Leftarrow P_2$.

Since the interfaces are required to be identical in all three cases, we introduce the following convention:

$$\Delta : P_1 \equiv P_2 \text{ abbreviates } \Delta : P_1 \equiv \Delta : P_2\,,$$

and analogously for the relations $\equiv\!>$ and $<\!\equiv$.

We now sketch the predicative semantics of specifications, programs and mixed terms [He90] [OR91]. In this semantics each of these syntactic objects is identified with a system, i.e. a pair of the form $\Delta : P$ where P is a predicate with the free variables determined by Δ as described above.

5.1 Predicative Semantics of Specifications

The predicative semantics of an SL_0 specification $S =$ **spec** Δ TA V CA **end** is given as follows:

$$\begin{aligned} S \equiv \Delta : \;\; & tcp(\Delta) \wedge \\ & \exists \overline{x}' \in \mathcal{I}[\![ty_{\overline{x}}]\!]\; \exists \overline{v} \in \mathcal{I}[\![ty_{\overline{v}}]\!]\; \exists \overline{v}' \in \mathcal{I}[\![ty_{\overline{v}}]\!] \bullet (\overline{v} = init_{\overline{v}} \wedge\; P\;)\,. \end{aligned}$$

Here $\overline{x}$ is the list of all global variables occurring in Δ the $\overline{x}'$ is the corresponding list of primed versions of these variables, and $\overline{v}$ is the list of all local variables occurring in V and $init_{\overline{v}}$ is the corresponding list of initial values specified in V. By $ty_{\overline{x}}$ we denote the list of types of the variables in $\overline{x}$ and by $\mathcal{I}[\![ty_{\overline{x}}]\!]$ the corresponding value sets, and analogously for $\overline{v}$. Existential quantification over $\overline{x}'$ expresses that the final values of the global variables are irrelevant and existential quantification over $\overline{v}$ and $\overline{v}'$ reflects the locality of these variables. P is a predicate with

$$free(P) \subseteq \{st, tr, Rdy\} \cup \{\overline{x,v}\} \cup \{\overline{x,v}'\}$$

where $\overline{x,v}$ is the combined list of all global and local variables. The predicate P consists of three conjuncts that define the status, the allowed traces and the required ready sets of S:

$$P =_{df} \boxed{st = stable \qquad \text{"status"}}$$

$$\wedge$$

$$\boxed{chan(tr) \in \mathcal{L}[\![TA]\!] \;\wedge\; \overline{x,v} \stackrel{tr}{\Longrightarrow} \overline{x,v'} \qquad \text{"traces"}}$$

$$\wedge$$

$$\boxed{\bigwedge_{ch \in Chans(\Delta)} (ch \in Rdy \Leftrightarrow chan(tr).ch \in \mathcal{L}[\![TA]\!] \;\wedge\; wh_{ch}[\overline{x,v'}/\overline{x,v}]) \qquad \text{"ready sets"}}$$

A semantic characteristic of an SL_0 specification is that its status is always *stable*. The idea is here to specify systems that are ready for a continuous and reliable communication with their environment. Such systems must not terminate or diverge.

To explain the requirements for the traces, we use the operator $chan(\cdot)$ for the trace part and the transition relation $\overline{x,v} \stackrel{tr}{\Longrightarrow} \overline{x,v'}$ for the state part. The operator $chan(\cdot)$ when applied to a trace $tr \in Comm(\Delta)^*$ strips off all communication values and yields the corresponding *channel word*, i.e. $chan(tr) \in Chan(\Delta)^*$. A trace tr satisfies the trace part of S if the channel word $chan(tr)$ is in the language $\mathcal{L}[\![TA]\!]$ associated with the set TA of trace assertions. This language is defined by looking at the individual trace assertions in TA:

$$\mathcal{L}[\![TA]\!] \;=\; \{\, w \in Chan(\Delta)^* \mid \bigwedge_{ta \in TA} chan(tr){\downarrow}\alpha_{ta}\mathcal{L}[\![re_{ta}]\!] \,\} \,.$$

Thus a channel word w is in $\mathcal{L}[\![TA]\!]$ if for each trace assertion ta in TA the projection of the channel word $chan(tr)$ onto the alphabet α_{ta} is in the language denoted by the regular expression re_{ta}.

Note that this condition does not in any way restrict the communication values of tr. To specify these values, we refer to the transition relation $\overline{x,v} \stackrel{tr}{\Longrightarrow} \overline{x,v'}$. Intuitively, it explains how a communication trace tr drives the system from the initial state represented by the values of the variables $\overline{x,v}$ to the current state represented by the values of the primed variables $\overline{x,v'}$. For each communication in tr the resulting state and communicated value are specified in the communication assertions of the state part of S.

The requirements for the ready sets are as follows. A channel ch is ready for communication if the extension of the channel word $chan(tr)$ by ch is in the language $\mathcal{L}[\![TA]\!]$ and if all when-predicates of the communication assertions evaluate to true in the current state, i.e. with variables $\overline{x,v'}$ substituted for $\overline{x,v}$ in the predicate wh_{ch}.

The transition relation is defined by the following recursive predicate:

$$\begin{aligned}\overline{x,v} \stackrel{tr}{\Longrightarrow} \overline{x,v'} \;=_{df}\; \mu X \bullet (\; (\; & tr = <> \wedge \overline{x,v} = \overline{x,v'}\;) \\ \vee \bigvee_{ch \in Chans(\Delta)} & (\; \exists\, @ch \in \mathcal{I}[\![ty_{ch}]\!],\; tr_1 \in Comm(\Delta)^*,\; \overline{W_{ch}'} \in \mathcal{I}[\![ty_{\overline{W_{ch}'}}]\!] \bullet \\ & \quad tr = < ch, @ch > .\; tr_1 \\ & \quad \wedge\, wh_{ch} \wedge th_{ch} \\ & \quad \wedge\, X[tr_1/tr, \overline{W_{ch}'}/\overline{W_{ch}}] \qquad\qquad))\end{aligned}$$

Thus if the trace tr is empty, the values of $\overline{x,v}$ and $\overline{x,v'}$ coincide. Otherwise tr consists of initial communication on a channel ch satisfying the predicates wh_{ch} and th_{ch} of the communication assertions of ch, and of a remainder tr_1 that satisfies the whole predicate again.

5.2 Predicative Semantics of Programs and Mixed Terms

Programs and mixed terms denote systems that may be stable, terminate or diverge. Thus in general the behaviour predicate contains three parts describing the state-trace-readiness observations of the system when the status evaluates to *stable*, *term* and *div*.

First of all, the predicative semantics of programs and mixed terms allows us to remove the **system-end** brackets:

$$\texttt{system}\ \Delta\ P\ \texttt{end}\ \equiv\ \Delta : P.$$

Here P is a process or system expression. Thus it remains to define what P means in terms of predicates, i.e. to state equations of the form

$$\Delta : P\ \equiv\ \Delta : Q$$

where Q is a predicate. We proceed by induction on the structure of P and thus consider each of the programming operators like STOP, SEQ, PAR and WHILE of PL and MIX separately. Semantically, these operators map systems to systems. Thus for each n-ary operator OP we state a definition of the form

$$\texttt{OP}[\Delta_1 : P_1, ..., \Delta_n : P_n] \equiv\ \Delta : Q$$

where $P_1, ..., P_n$ and Q are all predicates.

As examples of 0-ary operators we consider STOP, SKIP and input:

$$\Delta : \texttt{STOP}\ \equiv\ tcp(\Delta) \wedge st = stable \wedge tr = <> \wedge Rdy = \emptyset\ ,$$

$$\Delta : \texttt{SKIP}\ \equiv\ tcp(\Delta) \wedge st = term \wedge tr = <> \wedge \bigwedge_{x \in Vars(\Delta)} x' = x\ ,$$

$$\begin{aligned} \Delta : ch?x \equiv\ & tcp(\Delta) \wedge \\ & st = stable \wedge tr = <> \wedge Rdy = \{ch\} \\ & \vee\ st = term \wedge \exists m \bullet (tr = < ch, m > \wedge x' = m \wedge \bigwedge_{v \in Vars(\Delta) - \{x\}} v' = v)\ . \end{aligned}$$

As a more complex example we exhibit the full semantic definition of the n-ary operator SYN for the synchronisation of systems:

$$\begin{aligned}
&\texttt{SYN}[\Delta_1 : P_1, \ldots, \Delta_n : P_n]\ \equiv \\
&\quad \Delta :\ tcp(\Delta) \wedge \\
&\quad \exists t_1, \ldots, t_n \bullet (\ \textstyle\bigwedge_{i=1}^{n} t_i = tr{\downarrow}Chans(\Delta_i) \\
&\qquad\qquad \wedge (\ st = stable \\
&\qquad\qquad\quad \wedge \exists R_1, \ldots, R_n, st_1, \ldots, st_n \bullet \\
&\qquad\qquad\quad (\ (\ \textstyle\bigvee_{i=1}^{n} st_i = stable\ ) \\
&\qquad\qquad\quad \wedge \textstyle\bigwedge_{i=1}^{n} (\ st_i = stable \vee st_i = term \wedge R_i = \emptyset\ ) \\
&\qquad\qquad\quad \wedge Rdy = \textstyle\bigcap_{i=1}^{n} (\ R_i \cup (Chans(\Delta) - Chans(\Delta_i))\ ) \\
&\qquad\qquad\quad \wedge \textstyle\bigwedge_{i=1}^{n} (\ \exists \overline{Vars(\Delta_i)}' \bullet P_i[t_i/tr, R_i/Rdy, st_i/st]\ )\ \ ) \\
&\qquad\qquad \vee\ st = term \wedge \textstyle\bigwedge_{i=1}^{n} (\ \exists Rdy \bullet P_i[t_i/tr]\ )\qquad) \\
&\qquad\quad \vee \textstyle\bigwedge_{i=1}^{n} t_i \leq tr{\downarrow}Chans(\Delta_i) \\
&\qquad\quad \wedge \exists R_1, \ldots, R_n, st_1, \ldots, st_n \bullet \\
&\qquad\qquad (\ (\ \textstyle\bigvee_{i=1}^{n} st_i = div\ ) \\
&\qquad\qquad \wedge \textstyle\bigwedge_{i=1}^{n} (\ \exists \overline{Vars(\Delta_i)}' \bullet P_i[t_i/tr, R_i/Rdy, st_i/st]\ )\ )\quad)
\end{aligned}$$

where $\Delta = \bigcup_{i=1}^{n} \Delta_i$ and $Writes(\Delta_i) \cap Vars(\Delta_j) = \emptyset$ holds for all $i \neq j$, i.e. if one argument requires write access to a global variable then all other arguments must not access this variable.

Intuitively, the operator **SYN** requires the synchronisation of all communications that can occur in more than one of its n argument systems. In contrast to the parallel composition operator **PAR** of the programming language these synchronised communications are not yet hidden from the environment. Also, the operator **SYN** allows multiway synchronisation whereas the operator **PAR** allows only binary synchronisation.

There is a small problem when applying this semantics to programs because in programs the occam-like operators are applied to processes but not to systems, i.e. the interfaces are missing in the operator arguments.

To solve this difficulty, we introduce the following *inheritance rule* for interfaces: each process argument of an operator inherits the global operator interface. Formally, for processes $P_1, \ldots, P_n$ the pair

$$\Delta : \mathtt{OP}[P_1, \ldots, P_n] \text{ abbreviates } \mathtt{OP}[\Delta : P_1, \ldots, \Delta : P_n].$$

The case where some of the arguments of OP are processes and some are systems is treated similarly.

6 Design Rules

A program **prog** *satisfies* or *implements* a specification **spec** if

$$\mathbf{prog} \equiv> \mathbf{spec}$$

holds, i.e. if **prog** and **spec** have the same interface and if the behaviour predicate of **progr** implies the behaviour predicate of **spec**.

We present now some rules of a design calculus that allows us to transform a given specification stepwise into a communicating program satisfying that specification. The intermediate steps of such a design will be represented by mixed terms. We write such designs in a top-down fashion:

$$\begin{array}{c} \mathbf{spec} \\ \Uparrow \\ \text{mixed terms} \\ \Uparrow \\ \mathbf{prog} \end{array}$$

The initial step of such a design collects the interface and declarations of the given specification **spec**; it is formalized by the following *system rule*:

$\Delta = \Delta_0 \cup write(V \ \cup \ @variables(\Delta_0))$
spec Δ_0 TA V CA **end** $\Uparrow$ **system** Δ_0 $@variables(\Delta_0)$ V **spec** Δ TA CA **end** **end**

Here the set $@variables(\Delta_0)$ contains for each channel ch in Δ_0 a declaration of a corresponding local variable named $@ch$. The new interface Δ is obtained from Δ_0 by adding the set $write(V \cup @variables(\Delta_0))$. The operator $write(\cdot)$ changes a set of local variable declarations into a corresponding set of global write variables.

Thus we are left with transforming specifications of the form **spec** Δ TA CA **end** where all variables are global. The idea is that the trace assertions in TA yield the synchronisation skeleton of a program and that the communication assertions in CA yield the sequential parts that complete this skeleton to a communicating program.

In general, different applications of the design rules will produce different programs from the same initial specification. For producing sequential programs we have identified the following groups of design rules:

- rules of the expansion strategy,
- rules for syntax-directed transformation,
- rules for merging trace assertions,
- rules for recursion elimination in favour of `WHILE` loops.

For producing parallel programs we need the following:

- rules for parallel decomposition using `SYN`,
- rules for hiding of channel,
- rules for disjoint and general renaming of channels.

Additionally we need a collection of algebraic laws for each of the programming operators as in [RH88]. In the following we shall discuss some of these rules.

6.1 Expansion Strategy

In this design strategy one determines for each given specification **spec** Δ TA CA **end** the set of channels on which an initial communication is possible according to the trace assertions in TA. To this end, we define

$$init(TA) = \{ch \mid ch \in \mathcal{L}[\![TA]\!]\}.$$

If $init(TA)$ is empty, the specification can be implemented by `STOP`. This is formalized by the following *stop rule*:

$$<> \in \mathcal{L}[\![TA]\!] \text{ and } init(TA) = \emptyset$$

$$\textbf{spec } \Delta \ TA \ CA \textbf{ end}$$

$$\Uparrow$$

$$\texttt{STOP}$$

If $init(TA)$ is non-empty, we distinguish whether it contains only one output channel or one or more input channels. In the first case we apply the following *output rule*:

$<> \in \mathcal{L}[TA]$ and $init(TA) = \{ch\} \subseteq Outputs(\Delta)$
spec Δ TA CA **end** $\Uparrow$ IF[$wh_{ch} \rightarrow$ SEQ[$impl(th_{ch})$, $ch!@ch$, **spec** Δ TA **after** ch CA **end**]]

Here the specification **spec** Δ TA CA **end** is expanded into a mixed term consisting of an IF operator applied to a sequential composition of a program $impl(th_{ch})$ implementing the state transition specified by the effect predicate th_{ch}, an output on the channel ch, and a new specification

spec Δ TA **after** ch CA **end**.

The expression TA **after** ch inside this specification describes the set of all continuations of channel words in TA after ch has occurred, i.e. we have for all such words w:

$$w \in \mathcal{L}[TA \text{ after } ch] \text{ iff } ch.w \in \mathcal{L}[TA].$$

By induction on the structure of the regular expressions inside TA, one can calculate a new set of trace assertions TA' with $\mathcal{L}[TA \text{ after } ch] = \mathcal{L}[TA']$ and thus eliminate the **after** operator.

If $init(TA)$ consists of n input channels, we apply the following *input rule*:

$<> \in \mathcal{L}[TA]$ and $init(TA) = \{ch_1, ..., ch_n\} \subseteq Inputs(\Delta)$ with $n \geq 1$
spec Δ TA CA **end** $\Uparrow$ ALT[wh_{ch_1} & $ch_1?@ch_1 \rightarrow$ SEQ[$impl(th_{ch_1})$, **spec** Δ TA **after** ch_1 CA **end**] .... wh_{ch_n} & $ch_n?@ch_n \rightarrow$ SEQ[$impl(th_{ch_n})$, **spec** Δ TA **after** ch_n CA **end**]]

Here the specification **spec** Δ TA CA **end** is expanded into a mixed term consisting of an ALT construct with n input guards one for each of the channels $ch_1, ..., ch_n$. Due to the restrictions of occam the ALT operator cannot be applied to output guards. Therefore we have no corresponding design rule for the case of more than one output.

Thus each application of the output or the input rule generates new specifications of the form **spec** Δ TA **after** ch CA **end** to which we apply the above rules again. The results of successive expansion steps can be combined by using the transitivity of the relation $\equiv>$ and by applying the following *context rule*:

X has the same interface as *mixed_term_1* and *mixed_term_2*.

$$mixed\_term\_1$$

$$\Uparrow$$

$$mixed\_term\_2$$

$$P\{mixed\_term\_1/X\}$$

$$\Uparrow$$

$$P\{mixed\_term\_2/X\}$$

Here P is the *context*, i.e. a mixed term containing a name X for which systems can be substituted, and where $P\{mixed\_term\_1/X\}$ and $P\{mixed\_term\_2/X\}$ are the results of substituting *mixed_term_1* or *mixed_term_2* for X in P.

The aim of successively expanding a specification S is to discover a recursive implication of the form

$$P\{S/X\} \equiv> S$$

where P is a mixed term containing a name X for which S can be substituted and where $P\{S/X\}$ is the result this substitution. Then we can implement the specification S by the recursive mixed term REC $X \bullet P$ provided it is guarded. This is the contents of the following *recursion rule*:

X has the interface Δ and REC $X \bullet P$ is guarded.

$$\textbf{spec}\ \Delta\ TA\ CA\ \textbf{end}$$

$$\Uparrow$$

$$P\{\ \textbf{spec}\ \Delta\ TA\ CA\ \textbf{end}\ /\ X\ \}$$

$$\textbf{spec}\ \Delta\ TA\ CA\ \textbf{end}$$

$$\Uparrow$$

$$\text{REC}\ X \bullet\ P$$

6.2 Example and Further Rules

As an example let us apply the above expansion strategy to the **autopilot** specification. The result is the following mixed term written in indented form:

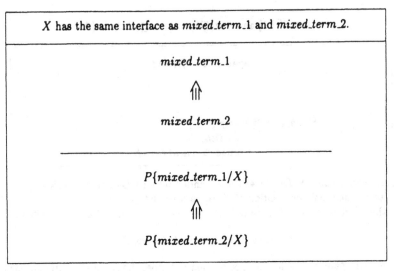

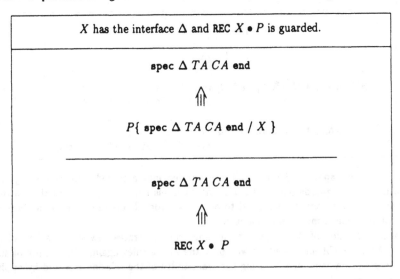

```
                                   autopilot

                                       ⇑

system
  input s of -1..1
  output a of int
  var @s of int -1..1 init 0
  var @a of int init 0
  var ps of int init 0
  var cs of int init 0
  REC X . ALT
            true & s?@s --> SEQ
                              ps,cs :=cs,@s
                              IF
                                true --> SEQ
                                           IF
                                             ps =  0 --> @a := 2 * cs
                                             ps <> 0 --> @a := cs
                                           a!@a
                                           X

end
```

To obtain a program in the language PL, the recursion operator has to be eliminated in favour of the WHILE operator. In the above example, we can apply the following simple version of a *recursion elimination rule*:

P does not contain any REC operator.
Δ : REC $X \bullet P$ ⇑   WHILE (true, P { SKIP/ X })

In general, the transformation of recursion elimination is more complex and introduces boolean *control variables* [Paw91].

The resulting WHILE program can be simplified further by applying the following algebraic laws for the operators ALT, IF, SEQ and variable declaration, e.g. from [RH88]:

- elimination of the boolean expression true:

$$\text{IF}[\text{true} \rightarrow \textit{system}] \equiv \textit{system}$$

$$\text{ALT}[\text{true}\ \&\ \textit{input} \rightarrow \textit{system}] \equiv \text{SEQ}[\textit{input}, \textit{system}]$$

- associtivity of SEQ:

$$\text{SEQ}[\textit{system}_1, \text{SEQ}[\textit{system}_2, ..., \textit{system}_n]] \equiv \text{SEQ}[\textit{system}_1, ..., \textit{system}_n]$$

- renaming of local variables:

$$\texttt{var}\ x\ \texttt{of}\ type\ \texttt{init}\ expr\ system \equiv \texttt{var}\ y\ \texttt{of}\ type\ \texttt{init}\ expr\ system\{y/x\}$$

provided y does not occur in *system*.

By applying these rules, we can produce exactly the program **pilotprog** of Section 3 as an implementation of **autopilot**. Thus we have derived:

$$\texttt{pilotprog} \equiv\!> \texttt{autopilot}\ .$$

For the **autopilot** specification we could have used the more specialized *syntax-directed transformation* of [Ros90] as an alternative. This transformation is applicable to specifications containing only one trace assertion with a regular expression re of a restricted format; it proceeds by induction on the structure of re as follows:

- every letter in re is transformed into an input or output,
- every . in re is transformed into a SEQ construct,
- every + in re is transformed into an ALT construct,
- every * in re is transformed into a WHILE loop.

The result is a communicating WHILE program *without* control variables. For arbitrary regular expressions this transformation would yield incorrect programs and is therefore not applicable. We refer to [RS91] for more details.

In the example of the **autopilot** specification the syntax-directed transformation is applicable and the regular expression

$$\texttt{pref}(s.a)^*$$

yields a program structure of the following form:

```
system
  ...

  WHILE true
    SEQ
        ... s? ...
        ... a! ...
end
```

Again, an application of algebraic laws is needed to obtain the program **pilotprogr** of Section 3.

6.3 Parallel Decomposition

The expansion strategy is always applicable but it produces only sequential programs as implementations of specifications. Often we wish to implement a specification as a parallel program. To this end, we shall decompose specifications using the synchronisation operator SYN. The predicative semantics of specifications and the SYN operator fit together well to yield the following very simple *synchronisation rule*:

• Δ_i contains all channels and global variables of TA_i and CA_i for $i = 1, ..., n$ • $\Delta = \bigcup_{i=1}^{n} \Delta_i$ is a consistent interface   • $Writes(\Delta_i) \cap Vars(\Delta_j) = \emptyset$ for all $i \neq j$
spec Δ $TA_1 ... TA_n$ $CA_1 ... CA_n$ **end** $\Uparrow$ SYN[**spec** Δ_1 TA_1 CA_1 **end**   ....   **spec** Δ_n TA_n CA_n **end**]

Since the operator SYN is not in present in the programming language PL, an application of this synchronisation rule can occur only in an intermediate step in the design of parallel programs from specifications. To introduce the parallel composition operator PAR of the programming language, the hiding operator HIDE needs to be applied to the channels that are synchronised with the operator SYN. Corresponding rules for PAR and HIDE are currently under development.

7 Conclusion

In this paper we treated only a toy example of a communicating system: the autopilot. In the ProCoS project more realistic examples have been studied. Among them is the control system for a gas burner. The informal requirements for this system have been collected in collaboration with a Danish manufacturer. These requirements have then been formalised in the specification language SL_0 [Jen90]. At present the transformational design of occam-like programs from this specification is investigated.

In Oldenburg we are currently developing a more extensive list of design rules, in particular for the design of parallel programs. All these rules have to be shown correct with respect to the underlying predicative semantics. The correctness of the rules of the expansion strategy has been shown in [San91].

A topic for future research is the integration of time into the design calculus. At present several unconnected pieces have been developed in the ProCoS project: an extension of trace assertions by discrete time events that are suitable to model delays and time-outs [Sch91]; a predicative semantics of occam programs with continuous real time [He91]; and a so-called *duration calculus* [ZHR90].

References

[Bjo89] D. Bjørner, A ProCoS project description, ESPRIT BRA 3104, Bulletin of the EATCS 39 (1989) 60-73.

[CH74] R.H. Campbell, A.N. Habermann, The specification of process synchronisation by path expressions, Lecture Notes in Comput. Sci. 16 (Springer-Verlag, 1974).

[He90] He Jifeng, Specification-oriented semantics for the ProCoS level 0 language, ProCoS Doc. Id. PRG/OU HJF 5/1, Oxford Univ., 1990.

[He91] He Jifeng, Specification-oriented semantics for the ProCoS programming language PL^{time}, ProCoS Doc. Id. PRG/OU HJF 7/2, Oxford Univ., 1991.

[Heh84] E.C.R. Hehner, Predicative programming, Comm. ACM 27 (2), 1984.

[Hoa85] C.A.R. Hoare, Programs are predicates, in: C.A.R. Hoare, J.C. Shepherdson (Eds.), Mathematical Logic and Programming Languages (Prentice-Hall, London, 1985) 141-155.

[IN88] INMOS Ltd., occam 2 Reference Manual (Prentice Hall, 1988).

[JROR90] K.M. Jensen, H. Rischel, E.-R. Olderog, S. Rössig, Syntax and informal semantics for the ProCoS specification language 0, ProCoS Doc. Id. ID/DTH KMJ 4/2, Tech. Univ. Denmark, 1990.

[Jen90] K.M. Jensen, Specification of a gas-burner, ProCoS Doc. Id. ID/DTH KMJ 10/1.2, Tech. Univ. Denmark, 1990.

[Lam83] L. Lamport, Specifying concurrent modules, ACM TOPLAS 5 (1983) 190-222.

[Old91] E.-R. Olderog, Nets, Terms and Formulas: Three Views of Concurrent Processes and Their Relationship (Cambridge University Press, 1991).

[OH86] E.-R. Olderog, C.A.R. Hoare, Specification-oriented semantics for communicating processes, Acta Inform. 23 (1986) 9-66.

[OR91] E.-R. Olderog, S. Rössig, Predicative semantics of MIX, ProCoS Doc. Id. OLD ERO 3/1, Univ. Oldenburg, 1991.

[Par76] D. Park, Finiteness is mu-ineffable, Theoret. Comput. Sci. 3 (1976) 173-181.

[Paw91] W. Pawłowski, Automatic transformation $SL_0 \rightarrow PL$, ProCoS Draft Note, Techn. Univ. Denmark, 1991.

[Ros90] S. Rössig, Transformation of SL_0 specifications into PL programs, ProCoS Doc. Id. OLD SR 1/4, Univ. Oldenburg, 1990.

[RS91] S. Rössig, M. Schenke, Specification and stepwise development of communicating systems, to appear in: Proc. VDM '91 Symposium, Noordwijkerhout, The Netherlands, Lecture Notes in Comput. Sci., Springer-Verlag, 1991).

[RH88] A.W. Roscoe, C.A.R. Hoare, The laws of occam programming, Theoret. Comput. Sci. 60 (1988) 177-229.

[San91] J. Sander, Korrektheit der Expansions-Strategie für die Transformation von SL_0-Spezifikationen in PL-Programme, Studienarbeit, Univ. Oldenburg, 1991.

[Sch91] M. Schenke, The bracket model - a discrete model for timed processes, ProCoS Doc. Id. OLD MS 2/2, Univ. Oldenburg, 1991.

[ZHR90] Zhou ChaoChen, C.A.R. Hoare, A.P. Ravn, A duration calculus for real time requirements in embedded systems, ProCoS Doc. Id. PRG/OU ZCC 2, Oxford Univ., 1990.

[Zwi89] J. Zwiers, Compositionality, Concurrency, and Partial Correctness - Proof Theories for Networks of Processes and Their Relationship, Lecture Notes in Comput. Sci. 321 (Springer-Verlag, 1989).

A Theory of Testing for ACP*

Luca Aceto
INRIA-Sophia Antipolis
F-06560 Valbonne Cedex, France

Anna Ingólfsdóttir
Aalborg University Centre
Aalborg, Denmark

Abstract

This paper introduces a process algebra which incorporates the auxiliary operators of ACP, [BK85], and is tailored towards algebraic verifications in the theory of testing equivalence. The process algebra we consider is essentially a version of ACP with the empty process in which the nondeterministic choice operators familiar from TCSP, [BHR84], and TCCS, [DH87], are used in lieu of the internal action τ and the single choice operator favoured by CCS, [Mil89], and ACP. We present a behavioural semantics for the language based upon a natural notion of testing equivalence, [DH84], and show that, contrary to what happens in a setting with the internal action τ, the left-merge operator is compatible with it. A complete equational characterization of the behavioural semantics is given for finite processes, thus providing an algebraic theory supporting the use of the auxiliary operators of ACP in algebraic verifications for testing equivalence. Finally we give a fully-abstract denotational model for finite processes with respect to the testing preorder based on a variation on Hennessy's Acceptance Trees suitable for our language.

1 Introduction

Algebraic techniques have recently found considerable application in the study of the semantics of concurrent, communicating systems. Following Milner's original insight that "concurrent processes have an algebraic structure", several algebraic languages for the description of concurrent processes, the so-called *Process Algebras*, have been proposed in the literature, e.g. CCS, [Mil89], CSP, [Hoare85], ACP, [BK85], and MEIJE, [AB84]. Such languages give a syntax for concurrent processes which may be used not only for describing actual systems, but also their specifications. It follows that an important component for these languages is a notion of equivalence between descriptions, which allows us to state formally that two syntactic descriptions of concurrent processes denote essentially the same abstract behaviour. Semantic processes are then taken to be equivalence classes of process terms with respect to the chosen notion of equivalence. Following Milner's paradigm, such notions of equivalence are usually behaviourally motivated; some well-known examples of behavioural equivalences

*This work has been supported by a grant from the United Kingdom Science and Engineering Research Council and by the Esprit BRA project CONCUR.

for process description languages are *trace equivalence*, [Hoare85], *testing equivalence*, [DH84], [H88], *failures equivalence*, [BHR84], and *bisimulation equivalence*, [Pa81], [Mil89].

A useful byproduct of the algebraic nature of process algebras is that the above mentioned notions of behavioural equivalence have been given complete equational characterizations over (subsets of) these languages, [HM85], [DH84], [BK85], [H88]. The main import of such axiomatic characterizations is that they allow us to give proofs of behavioural equivalence between process descriptions purely at the syntactic level, i.e. without having to be concerned with the underlying semantic model at all. Indeed, equational laws may be used to describe in a concise and elegant way the intended semantics for concurrent processes, as it is done in the *Algebra of Communicating Processes* (or ACP) of Bergstra and Klop, [BK85]. ACP consists of a family of axiom systems suitable for specifying and verifying concurrent processes in various semantic settings. The axiom systems of the ACP family have been applied in extensive case studies, including verifications of non-trivial concurrent systems, [GlV88], [Va90b], and to give formal semantics to high level concurrent programming languages, [Va90a], thus highlighting the usefulness of algebraic techniques in the study of concurrent systems and the applicability of the techniques developed in the ACP literature.

Two main features of ACP are the smooth algebraic treatment of a general sequential composition operator and the introduction of auxiliary operators, the *left-merge*, $\lfloor\!\lfloor$, and the *communication-merge*, $|_c$, for the algebraic treatment of the ACP parallel composition operator. The auxiliary operators of ACP drastically simplify equational proofs and have some "desirable metamathematical properties", [GlV88]. For instance, as shown in [BK85], the left-merge and the communication-merge can be used to give *finite* axiomatizations for the theories of observational congruence over CCS, [Mil89], and rooted τ-bisimulation over ACP, [BK85]. This has been shown to be impossible without the introduction of auxiliary operators in [Mol89], at least in a setting without τ-actions. Moreover, the auxiliary operators have greater suitability for term rewriting analysis than the parallel composition operator, [GlV88]. The properties of the left-merge and communication-merge operators have been extensively studied in the literature on ACP, mostly with respect to semantic models based on bisimulation-like equivalences. Bisimulation equivalence, [Pa81], [Mil89], is widely regarded as a very natural notion of behavioural equivalence for concurrent systems and has very appealing logical and equational characterizations [HM85], [Mil89]. However, bisimulation equivalence makes too many distinctions among processes in applications in which one is mostly interested in the deadlock behaviour of processes, rather than in their whole branching structure. In these applications, weaker notions of equivalence (or implementation preorders) like testing/failures equivalences, [DH84], [BHR84], [H88], are more suitable as formal means of establishing the correctness of implementations with respect to specifications. First attempts at proposing axiom systems of the ACP family suitable for verifications in failures semantics have been presented in [BKO87] for a language without parallel features. However, such axiom systems can *not* be conservatively extended to the whole signature of ACP_τ; in fact, as pointed out in [GlV88], the left-merge operator does *not* preserve testing/failures equivalences in a setting with the silent action τ of CCS. For instance, the law

$$\tau;(\tau;x+y) \quad = \quad \tau;x+y$$

is valid in testing/failures semantics and, by considering the instance of this law obtained by taking $x = a$ and $y = b$, we have that $\tau;(\tau;a+b) = \tau;a+b$. However, the processes $p = (\tau;(\tau;a+b))\lfloor c$ and $q = (\tau;a+b)\lfloor c$ are not even trace equivalent. In fact, p is capable of performing the sequence of actions cb whilst q cannot (see [GlV88], pages 19-21).

The inconsistency of the left-merge operator with respect to testing/failures equivalences has at least two unpleasant consequences:

1. it seems to imply that the useful auxiliary operators of ACP cannot be used in algebraic verifications with respect to testing/failures equivalences, and

2. it casts some doubts on the possibility of giving algebraic characterizations of non-interleaving versions of testing/failures equivalences; in fact, the left-merge operator plays a fundamental rôle in several axiomatizations of non-interleaving equivalences presented in the literature, see e.g. [CH89].

A very general solution to this problem has been proposed in [GlV88] by means of the *module approach*. There the authors propose an algebra of modules, which are generalizations of theories suitable for composing algebraic specifications, and a logic for reasoning about them. Their general techniques may be used to perform algebraic verifications on two levels: the level of bisimulation semantics, where the left-merge operator can be used, and the level of testing/failures semantics. As the testing/failures model can be obtained as a homomorphic image of the bisimulation one, certain formulae proved using the axioms involving the auxiliary operators in bisimulation semantics (the "positive" ones not containing the auxiliary operators [GlV88]) will remain valid in the testing/failures world.

In this paper we shall propose a more *ad hoc* solution to the above-discussed problem by introducing a process algebra which incorporates the auxiliary operators of ACP and is explicitly tailored towards algebraic verifications in the world of testing/failures semantics. The algebraic language which will be studied in this paper is based on the signature of ACP_τ. However, in view of the above discussion, the constant for the silent action τ and the single nondeterministic choice operator, favoured by CCS and ACP, will be replaced by the operators for internal and external nondeterminism familiar from the theory of CSP, [BHR84], [Hoare85], and TCCS, [DH87], [H88]. Following [DH87], [H88], we shall give a standard Plotkin-style operational semantics for our language and show how a natural notion of testing equivalence may be defined over it. The auxiliary operators of ACP will turn out to be compatible with the semantic theory for processes induced by the testing equivalence and this will allow us to use them in providing an algebraic characterization of the behavioural semantics for processes. The algebraic theory of processes will also prove its worth in suggesting a natural denotational model for our language with respect to the testing preorder. This model is based on a variation on Hennessy's Acceptance Trees [H88].

For lack of space we have omitted from this presentation all the proofs; most of these may be found in [Ace90].

2 The language and its operational semantics

The language we shall consider is a rather rich *process algebra* which incorporates many of the features of the signature of ACP_τ, [BK85], the empty process, [Vra86], and the nondeterministic choice operators familiar from the theory of CSP [BHR84], [Hoare85], and "CCS without τ's", [DH87], [H88]. The algebra is parameterized on A, a countable set of *observable actions* ranged over by $a, b, c, \ldots$, and Var, a countable set of *variables* ranged over by $x, y, \ldots$. In order to describe the synchronization of actions, we shall assume, following the ACP literature [BG87], a given partial *communication function* $\gamma : A \times A \rightharpoonup A$ which is commutative and associative, i.e. for all $a, b, c \in A$,

$$\gamma(a,b) \simeq \gamma(b,a) \text{ and } \gamma(a,\gamma(b,c)) \simeq \gamma(\gamma(a,b),c),$$

where $\simeq$ denotes Kleene equality. In what follows, we shall write $\gamma(a,b) \downarrow$ if γ is defined over the pair of actions (a,b) and $\gamma(a,b) \uparrow$ otherwise. If $\gamma(a,b) \simeq c$ then we say that actions a and b may synchronize and action c is the result of their synchronized occurrence. Note that, unlike τ in CCS, action c is potentially available for further synchronizations.

For each action $a \in A$, the signature of the process algebra will contain a constant, denoted by a with abuse of notation, representing a process capable of performing action a and then terminating successfully. The constant Ω will denote the process that may only diverge internally; δ will stand for a deadlocked process, a process that cannot perform any action. The *empty process* ε will stand for a process which may only terminate successfully. Following [BHR84], [BG87], we shall assume that processes communicate the successful completion of their evolution to the environment by performing a special action $\surd$, read "tick", not occurring in A. See [AH88] for an alternative approach. The combinators used to build new systems from existing ones are the following:

- $+$ for *external choice*. Intuitively, $p + q$ will stand for a process which will behave either like p or like q with the environment having some sort of control over which choice will be taken;
- $\oplus$ for *internal choice*. $p \oplus q$ will denote a process that may autonomously decide to behave either like p or like q— the choice of which option is taken cannot be influenced by the environment;
- ; for *sequential composition*. Intuitively, $p;q$ will be a process which will start the execution of q only when p has successfully completed its execution;
- | for *parallel composition*. Intuitively, $p|q$ denotes a process which is capable of performing any interleaving of the actions that p and q may perform. Moreover, $p|q$ may perform synchronizations of actions of p and q, as described by the communication function γ;

- $\not|$ for *left-merge*. The process $p \not| q$ behaves like $p|q$, but with the restriction that the first observable move of $p \not| q$ has to come from p;

- $|_c$ for *communication-merge*. The process $p|_c q$ behaves like $p|q$, but with the restriction that the first observable move from $p|_c q$ has to be a synchronization;

- $\tau_I(\cdot)$, $I \subseteq A$, for *hiding*. Intuitively, $\tau_I(p)$ will denote a process that behaves like p, but with all the actions in I made internal, i.e. unavailable for communication with the environment.

Formally:

Definition 2.1 (The Language) *Let $\Sigma = \{\Sigma_n\}_{n \in \omega}$ be the signature given below:*

$$\begin{aligned} \Sigma_0 &= \{\Omega, \delta, \varepsilon\} \cup A \\ \Sigma_1 &= \{\tau_I(\cdot) \mid I \subseteq A\} \\ \Sigma_2 &= \{+, \oplus, ;, |, \not|, |_c\} \\ \Sigma_n &= \emptyset \quad \text{for all } n > 2. \end{aligned}$$

The set $REC_\Sigma(\mathtt{Var})$ of recursive terms *over Σ and* Var *is given by the following syntax:*

$$t ::= f(t_1, \ldots, t_k) \; (f \in \Sigma_k) \mid x \mid rec\, x.\, t,$$

where $x \in \mathtt{Var}$. $REC_\Sigma(\mathtt{Var})$ will be ranged over by $t, u \ldots$. We shall assume the usual notions of free and bound variables in a term, with $rec\, x.$ _ as the binding construct. In what follows, REC_Σ $(p, q, \ldots \in REC_\Sigma)$ will denote the set of closed terms, *or* processes, *and $FREC_\Sigma$ $(d, e \ldots \in FREC_\Sigma)$ the set of* finite processes, *i.e. those not containing occurrences of $rec\, x.$ _.*

As pointed out above, the signature of the above given algebra is based on that of ACP_τ; the major departure from Bergstra and Klop's calculus is in the presence of the internal and external nondeterminism operators in lieu of a constant for the internal move τ and a CCS-like nondeterministic choice operator. Moreover, the language contains an explicit $rec\, x.$ _ construct for describing processes with an infinite behaviour and allows for the description of underspecified and divergent processes by means of the constant Ω. Following [DH87], [H88], we shall now define an operational semantics for the language REC_Σ. Let $\surd$ be a distinguished action symbol not occurring in A; $A_\surd =_{def} A \cup \{\surd\}$ will be ranged over by $u, v \ldots$. In what follows, $\surd$ will be the observable action processes perform upon successful completion of their execution. The operational semantics for the language REC_Σ consists of a Plotkin-style, [Pl81], structured operational semantics. This is given by a family of transition relations $\{\xrightarrow{u} \mid u \in A_\surd\}$, which are intended to capture the evolution of processes under the performance of observable actions, and by a transition relation $\rightarrowtail$ for describing the internal evolution of processes. A divergence predicate over REC_Σ, $\uparrow$, will then be defined by using the operational semantics; intuitively, for each process p, $p \uparrow$ iff p may embark on an infinite internal computation without interacting with its environment.

(O1)	$a \xrightarrow{a} \varepsilon$		
(O2)	$\varepsilon \xrightarrow{\surd} \delta$		
(O3)	$p \xrightarrow{a} p'$	implies	$p;q \xrightarrow{a} p';q$
(O4)	$p \xrightarrow{u} p'$	implies	$p+q \xrightarrow{u} p'$
			$q+p \xrightarrow{u} p'$
(O5)	$p \xrightarrow{a} p'$	implies	$p\|q \xrightarrow{a} p'\|q,\ q\|p \xrightarrow{a} q\|p'$
			$p\lfloor q \xrightarrow{a} p'\|q$
(O6)	$p \xrightarrow{\surd} p'$ and $q \xrightarrow{\surd} q'$	imply	$p\|q \xrightarrow{\surd} p'\|q'$
			$p\|_c q \xrightarrow{\surd} p'\|q'$
(O7)	$p \xrightarrow{a} p', q \xrightarrow{b} q'$ and $\gamma(a,b) \simeq c$	imply	$p\|q \xrightarrow{c} p'\|q'$
			$p\|_c q \xrightarrow{c} p'\|q'$
(O8)	$p \xrightarrow{u} p'$ and $u \notin I$	imply	$\tau_I(p) \xrightarrow{u} \tau_I(p')$

Figure 1: Axioms and rules for $\xrightarrow{u}$

For each $u \in A_\surd$, let $\xrightarrow{u}$ denote the least binary relation over REC_Σ which satisfies the axioms and rules in Figure 1. Intuitively, for processes $p, q \in REC_\Sigma$, $p \xrightarrow{u} q$ if p may perform action u and thereby be transformed into q. If $u = \surd$ then we say that p can terminate successfully. The internal evolution of the processes in REC_Σ is expressed by $\rightarrowtail$, the least binary relation over REC_Σ which satisfies the axioms and rules in Figure 2. Intuitively, $p \rightarrowtail q$ if p may evolve into q without interacting with its environment.

A few comments on the defining rules of the transition relations are now in order. The operational interpretation of most of the operators is well-known from the literature, see e.g. [H88]. However, subtleties arise in giving an operational semantics to the sequential composition operator and the ACP auxiliary operators, the left-merge and the communication-merge. In the operational interpretation of the sequential composition operator, moves signalling the successful completion of the execution of process p in the context $[\cdot];q$ are interpreted as *internal moves* triggering the execution of q (rule (I5) in Figure 2). Several other possibilities for defining an operational semantics for ; are discussed in [AH88], [BV89]. In particular, the reference [BV89] gives a clear account of different proposals, mostly in the field of *bisimulation semantics*, [Pa81]. The rules for the left-merge operator prescribe that the first observable move of process $p\lfloor q$ has to come from p and that q is blocked until p performs such a move. In particular, contrary to what happens to τ-moves in the theory of ACP$_\tau$, silent moves do *not* resolve the left-merge operator (rule (I7) in Figure 2). This is consistent with the idea that internal transitions do not change the structure of terms, [H88]. The rules defining the operational semantics for the communication-merge reflect the intuition that the first observable move of a process $p|_c q$

$(I1)$	$p \oplus q \rightarrowtail p$		
	$p \oplus q \rightarrowtail q$		
$(I2)$	$\Omega \rightarrowtail \Omega$		
$(I3)$	$rec\, x.\, t \rightarrowtail t[rec\, x.\, t/x]$		
$(I4)$	$p \rightarrowtail p'$	implies	$p;q \rightarrowtail p';q$
$(I5)$	$p \xrightarrow{\surd} p'$	implies	$p;q \rightarrowtail q$
$(I6)$	$p \rightarrowtail p'$	implies	$p+q \rightarrowtail p'+q$
			$q+p \rightarrowtail q+p'$
$(I7)$	$p \rightarrowtail p'$	implies	$p\vert q \rightarrowtail p'\vert q,\ q\vert p \rightarrowtail q\vert p'$
			$p\not\vert q \rightarrowtail p'\not\vert q$
			$p\vert_c q \rightarrowtail p'\vert_c q,\ q\vert_c p \rightarrowtail q\vert_c p'$
$(I8)$	$p \rightarrowtail p'$	implies	$\tau_I(p) \rightarrowtail \tau_I(p')$
$(I9)$	$p \xrightarrow{a} p'$ and $a \in I$	imply	$\tau_I(p) \rightarrowtail \tau_I(p')$

Figure 2: Axioms and rules for $\rightarrowtail$

must be a synchronization move. Note that a special case of "synchronization" is obtained when p and q may both perform a $\surd$-move (rule (O6) in Figure 1). However, silent transitions are allowed to occur asynchronously.

A *divergence predicate* over REC_Σ, $\uparrow$, may now be defined by using the above-given internal transition relation. For each $p \in REC_\Sigma$, we shall write $p \uparrow$ iff there exists a sequence $\langle p_i \mid i \geq 0 \rangle$ such that

$$p \equiv p_0 \rightarrowtail p_1 \rightarrowtail p_2 \rightarrowtail \cdots.$$

Intuitively, $p \uparrow$ iff p may embark on an infinite internal computation. We shall write $p \downarrow$, read "p converges", iff not $p \uparrow$. A process p is *stable* iff $p \not\rightarrowtail$, i.e. if p cannot perform internal transitions. The operational semantics for the language REC_Σ is then given by the Labelled Transition System, [Kel76],

$$\langle REC_\Sigma, \{\xrightarrow{u} \mid u \in A_\surd\}, \rightarrowtail\rangle.$$

The weak transition relations, which allow to abstract from internal moves in the behaviour of processes, are defined following standard lines by induction on the length of $\sigma \in A_\surd^*$ as follows:

- $\stackrel{\lambda}{\Longrightarrow} = \rightarrowtail^*$, where λ denotes the empty string;
- $\stackrel{u}{\Longrightarrow} = \stackrel{\lambda}{\Longrightarrow} \circ \xrightarrow{u} \circ \stackrel{\lambda}{\Longrightarrow}$, for $u \in A_\surd$; and
- $\stackrel{u.\sigma}{\Longrightarrow} = \stackrel{\sigma}{\Longrightarrow} \circ \stackrel{u}{\Longrightarrow}$, for $u \in A_\surd$ and $\sigma \in A_\surd^*$.

The set of *termination traces* $T_{\surd}$ is given by $T_{\surd} =_{def} \{\sigma\surd \mid \sigma \in A^*\}$. Let $\mathcal{T} = A^* \cup T_{\surd}$; it is easy to see that, for each $p \in REC_\Sigma$ and $\sigma \in A^*_{\surd}$, $p \stackrel{\sigma}{\Longrightarrow}$ implies $\sigma \in \mathcal{T}$. In view of this observation, in what follows we shall restrict ourselves to considering strings in $\mathcal{T}$. In the remainder of the paper we shall make extensive use of convergence predicates parameterized over strings $\sigma \in \mathcal{T}$. Formally, for each $\sigma \in \mathcal{T}$, the predicate $\downarrow \sigma$ over REC_Σ is defined by induction on the length of σ by:

- $p \downarrow \lambda$ iff $p \downarrow$, and
- $p \downarrow u.\sigma$ iff $p \downarrow$ and, for each p', $p \stackrel{u}{\Longrightarrow} p'$ implies $p' \downarrow \sigma$.

We shall write $p \uparrow \sigma$, read p diverges upon the performance of σ, iff not $p \downarrow \sigma$.

3 Testing processes

In the previous section, we defined an operational semantics for the language REC_Σ in terms of a Labelled Transition System $\langle REC_\Sigma, \{\stackrel{u}{\longrightarrow} \mid u \in A_{\surd}\}, \rightarrowtail \rangle$. The operational interpretation of processes will be used in this section to define a notion of behavioural equivalence over REC_Σ based upon the ideas underlying the testing equivalences proposed and studied in [DH84], [DH87], [H88]. The interested reader is referred to these references for motivations of the general testing philosophy and a discussion of the, mostly standard, definitions which will be given in what follows.

The application of the testing methodology, [DH84], [H88], requires the isolation of a suitable set of *observers*, or *tests*; as pointed out in the above-given references, a natural choice is to consider processes themselves as observers because concurrent processes evolve in an environment made up of other concurrent processes. In what follows, we shall consider as observers the set of processes $\mathcal{O}$ $(o, o' \ldots \in \mathcal{O})$ built using the same formation rules for REC_Σ and the following constant symbols not occurring in Σ:

- w, an action used to report *success* in experimentations, and
- θ, an action which will be used to test for successful termination.

An operational semantics for the set of observers $\mathcal{O}$ may then be given by extending the rules in Figures 1-2 with axioms

- $\eta \stackrel{\eta}{\longrightarrow} \varepsilon$, for each $\eta \in \{w, \theta\}$.

Following [H88], the set $\mathcal{O} \times REC_\Sigma$ may now be turned into an *experimental transition system* by defining a transition relation $\longrightarrow \subseteq (\mathcal{O} \times REC_\Sigma)^2$ as follows: ((o,p) is more suggestively written $o \parallel p$)

$$
o \parallel p \longrightarrow o' \parallel p' \text{ iff } \begin{array}{l} (1)\ p \rightarrowtail p' \text{ and } o \equiv o', \text{ or} \\ (2)\ o \rightarrowtail o' \text{ and } p \equiv p', \text{ or} \\ (3)\ p \stackrel{a}{\longrightarrow} p' \text{ and } o \stackrel{a}{\longrightarrow} o', \text{ for some } a \in A, \text{ or} \\ (4)\ p \stackrel{\surd}{\longrightarrow} p' \text{ and } o \stackrel{\theta}{\longrightarrow} o'. \end{array}
$$

A *computation* from $o \parallel p$ is a maximal sequence (finite or infinite)

$$o \parallel p \equiv o_0 \parallel p_0 \longrightarrow o_1 \parallel p_1 \longrightarrow o_2 \parallel p_2 \longrightarrow \cdots.$$

A computation is *successful* iff there exists $n \geq 0$ such that $o_n \xrightarrow{w}$. Then, for every $p \in REC_\Sigma$, $o \in \mathcal{O}$,

$$p \ \underline{\text{must}}\ o \text{ iff every computation from } o \parallel p \text{ is successful.}$$

Definition 3.1 (Testing Preorder) *For all $p, q \in REC_\Sigma$, $p \sqsubseteq_M q$ iff, for all $o \in \mathcal{O}$, p $\underline{\text{must}}$ o implies q $\underline{\text{must}}$ o.*

The reader is referred to [H88] for motivations of the above definitions. The preorder $\sqsubseteq_M$ and its kernel $\simeq_M$ will constitute the semantic theory for the language REC_Σ studied in the remainder of the paper. A few examples of processes which are distinguished according to $\sqsubseteq_M$ are now in order.

Example 3.1 (a) *$\delta \not\sqsubseteq_M \varepsilon$. In fact, for $o \equiv (w \oplus w) + \theta$, δ $\underline{\text{must}}$ o whilst ε $\underline{\text{m̸ust}}$ o. It is easy to see that δ $\underline{\text{must}}$ o because the only computation from $o \parallel \delta$ is*

$$o \parallel \delta \longrightarrow w + \theta \parallel \delta,$$

which is successful as $w + \theta \xrightarrow{w}$. On the other hand, $o \parallel \varepsilon \longrightarrow \varepsilon \parallel \delta$ is an unsuccessful computation from $o \parallel \varepsilon$.

(b) *$\varepsilon \not\sqsubseteq_M \delta$. In fact, for $o \equiv \theta; w$, we have that ε $\underline{\text{must}}$ o whilst δ $\underline{\text{m̸ust}}$ o.*

(c) *$\delta \not\sqsubseteq_M \Omega$. In fact, for $o \equiv (w \oplus w)$, δ $\underline{\text{must}}$ o, but Ω $\underline{\text{m̸ust}}$ o.*

It is easy to see that, for all $p \in REC_\Sigma$, $\Omega \sqsubseteq_M p$. In order to study the properties of the behavioural preorder $\sqsubseteq_M$ in more detail, it will be convenient to obtain an alternative, observer-independent characterization for it. The details of such a characterization of $\sqsubseteq_M$ follow closely the ones of similar results presented in [H88]. The following definition introduces some notation which will be used in defining the alternative characterization of $\sqsubseteq_M$.

Definition 3.2 (Initials, Derivations and Acceptance Sets) *Let $p \in REC_\Sigma$ and $\sigma \in \mathcal{T}$. Then:*

(1) *$I(p) = \{u \in A_\surd \mid p \stackrel{u}{\Longrightarrow}\}$ is the set of* initials *of p;*

(2) *$D(p, \sigma) = \{q \mid p \stackrel{\sigma}{\Longrightarrow} q\}$ is the set of σ-*derivatives *of p, and*

(3) *$\mathcal{A}(p, \sigma) = \{I(q) \mid q \in D(p, \sigma)\}$ is the* acceptance set *of p after σ.*

Definition 3.3 *For each $p, q \in REC_\Sigma$, $p \ll_M q$ iff, for all $\sigma \in \mathcal{T}$, $p \downarrow \sigma$ implies*

(1) *$q \downarrow \sigma$, and*

(2) *for every $X \in \mathcal{A}(q, \sigma)$ there exists $Y \in \mathcal{A}(p, \sigma)$ such that $Y \subseteq X$.*

Theorem 3.1 (Alternative Characterization) *For all $p, q \in REC_\Sigma$, $p \sqsubseteq_M q$ iff $p \ll_M q$.*

Using the above result, we shall now prove that $\sqsubseteq_M$ is a Σ-precongruence over REC_Σ by making an essential use of the preorder $\ll_M$.

Theorem 3.2 *$\ll_M$, and hence also $\sqsubseteq_M$, is a Σ-precongruence over REC_Σ.*

(+1)	$x+(y+z)=(x+y)+z$	(⊕1)	$x\oplus(y\oplus z)=(x\oplus y)\oplus z$
(+2)	$x+y=y+x$	(⊕2)	$x\oplus y=y\oplus x$
(+3)	$x+x=x$	(⊕3)	$x\oplus x=x$
(+4)	$x+\delta=x$	(⊕4)	$a;x\oplus a;y=a;(x\oplus y)$
$(SEQ1)$	$x;(y;z)=(x;y);z$	$(+\oplus 1)$	$a;x+a;y=a;x\oplus a;y$
$(SEQ2a)$	$\varepsilon;x=x$	$(+\oplus 2)$	$x+(y\oplus z)=(x+y)\oplus(x+z)$
$(SEQ2b)$	$a;\varepsilon=a$	$(+\oplus 2)$	$x+(y\oplus z)=(x+y)\oplus(x+z)$
$(SEQ3)$	$(x\oplus y);z=(x;z)\oplus(y;z)$	$(+\oplus 3)$	$x\oplus(y+z)=(x\oplus y)+(x\oplus z)$
$(SEQ4)$	$(\sum_{i\in I}a_i;x_i);y=\sum_{i\in I}(a_i;x_i);y$		
$(SEQ5)$	$(x+\varepsilon);y=(x;y+y)\oplus y$	(S)	$x\oplus y\leq x$

Figure 3: Inequations for sequential, nondeterministic processes

4 Algebraic characterization

The aim of this section is to give a complete equational characterization of the preorder $\sqsubseteq_M$ over the set of finite processes. The equations which will be used to characterize $\sqsubseteq_M$ over $FREC_\Sigma$ are inspired by those presented in [DH87], [H88]; however, special care has to be used in order to capture the interplay among the sequential composition operator, the nondeterministic choice operators + and ⊕ and the empty process ε. Most of the equations expressing properties of the ACP auxiliary operators, left-merge and communication-merge, are slight adaptations of well-known identities from various flavours of the theory of ACP with the empty process, [Vra86,BG87], while those for the hiding operators $\tau_I(\cdot)$ are closely related to the ones proposed in [DeN85] for a complete axiomatization of failures equivalence over TCSP. The set of inequations E which will be considered in this section is given in Figures 3-5.

Notation: The summation notation $\sum_{i\in I}x_i$ used in the inequations and in the remainder of the section is justified by axioms (+1)-(+2) in Figure 3. The notation $\{+\varepsilon\}$ denotes an optional summand and, by convention, $\sum_{i\in\emptyset}x_i\equiv\delta$.

We shall now comment briefly on the above equations. The axioms expressing basic properties of + and ⊕ and the interaction between the two flavours of nondeterminism present in the language REC_Σ are taken from the standard theory of testing, [H88]. Axiom (SEQ4) is a weaker version of

(Ω)	$\Omega \leq x$
$(\Omega 1)$	$x + \Omega \leq \Omega$
$(\Omega 2)$	$\Omega; x \leq \Omega$
$(\Omega 3)$	$\Omega \lfloor\!\lfloor x \leq \Omega$
$(\Omega 4)$	$\Omega \vert_c x \leq \Omega$
$(\Omega 5)$	$\tau_I(\Omega) \leq \Omega$
$(\Omega 6)$	$\Omega \vert x \leq \Omega$
$(\Omega 7)$	$x \vert \Omega \leq \Omega$
$(H1)$	$\tau_I(x \oplus y) = \tau_I(x) \oplus \tau_I(y)$
$(H2)$	$\tau_I(\sum_{i \in H} a_i; x_i\{+\varepsilon\}) = \sum_{i \in H} a_i; \tau_I(x_i)\{+\varepsilon\}$ if $\{a_i \mid i \in H\} \cap I = \emptyset$
$(H3)$	$\tau_I(a; x + y) = \tau_I(x) \oplus \tau_I(x + y)$ if $a \in I$

Figure 4: Inequations for Ω and hiding

the law

$$(x + y); z \quad = \quad (x; z) + (y; z). \tag{1}$$

This law is present in many of the axiom systems of the ACP family, see e.g. [BK85] and [BKO87], but is *not* sound with respect to $\simeq_M$. For instance, it is easy to check that

$$p \equiv (a + \varepsilon); (b \oplus c) \not\simeq_M (a; (b \oplus c)) + (\varepsilon; (b \oplus c)) \equiv q.$$

Axiom (SEQ5) expresses the interplay between the empty process ε and the sequential composition operator. It is intuitively justified by recalling that moves signalling the successful termination of a process p in the context $[\cdot]; q$ are interpreted as internal moves triggering the execution of q. Thus a process of the form $(x + \varepsilon); y$ may internally decide to behave like y. The $\oplus$-summand $x; y + y$ expresses the initial capabilities of $(x + \varepsilon); y$ with respect to the performance of observable actions.

Axiom (PAR3) is a weaker version of the standard ACP axiom

$$x \vert y \quad = \quad x \lfloor\!\lfloor y + y \lfloor\!\lfloor x + x \vert_c y \tag{2}$$

which applies to stable processes only. Indeed, the general law (2) is *not* sound with respect to $\simeq_M$. In fact, consider $(a \oplus b) \vert c$ with $\gamma(a, c) \simeq c_1$ and $\gamma(b, c) \simeq c_2$, with $c_1 \not\simeq c_2$. Then we have that

$$p \equiv (a \oplus b) \vert c \not\simeq_M (a \oplus b) \lfloor\!\lfloor c + c \lfloor\!\lfloor (a \oplus b) + (a \oplus b) \vert_c c \equiv q.$$

$$
\begin{array}{ll}
(PAR1) & (x \oplus y)|z = (x|z) \oplus (y|z) \\
(PAR2) & x|(y \oplus z) = (x|y) \oplus (x|z) \\
(PAR3) & \text{Let } x \equiv \sum_{i \in I} a_i; x_i \{+\varepsilon\} \text{ and } y \equiv \sum_{j \in J} b_j; y_j \{+\varepsilon\}. \text{ Then:} \\
 & x|y = x \lfloor y + y \lfloor x + x|_c y
\end{array}
$$

$$
\begin{array}{ll}
(LM1) & (x+y) \lfloor z = x \lfloor z + y \lfloor z \\
(LM2) & (x \oplus y) \lfloor z = x \lfloor z \oplus y \lfloor z \\
(LM3) & a; x \lfloor y = a; (x|y) \\
(LM4) & \delta \lfloor x = \delta \\
(LM5) & \varepsilon \lfloor x = \delta
\end{array}
$$

$$
\begin{array}{ll}
(CM1) & (x+y)|_c z = x|_c z + y|_c z \quad \text{if } z \equiv \sum_{i \in I} a_i; z_i \{+\varepsilon\} \\
(CM2) & (x \oplus y)|_c z = x|_c z \oplus y|_c z \\
(CM3) & x|_c y = y|_c x \\
(CM4) & \delta|_c \delta = \delta|_c \varepsilon = \delta|_c a; x = \delta \\
(CM5) & \varepsilon|_c \varepsilon = \varepsilon \\
(CM6) & \varepsilon|_c a; x = \delta \\
(CM7) & a; x|_c b; y = \begin{cases} c; (x|y) & \text{if } \gamma(a,b) \simeq c \\ \delta & \text{if } \gamma(a,b) \uparrow \end{cases}
\end{array}
$$

Figure 5: Inequations for the parallel combinators

Axiom (CM1) is a weaker version of the ACP law

$$(x+y)|_c z \quad = \quad x|_c z + y|_c z. \tag{3}$$

The condition on the form of z is necessary for the soundness of (CM1) with respect to $\simeq_M$. For instance, let $x \equiv a$, $y \equiv b$ and $z \equiv (a' \oplus b')$ in (3) and assume that $\gamma(a,a') \simeq c_1$, $\gamma(b,b') \simeq c_2$, $\gamma(a,b') \simeq c_3$ and $\gamma(b,a') \simeq c_4$. Then it is easy to see that

$$p \equiv (x+y)|_c z \not\lesssim_M x|_c z + y|_c z \equiv q.$$

Let $\leq_E$ denote the least Σ-precongruence over REC_Σ which satisfies the set of axioms E.

Theorem 4.1 (Soundness and Completeness) *For each $p, q \in REC_\Sigma$, $p \leq_E q$ iff $p \sqsubseteq_M q$.*

The proof of completeness of $\leq_E$ with respect to $\sqsubseteq_M$ relies, as usual, on the isolation of suitable *normal forms* for processes. The notion of normal form which is used in the proof of the above theorem is derived from the one studied in [H88] for must-testing. In order to clarify the model for $FREC_\Sigma$ proposed in §5, we shall now give the formal definition of the set of normal forms. The following standard notions will be used in the definition of normal forms; the interested reader is referred to [H88] for motivations.

Definition 4.1 (Saturated Sets) *Let $\mathcal{B}$ be a nonempty, finite set of finite subsets of $A_\surd$. Then:*

(1) *$\mathcal{B}$ is said to be* saturated *iff*

- $\bigcup \mathcal{B} \in \mathcal{B}$ *and*
- $X \in \mathcal{B}$ *and* $X \subseteq Y \subseteq \bigcup \mathcal{B}$ *imply* $Y \in \mathcal{B}$.

(2) *The convex, union closure of $\mathcal{B}$, $c(\mathcal{B})$, is the least set satisfying:*

- $X \in \mathcal{B}$ *implies* $X \in c(\mathcal{B})$,
- $X, Y \in c(\mathcal{B})$ *imply* $X \cup Y \in c(\mathcal{B})$ *and*
- $X, Y \in c(\mathcal{B})$ *and* $X \subseteq Z \subseteq Y$ *imply* $Z \in c(\mathcal{B})$.

We are now ready to define the notion of normal form used in the proof of the completeness theorem.

Definition 4.2 (Normal Forms) *The set of* normal forms *is the least set of terms satisfying:*

- *Ω is a normal form,*
- *if $\mathcal{A}$ is a saturated set over $A_\surd$ and for every $a \in \bigcup \mathcal{A} \setminus \{\surd\}$ there is a nf $n(a)$ then $\bigoplus \{n(X) \mid X \in \mathcal{A}\}$ is a nf, where $n(X) = \sum\{a; n(a) \mid a \in X \setminus \{\surd\}\}\{+\varepsilon \mid \text{if } \surd \in X\}$. The summation notations over $\oplus$ and $+$ are justified by axioms $(\oplus 1)$-$(\oplus 2)$ and $(+1)$-$(+2)$, respectively.*

Note that, by taking $\mathcal{A} = \{\emptyset\}$, we obtain that δ is a normal form. Moreover, for each $a \in \bigcup \mathcal{A}$, a normal form $n = \bigoplus \{n(X) \mid X \in \mathcal{A}\}$ has a unique a-derivative up to $\rightarrowtail \xrightarrow{a}$, namely $\varepsilon; n(a)$. This implies that, for instance, the term $p = a; b + a; \varepsilon$ is *not* a normal form. The normal form for p is the term $a; (b \oplus (\delta + \varepsilon) \oplus (b + \varepsilon))$.

5 Denotational Semantics

In this section we will give a mathematical model for the sublanguage $FREC_\Sigma$ in terms of a $\Sigma - po$ algebra which is a slight modification of the strong Acceptance Trees, AT_s, presented in [H88]. We assume that the reader is familiar with the theory of ordered algebras and algebraic semantics, which may be found in e.g. [Gue81] and [H88]. For the sake of completeness, we recall that a Σ-po algebra is a triple $\langle A, \Sigma_A, \leq_A \rangle$, where $\langle A, \Sigma_A \rangle$ is a Σ-algebra, $\langle A, \leq_A \rangle$ is a poset and the operators in Σ_A are monotonic with respect to $\leq_A$. We refer to $\langle A, \Sigma_A, \leq_A \rangle$ as A if no confusion arises. We will now introduce the Σ-po algebra of *Sequential Acceptance Trees* and prove that it is a fully abstract model with respect to $\sqsubseteq_M$ over $FREC_\Sigma$. For further motivation and technical details we refer the interested reader to [H88]. Before giving the definition of our model, we recall, for the sake of clarity, the basic ideas of Hennessy's original model.

Basically the model of Finite Acceptance Trees, fAT, in [H88] is obtained by taking the set of normal forms for testing equivalence, [DH84], as carrier set of a Σ-po algebra and equipping it with the preorder defined by the alternative characterization of the testing preorder. The only non-trivial task left is to define the operators in Σ over such a carrier set, i.e. to define them in such a way that applying them to normal forms yields normal forms.

For each set A, we will use $sat(A)$ to denote the set of saturated sets over A. For sets X, Y, $[X \longrightarrow Y]$ will denote the set of all functions from X onto Y. Moreover, we use the notation $[a_1 \rightarrow A_1, \cdots, a_n \rightarrow A_n]$ for the function which maps a_i to A_i, $i = 1, \cdots, n$. Then (the carrier of) fAT is formally defined as the least set which satisfies

1. $\bot \in fAT$
2. if $\mathcal{A} \in sat(A)$ and $f \in [\bigcup(\mathcal{A}) \longrightarrow fAT]$ then $(\mathcal{A}, f) \in fAT$.

Intuitively, the elements of fAT are finite, deterministic trees whose arcs are labelled on A and, for each $(\mathcal{A}, f)$ and $a \in \bigcup(\mathcal{A})$, $f(a)$ is the unique sub-tree of $(\mathcal{A}, f)$ reachable from its root by an a-labelled arc. The partial order $\leq_{fAT}$ over fAT is the least one which satisfies

1. $\forall T \in fAT. \bot \leq_{fAT} T$
2. $(\mathcal{A}, f) \leq_{fAT} (\mathcal{B}, g)$ if
   1)$\mathcal{B} \subseteq \mathcal{A}$
   2)$\forall a \in \bigcup \mathcal{B}. f(a) \leq_{fAT} g(a)$

The interpretation of Ω and of any divergent process is $\bot$ and that of the deadlocked process δ is $\Delta = (\{\emptyset\}, [])$. In our case we can follow the same idea and use the normal forms described in the previous section as the objects of the model. The main changes are due to the following requirements, which arise naturally from the behavioural semantics:

1. The new operator, ε, is interpreted as $E = (\{\{\surd\}\}, [\surd \longrightarrow \Delta])$.

2. $\surd$ can only occur as a label on a branch leading to Δ.

This leads to the following definition of finite sequential Acceptance Trees:

Definition 5.1 *The set of finite sequential Acceptance Trees, AT^{seq}, is defined as the least set satisfying the following:*

1. $\bot \in AT^{seq}$

2. If $\mathcal{A} \in sat(A_\surd)$ *and* $f : \bigcup(\mathcal{A}) \longrightarrow AT^{seq}$ *is such that* $\surd \in \bigcup(\mathcal{A})$ *implies* $f(\surd) = \Delta$*, then* $(\mathcal{A}, f) \in AT^{seq}$.

Note Δ and E, as defined above, belong to AT^{seq}. The partial order on AT^{seq}, $\leq_{AT^{seq}}$, is now defined exactly as the one on fAT given above. We will now endow the poset $\langle AT^{seq}, \leq_{AT^{seq}}\rangle$ with Σ-algebra structure in such a way that all the operations $op_{AT^{seq}}$, $op \in \Sigma$, will be monotonic with respect to $\leq_{AT^{seq}}$. For the sake of simplicity, we will drop the subscript in $op_{AT^{seq}}$ if no confusion can arise.

Definition of the Operators in AT^{seq}

$\Omega_{AT^{seq}}$: $\Omega_{AT^{seq}} = \perp$

$\delta_{AT^{seq}}$: $\delta_{AT^{seq}} = \Delta$

$\varepsilon_{AT^{seq}}$: $\varepsilon_{AT^{seq}} = E$

$a_{AT^{seq}}$: $a_{AT^{seq}} = (\{\{a\}\}, [a \rightarrow E])$

$\oplus_{AT^{seq}}$:

1. $T \oplus \perp = \perp \oplus T = \perp$
2. $(\mathcal{A}, f) \oplus (\mathcal{B}, g) = (c(\mathcal{A} \cup \mathcal{B}), f \oplus g)$

   $$\text{where } (f \oplus g)(a) = \begin{array}{ll} f(a) \oplus g(a) & \text{if } a \in dom(f) \cap dom(g) \\ f(a) & \text{if } a \in dom(f) \setminus dom(g) \\ g(a) & \text{if } a \in dom(g) \setminus dom(f) \end{array}$$

$+_{AT^{seq}}$:

1. $T + \perp = \perp + T = \perp$
2. $(\mathcal{A}, f) + (\mathcal{B}, g) = (\mathcal{A}\mu\mathcal{B}, f \oplus g)$, where $\mathcal{A}\mu\mathcal{B} = \{A \cup B \mid A \in \mathcal{A} \text{ and } B \in \mathcal{B}\}$.

Note that $\mathcal{A}\mu\mathcal{B}$ is saturated whenever $\mathcal{A}$ and $\mathcal{B}$ are; also, commutativity and associativity of the operators $\oplus$ and $+$ follow immediately from this definition. Moreover, for all sets A and B,

$$(\{A\}, f) = (\{A \setminus B\}, f_{A \setminus B}) + (\{A \cap B\}, f_{A \cap B})$$

where $f_{A \setminus B}$ and $f_{A \cap B}$ denote the restriction of the function f to the set $A \setminus B$ and $A \cap B$, respectively. This justifies the following way of writing Acceptance Trees:

$$(\mathcal{A}, f) = \sum \{\sum\{(\{\{a\}\}, f_a) | a \in A\} | A \in \mathcal{A}\}$$

where $f_a =_{def} f_{\{a\}} = [a \longrightarrow f(a)]$ and, by convention, the inner sum reduces to Δ, when the index set A is empty. We will use this representation for acceptance trees in the definitions of the missing operators. Following the notation introduced in the previous section, $\{+T\}$ and $\{\oplus T\}$ will denote optional summands.

$;_{AT^{seq}}$:

1. $\perp; T = \perp$

2. $(\mathcal{A},f);T = \sum \{(\sum\{(\{\{a\}\}, f_a;T)|a \in A \setminus \{\surd\}\}\{+T| \text{ if } \surd \in A\})\{\oplus T| \text{ if } \surd \in A\}|A \in \mathcal{A}\}$,

where $f_a;T =_{def} [a \rightarrow f(a);T]$. Note that by this definition, which is essentially a reformulation over acceptance trees of axioms (SEQ4) and (SEQ5) in Figure 3, $\Delta;T = \Delta$, $E;T = T$ and $a;E = a$. Moreover, we have that

$$(\mathcal{A},f) = \sum \{\sum\{a;T_a|a \in A\}|A \in \mathcal{A}\}$$

where $T_a =_{def} f(a)$ and $\surd;\Delta =_{def} E$. Note the very strong similarity between this representation of acceptance trees and the normal forms for finite processes. In the definition of the remaining operators we will use this characterization of AT^{seq}.

$\lfloor\!\lfloor_{AT^{seq}}$:

1. $\bot \lfloor\!\lfloor T = \bot$
2. $\sum \{\sum\{a;T_a|a \in A\}|A \in \mathcal{A}\} \lfloor\!\lfloor T = \sum \{\sum\{a;(T_a|T)|a \in A \setminus \{\surd\}\}|A \in \mathcal{A}\}$

$|_{c_{AT^{seq}}}$:

1. $\bot|_c U = U|_c \bot = \bot$
2. $\sum \{\sum\{a;T_a|a \in A\}|A \in \mathcal{A}\}|_c \sum \{\sum\{b;U_b|b \in B\}|B \in \mathcal{B}\} =$
   $\sum \{\sum(\{c;(T_a|U_b)| a \in A, b \in B, \gamma(a,b) = c\}\{+E \mid \text{ if } \surd \in A \cap B\})|A \in \mathcal{A}, B \in \mathcal{B}\}$

$|_{AT^{seq}}$:

$T|U = T\lfloor\!\lfloor U + U\lfloor\!\lfloor T + T|_c U$

$\tau_{I_{AT^{seq}}}$:

1. $\tau_I(\bot) = \bot$
2. $\tau_I(\sum \{\sum\{a;T_a|a \in A\}|A \in \mathcal{A}\}) = \sum \{\tau_I(\sum\{a;T_a|a \in A\})|A \in \mathcal{A}\}$, *where*
   $\tau_I(\sum\{a;T_a|a \in A\}) = \sum\{a;\tau_I(T_a)|a \in A\}$ *if* $I \cap A = \emptyset$
   $\tau_I(\sum\{a;T_a|a \in A\}) = \sum \{\tau_I(T_a)|a \in A \cap I\}$
   $\oplus\tau_I(\sum\{T_a|a \in A \cap I\} + \sum\{a;T_a|a \in A \setminus I\})$ *otherwise*

The definition of τ_I bears a strong similarity with axioms (H1)-(H3) in Figure 4. The following result states that we have indeed defined a Σ-algebra structure on AT^{seq} which is compatible with $\leq_{AT^{seq}}$.

Theorem 5.1 *$\langle AT^{seq}, \Sigma_{AT^{seq}}, \leq_{AT^{seq}}\rangle$ is a Σ-po algebra.*

We can now prove the full abstractness of the model with respect to the testing preorder $\sqsubseteq_M$ following [HI89].

Theorem 5.2 (Full Abstraction) *The Σ-po algebra $\langle AT^{seq}, \Sigma_{AT^{seq}}, \leq_{AT^{seq}}\rangle$ is a fully-abstract model for $FREC_\Sigma$ with respect to $\sqsubseteq_M$.*

The extension of the equational characterization of $\sqsubseteq_M$ given in §4 and of the full-abstraction result to the whole of REC_Σ is a routine application of the techniques presented in [H88] and [HI89].

6 References

[AB84] D. Austry and G. Boudol, Algebre de Processus et synchronisations, TCS 30(1), pp. 91-131

[Ace90] L. Aceto, A theory of Testing for ACP, Report 3/90, Dept. of Computer Science, University of Sussex, May 1990

[AH88] L. Aceto and M. Hennessy, Termination, Deadlock and Divergence, Report 6/88, Dept. of Computer Science, University of Sussex, 1988. To appear in the Journal of the ACM.

[BG87] J. C. M. Baeten and R. J. van Glabbeek, Abstraction and Empty Process in Process Algebra, Report CS-R8721, CWI Amsterdam, 1987 (to appear in Fundamenta Informaticae)

[BHR84] S. D. Brookes, C. A. R. Hoare and A. W. Roscoe, A Theory of Communicating Sequential Processes, JACM 31,3, pp. 560-599, 1984

[BK85] J. A. Bergstra and J. W. Klop, Algebra of Communicating Processes with Abstraction, TCS 37, 1, pp. 77-121, 1985

[BKO87] J. A. Bergstra, J. W. Klop and E.-R. Olderog, Failures Without Chaos: a New Process Semantics for Fair Abstraction, Formal Description of Programming Concepts-III (M. Wirsing ed.), North-Holland, 1987

[BV89] J. C. M. Baeten and F. Vaandrager, An Algebra for Process Creation, Report CS-R8907, CWI, Amsterdam, 1989

[CH89] I. Castellani and M. Hennessy, Distributed Bisimulations, JACM, October 1989

[DeN85] R. de Nicola, Two Complete Sets of Axioms for a Theory of Communicating Sequential Processes, Information and Control 64(1-3), pp. 136-176, 1985

[DH84] R. De Nicola and M. Hennessy, Testing Equivalences for Processes, TCS 34,1, pp. 83-134, 1987

[DH87] R. de Nicola and M. Hennessy, CCS without τ's, in *Proceedings TAPSOFT 87*, LNCS 249, pp. 138-152, Springer-Verlag, 1987

[GlV88] R. van Glabbeek and F. Vaandrager, Modular Specifications in Process Algebra– with Curious Queues, Report CS-R8821, CWI, Amsterdam, 1988

[Gue81] I. Guessarian, *Algebraic Semantics*, LNCS 99, Springer-Verlag, 1981

[H88] M. Hennessy, *Algebraic Theory of Processes*, MIT Press, 1988

[HI89] M. Hennessy and A. Ingólfsdóttir, A Theory of Communicating Processes with Value Passing, Report 3/89, University of Sussex, 1989

[HM85] M. Hennessy and R. Milner, Algebraic Laws for Nondeterminism and Concurrency, JACM 32,1, pp. 137-161, 1985

[Hoare85] C. A. R. Hoare, *Communicating Sequential Processes*, Prentice-Hall, 1985

[Kel76] R. Keller, Formal Verification of Parallel Programs, C. ACM 19,7, pp. 561-572, 1976

[Mil89] R. Milner, *Communication and Concurrency*, Prentice-Hall, 1989

[Mol89] F. Moller, *Axioms for Concurrency*, Ph. D. Thesis, University of Edinburgh, 1989

[Pa81] D. Park, Concurrency and Automata on Infinite Sequences, Lecture Notes in Computer Science vol. 104, Springer-Verlag, 1981

[Pl81] G. Plotkin, A Structural Approach to Operational Semantics, Report DAIMI FN-19, Computer Science Dept. , Aarhus University, 1981

[Va90a] F. Vaandrager, Process Algebra Semantics of POOL, to appear in *Applications of Process Algebra* (J.C.M. Baeten ed.), pp. 173-236, 1990

[Va90b] F. Vaandrager, Two Simple Protocols, to appear in *Applications of Process Algebra* (J.C.M. Baeten ed.), pp. 237-260, 1990

[Vra86] J. L. M. Vrancken, The Algebra of Communicating Processes with Empty Process, Report FVI 86-01, Dept. of Computer Science, University of Amsterdam, 1986

Real Space Process Algebra

J.C.M. Baeten
Department of Software Technology, CWI, P.O.Box 4079, 1009 AB Amsterdam, The Netherlands
Programming Research Group, University of Amsterdam, P.O.Box 41882, 1009 DB Amsterdam, The Netherlands

J.A. Bergstra
Programming Research Group, University of Amsterdam, P.O.Box 41882, 1009 DB Amsterdam, The Netherlands
Department of Philosophy, Utrecht University, Heidelberglaan 2, 3584 CS Utrecht, The Netherlands

We extend the real time process algebra of [BB91] to real space-time process algebra, where actions are not just parametrized by a time coordinate, but also by three spatial coordinates. We describe two versions: classical space-time, where all equations are invariant under Galilei transformations, and relativistic space-time, where all equations are invariant under Lorentz transformations. The latter case in turn splits into two subcases: the temporal interleaving model and the true concurrency model.

1980 Mathematics Subject Classification (1985 revision): 68Q45, 68Q55, 68Q65, 68Q50.
1987 CR Categories: F.4.3, D.2.10, D.3.1, D.3.3.
Key words & Phrases: process algebra, real time, real space-time, Galilei transformation, Lorentz transformation, interleaving, true concurrency.
Note: Partial support received by ESPRIT basic research action 3006, CONCUR, and by RACE contract 1046, SPECS. This document does not necessarily reflect the views of the SPECS consortium.

1. INTRODUCTION.

We quote from PEACKOCK [P30]:

> Algebra may be considered, in its most general form, as *the* science which treats of the combinations of arbitrary signs and symbols by means of defined through arbitrary laws ...

Based on this fairly liberal but certainly classical description of algebra the axiom system ACP (Algebra of Communicating Processes) of BERGSTRA & KLOP [BK84, 85, 86] can be viewed as a part of algebra. In [BB91], the system ACP was extended with real time by having all actions parametrized by some $t \in \mathbf{R}^{\geq 0}$. This constitutes a departure from algebra in the sense that the real numbers are not a purely algebraic concept. As it turns out in the construction of real time process algebra (ACPρ) from ACP, all that matters is that time is organized as a totally ordered set.

In this report we will exploit the fact that ACPρ can be generalized to a setting in which time constitutes a partially ordered set. Rather than working with a partial ordering in general, we concentrate on two examples of such partial orderings that have a particularly useful interpretation.

i. $\langle P^f(\mathbf{R}^3) \times \mathbf{R}, <_c\rangle$, the set of finite nonempty subsets of $\mathbf{R}^3$ with a time coordinate, with $(v,t) <_c (w,r)$ iff $t < r$. We interpret an element (v,t) of $P^f(\mathbf{R}^3) \times \mathbf{R}$ as a set of points in classical space-time, all having the same time coordinate t.

ii. $\langle \mathbf{R}^4, <\rangle$ with $x < y$ if $x \neq y$ and y is in the light cone of x in the sense of special relativity, taking the fourth coordinate as the time component.

In this way we obtain real space-time process algebra, which we abbreviate to real space process algebra.

This report deals exclusively with the design of appropriate axiom systems for the description of the various real space process algebras leaving the illustration of its practical use by means of examples as an issue of secondary importance for the moment. Moreover we consider finite processes only. In particular this means that we do not consider recursion and integration.

For motivation and examples of the use of ACP and related systems we refer to [BK84, 85, 86] or [BW90]. Motivation and illustrating examples on real time process algebra can be found in [BB91].

2. REAL TIME PROCESS ALGEBRA

We start with a review of real time process algebra as introduced in [BB91]. We make a few small changes, thereby modifying ACPρ into ACPδρ, in order to facilitate extensions to real space process algebra further on. This does not imply that the theory ACPρ from [BB91] is considered problematic in any way; in fact it may be more useful in 'practice' than the axiom systems to be discussed below.

2.1 BASIC PROCESS ALGEBRA.

Process algebra starts from a given *action alphabet* A (usually finite). Elements a,b,c of A are called *atomic actions*, and are constants of the sort P of *processes*. The theory Basic Process Algebra (BPA) has two binary operators +,·: P × P → P; + stands for alternative composition and · for sequential composition. BPA has the first five axioms from table 1.

If we add to BPA a special constant δ in P (not in A) standing for *inaction*, comparable to NIL or 0 of CCS (see MILNER [M80, 89] or HENNESSY [HE88]) or STOP of CSP (see HOARE [H85]), we obtain the theory BPAδ. The two axioms for δ are the last two in table 1.

$X + Y = Y + X$	A1
$(X + Y) + Z = X + (Y + Z)$	A2
$X + X = X$	A3
$(X + Y) \cdot Z = X \cdot Z + Y \cdot Z$	A4
$(X \cdot Y) \cdot Z = X \cdot (Y \cdot Z)$	A5
$X + \delta = X$	A6
$\delta \cdot X = \delta$	A7

Table 1. BPAδ.

When we add real time to this setting, our basic actions are not from the set $A_\delta = A \cup \{\delta\}$, but from the set

$$AT = \{a(t) \mid a \in A_\delta, t \in \mathbf{R}\} \cup \{\delta\}.$$

The process a(t) performs action a at time t, and then terminates. The process δ(t) deadlocks at time t. The process δ cannot do anything, in particular it cannot wait. Again, these actions can be combined by +,·. In this paper we take times t from **R** rather than from $\mathbf{R}^{\geq 0} = \{r \in \mathbf{R} \mid r \geq 0\}$. As a consequence, the law a(0) = δ(0) of [BB91] has to be removed. Instead of the identification δ(0) = δ of [BB91], we take a slightly more abstract view and introduce the identification δ(t) = δ for all t ∈ **R**, thus disregarding the operational difference between various deadlocks. The axiom system ACPρ of [BB91] still has its value and we do not propose to change it. Rather, we will introduce a second theory ACPδρ. This happens with the introduction of BPAδρ. We have:

$$BPA\delta\rho = BPA\rho - \{a(0) = \delta(0)\} + \{\delta(t) = \delta\}.$$

As mentioned above, the law ATA1 of [BB91] (reading $a(0) = \delta$) was changed. The letter A the names of the axioms start with, refers to *absolute time* (versions with relative time were also considered in [BB91], but are not treated here).

As in [BB91], we have the additional operation $\gg$, the *(absolute) time shift*. $t \gg X$ denotes the process X starting at time t. This means that all actions that have to be performed at or before time t are turned into deadlocks because their execution has been delayed too long.

Due to the presence of the law $\delta(t) = \delta$, axioms ATA2,3,4 of [BB91] are derivable from the other axioms of BPA$\delta\rho$, and so a simplification is possible. In table 2, we have $a \in A_\delta$.

$\delta(t) = \delta$	ATA1*
$a(t) \cdot X = a(t) \cdot (t \gg X)$	ATA5
$t < r \;\Rightarrow\; t \gg a(r) = a(r)$	ATB1
$t \geq r \;\Rightarrow\; t \gg a(r) = \delta$	ATB2*
$t \gg (X + Y) = (t \gg X) + (t \gg Y)$	ATB3
$t \gg (X \cdot Y) = (t \gg X) \cdot Y$	ATB4

Table 2. BPA$\delta\rho$.

2.2 Algebra of Communicating Processes.

An axiomatization of parallel composition with communication uses the left merge operator $⌊\!⌊$, the communication merge operator $|$, and the encapsulation operator ∂_H of [BK84]. Moreover, two extra auxiliary operators introduced in [BB91] are needed: the ultimate delay operator and the bounded initialization operator.

$a \mid b = b \mid a$	C1	$U(a(t)) = \{r \in \mathbf{R} \mid r \geq t\}$	ATU1
$a \mid (b \mid c) = (a \mid b) \mid c$	C2	$U(\delta) = \mathbf{R}$	ATU2
$\delta \mid a = \delta$	C3	$U(X + Y) = U(X) \cap U(Y)$	ATU3
$t \neq r \;\Rightarrow\; a(t) \mid b(r) = \delta$	ATC1	$U(X \cdot Y) = U(X)$	ATU4
$a(t) \mid b(t) = (a \mid b)(t)$	ATC2		
		$t \in V \;\Rightarrow\; a(t) \gg V = \delta$	ATB5
$X \parallel Y = X ⌊\!⌊ Y + Y ⌊\!⌊ X + X \mid Y$	CM1	$t \notin V \;\Rightarrow\; a(t) \gg V = a(t)$	ATB6
$a(t) ⌊\!⌊ X = (a(t) \gg U(X)) \cdot X$	ATCM2	$(X + Y) \gg V = (X \gg V) + (Y \gg V)$	ATB7
$(a(t) \cdot X) ⌊\!⌊ Y = (a(t) \gg U(Y)) \cdot (X \parallel Y)$	ATCM3	$(X \cdot Y) \gg V = (X \gg V) \cdot Y$	ATB8
$(X + Y) ⌊\!⌊ Z = X ⌊\!⌊ Z + Y ⌊\!⌊ Z$	CM4		
$(a(t) \cdot X) \mid b(r) = (a(t) \mid b(r)) \cdot X$	CM5'	$\partial_H(a) = a \quad \text{if } a \notin H$	D1
$a(t) \mid (b(r) \cdot X) = (a(t) \mid b(r)) \cdot X$	CM6'	$\partial_H(a) = \delta \quad \text{if } a \in H$	D2
$(a(t) \cdot X) \mid (b(r) \cdot Y) = (a(t) \mid b(r)) \cdot (X \parallel Y)$	CM7'	$\partial_H(a(t)) = (\partial_H(a))(t)$	ATD
$(X + Y) \mid Z = X \mid Z + Y \mid Z$	CM8	$\partial_H(X + Y) = \partial_H(X) + \partial_H(Y)$	D3
$X \mid (Y + Z) = X \mid Y + X \mid Z$	CM9	$\partial_H(X \cdot Y) = \partial_H(X) \cdot \partial_H(Y)$	D4

Table 3. Remaining axioms of ACP$\delta\rho$.

The ultimate delay operator U takes a process expression X in CPE, and returns a subset of $\mathbf{R}$. The intended meaning is that U(X) is the set of times at which X must have started, the set of times to which X cannot wait without performing any actions or deadlocking. In [BB91], a slightly different definition is used, and the infimum of the present set is taken, which explains the phrase 'ultimate delay'. In the present approach, we avoid the use of the symbol ω and we prepare for the use of a partially ordered time structure. The bounded initialization operator is also denoted by $\gg$, and is the counterpart of the operator with the same name that we saw in the axiomatization of BPA$\delta\rho$. With $X \gg V$ we denote the process X with its behaviour restricted to the extent that its first action must be performed at a time not in $V \subseteq \mathbf{R}$.

The axioms of ACP$\delta\rho$ are in tables 1 through 3. In table 3, $H \subseteq A$, $a,b,c \in A_\delta$.

A *closed process expression* (CPE) over the signature of ACP$\delta\rho$ with atoms A is an expression that does not contain variables for atoms, processes or real numbers. We allow every real number as a constant, which means there are uncountably many such closed process expressions. For finite closed process expressions an initial algebra can be defined. This is the initial algebra model of ACP$\rho\delta(A)$. This structure identifies two closed expressions whenever these can be shown identical by means of application of the axioms. We will look at an operational model next. We denote the set of actions over A without variables by IA (the set of instantiated actions).

2.3 OPERATIONAL SEMANTICS.

We describe an operational semantics for ACP$\delta\rho$ following KLUSENER [K91]. His operational semantics is a simplification of the one in [BB91]. In fact the operational semantics of [K91] is more abstract than the one given in [BB91]. We have two relations

$$\text{step} \subseteq \text{CPE} \times IA \times \text{CPE} \qquad\qquad \text{terminate} \subseteq \text{CPE} \times IA.$$

The extension of these relations is found as the least fixed point of a simultaneous inductive definition. We write

$x \xrightarrow{a(r)} x'$	for	$\text{step}(x, a(r), x')$, and
$x \xrightarrow{a(r)} \surd$	for	$\text{terminate}(x, a(r))$.

Notice that these relations are only defined for $a \in A$, so $a \neq \delta$.

The inductive rules for the operational semantics are similar to those used in structural operational semantics. In table 4, we have $a,b,c \in IA$, $r,s \in \mathbf{R}$, $x,x',y \in \text{CPE}$.

We see that the action rules for parallel composition make use of the ultimate delay operator. This operator was introduced axiomatically in 2.2, but can also be easily determined for a transition system, since we will always have that $U(x) = \{t \in \mathbf{R} \mid t \geq r \text{ for all } r \text{ with } x \xrightarrow{a(r)} x' \text{ or } x \xrightarrow{a(r)} \surd\}$. Thus, we can avoid the use of the axioms in the description of the structured operational semantics.

2.4 BISIMULATIONS.

Again we consider the class CPE of closed process expressions over ACP$\delta\rho$. A *bisimulation* on CPE is a binary relation R such that

i. for each p and q with $R(p, q)$: if there is a step $a(s)$ possible from p to p', then there is a CPE q' such that $R(p', q')$ and there is a step $a(s)$ possible from q to q'.

ii. for each p and q with $R(p, q)$: if there is a step $a(s)$ possible from q to q', then there is a CPE p' such that $R(p', q')$ and there is a step $a(s)$ possible from p to p'.

iii. for each p and q with $R(p, q)$: a termination step $a(s)$ is possible from p iff it is possible from q.

We say expressions p and q are *bisimilar*, denoted $p \leftrightarrow q$, if there exists a bisimulation on CPE with $R(p,q)$. In [K91] it is shown that bisimulation is a congruence relation on CPE, and that CPE/$\leftrightarrow$ is a model for BPA$\delta\rho$. Indeed, this model is isomorphic to the initial algebra. The advantage of this operational semantics is, that it allows extensions to models containing recursively defined processes.

$$a(r) \xrightarrow{a(r)} \surd$$

$$\frac{x \xrightarrow{a(r)} x'}{x+y \xrightarrow{a(r)} x',\ y+x \xrightarrow{a(r)} x'} \qquad \frac{x \xrightarrow{a(r)} \surd}{x+y \xrightarrow{a(r)} \surd,\ y+x \xrightarrow{a(r)} \surd}$$

$$\frac{x \xrightarrow{a(r)} x'}{x \cdot y \xrightarrow{a(r)} x' \cdot y} \qquad \frac{x \xrightarrow{a(r)} \surd}{x \cdot y \xrightarrow{a(r)} r \gg y}$$

$$\frac{x \xrightarrow{a(r)} x',\ r > s}{s \gg x \xrightarrow{a(r)} x'} \qquad \frac{x \xrightarrow{a(r)} \surd,\ r > s}{s \gg x \xrightarrow{a(r)} \surd}$$

$$\frac{x \xrightarrow{a(r)} x',\ r \notin U(y)}{x \| y \xrightarrow{a(r)} x' \| (r \gg y),\ x \lfloor\!\lfloor y \xrightarrow{a(r)} x' \| (r \gg y),\ y \| x \xrightarrow{a(r)} (r \gg y) \| x'}$$

$$\frac{x \xrightarrow{a(r)} \surd,\ r \notin U(y)}{x \| y \xrightarrow{a(r)} r \gg y,\ x \lfloor\!\lfloor y \xrightarrow{a(r)} r \gg y,\ y \| x \xrightarrow{a(r)} r \gg y}$$

$$\frac{x \xrightarrow{a(r)} x',\ y \xrightarrow{b(r)} y',\ a \mid b = c \neq \delta}{x \| y \xrightarrow{c(r)} x' \| y',\ x \mid y \xrightarrow{c(r)} x' \| y'} \qquad \frac{x \xrightarrow{a(r)} \surd,\ y \xrightarrow{b(r)} \surd,\ a \mid b = c \neq \delta}{x \| y \xrightarrow{c(r)} \surd,\ x \mid y \xrightarrow{c(r)} \surd}$$

$$\frac{x \xrightarrow{a(r)} x',\ y \xrightarrow{b(r)} \surd,\ a \mid b = c \neq \delta}{x \| y \xrightarrow{c(r)} x',\ y \| x \xrightarrow{c(r)} x',\ x \mid y \xrightarrow{c(r)} x',\ y \mid x \xrightarrow{c(r)} x'}$$

$$\frac{x \xrightarrow{a(r)} x',\ r \notin V}{x \gg V \xrightarrow{a(r)} x'} \qquad \frac{x \xrightarrow{a(r)} \surd,\ r \notin V}{x \gg V \xrightarrow{a(r)} \surd}$$

$$\frac{x \xrightarrow{a(r)} x',\ a \notin H}{\partial_H(x) \xrightarrow{a(r)} \partial_H(x')} \qquad \frac{x \xrightarrow{a(r)} \surd,\ a \notin H}{\partial_H(x) \xrightarrow{a(r)} \surd}$$

Table 4. Action rules for ACPδρ.

2.5 GRAPH MODEL.

A graph model (or, more accurately, a *tree* model) of ACPδρ can be constructed as follows.

Process trees are finite directed rooted trees with edges labeled by timed atomic actions and endpoint possibly labeled by δ, satisfying the condition that for each pair of consecutive transitions $s_1 \xrightarrow{a(r)} s_2 \xrightarrow{b(t)} s_3$ it is required that $r < t$.

Now $+, \cdot, \|, \lfloor\!\lfloor, \mid, \partial_H, \gg, U, \gg$ can be defined on these graphs in a straightforward manner:

- For +, take the disjoint union of the graphs and identify the roots. If exactly one of the two graphs is the one point δ-graph, remove its label.
- $t \gg g$ is obtained by removing every edge from the root with label $a(r)$ satisfying $t \gg a(r) = \delta$. If this gives a new endpoint, it is labeled by δ.

- $g \cdot h$ is constructed as follows: identify each non-δ endpoint s of g with the root of a copy of $t \gg h$, where t is the time of the edge leading to s.
- $U(g) = \{t \in \mathbf{R} \mid t \geq r$ for all $r \in \mathbf{R}$, $a \in A$ and $s \in g$ with $root(g) \xrightarrow{a(r)} s\}$.
- Let for $s \in g$ $(g)_s$ denote the subgraph of g with root s. Then $g \| h$ is defined as follows:
- the set of states is the cartesian product of the state sets of g and h, the root the pair of roots.
- transitions: if $s \xrightarrow{a(r)} s'$ and $r \notin U((h)_t)$ then $\langle s,t\rangle \xrightarrow{a(r)} \langle s',t\rangle$;
  if $t \xrightarrow{a(r)} t'$ and $r \notin U((g)_s)$ then $\langle s,t\rangle \xrightarrow{a(r)} \langle s,t'\rangle$;
  if $s \xrightarrow{a(r)} s'$ and $t \xrightarrow{b(r)} t'$ and $a \mid b = c \neq \delta$ then $\langle s,t\rangle \xrightarrow{c(r)} \langle s',t'\rangle$.

Note that the conditions imply that the resulting graph is actually a tree.

- the construction of $g \gg V$, $g \mathbin{⌊\!\!⌊} h$, $g \mid h$ and $\partial_H(g)$ is now straightforward.

Bisimulation on these graphs is defined as e.g. in BAETEN & WEIJLAND [BW90]. One may prove in a standard fashion that bisimulation is a congruence for all operators of ACP$\delta\rho$.

Our reason for spelling out the model construction is that it is useful in all other cases arising in this paper as well.

2.10 ZERO OBJECT.

It is interesting to see that we can simplify the system ACP$\delta\rho$ considerably if we take an even more abstract view of the process δ. We do this by adding the additional equation $x \cdot \delta = \delta$. Further on, in the setting of relativistic true concurrency real space process algebra, it seems to be the only option left open to us.

By adding the equation $x \cdot \delta = \delta$, δ is converted into the constant 0 of [BB90]. The axiom system ACP_0' replaces δ by 0. (Notice that ACP_0 denotes the axiom system from [BB90] that combines δ and 0.)

$a \mid b = b \mid a$	C1	$X + Y = Y + X$	A1
$a \mid (b \mid c) = (a \mid b) \mid c$	C2	$(X + Y) + Z = X + (Y + Z)$	A2
$0 \mid a = 0$	CZ3	$X + X = X$	A3
		$(X + Y) \cdot Z = X \cdot Z + Y \cdot Z$	A4
$X \| Y = X \mathbin{⌊\!\!⌊} Y + Y \mathbin{⌊\!\!⌊} X + X \mid Y$	CM1	$(X \cdot Y) \cdot Z = X \cdot (Y \cdot Z)$	A5
$a \mathbin{⌊\!\!⌊} X = a \cdot X$	CM2	$X + 0 = X$	A6 - Z2
$a \cdot X \mathbin{⌊\!\!⌊} Y = a \cdot (X \| Y)$	CM3	$0 \cdot X = 0$	A7 - Z3
$(X + Y) \mathbin{⌊\!\!⌊} Z = X \mathbin{⌊\!\!⌊} Z + Y \mathbin{⌊\!\!⌊} Z$	CM4	$X \cdot 0 = 0$	Z1
$a \cdot X \mid b = (a \mid b) \cdot X$	CM5		
$a \mid b \cdot X = (a \mid b) \cdot X$	CM6	$\partial_H(a) = a$ if $a \notin H$	D1
$a \cdot X \mid b \cdot Y = (a \mid b) \cdot (X \| Y)$	CM7	$\partial_H(a) = 0$ if $a \in H$	DZ2
$(X + Y) \mid Z = X \mid Z + Y \mid Z$	CM8	$\partial_H(X + Y) = \partial_H(X) + \partial_H(Y)$	D3
$X \mid (Y + Z) = X \mid Y + X \mid Z$	CM9	$\partial_H(X \cdot Y) = \partial_H(X) \cdot \partial_H(Y)$	D4

Table 5. ACP_0'.

If we now look at ACP0ρ, by again replacing all δ's by 0 in ACP$\delta\rho$, we can simplify considerably by not using the laws ATCM2,3 but the original laws CM2,3. This can be done because summands that have a wrong time sequence will be removed altogether by 0. Thus we see

$$a(1) \| b(2) = a(1) \mathbin{⌊\!\!⌊} b(2) + b(2) \mathbin{⌊\!\!⌊} a(1) + a(1) \mid b(2) = a(1) \cdot b(2) + b(2) \cdot a(1) + 0 =$$

$= a(1)\cdot b(2) + b(2)\cdot(2 \gg a(1)) = a(1)\cdot b(2) + b(2)\cdot 0 = a(1)\cdot b(2) + 0 = a(1)\cdot b(2)$.

As a consequence, the ultimate delay operator and the bounded initialization operator are not needed anymore for an axiomatization. Thus, ACP0ρ = A1-5 + Z1-3 + ZTA1 + ATA5 + ZTB2 + ATB1,3,4 + C1,2 + CZ3 + ATC1,2 + CM1,4,8,9 + CM2'-7' + D1-4 + ATD. These axioms can be found in tables 2, 3, 5 and 6 below.

$0(t) = 0$	ZTA1
$t \geq r \;\Rightarrow\; t \gg a(r) = 0$	ZTB2
$a(t) \mathbin{⫫} X = a(t)\cdot X$	CM2'
$a(t)\cdot X \mathbin{⫫} Y = a(t)\cdot(X \parallel Y)$	CM3'

Table 6. Additional axioms for ACP0ρ.

3. CLASSICAL RSPA.

In Classical Real Space Process Algebra (RSPA-C) we will add space coordinates to all atomic actions. Apart from this, we get a straightforward extension of the theory in section 2. The set of atomic actions is now

$$AST = \{a(x,y,z;t) \mid a \in A_\delta,\, x,y,z,t \in \mathbb{R}\} \cup \{\delta\}.$$

Instead of $a(x,y,z;t)$, we often write $a(\vec{x};t)$, sometimes also $a(\vec{x})(t)$.

3.1 MULTI-ACTIONS.

Multi-actions are process terms generated by actions from AST and the communication function $\mid$. All multi-actions can be written in a normal form modulo commutativity and associativity. These have the following form:

$$a_1(\vec{x}_1;t) \mid a_2(\vec{x}_2;t) \mid \ldots \mid a_n(\vec{x}_n;t),$$

where $n \geq 1$, all $a_i \neq \delta$ and all $\vec{x}_i$ are pairwise different. For these normal forms, we use the notation

$$(a_1(\vec{x}_1) \,\&\, a_2(\vec{x}_2) \,\&\, \ldots \,\&\, a_n(\vec{x}_n))(t),$$

but we do not introduce & as a function because it would be a partial one. Semantically, in RSPA-C, the multi-actions play the role of the timed actions in RTPA. We use the following axioms to reduce every communication term to normal form. In table 7, we have $a,b,c \in A_\delta$, and u,v,w are multi-actions.

$a \mid b = b \mid a$	C1
$a \mid (b \mid c) = (a \mid b) \mid c$	C2
$\delta \mid a = \delta$	C3
$t \neq r \;\Rightarrow\; a(\vec{p};t) \mid b(\vec{q};r) = \delta$	ASC1
$a(\vec{p};t) \mid b(\vec{p};t) = (a \mid b)(\vec{p};t)$	ASC2
$u \mid v = v \mid u$	ASC3
$u \mid (v \mid w) = (u \mid v) \mid w$	ASC4
$\delta \mid u = \delta$	ASC5

Table 7. Communication function for RSPA-C.

3.2 REAL SPACE PROCESS ALGEBRA.

Classical real space process algebra now has exactly the same axioms as real time process algebra, only the letters a,b now do not range over A respectively A_δ, but over expressions of the form $a_1(\vec{x}_1)$ & $a_2(\vec{x}_2)$ & ... & $a_n(\vec{x}_n)$ as above. Note that axiom ATA1* now reads $\delta(\vec{p};t) = \delta$. Further, BPA$\delta\rho\sigma$ contains axioms A1-7, ATA5 and ATB1-4 with a ranging over expressions $a_1(\vec{x}_1)$ & ... & $a_n(\vec{x}_n)$.

The axioms for ultimate delay are again ATU1-4 (with in ATU1 a ranging over the larger set). Parallel composition is dealt with likewise, obtaining the axiom system ACP$\delta\rho\sigma$ by adding axioms CM1,4-9, ATCM2,3, D1-4, ATD. Similarly, we obtain ACP0$\rho\sigma$.

The operational semantics for RSPA-C is just like in the temporal case, in section 2. Transitions are labeled with multi-actions, and these play exactly the same role as the timed actions in the case of ACP$\delta\rho$. Similarly we may define a graph model for ACP$\delta\rho\sigma$. In both cases bisimulation can be defined in the same way.

3.3 LEMMA.

ACP$\delta\rho\sigma$, with the set of atomic actions limited to $\{a(\vec{p};t) \mid a \in A_\delta, t \in \mathbb{R}\}$ for a fixed $\vec{p}$, is equivalent to ACP$\delta\rho$.

In words, classical real space process in one point is the same as real time process algebra. The proof of this fact is easy, as all axioms are the same, and with axioms ASC1-2, all multi-actions reduce to single actions.

Relating this axiom system ACP$\delta\rho\sigma$ to the system of [BB91] the following can be said. In [BB91], the system ACPρ has timed δ's and it is extended to incorporate multi-actions at different locations using the equation $\delta(\vec{p};t) = \delta(t)$. Thus, in the setting of ACPρ one can maintain the time of time-space deadlocks in a context with multi-atoms. This mechanism of [BB91] can be called ACP$\rho\sigma$, it has its justification because it preserves more detailed information about the timing of deadlocks.

4. PHYSICS PRELIMINARIES.

We will very briefly mention some notions from physics that will be relevant in the following section. For more information, any text book covering special relativity theory will suffice, see e.g. [B21].

4.1 COORDINATE TRANSFORMATIONS.

First, let us consider a *Galilei transformation*. A Galilei transformation $\mathcal{G}_{\vec{z}}$ over a vector $\vec{z}$ is a translation in the direction of $\vec{z}$ with the length of this vector per unit of time. Thus, if the origins of the two systems coincide, then we get the formula $\mathcal{G}_{\vec{z}}(\vec{p};t) = (\vec{p} - \vec{z}\cdot t;\ t)$.

If the mapping T is projection onto the time coordinate, i.e. $T(\vec{p};t) = t$, then obviously

$$T(\mathcal{G}_{\vec{z}}(\vec{p};t)) = T(\vec{p};t).$$

Thus, in *classical* (Newtonian) mechanics, time is absolute (independent of a linear observer). In special relativity, the same transformation is described by means of a Lorentz transformation.

For the *Lorentz transformation* $\mathcal{L}_{\vec{z}}$, time is not absolute anymore. Thus, it can occur that there are two points in $\mathbf{R}^4$ $\alpha = (\vec{p};t)$ and $\beta = (\vec{q};t)$ (so $T(\alpha) = T(\beta)$), and there are two vectors $\vec{z}$ and $\vec{w}$ in $\mathbf{R}^3$ such that

$$T(\mathcal{L}_{\vec{z}}(\alpha) < T(\mathcal{L}_{\vec{z}}(\beta)) \text{ but } T(\mathcal{L}_{\vec{w}}(\alpha)) > T(\mathcal{L}_{\vec{w}}(\beta)).$$

In fact, for all α,β with $\alpha \neq \beta$ and $T(\alpha) = T(\beta)$ such $\vec{z}$ and $\vec{w}$ can be found. This leads us to consider a new ordering on $\mathbf{R}^4$.

4.2 LIGHT CONES.

We define for $\alpha,\beta \in \mathbf{R}^4$: $\alpha < \beta$ iff for all $\vec{z} \in \mathbf{R}^3$ we have $T(\mathcal{L}_{\vec{z}}(\alpha) < T(\mathcal{L}_{\vec{z}}(\beta))$.
This is a partial ordering on $\mathbf{R}^4$. We write $\alpha \# \beta$ if α and β are incomparable in this ordering. The set $\{\beta \in \mathbf{R}^4 \mid \beta \geq \alpha\}$ is called the *light cone* of α. The intuition behind this is that if β is in the light cone of α, then it is possible to travel from α to β with a speed less than or equal to the speed of light.

4.3 REAL SPACE PROCESS ALGEBRA.

A Galilei transformation can be applied to a closed process expression over RSPA-C using the following inductive definition:

$\mathcal{G}_{\vec{z}}(a(\vec{p};t)) = a(\mathcal{G}_{\vec{z}}(\vec{p};t))$
$\mathcal{G}_{\vec{z}}(x \square y) = \mathcal{G}_{\vec{z}}(x) \square \mathcal{G}_{\vec{z}}(y)$ for $\square = +, \cdot, \|$
$\mathcal{G}_{\vec{z}}(\partial_H(x)) = \partial_H(\mathcal{G}_{\vec{z}}(x))$
$\mathcal{G}_{\vec{z}}(t \gg x) = t \gg (\mathcal{G}_{\vec{z}}(x))$
$\mathcal{G}_{\vec{z}}(x \gg V) = \mathcal{G}_{\vec{z}}(x) \gg V.$

$\mathcal{G}_{\vec{z}}$ acts on a transition system for ACP$\delta\rho\sigma$ by transforming each action occurring in a label. One may easily prove that $g \leftrightarrows h$ implies $\mathcal{G}_{\vec{z}}(g) \leftrightarrows \mathcal{G}_{\vec{z}}(h)$ and that $\mathcal{G}_{\vec{z}}$ commutes with all operators in the graph model.

4.4 AN INCOMPATIBILITY.

Now an important observation is that classical real space process algebra is not compatible with Lorentz transformations. First of all assume that $\mathcal{L}_{\vec{z}}(a(\vec{p};t)) = a(\mathcal{L}_{\vec{z}}(\vec{p};t))$ and $\mathcal{L}_{\vec{z}}(x \| y) = \mathcal{L}_{\vec{z}}(x) \| \mathcal{L}_{\vec{z}}(y)$. Now we will use the fact that $\mathcal{L}_{\vec{z}}$ does not preserve the partial ordering on $P^f(\mathbf{R}^3) \times \mathbf{R}$, described in the introduction, that underlies ACP$\delta\rho\sigma$.

Let $\alpha \# \beta$ and consider $p = a(\alpha)\cdot b(\beta)$. Suppose without loss of generality that $T(\alpha) < T(\beta)$. Choose $\vec{z}$ such that $T(\mathcal{L}_{\vec{z}}(\alpha)) > T(\mathcal{L}_{\vec{z}}(\beta))$. Write $\alpha' = \mathcal{L}_{\vec{z}}(\alpha)$, $\beta' = \mathcal{L}_{\vec{z}}(\beta)$. Then we find:

$$a(\alpha) \| b(\beta) = a(\alpha)\cdot b(\beta) \text{ and } a(\alpha') \| b(\beta') = b(\beta')\cdot a(\alpha') \text{ and thus}$$
$$\mathcal{L}_{\vec{z}}(a(\alpha)\cdot b(\beta)) = \mathcal{L}_{\vec{z}}(a(\alpha) \| b(\beta)) = a(\alpha') \| b(\beta') = b(\beta')\cdot a(\alpha'),$$

which contradicts the required distribution over $\cdot$. Hence RSPA-C is not *Lorentz-invariant*, and a different axiomatization is needed for a Lorentz-invariant form of real space process algebra. We will discuss such an axiomatization in the following section.

5. RELATIVISTIC RSPA.

In Relativistic Real Space Process Algebra (RSPA-R) we consider actions parametrized by elements of $\mathbf{R}^4$. The set of atomic actions is now

$$AST = \{a(x,y,z,t) \mid a \in A_\delta, x,y,z,t \in \mathbf{R}\} \cup \{\delta\}.$$

Instead of $a(x,y,z,t)$, we often write $a(\alpha)$.

5.1 BASIC RELATIVISTIC REAL SPACE PROCESS ALGEBRA.

Here, we consider BPAδρσ in a relativistic setting. Since time and space cannot be separated anymore, we will replace an expression of the form $t \gg X$ by an expression $\alpha \gg X$ for $\alpha \in \mathbf{R}^4$. Similarly, we obtain BPA0ρσr, by changing δ into 0 in axioms STA1, STB2. The operational semantics for BPAδρσr is as expected, replacing labels a(t) by labels a(α). Also, bisimulation is defined similarly.

$\delta(\alpha) = \delta$	STA1
$a(\alpha) \cdot X = a(\alpha) \cdot (\alpha \gg X)$	STA5
$\alpha < \beta \;\Rightarrow\; \alpha \gg a(\beta) = a(\beta)$	STB1
$\neg(\alpha < \beta) \;\Rightarrow\; \alpha \gg a(\beta) = \delta$	STB2
$\alpha \gg (X + Y) = (\alpha \gg X) + (\alpha \gg Y)$	STB3
$\alpha \gg (X \cdot Y) = (\alpha \gg X) \cdot Y$	STB4

Table 8. BPAδρσr = BPAδ + STA1,5 + STB1-4.

5.2 ULTIMATE DELAY.

The definition of the ultimate delay operator now uses the light cone of a point in four-space.

$U(a(\alpha)) = \{\beta \in \mathbf{R}^4 \mid \beta \geq \alpha\}$	STU1
$U(\delta) = \mathbf{R}^4$	STU2
$U(X + Y) = U(X) \cap U(Y)$	STU3
$U(X \cdot Y) = U(X)$	STU4

Table 9. Ultimate delay operator.

5.3 PARALLEL COMPOSITION.

First, we consider what happens when we take exactly the same axioms for parallel composition as before. First, the bounded initialization operator is defined as before, but now has signature $P \times Pow(\mathbf{R}^4) \to P$.

Then, we look at axioms for the communication function. We cannot consider multi-actions of simultaneously happening actions at different locations anymore, because simultaneity is not Lorentz-invariant: simultaneity of two actions is only due to the 'lucky' choice of an inertial system. This explains the replacement of axiom ASC1 by the following axiom STC1:

$\alpha \neq \beta \;\Rightarrow\; a(\alpha) \mid b(\beta) = \delta$ STC1

$a(\alpha) \mid b(\alpha) = (a \mid b)(\alpha)$ STC2.

Then, the axiom system ACPδρσr is obtained by taking BPAδρσr + STU1-4 + STB5-8 + C1-3 + STC1,2 and adding the axioms CM1,4-9, ATCM2,3, D1-4, ATD as in 2.7, but replacing all symbols t,r by α,β.

The operational rules for parallel composition are as before. Process graphs are just as in the RSPA-C case, be it that now for a pair of consecutive transitions $s \xrightarrow{a(\alpha)} s' \xrightarrow{b(\beta)} s''$ it is needed that $\alpha < \beta$.

5.4 LORENTZ INVARIANCE.

We can define a Lorentz transformation of a process in the obvious way:

$\mathcal{L}_{\vec{v}}(a(\alpha)) = a(\mathcal{L}_{\vec{v}}(\alpha))$.

$\mathcal{L}_{\vec{v}}(x \,\square\, y) = \mathcal{L}_{\vec{v}}(x) \,\square\, \mathcal{L}_{\vec{v}}(y)$ for $\square = +, \cdot, \|$

$\mathcal{L}_{\vec{v}}(\partial_H(x)) = \partial_H(\mathcal{L}_{\vec{v}}(x))$
$\mathcal{L}_{\vec{v}}(\alpha \gg x) = \mathcal{L}_{\vec{v}}(\alpha) \gg \mathcal{L}_{\vec{v}}(x)$
$\mathcal{L}_{\vec{v}}(x \gg V) = \mathcal{L}_{\vec{v}}(x) \gg \mathcal{L}_{\vec{v}}(V)$.

We claim that with this definition, all closed process identities provable from ACPδρσ are still provable after a Lorentz transformation of both sides of the equality sign. Thus, we can say that ACPδρσ is Lorentz invariant.

Notice that a transition system obtained from a finite closed process expression using the transition rules above is a finite graph with actions as edge labels and such that along every path through the graph, each action is in the light cone of the previous action.

It is also straightforward to define a Lorentz transformation of a transition system: just transform all action labels. We find that bisimulation is Lorentz invariant, and that modulo bisimulation, all operators commute with $\mathcal{L}_{\vec{v}}$.

5.5 TEMPORAL INTERLEAVING.

Now let us consider an example, to see how these axioms work out. Suppose $\alpha \# \beta$. Then we find:

$$\begin{aligned} a(\alpha) \| b(\beta) &= a(\alpha) ⌊⌊ b(\beta) + b(\beta) ⌊⌊ a(\alpha) + a(\alpha) \mid b(\beta) = \\ &= (a(\alpha) \gg U(b(\beta)) \cdot b(\beta) + (b(\beta) \gg U(a(\alpha)) \cdot a(\alpha) + \delta = \\ &= (a(\alpha) \gg \{\gamma \mid \gamma \geq \beta\}) \cdot b(\beta) + (b(\beta) \gg \{\gamma \mid \gamma \geq \beta\}) \cdot a(\alpha) = \\ &= a(\alpha) \cdot b(\beta) + b(\beta) \cdot a(\alpha) = \\ &= a(\alpha) \cdot (\alpha \gg b(\beta)) + b(\beta) \cdot (\beta \gg a(\alpha)) = \\ &= a(\alpha) \cdot \delta + b(\beta) \cdot \delta. \end{aligned}$$

We see that ACPδρσ describes a *mono-processor* execution of a parallel composition: there is a single processor executing $X \| Y$, that travels (maybe with the speed of light) from one action to the next. This explains the δ's in the expression above. We see that this semantics for parallel composition is opposed to a so-called 'true concurrency' interpretation, where actions at different locations can happen independently. This example also shows that the system ACP0ρσ has unwanted behaviour: if $\alpha \# \beta$ then the expression $a(\alpha) \| b(\beta)$ will equal 0. Therefore, we will not consider a system with temporal interleaving and the constant 0.

It should be noticed that the equation $a(\alpha) \| b(\beta) = a(\alpha) \cdot b(\beta) + b(\beta) \cdot a(\alpha)$ in fact excludes a parallel execution of $a(\alpha)$ and $b(\beta)$ if $\alpha \# \beta$. Therefore a more appropriate semantics cannot satisfy the expansion theorem. Thus, we will consider a true concurrency semantics, giving up the expansion theorem.

5.6 MULTIPLE PROCESSORS, TRUE CONCURRENCY.

As said above, the axiom system ACPδρσ is sound for a description of single processor execution of concurrent processes. We call this the *temporal interleaving* semantics for real space process algebra. Moreover, the equations of ACPδρσ are Lorentz invariant with respect to the outlined bisimulation model. In this case the system $a(\alpha) \| b(\beta)$ for $\alpha \# \beta$ equals $a(\alpha) \cdot \delta + b(\beta) \cdot \delta$. It follows that $a(\alpha)$ and $b(\beta)$ exclude one another. Assuming that different actions can be performed by different processors it is not at all the case that both actions in $a(\alpha) \| b(\beta)$ exclude one another (if $\alpha \# \beta$). Thus, a multi-processor (or true concurrency) interpretation of merge will be different from the temporal interleaving one. In fact the equation $a(\alpha) \| b(\beta) = a(\alpha) \cdot b(\beta) + b(\beta) \cdot a(\alpha)$ will *not* hold for $\alpha \# \beta$. To put it another way, a Lorentz invariant formulation of multiple processor execution of concurrent systems negates the expansion theorem, and thereby leads to 'true concurrency'.

Looking for a Lorentz invariant formulation of truly concurrent merge in the setting of ACP, we found that ACP itself contains an obstacle that has to be removed. Although we cannot prove this rigorously, it seems that ACP as such has a classical (non-relativistic) bias built in. This bias has to do with the constant δ and can be removed by changing δ into 0. Thus, we will only consider this case with the constant 0.

5.7 SYNTAX.

To recapitulate, we have the following syntax:

P	the sort of processes
A	a finite set of action labels
0	constant; $A_0 = A \cup \{0\}$
$a(\alpha)$	for every $\alpha \in \mathbf{R}^4$ and $a \in A_0$, $a(\alpha) \in P$ is an atomic action
$\mid$	communication function: $A_0 \times A_0 \to A_0$, commutative, associative, 0 as zero element
$+, \cdot, \Vert$	binary operators $P \times P \to P$
$\gg$	binary operator $\mathbf{R}^4 \times P \to P$
$\gg$	binary operator $P \times Pow(\mathbf{R}^4) \to P$
∂_H	unary operators $P \to P$ (for each $H \subseteq A$).

Now we will first consider a truly concurrent operational semantics for this syntax.

5.8 DEFINITION.

A *multiple processor transition system* is a rooted, edge-labeled finite graph such that the edge labels are actions in $A(\mathbf{R}^4)$ and such that for every path the sequence of edge labels $a_0(\alpha_0)\ a_1(\alpha_1) \dots a_n(\alpha_n)$ is such that for all $i < j$ it is not the case that $\alpha_j \leq \alpha_i$. In words: no action in the graph causally precedes an earlier action. Moreover, there is an additional requirement: if there are two paths in the graph that have the same starting point and the same end point, then these paths have the same multi-set of edge labels. Note that we do not restricts ourselves to *trees* any more. We call the trivial one-point graph the *zero graph*.

The Lorentz transformation of a multiple processor transition system is obtained by transforming all edge labels. Since a Lorentz transformation does not change the ordering on $\mathbf{R}^4$, the image is again a multiple processor transition system. Bisimulation is defined as usual.

5.9 PROPOSITION.

If $g \leftrightarrow h$ then $\mathcal{L}_\gamma(g) \leftrightarrow \mathcal{L}_\gamma(h)$.

5.10 ULTIMATE DELAY.

Let g be a multiple processor transition system. For a node s of g we denote the subgraph with root s by $(g)_s$. Now let s be a node of g, then $U((g)_s)$ is defined as follows:

- if $(g)_s$ is the zero graph then $U((g)_s) = \mathbf{R}^4$;
- otherwise, suppose s has outgoing edges labeled $a_i(\alpha_i)$ to nodes s_i $(1 \leq i \leq k)$. Then

$$U((g)_s) = \bigcap_{1 \leq i \leq k} (\{\beta \in \mathbf{R}^4 \mid \beta \geq \alpha_i\} \cup U((g)_{s_i})).$$

Next, we can define the operators on multiple processor transition systems.

5.11 DEFINITION.

Let g,h be two multiple processor transition systems.

- graph g+h is obtained by identifying the roots of g and h; this new node is the root.
- graph g·h is obtained as follows: if g or h is the zero graph, then g·h is the zero graph; otherwise, append a copy of h at each endpoint of g (identifying the root of h with the endpoint of g); then remove each branch in h containing an edge with action label $b(\beta)$ for which $\alpha_1 \gg (\alpha_2 \gg \dots (\alpha_n \gg b(\beta)\dots)) = 0$, where $\{\alpha_1, \dots, \alpha_n\}$ is the multi-set of locations appearing in a path leading to this endpoint.
- graph $\partial_H(g)$ is obtained by removing every branch containing an edge with a label $a(\alpha)$ with $a \in H$.
- graph $g \| h$ is the cartesian product of graphs g and h, with:

    there is an edge $(s,t) \xrightarrow{a(\alpha)} (s^*,t)$ in $g\|h$ if there is an edge $s \xrightarrow{a(\alpha)} s^*$ in g and $\alpha \notin U((h)_t)$

    there is an edge $(s,t) \xrightarrow{b(\alpha)} (s,t^*)$ in $g\|h$ if there is an edge $t \xrightarrow{b(\alpha)} t^*$ in h and $\alpha \notin U((g)_s)$

    there is an edge $(s,t) \xrightarrow{c(\alpha)} (s^*,t^*)$ in $g\|h$ if there are edges $s \xrightarrow{a(\alpha)} s^*$ in g and $t \xrightarrow{b(\alpha)} t^*$ in h with $a \mid b = c \neq 0$.
- graph $\alpha \gg g$ is obtained by removing every branch containing an edge with label $a(\beta)$ with $\alpha \gg a(\beta) = 0$.

We can check that in each case, the resulting graph is again a multiple processor transition system.

5.12 PROPOSITION.

Bisimulation is a congruence on the set of multiple processor transition systems with operators defined as in 5.11.

5.13 AN AXIOMATIZATION.

We can give an axiomatization for the multiple processor theory, called ACP0ρσm, with the use of the auxiliary operators $a(\alpha) \circ$ (for each $a \in A$ and $\alpha \in \mathbf{R}^4$), $\ggg$. The first is a kind of *prefix multiplication*, a unary operator for each atomic action. Whereas the 'closed' multiplication sign · denotes a causal dependency, the 'open' multiplication ∘ does not: we have that actions following ∘ *may not causally precede* the action in front of the ∘ sign. In addition to the time shift operator $\gg$, we have the *weak time shift operator* $\ggg$. $\alpha \ggg X$ is a variant of $\alpha \gg X$, that differs in case points in four-space are incomparable. We also use operators $\lfloor\!\lfloor, \mid$, but here they do not imply causal dependencies (but rather causal independencies). Since we have a system with 0, we do not need the ultimate delay operator or the bounded initialization operator.

5.14 REMARK.

Although for $\alpha \# \beta$ we now have $a(\alpha) \| b(\beta) = a(\alpha) \circ b(\beta) + b(\beta) \circ a(\alpha)$, one cannot say that ACP0ρσm implies arbitrary interleaving, because ∘ is not ·. ∘ does not correspond to sequential composition of systems, rather $a(\alpha) \circ b(\beta)$ is $a(\alpha) \| b(\beta)$ under the additional constraint that $b(\beta)$ does not causally preceed $a(\alpha)$. A philosophical difficulty arises as follows: consider $\alpha,\beta \in \mathbf{R}^4$ with $\alpha \# \beta$. Then $a(\alpha) \circ b(\beta)$ and $b(\beta) \circ a(\alpha)$ show the same behaviour for any observer. Still, they are not identified. It follows that ∘ is a truly hidden function. The additional structure imposed by this operator is not always based on an observable (behavioural) criterion. Rather, ∘ is to be seen (as $\lfloor\!\lfloor$ and $\mid$ in this case) as an auxiliary operator that mainly has a formal role to play.

$X + Y = Y + X$	A1	$a \mid b = b \mid a$	C1
$(X + Y) + Z = X + (Y + Z)$	A2	$a \mid (b \mid c) = (a \mid b) \mid c$	C2
$X + X = X$	A3	$0 \mid a = 0$	CZ3
$(X + Y)\cdot Z = X\cdot Z + Y\cdot Z$	A4		
$(X\cdot Y)\cdot Z = X\cdot(Y\cdot Z)$	A5	$\alpha \neq \beta \Rightarrow a(\alpha) \mid b(\beta) = 0$	STC1
$X + 0 = X$	A6 - Z2	$a(\alpha) \mid b(\alpha) = (a \mid b)(\alpha)$	STC2
$0\cdot X = 0$	A7 - Z3		
$X\cdot 0 = 0$	Z1	$X \parallel Y = X \mathbin{\lfloor\!\lfloor} Y + Y \mathbin{\lfloor\!\lfloor} X + X \mid Y$	CM1
$a(\alpha)\circ 0 = 0$	OZ1	$a(\alpha) \mathbin{\lfloor\!\lfloor} X = a(\alpha)\circ X$	CM2'
$0\circ X = 0$	OZ2	$a(\alpha)\circ X \mathbin{\lfloor\!\lfloor} Y = a(\alpha)\circ(X \parallel Y)$	CM3'
$0(\alpha) = 0$	MTA1	$(X + Y) \mathbin{\lfloor\!\lfloor} Z = X \mathbin{\lfloor\!\lfloor} Z + Y \mathbin{\lfloor\!\lfloor} Z$	CM4
$a(\alpha) \circ X = a(\alpha) \circ (\alpha \ggg X)$	MTA5	$a(\alpha)\circ X \mid b(\beta) = (a(\alpha) \mid b(\beta))\circ X$	MTCM5
$a(\alpha) \cdot X = a(\alpha) \circ (\alpha \gg X)$	OA1	$a(\alpha) \mid b(\beta)\circ X = (a(\alpha) \mid b(\beta))\circ X$	MTCM6
$(a(\alpha) \circ X) \cdot Y = a(\alpha) \circ (X \cdot (\alpha \gg Y))$	OA2	$a(\alpha)\circ X \mid b(\beta)\circ Y = (a(\alpha) \mid b(\beta))\circ(X \parallel Y)$	MTCM7
$\alpha < \beta \;\Rightarrow\; \alpha \gg a(\beta) = a(\beta)$	STB1	$(X + Y) \mid Z = X \mid Z + Y \mid Z$	CM8
$\alpha \# \beta \Rightarrow \alpha \gg a(\beta) = 0$	STB1/2	$X \mid (Y + Z) = X \mid Y + X \mid Z$	CM9
$\alpha \geq \beta \;\Rightarrow\; \alpha \gg a(\beta) = 0$	STB2		
$\alpha \gg (X + Y) = (\alpha \gg X) + (\alpha \gg Y)$	STB3		
$\alpha \gg (X \cdot Y) = (\alpha \gg X) \cdot Y$	STB4	$\partial_H(a) = a \qquad \text{if } a \notin H$	D1
$\alpha \gg (a(\beta) \circ X) = (\alpha \gg a(\beta)) \circ (\alpha \gg X)$	OTB1	$\partial_H(a) = 0 \qquad \text{if } a \in H$	DZ2
$\alpha < \beta \;\Rightarrow\; \alpha \ggg a(\beta) = a(\beta)$	MTB1	$\partial_H(a(\alpha)) = \partial_H(a)(\alpha)$	STD
$\alpha \# \beta \Rightarrow \alpha \ggg a(\beta) = a(\beta)$	MTB1/2	$\partial_H(X + Y) = \partial_H(X) + \partial_H(Y)$	D3
$\alpha \geq \beta \;\Rightarrow\; \alpha \ggg a(\beta) = 0$	MTB2	$\partial_H(X \cdot Y) = \partial_H(X) \cdot \partial_H(Y)$	D4
$\alpha \ggg (X + Y) = (\alpha \ggg X) + (\alpha \ggg Y)$	MTB3	$\partial_H(a(\alpha) \circ X) = \partial_H(a(\alpha)) \circ \partial_H(X)$	D5
$\alpha \ggg (X \cdot Y) = (\alpha \ggg X) \cdot Y$	MTB4		
$\alpha \ggg (a(\beta) \circ X) = (\alpha \ggg a(\beta)) \circ (\alpha \ggg X)$	OTB2		

Table 10. ACP0ρσrm.

We also remark that the notion of a state is not self evident in this theory. Given the transition $a(\alpha) \parallel b(\beta) \xrightarrow{a(\alpha)} b(\beta)$ one might say that $b(\beta)$ is a state of the process $a(\alpha) \parallel b(\beta)$. But if $\alpha \# \beta$ then for some observer, β precedes α in time. This observer cannot possibly observe the state $b(\beta)$. Thus, states are formal mathematical entities rather than 'real' observable quantities.

5.15 NOTE.

Notice that the law $a(\alpha) \cdot X = a(\alpha) \circ (\alpha \gg X)$ (OA1) of the table above implies the law $a(\alpha) \cdot X = a(\alpha) \cdot (\alpha \gg X)$, for all closed terms. For, it is straightforward to derive $\alpha \gg X = \alpha \gg (\alpha \gg X)$ for all closed terms by structural induction, and using this, we obtain:

$$a(\alpha) \cdot X = a(\alpha) \circ (\alpha \gg X) = a(\alpha) \circ (\alpha \gg (\alpha \gg X)) = a(\alpha) \cdot (\alpha \gg X).$$

5.16 NOT EQUAL TO ZERO.

We can add a predicate $\neq 0$ as in [BB90]. Axioms for this unary predicate on processes are in table 11.

$a \neq 0 \;\Rightarrow\; a(\alpha) \neq 0$	MNZ1
$\alpha \gg x \neq 0 \;\Rightarrow\; a(\alpha)\cdot x \neq 0$	MNZ2
$\alpha \ggg x \neq 0 \;\Rightarrow\; a(\alpha)\circ x \neq 0$	MNZ3
$x \neq 0 \;\Rightarrow\; x + y \neq 0$	MNZ4

Table 11. Nonzero predicate.

5.17 ACTION RULES.

We can give action rules for ACP0ρσrm, but not in a modular fashion as done for systems above. The reason for this is, that the steps that a process e.g. x·y can take, are not completely determined by the steps that x can take, but also on the fact whether y will evaluate to 0 starting at a point where x terminates. Thus, action rules can only defined *on top of* the axioms, as in [BB90].

5.18 CONCLUSION.

We have obtained an important *non-interleaving* model of the ACP syntax. An expansion theorem for this model has a very different interpretation. We conclude that the ACP axiomatization of || using ⫽ and | is still possible in the case of relativistic multi-processor systems, and a truly concurrent Lorentz invariant operational semantics can be found.

Of course many problems are left open, e.g. can one find a *complete* axiomatization of the theory of closed finite process identities in the multi-processor bisimulation model outlined above.

REFERENCES.

[BB91] J.C.M. BAETEN & J.A. BERGSTRA, *Real time process algebra,* Formal Aspects of Computing 3 (2), 1991, pp. 142-188 (original version: report P8916, Programming Research Group, University of Amsterdam 1989).

[BB90] J.C.M. BAETEN & J.A. BERGSTRA, *Process algebra with a zero object,* in: Proc. CONCUR 90, Amsterdam (J.C.M. Baeten & J.W. Klop, eds.), Springer LNCS 458, 1990, pp. 83-98.

[BW90] J.C.M. BAETEN & W.P. WEIJLAND, *Process algebra,* Cambridge Tracts in TCS 18, Cambridge University Press 1990.

[BK84] J.A. BERGSTRA & J.W. KLOP, *Process algebra for synchronous communication,* Inf. & Control 60, 1984, pp. 109-137.

[BK85] J.A. BERGSTRA & J.W. KLOP, *Algebra of communicating processes with abstraction,* TCS 37, 1985, pp. 77-121.

[BK86] J.A. BERGSTRA & J.W. KLOP, *Process algebra: specification and verification in bisimulation semantics,* in: Math. & Comp. Sci. II (M. Hazewinkel, J.K. Lenstra & L.G.L.T. Meertens, eds.), CWI Monograph 4, North-Holland, Amsterdam 1986, pp. 61-94.

[B21] M. BORN, *Die Relativitätstheorie Einsteins,* Springer Verlag 1921.

[HE88] M. HENNESSY, *Algebraic theory of processes,* MIT Press 1988.

[H85] C.A.R. HOARE, *Sequential communicating processes,* Prentice Hall, 1985.

[K91] A.S. KLUSENER, *Completeness in real time process algebra,* report CS-R9106, CWI Amsterdam 1991. Extended abstract in this volume.

[M80] R. MILNER, *A calculus of communicating systems,* Springer LNCS 92, 1980.

[M89] R. MILNER, *Communication and concurrency,* Prentice Hall, 1989.

[P30] G. PEACKOCK, *A treatise of algebra,* Cambridge 1830.

The Failure of Failures in a Paradigm for Asynchronous Communication *

F.S. de Boer[1], J.N. Kok[2], C. Palamidessi[2,3], J.J.M.M. Rutten[3]

[1]Department of Computer Science, Technical University Eindhoven,
P.O. Box 513, 5600 MB Eindhoven, The Netherlands

[2]Department of Computer Science, Utrecht University,
P.O. Box 80089, 3508 TB Utrecht, The Netherlands

[3]Centre for Mathematics and Computer Science,
Kruislaan 413, 1098 SJ Amsterdam, The Netherlands

e.mail: {frb, joost, katuscia, janr}@cwi.nl

Abstract

We develop a general framework for a variety of concurrent languages all based on asynchronous communication, like data flow, concurrent logic, concurrent constraint languages and CSP with asynchronous channels. The main characteristic of these languages is that processes interact by reading and modifying the state of some common data structure. We abstract from the specific features of the various communication mechanisms by means of a uniform language where actions are interpreted as partially defined transformations on an abstract set of states. Suspension is modelled by an action being undefined in a state. The languages listed above can be seen as instances of our paradigm, and can be obtained by fixing a specific set of states and interpretation of the actions.

The computational model of our paradigm is described by a transition system in the style of Plotkin's SOS. A compositional model is presented that is based on traces (of pairs of states). This sharply contrasts with the synchronous case, where some additional branching information is needed to describe deadlock. In particular, we show that our model is more abstract than the standard failure set semantics (that is known to be fully abstract for the classical synchronous paradigms).

We also investigate the problem of full abstraction, with respect to various observation criteria. To tackle this problem, we have to consider the particular features of the specific languages. We study some cases, for which we give a fully abstract semantics.

1 Introduction

In this paper we propose a general paradigm for asynchronously communicating processes. Such a paradigm should encompass such diverse systems as described by concurrent logic languages [Sha89], concurrent constraint languages [Sar89], imperative languages in which processes communicate by

*Part of this work was carried out in the context of ESPRIT Basic Research Action (3020) Integration. The research of F.S. de Boer was partially supported by the Dutch REX (Research and Education in Concurrent Systems) project and the Basic Research Action SPEC.

means of shared variables [HdBR90], or asynchronous channels [JJH90], and dataflow languages [Kah74].

These systems have in common that processes communicate via some shared data structure. The asynchronous nature of the communication consists in the way access to this shared data structure is modelled: the data structure is updated by means of write primitives which have free access whereas the read primitives may suspend in case the data structure does not contain the information required by it. The execution of the read and write primitives are independent in the sense that they can take place at different times. This marks an essential difference with synchronously communicating processes, like CSP [Hoa78], where reading from and writing to a channel has to take place at the same time.

Our paradigm consists of a concurrent language $\mathcal{L}$ which assumes given a set of basic (or atomic) actions. Statements are constructed from these actions by means of sequential composition, the plus operator for nondeterministic choice, and the parallel operator. (For simplicity, only finite behaviour is considered; recursion can be added straightforwardly.) Furthermore we assume given an abstract set of states. The basic actions are interpreted by means of an interpretation function I as partially defined state transformations. A pure read action a (like, e.g., a test) will have the property that $I(a)$ is a partial function; it suspends in a state in which $I(a)$ is undefined. A suspended process is forced to wait until actions of other processes produce a state in which it is enabled. A pure write action a is characterized by the fact that $I(a)$ is a totally defined function. It can always proceed autonomously. In general, an action can embody both a read and a write component. (See Example 1 of Section 2.)

Many languages for asynchronously communicating processes can be obtained as instances of our paradigm by choosing the appropriate set of actions, the set of states and the interpretation function for the basic actions. For example, the imperative language described in [HdBR90], based on shared variables, can be modelled by taking as states functions from variables to values, as actions the set of assignments, and then the usual interpretation of an assignment as a state transformation. Languages based on the *blackboard model* [EHLR80], like Linda [Gel86] and Shared Prolog [BC89] can be modelled analogously, by taking as states the configurations of a centralized data structure (the blackboard) and as actions checks and updates of the blackboard. Another example is the class of concurrent constraint languages [Sar89]. These are modelled by interpreting the abstract set of states as a constraint system and the actions as ask/tell primitives. Concurrent logic languages, like Flat Concurrent Prolog [Sha89], can be obtained by interpreting the states as the bindings established on the logical variables, and the actions as the unification steps. An asynchronous variant of CCS [Mil80, Mil83] is modelled by considering the state as a set (or a multi-set) of actions. Performing an action then corresponds to adding it to the set, while performing the complementary action corresponds to testing whether the action is already in the set. Finally, a variant of CSP [Hoa78], based on asynchronous channels (see also [JJH90]), can be obtained by taking as states the configurations of the channels and as actions the input-output primitives on these channels.

The basic computation model of the paradigm $\mathcal{L}$ is described by means of a labelled transition system in the style of Plotkin's SOS. It specifies for every statement what steps it can take. Each step results in a state transformation, which is registered in the label: as labels we use pairs of states. Based on this transition system, various notions of observables for our language are defined. One of the main results of this paper is a compositional characterization of these notions of observables, which is defined independently of the particular choice for the sets of actions and the set of states. Thus a general compositional description of all the possible mechanisms for asynchronous communication is provided, so unifying the semantic work done in such apparently diverse fields as concurrent logic programming, dataflow, and imperative programming based on asynchronous communication.

The most striking feature of our compositional semantics is that it is essentially based on traces, namely sequences of pairs of states. A pair encodes the state transformation occurred during a transition step (initial state - final state). These sequences are not necessarily connected, i.e. the final state of a pair can be different from the initial state of the following pair. These "gaps" represent, in a sense, the possible steps made by the environment. Since there is no way to synchronize on actions, the behaviour of processes just depends upon the state. Therefore, such a set of sequences encodes all the information necessary for a compositional semantics.

The compositional model for our paradigm is so simple that it might look trivial. We should like to point out that it is not. Its interest is formed by the mere fact that it is as simple as it is. In particular, its definition is based on traces and does not need additional structures like failure sets, which are needed for describing deadlock in the case of synchronously communicating processes. We show that our model is more abstract than the classical failure set semantics, and for that reason more suitable for describing asynchronous communication.

Another contribution of the paper is the identification of two classes of interpretations, for which a full-abstraction result is obtained. The first class, the elements of which are called *complete*, characterizes in an abstract setting the imperative paradigm. The second class characterizes asynchronous communication of the concurrent constraint paradigm; such interpretations are called *monotonic*.

For complete interpretations it is shown that our model is fully abstract with respect to a notion of observables consisting of (sets of) sequences of states. For monotonic interpretations, full abstraction is considered with respect to another notion of observables, which abstracts from state repetitions ("finite stuttering"). This case is more complicated. The basic compositional model is not fully abstract. It is shown that a fully abstract model can be obtained by applying an abstraction operator to the first model. This abstraction consists of taking the closure of sets of sequences under a number of conditions. Interestingly, these closure conditions are reminiscent of the way one can view rooted tau-bisimulation [BK88] (or weak observational congruence, in the vocabulary of [Mil80]) as ordinary strong bisimulation, by adding certain rules to the transition system. In the present situation, a subtle refinement of that approach is required, due to the non-uniform nature of our models.

1.1 Comparison with related work

In spite of the general interest for asynchronous communication as the natural mechanism for concurrency in many different programming paradigms, not much work has been done in the past, neither for defining a uniform framework, nor for providing the appropriate semantics tools for reasoning about such a mechanism in an abstract way. In most cases, asynchronous languages have been studied as special instances of the synchronous paradigm. For example, in [GCLS88, GMS89] the semantics of FCP is defined by using the failure set semantics of TCSP [BHR84], and [SR90] uses for a concurrent constraint language the bisimulation equivalence on trees of CCS [Mil80]. Only recently [dBP90b, dBP91] it has been shown that concurrent logic and constraint languages do not need to code the branching structure in the semantic domain: linear sequences of assume/tell-constraints are sufficiently expressive for defining a compositional model (both for the success and for the deadlock case). The paradigm and the semantics presented here can be seen as a generalization of this approach, abstracting from the specific details related to concurrent logic and constraint languages, and showing that it can be applied to a much wider range of languages. In fact, the models of [dBP90b, dBP91] can be obtained as special instances of our language: see Example 2 of Section 2.

In the field of data flow, compositional models based on linear sequences have been developed (for example in [Jon85]) and have been shown to be fully abstract (see [Kok87] for the first result not depending on fairness notions). For an overview consult [Kok89]. A related paradigm (abstract processes communicating via asynchronous channels) has been recently studied in [JHJ90]. Also in this paper the authors propose a linear semantics of input-output events, as opposed to the failure set semantics. Again, this model can be obtained as an instance of ours by interpreting the events as state transformations.

Finally, in [HdBR90], a semantics based on sequences of pair of states, similar to the one we study in this paper, has been developed for an imperative language and shown correct and fully abstract with respect to successful computations.

The main contribution of this paper is the generalization of the results obtained in [dBP90b, dBP91, JHJ90, HdBR90] to a paradigm for asynchronous communication, and thus providing a uniform framework for reasoning about this kind of concurrency.

1.2 Plan of the paper

In the next section we start by presenting our paradigm. We give the syntax and the computational model (characterizing the observational behaviour) of the language, and show that many formalisms for asynchronous processes can be obtained as instances of it. Next a compositional model is introduced that is correct with respect to the observational model. In Section 3 we compare this compositional semantics with the standard notion of failure set semantics. We show that our model is more abstract and we characterize the redundancy present in the latter (when applied to asynchronous languages). The issue of full abstraction is addressed in Section 4. We give conditions on the interpretations, corresponding to various classes of languages, under which a number of full abstraction results (possibly after some closure operation) can be obtained. Section 5 briefly sketches some future research.

2 The language and its semantics

Let $(a \in)A$ be a set of *atomic actions*. We define the set $(s \in)\mathcal{L}$ of statements as follows:

$$s ::= a \mid s; t \mid s + t \mid s \parallel t$$

Moreover, $\mathcal{L}$ contains a special E, the terminated statement. The symbols ';', '+' and '$\parallel$' represent the sequential, the choice and the parallel operator, respectively. Note that we do not include any constructs for recursion. In this paper, only finite behaviour is studied for the sake of simplicity. All the results that follow can be extended as to cover also infinite behavior[1].

The actions of our language are interpreted as transformations on a set $(\sigma \in)\Sigma$ of abstract *states*. We assume given an interpretation function I of type

$$I : A \rightarrow \Sigma \rightarrow_{partial} \Sigma$$

that maps atomic actions to partially defined state transformations. If $I(a)(\sigma)$ is undefined, the action is blocked in the current state σ. This need not neccesarily lead to a global deadlock of the whole system, because some other component of the program may be enabled to take a next step. Note that therefore the operator plus models global nondeterminism rather than local choice: the choice can be influenced by the environment.

The computational model of $\mathcal{L}$ is described by a *labelled transition system* $(\mathcal{L}, Label, \rightarrow)$. The set $(\lambda \in)Label$ of labels is defined by $Label = \Sigma \times \Sigma$. A label represents the state transformation caused by the action performed during the transition step.

Instead of pairs of states, one could also take functions from Σ to Σ as labels. We prefer to use pairs of states because in that way a semantics is obtained that is more abstract. This is due to the fact that using sets of (sequences of) pairs will yield more identifications of statements than using sets of (sequences of) functions. (The reader is invited to find a simple example.)

The transition relation $\rightarrow \subseteq \mathcal{L} \times Label \times \mathcal{L}$ is defined as the smallest relation satisfying the following axiom and rules:

- If $I(a)(\sigma)$ is defined then

$$a \xrightarrow{(\sigma, I(a)(\sigma))} E$$

- If $s \xrightarrow{\lambda} s'$ then

$$s; t \xrightarrow{\lambda} s'; t \quad s + t \xrightarrow{\lambda} s' \quad t + s \xrightarrow{\lambda} s' \quad s \parallel t \xrightarrow{\lambda} s' \parallel t \quad t \parallel s \xrightarrow{\lambda} t \parallel s'$$

[1]In particular, the co-domains of our semantic models should then be turned into *complete* spaces of some kind in order to obtain infinite behaviour as limit of a sequence of finite approximations. A suitable framework would be the family of complete metric spaces (see [dBZ82]).

If $s' = E$ then read t for s'; t, $s' \parallel t$ and $t \parallel s'$ in the clauses above.

Note that the transition relation depends on I.

There are various reasonable notions of observables for $\mathcal{L}$ that we can derive from the transition system above. Given an initial state σ, the first observation criterion we consider, Obs_1, assigns to a statement a set of sequences of states. Each such sequence represents a possible computation of the statement, listing *all* intermediate states through which the computation goes. (Such a sequence may end in δ, indicating *deadlock*, if no transitions are possible anymore and the end of the statement has not yet been reached.) As an example, we have that if

$$s \xrightarrow{(\sigma_0,\sigma_1)} s_1 \xrightarrow{(\sigma_1,\sigma_2)} \cdots \xrightarrow{(\sigma_{n-2},\sigma_{n-1})} s_{n-1} \xrightarrow{(\sigma_{n-1},\sigma_n)} s_n = E$$

then $\sigma_0 \cdot \sigma_1 \cdots \sigma_n \in Obs_1[\![s]\!](\sigma_0)$. Note that in the definition of Obs_1, only *connected* transition sequences are considered: the labels of subsequent transitions have the property that the last element of the first label equals the first element of the second.

The second observation criterion we consider, Obs_2, is slightly more abstract than Obs_1: it also yields sequences of intermediate states, but omits subsequent repetitions of identical states. Thus it abstracts from so-called *finite stuttering*.

The third observation criterion is the most abstract one: it only registers final states for successfully terminating computations, and a pair of the final state together with δ for deadlocking computations.

Definition 2.1 *Let Σ^+ denote the set of all finite non-empty sequences of states. We put $\Sigma_\delta^+ = \Sigma^+ \cup \Sigma^+ \cdot \{\delta\}$ and $\Sigma_\delta = \Sigma \cup \{\delta\}$. Let $\mathcal{P}(\cdot)$ be the set of subsets of $(\cdot)$. We define*

$$Obs_1 : \mathcal{L} \rightarrow \Sigma \rightarrow \mathcal{P}(\Sigma_\delta^+)$$

$$Obs_2 : \mathcal{L} \rightarrow \Sigma \rightarrow \mathcal{P}(\Sigma_\delta^+)$$

$$Obs_3 : \mathcal{L} \rightarrow \Sigma \rightarrow \mathcal{P}(\Sigma_\delta)$$

as follows. We put, for $i = 1, 2$,

$$Obs_i[\![E]\!](\sigma) = \{\sigma\}$$

and for $s \neq E$,

$$Obs_1[\![s]\!](\sigma) = \bigcup\{\sigma \cdot Obs_1[\![s']\!](\sigma') : s \xrightarrow{(\sigma,\sigma')} s'\} \cup \{\sigma \cdot \delta : \forall \sigma' \forall s', \neg(s \xrightarrow{(\sigma,\sigma')} s')\}$$

$$\begin{aligned} Obs_2[\![s]\!](\sigma) = \; & \bigcup\{\sigma \cdot Obs_2[\![s']\!](\sigma') : s \xrightarrow{(\sigma,\sigma')} s' \wedge \sigma \neq \sigma'\} \cup \\ & \bigcup\{Obs_2[\![s']\!](\sigma) : s \xrightarrow{(\sigma,\sigma)} s'\} \cup \{\sigma \cdot \delta : \forall \sigma' \forall s', \neg(s \xrightarrow{(\sigma,\sigma')} s')\} \end{aligned}$$

Finally, we put $Obs_3 = \lambda s.\lambda\sigma.\gamma(Obs_1[\![s]\!](\sigma))$, with $\gamma : \mathcal{P}(\Sigma_\delta^+) \rightarrow \mathcal{P}(\Sigma_\delta)$ defined by

$$\gamma(X) = \{\sigma : w \cdot \sigma \in X, \text{ for some } w\} \cup \{\delta : w \cdot \delta \in X, \text{ for some } w\}$$

Note that the definitions of Obs_1 and Obs_2 are recursive. Since we do not treat infinite behaviour, they can be justified by a simple induction on the structure of statements. The relation between Obs_1 and Obs_2 is immediate: If we define, for a word $w \in \Sigma_\delta^+$, $del(w)$ to be the word obtained from w by deleting all subsequent occurrences of identical states, and $\beta : \mathcal{P}(\Sigma_\delta^+) \rightarrow \mathcal{P}(\Sigma_\delta^+)$ by

$$\beta(X) = \{del(w) : w \in X\}$$

then we have: $Obs_2 = \beta \circ Obs_1$.

Now we illustrate the generality of the language $\mathcal{L}$ and its semantics presented above. It does not constitute one language with a fixed semantics but rather an entire family, each member of which depends on the particular choice of A, Σ and I. We present a list of five examples.

Example 1: An imperative language

Let A be the set of assignments $x := e$, where $x \in Var$ is a variable and $e \in Exp$ is an expression. Assume that the evaluation $\mathcal{E}(e)(\sigma)$ of expression e in state σ is simple in that it does not have side effects and is instantaneous. Let the set of states be defined by

$$\Sigma = Var \rightarrow Val$$

where Val is some abstract set of values. Then define I by

$$I(x := e)(\sigma)(y) = \begin{cases} \sigma(y) & \text{if } y \neq x \\ \mathcal{E}(e)(\sigma) & \text{if } y = x \end{cases}$$

With this choice for A, Σ and I, the models Obs_1 and O (to be introduced below) for $\mathcal{L}$ are essentially the same as the operational and denotational semantics presented for a concurrent language with assignment in [HdBR90]

One could include in this language a suspension mechanism by associating with each assignment a boolean expression, which must be true to enable the execution of the assignment (otherwise it suspends). A basic action is then an object of the form $b.x := e$. Its interpretation is:

$$I(b.x := e)(\sigma)(y) = \begin{cases} \sigma(y) & \text{if } \mathcal{E}(b)(\sigma) \text{ and } y \neq x \\ \mathcal{E}(e)(\sigma) & \text{if } \mathcal{E}(b)(\sigma) \text{ and } y = x \\ \text{undefined} & \text{otherwise} \end{cases}$$

Example 2: Concurrent constraint languages

Constraint programming is based on the notion of computing with systems of partial information. The main feature is that the state is seen as a constraint on the range of values that variables can assume, rather than a function from variables to values (valuation) as in the imperative case. In other words, the state is seen as a (possibly infinite) set of valuations. Constraints are just finite representations of these sets. For instance, a constraint can be a first order formula, like $\{x = f(y)\}$, representing the set $\{\{y = a, x = f(a)\}, \{y = b, x = f(b)\}, \ldots\}$. As discussed in [Sar89, SR90], this notion of state leads naturally to a paradigm for concurrent programming. All processes share a common *store*, i.e. a set of variables and the constraints established on them until that moment. Communication is achieved by adding (telling) some constraint to the store, and by checking (asking) if the store entails (implies) a given constraint. Synchronization is based on a blocking ask: a process waits (suspends) until the store is "strong" enough to entail a certain constraint.

A typical example of a constraint system is a decidable first-order theory, a constraint in this case being simply a first-order formula. Given a first-order language L and a theory T in L define A to be the set of ask and tell primitives, i.e., $A = \{ask(\vartheta), tell(\vartheta) : \vartheta \in L\}$. Let the set of states be defined by

$$\Sigma = \{\vartheta : \vartheta \in L\}$$

The interpretation function I is given by

$$I(ask(\vartheta))(\vartheta') = \begin{cases} \vartheta' & \text{if } T \cup \vartheta' \vdash \vartheta \\ \text{undefined} & \text{otherwise} \end{cases}$$

and

$$I(tell(\vartheta))(\vartheta') = \vartheta \wedge \vartheta'$$

Example 3: Asynchronous CCS
Let $(a \in) Act$ be a set of atomic actions and $\bar{Act} = \{\bar{a} : a \in Act\}$ a set of actions corresponding with the ones in Act. Let

$$A = Act \cup \bar{Act}, \quad \Sigma = \mathcal{P}(A)$$

Define I by $I(a)(\sigma) = \sigma \cup \{a\}$ and

$$I(\bar{a})(\sigma) = \begin{cases} \sigma & \text{if } a \in \sigma \\ \text{undefined} & \text{if } a \notin \sigma \end{cases}$$

With this interpretation, an asynchronous variant of CCS is modelled in the following sense. Actions $a \in Act$ are viewed as send actions; they can always proceed. The actions $\bar{a} \in \bar{Act}$ are the corresponding receive actions: an action $\bar{a}$ can only take place when at least one a action has been performed.

Another interpretation would be to take as states *multisets* of actions rather than plain sets. Thus one could register the number of a actions that have been performed, and decrease this number each time an $\bar{a}$ action is executed.

Example 4: Concurrent Prolog
For our fourth example we refer to [dBK90], where a mapping is defined from the language Concurrent Prolog [Sha83] to a language similar to ours.

Example 5: Asynchronous CSP
We consider an asynchronous version of CSP as described in [JJH90, JHJ90]. Let $(x \in) Var$ be a set of variables, $(h \in) IExp$ a set of integer expressions, $(b \in) BExp$ a set of Boolean expressions, and $(\alpha \in) CName$ a set of channel names. Let the set of atomic actions a be defined by

$$A = BExp \cup \{\alpha?x : \alpha \in CName, \ x \in Var\} \cup \{\alpha!h : \alpha \in CName, \ h \in IExp\}$$

Let Val be a set of values. We take as set of states

$$\Sigma = (Var \rightarrow Val) \times (CName \rightarrow Val^*)$$

The interpretation function is defined as follows:

$$I(b)(\sigma) = \begin{cases} \sigma & \text{if } \mathcal{E}(b)(\sigma) = true \\ \text{undefined} & \text{otherwise} \end{cases}$$

$$I(\alpha?x)(\sigma) = \begin{cases} \sigma\langle head(\sigma(\alpha))/x, tail(\sigma(\alpha))/\alpha\rangle & \text{if } \sigma(\alpha) \text{ is non empty} \\ \text{undefined} & \text{otherwise} \end{cases}$$

$$I(\alpha!h)(\sigma) = \sigma\langle\sigma(\alpha) \cdot \mathcal{E}(h)(\sigma)/\alpha\rangle$$

Note that a guarded command of the form $g_1 \rightarrow S_1 \Box \ldots \Box g_n \rightarrow S_n$ $(g_1, \ldots g_n \in A)$ will be translated as $g_1; S_1 + \ldots + g_n; S_n$.

A similar construction can be made for static dataflow along the lines of [JK89], in which a state based model for dataflow nets is given. (Already referring to the discussion in the next section, we observe that in the world of dataflow, it is already known for a long time that trace models are compositional (and even fully abstract).)
End of examples.

Next we introduce a semantics O that describes the behaviour of $\mathcal{L}$ in a compositional manner. It is introduced using the transition system, and is later shown to be compositional. (This way of introducing O has the advantage that its *correctness* can be easily proved (see Theorem 2.5).)

Definition 2.2 *First a semantic domain $(X, Y \in)P$ is introduced. It is defined by*

$$P = \mathcal{P}_{ne}(Q) \quad \text{(non-empty subsets of } Q)$$

$$Q = (\Sigma \times \Sigma)^* \cup (\Sigma \times \Sigma)^* \cdot (\Sigma \times \{\delta\})$$

Next $O : \mathcal{L} \rightarrow P$ is defined as follows. We put $O[\![E]\!] = \{\epsilon\}$ and, for $s \neq E$,

$$O[\![s]\!] = \bigcup \{(\sigma, \sigma') \cdot O[\![s']\!] : s \xrightarrow{(\sigma,\sigma')} s'\} \cup \{(\sigma, \delta) : \forall \sigma' \forall s', \neg(s \xrightarrow{(\sigma,\sigma')} s')\}$$

The function O yields sets of sequences of *pairs* of states, rather than just states. The intuition behind such a pair (σ, σ') is that if the current state is σ, then the computation at hand can transform this state into σ'. For instance, if

$$s \xrightarrow{(\sigma_1,\sigma_1')} s_1 \xrightarrow{(\sigma_2,\sigma_2')} \cdots \xrightarrow{(\sigma_{n-1},\sigma_{n-1}')} s_{n-1} \xrightarrow{(\sigma_n,\sigma_n')} s_n = E$$

then $(\sigma_1, \sigma_1') \cdots (\sigma_n, \sigma_n') \in O[\![s]\!]$. An important difference between the functions Obs_i and O is that in the definition of the latter, the transition sequences need not be connected: for instance, in the above example σ_1' may be different from σ_2.

The main interest of O lies in the fact that it is *compositional*. This we show next. To this end, semantic interpretations of the operators ; , +, $\|$, denoted by the same symbols, are introduced.

Definition 2.3 *Three operators* ; , +, $\|$: $P \times P \rightarrow P$ *are introduced as follows.*

- $X_1; X_2 = \bigcup \{w_1 \hat{;} w_2 : w_1 \in X_1 \wedge w_2 \in X_2\}$,
  where $\hat{;} : Q \times Q \rightarrow P$ *is defined by*

$$w_1 \hat{;} w_2 = \begin{cases} \{w_1\} & \text{if } w_1 = w \cdot (\sigma, \delta) \\ \{w_1 \cdot w_2\} & \text{otherwise} \end{cases}$$

- $X_1 + X_2 = ((X_1 \cup X_2) \cap ((\Sigma \times \Sigma) \cdot Q)) \;\cup\; (X_1 \cap X_2 \cap (\Sigma \times \{\delta\}))$
- $X_1 \parallel X_2 = \bigcup \{w_1 \hat{\|} w_2 : w_1 \in X_1 \wedge w_2 \in X_2\}$,
  where $\hat{\|}, ⌊⌊ : Q \times Q \rightarrow P$ *are defined by induction on the length of words* $w_1, w_2 \in Q$ *by*
  - $w_1 \hat{\|} w_2 = w_1 ⌊⌊ w_2 \cup w_2 ⌊⌊ w_1$
  - $$w_1 ⌊⌊ w_2 = \begin{cases} (\sigma_1, \sigma_2) \cdot (w_1' \hat{\|} w_2) & \text{if } w_1 = (\sigma_1, \sigma_2) \cdot w_1' \\ (\sigma, \delta) & \text{if } (w_1 = (\sigma, \delta) = w_2) \text{ or } (w_1 = (\sigma, \delta) \text{ and } w_2 = \epsilon) \\ w_2 & \text{if } w_1 = \epsilon \\ \emptyset & \text{otherwise} \end{cases}$$

The definition of the sequential composition ; is straightforward.

The definition of the choice operator + is slightly more intricate. The value of $X_1 + X_2$ consists of all sequences of both sets that do not start with a deadlock pair (i.e., a pair of which the second element is δ), together with those pairs (σ, δ) that occur in both sets. This is motivated by the fact that operationally, the nondeterministic composition of two statements will yield a deadlock only if both statements yield deadlock separately.

The merge operator $\|$, applied to two sets of sequences X_1 and X_2, takes all the possible interleavings $w_1 \hat{\|} w_2$ of words $w_1 \in X_1$ and $w_2 \in X_2$. The set $w_1 \hat{\|} w_2$ is the union of two so-called left merges: $w_1 ⌊⌊ w_2$ and $w_2 ⌊⌊ w_1$. In $w_1 ⌊⌊ w_2$, every word starts with a step from the left component w_1. This definition of the merge ensures that deadlocking steps are delayed as long as possible. Thus we have, for instance,

$$\{(\sigma, \sigma)\} \parallel \{(\sigma, \delta)\} = \{(\sigma, \sigma) \cdot (\sigma, \delta)\}$$

Now we are ready for the following theorem.

Theorem 2.4 (Compositionality of $\mathcal{O}$) *For all $s, t \in \mathcal{L}$, $* \in \{;, +, \|\}$,*

$$\mathcal{O}[s * t] = \mathcal{O}[s] * \mathcal{O}[t]$$

Finally, it is shown that $\mathcal{O}$ is *correct* with respect to the observation functions Obs_i, for $i = 1, 2, 3$. That is, if two statements are distinguished by any of these functions, then $\mathcal{O}$ should distinguish them as well. We show that $\mathcal{O}$ is correct with respect to Obs_1, from which the other two cases will follow. The relation between Obs_1 and $\mathcal{O}$ can be made precise using the following abstraction operator. Let $\alpha : P \to \Sigma \to \mathcal{P}(\Sigma_\delta^+)$ be defined by

$$\alpha(X)(\sigma) = \bigcup\{\alpha(x)(\sigma) : x \in X\}$$

where

$$\alpha(x)(\sigma) = \begin{cases} \{\sigma\sigma_1 \cdots \sigma_n\} & \text{if } x = (\sigma, \sigma_1)(\sigma_1, \sigma_2)\cdots(\sigma_{n-1}, \sigma_n) \\ \{\sigma\sigma_1 \cdots \sigma_{n-1}\delta\} & \text{if } x = (\sigma, \sigma_1)(\sigma_1, \sigma_2)\cdots(\sigma_{n-1}, \delta) \\ \emptyset & \text{otherwise} \end{cases}$$

The operator α selects from a set X, given an initial state σ, all connected sequences starting with σ. (It should be noted that also this operator is defined "element-wise".)

Theorem 2.5 (Correctness of $\mathcal{O}$) $\alpha \circ \mathcal{O} = Obs_1$

As a corollary, the correctness of Obs_2 and Obs_3 is immediate:

$$Obs_2 = \beta \circ Obs_1 = \beta \circ \alpha \circ \mathcal{O}$$

$$Obs_3 = \gamma \circ Obs_1 = \gamma \circ \alpha \circ \mathcal{O}$$

3 Comparison with failure semantics

The reader familiar with the various semantic models for synchronous concurrency (as exemplified by languages like, e.g., CCS [Mil80] and TCSP [BHR84]) might be surprised and might even be made somewhat suspicious by the simplicity of the model $\mathcal{O}$. It is well known that the most abstract semantics for CCS, called *fully* abstract, that is still compositional and correct (with respect to the standard trace semantics) is *failure* semantics, and that the trace semantics for CCS is *not* compositional. (See [BHR84] and [BKO88].) How come that for the present language failure semantics is not needed and already a trace-like model ($\mathcal{O}$) is compositional?

Failure semantics assigns to statements sets of streams of actions possibly ending in a so-called failure set of actions. The intended meaning of a stream of actions ending in a failure set is the following: after having performed the actions in the stream, the statement can refuse the actions present in the failure set. That is, if the environment offers one or more (possibly all) of these actions, then the parallel composition of the environment and this statement will deadlock. Note that the environment can offer (by means of the plus operator for nondeterministic choice) more than one action at the same time.

For our language $\mathcal{L}$, one could try to mimic this approach and define a failure semantics as well. The first thing to be observed is that it would not make sense to have sets of *actions* for the failure sets, because an action may or may not deadlock depending on the current state ($I(a)$ is in general a *partial* function). Therefore it would be better to take sets of *states*, namely those that would yield a deadlock when generated by the environment. Now the main difference between the synchronous and the asynchronous case is essentially that, in the asynchronous case, there is a fundamental difference between the role of the actions, on the one hand, and the states, on the other: Consider a statement

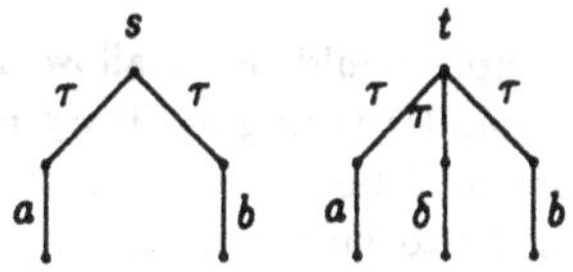

Figure 1: In case of asynchronous communication, s and t cannot be distinguished by any context.

s in an environment. At any moment in the computation the way in which this environment can influence the possible behaviour of s is not so much determined by the fact that the environment can choose among a set of actions. What *is* relevant is the fact that corresponding to each such choice there will be a new state, which *does* influence the activity of s: in this new state, s may or may not be able to perform some action that is enabled. In other words, although the environment can perform different *actions*, it cannot simultaneously offer different *states*. At every moment in the computation there is only one relevant state (the "current" state).

The above should, at least at an intuitive level, make clear that it is sufficient to use failure sets that contain only one element. This, however, means abandoning the idea of failure *sets* altogether. The result is our semantic model $\mathcal{O}$ based on streams of pairs of states that can possibly end in a pair (σ, δ). The correspondence with the failure set semantics (containing only one element) is given by interpreting such a pair (σ, δ) at the end of a stream as a failure set with one element, σ. If the environment offers the state σ, then the statement will deadlock.

Let us inspect a brief example to make this point more clear. Suppose that

$$A = \{a, b, \tau, \delta\}, \quad \Sigma = \{1,2\}$$

and that $I: A \to \Sigma \to_{partial} \Sigma$ is defined by

$$I(a)(i) = \begin{cases} 1 & \text{if } i = 1 \\ \text{undefined} & \text{if } i = 2 \end{cases} \qquad I(b)(i) = \begin{cases} 2 & \text{if } i = 2 \\ \text{undefined} & \text{if } i = 1 \end{cases}$$

$$I(\tau)(i) = i, \text{ for } i = 1,2, \quad I(\delta)(i) = \text{ undefined, for } i = 1,2$$

Next consider two statements

$$s = \tau; a + \tau; b, \quad t = \tau; a + \tau; b + \tau; \delta$$

(see Figure 1).

Without giving any formal definitions, the failure semantics for s and t would be as follows (using $(*,*)$ to indicate either $(1,1)$ or $(2,2)$):

$$\mathit{failure}(s) = \{\emptyset, (*,*)(1,1), (*,*)(2,2), (*,*)\{1\}, (*,*)\{2\}, (*,*)\emptyset\}$$

$$\mathit{failure}(t) = \{\emptyset, (*,*)(1,1), (*,*)(2,2), (*,*)\{1\}, (*,*)\{2\}, (*,*)\{1,2\}, (*,*)\emptyset\}$$

(Note that elements like $(*,*)\emptyset$ are present in $\mathit{failure}(s)$ and $\mathit{failure}(t)$ because these are closed, as in the standard failure semantics, under taking arbitrary subsets of failure sets: if wX is an element and $Y \subseteq X$, then also wY is an element.)

Clearly, the two statements are distinguished because of the component $\tau; \delta$ in t, which does not occur in s: This explains the presence of $(*,*)\{1,2\}$ in $\mathit{failure}(t)$. However, a moment's thought is sufficient to see that both s and t will have the same deadlock behaviour in all possible environments. For, any of the deadlock possibilities represented in t by $(*,*)\{1,2\}$ occurs also in the meaning of s, namely in the form of $(*,*)(1,1)$ and $(*,*)(2,2)$. Therefore s and t need not be distinguished. As we can see, $\mathcal{O}$ does not distinguish between the two statements:

$$\mathcal{O}[\![s]\!] = \mathcal{O}[\![t]\!] = \{(*,*)(1,1),\ (*,*)(2,2),\ (*,*)(1,\delta),\ (*,*)(2,\delta)\}$$

A remedy suggested by the above example would be to allow, in addition to the usual closure under arbitrary subsets, also the closure under taking arbitrary unions of failure sets. It can be easily shown formally that such a closure condition would yield a correct compositional model. In fact, the resulting model would be isomorphic to our semantics $\mathcal{O}$: allowing arbitrary unions of failure sets is equivalent to having one-element failure sets. Thus we find back the observation made above at an intuitive level.

We can conclude that for our asynchronous language $\mathcal{L}$ the failure model is not abstract enough (let alone be *fully* abstract), since it distinguishes more statements that necessary. Instead, a stream-like model $\mathcal{O}$, which is also compositional but more abstract, is more suited. The question of a fully abstract model for $\mathcal{L}$ that is correct with respect to *Obs* will be treated in the next section.

4 Full abstraction

In this section we discuss the problem of the full abstraction of the compositional semantics $\mathcal{O}$ (with respect to the different notions of observability) for two classes of interpretations.

4.1 Complete interpretations

The first class is intended to characterize the asynchronous communication of the imperative paradigm. Such interpretations are called *complete* and satisfy the following two properties:

- For every $\sigma, \sigma' \in \Sigma$ there exists an atomic action $a \in A$ (also denoted by $a(\sigma, \sigma')$) such that

  $$I(a)(\sigma^\bullet) = \begin{cases} \sigma' & \text{if } \sigma^\bullet = \sigma \\ \text{undefined} & \text{if } \sigma^\bullet \neq \sigma \end{cases}$$

  If the current state is σ then the action $a(\sigma, \sigma')$ changes it to σ'; otherwise the actions blocks.

- For every $s, t \in \mathcal{L}$ and every $\sigma, \sigma' \in \Sigma$ there exists a state $\mu \in \Sigma$ (also denoted by $\mu(\sigma, \sigma')$) such that (σ, μ) and (μ, σ') do not occur in $\mathcal{O}[\![s]\!] \cup \mathcal{O}[\![t]\!]$.

Example We consider a variant of Example 1 of Section 2 with multiple assignment. Let A be the set of atomic actions that can instantaneously test and perform multiple assignment. It is easy to see that the first property is satisfied. For the second one, consider statements s and t. Let $y \in Var$ be a variable that does not occur in either s or t. (Thus s and t do not change the value of y.) Let $\sigma, \sigma' \in \Sigma$. Choose $v \in Val$ different from $\sigma(y)$ and $\sigma'(y)$. (Both *Var* and *Val* are assumed to be infinite.) Then define

$$\tau(\sigma, \sigma')(x) = \begin{cases} \sigma(x) & \text{if } x \neq y \\ v & \text{if } x = y \end{cases}$$

Now (σ, τ) and (τ, σ') do not occur in $\mathcal{O}[\![s]\!] \cup \mathcal{O}[\![t]\!]$.
End of example.

4.2 Monotonic interpretations

The second class we consider here is intended to characterize the asynchronous communication of the concurrent constraint paradigm. (For a short explanation see Example 2 of Section 2.) The elements of a constraint system are naturally ordered with respect to (reverse) logical implication. The effect of both the ask and tell primitives is *monotonic* with respect to the store, in fact tell only adds constraints to the store, while ask does not modify it. Since it is modelled by implication, also the successful execution of ask depends monotonically on the store, i.e., if a certain ask is defined on σ, it will be defined in all the constraints greater than σ. Both ask and tell are *extending*, i.e. their action on the store can only increase the store. Another characteristic is that both ask and tell are *strongly idempotent*: if their execution results in a certain store σ, to execute them again in the same store σ, or in a greater store, will have no effect. These properties easily derive from the definition of ask and tell (see Section 2). Notice that a consequence of them is that the store will monotonically increase during the computation.

We now formalize these features in our framework. Given a set of states Σ, where a state represents a store (constraint), and a partial order $\sqsubseteq$ on Σ, where $\sigma \sqsubseteq \sigma'$ should be read as "σ' encodes more information than (or the same as) σ", the behaviour of the ask and tell primitives is characterized by the following requirements on the interpretation function I:

- $\sigma \sqsubseteq \sigma' \Rightarrow I(a)(\sigma) \sqsubseteq I(a)(\sigma')$ (monotonicity)
- $I(a)(\sigma) \sqsubseteq \sigma' \Rightarrow I(a)(\sigma') = \sigma'$ (strong idempotency)
- $\sigma \sqsubseteq I(a)(\sigma)$ (extension)

for every action a, states σ and σ'. (Note that these notions are independent.)

Furthermore, for the construction of the fully abstract semantics, we require the following assumption on the expressiveness of the atomic actions:

> **(Assumption)** For every $\sigma \sqsubseteq \sigma' \in \Sigma$ there exists an atomic action a such that
>
> 1. $I(a)(\sigma) = \sigma'$, and
> 2. for every $\sigma'' \sqsubseteq \sigma$ $(\sigma'' \neq \sigma)$, $I(a)(\sigma'')$ is undefined.

This assumption will be used to construct a distinguishing context in the full abstraction proof. Actually, what we exactly need, is the language to allow the construction of a compound statement having the same semantics $\mathcal{D}$ (see Section 4.4) as the action a above. In concurrent constraint languages, the above assumption corresponds to requiring the atomic actions to contain both the tell (1) and the ask (2) component (like, for instance, the guards of the language in [dBP90a]). Some concurrent constraint languages (see, for instance, the languages in [SR90, dBP91]) do not allow this. However, it is possible there to construct a statement of two consecutive actions performing the check for entailment (ask) and the state transformation (tell), and we can prove that it has the same semantics $\mathcal{D}$ as if it were atomic.

An interpretation satisfying the above requirements is called *monotonic*.

In the rest of this section, two full abstraction results are presented. The first one concerns the full abstraction of O with respect to Obs_1. Next we consider the second observation function Obs_2. For this, O is not fully abstract. We develop a more abstract compositional semantics $\mathcal{D}$ by applying certain closure operators to O, and we show that $\mathcal{D}$ is fully abstract with respect to Obs_2 both for complete and monotonic interpretations.

4.3 Full abstraction of O with respect to Obs_1 for complete interpretations

In this section we state the full abstraction of O for complete interpretations.

Theorem 4.1 *For complete interpretations I, O is fully abstract with respect to Obs_1. That is, for all $s, t \in \mathcal{L}$,*

$$O[\![s]\!] = O[\![t]\!] \Leftrightarrow \forall C(\cdot),\ Obs_1[\![C(s)]\!] = Obs_1[\![C(t)]\!]$$

(Here $C(\cdot)$ is a unary context, which yields for each statement u a statement $C(u)$.)

4.4 Full abstraction with respect to Obs_2

It is not difficult to see that O is not fully abstract with respect to Obs_2. In fact, O encodes the states encountered step by step in the computation, (so, also the repetitions of the same state), while in Obs_2 only the transitions between two different states are visible. To obtain a fully abstract semantics we have therefore to abstract from "silent steps", namely those steps that do not cause any change in the state. We do so by saturating the semantics O, closing it under the following conditions:

Definition 4.2 (Closure conditions) *Let $X \in P$ be a set of sequences of pairs of states.*

$$\begin{array}{llll}
\textbf{C1} & w_1 \cdot w_2 \in X & \Rightarrow w_1 \cdot (\sigma,\sigma) \cdot w_2 \in X & (w_1 \neq \epsilon) \\
\textbf{C2} & w \in X & \Rightarrow (\sigma,\sigma) \cdot w \in X & ((\sigma,\delta) \notin X) \\
\textbf{C3} & w_1 \cdot (\sigma,\sigma) \cdot (\sigma,\sigma') \cdot w_2 \in X & \Rightarrow w_1 \cdot (\sigma,\sigma') \cdot w_2 \in X & \\
\textbf{C4} & w_1 \cdot (\sigma,\sigma') \cdot (\sigma',\sigma') \cdot w_2 \in X & \Rightarrow w_1 \cdot (\sigma,\sigma') \cdot w_2 \in X & \\
\textbf{C5} & w_1 \cdot (\sigma,\sigma) \cdot (\sigma,\delta) \in X & \Rightarrow w_1 \cdot (\sigma,\delta) \in X & (w_1 \neq \epsilon)
\end{array}$$

Furthermore, let $Close(X)$ denote the smallest set containing X and closed under the conditions **C1, C2, C3, C4** *and* **C5**.

The conditions **C1** and **C2** allow for the addition of silent steps, whereas **C3**, **C4** and **C5** allow for the removal of silent steps. Note that we do not allow the addition of (σ,σ) at the beginning of a sequence w in case $(\sigma,\delta) \in X$ because this would yield incorrect results with respect to a plus context: the deadlock possibility (σ,δ) would be removed because of the presence of $(\sigma,\sigma) \cdot w$.

It is interesting to note that it is possible to express these closure conditions inside the transition system itself. For instance, the counterpart for **C3** would be a transition rule of the form

$$\text{If } s \xrightarrow{(\sigma,\sigma)} s' \text{ and } s' \xrightarrow{(\sigma,\sigma')} s'' \text{ then } s \xrightarrow{(\sigma,\sigma')} s''$$

This is reminiscent of the way one can mimic rooted tau-bisimulation [BK88] (or weak observational congruence, in the vocabulary of [Mil80]) with ordinary strong bisimulation by adding rules like, for instance,

$$\text{If } s \xrightarrow{\tau} s' \text{ and } s' \xrightarrow{a} s'' \text{ then } s \xrightarrow{a} s''$$

(See [BK88, vG87].) The present case is by its non-uniform nature essentially more intricate. We intend to investigate this point further in the future.

Definition 4.3 *We define the semantics $\mathcal{D}$ as follows: $\mathcal{D}[s] = Close(O[s])$*

First we note that $\mathcal{D}$ is correct:

Theorem 4.4 (Correctness of $\mathcal{D}$) $\beta \circ \alpha \circ \mathcal{D} = Obs_2$.

The following theorem states the compositionality of $\mathcal{D}$.

Theorem 4.5 (Compositionality of $\mathcal{D}$) *We have*

$$\begin{array}{lll}
\mathcal{D}[s_1; s_2] & = & Close(\mathcal{D}[s_1]; \mathcal{D}[s_2]) \\
\mathcal{D}[s_1 + s_2] & = & \mathcal{D}[s_1] + \mathcal{D}[s_2] \\
\mathcal{D}[s_1 \parallel s_2] & = & Close(\mathcal{D}[s_1] \parallel \mathcal{D}[s_2])
\end{array}$$

The proof of the full abstraction of $\mathcal{D}$ with respect to Obs_2, for complete interpretations, essentially follows the same line of reasoning as presented above (for the full abstraction of $\mathcal{O}$ with respect to Obs_1).

For monotonic interpretations, we first notice that we can, without loss of generality, restrict the the domain of $\mathcal{O}$ and $\mathcal{D}$ to increasing sequences. In fact, since during a computation the state increases monotonically, only increasing sequences can be combined so to give connected results.

Next, we show that $\mathcal{D}$ satisfies the following additional closure property:

Proposition 4.6 *For monotonic interpretations we have*

$$\textbf{C6} \quad w_1 \cdot (\sigma_1, \sigma_2) \cdot w_2 \in \mathcal{D}[s] \;\Rightarrow\; w_1 \cdot (\sigma, \sigma) \cdot w_2 \in \mathcal{D}[s]$$

for every s, with $\sigma_2 \sqsubseteq \sigma$.

Proof By the requirement of (strong) idempotency of atomic actions. □

We are now ready to prove the full abstraction of $\mathcal{D}$ for monotonic interpretations.

Theorem 4.7 *For monotonic interpretations I, $\mathcal{D}$ is fully abstract with respect to Obs_2. That is, for all $s, t \in \mathcal{L}$,*

$$\mathcal{D}[s] = \mathcal{D}[t] \Leftrightarrow \forall C(.),\ Obs_2[C(s)] = Obs_2[C(t)].$$

(Here $C(.)$ is a unary context, which yields for each statement u the statement $C(u)$.)

5 Future work

As was shown in Section 3, the equivalence induced by the compositional semantics for asynchronous processes is coarser than the equivalence associated with failure set semantics, and, a fortiori, the equivalences associated to the various notions of bisimulation. It would be interesting to investigate if it is possible to give an axiomatic characterization of this equivalence.

With respect to the issue of full abstraction, a number of questions remain to be answered. For instance, we have not yet investigated full abstraction for Obs_3, in which only the initial and final states are visible. For complete interpretations, this is expected to be an easy extension; for monotonic ones, some new closure conditions will have to be applied.

Our language $\mathcal{L}$ does not have a construct for recursion; this should be added. We should also like to investigate the extension of the language with an operator for hiding in combination with the possibility of distinguishing between local and global states.

Acknowledgements We would like to thank Jan-Friso Groote, Peter Knijnenburg, Alban Ponse, Fer-Jan de Vries and Jeroen Warmerdam for their detailed comments on preliminary versions of this paper. We thank the members of the Amsterdam Concurrency Group, including Jaco de Bakker, Franck van Breughel, Arie de Bruin, Peter Knijnenburg, Erik de Vink and Jeroen Warmerdam for helpful comments and stimulating discussions.

References

[BC89] A. Brogi and P. Ciancarini. The concurrent language Shared Prolog. Technical Report TR-8/89, Dipartimento di Informatica, Università di Pisa, 1989.

[BHR84] S.D. Brookes, C.A.R. Hoare, and W. Roscoe. A theory of communicating sequential processes. *J. Assoc. Comput. Mach.*, 31:560–599, 1984.

[BK88] J.A. Bergstra and J.W. Klop. A complete inference system for regular processes with silent moves. In F.R. Drake and J.K. Truss, editors, *Proceedings Logic Colloquium 1986*, pages 21–81, Hull, 1988. North-Holland.

[BKO88] J.A. Bergstra, J.W. Klop, and E.-R. Olderog. Readies and failures in the algebra of communicating systems. *SIAM J. Comp.*, 17(6):1134–1177, 1988.

[dBK90] J.W. de Bakker and J.N. Kok. Comparative metric semantics for Concurrent Prolog. *Theoretical Computer Science*, 75:15–43, 1990.

[dBP90a] F.S. de Boer and C. Palamidessi. Concurrent logic languages: Asynchronism and language comparison. In *Proc. of the North American Conference on Logic Programming*, Series in Logic Programming, pages 175–194. The MIT Press, 1990. Full version available as technical report TR 6/90, Dipartimento di Informatica, Università di Pisa.

[dBP90b] F.S. de Boer and C. Palamidessi. On the asynchronous nature of communication in concurrent logic languages: A fully abstract model based on sequences. In J.C.M. Baeten and J.W. Klop, editors, *Proc. of Concur 90*, volume 458 of *Lecture Notes in Computer Science*, pages 99–114, The Netherlands, 1990. Springer-Verlag. Full version available as report at the Technische Universiteit Eindhoven.

[dBP91] F.S. de Boer and C. Palamidessi. A fully abstract model for concurrent constraint programming. In S. Abramsky and T.S.E. Maibaum, editors, *Proc. of TAPSOFT/CAAP*, volume 493 of *Lecture Notes in Computer Science*. Springer-Verlag, 1991. Revised and Extended version in Technical Report CS-9110, Department of Computer Science, University of Utrecht, The Netherlands.

[dBZ82] J.W. de Bakker and J.I. Zucker. Processes and the denotational semantics of concurrency. *Information and Control*, 54:70–120, 1982.

[EHLR80] D. Erman, F. HayesRoth, V. Lesser, and D. Reddy. The Hearsay2 speech understanding system: Integrating knowledge to resolve uncertainty. *ACM Computing Surveys*, 12:213–253, 1980.

[GCLS88] R. Gerth, M. Codish, Y. Lichtenstein, and E. Shapiro. Fully abstract denotational semantics for Concurrent Prolog. In *Proc. of the Third IEEE Symposium on Logic In Computer Science*, pages 320–335. IEEE Computer Society Press, New York, 1988.

[Gel86] D. Gelenter. Generative communication in linda. *ACM TOPLAS*, 7(1):80–112, 1986.

[GMS89] H. Gaifman, M. J. Maher, and E. Shapiro. Reactive Behaviour semantics for Concurrent Constraint Logic Programs. In E. Lusk and R. Overbeck, editors, *North American Conference on Logic Programming*, 1989.

[HdBR90] E. Horita, J.W. de Bakker, and J.J.M.M. Rutten. Fully abstract denotational models for nonuniform concurrent languages. Technical Report CS-R9027, Centre for Mathematics and Computer Science, Amsterdam, 1990.

[Hoa78] C.A.R. Hoare. Communicating sequential processes. *Communications of the ACM*, 21(8):666–677, 1978.

[JHJ90] M.B. Josephs, C.A.R. Hoare, and He Jifeng. A theory of asynchronous processes. Technical report, Oxford University Computing Laboratories, 1990.

[JJH90] He Jifeng, M.B. Josephs, and C.A.R. Hoare. A theory of synchrony and asynchrony. In *Proc. of IFIP Working Conference on Programming Concepts and Methods*, pages 459–478, 1990.

[JK89] B. Jonsson and J.N. Kok. Comparing two fully abstract dataflow models. In *Proc. Parallel Architectures and Languages Europe (PARLE)*, number 379 in Lecture Notes in Computer Science, pages 217–235, 1989.

[Jon85] B. Jonsson. A model and a proof system for asynchronous processes. In *Proc. of the 4th ACM Symp. on Principles of Distributed Computing*, pages 49–58, 1985.

[Kah74] G. Kahn. The semantics of a simple language for parallel programming. In *Information Processing 74: Proc. of IFIP Congress*, pages 471–475, New York, 1974. North-Holland.

[Kok87] J.N. Kok. A fully abstract semantics for data flow nets. In J.W. de Bakker, A.J. Nijman, and P.C. Treleaven, editors, *Proc. Parallel Architectures and Languages Europe (PARLE)*, volume 259 of *Lecture Notes in Computer Science*, pages 351–368. Springer Verlag, 1987.

[Kok89] J.N. Kok. Traces, histories and streams in the semantics of nondeterministic dataflow. In *Proceedings Massive Parallellism: Hardware, Programming and Applications*, 1989. Also available as report 91, Abo Akademi, Finland, 1989.

[Mil80] R. Milner. *A Calculus of Communicating Systems*, volume 92 of *Lecture Notes in Computer Science*. Springer-Verlag, New York, 1980.

[Mil83] Robin Milner. Calculi for synchrony and asynchrony. *Theoretical Computer Science*, 25:267–310, 1983.

[Sar89] V.A. Saraswat. *Concurrent Constraint Programming Languages*. PhD thesis, january 1989. To be published by the MIT Press.

[Sha83] E.Y. Shapiro. A subset of concurrent prolog and its interpreter. Technical Report TR-003, ICOT, 1983.

[Sha89] E.Y. Shapiro. The family of concurrent logic programming languages. *ACM Computing Surveys*, 21(3):412–510, 1989.

[SR90] V.A. Saraswat and M. Rinard. Concurrent constraint programming. In *Proc. of the seventeenth ACM Symposium on Principles of Programming Languages*, pages 232–245. ACM, New York, 1990.

[vG87] R.J. van Glabbeek. Bounded nondeterminism and the approximation induction principle in process algebra. In F.J. Brandenburg, G. Vidal-Naquet, and M. Wirsing, editors, *Proceedings STACS 1987*, volume 247 of *Lecture Notes in Computer Science*, pages 336–347. Springer-Verlag, 1987.

Embedding as a tool for Language Comparison: On the CSP hierarchy

Frank S. de Boer[1] and Catuscia Palamidessi[2]

[1]Technische Universiteit Eindhoven,
P.O. Box 513, 5600 MB Eindhoven, The Netherlands
email: wsinfdb@tuewsd.win.tue.nl

[2]Centre for Mathematics and Computer Science,
P.O. Box 4079, 1009 AB Amsterdam, The Netherlands
email: katuscia@cwi.nl
and
Department of Computer Science, Utrecht University
P.O. Box 80089 3508 TB Utrecht, The Netherlands

Abstract

The concept of embedding has recently been introduced as a formal tool to study the relative expressive power of (concurrent) programming languages. We use the notion of "modular embedding" to compare various dialects of CSP and ACSP (Asynchronous CSP), which differ on the kind of communication primitives allowed in the guards: all, only input, or none. Concerning the synchronous paradigm, we show that CSP is strictly more powerful than $CSP_{\mathcal{I}}$ (the version of CSP with no output guards), and that $CSP_{\mathcal{I}}$ is strictly more powerful than $CSP_{\emptyset}$ (the version of CSP with no communication primitives in the guards). The first separation result does not hold in the asynchronous variants of these languages: since asynchronous output guards cannot be influenced by the environment (they can always proceed), it is irrelevant to have or not to have them in the language. Therefore, ACSP and $ACSP_{\mathcal{I}}$ are equivalent. Still, they are strictly more expressive than $ACSP_{\emptyset}$. Finally, we come to compare the synchronous and asynchronous paradigms. The asynchronous communication can be modeled synchronously by means of "buffer" processes. On the other hand, synchronous communication (when not fully used to control non-determinism) can be modeled asynchronously by means of acknowledgement messages. As a consequence, $CSP_{\mathcal{I}}$, ACSP, and $ACSP_{\mathcal{I}}$ are equivalent. An interesting corollary of these results is that ACSP is strictly less powerful than CSP.

C.R. Categories: D.1.3, D.3.1, F.1.2, F.3.2, F.4.1.

Key Words and Phrases: concurrent logic languages, compositional semantics, embedding.

Note: Part of this work was carried out in the context of the ESPRIT Basic Research Action (3020) Integration. The research of Frank S. de Boer was supported by the Dutch REX (Research and Education in Concurrent Systems) project. The stay of Catuscia Palamidessi at the Centre for Mathematics and Computer Science was partially supported by the Italian CNR (Consiglio Nazionale delle Ricerche).

1 Introduction

From a mathematical point of view, all "reasonable" programming languages are equivalent, since all of them can compute the same class of functions. Yet, it is common practice to speak about the "power" of a language on the basis of the expressibility or non expressibility of programming constructs. In the field of sequential languages there has been already since a long time a line of research aiming to formalize the notion of "expressive power" [5, 10, 14, 16, 17, 18, 22]. The various approaches agree in considering a language L more expressive than L' if the constructs of L' can be translated in L without requiring a "global reorganization of the entire program" [10], i.e., compositionally. Of course, the translation must preserve the meaning, at least in the weak sense of preserving termination [10]. In case of nondeterministic sequential languages, termination is usually dealt with existentially (i.e. failing or infinite computations are ignored, if there is at least a successfully terminating one). In this sense the nondeterministic Turing machines are equivalent to the deterministic ones.

When we move to the field of concurrent languages, the notion of termination must be reconsidered. This is because the nondeterminism plays an essentially different role: each possible computation represents a possible different evolution of a system of interacting processes, and must be considered independently from the other ones (backtracking is usually not possible, or to difficult to implement). Also, there is an additional termination case: *deadlock*, representing the situation in which each process is stuck waiting for some condition to be established by the others. Essentially due to this "richer" concept of termination, the models (and the notion of meaning itself) for concurrent languages are usually far more complicated. From the point of view of language comparison, this richer notion of meaning gives additional "freedom" for the definition of the notion of expressivity [20, 7, 8, 6, 21, 9, 1, 2, 15, 23].

In [23] the expressive power of a concurrent languages is investigated under various criteria, increasingly more refined:

- the capability to simulate Turing machines,
- the capability to specify effective process graphs (up to some notion of equivalence), and
- the capability to express effective operations on graphs (as contexts of the language).

While all "reasonable" languages are universal up to the first criterion, this is not the case for the other two. In particular, [23] shows that there cannot be a concurrent language (with an effective operational semantics) able to express all effective process graphs, up to trace equivalence. This generalizes a result of [1], proving the same but for (strong) bisimulation equivalence. Positive results for the second criterion include [1], showing the universality of ACP_τ (up to weak bisimulation), and [9], showing the universality of MEIJE-SCCS with unguarded recursion (up to strong bisimulation). This last result does not contradict the results of [1, 23], since unguarded recursion induces an infinitely branching (hence not effective) operational semantics. Even more surprisingly, [9] shows that MEIJE-SCCS are universal with respect to all the operators definable via transition rule of a certain, very general, format. In [15] an interesting result is shown for the class of finite process graphs: all of them can be expressed (up to every equivalence between traces and bisimulation, under τ abstraction) as parallel composition of a finite number of instances of three elementary processes (a three-ways synchronizer, an arbiter, and an alternator). As a consequence, it is shown that all finite-state asynchronous operators (including for instance the CSP external nondeterministic choice, parallel, and hiding) can be expressed as contexts in that simple language. With respect to the second criterion, [2] provides a detailed classification of various ACP sublanguages, showing how each operator contributes to increase the expressive power.

In this paper the notion of expressivity is considered only relatively, i.e. in the comparison of one language with respect to another. The method of comparison we adopt is, in part, based on the same idea of the third criterion illustrated above, in the sense that it requires (some) of the operators of a language to be expressible (as operators) in the other language. One difference is that we do not require a statement in a language and its correspondent in the other language to have the same semantics, even not up to isomorphism. We only require an injection (abstraction) from the second to the first. To our opinion, this second (more liberal) requirement better capture the intuition of expressing a language into another, since it allows to abstract from "details" that may be necessary for the implementation (like additional information about control).

We consider the notion of *modular embedding*, introduced in [7] as a method to compare the expressive power of concurrent logic languages. This notion has been refined in [8] and shown to be general enough to establish a hierarchy on a broader class of languages: the Concurrent Constraint family [19]. In this paper, we apply the method to compare various dialects of the CSP paradigm [4, 12]. We show that CSP is strictly more powerful than $CSP_\mathcal{I}$ (the sublanguage with no *output guards*), and that $CSP_\mathcal{I}$ is strictly more powerful than $CSP_\emptyset$ (the sublanguage with no *communication primitives* in the guards). This presents a strict analogy with the concurrent constraint case: the choices guarded by *tell* operations cannot be simulated by choices guarded by *ask* operations, and the latter cannot be simulated by the unguarded choice [8].

If we now consider the asynchronous variant of the CSP family, ACSP [12, 13], we may expect that these separation results are reflected there, but this is not the case. As we show in this paper, $ACSP_\emptyset$ is still less powerful, but ACSP and $ACSP_{\mathcal{I}}$ are equivalent. This is due to the asymmetric behavior of input and output guards in ACSP: an output can always proceed, independently from the actions performed by the other processes in the environment. Therefore output guards cannot control nondeterminism. They don't really increase the expressive power of the language. This is already suggested in [13], in fact output guards are not even considered there.

This asymmetry already suggests that shifting to asynchrony causes a loss of power, and, in fact, we show that ACSP is equivalent to $CSP_{\mathcal{I}}$, so proving that CSP is strictly more powerful than ACSP.

1.1 The method

We summarize here the method for language comparison, called modular embedding, as defined in [8].

A natural way to compare the expressive power of two languages is to see whether all programs written in one language can be "easily" and "equivalently" translated into the other one, where equivalent is intended in the sense of the same observable behavior. This notion has recently become popular with the name of *embedding* [20, 7, 8, 21]. The basic definition of embedding, given by Shapiro [20], is the following. Consider two languages, L and L'. Assume given the semantic functions (*observation criteria*) $\mathcal{S} : L \to Obs$ and $\mathcal{S}' : L' \to Obs'$, where Obs, Obs' are some suitable domains. Then L *can embed* L' if there exists a mapping $\mathcal{C}$ (*compiler*) from the statements of L' to the statements of L, and a mapping $\mathcal{D}$ (*decoder*) from Obs to Obs' such that for every statement $A \in L'$, the following equation holds

$$\mathcal{D}(\mathcal{S}[\![\mathcal{C}(A)]\!]) = \mathcal{S}'[\![A]\!]$$

In other words, the diagram of Figure 1 commutes.

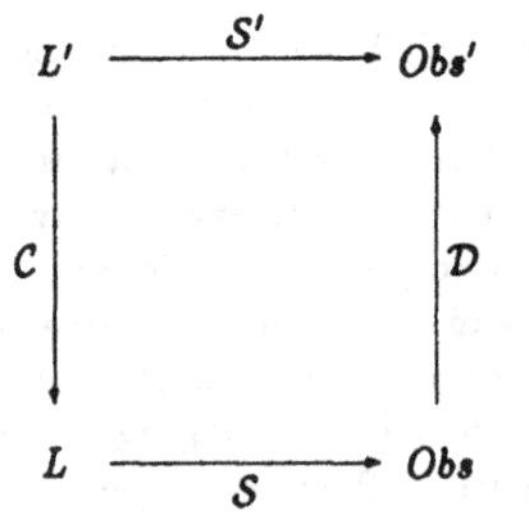

Figure 1: basic embedding.

This notion however is too weak (as Shapiro himself remarked) since the above equation is satisfied by any Turing-complete language. Actually, L does not even need to be Turing-complete, it is sufficient that it contains infinitely many observably different programs. We can then take a $\mathcal{C}$ such that $\mathcal{S} \circ \mathcal{C}$ does not identify more programs than $\mathcal{S}'$, and define $\mathcal{D}$ as the function such that the diagram of Figure 1 commutes. In [21] it is shown how finite automata can "embed" (in this weak sense) Turing machines.

In order to use the notion of embedding as a tool for comparison of concurrent languages we have therefore to add some restrictions on $\mathcal{C}$ and $\mathcal{D}$. We do this by requiring $\mathcal{C}$ and $\mathcal{D}$ to satisfy certain properties that, to our opinion, are rather "reasonable" in a concurrent framework.

A first remark is the following. In a concurrent language, where indeterminism plays an important role, the domain of the observables (Obs) is in general a powerset (i.e. the elements S of Obs are sets). In fact, each element must represent the outcomes of all possible computations. Moreover, each outcome will be observed independently from the other possible ones. Therefore it is reasonable to require $\mathcal{D}$ to be defined *elementwise* on the sets that are contained in Obs.

Formally:

P1 $\forall S \in Obs.\, \mathcal{D}(S) = \{\mathcal{D}_{el}(s) : s \in S\}$

for some appropriate $\mathcal{D}_{el}$. Yet, this restriction doesn't increase significantly the discriminating power of the notion of embedding. In fact, we can always define C so that, for each statement A, each element of $\mathcal{S}[C(A)]$ encodes A, and then define an appropriate decoder. See [8, §4] for a concrete example of such an embedding.

Another observation is the following. When compiling a concurrent process, it might not be feasible to have all the information about the processes that will be present in the environment at run time. Therefore it is reasonable to require the "separate compilation" of the parallel processes, or, in other words, the *compositionality* of the compiler with respect to the parallel operator.

Additionally, it is useful to compile a process in a compositional way with respect to the possible nondeterministic choices, so to have the possibility to add alternatives (for instance, communication offers) without the need of recompilation. These properties can be formulated as follows:

P2 $C(A \parallel' B) = C(A) \parallel C(B)$ *and* $C(A +' B) = C(A) + C(B)$

for every pair of processes A and B in L'. (Here $\parallel$, $\parallel'$, $+$, and $+'$ represent the parallel operators and the nondeterministic choice operators in L and L' respectively.)

A final point is that the embedding must preserve the behavior of the original process with respect to deadlock (and/or failure) and success. Intuitively, a system which is not deadlock-free cannot be considered equivalent to a system which is. Therefore we require the termination mode of the target language not to be affected by the decoder (*termination invariance*). In other words, a deadlock [failure] in $\mathcal{S}[C(A)]$ must correspond to a deadlock [failure] in $\mathcal{S}'[A]$, and a success must correspond to a success. Formally

P3 $\forall S \in Obs. \forall s \in S.\ tm'(\mathcal{D}_{el}(s)) = tm(s)$

where tm and tm' extract the information concerning the termination mode from the observables of L and L' respectively.

An embedding is called *modular* if it satisfies the three properties **P1**, **P2** and **P3** discussed above. (In the following we will omit the term "modular" when it is clear from the context.)

The existence of a modular embedding from L' into L will be denoted by $L' \leq L$. It is immediate to see that $\leq$ is a preorder relation, in fact the reflexivity is given by the possibility of defining C and $\mathcal{D}$ as the identity functions, and the transitivity is shown by the commutative diagram in Figure 2.

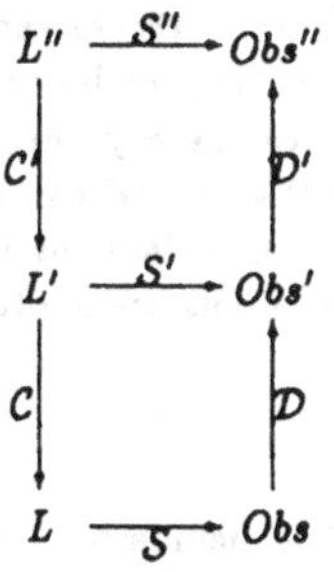

Figure 2: transitivity of $\leq$.

Note that, if $L' \subseteq L$, then $L' \leq L$. In fact, it is sufficient to define C and $\mathcal{D}$ as (the extension of) the identity functions.

1.2 Related works

Bougé [3] has presented similar separation results for three CSP-dialects which closely correspond to three of the languages we study: CSP, $\mathrm{CSP}_{\mathcal{I}}$, and $\mathrm{CSP}_{\emptyset}$. (The main difference is that he considers the original definition of CSP, as given in [11].)

His method is based on showing that, given some communication graph, one dialect admits symmetric solutions to the *election problem*, while another dialect doesn't. These solutions are required to satisfy certain conditions about termination which closely correspond to our notion of termination invariance. These results can be interpreted as stating the non-existence of a translation, when the compiler is required to preserve parallelism and the topology of the network.

The notion of embedding was first proposed by Shapiro as a method for language comparison in [20], and refined in various vays in [7, 8, 21, 6] by adding conditions so to make it non-trivial. As already explained, we follow here the approach of [7, 8], where the notion of modular embedding was first defined and applied to show separation results in the Concurrent Constraint family. Based upon the same notion we establish in this paper a hierarchy of the CSP languages similar to the one of the Concurrent Constraint family. This is quite surprising, because the Concurrent Constraint languages are based on asynchronous communication, so one would rather expect a similarity with the ACSP hierarchy.

In [21] three different notions of embedding are investigated. The first one (sound embedding) is equivalent to the original definition in [20] plus the requirement of compositionality with respect to the parallel operator. (Therefore it is equivalent to our notion, dropping the conditions on the decoder and the compositionality w.r.t. the choice operator. Notice that our notion of embedding thus leads to a subcategory of the category of sound embeddings.) The second one (faithful embedding) requires additionally the compiler to translate (observable) equivalent statements into equivalent ones. The third notion considered (fully abstract embedding) requires the compiler to preserve the (non-)equivalence of statements with respect to the fully abstract semantics. These two last notions are not comparable with our approach.

In [6] the notion of modular embedding is used to compare the expressive power of a general asynchronous paradigm $\mathcal{L}$ with respect to a synchronous paradigm (CCS). It is shown that CCS can be embedded into $\mathcal{L}$, by choosing an appropriate interpretation for the basic actions of $\mathcal{L}$ (CCS and $\mathcal{L}$ are *uniform* languages, i.e. the basic actions are uninterpreted). This is not in contrast with the non-embeddability of CSP into ACSP, because ACSP is only a particular instance of $\mathcal{L}$. In order to point out the differencies between synchronous and asynchronous forms of communication, it is investigated under which further conditions CCS cannot be embedded into $\mathcal{L}$.

1.3 Plan of the paper

This paper is organized as follows. Next section introduces the family $\mathrm{CSP}_{\mathcal{G}}$ as a class of CSP-like languages parametrized on $\mathcal{G}$, the set of communication primitives that can occur in the guards. The behavior of $\mathrm{CSP}_{\mathcal{G}}$ processes is specified via a transition system, from which we derive the notion of observables and a compositional semantics. In Section 3 we study the hierarchy on the members of this class: by using the compositional semantics we show that CSP cannot be embedded in $\mathrm{CSP}_{\mathcal{I}}$, and that $\mathrm{CSP}_{\mathcal{I}}$ cannot be embedded in $\mathrm{CSP}_{\emptyset}$. In Section 4 we introduce the asynchronous variant of this family, $\mathrm{ACSP}_{\mathcal{G}}$, and its compositional model. In Section 5 we show that ACSP can be embedded in $\mathrm{ACSP}_{\mathcal{I}}$, but not in $\mathrm{ACSP}_{\emptyset}$. Finally, the synchronous and the asynchronous CSP families are compared, and we discuss the scope of the results. Due to space limitations, some of the proofs are omitted.

2 The class $\mathrm{CSP}_{\mathcal{G}}$

In this section we present the $\mathrm{CSP}_{\mathcal{G}}$ family. The members of this class are simplified versions of CSP dialects [4, 12]. We abstract from some of the traditional CSP constructs, like renaming. Also, we don't consider recursion (we deal only with finite processes), but the results we present can be generalized to the full version of the languages.

2.1 The syntax

Let $(c, d, \ldots \in)$ *Chan* be a set of *channel names*. Let $(x, y, \ldots \in)$ *Var* be a set of *variables*, $(t, u, \ldots \in)$ *Term* an abstract set of terms (expressions) on these variables, and $(v, w, \ldots \in)$ *Val* an abstract set of values. The set of basic actions is given by $\mathcal{I} \cup \mathcal{O} \cup \mathcal{A}$, where

$$(i \in) \mathcal{I} = \{c?x : c \in \mathit{Chan}, x \in \mathit{Var}\}$$

are the *input* actions,

$(o \in)\ \mathcal{O} = \{c!t : c \in Chan, t \in Term\}$

are the *output* actions, and $(a \in)\ A$ are internal actions. Note that we abstract from the structure of internal actions. We only assume the existence of an internal move, *Skip*, which does not have any observable effect.

The set $(g \in)\ \mathcal{G}$ specifies the *communication primitives* used in the guards. We restrict to the following cases: $\mathcal{G} = \emptyset$, $\mathcal{G} = \mathcal{I}$, or $\mathcal{G} = \mathcal{I} \cup \mathcal{O}$. The set of statements in $\mathrm{CSP}_{\mathcal{G}}$, with typical elements $A, B, \ldots$, is described by the following grammar

$$A ::= Stop \mid c!t; A \mid c?x; A \mid a; A \mid A \parallel A \mid G$$

$$G ::= g \rightarrow A \mid a \rightarrow A \mid G + G$$

The symbols ; and $\parallel$ represent the sequential and the parallel composition respectively. A process $g \rightarrow A$ first executes g (if possible) and then it behaves like A. The *guard* g belongs to $\mathcal{G}$ and its execution depends upon the actions performed by the external environment. The language presents two forms of nondeterministic choice $+$: the guarded (external) nondeterminism, like for instance in $(g_1 \rightarrow A_1) + (g_2 \rightarrow A_2)$, where only a branch whose guard is enabled can be selected, and the unguarded (internal) nondeterminism, like for instance in $(a_1 \rightarrow A_1) + (a_2 \rightarrow A_2)$, where a branch will be selected independently from the external environment.

Note that we don't impose explicitly one-to-one communication. All the results we present (apart from $\mathrm{CSP}_{\mathcal{I}} \leq \mathrm{ACSP}_{\mathcal{I}}$ and $\mathrm{CSP}_{\emptyset} \leq \mathrm{ACSP}_{\emptyset}$) do not depend on this assumption.

2.2 The operational model of $\mathrm{CSP}_{\mathcal{G}}$

The operational model of $\mathrm{CSP}_{\mathcal{G}}$ is uniformly described by a labeled transition system

$$T = (Conf, \bigcup_{e \in E} \xrightarrow{e})$$

where $(e \in)\ E$ denotes the set of events of the form $c?v, c!v$ (*external* or *visible* steps), with $v \in Val$, and τ (*internal* or *invisible* step),. The configurations *Conf* are pairs consisting of a statement A and a state σ ($\in State$), namely a mapping from *Var* to *Val*. The notion of state is introduced here just to assign a meaning to internal actions, it cannot be used to communicate (there is no shared memory). In order to simplify the description of the transition system, we assume that the components of a set of parallel processes do not share variables with the same name. This syntactical restriction on the language allows us to represent the collection of all local states by just one "global" state. The meaning of internal actions we assume to be given by an *interpretation function* I. Namely, $I(a)(\sigma)$ is the state resulting by executing a in σ. (Actually, the execution of a only depends upon and affects the component of σ local to the process executing a.) The interpretation of *Skip* is the identity, i.e. $I(Skip)(\sigma) = \sigma$. Given a state σ and a term t, the value of t is denoted by $\sigma(t)$. The state resulting from σ by assigning v to x is denoted by $\sigma\{v/x\}$.

The transition relations are described in Table 1. The first rule describes the meaning of an internal action as a state transformation. The statement *Stop* denotes termination. An input action $c?y$ is described by means of a transition labeled by an event $c?v$, which records the fact that the value v has been received. Similarly, an output action $c!t$ is described by means of a transition labeled by an event $c!v$, where v is the value of the term t. The other rules are the usual rules for compound statements (note that parallelism is described as interleaving).

The result of a computation consists of the final state together with the termination mode, ss or dd, indicating successful termination or deadlock, respectively. This is formally represented by the notion of *observables*.

Definition 2.1 *The observables of the class* $\mathrm{CSP}_{\mathcal{G}}$ *are given by the function* $\mathcal{S}_{\mathcal{G}} : \mathrm{CSP}_{\mathcal{G}} \rightarrow Obs$ *with* $Obs = State \rightarrow (State \times \{ss, dd\})$.

$$\begin{aligned} \mathcal{S}_{\mathcal{G}}[\![A]\!](\sigma) = \ & \{\langle \sigma', ss\rangle : \langle A, \sigma\rangle \xrightarrow{\tau}{}^{*} \langle Stop, \sigma'\rangle\} \\ & \cup \\ & \{\langle \sigma', dd\rangle : \langle A, \sigma\rangle \xrightarrow{\tau}{}^{*} \langle B, \sigma'\rangle \not\xrightarrow{\tau} \wedge B \neq Stop\} \end{aligned}$$

Table 1: The Transition System T

R0	$\langle a; A, \sigma\rangle \xrightarrow{\tau} \langle A, I(a)(\sigma)\rangle$	
R1	$\langle c?x; A, \sigma\rangle \xrightarrow{c?v} \langle A, \sigma\{v/x\}\rangle$	where $v \in Val$
R2	$\langle c!t; A, \sigma\rangle \xrightarrow{c!v} \langle A, \sigma\rangle$	where $\sigma(t) = v$
R3	$\dfrac{\langle g; Stop, \sigma\rangle \xrightarrow{e} \langle Stop, \sigma'\rangle}{\langle g \rightarrow A, \sigma\rangle \xrightarrow{e} \langle A, \sigma'\rangle}$	where $g \in \mathcal{G} \cup \mathcal{A}$
R4	$\dfrac{\langle A, \sigma\rangle \xrightarrow{e} \langle A', \sigma'\rangle \mid \langle Stop, \sigma'\rangle}{\begin{array}{l}\langle A \parallel B, \sigma\rangle \xrightarrow{e} \langle A' \parallel B, \sigma'\rangle \mid \langle B, \sigma'\rangle \\ \langle B \parallel A, \sigma\rangle \xrightarrow{e} \langle B \parallel A', \sigma'\rangle \mid \langle B, \sigma'\rangle \\ \langle A+B, \sigma\rangle \xrightarrow{e} \langle A', \sigma'\rangle \mid \langle Stop, \sigma'\rangle \\ \langle B+A, \sigma\rangle \xrightarrow{e} \langle A', \sigma'\rangle \mid \langle Stop, \sigma'\rangle\end{array}}$	
R5	$\dfrac{\langle A, \sigma\rangle \xrightarrow{c?v} \langle A', \sigma'\rangle \quad \langle B, \sigma\rangle \xrightarrow{c!v} \langle B', \sigma\rangle}{\langle A \parallel B, \sigma\rangle \xrightarrow{\tau} \langle A' \parallel B', \sigma'\rangle}$	

where $\xrightarrow{\tau}{}^{*}$ *denotes the reflexive and transitive closure of* $\xrightarrow{\tau}$.

Note that the observables are defined in a uniform way for all the members of the class, and on the same domain *Obs*. In the following, we will omit the subscript $\mathcal{G}$ when it is clear from the context which language we are referring to.

On the basis of the transition system T we now define a compositional semantics $\mathcal{M}_{\mathcal{G}}$ for $\mathrm{CSP}_{\mathcal{G}}$. The semantical domain of $\mathcal{M}_{\mathcal{G}}$, denoted by $(p, q \in)\ P$, is the same for all $\mathcal{G}$'s and it is the set of synchronization trees with finite depth whose arcs are labeled on $State \times E \times State$. More formally, P is the smallest set that satisfies the following conditions:

- $\emptyset \in P$
- If $\phi_1, \ldots, \phi_n, \ldots \in State \times E \times State$, and $p_1, \ldots, p_n, \ldots \in P$ then $\{\phi_1 \cdot p_1, \ldots, \phi_n \cdot p_n, \ldots\} \in P$

Definition 2.2 *The semantics* $\mathcal{M}_{\mathcal{G}} : \mathrm{CSP}_{\mathcal{G}} \rightarrow P$ *is defined as*

$$\mathcal{M}_{\mathcal{G}}[A] = \begin{cases} \emptyset & \textit{if } A = Stop \\ \{\langle \sigma, e, \sigma'\rangle \cdot \mathcal{M}_{\mathcal{G}}[B] : \langle A, \sigma\rangle \xrightarrow{e} \langle B, \sigma'\rangle\} & \textit{otherwise} \end{cases}$$

Also for $\mathcal{M}_{\mathcal{G}}$ we have a uniform definition, and we will omit the subscript $\mathcal{G}$.

The correctness $\mathcal{M}$ is shown by defining the following abstraction operator $\mathcal{R}$, that extracts the observables of a process from its denotation in $\mathcal{M}$. This is done by collecting the final state plus termination mode of all those maximal paths labeled by τ steps and consecutive states. Such a path is maximal if either it ends in a leaf, in which case it represents a successful terminating execution, or it cannot be extended by a τ step, thus representing a deadlocking execution.

Definition 2.3
The operator $\mathcal{R} : P \rightarrow Obs$ *is given by*

$$\mathcal{R}(p)(\sigma) = \begin{cases} \{\langle \sigma, ss\rangle\} & \textit{if } p = \emptyset \\ \{\langle \sigma, dd\rangle\} & \textit{if } p \neq \emptyset \textit{ and } \forall \sigma', q. \langle \sigma, \tau, \sigma'\rangle \cdot q \notin p \\ \bigcup\{\mathcal{R}(q)(\sigma') : \langle \sigma, \tau, \sigma'\rangle \cdot q \in p\} & \textit{otherwise} \end{cases}$$

Theorem 2.4 (Correctness of $\mathcal{M}$) *The observables $\mathcal{S}$ can be obtained by $\mathcal{R}$-abstraction from $\mathcal{M}$, namely $\mathcal{S} = \mathcal{R} \circ \mathcal{M}$.*

The compositionality of $\mathcal{M}$ is shown by defining semantic operators corresponding to the operators of the language. The choice operator is just defined as union and the sequential operator as tree concatenation. The parallel operator $\tilde{\|}$ is defined as usual in terms of the left merge and the synchronization merge, where the synchronization merge transforms the arcs $\langle\sigma, c!v, \sigma\rangle$ and $\langle\sigma, c?v, \sigma'\rangle$ into $\langle\sigma, \tau, \sigma'\rangle$.

3 The CSP hierarchy

In this section we study the relations between the members of the CSP family. We consider $\text{CSP}_\emptyset$, $\text{CSP}_\mathcal{I}$ and $\text{CSP}_{\mathcal{I}\cup\mathcal{O}}$. For the sake of convenience, the latter will be denoted by CSP.

Since the languages $\text{CSP}_\emptyset$, $\text{CSP}_\mathcal{I}$ and CSP are sublanguages of each other, we have the following proposition.

Proposition 3.1 $\text{CSP}_\emptyset$ *can be embedded in* $\text{CSP}_\mathcal{I}$ *and* $\text{CSP}_\mathcal{I}$ *can be embedded in* CSP, *namely:* $\text{CSP}_\emptyset \leq \text{CSP}_\mathcal{I} \leq \text{CSP}$.

The rest of the section will be devoted to show that this ordering is strict, namely $\text{CSP} \not\leq \text{CSP}_\mathcal{I} \not\leq \text{CSP}_\emptyset$.

We will use the following properties on the compositional semantics and on the abstraction operator. They can easily be shown by definition of $\mathcal{R}$ and $\tilde{\|}$.

Proposition 3.2

1. $\forall p.\ \mathcal{R}(p)(\sigma) \neq \emptyset$
2. $\forall \sigma, \sigma', p, q.$ *if* $\langle\sigma, \tau, \sigma'\rangle \cdot p \in q$ *then* $\mathcal{R}(\langle\sigma, \tau, \sigma'\rangle \cdot p)(\sigma) \subseteq \mathcal{R}(q)(\sigma)$
3. $\forall p, q, q'.\ p\tilde{\|}(q \cup q') = p\tilde{\|}q \cup p\tilde{\|}q'$

The first property says that the abstraction operator $\mathcal{R}$ always delivers a non-empty set of results for any synchronization tree. The second property states that a subtree starting with a τ branch will deliver a subset of the results delivered by the complete tree. Note that this is not the case for subtrees starting with a communication action: they give a deadlock, whereas the full tree may offer other alternatives, so avoiding deadlock. Finally, the last property states the distributivity of $\tilde{\|}$ with respect to the union.

We first show that CSP cannot be embedded into $\text{CSP}_\mathcal{I}$.

Theorem 3.3 $\text{CSP} \not\leq \text{CSP}_\mathcal{I}$.

Proof Assume, by contradiction, that $\text{CSP} \leq \text{CSP}_\mathcal{I}$ via $\mathcal{C}$ and $\mathcal{D}$. Let

$$A_1 = c_1!v_1 \rightarrow Stop,\quad A_2 = c_2?x_2 \rightarrow Stop,$$

and

$$B_1 = c_1?x_1 \rightarrow Stop,\quad B_2 = c_2!v_2 \rightarrow Stop.$$

with $c_1 \neq c_2$. Let $A = A_1 + A_2$, and $B = B_1 + B_2$, and consider $A \| B$.

We have that

$$\mathcal{S}[A \| B](\epsilon) = \{\langle\{v_1/x_1\}, ss\rangle, \langle\{v_2/x_2\}, ss\rangle\} \tag{1}$$

where ϵ denotes the empty (initial) state. Because of **P2** and the compositionality of $\mathcal{M}$, we have

$$\mathcal{M}[\mathcal{C}(A \| B)] = (\mathcal{M}[\mathcal{C}(A_1)] \cup \mathcal{M}[\mathcal{C}(A_2)])\ \tilde{\|}\ (\mathcal{M}[\mathcal{C}(B_1)] \cup \mathcal{M}[\mathcal{C}(B_2)]) \tag{2}$$

Because of **P3** and the fact that in $\text{CSP}_\mathcal{I}$ the semantics of a choice cannot contain an initial node labeled by an output event (a choice cannot be guarded by an output event) we then have

$$\exists \sigma, p.\ \langle\epsilon, \tau, \sigma\rangle \cdot p \in \mathcal{M}[\mathcal{C}(A_1)] \cup \mathcal{M}[\mathcal{C}(A_2)] \cup \mathcal{M}[\mathcal{C}(B_1)] \cup \mathcal{M}[\mathcal{C}(B_2)]$$

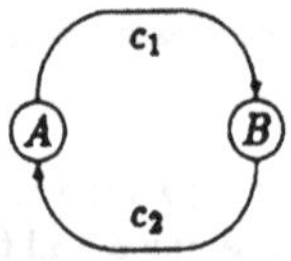

Figure 3: $A \parallel B$

We consider the following case (the other ones being analogous):

$$\langle \epsilon, \tau, \sigma \rangle \cdot p \in \mathcal{M}[\![\mathcal{C}(A_1)]\!]. \tag{3}$$

We show that there exists an element $\langle \vartheta, dd \rangle \in \mathcal{S}[\![\mathcal{C}(A \parallel B)]\!](\epsilon)$, that, together with (1), contradicts **P3**.

By Proposition 3.2(1),

$$\exists \langle \vartheta, \alpha \rangle \in \mathcal{R}(\langle \epsilon, \tau, \sigma \rangle \cdot p \,\tilde{\parallel}\, \mathcal{M}[\![\mathcal{C}(B_2)]\!])(\epsilon)$$

where $\langle \epsilon, \tau, \sigma \rangle \cdot p$ is the element considered in (3). By Proposition 3.2(2),

$$\mathcal{R}(\langle \epsilon, \tau, \sigma \rangle \cdot p \,\tilde{\parallel}\, \mathcal{M}[\![\mathcal{C}(B_2)]\!])(\epsilon) \subseteq \mathcal{R}(\mathcal{M}[\![\mathcal{C}(A_1)]\!] \,\tilde{\parallel}\, \mathcal{M}[\![\mathcal{C}(B_2)]\!])(\epsilon)$$

Since $A_1 \parallel B_2$ always deadlock, we have by **P1**, **P2** and **P3** that $\alpha = dd$. Therefore

$$\begin{aligned} \langle \vartheta, dd \rangle &\in \mathcal{R}(\langle \epsilon, \tau, \sigma \rangle \cdot p \,\tilde{\parallel}\, \mathcal{M}[\![B_2]\!])(\epsilon) \\ &\subseteq \mathcal{R}(\mathcal{M}[\![\mathcal{C}(A \parallel B)]\!])(\epsilon) && \text{(by Proposition 3.2 (2 and 3) and by (2))} \\ &= \mathcal{S}[\![\mathcal{C}(A \parallel B)]\!](\epsilon) && \text{(by Theorem 2.4 (correctness))} \end{aligned}$$

□

In a similar way we can prove that CSP$_\mathcal{I}$ cannot be embedded in CSP$_\emptyset$:

Theorem 3.4 CSP$_\mathcal{I} \not\leq$ CSP$_\emptyset$.

4 The class ACSP$_\mathcal{G}$

In this section we present the ACSP$_\mathcal{G}$ family. The members of this class are simplified versions of ACSP dialects [13] with the difference that we consider, for the sake of uniformity with the synchronous case, also output guards (not present in [13]).

The syntax of the languages of the ACSP$_\mathcal{G}$ family is defined in the same way as for CSP$_\mathcal{G}$ but for the communication actions: outputting a value v along a channel c is now indicated by $c!!v$, and receiving a value by $c??x$.

$$A ::= Stop \mid c!!t; A \mid c??x; A \mid a; A \mid A \parallel A \mid G$$

$$G ::= g \rightarrow A \mid a \rightarrow A \mid G + G$$

Semantically, we do not require synchronization on complementary events: outputting a value v along a channel c does not need to take place at the same time as a corresponding input action $c??x$. The only restriction is that an input action on a channel c can take place only if at least one output action on c has been performed (by another process), and the corresponding value has not yet been "consumed" by another input action on c. In other words, a channel is seen as a buffer. Outputting a value corresponds to adding it to the buffer, and inputting a value corresponds to reading and retrieving a value present in the buffer. There are various design options concerning the buffers. First of all, a buffer can be *ordered* or *unordered*. In the first case there are various strategies, FIFO, LIFO etc. The most "natural" is the FIFO: an input reads and consumes the first value sent and not yet consumed. This is the solution adopted in standard ACSP [12, 13]. For the sake of simplicity, we consider here unordered buffers (bags). However, the results we present can be adapted to the ordered buffers (the only non-obvious case is $ACSP_{\mathcal{I}} \leq CSP_{\mathcal{I}}$, for which we have to require explicitly that communication is one-to-one).

The state of a channel modeled as a bag is a multiset of values. An output action adds the corresponding value, whereas an input action reads and retrieves a value nondeterministically selected . An input action suspends in case the channel is empty.

The operational model of $ACSP_{\mathcal{G}}$ is based upon a transition system T' that is defined in the same way as T (the transition system for $CSP_{\mathcal{G}}$) but for the last rule (synchronous communication) which is omitted. Formally:

$$T' = (Conf, \bigcup_{e \in E} \xrightarrow{e})$$

where *Conf* is defined as in T and the transition relations $\xrightarrow{e}$ are defined by the rules **R0-R4** of Table 1. (Replacing, of course, $c?$ by $c??$ and $c!$ by $c!!$.)

The semantics $\mathcal{M}$ defined for $CSP_{\mathcal{G}}$ can be adopted also for $ACSP_{\mathcal{G}}$ because T' is just a sub-transition system of T. (Of course, $c?$ and $c!$ have to be replaced by $c??$ and $c!!$. The new model will be denoted by $\mathcal{M}'$.) The compositionality of $\mathcal{M}'$ is shown in a similar way, the only difference being the definition of the parallel operator, which is defined only in terms of the leftmerge, i.e., we do not have the synchronization merge. To extract the observables from the denotation of a program we have to modify the definition of the abstraction operator $\mathcal{R}$. For this purpose we add a parameter which assigns to each channel a multiset of values. The execution of an output action then will consists in adding the value sent to the channel, and the execution of an input action in retrieving a value from the channel. The set of assignments of multisets to channels is denoted by $(b \in)B = Chan \to \mathcal{P}_m(Val)$, where $\mathcal{P}_m(Val)$ denotes the set of multisets of values. Given a multiset m and a value v the multisets $m \setminus v$ and $m \cup v$ denote the result of deleting a copy of v from m, and adding a copy of v, respectively.

Definition 4.1
The operator $\mathcal{R}' : P \to B \to State \to (State \times \{ss, dd\})$ *is given by*

$$\begin{aligned}\mathcal{R}'(p)(b)(\sigma) = \; & \{\mathcal{R}'(q)(b)(\sigma') : \langle \sigma, \tau, \sigma' \rangle \cdot q \in p\} \\ & \cup \\ & \{\mathcal{R}'(q)(b\{b(c) \cup v/c\})(\sigma') : \langle \sigma, c!!v, \sigma' \rangle \cdot q \rangle \in p\} \\ & \cup \\ & \{\mathcal{R}'(q)(b\{b(c) \setminus v)/c\})(\sigma') : \langle \sigma, c??v, \sigma' \rangle \cdot q \in p \wedge v \in b(c)\} \\ & \cup \\ & \{\langle \sigma, dd \rangle : \{\langle \sigma, e, \sigma' \rangle : \langle \sigma, e, \sigma' \rangle \cdot q \in p \text{ and if } e = c??v \text{ then } v \in b(c)\} = \emptyset\}\end{aligned}$$

Here p is assumed to be not empty, for $p = \emptyset$ *we define* $\mathcal{R}'(\emptyset)(b)(\sigma) = \{\langle \sigma, ss \rangle\}$.

Definition 4.2 *The observables of the class* $ACSP_{\mathcal{G}}$ *are given by the function* $\mathcal{S}' : ACSP_{\mathcal{G}} \to State \to (State \times \{ss, dd\})$ *defined as follows:*

$$\mathcal{S}' = \mathcal{R}' \circ \mathcal{M}'(\emptyset)$$

where $\emptyset$ *represents the function that assigns to every channel a empty multiset (at the beginning of the computation, all buffers are assumed to be empty).*

5 The ACSP hierarchy

In this section we study the relation between $ACSP_{\emptyset}$, $ACSP_{\mathcal{I}}$ and $ACSP_{\mathcal{I} \cup \mathcal{O}}$ (denoted by ACSP).

As in the synchronous class, we have the obvious embeddings due to the subset relations:

Proposition 5.1 $ACSP_{\emptyset} \leq ACSP_{\mathcal{I}} \leq ACSP$.

The relation between $ACSP_{\emptyset}$ and $ACSP_{\mathcal{I}}$ is strict, namely:

Theorem 5.2 $\mathrm{ACSP}_{\mathcal{I}} \not\leq \mathrm{ACSP}_{\emptyset}$

Proof Consider the processes $A_1 = c_1??x_1 \rightarrow Stop$, $A_2 = c_2??x_2 \rightarrow Stop$, and $B = c_1!!v; Stop$. with $c_1 \neq c_2$, and let $A = A = A_1 + A_2$. We have that

$$\mathcal{S}[A \parallel B](\epsilon) = \{(\{v_1/x_1\}, ss)\}. \tag{4}$$

The rest of the proof proceeds as in Theorem 3.4, by showing that there exists an element $(\vartheta, dd) \in \mathcal{S}[C(A \parallel B)](\epsilon)$, which, together with (4), contradicts **P3**. □

One might now expect a separation between ACSP and $\mathrm{ACSP}_{\mathcal{I}}$, like the one for CSP and $\mathrm{CSP}_{\mathcal{I}}$, but this is not the case. In fact, there is an asymmetry between ACSP and CSP: the output actions, in ACSP, do not synchronize with the corresponding input actions, they can always proceed independently from the other processes. As a consequence, a choice guarded by output actions is an *internal choice*. This suggests how to compile ACSP into $\mathrm{ACSP}_{\mathcal{I}}$: it is sufficient to transform the output guarded statements in sequential statements guarded by a *Skip* action. All the others operators are left unchanged.

Definition 5.3 (A compiler C from ACSP into $\mathrm{ACSP}_{\mathcal{I}}$) . *The only non-trivial case is given by the translation of the statement* $c!! \rightarrow A$:

$$C(c!!t \rightarrow A) = Skip \rightarrow c!!t; C(A)$$

The compiler C, and the decoder $\mathcal{D}$ defined as the identity function, obviously satisfy the conditions **P1-P3**. Furthermore, they constitute an embedding of ACSP into $\mathrm{ACSP}_{\mathcal{I}}$.

Theorem 5.4 $\mathrm{ACSP} \leq \mathrm{ACSP}_{\mathcal{I}}$.

The proof is based on the following lemma, which shows the correctness of the compiler defined above.

Lemma 5.5 *For every statement A in* ACSP, $b \in Chan \rightarrow \mathcal{P}_m(Val)$, *state* σ, *we have*

$$\mathcal{R}'(\mathcal{M}'[A])(b)(\sigma) = \mathcal{R}'(\mathcal{M}'[C(A)])(b)(\sigma)$$

Proof Induction on the structural complexity of A. □

6 Comparing CSP and ACSP

The main result of this section is the separation between CSP and ACSP. This result follows from the relations established so far and the the fact that $\mathrm{ACSP}_{\mathcal{I}}$ can be embedded into $\mathrm{CSP}_{\mathcal{I}}$, that we show now.

The only non-trivial case, in the definition of a compiler, is the translation of communication actions. The asynchronism between an output action and the corresponding input action can be simulated, in the synchronous framework, in the following way. For every process which performs an output action on c we create a parallel process which behaves like a sort of one-position buffer: it inputs the value and outputs it later on. In order to prevent the sender to communicate directly with the receiver (that would cause the buffer to become blocked) the original output and the input of the buffer will take place on a different channel b_c.

Note that this solution would work also in case of (recursively defined) infinite processes, but we must then assume that communication is many-to-many (since many parallel one-position buffer processes inputting on b_c or outputting on c can be created), and it works only for bag-like channels (since the parallel one-position buffers may interleave the output actions in arbitrary ways). However, if we assume one-to-one communication, there is an alternative way to simulate asynchronous communication in $\mathrm{CSP}_{\mathcal{I}}$ by means of ordered buffers (see [4, 12]). In case of infinite processes the buffers will have to be unbounded (i.e. the corresponding processes can be infinite).

Definition 6.1 (A compiler C from $\mathrm{ACSP}_{\mathcal{I}}$ into $\mathrm{CSP}_{\mathcal{I}}$) .

- $C(Stop) = Stop$
- $C(c!!t; A) = (b_c!t; C(A)) \parallel (b_c?x \rightarrow c!x)$ *where b_c is a new channel not occurring in* $C(A)$.

- $\mathcal{C}(c??x; A) = c?x; \mathcal{C}(A)$
- $\mathcal{C}(a; A) = a; \mathcal{C}(A)$
- $\mathcal{C}(A_1 \parallel A_2) = \mathcal{C}(A_1) \parallel \mathcal{C}(A_2)$
- $\mathcal{C}(A_1 + A_2) = \mathcal{C}(A_1) + \mathcal{C}(A_2)$
- $\mathcal{C}(c??x \to A) = c?x \to \mathcal{C}(A)$
- $\mathcal{C}(a \to A) = a \to \mathcal{C}(A)$

The compiler $\mathcal{C}$, and the decoder $\mathcal{D}$ defined as the identity function, obviously satisfy the conditions **P1-P3**. Furthermore, they constitute an embedding of $\text{ACSP}_{\mathcal{I}}$ into $\text{CSP}_{\mathcal{I}}$.

Note that it is not necessary to use a input guard in the definition of the buffer process, we could just use a sequential statement, namely $\mathcal{C}(c!!t; A) = (b_c!t; \mathcal{C}(A)) \parallel (b_c?x; c!x)$. This leads immediately to the definition of a compiler of $\text{ACSP}_{\emptyset}$ in $\text{CSP}_{\emptyset}$.

Theorem 6.2 $\text{ACSP}_{\mathcal{I}} \leq \text{CSP}_{\mathcal{I}}$, *and* $\text{ACSP}_{\emptyset} \leq \text{CSP}_{\emptyset}$.

The proof is based on the following lemma, which shows the correctness of the compiler(s) defined above.

Lemma 6.3 *For every statement A of* $\text{ACSP}_{\mathcal{I}}$ *(*$\text{ACSP}_{\emptyset}$*), $b \in Chan \to \mathcal{P}_m(Val)$, state σ, we have*

$$\mathcal{R}'(\mathcal{M}'[\![A]\!])(b)(\sigma) = \mathcal{R}(\mathcal{M}[\![\mathcal{C}(A) \parallel A_b]\!])(\sigma)$$

where $A_b = \|_c \|_{v \in b(c)}\, c!v$.

Proof Induction on the structural complexity of A. □

Now we can prove the following theorem which separates CSP from ACSP:

Theorem 6.4 CSP $\not\leq$ ACSP.

Proof Suppose that CSP $\leq$ ACSP. Since ACSP $\leq \text{ACSP}_{\mathcal{I}} \leq \text{CSP}_{\mathcal{I}}$, we would have that CSP $\leq \text{CSP}_{\mathcal{I}}$, which contradicts Theorem 3.3. □

Note that on the other hand we have ACSP $\leq$ CSP.

There are still two questions: at which level $\text{ACSP}_{\mathcal{I}}$ and $\text{ACSP}_{\emptyset}$ are situated, with respect to $\text{CSP}_{\mathcal{I}}$ and $\text{CSP}_{\emptyset}$? The answer to these questions depends on the assumption that communication is one-to-one. If this is the case, then $\text{ACSP}_{\mathcal{I}}$ can embed $\text{CSP}_{\mathcal{I}}$, and $\text{ACSP}_{\emptyset}$ can embed $\text{CSP}_{\emptyset}$. In fact, synchronous communication can be simulated asynchronously via acknowledgement messages [21]: every process which performs an input action will send an acknowledgement, and each process which performs an output action will wait for the corresponding acknowledgement. Of course, this technique does not work when the communication is many-to-many: one sender could "steal" the acknowledgement directed to an other process.

Definition 6.5 (A compiler $\mathcal{C}$ from $\text{CSP}_{\mathcal{I}}$ into $\text{ACSP}_{\mathcal{I}}$) .

- $\mathcal{C}(Stop) = Stop$
- $\mathcal{C}(c!t; A) = c!!t; ack_c??x; \mathcal{C}(A)$
- $\mathcal{C}(c?x; A) = c??x; ack_c!!ok; \mathcal{C}(A)$
- $\mathcal{C}(a; A) = a; \mathcal{C}(A)$
- $\mathcal{C}(A_1 \parallel A_2) = \mathcal{C}(A_1) \parallel \mathcal{C}(A_2)$
- $\mathcal{C}(A_1 + A_2) = \mathcal{C}(A_1) + \mathcal{C}(A_2)$
- $\mathcal{C}(c?x \to A) = c??x \to ack_c!!ok; \mathcal{C}(A)$

- $\mathcal{C}(a \to A) = a \to \mathcal{C}(A)$

The compiler $\mathcal{C}$ from $\mathrm{CSP}_{\emptyset}$ into $\mathrm{ACSP}_{\emptyset}$ can be obtained just by dropping the last but one line in the previous definition.

The compiler $\mathcal{C}$, and the decoder $\mathcal{D}$ defined as the identity function, obviously satisfy the conditions **P1-P3**. Furthermore, they constitute an embedding of $\mathrm{ACSP}_{\mathcal{I}}$ into $\mathrm{CSP}_{\mathcal{I}}$ ($\mathrm{CSP}_{\emptyset}$ in $\mathrm{ACSP}_{\emptyset}$).

Theorem 6.6 *If the communication is one-to-one, then* $\mathrm{CSP}_{\mathcal{I}} \leq \mathrm{ACSP}_{\mathcal{I}}$, *and* $\mathrm{CSP}_{\emptyset} \leq \mathrm{ACSP}_{\emptyset}$.

The proof is based on the following lemma, which shows the correctness of the compiler(s).

Lemma 6.7 *For every statement A of* $\mathrm{CSP}_{\mathcal{I}}$ *(*$\mathrm{CSP}_{\emptyset}$*) and state σ we have*

$$\mathcal{R}(\mathcal{M}[\![A]\!])(\sigma) = \mathcal{R}'(\mathcal{M}'[\![\mathcal{C}(A)]\!])(\emptyset)(\sigma)$$

Proof Induction on the structural complexity of A. □

7 Conclusions and future work

We have applied our notion of embedding to establish a hierarchy between various sublanguages of CSP and ACSP, see Figure 4.

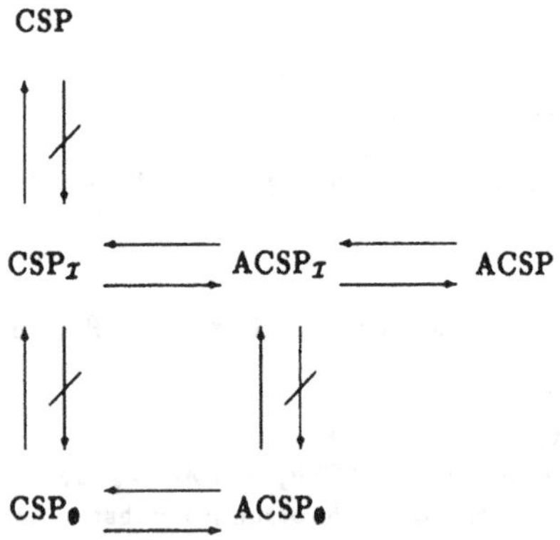

Figure 4: The CSP-ACSP hierarchy.

It is worthwhile to remark that the diagram actually should hold for every "reasonable" notion of embedding. In particular, $\mathrm{CSP}_{\emptyset} \leq \mathrm{CSP}_{\mathcal{I}} \leq \mathrm{CSP}$ and $\mathrm{ACSP}_{\emptyset} \leq \mathrm{ACSP}_{\mathcal{I}} \leq \mathrm{ACSP}$ hold for every notion of embedding subsuming the sublanguage relation, and $\mathrm{CSP} \not\leq \mathrm{CSP}_{\mathcal{I}} \not\leq \mathrm{CSP}_{\emptyset}$ is justified by the existence of algorithms expressible in one language and not in the other [3]. Furthermore, $\mathrm{ACSP} \leq \mathrm{ACSP}_{\mathcal{I}}$ holds because the local nature of asynchronous output guards makes them superfluous [13]. Finally, $\mathrm{ACSP}_{\mathcal{I}}$ can be implemented in $\mathrm{CSP}_{\mathcal{I}}$ by means of buffering techniques [12]. Thus, the difference in the expressivity of CSP and ACSP seems to be a general result.

If we compare the results of this paper with the ones in [8], it is quite surprising to see that the Concurrent Constraint hierarchy strictly corresponds to the CSP hierarchy. Since Concurrent Constraint is an asynchronous paradigm, we would rather expect a correspondence with the ACSP family! To our opinion, this is due to the fact that Concurrent Constraint has the possibility to express choices guarded by tell primitives, which enforce a test for consistency, so depending upon the previous tell actions done by the environment. This mutual dependency of the same kind of action cannot be expressed in any way in ACSP (input only depends on output, and output does not depend on any other action). In CSP we have an indirect mutual dependency (input on output and output on input). Why exactly this mutual dependency determinates a growth in the expressive power, has still to be understood.

The characteristic features of our notion of embedding are compositionality of the compiler and termination invariance of the decoder. Actually, the requirement **P2** on the compiler is actually more restrictive than simple compositionality w.r.t. $+$ and $\|$ (i.e., the translation of these operators in a combination of operators), and it can be justified as follows. Since the languages we study extensions of each other, and the differences between them consist of the kind of the guard g in the guarded statement $g \rightarrow A$, we can phrase the problem of the expressive power of these languages as the question:

can a guard operator $g \rightarrow$ in L' be expressed in terms of the operators of L?

In other words,the question is whether a guard operator $g \rightarrow$ in L' can be translated into a context $c_g[\,]$ in L such that for every process A in L' we have

$$\mathcal{D}(\mathcal{O}[A']) = \mathcal{O}[A]$$

where A' is obtained by replacing every occurrence of a guard operator $g \rightarrow$ by $c_g[\,]$. (A similar formalization of language comparison is also studied in [10]). This amounts to require the existence of a translation that only transforms the guard operators and is invariant with respect to $+$ and $\|$. Such a translation can be seen as a particular case of a compiler that satisfies **P2**.

It would be interesting to study the consequences of adopting a weaker notion of compositionality. More generally a systematic study on the kind of restrictions imposed by the different requirements seems to be of interest. To this end several case studies can be considered. For example, is there (and should there be) a difference in expressive power between many-to-many channels and one-to-one channels, and how does the expressive power of CSP relate to other asynchronous languages (like the concurrent logic languages)?

Acknowledgements We thank Jan-Willem Klop, Joost Kok, Jan Rutten and Ehud Shapiro for stimulating discussions and encouragements. We thank the members of the C.W.I. concurrency group, J.W. de Bakker, F. Breugel, A. de Bruin, J.M. Jacquet, P. Knijnenburg, J. Kok, J. Rutten, E. de Vink and J. Warmerdam for their comments on preliminary versions of this paper. We acknowledge the department of Software Technology of CWI, and the Department of Computer Science at Utrecht University, for providing a stimulating working environment. Finally, we thank Krzysztof Apt for having suggested us relevant literature on the subject.

References

[1] J.C.M. Baeten, J.A. Bergstra, and J.-W. Klop. On the consistency of Koomen's fair abstraction rule. *Theoretical Computer Science*, 51(1,2):129–176, 1987.

[2] J.A. Bergstra and J.-W. Klop. Process algebra: specification and verification in bisimulation semantics. In *Mathematics and Computer Science II*, CWI Monographs, pages 61 – 94. North-Holland, 1986.

[3] L. Bougé. On the existence of symmetric algorithms to find leaders in networks of communicating sequential processes. *Acta Informatica*, 25:179–201, 1988.

[4] S.D. Brookes, C.A.R. Hoare, and W. Roscoe. A theory of communicating sequential processes. *Journal of ACM*, 31:499–560, 1984.

[5] A.K. Chandra and Z. Manna. The power of programming features. *J. Computer Languages*, 1:219–232, 1975.

[6] F.S. de Boer, J.N. Kok, C. Palamidessi, and J.J.M.M. Rutten. The failure of failures: Towards a paradigm for asynchronous communication. Technical Report RUU-CS-90-40, Department of Computer Science, University of Utrecht, 1990. A short version of this paper will appear in Proc. of CONCUR 91.

[7] F.S. de Boer and C. Palamidessi. Concurrent logic languages: Asynchronism and language comparison. In *Proc. of the North American Conference on Logic Programming*, Series in Logic Programming, pages 175–194. The MIT Press, 1990. Full version available as technical report TR 6/90, Dipartimento di Informatica, Università di Pisa.

[8] F.S. de Boer and C. Palamidessi. Embedding as a tool for language comparison. Technical Report CS-R9102, Centre for Mathematics and Computer Science (CWI), Amsterdam, 1991.

[9] R. de Simone. Higher-level synchronising devices in MEIJE-SCCS. *Theoretical Computer Science*, 37(3):245–267, 1985.

[10] M. Felleisen. On the expressive power of programming languages. In N. Jones, editor, *Proc. of the European Symposium on Programming*, volume 432 of *Lecture Notes in Computer Science*, pages 134 – 151. Springer-Verlag, 1990. Full version to appear in *Science of Computer Programming*.

[11] C.A.R. Hoare. Communicating sequential processes. *Communications of the ACM*, 21(8):666–677, 1978.

[12] He Jifeng, M.B. Josephs, and C.A.R. Hoare. A theory of synchrony and asynchrony. In *Proc. of IFIP Working Conference on Programming Concepts and Methods*, pages 459–478, 1990.

[13] M.B. Josephs, C.A.R. Hoare, and He Jifeng. A theory of asynchronous processes. Technical report, Oxford University Computing Laboratories, 1990.

[14] P.J. Landin. The next 700 programming languages. *Communications of the ACM*, 3(9):157–166, 1966.

[15] J. Parrow. The expressive power of parallelism. In *Proc. of PARLE 89*, volume 366 of *Lecture Notes in Computer Science*, pages 389–405. Springer-Verlag, 1989. Revised and extended version in SICS Research Report R90016.

[16] M.S. Paterson and C.E. Hewitt. Comparative schematology. In *Conf. Rec. ACM Conference on Concurrent Systems and Parallel Computation*, pages 119–127, 1970.

[17] J.C. Reynolds. GEDANKEN - a symple typeless language based on the principle of completeness and the reference concept. *Communications of the ACM*, 5(13):308–319, 1970.

[18] J.C. Reynolds. The essence of Algol. In J. de Bakker and van Vliet, editors, *Algorithmic Languages*, pages 345–372. North-Holland, Amsterdam, 1981.

[19] V.A. Saraswat and M. Rinard. Concurrent constraint programming. In *Proc. of the seventeenth ACM Symposium on Principles of Programming Languages*, pages 232–245. ACM, New York, 1990.

[20] E.Y. Shapiro. The family of concurrent logic programming languages. *ACM Computing Surveys*, 21(3):412–510, 1989.

[21] E.Y. Shapiro. Separating concurrent languages with categories of language embeddings. In *Proc. of STOCS*, 1991. To appear.

[22] G.L.Jr. Steele and G.J. Sussman. Lambda: The ultimate imperative. Technical Report Memo 353, MIT AI Lab., 1976.

[23] F. Vaandrager. Expressiveness results for process algebra. Technical report, MIT Lab. for Comp. Sci., Cambridge, USA, 1991.

A Conditional Operator for CCS

Juanito Camilleri *jacl@cl.cam.ac.uk*
Computer Laboratory, University of Cambridge,
New Museums Site, Cambridge CB2 3QG, England

Abstract

This paper investigates an extension of Milner's CCS with a conditional operator called *unless* [Cam90]. The agent $\mathcal{K} \rhd E$, pronounced E unless $\mathcal{K}$, behaves as E unless the environment is ready to perform any action in the set $\mathcal{K}$. This dependency on the set of actions the environment is ready to perform goes beyond that encountered in traditional CCS. Its expression is realised by an operational semantics in which transitions carry ready-sets (of the environment) as well as the normal action symbols from CCS. A notion of strong bisimulation is defined on conditional agents via this semantics. It is a congruence and satisfies new equational laws (including a new expansion law) which are shown to be complete for finite agents with the unless operator. The laws are conservative over agents of traditional CCS. The *unless* operator provides a rudimentary means of expressing bias (or priority) in the behaviour of agents; it is more expressive than the prisum operator presented in [CW91] and [Cam90].

1 Introduction

This paper augments Milner's CCS with a conditional operator called *unless*. The *unless* operator can be used to express the behaviour of an agent depending on which actions can take place next in the environment. We will show how the operator provides a syntactic means of expressing a priority structure on actions and moreover, that it can encode a form of multi-way synchronisation. The work presented here can be adopted as a formal semantic foundation for existing programming language constructs that embody the notion of priority between actions [Cam90] [Cam89].

The expressiveness of *unless* can specify a priority structure on actions that is both *dynamic* and *local*. Dynamic in the sense that the priority structure can change as execution proceeds. Local in the sense that the priority structure expressed need not be linear and therefore components of a system may behave independently according to a local bias.

Consider, for example, a reactive system *Sys* (see Fig.1). An agent A is busy-waiting for the environment to be able to perform $\overline{act}$. In the meantime, another agent B is *dormant*—i.e., it cannot react while A is busy-waiting. As soon as the environment can perform an $\overline{act}$ action, A is required to stop waiting immediately and it is expected to proceed to handshake with B. Following the communication, A is required to stop while B first reacts and then stops. This scenario can be specified very naturally using the *unless* operator. Suppose the agent $\mathcal{K} \rhd E$ behaves as E unless the environment is ready to perform any action in $\mathcal{K}$, then the system *Sys* can then be described as follows:

$$\begin{array}{lcl} Sys & \stackrel{def}{=} & (A \mid B)\backslash a \\ A & \stackrel{def}{=} & act.\overline{a}.0 \ + \ \{\overline{act}\} \rhd \tau.A \\ B & \stackrel{def}{=} & a.react.0 \end{array}$$

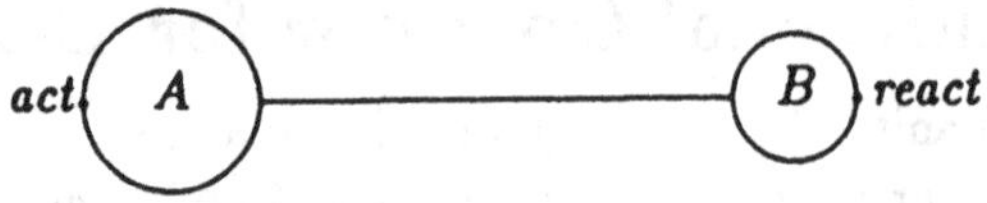

Figure 1: A simple reactive system.

In Section 5.1, we will show that the behaviour of *Sys* is equivalent to *Spec* defined as follows:

$$Spec \stackrel{def}{=} act.\tau.react.0 \; + \; \{\overline{act}\} \triangleright \tau.Spec$$

In other words, the unless operator allows agent A to give precedence to action *act* over the τ loop that represents busy-waiting. The semantics of *unless* guarantees that A stops busy-waiting as soon as the environment is ready to perform $\overline{act}$. This example illustrates the expressiveness of the *unless* operator; by relying on fairness and the conventional operators of CCS, one can only guarantee that if the environment can perform $\overline{act}$, then *eventually* the agent will stop busy-waiting. In system *Sys* however, we required the response to $\overline{act}$ to be immediate.

Now let us change the scene slightly. Suppose we do not insist that A stops busy-waiting as soon as the environment can perform an $\overline{act}$ action. We also require however, agent B to *react* immediately after A performs *act*—i.e., this should happen without an intermediate handshake between the two agents. In other words, the system comprising A and B should have the specification $Spec_0$ defined as follows:

$$Spec_0 \stackrel{def}{=} act.react.0 \; + \; \tau.Spec_0$$

In CCS, the silent action τ plays two roles. First, it can be viewed as an unobservable *skip* operation. Second, it denotes a handshake between two complementary actions. The silent action τ in $Spec_0$ adopts the former use.

In this paper, we introduce a new symbol ι (iota) distinct from any other action; ι is referred to as *idling*. It is intended that *idling* represents a special kind of *skip* operation; namely a skip operation that may be *detected* by the environment. We use the word 'detected' and not 'observed' to emphasise that ι is not intended to have a complement in the traditional sense. Now consider an agent of the form $\{\iota\} \triangleright E$: this agent behaves as E unless *idling* can be detected in the environment.

Sometimes, one needs to suppress or localise an agent's ability to detect idling. For this purpose a new operator $\langle\,\rangle$ is introduced to the language of expressions; the operator is called *masking*. Agent $\langle E\rangle$ behaves as E when E cannot detect *idling* in its environment. Masking does not affect an agent's ability to perform idling. To summarise, we say that an agent A *detects idling* in another agent B, if A is not masked and *idling* occurs as a prefix in one of the sub-agents of B.

Now suppose we replace the silent action in $Spec_0$ by an idling action to yield:

$$Spec_1 \stackrel{def}{=} act.react.0 \; + \; \iota.Spec_1$$

Intuitively, we expect this specification to be equivalent to Sys_1 defined as follows:

$$
\begin{array}{lcl}
Sys_1 & \stackrel{def}{=} & (A \mid B) \\
A & \stackrel{def}{=} & act.0 + \iota.A \\
B & \stackrel{def}{=} & \{\iota\} \rhd react.0
\end{array}
$$

The combined use of conditional agents with idling allows B to detect A's ability to idle. Masking $(A \mid B)$ makes B's dependency on idling local to $(A \mid B)$. In Sys_1, B is unable to *react* until A performs *act*, and agent B will *react* immediately after A performs *act*.

One may question whether the effect of the *unless* operator can be implemented. In existing programming languages, handshaking between processes is implemented using channels through which data may be exchanged, however at times, handshaking is used merely to synchronise the behaviour of two processes without the exchange of data. The conditional operator presented here provides another means of synchronisation which does not entail data exchange; the operator provides the means for an agent to infer information about, and so behave depending on, the state of its environment. Moreover, the introduction of *idling* to the algebra allows one to specify the behaviour of a process depending on its ability to detect idling in its environment.

The unless operator seems to lend itself to implementation. Consider the process $\{a_0, \ldots, a_n\} \rhd E$. The process remains dormant while any of the channels a_0 to a_n are ready to participate in a handshake, otherwise it behaves like process E. One can implement detectable idling by associating a status flag with each process. The flag becomes true when a process that is idling requires its environment to detect this fact; the flag is false otherwise. The flag can be viewed as a dummy channel that cannot transport data, but, merely records the status of the process. A process can detect idling in its environment if it can detect idling in one of the components of its environment. Masking a process would in effect force it to ignore the environment's ability to perform an idling action; the process would just assume that its environment cannot idle.

2 CCS with *unless*, *masking* and *idling*

Suppose we simply augment CCS with terms of the form $\mathcal{K} \rhd E$ where $\mathcal{K}$ is a set of actions and E is any expression in the augmented language. We would then allow expressions such as $((a.0 + \{\overline{a}\} \rhd b.0) \mid (\overline{b}.0 + \{b\} \rhd \overline{a}.0)) \setminus \{a, b\}$. Can this agent perform a τ action? One can argue both ways. Partly to avoid deciding such questions, and partly to allow a simple expansion law (see Fig.5), we restrict the syntax of agent expressions. We will break the symmetry in CCS that exists between actions a and their complements $\overline{a}$, and distinguish between i-actions and o-actions:

- an i-action is a named action in $\mathcal{A}$ with typical elements $a, b, c, \ldots$,
- an o-action is a co-named action in $\overline{\mathcal{A}}$ with typical elements $\overline{a}, \overline{b}, \overline{c}, \ldots$,
- a *silent action* is represented by τ and *idling* is represented by ι.

We shall denote by *Act* the set of *actions* $\mathcal{A} \cup \overline{\mathcal{A}} \cup \{\tau, \iota\}$ ranged over by α. We shall understand the operation $\overline{(\,)}$ to act so $a \mapsto \overline{a}$, $\overline{a} \mapsto a$. The operation $\overline{(\,)}$ acts as identity on both τ and ι.

CCS augmented with the unless and masking operators is called CCS$^{\triangleright}$. Let $\mathcal{E}^{\triangleright}$ be the set of agent expressions with typical elements $E, F \ldots$, and let $\mathcal{G}^{\triangleright}$ be the set of conditional expressions with typical elements $G, H \ldots$. Let X range over the set of agent variables and P, Q and N range over the set of closed terms $\mathcal{P}^{\triangleright}$. The syntax of CCS$^{\triangleright}$ expressions is defined as follows:

$$G ::= X \mid 0 \mid a.E \mid \tau.E \mid G \backslash L \mid G[f] \mid G + G \mid fix(X = G) \mid \mathcal{K} \triangleright G \mid \langle G \rangle$$
$$E ::= X \mid 0 \mid \alpha.E \mid E \backslash L \mid E[f] \mid E + E \mid E|E \mid fix(X = E) \mid \langle E \rangle \mid G$$

We assume that the relabelling function f in $E[f]$ is injective and maps $\mathcal{A}$ to $\mathcal{A}$ and $\overline{\mathcal{A}}$ to $\overline{\mathcal{A}}$. Furthermore, let L in $E \setminus L$ be a subset of $\mathcal{A}$. In other words, we do not allow idling to be restricted, but of course, a term's ability to detect idling in its environment can be suppressed using the masking operator as illustrated in the introduction.

The condition-set $\mathcal{K}$ is a subset of $\overline{\mathcal{A}} \cup \{\iota\}$. Notice that o-action prefixes and *idling* prefixes are prohibited in conditional terms G in $\mathcal{G}^{\triangleright}$. The term $\mathcal{K} \triangleright G$ is expected to behave as follows:

- if $\overline{a} \in \overline{\mathcal{A}}$ is also an element of $\mathcal{K}$, then G can perform an i-action provided the environment is not ready to perform $\overline{a}$,
- if *idling* ι is an element of $\mathcal{K}$, then G can perform an i-action provided idling cannot be detected in the environment.

Finally, let recursion be guarded.

3 Operational semantics

The behaviour of CCS$^{\triangleright}$ agents is formalised by a transition relation $\vdash_R E \xrightarrow{\alpha} E'$ to be understood as meaning: in an environment which is ready to perform the actions R, the agent E can perform an action α to become the agent E'. The ready-set R is a subset of $\overline{\mathcal{A}} \cup \{\iota\}$. The transition relation will be defined in terms of a *ready-function*. Given an agent E, the ready-function yields the set containing those actions in $\overline{\mathcal{A}} \cup \{\iota\}$ that E can do next in any environment. The ready-function is defined by the rules of Fig.2.

The rules defining the transition relation are presented in Fig.3. Since the other rules are similar to those of CCS, we comment only on the rules for prefixing with *idling*, *unless*, masking and composition. Rule Pre_ι states that a term which is prefixed by *idling* can perform ι irrespective of the ready-set of the environment. Rule Cond states that $\mathcal{K} \triangleright G$ can perform α in an environment that is ready to perform R, provided G can perform α and none of the actions in $\mathcal{K}$ are elements of R. The rule Mask states that a masked agent is not able to detect idling in its environment, however masking does not suppress an agent's ability to perform an *idling* action. Now consider the rule Com_ϵ for composition under the assumptions that E re R_0 and F re R_1. The rule takes account of the fact that the assumption that the environment of $E|F$ is ready to do R amounts to the assumption on E that its environment is ready with $R \cup R_1$, and similarly that F's environment is ready with $R \cup R_0$. If under these assumptions E and F can perform complementary actions then their composition can synchronise. The rule Com_ϵ has a pleasing symmetry,

$$\mathsf{re}\,(\mathrm{i})\quad \mathcal{K} \rhd G \;\mathsf{re}\; \emptyset \qquad\qquad \mathsf{re}\,(\mathrm{ii})\quad \frac{E \;\mathsf{re}\; R}{\langle E\rangle \;\mathsf{re}\; R}$$

$$\mathsf{re}\,(\mathrm{iii})\quad 0 \;\mathsf{re}\; \emptyset \qquad\qquad \mathsf{re}\,(\mathrm{iv})\quad a.E \;\mathsf{re}\; \emptyset$$

$$\mathsf{re}\,(\mathrm{v})\quad \iota.E \;\mathsf{re}\; \{\iota\} \qquad\qquad \mathsf{re}\,(\mathrm{vi})\quad \tau.E \;\mathsf{re}\; \emptyset$$

$$\mathsf{re}\,(\mathrm{vii})\quad \overline{a}.E \;\mathsf{re}\; \{\overline{a}\}$$

$$\mathsf{re}\,(\mathrm{viii})\quad \frac{E_0 \;\mathsf{re}\; R_0 \qquad E_1 \;\mathsf{re}\; R_1}{E_0 + E_1 \;\mathsf{re}\; R_0 \cup R_1} \qquad\qquad \mathsf{re}\,(\mathrm{ix})\quad \frac{E \;\mathsf{re}\; R}{E \setminus L \;\mathsf{re}\; R - \overline{L}}\;(L \subseteq \mathcal{A})$$

$$\mathsf{re}\,(\mathrm{x})\quad \frac{E[fix(X = E)/X] \;\mathsf{re}\; R}{fix(X = E) \;\mathsf{re}\; R} \qquad\qquad \mathsf{re}\,(\mathrm{xi})\quad \frac{E \;\mathsf{re}\; R}{E[f] \;\mathsf{re}\; f(R)}$$

$$\mathsf{re}\,(\mathrm{xii})\quad \frac{E \;\mathsf{re}\; R_0 \qquad F \;\mathsf{re}\; R_1}{E|F \;\mathsf{re}\; R_0 \cup R_1}$$

Figure 2: The definition of the ready-function.

though note that by virtue of Prop.3.1 the requirements of Com_c, $\mathrm{Com}_\bullet$ and $\mathrm{Com}_\flat$ can be relaxed when they involve o-actions or *idling*. Consequently, these rules could be replaced by two rules taking account of the fact that transitions associated with o-actions or *idling* do not depend on ready-sets of the environment.

Proposition 3.1 *For terms E, E' and all $R, S \subseteq \overline{\mathcal{A}} \cup \{\iota\}$, $\alpha \in \overline{\mathcal{A}} \cup \{\iota\}$,*

$$\vdash_R E \xrightarrow{\alpha} E' \iff \vdash_S E \xrightarrow{\alpha} E'.$$

Proposition 3.2 *The ready-relation* re *is a function in the sense that $E \,\mathrm{re}\, R$ and $E \,\mathrm{re}\, R'$ implies $R = R'$. Moreover*

$$E \,\mathrm{re}\, S \iff S = \{\alpha \in \overline{\mathcal{A}} \cup \{\iota\} \ : \ \forall R \exists E'. \vdash_R E \xrightarrow{\alpha} E'\}$$

Notation: In future we will use $\mathrm{re}(E)$ for the ready-set of E—justified because the ready-relation is a function.

CCS$^\triangleright$ essentially extends CCS; once we restrict to unconditional (i.e., *unless-free*), unmasked (i.e., *masking-free*) and *idling-free* agents, the transition relations agree but for the extra decoration of ready-sets on the relations.

Proposition 3.3 *For a term E, that is unless-free, masking-free and idling-free,*
$E \xrightarrow{\alpha} E'$ in CCS *iff*
$\vdash_R E \xrightarrow{\alpha} E'$ in CCS$^\triangleright$ *for all $R \subseteq \overline{\mathcal{A}} \cup \{\iota\}$ such that, if $\alpha \in \mathcal{A}$ then $\overline{\alpha} \in R$.*

4 Strong bisimulation

We take a generalisation of Milner's strong bisimulation as our central equivalence between agents.

Definition 4.1 A relation $\mathcal{Q} \subseteq \mathcal{P}^\triangleright \times \mathcal{P}^\triangleright$ is a strong bisimulation with respect to the operational semantics, if $(P, Q) \in \mathcal{Q}$ implies, for all $\alpha \in Act$ and for all $R \subseteq \overline{\mathcal{A}} \cup \{\iota\}$,

1. whenever $\vdash_R P \xrightarrow{\alpha} P'$ then, for some Q', $\vdash_R Q \xrightarrow{\alpha} Q'$ and $(P', Q') \in \mathcal{Q}$,

2. whenever $\vdash_R Q \xrightarrow{\alpha} Q'$ then, for some P', $\vdash_R P \xrightarrow{\alpha} P'$ and $(P', Q') \in \mathcal{Q}$.

Definition 4.2 Let the relation $\sim$ on agents be defined by:

$$P \sim Q \text{ iff } (P, Q) \in \mathcal{Q} \text{ for some strong bisimulation } \mathcal{Q}.$$

As emphasised by Park, it follows by basic fixed-point theory that $\sim$ is an equivalence relation and the largest strong bisimulation, and as such it is amenable to the proof technique: to show $P \sim Q$ it is sufficient to exhibit a strong bisimulation containing (P, Q).

This technique is used to show that equivalence is a congruence, i.e., it is substitutive under the constructs of CCS$^\triangleright$ as well as under recursive definition. The proof follows the standard lines of [Mil89], though with this more intricate operational semantics, it is necessary to check that the strong equivalence of two agents implies that they have the same ready-sets (this is needed in proving the congruence of $\sim$ with respect to parallel composition):

$$\textsf{Pre}_a \quad \vdash_R a.E \xrightarrow{a} E \ \text{ if } \bar{a} \in R \qquad\qquad \textsf{Pre}_b \quad \vdash_R \iota.E \xrightarrow{\iota} E$$

$$\textsf{Pre}_c \quad \vdash_R \bar{a}.E \xrightarrow{\bar{a}} E \qquad\qquad \textsf{Pre}_d \quad \vdash_R \tau.E \xrightarrow{\tau} E$$

$$\textsf{Mask} \quad \frac{\vdash_{R-\{\iota\}} E \xrightarrow{\alpha} E'}{\vdash_R \langle E \rangle \xrightarrow{\alpha} \langle E' \rangle}$$

$$\textsf{Cond} \quad \frac{\vdash_R G \xrightarrow{\alpha} E'}{\vdash_R \mathcal{K} \triangleright G \xrightarrow{\alpha} E'} \quad (\mathcal{K} \cap R = \emptyset)$$

$$\textsf{Sum}_a \quad \frac{\vdash_R E \xrightarrow{\alpha} E'}{\vdash_R E + F \xrightarrow{\alpha} E'} \qquad\qquad \textsf{Sum}_b \quad \frac{\vdash_R F \xrightarrow{\alpha} F'}{\vdash_R E + F \xrightarrow{\alpha} F'}$$

$$\textsf{Res} \quad \frac{\vdash_{R-\overline{L}} E \xrightarrow{\alpha} E'}{\vdash_R E \setminus L \xrightarrow{\alpha} E' \setminus L} \ (\alpha \notin \overline{L}) \qquad\qquad \textsf{Rel} \quad \frac{\vdash_R E \xrightarrow{\alpha} E'}{\vdash_{f(R)} E[f] \xrightarrow{f(\alpha)} E'[f]}$$

$$\textsf{Com}_a \quad \frac{\vdash_{R \cup R_1} E \xrightarrow{\alpha} E' \qquad F \ \textsf{re} \ R_1}{\vdash_R E|F \xrightarrow{\alpha} E'|F} \quad (\alpha \in \mathcal{A} \Longrightarrow \bar{\alpha} \in R)$$

$$\textsf{Com}_b \quad \frac{\vdash_{R \cup R_0} F \xrightarrow{\alpha} F' \qquad E \ \textsf{re} \ R_0}{\vdash_R E|F \xrightarrow{\alpha} E|F'} \quad (\alpha \in \mathcal{A} \Longrightarrow \bar{\alpha} \in R)$$

$$\textsf{Com}_c \quad \frac{\vdash_{R \cup R_1} E \xrightarrow{\alpha} E' \quad E \ \textsf{re} \ R_0 \quad \vdash_{R \cup R_0} F \xrightarrow{\bar{\alpha}} F' \quad F \ \textsf{re} \ R_1}{\vdash_R E|F \xrightarrow{\tau} E'|F'} \quad (\alpha \notin \{\tau, \iota\})$$

$$\textsf{Rec} \quad \frac{\vdash_R E[fix(X = E)/X] \xrightarrow{\alpha} E'}{\vdash_R fix(X = E) \xrightarrow{\alpha} E'}$$

Figure 3: The definition of the transition relation.

Lemma 4.1 *If $P \sim Q$ then* $\mathrm{re}(P) = \mathrm{re}(Q)$.

Proposition 4.2 *Let $P_1 \sim P_2$, then*
(1) $\alpha.P_1 \sim \alpha.P_2$ *(3)* $\mathcal{K} \rhd P_1 \sim \mathcal{K} \rhd P_2$ *(5)* $P_1|Q \sim P_2|Q$ *(7)* $P_1[f] \sim P_2[f]$
(2) $P_1 + Q \sim P_2 + Q$ *(4)* $P_1 \setminus L \sim P_2 \setminus L$ *(6)* $\langle P_1 \rangle \sim \langle P_2 \rangle$

Thus strong equivalence is preserved by prefixing, summation, unless, parallel composition, restriction, relabelling and masking. We remark that, due to the syntactic restriction on conditional terms, P_1 and P_2 in statement *(3)* must be terms in $\mathcal{G}^{\rhd}$, otherwise $\mathcal{K} \rhd P_1, \mathcal{K} \rhd P_2$ etc. would not be terms in $\mathcal{E}^{\rhd}$. For example, let $E \equiv (\overline{a}.0 + b.0) \setminus a$ and $F \equiv b.0$—i.e., suppose that F is an element of $\mathcal{G}^{\rhd}$ and E is not. Although $E \sim F$, $\mathcal{K} \rhd E \not\sim \mathcal{K} \rhd F$ for $\mathcal{K} \subseteq \overline{\mathcal{A}} \cup \{\iota\}$.

Hitherto, strong equivalence has been defined only for closed expressions. To remedy this, we extend the definition of $\sim$ to open terms as follows. Let *substitution* σ map term variables to closed terms such that $E\sigma$ represents the closed term resulting from the substitution of all free variables X in E by $\sigma(X)$.

Definition 4.3 Let E and F be agent terms, possibly with free variables. Then define $E \sim F$ to hold exactly when for all substitutions σ, $E\sigma \sim F\sigma$.

It is a simple matter to extend Prop.4.2 to open terms. Prop.4.3 shows, moreover, that recursion preserves strong equivalence.

Proposition 4.3 *If $E \sim F$ then $fix(X = E) \sim fix(X = F)$*

Theorem 4.4 *$\sim$ is a congruence with respect to the operators of* $\mathrm{CCS}^{\rhd}$.

Finally we note that the extension of CCS with *unless*, *masking* and *idling*, does not lead to any new identifications between closed terms of CCS:

Proposition 4.5 *For terms E, E' that are unless-free, masking-free and idling-free, E and E' are strongly equivalent in the sense of Milner iff $E \sim E'$ in* $\mathrm{CCS}^{\rhd}$.

This means that the equational laws of the next section are conservative over CCS terms: terms of CCS will only be provably equal iff they formerly were so in CCS.

5 Equational laws

We now present a set of equational laws which are complete with respect to finite $\mathrm{CCS}^{\rhd}$ terms (A term is *finite* if it contains no variables). First, the usual rules of equational reasoning (reflexivity, symmetry, transitivity and Liebnitz' rule, *viz.*"substitution of equals for equals") hold as $\sim$ is a congruence. Further rules are presented in Fig.4. These consist of Milner's laws for strong equivalence together with new laws for the *unless* operator, notably **U1-U6** and new laws for masking namely **M1-M4**.

Law **U1** states that the agent G, conditional on nothing, behaves as G. Law **U2** states that the **0** agent, conditional on anything, behaves as **0**. Similarly, $\mathcal{K} \rhd a.E$ behaves as **0** when $\overline{a}$ is in $\mathcal{K}$ (see law **U3**). Laws **U4-U6** are more interesting. **U4** states that G

A1	$P+Q=Q+P$	**A3**	$P+(Q+R)=(P+Q)+R$
A2	$P+P=P$	**A4**	$P+0=P$
U1	$\{\} \triangleright G=G$	**U4**	$(\mathcal{K} \triangleright G)+(\mathcal{K} \triangleright H)=\mathcal{K} \triangleright (G+H)$
U2	$\mathcal{K} \triangleright 0=0$	**U5**	$(\mathcal{K}_0 \triangleright (\mathcal{K}_1 \triangleright G))=(\mathcal{K}_0 \cup \mathcal{K}_1) \triangleright G$
U3	$\mathcal{K} \triangleright a.G=0$ if $\overline{a} \in \mathcal{K}$	**U6**	$\mathcal{K}_0 \triangleright G + \mathcal{K}_1 \triangleright G = \mathcal{K}_0 \triangleright G$ if $\mathcal{K}_0 \subseteq \mathcal{K}_1$
C1	$P\|Q=Q\|P$	**C3**	$P\|(Q\|R)=(P\|Q)\|R$
C2	$P\|0=P$		
R1	$0[f]=0$	**R3**	$(\alpha.P)[f]=f(\alpha).(P[f])$
R2	$(P+Q)[f]=P[f]+Q[f]$	**R4**	$(\mathcal{K} \triangleright G)[f]=f(\mathcal{K}) \triangleright G[f]$
M1	$\langle 0 \rangle = 0$	**M3**	$\langle P+Q \rangle = \langle P \rangle + \langle Q \rangle$
M2	$\langle \alpha.P \rangle = \alpha.\langle P \rangle$	**M4**	$\langle \mathcal{K} \triangleright \alpha.P \rangle = (\mathcal{K} - \{\iota\}) \triangleright (\alpha.\langle P \rangle)$

L1 $0 \setminus L = 0$

L2 $$(\alpha.P) \setminus L = \begin{cases} 0 & \text{if } \alpha \in L \cup \overline{L} \\ \alpha.(P \setminus L) & \text{otherwise} \end{cases}$$

L3 $(P+Q) \setminus L = (P \setminus L) + (Q \setminus L)$

L4 $(\mathcal{K} \triangleright G) \setminus L = \mathcal{K} \triangleright (G \setminus L)$

Rec1 $fix(X=E)=E[fix(X=E)/X]$
Rec2 $F=fix(X=E)$ if $F=E[F/X]$

Figure 4: Equational laws satisfied by $\sim$.

unless $\mathcal{K}$ or H unless $\mathcal{K}$ behaves as $G + H$ unless $\mathcal{K}$. **U5** states that G unless $\mathcal{K}_1$ and $\mathcal{K}_0$ behaves as G unless $\mathcal{K}_0 \cup \mathcal{K}_1$. Finally, **U6** confirms that G unless $\mathcal{K}_0$ or G unless $\mathcal{K}_1$ behaves as G unless $\mathcal{K}_0$ provided $\mathcal{K}_0$ is a subset or equal to $\mathcal{K}_1$. Laws **M1-M3** are straightforward. Law **M4** states that masking the agent $\mathcal{K} \rhd \alpha.P$ will force it to behave as $(\mathcal{K} - \{\iota\}) \rhd (\alpha.\langle P \rangle)$. Recall that since $\mathcal{K} \rhd \alpha.P \in \mathcal{G}^{\rhd}$, then α in law **M4** is assumed to be an element of $\mathcal{A} \cup \{\tau\}$.

Excluding **Rec1** and **Rec2**, the laws of Fig.4 with the addition of the expansion law **INT** (Fig.5) are complete for finite terms. The expansion law operates on terms in *conditional* form.

Definition 5.1 A term is said to be in *conditional form*:

$$\sum_{m \in M} \mathcal{K}_m \rhd \alpha_m.P_m \text{ if for all } m \in M,\ P_m \text{ are in conditional form.} \tag{1}$$

When the indexing set M is empty, we have the **0** agent in conditional form. When E is in conditional form, the prefix $\alpha.E$ is in conditional form if the indexing set M is singleton and $\mathcal{K}_m$ is empty for $m \in M$. The summation, composition, restriction, masking and relabelling of terms in conditional form can be reduced to a term in conditional form using the laws in Fig.4 and the expansion law in Fig.5. In the case of expressions that are unless-free, masking-free and idling-free, the expansion law reduces to the one from CCS.

Notation The sum $\sum_{i \in I} E_i$ is indexed by a finite ordered set I. Because summation is commutative and associative with respect to $\sim$, we do not care about the precise order on the indexing set. We shall understand $\sum_{P(G_i)} G_i$, where P is a predicate, as an abbreviation for the sum $\sum_{i \in I'} G_i$ indexed by $I' = \{i \in I \mid P(G_i)\}$.

Theorem 5.1 *(Soundness) The equational laws of Fig.4 are valid (i.e., for each law $P = Q$ it is true that $P \sim Q$). The expansion law of Fig.5 is sound (in the sense of preserving valid equations). Any equation deduced by equational reasoning from these laws is valid as long as both sides of the equation are terms in $\mathcal{E}^{\rhd}$.*

The proof of completeness uses a more refined notion of conditional form:

Definition 5.2 A term P, in the conditional form $\sum_{m \in M} \mathcal{K}_m \rhd \alpha_m.P_m$ is said to be in *strong conditional form* if

- $\forall m \in M.\ \overline{\alpha}_m \notin \mathcal{K}_m$, and
- $\forall m, m' \in M.\ \alpha_m.P_m \equiv \alpha_{m'}.P_{m'} \Longrightarrow \mathcal{K}_m \not\subseteq \mathcal{K}_{m'} \ \wedge\ \mathcal{K}_{m'} \not\subseteq \mathcal{K}_m.$

The importance of a strong conditional form, is that any prefix component $\alpha_m.P_m$ is associated with transitions that the strong conditional form can make.

Theorem 5.2 *For finite terms P, Q in $\mathcal{E}^{\rhd}$, $P \sim Q$ if and only if $P = Q$.*

Proof

Soundness follows from Theorem 5.1. Conversely, suppose $P \sim Q$. One can argue without loss of generality that P and Q are in conditional form. Using laws **U1** to **U6**, P and

Let $P \equiv \sum_{m\in M} \mathcal{K}_m \rhd \alpha_m.P_m$ and $Q \equiv \sum_{n\in N} \mathcal{J}_n \rhd \beta_n.Q_n$

be two terms in conditional form. Then

$$
\begin{aligned}
P|Q \;=\; & \sum_{m\in M} \{\mathcal{K}_m \rhd \alpha_m.(P_m|Q) : \forall n \in N.\ \beta_n \notin \mathcal{K}_m\} \;+\\
& \sum_{n\in N} \{\mathcal{J}_n \rhd \beta_n.(P|Q_n) : \forall m \in M.\ \alpha_m \notin \mathcal{J}_n\} \;+\\
& \sum_{\overline{\beta_n}=\alpha_m\in\mathcal{A}} \{\mathcal{K}_m \rhd \tau.(P_m|Q_n) : \forall n \in N.\ \beta_n \notin \mathcal{K}_m\} \;+\\
& \sum_{\overline{\alpha_m}=\beta_n\in\mathcal{A}} \{\mathcal{J}_n \rhd \tau.(P_m|Q_n) : \forall m \in M.\ \alpha_m \notin \mathcal{J}_n\}
\end{aligned}
$$

Figure 5: The expansion law **INT**.

Q and their subterms can be converted to terms in strong conditional form. Therefore, without loss of generality, we show that $P \sim Q \Rightarrow P = Q$ where P and Q and their subterms are in strong conditional form written as:

$$P \equiv \sum_{m\in M} \mathcal{K}_m \rhd \alpha_m.P_m \quad \text{and} \quad Q \equiv \sum_{n\in N} \mathcal{J}_n \rhd \beta_n.Q_n$$

If one shows that $Q = Q + \mathcal{K}_{m_0} \rhd \alpha_{m_0}.P_{m_0}$ for all $m_0 \in M$, it then follows that $Q + P = Q$ and by a symmetric argument that $P + Q = P$. Hence $P = Q$. Suppose $\mathcal{K}_{m_0} \rhd \alpha_{m_0}.P_{m_0}$ is a summand of P for some $m_0 \in M$, then for $R = (\overline{\mathcal{A}} \cup \{\iota\}) - \mathcal{K}_{m_0}$,

$$\vdash_R P \xrightarrow{\alpha} P'$$

where $\alpha = \alpha_{m_0}$ and $P' \equiv P_{m_0}$. Since $P \sim Q$ and P, Q and their subterms are in strong conditional form, then there exists $n_0 \in N$, and a term Q' such that

$$\vdash_R Q \xrightarrow{\alpha} Q', \quad P' \sim Q', \quad \alpha = \beta_{n_0}, \quad Q' \equiv Q_{n_0} \quad \text{and} \quad \mathcal{J}_{n_0} \cap R = \emptyset$$

Therefore $\mathcal{J}_{n_0} \subseteq \mathcal{K}_{m_0}$. By law **U6**,

$$Q = Q + \mathcal{K}_{m_0} \rhd (\beta_{n_0}.Q_{n_0}).$$

Since, inductively, $P' = Q'$ and $\alpha_{m_0} = \beta_{n_0}$, then

$$Q = Q + \mathcal{K}_{m_0} \rhd (\alpha_{m_0}.P_{m_0}).$$

This can be shown for all $m_0 \in M_0$. Therefore $Q = Q + P$. A converse argument shows that $P = P + Q$. Therefore $P = Q$. ∎

5.1 Applying the equational laws on the reactive systems

Recall the reactive system Sys defined in the introduction as follows:

$$\begin{array}{lcl} Sys & \stackrel{def}{=} & (A \mid B)\backslash a \\ A & \stackrel{def}{=} & act.\overline{a}.0 \ + \ \{\overline{act}\} \rhd \tau.A \\ B & \stackrel{def}{=} & a.react.0 \end{array}$$

Since A and B are in conditional form, applying **INT** to Sys yields:

$$(act.(\overline{a}.0|B) \ + \ \{\overline{act}\} \rhd \tau.(A|B) \ + \ a.(A|react.0))\backslash a$$

Applying **L3**, **L2** and **A4** yields:

$$act.((\overline{a}.0|B)\backslash a) \ + \ (\{\overline{act}\} \rhd \tau.(A|B))\backslash a$$

Applying **L4** and **INT**:

$$act.((\overline{a}.(0|B) \ + \ a.(\overline{a}.0|react.0) \ + \ \tau.(0|react.0))\backslash a) \ + \ \{\overline{act}\} \rhd (\tau.(A|B)\backslash a)$$

Further application of **C1**, **C2**, **L2** and **L3**, yields:

$$act.\tau.react.0 \ + \ \{\overline{act}\} \rhd \tau.((A|B)\backslash a)$$

Therefore, one can express the behaviour of Sys as $Spec$ defined as follows:

$$Spec \stackrel{def}{=} act.\tau.react.0 \ + \ \{\overline{act}\} \rhd \tau.Spec$$

Now recall the reactive system Sys_1 defined as follows:

$$\begin{array}{lcl} Sys_1 & \stackrel{def}{=} & \langle A \mid B \rangle \\ A & \stackrel{def}{=} & act.0 \ + \ \iota.A \\ B & \stackrel{def}{=} & \{\iota\} \rhd react.0 \end{array}$$

Since A and B are in conditional form, applying **INT** to Sys_1 yields:

$$\langle act.(0|B) \ + \ \iota.(A|B) \rangle$$

Applying **C1**, **C2** and the definition of B yields:

$$\langle act.(\{\iota\} \rhd react.0) \ + \ \iota.(A|B) \rangle$$

Applying **M3**, and **M2** twice yields:

$$act.\langle \{\iota\} \rhd react.0 \rangle \ + \ \iota.\langle A|B \rangle$$

Applying **M4** yields:

$$act.(\{\} \rhd react.\langle 0 \rangle) \ + \ \iota.\langle A|B \rangle$$

Applying **U1** and **M1** yields:

$$act.react.0 \ + \ \iota.\langle A|B \rangle$$

Therefore as expected, one can express the behaviour of Sys_1 as $Spec_1$ defined as follows:

$$Spec_1 \stackrel{def}{=} act.react.0 \ + \ \iota.Spec_1$$

$$Meal \stackrel{def}{=} (Food \mid D_0 \mid D_1 \mid D_2 \mid Butler) \setminus \{gong, eat\}$$

$$D_0 \stackrel{def}{=} gong.(\{\overline{gong}\} \rhd port.0) + \{\overline{gong}\} \rhd eat.D_0$$

$$D_1 \stackrel{def}{=} gong.(\{\overline{gong}\} \rhd port.0) + \{\overline{gong}\} \rhd eat.D_1$$

$$D_2 \stackrel{def}{=} gong.(\{\overline{gong}\} \rhd port.0) + \{\overline{gong}\} \rhd eat.D_2$$

$$Butler \stackrel{def}{=} timeup.\overline{gong}.\overline{gong}.\overline{gong}.0$$

$$Food \stackrel{def}{=} \overline{eat}.Food$$

Figure 6: The dons' meal.

6 The dining-dons example

Three Cambridge dons are sharing a limitless source of food. A butler waits patiently while the meal proceeds. When the butler notices that time is up, the dons are required to stop eating immediately, and the butler strikes a gong three times to declare the meal 'over'. The meal is defined in Fig.6. Before *timeup* occurs:

- Any don can help himself or herself to food.
- The food never runs out and the butler waits patiently.

After *timeup* occurs, the dons cannot drink port before three gong-strikes. In fact, one can prove (see [Cam90]) that the behaviour can only proceed as follows:

$$\tau.\tau.\tau.port.port.port.0$$

Informally, suppose *timeup* occurs. This can only be followed by a $gong/\overline{gong}$ interaction between the butler and one of the dons—for example don D_0. After this first interaction D_0 is in the state:

$$\{\overline{gong}\} \rhd port.0$$

while the butler is in state:

$$\overline{gong}.\overline{gong}.0$$

Since the butler is still prefixed by a $\overline{gong}$ action, D_0 is prevented from drinking port while D_1 and D_2 are prevented from eating. Once again, only a $gong/\overline{gong}$ interaction may take place, this time between the butler and either don D_1 or don D_2. Suppose the butler interacts with don D_2, then the state of the butler becomes $\overline{gong}.0$, and don D_2 like D_0 has state $\{\overline{gong}\} \rhd port.0$. The remaining $\overline{gong}$ prefix of the butler prevents D_0 and D_2 from drinking port until the final $gong/\overline{gong}$ interaction takes place between the butler and D_1. This done, the butler stops and as there are no $\overline{gong}$ prefixes left in their environment, the dons are now free to have port.

This example illustrates the use of *unless* to encode a form of multi-way synchronisation; notice that all the dons stop eating as soon as *timeup* occurs. The dons represent agents that share some resource. The butler represents a sensor. When the sensor detects an interrupt, the agents stop their normal behaviour. The sensor then ensures that each agent commences some routine to recover from the interrupt. The unless operator prevents one of the agents to proceed with recovery before the sensor has initialised recovery in the other agents.

7 Related Work

This work arose as a continuation of [Cam89] which presented an operational semantics of Occam. The work outlined here is presented in more detail in [Cam90]. We know of no other successful attempt to both semantically define and, with this as a basis, provide a complete proof system for a CCS-like language with a conditional operator. We contribute a new set of laws for conditional agents, complete for finite agents, as part of a well-rounded and, we believe, convincing theory.

There have been other attempts to give a semantic basis to reasoning about priority [BBK85] [Bar89] [CH88] [BK90] [Gro90] [GL90] [SS90] [Tof90] (see [Cam90] for more details). These attempts fall under two main categories:

- those that associate priority with choice [Cam89] [Bar89] [Cam90] [SS90] [Tof90] [CW91], and
- those that associate priority with events [CH88] [BK90] [GL90].

The conditional operator presented here falls under the first category. It is more rudimentary than the priority choice operator presented in [Cam90] and [CW91]; any agent containing priority choice can be re-expressed using the *unless* operator (the converse does not hold). Moreover, as stated in the introduction, the conditional operator:

- allows global dynamic ordering of actions,
- allows local partial ordering of actions,
- allows the behaviour of an agent to be dependent on the possible behaviour of the environment,
- can be used to encode a form of multiway synchronisation,
- reflects syntactically the priority structure of actions in each state, and
- lends itself to implementation—it is closely related to existing priority constructs in programming languages [Cam89] [Cam90].

References

[Bar89] G. Barrett. The semantics of priority and fairness in occam, April 1989. Proc. MFPS 5, New Orleans, USA.

[BBK85] J.C.M Baeten, J.A. Bergstra, and J.W. Klop. Syntax and defining equations for an interrupt mechanism in process algebra. Technical Report CS-R8503, Center for Mathematics and Comp. Sci, Amsterdam, February 1985.

[BK90] E. Best and M. Koutny. Partial order semantics of priority systems. Technical Report 6/90, Institute of Computer Science, University of Hildesheim, June 1990.

[Cam89] Juanito Camilleri. An operational semantics for occam. *International Journal of Parallel Programming*, 18(5), October 1989.

[Cam90] Juanito Camilleri. *Priority in Process Calculi*. PhD thesis, Department of Computer Science, University of Cambridge, October 1990.

[CH88] R. Cleaveland and M. Hennessy. Priorities in process algebras. Technical Report 2/88, Department of Computer Science, University of Sussex, March 1988.

[CW91] J. Camilleri and G. Winskel. CCS with Priority Choice. In *Sixth Annual IEEE Symposium on Logic in Computer Science*. Springer Verlag, July 1991.

[GL90] R. Gerber and I. Lee. CCSR: A calculus for communicating shared resources. In J.C.M. Baeten and J.W.Klop, editors, *ConCur'90*, number 458 in LNCS, pages 263–277. Springer Verlag, 1990.

[Gro90] Jan Friso Groote. Transition system specifications with negative premises. In J.C.M. Baeten and J.W.Klop, editors, *ConCur'90*, number 458 in LNCS, pages 332–341. Springer Verlag, 1990.

[Mil89] Robin Milner. *Communication and Concurrency*. International Series in Computer Science. Prentice Hall, 1989.

[SS90] S. Smolka and B. Steffen. Priority as extremal probability. In J.C.M. Baeten and J.W.Klop, editors, *ConCur'90*, number 458 in LNCS, pages 456–466. Springer Verlag, 1990.

[Tof90] C. Tofts. A synchronous calculus of relative frequency. In J.C.M. Baeten and J.W.Klop, editors, *ConCur'90*, number 458 in LNCS, pages 467–480. Springer Verlag, 1990.

Algebraic Formulations of Trace Theory

N.J.Drost
Programming Research Group, University of Amsterdam
P.O.Box 41882, 1009 DB Amsterdam, The Netherlands

Abstract

In this paper mathematical models are given for Trace Theory as described in [Rem85] and [Kal86]. They model a process by a trace structure: a pair consisting of an alphabet and a trace set over this alphabet. We show that in fact two incompatible process models are used, and we devise a new model that has all essential characteristics of the two former models. A complete axiomatization of this model is given. It is shown that a distinction between successful and unsuccessful termination is needed to effectuate associativity of parallel composition with communication in the presence of sequential composition. Two operators generating infinite processes are added, which makes a verification of the alternating bit protocol possible.

Key words and phrases: concurrency, process algebra, trace models, complete axiomatization, infinite processes, verification, alternating bit protocol.

1 Introduction

At the moment a great amount of research is going on in the field of concurrency. The complexity of systems of parallel processes communicating with each other makes the use of mathematical models for concurrent processes obligatory. A mathematical model M consists of a nonempty domain A of mathematical objects, and one or more functions $f : A^n \rightarrow A$ on this domain.

A mathematical model becomes an algebra by adding a signature $\sum$ of constant, variable, and function symbols to a model, plus a mapping of constant and function symbols to objects and functions in the model. Each closed algebraic term from this signature then refers to an object in the domain. Different terms may refer to the same object, and there may be objects to which no term refers.

Axioms may be added to be able to derive whether terms denote the same object (process). To ensure that all correct equalities are derivable, the set of axioms should be sound and complete.

Many models, algebras, and axiom sets for concurrent processes have been devised. Some examples are: CCS [Mil89], CSP [Hoa85], ACP_τ[BK85].

Algebras with the same signature may be partially ordered w.r.t. the identifications on terms that they induce. A model that equates many terms is considered as more primitive. Such a comparison is made by van Glabbeek [Gla90]. Important properties for this ordering are true concurrency versus interleaving, and presence versus absence of choice moments. The most primitive models in this partial ordering are models based on sets of traces. They contain no true concurrency and no choice moments. Many authors describe trace models, e.g. Hoare [Hoa85], Hoare and Olderog [HO86], Baeten and Weijland [BW90], Rem [Rem85], Kaldewaij [Kal86].

This paper focuses on the model of [Rem85] and [Kal86]. As their definitions seem to be incomplete and not fully algebraical, a complete algebraical description will be given of the model(s) underlying their approach, and a complete axiomatization. This yields a better insight in the properties of the constants and operators, and makes verifications possible.

In this paper all proofs are omitted. They can be found in [Dro90].

2 Trace structures

In this section a short description is given of some notions used by Rem [Rem85] and Kaldewaij [Kal86]. They use pairs (called trace structures), consisting of a set of traces (strings) and an alphabet, as representation of processes. The alphabet stands for the set of all possible actions of the process, and is a subset of a given alphabet A, which may be infinite. Each trace represents a possible execution of the process.

Alphabets will be denoted by $B, C, \ldots$, traces by $v, w, \ldots$, trace sets by $V, W, \ldots$, and trace structures by $S, T, \ldots$. The empty trace will be denoted as λ. The alphabet of a trace structure T is denoted by $\alpha(T)$ and its trace set by $\tau(T)$.

The trace set of a process must be prefix closed. The function prefix closure on trace sets is defined as: $\mathrm{pref}(V) = \{v \mid v \in A^* \wedge \exists w \in V : v \leq w\}$ with $v \leq w$ meaning: $\exists u \in A^* : vu = w$.

Processes will be denoted by P, Q, R.

Two operators are defined on trace structures:

1) Projection ($\lceil$) on an alphabet B. This is a primitive abstraction operator. In each trace all symbols outside B are removed.

2) Weave (**w**). This is an interleaving parallel composition operator. It also implements communication: actions from the intersection of the alphabets of both processes must match. It is defined as: $(B, V)\ \mathbf{w}\ (C, W) = (B \cup C, \{v \mid v \in (B \cup C)^* \wedge v\lceil B \in V \wedge v\lceil C \in W\})$

Kaldewaij also gives a program notation for defining a process. Such a program is also called a component. A component consists of commands. Commands are defined inductively:

Definition 2.1 *(Commands)*
ϵ is a command; each symbol $a \in A$ is a command.
If q and r are commands, then q^*, $q|r$, $q;r$, q,r are commands.

With command q the trace structure $\mathrm{TR}(q)$ is associated, which is not necessarily prefix closed:

Definition 2.2 *(Trace structures associated to commands)*

i) $\mathrm{TR}(\epsilon) = (\emptyset, \{\lambda\})$,
ii) $\mathrm{TR}(a) = (\{a\}, \{a\})$,
iii) $\mathrm{TR}(q^*) = (\alpha(\mathrm{TR}(q)), (\tau(\mathrm{TR}(q)))^*)$,
iv) $\mathrm{TR}(q|r) = (\alpha(\mathrm{TR}(q)) \cup \alpha(\mathrm{TR}(r)), \tau(\mathrm{TR}(q)) \cup \tau(\mathrm{TR}(r)))$,
v) $\mathrm{TR}(q;r) = (\alpha(\mathrm{TR}(q)) \cup \alpha(\mathrm{TR}(r)), \{uv \mid u \in \tau(\mathrm{TR}(q)) \wedge v \in \tau(\mathrm{TR}(r))\})$,
vi) $\mathrm{TR}(q,r) = \mathrm{TR}(q)\ \mathbf{w}\ \mathrm{TR}(r)$.

Commands are used as part of a component. The simplest form of a component is: **com** $c(B) : q$ **moc** where c is the name of the component, B is a finite alphabet, and q is a command.

With this component c a process $TR(c)$ is associated: $TR(c) = \mathrm{pref}(TR(q))$.

In fact two models are employed in Trace Theory. The first model is based on trace structures with prefix closed trace sets. Here, all possible partial executions are represented. For this model two basic operators are defined: projection (abstraction from internal actions), and weave (parallel composition with communication.

In the second model arbitrary trace sets are used. Here, a trace stands for a terminated run of the process, and will therefore be called a complete trace. The same operations are defined as in the first model, plus two extra: alternative and sequential composition.

The operator pref on arbitrary trace sets is in fact used to map trace structures with sets of complete traces to trace structures with prefix closed trace sets.

In the next section two algebras will be defined for these two models.

3 Algebras based on the definitions of trace theory

3.1 Introduction

In this section two algebras are defined for the two Trace Theory models. The first algebra, P, is based on prefix closed trace structures; the second algebra, CB, on trace structures with sets of complete traces. Sequential and alternative composition are added to the first model. An alternative definition for parallel composition is given.

The signatures of the algebras should at least contain constant symbols for processes. But as the result of a parallel composition is dependent on the alphabets of the argument processes, the alphabets of the processes must be deducible from the process terms. Therefore I use a many-sorted signature, with for each possible alphabet B in the model a sort B in the signature. Each sort has its own set of constants. Operators are strongly overloaded: the same symbol is used for operators which differ in the sorts of their arguments. The sort of a term t will be denoted by sort(t).

3.2 P: Prefix closed trace structures.

Signature:

Constants:

ϵ_B for each sort B,

a_B for each sort B with $a \in B$.

Functions:

$\lceil B : C \rightarrow B \cap C$ for all sorts B, C (projection),
$+ : B \times C \rightarrow B \cup C$ for all sorts B, C (alternative composition),
$. : B \times C \rightarrow B \cup C$ for all sorts B, C (sequential composition),
$\|_b : B \times C \rightarrow B \cup C$ for all sorts B, C (parallel composition).

The b in $\|_b$ stands for blocking merge. This will be explained later on.
Suppose $\mathcal{V}_B$ is an infinite set of variables of sort B and $\mathcal{V} = \bigcup_{B \subseteq A} \mathcal{V}_B$.

Definition 3.1 *The set $\mathcal{T}(\Sigma^P, \mathcal{V})$ of terms in the signature of P is inductively defined as:*
$\epsilon_B \in \mathcal{T}(\Sigma^P, \mathcal{V})$ *for each sort* B,
$a_B \in \mathcal{T}(\Sigma^P, \mathcal{V})$ *for each sort* B,
$x_B \in \mathcal{T}(\Sigma^P, \mathcal{V})$ *for each* $x_B \in \mathcal{V}_B$, *for each sort* B,
$t_C \lceil B \in \mathcal{T}(\Sigma^P, \mathcal{V})$ *for each sort* B, *and each term* $t_C \in \mathcal{T}(\Sigma^P, \mathcal{V})$ *of sort* C.
$t_B \Box t_C \in \mathcal{T}(\Sigma^P, \mathcal{V})$ *for each term* $t_B, t_C \in \mathcal{T}(\Sigma^P, \mathcal{V})$ *and* $\Box = +, ., $ *or* $\|$.

The set of closed terms in the signature of P is denoted as $\mathcal{T}(\Sigma^P)$.
Terms will be denoted by $s, t, t_1, t_2, \ldots$.
Notation:
The symbol . will often be omitted. Also brackets are often omitted. The priority order of the operators is from high to low: $.$, $\lceil$, $\|_b$, $+$.

The model of P:
Domain: Pairs (B, V) with $B \subseteq A$, $V \subseteq B^*$, prefix-closed, $V \neq \emptyset$. V may contain infinitely many traces. All traces in V are finite.
Interpretation of constant symbols: $[\![\epsilon_B]\!] = (B, \{\lambda\})$, $[\![a_B]\!] = (B, \{\lambda, a\})$.

In [Kal86] only definitions for projection and weave were given for trace structures with prefix closed trace sets. Here definitions for alternative and sequential composition are added. The definition for alternative composition is the same as given in [Kal86] for commands. The definition of sequential composition is rather problematical. The idea behind sequential composition is that a second process starts after a first process has finished. This is the case if the first process has executed a maximal trace. So in the definition added here a composite process only continues with actions from the second process if the actions executed previously constitute a maximal trace in the first process. For parallel composition with communication another definition is given. This is done because this definition is easier to adapt to slightly different intuitions about parallel composition. It will be proved that this new definition in fact defines the same operator on trace structures as the weave of [Kal86].
To define the parallel composition first a preliminary definition is given:
Let $a, b \in A$, $B \subseteq A$, $v, w \in A^*$.

Definition 3.2 *(Blocking merge)*

The function $bmerge_B : A^* \times A^* \rightarrow \mathcal{P}(A^*)$ *is defined as:*

$bmerge_B(\lambda, \lambda) = \{\lambda\}$
$bmerge_B(av, \lambda) = bmerge_B(\lambda, av) =$
  $a.bmerge_B(v, \lambda)$ *if* $a \notin B$
  $\emptyset$ *if* $a \in B$

$bmerge_B(av, bw) =$

$$
\begin{array}{ll}
a.bmerge_B(v, bw) \cup b.bmerge_B(av, w) & \textit{if } a, b \notin B \\
a.bmerge_B(v, bw) & \textit{if } a \notin B, b \in B \\
b.bmerge_B(av, w) & \textit{if } a \in B, b \notin B \\
a.bmerge_B(v, w) & \textit{if } a, b \in B \textit{ and } a = b \\
\emptyset & \textit{if } a, b \in B \textit{ and } a \neq b
\end{array}
$$

The function $bmerge_B$ merges two strings using the communication alphabet B. The function produces a set of traces. If the communication actions of the traces do not match, an empty set of traces is generated. A similar function is defined in [OH86].

The operators of P are now defined as follows:

Suppose $B \subseteq A$, (B, V) and $(C, W) \in$ P.
Then:

$$
\begin{array}{ll}
(B,V)\lceil C & = (B \cap C, \{v \lceil C \mid v \in V\}), \\
(B,V) + (C,W) & = (B \cup C, V \cup W), \\
(B,V).(C,W) & = (B \cup C, V \cup \{vw \mid v \in V \text{ and } w \in W \text{ and } \neg \exists u \in V : v < u\}) \\
(B,V) \|_b (C,W) & = (B \cup C, \bigcup_{v \in V, w \in W} bmerge_{B \cap C}(v, w)).
\end{array}
$$

Also two auxiliary operators are defined: $\alpha((B, V)) = B$, and $\tau((B, V)) = V$.

The operator $\|_b$ defines the same operation on trace structures as the operator **w** in [Kal86]:

Theorem 3.1 *Suppose* $B, C \subseteq A$, $V_1 \subseteq B^*$, *and* $V_2 \subseteq C^*$ *Then:*
$(B, V_1) \text{ w } (C, V_2) = (B, V_1) \|_b (C, V_2)$.

This theorem holds for all trace structures, not only prefix closed ones, if the definition of the operator $\|_b$ is extended to all trace structures.

Theorem 3.2 *Suppose* $B, C, D, E, F \subseteq A$, *and* x, y, z *are variables of sort* B, C, *and* D *respectively.*
Then the following equations hold in P:

A1 $x + y = y + x$	E1 $x_B \epsilon_B = x_B$
A2 $(x + y) + z = x + (y + z)$	E2 $\epsilon_C x_B = x_B \epsilon_C$
A3 $x + x = x$	E3 $\epsilon_B \epsilon_C = \epsilon_{B \cup C}$
A4 $x(y + z) = xy + xz$	E4 $\epsilon_B + \epsilon_C = \epsilon_{B \cup C}$
A5 $x(yz) = (xy)z$	E5 $a_B = a_{\{a\}} \epsilon_B$

M1 $\epsilon_B \|_b \epsilon_C = \epsilon_{B \cup C}$

M2 $\epsilon_C \|_b a_E x_B =$
$a_E(\epsilon_C \|_b x_B \epsilon_E)$ if $a \notin C$
$\epsilon_{B \cup C \cup E}$ if $a \in C$

P1 $\epsilon_C \lceil D = \epsilon_{C \cap D}$

P2 $a_C x \lceil D = a_C(x \lceil D)$ if $a \in D$
$x \lceil D$ if $a \notin D$

P3 $(x + y) \lceil D = x \lceil D + y \lceil D$

M3 $a_E x_B \|_b b_F y_C =$

$$
\begin{array}{ll}
a_E(x_B\epsilon_E \|_b b_F y_C) + b_F(a_E x_B \|_b y_C \epsilon_F) & \text{if } a \notin C \cup F, b \notin B \cup E \\
a_E(x_B\epsilon_E \|_b b_F y_C) & \text{if } a_E \notin C \cup F, b \in B \cup E \\
b_F(a_E x_B \|_b y_C \epsilon_F) & \text{if } a \in C \cup F, b \notin B \cup E \\
a_E(x_B\epsilon_E \|_b y_C \epsilon_F) & \text{if } a, b \in (B \cup E) \cap (C \cup F), a = b \\
\epsilon_{B \cup C \cup E \cup F} & \text{if } a, b \in (B \cup E) \cap (C \cup F), a \neq b
\end{array}
$$

M4 $(x_B + y_C) \|_b z_D = x_B \epsilon_C \|_b z_D + y \epsilon_B \|_b z_D$

M5 $x \|_b y = y \|_b x$

M6 $x \|_b (y \|_b z) = (x \|_b y) \|_b z$

The axioms of theorem 3.2 are in fact axiom schemes, because the sorts of the variables are arbitrary, and there is overloading of the operators. Axiom A3: $x+x=x$ for instance stands for a collection of axioms $x_B +_{B\times B \to B} x_B = x_B$ for each sort B. Axioms A2 and M6 seem to express associativity of $+$ and $\|_b$. This is no real associativity, because operators of different type are involved. For instance: axiom A2: $(x+y)+z = x+(y+z)$ stands for $(x_B +_{B\times C \to B\cup C} y_C) +_{(B\cup C)\times D \to B\cup C\cup D} z_D = x_B +_{B\times (C\cup D) \to B\cup C\cup D} (y_C +_{C\times D \to C\cup D} z_D)$. Still I will say that axioms A2 and M6 express associativity of $+$ and $\|_b$, and also that axiom A4 expresses left-distributivity of . over $+$.

In this model sequential composition is not right-distributive over alternative composition. Counterexample:
Suppose $P = (\{a,b\},\{\lambda,a\})$, $Q = (\{a,b\},\{\lambda,a,ab\})$, and $R = (\{c\},\{\lambda,c\})$.
Then $(P+Q).R = (\{a,b,c\},\{\lambda,a,ab,abc\})$,
but $P.R + Q.R = (\{a,b,c\},\{\lambda,a,ac,ab,abc\})$.
This is caused by the fact that in a sum of prefix closed trace sets termination information may disappear, because traces which were maximal in the former trace set now become a prefix of another trace in the new trace set.

3.3 CB: Algebra with Complete traces and Blocking merge

This algebra has a domain consisting of all trace structures, hence with trace sets that need not be prefix closed. Each trace stands for a complete execution of a process. Because the weave-operator of [Kal86], applied to non-prefix-closed trace structures, may produce a trace structure with an empty trace set, trace structures with an empty trace set are included in the domain of CB. The signature of CB contains constants δ_B for trace structures with an empty trace set.
The signature Σ^{CB} consists of: Constants: δ_B, ϵ_B, and a_B, Functions: $\lceil B$, $+$, ., and $\|_b$.
Model of CB:
Domain: pairs (B,V) with $B \subseteq A$, $V \subseteq B^*$. V need not be prefix closed, and may be empty.
Interpretation of constant symbols: $[\![\delta_B]\!] = (B,\emptyset)$, $[\![\epsilon_B]\!] = (B,\{\lambda\})$, $[\![a_B]\!] = (B,\{a\})$.
Functions:

Suppose $B \subseteq A$, (B,V) and $(C,W) \in$ CB. Then:

$$
\begin{array}{ll}
(B,V)\lceil C & = (B\cap C, \{v\lceil C \mid v \in V\}), \\
(B,V)+(C,W) & = (B\cup C, V\cup W), \\
(B,V).(C,W) & = (B\cup C, \{vw \mid v\in V \wedge w \in W\}),
\end{array}
$$

$(B,V)\|_b(C,W) = (B \cup C, \bigcup_{v\in V, w\in W} bmerge_{B\cap C}(v,w))$.

These functions are identical to the ones defined in [Kal86] for commands.

Theorem 3.3 *Suppose $B,C,D,E,F \subseteq A$, and x,y,z are variables of sort B, C, and D respectively. Then the following equations hold in CB:*
A1 to A5, E1 to E5, P1 to P4, M1, M4 to M6, and:

A4′	$(x+y)z = xz + yz$	D1	$x_B + \delta_C = x_B\epsilon_C$
P4	$xy\lceil D = (x\lceil D)(y\lceil D)$	D2	$\delta_C x_B = \delta_{B\cup C}$
P5	$\delta_C\lceil D = \delta_{C\cap D}$	D3	$x_B\delta_C = \delta_{B\cup C}$
M2	$\epsilon_C\|_b a_E x_B = ... \ \delta_{B\cup C\cup E}$ if $a \in C$		
M3	$a_E x_B\|_b b_F y_C = ... \ \delta_{B\cup C\cup E\cup F}$ if $a,b \in (B\cup E)\cap(C\cup F), a \neq b$		
M7	$\delta_C\|_b x_B = \delta_{B\cup C}$		

A remarkable axiom is D3: $x_B\delta_C = \delta_{B\cup C}$. Here a deadlock caused by unmatched communication actions erases all previous actions performed by the process. This is contrary to the intuition that processes perform actions independently until they need to synchronize. It is caused by the fact that a merge of two traces with nonmatching communications produces no traces at all, instead of a merge of both traces up to the first nonmatching pair of communication actions. Example: $(\{a,b,c\},\{ca\})\|_b(\{a,b,d\},\{db\}) = (\{a,b,c,d\},\emptyset)$

The two trace models P and CB are not compatible, for two reasons:
1) In P no indication of possible termination of a process is present. In CB a trace structure with trace set $\{a, ab\}$ denotes a process that may terminate after doing an a-action. In P a trace set $\{\lambda, a, ab\}$ contains no indication of termination after doing an a-action.
2) Although parallel composition is defined in P and in CB in the same way, it corresponds in these two models to different intuitions. In P two parallelly composed processes may perform actions in arbitrary order, until a synchronization action must be performed. If there is no matching synchronization action, the process stops. In CB a parallel composition of two processes with nonmatching sequences of synchronization actions simply performs no action at all. So in the next section modified versions of the two models are presented, which are compatible, and do not have the undesirable properties of the first two models.

4 Modified versions of the two algebras

In this chapter modified versions of the two algebras CB and P are defined. The first algebra, CN, is based on sets of complete traces, with a slightly changed definition of parallel composition. The second algebra, PT, is made by adding traces ending in a special termination symbol to prefix closed trace sets.

Signature of CN and PT:
Constants: ϵ_B, a_B. Functions: $\lceil B$, $+$, $.$, and $\|_n$.

Model of CN:

The merge of two traces is redefined in such a way that a merge of two traces with non-matching communication actions is equal to the merge of the subtraces up to the first pair of nonmatching communications.
Domain: Pairs (B, V) with $B \subseteq A, V \subseteq B^*, V \neq \emptyset$.
Interpretation of constant symbols: $[\epsilon_B] = (B, \{\lambda\})$, $[a_B] = (B, \{a\})$.

Operators:
$\lceil B$, $+$, and . are defined as in CB.
Parallel composition:
Suppose $B \subseteq A$, (B,V) and (C,W) $\in$ Dom(CN).
Then:
$(B, V) \|_n (C, W) = (B \cup C, \bigcup_{v \in V, w \in W} nmerge_{B \cap C}(v, w))$.
where $nmerge_B$ is equal to $bmerge_B$, except:
$nmerge_B(av, \lambda) = nmerge_B(\lambda, av) = \{\lambda\}$ if $a \in B$
$nmerge_B(av, bw) = \{\lambda\}$ if $a, b \in B$ and $a \neq b$

The model of PT:
The domain consists of prefix closed trace sets. Traces may end with a special termination symbol $\downarrow \notin A$. All maximal traces must end on $\downarrow$. The definition of sequential composition is changed in such a way that the second process may only start after each termination point of the first. So the domain is: Pairs (B, V) with $B \subseteq A$, $V \subseteq B^* \cup B^* \downarrow$, prefix-closed, $V \neq \emptyset$, and for all $t \in V$: there is a $t' \in V : t = t' \downarrow$ or $t < t'$.
Interpretation of constant symbols: $[\epsilon_B] = (B, \{\lambda, \lambda\downarrow\})$, $[a_B] = (B, \{\lambda, a, a\downarrow\})$.

Operators: projection and parallel composition as in P.
Sequential composition:
$(B, V).(C, W) = (B \cup C, \{v \in V \mid \neg \Downarrow v\} \cup \{vw \mid v\downarrow \in V \wedge w \in W\})$,
where the predicate $\Downarrow v$ (v ends with an $\downarrow$) is defined as:
$\Downarrow v \equiv \exists v' \in A^* : v = v' \downarrow$
Parallel composition:
$(B, V) \|_n (C, W) = (B \cup C, \bigcup_{v \in V, w \in W} nmerge_{B \cap C}(v, w))$,
where $nmerge_B$ is extended with:
$nmerge_B(\downarrow, \downarrow) = \{\downarrow\}$,
$nmerge_B(\lambda, \downarrow) = nmerge_B(\downarrow, \lambda) = \{\lambda\}$,
$nmerge_B(av, \downarrow) = nmerge_B(\downarrow, av) = a.nmerge_B(v, \downarrow)$ if $a \notin B$,
$\{\downarrow\}$ if $a \in B$,
$nmerge_B(av, bw) = \{\downarrow\}$ if $a, b \in B$ and $a \neq b$.

Theorem 4.1 *Suppose $B, C, D, E, F \subseteq A$, and x, y, z are variables of sort B, C, and D respectively. Then the following equations hold in CN and PT:*
A1 to A5, A4', P1 to P4, E1 to E5, M1, M4, M5, and:

M2 $\epsilon_C \|_n a_E x_B = \ldots \epsilon_{B \cup C \cup E}$ if $a \in C$
M3 $a_E x_B \|_n b_F y_C = \ldots \epsilon_{B \cup C \cup E \cup F}$ if $a, b \in (B \cup E) \cap (C \cup F), a \neq b$

In these two models parallel composition turns out not to be associative. Example:
$(a_{\{a,b\}}\|_n b_{\{a,b\}})\|_n c_{\{c\}} = \epsilon_{\{a,b\}}\|_n c_{\{c\}} = c_{\{a,b,c\}}$
$a_{\{a,b\}}\|_n(b_{\{a,b\}}\|_n c_{\{c\}}) = a_{\{a,b\}}\|_n(b_{\{a,b\}}c_{\{c\}} + c_{\{c\}}b_{\{a,b\}}) = \epsilon_{\{a,b,c\}} + c_{\{a,b,c\}}$.
This is caused by the fact that unsuccessful communication results in the empty process: $a_B x_C \|_n b_D y_E = \epsilon_{B\cup C\cup D\cup E}$ if $a, b \in (B\cup C)\cap(D\cup E)$ and $a \notin B$.
and adding the empty process to some process p need not result in the same process p: $x_B + \epsilon_B \neq x_B$ So if $x_B + \epsilon_B \neq x_B$ and associativity of parallel composition are desired, a new constant γ_B is needed with $x_B + \gamma_B = x_B$ and $a_B x_C \|_n b_D y_E = \gamma_{B\cup C\cup D\cup E}$, if $a, b \in (B\cup C)\cap(D\cup E)$ and $a \neq b$.

5 Successful and unsuccessful termination

In this section a last model is given, based on prefix closed trace structures, in which parallel composition is associative. As was argued in the previous section, a new constant (set of constants) δ_B is needed, with the property $x_B + \delta_B = x_B$. This constant corresponds to a process that immediately terminates unsuccessfully. Parallel composition of two processes starting with incompatible communication actions produces such a process. In a sequential composition of two processes no actions of the second process are executed if the first process terminates unsuccessfully. The property $x_B + \delta_B = x_B$ reflects the intuition that a process never terminates unsuccessfully if it may also choose another action.

5.1 PTL: Prefix closed trace sets, Termination, Lock

The signature Σ^{PTL} consists of:
Constants: ϵ_B, δ_B, and a_B; Functions: $\lceil B$, $+$, $\cdot$, and $\|_b$.
The model of PTL:
Domain: Pairs (B,V) with $B \subseteq A$, $V \in B^* \cup B^*\downarrow$, prefix closed, $V \neq \emptyset$.
Interpretation of constants: $[\![\delta_B]\!] = (B, \{\lambda\})$, $[\![\epsilon_B]\!] = (B, \{\lambda, \lambda\downarrow\})$, $[\![a_B]\!] = (B, \{\lambda, a, a\downarrow\})$.

Functions:

$\lceil$, $+$, and $\cdot$ have the same definition as the corresponding ones of PT.
Parallel composition is defined as follows:
$(B_1, V_1)\|(B_2, V_2) = (B_1 \cup B_2, \bigcup_{v_1 \in V_1, v_2 \in V_2} merge_{B_1 \cap B_2}(v_1, v_2))$,
where $merge_B(v_1, v_2) = nmerge_B(v_1, v_2)$, except:
$merge_B(\downarrow, av) = merge_B(av, \downarrow) = \{\lambda\}$ if $a \in B$,
$merge_B(av_1, bv_2) = \{\lambda\}$ if $a, b \in B, a \neq b$.

Theorem 5.1 *Suppose $B, C, D, E, F \subseteq A$, and x, y, z are variables of sort B, C, and D respectively. Then the following equations hold in PTL:*
A1 to A5, A4', d1, D2, E1 to E5, P1 to P5, M1, M4 to M6, and:

M2 $\epsilon_C \| a_E x_B = \ldots \ \delta_{B \cup C \cup E}$ if $a \in C$
M3 $a_E x_B \| b_F y_C = \ldots \ \delta_{B \cup C \cup E \cup F}$ if $a, b \in (B \cup E) \cap (C \cup F), a \neq b$
M7 $\delta_B \| \delta_C = \delta_{B \cup C}$
M8 $\delta_B \| \epsilon_C = \delta_{B \cup C}$
M9 $\delta_C \| a_D x_B = a_E(\delta_C \| x_B \epsilon_E)$ if $a \notin C$
$\delta_{B \cup C \cup E}$ if $a \in C$

These equations will be called Ax(PTL).

Lemma 5.2 *Let $B, C \subseteq A, V_1 \subseteq B^* \cup B^* \downarrow, V_2 \subseteq C^* \cup C^* \downarrow$, V_1 and V_2 prefix closed. Then:* $\bigcup_{v_1 \in V_1, v_2 \in V_2} merge_{B \cap C}(v_1, v_2) = \{v \mid v \lceil B \in V_1 \wedge v \lceil C \in V_2\}$.

Definition 5.1 *Suppose I is a finite index set with n elements and t_i is a PTL-term for each $i \in I$. Then: $\sum_{i \in I} t_i = (..(t_1 + t_2) + \ldots) + t_n$.*

Theorem 5.3 *(Expansion Theorem) Suppose: constant a_i has sort C_i, variable x_i has sort D_i, $B_i = C_i \cup D_i$, $B = \bigcup_{i \leq n} B_i$, $B' = \bigcup_{i \leq n-1} B_i$, $i \neq j \neq k \Rightarrow B_i \cap B_j \cap B_k = \emptyset$ (Handshaking). Then:*

$$a_1 x_1 \| \ldots \| a_n x_n = \sum_{i \leq n, j \neq i \leq n: a_i \notin B_j} a_i(a_1 x_1 \| \ldots \| x_i \epsilon_{B_i} \| \ldots \| a_n x_n) + \sum_{i \leq n, j \neq i \leq n: a_i = a_j} a_i(a_1 x_1 \| \ldots \| x_i \epsilon_{B_i} \| \ldots \| x_j \epsilon_{B_j} \| \ldots \| a_n x_n)$$

Definition 5.2 *The set BT of basic terms from $T(\Sigma^{PTL})$ is inductively defined as:*

$\epsilon_B, \delta_B \in BT$ *for all* $B \subseteq A$,
$t_1, t_2 \in BT \Rightarrow a_B.t_1 \in BT$ *for all* $B \subseteq A$; $t_1 + t_2 \in BT$.

Theorem 5.4 *(Elimination Theorem)*
For each $t \in T(PTL)$ there is an $s \in BT$ s.t. $Ax(PTL) \vdash t = s$.

Definition 5.3 *The set ST of standard terms from $T(\Sigma^{PTL})$ is inductively defined as:*

$\epsilon_B, \delta_B \in ST$ *for all* $B \subseteq A$
Suppose: I is a finite nonempty index set,
for all $i \in I$: $s_i \in ST$, $sort(s_i) = sort(a_i) = B$,
for all $i, j \in I$: $i \neq j \rightarrow a_i \neq a_j$,
Then: $\sum_{i \in I} a_i s_i \in ST$, $\sum_{i \in I} a_i s_i + \epsilon_B \in ST$.

Theorem 5.5 *For each $s \in BT$ there is an $r \in ST$ s.t. $Ax(PTL) \vdash s = r$.*

Theorem 5.6 *(Completeness of Ax(PTL) for PTL)*
Suppose $s, t \in T(PTL)$. Then
$PTL \models [s] = [t] \Rightarrow Ax(PTL) \vdash s = t$.

6 Infinite processes

Many processes, like protocols and the processes occurring in electronic circuits, are described as infinite processes. So it is desirable to extend the algebra of PTL with some means to describe infinite processes.

A process may be infinite in two ways:

Definition 6.1 *A process has the property* **infinitely running** *if it may perform an infinite execution.*

Definition 6.2 *A process has the property* **infinitely branching** *if it chooses from infinitely many different executions.*

Infinitely running processes are not present in models based on set of complete traces, like CB and CN, because there each trace stands for a complete run of a process. P contains no termination indications, so in many cases infinitely running and infinitely branching processes cannot be distinguished.
Example: $(\{a\}, \{\lambda, a, aa, aaa, \ldots\})$.
In PTL infinitely running and infinitely branching processes correspond to trace structures with different trace sets.
Example: Infinitely running: $(\{a, b\}, \{\lambda, a, ab, aba, abab, \ldots\})$.
Infinitely branching: $(\{a, b\}, \{\lambda, \downarrow, a, ab, ab\downarrow, aba, abab, abab\downarrow, \ldots\})$.
In fact the process of the last example is both infinitely branching and infinitely running. A process that is only infinitely branching may only be given using an infinite alphabet.

Terms denoting infinite processes may be denoted using new operators. In [Kal86] the operator *(Kleene star) is used for sets of complete traces. As each trace stands for a complete run of the process, this operator generates infinitely branching processes. Sets of complete traces are mapped to prefix closed sets using the function pref. Infinitely branching trace structures defined with * are then mapped to infinitely running processes.
Example: $\text{pref}(B, \{ab\}^*) = (B, \{\lambda, a, ab, aba, abab, \ldots\})$.
To be able to denote both infinitely branching and infinitely running processes, two new operators * and $^\infty$ are added to the signature of PTL. The definion of these operators on the domain of PTL is:

$$\begin{aligned}(B,V)^* &= (B, \{\downarrow\} \cup \{v_1 \ldots v_n \mid v_i{\downarrow} \in V \ (0 < i < n) \wedge v_n \in V \wedge n > 0\}) \text{ if } \exists v{\downarrow} \in V, \\ & \quad (B,V) \qquad \text{otherwise.} \\ (B,V)^\infty &= (B, \{v_1 \ldots v_n \mid v_i{\downarrow} \in V (0 < i < n) \wedge n > 0 \wedge v_n \in V \wedge \neg\exists v : v_n = v{\downarrow}\})\end{aligned}$$

Examples:
$(B, \{\lambda, a, ab, ab\downarrow\})^* = (B, \{\downarrow, \lambda, a, ab, ab\downarrow, aba, abab, abab\downarrow, \ldots\})$,
$(B, \{\lambda, a, ab, ab\downarrow\})^\infty = (B, \{\lambda, a, ab, aba, abab, \ldots\})$.
This new algebra is called PTL^∞.

Theorem 6.1 *The following equations hold in PTL^∞:*
Ax(PTL), and:

K1 $x_B{}^*\delta_\emptyset = x_B{}^\infty$	K4 $\epsilon_B{}^* = \epsilon_B$
K2 $x_B{}^* = x_B\lceil\emptyset + x_Bx_B{}^*$	K5 $(x_C{}^*)\lceil B = (x_C\lceil B)^*$
K3 $(x_B{}^*)^* = x_B{}^*$	K6 $(x_B{}^n)^*\delta_\emptyset = x_B{}^*\delta_\emptyset$

Equation K5 is useful for abstracting from internal actions in verifications. It is comparable to the principle KFAR (Koomen's Fair Abstraction Rule) of ACP_τ[BK86], as it removes infinite sequences of internal actions.

Corollary 6.2

i) $(x_B\delta_C)^* = x_B\delta_C$	iii) $x_B{}^\infty y_C = x_B{}^\infty\epsilon_C$	v) $\epsilon_B{}^\infty = \delta_B$
ii) $x_B{}^\infty = x_Bx_B{}^\infty$	iv) $(x_B{}^\infty)^\infty = x_B{}^\infty$	vi) $x_C{}^\infty\lceil B = (x_C\lceil B)^\infty$

A second way to describe infinite processes uses recursive specifications. A recursive specification $\mathcal{E}$ is a set of equations $\{X = t_X \mid X\in\mathcal{V}_\mathcal{E}\}$ with $\mathcal{V}_\mathcal{E}$ a set of variables and t_X a PTL-term where all variables are from $\mathcal{V}_\mathcal{E}$. X must have the same sort as t_X. A process of PTL is a solution of $\mathcal{E}$ if it satisfies the equations of $\mathcal{E}$. To find recursive equations with unique solutions some extra definitions are needed. These definitions are based on [BK84a] and [BM88].

Definition 6.3 *(Guarded terms)*

Suppose $\mathcal{E}$ is a recursive specification in the signature of PTL.
The set of guarded terms $\mathcal{GT}$ from PTL + $\mathcal{E}$ is inductively defined as:
$a_B\in\mathcal{GT}$,
Suppose $t\in\mathcal{T}(\Sigma^{PTL}, \mathcal{V}_\mathcal{E})$, and $g_1, g_2\in\mathcal{GT}$. Then: $g_1 + g_2\in\mathcal{GT}$, $g_1.t\in\mathcal{GT}$.
Suppose Ax(PTL),$\mathcal{E}\vdash t = g_1$. Then: $t\in\mathcal{GT}$.

Definition 6.4 *(Guarded equations)*

$X_B = t$ is a **guarded equation** iff t is a guarded term, or $t = t' + \epsilon_C$, and t' is a guarded term.

Definition 6.5 *(Guarded recursive specifications)*

Suppose $\mathcal{E} = \{X_i = t_i \mid i\in I\}$ is a recursive specification.
$\mathcal{E}$ is a **guarded recursive specification** iff all equations $X_i = t_i$ are guarded.

There are three important principles concerning recursive specifications [BK84b]:
1) Recursive Definition Principle(RDP): Every recursive specification has a solution.
Restricted version (RDP$^-$): Every guarded recursive specification has a solution.
2) Approximation Induction Principle (AIP): A process is determined by its finite prefix cuts.
3) Recursive Specification Principle (RSP): A guarded recursive specification has at most one solution.
AIP implies RSP, and RDP$^-$ plus RSP guarantee that guarded recursive specifications have unique solutions.
Prefix cut of a trace v is defined as: $\pi_n(\lambda) = \lambda$ for $n \geq 0$, $\pi_0(v) = \lambda$, $\pi_n(av) = a.\pi_{n-1}(v)$

for $n > 0$.
Prefix cut of a trace set is the set of prefix cuts of its traces: $\pi_n(V) = \{\pi_n(v) \mid v \in V\}$, and prefix cut of a trace structure is the structure with the same alphabet and the prefix cut of the trace set: $\pi_n((B, V)) = (B, \pi_n(V))$.

Theorem 6.3 *RDP⁻, AIP, and RSP hold in PTL.*

Fact 6.4 *Suppose $\mathcal{E}$ is a guarded recursive specification over PTL^∞ with recursion variables $X_1 \ldots X_n$ with known sorts. Then $X_1 \ldots X_n$ may be added to the language of PTL^∞, and the recursion equations may be added to the equations of PTL^∞.*

This extension will be denoted by $PTL^\infty(\mathcal{E})$.

A process which is the solution of a guarded equation of the form $X_B = sX_B + t$ can always be denoted by a term $t \in \mathcal{T}(\Sigma^{PTL^\infty})$:

Lemma 6.5 *Suppose $s, t \in \mathcal{T}(\Sigma^{PTL^\infty})$, $X_B = sX_B$ is guarded w.r.t. $Ax(PTL^\infty)$ and $\mathcal{E}$, $sort(s) = C$, $s|\emptyset = \epsilon_C$. Then: $X_B = sX_B + t \Rightarrow X_B = s^* t \epsilon_B$*

Corollary 6.6 $X_B = sX_B \Rightarrow X_B = s^\infty \epsilon_B$

7 Conclusions and discussion

The two models used in Trace Theory are incompatible with each other. In the model with prefix closed trace structures no definition of sequential composition is possible which corresponds to the sequential composition in the model based on complete traces. Sequential composition of processes is preferable to prefixing with atomic actions, because it allows a modular design of processes. In the model based on complete traces an unsuccessful communication erases also all actions that were performed earlier by both processes.

Combining the two models to a model without a distinction between successful and unsuccessful termination leads to non-associativity of parallel composition. This does not correspond to the behavior of real processes in parallel systems. The problem arises from the combination of sequential composition and only one form of termination. If two subprocesses of a process try to synchronize on non-matching atomic actions, the process stops. Other models of concurrency that have only one kind of termination have indeed only prefixing with atomic actions and no sequential composition, e.g. CCS [Mil89]. Such a model does not need different constants for the empty successfully and unsuccessfully terminating process, as it is not possible to sequentially compose arbitraty processes.

In [AH88] it was already noted that the NIL of CSP stands for both successful termination and deadlock, and that these are experimentally indistinguishable, due to the limited form of sequential composition: action prefixing. The constants δ and nil proposed in [AH88] have some very strange properties:
1) In a choice between terminating successfully or unsuccessfully, a process always terminates unsuccessfully: $\delta + nil = \delta$.
2) In a choice between terminating successfully and continuing, a process will always continue: $x + nil = x$.
This does not correspond with the intuitions adopted here.

Adding a distinction between successful and unsuccessful termination to the prefix closed model gives an algebra which has all essential properties of the first two models, and no unwanted features. This algebra should provide a sound basis for Trace Theory. If the $\downarrow$ is considered as an ordinary symbol, contained in the alphabet of every process, the definition of parallel composition is the same as the one given for trace structures with prefix closed trace sets in [Kal86]. Alternative and sequential composition correspond to the definitions in [Kal86] for commands.

In [BKO88] and [BW90] a trace model with prefix closed traces, possibly ending in a termination symbol, is described. It has constants for lock and atomic processes, and operators for alternative and sequential composition. The algebra PTL is in fact based on this model. The main extensions are:

- alphabets are added to trace sets,
- parallel composition with synchronization is added.

In his partial order on semantics for process languages van Glabbeek [Gla90] gives as simplest semantics trace semantics, followed by completed trace semantics. He uses a signature with operators for choice and action prefixing. The traces T(p) of a process p are defined as all possible action sequences of (partial) executions of the process, and the complete traces CT(p) of p as all action sequences of successfully terminated executions of a process. Two processes p and q are trace equivalent iff T(p)=T(q), and completed trace equivalent iff T(p)=T(q) and CT(p)=CT(q). So trace equivalence corresponds to algebra P and completed trace equivalence to PTL.

In the signature of PTL a constant δ for blocking is present, which makes deadlock a property of a process, not only of a group of processes, as in [Kal86]. It is sometimes argued that models based on sets of traces are not suitable as models for concurrency, because processes with deadlock are equaled to processes without deadlock [BW90]. This is a wrong claim, because in models based on trace sets no assumption is made about the moment of choice between two traces with equal prefixes. The processes $ab + a\delta$ and $a(b + \delta)$ both contain no deadlock, because it is assumed that a process never blocks if another action is still possible.

A real disadvantage of this kind of trace models is the crude type of abstraction, where internal actions are mapped to the empty action. This may remove an existing deadlock, as was already concluded in [BG89]. In most other process algebras, e.g. ACP[BK85] and CCS [Mil89], actions are mapped to a special internal action τ, which conforms to special laws.

The signature with constants ϵ, δ, a_B, and operators $+$, $.$, $\lceil$, and $\|$ only contains terms for finite processes. Two operators are added to generate also terms for infinite processes: * for infinitely branching and $^\infty$ for infinitely running processes. It turns out that $^\infty$ is in this model definable using * and δ. Also new constants, which denote the unique solution of a set of recursive process equations, may be added to the signature. The set of equations is then added to the axioms. This mechanism may be used to verify whether a composite process, whose components are defined using recursive equations, conforms to some global specification. The absence of deadlock must be checked before any abstraction of internal actions is done. During abstraction, cycles of internal actions are easily removed using the axioms for * and $^\infty$.

References

[AH88] Aceto, L., and M. Hennessy: Termination, Deadlock and Divergence. Report 6/88, Computer Science, Univ. of Sussex, Brighton BN1 9QH. 1988.

[BW90] Baeten, J.M.C. and W.P. Weijland: Process Algebra. Cambridge University Press, Cambridge. 1990.

[BG89] Baeten, J.M.G. and R.J. van Glabbeek: Abstraction and Empty Process in Process Algebra. Fund. Inf. XII, pp. 221-241. 1989.

[BM88] Bakker, J.W. de, and J.-J.Ch. Meyer: Metric Semantics for Concurrency. BIT 28, pp. 504-529. 1988.

[BK84a] Bergstra, J.A., and J.W. Klop: The algebra of Recursively Defined Processes and the the Algebra of Regular Processes. Proceedings 11th ICALP, LNCS 172, pp. 82-95. 1984.

[BK84b] Bergstra, J.A., and J.W. Klop: Verification of an Alternating Bit Protocol by means of Process Algebra. CWI report CS-R8404, Amsterdam. 1984.

[BK85] Bergstra, J.A., and J.W. Klop: Algebra of Communicating Processes with Abstraction. TCS 37(1): pp. 77-121. 1985.

[BKO88] Bergstra, J.A., J.W. Klop, and E.-R. Olderog: Readies and Failures in the Algebra of Communicating Processes. Siam J. Comput. 17(6): pp. 1134-1177. 1988.

[Dro90] Drost, N.: Algebraic Formulations of Trace Theory. Report P9004, Programming Research Group, Dept. of Math. and Comp. Sci., Univ. of Amsterdam. 1990.

[Gla90] Glabbeek, R.J. van: Comparative Concurrency Semantics, with Refinement of Actions. Ph.D.Thesis, Free University, Amsterdam. 1990.

[Hoa85] Hoare, C.A.R.: Communicating Sequential Processes. Prentice Hall, London. 1985.

[Kal86] Kaldewaij, A.: A Formalism for Concurrent Processes. Ph.D.Thesis, Technical University, Eindhoven. 1986.

[Mil89] Milner, R.: Communication and Concurrency. Prentice Hall, London. 1989.

[OH86] Olderog, E.-R. and C.A.R. Hoare: Specification-Oriented Semantics for Communicating Processes. Acta Inf. 23, pp. 9-66. 1986.

[Rem85] Rem, M.: Concurrent Computations and VLSI Circuits. in: M. Broy (ed.): Control Flow and Data Flow: Concepts of Distributed Programming, pp. 399-437. Springer, Berlin. 1985.

Compositional Synthesis of Live and Bounded Free Choice Petri Nets [1]

Javier Esparza
Institut für Informatik, Universität Hildesheim
Samelsonplatz 1, D-3200 Hildesheim (FRG)
e-mail:esparza@infhil.uucp

Manuel Silva
Depto. Ingeniería Eléctrica e Informática
Universidad de Zaragoza
C/ María de Luna 3, E-50015 Zaragoza (Spain)
e-mail:silva@etsii.unizar.es

Abstract. The paper defines two notions of composition of concurrent modules modelled by means of Petri nets: *synchronisations* and *fusions*. We study these two notions for the class of Free Choice nets, and characterise the compositions (within this class) that preserve liveness (absence of partial or global deadlocks) and boundedness (absence of overflows in finite stores). The characterisation shows which structures must be avoided in order to preserve the properties.

Keywords. Petri nets, Free Choice nets, compositional synthesis, liveness, boundedness.

1 Introduction

The development of compositional techniques for the analysis and synthesis of concurrent systems is an active field of research. This paper deals with this problem for systems modelled by means of Petri Nets. In particular, our goal is to give, for interesting composition operators, necessary and sufficient conditions on the structure of the net for the preservation of two properties: *liveness* and *boundedness*. Liveness is defined as the absence of partial or global deadlocks (from every reachable state all actions can

[1]This work was partially supported by the DEMON Esprit Basic Research Action 3148 and the Spanish Plan Nacional de Investigación, Grant TIC-0358/89.

be executed again). Boundedness means finiteness of the state space, and can be also interpreted as the absence of overflows in finite stores such as buffers.

However, the obtention of these conditions for general Petri Nets is an exceedingly ambitious goal, because the interplay between nondeterminism - choices - and concurrency makes very difficult to find relationships between the behaviour of a system and the structure of the net that models it. That is why we consider here the subclass of Free Choice nets (FC), in which this interplay is restricted: in FC nets, choices are not influenced by the environment, a concept similar to the internal nondeterminism of TCSP. This subclass has been studied in [BD 90,Hack 72,TV 84] among other papers.

Recently, [ES 90] gave a first complete theory for the *top-down* synthesis of live and bounded FC systems, which was subsequently used in [Espa 90] to derive new properties. In this work, we present a compositional synthesis theory for the class of nets underlying this class of systems: actually, the free choice nets that are structurally live and structurally bounded (SL&SB for short). In other words, we abstract from the initial markings. However, this is not a heavy constraint, since the markings that make these nets live and bounded can be easily calculated.

We start introducing two notions of composition: *synchronisations* and *fusions*. Synchronisations essentially merge transitions: they are closely related to the parallel operator of process algebras. Fusions, on the other hand, essentially merge places. We introduce later the concept of *well formed FC-synchronisations* as those preserving the free choice property (i.e. if the components of the synchronisation are FC so is the final result), and satisfying an additional graph theoretical condition. We show that an FC-synchronisation is SL&SB if and only if it is well formed.

This characterisation in terms of graph theoretical properties can be called "low level", since it is close to the graph structure of nets but difficult to interpret. We show that it is equivalent to a "high level" characterisation, which consist of the absence of two structures in the composed net, called *killing choices* and *synchronic mismatches*. These two structures have a clear and intuitive meaning.

Finally, we use the Duality Theorem of FC nets to derive for fusions similar results to the ones obtained for synchronisations.

Section 2 introduces the concepts of synchronisation and fusion. Sections 3 and 4 present the "low level" and "high level" characterisations of SL&SB FC-synchronisations. In section 5 the correspondent results for fusions are derived.

The basic definitions of net theory relevant for the paper can be found in [Espa 90]. For full proofs the reader is referred to [Espa 90b].

2 Composition of nets: Synchronisations and Fusions

To define synchronisations and fusions, we introduce the notions of *isomorphic* nets and *composition*.

Definition 2.1 *Two nets* $N_a = (P_a, T_a, F_a)$ *and* $N_b = (P_b, T_b, F_b)$ *are* isomorphic *iff there exists a bijection* $h: P_a \cup T_a \cup F_a \rightarrow P_b \cup T_b \cup F_b$ *such that:*

- $h(P_a) = P_b, h(T_a) = T_b, h(F_a) = F_b$
- $\forall (x,y) \in F_a: h((x,y)) = (h(x), h(y))$ ▪ 2.1

Definition 2.2 *Let* $\{N_1, \ldots, N_k\}$ *be a finite set of nets.* $N = (P, T, F)$ *is a* composition *of* $\{N_1, \ldots, N_k\}$ *iff:*

(a) there exists a set $\{\hat{N}_1, \ldots, \hat{N}_k\}$ *of subnets of* N *such that* $\forall i, 1 \leq i \leq k : N_i$ *is isomorphic to* $\hat{N}_i$

(b) $\cup_{i=1}^{k} \hat{N}_i = N$

The nets $N_1, \ldots, N_k$ *are* components *of* N. ▪ 2.2

The notion of composition is too general: very little can be said about the behaviour of the composition from the behaviours of the components. We consider now particular compositions with a better interpretation.

Definition 2.3 *A composition* N *of* $\{N_1, \ldots, N_k\}$ *(under isomorphisms* $h_1, \ldots h_k$*) is a* synchronisation *iff*

$$\forall i, 1 \leq i \leq k, \; \forall p \in \hat{P}_i: {}^\bullet p \cup p^\bullet \subseteq \hat{T}_i$$

N *is a* fusion *iff*

$$\forall i, 1 \leq i \leq k, \; \forall t \in \hat{T}_i: {}^\bullet t \cup t^\bullet \subseteq \hat{P}_i$$

where the dot notation refers to N. ▪ 2.3

Figure 1 shows a composition, a synchronisation and a fusion of two small nets. The drawing conventions are as follows. In the net composed by other two:

- white nodes belong to the first component but not to the second.
- shaded nodes belong to the second component but not to the first.
- dashed nodes belong to both components.

These conventions are used again in section 4.

Loosely speaking, the isomorphisms of synchronisations "preserve" the environment of places, while the isomorphisms of fusions "preserve" the environment of transitions. This means that the communication between the components is done through transitions in the case of synchronisations, and through places in the case of fusions. The first corresponds to communication by means of rendez-vous, and the second to the case

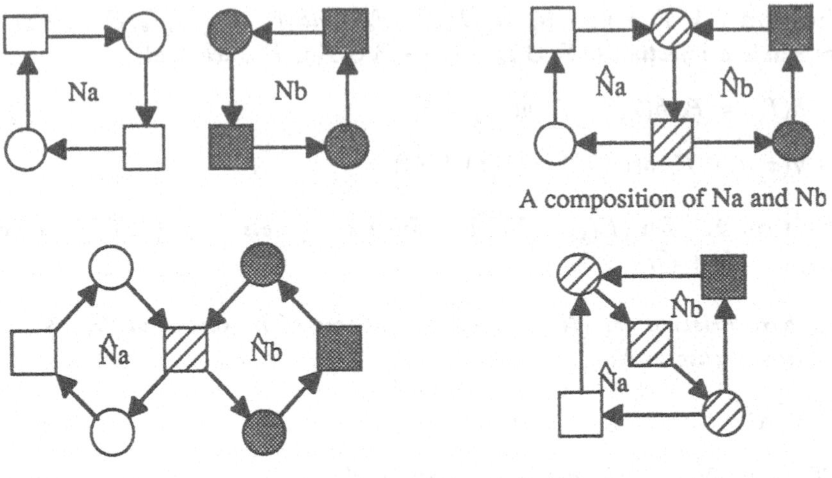

Figure 1: A composition, a synchronisation and a fusion of two small nets.

in which the components share some kind of resource, such as local memory, or share certain states.

In the sequel we consider only compositions of two nets. This is not an important restriction, because any composition of k nets can be done in a stepwise way composing first two nets N_1 and N_2, then composing the obtained net with N_3 and so on, that is, dividing it into $k-1$ compositions of two nets. The definitions are given from this point on for two nets, though theirs extension to the general case is always straightforward. We also change the notation, and denote the two components of the composition by N_a and N_b.

We are interested in the study of synchronisations producing FC nets, that we call *Free Choice Synchronisations.*

Definition 2.4 *A synchronisation N of $\{N_a, N_b\}$ is a* Free Choice synchronisation *(FC-synchronisation for short) iff N is FC.* ▪ 2.4

Free Choice synchronisations admit the following more useful characterisation, which follows easily from the definitions.

Proposition 2.5 *Let N be a synchronisation of $\{N_a, N_b\}$. N is a Free Choice synchronisation iff the two following conditions hold:*

(a) N_a and N_b are FC nets

(b) For every transition t in N: $({}^\bullet t \cap (P_a \setminus P_b) \neq \emptyset \wedge {}^\bullet t \cap (P_b \setminus P_a) \neq \emptyset) \Rightarrow ({}^\bullet t)^\bullet \subseteq \{t\}$.

Proof: It is easy to show that a net is Free Choice iff for all transitions t: $|{}^\bullet t| > 1 \Rightarrow ({}^\bullet t)^\bullet = \{t\}$.

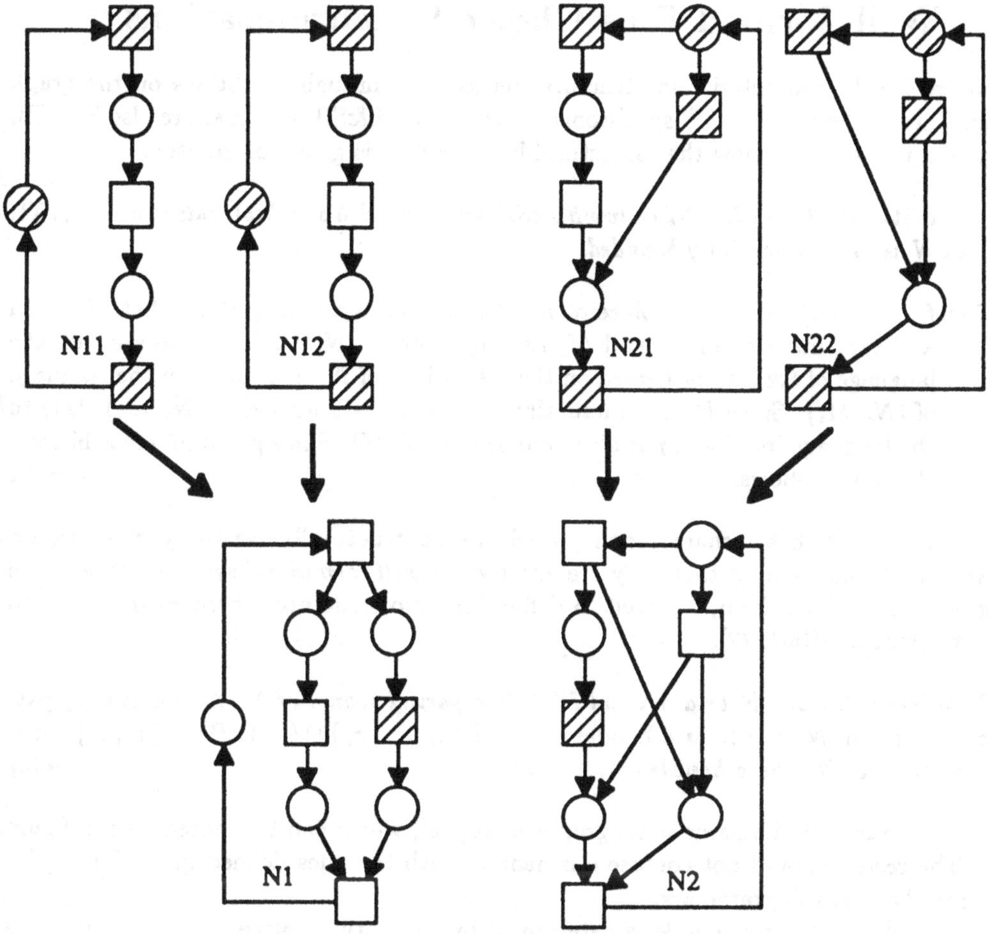

Figure 2: A synchronisation of four nets.

($\Rightarrow$) Assume N is Free Choice. (a) is obvious. To prove (b), notice that $({}^\bullet t \cap (P_a \setminus P_b) \neq \emptyset \wedge {}^\bullet t \cap (P_b \setminus P_a) \neq \emptyset)$ implies $|{}^\bullet t| > 1$.

($\Leftarrow$) Assume (a) and (b) hold. Take a transition t of N such that $|{}^\bullet t| > 1$. If ${}^\bullet t \subseteq P_a$, by the definition of synchronisation, $({}^\bullet t)^\bullet \subseteq T_a$. Since N_a is FC by (a), we have $({}^\bullet t)^\bullet = \{t\}$. Similarly if ${}^\bullet t \subseteq P_b$. If neither ${}^\bullet t \subseteq P_a$ nor ${}^\bullet t \subseteq P_b$, we have again $({}^\bullet t)^\bullet = \{t\}$ by (b). ■ 2.5

Figure 2 shows how an FC net can be constructed stepwisely by means of succesive FC-synchronisations. The four initial nets, N_{11}, N_{12}, N_{21}, N_{22}, are strongly connected state machines. N_{11} and N_{12} are synchronised to yield N_1 (the nodes identified by the isomorphisms are shaded). Analogously, N_{11} and N_{12} yield N_2. Finally, N_1 and N_2 are synchronised to yield N (not shown in the figure).

3 Well Formed Free Choice Synchronisations

Our goal is to characterise in structural terms (i.e. through conditions on the graph structure of the net) the FC-synchronisations of two SL&SB nets that are also SL&SB. In fact, it is easy to show that structural boundedness is given for granted.

Proposition 3.1 *Let N_a, N_b be two SL&SB nets, and N a synchronisation of $\{N_a, N_b\}$. Then N is also structurally bounded.*

Proof: (sketch) Let p be a place of N. Assume w.l.o.g. that $p \in P_a$. Let M be an arbitrary marking of N, and M_a its projection on N_a. It is easy to see that the language of (N, M) projected on the transitions of N_a is a subset of the language of (N_a, M_a). Since N_a is structurally bounded, p is bounded in (N_a, M_a). Due to the language inclusion, p is also bounded in (N, M). Since p and M are arbitrary, the result follows. ∎ 3.1

The difficulty lies in characterising which are the structurally live FC-synchronisations. We show in this section that they are exactly the *well formed* FC-synchronisations. In order to introduce them, we need to define first two structures: handles [ES 89], and T-components [Hack 72].

Definition 3.2 *Let N be a net and $N' \leq N$ a partial subnet of N. An elementary path $(x_1, \ldots, x_r)$ in N, $r \geq 2$, is a* handle *of N' iff $\{x_1, \ldots, x_r\} \cap (P' \cup T') = \{x_1, x_r\}$. It is also said that N'* has *a handle $(x_1, \ldots, x_r)$.* ∎ 3.2

The reason of the name is its graphical appeal, which can be appreciated in figure 3. The reader should not confuse our handles with the ones defined in [GJRT 83] for the study of graph grammars.

The character of a handle is determined by the nature (place or transition) of its first and last nodes. We classify them according to this criterion into four subclasses: *PP-*, *PT-*, *TP-* and *TT-handles* (see figure 3). The meaning is obvious.

The intuition lying behind figure 3 is that, when constructing a system through the iterative addition of handles, PP- and TT-handles are nicer for preserving liveness and boundedness than PT- or TP-handles, which "create problems" that have to be solved.

T-components are structures associated to the infinite behaviours of the net.

Definition 3.3 *Let $N = (P, T, F)$ be a net. A strongly connected T-graph $N_1 = (P_1, T_1, F_1) \subseteq N$ is a T-component of N iff $P_1 = {}^\bullet T_1 = T_1^\bullet$, where the dot notation refers to N.* ∎ 3.3

The basic property of T-components is that an occurrence sequence in which only the transitions of the T-component occur, and they occur exactly once, reproduces the original marking. Therefore, such a sequence can be executed infinitely many times.

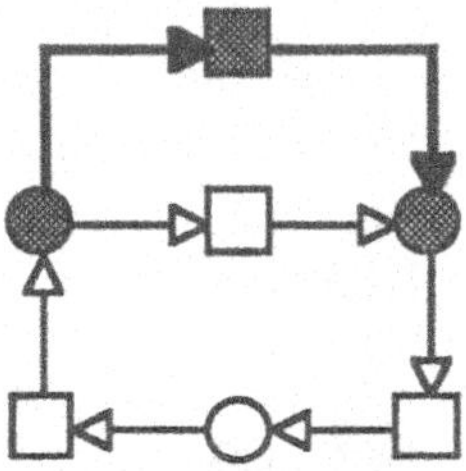

A PP-handle
(PP-handles represent
"well formed" choices)

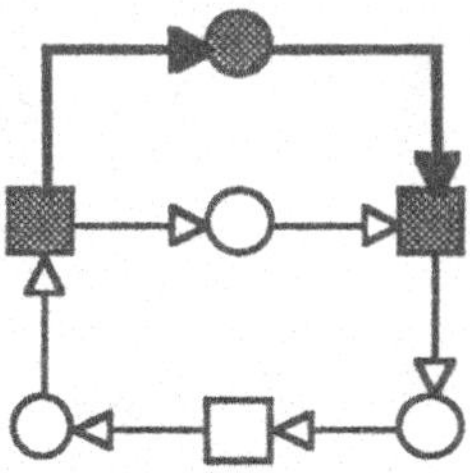

A TT-handle
(TT-handles represent
"well formed" concurrency)

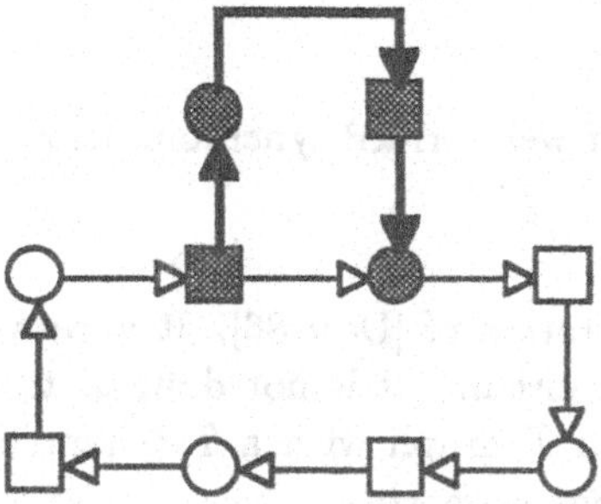

A TP-handle
(TP-handles can lead to unboundedness)

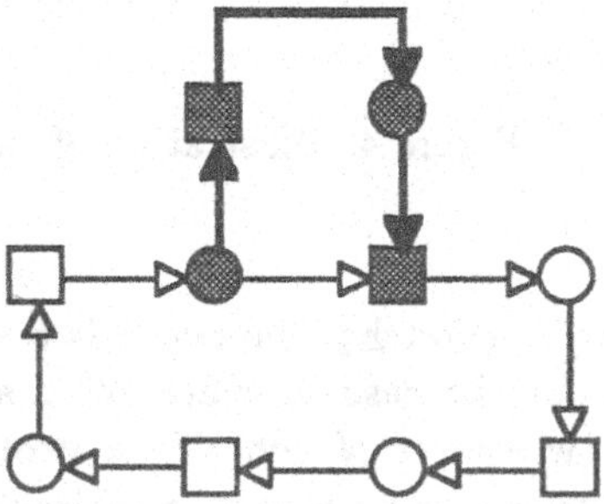

A PT-handle
(PT-handles can lead to non-liveness)

Figure 3: The four classes of handles.

Proposition 3.4 *Let (N, M_0) be a system and $N_1 = (P_1, T_1, F_1)$ a T-component of N. If there exists a sequence σ such that*

$$\vec{\sigma}(t) = \begin{cases} 1 & \text{if } t \in T_1 \\ 0 & \text{otherwise} \end{cases}$$

then $M_0[\sigma\rangle M_0$. ▪ 3.4

We can now define well formed FC-synchronisations.

Definition 3.5 *Let N_a and N_b be two SL&SB nets. N is a* well formed FC-synchronisation *of $\{N_a, N_b\}$ iff no T-component of N_a or N_b has a TP-handle in N.* ▪ 3.5

Using the following proposition, it is not difficult to prove that SL&SB FC-synchronisatior must be well formed:

Proposition 3.6 *Let N be an FC net and $N' \leq N$ a strongly connected T-graph with a TP-handle in N. Then N is not SL&SB.*

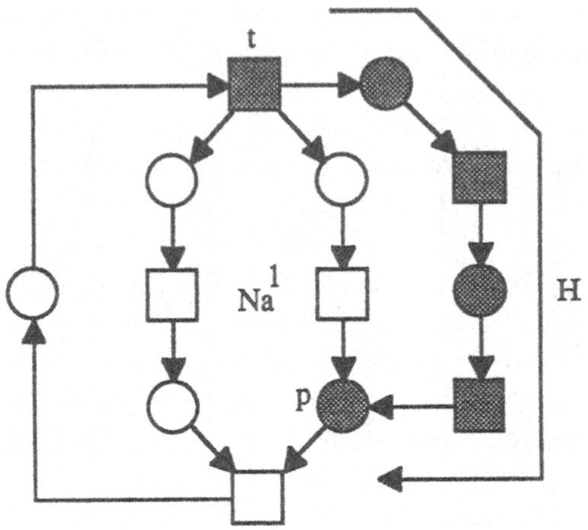

Figure 4: Illustration of the definition of well formed synchronisation.

Proof: (sketch) The result is a slight generalisation of [Dese 86]. It is proven there for the case in which N' is an elementary circuit. It is not difficult to see that whenever N contains a strongly connected T–graph with a TP–handle, it also contains an elementary circuit with the same property. ▪ 3.6

Since a T–component of N_a or N_b is a strongly connected T–graph of N, it follows that a non well formed FC–synchronisation cannot be *SL&SB*. We would like to give an informal argument to make this result plausible. Let N_1^a be a T–component of N_a with a TP–handle $H = (t, \ldots, p)$ in N. The intuitive idea is to use a policy for the occurrence of transitions. Denote by $N_1^a \cup H$ the net composed by N_1^a and H (see figure 4). Let p' be any place in $N_1^a \cup H$. Whenever one of its output transitions is enabled, *all* its output transitions are enabled because the net is Free Choice. The policy consists of always letting the transition in $N_1^a \cup H$ occur. Assume that the system is live. It can be proved that occurrence sequences exist which respect this policy and let t occur arbitrarily many times. These occurrence sequences increase arbitrarily the total number of tokens in the places of $N_1^a \cup H$. Hence, the system is not bounded for these markings, which contradicts proposition 3.1.

Well formedness is not only a necessary condition but also characterises SL&SB FC–synchronisations of SL&SB components:

Theorem 3.7 *Let N be an FC-synchronisation of $\{N_a, N_b\}$, where N_a and N_b are SL&SB. N is SL&SB iff it is well formed.*

Proof: (hint)

(⇒) See above.

(⇐) The proof is long and quite hard. It has two parts. First the result is proven for the particular case in which N_a is a strongly connected P–graph. It is shown that, if N is well formed, then it can be reduced to N_b using the reduction algorithm of [ES 90]. Since this reduction procedure preserves SL&SB and N_b is SL&SB by hypothesis, it follows that N is SL&SB. Using this first result, the general case is proven by means of a graph argument. ▪ 3.7

The reader can check that all the FC-synchronisations performed to obtain the net N of figure 2 are well formed, and that the resulting net is SL&SB.

We finish this section with two results. The first shows that every SL&SB FC net can be obtained through well formed synchronisations of strongly connected P-graphs (i.e. well formed synchronisations are, in some sense, complete).

We need introduce first the notion of P-component of a net.

Definition 3.8 *Let $N = (P, T, F)$ be a net. A strongly connected P-graph $N_1 = (P_1, T_1, F_1) \subseteq N$ is a P-component of N iff $T_1 = {}^\bullet P_1 = P_1^\bullet$, where the dot notation refers to N.* ▪ 3.8

Proposition 3.9 *Let N be an SL&SB FC net. There exists a set $\{N_1, \ldots, N_k\}$ of strongly connected P–graphs and a sequence $\{N^1, \ldots, N^k\}$ of nets such that:*

(1) $N^1 = N_1$

(2) $\forall i, 1 < i \leq (k-1)$: *$N^{i+1}$ is a well formed FC-synchronisation of $\{N^i, N_i\}$*

(3) $N^k = N$.

Proof: (sketch) By a well known result [Hack 72], every node of N belongs to some P–component. The nets N_1 to N_k are chosen isomorphic to some minimal set of P–components that cover the net. This guarantees that N can be obtained by synchronising N_1 to N_k. The result follows then from an important monotonicity property: if N^i is not SL&SB, then N^{i+1} is also not SL&SB. Now, if the synchronisation of $\{N^i, N_i\}$ were not well formed, N^{i+1} would not be SL&SB and, by the monotonicity result, neither would be N, against the hypothesis. ▪ 3.9

The net N of figure 2 can be obtained by synchronising first N_{11} and N_{12}, and synchronising then the result with N_{21} and N_{22} succesively.

The second result characterises, by means of a simple structural condition, the set of markings that make an SL&SB FC net live and bounded. This shows that by considering the structural problem first we did not impose a strong constraint.

Theorem 3.10 *Let N be an SL&SB FC net. (N, M_0) is live and bounded iff for every P-component $N_1 = (P_1, T_1, F_1)$ of N, at least one place of P_1 is marked at M_0.*

Proof: (hint) Follows from Commoner's theorem [Hack 72] and lemma 6.10 of [BT 87]. ▪ 3.10

The condition of theorem 3.10 can be checked in polynomial time by means of a graph algorithm.

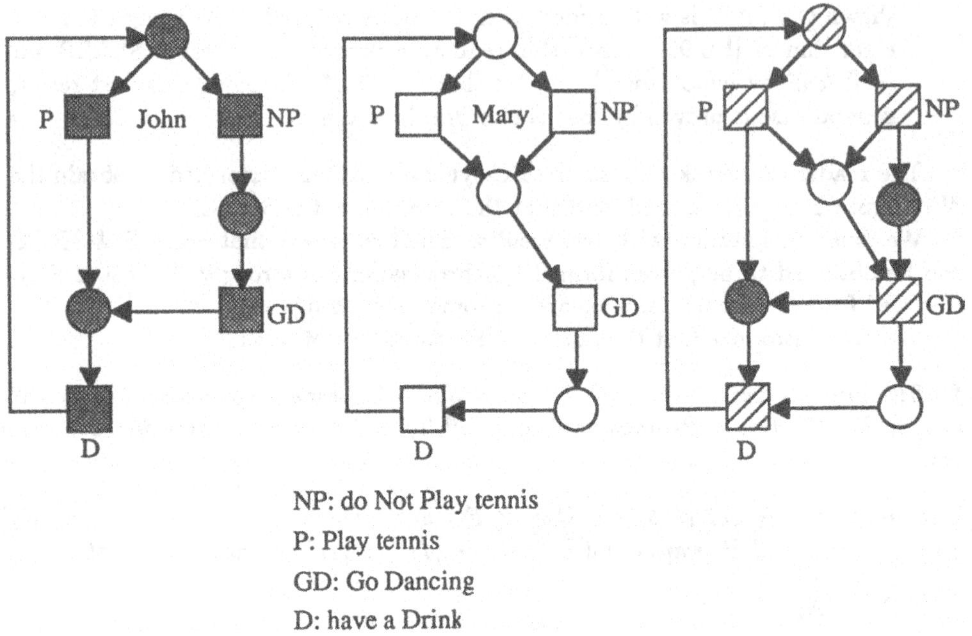

Figure 5: The pair of transitions (P, GD) is a synchronic mismatch.

4 High-level characterisation of structurally well-formed synchronisations

The definition of well formed synchronisations has one strong and one weak point. The strong point is its simplicity and suitability for calculations. The weak point, its absence of "meaning". If it is shown that a certain synchronisation is not well formed, the definition sheds no light on which kind of design error was committed. Due to this reason, we characterise here well formed synchronisations from a "high-level" point of view, by means of more complex structures in the graph theoretical sense, but closer to design concepts. In fact, we show that there are only two "bad structures" or structural design errors that may cause an FC-synchronisation to be non well formed.

Synchronic mismatches. In order to introduce this first design error, consider the two nets on the left of figure 5. They model the behaviour of John and Mary, two millionaires of Palm Beach. Every day John decides whether he will play tennis or not. If he does not play tennis, he goes dancing and then has a drink. If he does play tennis, then he is too tired to go dancing and just drinks. After the drink a new day comes and everything starts again.

Also Mary decides every day to play tennis or not. But, since she is in better shape than John, she always goes dancing after, and then has the drink. The question is: if John and Mary get married, and want to play tennis, go dancing and drink together, can the marriage reach a deadlock? The marriage corresponds to the FC-synchronisation on the right of the figure, and it is easy to see that the system can deadlock. The reason is that John can execute the action "do play tennis" an arbitrarily large number of times without executing "go dancing", while Mary cannot. Since the occurrence dependences of these two actions are different for the two components of the synchronisation we say that they do not "match".

To formalize the above problem, let us introduce a *synchronic relation*. Synchronic relations [Silv 87] are used to study dependences between the occurrences of transitions.

Definition 4.1 *Let (N, M_0) be a system with $N = (P,T,F)$ and $t_1, t_2 \in T$. We define the following relations over $T \times T$:*

(1) (t_1, t_2) *is in* k-bounded deviation relation *in* (N, M_0) *iff* $\forall M \in [M_0\rangle$ *and* $\forall \sigma$ *applicable at* M *(i.e.* $M[\sigma\rangle$*):* $\vec{\sigma}(t_2) = 0 \Rightarrow \vec{\sigma}(t_1) \leq k$.

(2) (t_1, t_2) *is in* bounded deviation relation (BD-relation) *in* (N, M_0) *iff* $\exists k \in I\!N$ *such that* (t_1, t_2) *is in k-bounded deviation relation.*

Let now $N = (P,T,F)$ be a net and $t_1, t_2 \in T$.

(3) (t_1, t_2) *is in* structural BD-relation *in* N *iff* $\forall M_0$: (t_1, t_2) *are in BD-relation.* ∎ 4.1

Definition 4.2 *Let N be a synchronisation of $\{N_a, N_b\}$ and $t_i, t_j \in T_a \cap T_b$. (t_i, t_j) is a* synchronic mismatch *iff it is in structural BD-relation in one and only one of N_a, N_b.* ∎ 4.2

In the case of John and Mary, the pair (P, GD) is in the structural BD-relation of Mary but not in the one of John. The pair is hence a synchronic mismatch.

Proposition 4.3 *Let N be an FC-synchronisation of $\{N_a, N_b\}$, where both N_a, N_b are SL&SB. If N contains a synchronic mismatch, then N is not SL&SB.*

Proof: (sketch) Assume w.l.o.g. that (t_i, t_j) is in the structural BD-relation for N_a but not for N_b. Using a result of [Silv 87], we have:

- every T-component of N_a containing t_i contains also t_j
- there exists a T-component N_b^1 of N_b that contains t_i but not t_j.

The proof is carried out by showing that N_b^1 has a TP–handle in N. Then, N is not well formed and by theorem 3.7 not SL&SB. It is proved that:

- There is an elementary path Π in N_a leading from a transition t of N_b^1 to t_j, such that its only node in N_b^1 is t.
  This part is non trivial. See [Espa 90b].

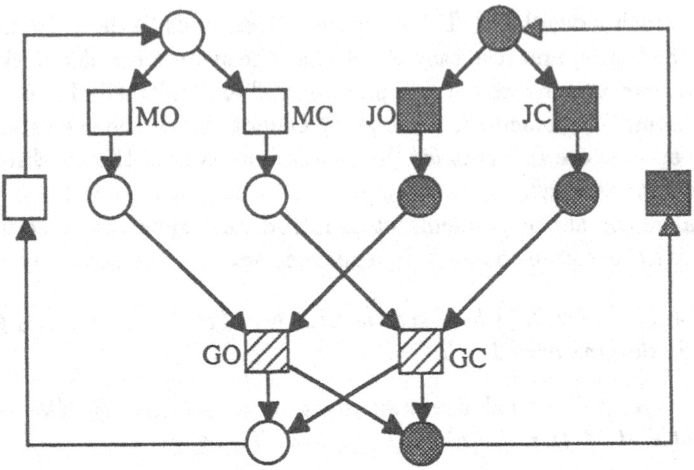

MO / JO: Mary / John decides to go to the Odeon

MC / JC : Mary / John decides to go to the Capitol

GO: John and Mary go to the Odeon

GC: John and Mary go to the Capitol

Figure 6: The two places on the top are killing choices.

- There is an elementary path Π' in N_b leading from t_j to a place p of N_b^1, such that its only node in N_b^1 is p.

  Since N_b is SL&SB, it is strongly connected [Best 87]. This guarantees the existence of an elementary path in N_b leading from t_j to a node of N_b^1, with only its last node in N_b^1. This last node is a place because N_b^1 is a T–component of N_b.

The TP–handle can be extracted from the concatenation of Π and Π'. ∎ 4.3

Killing choices. In order to introduce the second error, let us go back to John and Mary. They have changed of hobbies, and like now to go to the cinema every day. There are two cinemas for millionaires in Palm Beach, the "Odeon" and the "Capitol". John decides each day which of the two cinemas he wants to go to, and so does Mary.

John and Mary want to get married and go to the cinema together, but both want to decide, without consulting the other, which of the two cinemas they will go to. The corresponding synchronisation is shown in figure 6. Notice that the net contains no synchronic mismatches, but nevertheless leads to a deadlock for any marking. The deadlock is produced by the fact that the choices of John and Mary are *private*, but *concern the partner*. It is intuitively reasonable that these choices lead to non liveness for any marking. We call them *killing choices*.

Definition 4.4 *Let N be a FC-synchronisation of $\{N_a = (P_a, T_a, F_a), N_b = (P_b, T_b, F_b)\}$. A place $p \in P_a$ is a* killing choice *of N_a iff the following three conditions hold:*

(a) $p \notin P_b$

(b) There exists a T-component N_a^1 of N_a containing p and a transition $t_i \in T_a \cap T_b$.

(c) There exists an elementary path $B = (p, \ldots, t_j)$, $t_j \in T_a \cap T_b$, such that p is the only node of N_a^1 in B.

A killing choice of N_b is defined analogously. N contains a killing choice *iff it contains a killing choice of N_a or a killing choice of N_b.* ∎ 4.4

Notice that p is a place with more than one output transition, because it has at least one output transition in the T-component and another one out of it. In fact, N_a can decide freely at p whether the tokens are kept in the T-component or are taken out of it. The reader can check that the two top places of the net of figure 6 are killing choices.

We obtain the following result:

Proposition 4.5 *Let N_a and N_b be two SL&SB FC nets and N be an FC-synchronisation of $\{N_a, N_b\}$. If N contains a killing choice, then N is not SL&SB.*

Proof: (sketch) Assume w.l.o.g. that N contains a killing choice p of N_a. By definition, there exists a T-component N_a^1 of N_a containing p and t_i, but not t_j (where t_i, $t_j \in T_a \cap T_b$). The definition of killing choice does not impose further requirements on t_i , t_j. Nevertheless, it is inmediate to see the following:

- t_i can be chosen such that there exists an elementary path $\Pi = (t_i, \ldots, p)$ of N_a^1 whose only node in N_b is t_i.
- t_j can be chosen such that the only node of the path B in N_b is t_j (where B is the path required by the definition of killing choice).

As N_b is SL&SB, a well known result states that there exists a T–component of N_b containg t_i [Best 87]. Consider two cases:

Case 1. Every T-component of N_b containing t_i contains t_j.

In this case, N contains a synchronic mismatch and by proposition 4.3 it is not well formed.

Case 2. There exists a T-component N_b^1 of N_b that contains t_i but not t_j.

In this case, the concatenation of Π and B is an elementary path leading from N_b^1 to t_j whose only node in N_b^1 is t_i. Since N_b is SL&SB, it is strongly connected [Best 87]. Therefore there exists a path B' in N_b from t_j to N_b^1 whose only node in N_b^1 is the last one. This last node is a place because N_b^1 is a T-component of N_b. A TP-handle of N_b^1 can be extracted from the concatenation of Π, B and B'.

∎ 4.5

The completeness theorem. Killing choices and synchronic mismatches are structures that correspond to our intuitions of bad designs in the construction of a concurrent system. It is not surprising that they lead to deadlocks. The stronger result we present is that, loosely speaking, these are the only two possible errors. More precisely, all FC-synchronisations which are not SL&SB contain killing choices and/or synchronic mismatches:

Theorem 4.6 *Let N_a and N_b two SL&SB FC nets and N an FC-synchronisation of $\{N_a, N_b\}$. N is SL&SB iff it contains no synchronic mismatch and no killing choice.*

Proof: ($\Rightarrow$) Use propositions 4.3, 4.5.

($\Leftarrow$) If N is not well formed, we can assume w.l.o.g. that N_a^1 is a T-component of N_a with a TP-handle $H = (t, \ldots, p)$. It is possible to prove that H can be chosen as the concatenation of two paths Π_1 and B, where $\Pi_1 = (t, \ldots, t')$ is a handle of N_a and B is a path of N_a.
Consider now two cases:

Case 1. Every T-component of N_b containing t contains also t'.

Then (t, t') is a synchronic mismatch because t' is not a transition of N_a^1.

Case 2. There exists a T-component $N_b^1 = (P_b^1, T_b^1; F_b^1)$ containing t but not t'.

Let p' be the last node of Π_1 that belongs to N_b^1 (p' must be a place because N_b^1 is a T-component of N_b). The subpath $\Pi_1' = (p', \ldots, t')$ of Π_1 leads from N_b^1 to $t' \in T_a \cap T_b$ and its only node in N_b^1 is p'. Moreover, $p' \notin P_a$ because Π_1 is a handle of N_a. Then p' is a killing choice of N_b. ▪ 4.6

5 Fusions

Given a net N, N^{-d} denotes the reverse dual net of N. The following relationship between synchronisations and fusions follows easily from the definitions:

Proposition 5.1 *N is an FC-synchronisation of $\{N_a, N_b\}$ iff N^{-d} is an FC-fusion of $\{N_a^{-1}, N_b^{-1}\}$.* ▪ 5.1

Making use of this property and of the Duality theorem for FC nets, we can obtain for fusions similar results to the ones obtained for synchronisations. The Duality theorem states the following:

Theorem 5.2 *[Hack 72] Let N be a net. N is SL&SB FC iff N^{-d} is SL&SB FC.* ▪ 5.2

In order to check if an FC-fusion N of two SL&SB FC nets N_a, N_b is SL&SB as well, we just consider the reverse-dual net N^{-d}, which by proposition 5.1 is an FC-synchronisation. We can then check whether this FC-synchronisation is well formed. By theorem 3.7, this is the case exactly when N^{-d} is SL&SB and, by the Duality theorem, exactly when N is SL&SB.

It is possible to mimic our presentation of the results for synchronisations. An FC-fusion is defined to be *well formed* iff the FC-synchronisation of the reverse-dual components is well formed. Also the design errors can be introduced in the same way: an FC-fusion of two nets has a *killing joint* (respectively, a *fusion mismatch*) iff the FC-synchronisation of of the reverse-dual nets has a killing choice (respectively, a synchronic mismatch). We obtain the dual theorems corresponding to our two main results for synchronisations:

Theorem 5.3 *Let N be an FC-fusion of $\{N_a, N_b\}$ N is SL&SB iff it is well formed.* ▪ 5.3

Theorem 5.4 *Let N_a and N_b be two SL&SB FC nets and N an FC-fusion of $\{N_a, N_b\}$. N is SL&SB iff it contains no fusion mismatch and no killing joint.* ▪ 5.4

6 Conclusions

We have introduced two composition operators for Petri Nets. For the class of Free Choice nets, we have characterised by means of compositional structural conditions when these operators preserve SL&SB. We have interpreted this characterisation in terms of two design errors. These errors are close to the intuition, and suggest what to change in order to obtain a correct system.

Acknowledgements

We thank three anonymous referees for pointing out some mistakes and for helpful comments.

References

[BD 90] BEST, E.; DESEL, J.: *Partial Order Behaviour and Structure of Petri Nets.* Formal Aspects of Computing Vol.2 No.2, 123–138.

[Best 87] BEST, E.: *Structure Theory of Petri Nets: the Free Choice Hiatus.* Advanced Course on Petri Nets / Brauer, Reisig, Rozenberg (eds.), LNCS 254 and 255, pp. 168–205.

[BT 87] BEST, E.; THIAGARAJAN, P.S.: *Some Classes of Live and Safe Petri Nets.* Concurrency and Nets / Voss, K.; Genrich, H.J., Rozenberg, G. (eds.). — Berlin: Springer-Verlag, pp. 71–94.

[Dese 86] DESEL, J.: *A structural property of Free-choice systems.* Newsletter of the GI Special Interest Group in Petri Nets and Related System Models, No. 25, pp.16–20.

[Espa 90b] ESPARZA, J.: *Structure Theory of Free Choice nets.* Ph. D. Thesis, Departamento de Ingeniería Eléctrica e Informática, Universidad de Zaragoza, June.

[Espa 90] ESPARZA, J.: *Synthesis Rules for Petri Nets, and How They Lead to New Results.* CONCUR'90 / Baeten, Klop, (eds.), LNCS 458, pp.182–198.

[ES 91] ESPARZA, J.; SILVA, M.: *Handles in Petri Nets.* Hildesheimer Informatik Fachbericht, 3-91.

[ES 90] ESPARZA, J.; SILVA, M.: *Top-down Synthesis of Live and Bounded Free Choice nets.* Proceedings of the XIth. International Conference on Application and Theory of Petri nets. Paris, June, pp. 63-83. To appear in Advances in Petri Nets 91.

[GJRT 83] GENRICH, H.J.; JANNSENS, D.; ROSENBERG, G.; THIAGARAJAN, P.S.: *Petri Nets and Their Relation to Graph Grammars.* 2nd Int. Workshop on Graph Grammars and their Application to Computer Science. LNCS 153, pp. 115–129.

[Hack 72] HACK, M.H.T.: *Analysis of Production Schemata by Petri Nets.* Cambridge, Mass.: MIT, Dept. Electrical Engineering, MS Thesis. Corrected June 1974

[Silv 87] SILVA, M.: *Towards a Synchrony Theory for P/T Nets.* Concurrency and Nets / Voss, K.; Genrich, H.J., Rozenberg, G. (eds.). — Berlin: Springer-Verlag, pp. 71–94.

[TV 84] THIAGARAJAN, P.S.; VOSS, K.: *A Fresh look at free Choice Nets.* Information and Control, Vol. 61, No. 2, May, pp. 85–113.

The Observation Algebra of Spatial Pomsets*

Gian Luigi Ferrari†, Ugo Montanari‡

†IEI-CNR, Via Santa Maria 46, Italy
‡Dipartimento di Informatica, Università di Pisa, Corso Italia 40, Italy

Abstract

For sequential programming, the theory of functions provides a uniform metalanguage to describe behaviours by abstracting from the actual implementation of programs. For concurrent and distributed systems, instead, there is no well accepted metalanguage to describe the possible observations of the behaviour of programs. The proper treatment of observations is thus an important and complex issue of concurrency theory. In this paper we show that observations can be described in a uniform way by introducing certain algebras called *observation algebras*. They lift to an algebraic level the standard treatment of actions in the operational semantics of process algebras. Observations are described as terms of an algebra. As a consequence, we separate the *control* level (the operational semantics) from the *data* level (the observations). The chosen notion of observability can be obtained by suitably axiomatizing the operations of the observation algebra. We show how observation algebras can be naturally derived from process algebras. As a case study we consider Milner's CCS. We introduce an observation algebra for CCS and we show that the standard interleaving semantics can be obtained by axiomatizing the operations to yield actions. Furthermore, we give a complete axiomatization of an observation algebra whose elements are certain labelled partial orderings of events (pomsets) called *Spatial Pomsets*.

1 Introduction

Over the last few years many efforts in theoretical computer science have been devoted to define a comprehensive mathematical theory of concurrency. There are several controversies about the research in this field mainly because the motivations and the intuitions are derived from problems encountered in the practical programming activities, but there is no well accepted abstract model of parallel computing. A considerable number of models have been proposed. The approaches to semantics can be roughly divided into two groups: the *interleaving* approach (e.g.[Mil80,Mil89], [BHR84,Ho85], [AB84], [BK84], [He88]) and the *true concurrency* approach (e.g. [Re85], [Ma77], [NPW81], [Pr86], [BC88], [DM87]). The debate and the arguments of either these approaches are well known. The crucial point is that there is no agreement on the basic level of what a model of concurrency should be.

In the case of sequential programming the situation is quite different. In fact a sequential program can be viewed in an abstract way as a function which transforms its input data into its output data. The theory of functions supplies enough mathematical machinery to describe the abstract behaviour of sequential programs. The availability an abstract mathematical theory to describe abstract behaviours allows us to have a clean division between the observable behaviour (i.e. the input-output), and the control mechanisms (i.e. the computational rules which are

*Work partially supported by ESPRIT Basic Research Action 3011, CEDISYS, and by Progetto Finalizzato Informatica e Calcolo Parallelo, obiettivo LAMBRUSCO.

adopted to evaluate the value of a function on certain given data). In other words, the theory of functions provides a uniform metalanguage to describe the behaviour of programs by abstracting from their actual implementation.

Several models of concurrency are introduced and motivated by means of an observational scenario in terms of *button pushing experiments* [Mil81]. The observer interacts with a machine viewed as a black-box. In Milner's experimental set up each machine is equipped with a button for each basic experiment. The observer performs the experiment by pushing the corresponding button. The machine is also equipped with a display which is used to inform the observer that the machine is responding to the experiment. Certain combinators are then introduced on machines thus yielding an algebra of machines, usually called agents.

This experimental set up is rather intuitive. The main limitation is given by the identification between the basic experiments and the buttons of the machine. This identification leads to consider the experiments as the basic actions the machines are capable of performing. As a consequence there is no sensible difference between an action performed by a sequential machine, and the same action performed by a system of parallel machines. This assumption is at the basis of the interleaving semantics: the parallel execution of actions is represented by their non deterministic interleaving, i.e. a parallel machine is always simulated by a sequential but non deterministic machine. Hence, a total ordering between causally and/or spatially independent actions is imposed. This is the main criticism made by the true concurrency approach: the interleaving assumption that concurrency is not observable leads to describe a distributed system as a single processor performing multitasking, and thus the peculiar features of distributed systems are not faithfully represented.

Indeed, this criticism should not be moved against the experimental scenario but rather against the lack of structure of the experiments. Here, we extend Milner's experimental set up by assuming that the experiments are still basic actions but enriched with topological information stating the *locality* of the machine where the action takes place. In other words, the observer, beyond basic actions, knows the topological structure of the system of machines. Our approach has several analogies with the locality semantics independently introduced by [BCKH91]. Here, the linkage between actions and localities is *statically* derived from the structure of the processes; whereas in [BCKH91] localities are *dynamically* created to label the sites where the actions are observed.

Our starting point is the previous work [FGM91] on the (algebraic) equational characterization of bisimulation equivalences [Par81] for process algebras. In that paper a simple extension of Milner's *Calculus of Communicating Systems* (CCS) [Mil89] is proposed. The resulting process description language is called *Closed CCS* (CCCS). In CCS there is a prefix operator which from the atomic action μ and the agent E yields the agent $\mu.E$. Instead, in CCCS a generalized prefixing is allowed. The generalized prefixing takes an observation ω, an agent E and yields the agent $\omega.E$. The observations are elements of a special algebra called Observation Algebra. It is proved that bisimulation equivalences for CCCS are characterized by a complete set of axioms, and that the axiomatization does not depend on the actual algebra of observations. In fact by suitably interpreting the operations of the algebra of the observations to yield *specific* observations we still obtain sound and complete characterizations of the corresponding bisimulation equivalence.

A fundamental property of concurrency is the great variety of notions of observations of behaviours; in fact, depending on the application, one is interested in stressing one notion of behaviour more than others. For instance, at the user level one is interested in observing that the system has performed certain sequences of operations without any knowledge of parallism and distribution; hence interleaving semantics provide the right level of abstraction. Instead, information about distribution and causality can be profitely used at design level. For instance, if we imagine of deriving the design of a distributed system from its specification then we could be interested in having a measure of the degree of parallelism in order to map the specification into an architecture with a certain interconnection network.

In this paper we intend to show that observation algebras provide an uniform metalanguage to describe the observable behaviour of computations of concurrent and distributed systems. The behaviour of a system is represented by a term of an algebra. One advantage of this operation is the division between the *control* level (the computational rules, the operational semantics) and the *data* level (the observation of the behaviour of the system of processes). The control level is determined by the rules of the operational semantics of the language; instead the observability of the behaviour is determined by the chosen axiomatization of the observation algebra. By considering different interpretations of the operations of the algebra of observations we can consider a wide range of observations of behaviours: which aspects of the behaviour are of importance depends on the applications at hand. As a case study we consider CCS [Mil80,Mil89].

The operational semantics of CCS thus obtained can indeed be considered as a family of operational semantics one for each axiomatization of the algebra of observations. For instance, the standard interleaving treatment of actions can be retrieved by simply forgetting information about localities of actions.

A truly concurrent observational semantics is also provided. We introduce an algebra of labelled partial orders (pomsets) called *Spatial Pomsets*, where the events are labelled with spatial actions, i.e. actions containing information about localities. Spatial actions are exactly the basic experiments of the experimental scenario. We prove that the algebra of spatial pomsets is axiomatized by introducing permutation axioms on spatial actions. We introduce a relation, called *the concurrency relation*, on spatial actions. The idea is that the concurrency relation relates actions which take place on different localities, i.e. they are independent because they are performed by different components of the system. Spatial pomsets correspond to the equivalence classes of sequences of spatial actions modulo the equivalence induced by the concurrency relation.

As a byproduct of this result we have that our experimental scenario is powerful enough to distinguish pomsets. In this respect Pratt and Plotkin [PP90] have recently introduced an experimental scenario for observing arbitrary pomsets[1]. Their scenario involves the use of multiple observers (teams), and the use of an operation of action refinement. Instead, our experimental scenario is conceptually simpler: it just requires to know the localities where the actions take place.

In the theory of concurrency, the idea of describing the behaviour of a system as an equivalence class of sequences has been first exploited by Mazurkiewicz [Ma77,Ma89]. Mazurkiewicz's traces are a generalization of strings which allows modelling concurrency. A trace is an equivalence class of strings of actions up to commutativity of parallel independent actions. The similarity between spatial pomsets and traces is indeed very precise. We provide an obvious alternative characterization of spatial pomsets in terms of trace theory. Spatial Pomsets are isomorphic to the collection of traces over the concurrent alphabet whose symbols are spatial actions, and where the independence relation is given by the concurrency relation.

2 Process Algebras and Observation Algebras

In this section we introduce the notion of *Observation Algebra* as a mean to describe the observable behaviour of a system of processes. We assume some familiarity with CCS and related languages; we refer to [Mil89] for a general introduction to CCS. Let Δ (ranged over by α) be the alphabet of actions, and $\overline{\Delta}$ the alphabet of complementary actions ($\Delta = \overline{\overline{\Delta}}$). The set $\Lambda = \Delta \cup \overline{\Delta}$ will be ranged over by λ. Furthermore, let τ, $\tau \notin \Lambda$ be a special action to indicate internal moves, and let $\Lambda \cup \{\tau\}$ (ranged over by μ) be the set of CCS actions.

A CCS agent E has the following syntax:

$$E ::= nil \,,\ \mu.E \,,\ E\backslash\alpha \,,\ E[\Phi] \,,\ E_1 + E_2 \,,\ E_1 \mid E_2$$

[1] A simpler set up can be used to observe the so called series/parallel pomsets.

where Φ is a permutation on the set of CCS actions, preserving τ and complementation.

The standard operational semantics of CCS is given by axioms and inference rules [Plo81] which allow us to derive statements of the form $E_1 \xrightarrow{\mu} E_2$, where μ is the action (observation) associated to the transition. Basically, we have a deductive system where the transitions of the agent $\sigma(E_1, \ldots E_n)$, for some agent constructor σ, depend on the transitions of the agents $E_1, \ldots E_n$. Moreover, the deductive system explicitly uses information about the labels of transitions. For instance, an agent of the form $E_1 \backslash \alpha$ may evolve just by performing a transition which is not labelled with α or $\bar{\alpha}$ (consider the inference rule below)

$$\frac{E_1 \xrightarrow{\mu} E_2,\ \mu \notin \{\alpha,\ \bar{\alpha}\}}{E_1 \backslash \alpha \xrightarrow{\mu} E_2 \backslash \alpha}$$

A similar situation happens for the synchronization: only agents performing complementary actions may synchronize. As shown by De Simone [DeS85] the general pattern of behavioural rules which allows one to provide an operational semantics of process constructors in MEIJE-CCS languages is

$$\frac{\{p_i \xrightarrow{a_i} p_i' \mid i \in [1,k]\} \ \&\ R(a_1, \ldots, a_k, a)}{\sigma(p_1, \ldots p_n) \xrightarrow{a} p}$$

where $k \leq n$, R is a $(k+1)$-ary relation over the set of actions and p is a term of the language.

Here, in presenting the operational semantics of CCS we do not strictly follow De Simone's format; instead, we represent the use of information about the labels of transition by means of operations on the alphabet of actions. Thus, we write

$$E_1 \xrightarrow{\omega} E_2$$

to indicate that E_1 evolves to E_2 by ω, ω being a term of the algebra whose constants are actions. The operational semantics of CCS is presented in Table 1.

$$\mu.E \xrightarrow{\mu} E$$

$$\frac{E_1 \xrightarrow{\omega} E_2}{E_1 \backslash \alpha \xrightarrow{\omega \backslash \alpha} E_2 \backslash \alpha} \qquad \frac{E_1 \xrightarrow{\omega} E_2}{E_1[\Phi] \xrightarrow{\omega[\Phi]} E_2[\Phi]}$$

$$\frac{E_1 \xrightarrow{\omega} E_2}{E_1 + E \xrightarrow{\omega <+ -} E_2} \qquad \frac{E_1 \xrightarrow{\omega} E_2}{E + E_1 \xrightarrow{- +> \omega} E_2}$$

$$\frac{E_1 \xrightarrow{\omega} E_2}{E_1 \mid E \xrightarrow{\omega \rfloor -} E_2 \mid E} \qquad \frac{E_1 \xrightarrow{\omega} E_2}{E \mid E_1 \xrightarrow{- \lfloor \omega} E \mid E_2}$$

$$\frac{E_1 \xrightarrow{\omega} E_2,\ E_1' \xrightarrow{\omega'} E_2'}{E_1 \mid E_1' \xrightarrow{\omega \mid \omega'} E_2 \mid E_2'}$$

Table 1: The Operational Semantics of CCS

The operational semantics for CCS introduced in this way allows us to derive transitions which do not correspond to any transition of the classical interleaving semantics. For instance, the transition

$$\frac{\alpha.nil \xrightarrow{\alpha} nil,\ \beta.nil \xrightarrow{\beta} nil}{\alpha.nil \mid \beta.nil \xrightarrow{\alpha \mid \beta} nil \mid nil}$$

even if derivable, does not represent a *legal* or *observable* transition of the CCS term $\alpha.nil \mid \beta.nil$.

The set of observable transitions can be obtained by suitably axiomatizing the terms which label the transition relation. The idea is that the axioms embody the chosen notions about the observability of behaviours. The standard interleaving semantics of CCS is given below. We use the special symbol δ, $\delta \notin \Lambda \cup \{\tau\}$, to indicate the occurrence of an error.

- $\mu\backslash\alpha =$ if $\mu \in \{\alpha, \overline{\alpha}\}$ then δ else μ
- $\mu[\Phi] = \Phi(\mu)$,
- $\mu <+- = -+> \mu = \mu$,
- $\mu\rfloor - = -\lfloor\mu = \mu$,
- $\mu \mid \mu' =$ if $\mu = \overline{\mu'}$ then τ else δ,
- $\delta\backslash\alpha = \delta[\Phi] = \delta <+- = -+> \delta = \delta\rfloor - = -\lfloor\delta = \omega \mid \delta = \delta \mid \omega = \delta$

It is immediate to prove that the set of the interleaving CCS transitions corresponds to the set of transitions $E_1 \xrightarrow{\omega} E_2$ with $\omega \neq \delta$.

As a result of this discussion we have that we can safely replace the labels of transitions with an algebra of observations which is suitably axiomatized. One advantage of this operation is the separation between the *control* level (the operational semantics) and the *data* level (the observation of the behaviour of the system of processes). In fact the control level is determined by the axioms and inference rules of Table 1; instead the observability of the behaviour is determined by the introduction of an axiomatization of the observation algebra.

In this perspective, the elementary actions can be understood as the basic universe of data the processes may manipulate. The operations on the actions have the intuitive meaning of describing the physical structure of data. For instance, the term $\lambda\rfloor-$ expresses the data λ has been provided by some process in the left part of the system. In other words, term $\lambda\rfloor-$ contains topological information stating where the observed activity takes place. Similarly, the term $\lambda_1 \mid \lambda_2$ expresses that the data is a result of a synchronization of two components of the system one on the right and the other on the left. Further, the term $\lambda\backslash\alpha$ states a constraint on the availability of data: data of the form α or $\overline{\alpha}$ are private data of a subpart of the system and thus cannot be exported outside. More subtle is the case concerning nondeterminism. Intuitively, the term $\lambda <+-$ expresses that the data λ is the result of a choice. The crucial point is to understand whether or not the choice context should be observable. Assuming that the choice context is observable, the agents $\alpha.nil+\alpha.nil$ and $\alpha.nil$ have a different observable behaviour. In the first case the action α is always available within a choice context. This is not the case for the latter agent. Instead, assuming that the choice contexts are not visible, the two agents have the same observable behaviour.

In this paper we assume that choices made by the control mechanism are not observable, in other words the observer is not able to see the refused alternatives. However, the technical development we are proposing can be easily extended to deal with the observability of choices.

Consequently, the inference rules of the operational semantics of CCS concerning the non deterministic choice are modified as follows:

$$\frac{E_1 \xrightarrow{\omega} E_2}{E_1 + E \xrightarrow{\omega} E_2} \qquad\qquad \frac{E_1 \xrightarrow{\omega} E_2}{E + E_1 \xrightarrow{\omega} E_2}$$

Definition 1 *(Basic CCS Observation Algebras)*
A basic CCS observation algebra *(*B_{CCS}*)* Ω, *with elements called* observations *(denoted by* ω*), is any one- sorted algebra with the following syntax:*

$$\omega ::= \lambda\,,\ \delta\,,\ \omega\backslash\alpha\,,\ \omega[\Phi]\,,\ \omega\rfloor-\,,\ -\lfloor\omega\,,\ \omega \mid \omega'$$

$\lambda\backslash\alpha = \lambda, \lambda \notin \{\alpha, \overline{\alpha}\}$	$\lambda[\Phi] = \Phi(\lambda)$
$\alpha\backslash\alpha = \overline{\alpha}\backslash\alpha = \delta$	$\delta[\Phi] = \delta$
$(\omega\rfloor-)\backslash\alpha = \omega\backslash\alpha\rfloor-$	$(\omega\rfloor-)[\Phi] = \omega[\Phi]\rfloor-$
$(-\lfloor\omega)\backslash\alpha = -\lfloor\omega\backslash\alpha$	$(-\lfloor\omega)[\Phi] = -\lfloor\omega[\Phi]$
$(\omega \mid \omega')\backslash\alpha = \omega \mid \omega'$	$(\omega \mid \omega')[\Phi] = \omega[\Phi] \mid \omega'[\Phi]$
$\theta_1[\lambda_1] \mid \theta_2[\lambda_2] = \delta,$	if $\lambda_1 \neq \overline{\lambda_2}$
$\delta\rfloor- = -\lfloor\delta = \omega \mid \delta = \delta \mid \omega = \delta$	$(\omega_1 \mid \omega_2) \mid \omega_3 = \omega_1 \mid (\omega_2 \mid \omega_3) = \delta$

Table 2: The Axioms of Basic Observation Algebras

where $\lambda \in \Lambda$, δ is a special constant, $\delta \notin \Lambda$, $\alpha \in \Delta$, and Φ is a permutation of Λ such that $\Phi(\overline{\alpha}) = \overline{\Phi(\alpha)}$. A context of B_{CCS} is called θ-context *($\theta[]$) provided that it is built using only the operations $\rfloor-$ and $-\lfloor$. Furthermore, a basic observation algebra satisfies the axioms of Table 2.* □

We can comment briefly on the definition of basic observation algebra. The element δ acts as absorbing element for all the operations. The axioms express that the operations $\backslash\alpha$ and $[\Phi]$ have the meaning of restriction and relabelling. These operations distribute with respect to the other operations. We have already remarked that terms of the form $\omega\rfloor-$ $(-\lfloor\omega)$ describe the observation of an asynchronous evolution of a subcomponent of the system. Terms of the form $\omega \mid \omega'$ are used to indicate the occurrence of a synchronization. Notice that the operation of synchronization is binary (i.e. only two components of the system are involved and active in the communication) and follows the standard CCS synchronization mechanism. The attempts of synchronizing more than two components yields the error δ.

An example of CCS observation algebra is the initial algebra T_Ω, i.e. the initial algebra in the class of algebras satisfying the presentation of B_{CCS}.

Definition 2 *(Spatial Actions)*
Let T_S be the set of terms which can be expressed with the restricted signature S comprising $\lambda, \rfloor-, -\lfloor$ and $\mid$. □

Thus the terms of the restricted signature describe the possible experiments: actions enriched with topological information, i.e. *spatial actions*.

Theorem 3 *(Normal Form Observations)*
For any observation ω, $\omega \neq \delta$, in T_Ω there exists an observation ω' in T_S such that $\omega = \omega'$.

Proof. The proof is by induction on the structure of ω. Because the operations $\backslash\alpha$ and $[\Phi]$ distribute over the other operations we can always push them inside the structure of terms until an action λ is found. Now, applying the axioms for the basic cases we can remove the operations $\backslash\alpha$ and $[\Phi]$. Notice that when the operation $\backslash\alpha$ is applied to terms of the form $\omega \mid \omega'$, it can be directly removed. □

The existence of the normal form ensures that the operations $\backslash\alpha$ and $[\Phi]$ are indeed auxiliary. Hence spatial actions are precisely the basic experiments of the experimental set up.

Example 4 *(Interleaving Forgets Spatial Information)*
The elements of the interleaving observation algebra $\mathcal{I}$ are actions including τ, plus δ. The algebra $\mathcal{I}$ can be understood as the quotient of the initial algebra with respect to the axioms defining the interpretation of the operations. Each constant λ is interpreted by the corresponding action, and the interpretation of the operations is defined as follow.

$$\lambda\rfloor - = \lambda, \qquad -\lfloor\lambda = \lambda \qquad \lambda \mid \bar{\lambda} = \tau$$

The interleaving interpretation forgets information about the physical distribution: the experiments are just actions. Notice that with the above interpretation the algebra $\mathcal{I}$ becomes the synchronization algebra of CCS as defined by Winskel [Win82]. □

Each element of a basic observation algebra stands for an observation of a single step of the evolution of a system. The introduction of an operation of sequential composition allows us to deal with the observations of computations.

Definition 5 *(CCS Observation Algebras)*
Let Ω_C be any algebra obtained by enriching the signature of B_{CCS} with a binary operation $-;-$. This operation is subjected to the axioms of Table 3. □

$\omega;\delta = \delta;\omega = \delta$	$(\omega_1;\omega_2);\omega_3 = \omega_1;(\omega_2;\omega_3)$
$(\omega_1;\omega_2)\backslash\alpha = \omega_1\backslash\alpha;\omega_2\backslash\alpha$	$(\omega_1;\omega_2)[\Phi] = \omega_1[\Phi];\omega_2[\Phi]$
$(\omega_1;\omega_2)\rfloor - = \omega_1\rfloor -;\omega_2\rfloor -$	$-\lfloor(\omega_1;\omega_2) = -\lfloor\omega_1;-\lfloor\omega_2$
$(\omega_1;\omega_2) \mid \omega = \delta$	$\omega \mid (\omega_1;\omega_2) = \delta$

Table 3: The Axiomatization of the operation of sequential composition

The axiomatization of the operation of sequential composition expresses that the operation is strict with respect to the element δ, it is associative, and that all the operations except the $\mid$ distribute over computations. The axioms $(\omega_1;\omega_2) \mid \omega = \delta$ and $\omega \mid (\omega_1;\omega_2) = \delta$ state that we cannot synchronize computations.

The precedence among the operators is given, in decreasing order, by: $\backslash\alpha$, $[\Phi]$, $\mid$, $\rfloor-$, $-\lfloor$, $;$, thus the expression $\alpha\rfloor - \backslash\alpha \mid \beta[\Phi];\gamma\rfloor-$ means $(((\alpha\rfloor-)\backslash\alpha) \mid (\beta[\Phi]));(\gamma\rfloor-)$.

The operation of sequential composition between observations is reflected at control level (i.e. in the operational semantics) by the introduction of the following behavioural rule:

$$\frac{E_1 \xrightarrow{\omega} E' \;\&\; E' \xrightarrow{\omega'} E_2}{E_1 \xrightarrow{\omega;\omega'} E_2}$$

The initial algebra of computations $\mathcal{T}_{\Omega_C}$ is the algebra freely generated by the presentation of Ω_C. Because of the distributivity of the operations with respect to sequential composition, and because of computations cannot be synchronized we have that a normal form for computations can be obtained by considering the restricted signature S_C having just $\lambda, \rfloor-, -\lfloor, \mid$ and $;$.

Theorem 6 *For any computation ω, $\omega \neq \delta$, in $\mathcal{T}_{\Omega_C}$ there exists a computation $\omega' = \omega_1;\ldots;\omega_n$ in $\mathcal{T}_{S_C}$ such that $\omega = \omega'$, and for each i, ω_i does not contain the operation of sequential composition and it is in normal form.*

Proof. By the existence of the normal form for basic process algebras, and by the distributivity of the operations with respect to the operation of sequential composition. □

3 The Algebra of Spatial Pomsets

In this section we introduce an observation algebra whose elements are certain labelled partial orders called *Spatial Pomsets*. Before introducing the algebra of spatial pomsets we need some preliminary definitions. We start by recalling the definition of labelled partial orders.

Definition 7 *(Labelled Partial Orders)*
A labelled partial order *over a set of actions A is a structure $(E, \leq, \ell)$ where $(E, \leq)$ is a partially ordered set, and ℓ is a mapping from E to A which assigns to each element of E an action taken from A.* □

The elements of E are called *events*, and $\ell(e)$ is the action that happens at e. The ordering relation $\leq$ describes the causal links among events, i.e. $e_1 \leq e_2$ is intended to mean that the occurrence of the event e_1 causes the occurrence of e_2. Two events e_1, e_2 are *concurrent*, notation $e_1 \, co \, e_2$, provided that they are not related by the ordering relation, i.e. neither $e_1 \leq e_2$ nor $e_2 \leq e_1$. Finally, we use the symbol $\prec$ to indicate the immediate causality relation, i.e. $e_1 \prec e_2$ provided that $e_1 \leq e_2$, $e_1 \neq e_2$, and there does not exist any e such that $e_1 \leq e \leq e_2$.

Labelled partial orders are considered up to isomorphisms, i.e. label and order preserving bijections among their events. After Pratt [Pr86], a class of isomorphic labelled partial orders is usually called *pomset*.

One of the main problems of the partial ordering approach to the description of concurrent computations is that there is no operation of sequential composition for partial orders which preserves all informations on causal dependencies. The only exception is provided by the simple case of series parallel pomsets where all the actions in the first pomset cause all the actions of the second pomset. In this paper we equip pomsets with a sophisticated operation of sequential composition, where the actions of the first pomset may cause actions of the second pomset only when their occurences fill a common part of the space. To this aim we introduce a more refined view of pomsets which is obtained by considering *spatial actions* as set of event labels . We first introduce a relation, called *the concurrency relation*, $\diamond$, over spatial actions. Intuitively, actions performed in different parts of the space are related by $\diamond$.

Definition 8 *(The Concurrency Relation)*
The concurrency relation, $\diamond$, *is the least binary symmetric relation over spatial actions satisfying the clauses below:*

$$\omega_1\rfloor - \diamond - \lfloor\omega_2$$

$$\frac{\omega_1 \diamond \omega_2}{\omega_1\rfloor - \diamond \, \omega_2\rfloor -} \qquad\qquad \frac{\omega_1 \diamond \omega_2}{-\lfloor\omega_1 \diamond - \lfloor\omega_2}$$

$$\frac{\omega_1 \diamond \omega_2}{\omega_1\rfloor - \diamond \, \omega_2 \mid \omega} \qquad\qquad \frac{\omega_1 \diamond \omega_2}{-\lfloor\omega_1 \diamond \omega \mid \omega_2}$$

$$\frac{\omega_1 \diamond \omega_2 \;\&\; \omega_1' \diamond \omega_2'}{\omega_1 \mid \omega_1' \diamond \omega_2 \mid \omega_2'}$$

□

The first clause expresses the commutativity between actions observed on different parts of the space. The rest of the clauses express the compatibility of the concurrency relation with respect to the spatial information. Let $\asymp$ be the complement of the concurrency relation $\diamond$; hence two spatial actions are related by $\asymp$ provided that they share some space. For instance, $\alpha\rfloor - \diamond - \lfloor\beta$, while $\alpha\rfloor - \asymp \beta\rfloor -$. Moreover, we have $\alpha\rfloor - \asymp (-\lfloor\gamma)\rfloor -$; instead, $\beta\rfloor - \mid \overline{\beta} \diamond (-\lfloor\gamma)\rfloor -$.

Definition 9 *(Spatial Pomsets)*
A spatial pomset p *is a pomsets over the set of spatial actions T_S such that*

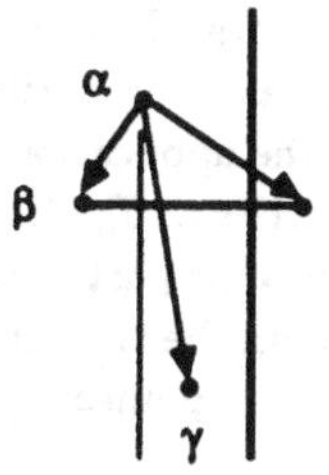

Figure 1: A Spatial Pomset.

(i) $e_1 \prec e_2$ *implies* $\ell(e_1) \asymp \ell(e_2)$,

(ii) $e_1 \; co \; e_2$ *implies* $\ell(e_1) \Diamond \ell(e_2)$. □

Thus a spatial pomset describes a computation of a distributed system by providing information both about causality and distribution. Intuitively, in the computation represented by the spatial pomset, if two events are related by the immediate causality relation then they overlap in space, i.e. theirs label are related by $\asymp$ (point (i) of Definition 9). Instead, if two events are concurrent then they are performed on non overlapping parts of the space, i.e. their labels are related by $\Diamond$ (point (ii) of Definition 9). Figure 1 illustrates a spatial pomset. Actions describing the occurrence of a synchronization are represented by linking together their components. The spatial information of the actions is directly drawn in the picture: it can be inferred by the positions of the events with respect to the simmetry lines. Finally, the partial ordering is represented by its Hasse diagram growing downward. In the example of Figure 1 the action $\alpha\rfloor-$ causes both the action $\beta\rfloor- \mid \overline{\beta}$, and the action $(-\lfloor\gamma)\rfloor-$. These actions are instead concurrent between them.

Definition 10 *(The Algebra of Spatial Pomsets)*
The algebra of Spatial Pomsets, $\mathcal{SP}$, contains the spatial pomsets generated by the following constants and operations. The set of constants Λ will be interpreted as the set of pomsets p_λ (the pomset with one event labelled by λ), and the constant δ by the element δ of the algebra; we assume that the element δ is absorbent with respect to all the operations. Let $p = (E, \leq, \ell)$ be a spatial pomset.

(i) If for each $e \in E$, $\ell(e)\backslash\alpha \neq \delta$, then $p\backslash\alpha = p$. Otherwise, $p\backslash\alpha = \delta$.

(ii) $p[\Phi] = (E, \leq, \ell')$ where for all the events e, $\ell'(e) = \ell(e)[\Phi]$

(iii) $p\rfloor- = (E, \leq, \ell')$, where for all the events e, $\ell'(e) = \ell(e)\rfloor-$. Symmetrically for the operation $-\lfloor p$.

(iv) The operation of synchronization, $p_1 \mid p_2$, yields a pomset only when both have a unique event, say e_1 and e_2, respectively, and $\ell_1(e_1) = \theta_1[\lambda]$, $\ell_2(e_2) = \theta_2[\overline{\lambda}]$. In this case, $p_1 \mid p_2$ consists of just an event e, whose label is $\ell_1(e_1) \mid \ell_2(e_2)$. Otherwise, $p_1 \mid p_2 = \delta$.

(v) Let $p_1 = (E_1, \leq_1, \ell_1)$ and $p_2 = (E_2, \leq_2, \ell_2)$ be spatial pomsets. Then $p_1; p_2 = (E, \leq, \ell)$ where:

- $E = E_1 \cup E_2$
- $\leq$ *is the reflexive and transitive closure of the relation*

$$\leq_1 \cup \leq_2 \cup \{(e_1, e_2) \mid e_1 \in E_1, e_2 \in E_2, \ell_1(e_1) \asymp \ell_2(e_2)\}$$

- $\ell = \ell_1 \cup \ell_2$. □

In the definition of the operations of the algebra of spatial pomsets we use the properties of spatial actions viewed as elements of the initial basic observation algebra $\mathcal{T}_\Omega$. For instance, in the definition of the operation $\backslash\alpha$ we first evaluate the application of the operator $\backslash\alpha$ to the labels of the events of the pomset. Because of the properties of $\mathcal{T}_\Omega$ the result is different from δ provided that there is no attempt at performing α or $\overline{\alpha}$ in some part of the space. In this case, the result of $p\backslash\alpha$ is p. Similarly, in the case of the $p[\Phi]$ to obtain the right labelling we evaluate the application of the operator $[\Phi]$ to the labels of the events of the pomset.

Theorem 11 *(Soundness & Completeness)*

(a) The collection of spatial pomsets is the closure of the constants p_λ with respect to the operations of the algebra $\mathcal{SP}$.

(b) The algebra of spatial pomsets is an observation algebra.

Proof.

(a) We first show that the operations are well defined, i.e. if the result of the application of an operator to a spatial pomset is different from δ then it is a spatial pomset. The proof is by case analysis. For the operations of $\backslash\alpha$, $[\Phi]$ and synchronization the result is immediate. In the case of the operation $\rfloor-$ it is enough to note that $\omega\Diamond\omega'$ implies $\omega\rfloor-\Diamond\omega'\rfloor-$. Symmetrically, for $-\lfloor$. The only difficult case concerns the operation of sequential composition. However, notice that an event of the first pomset causes an event of the second pomset provided that their labels are related by relation $\asymp$. This ensures that the resulting labelled partial ordering satisfies condition (i) and (ii) of the definition of spatial pomsets.

We have to show now that any spatial pomset can be obtained by using the operations. Let p be a spatial pomset, and let $e_1,\ldots,e_n$ be a total ordering of its events which is compatible with the partial ordering. The pomset p is obtained by considering the expression $p_1;p_2;\ldots;p_n$, where p_i is the pomset with just one event whose label is $\ell(e_i)$. Clearly, the pomsets p_i are generated from the constants p_λ applying the operations (except sequential composition) in a suitable way. Because the operations are well defined the result follows.

(b) Trivial, by construction the operations satisfy the axioms. □

An example of the operations of the algebra of spatial pomsets is reported in Figure 1. The pomset is the evaluation of the term $(\alpha\rfloor-;(\beta\rfloor-)\mid\overline{\beta};(-\lfloor\gamma)\rfloor-)\backslash\beta$. In the rest of this paper, we will use $\mathcal{P}(\omega)$ to indicate the spatial pomset which is the result of the evaluation of the term ω. More formally, $\mathcal{P}$ is the unique homomorphism from the initial algebra $\mathcal{T}_{\Omega_C}$ to the algebra $\mathcal{SP}$.

Theorem 12 *(Generation Ordering)*
Let ω, $\omega\neq\delta$, be a computation in normal form which evaluates to the spatial pomset p. Then the computation ω individuates over p an obvious total ordering of events which is compatible with the partial ordering.

Proof. Assume that $\omega=\omega_1;\ldots;\omega_n$. By hypothesis $p=\mathcal{P}(\omega_1;\ldots;\omega_n)$, and because $\mathcal{P}$ is an homomorphism of observation algebras $\mathcal{P}(\omega_1;\ldots;\omega_n)=\mathcal{P}(\omega_1);\ldots;\mathcal{P}(\omega_n)$. Since ω is in normal form, each ω_i does not contain the operator of sequential composition, and thus each $\mathcal{P}(\omega_i)$ individuates an event e_i of the spatial pomset. By construction $\{e_1<e_2<\ldots<e_n\}$ is a total ordering compatible with the partial ordering. □

As a final example, consider the following terms $(\alpha\rfloor-);(-\lfloor\beta)$ and $(-\lfloor\beta);(\alpha\rfloor-)$. They both evaluate to the same spatial pomset with two concurrent events, however the two terms are not identified by the axioms of Table 2 and 3.

4 Axiomatizing the Algebra of Spatial Pomsets

In this section we provide a complete axiomatization of the algebra of spatial pomsets.

Definition 13 *(Permutation Algebra)*
Let $\mathcal{P}_{\Omega_C}$ be the algebra of observations obtained as the quotient of the observation algebra $\mathcal{T}_{\Omega_C}$ with respect to the equational rule:

$$\frac{\omega_1 \diamond \omega_2}{\omega_1;\omega_2 = \omega_2;\omega_1}$$

□

In the following, we will use $=_{\mathcal{P}}$ to indicate the equality in the algebra $\mathcal{P}_{\Omega_C}$. For instance in the permutation algebra we have $(\alpha\rfloor -);(-\lfloor\beta) =_{\mathcal{P}} (-\lfloor\beta);(\alpha\rfloor -)$. Furthermore, $(\alpha\rfloor -) \mid (\overline{\alpha}\rfloor -);(-\lfloor\alpha) \mid (-\lfloor\overline{\alpha}) =_{\mathcal{P}} (-\lfloor\alpha) \mid (-\lfloor\overline{\alpha});(\alpha\rfloor -) \mid (\overline{\alpha}\rfloor -)$. In fact we have $\alpha\rfloor - \diamond - \lfloor\alpha$, and $\overline{\alpha}\rfloor - \diamond - \lfloor\overline{\alpha}$; by applying the last clause of the definition of concurrency relation we have: $(\alpha\rfloor - \mid \overline{\alpha}\rfloor -)\diamond(-\lfloor\alpha \mid -\lfloor\overline{\alpha})$, and from this the above equality follows.

Lemma 14 *Let $\omega_1;\omega_2$ be a two-step computation in normal form such that $\mathcal{P}(\omega_1;\omega_2)$ is a spatial pomset having just two concurrent events. Then $\mathcal{P}(\omega_1;\omega_2) = \mathcal{P}(\omega_2;\omega_1)$ and $\omega_1;\omega_2 =_{\mathcal{P}} \omega_2;\omega_1$.*

Proof. The proof is by induction on the structure of ω_1 and ω_2. Because the two-step computation evaluates to a spatial pomset having just two concurrent events, then the basic case is $\omega_1 = \lambda_1\rfloor -$ and $\omega_2 = -\lfloor\lambda_2$, for some $\lambda_i \in \Lambda$.

Because of the definition of concurrency relation we have $\lambda_1\rfloor - \diamond - \lfloor\lambda_2$. It is immediate to see that $\mathcal{P}(\omega_1;\omega_2) = \mathcal{P}(\omega_2;\omega_1)$, and, because of the definition of the algebra $\mathcal{P}_{\Omega_C}$ we have $\omega_1;\omega_2 =_{\mathcal{P}} \omega_2;\omega_1$.
To prove the inductive steps, it is sufficient to apply the clauses of the definition of the concurrency relation. In fact, by a soundness analysis it is easy to see that these clauses ensure to cover all the possible cases in which a two step computation in normal form can be written. □

Lemma 15 *Let $\omega = \omega_1;\ldots;\omega_n$, $\omega \neq \delta$, be a computation in normal form such that $\mathcal{P}(\omega) = p$. Let e, e' be two concurrent events of p individuted by the two consecutive steps ω_i, ω_{i+1} of ω, respectively. Then there always exists a computation in normal form $\omega' = \omega_1;\ldots;\omega_{i-1};\omega_{i+1};\omega_i;\ldots\omega_n$ such that $\mathcal{P}(\omega') = \mathcal{P}(\omega)$.*

Proof. Because $\mathcal{P}$ is a homomorphism of observation algebras

$$\mathcal{P}(\omega_1;\ldots;\omega_n) = \mathcal{P}(\omega_1);\ldots;\mathcal{P}(\omega_i);\mathcal{P}(\omega_{i+1});\ldots\mathcal{P}(\omega_n)$$

By applying Lemma 14 we have that $\mathcal{P}(\omega_i;\omega_{i+1}) = \mathcal{P}(\omega_{i+1};\omega_i)$ and $\omega_i;\omega_{i+1} =_{\mathcal{P}} \omega_{i+1};\omega_i$. Hence

$$\begin{aligned}\mathcal{P}(\omega) &= \mathcal{P}(\omega_1);\ldots;\mathcal{P}(\omega_i);\mathcal{P}(\omega_{i+1});\ldots\mathcal{P}(\omega_n)\\ &= \mathcal{P}(\omega_1);\ldots;\mathcal{P}(\omega_{i+1});\mathcal{P}(\omega_i);\ldots\mathcal{P}(\omega_n)\\ &= \mathcal{P}(\omega_1;\ldots;\omega_{i+1};\omega_i;\ldots\omega_n) = \mathcal{P}(\omega')\end{aligned}$$

Computation ω' is in normal form and has the required properties. □

Lemma 16 *Let $\omega = \omega_1;\ldots;\omega_n$ be a computation in normal form such that $\mathcal{P}(\omega) = p$. Let e_i, e_j be two concurrent events of p individuted by the two steps ω_i, ω_j of ω, $j > i$, respectively. Then for all k, $i < k < j$, the events e_k individuated by the steps ω_k are concurrent with either e_i or e_j.*

Proof. This follows directly from the fact that the computation ω individuates a total ordering of events which is compatible with the partial ordering. □

Theorem 17 *(Completeness)*
Let ω and ω' two computations in normal form which evaluates to the same spatial pomset p. Then $\omega =_{\mathcal{P}} \omega'$.

Proof. Because the two computations evaluate to the same spatial pomsets they do differ only for the generation ordering of concurrent events. Let e and e' be two concurrent events which are generated in a different order by the two computations. Without loss of generality, we can assume that e is generated at step i in ω, and at step i' in ω'. Similarly, e' is generated at step j in ω, and at step j' in ω'. Assume that $i < j$, this by hypothesis implies that $j' < i'$. Now, because of the previous lemma, we events generated in ω at step k, with $i < k < j$ are concurrent either with e or with e'. The same happens for the events generated in ω' at step k', $j' < k' < i'$. Now, perform the necessary exchanges of consecutive concurrent events. The previous lemmas ensures that we get the required equality. □

Theorem 18 *(Representation Theorem)*
The algebra $\mathcal{P}_{\Omega_C}$ is isomorphic to the algebra of spatial pomsets. □

The terms $(\alpha\rfloor-) \mid \overline{\alpha}$ and $(-\lfloor\alpha) \mid \overline{\alpha}$ are not identified in the permutation algebra, i.e. they do not evaluate to the same spatial pomset. In our experimental set up, in the first term we have a synchronization between the first and the third machine, instead in the second term the synchronization is between the second and the third machine. This distiction might be thought of as too artificial. However, it is easy to convince oneself that this must be the case when we have an incremental approach to the description of computations. In fact, assume that the above terms are the intermediate states of the computations $\alpha\rfloor- \mid \overline{\alpha};\beta\rfloor-\rfloor-$ and $-\lfloor\alpha \mid \overline{\alpha};\beta\rfloor-\rfloor-$. In the first computation the action β is caused by the synchronization; this is not the case in the second computation.

An obvious alternative characterization of the algebra of spatial pomsets in terms of the theory of traces can be provided: it is enough to forget about the operations of the algebra of spatial pomsets apart from the operation of sequential composition. The operation of sequential composition will play the role of the operation of concatenation of traces. We start by recalling the basic definitions of traces; we refer to [Ma77,Ma89] for a more comprehensive introduction.

Definition 19 *(Concurrent Alphabet)*
A concurrent alphabet *is a pair $A = (\Sigma, \mathcal{I})$ where Σ is a finite set (the alphabet of A), and $\mathcal{I}$ is a symmetric irreflexive relation, $\mathcal{I} \subseteq \Sigma^2$, called the independency relation.* □

Definition 20 *(Traces)*
Let A be a concurrent alphabet. Define $\equiv_A$ as the least congruence in the monoids of strings on Σ such that $a\,\mathcal{I}\,b$ implies $ab \equiv_A ba$. Thus $\sigma \equiv_A \sigma'$ if and only if σ can be trasformed to σ' by a finite number of exchanges of adjacent independent actions. The relation $\equiv_A$ is called trace equivalence. *The equivalence classes of $\equiv_A$ are called* traces *over the concurrent alphabet A.* □

The intuitive idea is that $a\,\mathcal{I}\,b$ holds provided that a and b are not causally related, i.e. they can be executed in any order. For instance, let $\Sigma = \{a, b, c\}$ be an alphabet of actions, and $b\,\mathcal{I}\,c$ (and symmetrically) the only independency. Then the equivalence class of the string $abbca$ is:

$$[abbca]_{\equiv} = \{abbca, abcba, acbba\}.$$

Let $(\mathcal{T}_S, \diamond)$ be the concurrent alphabet whose alphabet of symbols is the set of spatial actions, and where the independency relation is given by the concurrency relation $\diamond$. We can transform a computation in normal form into a trace over this concurrent alphabet just by considering the operation of sequential composition as the operation of cancatenation of traces. Let $\omega = \omega_1; \ldots ; \omega_n$ be a computation of $\mathcal{T}_{\Omega_C}$ in normal form, $\omega \neq \delta$. Let $Tr(\omega)$ be the trace defined as $Tr(\omega) = [\omega_1\omega_2\ldots\omega_n]_{\equiv}$. As an example, the trace corresponding to $\alpha\rfloor-;-\lfloor\beta$ is $\{(\alpha\rfloor-)(-\lfloor\beta),(-\lfloor\beta)(\alpha\rfloor-)\}$. The following characterization result is almost immediate.

Theorem 21 *(Spatial Pomsets as Traces)*
The collection of spatial pomsets is isomorphic to the traces over $(T_S, \diamond)$. □

5 Concluding Remarks

In this paper a new experimental scenario for concurrency theory has been introduced. This experimental set up has led to the definition of certain algebras called observation algebras. We have shown that observation algebras provide a uniform framework to define the observational semantics of process description languages. It should be remarked that a complete equational characterization of a bisimulation equivalence for CCS based on spatial pomset observations can be automatically obtained by adding the axiomatization of the algebra of Spatial Pomsets to the (complete) equational theory of the Observational Equivalence introduced in [FGM91].

In the case of process algebras, the semantics by *permutation* has been exploited by Boudol and Castellani [BC89,BC90], and by the authors [FM90,CFM90]. The key idea is to consider *Proved Transition Systems* where transitions are labelled with their proofs [BC89,BC90], or *Structured Transition Systems*, i.e. transition systems with algebraic structure on both states and transtions [FM90,CFM90], and then to take advantage of the information of proofs, or of the algebraic structure on transitions to identify CCS computations which can be obtained one from the other by permuting parallel independent transitions. The use of an experimental scenario based on spatial actions is conceptually simpler and greatly simplify the definition of the concurrency relation, and, hence, the permutation semantics.

Together with the definition of mathematical models, several efforts have been devoted to define logics for reasoning about the behaviour of concurrent and distributed systems. Specifications and verifications of properties of concurrent programs are usually treated using modal and temporal logics (e.g. [MP89], [La83], [CES86] [Sti89]). In our algebraic framework, logics which describe the observable behaviour of computations can be obtained by considering *Dynamic Logics* [Ha84]. Dynamic Logics are special modal logics where the modalities are parameterized by terms of an algebra of programs[2]. A simple example of propositional dynamic logic is provided by the *Hennessy-Milner Logic* (HML) [HM85]. HML is a dynamic logic where modalities are indexed by atomic actions, i.e. by basic programs or experiments. Hennessy and Milner have shown that the *Observational Equivalence* is completely characterized by HML: the equivalence induced by the logic coincide with the bisimulation equivalence. Clearly, similar results can be extended and reformulated in our framework.

Acknowledgement

We would like to thank Roberto Gorrieri for fruitful discussions and collaborations in joint works which have led to the development of the ideas of this paper.

References

[AB84] Austry, D. Boudol, G. *Algebre de Processus et Synchronization*, Theoretical Computer Science **30** (1), pp 91-131, 1984.

[BC88] Boudol, G., Castellani, I., *Concurrency and Atomicity*, Theoretical Computer Science **59** (1,2), pp. 25- 84, 1988.

[2]In the classical formulation the algebra of programs is a Kleene algebra.

[BC89] Boudol, G., Castellani, I., *Permutations of Transitions: An Event Structure Semantics for CCS*, In Proc. REX School, Workshop on Linear Time Branching Time and Partial Orders in Logics and Models for Concurrency, LNCS **354**, pp 411-437 1989.

[BC90] Boudol, G., Castellani, I., *Three Equivalent Semantics Semantics for CCS*, In Semantics of Systems of Concurrent Processes, LNCS **469**, pp 96-141, 1990.

[BCKH91] Boudol, G., Castellani, I., Kiehn, A., Hennessy, M., *Observing Localities*, To appear Proc. MFCS 1991, LNCS, 1991.

[BHR84] Brookes, S.D., Hoare, C.A.R., Roscoe, A.D., *A Theory of Communicating Sequential Processes*, Journal of ACM **31** (3), pp 560-599, 1984.

[BK84] Bergstra, J., Klop, W., *Process Algebra for Synchronous Communication*, Information and Control **60**, pp 109-137, 1984.

[CES86] Clarke, E., Emerson, A., Sistla, P. *Automatic Verifications of Finite State Concurrent Systems using Temporal Logic Specifications*, ACM, TOPLAS, **8**, pp 244-263, 1986.

[CFM90] Corradini, A., Ferrari, G., Montanari, U. *Transition Systems with Algebraic Structure as Models of Computations*, In Semantics of Systems of Concurrent Processes, LNCS **469**, pp 185-222, 1990.

[DM87] Degano, P., Montanari, U., *Concurrent Histories: A Basis for Observing Distributed Systems*, Journal of Computer and System Sciences **34**, pp 422-461, 1987.

[DeS85] De Simone, R., *Higher Level Synchronising Devices in MEIJE-SCCS*, Theoretical Computer Science, **37** (3), pp 245-267, 1985.

[FGM91] Ferrari, G., Gorrieri, R., Montanari, U., *An Extended Expansion Theorem*, In Proc. TAPSOFT 91, LNCS **494**, pp 29-48, 1991.

[FM90] Ferrari, G., Montanari, U., *Towards the Unification of Models for Concurrency*, Proc. CAAP'90, LNCS **431**, pp 162-176, 1990.

[Ha84] Harel, D. *Dynamic Logic*, In Handbook of Philosophical Logic, Vol II, (Gabbay-Guenthner Eds.), pp 497-604, 1984.

[Ho85] Hoare, C.A.R., *Communicating Sequential Processes*, Prentice Hall, 1985.

[He88] Hennessy, M. *An Algebraic Theory of Processes*, MIT Press, 1988.

[HM85] Hennessy, M., Milner, R., *Algebraic Laws for Nondeterminism and Concurrency*, Journal of ACM **32** (1), pp 137-141, 1985.

[La83] Lamport, L. *What Good is Temporal Logic*, IFIP-83, pp 657-668, 1983.

[Ma77] Mazurkiewicz, A. *Concurrent Program Schemes and their Interpretations*, Technical Report DAIMI PB-78, Aarhus University, 1977.

[Ma89] Mazurkiewicz, A. *Basic Notions of Trace Theory*,In Proc. REX School, Workshop on Linear Time Branching Time and Partial Orders in Logics and Models for Concurrency, LNCS **354**, pp 285-363, 1989.

[Mil80] Milner, R., *A Calculus of Communicating Systems*, LNCS **92**, 1980.

[Mil81] Milner, R. *A Modal Characterization of the Observable Machine Behaviour*, In Proc. CAAP 81, LNCS **112**, pp 25-34, 1981.

[Mil89] Milner, R., *Communication and Concurrency*, Prentice Hall, 1989.

[MP89] Manna, Z., Pnueli, A. *The Anchored Version of the Temporal Framework*, In Proc. REX School, Workshop on Linear Time Branching Time and Partial Orders in Logics and Models for Concurrency, LNCS **354**, pp 201-284 1989.

[Par81] Park, D., *Concurrency and Automata on Infinite Sequences*, in Proc. GI, LNCS **104**, pp 167-183, 1981.

[NPW81] Nielsen, M., Plotkin, G. Winskel, G. *Petri Nets, Event Structures and Domains* (Part I). Theoretical Computer Science, **13** (1), pp 85-108, 1981.

[Plo81] Plotkin, G. *A Structured Approach to Operational Semantics*, DAIMI FN-19, Computer Science Dept. University of Aarhus, 1981.

[PP90] Plotkin, G., Pratt, W., *Teams Can See Pomsets*, Preliminary Report, August 1990.

[Pr86] Pratt, V., *Modelling Concurrency with Partial Orders*, Int. Journal of Parallel Programming, **15** (1), pp 381-400, 1986.

[Re85] Reisig, W. *Petri Nets: An Introduction*, EATCS Monograph, Springer, 1985.

[Sti89] Stirling, C. *Modal and Temporal Logics*, To appear in Handbook of Logic in Computer Science, Vol I, (Gabbay- Maibaum Eds.) Oxford University Press.

[Win82] Winskel, G. *Event Structure Semantics for CCS and Related Languages*, Proc. ICALP 82, LNCS **140**, pp 561- 576, 1982.

Synchrony loosening transformations for Interacting Processes

Nissim Francez* Ira R. Forman†

1 Introduction

In this paper we consider *synchrony loosening transformations* (*SLTs*) for *multiparty interactions*. Refinement has been applied to several subjects. For example: *Data Refinement:* Replacing abstract data by more efficient concrete representation e.g. [23], [5], *Action Refinement:* Replacing a complex action by a combination of simpler actions (a common refinement), *Atomicity Refinement:* [6].

While the theory of stepwise refinement (by correctness preserving transformations) has reached a rather elaborate state by now (e.g., [4], which contains further references), very little, if anything, has been said about the refinement of synchronous, multiparty actions. Such actions occur only in the context of distributed programs and have been found to be a very useful design tool, as explained below.

Synchrony loosening transformations constitute a major design tool used in *Interacting Processes (IP)* [21]. The core of *IP* together with its operational semantics have been defined in [3], [20]. The latter presents an informal application of one synchrony loosening transformation to the design of an electronic fund transfer system. This paper considers several such transformations and proves that each preserves total-correctness. This is a powerful new application of proof systems: The proof of the source program, within some given proof system, is "massaged" to obtain a proof of the target program (with respect to the same specification), again within the given proof system. Thus, proof systems can be used for more than direct a posteriori program verification. The actual verification of the transformations is based on the formal proof system for (the core of) *IP*, presented in [19]. The main problem is the establishment of the *monotonicity* of the *SLTs* , whereby their application to subparts of a program in *any* context (or under certain contextual constraints) preserves the correctness of the whole program. This is the key property needed for *stepwise* refinement [4].

This paper covers total correctness only (including deadlock freedom). It is expected that the results will be strengthened to the effect that general temporal properties, expressible in *temporal-logic*, are preserved too, once a proof system for showing the satisfaction of such properties by *IP* programs is developed.

Our interest in *SLTs* stems from our wish to support the following design methodology for *reactive systems*:

- Start with a simple *IP* program that has perspicuous correctness because it employs "fat" multiparty interactions. Such interactions may synchronize an arbitrary number of *participating processes* (possibly all processes in the system) and during the interaction arbitrary expressions over the *combined state* may be computed by the participating processes. Such a program typically has a relatively small state space, thereby contributing to the ease of verification.

- Refine the initial program by (stepwise) application of *SLTs* , whereby the "fat" interaction is decomposed to "thinner" interactions. Such interactions may involve fewer participants and compute simpler expressions over the combined state. Usually, additional state information is introduced to facilitate these transformations. This step may be iterated until the synchrony level of the resulting design matches the one available in the implementation network and.

- Encapsulate the design in a *team abstraction* to facilitate reuse of abstraction. *Conflict Propagation* [20] is needed for this step to guarantee coordinated invocation (*enrolement* in the *IP* parlance) of the abstraction.

*Computer Science Dept., Technion, Haifa, Israel

†Microelectronics and Computer Technology Corp., Austin, Texas

- Orthogonally, inducing ***separation of concerns***, design control modification of the programs obtained by using ***superimposition*** [22].

We shall concern ourselves here only with the first two steps.

The closest to our view is that of [7] and [10], which do deal with joint actions refinement. However, the notion of participants synchronizing and forming a (temporary) combined state is lacking there. Their notion of a process, similar to *UNITY* [11], is a derived one, obtained by variable partitioning. In *IP* processes form abstract units of structure and have nothing to do with low-level implementation considerations.

Because various forms of synchronous multiparty interactions have appeared in the literature and because we believe in their strong potential in reactive systems design, we attribute great importance to extending the theory of action refinements to cover the additional aspect of synchrony loosening of such joint actions. The practical advantages of this design method have been shown by its application to *Raddle87* [2], a predecessor of *IP*, e.g., see [15], [16]. It was applied in the *IP* framework in [20]. It is also advocated in [24]. However, no where has a formal verification of the correctness preservation of *SLTs* been presented.

Further transformations may be employed to reduce the program to (completely) asynchronous message passing. To represent such solutions in *IP*, we would need to employ ***teams***, the ***abstraction*** mechanism in *IP*. Since such techniques of converting binary interactions to asynchronous message passing have been already studied, e.g., [9], we do not dwell more on this issue here.

Below, all references to axioms and proof rules refer to the version of ***cooperating proofs*** presented in [19].

2 Synchrony loosening transformations and their correctness

We start by providing a formal definition of *SLTs* . The purpose of this formalization is more to set up context and direct the intuition, since the transformations considered here are clearly synchrony loosening. For the sake of the definition we assume the notion of a ***context*** $C[\bullet]$. We refer to the argument position of a context as its ***hole***. We only consider contexts having the syntactic form of a concurrent composition, in which the hole has a part, referred to as a ***sub-hole***, in each concurrent component. When a concrete concurrent composition P is substituted for the hole, $C[P]$ becomes a complete program. The exact definition of this substitution is ommitted here for lack of space. There is a natural correspondance between computations of $C[P]$ and $C[P']$. For our purposes, all programs are *IP* programs, but the definitions hold under more general circumstances. Lamport's ***control predicates*** $in(P)$, $before(P)$ and $after(P)$ are used. Since we are dealing with concurrent computations, we use $in_i(P)$ to say that process P_i satisfies $in(P)$, and similarly for the other predicates.

Definition:

1. P' is ***less presynchronous*** than P, denoted by $P' <^{\overleftarrow{s}} P$, iff for every context $C[\bullet]$ the following two conditions are satisfied:
   - For every $i,\ j,\ i \neq j$, and for every execution of $C[P']$: if $in_i(P') \Longleftrightarrow in_j(P')$, then the corresponding computation of $C[P]$ satisfies $in_i(P) \Longleftrightarrow in_j(P)$.
   - There is an execution of $C[P']$ and $i,\ j,\ i \neq j$ such that $in_i(P') \wedge before_j(P')$, while in the corresponding computation of $C[P]$ $in_i(P) \Longleftrightarrow in_j(P)$ holds.
2. P' is ***less postsynchronous*** than P, denoted by $P' <^{\overrightarrow{s}} P$, iff for every context $C[\bullet]$ the following two conditions are satisfied:
   - For every $i,\ j,\ i \neq j$, and for every execution of $C[P']$: if $in_i(P') \Longleftrightarrow in_j(P')$, then the corresponding computation of $C[P]$ satisfies $in_i(P) \Longleftrightarrow in_j(P)$.
   - There is an execution of $C[P']$ such that $in_i(P') \wedge after_j(P')$, while in the corresponding computation of $C[P]$ $in_i(P) \Longleftrightarrow in_j(P)$ holds.
3. P' is ***weakly less synchronous*** than P, denoted by $P' <^{w} P$ iff P' is either less presynchronous than P or less postsynchronous than P.
4. P' is ***strongly less synchronous*** than P, denoted by $P' <^{s} P$ iff P' is both less presynchronous than P' and less postsynchronous than P'.

All transformations considered here produce strongly less synchronous outcomes, though weak synchrony loosening is useful too. Below, we shall take P to consist of merely one multiparty interaction, while P' might be a complicated combination of interactions with possibly less participants.

Next, we define the correctness of a *SLTs* . Actually, such transformations inherit the general definition of correctness, namely the ***preservation of specification satisfaction***. Here, the specifications of concern are those of ***total correctness***, denoted usually by $[p]\ P\ [q]$, where p and q are the precondition and post condition, respectively. This specification implies partial correctness $\{p\}\ P\ \{q\}$, termination, and ***deadlock freedom***. The latter is of special concern, because the loosening of synchrony is prone to introduce deadlock.

Definition: P' is a ***correct refinement*** of P, denoted by $P \leq P'$ iff for every p and q: $[p]\ P\ [q] \Rightarrow [p]\ P'\ [q]$.

Thus, we are interested in *SLTs* $\mathbf{T}$ such that $C[\mathbf{T}(P)] \leq C[P]$. In Back's refinement calculus (cited above) the weakest precondition is used for the same purpose. However, to date there is no satisfactory definition of weakest precondition semantics for distributed programs with explicit concurrent composition, though some first attempts may be found in [14]. Hence, in establishing the correctness of the *SLTs* considered below, ***cooperating proofs*** are used to establish partial correctness and deadlock freedom, and well-founded decreasing ***variants*** are used to establish termination.

Regarding deadlock freedom, synchrony loosening may introduce two kinds of deadlock.

Internal deadlocks: This is a deadlock *within* $\mathbf{T}(P)$. The absence of such deadlocks is shown below for each transformation, considered in isolation of any context.

External deadlock: This is a deadlock that occurs in some context $C[\mathbf{T}(P)]$, when some processes need not engage at all in the execution of $C[\mathbf{T}(P)]$, while the semantics of *IP* forces coordination in P. The absence of this kind of deadlock is part of the ***monotonicity*** of $\mathbf{T}$, dealt with in a separate section.

Note that this distinction does not rise in refinements of ***joint actions*** [8], in which there is no explicit synchronization of concurrent processes. In [20] we introduce ***conflict propagation*** to allow treating this difficulty.

3 Loosening by splitting

One of the simplest synchrony loosening transformation is ***splitting*** an interaction into two or more, based on the connectivity of its dependency graph [24]. We discuss in detail the binary case. The general case is similar.

Consider an interaction a with parts $P :: [\, \|_{i \in A}\ a[\bar{x}_i := \bar{e}_i]\,]$, and suppose that $A = B \cup C$ is a partition of A such that

- No expression $e \in \bar{e}_i,\ i \in B$, refers to a variable $x \in \bar{x}_j,\ j \in C$.
- No expression $e \in \bar{e}_j,\ j \in C$, refers to a variable $x \in \bar{x}_i,\ i \in B$.

and suppose that P should terminate and satisfy

$$\{p\}\ P\ \{q\} \tag{1}$$

Assume that the following local proof-outline is an application of the *iba* axiom.

$$\{p_i\}\ a[\bar{x}_i := \bar{e}_i]\ \{q_i\} \qquad (L_1)$$

Furthermore, cooperation with respect to a ***global invariant*** I is established using the *gia* axiom in:

$$\{I \wedge \bigwedge_{i \in A} p_i\} \left[\, \|_{i \in A}\ a[\bar{x}_i := \bar{e}_i] \right] \{\, I \wedge \bigwedge_{i \in A} q_i\} \qquad (C_1)$$

(suppressing the trivial bracketing required by the cooperation-rule). Note that I may refer to variables of *all* the participants of interaction a.

Together with an application of the concurrent-composition rule, (L_1) and (C_1) constitute a partial-correctness proof for P for specification (1).

The transformation $\mathbf{S}(P)$ does the following:

- The interaction a is split into two interactions $a_1,\ a_2$.

- The program P above is transformed into $\mathsf{S}(P) :: [\ \|_{i\in B}\ a_1 [\bar{x}_i := \bar{e}_i]\ \|\ \|_{i\in C}\ a_2 [\bar{x}_i := \bar{e}_i]]$

Operationally, in an execution of $\mathsf{S}(P)$ first one of the split interactions occurs, followed by the other (in any order). The main problem at this stage is the addition of an intermediate state (between the two split interaction), that might violate the invariant I. Intuitively, one feels that, given the separability of reference in interaction a, that additional state 'should not matter'. However, for embedding in an encompassing context, the invariant *may* relate variables in both B and C. For a simple example, consider the program

$$\begin{array}{l} P :: [P_1 :: x : \textbf{integer};\ a[x := y]\ \| \\ \quad\ \ P_2 :: y : \textbf{integer};\ a[\ ]\ \| \\ \quad\ \ P_3 :: u : \textbf{integer};\ a[u := v]\ \| \\ \quad\ \ P_4 :: v : \textbf{integer};\ a[\ ]\ ] \end{array}$$

Clearly, the dependency graph can be decomposed into $B = \{1,\ 2\}$, $C = \{3,\ 4\}$. Still, one might prove $\{y = v\}\ P\ \{x = u\}$. In [24], such an invariant renders the original synchrony of being *essential*. We return to this issue at the end of this section.

We now convert the above proof to a proof of $\{p\}\ \mathsf{S}(P)\ \{q\}$, thereby establishing its partial-correctness preservation. Note that termination here is trivial, as no iteration is introduced. Internal deadlock freedom is also trivial, as interaction-parts have neither alternatives nor guards. Thus, every part is continuously ready.

The first step is to decompose I into $I_B \wedge I_C \wedge I_A$, where I_B refers only to variables in B, I_C refers only to variables in C, and I_A may refer to all variables in A. Any of these conjuncts may be identically true.

Observation: For a postcondition q_i, $i\in B$, its justification can depend only on I_B, since its variables are updated only in terms of variables in B. Similarly, only I_C is needed to establish postconditions q_i, $i\in C$.

The next step is the introduction of *auxiliary variables* to represent control states in the program. Thus, each process P_i is augmented with a *new* variable, say z_i (not referred to within P). The initial value of z_i is 0, and it is reset by P_i to 1 after the respective split interaction (a_1 or a_2, depending on whether $i\in B$ or $i\in C$) is executed. To keep the trivial bracketing, the additional auxiliary assignment is placed in the interaction part itself. Thus, for the new local proof-outlines, the precondition of P_i is $p_i' \stackrel{df.}{\equiv} p_i \wedge z_i = 0$, while the new postcondition is $q_i' \stackrel{df.}{\equiv} q_i \wedge z_i = 1$. The justification of the new conjunct in the postcondition is directly established by the augmenting auxiliary assignment. The justification of the 'old' pre-post relationship is given.

With the aid of these auxiliary variables another global invariant I' is constructed "to remember" the effect of a split interaction in the new intermediate state and carry it to the final state (after both splits have taken place). This reestablishes I. The following abbreviations are used in the formulation of I':

- $\mathrm{eq}_A(\bar{z}) \stackrel{df.}{\equiv} \bigwedge_{i\in A} z_i\in\{0,\ 1\} \wedge z_1 = \cdots = z_n$
- $\mathrm{eq}_B(\bar{z}) \stackrel{df.}{\equiv} \bigwedge_{i\in B} z_i = 1 \wedge \bigwedge_{i\in C} z_i = 0$
- $\mathrm{eq}_C(\bar{z}) \stackrel{df.}{\equiv} \bigwedge_{i\in B} z_i = 0 \wedge \bigwedge_{i\in C} z_i = 1$

$$I' \stackrel{df.}{\equiv} I_B \wedge I_C \wedge (\ \mathrm{eq}_B(\bar{z}) \Rightarrow I^{\bar{x}_i}_{\bar{e}_i,\, i\in B}\ ) \wedge (\ \mathrm{eq}_C(\bar{z}) \Rightarrow I^{\bar{x}_i}_{\bar{e}_i,\, i\in C}\ ) \wedge (\ \mathrm{eq}_A(\bar{z}) \Rightarrow I)$$

By the variables disjointness assumption and split dependency graph,

$$[I^{\bar{x}_i}_{\bar{e}_i,\, i\in C}]^{\bar{x}_i}_{\bar{e}_i,\, i\in B} \equiv [I^{\bar{x}_i}_{\bar{e}_i,\, i\in B}]^{\bar{x}_i}_{\bar{e}_i,\, i\in C}$$

That is, the assignments of the a_1 and a_2 interactions have the same effect in any order.

We now have to show that I' accomplishes the required cooperation. There are four cases to consider.

Case 1: Interaction a_1 is executed first. We have to show that

$$\{I' \wedge \bigwedge_{i\in B} p_i'\}\ [\ \|_{i\in B}\ a_1 [\bar{x}_i := \bar{e}_i]]\ \{I' \wedge \bigwedge_{i\in B} q_i'\}$$

In this case $\bigwedge_{i\in A} z_i = 0$ holds initially, implying $\mathrm{eq}_A(\bar{z})$. Hence, I holds initially. Therefore, the justification of the local postconditions and of I_B, I_C is as given in the original proof. Upon termination, $eq_B(\bar{z})$ holds. However, $I^{\bar{x}_i}_{\bar{e}_i,\, i\in B}$ is provable by applying *gia* to a_1. The other conjuncts of I' hold vacuously.

Case 2: Interaction a_1 is executed second. We have to show that

$$\{I' \wedge \bigwedge_{i\in C} p'_i\} \; [\, \big\|_{i\in C} a_1 [\bar{x}_i := \bar{e}_i]] \; \{I' \wedge \bigwedge_{i\in C} q'_i\}$$

In this case $\mathrm{eq}_B(\bar{z})$ holds initially. By the observation mentioned above, the justification of local postconditions, as well as that of I_B, remains unaffected. The antecedent of the third conjunct of I' becomes true. However, after executing a_1 second, both split interactions have been executed. Since in the precondition we have $I^{\bar{x}_i}_{\bar{z}_i, i\in C}$, the combined effect is $[I^{\bar{x}_i}_{\bar{z}_i, i\in C}]^{\bar{x}_i}_{\bar{z}_i, i\in B}$ which is equivalent to $I^{\bar{x}_i}_{\bar{z}_i, i\in A}$. The latter preserves I by the originally given proof.

Note that we skipped the formal substitution manipulation needed to derive that argument by applying the assignment axiom, *gia* and the consequence rule.

Cases 3 and 4: Similar to cases 1 and 2, with a_2 replacing a_1 and C and B interchanged.

For example, in the program P considered above, the intermediate state is "remembered" by converting the initial $y = v$ to $z = v$, becoming the required $x = u$ after the second split interaction is finished.

As a final note, though the original invariant I is *not* preserved throughout the transformed program, it *need not be*, since it is not part of the specification; rather, it is an artifact of the proof. Thus, such transformations can be applied in some cases even when synchronization is "essential" in the terminology of [24]. We return to a more detailed discussion of conditions of applicability in the section on monotonicity.

4 Loosening by decoupling

Decoupling is one of simple but commonly used *SLTs* in which a ternary interaction is transformed into two binary ones. The temporal ordering on the two binary interactions is achieved by having them share a participant, in which the respective interaction-parts are sequentially composed. The same method could decouple an interaction with n participants into an interaction with m participants, $m < n$, followed by an interaction with $n - m + 1$ participants, imposing the temporal ordering in the same way. Also, an overlap of more than one participant can be similarly defined. We treat the ternary case only in order to simplify the notation.

The main application of this transformation is in replacing the preservation of a global invariant by its temporary relaxation and its later reestablishment.

Consider a concurrent composition $P :: [\, P_1 \| P_2 \| P_3 \,]$ that is supposed to terminate and satisfy

$$\{p\}\; P\; \{q\} \tag{2}$$

Let each process have the following form:

$$P_i :: \; a[\bar{x}_i := \bar{e}_i]\,, \; i = 1,\, 2,\, 3$$

where the collections of local variables $\bar{x}_i$ are pairwise disjoint. As a preliminary assumption (to be relaxed below), assume that $\bar{e}_1$ and $\bar{e}_2$ have no reference to variables in $\bar{x}_3$. Let $\bar{y}_1 \subseteq \bar{x}_1$ be the variables in P_1 referred to by expressions in $\bar{e}_3$.

Assume that the following local proof-outline is an application of the *iba* axiom.

$$\{p_i\}\; a[\bar{x}_i := \bar{e}_i]\; \{q_i\} \tag{L_2}$$

Furthermore, cooperation with respect to a *global invariant* I is established using the *gia* axiom in:

$$\{I \wedge \bigwedge_{1\le i\le 3} p_i\} \left[\big\|_{1\le i\le 3} a[\bar{x}_i := \bar{e}_i]\right] \{\, I \wedge \bigwedge_{1\le i\le 3} q_i\} \tag{C_2}$$

The transformation $\mathbf{D}$ transforms P according to the following rules:

- Interaction a is 'broken' into two interactions a_1 and a_2.
- The interaction parts of a in P_1 and P_3 are replaced by corresponding parts for a_1 and a_2. The part of a_1 in P_1 preserves the assignments in the corresponding part of a. However, in the part of a_2 in P_3, every reference to a variable, say v, in y_1 is replaced by a reference to a *new* variable u (in P_2). Let $\bar{u}$ be the collection of these variables, assumed in a one-to-one correspondence with $\bar{y}_1$.

$$
\begin{aligned}
\mathbf{D}(P) :: [\; & \\
& P_1 :: a_1 [\bar{u}_1 := \bar{y}_{2,1}];\ a_3 [\bar{v}_1 := \bar{y}_{3,1}];\ \bar{x}_1 := (\,\bar{e}_1\,)^{\bar{y}_{2,1},\,\bar{y}_{3,1}}_{\bar{u}_1,\,\bar{v}_1} \\
& \| \\
& P_2 :: a_1 [\bar{u}_2 := \bar{y}_{1,2}];\ a_2 [\bar{v}_2 := \bar{y}_{3,2}];\ \bar{x}_2 := (\,\bar{e}_2\,)^{\bar{y}_{1,2},\,\bar{y}_{3,2}}_{\bar{u}_2,\,\bar{v}_2} \\
& \| \\
& P_3 :: a_2 [\bar{u}_3 := \bar{y}_{2,3}];\ a_3 [\bar{v}_3 := \bar{y}_{1,3}];\ \bar{x}_3 := (\,\bar{e}_3\,)^{\bar{y}_{1,3},\,\bar{y}_{2,3}}_{\bar{u}_3,\,\bar{v}_3}\ ]
\end{aligned}
$$

Figure 1: General ternary to binary decoupling

- The interaction part for a in P_2 is replaced by an interaction part for a_1. This part contains all the assignments as the original part of a, as well as the new assignments $u := v$ for every $v \in \bar{y}_1$, u being the corresponding variable. This part is *sequentially composed* with an interaction part of a_2 with an empty set of assignments.

Thus, the transformed program has the form

$$\mathbf{D}(P) :: [\, P_1 :: a_1 [\bar{x}_1 ::= \bar{e}_1] \,\|\, P_2 :: a_1 [\bar{x}_2 := \bar{e}_2,\ \bar{u} := \bar{y}_1];\ a_2 [\,] \,\|\, P_3 :: a_2 [\bar{x}_3 := (\,\bar{e}_3\,)^{\bar{y}_1}_{\bar{u}}]\,]$$

In converting the given partial-correctness proof for P to one for $\mathbf{D}(P)$ the idea is similar to that of the splitting transformation. The invariant I'' needs to record a property of the arising intermediate state between the execution of a_1 and that of a_2 (note that they can not be executed this time in the other order). The same augmentation with auxiliary variables z_i, $i = 1, 3$, is done as for the splitting transformation.

$$I'' \stackrel{df.}{\equiv} (\, z_1 = z_2 = 1 \Rightarrow \bar{u} = \bar{y}_1 \wedge I^{\bar{x}_i}_{\bar{e}_i,\, i=1,2}) \wedge (\,(z_1 = z_2 = 0 \vee z_2 = z_3 = 1) \Rightarrow I)$$

We leave out the details of formally establishing cooperation with I''.

Note that termination here is still trivial. Internal deadlock freedom is also quite simple and omitted.

Next, we turn to relaxing the restriction initially imposed on variable references and assume that the dependency graph is a full graph (over three nodes). We consider here one possible decoupling, the others being similarly treated. Let $\bar{y}_{1,2} \subseteq \bar{x}_1$, $\bar{y}_{1,3} \subseteq \bar{x}_1$ be the variables of P_1 referred to by P_2 and P_3, respectively, and similarly for $\bar{y}_{2,1} \subseteq \bar{x}_2$, $\bar{y}_{2,3} \subseteq \bar{x}_2$ and $\bar{y}_{3,1} \subseteq \bar{x}_3$, $\bar{y}_{3,2} \subseteq \bar{x}_3$.

Each process P_i, $i = 1, 3$ is augmented with two lists of new temporary local variables $\bar{u}_i$ and $\bar{v}_i$. The ternary interaction a is broken into three binary interactions a_1, a_2, and a_3. In each binary interaction its two participants, say P_i and P_j, exchange variables. P_i copies $\bar{y}_{j,i}$ into $\bar{u}_i$ (or $\bar{v}_i$), while P_j copies $\bar{y}_{i,j}$ into $\bar{u}_j$ (or $\bar{v}_j$). The temporal ordering among the binary interactions is immaterial and fixed in some way. The different orders[1] define different but very similar decouplings. After all variable exchange interactions have taken place, each process P_i *locally* updates its "proper" state x_i by a variant of the original $\bar{e}_i$, in which $\bar{u}_i$ and $\bar{v}_i$ are substituted for the remote variables.

The resulting decoupling is presented in Figure 1.

To formulate the corresponding global invariant I''', we slightly modify the assignments to the auxiliary variables z_i. The new values are:

$$z_i \stackrel{df.}{=} \begin{cases} 0 & \text{before decoupled interactions (i.e., initially)} \\ 1 & \text{between decoupled interactions} \\ 2 & \text{after decoupled interactions} \\ 3 & \text{after local update} \end{cases}$$

The new invariant records all the additional intermediate states.

$$
\begin{aligned}
I''' \stackrel{df.}{\equiv} & \bigwedge_{k=1,3} z_k \in \{0, 1, 2, 3\} \wedge (z_1 = z_2 = z_3 \Rightarrow I) \wedge \\
& (z_1 = z_2 = 1 \Rightarrow \bar{u}_1 = \bar{y}_{2,1} \wedge \bar{u}_2 = \bar{y}_{1,2} \wedge I) \wedge \\
& (z_2 = 2 \wedge z_3 = 1 \Rightarrow \bar{u}_1 = \bar{y}_{2,1} \wedge \bar{u}_2 = \bar{y}_{1,2} \wedge \bar{u}_3 = \bar{y}_{2,3} \wedge \bar{v}_2 = \bar{y}_{3,2} \wedge I) \wedge \\
& (z_1 = 2 \wedge z_3 = 2 \Rightarrow \bar{u}_1 = \bar{y}_{2,1} \wedge \bar{u}_2 = \bar{y}_{1,2} \wedge \bar{u}_3 = \bar{y}_{2,3} \wedge \bar{v}_2 = \bar{y}_{3,2} \bar{v}_1 = \bar{y}_{3,1} \wedge \bar{v}_3 = \bar{y}_{1,3} \wedge I) \wedge \\
& \bigwedge_{k=1,3} I^{*}_{k}
\end{aligned}
$$

[1] For arbitrary $n > 3$, one might consider, similarly to [24], a nondeterministic iteration, leaving the order of execution to run-time.

where

$$I_1^\bullet \stackrel{df.}{\equiv} (z_1 = 3 \wedge z_2 = z_3 = 2 \Rightarrow (I)^{g_{2,1},g_{3,1}}_{a_1,e_1}) \wedge$$
$$(z_1 = z_2 = 3 \wedge z_3 = 2 \Rightarrow ((I)^{g_{2,1},g_{3,1}}_{a_1,e_1})^{g_{1,3},g_{3,2}}_{a_3,e_3})$$

and similarly for $I_2^\bullet$, $I_3^\bullet$.

The proof is obtained by observing that $(((I)^{g_{2,1},g_{3,1}}_{a_1,e_1})^{g_{1,3},g_{3,2}}_{a_3,e_3})^{g_{1,3},g_{2,3}}_{a_3,e_3}$ preserves I by the originally given proof.

5 Loosening by participation elimination

A transformation that looks most obvious, but turns to be very useful, removes a redundant participant from an interaction. A participant is redundant if neither are its variables referred to by other participants, nor is it referring to variables of any other participant. Thus, the part of a redundant participant in an interaction a has the form $a[\,]$ (with *no* assignments[2]). We again base the presention on a triple interaction, transformed into a binary interaction. The extension to arbitrary interaction with an arbitrary collection of redundant participants is straightforward.

Thus, let be the program $P :: \ [\, P_1 :: \ a[\bar{x}_1 := \bar{e}_1] \,\|\, P_2 :: \ a[\bar{x}_2 := \bar{e}_2] \,\|\, P_3 :: \ a[\,]\,]$. Then, we have

$$\mathbf{E}(P) :: \ [\, P_1 :: \ a[\bar{x}_1 := \bar{e}_1] \,\|\, P_2 :: \ a[\bar{x}_2 := \bar{e}_2] \,\|\, P_3 :: \ skip]$$

The invariant here remains I, and cooperation for the restricted interaction still holds due to the assumption on non-referencing.

Let us pause and summarize where we are. Three *SLTs* (S (splitting), D (decoupling) and E (elimination)) have been introduced. For each we described how the old invariant (used in the correctness proof of the untransformed program) is converted into a new invariant for the transformed program. Next, we present an application of the transformations given, and then continue with the introduction of yet another transformation.

The transformations are not applicable in every context; in the final section the applicability conditions (technically, the *monotonicity* of the transformations) is discussed.

6 An application

We consider a simplified solution to the problem of designing a debit card for an *Electronic Funds Transfer* system [20], ignoring the issues of team abstraction and replication. When a customer presents the card to a merchant for a purchase, the card is used to initiate a three party interaction *xaction*, in which funds are transferred from the customer's bank to the merchant's bank. The debit card system has three components: the point-of-sales terminals (*pos*), the computer that holds the customer accounts, and the computer that holds the merchant accounts. A debit card system has three basic requirements:

- All requests must transfer funds correctly.
- A customer account must never have a negative balance.
- All requests must eventually be processed.

More detailed presentations of this problem can be found in [18],[26].

We use the following global type, representing an account of a customer in a bank:

type *account* = **record** *id* : **integer**; *bal* : **real end**

Figure 2 contains the initial design. The design consists of a concurrent composition of three processes: *pos*, *cbank* and *mbank*. For simplicity we assume the account databases are already initialized and the sale request is set non-null by some outside mechanism, not explicitly shown, via the *next* – *action* interaction. In later figures, we supress this alternative. The essence of the design is captured in the three-party interaction *xaction*, which checks the balance of the customer and if sufficient, transfers the funds.

[2] Or more generally, $a[\bar{x} := \bar{e}]$, where $\bar{e}$ refers only to variables in $\bar{x}$, treated similarly.

```
[pos :: s : sale  := null, okay : boolean ;
*[ s ≠null &xaction ⟦okay := (c.bal ≥ sale.amount), s := null⟧ → skip
▯
s = null&next − action ⟦···⟧ → skip ]
▯
cbank :: c : account ;
*[ xaction ⟦ if c.balance ≥ sale.amount
             then c.balance := c.balance − sale.amount ⟧ → skip]
▯
mbank :: m : account ;
*[ xaction ⟦ if c.balance ≥ sale.amount
             then m.balance := m.balance + sale.amount ⟧ → skip]
]
```

Figure 2: Initial Debit Card System.

```
[pos :: s : sale  := null, okay : boolean ;
*[ s ≠null &approve ⟦okay := (c.balance ≥ sale.amount), s := null⟧ → [okay→xfer ⟦ ⟧
                                                                        ▯
                                                                        ¬okay&continue ⟦ ⟧→ skip] ]
▯
cbank :: c : account ;
*[ approve ⟦ ⟧ → [ xfer ⟦c.balance := c.balance − sale.amount ⟧
                  ▯
                  continue ⟦ ⟧→ skip] ]
▯
mbank :: m : account ;
*[ approve ⟦ ⟧ → [ xfer ⟦m.balance := m.balance + sale.amount ⟧
                  ▯
                  continue ⟦ ⟧→ skip] ]
]
```

Figure 3: First decomposition

Figure 3 expresses a decomposition, which is not synchrony loosening but prepares the ground for subsequent synchrony loosening. Its correctness can be established by similar means. Basically, the initial three party interaction *xaction* is decomposed into sequentially composed three party interactions. The one, *approve*, takes care of the approval test (non-negative balance). The second, *xfer*, takes care of the actual transfer in case of approval. The third takes care of joint inaction in case of disapproval. The reason for this decomposition is that a different participant is eliminated from each "fragment" of interaction *xaction*.

We now observe that the part of *approve* in the *mbank* process satisfies the requirement for participant elimination and apply the transformation, resulting in the program in Figure 4. Note that the part of the *cbank* process is ineligible for similar elimination though being empty, since the part of *pos* in the same interaction refers to the variable *c.balance* in *cbank*.

The next observation is that the part of *pos* in the *xfer* interaction is redundant and is eliminated. Due to the well-formedness syntactic rules, it is replaced by *skip*, resulting in the program in Figure 5. However, the replaced part was *conditional* on approval and controled enablement. To preserve the correct enablement, the part of *cbank* in the *approve* interaction repeats the approval computation, storing the result in a new boolean variable *okay*1. The latter is used for guarding the part of *cbank*, restoring the right enablement. The correctness preservation of such shift in enablement control is also easy to establish.

Finally, we notice that the part of *pos* in the *continue* interaction can be eliminated, as no full postsynchrony is required. Yet another trivial local simplification results in the program in Figure 6.

```
[pos :: s : sale := null, okay : boolean;
*[ s ≠null &approve ⟦okay := (c.balance ≥ sale.amount), s := null⟧ → [okay→xfer ⟦ ⟧
                                                                       ▯
                                                                       ¬okay&continue ⟦ ⟧→ skip] ]
∥
cbank :: c : account;
*[ approve ⟦ ⟧ → [ xfer ⟦c.balance := c.balance − sale.amount⟧
                   ▯
                   continue ⟦ ⟧→ skip] ]
∥
mbank :: m : account;
*[true → [ xfer ⟦m.balance := m.balance + sale.amount⟧
           ▯
           continue ⟦ ⟧→ skip] ]
]
```

Figure 4: First participant elimination

```
[pos :: s : sale := null, okay : boolean;
*[ s ≠null &approve ⟦okay := (c.balance ≥ sale.amount), s := null⟧ → [okay→ skip
                                                                       ▯
                                                                       ¬okay&continue ⟦ ⟧→ skip] ]
∥
cbank :: c : account; okay1 : boolean;
*[ approve ⟦okay1 := (c.balance ≥ sale.amount)⟧ → [ okay1&xfer ⟦c.balance := c.balance − sale.amount⟧
                                                    ▯
                                                    ¬okay1&continue ⟦ ⟧→ skip] ]
∥
mbank :: m : account;
*[true → [ xfer ⟦m.balance := m.balance + sale.amount⟧
           ▯
           continue ⟦ ⟧→ skip] ]
]
```

Figure 5: Second participant elimination

```
[pos :: s : sale := null, okay : boolean;
*[ s ≠null &approve ⟦okay := (c.balance ≥ sale.amount), s := null⟧ → skip]
∥
cbank :: c : account; okay1 : boolean;
*[ approve ⟦okay1 :=(c.balance ≥ sale.amount)⟧ →
                   [ okay1&xfer ⟦c.balance := c.balance − sale.amount⟧
                     ▯
                     ¬okay1&continue ⟦ ⟧→ skip] ]
∥
mbank :: m : account;
*[true → [ xfer ⟦m.balance := m.balance + sale.amount⟧
           ▯
           continue ⟦ ⟧→ skip] ]
]
```

Figure 6: Final EFT design

7 Loosening by rounds

Let us consider transformations of interactions involving a large collection of n participating processes P_i, $0 \leq i < n$, each computing in the interaction (the same) function f over a set of n elements, each local to one participant. The function satisfies the following[3] properties:

- $f(\{x\}) = x$
- $f(S_1 \cup S_2) = f(\{f(S_1), f(S_2)\})$

In each interaction-part in process[4] P_i, the value of the computed function f is assigned to a local variable x_i. The synchrony-loosening by rounds transformation **R** is introduced in two steps.

The first step consists of a transformation $\mathbf{R}^0$, which breaks the full dependency among the participants of a by introducing *rounds*, in each of which a pair of processes pairwise communicate (inducing a cyclical neighboring relation), computing an application of f to a set of two elements. The one is a cumulative evaluation of f to previously evaluated arguments, the other is a new element, equal to the cumulative evaluation of f by a neighbor process. Note that the set of participants still remains wholly synchronized. The next transformation, $\mathbf{R}^1$, loosens the synchrony based on the weakened communication dependency.

Let $P :: [\underset{0 \leq i < n}{\|} P_i :: a[\![x_i := f(\{x_1, \cdots, x_n\})]\!]]$, and suppose that

$$\{p \wedge \bigwedge_{0 \leq i < n} x_i = X_i\}\ P\ \{q \wedge \bigwedge_{0 \leq i < n} x_i = f(\{X_1, \cdots, X_n\})\} \tag{3}$$

is the specification of P. The part p of the precondition can be used to further restrict the values of the X_is, for example, to be distinct.

Assume that the following local proof-outlines of the processes consist of one application of the *iba* axiom,

$$\{p_i \wedge x_i = X_i\}\ a[\![x_i := f(\{x_1, \cdots, x_n\})]\!]\ \{q_i \wedge x_i = f(\{X_1, \cdots, X_n\})\} \tag{L_3}$$

In addition, assume that the following proof-section establishes cooperation with respect to an invariant I, using the *gia* axiom.

$$\begin{array}{c} \{I \wedge \bigwedge_{0 \leq i < n} x_i = X_i \wedge \bigwedge_{0 \leq i < n} p_i\} \\ \left[\underset{0 \leq i < n}{\|} a[\![x_i := f(\{x_1, \cdots, x_n\})]\!]\right] \\ \{\ I \wedge \bigwedge_{0 \leq i < n} x_i = f(\{X_1, \cdots, X_n\}) \wedge \bigwedge_{0 \leq i < n} q_i\} \end{array} \tag{C_3}$$

Together with an application of the concurrent-composition rule, (L_3) and (C_3) constitute a partial-correctness proof for P (with respect to the above specification).

The transformation $\mathbf{R}^0$ transforms the interaction a according to the rules below:

- Each process P_i is augmented with a *new* variable r_i, initialized to 1.
- The local part in a of P_i is replaced by an iteration, guarded by counting rounds, as follows:

$$\mathbf{R}^0(P_i) :: *[\langle\, r_i < n \& a[\![x_i := f(\{x_{i-1}, x_i\})]\!] \rightarrow r_i := r_i + 1 \,\rangle]$$

Recall that the extra bracketing '⟨' and '⟩' delimit the scope of the holding of the global invariant, as shown in the cooperation-proof below.

It is easy to establish total correctness of $\mathbf{R}^0(P)$ with respect to the same specification (3). The local loop-invariant for P_i is

$$LI_i^0 \stackrel{\text{df.}}{\equiv} x_i = f(\{X_{i+1-r_i}, \cdots, X_i\}) \wedge 1 \leq r_i \leq n \wedge (r_i = n \Rightarrow q_i)$$

[3] More general properties are also amenable to a similar treatment. We want to keep the description simple, and, hence, do not consider greater generality here.

[4] All index computations are cyclical, modulo n.

An assumption that $x_{i-1} = f(\{X_{i-r_{i-1}}, \cdots, X_{i-1}\})$ and the usual sequential rules reduce the invariance of LI_i^0 to the logical assertion

$$x_i = f(\{X_{i+1-r_i}, \cdots, X_i\}) \wedge 1 \leq r_i \leq n \wedge r_i < n$$

$$\Rightarrow$$

$$f(\{x_i, x_{i-1}\}) = f(\{X_{i+1-(r_i+1)}, \cdots, X_i\}) \wedge 1 \leq r_i + 1 \leq n$$

which clearly holds (under the above assumption), due to the union-distributivity of f. Note that upon local loop termination $r_i = n$ holds, and hence $x_i = f(\{X_{i+1-n}, \cdots, X_i\})$, which the same as $x_i = f(\{X_1, \cdots, X_n\})$.

For cooperation, we choose the global invariant $I^0 \stackrel{df.}{=} ((\bigwedge_{0 \leq i < n} r_i = n) \Rightarrow I) \wedge \bigwedge_{0 \leq i, j < n} r_i = r_j$. The second conjunct, asserting that all processes are in the same round, reflects the fact that synchrony was not yet loosened, though dependency was weakened.

It is easy to check, based on the assumption that I satisfied the cooperation requirement C_3, that I^0 satisfies the cooperation requirements for $\mathbf{R}^0(P)$. The first conjunct is invariant, since initially $r_i \neq n$ and $\bigwedge_{0 \leq i < n} r_i = 1$; once $r_i = n$ becomes true, the holding of I follows from the invariance of I in the given initial proof. The second conjunct is immediate, since both round counters are incremented posterior to interactions. Again, the manipulation of substitutions is omitted.

The invariant I^0 implies also the absence of deadlock in $\mathbf{R}^0(P)$, the latter occurring when at least one P_i has already exited its local loop (implying $r_i = n$), while the other P_js are still waiting to interact in interaction a (implying $r_j < n$, contradicting I).

Finally, termination of $\mathbf{R}^0(P_i)$ is proved by using the well-founded variant $n - r_i$, which decreases after every iteration in P_i, and by LI_i is bounded from below by 0.

We now turn to the second stage, embodied in the transformation $\mathbf{R}^1$, which replaces the "global" synchronizing interaction a by a family of *binary* interactions a_i, $0 \leq i < n$. Each process keeps track of the "distance" to the left to which its own application of f has spread (this turns out to coincide with the round number). In addition, each process keeps track of the distance of its own contribution to the spreading of the application of f by its right neighbor.

The transformation is specified by the following rules:

- Each process P_i is augmented with a *new* variable d_i (recording the second above mentioned "distance"), initialized to 0. The relation $d_i \leq r_i$ will be maintained as part of the new local loop invariant. The relation $r_i < n \Rightarrow r_i = d_{i-1} + 1$ will be maintained as part of the new global invariant.
- The body of process P_i is now the following:

$$\mathbf{R}^1(\mathbf{R}^0(P_i)) :: *[$$
$$r_i < n \& a_{i-1} [\![x_i := f(\{x_{i-1}, x_i\}),\ r_i := min(r_{i-1} + 1,\ n)]\!] \rightarrow skip$$
$$\|$$
$$d_i < r_i \& a_i [\![\,]\!] \rightarrow d_i := r_i$$
$$]$$

We now show that $\mathbf{R}^1$ preserves the specification of P.

For the local proofs, we choose the loop-invariant $LI_i^1 \stackrel{df.}{=} LI_i^0 \wedge d_i \leq r_i$. The proof-outline is shown in Figure 7.

The invariance of LI_i^0 is established for the first direction similarly as for $\mathbf{R}^0$. The second direction preserves it trivially. The second conjunct is preserved by the first direction by an assumption that r_i only increases (expressed via an *auxiliary variable* R_i), and is preserved by the second direction due to direct copying. We omit the formal manipulation of substitutions.

We now turn to the cooperation proofs.

First, we note that $\bigwedge_{0 \leq i, j < n} r_i = r_j$ is no longer an invariant, since $\mathbf{R}^1$ loosened the synchrony, and no strict round synchronization is present in the transformed program. Instead, we choose the following new global invariant I^1, which relates the two "distances" that the processes maintain.

$$
\begin{array}{ll}
\mathbf{R}^1(\mathbf{R}^0(P_i)) :: & *[\,\{\,LI_i^1 \wedge r_i = R_i\,\} \\
& \langle\, r_i < n \& a_{i-1} [\![x_i := f(\{x_{i-1}, x_i\}),\ r_i := min(r_{i-1}+1,\ n)]\!] \rightarrow skip \rangle\ \{r_i > R_i\} \\
& \| \\
& \langle\, d_i < r_i \& a_i [\![\,]\!] \rightarrow d_i := r_i \rangle\ \{d_i = r_i\} \\
&]
\end{array}
$$

Figure 7: Proof-outline for $\mathbf{R}^1$

$$
\begin{array}{l}
I^1 \stackrel{df.}{\equiv} ((\bigwedge_{0 \le i < n} r_i = n) \Rightarrow I^0) \wedge \\
\quad \bigwedge_{0 \le i < n} (\, r_i < n \Rightarrow d_{i-1} + 1 = r_i) \wedge \\
\quad \bigwedge_{0 \le i < n} r_{i+1} \le d_i + 1
\end{array}
$$

For lack of space, we omit the details of the invariance proof of I^1.

Next, we have to establish that $\mathbf{R}^1$ did not introduce a deadlock possibility. In any deadlock situation there must exist a non-terminated process, say P_i, the two neighbors of which have already terminated. Thus, a deadlock is characterized by the following assertion (D_3), which is shown to contradict the already established invariants. Note that here the third conjunct of I^1, not used so far, is used.

$$
(\, r_i < n \vee d_i < r_i \,) \wedge (\, r_{i-1} = d_{i-1} = n \,) \wedge (\, r_{i+1} = d_{i+1} = n \,) \qquad (D_3)
$$

- Assume first $r_i < n$. From the second conjunct of I^1 we get $d_{i-1} + 1 = r_i$. Hence, $d_{i-1} < n$, contradicting the second conjunct of (D_3).
- Assume next that $d_i < r_i$. From the third conjunct of I^1 we get $d_i > r_{i+1}$. Since by the third conjunct of (D_3) $r_{i+1} = n$, we get $r_i > n$, contradicting LI_i^1.

Finally, we show the proper termination of $\mathbf{R}^1(\mathbf{R}^0(P))$. As the ranking variant we take $2n - (r_i + d_i)$. It is bounded by 0 by the invariants. Whenever P_i executes its first direction r_i increases, and whenever it executes its second direction, d_i increases. In both cases the variant decreases.

Note that a very similar development can be based on different graph structures than rings. We mention one application later.

7.1 Applications of synchrony loosening by rounds

We now show that by instantiating the above scheme, known ring leader-election algorithms can be derived in a systematic way. The special-case derivation of such algorithms based on this design method was presented in [17], with an ad-hoc proof of each step of the refinement.

For a leader-election program L, we want to establish

$$
\{\bar{id} = \bar{id}^0 \wedge distinct(\bar{id}^0)\}\ L\ \{\bar{id} = \bar{id}^0 \wedge distinct(\bar{id}^0) \wedge\ leader_i \equiv (id_i = \min_{0 \le j < n} id_j^0)\}
$$

Here $distinct(\bar{y})$ is the *pairwise-nonequality* predicate defined by $\bigwedge_{0 \le j,\, k < n} (\, j \ne k \Rightarrow y_j \ne y_k\,)$.

The immediate solution $L = LEADER_0$ is obtained by taking (the integer valued) id_i as x_i of the general scheme, and *min* (the usual minimum function) as f. It is easy to see that *min* satisfies the requirements for f. For clarity, X_i is denoted as id_i^0. The precondition p_i is taken as *true* and r_i is denoted $round_i$. The schematic interaction a is instantiated to *elect*. The global invariant is $I = distinct(\bar{id})$.

$$
LEADER_0 :: \left[\Big\|_{0 \le i < n} elect [\![leader_i := (id_i = \min_{0 \le j < n} id_j)]\!] \right]
$$

The synchronous ring solution obtained after the $\mathbf{R}^0$ step is presented in Figure 8. To emphasize the function of the restricted interaction it is now called *pass*. The program employs one more assignment of the *unique* minimal *id* computed by the scheme to determine the leader. This extra step is easily verified and the details are omitted.

$LEADER_1 :: [P_1 \| \cdots \| P_n]$, where

$P_i :: minid_i := id_i; round_i := 1;$
$\quad *[round_i < n \ \& \ pass [minid_i := min(minid_{i-1}, minid_i)] \rightarrow round_i := round_i + 1];$
$\quad leader_i := (id_i = minid_i)$

Figure 8: First ring leader election program

$LEADER_2 :: [P_1 \| \cdots \| P_n]$, where
$P_i :: minid_i := id_i; round_i := 1; given_i := 0;$
$\quad *[round_i < n \& \ pass_i [minid_i := min(minid_{i-1}, minid_i),$
$\qquad round_i := min(round_{i-1}, n)]$
$\quad \|$
$\quad given_i < round_i \& pass_i [\,] \rightarrow given_i := round_i];$
$\quad leader_i := (id_i = minid_i)$

Figure 9: Second ring leader election program

By applying the second step $\mathbf{R}^1$, we get the following leader election program in Figure 9. The variable d_i is renamed as $given_i$.

By one small additional transformation, keeping track of *ids* passing via a node and interacting to forward them unless they are smaller than the latest minimum passed, one obtains the leader election algorithm in [12]. Further refinements, not related to synchrony loosening, may be employed to improve the message complexity.

Note that by a very similar refinement, conducted on a *full graph* instead of a ring, we can generate the *distributed maximum (or minimum)* algorithm presented in [25].

8 Monotonicity of synchrony loosening

In this section we consider the *monotonicity* of *SLTs* , a property of utmost importance for the usefulness of such transformation in the design methodology stated in the introduction. Basically, conditions for monotonicity capture the intuitive notion of *conditions of applicability*, i.e., conditions on contexts under which the transformation is applicable. Ideally, the transformations should be monotonic, thus applicable in any context. Unfortunately, the *SLTs* are not monotonic in general. We provide a useful and natural class of contexts for which they are monotonic.

Note that the situation here is more complicated than the corresponding situation in Back's *refinement calculus*, where context information can be characterized by a state-assertion and incorporated as a statement in the calculus. Here the contexts have more complicated characterizations. This complication originates from properties of concurrency that render the usual proof-systems for partial-corrrectnes as *non-compositional* (including the *cooperating proofs* system used here).

8.1 Violation of monotonicity

Before presenting conditions for monotonicity, we show some simple counter-examples, that may give the reader a feeling of what goes wrong. The three major "dangers" of synchrony loosening are:

- Introduction of external deadlock
- Introduction of nontermination
- Violation of an essential synchronization

All can be attributed intuitively to a weakening of the common knowledge obtained by the coordinated agreement imposed by the original, synchronous interaction.
The third, however, is not relevant for total-correctness specifications, because it can be shown (by a completeness proof similar to that in [1]) that no essential synchronizations are needed. Still, such synchronizations may

be important for more general safety and liveness properties.

Example: Introduction of external deadlock

Consider the following program $P :: [P_1 \parallel P_2 \parallel P_3 \parallel P_4]$, constituting a context for interaction a, where

$$P_1 :: [a[\,] \rightarrow skip \mid d[\,] \rightarrow skip]$$
$$P_2 :: [a[\,] \rightarrow skip \mid d[\,] \rightarrow skip]$$
$$P_3 :: [a[\,] \rightarrow skip \mid b[\,] \rightarrow skip \mid e[\,] \rightarrow skip]$$
$$P_4 :: [b[\,] \rightarrow skip \mid c[\,] \rightarrow skip]$$

Clearly, this program is deadlock free. Its computations are:

1. P_1, P_2 and P_3 do interaction a and P_4 does (local) action c
2. P_1 and P_2 do interaction d while P_3 and P_4 do interaction b
3. P_1 and P_2 do interaction d while P_3 does its local action e and P_4 doe its local action c.

Now, suppose we loosen the synchrony of interaction a by decoupling it to a_1 and a_2, resulting in $\mathbf{D}(P) :: [P_1 \parallel P_2 \parallel P_3 \parallel P_4]$, where
$P_1 :: [a_1[\,] \rightarrow skip \mid d[\,] \rightarrow skip]$
$P_2 :: [a_1[\,] \rightarrow a_2[\,] \mid d[\,] \rightarrow skip]$
$P_3 :: [a_2[\,] \rightarrow skip \mid b[\,] \rightarrow skip \mid e[\,] \rightarrow skip]$
$P_4 :: [b[\,] \rightarrow skip \mid c[\,] \rightarrow skip]$
We now have the deadlocking computation in which P_1 and P_2 interact via a_1, leaving P_2 waiting for a_2 forever, while P_3 and P_4 interact with b.

Example: Introduction of nontermination

Consider the following program $P :: [P_1 \parallel P_2 \parallel P_3]$, constituting a context for interaction a, where

$$P_1 :: f_1 := true;\ *[f_1 \& a[\,] \rightarrow skip \mid f_1 \rightarrow f_1 := false]$$
$$P_2 :: f_2 := true;\ *[f_2 \& a[\,] \rightarrow skip \mid f_2 \rightarrow f_2 := false]$$
$$P_3 :: f_3 := true;\ *[x > 0 \wedge f_3 \& a[\,] \rightarrow x := x - 1 \mid f_3 \rightarrow f_3 := false]$$

This program always terminates. It has two kinds of computations. In the one, after some number of executions of interaction a, one of P_i $i = 1, 3$, falsifies f_i and terminates, leaving the other two processes with having only the local action alternative, leading to termination. In the other interaction a is executed suffiently many times, falsifying the guard $x > 0$ in P_3, enforcing P_3 to choose its local action, leading to termination as above.

However, in splitting interaction a into a_1, a_2 with $\mathcal{P}_{a_1} = \{P_1, P_2\}$ (noting that the restrictions on variable references are satisfied), we get the program

$\mathbf{S}(P) ::$
$P_1 :: f_1 := true;\ *[f_1 \& a_1[\,] \rightarrow skip \mid f_1 \rightarrow f_1 := false]$
$P_2 :: f_2 := true;\ *[f_2 \& a_1[\,] \rightarrow skip \mid f_2 \rightarrow f_2 := false]$
$P_3 :: f_3 := true;\ *[x > 0 \wedge f_3 \& a_2[\,] \rightarrow x := x - 1 \mid f_3 \rightarrow f_3 := false]$

In this program, the guarding of iterating a_1 by $x > 0$ "is lost", and there is an infinite computation in which a_1 is repeated forever (independently of the number of times a_2 was executed).

Example: Violating essential synchrony

Consider the following simple variant of a *mutual exclusion* program, in which P_1 and P_2 interact with SEM, a semaphore-like process. The mutually exclusive critical sections are cs_i, $i = 1, 2$.

$P_1 :: x := 0;\ *[a_1[x := x + 1] \rightarrow cs_1;\ r_1[x := x - 1]]$
$\parallel$
$SEM :: *[a_1[\,] \rightarrow r_1[\,] \mid a_2[\,] \rightarrow r_2[\,]]$
$\parallel$
$P_2 :: y := 0;\ *[a_2[y := y + 1] \rightarrow cs_2;\ r_2[y := y - 1]]$

The invariant $0 \leq x+y \leq 1$ reflects the mutual exclusion. By eliminating the participation of any process, either from a_1 or from a_2 (both looking redundant), clearly the resulting program violates the exclusion property.

8.2 Sufficient conditions for monotonicity

We now turn to the provision of sufficient conditions for monotonicity of the *SLTs* presented above. Since in general a proof of a property of $C[P]$ need not contain a proof of a related property of P as a ***sub-proof***(due to non-compositionality of the proof systems), we have to resort to reasoning directly in terms of the *IP* semantics.

We start by defining some properties of contexts and their computations under substitutions.

Definition: A computation of $C[P]$ is ***hole grouped*** iff no two events (i.e., interaction executions) originating from P are separated by an event not originating from P.

Thus, in such a computation, whenever control "enters the hole" no action from outside the hole takes place until controll "exits the hole".

Definition: Two sub-holes of $C[\bullet]$ are *linked* in a substitution $C[P]$ iff for every computation π there is a bound on the difference between the number of times the filling of each hole is executed[5].

Thus, in a context linked for some substitution it is impossible to iterate an unbounded number of times the filling of one sub-hole while not executing the filling of the other sub-hole.

Definition: Two (collections of) sub-holes H_1, H_2 of $C[\bullet]$ are *separable* in a substitution $C[P]$ iff there exists a computation with a chain of linearly ordered, consecutive interaction executions b_i, $i = 1, m$ (for some $m \geq 1$), such that the following conditions hold:

- $H_1 \subseteq \mathcal{P}_{b_1}$ and H_1 executes its part in b_1 *before* entering the hole filling.
- $H_2 \subseteq \mathcal{P}_{b_m}$ and H_2 executes its part in b_m *after* exiting the hole filling.
- $H_i \cap \mathcal{P}_{b_j} = \emptyset, i = 1, 2,\ 1 < j < m$.

Note that $m = 1$ is possible, referred to as *direct* separability.

Lemma: (Hole-filler interleaving)

If the sub-holes of $C[\bullet]$ are pairwise linked and nonseparable for a substitution $C[P]$, then every computation of $C[P]$ is equivalent to a hole-grouped computation.

Sketch of proof: The proof idea, similar to several other similar propositions, e.g. in [7] or [13], is based on the ability to commute independent interactions. Suppose control reaches the hole and an interaction in P takes place. By the linking properties, eventually the other actions (in the various sub-hole substitutions) eventually take place too. By commuting them with independent interactions, they can be brought to be contiguous, otherwise a separable pair of holes for the given substitution must exist.

Proposition: If the holes for components B and C in $C[S(a\llbracket\cdots\rrbracket$ are linked and nonseparable, then $C[a\llbracket\cdots\rrbracket \leq C[S(a\llbracket\cdots\rrbracket)]$.

Sketch of proof: Assume $[p]\ C[a\llbracket\cdots\rrbracket\ [q]$. We have to show that $C[S(a\llbracket\cdots\rrbracket)]$ has no nonterminating computations, has no deadlock, and is partially correct with respect to p and q.

By assuming $C[S(a\llbracket\cdots\rrbracket)]$ to have a computation π violating the specification, by the hole-filler lemma it has an equivalent hole-grouped one. However, every hole-grouped computation of $C[S(a\llbracket\cdots\rrbracket)$ corresponds to one of $C[a\llbracket\cdots\rrbracket$ with a similar violation, contradicting the assumption of total correctness of $C[a\llbracket\cdots\rrbracket$.

With a very similar reasoning, we obtain

---

[5]The notion of linking was considered also in [24] with the following differences:

1. The linkage was not defined in terms of contexts, only directly for fillings, which left the scope of the definition unclear.
2. The bound there was at most 1, imposing a "none or all" requirement.
3. The definition there included also a (version of) the *separability* property, which we prefer to separate as an independent property.

Proposition: If the holes for components P_1 and P_3 in $C[\mathrm{D}(a [\![\cdots]\!]$ are linked and nonseparable, then $C[a [\![\cdots]\!] \leq C[\mathrm{D}(a [\![\cdots]\!])]$.
Proposition: If the holes for components P_i and P_j in $C[\mathrm{R}(a [\![\cdots]\!]$ are pairwise linked, then $C[a [\![\cdots]\!] \leq C[\mathrm{R}(a [\![\cdots]\!])]$. Note that the separability condition is not needed, since a process P_i can leave $\mathrm{R}(a [\![\cdots]\!]$ only after having interacted with every P_j, $j \neq i$.
Proposition: If the holes for components P_1 and P_2 in $C[\mathrm{E}(a [\![\cdots]\!]$ are nonseparable from the hole in P_3, then $C[a [\![\cdots]\!] \leq C[\mathrm{E}(a [\![\cdots]\!])]$.

9 Conclusion

We identified a collection of *synchrony loosening* transformations, supporting a refinement design method for multiparty interactions. Their correctness preservation (for total-correctness specification) was established by a proof system for such correctness properties for (the core of) the *IP* language. In addition, sufficient conditions for monotonicity of the synchrony loosening transformations were providid.

Further work might yield stronger such transformations and better applicability conditions once *fairness* assumptions are considered (see [3] for a discussion of fairness for multiparty interactions). Other transformations, enhancing the applicability of the above mentioned design method, dealing with other features of *IP* such as replication and superimposition [22] are under development.

We conjecture that one could formulate a *representation theorem*, characterizing *any* synchrony loosening transformation as simple combinations of a small number of other transformations, such as the *phasing* used in the application example, and one or two of the basic synchrony loosening transformations considered here. This is currently under investigation.

Acknowledgements

Most of this work was done during a Sabbatical leave of the first author at MCC, Austin, TX. At the Technion, the work of the first author was funded by a grant from the Israeli Academy of Sciences (basic research), on *Program verification and semantics of programming languages.* We thank Paul C. Attie, Ralph J. Back, and Shmuel Katz for various discussion regarding *SLTs* and the design method based on them.

References

[1] Krzysztof R. Apt. Ten years of Hoare's logic: A survey - part i. *ACM Transactions on Programming Languages and Systems*, 3(4):431 – 483, October 1981.

[2] Paul C. Attie. A guide to raddle87 semantics. Technical Report STP-340-87, MCC, January 11 1988.

[3] Paul C. Attie, Nissim Francez, and Orna Grumberg. Fairness and hyperfairness in multi-party interactions. In *17th ACM-POPL*, pages 292 – 305, San-Francisco, CA, January 17-19 1990.

[4] Ralph -J. R. Back. A calculus of refinement for program derivation. *Acta Informatica*, 25:593 – 624, 1988.

[5] Ralph -J. R. Back. Changing the data representation in the refinement calculus. In *21 Hawaii International Conference on Systems Science*, January 1989.

[6] Ralph -J. R. Back. Refining atomicity in parallel programs. In *PARLE conference on parallel architectures and languages in Europe*, Eindhoven, The Netherlands, June 1989. LNCS 366, Springer-Verlag.

[7] Ralph -J. R. Back. Refinement calculus, part II: Parallel and reactive systems. In *REX workshop on refinements of distributed systems*, pages 67 – 93. LNCS 430, Springer-Verlag, 1990.

[8] Ralph -J. R. Back and Reino Kurki-Suonio. Distributed cooperation with action systems. *TOPLAS*, 10(4):513–554, October 1988.

[9] Ralph -J. R. Back and Reino Kurki-Suonio. Decentralization of process nets with centralized control. *Distributed Computing*, 3:73 – 87, 1989.

[10] Ralph -J. R. Back and Kaisa Sere. Refinement of action systems. *Science of Computer Programming*, 13:133 – 180, 1989/90. Preliminary form in *Mathematics in program construction*, LNCS 375, Springer-Verlag.

[11] K. Mani Chandy and Jayadev Misra. *Parallel program design: A foundation*. Addison-Wesley, 1988.

[12] E. Chang and R. Roberts. An improved algorithm for decentralized extrema finding in circular configuration of processes. *Communications of the ACM*, 122(5):281–283, May 1979.

[13] Tzilla Elrad and Nissim Francez. Decomposition of distributed programs into communication-closed layers. *SCP*, 2:155 – 173, 1982.

[14] Tzilla Elrad and Nissim Francez. Weakest precondition semantics for communicating processes. *TCS*, 29(3):231 – 250, April 1984.

[15] Ira R. Forman. On the design of large distributed systems. In *First international conference on computer languages*, pages 84–95, October 1987.

[16] Ira R. Forman. Design by decomposition of multiparty interactions in *raddle87*. In *Fifth International Workshop on Software Specification and Design*, pages 2–10, Pittsburgh, Pa., May 19-20 1989.

[17] Ira R. Forman. Leader election: An exercise in Raddle design. Technical Report STP-270-87, MCC, Austin, TX, September 9, 1988.

[18] Ira R. Forman and W. Michael Evangelist. Eft: A case study in design using *raddle*. Technical Report STP-121-87, Microelectronics and Computer Technology Corp., April 1987.

[19] Nissim Francez. Cooperative proofs for distributed programs with multi-party interactions. *IPL*, 32:235 -242, September 22 1989.

[20] Nissim Francez and Ira R. Forman. Conflict propagation. In *IEEE International Conference on Computer Languages (ICCL'90)*, pages 155 – 168, New Orleans, LA, March 12-15 1990.

[21] Nissim Francez and Ira R. Forman. *Interacting Processes: A Multiparty Approach to Coordinated Distributed Programming*. Forthcoming book, 1990.

[22] Nissim Francez and Ira R. Forman. Superimposition for interacting processes. In *Proc. Concur'90: Theories of concurrency – unification and extension*, Amsterdam, The Netherlands, August 27 - 30 1990.

[23] C. A. R. Hoare. Proof of correctness of data representations. *Acta Informatica*, 1(19):271–281, 1972.

[24] Shmuel M. Katz, Ira R. Forman, and W. Michael Evangelist. Language constructs for distributed systems. In *IFIP TC2 Working Conference on Programming Concepts and Methods*, Sea of Galilee, Israel, April 2-5 1990.

[25] Gary Levin and David Gries. Proof techniques for communicating sequential processes. *Acta Informatica*, 15:281 – 302, 1981.

[26] M. Staskauskas. The formal specification and design of a distributed electronic funds-transfer system. *IEEE Trans. on Computers*, 37(12):1515–1528, December 1988.

A Compositional Model for Layered Distributed Systems

Kenneth J. Goldman*
Department of Computer Science
Washington University
St. Louis, MO 63130-4899 USA
kjg@cs.wustl.edu

Abstract

Composition and layering are important mechanisms for constructing modular descriptions of distributed systems. Composition is a symmetric operator that allows system components to communicate with each other across module boundaries. Layering is an asymmetric relationship that allows one system component to observe the state of another.

Both composition and layering are useful in formal models of distributed systems. For example, Lynch and Tuttle define a composition operator for the I/O automaton model that has associated *compositionality properties* guaranteeing, for example, that when an execution of a composition is projected on each of its components, the result is a set of executions of the components. Such compositionality properties are important for constructing modular correctness proofs for distributed algorithms. Chandy and Misra define a layering mechanism, called *superposition*, for the UNITY programming model. They define superposition as a program transformation that adds a layer on top of a program such that all properties of the original program are preserved, again supporting modular correctness proofs.

It would seem desirable to mix the notions of composition and layering in formal descriptions of complex distributed systems. However, UNITY provides a superposition operator, but its union operator for combining programs lacks compositionality properties. And the I/O automaton model provides compositionality properties, but offers no support for constructing the kinds of layered systems we have described. In this paper, the I/O automaton model of Lynch and Tuttle is extended to permit superposition of program modules. This results in a unified model that supports both composition and layering. We show that our superposition operator does not affect the set of executions of the underlying module, thus preserving all properties of that module. The extended model also includes a formal specification mechanism for layered systems that allows the set of correct behaviors of the higher layer to be expressed in terms of the states of the lower layer.

1 Introduction

Modular descriptions of distributed algorithms are sometimes most easily written in terms of several program layers. Higher layers are allowed to make use of lower layers, but lower layers are unaware of the higher layers. One layering mechanism, called *superposition*, is defined by Chandy and Misra for the UNITY programming language [2]. A UNITY program consists of a

*This research was conducted at the Massachusetts Institute of Technology Laboratory for Computer Science and was supported in part by the National Science Foundation under Grant CCR-86-11442, by the Office of Naval Research under Contract N00014-85-K-0168, by the Defense Advanced Research Projects Agency (DARPA) under Contract N00014-83-K-0125.

set of *statements* that access a global shared memory. At each step in the execution, a statement is selected and executed, possibly updating the memory. Superposition in UNITY is defined to be a program transformation that adds a layer on top of a program, while preserving all the properties of the underlying program. Essentially, the transformation modifies the underlying program by augmenting it with a set of new variables and additional statements. In order to preserve the properties of the underlying program, the additional statements must not write to the original variables (although they may read them). Unfortunately, modularity is lacking in UNITY because the interfaces between program modules are not described in terms of well-defined sets of actions, but only in terms of the program variables that they access. Therefore, one must reason about programs not in terms of actions that occur at module boundaries, but in terms of the memory locations that modules read and write. That is, one cannot treat a module as an abstraction with a certain set of behaviors, but must must always be concerned with the internal state of the module. In addition, UNITY has no notion of an action being an output of one component and an input to another. We would like such a separation for describing distributed systems.

Partly because of its separation of inputs and outputs, the I/O automaton model of Lynch and Tuttle [5] is particularly natural for describing distributed systems. It permits writing precise problem specifications, clear algorithm descriptions, and careful correctness proofs. Unlike UNITY, communication in this model takes place entirely in terms of actions shared across module boundaries. Each module has its own local state variables, unseen by other modules. The compositionality results of the model make it possible to reason locally about system components in order to prove properties about executions of the entire system. However, the I/O automaton model does not provide a mechanism for constructing layered systems in which higher level modules can observe the states of lower level ones. Thus, UNITY has a superposition mechanism but little modularity, while I/O automata provide a great deal of modularity but no superposition mechanism.

In this paper, we extend the I/O automaton model to permit superposition of program modules. Rather than viewing superposition as a program transformation, we view it as a particular method for hierarchically combining separate program modules. When one module is superposed on another, the higher level module is allowed to observe (but not modify) the state of the underlying module, while the state of the higher level is unknown to the underlying module. We define an operator for superposing one I/O automaton on another, and show that superposition does not affect the set of executions of the underlying module, thus preserving all properties of that module. A formal specification mechanism is presented that allows the set of correct behaviors of the higher level module to be expressed in terms of the state of the underlying module.

With the superposition extensions presented in this paper, the I/O automaton model can now be used to model algorithms for problems in which layering is the most natural structure. For example, we have used the extended model to describe and prove correct the global snapshot algorithm of Chandy and Lamport [1]. In the problem specification, algorithm description and proof, composition and superposition each play an important role. This interaction is discussed briefly in the conclusion.[1]

A different approach to adding superposition to the I/O automaton model is presented by Nour [6]. In that work, a restricted class of I/O automata, called UNITY automata, is defined in order to express UNITY programs as I/O automata. A superposition operator is defined for

[1]For readers interested in the details, the complete problem specification, algorithm description and proof are contained in [4].

this restricted class. Since UNITY automata are restricted to have output actions only, it is not possible to model a superposition in which the higher level module may share actions with the lower level module. In the present work, we do not need such restrictions. In fact, our example algorithm makes important use of shared actions between layers.

The I/O automaton model previously has been extended by Goldman and Lynch to permit automata to make make atomic accesses to shared variables [3]. In that paper, the variables are modelled as being completely external to the automata sharing them, so an automaton must be prepared to observe any value in the memory whenever it executes an access. In this paper, variables are shared, but the sharing relationship is different. The higher level module sees the variables of the lower level module *at all times*. It is not necessary for the higher level automaton to execute a particular action in order to observe the values of those variables. Therefore, the set of actions "enabled" in the higher level module may change as the lower level module updates its variables. This sort of relationship cannot be modelled using the atomic shared memory extensions of Goldman and Lynch.

2 The I/O Automaton Model

The I/O Automaton model [5] encourages one to write precise statements of the problems to be solved by modules in concurrent systems, allows very careful algorithm descriptions, and can be used to construct rigorous correctness proofs. In addition, the model can be used for carrying out complexity analysis and for proving impossibility results. The following introduction to the model is adapted from [5], which explains the model in more detail, presents examples, and includes comparisons to other models. Readers already familiar with the I/O automaton model may skip this section without loss of continuity.

2.1 I/O Automata

I/O automata are best suited for modelling systems in which the components operate asynchronously. Each system component is modeled as an I/O automaton, which is essentially a nondeterministic (possibly infinite state) automaton with an action labeling each transition. An automaton's actions are classified as either 'input', 'output', or 'internal'. An automaton can establish restrictions on when it will perform an output or internal action, but it is unable to block the performance of an input action. An automaton is said to be *closed* if it has no input actions; it models a closed system that does not interact with its environment.

Formally, an *action signature* S is a partition of a set $acts(S)$ of *actions* into three disjoint sets $in(S)$, $out(S)$, and $int(S)$ of *input actions*, *output actions*, and *internal actions*, respectively. We denote by $ext(S) = in(S) \cup out(S)$ the set of *external actions*. We denote by $local(S) = out(S) \cup int(S)$ the set of *locally-controlled actions*. An I/O automaton consists of five components:

- an action signature $sig(A)$,
- a set $states(A)$ of *states*,
- a nonempty set $start(A) \subseteq states(A)$ of *start states*,
- a transition relation $steps(A) \subseteq states(A) \times acts(A) \times states(A)$ with the property that for every state s' and input action π there is a transition (s', π, s) in $steps(A)$, and
- an equivalence relation $part(A)$ partitioning the set $local(A)$ into at most a countable number of equivalence classes.

The equivalence relation *part*(A) will be used in the definition of fair computation. Each class of the partition may be thought of as a separate process. We refer to an element (s', π, s) of *steps*(A) as a *step* of A. If (s', π, s) is a step of A, then π is said to be *enabled* in s'. Since every input action is enabled in every state, automata are said to be *input-enabled*. This means that the automaton is unable to block its input.

An *execution* of A is a finite sequence $s_0, \pi_1, s_1, \ldots, \pi_n, s_n$ or an infinite sequence $s_0, \pi_1, s_1, \pi_2, \ldots$ of alternating states and actions of A such that $(s_i, \pi_{i+1}, s_{i+1})$ is a step of A for every i and $s_0 \in start(A)$. The *schedule* of an execution α is the subsequence of α consisting of the actions appearing in α. The *behavior* of an execution or schedule α of A is the subsequence of α consisting of *external* actions. The sets of executions, finite executions, schedules, finite schedules, behaviors, and finite behaviors are denoted *execs*(A),it finexecs(A), *scheds*(A), *finscheds*(A), *behs*(A), and *finbehs*(A), respectively. The same action may occur several times in an execution or a schedule; we refer to a particular occurrence of an action as an *event*.

2.2 Composition

We can construct an automaton modelling a complex system by composing automata modelling the simpler system components. When we compose a collection of automata, we identify an output action π of one automaton with the input action π of each automaton having π as an input action. Consequently, when one automaton having π as an output action performs π , all automata having π as an action perform π simultaneously (automata not having π as an action do nothing).

Since we require that most one system component controls the performance of any given action, we must place some compatibility restrictions on the collections of automata that may be composed. A countable collection $\{S_i\}_{i\in I}$ of action signatures is said to be *strongly compatible* if for all $i, j \in I$ satisfying $i \neq j$ we have

1. $out(S_i) \cap out(S_j) = \emptyset$,
2. $int(S_i) \cap acts(S_j) = \emptyset$, and
3. no action is contained in infinitely many sets $acts(S_i)$.

We say that a collection of automata are *strongly compatible* if their action signatures are strongly compatible.

The *composition* $S = \prod_{i\in I} S_i$ of a countable collection of strongly compatible action signatures $\{S_i\}_{i\in I}$ is defined to be the action signature with

- $in(S) = \cup_{i\in I} in(S_i) - \cup_{i\in I} out(S_i)$,
- $out(S) = \cup_{i\in I} out(S_i)$, and
- $int(S) = \cup_{i\in I} int(S_i)$.

The *composition* $A = \prod_{i\in I} A_i$ of a countable collection of strongly compatible automata $\{A_i\}_{i\in I}$ is the automaton defined as follows:[2]

- $sig(A) = \prod_{i\in I} sig(A_i)$,

[2]Here *start*(A) and *states*(A) are defined in terms of the ordinary Cartesian product, while *sig*(A) is defined in terms of the composition of actions signatures just defined. Also, we use the notation $\vec{s}[i]$ to denote the ith component of the state vector $\vec{s}$.

- $states(A) = \prod_{i \in I} states(A_i)$,
- $start(A) = \prod_{i \in I} start(A_i)$,
- $steps(A)$ is the set of triples $(\vec{s_1}, \pi, \vec{s_2})$ such that, for all $i \in I$, if $\pi \in acts(A_i)$ then $(\vec{s_1}[i], \pi, \vec{s_2}[i]) \in steps(A_i)$, and if $\pi \notin acts(A_i)$ then $\vec{s_1}[i] = \vec{s_2}[i]$, and
- $part(A) = \cup_{i \in I} part(A_i)$.

Given an execution $\alpha = \vec{s_0}\pi_1\vec{s_1} \ldots$ of A, let $\alpha|A_i$ (read "α projected on A_i") be the sequence obtained by deleting $\pi_j\vec{s_j}$ when $\pi_j \notin acts(A_i)$ and replacing the remaining $\vec{s_j}$ by $\vec{s_j}[i]$.

2.3 Fairness

Of all the executions of an I/O automaton, we are primarily interested in the 'fair' executions — those that permit each of the automaton's primitive components (i.e., its classes or processes) to have infinitely many chances to perform output or internal actions. The definition of automaton composition says that an equivalence class of a component automaton becomes an equivalence class of a composition, and hence that composition retains the essential structure of the system's primitive components. In the model, therefore, being fair to each component means being fair to each equivalence class of locally-controlled actions. A *fair execution* of an automaton A is defined to be an execution α of A such that the following conditions hold for each class C of $part(A)$:

1. If α is finite, then no action of C is enabled in the final state of α.
2. If α is infinite, then either α contains infinitely many events from C, or α contains infinitely many occurrences of states in which no action of C is enabled.

We denote the set of fair executions of A by *fairexecs*(A). We say that β is a *fair behavior* of A if β is the behavior of a fair execution of A, and we denote the set of fair behaviors of A by *fairbehs*(A). Similarly, β is a *fair schedule* of A if β is the schedule of a fair execution of A, and we denote the set of fair schedules of A by *fairscheds*(A).

2.4 Problem Specification

A 'problem' to be solved by an I/O automaton is formalized as a set of (finite and infinite) sequences of external actions. An automaton is said to *solve* a problem P provided that its set of fair behaviors is a subset of P. Although the model does not allow an automaton to block its environment or eliminate undesirable inputs, we can formulate our problems (i.e., correctness conditions) to require that an automaton exhibits some behavior only when the environment observes certain restrictions on the production of inputs.

We want a problem specification to be an interface together with a set of behaviors. We therefore define a *schedule module* H to consist of two components, an action signature $sig(H)$, and a set $scheds(H)$ of *schedules*. Each schedule in $scheds(H)$ is a finite or infinite sequence of actions of H. Subject to the same restrictions as automata, schedule modules may be composed to form other schedule modules. The resulting signature is defined as for automata, and the schedules $scheds(H)$ is the set of sequences β of actions of H such that for every module H' in the composition, $\beta|H'$ is a schedule of H'.

It is often the case that an automaton behaves correctly only in the context of certain restrictions on its input. A useful notion for discussing such restrictions is that of a module 'preserving' a property of behaviors. A set of sequences $\mathcal{P}$ is said to be *prefix-closed* if $\beta \in \mathcal{P}$ whenever both β is a prefix of α and $\alpha \in \mathcal{P}$. A module M (either an automaton or schedule module) is said to be *prefix-closed* provided that *finbehs*(M) is prefix-closed. Let M be a prefix-closed module and let $\mathcal{P}$ be a nonempty, prefix-closed set of sequences of actions from a set Φ satisfying $\Phi \cap int(M) = \emptyset$. We say that M *preserves* $\mathcal{P}$ if $\beta\pi|\Phi \in \mathcal{P}$ whenever $\beta|\Phi \in \mathcal{P}$, $\pi \in out(M)$, and $\beta\pi|M \in finbehs(M)$. Informally, a module *preserves* a property $\mathcal{P}$ iff the module is not the first to violate $\mathcal{P}$: as long as the environment only provides inputs such that the cumulative behavior satisfies $\mathcal{P}$, the module will only perform outputs such that the cumulative behavior satisfies $\mathcal{P}$. One can prove that a composition preserves a property by showing that each of the component automata preserves the property.

3 Superposition Extensions

In this section, we present definitions that extend the I/O automaton model for superposition of program modules. We begin by defining what it means for an automaton to be "unconstrained" for a particular set of variables, and use this definition to state the requirements for one automaton to be "superposable" on another. We then define the superposition operator, and show that the superposition of one I/O automaton on another produces a new I/O automaton. Therefore, all the standard definitions and results for I/O automata (for fairness, compositionality, etc.) immediately carry over to superposed automata. Furthermore, we show that any fair execution of a superposed automaton, when projected on the underlying module, is a fair execution of the underlying module. In addition, if no output actions of the higher level module are input actions of the underlying module, then every execution of the underlying module is a projection of some execution of the superposed automaton. These results correspond to the UNITY notion that superposition preserves all properties of the underlying algorithm. In addition, we show that when an automaton A is superposed on some other automaton, then the set of schedules of the resulting automaton, when projected on the signature of A, is a subset of the schedules of A alone. Finally, we present a new problem specification mechanism that is analogous to schedule modules for ordinary I/O automata, but that allows one to specify the allowable behaviors of a higher level module in terms of the *state* of the lower level module.

Throughout this paper, we refer to the state of an automaton as being divided into sets of variables, where each set of variables takes on values from a particular domain. For example, we may say that the state of automaton A is divided into two sets of variables X and Y with domains *dom*(X) and *dom*(Y), respectively. In this case, we use an ordered pair (x, y) to name a particular state of A, where $x \in dom(X)$ and $y \in dom(Y)$, and we take the set of possible states of A to be the cartesian product $dom(X) \times dom(Y)$. If s is a particular state of A, we let $s|X$ denote the values of the variables of X in state s.

All extensions defined in the section are simply additions to the I/O automaton model. We do not redefine any concepts of the original model, so all of its properties carry over to the extended model.

3.1 Unconstrained Automata

When we superpose one module on another, we would like the higher level module not to interfere with the lower level one. In particular, we do not want the higher level module to place constraints on how the lower level module may modify its own variables. Therefore, we will define superposition to apply only when the higher level module is "unconstrained" for the variables of the lower level module. We first define formally what it means for an automaton to be unconstrained for a set of variables. Let X be a set of variables with domain *dom(X)*. An *unconstrained automaton* A for X is an I/O automaton such that there exists a set P of variables with a set of possible initial values *init(P)* such that:

- $states(A) = dom(P) \times dom(X)$,
- $start(A) = init(P) \times dom(X)$, and
- for every step $((p', x'), \pi, (p, x))$ in $steps(A)$, for all $\hat{x} \in dom(X)$, $((p', x'), \pi, (p, \hat{x}))$ is in $steps(A)$.

Informally, the extra condition on the transition relation says that automaton A places no restrictions on the values of the variables in X following any action. Note, however, that the set of locally controlled actions enabled in a given state of A may depend on the values of X variables in that state.

Since an unconstrained automaton is an I/O automaton, all the standard I/O automaton definitions for executions, schedules, behaviors, and composition carry over to unconstrained automata. One may think of an "ordinary" I/O automaton as an unconstrained automaton for $X = \emptyset$.

One way to model a layered multicomponent system is to individually superpose pairs of automata and then compose. An equally valid method is to create two entire system layers through composition, and then superpose. In using the latter method, we would like the composition of an unconstrained automaton for X and an unconstrained automaton for Y, with $X \cap Y = \emptyset$, to be an unconstrained automaton for $X \cup Y$. However, this is not the case. Even if the components of the higher layer are each appropriately unconstrained, their composition is not.[3] Therefore, we define a relaxation operator $\mathcal{U}$ that builds an unconstrained automaton from an ordinary one. Let A be an I/O automaton whose state is divided into two sets of variables P and X with domains $dom(P)$ and $dom(X)$ respectively. We define the *relaxation of A with respect to X*, denoted $\mathcal{U}(A, X)$, to be the automaton B as follows:

- $sig(B) = sig(A)$,
- $states(B) = states(A)$,
- $start(B) = \{(p, \hat{x}) : \hat{x} \in dom(X) \wedge \exists x \in dom(X), (p, x) \in start(A)\}$,
- $steps(B) = \{((p', x'), \pi, (p, \hat{x})) : \hat{x} \in dom(X) \wedge \exists x \in dom(X), ((p', x'), \pi, (p, x)) \in steps(A)\}$, and
- $part(B) = part(A)$.

The relaxation operator $\mathcal{U}$ simply constructs the new automaton by adding enough start states and steps to make it unconstrained for X. The following lemma follows immediately from the definitions.

Lemma 1: Let A be an I/O automaton whose state is divided into two sets of variables, P and X. Then $\mathcal{U}(A, X)$ is an unconstrained automaton for X.

[3] For example, suppose A_X is an unconstrained automaton for X and A_Y is an unconstrained automaton for Y. In the composition of A_X and A_Y, the values of the variables of X are changed only in steps involving actions of A_X. Therefore, any action of A_Y that is not an action of A_X is constrained to leave the values of the variables in X unchanged. Thus, the composition of A_X and A_Y is not unconstrained for $X \cup Y$.

The following result allows us to prove properties of the schedules of individual unconstrained automata with the knowledge that these properties will carry over to all schedules of the relaxation of the composition.

Lemma 2: Let $\{X_i\}_{i\in\mathcal{I}}$ be a set of disjoint sets of variables, and let $\{A_i\}_{i\in\mathcal{I}}$ be a collection of strongly compatible automata, where each A_i is unconstrained for X_i. Let A be the composition $\Pi_{i\in\mathcal{I}}A_i$, and let A_u be the automaton $\mathcal{U}(A, \bigcup_{i\in\mathcal{I}} X_i)$. Then $scheds(A_u) = scheds(A)$ and $fairscheds(A_u) = fairscheds(A)$.

Proof: We know that $scheds(A) \subseteq scheds(A_u)$, since $start(A) \subseteq start(A_u)$ and $steps(A) \subseteq steps(A_u)$ by definition. We show that $scheds(A_u) \subseteq scheds(A)$ using the following construction. Let α_u be an execution of A_u, and let α be identical to α_u, except that $\forall i \in \mathcal{I}, \forall n > 0$, if s_u is the nth state of α_u and s is the nth state of α, then $s|X_i = s'_u|X_i$, where s'_u is the state of α_u immediately preceding the first action of A_i following s_u (if no action of A_i follows s_u, then s'_u is the state immediately after the the last action of A_i in α_u; if no action of A_i occurs in α_u, then s'_u is the initial state of α_u). Note that the value of $s|X_i$ is identical for all states s between to successive actions of A_i in α, and is equal to the value of X_i just before the next step of A_i in α_u.

Clearly $sched(\alpha) = sched(\alpha_u)$. To show that α is a schedule of A, we must show that (1) if s_0 is the first state of α, then $s_0 \in start(A)$, and (2) every step (s', π, s) in α is in $steps(A)$. For condition (1), since each component A_i is unconstrained for X_i, we know that the initial value for x_i may be any value in $dom(X_i)$. Therefore, $s_0 \in start(A)$. For condition (2), we note that if (s', π, s) is the nth step of α, we know from the construction that if $\pi \in acts(A_i)$, then $s'|A_i = s'_u|A_i$, where s'_u is the nth state of α_u, and that π is enabled in state s'_u. Therefore, π is enabled in state s'. And since A_i is unconstrained for X_i, any value is possible for X_i in the resulting state. Furthermore, we know from the construction that if $\pi \notin acts(A_i)$, then $s|A_i = s'|A_i$. Therefore, (s', π, s) is a step of A.

The fairness result follows from the above arguments and the fact that $part(A_u) = part(A)$ by definition of the relaxation operator. ∎

3.2 Superposition

In this section, we define the conditions under which one module may be superposed on another, and then define the superposition operator itself.

Requirements for Superposition: In order to provide a sensible semantics for the superposition operator, we define the superposition of one automaton on another only when the two automata satisfy certain compatibility conditions, defined as follows. Let X be a set of variables with domain $dom(X)$. We say that automaton A is *superposable* on automaton B with respect to X iff

1. A is unconstrained for X,
2. $states(B) = dom(X)$, and
3. $sig(A)$ and $sig(B)$ are strongly compatible.

Loosely speaking, the first condition ensures that module B may freely modify its own variables in the superposition. The second condition says that the set of states of the underlying automaton must match the domain for the set of variables on which A is unconstrained. The third condition is the usual restriction for composition of automata.

Superposition Operator: We would like superposition to capture the idea that the higher level automaton is allowed to observe (but not modify) the state of the lower level automaton, and that the lower level automaton is unaware of the variables of the higher level automaton. We want the actions of the superposed automaton to include the actions of both the high level and low level automata, and we wish to allow the possibility of actions that are shared by both automata. This motivates the following definition.

Let X be a set of variables with domain *dom*(X), and let A and B be automata such that A is superposable on B with respect to X. We define the *superposition of A on B with respect to X*, denoted $C = S(A, B, X)$, as follows:

- $sig(C) = sig(A) \times^{4} sig(B)$,
- $states(C) = states(A)$,
- $start(C) = \{(p, x) \in start(A) : x \in start(B)\}$,
- $steps(C) =$ all steps $((p', x'), \pi, (p, x))$ such that the following conditions hold:
    1. $\pi \in sig(C)$
    2. if $\pi \in sig(A)$, then $((p', x'), \pi, (p, x)) \in steps(A)$
    3. if $\pi \in sig(B)$, then $(x', \pi, x) \in steps(B)$
    4. if $\pi \notin sig(A)$, then $p = p'$
    5. if $\pi \notin sig(B)$, then $x = x'$, and
- $part(C) = part(A) \cup part(B)$.

Informally, the signature of the superposed automaton C is the composition of the signatures of A and B. The states of C are the same as the states of A, and the set of start states of C is the set of all start states of A such that the values of X agree with some start state of B. The most interesting part of the superposition definition is the construction of the set of steps. It says that any step of C for an action of A must also be a step of A. Similarly, any step of C for an action of B must be a step of B, when projected on the variables in X. Essentially, the actions of A and B are enabled just as before, with automaton B placing constraints on the values of the variables in X. The last two conditions of the *steps*(C) construction simply prevent steps involving only B from modifying the private variables of A, and steps involving only A from modifying the variables in X. That is, if a step of C does *not* involve an action of A, then the private state variables of A must not be modified by the step. Similarly, if a step of C does *not* involve an action of B, then the values of the variables in X are unchanged by the step.

In a step for an action shared by A and B, the private state of A is modified according to the transition relation of A, while the state of X is modified according to the transition relation of B. This should agree with one's intuition about the semantics for such shared actions.

The following lemma states that a superposition of one I/O automaton on another results in a new I/O automaton. This implies that all the standard definitions and results for I/O automata, notably for composition and fairness, immediately carry over to superposed automata.

Lemma 3: Let X be a set of variables with domain *dom*(X), and let A and B be automata such that A is superposable on B with respect to X. Then $C = S(A, B, X)$ is an I/O automaton.

[4] Usual signature composition.

Proof: We must show that inputs of C are always enabled. That is, we must show that for all states $s' \in states(C)$ and for all actions $\pi \in in(C)$, there exists a state $s \in states(C)$ such that $(s, \pi, s) \in steps(C)$. Let $s' = (p', x')$. There are three cases for $\pi \in in(C)$. For each case, we exhibit an appropriate new state s:

1. $\pi \in sig(A)$ and $\pi \notin sig(B)$. Since A is an unconstrained automaton, we know that $\exists p \in private(A)$ such that $\forall \hat{x} \in dom(X)$, $((p', x'), \pi, (p, \hat{x})) \in steps(A)$. Specifically, if we let $\hat{x} = x'$, then we are done.

2. $\pi \notin sig(A)$ and $\pi \in sig(B)$. Since B is an I/O automaton, we know that $\exists x \in states(B)$ such that $(x', \pi, x) \in steps(B)$. Therefore, since $\pi \notin sig(A)$, $((p', x'), \pi, (p', x)) \in steps(C)$.

3. $\pi \in sig(A)$ and $\pi \in sig(B)$. Since A is an unconstrained automaton, we know that $\exists p \in private(A)$ such that $\forall \hat{x} \in dom(X)$, $((p', x'), \pi, (p, \hat{x})) \in steps(A)$. Furthermore, since B is an I/O automaton, we know that $\exists x \in states(B)$ such that $(x', \pi, x) \in steps(B)$. Therefore, letting $\hat{x} = x$ completes the proof.

In each case, π is enabled from s'. ∎

The following two results formalize the notion that properties of the underlying algorithm are preserved in the superposition.

Lemma 4: Let X be a set of variables with domain $dom(X)$. Let A and B be automata such that A is superposable on B with respect to X, and let $C = S(A, B, X)$. Then $execs(C)|B \subseteq execs(B)$ and $fairexecs(C)|B \subseteq fairexecs(B)$.

Proof: Let α be a (fair) execution of C. By definition of superposition, if (s', π, s) is a step of α and $\pi \notin acts(B)$ then $s|X = s'|X$. Therefore, $\alpha|B$ is a (fair) execution of B. (The fairness result follows from the fact that $part(B) \subseteq part(C)$, so any execution fair to the classes of C must also be fair to the classes of B.) ∎

In general, it is not the case that every execution of the lower level automaton is a projection of an execution of the superposed automaton. For example, lower level automaton B may have π as an input action, so its set of executions include executions in which π occurs multiple times. If automaton A is defined to have π as an output action such that π occurs at most once in every execution of A, then none of the executions of B in which π occurs more than once are projections of executions of the superposition of A on B. However, when no output actions of the higher level automaton are inputs to the lower level automaton, the converse of Lemma 4 holds, and we have the following result.

Lemma 5: Let X be a set of variables with domain $dom(X)$. Let A and B be automata such that A is superposable on B with respect to X, and let $C = S(A, B, X)$. If $in(B) \cap out(A) = \emptyset$, then $execs(C)|B = execs(B)$ and $fairexecs(C)|B = fairexecs(B)$.

Proof: Lemma 4 tells us that $execs(C)|B \subseteq execs(B)$ and $fairexecs(C)|B \subseteq fairexecs(B)$. Let β be a (fair) execution of B. Since $in(B) \cap out(A) = \emptyset$, we know that the higher level component A has no control over which actions of $acts(B)$ occur in an execution of C. Furthermore, only the actions of B may change the variables in X in the superposition. Therefore, since a locally controlled action of B is enabled from state s in C iff it is enabled from state $s|X$ in B, there must exist some (fair) execution γ of C such that $\gamma|B = \beta$. Thus, $execs(B) \subseteq execs(C)|B$ and $fairexecs(B) \subseteq fairexecs(C)|B$. ∎

The next result says that when an automaton A is superposed on some other automaton, then the set of schedules of the resulting automaton, when projected on the signature of A, is a subset of the schedules of A alone. This is very important because it allows us to prove safety properties about A alone with the knowledge that these properties will hold when A is superposed on some other automaton.

Lemma 6: Let X be a set of variables with domain $dom(X)$. Let A and B be automata such that A is superposable on B with respect to X, and let $C = \mathcal{S}(A, B, X)$. Then $scheds(C)|sig(A) \subseteq scheds(A)$.

Proof: Let γ be an execution of C. We construct α from γ by the following steps:

1. Remove from γ all actions not in $sig(A)$. This may create sequences of states not separated by actions.

2. Replace the sequence of states between each pair of successive actions by the last state in that sequence.

Clearly, α is an alternating sequence of states of A and actions of A. To show that $\alpha \in execs(A)$, we must show that the first state of α is in $start(A)$ and that if $\sigma = ((p', x'), \pi, (p, x))$ is a step in α, then $\sigma \in steps(A)$. For both of these, we use the following fact.

Fact: If a sequence of states from γ is replaced in step 2 of the construction by the single state (p, x), then every state in that sequence has p as the value of the private state of A.

Proof of Fact: In γ, each of these states is separated by an action not in the signature of A. From the definition of superposition, we know that any step in γ not involving an action of A does not change the values of the private variables of A. Since (p, x) is the last state in the sequence, every state in the sequence must have p as its first component.

From the above fact, we know that the first state of γ and the first state of α agree on the values of the private variables of A. Since A is unconstrained, any value in $dom(X)$ is an allowable value for the second component of the start state. Therefore, the first state of α is a start state of A.

If $\sigma = ((p', x'), \pi, (p, x))$ is a step in γ, then we know that π occurs from state (p', x') in α. Furthermore, from the above fact, we know that π results in state $(p, \hat{x})$ in γ for some $\hat{x} \in dom(X)$. So, we know that $steps(A)$ contains the step $((p', x'), \pi, (p, \hat{x}))$ for some $\hat{x} \in dom(X)$. Therefore, since A is unconstrained for X, we know that $steps(A)$ contains the step $((p', x'), \pi, (p, \hat{x}))$ for all $\hat{x} \in dom(X)$, and specifically for $\hat{x} = x$. This completes the proof. ∎

Note that not all schedules of A are necessarily possible in the superposition, since certain states reachable in A alone may not be reachable in the superposition. For example, suppose a particular action π of A is enabled only when a variable $x \in X$ has a particular value v, and suppose that the automaton B on which A is superposed is defined to never set $x = v$. Since A alone may set x to any value (by the definition of unconstrained for X), the action π may occur in behaviors of A. However, by the definition of superposition, there is no step of $\mathcal{S}(A, B, X)$ that results in $x = v$, so π is never enabled. This is a perfectly natural and desirable property of superposition, for it says that the state of the lower layer affects the behavior of the higher layer.

Another interesting fact is that *fairscheds*$(C)|sig(A)$ and *fairscheds*(A) are incomparable. We know from the above paragraph that *fairscheds*$(A) \not\subseteq$ *fairscheds*$(C)|sig(A)$. But it is also the case that *fairscheds*$(C)|sig(A) \not\subseteq$ *fairscheds*(A), as witnessed by the following example. Suppose that A has only two actions, π_1 and π_2, each in its own class of the partition. Furthermore, suppose that both events are enabled exactly when $x = 0$. Now, suppose that B has exactly one action π_3, that toggles the value of x between 0 and 1, and is always enabled. In the superposition of A on B, a fair schedule would be $\pi_1, \pi_3, \pi_3, \pi_1, \pi_3, \pi_3, \pi_1, \ldots$, in which the class containing π_2 is given a chance to take a step only when $x = 1$. However, the infinite schedule $\pi_1, \pi_1, \pi_1, \ldots$ is *not* a fair schedule of A alone: Since the schedule consists of infinitely many π_1 actions, it must be that π_1 is enabled from every state of the corresponding execution. Therefore, $x = 0$ in all states of that execution. But π_2 is also enabled whenever $x = 0$, yet the class containing π_2 is never given a chance to take a step, so the schedule is not fair.

The reason for the above fact is that the preconditions for the locally controlled actions of A are allowed to depend upon the values of the variables in X. Keeping this in mind, consider the following additional condition on unconstrained automata. If A is an unconstrained automaton for X, then A is said to be *completely unconstrained for* X iff for for all actions $\pi \in sig(A)$, if $((p', x'), \pi, (p, x)) \in steps(A)$ then for all $\hat{x} \in dom(X)$, there exists a state $(\hat{p}, x) \in states(A)$ such that $((p', \hat{x}), \pi, (\hat{p}, x)) \in steps(A)$. In other words, whether or not an action of A is enabled can depend only upon the values of its private variables. The only way for A to make any use of the variables of X would be for it to modify its own local variables according to what it observes in X, causing other actions of A to become enabled or disabled. Modifying the definition of superposable to require the higher level automaton to be completely unconstrained for X would allow us to prove that *fairscheds*$(C)|sig(A) \subseteq$ *fairscheds*(A), but would result in a significant loss of expressive power. So, rather than require this condition outright, we state the following lemma, which says that *if* an automaton happens to be completely unconstrained, then the containment result holds for its fair schedules. This gives us more flexibility in the use of the model.

Lemma 7: Let X be a set of variables with domain $dom(X)$. Let A and B be automata such that A is completely unconstrained for X and A is superposable on B with respect to X. Let $C = S(A, B, X)$. Then *fairscheds*$(C)|sig(A) \subseteq$ *fairscheds*(A).

Proof: Analogous to that of Lemma 6, but noting that the actions of A are enabled independently of the value of X and applying the definition of fairness. ∎

The definition of an unconstrained automaton A for X requires that the value of X may be changed arbitrarily with each step of A. However, a more natural way to describe the behaviors of a module to be superposed on another module might be to allow the values of X to change *between* the steps of A as well. For this, we define the notion of an "extended execution" in which several states may occur between two successive actions. If A is an unconstrained automaton for X, we define an *extended execution* of A to be a sequence α of states in $states(A)$ and actions in $acts(A)$, beginning with a state in $start(A)$, such that:

1. if a state-action-state sequence $s'\pi s$ appears in α, then (s', π, s) is in $steps(A)$,

2. if two states s' and s appear consecutively in α, then they differ only in the value of X, and

3. no two actions appear consecutively in α.

We define fairness for extended executions exactly as for ordinary executions. We let *extexecs*(A) and *fairextexecs*(A) denote the sets of extended executions and fair extended executions of A, respectively. If α is a sequence of states and actions and Π is a set of actions, we define the notation $\alpha\|\Pi$ to be the sequence that results from deleting from α exactly those actions not in Π. Using extended executions instead of ordinary executions, we get the desired fairness result:

Lemma 8: Let X be a set of variables with domain *dom*(X). Let A and B be automata such that A is superposable on B with respect to X, and let $C = \mathcal{S}(A, B, X)$. Then *execs*$(C)\|$*sig*$(A) \subseteq$ *extexecs*(A) and *fairexecs*$(C)\|$*sig*$(A) \subseteq$ *fairextexecs*(A).

Proof: Let α be an execution of C. From the definition of superposition, we know that α begins with a state in *start*(A), and that any step (s', π, s) occurring in α with $\pi \in$ *sig*(A) must be a step of A. Also by the definition of superposition, for any step (s', π, s) where π is *not* in *sig*(A), s' and s must differ only in the value of X. Therefore, $\alpha\|$*sig*(A) is an extended execution of A by definition. If α is fair, then since α and $\alpha|$*sig*(A) contain the same sequence of states, and since *part*$(A) \subseteq$ *part*(C), we know that $\alpha\|$*sig*(A) is a fair extended execution of A. ∎

3.3 Partial Execution Modules

It is important to have a formal mechanism for specifying the problem to be solved by an automaton. Schedule modules, as described in Section 2.4, permit us to specify the allowable schedules of a module in terms of the actions that occur the boundary with its environment. However, if an automaton A is to be superposed on top of some underlying automaton B, then we would like to specify the allowable behaviors of A not only in terms of the actions that occur at its external interface, but also in terms of the internal state of B. To accomplish this, we define a new specification mechanism called a "partial execution module."

Let X be a set of variables with domain *dom*(X), and let Π be a set of actions. A *partial execution* for Π and X is defined to be a sequence of states and actions, beginning with a state, such that each state is in *dom*(X), each action is in Π, and each action is immediately followed by a state. Note that a partial execution may contain several states between two consecutive actions. A *partial execution module* H consists of

- *sig*(H), an external action signature,
- *vars*(H), a set of variables with domain *dom*(*vars*(H)), and
- *pexecs*(H), a set of partial executions for *sig*(H) and *vars*(H).

A partial execution module H defines a problem to be solved by an unconstrained automaton for *vars*(H) with external signature *sig*(H). In order to define what it means for an automaton to "solve" H, we need a way to extract partial executions from extended executions: Let X be a set of variables with domain *dom*(X), let Π be a set of actions, and let α be an extended execution of any automaton that is unconstrained for X. We define $\alpha|(\Pi, X)$, the *partial execution for* Π *and* X *in* α, to be the same as α, except that each state s is replaced by its projection on X and each action not in Π is deleted. If A is an unconstrained automaton for X with external signature Π, we define *pexecs*(A, X) to be the set $\{\alpha|(\Pi, X) : \alpha \in$ *fairextexecs*$(A)\}$.

An automaton A is said to *solve* a partial execution module H iff *pexecs*$(A,$ *vars*$(H)) \subseteq$ *pexecs*(H).

3.4 Superposition for Partial Executions

Lynch and Tuttle define composition for both automata and schedule modules. So far, we have defined the superposition of one automaton on another, but have not yet defined an analogous operator for superposing a partial execution module on another module. We now complete the theory by defining the superposition of a set of partial executions on a set of ordinary executions.

Let X be a set of variables and let Π and Δ be sets of actions. Let ∂ be a set of partial executions for Π and X, and let Φ be a set of alternating sequences of states in of $dom(X)$ and actions in Δ. Let $\mho$ be the set of all alternating sequences of states of X and actions of $\Pi \cup \Delta$. We now define the *superposition of ∂ on Φ with respect to X*. Overloading the S notation, we define

$$S(\partial, \Phi, X) = \{\alpha \in \mho : \alpha \| \Pi \in \partial \wedge \alpha | \Delta \in \Phi\}.$$

In other words, for each element α of $S(\partial, \Phi, X)$, deleting all actions from α except those in Π results in a partial execution in ∂, and projecting α on the actions of Δ results in an execution in Φ.

The following result says that the set of fair behaviors of a superposition of A on B with respect to X is the same as the set of behaviors resulting from the superposition of $pexecs(A, X)$ on the fair executions of B.

Lemma 9: Let X be a set of variables. If automaton A is superposable on automaton B with respect to X, then $fairbehs(S(A, B, X)|(\Pi, X)) = behs(S(pexecs(A), fairexecs(B), X))$.

Proof: If β is a fair behavior of $S(A, B, X)$, let α be the corresponding execution. By Lemma 8, $\alpha \| sig(A)$ is a fair extended execution of A, so $\alpha|(sig(A), X) \in pexecs(A)$. And by Lemma 4, $\alpha|B \in fairexecs(B)$, so $fairbehs(S(A, B, X)|(\Pi, X)) \subseteq behs(S(pexecs(A), fairexecs(B),$.

To show the other direction, let α be an element of $S(pexecs(A), fairexecs(B), X)$. From the definition of superposition of partial executions, we know that $\alpha \| \Pi \in pexecs(A)$. Therefore, there exists a fair extended execution α' of A such that $\alpha = \alpha'|(ext(A), X)$. Also from the definition of superposition of partial executions, we know that $\alpha|\Delta \in fairexecs(B)$. Since the states of α an α' are identical with respect to X, we know that for each step (s', π, s) of $\alpha|\Delta$, there exists in α' a pair of consecutive states $\hat{s}'$ and $\hat{s}$ such that $\hat{s}'|X = s'$ and $\hat{s}|X = s$. We construct α'' by inserting each action of $\alpha|\Delta$ between the corresponding pair of states in α'. To complete the proof, we must show that α'' is a fair execution of $S(A, B, X)$. We know that α'' begins with an initial state of A. Now, we consider the four possible cases for each step (s', π, s) in α'':

1. If $\pi \in sig(A)$, then $(s', \pi, s) \in steps(A)$, since α' is an extended execution of A.
2. If $\pi \in sig(B)$, then $(s'|X, \pi, s|X) \in steps(B)$, because of our construction of α'' from α and the fact that $\alpha|\Delta$ is an execution of B.
3. If $\pi \notin sig(A)$, then s' and s differ only in the value of X by definition of an extended execution.
4. If $\pi \notin sig(B)$, then $s'|X = s|X$, again because $\alpha|\Delta$ is an execution of B.

Therefore, α'' is an execution of $S(A, B, X)$. To show that α'' is fair, we note that $part(S(A, B, X))$ $part(A) \cup part(B)$ by the definition of superposition, and we consider the classes of A and B separately. We know that α' is a fair extended execution of A. Therefore, since $\alpha''\|A = \alpha'$, α'' is fair to the classes of A. Similarly, since $\alpha|\Delta$ is a fair execution of B, and $\alpha''|B = \alpha|\Delta$, we know that α is fair to the classes of B. ∎

4 Conclusion

In this paper, we extended the I/O automaton model to permit superposition of program modules. This provides a unified model that permits one to reason locally about components of a distributed system, and to combine those modules through either composition or superposition (or both) in such a way that the essential properties of the components are preserved in the resulting system.

Extended with the superposition operator, the I/O automaton model can now be used to model algorithms for problems in which layering is the most natural structure. For example, we have used the extended model to describe and prove correct the global snapshot algorithm of Chandy and Lamport[1]. We define the global snapshot problem as a partial execution module, and then describe the global snapshot algorithm as an automaton to be superposed on an arbitrary application program. Both composition and superposition are important in this example because the snapshot automaton is, in fact, the composition of a collection of automata, one superposed on each component of the distributed application. Each of these automata acts as a "filter" of the incoming and outgoing messages of the application program. Since superposition permits each of these automata to observe the state of the corresponding component of the application, the existence of the global snapshot algorithm is entirely transparent to the application program. Without the superposition operator, it would have been necessary to modify the application program to explicitly communicate its state to the snapshot algorithm at the appropriate point in the global snapshot protocol. The correctness proof, which appears in [4], shows that the global snapshot automaton solves the partial execution module and makes important use of the compositionality results of the model.

Acknowledgements

I thank Nancy Lynch for many useful comments and Hagit Attiya for several helpful discussions.

References

[1] K. Mani Chandy and Leslie Lamport. Distributed snapshots: Determining global states of distributed systems. *ACM Transactions on Computer Systems*, 3(1):63–75, February 1985.

[2] K. Mani Chandy and Jayadev Misra. *A Foundation of Parallel Program Design*. Addison–Wesley, Reading, MA, 1988.

[3] Kenneth Goldman and Nancy Lynch. Modelling shared state in a shared action model. In *Proceedings of the 5th Annual IEEE Symposium on Logic in Computer Science*, June 1990.

[4] Kenneth J. Goldman. Distributed algorithm simulation using Input/Output Automata. Technical Report MIT/LCS/TR–490, MIT Laboratory for Computer Science, July 1990. Ph.D. Thesis.

[5] Nancy A. Lynch and Mark R. Tuttle. An introduction to Input/Output Automata. *CWI-Quarterly*, 2(3), 1989.

[6] Magda F. Nour. An automata-theoretic model for UNITY. Technical Report MIT/LCS/TM-400, MIT Laboratory for Computer Science, June 1989. Senior Thesis.

Process Algebra with Guards

Combining Hoare Logic with Process Algebra

(Extended Abstract)

Jan Friso Groote & Alban Ponse

Department of Software Technology, CWI

P.O. Box 4079, 1009 AB Amsterdam, The Netherlands

e-mail: jfg@cwi.nl - alban@cwi.nl

Abstract

We extend process algebra with guards, comparable to the guards in guarded commands or conditions in common programming constructs. The extended language is provided with an operational semantics based on transitions between pairs of a process and a data-state. The data-states are given by a data environment that also defines in which data-states guards hold and how actions (non-deterministically) transform these states. The operational semantics is studied modulo strong bisimulation equivalence. For basic process algebra (without operators for parallelism) we present a small axiom system that is complete with respect to a general class of data environments. In case a data environment S is known, we add three axioms to this system, which is then again complete, provided weakest preconditions are expressible and S is sufficiently deterministic.

Then we study process algebra with parallelism and guards. A two phase-calculus is provided that makes it possible to prove identities between parallel processes. Also this calculus is complete. In the last section we show that partial correctness formulas can easily be expressed in this setting and we use process algebra with guards to prove the soundness of Hoare logic for linear processes by translating proofs in Hoare logic into proofs in process algebra.

Note: The first author is supported under ESPRIT Basic Research Action no. 3006 (CONCUR) and both authors are supported under RACE project no. 1046 (SPECS) but this document does not necessarily reflect the view of the SPECS consortium.

1 Introduction

Hoare logic has been introduced in 1969 as a proof system for the correctness of programs [Hoa69]. Since then it has been applied to many problems, and it has been thoroughly studied (see [Apt81] for an overview). In Hoare logic a program is considered to be a state transformer; the initial state is transformed to a final state. The correctness of a program is expressed by pre- and post-conditions.

More recently, the behaviour of processes has attracted attention. This has led to several process calculi (CCS [Mil80], CSP [Hoa85], ACP [BK84, BW90] and MEIJE [AB84]).

In these calculi the correctness of processes is generally expressed by equations, often saying that a specification and an implementation are equivalent in some sense. The equivalences that are used are mainly based on observations: two processes are equal if some observer cannot distinguish between the two.

It seems a natural and useful question how Hoare logic and process algebra can be integrated. In this paper we provide an answer in two steps. First we extend process algebra with *guards*. Depending on the state, a guard can either be transparent such that it can be passed, or it can block and prevent subsequent processes from being executed. Typical for our approach is that a guard *itself* represents a process. With this construct we can easily express the guarded commands of DIJKSTRA [Dij76] and many other conditional constructs in programming and specification languages. The guards in our framework have several nice properties, e.g. they constitute a Boolean algebra. Partial correctness formulas $\{\alpha\}\, p\, \{\beta\}$ can be expressed by algebraic equations of the form $\alpha p = \alpha p \beta$ where α and β are guards (cf. [MA86]).

We provide process algebra with guards with an operational semantics involving data-state transformations. From now on we use the term 'data-state' to avoid confusion with the notion of a state in process algebra. We consider the processes modulo strong bisimulation equivalence [Mil80] and we come up with two axiomatisations for Basic Process Algebra (without parallelism).

Parallel operators fit easily in the process algebra framework. In Hoare logic, however, parallelism turns out to be rather intricate; proof rules for parallel operators are often substantial [OG76]. In our setup we cannot avoid the difficulties caused by parallel operators in Hoare logic, but we can deal with them in a simple algebraic way.

In the last section of this paper we relate Hoare logic and process algebra. The soundness of a Hoare logic for processes defined by linear recursion [Pon89] can be proved within our algebraic framework.

For proofs omitted here we refer to the full version of this paper [GP90].

Acknowledgement

We thank Jos Baeten, Jan Bergstra, Frank de Boer, Tony Hoare, Catuscia Palamidessi, Fer-Jan de Vries and the referees for their helpful comments.

2 Basic Process Algebra with guards

We extend basic process algebra (BPA [BK84]) with guards. Basic process algebra consists of a given set A of atomic actions with typical elements $a, b, \ldots$ and the operators $+$ (alternative composition) and $\cdot$ (sequential composition). Atomic actions are viewed as nondeterministic data-state transformers. We assume that we have some set G_{at} of *atomic guards*. Guards are viewed as elementary processes that block or are transparent depending on the data-state of the process. We extend the signature $\Sigma(\text{BPA})$ to the signature $\Sigma(\text{BPA}_G)$ by adding *basic guards* that have as syntax:

$$\phi \ ::= \ \delta \mid \epsilon \mid \neg\phi \mid \psi \in G_{at}$$

where $\neg$ is the negation operator on guards, δ is the guard that always blocks and ϵ is the guard that can always be passed. These last two constants are already well-known in process algebra.

Let $V = \{x, y, z, ...\}$ be a set of variables. Process terms over $\Sigma(\text{BPA}_G)$, or shortly terms, are constructed from the variables in V and the elements of $\Sigma(\text{BPA}_G)$. In terms we generally omit the function symbol $\cdot$ and we adopt the convention that $\cdot$ binds stronger than $+$. We use letters $t, t', ...$ to denote open terms and letters $p, q, ...$ to denote closed terms. $Var(t)$ denotes the set of variables occurring in the term t. We use substitutions as mappings from variables to terms, referred to by letters $\sigma, \rho, ...$ Substitutions are extended to terms in the usual way. We use equations between terms, notation $t = t'$, and equational provability, notation $E \vdash t = t'$, from a set of equations E. Furthermore, we introduce *summand inclusion*: for any two terms t, t' over $\Sigma(\text{BPA}_G)$ we write $t \subseteq t'$ for $t + t' = t'$ and $t' \supseteq t$ for $t' = t + t'$. In both cases we say that t is a *summand* of t'.

The set of axioms BPA_G^4 in table 1 describes the basic identities between terms over $\Sigma(\text{BPA}_G)$. The axioms A1 – A9 are the ordinary $\text{BPA}_{\delta\epsilon}$-axioms [BW90]. The axioms G1 – G4 describe the fundamental identities between guards. G1 and G2 express that a basic guard always behaves dually to its negation: ϕ holds in a data-state s iff $\neg\phi$ does not and vice versa. The axiom G3 states that $+$ does not change the interpretation of a basic guard ϕ. It does not matter whether the choice is exercised before or after the evaluation of ϕ. The last new axiom G4 can be explained as follows: the process $a(\phi x + \neg\phi y)$ behaves either like ax or ay, depending on whether ϕ or $\neg\phi$ can be passed in the data-state resulting from the execution of a. As a consequence the process $a(\phi x + \neg\phi y)$ should be a provable summand of $ax + ay$. The a in this axiom may not be replaced by a larger process expression. If it is for instance replaced by the expression $a \cdot b$ then after a has happened, it is in general not clear whether ϕ or $\neg\phi$ will hold after b. Hence $ab(\phi x + \neg\phi y)$ need not be a summand of $abx + aby$. Note that the axiom G4 is not derivable from the first three 'guard'-axioms. The superscript 4 in BPA_G^4 indicates that there are four axioms referring to guards. We will not always consider all of these. In particular the system BPA_G^3, containing all BPA_G^4-axioms except G4 will play a role in this paper.

$x + y = y + x$	A1	$\phi \cdot \neg\phi = \delta$	G1
$x + (y + z) = (x + y) + z$	A2	$\phi + \neg\phi = \epsilon$	G2
$x + x = x$	A3	$\phi(x + y) = \phi x + \phi y$	G3
$(x + y)z = xz + yz$	A4		
$(xy)z = x(yz)$	A5		
$x + \delta = x$	A6		
$\delta x = \delta$	A7	$a(\phi x + \neg\phi y) \subseteq ax + ay$	G4
$\epsilon x = x$	A8		
$x\epsilon = x$	A9		

Table 1: The axioms of BPA_G^4 where $\phi \in G$ and $a \in A$

Up till now we only defined 'basic' and 'atomic' guards. We use the general name *guards* $\alpha, \beta, ...$ for terms over $\Sigma(\text{BPA}_G)$ that contain only basic guards and the sequential and alternative composition operators. In order to have the Boolean operator $\neg$ on guards, we introduce the *abbreviations*

$$\neg(\alpha\beta) \quad \text{for} \quad \neg\alpha + \neg\beta$$
$$\neg(\alpha + \beta) \quad \text{for} \quad \neg\alpha\neg\beta.$$

For guards we have the following theorem (cf. [Sio64]):

Theorem 2.1. *Let G_{at} be a set of atomic guards.* BPA_G^3 *is an equational basis for the Boolean algebra* $(G_{at}, +, \cdot, \neg)$. □

We extend our process language with a mechanism that enables us to specify infinite processes by recursive equations.

Definition 2.2. A *recursive specification* $E = \{x = t_x \mid x \in V_E\}$ *over* the signature $\Sigma(\mathrm{BPA}_G)$ is a set of equations where V_E is a (possibly infinite) set of variables and t_x a term over $\Sigma(\mathrm{BPA}_G)$ such that $Var(t_x) \subseteq V_E$. □

A *solution* of a recursive specification $E = \{x = t_x \mid x \in V_E\}$ is an interpretation of the variables in V_E as processes, such that the equations of E are satisfied. For instance the recursive specification $\{x = x\}$ has any process as a solution for x and $\{x = ax\}$ has the infinite process "a^ω" as a solution for x. We introduce the following syntactical restriction on recursive specifications.

Definition 2.3. Let t be a term over a signature $\Sigma(\mathrm{BPA}_G)$. An occurrence of a variable x in t is *guarded* iff t has a subterm of the form $a \cdot M$ with $a \in A \cup \{\delta\}$, and this x occurs in M. Let $E = \{x = t_x \mid x \in V_E\}$ be a recursive specification over $\Sigma(\mathrm{BPA}_G)$. We say that E is a *guarded* specification iff all occurrences of variables in the terms t_x are guarded. □

Remark 2.4. The terminology *guarded* recursive specification is established and should therefore be respected. The adjective "guarded" has nothing to do with the "guards" that form the main subject of this paper. *(End remark.)*

Now the signature $\Sigma(\mathrm{BPA}_G)_{\mathrm{REC}}$, in which we are interested, is defined by:

Definition 2.5. The signature $\Sigma(\mathrm{BPA}_G)_{\mathrm{REC}}$ is obtained by extending $\Sigma(\mathrm{BPA}_G)$ in the following way: for each guarded specification $E = \{x = t_x \mid x \in V_E\}$ over $\Sigma(\mathrm{BPA}_G)$ a set of constants $\{<x \mid E> \mid x \in V_E\}$ is added, where the construct $<x \mid E>$ denotes the x-component of a solution of E. □

We introduce some more notations: let $E = \{x = t_x \mid x \in V_E\}$ be a guarded specification over $\Sigma(\mathrm{BPA}_G)$, and t some term over $\Sigma(\mathrm{BPA}_G)_{\mathrm{REC}}$. Then $<t \mid E>$ denotes the term in which each occurrence of a variable $x \in V_E$ in t is replaced by $<x \mid E>$, e.g. the expression $<aax \mid \{x = ax\}>$ denotes the term $aa<x \mid \{x = ax\}>$.

For the constants of the form $<x \mid E>$ there are two axioms in table 2. In these axioms the letter E ranges over guarded specifications. The axiom REC states that the constant $<x \mid E>$ ($x \in V_E$) is a solution for the x-component of E. The conditional axiom RSP (Recursive Specification Principle) expresses that E has at most one solution for each of its variables: whenever we can find processes p_x ($x \in V_E$) satisfying the equations of E, then $p_x = <x \mid E>$.

In this paper we let $\Sigma(\mathrm{BPA}_G)_{\mathrm{REC}}$-processes operate on *data-states*. We adopt an abstract view and assume that data-states are given by a set S. Atomic actions are considered as non-deterministic data-state *transformers*. This is modelled by a function *effect* that, given some atomic action a and a data-state s, returns the data-states which may result from the execution of a in s. We demand that the function *effect* never

$<x\,|\,E> = <t_x\,|\,E>$ if $x = t_x \in E$ and E guarded		REC
$\dfrac{\sigma(E)}{\sigma(x) = <x\,|\,E>}$	if $x \in V_E$ and E guarded and σ is a substitution	RSP

Table 2: Axioms for guarded recursive specifications

returns the empty set, ensuring that an atomic action can always be executed. We need the guards if we want to prevent actions from happening in certain data-states. The predicate *test* determines whether an atomic guard holds in some data-state.

Definition 2.6. A data environment $\mathcal{S} = \langle S, \textit{effect}, \textit{test}\rangle$ over a set A of atomic actions and a set G_{at} of atomic guards is specified by

- A non-empty set S of data-states,
- A function $\textit{effect} : S \times A \to (\mathcal{P}(S) - \{\emptyset\})$,
- A predicate $\textit{test} \subseteq G_{at} \times S$.

Here $\mathcal{P}(S)$ is the powerset of S. □

Whenever $\textit{test}(\phi, s)$ holds, this means that in data-state s the atomic guard ϕ may be passed. In this case we say that ϕ *holds* in s. In order to interpret basic guards, we extend the predicate *test* in the obvious way.

Definition 2.7. Let $\langle S, \textit{effect}, \textit{test}\rangle$ be some data environment. We extend the domain of *test* to $G \times S$ as follows:

- for all $s \in S$: $\textit{test}(\epsilon, s)$ holds and $\textit{test}(\delta, s)$ does not hold,
- for all $s \in S$ and $\phi \in G$: $\textit{test}(\neg\phi, s)$ holds iff $\textit{test}(\phi, s)$ does not hold.

□

We give an operational semantics in the style of PLOTKIN [Plo81]. The behaviour of a process p is defined by transitions between *configurations*.

Definition 2.8. Let S be a set of data-states. A *configuration* (p, s) *over* $(\Sigma(\text{BPA}_G), S)$ is a pair containing a closed term p over $\Sigma(\text{BPA}_G)$ and a data-state $s \in S$. The set of all configurations over $(\Sigma(\text{BPA}_G), S)$ is denoted by $C(\Sigma(\text{BPA}_G), S)$. □

Let $A_{\surd} \stackrel{\text{def}}{=} A \cup \{\surd\}$. The transition relation $\longrightarrow_{\Sigma(\text{BPA}_G)_{\text{REC}}, S}$ contains exactly all transitions between the configurations over $(\Sigma(\text{BPA}_G)_{\text{REC}}, S)$ that are derivable with the rules for ϕ, a, $+$, $\cdot$ and recursion in table 5. The $\surd$-transitions signal termination of a process. The possible behaviour of a term p in initial data-state s is given by all transitions reachable from (p, s) in $\longrightarrow_{\Sigma(\text{BPA}_G)_{\text{REC}}, S}$.

We identify *bisimilar* processes (see [Mil80]). But following the traditional approach in semantics based on data-state transformations, processes with different data-states in their configurations are not considered as equivalent. Therefore we adapt the standard notion of bisimilarity in the following way.

Definition 2.9. Let $\mathcal{S}$ be a data environment with data-state space S. A binary relation $R \subseteq C(\Sigma(\text{BPA}_G)_{\text{REC}}, \mathcal{S}) \times C(\Sigma(\text{BPA}_G)_{\text{REC}}, \mathcal{S})$ is an $\mathcal{S}$*-bisimulation* iff R satisfies the transfer property, i.e. for all $(p, s), (q, s) \in C(\Sigma(\text{BPA}_G)_{\text{REC}}, \mathcal{S})$ with $(p, s)R(q, s)$:

1. whenever $(p,s) \xrightarrow{a}_{\Sigma(\text{BPA}_G)_{\text{REC}},\mathcal{S}} (p', s')$ for some a and (p', s'), then, for some q', also $(q,s) \xrightarrow{a}_{\Sigma(\text{BPA}_G)_{\text{REC}},\mathcal{S}} (q', s')$ and $(p', s')R(q', s')$,
2. whenever $(q,s) \xrightarrow{a}_{\Sigma(\text{BPA}_G)_{\text{REC}},\mathcal{S}} (q', s')$ for some a and (q', s'), then, for some p', also $(p,s) \xrightarrow{a}_{\Sigma(\text{BPA}_G)_{\text{REC}},\mathcal{S}} (p', s')$ and $(p', s')R(q', s')$.

Two closed terms p, q over $\Sigma(\text{BPA}_G)_{\text{REC}}$ are $\mathcal{S}$*-bisimilar*, notation $p \leftrightarrows_{\mathcal{S}} q$, iff for all $s \in S$ there is some $\mathcal{S}$-bisimulation R such that $(p, s)R(q, s)$. □

Lemma 2.10. *For any data environment $\mathcal{S}$ the relation $\leftrightarrows_{\mathcal{S}}$ between closed terms over $\Sigma(\text{BPA}_G)_{\text{REC}}$ is a congruence with respect to the operators of $\Sigma(\text{BPA}_G)$.* □

Theorem 2.11. (Soundness) *Let p, q be closed terms over $\Sigma(\text{BPA}_G)_{\text{REC}}$. If* $\text{BPA}_G^4 + \text{REC} + \text{RSP} \vdash p = q$, *then $p \leftrightarrows_{\mathcal{S}} q$ for any data environment $\mathcal{S}$.* □

Theorem 2.12. (Completeness) *Let r_1, r_2 be closed terms over $\Sigma(\text{BPA}_G)$. If $r_1 \leftrightarrows_{\mathcal{S}} r_2$ for all data environments $\mathcal{S}$, then* $\text{BPA}_G^4 \vdash r_1 = r_2$. □

3 BPA with guards in a specific data environment

We have described process algebra with guards with respect to the general class of data environments. But often one wants to consider a data environment that is already determined, for instance in the case where atomic actions are assignments and guards are Boolean expressions. Therefore we now investigate bisimulation semantics for $\Sigma(\text{BPA}_G)_{\text{REC}}$ in a *specific* data environment.

$x + y = y + x$	A1	$\phi \cdot \neg\phi = \delta$	G1
$x + (y + z) = (x + y) + z$	A2	$\phi + \neg\phi = \epsilon$	G2
$x + x = x$	A3	$\phi(x + y) = \phi x + \phi y$	G3
$(x + y)z = xz + yz$	A4		
$(xy)z = x(yz)$	A5	$\phi_0 \cdot \ldots \cdot \phi_n = \delta$	SI
$x + \delta = x$	A6	if $\forall s \in S\ \exists i \leq n$ not $test(\phi_i, s)$	
$\delta x = \delta$	A7		
$\epsilon x = x$	A8	$wp(a, \phi)a\phi = wp(a, \phi)a$	WPC1
$x\epsilon = x$	A9	$\neg wp(a, \phi)a\neg\phi = \neg wp(a, \phi)a$	WPC2

Table 3: The axioms of $\text{BPA}_G(\mathcal{S})$ where $\phi, \phi_i \in G$ and $a \in A$

In table 3 we present the axiom system $\text{BPA}_G(\mathcal{S})$. It contains the first three axioms for guards and three new axioms depending on $\mathcal{S}$ (this explains the $\mathcal{S}$ in $\text{BPA}_G(\mathcal{S})$). The axiom SI (Sequence is Inaction) expresses that if a sequence of basic guards fails in each data-state, then it equals δ. Note that SI implies G1.

In the axioms WPC1 and WPC2 (Weakest Precondition under some Constraints) the expression $wp(a,\phi)$ represents the basic guard that is the *weakest precondition* of an atomic action a and an atomic guard ϕ. Weakest preconditions are semantically defined as follows:

Definition 3.1. Let A be a set of atomic actions, G_{at} a set of atomic guards and $\mathcal{S} = \langle S, \mathit{effect}, \mathit{test}\rangle$ be a data environment over A and G_{at}. A *weakest precondition* of an atomic action $a \in A$ and an atomic guard $\phi \in G_{at}$ is a basic guard $\psi \in G$ satisfying for all $s \in S$:

$$\mathit{test}(\psi, s) \text{ iff } \forall s' \in S\ (s' \in \mathit{effect}(a,s) \Longrightarrow \mathit{test}(\phi, s')).$$

If ψ is a weakest precondition of a and ϕ, it is denoted by $wp(a,\phi)$. Weakest preconditions are *expressible* with respect to A, G_{at} and $\mathcal{S}$ iff there is a weakest precondition in G of any $a \in A$ and $\phi \in G_{at}$. □

Definition 3.2. Let A be a set of atomic actions and G_{at} a set of atomic guards and let $\mathcal{S} = \langle S, \mathit{effect}, \mathit{test}\rangle$ be a data environment over A and G_{at}. We say that $\mathcal{S}$ is *sufficiently deterministic* iff for all $a \in A$ and $\phi \in G_{at}$:

$$\forall s, s', s'' \in S\ (s', s'' \in \mathit{effect}(a,s) \quad \Longrightarrow \quad (\mathit{test}(\phi, s') \Longleftrightarrow \mathit{test}(\phi, s''))).$$

□

Remark that a data environment $\mathcal{S}$ with a deterministic function *effect* is sufficiently deterministic. If $\mathcal{S}$ is a data environment such that weakest preconditions are expressible and that is sufficiently deterministic then the axioms WPC1 and WPC2 exactly characterise the weakest preconditions in an algebraic way: WPC1 expresses that $wp(a,\phi)$ is a precondition of a and ϕ and WPC2 states that $wp(a,\phi)$ is the *weakest* precondition of a and ϕ. If on the other hand weakest preconditions are expressible in $\mathcal{S}$, then the soundness of $\mathrm{BPA}_G(\mathcal{S})$ implies that $\mathcal{S}$ is also sufficiently deterministic.

Theorem 3.3. (Soundness) *Let $\mathcal{S}$ be a data environment such that weakest preconditions are expressible and that is sufficiently deterministic. Let r_1, r_2 be closed terms over $\Sigma(\mathrm{BPA}_G)_{\mathrm{REC}}$. If $\mathrm{BPA}_G(\mathcal{S}) + \mathrm{REC} + \mathrm{RSP} \vdash r_1 = r_2$ then $r_1 \leftrightarrows_{\mathcal{S}} r_2$.* □

Theorem 3.4. (Completeness) *Let $\mathcal{S}$ be a data environment such that weakest preconditions are expressible and that is sufficiently deterministic. Let r_1, r_2 be closed terms over $\Sigma(\mathrm{BPA}_G)$. If $r_1 \leftrightarrows_{\mathcal{S}} r_2$ then $\mathrm{BPA}_G(\mathcal{S}) \vdash r_1 = r_2$.* □

Example 3.5. Process algebra with guards can be used to express and prove partial correctness formulas in Hoare logic. In section 5 we elaborate on this idea. Here a simple example that is often used as an illustration of Hoare logic is presented and its correctness is shown.

First we transform $\mathrm{BPA}_G(\mathcal{S})$ into a small programming language with Boolean guards and assignments. Our language has the signature of $\Sigma(\mathrm{BPA}_G)$ and we have some set $\mathcal{V} = \{x, y, \ldots\}$ of data variables. Actions have the form:

$$x := e$$

with $x \in \mathcal{V}$ a variable ranging over the integers $\mathbb{Z}$ and e an integer expression. We assume that some interpretation $[\![\cdot]\!]$ from closed integer expressions to integers is given. Atomic guards have the form

$$e = f$$

where e and f are both integer expressions. For readability, we sometimes write angular brackets around guards and square brackets around assignments.

The components of the data environment $\mathcal{S} = \langle S, \mathit{effect}, \mathit{test}\rangle$ are straightforward to define:

$$S = \mathbb{Z}^{\mathcal{V}}$$

i.e. the set of mappings from $\mathcal{V}$ to the integers. We write ρ, σ for data-states in S, and we assume that the domain $\mathcal{V}$ of these mappings is extended to integer expressions in the standard way. The function *effect* is defined by:

$$\mathit{effect}(x := e, \rho) = \rho[[\![\rho(e)]\!]/x]$$

where $\rho[n/x]$ is as the mapping ρ, except that x is mapped to n. We define the predicate *test* by:

$$\mathit{test}(e = f, \rho) \iff ([\![\rho(e)]\!] = [\![\rho(f)]\!]).$$

Note that the effect function is deterministic, so $\mathcal{S}$ is certainly sufficiently deterministic. Weakest preconditions can easily be expressed:

$$wp(x := e, e_1 = e_2) = \langle e_1[e/x] = e_2[e/x]\rangle.$$

The axiom SI cannot be formulated so easily, partly because we have not yet defined integer expressions very precisely. We characterise SI by the scheme:

$$\langle e_0 = f_0\rangle \cdot \ldots \cdot \langle e_n = f_n\rangle = \delta$$

iff $\forall \rho \in S$ we can find $i \leq n$ such that $[\![\rho(e_i)]\!] \neq [\![\rho(f_i)]\!]$.

In this language we can express the following tiny program *SWAP* that exchanges the initial values of x and y without using any other variables.

$$SWAP \quad = \quad [x := x + y] \cdot [y := x - y] \cdot [x := x - y].$$

The correctness of this program can be expressed by the following equation:

$$\langle x = n\rangle\langle y = m\rangle SWAP = \langle x = n\rangle\langle y = m\rangle SWAP\langle x = m\rangle\langle y = n\rangle.$$

This equation says that if *SWAP* is executed in an initial data-state where $x = n$ and $y = m$, then after termination of *SWAP* it must hold, i.e. it can be derived, that $x = m$ and $y = n$. So *SWAP* indeed exchanges the values of x and y.

The correctness of *SWAP* can be proved as follows:

$$\langle x = n\rangle\langle y = m\rangle SWAP \overset{\text{SI}}{=} \langle (x + y) - y = n\rangle\langle (x + y) - ((x + y) - y) = m\rangle SWAP$$

$$\overset{\text{SI,WPC1}}{=} \langle x = n\rangle\langle y = m\rangle[x := x + y]\langle x - y = n\rangle\langle x - (x - y) = m\rangle[y := x - y][x := x - y]$$

$$\overset{\text{WPC1}}{=} \langle x = n\rangle\langle y = m\rangle[x := x + y][y := x - y]\langle y = n\rangle\langle x - y = m\rangle[x := x - y]$$

$$\overset{\text{WPC1}}{=} \langle x = n\rangle\langle y = m\rangle SWAP\langle x = m\rangle\langle y = n\rangle$$

(End example.)

4 Parallel processes and guards

We extend the language of $\Sigma(\mathrm{BPA}_G)$ to $\Sigma(\mathrm{ACP}_G)$ with four operators [BK84]: the *encapsulation operator* ∂_H, the *merge* $\|$, the *left-merge* $\lfloor\!\lfloor$ and the *communication-merge* $|$, suitable to describe the behaviour of parallel, communicating processes. Encapsulation is used to enforce communication between processes. Communication is modelled by a communication function $\gamma : A \times A \longrightarrow A_\delta$ that is commutative and associative. If $\gamma(a, b)$ is δ, then a and b cannot communicate, and if $\gamma(a, b) = c$, then c is the action resulting from the communication between a and b. All general definitions for $\Sigma(\mathrm{BPA}_G)$ carry over to $\Sigma(\mathrm{ACP}_G)$, especially, we write $\Sigma(\mathrm{ACP}_G)_{\mathrm{REC}}$ for $\Sigma(\mathrm{ACP}_G)$ extended with all constants denoting solutions of guarded recursive specifications over $\Sigma(\mathrm{ACP}_G)$.

For the terms over $\Sigma(\mathrm{ACP}_G)$ we have the axioms given in table 4 (note that the axiom G4 is absent). Most of these axioms are standard for ACP and, apart from G1, G2 and G3, only the axioms EM10, EM11 and D0 are new. The axiom EM10 (EM11) expresses that a basic guard ϕ in $\phi x \lfloor\!\lfloor y$ ($\phi x \mid y$) may prevent both x and y from happening.

Using ACP_G any closed term over $\Sigma(\mathrm{ACP}_G)$ can be proved equal to one without merge operators, i.e. a closed term over $\Sigma(\mathrm{BPA}_G)$.

Theorem 4.1. (Elimination) *Let p be a closed term over $\Sigma(\mathrm{ACP}_G)$. There is a closed term q over $\Sigma(\mathrm{BPA}_G)$ such that $\mathrm{ACP}_G \vdash p = q$.* □

ACP_G and BPA_G^4 or $\mathrm{BPA}_G(\mathcal{S})$ cannot be combined in bisimulation semantics as $\leftrightarrows_{\mathcal{S}}$ is not a congruence for the merge operators; if G4 is added to ACP_G we can derive the following:

$$\begin{aligned} \mathrm{ACP}_G + \mathrm{G4} \quad &\vdash \quad a(b \parallel d) + a(c \parallel d) + d(ab + ac) && (1)\\ &= \quad (ab + ac) \parallel d \\ &\overset{\mathrm{G4}}{=} \quad (ab + ac + a(\phi b + \neg\phi c)) \parallel d \\ &\supseteq \quad a(\phi bd + \neg\phi cd + d(\phi b + \neg\phi c)). && (2) \end{aligned}$$

So, in (2) it can be the case that after an a step ϕ holds, and we arrive in a state where we can do a b or a d step. Performing the d step can bring us in a state were $\neg\phi$ holds, so the only possible step left is a c step. This situation cannot be mimicked in (1). Therefore, every term with (2) as a summand is not bisimilar to (1) for any reasonable form of bisimulation. So $\mathrm{ACP}_G + \mathrm{G4}$ is not sound in any bisimulation semantics.

Because we still want to derive $\mathcal{S}$-bisimilarity between closed terms containing merge operators, we introduce a *two-phase* calculus that does not have these problems. Derivability in this calculus is denoted by $\vdash_c$.

Definition 4.2. Let p_1, p_2 be closed terms over $\Sigma(\mathrm{ACP}_G)_{\mathrm{REC}}$. We write

$$\mathrm{ACP}_G^4 \vdash_c p_1 = p_2$$

iff there are closed terms q_1, q_2 over $\Sigma(\mathrm{BPA}_G)_{\mathrm{REC}}$ such that $\mathrm{ACP}_G \vdash p_i = q_i \quad (i = 1, 2)$ and $\mathrm{BPA}_G^4 \vdash q_1 = q_2$.

Furthermore, we write

$$\mathrm{ACP}_G(\mathcal{S}) \vdash_c p_1 = p_2$$

iff there are closed terms q_1, q_2 over $\Sigma(\mathrm{BPA}_G)_{\mathrm{REC}}$ such that $\mathrm{ACP}_G \vdash p_i = q_i \quad (i = 1, 2)$ and $\mathrm{BPA}_G(\mathcal{S}) \vdash q_1 = q_2$.

We sometimes put REC + RSP in front of $\vdash_c$ which means that we may use REC and RSP in proving $p_i = q_i$ $(i = 1, 2)$ and $q_1 = q_2$. □

$x + (y + z) = (x + y) + z$	A1	$\phi \cdot \neg\phi = \delta$	G1
$x + y = y + x$	A2	$\phi + \neg\phi = \epsilon$	G2
$x + x = x$	A3	$\phi(x + y) = \phi x + \phi y$	G3
$(x + y)z = xz + yz$	A4		
$(xy)z = x(yz)$	A5		
$x + \delta = x$	A6		
$\delta x = \delta$	A7		
$\epsilon x = x$	A8		
$x\epsilon = x$	A9		
$a \mid b = \gamma(a, b)$	CF		
$x \parallel y = x \mathbin{\lfloor\!\lfloor} y + y \mathbin{\lfloor\!\lfloor} x + x \mid y$	EM1	$\phi x \mathbin{\lfloor\!\lfloor} y = \phi(x \mathbin{\lfloor\!\lfloor} y)$	EM10
$\epsilon \mathbin{\lfloor\!\lfloor} x = \delta$	EM2	$\phi x \mid y = \phi(x \mid y)$	EM11
$ax \mathbin{\lfloor\!\lfloor} y = a(x \parallel y)$	EM3		
$(x + y) \mathbin{\lfloor\!\lfloor} z = x \mathbin{\lfloor\!\lfloor} z + y \mathbin{\lfloor\!\lfloor} z$	EM4		
$x \mid y = y \mid x$	EM5	$\partial_H(\phi) = \phi$	D0
$\epsilon \mid \epsilon = \epsilon$	EM6	$\partial_H(a) = a$ if $a \notin H$	D1
$\epsilon \mid ax = \delta$	EM7	$\partial_H(a) = \delta$ if $a \in H$	D2
$ax \mid by = (a \mid b)(x \parallel y)$	EM8	$\partial_H(x + y) = \partial_H(x) + \partial_H(y)$	D3
$(x + y) \mid z = x \mid z + y \mid z$	EM9	$\partial_H(xy) = \partial_H(x)\partial_H(y)$	D4

Table 4: The axioms of ACP_G, $a, b \in A$, $H \subseteq A$ and $\phi \in G$

Let $\mathcal{S} = \langle S, \mathit{effect}, \mathit{test}\rangle$ be some data environment over a set A of atomic actions and a set G_{at} of atomic guards. In table 5 we display the set of transition rules to give an operational semantics to the closed terms over $\Sigma(\mathrm{ACP}_G)_{\mathrm{REC}}$. Let $\longrightarrow_{\Sigma(\mathrm{ACP}_G)_{\mathrm{REC}}, \mathcal{S}} \subseteq C(\Sigma(\mathrm{ACP}_G)_{\mathrm{REC}}, \mathcal{S}) \times A_{\surd} \times C(\Sigma(\mathrm{ACP}_G)_{\mathrm{REC}}, \mathcal{S})$ be the transition relation containing all transitions that are derivable by these rules. We define a different bisimulation equivalence, called *global $\mathcal{S}$-bisimilarity*, that is a congruence for the merge operators. The idea behind a global $\mathcal{S}$-bisimulation is that a context $p \parallel (.)$ around a process q can change the data-state of q at any time and global $\mathcal{S}$-bisimulation equivalence must be resistant against such changes. So, a configuration (p_1, s) is related to a configuration (p_2, s) if $(p_1, s) \xrightarrow{a} (q_1, s')$ implies $(p_2, s) \xrightarrow{a} (q_2, s')$ and, as the environment may change s', q_1 is related to q_2 in *any* data-state:

Definition 4.3. Let $\mathcal{S}$ be a data environment with data-state space S. A binary relation $R \subseteq C(\Sigma(\mathrm{ACP}_G)_{\mathrm{REC}}, \mathcal{S}) \times C(\Sigma(\mathrm{ACP}_G)_{\mathrm{REC}}, \mathcal{S})$ is a *global $\mathcal{S}$-bisimulation* iff R satisfies the following (global) version of the transfer property: for all $(p, s), (q, s) \in C(\Sigma(\mathrm{ACP}_G)_{\mathrm{REC}}, \mathcal{S})$ with $(p, s)R(q, s)$:

$\phi \in G \quad (\phi, s) \xrightarrow{\surd} (\delta, s) \quad \text{if } test(\phi, s)$

$a \in A \quad (a, s) \xrightarrow{a} (\epsilon, s') \quad \text{if } s' \in effect(a, s)$

$+$

$$\frac{(x, s) \xrightarrow{a} (x', s')}{(x + y, s) \xrightarrow{a} (x', s')} \qquad \frac{(y, s) \xrightarrow{a} (y', s')}{(x + y, s) \xrightarrow{a} (y', s')}$$

$$\frac{(x, s) \xrightarrow{a} (x', s')}{(xy, s) \xrightarrow{a} (x'y, s')} \text{ if } a \neq \surd \qquad \frac{(x, s) \xrightarrow{\surd} (x', s') \quad (y, s) \xrightarrow{a} (y', s'')}{(xy, s) \xrightarrow{a} (y', s'')}$$

$\|$

$$\frac{(x, s) \xrightarrow{a} (x', s')}{(x \parallel y, s) \xrightarrow{a} (x' \parallel y, s')} \text{ if } a \neq \surd \qquad \frac{(y, s) \xrightarrow{a} (y', s')}{(x \parallel y, s) \xrightarrow{a} (x \parallel y', s')} \text{ if } a \neq \surd$$

$$\frac{(x, s) \xrightarrow{a} (x', s') \quad (y, s) \xrightarrow{b} (y', s'')}{(x \parallel y, s) \xrightarrow{\gamma(a,b)} (x' \parallel y', s''')} \quad \text{if } \gamma(a, b) \neq \delta,\ a, b \neq \surd, \text{ and } s''' \in effect(\gamma(a, b), s)$$

$$\frac{(x, s) \xrightarrow{\surd} (x', s') \quad (y, s) \xrightarrow{\surd} (y', s')}{(x \parallel y, s) \xrightarrow{\surd} (x' \parallel y', s')}$$

$\lfloor\!\lfloor$

$$\frac{(x, s) \xrightarrow{a} (x', s')}{(x \lfloor\!\lfloor y, s) \xrightarrow{a} (x' \parallel y, s')} \text{ if } a \neq \surd$$

$|$

$$\frac{(x, s) \xrightarrow{a} (x', s') \quad (y, s) \xrightarrow{b} (y', s'')}{(x \mid y, s) \xrightarrow{\gamma(a,b)} (x' \parallel y', s''')} \quad \text{if } \gamma(a, b) \neq \delta,\ a, b \neq \surd, \text{ and } s''' \in effect(\gamma(a, b), s)$$

$$\frac{(x, s) \xrightarrow{\surd} (x', s') \quad (y, s) \xrightarrow{\surd} (y', s')}{(x \mid y, s) \xrightarrow{\surd} (x' \parallel y', s')}$$

∂_H

$$\frac{(x, s) \xrightarrow{a} (x', s')}{(\partial_H(x), s) \xrightarrow{a} (\partial_H(x'), s')} \text{ if } a \notin H \subseteq A$$

recursion

$$\frac{(<t_x \mid E>, s) \xrightarrow{a} (y, s')}{(<x \mid E>, s) \xrightarrow{a} (y, s')} \text{ if } x = t_x \in E$$

Table 5: Transition rules ($a, b \in A_{\surd}$, $H, I \subseteq A$)

1. whenever $(p, s) \xrightarrow{a}_{\Sigma(\mathrm{ACP}_G)_{\mathrm{REC}}, \mathcal{S}} (p', s')$ for some a and (p', s'), then, for some q', also $(q, s) \xrightarrow{a}_{\Sigma(\mathrm{ACP}_G)_{\mathrm{REC}}, \mathcal{S}} (q', s')$ and $\forall s'' \in S\ ((p', s'')R(q', s''))$,

2. whenever $(q, s) \xrightarrow{a}_{\Sigma(\mathrm{ACP}_G)_{\mathrm{REC}}, \mathcal{S}} (q', s')$ for some a and (q', s'), then, for some p', also $(p, s) \xrightarrow{a}_{\Sigma(\mathrm{ACP}_G)_{\mathrm{REC}}, \mathcal{S}} (p', s')$ and $\forall s'' \in S\ ((p', s'')R(q', s''))$.

Two closed terms p, q over $\Sigma(\mathrm{ACP}_G)_{\mathrm{REC}}$ are *globally $\mathcal{S}$-bisimilar*, notation $p \,\underline{\leftrightarrows}_{\mathcal{S}}\, q$, iff for each $s \in S$ there is a global $\mathcal{S}$-bisimulation relation R with $(p, s)R(q, s)$. □

By definition of global $\mathcal{S}$-bisimilarity we have for closed terms p, q over $\Sigma(\mathrm{ACP}_G)_{\mathrm{REC}}$

$$p \,\underline{\leftrightarrows}_{\mathcal{S}}\, q \quad \Longrightarrow \quad p \leftrightarrows_{\mathcal{S}} q.$$

Our goal, i.e. global $\mathcal{S}$-bisimilarity being a congruence relation, has been achieved:

Lemma 4.4. *For any data environment $\mathcal{S}$ the relation $\underline{\leftrightarrows}_{\mathcal{S}}$ is a congruence with respect to the operators of $\Sigma(\mathrm{ACP}_G)$.* □

Theorem 4.5. (Soundness) *Let p, q be closed terms over $\Sigma(\mathrm{ACP}_G)_{\mathrm{REC}}$.*

1. *If $\mathrm{ACP}_G + \mathrm{REC} + \mathrm{RSP} \vdash p = q$, then $p \,\underline{\leftrightarrows}_{\mathcal{S}}\, q$ for any data environment $\mathcal{S}$.*

2. *If $\mathrm{ACP}_G^4 + \mathrm{REC} + \mathrm{RSP} \vdash_c p = q$, then $p \leftrightarrows_{\mathcal{S}} q$ for any data environment $\mathcal{S}$.*

3. *Let $\mathcal{S}$ be a data environment such that weakest preconditions are expressible and that is sufficiently deterministic. If $\mathrm{ACP}_G(\mathcal{S}) + \mathrm{REC} + \mathrm{RSP} \vdash_c p = q$, then $p \leftrightarrows_{\mathcal{S}} q$.* □

Theorem 4.6. (Completeness) *Let r_1, r_2 be closed terms over $\Sigma(\mathrm{ACP}_G)$.*

1. *If $r_1 \,\underline{\leftrightarrows}_{\mathcal{S}}\, r_2$ for all data environments $\mathcal{S}$, then $\mathrm{ACP}_G \vdash r_1 = r_2$.*

2. *If $r_1 \leftrightarrows_{\mathcal{S}} r_2$ for all data environments $\mathcal{S}$, then $\mathrm{ACP}_G^4 \vdash_c r_1 = r_2$.*

3. *Let $\mathcal{S}$ be a data environment such that weakest preconditions are expressible and that is sufficiently deterministic. If $r_1 \leftrightarrows_{\mathcal{S}} r_2$, then $\mathrm{ACP}_G(\mathcal{S}) \vdash_c r_1 = r_2$.* □

5 Partial correctness and Hoare logic

We show that we can capture Hoare logic in a completely algebraic way. Given a set A of atomic actions and a set G_{at} of atomic guards, we here consider partial correctness formulas of the form $\{\alpha\}\, p\, \{\beta\}$ with as intuitive meaning that whenever the assertion α holds before the execution of p and p terminates, then the assertion β holds after the execution of p.

So guards serve as assertions and closed terms over $\Sigma(\mathrm{ACP}_G)_{\mathrm{REC}}$ are considered as programs. This is on a rather abstract level and suitable to express many programming primitives and constructs. We only consider data environments that are sufficiently deterministic and such that weakest preconditions are expressible. These are no serious restrictions that occur often in some related form in the study of Hoare logic (cf. [Apt81]).

We define the interpretation of our assertions in $\mathcal{S}$ using $\surd$-transitions.

Definition 5.1. Let α be an assertion and $\mathcal{S} = \langle S, \mathit{effect}, \mathit{test}\rangle$ some data environment. We say that α *holds in* $s \in S$, notation $\mathcal{S} \models \alpha[s]$, iff $(\alpha, s) \xrightarrow{\surd} (\delta, s)$. □

Let $\xrightarrow{\sigma}\!\!\!\!\twoheadrightarrow$ be the transitive and reflexive closure of $\longrightarrow_{\Sigma(\mathrm{ACP}_G)_{\mathrm{REC}}}$. The interpretation of a partial correctness formula in $\mathcal{S}$ is defined as follows:

Definition 5.2. Let $\mathcal{S}$ be a data environment and let p be a term over $\Sigma(\mathrm{ACP}_G)_{\mathrm{REC}}$. A partial correctness formula $\{\alpha\}\, p\, \{\beta\}$ *is valid in* $\mathcal{S}$, notation $\mathcal{S} \models \{\alpha\}\, p\, \{\beta\}$, iff for all $s \in S$ and all $\sigma \in A^*$:

$$\mathcal{S} \models \alpha[s] \text{ and } (p, s) \xrightarrow{\sigma\surd}\!\!\!\!\twoheadrightarrow (p', s') \implies \mathcal{S} \models \beta[s'].$$

□

The following correspondence theorem gives us the means to use process algebra for proving partial correctness formulas.

Theorem 5.3. *Let $\mathcal{S}$ be a data environment. For all partial correctness formulas $\{\alpha\}\, p\, \{\beta\}$ over $\mathcal{S}$ with p a term over $\Sigma(\mathrm{ACP}_G)_{\mathrm{REC}}$ it holds that*

$$\mathcal{S} \models \{\alpha\}\, p\, \{\beta\} \iff \alpha p \leftrightarrows_{\mathcal{S}} \alpha p \beta.$$

□

In table 6 we present a proof system H in a natural deduction format for deriving partial correctness formulas over $\Sigma(\mathrm{BPA}_G)_{\mathrm{REC}}$ (cf. [Pon89]). Notice that the rules of H refer to terms over $\Sigma(\mathrm{BPA}_G)_{\mathrm{REC}}$ that need not be closed. Let Γ be a set of assertions and partial correctness formulas. We write $\Gamma \vdash_H \{\alpha\}\, t\, \{\beta\}$ iff we can derive $\{\alpha\}\, t\, \{\beta\}$ in H using elements of Γ as hypotheses.

In rule I the expression $wp(a, \alpha)$ serves as an abbreviation for weakest preconditions on guards: $wp(a, \neg\alpha)$ stands for $\neg wp(a, \alpha)$, $wp(a, \alpha + \beta)$ abbreviates $wp(a, \alpha) + wp(a, \beta)$ and we write $wp(a, \alpha\beta)$ for $wp(a, \alpha)wp(a, \beta)$.

Rule V, *consequence*, is a standard proof rule in Hoare logic. The intended interpretation of an expression $\alpha \to \beta$ is as expected: $\mathcal{S} \models \alpha \to \beta$ iff for all $s \in S$ $(\mathcal{S} \models \alpha[s] \implies \mathcal{S} \models \beta[s])$. An expression $\alpha \to \beta$ corresponds to the algebraic equations $\alpha \cdot \beta = \alpha$ or $\alpha + \beta = \beta$.

Rule VI, an instance of *Scott's induction rule* (see eg. [Apt81]), is suitable to derive partial correctness formulas with recursive terms over $\Sigma(\mathrm{BPA}_G)_{\mathrm{REC}}$. This rule allows *cancellation* of hypotheses, indicated by the square brackets in its premises: let $E = \{x = t_x \mid x \in V_E\}$ be a guarded recursive specification and α_x, β_x $(x \in V_E)$ be guards. If for all $y \in V_E$ we can derive (indicated by the dots in the rule) $\{\alpha_y\}\, t_y\, \{\beta_y\}$ from a set of hypotheses Γ_y containing *no* other partial correctness formulas with free variables in V_E than those in $\{\{\alpha_x\}\, x\, \{\beta_x\} \mid x \in V_E\}$, then for any $z \in V_E$ the partial correctness formula $\{\alpha_z\} \langle z \mid E\rangle \{\beta_z\}$ can be derived from

$$\bigcup_{x \in V_E} \Gamma_x - \{\{\alpha_x\}\, x\, \{\beta_x\} \mid x \in V_E\}.$$

We present a soundness result for H provided that recursive specifications have a finite number of equations and are *linear*:

I	*axioms for $a \in A$*	$\{wp(a,\alpha)\}\, a\, \{\alpha\}$
II	*axioms for $\phi \in G$*	$\{\alpha\}\, \phi\, \{\alpha \cdot \phi\}$
III	*alternative composition*	$\dfrac{\{\alpha\}\, t\, \{\beta\} \quad \{\alpha\}\, t'\, \{\beta\}}{\{\alpha\}\, t + t'\, \{\beta\}}$
IV	*sequential composition*	$\dfrac{\{\alpha\}\, t\, \{\alpha'\} \quad \{\alpha'\}\, t'\, \{\beta\}}{\{\alpha\}\, t \cdot t'\, \{\beta\}}$
V	*consequence*	$\dfrac{\alpha \rightarrow \alpha' \quad \{\alpha'\}\, t\, \{\beta'\} \quad \beta' \rightarrow \beta}{\{\alpha\}\, t\, \{\beta\}}$
VI	*Scott's induction rule*	For $E = \{x = t_x \,\vert\, x \in V_E\}$ a *guarded* rec. specification $\dfrac{\begin{array}{c}[\{\{\alpha_x\}\, x\, \{\beta_x\} \,\vert\, x \in V_E\}] \\ \vdots \\ \{\alpha_y\}\, t_y\, \{\beta_y\} \qquad \text{for all } y \in V_E\end{array}}{\{\alpha_z\} <z \,\vert\, E> \{\beta_z\}} \quad z \in V_E$

Table 6: The proof system H

Definition 5.4. A process term is called *linear* over $V' \subseteq V$ iff

$$t \ ::= \ p \ | \ x \ | \ pt \ | \ tp \ | \ t + t$$

where p is a closed term over $\Sigma(\text{BPA}_G)$ and $x \in V'$. We call a recursive specification $E = \{x = t_x \,|\, x \in V_E\}$ *linear* whenever the terms t_x are linear over V_E. □

Theorem 5.5. (Soundness of H) *Let p be a closed term over $\Sigma(\text{BPA}_G)_{\text{REC}}$ in which all occurrences of the form $<x \,|\, E>$ refer to a (guarded) recursive specification E over $\Sigma(\text{BPA}_G)$ that is linear and contains only finitely many equations.*
Let $Tr_S = \{\alpha \rightarrow \beta \,|\, S \models \alpha \rightarrow \beta\}$. Then

$$\begin{array}{rcl} Tr_S \vdash_H \{\alpha\}\, p\, \{\beta\} & \Longrightarrow & \text{BPA}_G(S) + \text{REC} + \text{RSP} \vdash \alpha p = \alpha p \beta \\ & \Longrightarrow & \alpha p \leftrightarrows_S \alpha p \beta \\ & \Longleftrightarrow & S \models \{\alpha\}\, p\, \{\beta\}. \end{array}$$

Proof. The main part of this theorem is proved by giving a canonical translation from proofs in Hoare logic into proofs in process algebra. □

References

[AB84] D. Austry and G. Boudol. Algèbre de processus et synchronisations. *Theoretical Computer Science*, 30(1):91–131, 1984.

[Apt81] K.R. Apt. Ten years of Hoare's logic, a survey, part I. *ACM Transactions on Programming Languages and Systems*, 3(4):431–483, 1981.

[BK84] J.A. Bergstra and J.W. Klop. The algebra of recursively defined processes and the algebra of regular processes. In J. Paredaens, editor, *Proceedings* 11th *ICALP*, Antwerp, volume 172 of *Lecture Notes in Computer Science*, pages 82–95. Springer-Verlag, 1984.

[BW90] J.C.M. Baeten and W.P. Weijland. *Process Algebra*. Cambridge Tracts in Theoretical Computer Science 18. Cambridge University Press, 1990.

[Dij76] E.W. Dijkstra. *A Discipline of Programming*. Prentice-Hall International, Englewood Cliffs, 1976.

[GP90] J.F. Groote and A. Ponse. Process algebra with guards. Report CS-R9069, CWI, Amsterdam, 1990.

[Hoa69] C.A.R. Hoare. An axiomatic basis for computer programming. *Communications of the ACM*, 12(10), October 1969.

[Hoa85] C.A.R. Hoare. *Communicating Sequential Processes*. Prentice-Hall International, Englewood Cliffs, 1985.

[MA86] E.G. Manes and M.A. Arbib. *Algebraic Approaches to Program Semantics*. Texts and Monographs in Computer Science. Springer-Verlag, 1986.

[Mil80] R. Milner. *A Calculus of Communicating Systems*, volume 92 of *Lecture Notes in Computer Science*. Springer-Verlag, 1980.

[OG76] S. Owicki and D. Gries. An axiomatic proof technique for parallel programs. *Acta Informatica*, pages 319–340, 1976.

[Plo81] G.D. Plotkin. A structural approach to operational semantics. Report DAIMI FN-19, Computer Science Department, Aarhus University, 1981.

[Pon89] A. Ponse. Process expressions and Hoare's logic. Technical Report CS-R8905, CWI, Amsterdam, March 1989. To appear in *Information and Computation*.

[Sio64] F.M. Sioson. Equational bases of Boolean algebras. *Journal of Symbolic Logic*, 29(3):115–124, September 1964.

Model Checking and Modular Verification*

Orna Grumberg
Computer Science Department
The Technion
Haifa 32000, Israel
orna@techsel (BITNET)

David E. Long
School of Computer Science
Carnegie Mellon University
Pittsburgh, PA 15213
long+@cs.cmu.edu (Internet)

Abstract

We describe a framework for compositional verification of finite state processes. The framework is based on two ideas: a subset of the logic CTL for which satisfaction is preserved under composition; and a preorder on structures which captures the relation between a component and a system containing the component. Satisfaction of a formula in the logic corresponds to being below a particular structure (a tableau for the formula) in the preorder. We show how to do assume-guarantee style reasoning within this framework. In addition, we demonstrate efficient methods for model checking in the logic and for checking the preorder in several special cases. We have implemented a system based on these methods, and we use it to give a compositional verification of a CPU controller.

1 Introduction

Temporal logic model checking procedures are useful tools for the verification of finite state systems [3, 11, 19]. However, these procedures have traditionally suffered from the state explosion problem. This problem arises in systems which are composed of many parallel processes; in general, the size of the state space grows exponentially with the number of processes. By introducing symbolic representations for sets of states and transition relations and using a symbolic model checking procedure, systems with very large state spaces (10^{100} or more states) can be verified [1, 7]. Further, the time and space requirements with these techniques may in practice be polynomial in the number of *components* of the system. Unfortunately, the symbolic procedures still have limits,

*This research was sponsored in part by the Avionics Laboratory, Wright Research and Development Center, Aeronautical Systems Division (AFSC), U.S. Air Force, Wright-Patterson AFB, Ohio 45433-6543 under Contract F33615-90-C-1465, ARPA Order No. 7597 and in part by the National Science Foundation under Contract No. CCR-9005992 and in part by the U.S.-Israeli Binational Science Foundation.

The views and conclusions contained in this document are those of the authors and should not be interpreted as representing the official policies, either expressed or implied, of the U.S. government.

and many realistic problems are not tractable due to their size. Thus, we are motivated to search for additional methods of handling the state explosion problem, methods which work well in conjunction with the symbolic techniques.

An obvious method for trying to avoid the state explosion problem is to use the natural decomposition of the system. The goal is to verify properties of individual components, infer that these hold in the complete system, and use them to deduce additional properties of the system. When verifying properties of the components, it may also be necessary to make assumptions about the environment. This approach is exemplified by Pnueli's assume-guarantee paradigm [21]. A formula in his logic is a triple $\langle\varphi\rangle M \langle\psi\rangle$ where φ and ψ are temporal formulas and M is a program. The formula is true if M plus its environment satisfies ψ whenever the environment satisfies φ. A typical proof shows that $\langle\varphi\rangle M\langle\psi\rangle$ and $\langle true\rangle M'\langle\varphi\rangle$ hold and concludes that $\langle true\rangle M \parallel M'\langle\psi\rangle$ is true.

In order to automate this approach, a model checker must have several properties. It must be able to check that a property is true of *all* systems which can be built using a given component. More generally, it must be able to restrict to a given class of environments when doing this check. It must also provide facilities for performing temporal reasoning. Most existing model checkers were not designed to provide these facilities. Instead, they typically assume that they are given complete systems.

An elegant way to obtain a system with the above properties is to provide a preorder with appropriate properties on the finite state models and to use a logic whose semantics relate to the preorder. The preorder should preserve satisfaction of formulas of the logic, i.e., if a formula is true for a model, it should also be true for any model which is smaller in the preorder. In addition, composition should preserve the preorder, and a system should be smaller in the preorder than its individual components. Finally, satisfaction of a formula should correspond to being smaller than a particular model (a tableau for the formula) in the preorder. In such a framework, the above reasoning sequence might be expressed as: T is the tableau of φ, $M \| T \models \psi$, $M' \preceq T$, and hence $M \| M' \models \psi$. Note that assumptions may be given either as formulas or directly as finite state models, whichever is more concise or convenient. More complex forms of reasoning such as induction [17] are also possible within this framework.

In choosing a computational model, a logic and a preorder to obtain a system such as this, we are guided by the following considerations. First, we must be able to realistically model physical systems such as circuits. Second, there should be efficient procedures for model checking and for checking the preorder. Finally, it should be possible to implement these procedures effectively using symbolic techniques.

In this paper, we propose a preorder for use with a subset of the logic CTL* [10]. This subset is strictly more expressive than LTL. Further, the induced subset of CTL is expressive enough for most verification tasks and has an efficient model checking algorithm. We also give a tableau construction for this CTL subset. The construction provides a means of temporal reasoning and makes it possible to use formulas as assumptions. Our preorder and the semantics of our logics both include a notion of fairness. This is essential for modeling systems such as communication protocols. We show how to use our results to verify systems composed of Moore machines. Moore machines have an explicit notion of input and output and are particularly suitable for modeling synchronous circuits. Finally, we suggest efficient methods for checking the preorder in several interesting cases. We have implemented a system based on these results; the system supports efficient compositional verification and temporal reasoning.

Our paper is organized as follows. Section 2 surveys some related work. In section 3, we present the logic and its semantics (for Kripke structures). The preorder and some of its properties are given in section 4. The next section defines the semantics of the logic for Moore machines. Given a Moore machine and a formula, we show how to efficiently check whether for all environments, the Moore machine in the environment satisfies the formula. Section 6 presents the tableau construction and demonstrates how to use it for temporal reasoning. Methods for checking the preorder are discussed in section 7. Section 8 gives a compositional verification of a simple CPU controller. We conclude with a summary and some directions for future work.

2 Related work

Much of the work on reducing the complexity of automatic verification can be grouped into two classes. The first class includes methods to build a reduced global state graph or to expand only the needed portion of the global state graph.

Local model checking algorithms [6, 24] based on logics like the μ-calculus use a tableau-based procedure to deduce that a specific state (the initial state of the system) satisfies a given logical formula. The state space can be generated as needed in such an algorithm, and for some formulas, only a small portion of the space may have to be examined. The main drawback of these algorithms is that often the entire space is generated (for example, when checking that a property holds globally). It is also not clear whether the algorithms can take good advantage of symbolic representations.

Graf and Steffen [12] describe a method for generating a reduced version of the global state space given a description of how the system is structured and specifications of how the components interact. Clarke, Long and McMillan [4] describe a similar attempt. Both methods will still produce large state graphs if most of the states in the system are not equivalent, and much of the verification must be redone if part of the system changes. Shtadler and Grumberg [22] show how to verify networks of processes whose structure is described by grammars. In this approach, which involves finding the global behavior of each component, networks of arbitrary complexity can be verified by checking one representative system. For many systems, however, the number of states may still be prohibitive, and it is not clear whether the method can use symbolic representations.

The second class of methods are compositional; properties of the individual components are verified, and properties of the global system are deduced from these. A representation of the global state space is not built.

Josko [14] gives an algorithm for checking whether a system satisfies a CTL specification in all environments. His algorithm also allows assumptions about the environment to be specified in a restricted linear-time logic. The system is able to handle assume-guarantee reasoning. The method is fairly *ad hoc* however, and more complex forms of reasoning such as induction cannot be easily incorporated into the system.

Within the framework of CCS [20], there have been a number of suggestions for compositional reasoning. Larsen [18] investigates the expressive power of formalisms for specifying the behavior of a process in a system. He suggests equivalence, refinement and satisfaction (of a formula) as three interesting relations between an implementation and its specification. However, he does not discuss the applicability of these ideas to verification, nor does he suggest how they can be implemented. Walker [25] demonstrates how to use a preorder plus knowledge of how a system should operate to simplify the verification of bisimulation equivalence. Winskel [26] proposes a method for decomposing specifications into properties which the components of a system must satisfy for the specification to hold. The approach is very appealing, but unfortunately, dealing with parallel composition is difficult. It is not apparent whether any of these methods will work well with symbolic representations.

Kurshan [15] describes a verification methodology based on testing containment of ω-regular languages. Homomorphic reductions are used to map implementations to specifications, and the specifications may be used as implementations at the next level of abstraction. Dill [9] proposes an elegant form of trace theory which can be used in a similar manner, but the framework does not handle liveness properties well. Both approaches depend on specifications being deterministic for efficiency, and neither approach makes provisions for using logical formulas as specifications or assumptions.

Shurek and Grumberg [23] describe criteria for obtaining a modular framework, and illustrate the idea using CTL* with only universal path quantifiers. This system is closest to the work presented here, but they give no provisions for handling fairness efficiently, using formulas as assumptions, or supporting temporal reasoning. Models in their system are also associated with a fixed decomposition into components; hence it is unclear how to perform inductive reasoning in the framework.

3 Temporal logic

The logics presented in this section are branching-time temporal logics. In order to be able to efficiently decide whether a formula is true in all systems containing a given component, we eliminate the existential path quantifier from the logics. Thus, a formula may include only the universal quantifier over paths, but unlike in linear-time temporal logic, nesting of path quantifiers is allowed. To ensure that existential path quantifiers do not arise via negation, we will assume that formulas are expressed in negation normal form. In other words, negations are applied only to atomic propositions. The logics are interpreted over a form of Kripke structure with fairness constraints. Path quantifiers range over the fair paths in the structures.

Definition 1 ($\forall$CTL*) *The logic $\forall CTL^*$ is the set of state formulas given by the following inductive definition.*

1. *The constants true and false are state formulas. For every atomic proposition p, p and $\neg p$ are state formulas.*
2. *If φ and ψ are state formulas, then $\varphi \wedge \psi$ and $\varphi \vee \psi$ are state formulas.*
3. *If φ is a path formula, then $\forall(\varphi)$ is a state formula.*
4. *If φ is a state formula, then φ is a path formula.*
5. *If φ and ψ are path formulas, then so are $\varphi \wedge \psi$, $\varphi \vee \psi$.*
6. *If φ and ψ are path formulas, then so are*
   (a) $\mathbf{X}\,\varphi$,
   (b) $\varphi\,\mathbf{U}\,\psi$, *and*
   (c) $\varphi\,\mathbf{V}\,\psi$.

We also use the following abbreviations: $\mathbf{F}\,\varphi$ and $\mathbf{G}\,\varphi$, where φ is a path formula, denote ($true\ \mathbf{U}\,\varphi$) and ($false\ \mathbf{V}\,\varphi$) respectively.

∀CTL is a restricted subset of ∀CTL* in which the ∀ path quantifier may only precede a restricted set of path formulas. More precisely, ∀CTL is the logic obtained by eliminating rules 3 through 6 above and adding the following rule.

3'. If φ and ψ are state formulas, then $\forall \mathbf{X}\, \varphi$, $\forall(\varphi \mathbf{U}\, \psi)$, and $\forall(\varphi \mathbf{V}\, \psi)$ are state formulas.

In practice, we have found that many of the formulas which are used in specifying and verifying systems are expressible in ∀CTL, and almost all are expressible in ∀CTL*. An example formula which is not expressible in ∀CTL* is a weak form of absence of deadlock: $\forall \mathbf{G}\, \exists \mathbf{F}\, p$ states that it should always be possible to reach a state where p holds.

We will give the semantics of the logic using a form of Kripke structure with fairness constraints.

Definition 2 (structure) *A structure $M = \langle S, S_0, \mathcal{A}, \mathcal{L}, R, \mathfrak{F}\rangle$ is a tuple of the following form.*

1. *S is a finite set of states.*
2. *$S_0 \subseteq S$ is a set of initial states.*
3. *$\mathcal{A}$ is a finite set of atomic propositions.*
4. *$\mathcal{L}$ is a function that maps each state to the set of atomic propositions true in that state.*
5. *$R \subseteq S \times S$ is a transition relation.*
6. *$\mathfrak{F}$ is a Streett acceptance condition, represented by pairs of sets of states.*

Definition 3 *A path in M is an infinite sequence of states $\pi = s_0 s_1 s_2 \ldots$ such that for all $i \in \mathbb{N}$, $R(s_i, s_{i+1})$.*

Definition 4 *Define $\inf(\pi) = \{\, s \mid s = s_i$ for infinitely many $i\,\}$. π is a fair path in M iff for every $(P, Q) \in \mathfrak{F}$, if $\inf(\pi) \cap P \neq \emptyset$, then $\inf(\pi) \cap Q \neq \emptyset$.*

The notation π^n will denote the suffix of π which begins at s_n. We now consider the semantics of the logic ∀CTL* with atomic propositions drawn from the set $\mathcal{A}$.

Definition 5 (satisfaction of a formula) *Satisfaction of a state formula φ by a state s ($s \models \varphi$) and of a path formula ψ by a fair path π ($\pi \models \psi$) is defined inductively as follows.*

1. *$s \models true$, and $s \not\models false$. $s \models p$ iff $p \in \mathcal{L}(s)$. $s \models \neg p$ iff $p \notin \mathcal{L}(s)$.*
2. *$s \models \varphi \wedge \psi$ iff $s \models \varphi$ and $s \models \psi$. $s \models \varphi \vee \psi$ iff $s \models \varphi$ or $s \models \psi$.*
3. *$s \models \forall(\varphi)$ iff for every fair path π starting at s, $\pi \models \varphi$.*
4. *$\pi \models \varphi$, where φ is a state formula, iff the first state of π satisfies the state formula.*
5. *$\pi \models \varphi \wedge \psi$ iff $\pi \models \varphi$ and $\pi \models \psi$. $\pi \models \varphi \vee \psi$ iff $\pi \models \varphi$ or $\pi \models \psi$.*
6. (a) *$\pi \models \mathbf{X}\varphi$ iff $\pi^1 \models \varphi$.*
   (b) *$\pi \models \varphi \mathbf{U} \psi$ iff there exists $n \in \mathbb{N}$ such that $\pi^n \models \psi$ and for all $i < n$, $\pi^i \models \varphi$.*
   (c) *$\pi \models \varphi \mathbf{V} \psi$ iff for all $n \in \mathbb{N}$, if $\pi^i \not\models \varphi$ for all $i < n$, then $\pi^n \models \psi$.*

$M \models \varphi$ indicates that for every $s_0 \in S_0$, $s_0 \models \varphi$.

Emerson and Halpern [10] compared the expressive power of the three logics LTL, CTL and CTL*. They showed that LTL and CTL have incomparable expressive power, while CTL* is strictly more expressive than either of the others. Eliminating the existential path quantifier from CTL and CTL* does not affect the relative expressive power of the logics. ∀CTL* trivially encompasses LTL and ∀CTL. The formula $\forall \mathbf{F} \forall \mathbf{G} p$ is a formula of ∀CTL that does not have an equivalent LTL formula. On the other hand, there is no ∀CTL formula that is equivalent to the LTL formula $\forall \mathbf{F} \mathbf{G} p$. Thus, LTL and ∀CTL are incomparable, and both are strictly less expressive than ∀CTL*.

4 Homomorphisms and composition of structures

In this section, we define the preorder which we use and examine some of its properties. We also show how these properties make assume-guarantee style reasoning possible.

Definition 6 (structure homomorphism) *Let M and M' be two structures with $\mathcal{A} \supseteq \mathcal{A}'$, and let t and t' be states in S and S', respectively. A relation $H \subseteq S \times S'$ is a homomorphism from (M,t) to (M',t') iff the following conditions hold.*

1. *$H(t,t')$.*
2. *For all s and s', $H(s,s')$ implies*
   (a) *$\mathcal{L}(s) \cap \mathcal{A}' = \mathcal{L}'(s')$; and*
   (b) *for every fair path $\pi = s_0 s_1 \ldots$ from $s = s_0$ in M there exists a fair path $\pi' = s'_0 s'_1 \ldots$ from $s' = s'_0$ in M' such that for every $i \in \mathbb{N}$, $H(s_i, s'_i)$.*

When H satisfies property 2, we say H is a homomorphism. H is a homomorphism from M to M' iff for every $s_0 \in S_0$ there is $s'_0 \in S'_0$ such that $H(s_0, s'_0)$. To indicate that two paths correspond as in item 2b above, we write $H(\pi, \pi')$.

Definition 7 *For $s \in S$ and $s' \in S'$, $(M,s) \preceq (M',s')$ iff there is a homomorphism from (M,s) to (M',s'). $M \preceq M'$ iff there exists a homomorphism from M to M'.*

When M and M' are understood, we sometimes write $s \preceq s'$. Intuitively, two states are homomorphic if their labels agree on the atomic propositions of the second structure and if for every fair path from the first state there is a corresponding fair path from the second state. Two structures are homomorphic if for every initial state of the first, there is a corresponding initial state of the second. One may view the second structure as a specification and the first as its implementation. Since a specification may hide some of the implementation details, it may have a smaller set of atomic propositions.

Definition 8 (composition of structures) *Let M and M' be two structures. The composition of M and M', denoted $M \parallel M'$, is the structure M'' defined as follows.*

1. $S'' = \left\{ (s,s') \,\middle|\, \mathcal{L}(s) \cap \mathcal{A}' = \mathcal{L}'(s') \cap \mathcal{A} \right\}$.
2. $S''_0 = (S_0 \times S'_0) \cap S''$.
3. $\mathcal{A}'' = \mathcal{A} \cup \mathcal{A}'$.
4. $\mathcal{L}''\big((s,s')\big) = \mathcal{L}(s) \cup \mathcal{L}'(s')$.
5. $R''\big((s,s'),(t,t')\big)$ *iff* $R(s,t)$ *and* $R'(s',t')$.

6. $\mathcal{F}'' = \left\{ \left((P \times S') \cap S'', (Q \times S') \cap S''\right) \,\middle|\, (P,Q) \in \mathcal{F} \right\}$
$\quad \cup \left\{ \left((S \times P') \cap S'', (S \times Q') \cap S''\right) \,\middle|\, (P',Q') \in \mathcal{F}' \right\}.$

The choice of this definition of composition is motivated by its correspondence with composition of Moore machines. Each transition of the composition is a joint transition of the components, and states of the composition are pairs of component states that agree on their common atomic propositions. We first note that this composition operator has the usual properties.

Theorem 1 *Composition of structures is commutative and associative (up to isomorphism).*

We now turn to the connections between the relation $\preceq$ and composition. First note that a path in $M \parallel M'$ is fair iff its restriction to each component results in a fair path. From this insight we obtain the following result.

Theorem 2

1. *$\preceq$ is a preorder.*
2. *For all M and M', $M \parallel M' \preceq M$.*
3. *For all M, M' and M'', if $M \preceq M'$ then $M \parallel M'' \preceq M' \parallel M''$.*
4. *For all M, $M \preceq M \parallel M$.*

Proof Because of space limitations, we only give a sketch here. Transitivity of $\preceq$ is shown by demonstrating that the relational product of homomorphisms from M to M' and from M' to M'' is a homomorphism from M to M''. For part 2, the map taking each state of $M \parallel M'$ to its first component is shown to be a homomorphism. To show part 3, we prove that $\left\{ \left((s,s''),(s',s'')\right) \,\middle|\, H(s,s') \right\}$ is a homomorphism from $M \parallel M''$ to $M' \parallel M''$ whenever H is a homomorphism from M to M'. For part 4, we demonstrate that $\left\{ \left(s,(s,s)\right) \,\middle|\, s \in S \right\}$ is a homomorphism from M to $M \parallel M$. □

Theorem 3 *Suppose $M \preceq M'$. Then for every $\forall CTL^*$ formula φ (with atomic propositions in A'), $M' \models \varphi$ implies $M \models \varphi$.*

Using theorems 2 and 3, we see that a standard CTL (CTL*) model checking algorithm [3], when restricted to ∀CTL (∀CTL*), can be viewed as determining whether a formula is true of all systems containing a given component. This is the key to compositional verification. With the theorems, it is also straightforward to justify the soundness of the assume-guarantee paradigm when assumptions are given as structures. (The connection between structures and formulas will be examined in section 6.) Discharging an assumption involves checking for the relation $\preceq$. Suppose that we wish to check that $M \parallel M' \models \varphi$ and that we have verified the following relationships:

$$M \preceq A$$
$$A \parallel M' \preceq A'$$
$$M \parallel A' \models \varphi.$$

In other words, M discharges assumption A, M' under assumption A discharges assumption A', and M under assumption A' satisfies the desired formula. From theorem 2, we have

$$\begin{aligned} M \parallel M' &\preceq M \parallel M \parallel M' \\ &\preceq M \parallel A \parallel M' \\ &\preceq M \parallel A'. \end{aligned}$$

Then theorem 3 implies that $M \parallel M' \models \varphi$. The theorems also show that any system containing $M \parallel M'$ will satisfy φ. Note that φ is not necessarily true in either M or M' and may involve atomic propositions from both M and M'.

5 Moore machines

We have seen that the structures defined earlier (definition 2) can be used for compositional reasoning about synchronous systems. However, such systems are typically given using a more common finite state model such as Moore machines [13]. Moore machines are models of computation with an explicit notion of inputs and outputs. Since the inputs originate from an external, uncontrolled environment, the machine can always receive any combination of input values. Moore machines are synchronous; in a composition of Moore machines, each machine makes a single step at every point. Thus, they are most suitable for modeling synchronous circuits. In this section, we show a natural correspondence between Moore machines with an empty set of inputs and the structures defined earlier. We use this correspondence to define the semantics of ∀CTL* with respect to Moore machines, and we show how to use compositional reasoning to verify a system composed of Moore machines.

Definition 9 (Moore machine) *A Moore machine* $M = \langle S, S_0, I, O, \mathcal{L}, R\rangle$ *is a tuple of the following form*

1. S *is a finite set of states.*
2. $S_0 \subseteq S$ *is a set of initial states.*
3. I *is a finite set of input propositions.*
4. O *is a finite set of output propositions.*
5. $\mathcal{L}$ *is a function that maps each state to the set of output propositions true in that state.*
6. $R \subseteq S \times 2^I \times S$ *is the transition relation.*

We require that $I \cap O = \emptyset$ *and that for every* $s \in S$ *and* $v \subseteq I$, *there exists some* $t \in S$ *such that* $R(s, v, t)$. *We also let* $\mathcal{A}$ *denote* $I \cup O$.

Definition 10 (composition of Moore machines) *Let* M *and* M' *be Moore machines with* $O \cap O' = \emptyset$. *The composition of* M *and* M', *denoted* $M \| M'$, *is the Moore machine* M'' *defined as follows.*

1. $S'' = S \times S'$.
2. $S''_0 = S_0 \times S'_0$.
3. $I'' = (I \cup I') \setminus (O \cup O')$.

4. $O'' = O \cup O'$.
5. $\mathcal{L}''\big((s,s')\big) = \mathcal{L}(s) \cup \mathcal{L}'(s')$.
6. $R''\big((s,s'),v,(t,t')\big)$ *iff* $R\big(s,(v \cup \mathcal{L}'(s')) \cap I, t\big)$ *and* $R'\big(s',(v \cup \mathcal{L}(s)) \cap I', t'\big)$.

We now turn to the question of how to define satisfaction of a specification by a Moore machine M. The key consideration is that we wish to have a compositional method of reasoning. Thus, *M satisfying a specification should mean that M plus any environment satisfies that specification.* We will achieve this by considering the behavior of complete systems involving M.

Definition 11 *A Moore machine M is called closed if $I = \emptyset$.*

Intuitively, the behavior of a closed machine cannot be altered. For such a machine, there is a structure which naturally corresponds to it. We define this structure precisely now. The definition here is actually slightly more general in that it assigns a structure to non-closed machines as well.

Definition 12 (structure for a Moore machine) *The structure M' corresponding to the Moore machine M is denoted by $K(M)$ and is defined as follows.*

1. $S' = S \times 2^I$.
2. $S'_0 = S_0 \times 2^I$.
3. $\mathcal{A}' = \mathcal{A} = I \cup O$.
4. $\mathcal{L}'\big((s,v)\big) = \mathcal{L}(s) \cup v$.
5. $R'\big((s,v_1),(t,v_2)\big)$ *iff* $R(s,v_1,t)$.
6. $\mathcal{F}' = \emptyset$.

Definition 13 *A Moore machine M' is called a closing environment for M if $O \cap O' = \emptyset$, $I \subseteq O'$ and $I' \subseteq O$.*

Definition 14 (satisfaction in a Moore machine) *If M is a Moore machine and φ is a $\forall CTL^*$ formula with atomic propositions over $\mathcal{A}$, then $M \models \varphi$ iff for every closing environment M' for M, $K(M \parallel M') \models \varphi$.*

We must now demonstrate how to efficiently check whether $M \models \varphi$.

Lemma 1 *If M and M' are Moore machines with $O \cap O' = \emptyset$, then $K(M \parallel M')$ is isomorphic to $K(M) \parallel K(M')$.*

Proof The mapping ϕ between $K(M \| M')$ and $K(M) \| K(M')$ is given by $\phi\big(((s,s'),v)\big) = \big((s,(v \cup \mathcal{L}'(s')) \cap I),(s',(v \cup \mathcal{L}(s)) \cap I')\big)$. □

Definition 15 *If M is a Moore machine, the maximal closing environment for M, denoted $E(M)$, is the Moore machine M' defined as follows.*

1. $S' = 2^I$.
2. $S'_0 = S'$.
3. $I' = \emptyset$.

4. $O' = I$.
5. $\mathcal{L}'(s') = s'$.
6. $R'(s', \emptyset, t')$ *is identically true.*

The maximal environment (for M) represents an environment which can do anything at each step. Intuitively, a possible behavior of M in an arbitrary environment must also be a possible behavior of M in the maximal environment. The logics we use specify properties that should hold for every possible behavior of a system. Hence, if M plus its maximal environment satisfies a formula, then M in any environment should satisfy that formula.

Lemma 2 *Suppose M' is a closing environment for M, and suppose $M'' = E(M)$. Then $K(M') \preceq K(M'')$.*

Lemma 3 *Let M be a Moore machine. Then $K(M)$ is isomorphic to $K(M \parallel E(M))$.*

Theorem 4 *If M is a Moore machine, then $M \models \varphi$ iff $K(M) \models \varphi$.*

Thus, to determine if a system $M_1 \parallel M_2 \parallel \ldots \parallel M_n$ satisfies a formula φ, we instead check that $K(M_1 \parallel M_2 \parallel \ldots \parallel M_n)$ satisfies φ. By lemma 1, this is equivalent to checking that $K(M_1) \parallel K(M_2) \parallel \ldots \parallel K(M_n)$ satisfies the formula. As illustrated in the previous section, we can use the assume-guarantee paradigm to try to verify this latter relation. Thus, during an actual verification we will be working with structures even though the thing we want to verify is a property of a composition of Moore machines.

6 The tableau construction

In this section, we give a tableau construction for $\forall$CTL formulas (for a similar construction for LTL, see Burch *et al.* [1]). We show that the tableau of a formula is a maximal model for the formula under the relation $\preceq$. Thus, the structure generated in the construction can be used as an assumption by composing the structure with the desired system before applying the model checking algorithm. Discharging the assumption is simply a matter of checking that the environment satisfies the formula. We also indicate how the tableau can be used to do temporal reasoning. For the remainder of this section, fix a $\forall$CTL formula ψ.

Definition 16 *The set* sub(φ) *of subformulas of the formula φ is defined by the following equations.*

1. *If $\varphi = true$ or $\varphi = false$ or $\varphi = p$, an atomic proposition, then* $\mathrm{sub}(\varphi) = \{\varphi\}$. *If $\varphi = \neg p$, a negated atomic proposition, then* $\mathrm{sub}(\varphi) = \{\varphi, p\}$.
2. *If $\varphi = \varphi_1 \wedge \varphi_2$ or $\varphi = \varphi_1 \vee \varphi_2$, then* $\mathrm{sub}(\varphi) = \{\varphi\} \cup \mathrm{sub}(\varphi_1) \cup \mathrm{sub}(\varphi_2)$.
3. (a) *If $\varphi = \forall \mathbf{X} \varphi_1$, then* $\mathrm{sub}(\varphi) = \{\varphi\} \cup \mathrm{sub}(\varphi_1)$.
   (b) *If $\varphi = \forall(\varphi_1 \mathbf{U} \varphi_2)$, then* $\mathrm{sub}(\varphi) = \{\varphi\} \cup \mathrm{sub}(\varphi_1) \cup \mathrm{sub}(\varphi_2)$.
   (c) *If $\varphi = \forall(\varphi_1 \mathbf{V} \varphi_2)$, then* $\mathrm{sub}(\varphi) = \{\varphi\} \cup \mathrm{sub}(\varphi_1) \cup \mathrm{sub}(\varphi_2)$.

Definition 17 *The set* el(φ) *of elementary formulas of the formula φ is defined by the following equations.*

1. *If* $\varphi = true$ *or* $\varphi = false$, *then* $\mathrm{el}(\varphi) = \emptyset$. *If* $\varphi = p$, *an atomic proposition, or* $\varphi = \neg p$, *then* $\mathrm{el}(\varphi) = \{p\}$.
2. *If* $\varphi = \varphi_1 \wedge \varphi_2$ *or* $\varphi = \varphi_1 \vee \varphi_2$, *then* $\mathrm{el}(\varphi) = \mathrm{el}(\varphi_1) \cup \mathrm{el}(\varphi_2)$.
3. (a) *If* $\varphi = \forall\mathbf{X}\,\varphi_1$, *then* $\mathrm{el}(\varphi) = \{\forall\mathbf{X}\,\varphi_1\} \cup \mathrm{el}(\varphi_1)$.
   (b) *If* $\varphi = \forall(\varphi_1\,\mathbf{U}\,\varphi_2)$, *then* $\mathrm{el}(\varphi) = \{\forall\mathbf{X}\,\mathit{false}, \forall\mathbf{X}\,\forall(\varphi_1\,\mathbf{U}\,\varphi_2)\} \cup \mathrm{el}(\varphi_1) \cup \mathrm{el}(\varphi_2)$.
   (c) *If* $\varphi = \forall(\varphi_1\,\mathbf{V}\,\varphi_2)$, *then* $\mathrm{el}(\varphi) = \{\forall\mathbf{X}\,\mathit{false}, \forall\mathbf{X}\,\forall(\varphi_1\,\mathbf{V}\,\varphi_2)\} \cup \mathrm{el}(\varphi_1) \cup \mathrm{el}(\varphi_2)$.

The special elementary subformula $\forall\mathbf{X}\,\mathit{false}$ denotes the nonexistence of a fair path; $s \models \forall\mathbf{X}\,\mathit{false}$ indicates that no fair path begins at s.

Definition 18 (tableau of a formula) *The tableau of* ψ, *denoted* $\mathcal{T}(\psi)$, *is the structure* $\langle S, S_0, \mathcal{A}, \mathcal{L}, R, \mathfrak{F}\rangle$ *defined as follows.*

1. $S = 2^{\mathrm{el}(\psi)}$.
2. $S_0 = \Phi(\psi)$, *where* Φ *is the map from* $\mathrm{el}(\psi) \cup \mathrm{sub}(\psi) \cup \{\mathit{true}, \mathit{false}\}$ *to* S *defined by the following equations.*
   (a) $\Phi(\mathit{true}) = S$, $\Phi(\mathit{false}) = \emptyset$. *If* $\varphi \in \mathrm{el}(\psi)$, *then* $\Phi(\varphi) = \{\, s \mid \varphi \in s \,\}$. *If* $\varphi = \neg\varphi_1$, *then* $\Phi(\varphi) = S \setminus \Phi(\varphi_1)$.
   (b) *If* $\varphi = \varphi_1 \wedge \varphi_2$, *then* $\Phi(\varphi) = \Phi(\varphi_1) \cap \Phi(\varphi_2)$. *If* $\varphi = \varphi_1 \vee \varphi_2$, *then* $\Phi(\varphi) = \Phi(\varphi_1) \cup \Phi(\varphi_2)$.
   (c) i. *If* $\varphi = \forall(\varphi_1\mathbf{U}\varphi_2)$, *then* $\Phi(\varphi) = \Big(\Phi(\varphi_2) \cup \big(\Phi(\varphi_1) \cap \Phi(\forall\mathbf{X}\,\varphi)\big)\Big) \cup \Phi(\forall\mathbf{X}\,\mathit{false})$.
       ii. *If* $\varphi = \forall(\varphi_1\mathbf{V}\varphi_2)$, *then* $\Phi(\varphi) = \Big(\Phi(\varphi_2) \cap \big(\Phi(\varphi_1) \cup \Phi(\forall\mathbf{X}\,\varphi)\big)\Big) \cup \Phi(\forall\mathbf{X}\,\mathit{false})$.
3. $\mathcal{A} = \{\, p \mid p \in \mathrm{el}(\psi) \,\}$.
4. $\mathcal{L}(s) = \{\, p \mid p \in s \,\}$.
5. $R(s,t)$ *iff for each formula* $\forall\mathbf{X}\,\varphi$ *in* $\mathrm{el}(\psi)$, $\forall\mathbf{X}\,\varphi \in s$ *implies* $t \in \Phi(\varphi)$.
6. $\mathfrak{F} = \Big\{ \big(\Phi(\forall\mathbf{X}\,\forall(\varphi_1\,\mathbf{U}\,\varphi_2)), \Phi(\varphi_2)\big) \;\Big|\; \forall\mathbf{X}\,\forall(\varphi_1\,\mathbf{U}\,\varphi_2) \in \mathrm{el}(\psi) \Big\}$.

Lemma 4 *For all subformulas* φ *of* ψ, *if* $s \in \Phi(\varphi)$, *then* $s \models \varphi$.

Now let $M = \mathcal{T}(\psi)$, and fix a structure M'.

Lemma 5 *Define a relation* $H \subseteq S' \times S$ *by*

$$H = \Big\{ (s', s) \;\Big|\; s = \{\, \varphi \mid \varphi \in \mathrm{el}(\psi), s' \models \varphi \,\} \Big\}.$$

If $H(s', s)$, *then for every subformula or elementary formula* φ *of* ψ, $s' \models \varphi$ *implies* $s \in \Phi(\varphi)$.

Lemma 6 *The relation* H *given above is a homomorphism.*

Theorem 5 $M' \models \psi$ *iff* $M' \preceq \mathcal{T}(\psi)$.

The tableau construction can also be used to reason about formulas. We are typically interested in whether every model of a formula φ is also a model of some other formula ψ. Let $\varphi \models \psi$ denote this semantic relation.

Proposition 1 $\varphi \models \psi$ *iff* $\mathcal{T}(\varphi) \models \psi$.

We will sometimes extend the set of elementary formulas of a formula by adding additional atomic propositions. For example, if we wished to check whether *true* implied p, we would extend the set of atomic propositions for *true* to include p (another way to view this is to imagine rewriting *true* as $\mathit{true} \wedge (p \vee \neg p)$. The formula ψ has a nontrivial model iff it is not the case that $\psi \models \forall\mathbf{X}\,\mathit{false}$. ψ is true in every model iff $\mathit{true} \models \psi$.

7 Checking for homomorphism

In this section, we discuss the problem of determining whether there exists a homomorphism between two structures M and M'. Our goal is to efficiently determine if $M \preceq M'$. First note that if H_1 and H_2 are homomorphisms, then $H_1 \cup H_2$ is a homomorphism. Also, $\emptyset$ is trivially a homomorphism. These facts imply that there is a maximal homomorphism under set inclusion. We will actually give an algorithm for computing this maximal homomorphism.

We also note the following facts.

1. If s is a state of M and no fair paths start at s, then s is homomorphic to exactly those states s' in M' for which $\mathcal{L}(s) \cap \mathcal{A}' = \mathcal{L}'(s')$.
2. If s' is a state of M' and no fair paths start at s', then s' is homomorphic exactly to those states s in M which are the start of no fair path and for which $\mathcal{L}(s) \cap \mathcal{A}' = \mathcal{L}'(s')$.

States which are the start of no fair path can be detected in polynomial time [11] and eliminated in a preprocessing step. Hence, without loss of generality, we can assume that every state in M and M' is the start of some fair path. We now describe polynomial time algorithms for checking the preorder in several important special cases.

Suppose that M' has a trivial acceptance condition, i.e., $\mathcal{F}' = \emptyset$.

Definition 19 *Define a sequence of relations H_i as follows.*

1. $H_0 = \left\{ (s, s') \,\middle|\, \mathcal{L}(s) \cap \mathcal{A}' = \mathcal{L}'(s') \right\}$
2. $H_{i+1} = H_i \cap \left\{ (s, s') \,\middle|\, \forall t[R(s,t) \rightarrow \exists t'(R'(s',t') \wedge H_i(t,t'))] \right\}$

Define H_ω to be the first H_i such that $H_i = H_{i+1}$ (such an i exists since $H_{j+1} \subseteq H_j$ for all j and each H_j is finite).

Theorem 6 *For every $s \in S$ and $s' \in S'$, $s \preceq s'$ iff $H_\omega(s, s')$.*

We note that $H_\omega = H_i$ for some i which is at most $|S| \cdot |S'|$. Each H_{j+1} can also be computed in polynomial time from H_j; hence H_ω can be computed in polynomial time.

Another important case is when M' is deterministic, i.e., if $R'(s', t')$ and $R'(s', u')$, then $\mathcal{L}'(t') \neq \mathcal{L}'(u')$. For this case, $s \preceq s'$ iff the language of s is contained in the language of s' (the language for a state s is the set of sequences of labelings which occur along the fair paths starting at s). This relation can be checked in polynomial time using the techniques of Clarke, Draghicescu and Kurshan [2].

Finally, if M' is the result of a tableau construction, say $M' = \mathcal{T}(\psi)$, then as shown in the previous section, checking whether $M \preceq M'$ reduces to the problem of checking whether $M \models \psi$.

8 An example

We have implemented a BDD-based model checker based on the theory developed in the previous sections. The model checker is written in a combination of T (Yale's dialect of Scheme) and C. It includes facilities for model checking, temporal reasoning (via the tableau construction), and checking for homomorphism. To illustrate the system, we use the controller of a simple CPU as an example. The controller is written in a state machine description language called CSML [5] which is compiled into Moore machines. We give only a brief description of the CPU here; Clarke, Long and McMillan [5] give details. The CPU is a simple stack-based machine, i.e., part of the CPU's memory contains a stack from which instruction operands are popped and onto which results are pushed. There are two parts to the CPU controller. The first part is called the access unit and is responsible for all the CPU's memory references. The second part, called the execution unit, interprets the instructions and controls the arithmetic unit, shifter, etc. These two parts operate in parallel. The access unit and execution unit communicate via a small number of signals. Three of the signals, *push*, *pop* and *fetch*, are inputs of the access unit and indicate that the execution unit wants to push or pop something from the stack or to get the next instruction. For each of these signals there is a corresponding ready output from the access unit. The execution unit must wait for the appropriate ready signal before proceeding. One additional signal, *branch*, is asserted by the execution unit when it wants to jump to a new program location.

In order to increase performance, the access unit attempts to keep the value on the top of the stack in a special register called the TS register. The goal is to keep the execution unit from having to wait for the memory. For example, when the TS register contains valid data, a pop operation can proceed immediately. In addition, when a value is pushed on the stack, it is moved into this register and copied to memory at some later point. The access unit also loads instructions into a queue when possible so that fetches do not require waiting for the memory. This queue is flushed whenever the CPU branches.

Clarke, Long and McMillan gave a number of correctness conditions for the controller. We demonstrate here how these formulas can be verified in a compositional fashion. From the form of the conditions, we divide them into three classes. The first class consists of simple safety properties; we omit the description of their verification here.

The conditions in the second class are slightly more complex. These properties are safety properties which specify what sequences of operations are allowed. They depend on the access unit asserting the various ready signals at appropriate times and on the memory acknowledge signal being well-behaved. In order to verify the properties, we made a simple model of the memory (see figure 1). For conciseness, the figure shows a Moore machine; the actual model used is obtained by adding the fairness constraint shown in the figure to the structure corresponding to this Moore machine. By composing this model with the access unit, we were able to verify all of the properties except one. To verify the exception, an additional assumption $\forall\mathbf{G}(\neg push \vee \neg pop)$ was required. The model checker verified that the property was true under this assumption by building the tableau for the assumption, composing it with the access unit and memory model, and checking the property.

The final class of criteria consists of a single liveness property: $\forall\mathbf{G}\,\forall\mathbf{F}(fetch \wedge fetchrdy)$. This formula states that the CPU always fetches another instruction. In the full paper, we demonstrate two different ways of verifying this property. One way involves making a model of the execution unit. Here, we show how to perform the verification using a series of $\forall$CTL assumptions.

The idea will be to check the property for the execution unit. In order for the formula to be true, the access unit must eventually respond to push and pop requests and must fill the instruction queue when appropriate. We can only guarantee that the access unit meets these conditions if we know that the execution unit does not try to do two operations at once and that it will not remove a request before the corresponding operation can

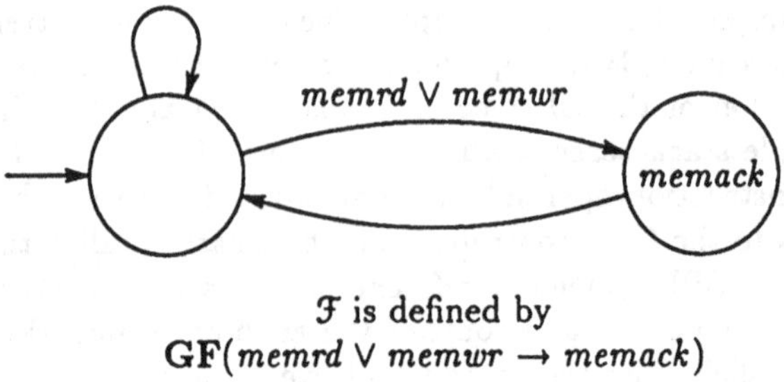

Figure 1: Memory abstraction

complete. We begin with these properties.

$$\forall\mathbf{G}\Big(\neg(\mathit{fetch} \wedge \mathit{push}) \wedge \neg(\mathit{fetch} \wedge \mathit{pop}) \wedge \cdots \wedge \neg(\mathit{pop} \wedge \mathit{branch})\Big) \tag{1}$$

$$\forall\mathbf{G}\Big(\mathit{push} \rightarrow \forall(\mathit{pushed}\ \mathbf{V}\ \mathit{push})\Big) \tag{2}$$

$$\forall\mathbf{G}\Big(\mathit{pop} \rightarrow \forall(\mathit{popped}\ \mathbf{V}\ \mathit{pop})\Big) \tag{3}$$

The first of these specifies that every pair of operations the execution unit can perform are mutually exclusive. The other two formulas state that if the execution unit makes a push or pop request, then it does not deassert the request until the operation completes. The model checker verified that these properties hold in the execution unit alone, and (using the tableau construction) that the first property implies the assumption $\forall\mathbf{G}(\neg \mathit{push} \vee \neg \mathit{pop})$ used above. Now using formulas 1 and 2 as assumptions, we checked that the system composed of the access unit and the memory model satisfied the formula

$$\forall\mathbf{G}\Big(\mathit{push} \rightarrow \forall(\mathit{push}\ \mathbf{U}\ \mathit{pushed})\Big). \tag{4}$$

This specification states that every push operation will be completed. Similarly, using formulas 1 and 3 as assumptions, we verified

$$\forall\mathbf{G}\Big(\mathit{pop} \rightarrow \forall(\mathit{pop}\ \mathbf{U}\ \mathit{popped})\Big). \tag{5}$$

The system composed of the access unit and the memory model also satisfies the formula $\forall\mathbf{G}\,\forall\mathbf{F}(\mathit{fetchrdy} \vee \mathit{branch})$ (at any point, either the access unit will eventually fill the instruction queue or a branch will occur). Finally, using this formula and formulas 4 and 5 as assumptions, the model checker verified that the execution unit satisfies $\forall\mathbf{G}\,\forall\mathbf{F}(\mathit{fetch} \wedge \mathit{fetchrdy})$. To complete the verification and conclude that the entire specification was true of a system, we would have to check that the actual memory was homomorphic to the model we used.

9 Conclusion

We have identified a subset, ∀CTL*, of CTL* which is appropriate for compositional reasoning. For this subset, satisfaction is preserved under composition; hence a standard model checking algorithm can be used to answer the question: Is a formula true for all systems containing a specified component? We have also proposed a preorder $\preceq$ which is appropriate for ∀CTL*. The preorder captures the relation between a component and a system containing that component. It provides the basis for using an assume-guarantee style of reasoning with the logic. Assumptions which are given as structures are discharged by checking the preorder. We have given a tableau construction for the ∀CTL subset of ∀CTL*. Satisfaction of a ∀CTL formula corresponds to being below the tableau of the formula in the preorder. The construction makes it possible to use ∀CTL formulas as assumptions and to do temporal reasoning. ∀CTL also has an efficient model checking algorithm. We have implemented a symbolic verification system based on these results and have used it to verify some nontrivial systems in a compositional fashion.

There are several directions for future work. Intuitively, the ∀CTL* subset of CTL* should be maximal in the sense that any formula for which satisfaction is preserved under composition should be equivalent to a formula of ∀CTL*, but we have not proved this. Another idea is to look at different logics with the same flavor, such as ∀CTL* extended with automata operators or the μ-calculus with only $[\cdot]$ modalities. It would also be interesting to try to extend the tableau construction of section 6 to all of ∀CTL*. In order to accomplish this however, it will almost certainly be necessary to use a more complex type of structure than that given in definition 2. Another question is whether it is possible to apply our ideas to branching-time logics with existential path quantifiers. For example, is there a reasonable algorithm which will determine whether a CTL formula is true in all systems containing a given component? It is fairly easy to come up with algorithms which are sound, but completeness seems more difficult to achieve. We also wish to examine the problem of efficiently checking the preorder for arbitrary structures. Finally, it is essential to try to apply the compositional reasoning methods we have considered to more complex systems in order to evaluate the techniques.

References

[1] J. R. Burch, E. M. Clarke, K. L. McMillan, D. L. Dill, and J. Hwang. Symbolic model checking: 10^{20} states and beyond. In *Proceedings of the Fifth Annual Symposium on Logic in Computer Science*. IEEE Computer Society Press, June 1990.

[2] E. M. Clarke, I. A. Draghicescu, and R. P. Kurshan. A unified approach for showing language containment and equivalence between various types of ω-automata. In A. Arnold and N. D. Jones, editors, *Proceedings of the 15th Colloquium on Trees in Algebra and Programming*, volume 407 of *Lecture Notes in Computer Science*. Springer-Verlag, May 1990.

[3] E. M. Clarke, E. A. Emerson, and A. P. Sistla. Automatic verification of finite-state concurrent systems using temporal logic specifications. *ACM Transactions on Programming Languages and Systems*, 8(2):244–263, 1986.

[4] E. M. Clarke, D. E. Long, and K. L. McMillan. Compositional model checking. In *Proceedings of the Fourth Annual Symposium on Logic in Computer Science*. IEEE Computer Society Press, June 1989.

[5] E. M. Clarke, D. E. Long, and K. L. McMillan. A language for compositional specification and verification of finite state hardware controllers. In J. A. Darringer and F. J. Rammig, editors, *Proceedings of the Ninth International Symposium on Computer Hardware Description Languages and their Applications*. North-Holland, June 1989.

[6] R. Cleaveland. Tableau-based model checking in the propositional mu-calculus. *Acta Informatica*, 27:725–747, 1990.

[7] O. Coudert, C. Berthet, and J. C. Madre. Verifying temporal properties of sequential machines without building their state diagrams. In Kurshan and Clarke [16].

[8] J. W. de Bakker, W.-P. de Roever, and G. Rozenberg, editors. *Proceedings of the REX Workshop on Stepwise Refinement of Distributed Systems, Models, Formalisms, Correctness*, volume 430 of *Lecture Notes in Computer Science*. Springer-Verlag, May 1989.

[9] D. L. Dill. *Trace Theory for Automatic Hierarchical Verification of Speed-Independent Circuits*. ACM Distinguished Dissertations. MIT Press, 1989.

[10] E. A. Emerson and J. Y. Halpern. "Sometimes" and "Not Never" revisited: On branching time versus linear time. *Journal of the ACM*, 33:151–178, 1986.

[11] E. A. Emerson and C.-L. Lei. Efficient model checking in fragments of the propositional mu-calculus. In *Proceedings of the Second Annual Symposium on Logic in Computer Science*. IEEE Computer Society Press, June 1986.

[12] S. Graf and B. Steffen. Compositional minimization of finite state processes. In Kurshan and Clarke [16].

[13] J. E. Hopcroft and J. D. Ullman. *Introduction to Automata Theory, Languages, and Computation*. Addison-Wesley, 1979.

[14] B. Josko. Verifying the correctness of AADL-modules using model checking. In de Bakker et al. [8].

[15] R. P. Kurshan. Analysis of discrete event coordination. In de Bakker et al. [8].

[16] R. P. Kurshan and E. M. Clarke, editors. *Proceedings of the 1990 Workshop on Computer-Aided Verification*, June 1990.

[17] R. P. Kurshan and K. L. McMillan. A structural induction theorem for processes. In *Proceedings of the Eighth Annual ACM Symposium on Principles of Distributed Computing*. ACM Press, August 1989.

[18] K. G. Larsen. The expressive power of implicit specifications. To appear in Proceedings of the Eighteenth International Colloquium on Automata, Languages, and Programming.

[19] O. Lichtenstein and A. Pnueli. Checking that finite state concurrent programs satisfy their linear specification. In *Proceedings of the Twelfth Annual ACM Symposium on Principles of Programming Languages*, January 1985.

[20] R. Milner. *A Calculus of Communicating Systems*, volume 92 of *Lecture Notes in Computer Science*. Springer-Verlag, 1980.

[21] A. Pnueli. In transition for global to modular temporal reasoning about programs. In K. R. Apt, editor, *Logics and Models of Concurrent Systems*, volume 13 of *NATO ASI series. Series F, Computer and system sciences*. Springer-Verlag, 1984.

[22] Z. Shtadler and O. Grumberg. Network grammars, communication behaviors and automatic verification. In J. Sifakis, editor, *Proceedings of the 1989 International Workshop on Automatic Verification Methods for Finite State Systems, Grenoble, France*, volume 407 of *Lecture Notes in Computer Science*. Springer-Verlag, June 1989.

[23] G. Shurek and O. Grumberg. The modular framework of computer-aided verification: Motivation, solutions and evaluation criteria. In Kurshan and Clarke [16].

[24] C. Stirling and D. J. Walker. Local model checking in the modal mu-calculus. In J. Diaz and F. Orejas, editors, *Proceedings of the 1989 International Joint Conference on Theory and Practice of Software Development*, volume 351–352 of *Lecture Notes in Computer Science*. Springer-Verlag, March 1989.

[25] D. Walker. Bisimulations and divergence. In *Proceedings of the Third Annual Symposium on Logic in Computer Science*. IEEE Computer Society Press, June 1988.

[26] G. Winskel. Compositional checking of validity on finite state processes. Draft copy.

GEOMETRIC LOGIC, CAUSALITY AND EVENT STRUCTURES

Jeremy Gunawardena,

Hewlett-Packard Laboratories,

Filton Road, Stoke Gifford,

Bristol BS12 6QZ, United Kingdom.

jhcg@hplb.hpl.hp.com jhcg@hpl.hp.co.uk

Abstract

The conventional approach to causality is based on partial orders. Without additional structure, partial orders are only capable of expressing AND causality. In this paper we investigate a syntactic, or logical, approach to causality which allows other causal relationships, such as OR causality, to be expressed with equal facility. In earlier work, [3], we showed the benefits of this approach by giving a causal characterisation, in the finite case, of Milner's notion of confluence in CCS. This provides the justification for the more systematic study of causality, without finiteness restrictions, which appears here. We identify three general principles which a logic of causality should satisfy. These principles summarise some basic intuitions about events and causality. They lead us to geometric logic - the "logic of finite observations" - as a candidate for a logic of causality. We introduce the formalism of geometric automata based on this choice; a geometric automaton is a set E together with a pair of endomorphisms of the free frame (locale) generated by E. Our main result is to show that Winskel's general event structures are a special case of geometric automata. This is analogous to the transition from topological data (sets of points) to algebraic structures (lattices of open subsets) in "pointless topology", [6]. This result links our ideas on causality with Winskel's theory of events in computation; it provides a syntax for describing event structures and it opens the way to giving a causal interpretation of event structure phenomena. We show further that geometric automata give rise to domains of configurations which generalise the event domains of Winskel and Droste.

1 Introduction

In this paper we develop a syntactic approach to causality. We seek to find a language (a logic or algebra) in which causal relationships can be described and to embody this in a formalism for reasoning about reactive systems.

Causality is conventionally represented by a partially ordered set (poset). The poset whose Hasse diagram is shown in Figure 1 can be rendered into syntactic form as shown in Figure 2. The arrow symbol, $\rightarrow$, can be read as "is-caused-by". The special symbol T, for the moment un-interpreted, but with obvious logical connotations, indicates that the corresponding event is initial in the partial order. $\wedge$ has its usual meaning of logical AND. It is clear that any partial order could be translated into such a table, possibly infinite, using only the connective AND. We summarise this by saying that posets express only AND causality.

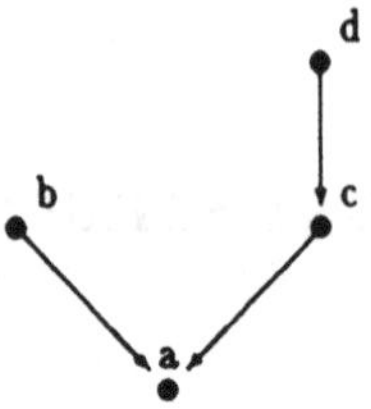

Figure 1: Hasse diagram of a poset

a	$\rightarrow$	$b \wedge c$
b	$\rightarrow$	T
c	$\rightarrow$	d
d	$\rightarrow$	T

Figure 2: Syntactic version of the poset

One advantage of the syntactic approach is that we can easily express other forms of causality, such as OR causality. We are accustomed to think of AND and OR as dual connectives of comparable importance. The table below seems as meaningful as the one in Figure 2.

a	$\rightarrow$	T
b	$\rightarrow$	T
c	$\rightarrow$	$a \vee b$

(We shall define an operational semantics for such tables in §3; the behaviour of this one should be reasonably clear.) In an earlier paper we used tables like these to give a causal characterisation, [3, Theorem 1.1], of Milner's notion of confluence in CCS, [7, Chapter 11]. This application provides a justification for the more systematic treatment of causality in the present paper. The reader is referred to [3, §1] for a discussion of OR causality and its significance in concurrency theory.

The tables which we constructed above in an informal way can be seen more formally as pairs (E, ρ) where E is some set of events and $\rho : E \rightarrow \mathcal{L}(E)$ is a function ("is caused by") from E to some logic, $\mathcal{L}(E)$ generated by the symbols in E. It seems to require at least the binary connectives AND, and OR and the unary connective T. From a logical viewpoint we shall be concerned with the model theory rather than the proof theory and we will work exclusively with the Lindenbaum algebra of $\mathcal{L}$. However, we find it convenient to continue to use the word "logic" in preference to "algebra" partly to avoid the associations with "process algebra". The syntax which is developed here allows us to describe causal relationships; it does not provide us with process constructors.

One objective of this paper is to understand the requirements for a logic of causality. In §2 we state three general principles which a logic of causality should satisfy. These principles summarise our foundational intuitions about events and causality. They limit the possible choices of logic and allow us to measure the expressibility of any particular logic.

In our earlier paper, [3], we restricted attention to the case of finitely many events and took the path of least resistance by choosing classical Boolean logic as the logic of causality. This gave rise to "tables" which we called causal automata. In the infinite case the choice of logic must be made with greater care and throws up some interesting problems which are still not completely resolved.

In §3 we show that geometric logic - the "logic of finite observations", [12] - is a suitable candidate for a logic of causality and we introduce a formalism based on this called geometric automata. Geometric logic, or its algebrisation, the theory of frames (locales), is the subject matter of "pointless topology", [6]. The significance of this to computer science was first noted by Smyth, [9], and followed up in Abramsky's programme, [1]. We define the concepts needed for the present paper but refer to Vickers' introductory treatment, [12], and Johnstone's treatise, [5], for details. A geometric automaton is simply a set, E, together with a pair of endomorphisms of the free frame generated by E.

A key result in §3 is Proposition 3.1 which gives a topological interpretation of the free frame. This is the essential ingredient in proving our main result, in §4, that Winskel's general event structures, [14], are a special case of geometric automata. This is an instance of the transition from topological data (sets of points) to algebraic structures (lattices of open subsets) which is fundamental to locale theory, [6]. This result links our ideas on causality with Winskel's theory of events in computation, [13]; it provides a syntax for event structures and it opens the way to giving a causal interpretation of event structure phenomena. We also show that geometric automata give rise to domains of configurations which are more general than the event domains of Winskel and Droste, [2].

In the concluding section we discuss briefly some open problems and some interesting directions for further study.

2 Requirements for A Logic of Causality

In this section we discuss three general principles for a logic of causality. These principles encapsulate some basic intuitions about events and causality. They should not be regarded as cast in stone, but rather as defining the parameters of the present investigation.

2.1 The principle of events

This principle of events asserts that causality exists at the level of action occurrences (events) and not at the level of actions. As I type this line of text at my word-processor I perform various actions. For instance, the action of pressing the "a" key. Each time this action occurs, a separate event is generated (a new ASCII character is added to my text file). I could, if I was sufficiently painstaking, enumerate these events from the very first time that I pressed the "a" key during this session of typing. Each time the action occurs, the reasons for it and the context in which it happens are different. The principle of events merely points out that in describing causal relationships we must do so at event level and not at action level because different action occurrences may have different causes.

All this may seem rather obvious. However, it means that when we look at a reactive system and attempt to describe it from this causal viewpoint we have to be able to see the individual events. The system must be transparent and not a black box. If we observe the system in operation in this way we will necessarily see a sequence of distinct events.

Definition 2.1 *A string $s \in E^*$ over some alphabet E is said to be pure if each symbol in E appears at most once in s.*

We will use the notation E^{*p} for the set of pure strings over E. Recall that a subset $T \subseteq E^*$ is a trace set if T is non-empty and prefix-closed: $\varepsilon \in T$ and $st \in T \Rightarrow s \in T$. Note that E^{*p} is itself a trace set. A pure trace set is a trace set contained in E^{*p}.

Transparent systems generate pure trace sets. Not only do we regard each symbol on a trace as a separate event but we regard the same symbol on different traces as the same event. Hence the trace set $\{\varepsilon, a, b, ab, ba\}$ can be unambiguously reconstructed into the reactive system which has two events a and b which are concurrent. There are other reactive systems which might appear to generate the same set of traces, for instance one where there is a choice between thé two interleavings of a and b. But transparently, this system has four events, although only two actions. We would actually see traces like $\{\varepsilon, u, v, uw, vx\}$ where, say, events u and x are occurrences of action a and events v and w are occurrences of b.

It appears from this discussion that pure trace sets are equivalent to transparent reactive systems and we might as well throw away the systems and work with the trace sets. If our aim is to set up a formalism based on a logic for causality then the power of the logic - its expressibility - should be assessed by determining the class of pure trace sets which the formalism generates. This is the mathematical content of the principle of events.

Actions can be recovered from their underlying events through a labelling function as is done for labelled event structures and pomsets. This amounts to a process of abstraction: different events are deemed to represent the same action. In this paper we shall not be concerned with labelled automata.

2.2 The principle of irrelevance of history

Consider the pure trace set $T_1 = \{\varepsilon, a, b, ab, ba, abc, bad\}$. The events c and d depend on the order in which the events a and b have occurred. If a happens before b then c occurs but not d and vice-versa. In other words, history is relevant. To describe this in our logic of causality it seems inescapable that we would need logical formulae $f \in \mathcal{L}(E)$ whose truth depends on sequences of events. This would appear to be a more discriminating and complex logic than one based on sets of events. In this paper we choose to avoid this possibility; for us, history will not be relevant. We stress that this is purely for reasons of convenience. We believe that history is very relevant and that we must come to terms with it in the future if we are to fully understand causality. By treating first the simpler problem we hope to lay the foundation for a study of the more complex one. We shall mention some of the directions that might be taken in §5.

The principle of irrelevance of history has two mathematical consequences. Firstly, it tells us something about the model theory of our logic. The truth of a logical formula will be determined by sets, as opposed to sequences, of events. Hence we expect a pairing between sets of events, $S \in 2^E$, and formulae, $f \in \mathcal{L}(E)$:

$$S(f) = \begin{cases} \mathsf{T} \\ \mathsf{F}. \end{cases}$$

Secondly, it rules out of consideration certain pure trace sets, such as the one above, in assessing our logic. How can we describe the trace sets for which history is irrelevant?

We need some notation for strings to start with. The prefix ordering on strings, $s, t \in E^*$, will be denoted $s \leq t$. The notation $s \sim t$ will indicate that s and t are permutations of each other. If T is a trace set and $s \in T$, then $[s]$ will indicate the equivalence class of s up to permutation in T:

$$[s] = \{t \in T | t \sim s\}.$$

On such equivalence classes, which form the set $T/\sim$, one can define the prefix ordering up to permutation: $[s] \preceq [t]$ if, and only if, $\exists s_1 \in [s], t_1 \in [t]$ such that $s_1 \leq t_1$. It is easy to see that this relation on $T/\sim$ is reflexive and anti-symmetric. It is not, however, always transitive, as the trace set T_1 above makes clear: $[a] \preceq [ab]$ and $[ab] \preceq [bad]$ but $[a] \not\preceq [bad]$. This captures exactly what we mean by history-relevance.

Definition 2.2 *A trace set T is transitive if the prefix ordering up to permutation is transitive. That is, if $(T/\sim, \preceq)$ is a partial order.*

For the rest of this paper we shall concentrate on pure, transitive trace sets. The partial order $(T/\sim, \preceq)$ will turn out to be particularly significant when we consider domains of configurations.

2.3 The principle of finite causes

It is clear that our logic of causality must have a connective resembling **AND**. When there are infinitely many events available this raises the possibility of an infinitary conjunction:

$$e \rightarrow \bigwedge\{e_1, e_2, \cdots, e_n, \cdots\}.$$

The problem with this is clear: the event e could not take place until infinitely many events had occurred. An infinitary disjunction, on the other hand, is much better behaved:

$$e \rightarrow \bigvee\{e_1, e_2, \cdots, e_n, \cdots\}.$$

Here e could occur after any of the e_i, a form of infinite choice. It is interesting that the intuitive duality between **AND** and **OR** which we argued for in §1 disappears in an infinite context.

The principle of finite causes is customarily invoked - in event structures for instance - as a way of avoiding infinitary conjunction. We could, of course, simply rule out the use of infinitary conjunction in our logic of causality. However it is more insightful to state the principle of finite causes in terms of the model theory in the following way: the validity of any formula in our logic should be determined by its value on just the finite sets of events. More precisely, if $Fin(E) \subseteq 2^E$ denotes the set of finite subsets of E, and $f, g \in \mathcal{L}(E)$ are formulae in our logic such that

$$\{S \in Fin(E) | S(f) = \mathsf{T}\} = \{T \in Fin(E) | T(g) = \mathsf{T}\}$$

then $f = g$ in $\mathcal{L}(E)$. This has the effect of directing our attention towards the set $Fin(E)$. Its structure seems to be of great significance in understanding logics of causality.

This completes our discussion of the principles required by a logic of causality. In the next section we introduce the particular candidate, geometric logic, which we will study in the rest of the paper.

3 Geometric Automata

The principle of finite causes draws our attention to the discrepancy between infinitary OR and infinitary AND. This should warn us that the customary dualities of classical Boolean logic are threatened in the infinite case. A similar phenomenon has been observed in geometric logic, the "logic of finite observations", [12, Chapter 2], for much the same reasons. This suggests that we examine geometric logic as a candidate for a logic of causality.

Geometric logic is an infinitary intuitionistic logic. The Lindenbaum algebra of a geometric theory is referred to as a frame. [6, 12]. Recall that if $(F, \leq)$ is a poset then a subset $S \subseteq F$ has a meet (greatest lower bound), $m = \bigwedge S$, if, $m \leq x$ for all $x \in S$ (m is a lower bound) and, if $m' \in F$ has the same property, then $m' \leq m$ (m is the greatest lower bound). A similar definition holds for the join (least upper bound) of S, denoted $\bigvee S$. Note that $x \leq y$ if, and only if, $x \wedge y = x$; similarly, $x \leq y$ if, and only if, $x \vee y = y$.

Definition 3.1 *A frame F is a poset in which* (1) *all finite meets exist;* (2) *arbitrary joins exist;* (3) *binary meets distribute over arbitrary joins, $a \wedge \bigvee_{i \in I}\{b_i\} = \bigvee_{i \in I}\{a \wedge b_i\}$.*

Historically, frames arose not from logic but from topology: they were the posets of open subsets of a topological space, In a topological space, meet corresponds to intersection of open subsets and join to union; the distributive law comes for free. The move away from topology as "sets of points" to topology as "lattices of opens" (pointless topology or locale theory) is ably documented in Johnstone's survey, [6].

We denote $\bigwedge \emptyset$, the greatest element of F, by T, and $\bigvee \emptyset$, the least element, by F. The simplest non-degenerate frame, the Sierpinski frame, is the poset $2 = \{\mathsf{F}, \mathsf{T}\}$ where, of course, $\mathsf{F} \leq \mathsf{T}$. If F and G are frames, a frame homomorphism is a function $f : F \rightarrow G$ which preserves meets and joins and hence preserves the partial order and T and F. Frames and frame homomorphisms form a category, **Frm**. Taking the poset of open subsets is a (contravariant) functor from the category, **Top**, of topological spaces and continuous maps, to **Frm**. (In pointless topology one prefers to work in $\mathbf{Frm}^{op}$, the category of locales, [6], but this distinction need not concern us here.)

When compared with complete Boolean algebras and complete Heyting algebras, frames have a better algebraic theory. Despite the infinitary operation, they can still be constructed by generators and relations. (**Frm** is algebraic over **Set**, [5, §II.1.2].) Given a set E there exists a free frame generated by E, denoted $Fr(E)$. $Fr : \mathbf{Set} \rightarrow \mathbf{Frm}$ is the left adjoint to the forgetful functor and $Fr(E)$ is defined up to isomorphism by the following universal property. There exists a set function $i : E \rightarrow Fr(E)$ which is initial in the following sense: given any other set function $f : E \rightarrow G$ from E to some frame G, there exists a unique frame homomorphism $\bar{f} : Fr(E) \rightarrow G$ such that $f = \bar{f}i$. We shall drop the function i and identify elements of E with their images $i(e) \in Fr(E)$. Similarly, we shall use the same notation for the set function f and its lifting to a frame homomorphism.

In marked contrast to frames there is no free complete Boolean algebra or free complete Heyting algebra on countably infinitely many generators, [5, §I.4.10], a problem which will confront us later. For the moment our first concern is with the structure of $Fr(E)$.

If $(X, \leq)$ is a poset, $x\uparrow$ will denote the upward closure of $x \in X$: $x\uparrow = \{y \in X \mid x \leq y\}$. This can be extended to subsets: if $S \subseteq X$, then $S\uparrow = \bigcup_{x \in S}\{x\uparrow\}$. A subset S is upward closed if $S = S\uparrow$. Downward closures will be denoted $x\downarrow$, $S\downarrow$. The collection of upward (downward) closed subsets of $(X, \leq)$ forms a topology on X, the Alexandrov topology, [12, §3.6.2], denoted $X\uparrow$ ($X\downarrow$).

Of particular interest to us are topologies on $Fin(E)$ which we consider as a partial order under inclusion of subsets. Let $\theta : E \to Fin(E)\uparrow$ be defined by $\theta(e) = \{e\}\uparrow$. As discussed above, this lifts uniquely to a frame homomorphism on $Fr(E)$.

Proposition 3.1 *$\theta : Fr(E) \to Fin(E)\uparrow$ is an isomorphism of frames.*

Proof: Johnstone's proof that **Frm** is algebraic over **Set**, [5, §II.1.2], shows that $Fr(E)$ may be represented, up to isomorphism, as $MSL(E)\downarrow$ where $MSL(E)$ is the free meet semi-lattice generated by E. In this representation, a generator $e \in E$ corresponds to $e\downarrow$ in $MSL(E)\downarrow$. Now $MSL(E)$ is simply $Fin(E)^{op}$ as a poset and hence $MSL(E)\downarrow$ can be identified with $Fin(E)\uparrow$. Under this identification, the generator e corresponds to $\{e\}\uparrow$. The result follows.

QED

The real content of this result is, of course, Johnstone's construction of the free frame. However, the result has a special significance for us: it is the "crucial characteristic property of {AND, OR} causality", [3, Lemma 3.1], placed in its correct setting and it is the key to our causal interpretation of event structures in §4.

In order to relate frames to the discussion in §2 we need to reintroduce the logical dimension which has been missing so far. In the trivial frame, 2, the operations of meet and join are identical to AND and OR if T and F are interpreted as "true" and "false". Let E be a set and $v : E \to 2$ be any set function. By the universal property of free frames, v lifts to a frame homomorphism $v : Fr(E) \to 2$. This corresponds to a valuation on $Fr(E)$ in which the elements $e \in E$ with $v(e) = \mathsf{T}$ are given the value "true", all other elements of E are valued "false" and meet and join are interpreted as AND and OR. We shall identify a function $v : E \to 2$ with the characteristic function of the subset $\{e \in E \mid v(E) = \mathsf{T}\}$ so that statements like $v \subseteq w$ have an obvious meaning. If $S \subseteq E$ then v_S will denote the corresponding valuation. We have a pairing

$$v(f) = \begin{cases} \mathsf{T} \\ \mathsf{F}. \end{cases}$$

between subsets $v \in 2^E$ and formulae $f \in Fr(E)$. This is what we expect from the principle of irrelevance of history as discussed in §2.2.

Lemma 3.1 *For any $f \in Fr(E)$, $\theta(f) = \{v \in Fin(E) \mid v(f) = \mathsf{T}\}$.*

Proof: Let $\theta_1 : Fr(E) \to Fin(E)\uparrow$ be defined by $\theta_1(f) = \{v \in Fin(E) \mid v(f) = \mathsf{T}\}$. Since the frame operations in $Fin(E)\uparrow$ are set theoretic, it is easy to check that $\theta_1(f \wedge g) = \theta_1(f) \cap \theta_1(g)$ and $\theta_1(\bigvee_{i \in I}\{f_i\}) = \bigcup_{i \in I}\{\theta_1(f_i)\}$. Hence θ_1 is a homomorphism of frames. By the universal property of $Fr(E)$ it is sufficient to check that $\theta = \theta_1$ on elements of E. For $e \in E$, and any valuation $v : E \to 2$, $v(e) = \mathsf{T}$ if, and only if, $e \in v$. That is, if, and only if, $v \in \{e\}\uparrow$. It follows that $\theta(e) = \{e\}\uparrow = \{v \in Fin(E) \mid v(e) = \mathsf{T}\} = \theta_1(e)$. Hence $\theta = \theta_1$ and the result follows.

QED

The Lemma shows immediately that the principle of finite causes, §2.3, is obeyed. It appears that $Fr(E)$ is a good candidate for $\mathcal{L}(E)$. However, as it stands, a table of the form $\rho : E \to Fr(E)$ would be incapable of representing the trace set $\{\varepsilon, a, b\}$. Indeed, when E is finite, such tables are exactly the {AND, OR} automata of [3] which represent only the confluent trace sets, [3, Proposition 3.1]. This brings us to the major problem of a causal logic: dealing with choice or conflict. (We will return to the question of expressibility of the logic later in this section.)

It seems clear that conflict is related logically to negation. If we attempt to incorporate negation into geometric logic we move inexorably towards a full Boolean algebra. Of course, frames have a negation anyway, the pseudocomplement of the corresponding complete Heyting algebra, [5, §I.1.11], [12, §3.10]. As one might expect, this has quite the wrong interpretation in the model theory: the pseudocomplement of an upwards closed subset is always empty. The correct interpretation comes from looking at both the upward and downward closed subsets of $Fin(E)$, corresponding to formulae in $Fr(E)$ and their "negations". The smallest topology containing both $Fin(E)\uparrow$ and $Fin(E)\downarrow$ is evidently the discrete topology on $Fin(E)$: the complete Boolean algebra $2^{Fin(E)}$. In the finite case this is free; in the infinite case we know that it cannot be, as pointed out earlier. It is not at all clear how $2^{Fin(E)}$ can be presented algebraically.

In this paper we shall sidestep this problem by dealing with choice in the operational semantics of the table formalism rather than within the logic of causality. This trick is entirely contrary to the spirit of the present paper but is justified because of the insight it gives into event structures. Because of the general acceptance of event structures as a formalism for dealing with concurrency, [11, 10, 14], and their importance as a link to the domain theory of Scott, [2, 8, 13], we feel that a causal interpretation of them is interesting enough to defer a purely logical treatment of conflict.

Definition 3.2 *A geometric automaton, G, is a triple, (E, ρ, σ) where E is a set of events and $\rho, \sigma : E \to Fr(E)$ are a pair of functions from E to the free frame generated by E.*

We will sometimes use subscripts, E_G, ρ_G, σ_G to avoid confusion. E is the carrier of G and ρ and σ are, respectively, the positive and negative causality functions. Conflict arises from the tension between them as the following operational semantics makes clear. Recall that for any set E, $v_\emptyset$ is the all-false valuation: $v_\emptyset(e) = \mathsf{F}$ for all $e \in E$.

Definition 3.3 *Let $G = (E, \rho, \sigma)$ be a geometric automaton. The event $e \in E$ is said to be enabled in G if $v_\emptyset(\rho(e)) = \mathsf{T}$ and $v_\emptyset(\sigma(e)) = \mathsf{F}$.*

Note that, by Proposition 3.1 and Lemma 3.1, $v_\emptyset(f) = \mathsf{T}$ if, and only if, $f = \mathsf{T}$.

Definition 3.4 *The automaton* $G = (E, \rho, \sigma)$ *offers the event* e *and evolves into the automaton* $G' = (E', \rho', \sigma')$, *denoted in the usual way by* $G \xrightarrow{e} G'$, *if, and only if, the following conditions hold:* (1) e *is enabled in* G; (2) $E' = E - \{e\}$; (3) $\rho' = \rho[\mathsf{T}/e]$; (4) $\sigma' = \sigma[\mathsf{T}/e]$.

The use of $v_\emptyset$ corresponds to setting each of the generators in E to F; informally, no event has yet been offered. Those events which can be offered are the enabled ones: those for which the positive causality is "on", T, and the negative causality is "off", F. When e is offered, we substitute for this generator the value T, as in condition 3 above, and a new automaton emerges.

An example may help to make the semantics less abstract. Consider the automaton G shown below, where the positive causality is written in the first column of the table and the negative causality in the last column.

$$G = \boxed{\begin{array}{ccc} \mathsf{T} & a & \mathsf{F} \\ \mathsf{T} & b & \mathsf{F} \\ a \vee b & c & a \wedge b \end{array}}$$

According to Definition 3.3, the only enabled events are a and b. If a is offered, the automaton evolves into

$$H = \boxed{\begin{array}{ccc} \mathsf{T} & b & \mathsf{F} \\ \mathsf{T} & c & b \end{array}}$$

since $\mathsf{T} \vee b = \mathsf{T}$ and $\mathsf{T} \wedge b = b$. The event c has now become enabled. If c is offered, then we evolve to the automaton

$$K = \boxed{\begin{array}{ccc} \mathsf{T} & b & \mathsf{F} \end{array}}$$

which can then proceed to offer b. On the other hand, if H had offered b instead of c, we would evolve to the automaton

$$L = \boxed{\begin{array}{ccc} \mathsf{T} & c & \mathsf{T} \end{array}}$$

in which c is no longer enabled. The automaton L is dead and can offer no events. The behaviour of G if it offers b to begin with is symmetrical. The traces of G are seen to be $\{\varepsilon, a, b, ac, bc, ab, ba, acb, bca\}$.

An automaton H is said to be derived from G if there are a sequence of automata $G_1, \cdots, G_n$, where $n \geq 1$, such that,

$$G = G_1 \xrightarrow{e_1} G_2 \xrightarrow{e_2} \cdots \xrightarrow{e_{n-1}} G_n = H.$$

The set of derived automata of G is denoted $Der(G)$. Note that $G \in Der(G)$, corresponding to the case $n = 1$, when $G = H$. $Der(G)$ forms a labelled transition system, $\mathsf{LTS}(G)$, under the operational semantics defined above:

$$\mathsf{LTS}(G) = (Der(G), E_G, \xrightarrow{e}),$$

where $\xrightarrow{e} \subseteq Der(G) \times E_G \times Der(G)$. The string $e_1 e_2 \cdots e_{n-1} \in (E_G)^{*p}$ is referred to as a trace of G. The empty string, ε, corresponds to the case $n = 1$. The set of traces is denoted $traces(G)$; it is clearly a pure trace set as defined in §2.1. Since we have carefully avoided history relevance, the following result is hardly surprising.

Lemma 3.2 *If G is a geometric automaton then traces(G) is a pure transitive trace set.*

However, not all such trace sets arise in this way. It is not hard to show that the following pure transitive trace set $\{\varepsilon, a, c, ab, cd, abc, cda, abcd, cdab\}$ cannot be the traces of any geometric automaton. Hence geometric logic, despite the trick of negative causality, is not as expressive of causal behaviour as we would ideally like. In this respect we mention without proof that any finite pure transitive trace set is the traces of some causal automaton (ie: where full Boolean logic is used). This draws our attention once again to problem of the structure of $2^{Fin(E)}$ when E is infinite.

An alternative discussion of the operational semantics of geometric automata may be found in [4]. It is equivalent to the one given above but recasts the behaviour in terms of the concepts of "observation" and "state". It is, in some ways, a more attractive treatment but it is unsuited to discussing event structures and we have chosen not to adopt it here.

This completes the introductory material on geometric automata. Before embarking on the next section it will be convenient to record a lemma which we will need later. Suppose that $e \in E$ and $F = E - \{e\}$. If $c \subseteq Fin(E)$ let $r_e(c)$ be defined by

$$r_e(c) = \{S \in Fin(F) \mid \text{either } S \in c, \text{ or, } S \cup \{e\} \in c\}.$$

It is easy to check that if c is upward closed then so is $r_e(c)$ so that we have a function $r_e : Fin(E)\uparrow \to Fin(F)\uparrow$. Note that r_e also preserves downward closed subsets.

Lemma 3.3 *r_e is a homomorphism of frames. Furthermore, the diagram below commutes*

$$\begin{array}{ccc} Fin(E)\uparrow & \xleftarrow{\theta_E} & Fr(E) \\ \downarrow r_e & & \downarrow [\mathsf{T}/e] \\ Fin(F)\uparrow & \xleftarrow{\theta_F} & Fr(F). \end{array}$$

Proof: The frame operations in $Fin(E)\uparrow$ and $Fin(F)\uparrow$ are set theoretic and it is easy to check that $r_e(c \cap d) = r_e(c) \cap r_e(d)$ and $r_e(\bigcup_{i\in I}\{c_i\}) = \bigcup_{i\in I}\{r_e(c_i)\}$, where $c, d, c_i \in Fin(E)\uparrow$.

The function $[\mathsf{T}/e] : Fr(E) \to Fr(F)$ is also a homomorphism of frames: it is the lifting to $Fr(E)$ of the function $E \to Fr(F)$ which is the identity on $x \neq e$ and takes e to T. Hence it is sufficient, by the universal property of $Fr(E)$, to check the commutativity of the diagram on the elements $x \in E$. If $x \neq e$ then $\theta_F(x[\mathsf{T}/e]) = \theta_F(x) = \{x\}\uparrow^F = r_e(\{x\}\uparrow^E) = r_e(\theta_E(x))$. (We have used superscripts to indicate in which set the upward closure is taking place.) If $x = e$, then $\theta_F(e[\mathsf{T}/e]) = \theta_F(\mathsf{T}) = \emptyset\uparrow^F = r_e(\{e\}\uparrow^E) = r_e(\theta_E(e))$.

QED

4 Event Structures

In this section we show how an event structure can be interpreted as a special type of geometric automaton. We recall the definition of an event structure from [14, §1.1.1].

Definition 4.1 *An event structure, S, is a triple $S = (E, Con, \vdash)$ where (1) E is a set of events; (2) $Con \subseteq Fin(E)$, the consistency predicate, satisfies: if $v \in Con$ and $w \subseteq v$ then $w \in Con$; (3) $\vdash \subseteq Fin(E) \times E$, the enabling relation, satisfies: if $v \vdash e$ and $v \subseteq w$ then $w \vdash e$.*

(We use subscripts, E_S, Con_S, $\vdash_S$, where necessary, to avoid confusion.)

We have made one alteration to Winskel's original definition. The enabling relation, $\vdash$, is taken to lie in $Fin(E) \times E$ rather than $Con \times E$. In effect, if $v \in Con$ and $v \vdash e$, then we adjoin to the enabling relation in $Con \times E$ any $w \in Fin(E)$, such that $v \subseteq w$. This cannot create any new enablings of e from among the consistent subsets because of 4.1(3). The reader can easily check that this change makes no difference to the configurations of the event structure. Note that 4.1(2) merely states that Con is downward closed and 4.1(3), because of the change made above, states that $\{v \in Fin(E) \mid v \vdash e\}$ is upward closed for all $e \in E$.

Winskel's definition of the behaviour of an event structure is in terms of its configurations, [14, §1.1.2]. The configurations form a Scott domain, $\mathcal{D}(E)$, under inclusion of subsets. The behaviour of a geometric automaton, however, is expressed in terms of a labelled transition system. We need common ground in order to compare the two formalisms and so we present a transition system semantics for event structures. We then explain how the domain of configurations can be recovered from it.

Definition 4.2 *Let $S = (E, Con, \vdash)$ be an event structure. The event $e \in E$ is said to be enabled in S if $\emptyset \vdash e$ and $\{e\} \in Con$.*

Definition 4.3 *The event structure $S = (E, Con, \vdash)$ offers the event e and evolves into the event structure $S' = (E', Con', \vdash')$, denoted $S \xrightarrow{e} S'$, if, and only if, the following conditions hold: (1) e is enabled in S; (2) $E' = E - \{e\}$; (3) $Con' = r_e(Con)$; (4) $\forall x \in E'$, $\{v \in Fin(E') \mid v \vdash' x\} = r_e(\{w \in Fin(E) \mid w \vdash x\})$.*

Since r_e preserves upward or downward closed subsets of $Fin(E)$, as discussed in §3, this definition does indeed yield an event structure. In a similar way to geometric automata, we get a set of derived event structures, $Der(S)$, a labelled transition system, $\mathsf{LTS}(S) = (Der(S), E_S, \xrightarrow{e})$, and a set of traces, $traces(S)$.

Lemma 4.1 *If S is an event structure then $traces(S)$ is a pure transitive trace set.*

If S is an event structure and $s \in traces(S)$ then s gives rise to a (finite) subset of E_S, $[s]$, by simply forgetting the ordering of symbols in the trace. If $s, t \in traces(S)$ are permutations of each other then clearly $[s] = [t]$. Hence $[-]$ is a function from $traces(S)/\sim$ to $Fin(E_S)$. The configurations of an event structure are also subsets of E_S. Let $\mathcal{D}_0(E_S)$ denote the partial order of finite (compact) elements, [14, §1.1.15], of $\mathcal{D}(E_S)$. We know that the finite elements are exactly the finite configurations, [14, Theorem 1.1.16], and so $\mathcal{D}_0(E_S) \subseteq Fin(E_S)$ and inherits the partial order coming from inclusion of subsets.

Proposition 4.1 *If S is an event structure then $[-]$ induces an isomorphism of partial orders*

$$[-] : (traces(S)/\sim, \preceq) \to \mathcal{D}_0(E_S).$$

This makes it clear how the labelled transition system semantics defined above relates to Winskel's semantics in terms of configurations. Since $\mathcal{D}(E_S)$ is an algebraic directed complete partial order, [14, Theorem 1.1.6], we can recover the full domain from its finite elements by ideal completion, [12, Proposition 9.1.4]. This construction of the domain of configurations appears to be new although it seems implicit in [10, Theorem 5.1]. It has little to recommend it, in so far as event structures are concerned, because it is unnecessarily complicated and fails to give the infinite configurations. Its proper significance is only revealed in the context of geometric automata.

Definition 4.4 *If $S = (E, Con, \vdash)$ is an event structure, define the geometric automaton $\Delta(S) = G$ where:* (1) $E_G = E$; (2) $\rho_G(e) = \theta^{-1}(\{v \in Fin(E) \mid v \vdash e\})$; (3) $\sigma_G(e) = (\theta^{-1}(\overline{Con}))[\mathsf{T}/e]$.

(Here, $\overline{Con}$ denotes the complement of Con in $Fin(E)$. Evidently, $\overline{Con}$ is upwards closed.)

Event structures, as originally formulated by Winskel, have a topological character. Geometric automata are a reformulation in algebraic terms in keeping with the transition from topological data (sets of points) to algebraic structures (lattices of open subsets) which is fundamental to locale theory, [6]. Proposition 3.1 is the key to making this work as the definition above shows. The trick of using positive and negative causality for geometric automata is already implicit in the definition of event structures. Of course, we still have to show that the behaviour of an event structure S is the same as that of $\Delta(S)$. This is accomplished in the following lemmas.

Lemma 4.2 *If S is an event structure then e is enabled in S if, and only if, e is enabled in $\Delta(S)$.*

Proof: Let $S = (E, Con, \vdash)$ and $\Delta(S) = (E, \rho, \sigma)$ and abbreviate "if, and only if," to iff. By Definitions 4.4(2) and 4.1(3), $\emptyset \vdash e$ iff $\theta(\rho(e)) = \emptyset\uparrow$. That is, by Lemma 3.1, iff $v_\emptyset(\rho(e)) = \mathsf{T}$.

Now let $F = E - \{e\}$. By Lemma 3.3 $(\theta_E^{-1}(\overline{Con}))[\mathsf{T}/e] = \theta_F^{-1}(r_e(\overline{Con}))$. Now $\{e\} \in Con$ iff $\{e\} \notin \overline{Con}$ iff $r_e(\overline{Con}) \neq \emptyset\uparrow$. Hence, by Definition 4.4(3) and Lemma 3.1, $\{e\} \in Con$ iff $v_\emptyset(\sigma(e)) = \mathsf{F}$.

The result now follows from Definitions 3.3 and 4.2.

QED

Lemma 4.3 *If S is an event structure and $S \xrightarrow{e} T$ then $\Delta(S) \xrightarrow{e} \Delta(T)$. Conversely, if G is a geometric automaton of the form $G = \Delta(S)$ and $G \xrightarrow{e} H$, then $H = \Delta(T)$ and $S \xrightarrow{e} T$.*

We can now put together the main result of this paper.

Theorem 4.1 *Δ gives a bijective correspondence between event structures and geometric automata, G, with the property that $\exists f \in Fr(E_G)$ such that $\forall e \in E_G$, $\sigma_G(e) = f[\mathsf{T}/e]$. Furthermore, for an event structure $S = (E, Con, \vdash)$, Δ induces an isomorphism of transition systems labelled over E between* $\mathsf{LTS}(S)$ *and* $\mathsf{LTS}(\Delta(S))$.

Proof: If $G = (E, \rho, \sigma)$ is an automaton of the appropriate form, let $\Lambda(G) = (E, Con, \vdash)$ be defined by $Con = \overline{\theta(f)}$, where $f \in Fr(E)$ is the element in the statement of the theorem, and $\vdash = \{(v, e) \in$

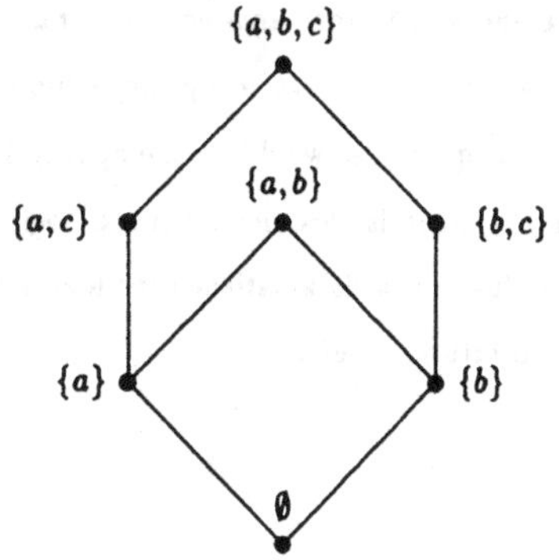

Figure 3: Domain of configurations

$Fin(E) \times E \mid v \in \theta(\rho(e))\}$. It now follows from Proposition 3.1 that $\Delta(\Lambda(G)) = G$ and, for an event structure S, that $\Lambda(\Delta(S)) = S$. This proves the first part. The second part follows easily from Lemma 4.3.

QED

The result shows that event structures are a special case of geometric automata: those with "constant" negative causality. With this in place we now have an obvious way to generalise Winskel's domain of configurations. If X is a poset, $Idl(X)$ denotes its ideal completion in the sense of [12, Definition 9.1.1].

Definition 4.5 *If G is a geometric automaton, its domain of configurations, denoted $\wp(G)$, is defined by $\wp(G) = Idl(traces(G)/\sim, \preceq)$.*

If follows from Proposition 4.1 that for an event structure S, $\wp(\Delta(S)) \cong \mathcal{D}(S)$. In an event structure the partial order on configurations comes from inclusion of subsets. For geometric automata this is no longer the case: a configuration may be properly contained in another one but the automaton may not be able to evolve from the smaller state to the larger. The inclusion ordering does not reflect the behaviour of the automaton. The correct partial order is that inherited from the prefix ordering on traces. For example, the automaton G discussed in §3 has the domain shown in Figure 3. We see that the configuration $\{a, b\}$ cannot evolve into $\{a, b, c\}$.

This example is also interesting because the domain of configurations is not consistently complete: the configurations $\{a\}$ and $\{b\}$ have an upper bound but no least upper bound. This shows that geometric automata give rise to more general domains than those coming from event structures, which Droste refers to as event domains, [2].

5 Conclusion

The main thrust of this paper has been the importance of studying causality from a logical standpoint. We have shown that the (first) crucial problem in this study is the logical treatment of conflict or choice. The solution adopted here enables us to give a simple interpretation of Winskel's general event structures but it cannot be considered as a complete and satisfactory answer in general.

The other interesting direction for further work is to drop the assumption of irrelevance of history. In this respect, our use of locales suggests that quantales would be the appropriate algebraic framework for history sensitive causality. The corresponding logic is (geometric) linear logic. Perhaps Girard's deconstruction of negation may also provide some clues towards a satisfactory logical treatment of conflict. We hope to address some of these speculations in future papers.

Acknowledgements

The work outlined here was undertaken as part of project CERES at Hewlett-Packard's Research Laboratory in Bristol, England. I am grateful to an anonymous ICALP referee of an earlier paper for pointing out the importance of infinitary OR. Martin Hyland raised the possibility of using logics other than Boolean logic. These clues were the starting point of the present study. Peter Johnstone kindly rescued me from my own stupidity and set me straight on the proof of Proposition 3.1, for which I am most grateful. My thanks also to the referees of the present paper for pointing out some errors and for their comments on presentation.

References

[1] S. Abramsky. Domain theory in logical form. *Annals of Pure and Applied Logic*, 1989.

[2] M. Droste. Event structures and domains. *Theoretical Computer Science*, 68:37–47, 1989.

[3] J. Gunawardena. Causal Automata I: Confluence $\equiv \{AND, OR\}$-Causality. In M. Z. Kwiatkowska, M. W. Shields, and R. M. Thomas, editors, *Semantics for Concurrency*, pages 137–156. Springer Workshops in Computing, 1990. To appear in TCS.

[4] J. Gunawardena. Eventless structures? (extended abstract). In *Third Workshop on Concurrency and Compositionality*, Goslar, March 1991.

[5] P. T. Johnstone. *Stone Spaces*, volume 3 of *Studies in Advanced Mathematics*. Cambridge University Press, 1982.

[6] P. T. Johnstone. The point of pointless topology". *Bulletin American Mathematical Society*, 8(1):41–53, 1983.

[7] R. Milner. *Communication and Concurrency*. International Series in Computer Science. Prentice-Hall, 1989.

[8] M. Nielsen, G. Plotkin, and G. Winskel. Petri nets, event structures and domains. *Theoretical Computer Science*, 13:85–108, 1981.

[9] M. Smyth. Powerdomains and predicate transformers: a topological view. In J. Diaz, editor, *Automata, Languages and Programming*. Springer LNCS 154, 1983.

[10] P. S. Thiagarajan. Some behavioural aspects of net theory. In T. Lepistö and A. Salomaa, editors, *Automata, Languages and Programming*. Springer LNCS 317, 1988.

[11] R. van Glabbeek and U. Goltz. Equivalence notions for concurrent systems and refinement of actions. Arbeitspapiere 366, GMD, February 1989.

[12] S. Vickers. *Topology via Logic*, volume 5 of *Cambridge Tracts in Theoretical Computer Science*. Cambridge University Press, 1989.

[13] G. Winskel. *Events in Computation*. PhD thesis, University of Edinburgh, 1980.

[14] G. Winskel. Event structures. In W. Brauer, W. Reisig, and G. Rozenberg, editors, *Advances in Petri Nets*. Springer LNCS 255, 1987.

Extended Horn Clauses: the Framework and some Semantics[1]

Jean-Marie Jacquet[2] and Luís Monteiro[3]

Abstract

The purpose of this paper is twofold: to introduce a new extension of concurrent logic programming languages aiming at handling synchronicity and to present and compare several semantics for it. The extended framework essentially rests on an extension of Horn clauses, including multiple atoms in their heads and a guard construct, as well as a new operator between goals. The semantics discussed consist of four semantics. They range in the operational, declarative and denotational types and are issued both from the logic programming tradition and the imperative tradition. They are composed of an operational semantics, describing the (classical) success set and failure set, of two declarative semantics, extending the Herbrand interpretation and the immediate consequence operator to the extended framework, and of a denotational semantics, defined compositionally and on the basis of histories possibly involving hypothetical statements. The mathematical tools mainly used are complete lattices and complete metric spaces.

1 Introduction

So-called or-parallelism and and-parallelism are the two main ways of introducing parallel executions in logic programming. Basically, the former consists of reducing an atom by using all unifiable clauses in parallel and by reducing concurrently the induced instances of the clause bodies. The latter consists of reducing a conjunction of atoms by reducing all atoms in parallel. In that framework, communication between concurrent reductions is achieved by means of the sharing of variables between several conjoined atoms. It is often further ruled by suspension mechanisms that force the reduction of some subgoals to wait until the reduction of other subgoals has sufficiently instantiated the shared variables. Examples of such mechanisms are Concurrent Prolog read-only annotations ([20]), Parlog mode declarations ([12]) and GHC suspension rules ([21]). As pointed out in [7], a form of asynchronous communication results. In most classical logic programming languages (e.g. Concurrent Prolog, Parlog, GHC, cc languages ([19]), ...), there is however no other means to tackle synchronous communication than that of coding it by means of auxiliary manager procedures and of asynchronous communication. This paper investigates a way of introducing synchronous communication directly. For that purpose, Horn clauses are extended in so-called extended Horn clauses and the SLD-resolution principle is extended accordingly. The aim of this paper is to sketch the resulting framework as well as to present and compare various semantics for it.

As a snapshot, the extended Horn clauses take the form

$$H_1 \diamond \cdots \diamond H_m \leftarrow G \mid G_1 \diamond \cdots \diamond G_m$$

where $H_1, \ldots, H_m$ are atoms and $G, G_1, \ldots, G_m$ are conjunctions of atoms combined with the operators " ; ", " $\|$ " and " & ". All atoms may share variables. Compared with classical Horn clauses, the main innovations are thus

i) the presence of multiple atoms in the head of a clause,
ii) the presence of a special goal G,
iii) the possibility to combine atoms with several operators to form goals.

---

[1] Part of this work was carried out in the context of ESPRIT Basic Research Action (3020) Integration.
[2] Centre for Mathematics and Computer Science, P.O. Box 4079, 1009 AB Amsterdam, The Netherlands
[3] Departamento de Informática, Universidade Nova de Lisboa, 2825 Monte da Caparica, Portugal

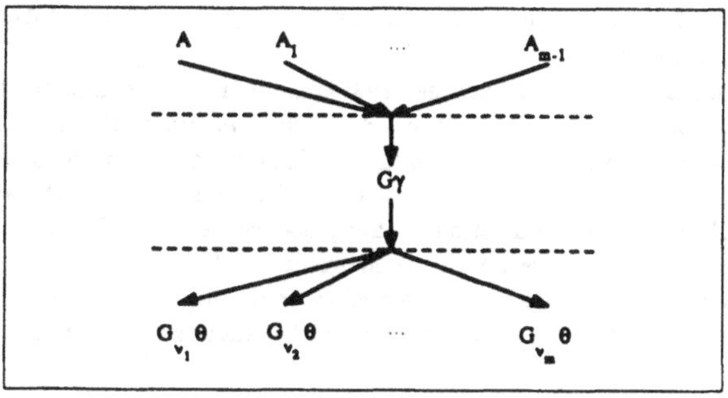

Figure 1: Synchronized reductions with extended Horn clauses

Particularly notice that the number of head atoms H_i equals the number of conjunctions G_i.

These extensions induce an extension of the SLD-resolution rule. Basically, the conjunction G acts as an additional test to the usual unification one: in order to use a clause for reduction, the instantiation of its G part by the corresponding mgu should in fact be completely reduced and this in isolation i.e. independently of concurrent processes.

The operators " ; " and " || " are used for sequential and parallel compositions, respectively. The operators " & " and " $\diamond$ " are employed, in a dual way, to specify synchronization. The operator " & " acts at the goal level and forces the reduction of conjuncts to be performed simultaneously. In a dual manner, the operator " $\diamond$ " acts at the clause level and forces the reduction of an atom A to wait for the presence of other (concurrent) atoms $A_1, \ldots, A_{m-1}$ such that the m-tuple $< A, A_1, \cdots, A_{m-1} >$ unifies with one permutation of the m-tuple $< H_1, \cdots, H_m >$, say $< H_{\nu_1}, \cdots, H_{\nu_m} >$. In that case, assuming the induced instance of G can be reduced successfully, say with the computed answer substitution θ, all atoms are simultaneously reduced to the instances by θ of the corresponding G_{ν_i}'s. This is schematized in figure 1.

Actually, the reduction possibilities are even richer in that it is allowed to group several clauses, previously renamed to avoid variable clashes, say

$$(L_1 \diamond \cdots \diamond L_p \leftarrow A \mid S_1 \diamond \cdots \diamond S_p), \cdots, (M_1 \diamond \cdots \diamond M_q \leftarrow B \mid T_1 \diamond \cdots \diamond T_q),$$

to form a clause

$$L_1 \diamond \cdots \diamond L_p \diamond \cdots \diamond M_1 \diamond \cdots \diamond M_q \leftarrow (A \parallel \cdots \parallel B) \mid S_1 \diamond \cdots \diamond S_p \diamond \cdots \diamond T_1 \diamond \cdots \diamond T_q$$

to consider in the same right as the one above.

Though simple, this extension to the classical logic programming framework is quite suited for handling synchronicity in logic programming. This fact is advocated in section 2. It is also shown that, as a side effect, extended Horn clauses provide a nice way of describing communication between objects and, hence, constitutes a means towards the integration of logic programming and object-oriented programming.

This paper also describes several semantics of extended Horn clauses, precisely of the concurrent language induced by the and-parallelism, the or-parallelism and the above operators. Four semantics are presented. They are composed of one operational semantics O_d, two declarative semantics, $Decl_m$ and $Decl_f$, and one denotational semantics Den. The three first ones take place in the logic programming tradition. The latter is issued from the imperative tradition, especially from its metric branch.

The operational semantics O_d rests on a derivation relation. It describes the derivations in a top-down manner and associates a computed answer substitution with each of them. It thus corresponds to the classical success set and failure set characterizations of programs.

The two declarative semantics $Decl_m$ and $Decl_f$ are based on model and fixed-point theory, respectively. They generalize the notions of Herbrand interpretation and consequence operator for classical Horn clause logic in order to take into account the conjoined dependency of the truth of formulae. As suggested, an effort has been made to keep these semantics as simple as possible as well as in the main streams of logic programming semantics. However, extended Horn clauses and synchronized executions raise new problems, for which fresh solutions are proposed.

The denotational semantics Den, defined as usual compositionally, completes the previous semantics by describing the behavior of compound goals in a closer way, including the modelling of parallelism just exposed, and by distinguishing various sources of failure: failure induced by the absence of suitable clauses (real failure), failure induced by infinite computations and failure induced by the absence of suitable concurrent goals that would allow synchronization to take place (suspension). In particular, the latter point is tackled by handling suitable hypotheses about the environment of goals.

Extended Horn clauses have already been presented in similar forms in [2], [3], [4], [8], [10], [16], [17] and [19]. The work reported here differs from them both from the language point of view and from the semantic point of view.

From the language point of view, our language differs in three main respects.

Firstly, it allows *arbitrary* sequential and parallel compositions inside goals as well as an unrestricted form of variable sharing. In particular, the duality of the expression of the synchronization in the goals and in the clause is peculiar to our work. In contrast with [2], we do not allow a forking primitive to take place in the body of clauses. However, this can be achieved easily in our model through or-parallelism.

Secondly, a notion of guard has been introduced; it is not present in any other work.

Thirdly, clauses always have the same number of heads and bodies. The reason for this requirement is that the reduction of a head by the corresponding body is seen as one step in the execution of the process corresponding to the head. As each process must have a continuation, even if to terminate, the continuation is represented by the corresponding body. It should be noted that this requirement, besides allowing to deal with unrestricted sequential composition, does not represent a real limitation as compared to the aforementioned languages. For example, the clauses $A_1 + A_2 \leftarrow A_3$ and $A_1 + A_2 \leftarrow A_3 + A_4 + A_5$ of Rose ([3]) may be rewritten respectively as $A_1 \diamond A_2 \leftarrow \Delta \mid A_3 \diamond \Delta$ and $A_1 \diamond A_2 \leftarrow \Delta \mid A_3 \diamond A_4 \parallel A_5$, with Δ denoting the empty conjunction of atoms.

From the semantic point of view, our work differs both from related work issued from the logic programming tradition and from the metric imperative tradition. To our best knowledge, semantics for extended Horn clauses have only been proposed in [2], [3], [10] and [16].

The semantics presented in [2] essentially refers to a new logic, called linear logic ([11]). It thus differs from our declarative and metric-based semantics.

In [3] and [10], the study of the declarative semantics is also conducted in terms of an extension of the Herbrand base containing parallel goals. Those goals, in the absence of a sequential composition operator, are parallel compositions of atomic formulae. By contrast, the extended Herbrand base appropriate to our language must consider parallel compositions of *arbitrary* goals. Another technical difference with our approach is our systematic use of t-contexts as an auxiliary tool in the definitions of both the operational and the declarative semantics. The main reason for introducing t-contexts was the need to find a concise way to specify the selection of atomic formulae in goals and their replacement by other goals. As can be appreciated from our semantic study, the use of t-contexts greatly simplifies the presentation of the semantic concepts of derivability and satisfiability. The declarative semantics presented here is also a clarified version of that presented in [16].

The operational semantics O_d differs from that of [3] and [10] by the use of the notion of t-context. It differs from [16] by the use of a semantic variant of the considered program P that allows several independent reductions to occur at the same time. The denotational semantics Den has no counterpart in [3], [10] and [16]. Although it is of classical metric inspiration, it still presents some originality with related work ([6], [5], [14], ...) which arises essentially from the two following points :

i) our concern with extended Horn clauses, which has not been done before and which requires new solutions; in particular, it should be noticed that the form of communication provided by the " $\diamond$ " and " & " operators is different from the monotonic asynchronous one of concurrent logic programming languages and from the synchronous one of CCS and CSP;
ii) our use of local states and of reconciliation to combine them.

Finally, the comparative study of semantics for extended Horn clauses issued both from the logic programming and from the imperative programming traditions is peculiar to our work.

The semantic tools mainly used in this paper are of two types: complete lattices and complete metric spaces. Despite this variety, the semantics have been related throughout the paper.

The remainder of this paper is organized into 9 sections. Section 2 suggests the interest of extended Horn clauses through the coding of various producer/consumer schemes and of several examples integrating the logic and object-oriented styles of programming. Section 3 describes the basic constructs of the language and explains our terminology. Section 4 recalls the basic semantic tools used in the paper. Section 5 introduces a semantic translation simplifying the presentation of the semantics. Section 6 defines the auxiliary concepts of t-context and program completion. Section 7 presents the operational semantics O_d. Section 8 discusses the declarative models $Decl_m$ and $Decl_f$ and connects them with the operational semantics O_d. Section 9 specifies the denotational semantics Den and compares it with the operational semantics O_d and, consequently, in view of previous results, to the other semantics. Finally, section 10 sums up the relationships established in the paper and gives our conclusions.

2 Examples

2.1 Producer-consumer schemes

As first examples of the expressiveness power of extended Horn clauses, let us code, by using them, synchronous communication in various producer/consumer schemes. Assume we are given a producer, say **prod**, and a consumer, say **cons**, behaving successively as follows:

i) execute some internal actions, say `int_prod(M,X)` and `int_cons(Y)`, respectively; the former producing some message M;
ii) communicate synchronously the message M and treat it;
iii) apply some (undefined) resumption actions, say `prod_res(M,U)` and `cons_res(M,V)`, respectively.

As can be deduced from our sketchy description of section 1, this behavior can be simulated by the evaluation of the query **prod** || **cons** for the program[4]

```
prod ← int_prod(M,X) ; pexch(M)
cons ← int_cons(Y) ; cexch(M)
pexch(M) ◇ cexch(M) ← treat(M) | prod_res(M,U) ◇ cons_red(M,V)
```

Indeed, the parallel composition " || " makes the atoms **prod** and **cons** reduce concurrently. This is achieved by means of the first and the second clauses, respectively. As a result, the two atoms are reduced to the sequential compositions `int_prod(`M_1`,`X_1`) ; pexch(`M_1`)` and `int_cons(`Y_2`) ; cexch(`M_2`)`, respectively, with M_1, M_2, X_1, Y_2 renamings of the variables M, X and Y. The reduction of the first conjunction consists of reducing `int_prod(`M_1`,`X_1`)`, which is not defined by the above program segment but is assumed to instantiate M_1, and then of reducing the induced instance of `pexch(`M_1`)`. Similarly, the reduction of the second conjunction consists of reducing `int_cons(`Y_2`)`, which is undefined here too, and then of reducing `cexch(`M_2`)`. Because of the parallel composition of **prod** and **cons**, the reductions of `int_prod(`M_1`,`X_1`)` and of `int_cons(`Y_2`)` can be performed in any order. However, because of the extended form of the third clause, the reduction of `pexch(`M_1`)` can only start in the presence of an atom `cexch(`M^*`)`, with M_1 and M^* unifiable, i.e. when the reduction of **cons** has reached the point of the reduction of `cexch(`M_2`)`. And vice-versa for the reduction of `cexch(`M_2`)` with respect to the atom `pexch(`M_1`)`. Furthermore, this synchronization in the reductions involves the common reduction of the (induced instance of) the atom `treat(M)` simulating the treatment of the message M. When this is done, and only then, the reduction of the induced instances of `prod_res(`M_3`,`U_3`)` and `cons_res(`M_3`,`V_3`)`, with M_3, U_3 and V_3 renamings of the variables M, U, V, are launched concurrently as the continuation of the reductions of `pexch(`M_1`)` and `cexch(`M_2`)`, that is of **prod** and **cons**, respectively.

The reader will appreciate the ease of coding in this example, as opposed to that obtained by using the asynchronous communication of usual concurrent logic programming languages. It is also worth noting that the synchronization between the producer and the consumer takes place from the communication of the message M to the end of the treatment of this message through `treat(M)`. As limit cases, one could think of an empty treatment of M or of empty continuations `prod_res(M)` and `cons_res(M)`. The first limit case

[4]Although any Horn clause $H \leftarrow B$ can be rewritten in an equivalent extended form $H \leftarrow \Delta \mid B$, we will stick, for the time being, to the classical Horn clause notation and reserve the extended form for clauses involving strictly more than one atom in their head.

corresponds to the situation where synchronization just acts on the communication of M. The second limit case is more in the philosophy of work such as [2], [3], [8], [10]; the synchronization then consists of the synchronous communication and the achievement of a common ending task.

One could be tempted to rewrite the above program as

```
prod ← int_prod(M,X) ; pexch(M) ; prod_res(M)
cons ← int_cons(Y) ; cexch(M) ; cons_red(M)
pexch(M) ◇ cexch(M) ← treat(M) | Δ ◇ Δ
```

and to infer therefrom that it is possible, in general, to rewrite extended Horn clauses in the format of the latter limit case. This is however not always feasible from a practical point of view, as suggested by the airline reservation system described below.

As final remarks, let us note that it is, of course, possible to refine the above basic scheme in several ways. For instance, one could add extra arguments to the predicates and complicate the definition of the predicates prod_res and cons_res at will.

2.2 Towards an integration of logic and object-oriented programming

Another interesting application of extended Horn clauses concerns the integration of logic and object-oriented programming. The behavior of objects is classically represented in logic programming by the evaluation of a call to a procedure defined recursively, the successive values of the arguments representing the successive states of the object. Following this line, the treatment of a message mess(M) by an object obj(S) by means of a method method(M) can be schematized by one of the two following clauses:

```
obj(S) ◇ mess(M) ← method(M) | obj(NewS) ◇ Δ
obj(S) ◇ mess(M) ← method(M) | obj(NewS) ◇ mess(M)     .
```

according as the message mess(M) is consumed or not. In that framework, the object conceptually moves from the state S to the new state NewS.

An instance of this scheme is given by the following description[5] of the class of stacks:

```
stack(Id,S) ◇ push(Id,X) ← Δ | stack(Id,[X|S]) ◇ Δ
stack(Id,[X|S]) ◇ pop(Id,X) ← Δ | stack(Id,S) ◇ Δ
stack(Id,[X|S]) ◇ top(Id,X) ← Δ | stack(Id,[X|S]) ◇ Δ     .
```

Stacks are identified there by the Id argument of the stack predicate and their state, implemented as a list, moves respectively from S, [X|S], [X|S] to [X|S], S, [X|S] according as a push, pop or top message is received. The treatment of these messages is quite straightforward so that all the guards are reduced to Δ. Nevertheless, it is easy to slightly complicate the problem in order to end up with more elaborated guards. For instance, one could require that the treatment of a push message includes, in addition, the check that the argument X is of some type t. In that case, the first clause of the stack procedure becomes

```
stack(Id,S) ◇ push(Id,X) ← t(X) | stack(Id,[X|S]) ◇ Δ.
```

The classical airline reservation system provides another interesting instance of the above scheme. The task consists here of simulating an airline reservation system composed of n agencies communicating with a global database about m flights. Using extended Horn clauses, this can be achieved by evaluating the query

```
agency(Id1) || ··· || agency(Idn) || airline_syst(DB_init)
```

where agency(Idj) represents the jth agency, identified by Idj, and where DB_init represents the initial information about the m flights. The exact description of the agencies is out of the scope of this paper. For our illustrative purposes, it is sufficient to assume that some internal actions successively generates queries for the database and behaves correctly according to the answers. We will consider two kinds of messages: reserve(Flight_id,Nb_seats,Ans) and ask_seats(Flight_id,Free_seats). Their goals are respectively

[5] This description has actually been inspired by that of [4].

i) to ask for the reservation of Nb_seats in the flight Flight_id, which yields the answer Ans;
ii) to ask the number of free seats in the flight Flight_id.

According to the above scheme and using the auxiliary predicates make_reservation and free_seats, with obvious meanings, the treatment of these messages can be coded as follows.

```
airline_syst(DB) ◇ reserve(Flight_id,Nb_seats,Ans) ←
    make_reservation(Flight_id,Nb_seats,DB,New_DB,Ans) | airline_syst(New_DB) ◇ Δ
airline_syst(DB) ◇ ask_seats(Flight_id,Free_seats) ←
    free_seats(Flight_id,Free_seats) | airline_syst(DB) ◇ Δ
```

The following points are worth noting. Firstly, accessing the database is achieved without explicitly handling lists of messages and without using merge processes, as usual in concurrent logic programming languages. Secondly, mutual exclusive access to the database is ensured by the synchronous mechanism. In that, our solution also contrasts with the classical concurrent logic one which involves commitment and merge processes. Finally, in opposition to the functional languages, answers are back communicated implicitly thanks to the unification mechanism and this without the use of identifiers.

2.3 More examples

Other examples, including semaphores, the seminal dining philosophers problem, generative communication in a Linda style, can be programmed with similar ease in the extended Horn clause framework. We refer the interested reader to [3], [8], [10], [16], [17], [19] for such or similar programming.

3 The language

As usual in logic programming, the extended language, subsequently referred to as *ELP*, comprises denumerably infinite sets of *variables*, *functions* and *predicates*. They are referred to as *Svar*, *Sfunct* and *Spred*, respectively. The notions of term, atom, substitution, unification, ... are defined therefrom as usual. We assume the reader to be familiar with them and will not recall them here. Rather, we now specify the extensions of goals and Horn clauses sketched in Section 1.

Definition 1

1) The extended goals *are defined inductively as follows:*

i) Δ *is an extended goal (representing the empty goal),*

ii) any atom is an extended goal,

iii) if $\overline{G}_1$ *and* $\overline{G}_2$ *are extended goals, then* $(\overline{G}_1 ; \overline{G}_2)$, $(\overline{G}_1 \parallel \overline{G}_2)$ *and* $(\overline{G}_1 \,\&\, \overline{G}_2)$ *are extended goals. Extended goals are typically denoted by the* $\overline{G}$ *letter, possibly subscripted. Their set is subsequently referred to as* Segoal.

2) The extended Horn clauses *are defined as clauses of the form*

$$H_1 \diamond \cdots \diamond H_m \leftarrow \overline{G} \mid \overline{G}_1 \diamond \cdots \diamond \overline{G}_m$$

where the H_i*'s are atoms and the* $\overline{G}$ *and* $\overline{G}_i$*'s are extended goals. By extension, these atoms and goals are still called the heads and bodies of the extended clause, respectively.*

3) The extended programs *or* programs, *for short, are sets of extended Horn clauses. Their set is subsequently referred to as* Sprog. ■

Particularly notice from the above definition that clauses are considered, from now on, in their extended form only. This is justified by uniformity purposes in subsequent treatments. As a consequence, any Horn clause $H \leftarrow B$ is now rewritten in its equivalent form $H \leftarrow \Delta \mid B$.

4 Mathematical preliminaries

4.1 Sets and multi-sets

Executions may result in computing a same answer or a same computation path several times. Multi-sets, allowing an element to be repeated, are used subsequently to capture this repetition. To clearly distinguish them from sets, they are denoted by bold brackets, as in **{**a, a, b**}**, whereas sets are denoted by simple brackets, as in $\{a, b\}$. The union symbol is kept unchanged but its use is disambiguated by the nature of its operands. To avoid any ambiguity, let us further precise that, given two multi-sets S and T, we denote by $S \cup T$ the collection of all elements of S and T repeated as many times as they occur in S and T.

The usual notations $\mathcal{P}(E)$ and $\mathcal{M}(E)$ are used to denote, respectively, the set of sets and multi-sets, with elements from E. The notations $\mathcal{P}_\pi(E)$ and $\mathcal{M}_\pi(E)$ are moreover employed to denote those sets and multi-sets verifying the property π. For instance, $\mathcal{P}_{ncl}(E)$ denotes the set of the non-empty and closed sets with elements from E.

4.2 Reconciliation of substitutions

Full use of and-parallelism requires a way of combining substitutions issued from the concurrent reductions of subgoals of an extended goal in order to form answer substitutions for the whole extended goal. It has been provided under the name of *reconciliation of substitutions* in [13] and has been extensively studied there. Concurrently, an equivalent notion, named parallel composition of substitutions, has been developed in [18]. We briefly recall this notion here for the sake of completeness. The reader is referred to the above two references for more details.

The reconciliation of substitutions is based on the interpretation of substitutions in equational terms. Precisely, any substitution $\theta = \{X_1/t_1, \ldots, X_m/t_m\}$ is associated with the system of the equations $X_1 = t_1$, $\ldots$, $X_m = t_m$, subsequently referred to as *syst(θ)*. Reconciling substitutions then consists of solving the system composed of the associated equations.

Concepts of unifiers and mgus can be defined for these systems in a straightforward way. It is furthermore possible to relate the unification of systems of equations with that of terms in such a way that all the properties of the unification of terms transpose to the unification of systems of equations. In particular, mgus of systems can be proved to be equal modulo renaming. We consequently use, in the following, the classical abuse of language and speak of *the* mgu of a unifiable system. It is referred to as *mgu_syst(S)*, where S is the system under consideration.

We are now in a position to define the notion of reconciliation of substitutions.

Definition 2 *The substitutions $\theta_1, \ldots, \theta_m$ $(m \geq 1)$ are reconcilable iff the system composed of the equations of syst(θ_1), ..., syst(θ_m) is unifiable. When so, its mgu is called the* reconciliation *of the substitutions. It is denoted by $\rho(\theta_1, \ldots, \theta_m)$.* ∎

The equational interpretation of substitutions requires, at some point, the idempotence of the substitutions. This is not a real restriction since any unifiable terms or systems of equations admit an idempotent mgu. It is furthermore to our point of view the natural one. For ease of the discussion, we will take the convention of using, from now on, idempotent substitutions only. Their set is referred to as *Ssubst*.

4.3 Complete lattices and metric spaces

Complete lattices and metric spaces will be used as important semantic tools. The reader is assumed to be familiar with them as well as with their related notions of convergent sequences, directed and closed subsets, completeness, continuous and contracting functions, ... He is also assumed to be familiar with Tarski's lemma, describing the set of prefixed points of continuous functions of complete lattices, and Banach's theorem, stating the existence of a unique fixed point of contractions in complete metric spaces. He is referred to [15] and [9], when need be. Furthermore, lack of space prevents us from describing all the metrics used in this paper. We will however employ the classical ones and refer to [5] for such a description.

5 Semantic translation

As pointed out in section 1, synchronization can be specified in two places: in goals, by means of the operator " & ", and in clauses, by means of the operator " $\diamond$ ". These two operators thus act in a dual way. It turns out, however, that it is possible to simulate the former by the latter, of a more dynamic nature. For instance, assuming that the predicates `a(X)` and `b(X)` are defined by the only two clauses

$$\texttt{a(Y)} \leftarrow \Delta \mid \texttt{r(Y)}$$
$$\texttt{b(Z)} \leftarrow \Delta \mid \texttt{s(Z)} \quad ,$$

the reduction of the conjunction a(X) & b(X) may be simulated by the reduction of $p_a(X) \parallel p_b(X)$ with p_a and p_b two new predicates defined by the only clause

$$p_a(X) \diamond p_b(X) \leftarrow \Delta \mid r(X) \diamond s(X)$$

Note that, with this device, we still have the possibility of using a(Y) and b(Z) separately.

The operator " & " is thus in some sense redundant with respect to the operator " $\diamond$ ". However, we believe that, from a language point of view, specifying synchronization in both goals and clauses is desirable and, therefore, we provide both constructs in the language. Nevertheless, this redundancy allows us to design semantics in two ways. One consists of translating the programs in the sublanguage of ELP without the operator " & " and of designing semantics for this sublanguage. The other one consists of designing semantics directly for the whole language. We have adopted here the first approach because it allows us to expose the semantics in a simpler framework - and thus in a clearer way - and because the semantics developed using the second approach can be obtained therefrom by simple extensions.

6 Auxiliary concepts

6.1 The t-contexts

Forcing atoms to synchronize introduces a need for a means to express which atoms in an extended goal are allowed to synchronize and for a means to create the goals resulting from the synchronized reductions. These means are provided by the notion of t-context. Basically, a t-context consists of a partially ordered structure where the place holder $\Box$ has been inserted in some top-level places i.e. places not constrained by the previous execution of other atoms. Atoms that can synchronize are then those that can be substituted by a place holder $\Box$ in a t-context. Furthermore, the extended goals resulting from the synchronized reductions are obtained by substituting the place holder by the corresponding bodies $\overline{G}_i$'s of the extended Horn clause used.

The precise definition of the t-contexts is as follows.

Definition 3 *The t-contexts are the functions inductively defined on the extended goals by the following rules.*

i) A nullary t-context is associated with any extended goal. It is represented by the extended goal and is defined as the constant mapping from Segoal^0 to this goal with the goal as value.

ii) $\Box$ is a unary t-context that maps any extended goal to itself. For any extended goal $\overline{G}$, this application is subsequently referred to as $\Box[\overline{G}]$.

iii) If c is an n-ary t-context and if $\overline{G}$ is an extended goal, then $(c\,;\overline{G})$ is an n-ary t-context. Its application is defined as follows : for any extended goals $\overline{G}_1, \ldots, \overline{G}_n$,

$$(c\,;\overline{G})[\overline{G}_1,\cdots,\overline{G}_n] = (c[\overline{G}_1,\cdots,\overline{G}_n]\,;\overline{G})$$

iv) If c_1 and c_2 are m-ary and n-ary t-contexts and if $n+m>0$, then $c_1 \parallel c_2$ is an (m+n)-ary t-context. Its application is defined as follows : for any extended goals $\overline{G}_1, \ldots, \overline{G}_{m+n}$,

$$(c_1 \parallel c_2)[\overline{G}_1,\cdots,\overline{G}_{m+n}] = (c_1[\overline{G}_1,\cdots,\overline{G}_m]) \parallel (c_2[\overline{G}_{m+1},\cdots,\overline{G}_{m+n}])$$

In the above rules, we further state that the structure (Segoal, ; , $\parallel$,Δ) is a bimonoid. Moreover, in the following, we will simplify the extended goals resulting from the application of t-contexts accordingly. ∎

The following points in the above definition are worth noting.

- Rule iii) forces the place holder $\Box$ to occur only in a position corresponding to atoms that can be reduced in the first reduction step of an associated extended goal.
- Rule iv) forces a composed t-context $c_1 \parallel c_2$ to include one place holder in at least one c_i although both can contain one. This corresponds to the fact that, to allow a composed goal $\overline{G}_1 \parallel \overline{G}_2$ to perform one reduction step, at least one of the conjunct $\overline{G}_i$ must perform one reduction step although both can do so simultaneously.

6.2 Program expansion

The extended clauses to consider to reduce extended goals are those obtained from the clauses of the (written) program by permuting them and by grouping them. To avoid handling this permutation and groupment explicitly, we now associate to any program P the program P^{*} that performs this task implicitly.

Definition 4 *For any program P, the* expansion *of P, denoted P^{*}, is defined as the following program:*

i) any clause of P is a clause of P^{*};

ii) if $(L_1 \diamond \cdots \diamond L_p \leftarrow \overline{A} \mid \overline{S}_1 \diamond \cdots \diamond \overline{S}_p)$ and $(M_1 \diamond \cdots \diamond M_q \leftarrow \overline{B} \mid T_1 \diamond \cdots \diamond T_q)$ are clauses of P^{*}, renamed to avoid variable clashes, then

$$L_1 \diamond \cdots \diamond L_p \diamond M_1 \diamond \cdots \diamond M_q \leftarrow (\overline{A} \parallel \overline{B}) \mid \overline{S}_1 \diamond \cdots \diamond \overline{S}_p \diamond T_1 \diamond \cdots \diamond T_q$$

is a clause of P^{*};

iii) if $(H_1 \diamond \cdots \diamond H_m \leftarrow \overline{G} \mid \overline{G}_1 \diamond \cdots \diamond \overline{G}_m)$ is a clause of P^{*} and if $(\nu_1, \ldots, \nu_m)$ is a permutation of $(1, \ldots, m)$, then $(H_{\nu_1} \diamond \cdots \diamond H_{\nu_m} \leftarrow \overline{G} \mid \overline{G}_{\nu_1} \diamond \cdots \diamond \overline{G}_{\nu_m})$ is a clause of P^{*}. ∎

7 Operational semantics

A first semantics of ELP may be expressed operationally in terms of a derivation relation, written as $P \vdash \overline{G}\ with\ \theta$ that, basically, expresses the property that, given the program P, the extended goal $\overline{G}$ has a successful derivation producing the substitution θ. It is defined by means of rules of the form

$$\frac{Assumptions}{Conclusion} \quad if\ Conditions,$$

asserting the Conclusion whenever the Assumptions and Conditions hold. Note that Assumptions and Conditions may be absent from some rules. Precisely, the derivation relation is defined as the smallest relation of *Sprog* × *Segoal* × *Ssubst* satisfying the following rules (N-I) and (E-I). As usual, the above notation is used instead of the relational one with the aim of suggestiveness.

Definition 5 (The derivation relation)

Null formula

(N-I) $$\frac{}{P \vdash \Delta\ with\ \epsilon}$$

Extended formula

(E-I) $$\frac{P \vdash \overline{G}\theta\ with\ \sigma \qquad P \vdash c[\overline{G_1}, \ldots, \overline{G_m}]\theta\sigma\ with\ \gamma}{P \vdash c[A_1, \ldots, A_m]\ with\ \theta\sigma\gamma}$$

$$\text{if} \begin{cases} (H_1 \diamond \cdots \diamond H_m \leftarrow \overline{G} \mid \overline{G_1} \diamond \cdots \diamond \overline{G_m}) \in P^{*}\ ^{6} \\ < A_1, \cdots, A_m >\ and\ < H_1, \cdots, H_m >\ unify\ with\ mgu\ \theta \end{cases}$$

∎

The derivation operational semantics can be derived therefrom as follows.

Definition 6 (The derivation operational semantics) *Define the derivation operational semantics as the following function $O_d : Sprog \rightarrow Segoal \rightarrow \mathcal{P}(Ssubst)$: for any $P \in Sprog$, $\overline{G} \in Segoal$, $O_d(P)(\overline{G}) = \{\theta : P \vdash \overline{G}\ with\ \theta\}$.* ∎

[6] As usual, a suitable renaming of the clauses is assumed.

8 The declarative semantics

One of the distinctive features of a logic programming language is that its semantics can be understood in at least two complementary ways, inherited from logic. The operational semantics, based on proof theory, describes the method for executing programs. The declarative semantics, based on model theory, explains the meaning of programs in terms of the set of their logical consequences. Any claim to the effect that a given language is a logic programming language must be substantiated by providing suitable logic-based semantic characterizations. The operational semantics of the language ELP under consideration in this paper has been studied in the previous section. The present section is devoted to the discussion of the declarative semantics.

One might at first think that the usual notion of (Herbrand) interpretation for Horn clause logic carries through to ELP. Thus an interpretation would be a set of ground atomic formulae, with the intended meaning that the formulae in the set are true under the interpretation. The truth of compound formulae would then be derived in a compositional manner. The problem with this is that the parallel composition is not a propositional operation in that its truth or falsity can not be derived from that of its arguments. More precisely, if both arguments are true then their parallel composition is also true, but if one or both are false then the parallel composition may be true or false. For example, A and B are false both for the empty program and for the program consisting of the clause $A \diamond B \leftarrow \Delta \mid \Delta \diamond \Delta$ alone. However, $A \parallel B$ is false for the first program and true for the second one.

Note that the sequential composition is not affected by a similar problem. Indeed, a sequential composition of goals is true if and only if the component goals are true, so that declaratively the sequential composition is just the logical conjunction. In any case we can not hope to be able to specify which formulae are true by giving only the true atomic formulae. We are thus led to consider an extended Herbrand base containing parallel compositions of ground extended goals, and take its subsets as our interpretations.

Definition 7 *The* extended Herbrand base *EB is the set of all ground atomic formulae A together with all parallel compositions* $\overline{G}_1 \parallel \overline{G}_2$ *of nonempty ground extended goals* $\overline{G}_1$ *and* $\overline{G}_2$. *An* interpretation *is a subset I of EB.* ∎

Definition 8 *Given a formula F, its truth in I, written* $\models_I F$, *is defined inductively by the following rules:*

i) If F is a clause or an extended goal, $\models_I F$ *if* $\models_I F_0$ *for every ground instance* F_0 *of F.*
ii) For a ground clause, $\models_I (A_1 \diamond \cdots \diamond A_n \leftarrow \overline{G} \mid \overline{G}_1 \diamond \cdots \diamond \overline{G}_n)$ *if, for every n-ary ground t-context c,* $\models_I c[A_1, \ldots, A_n]$ *whenever* $\models_I (\overline{G} \mid c[\overline{G_1}, \ldots, \overline{G_n}])$.
iii) $\models_I \Delta$.
iv) If $\overline{G}$ *and* $\overline{H}$ *are ground goals,* $\models_I (\overline{G} \,;\, \overline{H})$ *if* $\models_I \overline{G}$ *and* $\models_I \overline{H}$.
v) If $\overline{G}$ *and* $\overline{H}$ *are ground goals,* $\models_I (\overline{G} \mid \overline{H})$ *if* $\models_I \overline{G}$ *and* $\models_I \overline{H}$.
vi) If $\overline{G}$ *and* $\overline{H}$ *are ground goals,* $\models_I (\overline{G} \parallel \overline{H})$ *if* $(\overline{G} \parallel \overline{H}) \in I$ *or* $\models_I \overline{G}$ *and* $\models_I \overline{H}$.
vii) If A is a ground atomic formula, $\models_I A$ *if* $A \in I$. ∎

Definition 9 *An interpretation I is a* model *of a program P if* $\models_I C$ *for every clause* $C \in P$. *An extended goal* $\overline{G}$ *is said to be a* consequence *of P, written* $P \models \overline{G}$, *if* $\models_I \overline{G}$ *for every model I of P. The* success set *of* $\overline{G}$ *with respect to P is the set* $SS_D(\overline{G}) = \{\theta : P \models \overline{G}\theta\}$ *of all substitutions θ such that* $\overline{G}\theta$ *is a consequence of P.* ∎

We are now in a position to define the model declarative semantics.

Definition 10 (Model declarative semantics) *Define the model declarative semantics as the following function* $Decl_m : Sprog \rightarrow Segoal \rightarrow \mathcal{P}(Ssubst)$: *for any* $P \in Sprog$, $\overline{G} \in Segoal$, $Decl_m(P)(\overline{G}) = SS_D(\overline{G})$. ∎

If I and J are interpretations and F is a formula, it is easy to see by induction on the structure of F that $\models_{I \cap J} F$ if and only if $\models_I F$ and $\models_J F$. If we take for F the clauses of P, we conclude that the intersection of two models of P is again a model. This statement can obviously be generalized to the intersection of an arbitrary number of models. Since EB is a model, it follows that any program has a least model.

Proposition 11 *Every program P has a least model* M_P. ∎

The importance of M_P is that it allows to simplify the definition of success set: instead of requiring that $\overline{G}\theta$ be true in all models of P it is enough that it is true in M_P. Indeed, this is a consequence of the easy fact that if I and J are interpretations such that $I \subseteq J$ then $\models_I \overline{G}$ implies $\models_J \overline{G}$.

Proposition 12 $SS_D(\overline{G}) = \{\theta :\models_{M_P} \overline{G}\theta\}$. ∎

The least model M_P can also be characterized as the least fixed point of a continuous transformation $T_P : \mathcal{P}(EB) \rightarrow \mathcal{P}(EB)$, called as usual the *immediate consequence operator*. For every interpretation I, $T_P(I)$ is the set of all ground extended goals of the form $c[A_1, \ldots, A_n] \in EB$ such that $\models_I \overline{G}$ and $\models_I c[\overline{G_1}, \ldots, \overline{G_n}]$, for an n-ary ground t-context c and a ground instance $A_1 \diamond \cdots \diamond A_n \leftarrow \overline{G} \mid \overline{G_1} \diamond \cdots \diamond \overline{G_n}$ of a clause in $P^{\bullet}$.

Proposition 13 *The operator T_P is continuous and M_P is the least fixed point of T_P.* ∎

The *fixed-point* semantics of P associates with each $\overline{G}$ the set of all θ such that $\overline{G}\theta$ is true in the least fixed point $lfp(T_P)$ of T_P.

Definition 14 (Fixed-point declarative semantics) *Define the fixed-point declarative semantics as the following function $Decl_f : Sprog \rightarrow Segoal \rightarrow \mathcal{P}(Ssubst)$: for any $P \in Sprog$, $\overline{G} \in Segoal$, $Decl_f(P)(\overline{G}) = \{\theta :\models_{lfp(T_P)} \overline{G}\theta\}$.* ∎

Proposition 13 establishes the equivalence between the declarative and the fixed-point semantics of P.

Proposition 15 $Decl_m = Decl_f$. ∎

Finally, the equivalence between the operational and the declarative semantics can be stated as follows.

Proposition 16 *For every program P and every extended goal $\overline{G}$,*

i) if $P \vdash \overline{G}$ with θ, for some substitution θ, then $P \models \overline{G_0}$ for every ground instance $\overline{G_0}$ of $\overline{G}\theta$;
ii) if $P \models \overline{G}\tau$ for some substitution τ, then $P \vdash \overline{G}$ with θ, for some substitution θ such that $\overline{G}\tau \geq \overline{G}\theta$.

In particular, let $\alpha_1 : \mathcal{P}(Ssubst) \rightarrow \mathcal{P}(Ssubst)$ be the following function: for any $\Theta \in \mathcal{P}(Ssubst)$,

$$\alpha_1(\Theta) = \{\theta\gamma_{|S} : \theta \in \Theta, \gamma \in Ssubst, dom(\theta) \subseteq S\}$$

where $\theta\gamma_{|S}$ is the restriction of $\theta\gamma$ to the variables of S and $dom(\theta)$ denotes the domain of θ. Then, the equality

$$Decl_m(P)(\overline{G}) = Decl_f(P)(\overline{G}) = \alpha_1(O_d(P)(\overline{G}))$$

holds for any $P \in Sprog$, $\overline{G} \in Segoal$. ∎

9 The denotational semantics

This section introduces our last semantics. It is defined compositionally and makes no use of transition systems as well as no reference to any declarative paradigm. It is called denotational in view of these properties.

Compositionality of the semantics requires to determine the semantics of a compound goal in terms of the semantics of its components. However, as pointed out in section 8, this is not straightforward to realize for ELP. The problem is essentially that the failure or the suspension of a compound goal cannot be inferred directly from the failure or the suspension of its components considered individually. One way of solving this problem consists of taking into account environments composed of concurrent atoms (if any) that would unsuspend the suspended derivations of the components. To be more specific, with respect to the one clause program $A \diamond B \leftarrow \Delta \mid \Delta \diamond \Delta$ our idea is to deliver as semantics for A not failure nor a simple suspension but a suspension mark together with the derivation obtained by assuming the presence of B in concurrence with A. Giving a similar semantics for B, it is not difficult to imagine that it is possible to combine the semantics of A and of B to obtain that of $A \parallel B$. In general, the denotational semantics, to be presented subsequently, makes hypotheses about the environment of the reduction of a goal in order to unsuspend suspended derivations. Technically speaking, these hypotheses are inserted as members of the histories; they take the form $hyp[(A,\Sigma),(B,\Upsilon)]$ with the reading that given that A is composed of the atoms that can be reduced in the treated goal and given that Σ is composed of the associated substitutions in the derivation (representing the results computed sofar by the parallel components of the considered goal), the presence of concurrent atoms of B associated with the substitutions of Υ allows the considered suspended reduction to resume. As extended goals and the head of extended clauses may contain multiple occurrences of an atom, the A, B, Σ and Υ are designed as multi-sets.

The above example might lead to think that the presence of hypotheses in the histories suppress the grounds for existence of suspension marks. This is not true as shown by the program composed of the two clauses $A \diamond B \leftarrow \Delta \mid \Delta \diamond \Delta$ and $A \diamond B \diamond C \leftarrow \Delta \mid \Delta \diamond \Delta \diamond \Delta$. The hypothetical way of reasoning includes an hypothetical derivation assuming the existence of C in the semantics of $A \parallel B$. Nevertheless, despite it, the reduction of $A \parallel B$ does not suspend. Hence, any suspended reduction needs still to be associated with one reduction ending with one suspension mark. It takes the form $susp[\{(A_1,\sigma_1),\ldots,(A_m,\sigma_m)\},B]$ where the (A_i,σ_i) 's are the top-level atoms of the considered goal with their associated substitutions and where B is the set of the heads of the clauses that would allow the reduction to resume in case suitable atoms would be placed in concurrence with the treated goal.

A final technicality is involved in the denotational semantics. Treating in a compositional way a sequentially composed goal requires to be able to give the semantics of the second component of the goal in view of the results (i.e. substitutions) computed by the first component of the goal. Hence, the denotational semantics should deliver, for any given program and any given extended goal, not some set of histories but some function that maps any substitution to such a set. In order to ease the determination of the results, the termination mark in success is furthermore enriched by the set of substitutions computed during the considered derivation.

The following definition precises the concepts just introduced.

Definition 17

1) *An* hypothetical statement *is a construct of the form* $\mathrm{hyp}[(\mathrm{A},\Sigma),(\mathrm{B},\Upsilon)]$ *where A and B are multi-sets of atomic formulae and where* Σ *and* Υ *are multi-sets of substitutions. In the following, hypothetical statements are typically denoted by the* hh *symbol and their set is referred to as* Shyp.

2) *A* suspension statement *is a construct of the form* $\mathrm{susp}[\{(\mathrm{A}_1,\sigma_1),\ldots,(\mathrm{A}_m,\sigma_m)\},\mathrm{B}]$ *where the* A_i*'s are atomic formulae, the* σ_i*'s are substitutions and B is a set of multi-sets of atomic formulae. In the following, suspension statements are typically denoted by the* ss *symbol and their set is referred to as* Ssusp.

3) *Let* Sterm *be the set composed of the element* fail *and constructs of the form* $\mathrm{succ}(\Theta)$ *where* Θ *is a set of substitutions. The set of denotational histories,* Sdhist *is defined as the solution of the following recursive equation:*

$$Sdhist = Sterm \cup Ssusp \cup (Ssubst \times Sdhist) \cup (Shyp \times Ssubst \times Sdhist) \times Sdhist$$

(see [6] or [1] for the resolution of this equation). Histories are thus streams written as $(e_1,(e_2,(e_3,\cdots)))$ *thanks to the cartesian products. They are often rewritten in the simpler form* $e_1.e_2.e_3.\cdots$ *to avoid the intricate use of brackets. However, the structure of hypotheses followed by substitutions followed by guard evaluations will be conserved and written as triplets.*

Histories are typically denoted by the h *letter. Histories of the form* $< hh,\theta,g > .h$ *with* $hh \in Shyp$, $\theta \in Ssubst$ *and* $g,h \in Shist$ *are subsequently called* hypothetical histories. *Histories containing no hypothetical statement are called real histories. Their set is referred to as* Srhist. *Histories containing no suspension statements are called* unsuspended histories. *Their set is referred to as* Suhist.

4) *A set of histories S is coherent iff for any suspended history of S of the form*

$$hp.susp[\{(A_1,\sigma_1),\cdots,(A_m,\sigma_m)\},C]$$

there is in S an history of the form $hp. < hyp[(A,\Sigma),(B,\Gamma)],\theta,g > .hs$ *such that* $A = \{A_{\nu_1},\cdots,A_{\nu_p}\}$ *and* $\Sigma = \{\sigma_{\nu_1},\cdots,\sigma_{\nu_p}\}$, *for some subsequence* $(\nu_1,\cdots,\nu_p)$ *of* $(1,\cdots,m)$.

5) *The semantic domain* Sem *is defined as the (complete metric) space* $\mathcal{P}_{ncl}(Sdhist)$ *of non-empty, coherent and closed subsets of Sdhist.* ■

Semantic counterparts for the operators " ; " and " | " can be defined quite directly. The recursive nature of streams might suggest recursive definitions. However, their possible infinite nature makes direct definitions incorrectly stated. This problem is circumvented by using a higher-order function Ψ_{seq} of the same recursive nature but that turns out to be a well-defined contraction.

Definition 18 *Define the operator* $\Psi_{seq} : [(Sdhist \times (Ssubst \rightarrow Sem)) \rightarrow Sem] \rightarrow [(Sdhist \times (Ssubst \rightarrow Sem)) \rightarrow Sem]$ *as follows : for any* $F \in [(Sdhist \times (Ssubst \rightarrow Sem)) \rightarrow Sem]$, $f \in (Ssubst \rightarrow Sem)$, $\Theta \subseteq Ssubst$, $ss \in Ssusp$, $e \in \mathcal{M}(Ssubst) \cup Shyp$, $h \in Shist$,

i) $\Psi_{seq}(F)(fail, f) = \{fail\}$

ii) $\Psi_{seq}(F)(succ(\Theta), f) = \begin{cases} f(\theta) & \text{if } \Theta \text{ is reconcilable with reconciliation } \theta \\ \{fail\} & \text{otherwise} \end{cases}$

iii) $\Psi_{seq}(F)(ss, f) = \{ss\}$

iv) $\Psi_{seq}(F)(e.h, f) = \{e.h^* : h^* \in F(h, f)\}$. ∎

Proposition 19 *The function* Ψ_{seq} *is well-defined and is a contraction.* ∎

Definition 20

1) *Define the operator* $\widetilde{;}_{str} : (Sdhist \times (Ssubst \rightarrow Sem)) \rightarrow Sem$ *as the fixed point of* Ψ_{seq}.

2) *Define the operator* $\widetilde{;} : ((Ssubst \rightarrow Sem) \times (Ssubst \rightarrow Sem)) \rightarrow (Ssubst \rightarrow Sem)$ *as follows: for any* $f_1 : (Ssubst \rightarrow Sem)$, $f_2 : (Ssubst \rightarrow Sem)$ *and for any* $\sigma \in Ssubst$,

$$(f_1 \,\widetilde{;}\, f_2)(\sigma) = \{h : h_1 \in f_1(\sigma), h \in h_1 \,\widetilde{;}_{str}\, f_2\}$$

∎

Definition 21 *The counterpart of the operator "*$\widetilde{;}_{str}$*" on* $Sdhist \times Sdhist \rightarrow Sdhist$ *is defined similarly to definitions 18 and 20 and is denoted by "*$\widetilde{\odot}$*"* ∎

The operator " | " has the sequential nature of the operator " ; " but further constraints its left-hand side argument to be evaluated on its own. This latter feature is semantically modeled by preventing the argument evaluation to make hypotheses about its (non-existing) environment and by prohibiting suspended executions (of this evaluation) to be resumed thanks to the environment. Technically speaking, these two points are respectively achieved by eliminating hypothetical histories from the denotational semantics of the argument and by emptying the second argument of suspension marks of histories of this semantics. These are essentially the goals attached to the following function *guard*. For ease of subsequent use, it is defined at the level of functions of $Ssubst \rightarrow \mathcal{P}(Sdhist)$ rather than at the level of sets of $\mathcal{P}(Sdhist)$.

Definition 22 *Define the function* $guard : [Ssubst \rightarrow \mathcal{P}(Sdhist)] \rightarrow [Ssubst \rightarrow \mathcal{P}(Sdhist)]$ *as follows: for any* $f \in [Ssubst \rightarrow \mathcal{P}(Sdhist)]$, *any* $\sigma \in Ssubst$,

$$guard(f)(\sigma) = (f(\sigma) \cap Srhist \cap Suhist) \cup \{h.susp(\mathbf{A}, \emptyset) : h.susp(\mathbf{A}, B) \in f(\sigma)\}.$$

∎

It is possible to prove that the function guard conserves the non-empty, closed and coherent features of the elements of Sem. The operator " $\widetilde{|}$ " can thus be defined in terms of the operator " $\widetilde{;}$ " and the function guard.

Definition 23 *Define* $\widetilde{|} : ((Ssubst \rightarrow Sem) \times (Ssubst \rightarrow Sem)) \rightarrow (Ssubst \rightarrow Sem)$ *as follows: for any* $f_1, f_2 \in (Ssubst \rightarrow Sem)$, $f_1 \,\widetilde{|}\, f_2 = guard(f_1) \,\widetilde{;}\, f_2$. ∎

The construction of hypothetical histories requires an operator like the " | " operator but that conserves the marks of the guards. It is defined as the following operator " ⇒ ".

Definition 24 *Define the function* $\Rightarrow : (Shyp \times Ssubst \times (Ssubst \rightarrow Sem) \times (Ssubst \rightarrow Sem)) \rightarrow (Ssubst \rightarrow Sem)$ *as follows: for any* $hh \in Shyp$, $f_1, f_2 : (Ssubst \rightarrow Sem)$, $\sigma, \theta \in Ssubst$,

$$\begin{aligned}(f_1 \Rightarrow_{hh,\theta} f_2)(\sigma) = \; & \{< hh, \theta, g > .fail : g \in guard(f_1)(\sigma), g \text{ is infinite}\} \\ & \cup \{< hh, \theta, g.ss > .fail : g.ss \in guard(f_1)(\sigma)\} \\ & \cup \{< hh, \theta, g.fail > .fail : g.fail \in guard(f_1)(\sigma)\} \\ & \cup \{< hh, \theta, g.succ(\Omega) > .h : g.succ(\Omega) \in guard(f_1)(\sigma), \\ & \qquad \Omega \text{ is reconcilable with reconciliation } \omega, h \in f_2(\omega)\} \\ & \cup \{< hh, \theta, g.succ(\Omega) > .fail : g.succ(\Omega) \in guard(f_1)(\sigma), \\ & \qquad \Omega \text{ is not reconcilable}\}\end{aligned}$$

∎

In order to define the semantic counterpart " $\widetilde{\|}$ " of the parallel composition operator, let us first introduce two auxiliary operators. The first one, the operator " $\widehat{\|}_{susp}$ " determines how the ending suspension marks of derivations should be combined in parallel.

Definition 25 *Define the auxiliary operator* $\widehat{\|}_{susp}$ *on suspension statements as follows.*

$$susp[T_1, S_1] \ \widehat{\|}_{susp} \ susp[T_2, S_2] = \begin{cases} \emptyset & \text{if } C \text{ holds} \\ \{susp[T_1 \cup T_2, S_1 \cup S_2]\} & \text{otherwise} \end{cases}$$

where C *stands for the following condition : there is* $\{(A_1, \sigma_1), \ldots, (A_m, \sigma_m)\} \subseteq T_1$, $m > 0$, $\{(B_1, \tau_1), \ldots, (B_n, \tau_n)\} \subseteq T_2$, $n > 0$ *and* $\{H_1, \ldots, H_{m+n}\} \in S_1 \cap S_2$ *such that* $\{\sigma_1, \ldots, \sigma_m, \tau_1, \ldots, \tau_n\}$ *is reconcilable, say with reconciliation* θ, *and such that* $< A_1, \ldots, A_m, B_1, \ldots, B_n > \theta$ *and* $< H_1, \ldots, H_{m+n} >$ *are unifiable* ∎

The other auxiliary operator " $\widehat{\|}_{syhyp}$ " specifies how hypothetical histories should be combined in a synchronized parallel fashion.

Definition 26 *Define the operator* $\widehat{\|}_{syhyp}$ *on hypothetical histories and functions of* $(Sdhist \times Sdhist \rightarrow Sem)$ *as follows:*

$$< hyp[(A, \Sigma), (B, \Gamma)], \theta_1, g_1 > .h_1 \ \widehat{\|}^F_{syhyp} \ < hyp[(C, \Upsilon), (D, \Psi)], \theta_2, g_2 > .h_2$$
$$= \begin{cases} \{< hyp[(V, \Omega), (W, \Phi)], \theta_1, g_1 > .h : Desc\} & \text{if } Cond_1 \text{ and } Cond_2 \text{ holds} \\ \{\theta_1 . g_1 \odot h\} & \text{if } Cond_1 \text{ holds and } Cond_2 \text{ does not hold} \\ \emptyset & \text{otherwise} \end{cases}$$

where $Cond_1$, $Cond_2$ *and* $Desc$ *stand for the following conditions:*

- $Cond_1$: *i)* $\theta_1 = \theta_2$ *ii)* $g_1 = g_2$ *iii)* $A \subseteq D$ *iv)* $\Sigma \subseteq \Psi$ *v)* $C \subseteq B$ *vi)* $\Upsilon \subseteq \Gamma$ *vii)* $A \cup B = C \cup D$ *viii)* $\Sigma \cup \Gamma = \Upsilon \cup \Psi$
- $Cond_2$: *i)* $B \backslash C \neq \emptyset$ *ii)* $\Gamma \backslash \Upsilon \neq \emptyset$
- $Desc$: *i)* $V = A \cup C$ *ii)* $\Omega = \Sigma \cup \Upsilon$ *iii)* $W = B \backslash C$ *iv)* $\Phi = \Gamma \backslash \Upsilon$ *v)* $h \in F(h_1, h_2)$ ∎

We are now in a position to define the semantic counterpart " $\widetilde{\|}$ " of the operator " $\|$ ". As before, a suitable operator is used to provide a correct recursive definition. It is defined on histories rather than on sets of histories for the ease of the presentation.

Definition 27 *Define the function* $\Psi_{para} : (Sdhist \times Sdhist \rightarrow \mathcal{P}_{cl}(Sdhist)) \rightarrow (Sdhist \times Sdhist \rightarrow \mathcal{P}_{cl}(Sdhist))$ *as follows : for any* $F \in (Sdhist \times Sdhist \rightarrow \mathcal{P}_{cl}(Sdhist))$, *for any* $g, g_1, g_2, h, h_1, h_2 \in Sdhist$, $ss, ss_1, ss_2 \in Ssusp$, $hh, hh_1, hh_2 \in Shyp$, $\theta, \theta_1, \theta_2 \in Ssubst$, $\Theta, \Theta_1, \Theta_2 \subseteq Ssubst$,

i) $\Psi_{para}(F)(fail, h) = \Psi_{para}(F)(h, fail) = \{fail\} \cup \{\theta.h^* : \theta.h_r \in h, h^* \in F(fail, h_r)\}$
$\qquad \cup \{< hh, \theta, g > .h^* : < hh, \theta, g > .h_r \in h, h^* \in F(fail, h_r)\}$

ii) $\Psi_{para}(F)(succ(\Theta_1), succ(\Theta_2)) = \{succ(\Theta_1 \cup \Theta_2)\}$

iii) $\Psi_{para}(F)(succ(\Theta), ss) = \Psi_{para}(F)(ss, succ(\Theta)) = \{ss\}$

iv) $\Psi_{para}(F)(succ(\Theta_1), \theta_2.h) = \Psi_{para}(F)(\theta_2.h, succ(\Theta_1)) = \{\theta_2.h^* : h^* \in F(succ(\Theta_1), h)\}$

v) $\Psi_{para}(F)(succ(\Theta), < hh, \theta, g > .h) = \Psi_{para}(F)(< hh, \theta, g > .h, succ(\Theta))$
$\qquad = \{< hh, \theta, g > .h^* : h^* \in F(succ(\Theta), h)\}$

vi) $\Psi_{para}(F)(ss_1, ss_2) = ss_1 \ \widehat{\|}_{susp} \ ss_2$

vii) $\Psi_{para}(F)(ss, \theta.h) = \Psi_{para}(F)(\theta.h, ss) = \{\theta.h^* : h^* \in F(ss, h)\}$

viii) $\Psi_{para}(F)(ss, < hh, \theta, g > .h) = \Psi_{para}(F)(< hh, \theta, g > .h, ss) = \{< hh, \theta, g > .h^* : h^* \in F(ss, h)\}$

ix) $\Psi_{para}(F)(< hh_1, \theta_1, g_1 > .h_1, < hh_2, \theta_2, g_2 > .h_2) = < hh_1, \theta_1, g_1 > .h_1 \ \widehat{\|}^F_{syhyp} \ < hh_2, \theta_2, g_2 > .h_2$
$\qquad \cup \ \{< hh_1, \theta_1, g_1 > .h^* : h^* \in F(h_1, < hh_2, \theta_2, g_2 > .h_2\}$
$\qquad \cup \ \{< hh_2, \theta_2, g_2 > .h^* : h^* \in F(< hh_1, \theta_1, g_1 > .h_1, h_2\}$

x) $\Psi_{para}(F)(< hh_1, \theta_1, g_1 > .h_1, \theta_2.h_2) = \Psi_{para}(F)(\theta_2.h_2, < hh_1, \theta_1, g_1 > .h_1)$
$\qquad = \{\theta_2.h : h \in F(< hh_1, \theta_1, g_1 > .h_1, h_2)\} \cup \{< hh_1, \theta_1, g_1 > .h : h \in F(h_1, \theta_2.h_2)\}$

xi) $\Psi_{para}(F)(\theta_1.h_1, \theta_2.h_2) = \{\theta_1.h : h \in F(h_1, \theta_2.h_2)\} \cup \{\theta_2.h : h \in F(\theta_1.h_1, h_2)\}$

∎

Proposition 28 *The function Ψ_{para} is a contraction.* ∎

Definition 29

1) *Define the operator* $\widehat{\|}_{str}$: $Sdhist \times Sdhist \rightarrow \mathcal{P}_{cl}(Sdhist)$ *as the unique fixed point of the contraction* Ψ_{para}

2) *Define the operator* $\widetilde{\|}$: $((Ssubst \rightarrow Sem) \times (Ssubst \rightarrow Sem)) \rightarrow (Ssubst \rightarrow Sem)$ *as follows: for any* $f_1, f_2 \in (Ssubst \rightarrow Sem)$ *and any* $\sigma \in Ssubst$,

$$(f_1 \,\widetilde{\|}\, f_2)(\sigma) = \bigcup\{h_1 \,\widehat{\|}_{str}\, h_2 : h_1 \in f_1(\sigma), h_2 \in f_2(\sigma)\}$$

∎

Given the semantical counterparts "$\widetilde{\|}$", "$\widetilde{;}$" and "$\widetilde{|}$" of the operators "$\|$", "$;$" and "$|$", defining the denotational semantics essentially consists of defining the semantics for the basic constructs, namely the empty goal and the extended goals composed of one atom. The semantics of the former goal is quite obvious: success is returned together with the empty substitution ϵ. The semantics of a goal of the latter form, say A placed in the context of the substitution σ, is of a fourthfold nature: it contains

i) derivations started by any clause $(H \leftarrow \overline{G} \mid \overline{B})$ that unifies with $A\sigma$; the corresponding histories are composed of the mgu θ of the corresponding unification (precisely, the set formed of this mgu) followed by the histories of the semantics of $\overline{G} \mid \overline{B}$ in the state $\sigma\theta$;
ii) hypothetical histories for any extended Horn clause C and any multiset of atoms and substitutions that put in concurrence with the goal would allow C to be used; they are composed of the corresponding hypothetical statement followed by the mgu θ corresponding to the unification with the treated clause, an history of the guard evaluation and one execution of the corresponding body part of C
iii) a suspension mark for such extended Horn clauses, if any;
iv) a fail mark in case none of the previous histories can be delivered in the semantics

As before, a suitable higher-order contraction is used to tackle recursivity adequately.

Definition 30 *Define the operator* Ψ_{den} : $[Sprog \rightarrow Segoal \rightarrow Ssubst \rightarrow Sem] \rightarrow [Sprog \rightarrow Segoal \rightarrow Ssubst \rightarrow Sem]$ *as follows : for any* F : $[Sprog \rightarrow Segoal \rightarrow Ssubst \rightarrow Sem]$, *any* $P \in Sprog$, *any* $\sigma \in Ssubst$, *any atom* A, *any* $\overline{G}_1, \overline{G}_2 \in Segoal$,

i) $\Psi_{den}(F)(P)(A)(\sigma) =$
$\{\, \theta.F(P)(\overline{G} \mid \overline{B})(\sigma\theta) : (H \leftarrow \overline{G} \mid \overline{B}) \in P, A\sigma \text{ and } H \text{ unify with mgu } \theta \,\}$
$\cup \bigcup\{[\, \Psi_{den}(F)(P)(\overline{G}) \Rightarrow_{hh,\tau\theta} F(P)(\overline{G}_1)](\tau\theta) : \; Cond_h \,\}$
$\cup \{\, susp[\{(A,\sigma)\}, C] : \; Cond_s \,\}$
$\cup \{\, fail : \; Cond_f \,\}$

ii) $\Psi_{den}(F)(P)(\Delta)(\sigma) = \{succ(\{\sigma\})\}$

iii) $\Psi_{den}(F)(P)(\overline{G}_1 \| \overline{G}_2)(\sigma) = [\, \Psi_{den}(F)(P)(\overline{G}_1) \,\widetilde{\|}\, \Psi_{den}(F)(P)(\overline{G}_2)](\sigma)$

iv) $\Psi_{den}(F)(P)(\overline{G}_1 \,;\, \overline{G}_2)(\sigma) = [\, \Psi_{den}(F)(P)(\overline{G}_1) \,\widetilde{;}\, F(P)(\overline{G}_2)](\sigma)$

v) $\Psi_{den}(F)(P)(\overline{G}_1 \mid \overline{G}_2)(\sigma) = [\, \Psi_{den}(F)(P)(\overline{G}_1) \,\widetilde{|}\, F(P)(\overline{G}_2)](\sigma)$

where $Cond_h$, $Cond_s$ *and* $Cond_f$ *stand for the following conditions*[7]

- $Cond_h$:
  i) $\{\sigma\} \cup \Theta$ *reconcile with reconciliation* τ,
  ii) $(H_1 \diamond \cdots \diamond H_{n+1} \leftarrow \overline{G} \mid \overline{G}_1 \diamond \cdots \diamond \overline{G}_{n+1}) \in P^*$,
  iii) $< A, B_1, \cdots, B_n > \tau$ *and* $< H_1, \cdots, H_{n+1} >$ *unify with mgu* θ
  iv) $n \geq 1$
  v) $hh = hyp[(\{A\}, \{\sigma\}), (\{B_1, \ldots, B_n\}, \Theta)]$
- $Cond_s$:
  i) there are $B_1, \ldots, B_n$ *with* $n \geq 1$ *and a clause* $(H_1 \diamond \cdots \diamond H_{n+1} \leftarrow \overline{G} \mid \overline{G}_1 \diamond \cdots \diamond \overline{G}_{n+1}) \in P^*$, *such that* $< A, B_1, \cdots, B_n > \sigma$ *and* $< H_1, \cdots, H_{n+1} >$ *unify*
  ii) C is the set of the multisets of the atoms of the heads of all such general Horn clauses
  iii) $A\sigma$ *unifies with no clause of* P^*
- $Cond_f$:
  For any clause $(H_1 \diamond \cdots \diamond H_{n+1} \leftarrow \overline{G} \mid \overline{G}_1 \diamond \cdots \diamond \overline{G}_{n+1}) \in P^*$, *and any* $B_1, \ldots, B_n$, $n \geq 0$, $< A, B_1, \cdots, B_n > \sigma$ *and* $< H_1, \cdots, H_{n+1} >$ *do not unify.*

∎

[7] As usual, a suitable renaming of the clauses is assumed.

Proposition 31 *The function* Ψ_{den} *is well-defined and is a contraction.* ∎

Definition 32 *Define the denotational semantics* $Den : [Sprog \rightarrow Segoal \rightarrow Ssubst \rightarrow Sem]$ *as the unique fixed point of* Ψ_{den} ∎

We conclude this section by relating the semantics Den and O_d. Obviously, Den contains more information than O_d so that relating them consists of finding a function α_2 such that $\alpha_2 \circ Den = O_d$. The appropriate function α_2 operates essentially by retaining the non-hypothetical and successful histories from Den and by delivering, for each of them, the substitution computed by it, if any. Its precise definition is as follows.

Definition 33 *Define the function* $\alpha_2 : \mathcal{P}(Sdhist) \rightarrow \mathcal{P}(Sdhist)$ *as follows: for any* $S \in \mathcal{P}(Sdhist)$,

$$\alpha_2(S) = \{\rho(\Theta) : h.succ(\Theta) \in S \cap Srhist, \Theta \text{ is reconcilable}\}$$ ∎

Proposition 34 *The function* $\alpha_2 \hat{\circ} Den : Sprog \rightarrow Segoal \rightarrow \mathcal{P}(Ssubst)$ *defined as*

$$(\alpha_2 \hat{\circ} Den)(P)(\overline{G}) = \alpha[Den(P)(\overline{G})(\epsilon)],$$

for any program P and extended goal $\overline{G}$, *equals* O_d. ∎

10 Conclusion

The paper has presented an extension of the Horn clause framework as well as four semantics for the extended framework, ranging in the operational, declarative and denotational types. Three of these semantics are inspired by the traditional logic programming paradigm. They consist of the operational semantics O_d, based on the derivation relation $\vdash$, and of the declarative semantics $Decl_m$ and $Decl_f$, based on model theory and fixed-point theory, respectively. The other semantics, namely the denotational semantics Den, is issued from the imperative tradition, and, more particularly, from its metric semantic branch ([6], [5], [14], ...). It describes computations, in a compositional way, via histories, possibly including hypotheses.

All these semantics have been related throughout the paper, thanks to propositions, 15, 16 and 34. The minimal relations have only been stated. From them, it is possible to deduce other relations, for instance to connect Den with $Decl_m$ and $Decl_f$. It is furthermore impossible to add nonredundant relations. For instance, it is impossible to guess the infinite derivations contained in Den in view of the only computed substitutions of O_d. It is also impossible to guess the substitutions computed in O_d from all substitutions pointed out declaratively in $Decl_m$ or $Decl_f$. However, it is worth noting that although they are associated with different semantics, it is possible to connect the derivation relation $\vdash$ and the model theory, as established by proposition 16.

The ELP language introduced in this paper provides a suitable mechanism to introduce synchronicity in concurrent logic programming and to combine, to some extend, logic programming and object-oriented programming. Our future research, under development, will be concerned with more elaborated versions, including, for instance, more object-oriented constructs. Also, we are trying to develop semantics closer to real computations in treating and-parallelism in a non-interleaving way and or-parallelism not just as non-deterministic choice.

Acknowledgments

The research reported herein has been partially supported by Esprit BRA 3020 (Integration). The first author likes to thank the members of the C.W.I. concurrency group, J.W. de Bakker, F. de Boer, F. van Breugel, A. de Bruin, E. Horita, P. Knijnenburg, J. Kok, E. Marchiori, C. Palamidessi, J. Rutten, D. Turi, E. de Vink and J. Warmerdam, for their weekly intensive discussions. The second author wish to thank the Instituto Nacional de Investigação Científica and the Junta Nacional de Investigação Científica e Tecnológica for partial support.

References

[1] P. America and J.J.M.M. Rutten. Solving reflexive domain equations in a category of complete metric spaces. *Journal of Computer and System Sciences*, 39(3):343–375, 1989.

[2] J.-M. Andreoli and R. Pareschi. Linear Objects: Logical Processes with Built-in Inheritance. In D.H.D. Warren and P. Szeredi, editors, *Proc. 7th Int. Conf. on Logic Programming*, pages 495–510, Jerusalem, Israel, 1990. The MIT Press.

[3] A. Brogi. And-Parallelism without Shared Variables. In D.H.D. Warren and P. Szeredi, editors, *Proc. 7th Int. Conf. on Logic Programming*, pages 306–321, Jerusalem, Israel, 1990. The MIT Press.

[4] J.S. Conery. Logical Objects. In R.A. Kowalski and K.A. Bowen, editors, *Proc. 5th Int. Conf. and Symp. on Logic Programming*, pages 420–434, Seattle, USA, 1988. The MIT Press.

[5] J.W. de Bakker. Comparative Semantics for Flow of Control in Logic Programming without Logic. Technical Report CS-R8840, Centre for Mathematics and Computer Science (CWI), Amsterdam, The Netherlands, 1988.

[6] J.W. de Bakker and J.I. Zucker. Processes and the Denotational Semantics of Concurrency. *Information and Control*, 54:70–120, 1982.

[7] F.S. de Boer and C. Palamidessi. On the Asynchronous Nature of Communication in Concurrent Logic Languages: a Fully Abstract Model based on Sequences. In J.C.M. Baeten and J.W. Klop, editors, *Proc. of Concur 90*, volume 458 of *Lecture Notes in Computer Science*, pages 99–114, Amsterdam, The Netherlands, 1990. Springer-Verlag.

[8] P. Degano and S. Diomedi. A First Order Semantics of a Connective Suitable to Express Concurrency. In *Proc. 2nd Workshop on Logic Programming*, pages 506–517, Albufeira, Portugal, 1983.

[9] R. Engelking. *General Topology*. Heldermann Verlag, 1989.

[10] M. Falaschi, G. Levi, and C. Palamidessi. A Synchronization Logic: Axiomatics and Formal Semantics of Generalized Horn Clauses. *Information and Control*, 60:36–69, 1984.

[11] J.Y. Girard. Linear Logic. *Theoretical Computer Science*, 50:1–102, 1987.

[12] S. Gregory. *Design, Application and Implementation of a Parallel Logic Programming Language*. PhD thesis, Department of Computing, Imperial College, London, Great-Britain, 1985.

[13] J.-M. Jacquet. *Conclog: a Methodological Approach to Concurrent Logic Programming*. PhD thesis, Facultés Universitaires Notre-Dame de la Paix, University of Namur, Belgium, 1989. to appear as Lecture Notes in Computer Science, Springer-Verlag.

[14] J.N. Kok and J.J.M.M. Rutten. Contractions in Comparing Concurrency Semantics. *Theoretical Computer Science*, 76:179–222, 1990.

[15] J.W. Lloyd. *Foundations of logic programming*. Springer-Verlag, second edition, 1987.

[16] L. Monteiro. An Extension to Horn Clause Logic allowing the Definition of Concurrent Processes. In *Proc. Formalization of Programming Concepts*, volume 107 of *Lecture Notes in Computer Science*, pages 401–407. Springer-Verlag, 1981.

[17] L. Monteiro. A Horn Clause-like Logic for Specifying Concurrency. In *Proc. 1st Int. Conf. on Logic Programming*, pages 1–8, 1982.

[18] C. Palamidessi. Algebraic Properties of Idempotent Substitutions. In M.S. Paterson, editor, *Proc. of the 17th International Colloquium on Automata, Languages and Programming*, volume 443 of *Lecture Notes in Computer Science*, pages 386–399, Warwick, England, 1990. Springer-Verlag.

[19] V.A. Saraswat. *Concurrent Constraint Programming Languages*. PhD thesis, Carnegie-Mellon University, 1989. To be published by The MIT Press.

[20] E.Y. Shapiro. A Subset of Concurrent Prolog and its Interpreter. Technical Report TR-003, Institute for New Generation Computer Technology (ICOT), Tokyo, 1983.

[21] K. Ueda. *Guarded Horn Clauses*. PhD thesis, Faculty of Engineering, University of Tokyo, Tokyo, Japan, 1986.

Action Systems and Action Refinement in the Development of Parallel Systems

An Algebraic Approach

Wil Janssen, Mannes Poel, & Job Zwiers

University of Twente,
Dep. of Computer Science
P.O. Box 217,
7500 AE Enschede,
The Netherlands
E-mail:{janssenw,infpoel,zwiers}@cs.utwente.nl

Abstract

A new notion of refinement and several other new operators are proposed that allow for a compositional algebraic characterization of action systems and serializability in distributed database systems. A simple design language is introduced and is provided with a semantics essentially based on partial order models.
Various algebraic transformation rules are introduced. They are applied in the design process of a simple system, starting from a specification of functional behaviour via the intermediate step in the form of a "true concurrency" based initial design to an actual implementation on a two processor architecture.

1 Introduction

Two different trends can be observed in recent developments around the specification, verification and design of parallel systems:

One school of thought derives from the *compositionality principle*. A basic assumption here is that complex systems are *composed* out of smaller parts. The compositionality principle requires that a *specification* of some composed system can be derived from *specifications* of the constituent parts, i.e. without knowledge of the internal (syntactic) structure of those parts. An essential requirement for a compositional or modular approach is that a system has a suitable *algebraic* structure, which forms the basis for the analysis of that system.

A second school of thought rejects the algebraic compositional style, claiming that a system should be regarded rather as a collection of (guarded) actions, without any apparent algebraic structure. Such *action systems* as they are called are used by for instance Chandy and Misra [CM] and by Back [Back]. The rationale in the book by Chandy and Misra [CM] is that the algebraic syntactic structure of programming languages is too close to the actual architectures of (parallel) machines and that this aspect should not influence the (initial) design of systems. Questioning of the usefulness of the syntactic structure for analysis and design of parallel systems is also present in the work on *communication closed layers* by Elrad and Francez [EF], and related work on the verification of distributed protocols by Gallager, Humblet and Spira [GHS], and Stomp and de Roever [SR]. Although the *physical* structure of a distributed protocol has the form of a parallel composition of sequential programs, the *logical* structure of a protocol can often be described as a sequential composition of a number of parallel *layers* corresponding to the different phases of the protocol, which does not fit in the syntactic program structure as indicated. A third example of noncompositional reasoning can be found in *serializability theory* as described in the literature on distributed databases ([BHG]).

The main contribution of this paper is that we show how action systems and communication closed layers and concurrent database transactions can be designed and analyzed *in an algebraic, compositional framework*. This is accomplished by introducing a *new notion of refinement of actions* in a model of parallelism strongly related to *partial orders of events*, namely *directed acyclic graphs*. The relationship between refinement and an operation called *conflict composition* is clarified. The latter operation can be seen as a syntactic means to describe "layers" as in [EF] et al. It is a weak form of sequential composition, with nicer algebraic properties however, allowing for useful *transformation rules* for parallel systems. We envisage the role of operations such as conflict composition as being an adequate language for what software engineers call the *initial design stage* of a system. Such operations allow one to make the step from specifications of observable behaviour to *algorithms*, without premature commitment to any particular system architecture. The latter should be taken into account only in the stages following the initial design. The transformation of an initial design employing operations specifying what is called "true concurrency" to an implementation on a given architecture, with for instance a fixed number of processors, is a highly interesting, but largely unsolved problem. [CM][Hooman] We bring together the various techniques in an example where we design a parallel program for calculating binomial coefficients. We show the initial design from a specification of the required functional behaviour, resulting in a maximal parallel solution, followed by transformation to a system suited for a limited number of processors. The example employs a specialization of our algebraic language tailored to a shared variables model. At certain transformation stages we combine algebraic laws with state-based reasoning.

After the short sketch above of the contents of the paper we would like to discuss refinement and related operations in some more detail.

Partial order based descriptions of concurrent systems and refinement of atomic actions in partial orders have been studied extensively [Pratt] [DNM] [NEL] [GG] [Pomello]. We start from such partial order models but impose some extra structure in the form of *conflicts*[1] between events. Conflicting events in a single run cannot occur simultaneously, they have to be ordered. Our notion of conflict is an abstraction of conflicts between transactions in distributed database systems, where transactions are said to be in conflict if they access some common database item. In essence such a notion of conflict occurs also in [Pratt] where it is called colocation of events. The rationale for introducing conflicts is that it allows for the formulation of an interesting notion of *refinement of actions*. Our refinement notion differs from action refinement as e.g. in [GG] in that the refinement of action a inherits only those causal relationships which are imposed by conflicts on the concrete (refined) level (fig. 1). For action refinement as in [GG] an action, say b, in the refinement of some higher level action a inherits *all* ordering relations from that a action.

This minimization of causal relationships allows one to model *serializable* executions of distributed database transactions $P_0, P_1, \cdots, P_n$, ([BHG]) as a refinement of executions of atomic actions $T_0, \cdots, T_n$ thus:

$$\mathbf{ref}\ T_0 = P_0, T_1 = P_1, \cdots, T_n = P_n\ \mathbf{in}$$

$$T_0 \parallel T_1 \parallel \cdots \parallel T_n$$

On the abstract level one sees sequential executions of the form $T_{i_0} ; T_{i_1} ; \cdots ; T_{i_n}$, where $\{i_1, \ldots, i_n\}$ is some permutation of $\{0, \ldots, n\}$. Refinement with inheritance of *all* causal relations would result in *serial* executions of the form

$$P_{i_0} ; \cdots ; P_{i_n}$$

Our notion of refinement however results in *serializable* executions which are of the form (using *conflict composition*) as

$$P_{i_0} \cdot P_{i_1} \cdot \cdots \cdot P_{i_n}$$

The *conflict composition* $P_1 \cdot P_2$ is defined as follows:
For computations P_1 and P_2, $P_1 \cdot P_2$ results in causally ordering only those elements between P_1

[1] Terminology differs here from what is used to describe event structure as in for instance [Winskel], where "conflicting" events cannot occur in a single run

and P_2 which are conflicting; however – unlike parallel composition – one only wants to introduce ordering from P_1 to P_2, indicating the asymmetric nature of the construct. Our notion of ***conflict composition*** is related to the notion of *D-local concatenation* in [Gaifman].

As this database example indicates, action refinement does *not* commute with sequential composition. In a general *partial order* framework, it turns out that conflict composition *does not* commute with refinement either because a problem arises with *transitivity* as we will illustrate now. Whereas on the abstract level sequential execution of atomic transactions can be dictated by conflicts, after refinement the order implied by transitivity on the abstract level is no longer justified. Take for example the transactions sketched in figure 1. On the abstract level we have a serial execution of

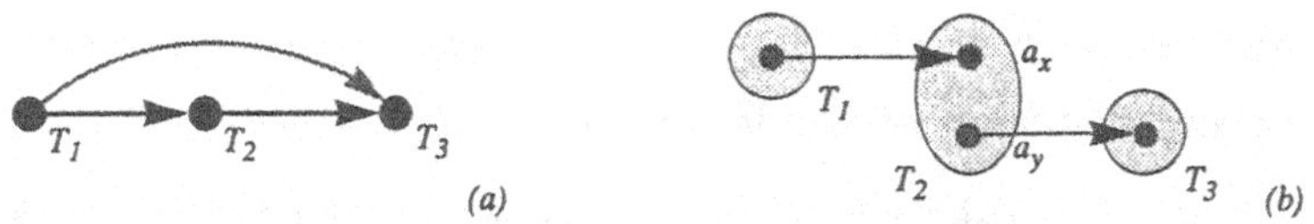

Figure 1: Refinement of database transactions

three transactions, where T_1 accesses some item x, T_2 accesses items x and y, and T_3 accesses an item y (fig. 1a). This is implemented by refining T_2 into two independent actions, accessing x and y. (fig. 1b) I.e., whereas when executing atomic actions causal order implies temporal order, after refinement this isn't necessarily the case; e.g. in the example above T_3 may very well be executed before T_1!

Our solution.to this problem is not to work with (transitive) partial orders, but with non-transitive orders, described as *directed acyclic graphs* (DAG's). For this class of models we show that action refinement has appropriate algebraic properties, such as commutativity with *sequential composition*, and the property that nested refinement is equivalent to simultaneous refinement.

We formulate algebraic laws for refinement and the different types of composition. An important paradigm in parallel program development, *"communication closed layers"* ([EF]), can now be algebraically characterized (for example in the case of two layers):

$$\text{(CCL)} \qquad (S_1 \cdot S_2) \parallel (T_1 \cdot T_2) = (S_1 \parallel T_1) \cdot (S_2 \parallel T_2)$$

provided no causal dependency between S_1 and T_2, and between S_2 and T_1 exists. The same law with conflict composition replaced by *sequential composition* does *not* hold.

For program development, algebraic equalities do not suffice. Two extra ingredients are required:

- *Reducing nondeterminism.* In accordance with this principle, $S_1 \cdot S_2$ should be a legal implementation of $S_1 \parallel S_2$, for every DAG in the semantics of $S_1 \cdot S_2$ is an element of the semantics of $S_1 \parallel S_2$.
- *Reducing the degree of parallelism.* E.g. when reducing the degree of parallelism to 1 (due to a single processor implementation), $S_1 ; S_2$ might also be seen as a legal implementation of $S_1 \parallel S_2$.

The structure of this paper is as follows: in the next section we introduce the algebraic process language, and a version of this language for shared variables based on guarded assignments and predicates that is used throughout the paper. Next we give a number of algebraic laws and implementation relations that are used in the design of a parallel algorithm to compute binomial coefficients. We also define a semantics for our language, justifying these laws and relations. We conclude with some final remarks and a discussion of possible future work.

2 A general process language

In this paper we use a process language based on a set of *actions* and the notion of *conflicts* between actions. Apart from well-known notions such as *sequential composition* and *parallel composition*, *iteration* and *choice* the language includes interesting operators like *refinement*, *atomicity* and *contraction*, and a more liberal form of sequential composition, named *conflict composition*.

This gives a language that allows us to express algebraic properties as well as programming constructs found in current programming languages. We also give an interpretation of the abstract actions and the conflict relation based on shared variables, with guarded assignments as basic actions. We will use the shared variables interpretation as a basis for the examples in this paper. It is however also possible to give other interpretations of these abstract notions as long as there is a sensible notion of *conflicts* between actions.

We first define the abstract syntax, which we extend to shared variables and actions described by predicates. Furthermore an intuition for the operators is given.

2.1 Syntax and intuition of the language

Assume we have a class of *actions* $\mathcal{A}ct$, with typical element a. We assume a symmetric relation *conflict* on actions.
It should be set at the outset that our *conflict* relation abstracts from the notion of conflicts between transactions in distributed databases, where conflicts are generated by accesses to some common database item. So, conflicting actions *can* occur in a single "run" of a system, but in that case they must be *causally ordered*.

The syntax of the language is the following:

$S \in \mathcal{P}rocess$

$$S ::= a \mid \textbf{empty} \mid \textbf{skip} \mid S_0 \parallel S_1 \mid S_0 \cdot S_1 \mid S_0 \,;\, S_1 \mid S_0 \textbf{ or } S_1 \mid S^{\odot} \mid S^{*} \mid \textbf{aug}(S) \mid \langle S \rangle \mid \textbf{contr}(S) \mid \textbf{ref } a = S_0 \textbf{ in } S_1$$

Most of the operators have an intuitively simple meaning. The most important operators are the three composition operators: *parallel composition* $S_0 \parallel S_1$, *conflict composition* $S_0 \cdot S_1$ and *sequential composition* $S_0 ; S_1$. In a sequential composition $S_0 ; S_1$ all actions in S_0 precede all actions in S_1. Conflict composition is a more liberal form of sequential composition where only *conflicting* actions are ordered. The iterated versions of conflict composition and sequential composition are denoted by $S^{\odot}$ and S^{*} respectively.
The **skip** statement acts as a unit element for all three types of composition, e.g.:

$$S_0 \parallel \textbf{skip} = \textbf{skip} \parallel S_0 = S_0$$

The process **empty** is the unit element for non-deterministic choice (**or**).

We also included a few non standard processes. The process $\langle S \rangle$ denotes execution of S where no interfering actions from other processes are allowed. The means that no action from some other process T may be "in between" two actions from S, where "being in between" refers to *causal ordering* of actions, not to *temporal ordering*.
Contrary to atomic brackets in interleaving models of concurrency, execution of S does allow for parallel activity, provided that such an action a either:

1. does not conflict at all with S actions, i.e. a and S are independent, or
2. causally precedes some S actions, but does not *follow* any, or
3. follows some S actions, but does not precede any.

Related to the atomic processes (and to refinement) is the *contract* operator. The process **contr**(S) denotes the atomic execution of S, mapped into *a single action*. Its main purpose is to relate the functional behaviours of processes, independent of their implementation. We do not allow the **contr** operator to appear within the scope of a refinement, as contraction can "hide" the actions to be refined in a single event.

In order to be able to relate processes with respect to their ordering relation, we have the *augment* operator **aug**(S). This denotes the process in which the ordering between actions of S is arbitrarily extended.

Finally we have refinement. The **ref** construct is a form of refinement where only *necessary ordering* is included in the refinement. In a process **ref** $a = S_0$ **in** S_1 the action a is executed *atomically* in S_1. All actions in S_0 that are in conflict with actions in S_1 are ordered according to the ordering of A in S_1, but non-conflicting actions are not.

2.2 An interpretation in a shared variables model

In our examples in this paper we use a version of the abstract language based on shared variables. To define this language we have to fill in the abstract notion of actions and the notion of conflict.

The basic actions are guarded multiple assignments, and abstract — uninterpreted — actions, and first order predicate logic formulae representing actions. Assume that we have given a finite set of variables ($x \in$) Var, a class of expressions ($f \in$) Exp and a class of boolean expressions ($b \in$) $Bexp$. For every variable $x \in \mathcal{V}ar$ we also have a "hooked" variable $\overleftarrow{x}$ that can be used in formulae to denote the initial value of x. The variables occurring in expression f or boolean expression b are denoted by $var(f)$ and $var(b)$. A set set of variables is denoted by vector notation, i.e. $\bar{x} \in \mathcal{P}(\mathcal{V}ar)$. All variables and expressions are of the same type, which is assumed to be "integer" in examples. Also assume that we have given a class of process names $\mathcal{P}roc$, with typical element A. The syntax of actions is:

$a \in Act$

$a ::= b \,\&\, \bar{x} := \bar{f} \;\mid\; A \;\mid\; \textit{read}\ \bar{y}, \textit{write}\ \bar{z} : \phi(\overleftarrow{x}, x)$

The intuition of an action $b \,\&\, \bar{x} := \bar{f}$ is that the process waits until the boolean guard b evaluates to true, thereafter simultaneously assigning f_i to x_i, for each x_i in $\bar{x}$. The action is executed as a single action, i.e. atomically.
Abstract actions A are left uninterpreted, but we assume they have a (syntactically determined) base denoting the variables read and written by the action.

We can define pure guards and simple assignments as $b \,\&\, x_b := x_b$, where x_b is a variable in $var(b)$, and $true \,\&\, \bar{x} := \bar{f}$ respectively.

The notion of *conflicts* can now be based on accesses to variables. There are several possibilities of doing so. We can define conflicts to be *read–read & read–write* conflicts, which means that any two actions that access a common variable are conflicting. In the examples however we take the more liberal notion of *read–write conflicts* only, which implies that two actions are not causally related if they read some common variable, but neither of them writes it.
Let a_1 be the assignment $b_1 \,\&\, \bar{x}_1 := \bar{f}_1$ and a_2 the assignment $b_2 \,\&\, \bar{x}_2 := \bar{f}_2$. We can define the *readset* $R(a)$ and the *writeset* $W(a)$ of an assignment a in the in the normal way, e.g. $R(a_1) = var(b_1) \cup var(\bar{f}_1)$ and $W(a_1) = \bar{x}_1$. We can define conflict in terms of these read- and writesets as follows:

$$conflict(\, a_1, a_2 \,) \stackrel{\text{def}}{=} (R(a_1) \cup W(a_1)) \cap W(a_2) \neq \emptyset \ \vee \ W(a_1) \cap (R(a_2) \cup W(a_2)) \neq \emptyset$$

As actions that occur simultaneously at the beginning of a process can all read some variable x we assume that all variables are initialized to some arbitrary value that is read by all of them.

In order to be able to relate processes and specifications we include first order predicate logic formulae as actions in the language. A first order logic predicate $\textit{read}\ \bar{y}, \textit{write}\ \bar{z} : \phi(\overleftarrow{x}, x)$ specifies an action where the variables $\overleftarrow{x}$, like in VDM, denote the initial values of variables in the action and x the final value [Jones]. The sets $\bar{y}$ and $\bar{z}$ determine the base related to the action, being the variables read and written. For example, the predicate

$\textit{read}\ x, \textit{write}\ x : \forall n\ (\overleftarrow{x} = n^2 \Rightarrow x = n)$

denotes an action calculation the square root of an integer (if it exists). In fact, even guarded assignments can be expressed as predicates. We have

$$(b \,\&\, x := f) \;=\; (\mathit{read}\,(\mathit{var}(b) \cup \mathit{var}(f)),\, \mathit{write}\; x : b[\overleftarrow{x}\;/x] \wedge x = f[\overleftarrow{x}\;/x])$$

where $b[\overleftarrow{x}\;/x]$ is the boolean expression b in which every free variable x is substituted by $\overleftarrow{x}$.

3 Algebraic laws and implementation relations

In this section we discuss a number of general algebraic laws that hold for our language. The purpose of these laws is *not* to give a complete algebraic axiomatization of the language, but instead they are essential in the construction and derivation of a process from a specification.
In first subsection we state simple algebraic laws concerning associativity, commutativity, and distributivity of the operators. The validity of these laws is a result of the definition of the semantics. Afterwards we will give some relevant laws for the refinement operator. Finally the algebraic law concerning the *communication closed layers* studied by Elrad and Francez [EF] is stated.
In the second section we will also define two important relations $\subseteq$ and $\sqsubseteq$ which are closely connected with the ideas of reduction of *nondeterminism* and reduction of *parallelism*, respectively.

3.1 Algebraic laws

First we will look at some laws concerning the choice operator and parallel, sequential, and conflict composition. It should be remarked that "=" denotes semantical equality. From the semantics, which is defined in the next section, trivially follows:

Lemma 3.1
Let P, Q and R be processes.

- Associativity and Distributivity

Let *op* be $\cdot$ or ; or $\|$ or **or** . Then:

$$(P\ op\ Q)\ op\ R \;=\; P\ op\ (Q\ op\ R)$$

$$P\ op\ (Q\ \mathbf{or}\ R) \;=\; (P\ op\ Q)\ \mathbf{or}\ (P\ op\ R)$$

$$(P\ \mathbf{or}\ Q)\ op\ R \;=\; (P\ op\ R)\ \mathbf{or}\ (P\ op\ Q)$$

- Commutativity

$$Q \,\|\, P = P \,\|\, Q$$

$$Q\ \mathbf{or}\ P = P\ \mathbf{or}\ Q$$

- Unit element

Let *op* be $\cdot$ or ; or $\|$. Then:

$$P\ op\ \mathbf{skip} \;= P$$

$$P\ \mathbf{or}\ \mathbf{empty} \;= P$$

□

For refinement the situation is more subtle, one of the reasons is that refinement can eliminate order introduced by sequential composition.

Theorem 3.2 *(Algebraic laws for refinement)*
Let Q and P be processes, the refinement operator **ref** obeys the following laws:

$$(\mathbf{ref}\ a = S\ \mathbf{in}\ a) = \langle S \rangle$$

$$(\mathbf{ref}\ a = S\ \mathbf{in}\ (Q\,;\,a)) = (Q \cdot \langle S \rangle)$$

$$(\mathbf{ref}\ a = S\ \mathbf{in}\ (a\,;\,Q)) = (\langle S \rangle \cdot Q)$$

Let op be one of the syntactic operators **or** , $\cdot$, or $\|$ then

$$(\mathbf{ref}\ a = S\ \mathbf{in}\ (P\ op\ Q)) = ((\mathbf{ref}\ a = S\ \mathbf{in}\ P)\ op\ (\mathbf{ref}\ a = S\ \mathbf{in}\ Q))$$

$$(\mathbf{ref}\ a = S\ \mathbf{in}\ \langle P \rangle) = (\langle\ \mathbf{ref}\ a = S\ \mathbf{in}\ P \rangle)$$

Under the assumption that the events a_0, a_1, are not contained in S_1 and S_0 respectively we have

$$(\mathbf{ref}\ a_0 = S_0\ \mathbf{in}\ (\mathbf{ref}\ a_1 = S_1\ \mathbf{in}\ P)) = (\mathbf{ref}\ a_1 = S_1\ \mathbf{in}\ (\mathbf{ref}\ a_0 = S_0\ \mathbf{in}\ P))$$

$$(\mathbf{ref}\ a = S\ \mathbf{in}\ P^{\odot}) = (\mathbf{ref}\ a = S\ \mathbf{in}\ P)^{\odot}$$

However in general

$$(\mathbf{ref}\ a = S\ \mathbf{in}\ P\,;\,Q) \neq ((\mathbf{ref}\ a = S\ \mathbf{in}\ P)\,;\,(\mathbf{ref}\ a = S\ \mathbf{in}\ Q))$$

□

By induction on the structure of a process we immediately deduce from the above theorem

Corollary 3.3
Let P be a process constructed by only using the syntactic operators $\|$ and $\cdot$, then

$$(\mathbf{ref}\ a = S\ \mathbf{in}\ P) = P[\langle S \rangle / a]$$

where $P[Q/a]$ denotes simply substituting Q for a in P as usual. □

The contract operator **contr** allows us to relate the functional behaviour of processes. One important algebraic law is that the *functional behaviour* of a process cannot change by replacing *conflict composition* by *sequential composition*, or in general by augmenting the ordering between actions.

Theorem 3.4 *(Contraction laws)*
Let P and Q be processes. We then have:

$$\mathbf{contr}(P \cdot Q) = \mathbf{contr}(P\,;\,Q) = \mathbf{contr}(\,\mathbf{contr}(P)\,;\ \mathbf{contr}(Q))$$

$$\mathbf{contr}(\,\mathbf{aug}(P)) = \mathbf{contr}(P)$$

The following laws also hold:

$$\mathbf{contr}(P\ \mathbf{or}\ Q) = \mathbf{contr}(P)\ \mathbf{or}\ \mathbf{contr}(Q)$$

$$\mathbf{contr}(\langle P \rangle) = \mathbf{contr}(P)$$

Furthermore contraction relates in the following way to refinement:

$$\mathbf{contr}(\,\mathbf{ref}\ a = P\ \mathbf{in}\ Q) = \mathbf{contr}(\,\mathbf{ref}\ a = \mathbf{contr}(P)\ \mathbf{in}\ Q) = \mathbf{contr}(P[\,\mathbf{contr}(S)/a])$$

□

Let S_0, S_1, T_0 and T_1 be processes such that there is no *conflict* between S_0 and T_1. Also assume that there is no *conflict* between S_1 and T_0. The system $(S_0 \cdot S_1) \| (T_0 \cdot T_1)$ has the general semantic structure, sketched in figure 2. It can be divided into two communication closed layers: the semantic structure of $(S_0 \| T_0) \cdot (S_1 \| T_1)$ is the same. (Intuitively this immediately clear.) The precise result is

Theorem 3.5 *(Communication Closed Layers)*
Let S_0, S_1, T_0 and T_1 be processes such that there is no *conflict* between S_0 (S_1) and T_1 (T_0) respectively. Then

$$(S_0 \cdot S_1) \| (T_0 \cdot T_1) = (S_0 \| T_0) \cdot (S_1 \| T_1)$$

□

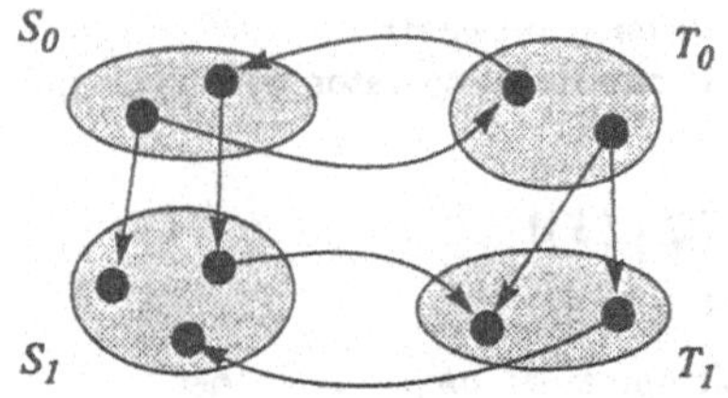

Figure 2: Communication closed layers

Taking one or more processes equal to **skip** leads to

Corollary 3.6
Let P, Q, and R be processes with no conflict between P and Q then

$$P \parallel (Q \cdot R) = Q \cdot (P \parallel R)$$
$$P \parallel (R \cdot Q) = (P \parallel R) \cdot Q$$
$$P \parallel Q = P \cdot Q$$

□

The law in Theorem 3.5 can however not be derived from these simpler laws. We continue with a number of useful implementation relations.

3.2 Implementation relations

In our setup the semantics of a process S, denoted by $[\![S]\!]$, is given by a set of possible *runs*. We can therefore define a *implementation relation*, sometimes called the satisfaction relation, based only on set inclusion and a *sequentialization relation* based on augmentation and set inclusion.

Definition 3.7 *(Implementation and Sequentialization)*
Let P and Q be processes, we say that process P *implements* process Q, denoted by

$$P \subseteq Q \text{ if and only if } [\![P]\!] \subseteq [\![Q]\!]$$

Process P *sequentializes* process Q, denoted by

$$P \sqsubseteq Q \text{ if and only if } [\![P]\!] \subseteq [\![\,\mathbf{aug}(Q)]\!]$$

i.e. if and only if $P \subseteq \mathbf{aug}(Q)$

□

Observe that the relations $\subseteq$ and $\sqsubseteq$ are transitive and are related as follows:

$$P \subseteq Q \Rightarrow P \sqsubseteq Q$$
$$(P \subseteq Q \sqsubseteq S \lor P \sqsubseteq Q \subseteq S) \Rightarrow (P \sqsubseteq S)$$

By augmenting a process Q to a process P, we cannot change it functional behaviour, only its degree of parallelism. This can be expressed as:

Proposition 3.8
Let P and Q be processes.

$$P \sqsubseteq Q \Rightarrow \mathbf{contr}(P) \subseteq \mathbf{contr}(Q)$$

□

For *interleaving models* of parallelism, one would have that $(P\,;\,Q) \subseteq (P \parallel Q)$. This is no longer the case for our models since $P\,;\,Q$ induces in general more ordering than $P \parallel Q$. However, we do have the following.

Proposition 3.9
For processes P and Q:

$$(P \cdot Q) \subseteq (P \parallel Q)$$

$$(P\,;\,Q) \sqsubseteq (P \cdot Q)$$

and thus by the observations above

$$(P\,;\,Q) \sqsubseteq (P \parallel Q)$$

□

In general there is no direct implementation relation between $(P\,;\,Q)$ and $(P \cdot Q)$, apart from the fact that $(P\,;\,Q)$ is an augment of $(P \cdot Q)$.

3.3 Mixed algebraic and state-based reasoning

Program verification for shared variables programming has been studied extensively.([OG], [Lamport], [MP]) It is not our intention to give a full account of such reasoning within our present framework. Rather we describe some useful transformation techniques where we combine algebraic reasoning with state-based reasoning.

A *local annotation* for a term S consists of first order formulae pre_S and $post_S$ called the (global) pre- and postcondition, together with, for each action a occurring in S, a pair $pre_a, post_a$. We require that the free variables of $pre_S, post_S$ are contained in $var(S)$, and similarly that the free variables in $pre_a, post_a$ are contained in $base(a)$. We denote an annotated term S by $\{pre_S\}\tilde{S}\{post_S\}$, where $\tilde{S}$ is like S accept that actions a have been replaced by $\{pre_a\}\ a\ \{post_a\}$. Such an annotation is called *valid* if for any execution of $\langle S\rangle$, starting with a (global) initial state satisfying pre_S, the event(s) corresponding to action a have an initial state satisfying pre_a and final state satisfying $post_a$ (for each action a). (Note that the restriction on free variables guarantees that we can assign a truth value to pre_a and $post_a$ in these local states indeed.) Moreover the global final state of the execution must satisfy $post_S$.

We indicate here how to prove correctness of a given local annotation for the special case that S is build up from action using *exclusively* conflict composition, sequential composition, iteration, and choice. For such S, let $S^{;}$ be the term obtained from S by replacing all conflict composition by sequential composition operations, and $\odot$ by $*$. The resulting term $S^{;}$ is a purely sequential program to which the well-known classical techniques for sequential program proving apply, such as Hoare's logic. In particular one can use a Hoare style *proof outline* $\{pre_S\}\tilde{S}^{;}\{post_S\}$ to show the correctness of the Hoare formula $\{pre_S\}S^{;}\{post_S\}$. Note that such a proof outline attaches first order assertions to all intermediate control points in $S^{;}$, each referring to the *global* state of $S^{;}$. In particular the proof outline attaches global assertions pre_a^G and $post_a^G$ to the points immediately before and after action a.

Claim: let $\{pre_S\}\tilde{S}\{post_S\}$ be a locally annotated term. Let $\{pre_S\}\tilde{S}^{;}\{post_S\}$ be the corresponding proof outline as indicated above which has been shown to be correct. Moreover assume that for each action a in S we have that

$$pre_a^G \Rightarrow pre_a$$

$$post_a^G \Rightarrow post_a.$$

Then the local annotation is valid. □

We use local annotations in the following program transformation technique. Let S be a term containing a subterm P of the form $P = Q \cdot R$. Assume that the only conflict between Q and R is caused by some action a_1 in Q and action a_2 in R. (The generalization to more conflicts is straightforward, if tedious.) Furthermore assume that we have a valid local annotation for S containing

$$\{\neg b\}a_1\{b\} \text{ and } \{b\}a_2\{\cdots\}$$

and that for all actions a in S except a_1 we have that

$$W(a) \cap var(b) = \emptyset$$

where $W(a)$ denotes the set of variables written by a.
Then we claim that by replacing P by $P' = Q \parallel R'$, where R' is R with action a_2 replaced by $b \& a_2$, in the local annotation results in again a valid annotation.

Proof: omitted.

Example. Let $S = (x := 2 \cdot y := x^2)$. If we have a valid local annotation containing

$$\{x = 0\}\ x := 2\ \{x > 0\}, \quad \{x > 0\}\ y := x^2\ \{\cdots\}$$

then we can replace the conflict composition within that annotation by

$$x := 2 \parallel (x > 0) \,\&\, y := x^2$$

4 An example of program development

We illustrate the algebraic laws and transformation techniques introduced above in the development of a simple program P calculating binomial coefficients. The idea is to calculate $\binom{n}{k}$ in shared variables $c(n,k)$ for indices $(n,k) \in I$, where I is the index set

$$I = \{(n,k) \mid 0 \leq n \leq m, 0 \leq k \leq n\}$$

and m is some number determining how "deep" we have to compute. We assume that the variables $c(n,k)$ are initialized to zero; an assumption that is made explicit in the following functional specification of P:

$$\mathbf{contr}(P) \subseteq (\bigwedge_I \overleftarrow{c}(n,k) = 0) \Rightarrow (\bigwedge_I c(n,k) = \binom{n}{k}) \tag{1}$$

(We abbreviate $\bigwedge_{(n,k)\in I} \varphi$ by $\bigwedge_I \varphi$.) The well-known recurrence relation:

$$\binom{n}{0} = \binom{n}{n} = 1, \text{ for } n \geq 0,$$

$$\binom{n}{k} = \binom{n-1}{k-1} + \binom{n-1}{k}, \text{ for } n > 0, 0 < k < n,$$

suggests that we calculate $c(n,k)$ by executing action $a(n,k)$, defined as

$$a(n,k) = c(n,k) := 1, \text{ for } k = 0 \text{ and } k = n$$

$$a(n,k) = c(n,k) := c(n-1,k-1) + c(n-1,k), \text{ for } 0 < k < n$$

It will be clear that for $0 < k < n$, action $a(n,k)$ is in conflict (only) with actions $a(n-1,k-1)$ and $a(n-1,k)$, and moreover that those two actions should *precede* $a(n,k)$. This is illustrated in fig. 3. We can impose this precedence relation by denoting P as a (conflict) composition of layers $L(k)$, each of which executes the actions $a(n,k)$, for $n = k, k+1, \cdots, m$. So:

$$P = L(0) \cdot L(1) \cdot L(2) \cdot \ldots \cdot L(m)$$

where

$$L(k) = a(k,k) \cdot a(k+1,k) \cdot \ldots \cdot a(m,k)$$

In [CM] this example is given as an action system where all actions $a(n,k)$ are executed infinitely often in an arbitrary order, eventually reaching a stable situation, thereby avoiding architectural bias. A problem is that such a description has no compositional (algebraic) structure. Moreover, if one would like to add *control flow* in order to transform towards a more efficient implementation, boolean variables and guards have to be added to encode this flow of control, which is somewhat unsatisfactory.

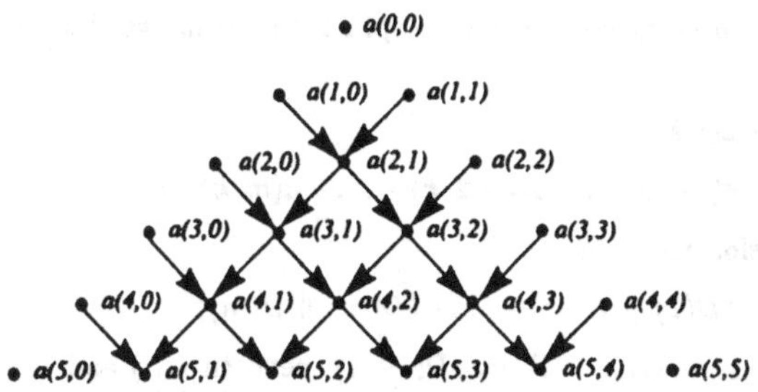

Figure 3:

Note that we have a structured (algebraic) description of the system without imposing unnecessary flow of control or architectural bias, however. Such an *initial design* can be transformed towards a design that suits a particular architecture as we show below. First however we prove *functional correctness* of our initial design, exploiting its compositional structure.

Action indices (i,j) occur *textually* in P in the order defined by

$$(i,j) \prec (k,l) \text{ iff } j < l \text{ or } (j = l \text{ and } i < k)$$

Note however that actions are not *executed* in this order; in fact, since we used conflict composition exclusively, action $a(i,j)$ and $a(k,l)$ will executed independently *except* when in conflict. In the latter case they execute in the order determined by "$\prec$." Note that $(n-1,k-1) \prec (n,k)$ and $(n-1,k) \prec (n,k)$, so indeed $a(n,k)$ will be preceded by $a(n-1,k-1)$ and $a(n-1,k)$.

To prove the correctness of (1) we must construct a local annotation of the form

$$\{(\bigwedge_I c(n,k) = 0)\}\ \tilde{P}\ \{(\bigwedge_I c(n,k) = \binom{n}{k})\} \qquad (*)$$

As discussed in section 3.3 it suffices here to consider the sequential program $\tilde{P}'$ obtained from P by replacing conflict composition by sequential composition, for which we must show:

$$\{(\bigwedge_I c(n,k) = 0)\}\ \tilde{P}'\ \{(\bigwedge_I c(n,k) = \binom{n}{k})\}$$

This is easily shown, using classical Hoare style logic for sequential programs. To be precise, the inductive assertion $\varphi(n,k)$ attached as precondition to action $a(n,k)$ can be chosen as follows: Let $J = \{(i,j) \in I \mid (i,j) \prec (n,k)\}$. Then

$$\varphi(n,k) \stackrel{\text{def}}{=} \bigwedge_J c(i,j) = \binom{i}{j} \wedge \bigwedge_{I-J} c(i,j) = 0$$

Apart from proving the functional correctness of the initial design, this also shows the validity of the *local* annotation $(*)$ if we annotate action $a(i,j)$ as:

$$\{c(i,j) = 0 \wedge c(i-1,j) > 0\}\ a(i,j)\ \{c(i,j) > 0\}$$

We use this local annotation in our next transformation step where we aim at gradually removing conflict composition in favour of parallel composition and sequential composition. We start with transforming each layer $L(k)$ into a number of parallel components, where the number of components depends upon the number of available processors. For simplicity we illustrate this for the case of two processors.

According to section 3.3 we can transform

$$a(k,k) \cdot \ldots \cdot \{\neg c(i,k) = 0\}\ a(i,k)\ \{c(i,k) > 0\}\ \cdot\ \{c(i,k) > 0\}\ a(i+1,k)\ \cdot \ldots \cdot a(m,k)$$

into

$$a(k,k) \cdot \ldots \cdot a(i,k) \parallel (c(i,k) > 0\ \&\ a(i+1,k)) \cdot \ldots \cdot a(m,k)$$

where i denotes the action in every layer where we split the layer in two. So we can transform $L(k)$ to $D(k) \parallel U(k)$ where

$$D(k) = a(k,k) \cdot \ldots \cdot a(i,k), \text{ and}$$
$$U(k) = (c(i,k) > 0) \,\&\, a(i+1,k)) \cdot a(i+2,k) \cdot \ldots \cdot a(m,k)$$

By doing so we have transformed P into

$$P_1 = (D(0) \parallel U(0)) \cdot (D(1) \parallel U(1)) \cdot \ldots \cdot (D(m) \parallel U(m))$$

Note that we have conflicts between $D(i)$ and $D(i+1)$, between $U(i)$ and $U(i+1)$, and between $D(i)$ and $U(i)$. However, no conflicts occur between $D(i)$ and $U(j)$ for $i \neq j$! So we can apply the *communication closed layers* law (3.5), and obtain the following program P_2:

$$P_2 = (D(0) \cdot D(1) \cdot \ldots \cdot D(m)) \parallel (U(0) \cdot U(1) \cdot \ldots \cdot U(m))$$

Finally we take into account that we have only two processors available. To this end we will intentionally decrease the amount of parallelism by introducing extra ordering between actions. Note that by law 3.8 this cannot effect the functional correctness. So we deduce

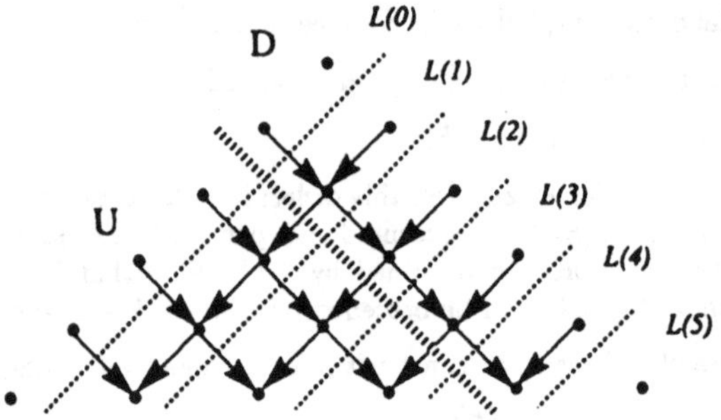

Figure 4:

$$\begin{aligned} P_2 &= (D(0) \cdot D(1) \cdot \ldots \cdot D(m)) \parallel (U(0) \cdot U(1) \cdot \ldots \cdot U(m)) \\ &\sqsupseteq \{\text{ proposition 3.9 }\} \\ & (D(0)\,;\, D(1)\,;\, \ldots\,;\, D(m)) \parallel (U(0)\,;\, U(1)\,;\, \ldots\,;\, U(m)) \\ &\sqsupseteq \{\text{ proposition 3.9 }\} \\ & (D'(0)\,;\, D'(1)\,;\, \ldots\,;\, D'(m)) \parallel (U'(0)\,;\, U'(1)\,;\, \ldots\,;\, U'(m)) \\ &\stackrel{\text{def}}{=} P_3 \end{aligned}$$

where $D'(k)$ is obtained from $D(k)$ by replacing every conflict composition by sequential composition, and analogously for $U'(k)$. We take P_3 as our final solution.

5 Semantics of the language

In this section we present a semantics for the language used in this paper. This semantics relies upon the distinction between process and environment actions, resulting in a definition of the composition operators based on intersection.

Computations, or single "runs" of a system, are modelled by a pair $(E, <)$, where E is a set of *events* and $<$ denotes the successor relation, or *causal order*. The pair $(E, <)$ must form a *directed acyclic graph* (DAG), which means that the transitive closure of the successor relation defines a *partial order*.

First we introduce the domain of computations and some notation. Then the semantics of processes is defined. Finally we gives a semantics for the shared variables interpretation of the language.

5.1 Preliminaries

In our framework a computation consists of a pair $(E, <)$ where E is a set of events from some domain $\mathcal{E}vent$ and $<$ is the successor relation or *causality relation*, i.e. if two events e_1 and e_2 are related ($e_1 < e_2$) then event e_1 must conceptually precede event e_2. This relation is irreflexive but not transitive; its transitive closure $<^+$ must be irreflexive too, which means that $(E, <^+)$ is an irreflexive partial order. For now, events are left uninterpreted.

Different events in a run can be occurrences of the same *action*, therefore E is a *multiset* of actions, rather than a set of actions. Formally speaking, we should define DAG-s over multisets as equivalence classes under isomorphism of 4-tuples $(E, \Sigma, <, \mu)$, where E is the set of events, $<$ the set of edges, Σ the set of possible actions and μ the labelling function mapping events to actions. If we assume all events can be distinguished we can restrict ourselves to the simpler model of pairs $(E, <)$.

In this paper we are only interested in *finite behaviour* of processes. Therefore the multiset E is always finite. It is also possible to give a model for diverging behaviour (which is done in [JPZ]) giving the possibility to discuss notions such as fairness. Here we restrict ourselves to the finite model.

A system can have many different runs due to nondeterminism or different initial states. The denotation of system is therefore a set of computations, where every computation denotes a possible run of the system.

We assume that a binary, symmetric relation *conflict* on events is given. Every pair of conflicting events must be ordered, as conflicting events can intuitively be seen as accesses to some common resource that have to take place under *mutual exclusion*.

A DAG $(E, <)$ has a certain *functional behaviour*. This functional behaviour can be represented as a *single event*, in some way analogously to the way a computation in the *interleaving framework* can be represented by a single state transformation. A computation in the interleaving framework consists of a *sequence of states*. This gives a contraction function with functionality $\mathcal{S}tate^* \rightarrow \mathcal{S}tate^2$:

$$(s_0, s_1, \ldots, s_{n-1}, s_n) \xrightarrow{contr} (s_0, s_n)$$

This can also be viewed as a function mapping a sequence of *pairs of states* (i.e. state transformers) to a single pair of states:

$$((s_0, s_1), (s_1, s_2), \ldots, (s_{n-1}, s_n)) \xrightarrow{contr} (s_0, s_n)$$

These state pairs can be viewed as *events*, i.e. $e_i = (s_i, s_{i+1})$, resulting in a mapping from a sequence of events to an event.

$$(e_0, e_1, \ldots, e_{n-1}) \xrightarrow{contr} e$$

This mapping for sequences of events can be generalized to our computations. We therefore want to define a function *contr* wich maps computations to events. This function is not defined for arbitrary DAG's, we need some notion of *well-formedness*. In the interleaving framework for example a sequence $((s_0, s_1), (s_2, s_3))$ such that $s_1 \neq s_2$ cannot be contracted to a single state transformation, as it has an inconsistent state pair.

A computation can be contracted if and only if it is *well-formed* and finite. (In this paper every computation is finite.) To define contraction we postulate a *partial function*

$$\rho : \mathcal{E}vent^2 \xrightarrow{p} \mathcal{E}vent$$

(analogously to the composition of binary relations). This function defines the contraction of a pair of events. Two events can be contracted to a single event if they are either *direct successors* or *unrelated*. I.e. e_1 and e_2 are contractable in a computation $(E, <)$ iff

$$\neg(\exists e \in E(e_1 <^+ e <^+ e_2 \vee e_2 <^+ e <^+ e_1))$$

If e_1 and e_2 are contractable and $\neg(e_2 <^+ e_1)$ then the function $\rho(e_1, e_2)$ is defined. The exact definition of the contraction depends upon the underlying model of events. We require ρ to be associative, and to be commutative for non-conflicting events.

We can define $contr(E,<)$ inductively as:

$$contr(\emptyset,\emptyset) \stackrel{\text{def}}{=} (\emptyset,\emptyset), \quad contr(\{e\},\emptyset) \stackrel{\text{def}}{=} (\{e\},\emptyset)$$

$$contr(E_1 \cup E_2, <_1 \cup <_2 \cup X) \stackrel{\text{def}}{=} contr(\{e_1,e_2\},<), \text{ if } <_1 \subseteq E_1^2, <_2 \subseteq E_2^2, X \subseteq (E_1 \times E_2)$$

where $e_1 = contr(E_1,<_1), e_2 = contr(E_2,<_2)$, and $<= \{(e_1,e_2)\}$ if $X \neq \emptyset$, else $<= \emptyset$. Informally, if we can split a computation into two "layers" without any ordering in opposite direction, we then can compute the contractions of the layers seperately and compose them.

Thus, in light of the remarks above, we define our domain of computations *Comp* as

$$\begin{aligned} Comp \stackrel{\text{def}}{=} \{ (E,<) \mid\ & E \subseteq \mathcal{E}vent \wedge < \subseteq (E \times E) \wedge \forall e \in E\,(e \not<^+ e) \wedge \\ & \forall e,e' \in E\,(conflict(e,e') \rightarrow (e < e' \vee e' < e)) \wedge \\ & (E,<) \text{ is well-formed } \} \end{aligned}$$

Our approach to define the semantics is to give the semantics of a process as computations consisting of two types of labelled events: *process* events and *environment* events. The process events give the semantics of the process in isolation, whereas the environment events model the (arbitrary) behaviour of other processes. An alternative would be to use process events only and to leave "gaps" to be filled by other processes. The approach taken in this paper enables us to define the semantics of e.g. atomic statements and refinement in an elegant way (see [JPZ] for comparison of the two semantics). This leads to a semantic function where we have to specify the name of the process and all processes in the environment. Formally:

$$[\![\cdot]\!] : Process \rightarrow (Pid \rightarrow (\mathcal{P}(Pid) \rightarrow \mathcal{P}(Comp)))$$

So the intention is that $[\![S]\!](P)(Env)$ is the set of all computations allowed by process P with body S in the context of a set of processes Env, where $P \notin Env$.
In the approach taken by [BKP] one would have a single environment label in the semantics. Our approach however facilitates the definition of parallel composition.

The semantics of a process *in isolation* (a complete system) can now be defined as function:

$$[\![S]\!] \stackrel{\text{def}}{=} [\![S]\!](P)(\emptyset)$$

Events are labelled with the name of the process that executes them. For an event e this label is denoted by $pid(e)$. We extend the definition of *pid* to computations:

$$pid(E,<) \stackrel{\text{def}}{=} \bigcup\{pid(e) \mid e \in E\}$$

Furthermore events are tagged with a name, corresponding with the action they belong to. This is used to recognize events in order to be able to refine them by other computations. The name of an event e is denoted by $name(e)$.

5.2 The semantics of processes

To ease the definition of the semantics of some processes we introduce some auxiliary processes, viz. the **step** and **maxpar** process. The former denotes a process where only a single process event is executed and the latter denotes all processes where the ordering relation between process and environment events is minimal in the sense that only *conflicting* events are ordered. This is a requirement that holds for every computation in the semantics of a process.
Their semantics can be defined as follows:

$$[\![\, \textbf{step} \,]\!](P)(Env) =$$

$$\{(E,<) \in Comp \mid \exists! e \in E(pid(e) = P) \wedge pid(E,<) \subseteq Env \cup \{P\} \}$$

where $\exists!$ denotes *unique* existence.

$$\begin{aligned} [\![\, \textbf{maxpar} \,]\!](P)(Env) = \{ & (E,<) \in Comp \mid pid(E,<) \subseteq Env \cup \{P\} \\ & \forall e,e' \in E\,((pid(e) = P \wedge pid(e') \neq P \wedge (e < e' \vee e' < e)) \rightarrow conflict(e,e'))\} \end{aligned}$$

Actions a have a semantics consisting of computation containing a single process event labelled a. We assume the set of possible events corresponding with an action a is determined by a characteristic predicate φ. This leads to the following definition.

$$[\![a]\!](P)(Env) \;=\; [\![\,\textbf{maxpar}\,]\!](P)(Env) \cap [\![\,\textbf{step}\,]\!](P)(Env) \cap \{(E,<) \in Comp \mid \exists e \in E\ (\varphi(e) \wedge name(e) = a)\}$$

The semantics of the **empty** process simply consists of the empty set of computations.

$$[\![\,\textbf{empty}\,]\!](P)(Env) = \emptyset$$

The semantics of **skip** is simple: the process P itself performs no actions, whereas the environment can perform arbitrary actions.

$$[\![\,\textbf{skip}\,]\!](P)(Env) = \{h \in Comp \mid pid(h) \subseteq Env\}$$

The **or** -operator represents nondeterministic choice. Its semantics therefore simply boils down to set theoretic union.

$$[\![S_0 \textbf{ or } S_1]\!](P)(Env) = [\![S_0]\!](P)(Env) \cup [\![S_1]\!](P)(Env)$$

Our semantics have been constructed to be able to define parallel composition in a straightforward way. The environment events should model the behaviour of other components in a parallel composition. When defining the semantics of $S_0 \parallel S_1$ the environment of S_0 should include the behaviour of S_1 and vice versa. Taking the parallel composition then simply boils down to taking the *intersection* of the respective semantics.

$$[\![S_0 \parallel S_1]\!](P)(Env) = ([\![S_0]\!](P_0)(Env_0) \cap [\![S_1]\!](P_1)(Env_1))[P/P_0, P/P_1]$$

In this definition P_0 and P_1 are "fresh" process names and $Env_0 = Env \cup \{P_1\}$ and $Env_1 = Env \cup \{P_0\}$. The *renaming* $U[P/P_0, P/P_1]$ operates pointwise on the computations in U. It relabels the events labelled P_0 or P_1 into events labelled P. This renaming is necessary as after the parallel composition we do not want to distinguish between events of the two components, whereas it is necessary to distinguish them as *process* or *environment* events.

The conflict composition can again be defined analogously to the parallel composition, where all conflicting events are ordered in the correct manner. To do so we define

$$conflict\_order(P_1, P_2) \stackrel{\text{def}}{=} \{(E,<) \in Comp \mid \forall e, e' \in E (pid(e) = P_1 \wedge pid(e') = P_2 \wedge conflict(e,e') \rightarrow e < e')\}$$

The semantics of conflict composition is now

$$[\![S_0 \cdot S_1]\!](P)(Env) = ([\![S_0]\!](P_0)(Env_0) \cap [\![S_1]\!](P_1)(Env_1) \cap conflict\_order(P_0, P_1))[P/P_0, P/P_1]$$

It is more difficult to give the semantics of sequential composition in an analogous way, due to the fact that the ordering between process events and environment events is *minimal*, i.e. only conflicting events are ordered. We can however define the semantics of sequential composition as an augment (extension of the ordering) of the semantics of conflict composition: in this case all process events from the two components must be ordered.
We define a function $\alpha_{P\rightarrow Q}$ that performs that augment, which can be defined as:

$$\alpha_{P\rightarrow Q}(E,<) \stackrel{\text{def}}{=} (E, < \cup X)$$

where X is the extension of the ordering, consisting of pairs of events labelled P and Q respectively, i.e.

$$X \stackrel{\text{def}}{=} \{(e,e') \mid e, e' \in E \wedge pid(e) = P \wedge pid(e') = Q\}$$

Note that this function does not always result in a DAG in general, it may lead to cycles. In our definition of the semantics of sequential composition however it does.
This results in the following semantics for sequential composition:

$$[\![S_0 \,;\, S_1]\!](P)(Env) = (\alpha_{P_0\rightarrow P_1}([\![S_0]\!](P_0)(Env_0) \cap [\![S_1]\!](P_1)(Env_1) \cap conflict\_order(P_0, P_1)))[P/P_0, P/P_1]$$

One can also define the semantics of sequential composition in a more direct way, by taking the disjoint union of the two computations and augmenting the resulting order in the correct way, meaning that process actions from the two components must all be ordered in the same direction, whereas other conflicting but yet unordered events can be ordered arbitrarily.

The iterated versions of the conflict and sequential composition can intuitively be seen as a non-deterministic choice of zero or more times executing a statement S, using the right form of composition. We therefore inductively define the following statements:

$$S^{[0]} \stackrel{\text{def}}{=} \textbf{skip} \qquad S^{[i+1]} \stackrel{\text{def}}{=} S^{[i]} ; S$$

$$S^{(0)} \stackrel{\text{def}}{=} \textbf{skip} \qquad S^{(i+1)} \stackrel{\text{def}}{=} S^{(i)} \cdot S$$

The semantics can now be defined as

$$[\![S^{*}]\!](P)(Env) = \bigcup_{i\geq 0} [\![S^{[i]}]\!](P)(Env)$$

$$[\![S^{\circledcirc}]\!](P)(Env) = \bigcup_{i\geq 0} [\![S^{(i)}]\!](P)(Env)$$

The intuition of atomic statements $\langle S\rangle$ is that during the execution of S no other processes may interfere; this does not preclude (conceptually) parallel events from other processes. This can be compared to refinement in the sense that the events in S can be seen as the result of the refinement of some abstract action A. This is the case if there are no cycles in the transitive ordering of A which is the case iff for every pair of process events e, e' there is no environment event e'' such that $e <^{+} e''$ and $e'' <^{+} e'$, giving $e <^{+} e'$.
We therefore define:

$$\begin{aligned}[\![\langle S\rangle]\!](P)(Env) \;=\; & [\![S]\!](P)(Env) \cap \\ & \{(E,<) \in \mathit{Comp} \mid \forall e,e',e'' \in E \\ & \quad (pid(e) = pid(e') = P \wedge pid(e'') \neq P \rightarrow \neg(e <^{+} e'' <^{+} e'))\}\end{aligned}$$

The semantics of the *contract* operator is related to the semantics of the atomic statements. Informally, a process $\textbf{contr}(S)$ denotes the atomic execution of S, mapped into *a single process event*, analogously to the contract function *contr*, but for process events only! We denote this process contraction function as $contr_P$. It is defined as:

$$contr_P(E,<) \stackrel{\text{def}}{=} ((E - E_P) \cup \{e_p\}, (< \cap (E - E_P)^2) \cup X)$$

where

$$E_P = \{e \in E \mid pid(e) = P\}, \quad e_p = contr(E_P, < \cap E_P^2)$$

$$X = \{(e, e_p) \mid e \in E - E_P \wedge \exists e' \in E_p (e < e')\} \cup \{(e_p, e) \mid e \in E - E_P \wedge \exists e' \in E_p (e' < e)\}$$

This function is only defined for computations $(E,<)$ such that

$$\neg(\exists e_1, e_2, e_3 \in E (pid(e_1) = pid(e_3) = P \neq pid(e_2) \wedge e_1 <^{+} e_2 <^{+} e_3))$$

i.e. the set of P-events in $(E,<)$ can be regarded as *atomic*.

This gives the following semantics:

$$\begin{aligned}[\![\textbf{contr}(S)]\!](P)(Env) \;=\; & [\![\textbf{maxpar}]\!](P)(Env) \cap [\![\textbf{step}]\!](P)(Env) \cap \\ & \{contr_P(h) \mid h \in [\![\langle S\rangle]\!](P)(Env)\}\end{aligned}$$

Augment closure can of be defined by simply augmenting the order arbitrarily:

$$[\![\textbf{aug}(S)]\!](P)(Env) = \{(E,<) \in \mathit{Comp} \mid \exists (E,<') \in [\![S]\!](P)(Env)\ (< = <' \cup X)\}$$

where X is *any* relation on $E \times E$ such that $<' \cup X$ satisfies the restrictions imposed by *Comp*. This is implicit by defining $(E,<) \in \mathit{Comp}$.

The refinement construct has a more intricate semantics. Informally the semantics of a process $\textbf{ref}\ a = S_0\ \textbf{in}\ S_1$ can be given as follows. First we compute the semantics of S_1, where the semantics of the action a is given by computations consisting of a single a-labelled process event. In the computations that are the result of this semantics, all abstract events named a are substituted by elements from the semantics of S_0, where the semantics of S_0 is computed in an *empty environment*, as to make sure that S_0 is executed *atomically*. This substitution is done in such a way that only *conflicting* events are ordered, and they are ordered in a manner corresponding to the ordering relation of the abstract event. The substitution should preserve the *functional behaviour* of the computation, i.e. the *contraction* of the computations that are substituted should be equal to the abstract event for which they are substituted. Figure 5 illustrates this definition of refinement. We

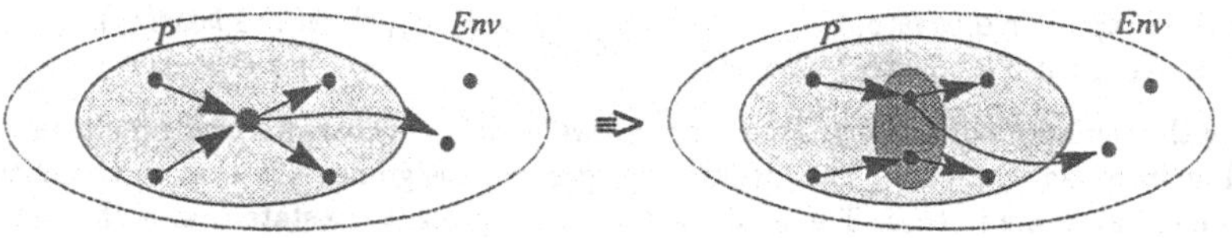

Figure 5: An example of refinement

can formalize this as follows. For computations $h_0 = (E_0, <_0)$ and $h_1 = (E_1, <_1)$, and process name a we define a refinement operator $h_0[a \Rrightarrow h_1]$ substituting elements from h_1 for abstract events named a in h_0. In this definition we assume that a occurs only once in a computation, the extension to multiple occurrences is straightforward but leads to a tedious definition.

For a multiset E let $e_a(E)$ denote the (unique) a-labelled event $e \in E$. Assume $e = e_a(E_0)$ exists and that $contr(h_1) = e$. We now define:

$$h_0[a \Rrightarrow h_1] \stackrel{\text{def}}{=} ((E_0 - \{e\}) \cup E_1, \ (<_0 \cap (E_0 - \{e\})^2) \cup <_1 \cup X)$$

where

$$\begin{aligned} X \ = \ & \{ (e_0, e_1) \mid e_0 \in E_0 - \{e\} \wedge e_1 \in E_1 \wedge e_0 <_0 e \wedge conflict(e_0, e_1) \} \cup \\ & \{ (e_1, e_0) \mid e_1 \in E_1 \wedge e_0 \in E_0 - \{e\} \wedge e <_0 e_0 \wedge conflict(e_0, e_1) \} \end{aligned}$$

We extend this definition to *sets* of computations D_0 and D_1 by pointwize extension:

$$\begin{aligned} D_0[a \Rrightarrow D_1] \ \stackrel{\text{def}}{=} \ & \{ h_0[a \Rrightarrow h_1] \mid h_0 \in D_0 \wedge h_1 \in D_1 \wedge e_a(h_0) \text{ exists } \wedge contr(h_1) = e_a(h_0) \} \cup \\ & \{ h_0 \in D_0 \mid e_a(h_0) \text{ does not exist } \} \end{aligned}$$

Now we can define the semantics of refinement as:

$$[\![\textbf{ ref } a = S_1 \textbf{ in } S_0]\!](P)(Env) = [\![S_1]\!](P)(Env)[a \Rrightarrow [\![S_0]\!](P)(\emptyset)]$$

5.3 The semantics of the shared variables model

When we work in some fixed model such as the shared variables model, we can give an interpretation to the set of events, the conflict relation and the contraction function ρ. In this section we give such an interpretation and a semantics for actions.

The events model *state transformations* caused by executing guarded assignments $b \,\&\, \bar{x} := \bar{f}$. Such events are described as labelled state transitions e of the form:

$$e = (s \xrightarrow{P_i, \beta} s')$$

The label consists of the name P_i of the process that caused the event and a base β which is a pair consisting of the set of variables that are read and the set of variables that are written by the event. We denote these by $pid(e)$ and $base(e)$. The base of e is also the domain of the (local) states s and s', i.e. $s : base(e) \rightarrow Val$ and $s' : base(e) \rightarrow Val$, where Val is some given domain of values of expressions. The first component of a base β (the read component) is denoted by β_R, the write component by β_W. The name of an event e is denoted by $name(e)$.

In the informal explanation of the language the concept of *conflicts* between actions was defined to be *read–write* conflicts only. For two events e and e' we can define the predicate *conflict* as:

$$\begin{aligned} conflict(e, e') \ \stackrel{\text{def}}{=} \ & ((base_R(e) \cup base_W(e)) \cap base_W(e') \neq \emptyset \ \vee \\ & (base_R(e') \cup base_W(e')) \cap base_W(e) \neq \emptyset) \end{aligned}$$

For our shared variables model we have to define a partial function ρ mapping pairs of events to a single event. The domain of ρ, $dom(\rho)$, is defined as:

$$\begin{aligned} dom(\rho) &= \{(e_1, e_2) \in \mathcal{E}vent^2 \mid \neg conflict(e_1, e_2) \wedge \forall x \in base_R(e_1) \cap base_R(e_2)(e_1(x) = e_2(x))\} \cup \\ &\quad \{(e_1, e_2) \in \mathcal{E}vent^2 \mid conflict(e_1, e_2) \wedge \forall x \in base(e_1) \cap base(e_2)(e_1'(x) = e_2(x))\} \end{aligned}$$

where $e(x)$ and $e'(x)$ denote the initial and final values of x respectively. The contraction $\rho(e_1, e_2)$ is now defined as: $\rho(e_1, e_2) = e$, where

$base(e) = (base_R(e_1) \cup base_R(e_2), base_W(e_1) \cup base_W(e_2))$ and $pid(e) = P$ and

$$e(x) \stackrel{\text{def}}{=} \begin{cases} e_1(x) & \text{if } x \in base(e_1) \\ e_2(x) & \text{if } x \in base(e_2) - base(e_1) \end{cases} \qquad e'(x) \stackrel{\text{def}}{=} \begin{cases} e_2'(x) & \text{if } x \in base(e_2) \\ e_1'(x) & \text{if } x \in base(e_1) - base(e_2) \end{cases}$$

We now give the semantics of actions. To do so we have to define a characteristic predicate for them. First of all guarded assignments. The intuition of guarded assignments is that in the initial state the guard should evaluate to true. The final state should represent the state that is the result of the multiple assignment. This gives a predicate φ defined as:

$$\begin{aligned} \varphi_{(b \,\&\, \bar{x} := \bar{f})}(e) &\stackrel{\text{def}}{=} base_R(e) = var(\bar{f}) \cup var(b) \wedge base_W(e) = \bar{x} \wedge b(e) \wedge \\ &\qquad \bar{x}'(e) = \bar{f}(e) \wedge \forall y \in base_R(e) - base_W(e)\ (y'(e) = y(e)) \end{aligned}$$

For abstract actions A we assume a base β is given, syntactically determined by the process it can be refined into. As we can only determine an upper bound for the base we assume the base of the event is a subset of β. Abstract events are left uninterpreted. Therefore, besides this base, no restrictions are placed on the functional behaviour of the actions, i.e. nothing is required for the initial and final states. This leads to a predicate φ_β:

$$\varphi_\beta(e) \stackrel{\text{def}}{=} base(e) \subseteq \beta$$

The semantics of predicates ϕ consists of all computations that consist of a single process action satisfying ϕ, with the base given by the *read* and *write* sets in ϕ. Let β be this base of ϕ. We can then define a predicate $\varphi_{\phi(\bar{x}, x)}$ characterizing these events as:

$$\varphi_{\phi(\bar{x}, x)}(e) \stackrel{\text{def}}{=} \phi(x(e), x'(e)) \ \wedge\ base(e) = \beta$$

This concludes the definition of our semantics.

6 Conclusion and future work

The introduction of refinement and operations such as conflict composition enable a compositional treatment of action systems, and allows for a smooth design process, from initial design to final implementation. We have provided several *algebraic* laws to characterize these new operations, and applied these laws in a transformation process, showing the feasibility of such a transformational approach. In the future we would like to supplement such algebraic laws by axioms and verification rules in the style of program logics like Hoare's logic. The approach taken in [ZR], where weakest preconditions are defined as adjoints of sequential composition operators, seems to be a good candidate for the axiomatization of the conflict composition operation. We are investigating a kind of "weakest precondition" [ZR] or "weakest prespecification" [HH] in the form of an adjoint to conflict composition.

The relation between our model and real-time is also a subject of current research. It appears that extending our model with an extra "temporal" ordering relation allows for an interesting notion of refinement in a real-time setting.

References

[Back] R.J.R. Back, A calculus of refinements for program derivations, *Acta Informatica* **25**, 1988.

[BKP] H. Barringer, R. Kuiper and A. Pnueli, Now you may compose temporal logic specifications, *Proc. of the 16th ACM Symposium on Theory of Computing*, Washington, 1984, pp. 51-63.

[BHG] P.A. Bernstein, V. Hadzilacos and N. Goodman, *Concurrency Control and Recovery in Database Systems*, Addison-Wesley, 1987.

[CM] K.M. Chandy and J. Misra, *Parallel Program Design: A Foundation*, Addison-Wesley, 1988.

[DNM] P. Degano, R. De Nicola and U. Montanari, Partial orderings descriptions and observations of nondeterministic concurrent processes, *Proc. of the REX workshop on Linear Time, Branching Time and Partial Order in Logics and Models for Concurrency*, 1988, LNCS 354, pp. 438-466.

[EF] T. Elrad and N. Francez, Decomposition of distributed programs into communication closed layers, *Science of Computer Programming 2*, 1982.

[Gaifman] H. Gaifman, Modeling Concurrency by Partial Orders and Nonlinear Transition Systems, *Proc. of the REX workshop on Linear Time, Branching Time and Partial Order in Logics and Models for Concurrency*, 1988, LNCS 354, pp. 467-488.

[GHS] R.T. Gallager, P.A. Humblet and P.M. Spira, A distributed algorithm for minimum-weight spanning trees, *ACM TOPLAS 5-1*, 1983.

[GG] R. J. van Glabbeek and U. Goltz, *Equivalence Notions for Concurrent Systems and Refinement of Actions*, Arbeitspapiere der GMD, Number 366, GMD, 1989

[HH] C.A.R. Hoare and He Jifeng , The weakest prespecification, *IPL*, 1987.

[Hooman] J. Hooman, *Specification and Compositional Verification of Real-Time Systems*, Ph.D. Thesis, Eindhoven University of Technology, 1991.

[Jones] C.B. Jones, *Systematic software development using VDM*, Prentice–Hall, 1986.

[JPZ] W. Janssen, M. Poel and J. Zwiers, *Consistent alternatives of parallelism with conflicts*, Memorandum INF-91-15, University of Twente.

[KP] S. Katz and D. Peled, Interleaving set temporal logic, *Proc. of the 6th ACM Symposium on Principles of Distributed Computing*, Vancouver, 1987, pp. 178-190.

[Lamport] L. Lamport, The Hoare Logic of concurrent programs, *Acta Informatica 14*, 1980.

[MP] Z. Manna and A. Pnueli, Verification of concurrent programs: the temporal framework, In R.S. Boyer and J.S. Moore (eds), *The Correctness Problem in Computer Science*, Academic Press, 1981.

[NEL] M. Nielsen, U. Engberg and K.S. Larsen, Fully abstract models for a process language with refinement, *Proc. of the REX workshop on Linear Time, Branching Time and Partial Order in Logics and Models for Concurrency*, 1988, LNCS 354, pp. 523-548.

[OG] S. Owicki and D. Gries, An axiomatic proof technique for parallel programs, *Acta Informatica 6*, 1976.

[Pomello] L. Pomello, Refinement of Concurrent Systems Based on Local State Transformations, *Proc. REX workshop on Stepwise Refinement of Distributed Systems*, 1989 LNCS 430, pp. 641-668.

[Pratt] V. Pratt, Modelling Concurrency with Partial orders, *International Journal of Parallel Programming 15*, 1986, pp. 33-71.

[SR] F.A. Stomp and W.P. de Roever, Designing distributed algorithms by means of formal sequentially phased reasoning, *Proc. of the 3rd International Workshop on Distributed Algorithms*, Nice, LNCS 392, Eds. J.-C. Bermond and M. Raynal, 1989, pp. 242-253.

[Winskel] G. Winskel, An introduction to event structures, *Proc. of the REX workshop on Linear Time, Branching Time and Partial Order in Logics and Models for Concurrency*, 1988, LNCS 354, pp. 364-397.

[ZR] J. Zwiers and W.P. de Roever, Predicates are Predicate Transformers: a unified theory for concurrency, *Proc. of the conference on Principles of Distributed Computing*, 1989.

INVARIANT SEMANTICS OF NETS WITH INHIBITOR ARCS

Ryszard Janicki
Department of Computer Science and Systems
McMaster University
Hamilton, Ontario, Canada, L8S 4K1

Maciej Koutny
Computing Laboratory
The University of Newcastle upon Tyne
Newcastle upon Tyne NE1 7RU, U.K.

Abstract

We here discuss an invariant semantics of concurrent systems which is a generalisation of the causal partial order (CPO) semantics. The new semantics is consistent with the full operational behaviour of inhibitor and priority nets expressed in terms of step sequences. It employs combined partial orders, or composets, where each composet is a relational structure consisting of a causal partial order and a weak causal partial order. In this paper we develop a representation of composets using a novel concept of comtrace, which is certain equivalence class of step sequences. The whole approach resembles to a significant extent the trace semantics introduced by Mazurkiewicz. Composets correspond to posets, comtraces correspond to traces, while step sequences correspond to interleaving sequences. The independency relation is replaced by two new relations. The first is simultaneity which is a symmetric relation comprising pairs of event which may be executed in one step. The other is serialisability which comprises pairs of events (e,f) such that if e and f can be executed in one step then they can also be executed in the order: *e followed by f*. We show that the comtraces enjoy essentially the same kind of properties as Mazurkiewicz traces, e.g., each comtrace is unambiguously identified by any step sequence which belongs to it. As a system model we consider Elementary Net Systems with Inhibitor Arcs (ENI-systems). We show that the comtrace model provides an invariant semantics for such nets and is in a full agreement with their operational semantics expressed in terms of step sequences. We finally show that the composets represented by comtraces can be generated by generalising the standard construction of a process of a 1-safe Petri net.

1. Introduction

In the development of mathematical models for concurrent systems, the concepts of partial and total order undoubtedly occupy a central position. Interleaving models use total orders of event occurrences, while so-called 'true concurrency' models use step sequences or causal partial orders (comp. [BD87, Ho85, Pr86]). Even more complex structures, such as failures [Ho85] or event structures [Wi82], are in principle based on the concept of a total or partial order. While interleavings and step sequences usually represent executions or observations and can be regarded as directly representing operational behaviour of a concurrent system, a causal partial order represents a set of executions or observations. The lack of ordering between two event occurrences in the case of a step sequence is interpreted as simultaneity, while in the case of a causal partial order it is interpreted as independency. This means that the event occurrences can be executed (observed) in either order or simultaneously. In other words, a causal partial order is an invariant describing an abstract history of a concurrent system. Both interleaving and true concurrency models have been developed to a high degree of sophistication and proved to be successful specification, verification and property proving tools. However, there are some problems, for instance the specification of priorities using partial orders alone is often problematic (see [La85, Ja87, JL88]). Another example is inhibitor nets (see [Pe81]) which are virtually admired by practitioners, and almost completely rejected by theoreticians, in our opinion mainly because their full concurrent behaviour cannot be properly defined in terms of causality based structures. We think that these kind of problems follow from the general assumption that all behavioural properties of a concurrent system can be adequately modelled in terms of causal partial orders or causality-based relations. We claim [JK90,91,91a,91b] that the structure of concurrency phenomena is richer and there are other invariants which can be used to represent an abstract history of a concurrent system.

In this paper we consider one of such invariants, called *weak causal partial order*. More precisely, we employ combined partial orders, or *composets*, to provide an invariant semantics of concurrent systems modelled by Elementary Net systems with inhibitor arcs. Each composet is a relational structure comprising a causal partial order and a *weak causal partial order*. We then introduce a representation of composets using a novel concept of *comtrace*, which is certain equivalence class of step sequences. The development of the comtrace model resembles to a significant extent that of Mazurkiewicz traces [Ma77, Ma86, AR88]. Composets correspond to posets, comtraces correspond to traces, while step sequences correspond to interleaving sequences. The independency relation used to define the equivalence classes of interleaving sequences in [Ma77] is replaced by two new relations on events, *simultaneity* and *serialisability*. The former specifies what events may be executed in one step; the latter comprises pairs of events (e,f) such that if $\{e,f\}$ is a possible execution step then e and f can also be executed in the order: *e followed by f* (but not necessarily in the order *f followed by e*).

The paper is organised as follows. In the next section we briefly present the motivation for the introduction of the new invariant semantics. In Section 3 we introduce composets. Section 4 contains the development of the comtrace model. The last section shows how the comtraces can provide an invariant semantics for the Elementary Net Systems with Inhibitor Arcs (ENI-systems).

2. Motivation

In this section we present an example which we believe clearly identifies an inability of the causal partial order (CPO) semantics to cope properly with some relevant aspects of non-sequential behaviour. We will use Petri nets [Pe81,Re85] to illustrate our discussion.

Our example closely follows the discussion in [Ja87,JL88,BK91]. We consider a concurrent system *Con* comprising two sequential subsystems *A* and *B* such that:

(1) *A* can execute event *a* and afterwards event *b*.

(2) *B* can either engage in event *b*, or engage in event *c*.

(3) The two sequential subsystems synchronise by means of the handshake communication.

(4) The specification of *Con* includes a priority constraint stating that whenever it is possible to execute event *b*, then event *c* must not be executed.

One can model *Con* as the Petri net N_{prior} of Figure 2.1. To obtain the step sequences generated by N_{prior}, we take the step sequences of net *N*, where *N* is N_{prior} without the priority constraint, and then delete those step sequences which are inconsistent with the priority specification. Since the step sequences of *N* are $steps(N)=\{\lambda,\{a\},\{c\},\{a,c\},\{a\}\{c\},\{c\}\{a\},\{a\}\{b\}\}$, the step sequences of are $steps(N_{prior})=\{\lambda, \{a\},\{c\},\{a,c\},\{c\}\{a\},\{a\}\{b\}\}$. Note that $\{a\}\{c\}\notin steps(N_{prior})$ since after executing *a*, event *b* becomes enabled and *c* cannot be executed. It is not difficult to see that $steps(N_{prior})$ cannot be consistent with any CPO semantics. The reason is that the simultaneous occurrence of *a* and *c* in $\{a,c\}$ would imply that $\{a\}\{c\}$ could also be executed. Note that in [BK91] it was observed that whether $\{a,c\}$ should be at all allowed as a valid behaviour of N_{prior} is intrinsically related to whether or not one can regard *a* as an event taking some time. Briefly, if *a* is instantaneous then $\{a,c\}$ should not be allowed, and then a CPO semantics consistent with the remaining step sequences in $steps(N_{prior})$ can be constructed along the lines described in [BK91]. If, however, *a* cannot be regarded as instantaneous (possibly because *a* is itself a compound event) then $\{a,c\}$ should be allowed, and one should look for an invariant model more expressive than CPO to describe the behaviour of N_{prior}.

In [JK90,91] it has been shown that to provide an invariant semantics consistent with the full set $steps(N_{prior})$ we need structures which are more expressive than CPO's. We proposed to use *combined partial orders* (or *composets*). A composet is a *structure* $co=(\Sigma,\rightarrow,\nearrow)$ such that $(\Sigma,\rightarrow)$ is the standard causality invariant, and $(\Sigma,\nearrow)$ is a *weak causality* invariant. The weak causality essentially means that if $a\nearrow b$ then in every step sequence consistent with *co*, *a precedes or is simultaneous with b.*

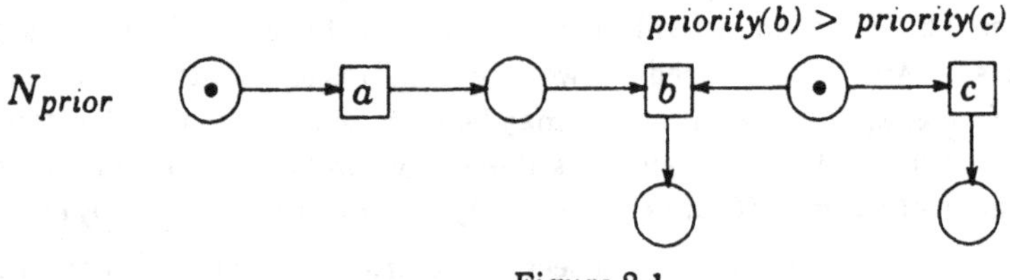

Figure 2.1

3. Composets

In this section, after presenting some notions concerning finite partial orders, we introduce main concepts of the composet model.

3.1 Basic Definitions

A *partially ordered set* (or poset) is a pair $po=(dom(po),\rightarrow_{po})$ such that $dom(po)$ is a finite set and $\rightarrow_{po}$ is an irreflexive and transitive relation. We will denote $a\leftrightarrow_{po}b$ if *a* and *b* are distinct elements of $dom(po)$ incomparable under $\rightarrow_{po}$. Figure 3.1(a) shows a poset such that $a\rightarrow_{po}b$ and $a\leftrightarrow_{po}c$ and $c\leftrightarrow_{po}b$. A *step sequence* (or stratified) poset is a poset *ssp* such that for all distinct $a,b,c\in dom(ssp)$, $a\leftrightarrow_{ssp}b\leftrightarrow_{ssp}c$ implies $a\leftrightarrow_{ssp}c$. In this case there is a unique sequence of non-empty sets $step(ssp)=B_1...B_k$ such that $\rightarrow_{ssp}=\bigcup_{i<j}B_i\times B_j$. A *total order* is a poset *to* such that $\leftrightarrow_{to}=\varnothing$. A step sequence poset *ssp* is *consistent* with poset *po*, $ssp\in steps(po)$, if $dom(po)=dom(ssp)$ and $\rightarrow_{po}\subseteq\rightarrow_{ssp}$. $total(po)$ comprises the total orders in $steps(po)$. In Figure 3.1, $step(ssp)=\{a\}\{b,c\}$ and $ssp,ssp_0\in steps(po)$.

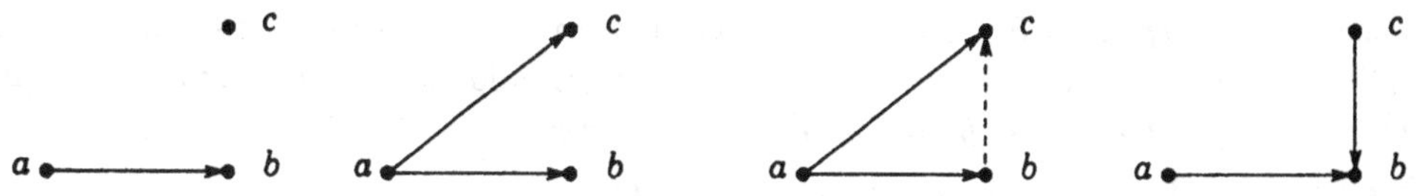

(a) *poset po* (b) *step sequence poset ssp* (c) *composet co* (d) *poset ssp_o*

Figure 3.1

Theorem 3.1.1 For every poset *po* there is exactly one (canonical) step sequence poset in *steps(po)*, denoted by *can(po)*, such that if $step(can(po))=B_1...B_k$ then for every $i\geq 2$ and every $b\in B_i$ there is $a\in B_{i-1}$ satisfying $a\rightarrow_{po}b$. (In Figure 3.1, $can(po)=ssp_o$.) □

A *composet* (or *combined partially ordered* set) is a triple $co=(\Sigma,\rightarrow,\nearrow)$ such that Σ is a finite set and $\rightarrow,\nearrow$ are binary relations on Σ satisfying the following conditions.

(C1) $\neg a\nearrow a$ (C3) $a\rightarrow b \Rightarrow \neg b\nearrow a$ (C5) $a\nearrow b \wedge b\rightarrow c \Rightarrow a\rightarrow c$
(C2) $a\rightarrow b \Rightarrow a\nearrow b$ (C4) $a\nearrow b \wedge b\nearrow c \Rightarrow a=c \vee a\nearrow c$ (C6) $a\rightarrow b \wedge b\nearrow c \Rightarrow a\rightarrow c$

Note that $(\Sigma,\rightarrow)$ is a poset. $\rightarrow$ is intended to represent causality, while $\nearrow$ weak causality. We will denote $dom(co)=\Sigma$ and $\rightarrow_{co}=\rightarrow$ and $\nearrow_{co}=\nearrow$. Figure 3.1(c) shows a composet such that $a\rightarrow_{co}b$ and $b\nearrow_{co}c$ and $a\rightarrow_{co}c$. (In the diagrams solid lines denote $\rightarrow_{co}$, while dashed arcs denote $\nearrow_{co}$. We do not draw the dashed arc between a and b if $a\rightarrow_{co}b$.) A composet co_1 is *included* in composet co_2, denoted $co_1\subseteq co_2$, if $dom(co_1)=dom(co_2)$ and $\rightarrow_{co_1}\subseteq\rightarrow_{co_2}$ and $\nearrow_{co_1}\subseteq\nearrow_{co_2}$.

Since composets satisfying $\rightarrow=\nearrow$ are isomorphic with partial orders, the theory of finite partial orders is in a natural way embedded in the composet model. Moreover, a number of notions and properties of partial orders can be lifted to the level of composets. One such notion is the operation of transitive closure. Let $q=(\Sigma,\rightarrow_o,\nearrow_o)$, where Σ is a finite set and $\rightarrow_o,\nearrow_o$ are two irreflexive relations on Σ. The *composet closure* of q is $q^\dagger=(\Sigma,\rightarrow,\nearrow)$, where $\rightarrow$ and $\nearrow$ are the smallest relations on Σ satisfying the following.

$a\rightarrow_o b \Rightarrow a\rightarrow b$ $a\nearrow_o b \Rightarrow a\nearrow b$ $a\nearrow b \wedge b\rightarrow c \Rightarrow a\rightarrow c$
$a\rightarrow b \Rightarrow a\nearrow b$ $a\nearrow b \wedge b\nearrow c \wedge a\neq c \Rightarrow a\nearrow c$ $a\rightarrow b \wedge b\nearrow c \Rightarrow a\rightarrow c$

We then introduce the notion of a *reinforced cycle* of q which is any sequence $a_1,a_2,...,a_n=a_1$ such that $a_i\rightarrow_o a_{i+1}$ or $a_i\nearrow_o a_{i+1}$ for all $i<n$, and $a_j\rightarrow_o a_{j+1}$ for at least one j.

Proposition 3.1.2 $q^\dagger$ is a composet if and only if q contains no reinforced cycles. □

The next result follows directly from Proposition 3.1.2 and shows two ways of augmenting composets. Note that *co* in Figure 3.1(c) could be augmented by adding either $b\rightarrow c$ or $c\nearrow b$.

Proposition 3.1.3 Let *co* be a composet and a,b be two distinct elements of *dom(co)*.
(1) If $\neg a\nearrow_{co}b$ then $(dom(co),\rightarrow_{co}\cup\{(b,a)\},\nearrow_{co})^\dagger$ is a composet.
(2) If $\neg a\rightarrow_{co}b$ then $(dom(co),\rightarrow_{co},\nearrow_{co}\cup\{(b,a)\})^\dagger$ is a composet. □

There is a similarity between the definition of a composet and the axioms for strong and weak precedence relation in [La86]. However, the way these two concepts are derived and the reasons for their introduction are quite different. Hence this similarity is either accidental or, as one might suspect, composets in a natural way generalise partial orders, and may be useful for various, perhaps unrelated, applications.

3.2 Composets and Step Sequence Posets

The relationship between composets and step sequence posets resembles that between partial and total orders. Let *co* be a composet and *ssp* be a step sequence poset such that *dom(ssp)*

$=dom(co)$ and $step(ssp)=B_1...B_k$. ssp is *consistent* with co, $ssp \in steps(co)$, if $\rightarrow_{co} \subseteq \rightarrow_{ssp}$ and $\nearrow_{co} \subseteq (\rightarrow_{ssp} \cup \leftrightarrow_{ssp})$. ssp is *canonical* for co if $ssp \in steps(co)$ and for every $i \geq 2$ and every $b \in B_i$ there is $a \in B_{i-1}$ such that $a \rightarrow_{co} b$. In Figure 3.1, $can(co)=ssp$.

Theorem 3.2.1 Let co be a composet and $po=(dom(co), \rightarrow_{co})$.
(1) There is a unique canonical step sequence poset for co, denoted by $can(co)$.
(2) $can(co)=can(po)$.
(3) $steps(co) \neq \emptyset$.

Proof: (3) follows directly from (1). Since every canonical step sequence for co is also canonical for po, it follows from Theorem 3.1.1 that to show (1) and (2) it suffices to prove that $ssp= can(po)$ is canonical for co, which will follow from $ssp \in steps(co)$. Let $step(ssp)=B_1...B_k$. Clearly, $\rightarrow_{co} \subseteq \rightarrow_{ssp}$. Suppose $a \nearrow_{co} b$ and $b \rightarrow_{ssp} a$. Then $a \in B_i$ for some $i \geq 2$. Hence, by $ssp=can(po)$, there is $c \in B_{i-1}$ such that $c \rightarrow_{co} a$. Thus $c \rightarrow_{co} b$ and, consequently, $c \rightarrow_{ssp} b$. Hence $b \in B_j$ for some $j \geq i$, contradicting $b \rightarrow_{ssp} a$. Thus $\nearrow_{co} \subseteq (\rightarrow_{ssp} \cup \leftrightarrow_{ssp})$. □

Proposition 3.2.2 Let a and b be two distinct elements of a composet co.
1. If $\neg a \nearrow_{co} b$ then there is $ssp \in steps(co)$ such that $b \rightarrow_{ssp} a$.
2. If $\neg a \rightarrow_{co} b$ then there is $ssp \in steps(co)$ such that $b \rightarrow_{ssp} a$ or $b \leftrightarrow_{ssp} a$.

Proof: By Proposition 3.1.3(1), $co_1=(dom(co), \rightarrow_{co} \cup \{(b,a)\}, \nearrow_{co})^{\dagger}$ is a composet. Clearly, $b \rightarrow_{ssp} a$ for all $ssp \in steps(co_1) \subseteq steps(co)$. Moreover, by Theorem 3.2.1(3), $steps(co_1) \neq \emptyset$. Hence (1) holds. To show (2) we proceed similarly, this time using Proposition 3.1.3(2). □

Every poset po is unambiguously identified by the set of its linearisations, *total*(po) [Sz30]. The same does not hold for composets. Consider co_1 and co_2 such that $dom(co_1)=dom(co_2)= \{a,b\}$ and $a \rightarrow_{co_1} b$ and $a \nearrow_{co_1} b$ and $a \nearrow_{co_2} b$. The two composets are different, yet in each case there is only one total order in $steps(co_i)$, namely to satisfying $a \rightarrow_{to} b$. To distinguish co_1 from co_2 we need to compare $steps(co_1)$ and $steps(co_2)$.

Theorem 3.2.3 Let co_1 and co_2 be composets. Then $co_1=co_2$ iff $steps(co_1)=steps(co_2)$.

Proof: It suffices to show that $steps(co_1) \subseteq steps(co_2)$ implies $co_2 \subseteq co_1$. From Theorem 3.2.1(3) it follows $dom(co_1)=dom(co_2)$. If $a \rightarrow_{co_2} b$ and $\neg a \rightarrow_{co_1} b$ then, by Proposition 3.2.2(2), there is $ssp \in steps(co_1)$ such that $b \rightarrow_{ssp} a$ or $b \leftrightarrow_{ssp} a$. Thus $ssp \notin steps(co_2)$, producing a contradiction with $steps(co_1) \subseteq steps(co_2)$. Hence $\rightarrow_{co_2} \subseteq \rightarrow_{co_1}$. Similarly, by using Proposition 3.2.2(1), we can show that $\nearrow_{co_2} \subseteq \nearrow_{co_1}$. □

Let Δ be a non-empty set of step sequence posets with a common domain Σ. The *intersection* of Δ is $co(\Delta)=(\Sigma, \rightarrow_\Delta, \nearrow_\Delta)=(\Sigma, \bigcap_{ssp \in \Delta} \rightarrow_{ssp}, \bigcap_{ssp \in \Delta} (\rightarrow_{ssp} \cup \leftrightarrow_{ssp}))$. For $\Delta=\{ssp_1, ssp_2\}$, where $step(ssp_1)=\{a\}\{b\}\{c\}$ and $step(ssp_2)= \{a\}\{b,c\}$, the intersection $co(\Delta)$ is co of Figure 3.1(c).

Proposition 3.2.4 $co(\Delta)$ is a composet.

Proof: C1, C2 and C3 are obvious. To show C4 we observe that $a \nearrow_\Delta b \wedge b \nearrow_\Delta c$ implies, for all $ssp \in \Delta$, $a \rightarrow_{ssp} b \rightarrow_{ssp} c \vee a \rightarrow_{ssp} b \leftrightarrow_{ssp} c \vee a \leftrightarrow_{ssp} b \rightarrow_{ssp} c \vee a \leftrightarrow_{ssp} b \leftrightarrow_{ssp} c$. Furthermore, from the definition of the step sequence poset we have: $a \rightarrow_{ssp} b \leftrightarrow_{ssp} c \Rightarrow a \rightarrow_{ssp} c$ and $a \leftrightarrow_{ssp} b \rightarrow_{ssp} c \Rightarrow a \rightarrow_{ssp} c$ and $a \leftrightarrow_{ssp} b \leftrightarrow_{ssp} c \Rightarrow a=c \vee a \leftrightarrow_{ssp} c$. Hence for all $ssp \in \Delta$, $a \rightarrow_{ssp} c \vee a \leftrightarrow_{ssp} c \vee a=c$. Thus $a \nearrow_\Delta c \vee a=c$, and C4 is satisfied. We then show C5 and C6 in a similar way. □

A fundamental result of [Sz30] says that by intersecting all the linearisations of a partial order one obtains the original partial order. A similar result holds also for composets.

Theorem 3.2.5 Let co be a composet. Then $co=co(steps(co))$.
(Note that the theorem is correctly formulated due to Theorem 3.2.1(3).)

Proof: Let $\Delta = steps(co)$. Clearly, $co \subseteq co(\Delta)$. If $a \rightarrow_{\Delta} b$ and $\neg a \rightarrow_{co} b$ then, by Proposition 3.2.2(2), there is $ssp \in \Delta$ such that $b \rightarrow_{ssp} a$ or $b \leftrightarrow_{ssp} a$, a contradiction with $a \rightarrow_{\Delta} b$. Hence $\rightarrow_{co} = \rightarrow_{\Delta}$. To show $\nearrow_{co} = \nearrow_{\Delta}$ we proceed similarly, this time using Proposition 3.2.2(1). □

To illustrate the similarities between the two notions, in Table 3.1 we relate some of the properties of finite partial orders and composets.

POSETS	*COMPOSETS*	
transitive closure is a poset iff there are no cycles	*composet closure is a composet iff there are no reinforced cycles*	*Proposition 3.1.2*
total(po) $\neq \emptyset$	*steps(co)* $\neq \emptyset$	*Theorem 3.2.1(3)*
intersecting total orders yields a poset	*intersecting step sequence posets yields a composet*	*Proposition 3.2.4*
intersecting total orders in total(po) yields po	*intersecting step sequence posets in steps(co) yields co*	*Theorem 3.2.5*
po has a canonical step sequence	*co has a canonical step sequence poset*	*Theorem 3.2.1(1)*

Table 3.1

4. Comtraces

Trace theory [Ma77, Ma86, AR88] deals with partial orders that can be interpreted as behaviours of, e.g., EN-systems or 1-safe Petri nets. We will now introduce a class of composets represented by *comtraces*, which generalise classical traces and can be interpreted as behaviours of, e.g., EN-systems with inhibitor arcs (see Section 5).

Let E be a non-empty set of *event names*, and let sim and ser be two binary relations on E such that sim is irreflexive and symmetric, and $ser \subseteq sim$. The elements of E will be interpreted as actions of a concurrent system. If $(e,f) \in sim$ then e and f can occur simultaneously, while $(e,f) \in ser$ implies that if e and f occurred simultaneously then it was also possible for e to occur before f. Thus sim represents *simultaneity*, while ser represents *serialisability*. We do not assume any special properties of the relation ser. In what follows E, sim and ser are fixed.

A non-empty finite set $A \subseteq E$ is a *step*, $A \in Step$, if for all distinct $e,f \in A$, $(e,f) \in sim$. Finite sequences of steps, called *step sequences*, are meant to represent single runs of a concurrent system. Let $\sim$ be a relation comprising all pairs $(t,u) \in Step^* \times Step^*$ such that $t = wAz$ and $u = wBCz$, for $A,B,C \in Step$ satisfying $B \cap C = \emptyset$ and $A = B \cup C$ and $B \times C \subseteq ser$. Intuitively, if $t \sim u$ then t is a run of the system if and only if u is also a possible run. Note that step A can be split into two consecutive steps, B and C, if every $b \in B$ and every $c \in C$ are serialisable. The reflexive transitive closure of $\sim$ will be denoted $\approx$, and any equivalence class of $\approx$ will be called a *comtrace*. A comtrace containing $t \in Step^*$ will be denoted $[t]$. As in trace theory, $[t]$ is intended to represent a non-sequential history of the concurrent system.

The original notion of trace [Ma77] deals only with sequences of occurrences of events. It has been generalised in [JK89] to step sequences with the resulting objects corresponding to comtraces with $sim = ser = ser^{-1}$. In such a case sim is called the *independency* relation and denoted by ind. Suppose that $ind = sim = ser = ser^{-1} = \{(a,b),(b,a)\}$. Then we have the following.

Classical trace of [Ma77]:	$[ab]_M=\{ab,ba\}$
Generalised trace of [JK89]:	$[\{a\}\{b\}]_G=\{\{a\}\{b\},\{b\}\{a\},\{a,b\}\}$
Comtrace:	$[\{a\}\{b\}]=\{\{a\}\{b\},\{b\}\{a\},\{a,b\}\}$.

We now relate step sequences of *Step** to step sequence posets introduced in Section 3. Let $t=A_1...A_k\in Step^*$. We define the set of *event occurrences* in t as $Occ(t)=\{(e,i)\mid e\in E\wedge 1\le i\le \#_e(t)\}$, where $\#_e(t)$ is the number of the sets A_i such that $e\in A_i$. Let $a=(e,i)\in Occ(t)$. The *position* of a in t, $pos_t(a)$, is the smallest j such that $\#_e(A_1...A_j)=i$. The *label* of a is defined as $l(a)=e$. Clearly, $l(a)\in A_{pos_t(a)}$. The partial order *induced* by t is defined as $ssp(t)=(Occ(t),\rightarrow)$, where $a\rightarrow b:\Leftrightarrow pos_t(a)<pos_t(b)$. Directly from the definition of $\sim$ we obtain the following.

Proposition 4.1 Let $t=A_1...A_k$ be a step sequence and $a,b\in Occ(t)$.
(1) $ssp(t)$ is a step sequence poset.
(2) $step(ssp(t))=B_1...B_k$, where $l(B_i)=A_i$ and $|B_i|=|A_i|$, for all i.
(3) If $t\sim u$ then $|(pos_t(a)-pos_t(b))-(pos_u(a)-pos_u(b))|\le 1$.
(4) If $pos_t(a)=pos_t(b)$ and $(l(a),l(b))\notin ser$ then $pos_u(b)\le pos_u(a)$ for all $u\in[t]$. □

In trace theory it is possible to construct, for every sequence $\tau\in E^*$, a partial order *po* which is the intersection of the total orders induced by the sequences in $[\tau]_M$. In the comtrace model a similar construction is possible. More precisely, given a step sequence $t\in Step^*$ one can construct a composet *co* satisfying $steps(co)=co(ssp([t]))$. The construction is based on the observation that if $pos_t(a)<pos_t(b)$ and $(l(a),l(b))\notin ser$ then $pos_u(a)<pos_u(b)$, for all $u\in[t]$. Indeed, if there were $w\in[t]$ such that $pos_w(b)<pos_w(a)$ then, by Proposition 4.1(3), there would be $u\in[t]$ such that $pos_u(a)=pos_u(b)$. Thus, if the observation does not hold, then $pos_u(a)=pos_u(b)$ for at least one $u\in[t]$. But this contradicts Proposition 4.1(4). Similarly, we may observe that if $pos_t(a)\le pos_t(b)$ and $(l(b),l(a))\notin ser$ then $pos_u(a)\le pos_u(b)$, for all $u\in[t]$. Thus in the first case we should have $a\rightarrow_{co}b$, while in the second case $a\nearrow_{co}b$. We define the *composet induced* by t as $co(t)=(Occ(t),\rightarrow_t,\nearrow_t)^+$, where for all distinct $a,b\in Occ(t)$,

$$a\rightarrow_t b:\Leftrightarrow (l(a),l(b))\notin ser\wedge pos_t(a)<pos_t(b)\quad\text{and}\quad a\nearrow_t b:\Leftrightarrow (l(b),l(a))\notin ser\wedge pos_t(a)\le pos_t(b).$$

Proposition 4.2 Let t be a step sequence. Then $co(t)$ is a composet and $ssp(t)\in steps(co(t))$.

Proof: Clearly, $\rightarrow_t$ and $\nearrow_t$ are irreflexive. Moreover, the only cycles in the graph of $(Occ(t),\rightarrow_t\cup\nearrow_t)$ are of the form $a_1,...,a_n=a_1$, where $pos_t(a_1)=...=pos_t(a_n)$. Hence $\neg\, a_i\rightarrow_t a_{i+1}$ for all $i<n$. Thus, by Proposition 3.1.2, $co(t)$ is a composet. Let a and b be two distinct elements in $Occ(t)$. From the definition of $\rightarrow_t$, $\nearrow_t$ and $^+$ it follows that $a\rightarrow_{co(t)}b\Rightarrow pos_t(a)<pos_t(b)\Rightarrow a\rightarrow_{ssp(t)}b$, and $a\nearrow_{co(t)}b\Rightarrow pos_t(a)\le pos_t(b)\Rightarrow a\rightarrow_{ssp(t)}b\vee a\leftrightarrow_{ssp(t)}b$. Hence $ssp(t)\in steps(co(t))$. □

The step sequence posets consistent with $co(t)$ are induced by step sequences.

Proposition 4.3 Let t be a step sequence. Then $steps(co(t))\subseteq ssp(Step^*)$.

Proof: Let $ssp\in steps(co(t))$ and $step(ssp)=B_1...B_k$. We will show that $u=l(B_1)...l(B_k)$ satisfies $u\in Step^*$ and $ssp=ssp(u)$. Suppose $a,b\in B_i$ are distinct elements such that $(l(a),l(b))\notin sim$. Then $(l(a),l(b))\notin ser$ and $(l(b),l(a))\notin ser$. If $pos_t(a)\ne pos_t(b)$ then $a\rightarrow_{co(t)}b$ or $b\rightarrow_{co(t)}a$. This and $ssp\in steps(co(t))$ implies $a\rightarrow_{ssp}b$ or $b\rightarrow_{ssp}a$, contradicting $a,b\in B_i$. Hence $pos_t(a)=pos_t(b)$, contradicting $t\in Step^*$. Thus $a,b\in B_i$ and $a\ne b$ implies $(l(a),l(b))\in sim$. In particular, this means that l is injective on each B_i. Hence $u\in Step^*$ and $dom(u)=dom(t)$. It is now easy to see that there is an isomorphism h for ssp and $ssp(u)$ satisfying $l(a)=l(h(a))$, for all a. Moreover, $(e,1)\rightarrow_{co(t)}(e,2)\rightarrow_{co(t)}...\rightarrow_{co(t)}(e,\#_e(t))$, for all $e\in E$, which means that $(e,1)\rightarrow_{ssp}(e,2)\rightarrow_{ssp}...\rightarrow_{ssp}(e,\#_e(t))$. On the other hand, $(e,1)\rightarrow_{ssp(u)}(e,2)\rightarrow_{ssp(u)}...\rightarrow_{ssp(u)}(e,\#_e(t))$. Thus h must be an identity mapping, which completes the proof. □

Our first major result, Theorem 4.7, implies that two step sequences induce the same composets if and only if they belong to the same comtrace.

Lemma 4.4 Let t and u be step sequences. Then $t \approx u$ implies $co(t) = co(u)$.

Proof: It suffices to show that if $t \sim u$ or $u \sim t$, then $\rightarrow_t \subseteq \rightarrow_u$ and $\nearrow_u \subseteq \nearrow_t$. It is easy to see that if this does not hold then there are a and b such that $pos_t(a) < pos_t(b)$ and $pos_u(b) \leq pos_u(a)$ and $(l(a), l(b)) \notin ser$. Thus, by Proposition 4.1(3), $pos_u(a) = pos_u(b)$. Hence, by Proposition 4.1(4), $pos_t(a) \geq pos_t(b)$, a contradiction. □

A *canonical* step sequence, $t \in Can$, is any $t = A_1 ... A_k \in Step^*$ such that if $i \geq 2$ then there is no step $B \subseteq A_i$ satisfying $A_{i-1} \times B \subseteq ser$ and $B \times (A_i - B) \subseteq ser$. The next result establishes a consistency between the two notions of canonical step sequence.

Proposition 4.5 Let $t \in Can$. Then $ssp(t) = can(co(t))$.

Proof: By Proposition 4.2, $ssp(t) \in steps(co(t))$. Let $t = A_1 ... A_k$ and $step(ssp(t)) = B_1 ... B_k$. By Theorem 3.2.1, it suffices to show that for every $i \geq 2$ and every $b \in B_i$ there is $a \in B_{i-1}$ such that $a \rightarrow_{co(t)} b$. If this does not hold then $B = \{b \in B_i \mid B_{i-1} \times \{b\} \cap \rightarrow_{co(t)} = \emptyset\} \neq \emptyset$, for some $i \geq 2$. Clearly, $A_{i-1} \times l(B) \subseteq ser$ which follows from the definition of $co(t)$. Suppose there is $a \in B$ and $b \in B_i - B$ such that $(l(a), l(b)) \notin ser$. Then $b \nearrow_{co(t)} a$. Moreover, by the definition of B, $c \rightarrow_{co(t)} b$ for some $c \in B_{i-1}$. Hence $c \rightarrow_{co(t)} a$, contradicting the definition of B. Thus we have $l(B) \times (A_i - l(B)) \subseteq ser$ and $A_{i-1} \times l(B) \subseteq ser$, contradicting $t \in Can$. □

Proposition 4.6 Let t be a step sequence. Then there is $u \in Can$ such that $t \approx u$.

Proof: Let $h : Step^* \rightarrow \{0,1,2,...\}$ be defined by $h(A_1 ... A_k) = 1 \times |A_1| + ... + k \times |A_k|$. There is $u \in [t]$ such that $h(u) \leq h(w)$ for all $w \in [t]$. We will show that $u \in Can$. Suppose $u = A_1 ... A_k$ and $u \notin Can$. Then there is $i \geq 2$ and a step $B \subseteq A_i$ such that $A_{i-1} \times B \subseteq ser$ and $B \times (A_i - B) \subseteq ser$. If $B = A_i$ then $w \sim u$ and $h(w) < h(u)$, where $w = A_1 ... A_{i-2}(A_{i-1} \cup A_i) A_{i+1} ... A_k$. If $B \neq A_i$ then $w \sim z$ and $u \sim z$ and $h(w) < h(u)$, where

$z = A_1 ... A_{i-2} A_{i-1} B (A_i - B) A_{i+1} ... A_k$ and $w = A_1 ... A_{i-2}(A_{i-1} \cup B)(A_i - B) A_{i+1} ... A_k$.

In either case we obtain a contradiction with the choice of u. □

Theorem 4.7 Let t and u be step sequences. Then $co(t) = co(u)$ iff $t \approx u$.

Proof: By Lemma 4.4, we only need to show the left-to-right implication. From Proposition 4.6 it follows that there are $t_o, u_o \in Can$ such that $t \approx t_o$ and $u \approx u_o$. By Lemma 4.4, $co(t_o) = co(u_o)$. By Proposition 4.5, $ssp(t_o) = can(co(t_o))$ and $ssp(u_o) = can(co(u_o))$. Hence, by Theorem 3.2.1, $ssp(t_o) = ssp(u_o)$. Thus $t_o = u_o$ and, consequently, $t \approx u$. □

We end this section proving two other major results. Theorem 4.9 says that the step sequence posets consistent with $co(t)$ are those generated by step sequences in $[t]$. Theorem 4.10 says that the composet induced by a comtrace is uniquely identified by any step sequence poset which is consistent with it.

Lemma 4.8 Let t and u be step sequences. Then $ssp(u) \in steps(co(t))$ implies $co(u) = co(t)$.

Proof: Let $a, b \in dom(u) = dom(t)$. We have $a \rightarrow_t b \Rightarrow a \rightarrow_{co(t)} b \Rightarrow a \rightarrow_{ssp(u)} b \Rightarrow pos_u(a) < pos_u(b)$. Moreover, $a \rightarrow_t b \Rightarrow (l(a), l(b)) \notin ser$. Hence $a \rightarrow_t b$ implies $a \rightarrow_u b$. Suppose $a \nearrow_t b$. Then $(l(b), l(a)) \notin ser$ and $a \nearrow_{co(t)} b$. Thus $a \rightarrow_{ssp(u)} b$ or $a \leftrightarrow_{ssp(u)} b$. Hence $(l(b), l(a)) \notin ser$ and $pos_u(a) \leq pos_u(b)$ which yields $a \nearrow_u b$. Consequently, $\rightarrow_t \subseteq \rightarrow_u$ and $\nearrow_t \subseteq \nearrow_u$. Suppose $a \rightarrow_u b$ and $\neg a \rightarrow_t b$. By $a \rightarrow_u b$, $(l(a), l(b)) \notin ser$. This and $\neg a \rightarrow_t b$ means that $pos_t(a) \geq pos_t(b)$. Hence $b \nearrow_t a$, producing a contradiction with $ssp(u) \in steps(co(t))$ and $a \rightarrow_{ssp(u)} b$ (which follows from $a \rightarrow_u b$). Suppose $a \nearrow_u b$ and $\neg a \nearrow_t b$. By $a \nearrow_u b$, $(l(b), l(a)) \notin ser$. This and $\neg a \nearrow_t b$ means that $pos_t(b) < pos_t(a)$. Hence $b \rightarrow_t a$, producing a contradiction with $ssp(u)\in steps(co(t))$ and $a\rightarrow_{ssp(u)}b \vee a\leftrightarrow_{ssp(u)}b$ (which follows from $a\nearrow_u b$). Thus $\rightarrow_u\subseteq\rightarrow_t$ and $\nearrow_u\subseteq\nearrow_t$. □

Theorem 4.9 Let t be a step sequence. Then $steps(co(t))=ssp([t])$.

Proof: If $u\in[t]$ then, by Theorem 4.7, $co(u)=co(t)$. This and Proposition 4.2 yields $ssp(u)\in steps(co(t))$. Hence $ssp([t])\subseteq steps(co(t))$. Suppose $ssp\in steps(co(t))$. By Proposition 4.3, there is $u\in Step^*$ such that $ssp=ssp(u)$. Thus, by Lemma 4.8, $co(u)=co(t)$. This and Theorem 4.7 yields $t\approx u$. Hence $ssp=ssp(u)\in ssp([t])$ which means that $steps(co(t))\subseteq ssp([t])$. □

Theorem 4.10 Let t and u be step sequences. Then $steps(co(t))\cap steps(co(u))\neq\emptyset$ implies $t\approx u$.

Proof: Let $ssp\in steps(co(t))\cap steps(co(u))$. By Proposition 4.3, there is $w\in Step^*$ such that $ssp=ssp(w)$. By Lemma 4.8, $co(u)=co(w)=co(t)$. This and Theorem 4.7 yields $t\approx u$. □

We end this section making a comment that comtraces form a monoid with the identity $[\lambda]$, where λ is the empty step sequence, and the concatenation operation defined by $[t]\circ[u]=[tu]$. It is not difficult to see that $\circ$ is indeed well defined, i.e., $[tu]=[vw]$, for all $v\in[t]$ and $w\in[u]$.

5. Elementary Net Systems with Inhibitor Arcs

Traces can provide a non-interleaving semantics of 1-safe Petri nets [Ma77] and EN-systems [NRT90]. In this section we will show how comtraces can provide a non-interleaving semantics for EN-systems with inhibitor arcs.

5.1 Basic Definitions

A *net with inhibitor arcs* is $N=(S,T,F,I)$, where S,T are finite disjoint sets, $F\subseteq(S\times T)\cup(T\times S)$ and $I\subseteq S\times T$, such that $(F\cup F^{-1})\cap I=\emptyset$ and $F\cap F^{-1}=\emptyset$ and $T\subseteq dom(F)\cap cod(F)$. The meaning of S, T and F is the same as in the standard net theory, while an inhibitor arc $(s,e)\in I$ means that e can be enabled only if s is unmarked. For every $x\in S\cup T$, $x^\bullet=\{y \mid (x,y)\in F\}$, ${}^\bullet x=\{y \mid (y,x)\in F\}$ and $x^\circ=\{y \mid (x,y)\in I\cup I^{-1}\}$. The dot-notation extends in usual way to sets of elements.

An *elementary net system with inhibitor arcs* (ENI-system) is $\Xi=(B,E,F,I,c_{in})$, where (B,E,F,I) is a net with inhibitor arcs, and $c_{in}\subseteq B$ is the initial case. (In general, any $c\subseteq B$ is a *case*.) The elements of E are called *events*, and of B *conditions*. EN-systems, i.e. those ENI-systems for which $I=\emptyset$, are meant to represent the simplest system model of net theory. They can also be used to provide an operational semantics for other system models after being equipped with a suitable labelling of events. For this reason it seems that ENI-systems could be seen as the simplest system model whose non-interleaving semantics would warrant relational structures richer than causal partial orders. As it has been shown in [NRT90] EN-systems can be given a trace semantics with the independency relation being based on the structural properties of the net. In Section 5.2 this approach will be generalised to ENI-systems whose semantics will be given in terms of comtraces. Figure 5.1(a) shows an ENI-system. Note that the inhibitor arc $(3,f)$ is identified by a small circle at one end. We will assume that Ξ is fixed throughout the rest of this section.

The operational semantics of Ξ is defined by means of a 'token game' which differs from that defined for EN-systems in that we additionally assume that an event can be enabled only if each condition with which it is joined by an inhibitor arc is unmarked. We first introduce an interleaving semantics of Ξ. Let $c\subseteq B$ and $e\in E$. Then e is *enabled* at c if ${}^\bullet e\subseteq c$ and $(e^\bullet\cup e^\circ)\cap c=\emptyset$. If e is enabled at c and $c'=c-{}^\bullet e\cup e^\bullet$ then c' can be *reached* from c through an occurrence of e. We denote this by $c[e>c'$. By a *firing sequence* of Ξ we mean any sequence of events $e_1...e_n$ such that there are cases $c_1,...,c_n$ satisfying $c_{in}[e_1>c_1[e_2>c_2...[e_n>c_n$. We also

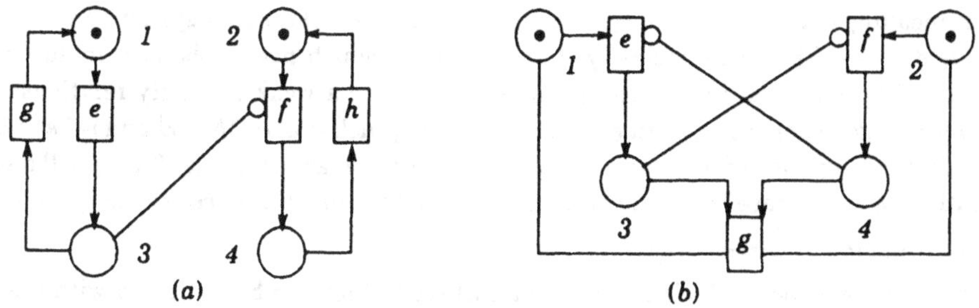

Figure 5.1: ENI-systems.

denote $c_n \in SC_\Xi$. Next we generalise the operational semantics to sequences of steps, each step being a set of events executed simultaneously. Let $U \subseteq B$ be a non-empty set such that $(e^\bullet \cup {}^\bullet e) \cap (f^\bullet \cup {}^\bullet f) = \emptyset$ for all distinct $e,f \in U$. U is *enabled* at case c if ${}^\bullet U \subseteq c$ and $(U^\bullet \cup U^\circ) \cap c = \emptyset$. Moreover, $c[U>c'$, where $c' = c - {}^\bullet U \cup U^\bullet$. By a *step sequence* of Ξ we mean any sequence of sets of events $U_1 \ldots U_n$ such that there are cases $c_1,\ldots,c_n$ satisfying $c_{in}[U_1> c_1[U_2>c_2 \ldots [U_n>c_n$. We then denote $c_{in}[U_1 \ldots U_n>c_n$ and $c_n \in C_\Xi$. The set of step sequences of Ξ will be denoted by $steps(\Xi)$. For the ENI-system of Figure 5.1(a), *feghfegh* is a firing sequence while *ef* is not; $\{e,f\}\{g,h\}\{e,f\}\{g,h\}$ is a step sequence while $\{e\}\{f,g\}$ is not; and $SC_\Xi = C_\Xi = \{1,3\} \times \{2,4\}$. Note that $SC_\Xi \subseteq C_\Xi$, while the reverse inclusion does not in general hold. E.g., for the ENI-system in Figure 5.1(b), $\{3,4\} \in C_\Xi - SC_\Xi$. The difference between the firing sequence and step sequence semantics of Ξ can be quite dramatic. The ENI-system of Figure 5.1(b) has only three firing sequences: λ, e and f, whereas there is infinitely many step sequences it can generate.

5.2 Comtraces of ENI-Systems

Traces of EN-systems are constructed by defining an independency relation *ind* on events which has the following property: If $(e,f) \in ind$ and the two events were executed simultaneously, then it is possible to execute them in any order. The situation is much more complicated if we consider ENI-systems. For example, the ENI-system of Figure 5.1(a) is such that we can execute e and f simultaneously, or f followed by e. However, e followed by f is not allowed. Thus, when dealing with ENI-systems we need to specify two relations: one identifying events which can be executed in one step, the other identifying events which can be serialised. We define $sim, ser \subseteq E \times E$ as follows:

$$(e,f) \in sim \;:\Leftrightarrow (e^\bullet \cup {}^\bullet e) \cap (f^\bullet \cup {}^\bullet f) = \emptyset \wedge (e^\circ \cap {}^\bullet f) \cup (f^\circ \cap {}^\bullet e) = \emptyset \,.$$

$$(e,f) \in ser \;:\Leftrightarrow (e,f) \in sim \wedge e^\bullet \cap f^\circ = \emptyset .$$

To show that comtraces provide an invariant semantics of ENI-systems we have two results which follow directly from the definition of *sim* and *ser*, the concurrent enabling rule, and the results presented in Section 4. The first is that a set of events is an enabled step if and only if all its events are enabled and form a step in the sense of the relation *sim*. The second is that it is possible to partition the step sequences of Ξ into comtraces. In what follows we use the same notation as in Section 4.

Theorem 5.2.1 Let $c \subseteq B$ and $U \subseteq E$ be a non-empty set.
(1) U is enabled at c if and only if $U \in Step$ and every $e \in U$ is enabled at c.
(2) $steps(\Xi) \subseteq Steps^*$. □

Theorem 5.2.2 Let $t,u \in Step^*$ and $t \approx u$.
(1) $t \in steps(\Xi) \Leftrightarrow u \in steps(\Xi)$.
(2) $steps(\Xi)$ can be partitioned into disjoint comtraces. □

The meaning of the strong and weak causality in the case of the ENI-system can be explained more directly. There are basically three situations which need to be accounted for (comp. Figure 5.4). The most interesting is one giving rise to a weak causality relationship. This happens, e.g., when we have an executable step $\{e,f\}$ such that $e^{\circ}\cap f^{\bullet}=\varnothing$ and $f^{\circ}\cap e^{\bullet}\neq\varnothing$. Then after executing e one of the places inhibiting f becomes marked, while $\{f\}\{e\}$ is still a valid execution. In such a case f can only be executed simultaneously or precede e, i.e., $f \nearrow e$.

5.3 Processes of ENI-systems

Every step sequence t of Ξ induces a composet $co(t)$ which can be identified with the step sequences in $[t]$ - the comtrace containing t. In this section we will show that it is possible to generate $co(t)$ by generalising the construction of processes of Petri nets [Re85, BD87, NRT90]. Below we assume that every condition $s\in B$ has a *complement*, i.e., there is exactly one condition $s^c\in B$ such that $(s^c)^{\bullet}={}^{\bullet}s$ and ${}^{\bullet}(s^c)=s^{\bullet}$ and $|\{s,s^c\}\cap c_{in}|=1$. Clearly, $(s^c)^c=s$.

Constructing a process of a Petri net can be understood as an unfolding of the net into an occurrence net such that event occurrences respect local environments of the events they are supposed to represent. To see whether this approach can be adopted for ENI-systems, we consider Ξ of Figure 5.2(a), and two step sequences, $t_1=\{g\}\{e\}\{f\}$ and $t_2=\{e\}\{f\}\{g\}$. Then, by unfolding Ξ according to t_1 and t_2, in both cases we obtain the same occurrence net, shown in Figure 5.2(b). However, t_1 and t_2 belong to different comtraces of Ξ ($[t_2]=\{t_2\}$ and $[t_1]=\{t_1,\{g,e\}\{f\}\}$) and should generate two different processes. A straightforward unfolding of the net does not, therefore, work properly. The reason for this is that in t_1 event g was enabled because 2 has not yet been marked with a token produced by the occurrence of e, while in t_2 event g was made enabled by the occurrence of f which removed the token from 2. Hence the two occurrences of g resulted from two essentially different 'non-holdings' of 2. In unfolding Ξ, however, we had at our disposal in both cases only one occurrence of 2, and could not distinguish between these two, clearly different, situations. The construction of a process will be modified by binding the occurrences of g to holdings of the complement condition 2^c. I.e., g can be enabled only if 2^c holds. We then will unfold Ξ into occurrence nets with *activator* arcs - indicated by black dots at one end. Essentially, an activator arc (s^c,e) will replace inhibitor arc (s,e). As a result, we generate two different processes for the step sequences t_1 and t_2, as shown in Figure 5.3.

Let $t=U_1...U_n\in steps(\Xi)$ be a step sequence fixed for the rest of this section. We define the *process* generated by t as $process(t)=N_n$, where N_n is the last net in the sequence $N_0,...,N_n$ constructed in the following way.

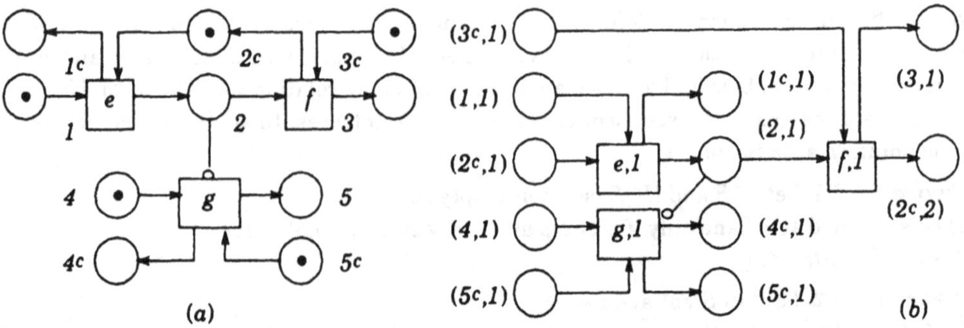

Figure 5.2: (*a*) ENI-system Ξ; (*b*) an attempt to construct a process of Ξ; $(2,1)$ denotes the first holding of 2, $(e,1)$ denotes the first occurrence of e, etc.

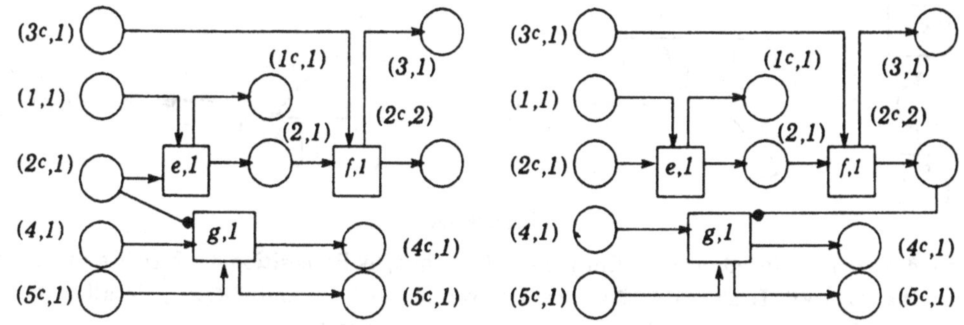

process generated by $t_1=\{g\}\{e\}\{f\}$ *process generated by* $t_2=\{e\}\{f\}\{g\}$

Figure 5.3

Construction Each net $N_k=(S_k,T_k,F_k,A_k)$, $k=0,1,\ldots,n$, is a net with *activator* arcs. The first three components of N_k are the same as in the definition of the net with inhibitor arcs, while $A_k\subseteq S_k\times T_k$ is the set of *activator arcs*. The elements of $S_k\cup T_k$ are of the form (x,i), where $x\in B\cup E$ and $i\geq 1$. We will denote $l(x,i)=x$ and $\#_{x,k}=|\{(x,i)\mid(x,i)\in S_k\cup T_k\}|$.

Step 0: $N_0=(\{(s,1)\mid s\in c_{in}\},\varnothing,\varnothing,\varnothing)$.

Step k+1: Given N_k and $U=U_{k+1}$ we construct N_{k+1} in the following way.

(1) $S_{k+1}=S_k\cup\{(s,1+\#_{s,k})\mid s\in U^\bullet\}$ and $T_{k+1}=T_k\cup\{(e,1+\#_{e,k})\mid e\in U\}$.

(2) $F_{k+1}=F_k\cup\{((s,\#_{e,k}),(e,1+\#_{e,k}))\mid e\in U\wedge(s,e)\in F\}$
$\cup\{((e,1+\#_{e,k}),(s,1+\#_{e,k}))\mid e\in U\wedge(e,s)\in F\}$.

(3) $A_{k+1}=A_k\cup\{((s^c,\#_{s^c,k}),(e,1+\#_{e,k}))\mid e\in U\wedge(s,e)\in I\}$. □

Let $k\leq n$. We observe that (S_k,T_k,F_k) is a process of the EN-system (B,E,F,c_{in}). Hence the following hold (comp. [Re85, BD87]). In what follows, $Max_k=\{(s,i)\in S_k\mid(s,i)^\bullet=\varnothing\}$.

(5.1) $po=(S_k\cup T_k,F_k{}^+)$ is a partial order.

(5.2) For every $(s,i)\in S_k$, $|^\bullet(s,i)|\leq 1$ and $|(s,i)^\bullet|\leq 1$.

(5.3) For every $s\in B$, the occurrences of s and s^c are totally ordered and alternating in po. Furthermore, $(s,i)\rightarrow_{po}(s,m)\Leftrightarrow i<m$.

(5.4) For every $e\in E$, the occurrences of e are totally ordered in po, and $(e,i)\rightarrow_{po}(e,m)\Leftrightarrow i<m$.

(5.5) l is injective on Max_k and $c_{in}[U_1\ldots U_k>l(Max_k)$.

(5.6) For every $(e,i)\in T_k$, l is injective on $(e,i)^\bullet\cup{}^\bullet(e,i)$ and $l((e,i)^\bullet)=e^\bullet$ and $l(^\bullet(e,i))={}^\bullet e$.

(5.7) If $(s,i)\in Max_k$ and $(r,m)\in Max_j$, where $k<j$ and $r=s$ or $r=s^c$, then $((s,i),(r,m))\in F_j{}^*$.

Note that if $s\in B$ and c is reachable from c_{in} then $|\{s,s^c\}\cap c|\leq 1$. Hence if $(e,i)\in T_k$ then $(s,e)\notin I$ or $(s^c,e)\notin I$. Thus from (5.5) it follows that for every $(e,i)\in T_k$ the following holds.

(5.8) l is injective on $(e,i)^\nabla$ and $l((e,i)^\nabla)=(e^o)^c$, where $(e,i)^\nabla=\{(s,m)\mid((s,m),(e,i))\in A_k\}$.

To show that the construction of *process(t)* is sound, we will prove that *co(t)* and a composet which is in a natural way induced by *process(t)* are identical. Define $co=(T_n,\rightarrow,\nearrow)^\dagger$, where

(5.9) $(e,i)\rightarrow(f,m)\ :\Leftrightarrow\ \exists q.\ ((e,i),q)\in F_n\wedge(q,(f,m))\in F_n\cup A_n$.

(5.10) $(e,i)\nearrow(f,m)\ :\Leftrightarrow\ \exists q.\ (q,(f,m))\in F_n\wedge(q,(e,i))\in A_n$. (see Figure 5.4)

Theorem 5.2.1 $co=co(t)$.

Proof: Clearly, $T_n=dom(co(t))$. From Construction and (5.1,9,10) we have the following.

(5.11) $(e,i)\rightarrow(f,m)\ \Rightarrow(e,f)\notin ser\wedge pos_t(e,i)<pos_t(f,m)$.

(5.12) $(e,i)\nearrow(f,m)\ \Rightarrow(f,e)\notin ser\wedge pos_t(e,i)\leq pos_t(f,m)$.

Clearly, $\rightarrow$ and $\nearrow$ are irreflexive. Furthermore, by (5.11,12), $\rightarrow\subseteq\rightarrow_t$ and $\nearrow\subseteq\nearrow_t$ (note that $\rightarrow_t$

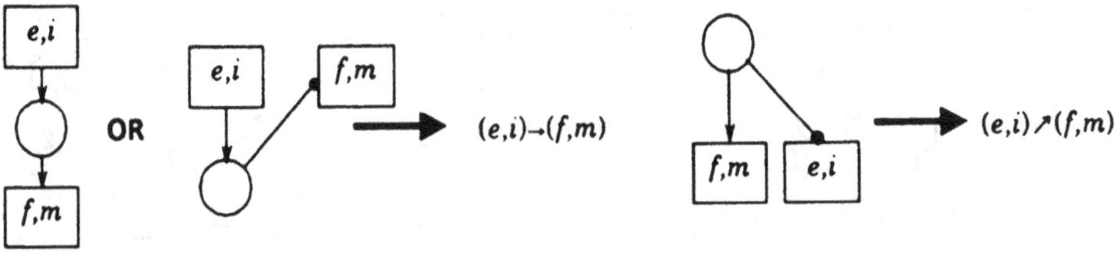

Figure 5.4

and $\nearrow_t$ were introduced in the definition of $co(t)$). Thus, by Proposition 3.1.2, co is a composet such that $co \subseteq co(t)$. To show $co(t) \subseteq co$ we will prove that $\to_t \subseteq \to_{co}$ and $\nearrow_t \subseteq \nearrow_{co}$. Recall that

(5.13) $(e,f) \in sim :\Leftrightarrow (e^\bullet \cup {}^\bullet e) \cap (f^\bullet \cup {}^\bullet f) = \emptyset \wedge (e^\circ \cap {}^\bullet f) \cup (f^\circ \cap {}^\bullet e) = \emptyset$.

(5.14) $(e,f) \in ser :\Leftrightarrow (e,f) \in sim \wedge e^\bullet \cap f^\circ = \emptyset$.

We first show that if $(e,i) \neq (f,m)$ then

(5.15) $(e,f) \notin sim \wedge pos_t(e,i) \leq pos_t(f,m) \Rightarrow pos_t(e,i) < pos_t(f,m)$

(5.16) $(e,f) \notin sim \wedge pos_t(e,i) < pos_t(f,m) \Rightarrow (e,i) \to_{co} (f,m)$.

Clearly, (5.15) holds. To show (5.16) we consider three cases (comp. (5.13)).

Case 1: $(e^\bullet \cup {}^\bullet e) \cap (f^\bullet \cup {}^\bullet f) \neq \emptyset$. Then from (5.1,2,3) it follows that $((e,i),(f,m)) \in F_n{}^+$, which implies $(e,i) \to^+ (f,m)$. Hence $(e,i) \to_{co} (f,m)$.

Case 2: $e^\circ \cap {}^\bullet f \neq \emptyset$. Let $s \in e^\circ \cap {}^\bullet f$. From (5.5,8) it follows that there is $(s^c,d) \in Max_{k-1}$, where $k = pos_t(e,i)$, such that $((s^c,d),(e,i)) \in A_k$. On the other hand, by (5.5,6) there is $(s,h) \in Max_{r-1}$, where $r = pos_t(f,m)$, such that $((s,h),(f,m)) \in F_r$. Thus, by (5.7), there is $(g,z) \in T_n$ such that $((s^c,d),(g,z)) \in F_n$ and $((g,z),(s,h)) \in F_n{}^+$. Hence we have $(e,i) \nearrow (g,z)$ and $(g,z) \to^+ (f,m)$, which yields $(e,i) \to_{co} (f,m)$.

Case 3: $f^\circ \cap {}^\bullet e \neq \emptyset$. Let $s \in f^\circ \cap {}^\bullet e$. By proceeding as in Case 2, we may show that there are d,r such that $((s,d),(e,i)) \in F_n$ and $((s^c,r),(f,m)) \in A_n$ and $((s,d),(s^c,r)) \in F_n{}^+$. Hence, by (5.1,2), $((e,i),(s^c,r)) \in F_n{}^+$. Consequently, there is $(g,z) \in T_n$ such that $((e,i),(g,z)) \in F_n{}^*$ and $(g,z) \to (f,m)$. Thus $(e,i) \to^+ (f,m)$ which means that $(e,i) \to_{co} (f,m)$.

Hence (5.16) holds. Suppose that $(e,i) \to_t (f,m)$. Then, by (5.14), $(e,f) \notin sim \vee e^\bullet \cap f^\circ \neq \emptyset$ and $pos_t(e,i) < pos_t(f,m)$. If $(e,f) \notin sim$ then, by (5.16), $(e,i) \to_{co} (f,m)$. If $e^\bullet \cap f^\circ \neq \emptyset$ then we proceed as follows. Let $s \in e^\bullet \cap f^\circ$. By proceeding as in Case 2 we can show that there are d and r such that $((e,i),(s,d)) \in F_n$ and $((s,d),(s^c,r)) \in F_n{}^+$ and $((s^c,r),(f,m)) \in A_n$. Hence there is $(g,z) \in T_n$ such that $((e,i),(g,z)) \in F_n{}^+$ and $((g,z),(s^c,r)) \in F_n$. Thus $(e,i) \to_{co} (f,m)$.

Suppose that $(e,i) \nearrow_t (f,m)$. Then, by (5.14), $(e,f) \notin sim \vee f^\bullet \cap e^\circ \neq \emptyset$, and $pos_t(e,i) \leq post_t(f,m)$. If $(e,f) \notin sim$ then, by (5.15,16), $(e,i) \to_{co} (f,m)$. Hence $(e,i) \nearrow_{co} (f,m)$.

If $s \in f^\bullet \cap e^\circ \neq \emptyset$ then, as in Case 2, one can show that there are d and r such that $((s^c,d),(e,i)) \in A_n$ and $((s^c,r),(f,m)) \in F_n$ and $((s^c,d),(s^c,r)) \in F_n{}^*$. It is now easy to see that if $(s^c,d) = (s^c,r)$ then $(e,i) \nearrow (f,m)$; and if $(s^c,d) \neq (s^c,r)$ then $(e,i) \nearrow (g,z) \to^+ (f,m)$, for some $(g,z) \in T_n$. In either case $(e,i) \nearrow_{co} (f,m)$. This completes the proof. ❑

The comtrace semantics of the ENI-systems can, indirectly, provide an invariant semantics for the priority nets defined as EN-systems augmented by a priority relation. It is not difficult to see that each such priority system is equivalent to an ENI-system (perhaps after applying some relabelling of events). For the priority net of Figure 2.1 an equivalent ENI-system is shown in Figure 5.5.

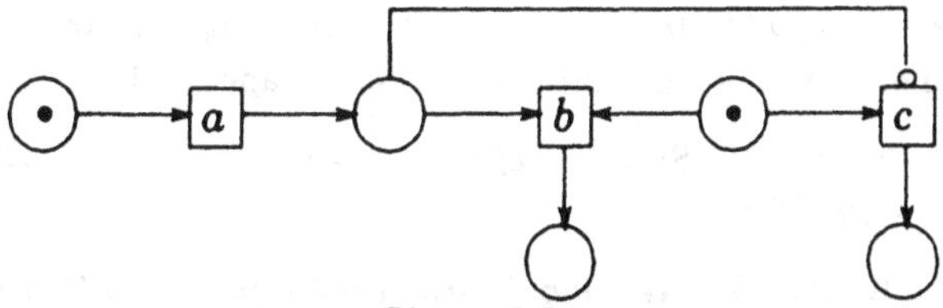

Figure 5.5

Concluding Remarks

In [Vo90] Vogler introduced 'step traces' - a generalisation of classical trace theory. Our first comment is that there is one important common characteristics shared by our approach and that of [Vo90], namely in both cases it is possible to have a step which is 'indivisible'. More precisely, dividing such a step leads to a run which is an observation of a different concurrent history of the system. Despite this similarity, composets cannot in general be modelled by step traces. For instance, there is no step trace generating exactly the step sequences in comtrace $[\{a\}\{b\}]=\{\{a,b\},\{a\}\{b\}\}$, for $sim=\{(a,b),(b,a)\}$ and $ser=\{(a,b)\}$. The comparison in the other direction is slightly more difficult as [Vo90] uses multisets rather than sets to model single steps. However, we conjecture that step traces with steps being sets rather than multisets of events, are equivalent to comtraces with a symmetric serialisability relation *ser*.

Acknowledgements

The authors would like to thank the referees for their comments and suggestions for improvement. This research was supported by a grant from NSERC No. OGP 0036539 and by ESPRIT Basic Research Action 3148 (project DEMON).

References

[AR88] Aalbersberg IJ., Rozenberg G., *Theory of Traces*, Theoretical Computer Science, 60 (1988), pp. 1-82.

[BD87] Best E., Devillers R., *Sequential and Concurrent Behaviour in Petri Net Theory*, Theoretical Computer Science, 55 (1987), pp. 87-136.

[BK91] Best E., Koutny M., *Petri Net Semantics of Priority Systems*, to appear in Theoretical Computer Science.

[Ho85] Hoare C.A.R., *Communicating Sequential Processes*, Prentice-Hall, 1985.

[Ja87] Janicki R., *A Formal Semantics for Concurrent Systems with a Priority Relation*, Acta Informatica 24, 1987, pp.33-55.

[JK89] Janicki R., Koutny M., *Towards a Theory of Simulation for Verification of Concurrent Systems*, in: PARLE'89, E. Odijk, M. Rem, J.-C. Syre (Eds.), Lecture Notes in Computer Science, vol.366, 73-88, 1989.

[JK90] Janicki R., Koutny M., *A Bottom-Top Approach to Concurrency Theory Part I: Observations, Invariants and Paradigms*, Technical Report 90-04, McMaster University, 1990.

[JK91] Janicki R., Koutny M., *Invariants and Paradigms of Concurrency Theory*, Proc. of Parle'91, Lecture Notes in Computer Science, to appear, 1991.

[JK91a] Janicki R., Koutny M., *Structure of Concurrency*, Proc. of the AMAST Conference, Iowa City, May 1991.

[JK91b] Janicki R., Koutny M., *Relational Structure Semantics of Concurrent Systems*, to appear in the Proc. of 13th IMACS Congress on Computation and Applied Mathematics, Dublin, July 1991.

[JL88] Janicki R., Lauer P.E., *On the Semantics of Priority Systems*, 17th Annual International Conference on Parallel Processing, Vol. 2, pp. 150-156, 1988, Pen. State Press.

[La85] Lamport L., *What It Means for a Concurrent Program to Satisfy a Specification: Why No One Has Specified Priority*, 12th ACM Symposium on Principles of Programming Languages, New Orleans, Louisiana, 1985, pp. 78-83.

[La86] Lamport L., *On Interprocess Communication, Part I: Basic formalism, Part II, Algorithms*, Distributed Computing 1 (1986), pp. 77-101.

[Ma77] Mazurkiewicz A., *Concurrent Program Schemes and Their Interpretations*, DAIMI-PB-78, Aarhus University, 1977.

[Ma86] Mazurkiewicz A., *Trace Theory*, Lecture Notes in Computer Science 255, Springer 1986, pp. 297-324.

[NRT90] Nielsen M., Rozenberg G., Thiagarajan P.S., *Behavioural Notions for Elementary Net Systems*, Distributed Computing 4 (1990), pp. 45-57.

[Pe81] Peterson J.L., *Petri Net Theory and the Modeling of Systems*, Prentice Hall, 1981.

[Pr86] Pratt V., *Modelling Concurrency with Partial Orders*, Int. Journal of Parallel Programming 15, 1 (1986), pp. 33-71.

[Re85] Reisig W., *Petri Nets*, Springer 1985.

[Sz30] Szpilrajn-Marczewski E., *Sur l'extension de l'ordre partial*, Fundamenta Mathematicae 16 (1930), pp. 386-389.

[Vo90] Vogler W., *A Generalization of Trace Theory*, Technical Report TUM-I9018, Techn. Univ. München, 1990, (to appear in RAIRO Theor. Inf. and Appl.).

[Wi82] Winskel G., *Event Structure Semantics for CCS and Related Language*, Lecture Notes in Computer Science 140, Springer 1982, pp. 561-567.

Abstract timed observation and process algebra

ALAN JEFFREY

ABSTRACT. In this paper, we investigate the notion of observation in a partially ordered time domain. We present an algebraic structure to represent such an observation, and use it to define a process algebra. It is then given an operational and denotational semantics, and we see that denotational equivalence is the same as may testing.

1 Introduction

Recently, there has been much interest in extending the concept of a process algebra to include time. Work has concentrated on adding a time domain to existing process algebras, such as Brookes, Hoare and Roscoe's Communicating Sequential Processes (CSP) [BHR84], Milner's Calculus of Communicating Systems (CCS) [Mil80, Mil89], and Bergstra and Klop's Algebra for Communicating Processes (ACP) [BK85, BW90]. Of these, the most developed is Reed and Roscoe's timed CSP [RR86, DS89], which the work in this paper is based upon. In addition, there are many extensions of CCS to include a notion of time—most notably those of Hennessy and Regan [HR90], Moller and Tofts [MT90] and Wang [Wan90, Wan91]; and the timed versions of ACP provided by Bergstra and Baeten [BB91b, BB90] and Niccolin and Sifakis [NS90].

These models all have in common the fact that they use a numeric domain (either $\mathbb{N}$ or $[0, \infty)$) as their notion of time. Bergstra and Baeten are slightly more general, and assume that their time domain is a totally ordered set, as I did when I generalised Wang's calculus [Jef91c].

However, with the exception of Bergstra and Baeten's real-space process algebra [BB90], all of the time domains investigated have been totally ordered. In this paper, we investigate a partially ordered notion of time, with a somewhat more general notion of observation than that previously used.

Partially ordered time domains have been used by Bergstra and Baeten to model extremely distributed systems, such as satellite communication systems [BB91a]. They also have applications to smaller systems where communication delays are important (such as the network layer of ethernet) and modelling relativistic phenomenon [Mur91a]. Murphy has investigated a timed model of partially ordered traces [Mur91b], but his time domain is the real numbers, and he uses the partial order to extract causal information.

Here, we shall investigate an algebraic structure which attempts to capture the notion of timed observation. From this, we construct a process algebra, and give it a

Presented at Concur 91.
Author's address: Department of Computer Sciences, S-412 96 Göteborg, Sweden.
Email: jeffrey@cs.chalmers.se.

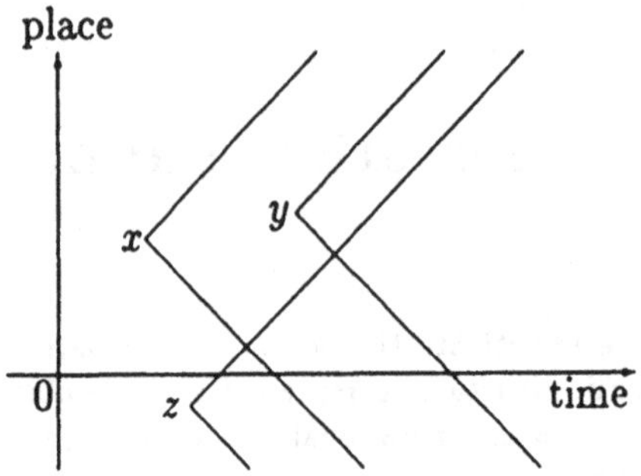

Figure 1: Some points with their light-cones

transition system semantics using observations as labels. We also present a variant of Reed and Roscoe's timed failures semantics [Ree88, DS89] and show that it is equivalent to de Nicola–Hennessy may testing equivalence [Hen88]. Similar work has been carried out independently by Schneider [Sch91], who shows that failures semantics for timed CSP processes is equivalent to may-testing.

This work is far from complete, and contains a number of malfeatures that are unfortunately hard-wired into the model. The most striking of these is the absence of a hiding operator, or any other method of expressing abstraction (such as non-injective alphabet transformation). This is due to a technical consideration about maximal progress, which cannot be covered by the notion of sequential composition given here. The other notable problem is that the delay operator $t \rightarrow P$ is not a simple transformation—it also removes all the behaviours of P that happened at times incomparable with time 0. This is because of our assumption that time is *relative* rather than *absolute*.

Both of these problems are addressed by the notion of an *observation space* [Jef91a], which is an algebraic structure for modelling absolute-time observations. This paper should be seen as a first attempt at modelling partially ordered time, which (although it is consistent) is overly cumbersome and doesn't capture many of the properties we are interested in. Hopefully both of these problems will be solved by looking at observation spaces.

2 Observation spaces

2.1 *Definition*

Since we are trying to develop a fairly general framework for timed concurrency, our basic notions should be as universal as possible. In this paper, we regard the notion of *timed observation* as important, and worth spending some time investigating in its own right.

We are dealing with a partially ordered notion of time, and it turns out that a good way of visualizing this is as a light-cone diagram. Picture a cartesian space, where a point (n, p) represents place p at time n. Then a vector in space-time is

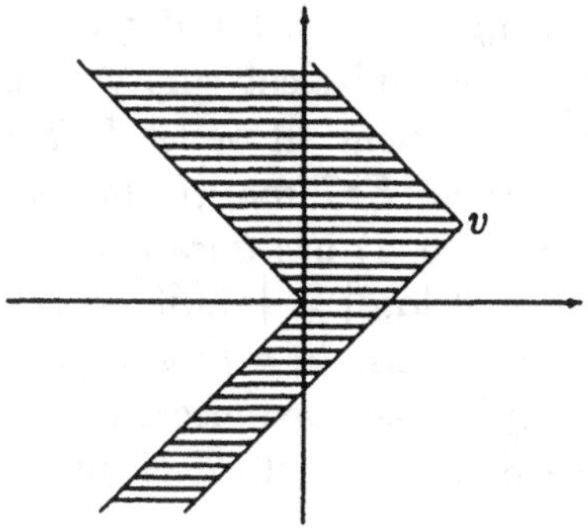

Figure 2: An observation (v, S)

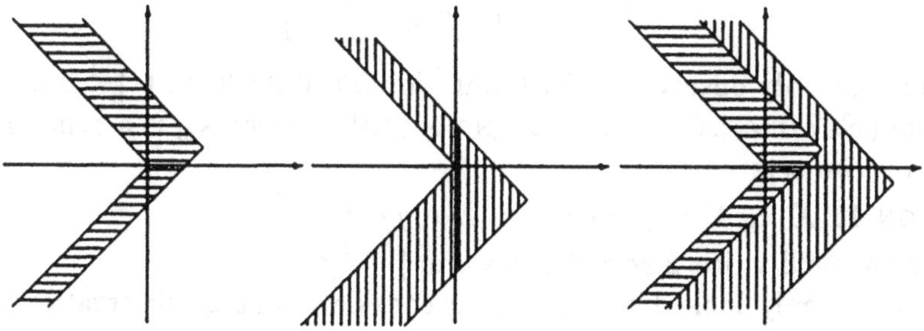

Figure 3: Composing α and β to get $\alpha;\beta$

a pair (n, p) such that $|p| \leq n$. For example, in Figure 1, there is a vector from x to y, but not between any other points. So, since information takes time to flow, information can go from x to y, but not between any other points, including from y to x.

So, in this example, an observation is a pair (v, S) where v is a space-time vector, and S consists of (x, l) pairs, where x is a point, and l comes from some set of labels, such that for any $(x, l) \in S$:

- there is a vector from x to v, so an observer at v could see behaviour at x, and
- there is no vector from x to $(0, 0)$, so the observer has not already seen the behaviour.

Each observation is of the form shown in Figure 2. For example, an empty observation is $(v, \emptyset)$—we will write 0 for the empty observation $((0, 0), \emptyset)$.

The distinctive L-shape of observations is important, as it allows us to *sequentially compose* observations, as shown in Figure 3.

$$(v_1, S_1);(v_2, S_2) = (v_1 + v_2, S_1 \cup \{(x + v_1, l) \mid (x, l) \in S_2\})$$

As ; is associative and has unit 0, $(\mathit{Example}, ;, 0)$ is a monoid, where *Example* is the set of all observations in our example. In addition, since every observation takes a positive amount of time, if $\alpha;\beta;\gamma = \alpha$ then $\alpha;\beta = \alpha$.

For every vector v there is an equivalent empty observation $(v, \emptyset)$, so we shall identify *times* with empty observations. If we let *ExTime* be the set of all empty observations in this example, then $(ExTime, ;, 0)$ forms a commutative monoid.

We can then say observation (v, S) has *duration* $(v, \emptyset)$. If we write $|\alpha|$ for the duration of α, then $|0| = 0$ and $|\alpha;\beta| = |\alpha|;|\beta|$, so $|\cdot|$ is a homomorphism from $(Example, ;, 0)$ to $(ExTime, ;, 0)$. Also $|t| = t$ for any time t.

Another important property of L-shaped pieces is that they can be *decomposed*, so if α has duration $t;u$ it can be split into β of duration t and γ of duration u, where $\alpha = \beta;\gamma$. So

$$\begin{aligned} |\cdot|^{-1}[t;u] &= \{\alpha \mid |\alpha| = t;u\} \\ &= \{\beta;\gamma \mid |\beta| = t \wedge |\gamma| = u\} \\ &= |\cdot|^{-1}[t] \times_{;} |\cdot|^{-1}[u] \end{aligned}$$

In addition, the only observation with duration 0 is 0 itself, so $|\cdot|^{-1}$ is a homomorphism from $(ExTime, ;, 0)$ to $(\mathbb{P}\,Example, \times_{;}, \{0\})$, where $\times_{\oplus}$ is a generalization of cross-product on sets.

DEFINITION 1. $X \times_{\oplus} Y = \{x \oplus y \mid x \in X \wedge y \in Y\}$

From now on, we'll write $Example_t$ to mean $|\cdot|^{-1}[t]$.

So far, we've only looked at the timing considerations of observations, and not looked at any behaviours they may contain. To begin with, we can define a partial order $\sqsubseteq_t$ on $Example_t$:

$$(v, S_1) \sqsubseteq_{(v,\emptyset)} (v, S_2) \;\Leftrightarrow\; S_1 \subseteq S_2$$

From the properties of $\subseteq$, this partial order is a complete distributive lattice with bottom $(v, \emptyset)$.

Since we're trying to produce a notion of concurrent observation, it would be nice to have a notion of concurrency. Given two observations α and β with duration t, we will combine them together to produce $\alpha \otimes_t \beta$. Given $\alpha \otimes_t \beta$ we would like to be able to reconstruct α and β, so $\otimes_t$ should be injective. It turns out to be technically useful for it to be surjective as well.

We can construct such a $\otimes_t$ if we assume the axiom of choice for our label set, so we can find injective functions f and g on labels such that $f \cup g$ is surjective. Then

$$(v, S_1) \otimes_{(v,\emptyset)} (v, S_2) = (v, f[S_1] \cup g[S_2])$$

For instance, $t \otimes_t t = t$, and (as long as both sides are defined):

$$\begin{aligned} (\alpha \otimes_t \beta);(\gamma \otimes_u \delta) &= \alpha;\gamma \otimes_{t;u} \beta;\delta \\ (\alpha \otimes_t \beta) \sqsubseteq_t (\gamma \otimes_t \delta) &\Leftrightarrow \alpha \sqsubseteq_t \gamma \wedge \beta \sqsubseteq_t \delta \end{aligned}$$

The first equation is quite interesting, as it tells us that we cannot observe *causality*. In a causal model (such as pomsets [Gis88]) α and δ would be causally dependent on the lhs but independent on the rhs. So this equation tells us that we are indeed looking at a model of *observation* rather than one of *behaviour*.

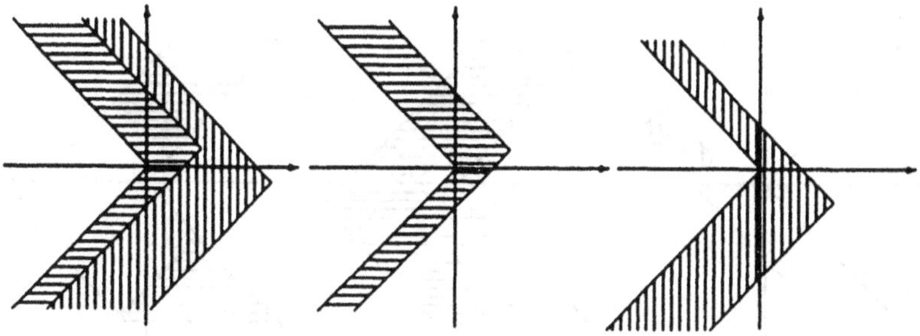

Figure 4: Decomposing α into $\alpha\nwarrow t$ and $\alpha\nearrow t$

This example is all very well (and has the advantage of allowing us to draw light-cone diagrams) but how much of it is important, and how much is overspecification? It turns out that the properties we shall require of our notion of observation are:

DEFINITION 2. *Obs, Time,* $|\cdot|$, $\sqsubseteq$, ;, $\otimes$ *and* 0 *are such that:*

- $(Obs, ;, 0)$ *is a monoid where* $\alpha;\beta;\gamma = \alpha \Rightarrow \alpha;\beta = \alpha$.
- $Time \subseteq Obs$, *and* $(Time, ;, 0)$ *is a commutative monoid.*
- $|\cdot|$ *is a homomorphism from* $(Obs, ;, 0)$ *to* $(Time, ;, 0)$ *such that* $|t| = t$.
- $|\cdot|^{-1}$ *is a homomorphism from* $(Time, ;, 0)$ *to* $(\mathbb{P}Obs, \times_;, \{0\})$.
- $(Obs_t, \sqsubseteq_t)$ *is a complete distributive lattice with bottom* t.
- ; *is continuous, and* $\alpha;\beta \sqsubseteq_{t;u} \gamma;\delta$ *iff* $\alpha \sqsubseteq_t \gamma$ *and* $\beta \sqsubseteq_u \delta$.
- $\otimes_t : Obs_t \times Obs_t \rightarrow Obs_t$ *is a bijective operator such that* $t \otimes_t t = t$.
- $\otimes_t$ *is continuous, and* $\alpha \otimes_t \beta \sqsubseteq_t \gamma \otimes_t \delta$ *iff* $\alpha \sqsubseteq_t \gamma$ *and* $\beta \sqsubseteq_t \delta$.
- $(\alpha \otimes_t \beta);(\gamma \otimes_u \delta) = \alpha;\gamma \otimes_{t;u} \beta;\delta$.

where $Obs_t = |\cdot|^{-1}(t)$.

For the rest of this paper we shall write $\alpha\beta$ for $\alpha;\beta$, $\alpha \sqsubseteq \beta$ for $\alpha \sqsubseteq_{|\alpha|} \beta$, and $\alpha \otimes \beta$ for $\alpha \otimes_{|\alpha|} \beta$. Let α, β, γ and δ range over *Obs*; t, u and v over *Time*; and a, b and c over $Obs \setminus Time$.

2.2 Other operators

From our definition of *Obs*, we can define some more operations on observations. To begin with, we can define a prefix ordering $\leq$, and show from the properties of ; that it is a partial order.

DEFINITION 3. $\alpha \leq \gamma$ *iff* $\exists \beta . \alpha\beta = \gamma$

We will write $A\!\downarrow$ for the downward $\leq$-closure of A, and $A\!\uparrow$ for all the observations of A followed by any time.

DEFINITION 4. $A\!\downarrow = \{\alpha \mid \exists \beta . \alpha\beta \in A\}$

DEFINITION 5. $A\!\uparrow = \{\alpha t \mid \alpha \in A \wedge t \in Time\}$

A/α is what's left of A after α.

DEFINITION 6. $A/\alpha = \{\beta \mid \alpha\beta \in A\}$

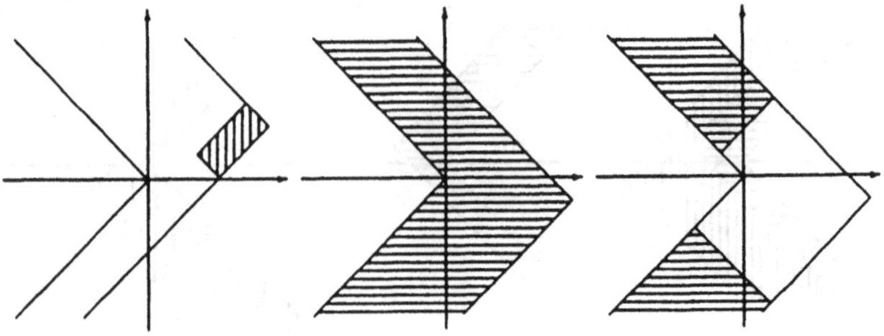

Figure 5: α, β, and $\alpha \bullet \beta$

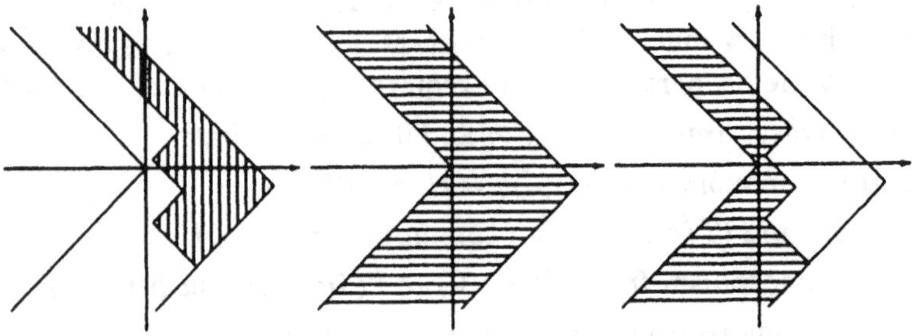

Figure 6: α, β and $\alpha \blacksquare \beta$

Given any observation α of duration tu, we can decompose α into all the behaviour before t $(\alpha \upharpoonleft t)$ and what's left $(\alpha \upharpoonright t)$, as shown in Figure 4.

DEFINITION 7. *If* $|\alpha| = tu$ *then* $|\alpha \upharpoonleft t| = t$, $|\alpha \upharpoonright t| = u$, *and* $(\alpha \upharpoonleft t)(\alpha \upharpoonright t) = \alpha$.

Using the fact that $|\cdot|^{-1}$ is a homomorphism, and the interaction of $\sqsubseteq$ and ; we can show that this is a unique definition.

We can also find out what an observation's behaviour is at any particular moment in time with $\alpha @ t$. This has the same duration as α, but only contains the observations at exactly that time—this is achieved by taking the limit of all the observations from intervals around t.

DEFINITION 8. $\alpha @ t = \bigsqcap(\{(\alpha \upharpoonleft u)(|\alpha| \upharpoonright u) \mid t < u\} \cup \{(|\alpha| \upharpoonleft u)(\alpha \upharpoonright u) \mid u < t\})$

Then we can say α has some behaviour at t iff $\alpha @ t \neq |\alpha|$.

DEFINITION 9. $\alpha\,!\,t$ *iff* $\alpha @ t \neq |\alpha|$

These combinators allow us to look at the timing information of an observation, but we would also like to look at what *causal* information an observation might have. Specifically, if we have observed $\alpha\beta$, is it possible that α caused β's behaviour, or that α caused β's *lack* of behaviour? This first question is familiar from looking at causal processes like $\alpha \rightarrow \beta$, but the second question is not—it comes about from the *negative causality* caused by choices like $\alpha \,\square\, \beta$—any behaviour of α will 'kill off' behaviour of β.

So $\vec{\alpha}$ (pronounced 'forward α') is all the behaviour from α that comes after time 0. This is used in defining positive causality. We will write $\vec{A}$ to mean $\{\vec{\alpha} \mid \alpha \in A\}$.

DEFINITION 10. $\vec{\alpha} = \bigsqcup\{\beta \sqsubseteq \alpha \mid t\beta \,!\, u \Rightarrow t \leq u\}$

To model negative causality, we define $\alpha \bullet \beta$ (pronounced 'α killed β') to be all the behaviour from β that comes after no behaviour in α, as seen in Figure 5.

DEFINITION 11. $\alpha \bullet \beta = \bigsqcup\{\gamma \sqsubseteq \beta \mid t\alpha \,!\, u \wedge t|\alpha|\beta \,!\, v \Rightarrow u \not\leq v\}$

In addition, if α and β are competing for the attention of the environment, and α wins, we need to know what is left of β—this is similar to $\alpha \bullet \beta$, but reflects what happens when α and β are competing simultaneously rather than α coming before β. See Figure 6 for an example. We also put in an extra condition saying that α will only kill β if α's behaviour isn't smaller than β's. This reflects the fact that if two observations are competing for attention, and one is larger than the other, then the larger one will win.

DEFINITION 12. $\alpha \blacksquare \beta = \bigsqcup\{\gamma \sqsubseteq \beta \mid t\alpha \,!\, u \wedge t\gamma \,!\, v \wedge t\alpha \,@\, u \not\sqsubset t\beta \,@\, u \Rightarrow u \not\leq v\}$

This gives us enough armoury to deal with causality and choice, so finally we'll consider a concept common to many timed process algebras, such as Timed CSP [Sch91] and Timed CCS [Wan91], that of *maximal progress*.

If an environment is prepared to accept α and β, and a process is prepared to offer α and β, which one happens? One possibility is that this should be resolved nondeterministically, but in the case that $\alpha \sqsubseteq \beta$ we would expect β to happen. In general, if there is some t such that $\alpha \backslash t \sqsubset \beta \backslash t$ then α can be *beaten* by β, written $\alpha \lhd \beta$. Note that $\lhd$ isn't necessarily a partial order.

DEFINITION 13. $\alpha \lhd \beta$ *iff* $\exists t \,.\, \alpha \backslash t \sqsubset \beta \backslash t$

We will write $max\, A$ for the $\lhd$-maximal members of A.

DEFINITION 14. $max\, A = \{\alpha \in A \mid \forall \beta \in A \,.\, \alpha \ntriangleleft \beta\}$

We will say Γ is $\lhd$-complete iff every $\sqsubseteq$-complete slice of Γ has $\lhd$-maximal members.

DEFINITION 15. *Γ is $\lhd$-complete iff for all $\sqsubseteq$-complete A, $max(\Gamma{\downarrow}{\uparrow} \cap A) \neq \emptyset$.*

We shall let Γ and Δ range over $\lhd$-complete sets.

3 Timed processes

3.1 Syntax

We can now give the syntax of our *Abstract-time Process Algebra* (*APA*). It is quite similar to Hoare's CSP [Hoa85] or Hennessy's CCS without τ [Hen88], but uses a parallelism operator more like that of SCCS [Mil83].

DEFINITION 16. *APA_{Obs} (normally just written APA) is given by:*

$$P \;::=\; STOP \mid RUN \mid \gamma : \Gamma \rightarrow P_\gamma \mid P \,\Box\, P \mid \textstyle\bigsqcap \mathcal{P} \mid P \otimes P \mid f[P] \mid \Delta \cap P \mid P/t$$

where

- *If $\alpha, \beta \in \Gamma$ and $\alpha\gamma = \beta\delta$ then $\alpha = \beta$.*
- *$\mathcal{P} \subseteq APA$ is nonempty and has cardinality less than APA.*
- *f is an injective continuous homomorphism on Obs.*

- $\Delta = \Delta\uparrow = \Delta\downarrow$.

DEFINITION 17. $\vec{P} = \vec{Obs} \cap P$

DEFINITION 18. $\alpha \bullet P = \{\beta \mid \beta = \alpha \bullet \beta\} \cap P$

STOP is the process that does nothing other than let time pass. It is similar to *STOP* from Timed CSP or 0 from Timed CCS.

RUN is the process that offers to do any observation. It is similar to *RUN* from untimed CSP or discrete timed CSP [Jef91b].

$\gamma : \Gamma \to P_\gamma$ is the process that offers observations from $\Gamma\downarrow$. If the environment accepts $\alpha \in \Gamma$ then it moves on to become $\vec{P}_\alpha$. It will always allow time to pass, even if the environment refuses to accept any of its offers.

Note that we insist that we move onto $\vec{P}_\alpha$ rather than just P_α. This means that we only allow the behaviours of P_α which come after α, to stop paradoxical processes.

The process $\gamma : \Gamma \to P_\gamma$ is similar to $a : A \to P_a$ from untimed CSP, or $A : \mathcal{A} \to P_A$ from discrete timed CSP.

$P \mathbin{\Box} Q$ is the process that offers the environment the choice between P's actions and Q's actions. If P does α and becomes P', Q does β and becomes Q', $\alpha = \beta \blacksquare \alpha$ and $\beta = \alpha \blacksquare \beta$, then $P \mathbin{\Box} Q$ does $\alpha \sqcup \beta$ and becomes $\beta \bullet P' \mathbin{\Box} \alpha \bullet Q'$.

So as long as α and β mutually kill each other, the process moves on. Note that we can't just kill one of the processes outright, and become P' or Q', as that would allow negative causality to flow faster than positive causality. It is perfectly possible for P and Q to mutually annihilate each other, but this is the penalty for relying on arbitration in a highly distributed world.

In the particular instance where all of P's initial behaviour and all of Q's initial behaviour are totally ordered, this problem does not arise, as the only way α and β could mutually kill one another is for one of them to be a time, and $t \bullet P$ is the same as P. So as long as we stick to 'sensible' uses of $\Box$ we won't have the problem of mutual annihilation.

This particular form of $\Box$ is, to my knowledge, unique. Real-space ACP has a similar problem with their + operation, which they resolve by allowing a 0 process which is a unit of nondeterminism and a zero of sequential composition. So whereas an inconsistent resolution of $\Box$ produces mutual annihilation in *APA*, in real-space ACP it produces 0, which represents a behaviour that 'never happened'.

$\prod \mathcal{P}$ is the process that nondeterministically may become any process from $\mathcal{P}$. This is the same as $\sqcap$ from CSP, or Hennessy's $\oplus$.

$P \otimes Q$ runs P in parallel with Q. If P can do α and Q can do β then $P \otimes Q$ can do $\alpha \otimes \beta$. This is similar to $\times$ from SCCS, except that our $\otimes$ is bijective, and doesn't have a group structure.

$f[P]$ applies the function f to the observations of P. If P offers the observation α, then $f[P]$ offers $f\,\alpha$.

$\Delta \cap P$ is the same as P, but restricted to observations taken from Δ. For example, $\vec{P}$ can only perform observations with behaviour after time 0, and $\alpha \bullet P$ can only perform observations which could have been killed by α.

P/t is the same as P, but brought forward in time by t. This is an 'anti-delay' operator which is obviously unimplementable, but is used to give the semantics of prefixing.

For example, we can define CSP parallelism in terms of $P \otimes Q$ and $f[P]$. $P \parallel Q$ will only allow an observation of both P and Q allow it.

$$\begin{aligned} P \parallel Q &= f_{\parallel}[\Delta_{\parallel} \cap (P \otimes Q)] \\ \Delta_{\parallel} &= \{\alpha \otimes \alpha \mid \alpha \in Obs\} \\ f_{\parallel}(\alpha \otimes \alpha) &= \alpha \end{aligned}$$

We will now go on to give two semantics for this language—one denotational and the other operational, and then show that they are in fact the same.

3.2 *Operational semantics*

We shall first of all give this language a *labelled transition system* semantics, in the style of Milner. This is a relation $\longrightarrow \subseteq APA \times Obs \times APA$ where $P \xrightarrow{\alpha} Q$ means 'P can do α and become Q'.

DEFINITION 19.

$$\frac{}{STOP \xrightarrow{t} STOP}$$

$$\frac{}{RUN \xrightarrow{\alpha} RUN}$$

$$\frac{}{\gamma : \Gamma \rightarrow P_{\gamma} \xrightarrow{\alpha} \vec{P}_{\alpha}} \; [\alpha \in \Gamma]$$

$$\frac{}{\gamma : \Gamma \rightarrow P_{\gamma} \xrightarrow{\alpha} \delta : \Gamma/\alpha \rightarrow P_{\alpha\delta}} \; [\alpha \in \Gamma\!\downarrow]$$

$$\frac{}{\gamma : \Gamma \rightarrow P_{\gamma} \xrightarrow{t} (\gamma : \Gamma \rightarrow P_{\gamma})/t} \; [t \notin \Gamma\!\uparrow]$$

$$\frac{P \xrightarrow{\alpha} P' \quad Q \xrightarrow{\beta} Q'}{P \,\Box\, Q \xrightarrow{\alpha \cup \beta} \beta \bullet P' \,\Box\, \alpha \bullet Q'} \; [\alpha = \beta \blacksquare \alpha, \beta = \alpha \blacksquare \beta]$$

$$\frac{}{\bigsqcap \mathcal{P} \xrightarrow{0} P} \; [P \in \mathcal{P}]$$

$$\frac{P \xrightarrow{\alpha} P' \quad Q \xrightarrow{\beta} Q'}{P \otimes Q \xrightarrow{\alpha \otimes \beta} P' \otimes Q'}$$

$$\frac{P \xrightarrow{\alpha} P'}{f[P] \xrightarrow{f\alpha} f[P']}$$

$$\frac{P \xrightarrow{\alpha} P'}{\Delta \cap P \xrightarrow{\alpha} \Delta/\alpha \cap P'} \; [\alpha \in \Delta]$$

$$\frac{P \xrightarrow{t\alpha} P'}{P/t \xrightarrow{\alpha} P'}$$

The closure of $\longrightarrow$ under ; is $\longrightarrow^*$.

DEFINITION 20. $\dfrac{P \xrightarrow{\alpha} P'}{P \xrightarrow{\alpha}{}^* P'} \qquad \dfrac{P \xrightarrow{\alpha}{}^* P' \xrightarrow{\beta}{}^* P''}{P \xrightarrow{\alpha\beta}{}^* P''}$

Having provided a transition system for APA, we still need to provide a notion of equality derived from the transition system. In this case, we will use a variant of de Nicola–Hennessy *testing* equivalence [Hen88]. We need a new observation space Obs_ω for tests, so a test T is a process from APA_{Obs_ω}.

DEFINITION 21. *$Obs_\omega \supset Obs$ is an observation space.*

Then Ω, ranged over by ω, is the set of all actions from Obs_ω which contain no behaviour from Obs.

DEFINITION 22. $\Omega = \{\omega \in Obs_\omega \setminus Obs \mid \nexists a \sqsubseteq \omega\}$.

For example, the successful test $SUCC$ nondeterministically performs any ω.

DEFINITION 23. $SUCC = \bigsqcap\{\gamma : \{\omega\} \rightarrow STOP \mid \omega \in \Omega\}$

We can place a process in parallel with a test using $P \Downarrow T$, which forces P and T to synchronize all of their actions, except ωs.

DEFINITION 24. $P \Downarrow T = f_\Downarrow[\Delta_\Downarrow \cap (P \otimes T)]$, *where*

$$\begin{aligned} \Delta_\Downarrow &= \{\alpha \otimes \alpha \mid \alpha \in Obs\} \cup \{\alpha \otimes (\alpha \sqcup \omega) \mid \alpha \in Obs, \omega \in \Omega\} \\ f_\Downarrow(\alpha \otimes \alpha) &= \alpha \\ f_\Downarrow(\alpha \otimes (\alpha \sqcup \omega)) &= \alpha \sqcup \omega \end{aligned}$$

Then a computation of $P \Downarrow T$ is a $\lhd$-maximal series of transitions.

DEFINITION 25. *A computation of P is a series of transitions $P \equiv P_0 \xrightarrow{\alpha_0} P_1 \xrightarrow{\alpha_1} \cdots \xrightarrow{\alpha_{n-1}} P_n$ such that $\alpha_i \in max\{\beta \mid P_i \xrightarrow{\beta} J\}$.*

Then P *may pass* T iff there is a computation of $P \Downarrow T$ that contains an ω.

DEFINITION 26. *P may T iff there is a computation of $P \Downarrow T$ such that one of the $\alpha_i \notin Obs$.*

So P and Q are *may-testing equivalent* iff P and Q may pass the same tests.

DEFINITION 27. *$P \simeq Q$ iff $\forall T \,.\, P$ may $T \Leftrightarrow Q$ may T*

It turns out that we don't need *must* testing [Hen88], as may testing is enough to produce timed failures equivalence, as also shown by Schneider [Sch91].

3.3 Denotational semantics

We can now give a denotational semantics to APA, in a similar style to Timed CSP's timed failures. A *timed failure* is a pair $(\alpha, \aleph)$ which represents 'the environment offered the process $\aleph$ and it chose to do $\alpha \in \aleph$'. Here, $\aleph$ is a *timed refusal*, and represents the observations the environment was prepared to observe.

DEFINITION 28. *$\aleph$ is a timed refusal iff $\aleph$ is $\lhd$-complete and $\aleph\uparrow\downarrow = \aleph\downarrow\uparrow$.*

DEFINITION 29. *$(\alpha, \aleph)$ is a timed failure iff $\alpha \in \aleph$.*

Definition 30. *F is a timed failures set iff*

- $\forall \aleph \,.\, \exists \alpha \,.\, (\alpha, \aleph) \in F$
- $(\alpha, \aleph) \in F \Rightarrow (\alpha, \{\alpha\}) \in F$
- $(\alpha, \aleph_1) \in F \wedge (\alpha, \aleph_1 \cup \aleph_2 \cup \aleph_3) \in F \Rightarrow (\alpha, \aleph_1 \cup \aleph_2) \in F$

These axioms for failures sets are all we need to prove the denotational semantics equivalent to may testing—if we were to investigate a complete axiomatization for APA, we would need more.

Definition 31.

$$
\begin{aligned}
[\![STOP]\!] &= \{(t, \aleph) \mid t \in \aleph\} \\
[\![RUN]\!] &= \{(\alpha, \aleph) \mid \alpha \in max\, \aleph\} \\
[\![\gamma : \Gamma \rightarrow P_\gamma]\!] &= \{(\alpha\beta, \aleph_1 \times_; \aleph_2) \mid \alpha \in \Gamma \cap max(\Gamma{\downarrow}{\uparrow} \cap \aleph_1) \wedge (\beta, \vec{\aleph}_2) \in [\![P_\alpha]\!]\} \\
&\quad \cup \{(\alpha, \aleph) \mid \alpha \in max(\Gamma{\downarrow}{\uparrow} \cap \aleph) \setminus \Gamma{\uparrow}\} \\
[\![P \,\square\, Q]\!] &= \{(\alpha \sqcup \beta, \aleph) \mid (\alpha, \{\beta\} \times_{\bullet} \aleph) \in [\![P]\!] \wedge (\beta, \{\alpha\} \times_{\bullet} \aleph) \in [\![Q]\!]\} \\
[\![\textstyle\bigsqcap \mathcal{P}]\!] &= \bigcup\{[\![P]\!] \mid P \in \mathcal{P}\} \\
[\![P \otimes Q]\!] &= \{(\alpha \otimes \beta, \aleph_1 \times_{\otimes} \aleph_2) \mid (\alpha, \aleph_1) \in [\![P]\!] \wedge (\beta, \aleph_2) \in [\![Q]\!]\} \\
[\![f[P]]\!] &= \{(f\,\alpha, \aleph) \mid (\alpha, f^{-1}[\aleph]) \in [\![P]\!]\} \\
[\![\Delta \cap P]\!] &= \{(\alpha, \aleph) \mid (\alpha, \Delta \cap \aleph) \in [\![P]\!]\} \\
[\![P/t]\!] &= \{(\alpha, \aleph) \mid (t\alpha, \{t\} \times_; \aleph) \in [\![P]\!]\}
\end{aligned}
$$

Lemma 32. $[\![P]\!]$ *is a timed failures set.*

Proof. A structural induction, requiring $\lhd$-completeness of Γ and Δ. □

We can now show that $[\![P]\!] = [\![Q]\!]$ iff $P \simeq Q$.

3.4 Equivalence of the semantics

We shall show our two semantics equivalent by proceeding in small steps. To begin with, we can construct a transition system $\longmapsto$ which turns the denotational semantics into an operational one.

Definition 33.

$$\frac{}{STOP \xmapsto{(t,\aleph)} STOP}\ [t \in \aleph]$$

$$\frac{}{RUN \xmapsto{(\alpha,\aleph)} RUN}\ [\alpha \in max\, \aleph]$$

$$\frac{}{\gamma : \Gamma \rightarrow P_\gamma \xmapsto{(\alpha,\aleph)} \vec{P}_\alpha}\ [\alpha \in \Gamma \cap max(\Gamma{\uparrow}{\downarrow} \cap \aleph)]$$

$$\frac{}{\gamma : \Gamma \rightarrow P_\gamma \xmapsto{(\alpha,\aleph)} \delta : \Gamma/\alpha \rightarrow P_{\alpha\delta}}\ [\alpha \in \Gamma{\downarrow} \cap max(\Gamma{\uparrow}{\downarrow} \cap \aleph)]$$

$$\frac{}{\gamma : \Gamma \rightarrow P_\gamma \xmapsto{(t,\aleph)} (\gamma : \Gamma \rightarrow P_\gamma)/t}\ [t \in max(\Gamma{\uparrow}{\downarrow} \cap \aleph) \setminus \Gamma{\uparrow}]$$

$$\frac{P \xmapsto{(\alpha,\{\beta\}\times_{\bullet}\aleph)} P' \quad Q \xmapsto{(\beta,\{\alpha\}\times_{\bullet}\aleph)} Q'}{P \,\square\, Q \xmapsto{(\alpha\sqcup\beta,\aleph)} \beta \bullet P' \,\square\, \alpha \bullet Q'}$$

$$\frac{}{\bigsqcap \mathcal{P} \xmapsto{(0,\{0\})} P}\,[P \in \mathcal{P}]$$

$$\frac{P \xmapsto{(\alpha,\aleph_1)} P' \quad Q \xmapsto{(\beta,\aleph_2)} Q'}{P \otimes Q \xmapsto{(\alpha\otimes\beta,\aleph_1 \times_{\bullet} \aleph_2)} P' \otimes Q'}$$

$$\frac{P \xmapsto{(\alpha,f^{-1}[\aleph])} P'}{f[P] \xmapsto{(f\alpha,\aleph)} f[P']}$$

$$\frac{P \xmapsto{(\alpha,\Delta\cap\aleph)} P'}{\Delta \cap P \xmapsto{(\alpha,\aleph)} \Delta/\alpha \cap P}$$

$$\frac{P \xmapsto{(t\alpha,\{t\}\times_{;}\aleph)} P'}{P/t \xmapsto{(\alpha,\aleph)} P'}$$

DEFINITION 34. $\dfrac{P \xmapsto{(\alpha,\aleph)} Q}{P \xmapsto{(\alpha,\aleph)}{}^{*} Q} \qquad \dfrac{P \xmapsto{(\alpha,\aleph_1)}{}^{*} Q \xmapsto{(\beta,\aleph_2)}{}^{*} R}{P \xmapsto{(\alpha\beta,\aleph_1\times_{;}\aleph_2)}{}^{*} R}$

Then we can show that $\longmapsto$ is the same as the denotational semantics.

LEMMA 35. $(\alpha,\aleph) \in [\![P]\!]$ *iff* $P \xmapsto{(\alpha,\aleph)}{}^{*}$.

PROOF. A structural induction, which uses the definition of a failures set, and the law $(\alpha \blacksquare \beta)(\alpha \bullet (\gamma \blacksquare \delta)) = \alpha\gamma \blacksquare \beta\delta$. □

Then we can produce a link between $\longmapsto$ and $\longrightarrow$.

DEFINITION 36. $P \xRightarrow{(\alpha,\aleph)} Q$ *iff* $P \xrightarrow{\alpha} Q$ *and* $\alpha \in max(tr\, P \cap \aleph)$.

DEFINITION 37. $\dfrac{P \xRightarrow{(\alpha,\aleph)} Q}{P \xRightarrow{(\alpha,\aleph)}{}^{*} Q} \qquad \dfrac{P \xRightarrow{(\alpha,\aleph_1)}{}^{*} Q \xRightarrow{(\beta,\aleph_2)}{}^{*} R}{P \xRightarrow{(\alpha\beta,\aleph_1\times_{;}\aleph_2)}{}^{*} R}$

LEMMA 38. $P \xmapsto{(\alpha,\aleph)} P'$ *iff* $P \xRightarrow{(\alpha,\aleph)} P'$

PROOF. An induction on the proofs of $P \xmapsto{(\alpha,\aleph)} P'$ and $P \xRightarrow{(\alpha,\aleph)} P'$. □

COROLLARY 39. $P \xmapsto{(\alpha,\aleph)}{}^{*} P'$ *iff* $P \xRightarrow{(\alpha,\aleph)}{}^{*} P'$

As a side-effect, since $(t,\{t\}) \in [\![P]\!]$ for any process P, this means our operational semantics is free of time-stops.

COROLLARY 40. $\forall t, P\,.\, P \xrightarrow{t}$

And in turn, this means that every process has to pass the successful test.

COROLLARY 41. $\forall P\,.\, P$ *may SUCC*

We can then define a test $T_{(\alpha,\aleph)}$ which tests whether a process can do α if offered $\aleph$.

DEFINITION 42. $T_{(\alpha,\aleph)} = \gamma : \aleph \rightarrow \begin{cases} SUCC & \text{if } \gamma = \alpha \\ STOP & \text{otherwise} \end{cases}$

Then we can show that may-testing is at least as powerful as $\Longrightarrow^*$.

LEMMA 43. *P may $T_{(\alpha,\aleph)}$ iff $P \xRightarrow{(\alpha,\aleph)}{}^*$*

PROOF. An induction on the derivation of $P \Downarrow T_{(\alpha,\aleph)} \xrightarrow{\omega}{}^*$ and $P \xRightarrow{(\alpha,\aleph)}{}^*$. This relies on every process passing $SUCC$. □

And so we have shown our first theorem, that may testing is at least as strong as failures equivalence.

THEOREM 44. *If $P \simeq Q$ then $[\![P]\!] = [\![Q]\!]$.*

The proof in the other direction is much simpler.

LEMMA 45. *P may T iff $(\alpha \sqcup \omega, Obs_{|\alpha|}) \in [\![P \Downarrow T]\!]$.*

PROOF. Follows directly from the previous lemmas. □

Since failures equivalence is a congruence, we have the other half of our proof.

THEOREM 46. *If $[\![P]\!] = [\![Q]\!]$ then $P \simeq Q$.*

References

[BB90] J. C. M. Baeten and J. A. Bergstra. Real space process algebra. Technical Report P9005, Programming Research Group, University of Amsterdam, 1990.

[BB91a] J. C. M. Baeten and J. A. Bergstra. Asynchronous communication in real space process algebra. In *Proc. Chalmers Workshop on Concurrency*. Department of Computer Sciences, Chalmers University, 1991.

[BB91b] J. C. M. Baeten and J. A. Bergstra. Real time proces algebra. *Formal Aspects of Computing*, 3:142–188, 1991.

[BHR84] S. D. Brookes, C. A. R. Hoare, and A. W. Roscoe. A theory of communicating sequential processes. *JACM*, 31(3):560–599, July 1984.

[BK85] J. A. Bergstra and J. W. Klop. Algebra of communicating processes with abstraction. *Theoretical Computer Science*, 37:77–121, 1985.

[BW90] J. C. M. Baeten and W. P. Weijland. *Process Algebra*, volume 18 of *Cambridge Tracts in Theoretical Computer Science*. Cambridge University Press, 1990.

[DS89] Jim Davies and Steve Schneider. An introduction to timed CSP. Technical monograph PRG-75, Oxford University Computing Laboratory, 1989.

[Gis88] Jay L. Gischer. The equational theory of pomsets. *Theoretical Computer Science*, 61:199–224, 1988.

[Hen88] M. Hennessy. *Algebraic Theory of Processes*. The MIT Press, 1988.

[Hoa85] C. A. R. Hoare. *Communicating Sequential Processes*. Prentice-Hall, 1985.

[HR90] M. Hennessy and T. Regan. A temporal process algebra. Technical Report 2/90, University of Sussex, Computer Science Department, 1990.

[Jef91a] Alan Jeffrey. An algebraic structure for timed observation. In *Proc. Chalmers Workshop on Concurrency*. Department of Computer Sciences, Chalmers University, 1991.

[Jef91b] Alan Jeffrey. Discrete timed CSP. PMG Memo 79, Department of Computer Sciences, Chalmers University, 1991.

[Jef91c] Alan Jeffrey. A linear time process algebra. To be presented at CAV 91, 1991.

[Mil80] Robin Milner. *A Calculus of Communicating Systems*. Springer-Verlag, 1980. LNCS 92.

[Mil83] Robin Milner. Calculi for synchrony and asynchrony. *Theoretical Computer Science*, pages 267–310, 1983.

[Mil89] Robin Milner. *Communication and Concurrency*. Prentice-Hall, 1989.

[MT90] F. Moller and C. Tofts. A temporal calculus of communicating systems. In *Proc. Concur 90*, pages 401–415. Springer-Verlag, 1990. LNCS 458.

[Mur91a] David Murphy. The physics of observation: A perspective for concurrency theorists. Submitted to the Bulletin of the EATCS, 1991.

[Mur91b] David Murphy. Testing, betting and true concurrency. To be presented at Concur 91, 1991.

[NS90] X. Nicollin and J. Sifakis. The algebra of timed processes ATP: Theory and application. Technical Report RT-C26, Laboratoire de Génie Informatique de Grenoble, 1990.

[Ree88] George M. Reed. *A Uniform Mathematical Theory for Real-time Distributed Computing*. D.Phil thesis, Oxford University, 1988.

[RR86] G. M. Reed and A. W. Roscoe. A timed model for communicating sequential processes. In *Proc. ICALP 86*, pages 314–323. Springer-Verlag, 1986. LNCS 226.

[Sch91] Steve Schneider. An operational semantics for timed CSP. In *Proc. Chalmers Workshop on Concurrency*, 1991.

[Wan90] Wang Yi. Real-time behaviour of asynchronous agents. In *Proc. Concur 90*, pages 502–520. Springer-Verlag, 1990. LNCS 458.

[Wan91] Wang Yi. CCS + time = an interleaving model for real time systems. To be presented at ICALP 91, 1991.

Simulations between Specifications of Distributed Systems *

Bengt Jonsson
Swedish Institute of Computer Science, Stockholm †
and Dept. of Computer Systems, Uppsala University

Abstract

In the stepwise development of a distributed system, the problem arises of verifying that a specification at a lower level of abstraction correctly implements a specification at a higher level of abstraction. Forward and backward simulation have been proposed as verification techniques for this problem. In this paper, we study forward and backward simulation in a framework where specifications are given as labeled transition systems with fairness requirements. We aim at clarifying the connection between simulations and the auxiliary variable constructions of Abadi and Lamport. In the paper, we also relax the earlier restriction that backward simulations be finitary. For a simple specification notation, similar to the action system formalism or Unity, we furthermore present proof rules that correspond to forward and backward simulations. Finally, we relate the forward and backward simulation techniques to subset-constructions that can be used in automata theory, e.g. for deciding language containment.

1 Introduction

Distributed computer systems can be specified at many levels of abstraction. For instance, a specification of a computer network can at one level describe an abstract file transfer service, and at another level include a description of a protocol for transmitting data over a physical link. Several correctness criteria and verification techniques have been proposed for determining whether a lower-level specification correctly implements a higher-level one.

Several correctness critera require that each computation of the lowel-level specification be equivalent to a computation of the higher-level one. Simulations have been proposed as a sound verification technique for such correctness criteria. Simulations reduce a verification problem which is stated in terms of computations, to properties of individual program statements. The usual form of simulation, which we shall call forward simulation, has successfully been used to verify many distributed algorithms and communication protocols (e.g. [Jon87b, Lam83, Lam89, LS90, LT87, Ora89, SL83, Sta84, WLL88]) and to verify refinements between data types [Hoa72, HJS87, Nip86]. Forward simulation is incomplete in itself, but when combined with its mirror-image backward simulation, completeness can be established for a rather large class of specifications [AL88, HJS87, Jos88, Jif89]. When the correctness criterion involves nonterminating computations, the backward simulation must be finitary, i.e., each lower-level state can be related to only finitely many higher-level states, in order to be sound. Consequently, the combination of forward and backward simulation is complete only for specifications with bounded nondeterminism.

*supported in part by the Swedish Board for Technical Development (STU) under contract No. 89-01220P as part of Esprit BRA project SPEC, No. 3096

†Address: SICS, Box 1263, S-164 28 Kista, SWEDEN, E-mail:bengt@sics.se

In this paper, we study the forward and backward simulation technique in the framework of labeled transition systems with fairness requirements. A specialization of this framework, I/O-automata, has been used to specify and verify distributed algorithms [Jon87b, LT87, Sta84, WLL88]. In our presentation, we aim at clarifying the connection between the forward and backward simulation as used in [HJS87, Jos88, Jif89] and the auxiliary variable constructions of [AL88]. The paper also contains the following contributions.

- We extend the backward simulation by relaxing the requirement of being finitary. Essentially, it is enough that each computation of the lower-level system contain infinitely many states whose image under the backward simulation is finitary. This extension has also been mentioned in [AL88]. By combining several infinitely often finitary backward simulations, the finitary requirement can be relaxed to cover several practically occurring cases.
- For a simple specification notation, which is similar to the action system formalism [BKS88, BS88] or Unity [CM88], we present proof rules that correspond to forward and backward simulations. Earlier presentations of backward simulation in [AL88, HJS87, Jos88, Jif89] are mostly semantic, and are not concerned with any particular notation for specifications.
- We relate the forward and backward simulation techniques to subset-constructions that are used in classical automata-theory, e.g. for deciding language containment. Subsets are also used by Gerth [Ger90] in a complete verification method for safety properties of communicating processes, and a related method is used by Klarlund and Schneider [KS89].

Forward simulations, mostly referred to as simulations, were defined by Milner [Mil], and have been used to verify distributed algorithms in the work of [Sta84, Sta88], Lynch and Tuttle [LT87], in our earlier work [Jon87a, Jon87b], by Lam and Shankar [LS90]. Forward and backward simulations have been used by Hoare, Jifeng and Sanders [HJS87, Jif89] and Josephs [Jos88] to refine data types and communication processes. They use the terms downward and upward simulations instead of forward and backward. Their framework considers only finite computations, whence they do not need to require backward simulations to be finitary. Refinement mappings, which are essentially functional forward simulations, have been used by Hoare [Hoa72] for data types and by Lamport [Lam83, Lam89] and Lam and Shankar [LS84] for distributed algorithms. Abadi and Lamport [AL88] have extended the refinement mappings by auxiliary variable constructions whose soundness follow using either forward or backward simulations. Gerth [Ger90] uses a single verification rule, corresponding to the subset-simulation, which in his framework is complete since he considers only safety properties.

The rest of the paper is organized as follows: In the next section, we define labeled transition systems and refinement. In Section 3, we present forward and backward simulations and prove separate and combined completeness results for them. In Section 4 we extend the backward simulation to unbounded nondeterminism under certain conditions. In Section 5 we present proof rules corresponding to forward and backward simulations for a simple notation. In Section 6 we relate the forward and backward simulations to subset-constructions in automata theory. Section 7 contains and example, and Section 8 contains conclusions.

2 Fair Transition Systems and Refinement

In this section, we define fair labeled transition systems and the refinement relation between them. Labeled or unlabeled transition systems have often been used for operational descriptions of computing systems, e.g. by Plotkin [Plo81] and Manna and Pnueli [MP81]. Essentially, a labeled transition system is a (not necessarily finite-state) automaton, consisting of states and labeled transitions.

We assume a set E of *communication events*, which does not include the *silent event* τ.

Definition 2.1 A *fair labeled transition system* (fts for short) is a tuple $\langle S, S^0, \longrightarrow, \mathcal{F}\rangle$, where

S is a set of *states*,

$S^0 \subseteq S$ is a nonempty set of *initial states*,

$\longrightarrow \subseteq S \times (E \cup \{\tau\}) \times S$ is a set of *labeled transitions*. We use $s \xrightarrow{e} s'$ to denote $\langle s, e, s'\rangle \in\longrightarrow$,

$\mathcal{F}$ is an at most countable set of pairs of form $\langle S^F, \longrightarrow^F\rangle$ where $S^F \subseteq S$ and $\longrightarrow^F \subseteq \longrightarrow$. Each pair $\langle S^F, \longrightarrow^F\rangle \in \mathcal{F}$ is called a *fairness requirement*.

A transition $s \xrightarrow{\tau} s'$ with the label τ is called a *silent transition*. A silent transition of form $s \xrightarrow{\tau} s$, with both states the same, is called a *null transition*. As a technical convenience, we require that each fts must contain the null-transition $s \xrightarrow{\tau} s$ for each of its states s. □

Intuitively, an fts represents a behavior which is given by its set of states, and how the state may change in transitions. Simultaneously with a transition, an event may occur. Comunication events are intended to represent observable interactions with the environment, e.g. the transmission of a message. The silent event τ signifies an internal transition which does not interact with the environment.

Example 2.2 We define a particular fts which represents a simple FIFO buffer, which receives messages from a channel *in* and transmits them onto channel *out* in the same order. We assume that the messages belong to a set M. The transmission of a message over *in* or *out* is a communication event denoted by $in(m)$ or $out(m)$, where $m \in M$. The buffer is represented by the fts $\langle S, S^0, \longrightarrow, \mathcal{F}\rangle$, where $S = M^*$ is the set of sequences of messages in M, where $S^0 = \{\langle\rangle\}$, where $\longrightarrow$ for each $s \in S$ and $m \in M$ contains the transition $s \xrightarrow{in(m)} s \bullet m$ which adds a message to the state, and the transition $m \bullet s \xrightarrow{out(m)} s$ which removes a message from the state (we use $\bullet$ to denote concatenation), and where $\mathcal{F} = \{\langle S^F, \longrightarrow^F\rangle\}$ with S^F being the set of states which are non-empty sequences, and with $\longrightarrow^F$ containing all transitions of form $m \bullet s \xrightarrow{out(m)} s$. The fairness requirement implies that the buffer will eventually output each message that it contains. □

Definition 2.3 Let $\mathcal{M}$ be a fts $\langle S, S^0, \longrightarrow, \mathcal{F}\rangle$. An *execution* of $\mathcal{M}$ is an infinite sequence of transitions

$$s^0 \xrightarrow{e^1} s^1 \xrightarrow{e^2} \cdots \xrightarrow{e^n} s^n \xrightarrow{e^{n+1}} \cdots$$

which starts in an initial state $s^0 \in S^0$. A *partial execution* of $\mathcal{M}$ is a finite sequence of transitions which starts in an initial state $s^0 \in S^0$. Let $\langle S^F, \longrightarrow^F\rangle$ be a fairness requirement in $\mathcal{F}$. An execution C of $\mathcal{M}$ *satisfies* $\langle S^F, \longrightarrow^F\rangle$ iff either infinitely many states of C are not in S^F, or C contains infinitely many occurrences of transitions in $\longrightarrow^F$. A *computation* of $\mathcal{M}$ is an execution which satisfies each fairness requirement in $\mathcal{F}$. The *trace* of an execution is the (finite or infinite) sequence of communication events (i.e., non-τ events) in the execution. A *trace* of a fts $\mathcal{M}$ is the trace of a computation of $\mathcal{M}$. A state is *reachable* if it occurs in some partial execution. □

The fairness used here is often referred to as weak fairness or justice. We could also have allowed the inclusion of strong fairness in the definition, but that would not affect the results in this paper. The requirement that executions and computations be infinite saves us separate treatment of finite and infinite executions in many definitions and proofs, without losing generality. A finite execution can be transformed into an infinite execution by adding an infinite suffix of null transitions.

Definition 2.4 Let $\mathcal{M}_C$ and $\mathcal{M}_A$ be fts's. We say that $\mathcal{M}_C$ *refines* $\mathcal{M}_A$, written $\mathcal{M}_C \sqsupseteq \mathcal{M}_A$ iff each trace of $\mathcal{M}_C$ is a trace of $\mathcal{M}_A$. □

It is easy to see that $\sqsupseteq$ is a reflexive and transitive relation on fts's.

3 Simulations

In this section, we consider the problem of verifying that a more concrete fts $\mathcal{M}_C$ correctly refines a more abstract fts $\mathcal{M}_A$. Recall that to establish $\mathcal{M}_C \sqsupseteq \mathcal{M}_A$, one must prove that each trace of $\mathcal{M}_C$ is also a trace of $\mathcal{M}_A$. In general, such a proof would require reasoning about entire computations, which is rather complex (results by Sistla [Sis88] and Vardi [Var87] show that this problem is Π^1_2-complete when the fts's are effectively given). Here we shall look at two verification techniques that reduce the verification problem to properties of individual transitions (corresponding to program statements). First in Section 3.1 we will temporarily disregard fairness requirements, which will reappear again in Section 3.2. This means that we will only look at techniques for verifying that for each execution of $\mathcal{M}_C$, there is a (possibly unfair) execution of $\mathcal{M}_A$ with the same trace.

The idea of the first technique is to show that, given an execution C_C of $\mathcal{M}_C$ with trace q, an execution C_A of $\mathcal{M}_A$ with trace q can be constructed step-by-step, starting from the beginning of the execution. In order to verify such a construction by reasoning about individual transitions, corresponding states of C_C and C_A must be related by a *forward simulation*. This technique has proven successful in several applications (e.g. [Jon87b, LS90, LT87, Ora89, Sta88]), and also its special case *refinement mapping* [KMPS91, Lam83]. The idea of the second technique is to construct C_A step-by-step from the end and work backwards. There is no "end" of a computation, so instead one works backwards from an arbitrary point of the computation. This proves the existence of an arbitrary finite prefix of C_A. The existence of C_A is then proven by a continuity argument, using Kōnig's lemma. Corresponding states of C_C and C_A must in this case be related by a *backward simulation*. This technique has been presented in various forms in [AL88, Jif89, Jos88, Mer90]. Neither of the techniques is complete, but their combination is complete for a rather large class of transition systems.

3.1 Forward Simulations and Backward Simulations

Definition 3.1 Let $\mathcal{M}_C = \langle S_C, S_C^0, \longrightarrow_C, \mathcal{F}_C\rangle$ and $\mathcal{M}_A = \langle S_A, S_A^0, \longrightarrow_A, \mathcal{F}_A\rangle$ be two fts's. A *forward simulation* between $\mathcal{M}_C$ and $\mathcal{M}_A$ is a relation R between S_C and S_A such that

1. for each initial state s_C^0 of $\mathcal{M}_C$ there is an initial state s_A^0 of $\mathcal{M}_A$ such that $s_C^0 \; R \; s_A^0$,
2. if $s_C \; R \; s_A$ and $s_C \stackrel{e}{\longrightarrow}_C s'_C$, then there is a state s'_A of $\mathcal{M}_A$ such that $s_A \stackrel{e}{\longrightarrow}_A s'_A$ and $s'_C \; R \; s'_A$.

□

Definition 3.2 Let $\mathcal{M}_C = \langle S_C, S_C^0, \longrightarrow_C, \mathcal{F}_C\rangle$ and $\mathcal{M}_A = \langle S_A, S_A^0, \longrightarrow_A, \mathcal{F}_A\rangle$ be two fts's. A *backward simulation* between $\mathcal{M}_C$ and $\mathcal{M}_A$ is a relation R between S_C and S_A such that

1. for each reachable state s_C of $\mathcal{M}_C$ there is a state s_A of $\mathcal{M}_A$ such that $s_C \; R \; s_A$.
2. if $s_C \; R \; s_A$ and $s'_C \stackrel{e}{\longrightarrow}_C s_C$ then there is a state s'_A of $\mathcal{M}_A$ such that $s'_A \stackrel{e}{\longrightarrow}_A s_A$ and $s'_C \; R \; s'_A$,
3. if $s_C \; R \; s_A$ and s_C is an initial state of $\mathcal{M}_C$ then s_A is an initial state of $\mathcal{M}_A$.

A backward simulation R is *finitary* if for each state s_C of $\mathcal{M}_C$, the set of states s_A of $\mathcal{M}_A$ such that $s_C \; R \; s_A$ is finite. □

Note that the two first conditions in the definition of a backward simulation are mirror-images of the two first conditions in the definition of forward simulation.

The following propositions show that, if we disregard the fairness requirements, forward simulation and finitary backward simulation are both sound verification techniques for establishing refinements between fts's.

Proposition 3.3 *If there exists a forward simulation between $\mathcal{M}_C$ and $\mathcal{M}_A$ then each trace of an execution of $\mathcal{M}_C$ is also a trace of an execution of $\mathcal{M}_A$.* □

Proposition 3.4 *If there exists a finitary backward simulation between $\mathcal{M}_C$ and $\mathcal{M}_A$ then each trace of an execution of $\mathcal{M}_C$ is also a trace of an execution of $\mathcal{M}_A$.* □

Proof: Subsumed by Proposition 4.2 □

3.2 Introducing Fairness Properties

We now extend the verification techniques of Section 3.1 to include fairness requirements. Essentially, when verifying that $\mathcal{M}_C \sqsupseteq \mathcal{M}_A$, one must in addition to finding a forward or backward simulation prove that the fairness requirements of $\mathcal{M}_A$ follow from those of $\mathcal{M}_C$. We propose to do this by combining the two transition systems by a superposition. The proof that the fairness requirements of $\mathcal{M}_A$ are satisfied can then be done using standard proof techniques for verifying liveness properties of reactive programs, e.g. of Manna and Pnueli [MP84, MP89], using well-founded induction.

Definition 3.5 Let $\mathcal{M}_C = \langle S_C, S_C^0, \longrightarrow_C, \mathcal{F}_C\rangle$ and $\mathcal{M}_A = \langle S_A, S_A^0, \longrightarrow_A, \mathcal{F}_A\rangle$ be fts's. A *superposition* of $\mathcal{M}_A$ onto $\mathcal{M}_C$ is an fts $\mathcal{M} = \langle S, S^0, \longrightarrow, \mathcal{F}\rangle$, where

$S = S_C \times S_A$; we define $\pi_i(\langle s_C, s_A\rangle) = s_i$ for $i = C, A$,

$S^0 \subseteq S_C^0 \times S_A^0$,

$\longrightarrow \subseteq \{\langle s_C, s_A\rangle \stackrel{e}{\longrightarrow} \langle s_C', s_A'\rangle \ : \ s_C \stackrel{e}{\longrightarrow}_C s_C' \ \wedge \ s_A \stackrel{e}{\longrightarrow}_A s_A'\}$;
we define $\pi_i(\langle s_C, s_A\rangle \stackrel{e}{\longrightarrow}_i \langle s_C', s_A'\rangle) = s_i \stackrel{e}{\longrightarrow} s_i'$ for $i = C, A$,

$\mathcal{F}$ contains for each fairness requirement $\langle S_C^F, \longrightarrow_C^F\rangle \in \mathcal{F}_C$
the pair $\langle \pi_C^{-1}(S_C^F), (\pi_C^{-1}(\longrightarrow_C^F) \cap \longrightarrow)\rangle$. □

Intuitively, the state of a superposition is a tuple written $\langle s_C, s_A\rangle$, where s_C is a state of $\mathcal{M}_C$ and s_A is a state of $\mathcal{M}_A$. Observe that the transitions of $\mathcal{M}$ are a *subset* of the possible combinations of transitions that synchronize over the same label. The superposition is intended to describe a particular way for transitions of $\mathcal{M}_A$ to synchronize with transitions of $\mathcal{M}_C$ when the computations of $\mathcal{M}_A$ mimic those of $\mathcal{M}_C$. The fairness requirements of $\mathcal{M}$ are straightforward mappings from those of $\mathcal{M}_C$. The definition of projection π_i is extended to sequences of transitions in the obvious manner.

Definition 3.6 Let $\mathcal{M}$ be a superposition of $\mathcal{M}_A$ onto $\mathcal{M}_C$. A relation R between the states S_C of $\mathcal{M}_C$ and the states S of $\mathcal{M}$ is said to *respect the first component* if $s_C \ R \ \langle s_C', s_A'\rangle$ implies $s_C = s_C'$. □

Definition 3.7 Let $\mathcal{M}$ be a superposition of $\mathcal{M}_A$ onto $\mathcal{M}_C$. We say that $\mathcal{M}$ is obtained from $\mathcal{M}_C$ by *adding $\mathcal{M}_A$ as a history variable* if there is a forward simulation R between $\mathcal{M}_C$ and $\mathcal{M}$ which respects the first component, and for each fairness requirement $\langle S_A^F, \longrightarrow_A^F\rangle$ of $\mathcal{M}_A$, each computation of $\mathcal{M}$ satisfies the fairness requirement $\langle \pi_A^{-1}(S_A^F), \pi_A^{-1}(\longrightarrow_A^F)\rangle$. We say that $\mathcal{M}$ is obtained from $\mathcal{M}_C$ by *adding $\mathcal{M}_A$ as a (finitary) prophecy variable* if there is a (finitary) backward simulation R between $\mathcal{M}_C$ and $\mathcal{M}$ which respects he first component, and for each fairness requirement $\langle S_A^F, \longrightarrow_A^F\rangle$ of $\mathcal{M}_A$, each computation of $\mathcal{M}$ satisfies the fairness requirement $\langle \pi_A^{-1}(S_A^F), \pi_A^{-1}(\longrightarrow_A^F)\rangle$. □

We can now state a main verification technique for establishing refinements between fts's.

Theorem 3.8 *Let $\mathcal{M}_C$ and $\mathcal{M}_A$ be fts's. If there exists an fts $\mathcal{M}$ which is obtained from $\mathcal{M}_C$ by adding $\mathcal{M}_A$ as either a history variable or a finitary prophecy variable, then $\mathcal{M}_C \sqsupseteq \mathcal{M}_A$.* □

Proof sketch: Proposition 3.3 implies that for each computation C_C of $\mathcal{M}_C$ there is an execution C of $\mathcal{M}$ with the same trace. The definitionn of superposition implies that C is in fact a computation of $\mathcal{M}$. The definitions of history and prophecy variables imply that $\pi_A(C)$ satisfies the fairness requirements of $\mathcal{M}_A$. Since $\pi_A(C)$ has the same trace as C, the theorem follows. □

That each computation of $\mathcal{M}$ satisfies some particular fairness requirement can be proven using standard techniques for proving liveness properties under fairness assumptions [MP89, Jon87b].

3.3 Completeness of Simulations

We shall in this section present three completeness results. The first, which concerns forward simulations, is a variant of a standard result of automata theory. The second, which concerns backward simulations, has earlier appeared in [Jon90]. The third concerns the combination of forward and backward simulations, and has in various forms appeared in [AL88, Jif89, Jos88]. In this section, we always assume that $\mathcal{M}_A$ in the relation $\mathcal{M}_C \sqsupseteq \mathcal{M}_A$ has no silent transitions, except null transitions. Thus our completeness results are valid only in the absence of non-null τ-transitions in the abstract fts.

Definition 3.9 If R is a relation between the states of $\mathcal{M}_C$ and $\mathcal{M}_A$, then *the superposition induced by* R is the superposition $\langle S, S^0, \longrightarrow, \mathcal{F}\rangle$, where S^0 contains all pairs $\langle s_C^0, s_A^0\rangle$ of initial states such that $s_C^0 \; R \; s_A^0$ and $\longrightarrow$ is the set of transitions $\langle s_C, s_A\rangle \overset{e}{\longrightarrow} \langle s'_C, s'_A\rangle$ such that $s_C \; R \; s_A$ and $s'_C \; R \; s'_A$ and $s_i \overset{e}{\longrightarrow}_i s'_i$ for $i = C, A$. □

Definition 3.10 An fts is *deterministic* if (1) it has only one initial state, (2) it has no transitions with event τ, except null transitions, and (3) for each state s and event e there is at most one transition of form $s \overset{e}{\longrightarrow} s'$. A fairness requirement $\langle S^F, \longrightarrow^F\rangle$ is called *simple* if there is some transition in $\longrightarrow^F$ from each state of S^F. The fts $\langle S, S^0, \longrightarrow, \mathcal{F}\rangle$ is *simple* if each fairness requirement in $\mathcal{F}$ is simple. □

Theorem 3.11 *For $i = C, A$ let $\mathcal{M}_i = \langle S_i, S_i^0, \longrightarrow_i, \mathcal{F}_i\rangle$ be fts's such that $\mathcal{M}_C$ is simple and $\mathcal{M}_A$ is deterministic. If $\mathcal{M}_C \sqsupseteq \mathcal{M}_A$, then $\mathcal{M}_A$ can be added as a history variable to $\mathcal{M}_C$.* □

Proof sketch: It is not difficult to see that there is a forward simulation R between $\mathcal{M}_C$ and $\mathcal{M}_A$. Let the superposition $\mathcal{M}$ be that which is induced by R. Define the forward simulation R_F between $\mathcal{M}_C$ and $\mathcal{M}$ by $s_C \; R_F \; \langle s_C, s_A\rangle$ iff $s_C \; R \; s_A$. For each trace of $\mathcal{M}_C$ there is a unique computation of $\mathcal{M}_A$ with that trace. Hence in each computation of $\mathcal{M}$, the fairness requirements of $\mathcal{M}_A$ must be satisfied. This and the fact that R_F is a forward simulation shows that $\mathcal{M}_A$ is added as a history variable. □

Definition 3.12 An fts $\mathcal{M}$ is *forest-like* if

1. for each reachable state s there is at most one non-null transition of form $s' \overset{e}{\longrightarrow} s$ which leads to s,
2. for each initial state s there is no non-null transition $s' \overset{e}{\longrightarrow} s$ from a reachable state s' of $\mathcal{M}$. □

Intuitively, if the non-null transitions between the reachable states of a forest-like transition system is displayed as a graph with states as nodes and transitions as edges, then the graph will have the form of a forest.

Definition 3.13 A fts $\mathcal{M}$ is said to be *image finite* if it has finitely many initial states and for each state s and event e there are only finitely many s' such that $s \xrightarrow{e} s'$ is a transition of $\mathcal{M}$. A fts $\mathcal{M}$ is *internally continuous* if each execution of $\mathcal{M}$ whose trace is a trace of $\mathcal{M}$ is also a computation of $\mathcal{M}$ □

Put differently, if C is an execution of an internally continuous fts, then whether or not C is a computation depends only on the trace of C.

Theorem 3.14 *For $i = C, A$ let $\mathcal{M}_i = \langle S_i, S_i^0, \longrightarrow_i, \mathcal{F}_i\rangle$ be fts's, where $\mathcal{M}_C$ is simple and forest-like, and $\mathcal{M}_A$ is image finite and internally continuous and has no τ-transitions, except null transitions. If $\mathcal{M}_C \sqsupseteq \mathcal{M}_A$, then $\mathcal{M}_A$ can be added as a finitary prophecy variable to $\mathcal{M}_C$.* □

Proof sketch: Define a relation R between S_C and S_A by $s_C\ R\ s_A$ iff for $i = C, A$ there exist computations C_i of $\mathcal{M}_i$ with the same sequences of events and an n such that s_i is the nth state of C_i. It is easy to see that R satisfies conditions 1 (depends on $\mathcal{M}_C$ being simple) and 3 in Definition 3.2. To check condition 2, assume that $s_C\ R\ s_A$, i.e., there are computations C_C and C_A with the same sequence of events such that s_i is the nth state of C_i. If now $s'_C \xrightarrow{e}_C s_C$ then, since $\mathcal{M}_C$ is forest-like, the transition $s'_C \xrightarrow{e}_C s_C$ must be the transition in C_C which leads to the nth state in C_C. Hence the transition $s'_A \xrightarrow{e'} s_A$ leading to the nth state in C_A satisfies $e' = e$ and $s'_C\ R\ s'_A$. We conclude that R is a backward simulation. Let the superposition be that which is induced by R. For each trace of $\mathcal{M}_C$ all executions of $\mathcal{M}_A$ with that trace must be computations of $\mathcal{M}_A$, since $\mathcal{M}_C \sqsupseteq \mathcal{M}_A$ and $\mathcal{M}_A$ is internally continuous. Hence in each computation of $\mathcal{M}$, the fairness requirements of $\mathcal{M}_A$ must be satisfied. □

Each of the techniques forward simulation and backward simulation is incomplete in itself. The following theorem shows that by combining the two techniques, we can obtain a rather strong completeness result.

Theorem 3.15 *For $i = C, A$ let $\mathcal{M}_i = \langle S_i, S_i^0, \longrightarrow_i, \mathcal{F}_i\rangle$ be fts's. Let $\mathcal{M}_C$ be simple and let $\mathcal{M}_A$ be image finite and internally continuous, and have no silent transitions except null transitions. If $\mathcal{M}_C \sqsupseteq \mathcal{M}_A$, then there exists an fts $\mathcal{M}_S$ which is obtained by adding a history variable to $\mathcal{M}_C$ such that $\mathcal{M}_S \sqsupseteq \mathcal{M}_A$ can be proven using the addition of a finitary prophecy variable in Theorem 3.8.* □

Proof sketch: Having the two preceding completeness theorems in mind, we can either construct $\mathcal{M}_S$ as a forest-like fts which is equivalent to $\mathcal{M}_C$ and then use Theorem 3.14, or construct a deterministic fts $\mathcal{M}_B$ which is equivalent to $\mathcal{M}_A$ and then use Theorem 3.11. We will thus give two proofs of this theorem.

Proof 1: Construct an fts $\mathcal{M}_B = \langle S_B, S_B^0, \longrightarrow_B, \mathcal{F}_B\rangle$, where S_B is the set of finite partial computations of $\mathcal{M}_C$, where S_B^0 is the set of partial computations with only an initial state, where $C_C \xrightarrow{e}_B (C_C \xrightarrow{e}_C s'_C)$ iff $s_C \xrightarrow{e}_C s'_C$ where s_C is the last state of C_C, and where $\mathcal{F}_B = \emptyset$. Define a relation R by $s_C\ R\ C_C$ iff s_C is the last state of C_C. Let $\mathcal{M}_S$ be the superposition of $\mathcal{M}_B$ onto $\mathcal{M}_C$ induced by R. It can be seen that $\mathcal{M}_B$ is added as a history variable to $\mathcal{M}_C$. Intuitively, the second component of the state of $\mathcal{M}_S$ is a history variable which records the computation that has been performed so far. It is easy to see that $\mathcal{M}_S$ is simple and forest-like, whence we can use Theorem 3.14 to conclude the proof.

Proof 2: Construct an fts $\mathcal{M}_B = \langle S_B, \{T^0\}, \longrightarrow_B, \emptyset\rangle$, where S_B is the set of finite subsets of states of $\mathcal{M}_A$, where T^0 is the set of initial states of $\mathcal{M}_A$, and where $T' \xrightarrow{e}_B T$ iff T is the set of states s_A of $\mathcal{M}_A$ for which there is a state $s'_A \in T'$ such that $s'_A \xrightarrow{e}_A s_A$. Since $\mathcal{M}_A$ is image finite, the set T is finite whenever T' is finite. It is easy to check that $\mathcal{M}_B$ is deterministic, and that there is a backward simulation R between $\mathcal{M}_B$ and $\mathcal{M}_A$ defined by $T\ R\ s_A$ iff $s_A \in T$. Moreover, R is finitary since all sets T are finite. Theorem 3.11 now proves that $\mathcal{M}_B$ can be added as a history variable to $\mathcal{M}_C$ to obtain $\mathcal{M}_S$. Using the backward simulation R, we can also add $\mathcal{M}_A$ as a prophecy variable to $\mathcal{M}_S$. The conditions about fairness requirements follow from the internal continuity of $\mathcal{M}_A$ in the same way as in the proof of Theorem 3.14. □

The combination of Proof 1 with the proof of Theorem 3.14 is analogous to the completeness proof in [AL88]. Proof 2 is, except for the fairness requirements, related to techniques from automata theory for deciding language-inclusion by making an automaton deterministic, and is analogous to a proof in [Jos88].

4 Non-Finitary Backward Simulations

A limitation of the backward simulation in Section 3 is that it must be finitary for soundness. This limitation makes the simulation technique unappliccable to several cases that occur in practice. In this section, we present an extension of the finitary backward simulation, which weakens the finitariness requirement. This extension has also been mentioned in [AL88]. The main idea of the extension is the observation that in the proof of soundness of backward simulation, it is not necessary that all states of a concrete computation correspond to finitely many abstract states; it is enough that infinitely many states do. Furthermore, by combining several such backward simulations we can obtain a relation where each concrete state corresponds to infinitely many abstract states.

Definition 4.1 A backward simulation R between two fts's is *infinitely often finitary* if each computation of $\mathcal{M}_C$ contains infinitely many states s_C for which there are only finitely many states s_A of $\mathcal{M}_A$ with $s_C \; R \; s_A$. In an analogous way we say that $\mathcal{M}$ is obtained from $\mathcal{M}_C$ by *adding $\mathcal{M}_C$ as an infinitely often finitary prophecy variable.* □

Assuming that the property of being related to only finitely many states of $\mathcal{M}_C$ can be formulated as a predicate over states of $\mathcal{M}_C$, standard proof methods for proving liveness properties can be used to verify that a backward simulation is infinitely often finitary. We now prove that the finitary requirement in Proposition 3.4 and Theorem 3.8 can be replaced by infinitely often finitary.

Proposition 4.2 *If there exists an infinitely often finitary backward simulation R between $\mathcal{M}_C$ and $\mathcal{M}_A$ then each trace of a computation of $\mathcal{M}_C$ is also a trace of an execution of $\mathcal{M}_A$.* □

Proof sketch: Consider a computation $C_C = s_C^0 \xrightarrow{e^1}_C s_C^1 \xrightarrow{e^2}_C \cdots \xrightarrow{e^n}_C s_C^n \xrightarrow{e^{n+1}}_C \cdots$ of $\mathcal{M}_C$. Let $i_1 < i_2 < i_3 < \cdots$ be the superscripts of the states in C_C that by the infinitely often finitary backward simulation R are related to only finitely many states of $\mathcal{M}_A$. For each $j \geq 2$ and state s_A^j of $\mathcal{M}_A$ such that $s_C^{i_j} \; R \; s_A^j$ we can, working backwards, construct a sequence of transitions $s_A^{j-1} \xrightarrow{e^{(i_{j-1}+1)}}_A \cdots \xrightarrow{e^{i_j}}_A s_A^j$ of $\mathcal{M}_A$ which has exactly the same sequence of events as the sequence between $s_C^{i_{j-1}}$ and $s_C^{i_j}$ in C_C, and such that $s_C^{i_{j-1}} \; R \; s_A^{j-1}$. When $j = 1$, we will have s_A^0 as an initial state of $\mathcal{M}_A$. Intending to use König's lemma, we construct a tree whose nodes are all states of $\mathcal{M}_A$ that are first or last states in any of the segments so constructed, and such that s_A^{j-1} is a parent of s_A^j if there is a segment from s_A^{j-1} to s_A^j. By König's lemma, since there are infinitely many states and the number of states at each level of the tree is finite, there is an infinite path in the tree. By our construction, we obtain an execution C_A of $\mathcal{M}_A$ by concatenating the sequences of transitions corresponding to the segments in this path. It is easy to see that C_A has the same trace as C_C. □

As an immediate corollary we can obtain the analogue of Theorem 3.8.

Proposition 4.3 *If there exists an fts $\mathcal{M}$ which is obtained from $\mathcal{M}_C$ by adding $\mathcal{M}_A$ as an infinitely often finitary prophecy variable, then $\mathcal{M}_C \sqsupseteq \mathcal{M}_A$.* □

Using Proposition 4.2, we can verify a refinement through any finite sequence of infinitely often finitary backward simulations. It is possible that the composition of the backward simulations in the sequence is never finitary. A natural application of this observation is the case when the state of the abstract fts is given by a finite set of variables, and where the restriction of the backward simulation to each variable is infinitely often finitary. We shall next prove a slightly more general form of such a method.

Let V be a set. A *V-state* is a mapping from V to some set of values. If s is a V-state and s' is a V'-state with $V \subseteq V'$, then we write $s \leq s'$ to denote that $s(v) = s'(v)$ for all $v \in V$. If S_A is a set of V-states, $v \in V$, and $R \subseteq S_C \times S_A$ for some set S_A is a relation, then the *v-image of $s_C \in S_C$ under R* is the set of $s_A(v)$ for which $s_C \; R \; s_A$.

Theorem 4.4 *Assume that $\mathcal{M}_C$ and $\mathcal{M}_A$ are fts's and that the states of $\mathcal{M}_A$ are V-states for some countable set V. Assume that R is a backward simulation between $\mathcal{M}_C$ and $\mathcal{M}_A$ such that*

1. *For each $v \in V$, each computation of $\mathcal{M}_C$ contains infinitely many occurrences of states s_C whose v-image under R is finite,*
2. *For each $s_C \in S_C$ there are only finitely many $v \in V$ such that the v-image of s_C under R contains more than one element,*

then each trace of $\mathcal{M}_C$ is the trace of an execution of $\mathcal{M}_A$. □

Proof Sketch: By adding one element of V at a time, we can prove the theorem by repeated applications of Proposition 4.2. □

5 A Notation for Fair Transition Systems

In this section, we define a simple notation for fair transition systems. We also give proof rules that correspond to the superposition, simulation and backwards simulation relations in Section 3. The notation is related to the work by Manna and Pnueli [MP89, Pnu86], by Chandy and Misra [CM88], and by Back and others [BS88, BKS88]. A difference is that our notation includes communication events as labels on transitions.

As a basis for our notation, we assume a language of terms and assertions, e.g. a many-sorted first-order language. We assume that each variable ranges over an appropriate domain, and that each constant, function, and predicate symbol has a fixed interpretation over the appropriate domains.

Let V be a set of variables. A *V-action* A is of the form

$$\textbf{event } eA \textbf{ when } gA \textbf{ do } \langle x_1, \ldots, x_n \rangle := \langle t_1, \ldots, t_n \rangle$$

where eA is a communication event, gA is an assertion, $x_1, \ldots, x_n$ are distinct variables in V, and $\langle t_1, \ldots, t_n \rangle$ are terms. The free variables of gA and $t_1, \ldots, t_n$ must be in V. We use bA to denote the multiple assignment $\langle x_1, \ldots, x_n \rangle := \langle t_1, \ldots, t_n \rangle$. The action **event** τ **when** *true* **do** $\langle\rangle := \langle\rangle$ is called the *null action*.

Definition 5.1 A *labeled action system* $\mathcal{N}$ is a tuple $\langle V, \Theta, \mathcal{A}, \mathcal{E} \rangle$, where

V is a set of variables, called the *state variables*,

Θ is an assertion, the *initial condition*, whose free variables are in V.

$\mathcal{A}$ is a set of V-*actions*, which includes the null action,

$\mathcal{E}$ is a countable collection of pairs $\langle g^F, \mathcal{A}^F\rangle$ where g^F is an assertion with free variables in V, and $\mathcal{A}^F$ is a subset of $\mathcal{A}$. □

Let V be a set of variables. A V-*state* is a mapping s from the variables in V to their domains. For an assertion ϕ whose free variables are in V, the V-state s is called a ϕ-*state* if ϕ is true under s. If A is a V-action, then an A-transition is a transition $s \xrightarrow{eA} s'$ where s and s' are V-states such that gA is true in s and s' is obtained from s by performing the multiple assignment statement bA in s.

Definition 5.2 If $\mathcal{N}$ is the labelled action system $\langle V, \Theta, \mathcal{A}, \mathcal{E}\rangle$, then the semantics of $\mathcal{N}$ is the fair transition system $\mathcal{T}(\mathcal{N}) = \langle S, S^0, \longrightarrow, \mathcal{F}\rangle$, where S is the set of V-states, S^0 is the set of V-states that are also Θ-states, $\longrightarrow$ is the set of all A-transitions for some $A \in \mathcal{A}$, and $\mathcal{F}$ contains for each pair $\langle g^F, \mathcal{A}^F\rangle$ in $\mathcal{E}$ the fairness requirement $\langle S^F, \longrightarrow^F\rangle$ where S^F is the set of g^F-states, and $\longrightarrow^F$ is the set of all A-transitions for some $A \in \mathcal{A}_F$. □

We can now give a definition of adding history and prophecy variables in the context of the notation of labelled action systems.

For multiple assignment statements $\overline{x}_C := \overline{t}_C$ and $\overline{x}_A := \overline{t}_A$, define $\overline{x}_C := \overline{t}_C \parallel \overline{x}_A := \overline{t}_A$ to be the multiple assignment statement $\overline{x}_C, \overline{x}_A := \overline{t}_C, \overline{t}_A$. Let A_C be a V_C-action, and let A_A be a V_A-action. A *superposition* of A_A onto A_C is an action of form

$$\textbf{event } eA_C \textbf{ when } gA_C \ \wedge\ gA_A \ \wedge\ \varphi \textbf{ do } bA_C \| bA_A$$

for some assertion φ. If for $i = C, A$, the labeled action systems $\mathcal{N}_i = \langle V_i, \Theta_i, \mathcal{A}_i, \mathcal{E}_i\rangle$ have disjoint sets of variables, then a *superposition* of $\mathcal{N}_A$ on $\mathcal{N}_C$ is an action system $\langle V, \Theta, \mathcal{A}, \mathcal{E}\rangle$, where $V = V_C \cup V_A$, where $\Theta = \Theta_C \ \wedge\ \Theta_A$, where $\mathcal{A}$ is a set of superpositions of actions in $\mathcal{A}_A$ onto actions in $\mathcal{A}_C$, and where $\mathcal{E}$ for each $\langle g_C^F, \mathcal{A}_C^F\rangle \in \mathcal{E}_C$ contains the pair $\langle g_C^F, \mathcal{A}^F\rangle$, where $\mathcal{A}^F$ is the set of actions in $\mathcal{A}$ that are obtained by superposing some action in $\mathcal{A}_A$ onto an action in $\mathcal{A}_C^F$. □

Proposition 5.3 *If $\mathcal{N}$ is a superposition of $\mathcal{N}_A$ onto $\mathcal{N}_C$, then $\mathcal{T}(\mathcal{N})$ is a superposition of $\mathcal{T}(\mathcal{N}_A)$ onto $\mathcal{T}(\mathcal{N}_C)$.* □

For an action A with bA being the multiple assignment statement $\overline{x} := \overline{t}$, let *substA* denote the substitution $\overline{t}/\overline{x}$ of $\overline{t}$ for $\overline{x}$. In the following, we present proof rules that correspond to forward and backward simulation. For simplicity, we will in this presentation disregard fairness requirements of the abstract system.

Proposition 5.4 *For $i = C, A$, let $\mathcal{N}_i = \langle V_i, \Theta_i, \mathcal{A}_i, \mathcal{E}_i\rangle$ be labeled action systems with $\mathcal{E}_A = \emptyset$. Let $\mathcal{N}$ be a superposition of $\mathcal{N}_A$ onto $\mathcal{N}_C$, and let R be an assertion over the state variables of $\mathcal{N}$. If*

1. $\Theta_C \implies (\exists V_A)[R \ \wedge\ \Theta_A]$,
2. *for each action A_C of $\mathcal{N}_C$, there is an index set I and actions B_i of $\mathcal{N}$ for each $i \in I$, each of which is a superposition of some action of $\mathcal{N}_A$ onto A_C, such that*

$$(R \ \wedge\ gA_C) \implies \bigvee_{i \in I}(gB_i \ \wedge\ R[substB_i]) \quad ,$$

then $\mathcal{T}(\mathcal{N})$ is obtained by adding $\mathcal{T}(\mathcal{N}_A)$ as a history variable to $\mathcal{T}(\mathcal{N}_C)$. Conversely, if $\mathcal{T}(\mathcal{N})$ is obtained by adding $\mathcal{T}(\mathcal{N}_A)$ as a history variable to $\mathcal{T}(\mathcal{N}_C)$, then there is an assertion R such that conditions 1. - 2. are satisfied. □

When asserting the existence of R, we mean that it exists in the semantic sense. Thus we avoid the question whether R can be expressed in out underlying assertion language.

Proposition 5.5 *For $i = C, A$, let $\mathcal{N}_i = \langle V_i, \Theta_i, \mathcal{A}_i, \mathcal{E}_i \rangle$ be labeled action systems with $\mathcal{E}_A = \emptyset$. Let $\mathcal{N}$ be a superposition of $\mathcal{N}_A$ onto $\mathcal{N}_C$, and let R be an assertion over the state variables of $\mathcal{N}$. If there exists an assertion R_C over the state variables of $\mathcal{N}_A$ which is an invariant in $\mathcal{N}_C$, such that*

1. $R_C \implies (\exists V_A)[R]$,
2. *for each action A_C of $\mathcal{N}_C$, there is an index set I and actions B_i of $\mathcal{N}$ for each $i \in I$, each of which is a superposition of some action of $\mathcal{N}_A$ onto A_C, such that*

$$(R[substA_C][V'_A/V_A] \wedge gA_C) \implies \bigvee_{i \in I} (\exists V_A)[gB_i \wedge (V_A[substB_i] = V'_A) \wedge R],$$

3. $\Theta_C \wedge R \implies \Theta$,

then $\mathcal{T}(\mathcal{N})$ is obtained by adding $\mathcal{T}(\mathcal{N}_A)$ as a prophecy variable to $\mathcal{T}(\mathcal{N}_C)$. Conversely, if $\mathcal{T}(\mathcal{N})$ is obtained by adding $\mathcal{T}(\mathcal{N}_A)$ as a history variable to $\mathcal{T}(\mathcal{N}_C)$, then there is an assertion R such that conditions 1. - 3. are satisfied. □

To establish the addition of history and prophecy variables in the case that the abstract system has fairness requirements, one must establish corresponding liveness properties of the superposition $\mathcal{N}$. This can be done using standard proof techniques for verifying liveness properties of reactive programs, e.g. [MP84, MP89].

6 Connections with Subset Constructions

In the case that the involved transition systems are finite-state, refinement becomes language inclusion between finite automata. A standard method for deciding language inclusion between the finite automata FA_1 and FA_2 is to make FA_2 deterministic by a subset-construction [HU79], as in Proof 2 of Theorem 3.15. In this section, we relate forward and backward simulations with a verification technique using subset constructions, which has also been used by Gerth [Ger90] and is related to the work by Klarlund and Schneider [KS89]. We will consider a slightly more general verification technique where the subset construction does not necessarily result in a determinstic transition system.

Definition 6.1 For $i = C, A$ let $\mathcal{M}_i = \langle S_i, S_i^0, \longrightarrow_i, \mathcal{F}_i \rangle$ be fts's. A relation R between states of $\mathcal{M}_C$ and sets of states of $\mathcal{M}_A$ (i.e., a subset of $S_C \times \mathcal{P}(S_A)$) is called a *subset-simulation* between $\mathcal{M}_C$ and $\mathcal{M}_A$ iff

1. whenever $s_C \; R \; T_A$ then T_A is nonempty,
2. for each initial state s_C of $\mathcal{M}_C$ there is a set T_A of initial states of $\mathcal{M}_A$ such that $s_C \; R \; T_A$,
3. whenever $s_C \; R \; T_A$ and $s_C \xrightarrow{e}_C s'_C$, there is a set T'_A of states of $\mathcal{M}_A$ such that
   (a) $s'_C \; R \; T'_A$, and
   (b) for each state s'_A in T'_A there is a state s''_A in T_A such that $s''_A \xrightarrow{e}_A s'_A$.

A subset-simulation R is *finitary* if T_A is finite whenever $s_C \; R \; T_A$. □

The soundness of finitary subset-simulation (and also infintiely often finitary) follows from the following correspondence with forward and backward simulations.

Theorem 6.2 *For $i = C, A$ let $\mathcal{M}_i = \langle S_i, S_i^0, \longrightarrow_i, \mathcal{F}_i \rangle$ be fts's. Then there exists a subset-simulation between $\mathcal{M}_C$ and $\mathcal{M}_A$ if and only if there exists a fts $\mathcal{M}_B$ such that there is a forward simulation between $\mathcal{M}_C$ and $\mathcal{M}_B$ and a backward simulation between $\mathcal{M}_B$ and $\mathcal{M}_A$. The theorem is also true if both subset-simulation and backward simulation are qualified by finitary.* □

Proof: Assume first that R is a subset-simulation between $\mathcal{M}_C$ and $\mathcal{M}_A$. Define $\mathcal{M}_B$ as the labeled transition system $\langle S_B, S_B^0, \longrightarrow_B, \mathcal{F}_B \rangle$, where

S_B is the set of non-empty subsets T_A of states of $\mathcal{M}_A$ such that $s_C \; R \; T_A$ for some s_C,

S_B^0 is those subsets in S_B that contain only initial states of $\mathcal{M}_A$,

$\longrightarrow_B$ is the set of triples $T_A \xrightarrow{e}_B T'_A$ such that for each state s'_A in T'_A there is a state s_A in T_A such that $s_A \xrightarrow{e}_A s'_A$.

We can now find a forward simulation between $\mathcal{M}_C$ and $\mathcal{M}_B$, which is precisely the subset-simulation R. There is also a backward simulation R_B between $\mathcal{M}_B$ and $\mathcal{M}_A$, defined by $T_A \; R_B \; s_A$ iff $s_A \in T_A$. The finitary case follows directly from the correspondence between R and R_B.

To prove the theorem in the other direction, assume that $\mathcal{M}_B$ is a labeled transition system such that there is a forward simulation R_F between $\mathcal{M}_C$ and $\mathcal{M}_B$ and a backward simulation R_B between $\mathcal{M}_B$ and $\mathcal{M}_A$. Define for each state s_B of $\mathcal{M}_B$ the set of states $T(s_B)$ of $\mathcal{M}_A$ as the set of states s_A such that $s_B \; R_B \; s_A$. Define a subset-simulation R by $s_C \; R \; T(s_B)$ iff $T(s_B)$ is nonempty, $s_C \; R_F \; s_B$, and s_C is reachable. It follows that R is a subset-simulation. □

Theorem 6.2 shows that forward and backward simulations are related to subset-constructions, the difference being that one does not need to represent $\mathcal{M}_B$ using subsets. This freedom of representation could be useful especially in hand-verification.

7 A Simple Example

In this section, we illustrate the use of nonfinitary backward simulation by a simple sketchy example, in which both forward simulation and finitary backward simulation fail.

Consider the two labeled action systems A (for abstract) and C (for concrete) in Figure 1. A contains two variables, i and j. The variable j determines in advance how many events of form *out* will be performed. Since j can be any nonnegative integer initially, there is no bound on how many events will be performed, as long as only finitely many are performed. C is an equivalent specification which performs the event *out* until the variable b becomes *false*. The number of *out* events is made finite by a fairness requiremet which forces b eventually to become *false*, thus stopping further events.

We shall prove that each trace of C is a trace of an execution of A by finding an infinitely often finitary backward simulation between A and C. The backward simulation between A and C identifies the variable i with k, and has the additional property $(j \geq 0) \land (\neg b \implies j = 0)$. Thus we define a relation R by

$$R \equiv (i = k) \land (j \geq 0) \land (\neg b \implies j = 0) \ .$$

We can construct superposition of A onto C by performing simultaneously the respective *out* actions.

Labeled Action System A
State Variables: i, j : integer
Initialization: $i = 0$, $j \geq 0$
Actions:

	event	condition	update
out	*out*	$j > 0$	$i, j := i+1, j-1$

Fairness: $\{(j > 0, out)\}$

Labeled Action System C
State Variables: k : integer
b : boolean
Initialization: $k = 0$
Actions:

	event	condition	update
out	*out*	b	$k := k+1$
stop	τ	*true*	$b :=$ *false*

Fairness: $\{(b, stop)\}$

Figure 1: Two specifications of a simple counter

To establish R as a backward simulation, we must for the action *out* prove that

$$[(i' = k+1) \wedge (j' \geq 0) \wedge (\neg b \implies j' = 0) \wedge b] \implies (\exists i, j) \left[\begin{array}{ll} & j > 0 \\ \wedge & i+1 = i' \\ \wedge & j-1 = j' \\ \wedge & i = k \\ \wedge & (\neg b \implies j = 0) \end{array} \right] ,$$

which if in the existential quantification we choose $i = i' - 1$ and $j = j' + 1$ simplifies to

$$[(i' = k+1) \wedge (j' \geq 0) \wedge b] \implies [j' + 1 > 0 \wedge i' - 1 = k] ,$$

which is obviously true. The action *stop* corresponds to a null action of A. We also see that R is infinitely often finitary since each computation of C eventually makes b false, and then 0 is the only possible value for j since $k = i$.

8 Conclusions

We have studied forward and backward simulations as verification techniques for verifying that one fair transition system correctly implements another one. We have tried to make a modular presentation of the simulations which shows the relationship between simulations, auxiliary variable constructions and techniques from automata-theory. We have extended backwards simulations to handle certain cases of unbounded nondeterminism, and presented proof rules for a simple specification notation.

It should be noted that our extension of the backward simulation by no means attains full completeness. Sistla [Sis88] argues that no reasonable verification method can be complete, since the verification problem is Π^1_2-complete when the labeled transition systems are effectively given.

In this paper, we have not considered exending the verification techniques to the case when the higher-level specification simulates a single transition of the lower-level specification by a sequence of transitions, most of which are silent. This case could be handled by extending the power of prophecy variables (as in [AL88]) or by working with extended transitions (as when going from strong bisimulation to weak bisimulation or branching bisimulation [dNV90]). We hope to treat this case also in our notation when continuing our work.

Acknowledgments

I am grateful to Martin Abadi, Ralph-Johan Back, Rob Gerth, Willem Paul de Roever, and Frits Vaandrager for comments and fruitful discussions.

References

[AL88] M. Abadi and L. Lamport. The existence of refinement mappings. In *Proc. 3rd IEEE Int. Symp. on Logic in Computer Science*, Edinburgh, 1988.

[BKS88] R.J.R. Back and R. Kurki-Suonio. Distributed cooperation with action systems. *ACM Trans. on Programming Languages and Systems*, 10(4):513–554, Oct. 1988.

[BS88] R.J.R. Back and K. Sere. Stepwise refinement of parallel algorithms. Technical Report A. 64, Åbo Akademi, Dept. of Computer Science and Mathematics, 1988.

[CM88] K.M. Chandy and J. Misra. *Parallel Program Design: A Foundation*. Addison-Wesley, 1988.

[dNV90] R. de Nicola and F.W. Vaandrager. Three logics for branching bisimulation. In *Proc. 5th IEEE Int. Symp. on Logic in Computer Science*, pages 118–129, 1990.

[Ger90] R. Gerth. Foundations of compositional program refinement – safety properties. Volume 430 of *Lecture Notes in Computer Science*, pages 777–808. Springer Verlag, 1990.

[HJS87] C.A.R. Hoare, H. Jifeng, and J.W. Sanders. Prespecification in data refinement. *Information Processing Letters*, 25:71–76, 1987.

[Hoa72] C.A.R. Hoare. Proof of correctness of data representation. *Acta Informatica*, 1(4):271–281, 1972.

[HU79] J.E. Hopcroft and J.D. Ullman. *Introduction to Automata Theory, Languages, and Computation*. Addison-Wesley, 1979.

[Jif89] H. Jifeng. Process simulation and refinement. *Formal Aspects of Computing*, 1:229–241, 1989.

[Jon87a] B. Jonsson. *Compositional Verification of Distributed Systems*. PhD thesis, Dept. of Computer Systems, Uppsala University, Sweden, Uppsala, Sweden, 1987. Available as report DoCS 87/09.

[Jon87b] B. Jonsson. Modular verification of asynchronous networks. In *Proc. 6th ACM Symp. on Principles of Distributed Computing, Vancouver, Canada*, pages 152–166, Vancouver, Canada, 1987. Extended Version as SICS Research Report R90010.

[Jon90] B. Jonsson. On decomposing and refining specifications of distributed systems. Volume 430 of *Lecture Notes in Computer Science*, pages 361–385. Springer Verlag, 1990.

[Jos88] M.B. Josephs. A state-based approach to communicating processes. *Distributed Computing*, 3:9–18, 1988.

[KMPS91] A. Kleinman, Y. Moscowitz, A. Pnueli, and E. Shapiro. Communication with directed logic variables. In *Proc. 18th ACM Symp. on Principles of Programming Languages*, 1991.

[KS89] N. Klarlund and F.B. Schneider. Verifying safety properties using infinite-state automata. Technical Report TR 89-1039, Cornell University, Ithaca, New York, 1989.

[Lam83] L. Lamport. Specifying concurrent program modules. *ACM Trans. on Programming Languages and Systems*, 5(2):190–222, 1983.

[Lam89] L. Lamport. A simple approach to specifying concurrent systems,. *Communications of the ACM*, 32(1):32–45, Jan. 1989.

[LS84] S.S. Lam and A.U. Shankar. Protocol verfication via projections. *IEEE Trans. on Software Engineering*, SE-10(4):325–342, July 1984.

[LS90] S.S. Lam and A.U. Shankar. Refinement and projection of relational specifications. Volume 430 of *Lecture Notes in Computer Science*, pages 454–486. Springer Verlag, 1990.

[LT87] N.A. Lynch and M.R. Tuttle. Hierarchical correctness proofs for distributed algorithms. In *Proc. 6th ACM Symp. on Principles of Distributed Computing, Vancouver, Canada*, pages 137–151, 1987.

[Mer90] M. Merritt. Completeness theorems for automata. Volume 430 of *Lecture Notes in Computer Science*, pages 544–560. Springer Verlag, 1990.

[Mil] R. Milner. An algebraic definition of simulation between programs. pages 481–489. Also as Report No. CS-205, Computer Science Department, Stanford University.

[MP81] Z. Manna and A. Pnueli. The temporal framework for concurrent programs. In Boyer and Moore, editors, *The Correctness Problem in Computer Science*, pages 215–274. Academic Press, 1981.

[MP84] Z. Manna and A. Pnueli. Adequate proof principles for invariance and liveness properties of concurrent programs. *Science of Computer Programming*, 4(4):257–289, 1984.

[MP89] Z. Manna and A. Pnueli. The anchored version of the temporal framework. In de Bakker, de Roever, and Rozenberg, editors, *Linear Time, Branching Time and Partial Order in Logics and Models for Concurrency*, volume 354 of *Lecture Notes in Computer Science*, pages 201–284. Springer Verlag, 1989.

[Nip86] T. Nipkow. Non-deterministic data types. *Acta Informatica*, 22:629–661, 1986.

[Ora89] F. Orava. Verifying safety and deadlock properties of networks of asynchronously communicating processes. In *Proc. 9th IFIP WG6.1 Symp. on Protocol Specification, Testing, and Verification*, Twente, Holland, 1989.

[Plo81] G. Plotkin. A structural approach to operational semantics. Technical Report DAIMI FN-19, Computer Science Department, Aarhus University, Denmark, 1981.

[Pnu86] A. Pnueli. Applications of temporal logic to the specification and verification of reactive systems: A survey of current trends. Volume 224 of *Lecture Notes in Computer Science*, pages 510–584. Springer Verlag, 1986.

[Sis88] A.P. Sistla. On verifying that a concurrent program satisfies a non-deterministic specification. Technical Report TR 88-378.01.1, Computer and Intelligent Systems Lab. GTE Laboratories, May 1988.

[SL83] A.U. Shankar and S.S. Lam. An HDLC protocol specification and its verification using image protocols. *ACM Transactions on Computer Systems*, 1(4):331–368, Nov. 1983.

[Sta84] E.W. Stark. *Foundations of a Theory of Specification for Distributed Systems*. PhD thesis, Massachussetts Inst. of Technology, 1984. Available as Report No. MIT/LCS/TR-342.

[Sta88] E.W. Stark. Proving entailment between conceptual state specifications. *Theoretical Computer Science*, 56:135–154, 1988.

[Var87] M.Y. Vardi. Verification of concurrent programs: The automata theoretic framework. In *Proc. 2nd IEEE Int. Symp. on Logic in Computer Science*, 1987.

[WLL88] J. Lundelius Welch, L. Lamport, and N. Lynch. A lattice-structured proof technique applied to a minimum spanning tree algorithm, July 1988.

Using Truth-Preserving Reductions to Improve the Clarity of Kripke-Models

Roope Kaivola
University of Helsinki
Department of Computer Science
Teollisuuskatu 23, SF-00510 Helsinki, Finland
tel. +358-0-708 4163
fax. +358-0-708 4441
email rkaivola@cc.helsinki.fi

Antti Valmari
Technical Research Centre of Finland
Computer Technology Laboratory
PO Box 201, SF-90571 Oulu, Finland
tel. +358-81-509 457
fax. +358-81-509 680
email ava@tko.vtt.fi

Abstract

We present an approach by means of which temporal logic models may be replaced by smaller ones without affecting the truth values of any formulas of a fairly standard linear-time temporal logic without a nexttime-operator. The main advantage of the approach is the increased readability of a model, as we can concentrate on some features of the model and hide irrelevant details. Two other advantages are the potential for increased model-checking speed, and the inherent compositionality of the method.

Our method is based on the observation that instead of recording the truth values of atomic propositions in the states of a model, it is enough to record the truth values in the initial state of the model and attach to each transition a label telling how the truth values of the atomic propositions change when that transition is taken. This allows us to handle a temporal logic model as a labelled transition system and apply process-algebraic reduction methods to it. Specifically, it is noted that the process-algebraic equivalence class defined by initial stability, stable failures and divergences, is truth-preserving w.r.t the logic applied in this paper.

1 Introduction

Although several methods for temporal logic model checking have been proposed [CES85, LP85, EL84], there has been relatively little discussion on truth-preserving equivalences between temporal logic models and on the corresponding truth-preserving minimisations of them [BCG87] [SW89]. In this paper we show how to apply process-algebraic reduction methods (in particular those discussed in [VT91]) to Kripke-models so that the reduction preserves the truth values of a given set of formulas of a (fairly standard) linear-time temporal logic without a nexttime-operator.

The main advantage of our approach is *readability*. By reducing a model after suitable hiding of irrelevant details we acquire a simpler, intuitively more understandable presentation of the working of a system. Our hope is that the practical examples in this paper speak for themselves in this respect.

Two other advantages of the approach are practical computational speed and compositionality. The known model-checking algorithms for linear temporal logics have a $O(|\mathcal{M}|\ 2^{|f|})$ time complexity [LP85], where $|\mathcal{M}|$ is the size of the model and $|f|$ that of the formula. If $|f|$ is large, it may be worthwhile to spend some effort in reducing the Kripke model before model checking. Although the reduction algorithm has exponential worst case complexity, experience with a related algorithm [CPS90] indicates that in practice the algorithm is fast most of the time. If the size of the Kripke model reduces from $|\mathcal{M}|$ to $|\mathcal{M}'|$, the savings in model checking time are $O((|\mathcal{M}| - |\mathcal{M}'|)2^{|f|})$, which is more than the time consumed by the reduction algorithm if $|f|$ is large.

Compositionality arises from the fact that the process algebraic semantics model we use in this paper has the following properties:

- Its corresponding equivalence is a congruence with respect to parallel composition, hiding and renaming.
- It records enough information for checking the truth values of formulas in our logic.

Because of these properties, it is possible to build a (reduced) Kripke model of a program in a compositional way: Kripke models (actually *labelled transition systems* or *ltss*) of individual processes or small groups of processes of the program are built, reduced using the reduction algorithm, composed together to (reduced) ltss of larger groups of processes and so on, until a reduced lts of the system as a whole is obtained. It is then transformed to a Kripke model using an algorithm presented in this paper. We prove that the process is truth-preserving with respect to our logic. Therefore the final reduced Kripke model can be used for model checking instead of the ordinary Kripke model of the program. But because the large ordinary Kripke model is never explicitly constructed, significant savings of effort may be achieved. The results should be considered initial, however, as we do not currently have a fully satisfactory way of hadling fairness assumptions during reduction. Other approaches to compositional model checking have been discussed in [CLM89].

The presentation proceeds as follows: we first examine informally how the execution of concurrent systems may be modelled by their state spaces, then recall the standard definitions of a linear temporal logic without nexttime, and show what features a reduction needs to preserve in order to be truth-preserving w.r.t our temporal logic. Then we recall some standard definitions of process algebras and show how applying certain process-algebraic reduction methods yields a truth-preserving reduction method. Finally, we discuss compositionality in the light of our approach.

2 Concurrent programs and state spaces

Without defining formally what the exact relation between a concurrent program and its execution model is, we note that very often the execution of a concurrent program is modelled by a directed graph, where a node represents a momentary global state of the program and an arc corresponds to the execution of an atomic action of the program. We denote the set of atomic actions by L. By global state we mean here information specifying the current values of all variables and the execution states of all concurrently executing processes.

We may meaningfully describe the global state of a program by statements, or propositions, referring to the values of the variables and to the execution state. Examples of atomic propositions could be $x = 0$, *process P is in execution state 3* etc. Each atomic proposition is either true or false in a given state. We denote the set of atomic propositions by $\mathcal{AP}$, and characterise a state by giving the subset of $\mathcal{AP}$ containing exactly the propositions true in that state.

Definition 2.1 A *state space* is a quadruple $T = (S, \Delta, V, s)$, where

- S is a *finite* set of states,
- $\Delta \subseteq S \times L \times S$ is a set of transitions,
- $V : S \rightarrow \mathcal{P}(\mathcal{AP})$ is a valuation expressing the atomic formulas true in a state, and
- $s \in S$ is the initial state. □

It is worth noticing that by ignoring the initial state and the atomic actions labelling the transitions, a state space may be seen as a Kripke-model.

Definition 2.2 A *truth set modifier* SM is a mapping $SM : \mathcal{P}(\mathcal{AP}) \rightarrow \mathcal{P}(\mathcal{AP})$. The set of all truth set modifiers is denoted by $\mathcal{TM}$. The *identity truth set modifier* τ is the identity mapping. □

The idea behind this definition is that a truth set modifier expresses how a certain change affects a state as characterised by the atomic propositions true in that state, i.e. what are the resulting truth values of atomic propositions after the change, as a function of their truth values before the change.

Definition 2.3 A *temporal semantics* $\mathcal{TS}$ for a set of atomic actions L is a mapping $\mathcal{TS} : L \rightarrow \mathcal{TM}$. □

Intuitively, $\mathcal{TS}(l)$ expresses the change effected by executing the atomic action l. What is more, $\mathcal{TS}(l)$ does not say anything about *when* an atomic action can be executed.

The definition of temporal semantics assumes that the atomic actions are deterministic in the sense that executing l in a state where the set of true atomic propositions is A always results in a state where the set of true atomic propositions is $\mathcal{TS}(l)(A)$. This is not a restriction, however, as nondeterminism may be presented in a higher level than that of the atomic actions.

In our approach the temporal semantics $\mathcal{TS}$ of atomic actions is more fundamental than a state space of a particular program. Actually, the state space should be defined in terms of the temporal semantics of atomic actions *and* the meaning of the higher-level program structures that specify when some atomic action may be executed. However, in order to skip the tedious task of introducing some toy programming language and its state space building rules here, we take the state space as given and just control that when an atomic action is executed, the change taking place is what it should be according to the temporal semantics. This is formalised by the concept of agreement:

Definition 2.4 A state space $T = (S, \Delta, V, s)$ *agrees* with temporal semantics $\mathcal{TS}$ iff for all $(s_1, l, s_2) \in \Delta$, $\mathcal{TS}(l)(V(s_1)) = V(s_2)$. (In other words, a state space and a temporal semantics agree, if the situation $V(s_2)$ caused by executing l in the situation $V(s_1)$ is the same in the state space as it should be according to the temporal semantics.) □

From this point onwards we always assume that state spaces and temporal semantics agree.

The state space of a program may contain information that is in some way irrelevant to us, i.e. it may record truth values of some atomic propositions we are not interested in. Normally it is easy just to discard this superfluous information. Here, however, we need to be somewhat cautious, lest the temporal semantics $\mathcal{TS}$ becomes non-well-defined. The following definitions outline how the extra information may be removed from the temporal semantics and the state space so that the temporal semantics remains well-defined and the agreement between the temporal semantics and the state space is not affected.

Definition 2.5 Let $\mathcal{AP}' \subseteq \mathcal{AP}$ and $T = (S, \Delta, V, s)$ be a state space. The *restriction of* T *to* $\mathcal{AP}'$ is defined as the state space $T' = (S, \Delta, V', s)$, where $V'(s') = V(s') \cap \mathcal{AP}'$ for all $s' \in S$. (In other words, in restricting the state space we discard all information concerning the truth values of the atomic propositions not in $\mathcal{AP}'$.) □

```
        P :                              Q :
1 :/* idle */                    1 :/* idle */
  y1 := true                       y2 := true
2 :wait until not y2             2 :if y1 then goto 4
3 :/* critical */                3 :/*  critical */
  y1 := false; goto 1              y2 := false; goto 1
                                 4 :y2 := false
                                 5 :wait until not y1
                                 6 :y2 := true; goto 2
```

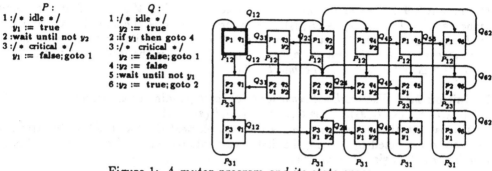

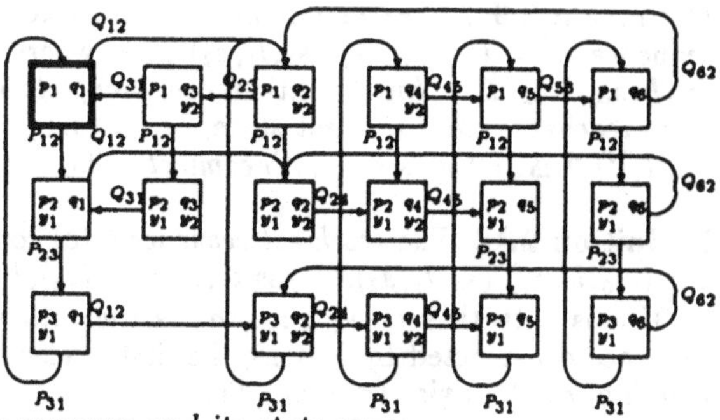

Figure 1: *A mutex-program and its state space*

Definition 2.6 Let $\mathcal{AP}' \subseteq \mathcal{AP}$ and $\mathcal{TS}$ be a temporal semantics for the set of atomic actions L. We say that *the restriction of $\mathcal{TS}$ to $\mathcal{AP}'$ is well-defined* iff for all $l \in L$ and for all $A_1, A_2 \subseteq \mathcal{AP}$ such that $A_1 \cap \mathcal{AP}' = A_2 \cap \mathcal{AP}'$ the following holds: $\mathcal{TS}(l)(A_1) \cap \mathcal{AP}' = \mathcal{TS}(l)(A_2) \cap \mathcal{AP}'$. If this is the case we define *the restriction of $\mathcal{TS}$ to $\mathcal{AP}'$* to be for every $l \in L$ the mapping $\mathcal{TS}'(l) : \mathcal{P}(\mathcal{AP}') \to \mathcal{P}(\mathcal{AP}'); A \mapsto (\mathcal{TS}(l)(A) \cap \mathcal{AP}')$ □

Theorem 2.7 Assume that T is a state space agreeing with $\mathcal{TS}$, $\mathcal{AP}' \subseteq \mathcal{AP}$ and the restriction $\mathcal{TS}'$ of $\mathcal{TS}$ to $\mathcal{AP}'$ is well-defined. Then the restriction T' of T to $\mathcal{AP}'$ agrees with $\mathcal{TS}'$

Proof: From definitions 2.4, 2.5 and 2.6. □

On the basis of these results we may restrict the temporal semantics and the given state space to a minimal set $\mathcal{AP}'$ such that $\mathcal{AP}'$ contains all the atomic propositions we are interested in and the restriction of $\mathcal{TS}$ to $\mathcal{AP}'$ is well-defined.

Example 2.8 In figure 1 there is a program which tries to guarantee mutual exclusion of a critical section to two concurrent processes. The language constructs are supposed to have their conventional meanings.

The meaningful statements referring to the program are of the forms $y_1 (y_2) = true$, and *process P (Q) is in state 1 ... 3 (1 ... 6)*. The set of corresponding atomic propositions can be taken to be $\mathcal{AP} = \{y_1, y_2, p_1, p_2, p_3, q_1, \ldots, q_6\}$.

We can classify the states of each process to three groups: idle, requested, or executing the critical section. The first group, idle, corresponds to states p_1 and q_1, the third group, executing the critical section, to states p_3 and q_3, and the second group to all the other states.

We use P_{ij} to denote the atomic action of process P leading from state p_i to p_j and similarly with Q. The set of atomic actions is thus $L = \{P_{12}, P_{23}, P_{31}, Q_{12}, Q_{23}, Q_{24}, Q_{31}, Q_{45}, Q_{56}, Q_{62}\}$. The temporal semantics $\mathcal{TS}$ is easy to define. As an example $\mathcal{TS}(P_{12}) : A \mapsto A \cup \{y_1, p_2\} \setminus \{p_1\}$, meaning intuitively that the atomic action of process P leading from state 1 to 2 sets y_1 and p_2 true, p_1 false, and leaves the rest of the atomic formulas intact. Other examples are $\mathcal{TS}(P_{23}) : A \mapsto A \cup \{p_3\} \setminus \{p_2\}$, $\mathcal{TS}(P_{31}) : A \mapsto A \cup \{p_1\} \setminus \{p_3, y_1\}$ and $\mathcal{TS}(Q_{24}) : A \mapsto A \cup \{q_4\} \setminus \{q_2\}$.

The figure 1 contains the state space of the program, too. A state is labelled by the atomic propositions true in that state and an arc by the corresponding atomic action. □

In the state space every complete path starting from the initial state and either continuing infinitely or leading to a state from which computation cannot continue specifies one possible complete execution sequence of the program. This justifies the following definition.

Definition 2.9 An *execution* in a state space $T = (S, \Delta, V, s)$ is a finite or infinite sequence $e = ((s_0, l_0, s_1), (s_1, l_1, s_2), \ldots)$, where $s_0 = s$ is the initial state and each $(s_i, l_i, s_{i+1}) \in \Delta$. An execution e is *complete* iff it is infinite or there is no further state reachable from the last state, i.e. if (s_{n-1}, l_{n-1}, s_n) is the last element of e, $\forall l, s' : (s_n, l, s') \notin \Delta$. Otherwise e is *incomplete*. □

Definition 2.10 The *truth set sequence* $ts(e)$ corresponding to an execution $e = ((s_0, l_0, s_1), (s_1, l_1, s_2), \ldots)$ is $ts(e) = (V(s_0), V(s_1), \ldots)$.

If σ is a truth set sequence, σ_n is the n:th element of σ and $\sigma^{(n)}$ is the truth set sequence constructed by leaving the first n elements out of σ. If σ is finite, $|\sigma|$ is the length of σ, otherwise $|\sigma| = \omega$. □

Definition 2.11 The *truth set modifier sequence* $tsm(e)$ corresponding to a temporal semantics $\mathcal{TS}$ and an execution $e = ((s_0, l_0, s_1), (s_1, l_1, s_2), \ldots)$ is $tsm(e) = (\mathcal{TS}(l_0), \mathcal{TS}(l_1), \ldots)$. The notions $\sigma^{(n)}$, σ_n and $|\sigma|$ are as before. □

Definition 2.12 The *truth set sequence induced by a truth set $INIT \subseteq \mathcal{AP}$ and a truth set modifier sequence tsm*, denoted $tss(INIT, tsm)$, is a sequence of truth sets such that

- $tss(INIT, tsm)_0 = INIT$,
- $tss(INIT, tsm)_{i+1} = tsm_i(tss(INIT, tsm)_i)$, and
- if tsm is finite, then $|tss(INIT, tsm)| = |tsm| + 1$, otherwise $|tss(INIT, tsm)| = \omega$.

□

Theorem 2.13 Let $T = (S, \Delta, V, s)$ be a state space, $\mathcal{TS}$ a temporal semantics agreeing with T, and e a complete execution in T, Then $tss(V(s), tsm(e)) = ts(e)$.
Proof: By induction on m from definitions 2.4, 2.9-2.12. □

The preceding theorem shows that in order to be able to reconstruct $ts(e)$ for any complete execution e, it is enough to record the truth values of atomic formulas in the initial state, i.e. $V(s)$, and the truth set modifier sequence corresponding to e.

3 Linear temporal logic

In this section we recall the definitions of a language, linear temporal logic, by means of which properties of truth set sequences may be described.

Definition 3.1 The *alphabet of propositional linear temporal logic $\mathcal{TL}$* consists of the set $\mathcal{AP}$ of atomic propositions and of the symbols $(,), \neg, \vee, \mathcal{U}$. The *well-formed formulas* (wffs) of $\mathcal{TL}$ are as follows:

- if $A \in \mathcal{AP}$, then A is a wff,
- if A and B are wffs, then $(\neg A)$, $(A \vee B)$ and $(A \mathcal{U} B)$ are wffs, and
- there are no other wffs.

We use the following abbreviations $\top \equiv_{df} (p \vee (\neg p))$ for some fixed $p \in \mathcal{AP}$, $(A \wedge B) \equiv_{df} (\neg((\neg A) \vee (\neg B)))$, $(A \Rightarrow B) \equiv_{df} ((\neg A) \vee B)$, $(\Diamond A) \equiv_{df} (\top \mathcal{U} A)$, $(\Box A) \equiv_{df} (\neg(\Diamond(\neg A)))$, and $A \mathcal{U}_w B \equiv_{df} (A \mathcal{U} B) \vee \Box A$. and use the ordinary precedence rules to reduce the number of parentheses needed in the expressions. □

Definition 3.2 A $\mathcal{TL}$-formula A is true in a truth set sequence $\sigma = (v_0, v_1, \ldots)$ i.e. $\models^\sigma A$, according to the following rules:

- If $A \in \mathcal{AP}$, then $\models^\sigma A$ iff $A \in v_0$.
- If A is of the form $\neg A_1$, then $\models^\sigma A$ iff not $\models^\sigma A_1$.

- If A is of the form $A_1 \vee A_2$, then $\models^\sigma A$ iff $\models^\sigma A_1$ or $\models^\sigma A_2$.
- If A is of the form $A_1 \mathcal{U} A_2$, then $\models^\sigma A$ iff there is $0 \leq i < |\sigma|$ such that $\models^{\sigma^{(i)}} A_2$ and for all $0 \leq j < i \models^{\sigma^{(j)}} A_1$.

A $\mathcal{TL}$-formula A is true in a state space T iff for every complete execution e in T, A is true in the truth set sequence $ts(e)$. □

The truth definitions of the operators have their conventional meanings, even though we defined the semantics of the logic in terms of truth set sequences instead of state sequences. The only points worth paying attention to are the reflexivity of $\mathcal{U}$ and the lack of a nexttime-operator.

If we are just interested in the validity of a fixed set of $\mathcal{TL}$-formulas $A_1, \ldots, A_n$, and not in that of all the other $\mathcal{TL}$-formulas, the state space may contain information irrelevant to us in the form of the truth values of the atomic propositions not occurring in $A_1, \ldots, A_n$. This may be removed by restricting the temporal semantics and the state space in the sense of definitions 2.5 and 2.6. In the following we implicitly assume that such a restriction has been done. This is not vital to the correctness of our method, but the more information the reduction method is allowed to ignore, the more efficient it becomes, and so it is highly recommendable to restrict the model to a minimal set.

In the rest of the chapter we show that we are allowed to overlook the transitions in the state space if they do not change the truth value of any atomic proposition and link this observation to the truth set modifier sequences of a state space.

Definition 3.3 Let $\sigma = (v_0, v_1, \ldots)$ be a truth set sequence. The *reduced form of* σ, denoted by $red(\sigma)$ is constructed by removing from σ all v_i such that $v_i = v_{i-1}$, i.e. by collapsing continuous sequences of identical elements v_i into one element. □

It is to be noted that the reduced form of an infinite truth set sequence may be finite.

Lemma 3.4 Let σ and σ' be truth set sequences such that $red(\sigma) = red(\sigma')$. Then a $\mathcal{TL}$-formula A is true in the truth set sequence σ iff it is true in the truth set sequence σ', i.e. $\models^\sigma A$ iff $\models^{\sigma'} A$.

Proof: Induction on the structure of A. □

The preceding result holds because our temporal logic is immune to stuttering and has no irreflexive or pure future time temporal operators. The result is essentially the same as in [Lam83] although it is not formally stated there. With minor modifications we could preserve the validity of formulas containing the pure future time operator *there are infinitely many instances in the future in which A holds*, too.

Corollary 3.5 Let T and T' be state spaces such that for every complete execution e in T there is a complete execution e' in T' such that $red(ts(e)) = red(ts(e'))$ and vice versa for all complete executions e' in T'. Then a $\mathcal{TL}$-formula A is true in the state space T iff it is true in the state space T'. □

Definition 3.6 The *reduced form* $rmod(m)$ of a truth set modifier sequence m is constructed by removing all identity truth set modifiers from it. □

Theorem 3.7 Let $T = (S, \Delta, V, s)$ be a state space, $\mathcal{TS}$ a temporal semantics agreeing with T, e a complete execution in T, and denote $V(s)$ by $INIT_T$. Then the truth set sequence induced by $INIT_T$ and the reduced form of the truth set modifier sequence corresponding to e has the same reduced form as the truth set sequence corresponding to e, i.e. $red(tss(INIT_T, rmod(tsm(e)))) = red(ts(e))$.

Furthermore, let T and T' be state spaces such that $INIT_T = INIT_{T'}$ and for every complete execution e in T there is a complete execution e' in T' such that $rmod(tsm(e)) = rmod(tsm(e'))$ and vice versa for all complete executions e' in T'. Then a $\mathcal{TL}$-formula A is true in the state space T iff it is true in the state space T'.
Proof: The first claim is immediate from 2.13, 3.3 and 3.6, and from the observation that for all $(s,l,s') \in \Delta$, if $\mathcal{TS}(l)$ is an identity truth set modifier, then $V(s) = V(s')$, i.e. by removing identity truth set modifiers we do not remove any truth sets which would differ from their predecessor. Remembering corollary 3.5, the second claim follows from the first one. □

4 State space reduction

In this section we apply the process algebraic techniques discussed in [VT91] in order to reduce the state space of a program so that the truth value of a $\mathcal{TL}$-formula A is preserved. To do this we first construct a *labelled transition system* from a state space.

Definition 4.1 The *labelled transition system induced by the state space* $T = (S, \Delta, V, s)$ is a quadruple $LTS = (S, \Sigma \cup \{\tau\}, \Delta_{lts}, s)$, where $\Sigma = \mathcal{TM} \setminus \{\tau\}$, $\Delta_{lts} \subseteq S \times (\Sigma \cup \{\tau\}) \times S$ and $(s,t,s') \in \Delta_{lts}$ iff there exists $l \in L$ such that $(s,l,s') \in \Delta$ and $t = \mathcal{TS}(l)$. □

Intuitively, we construct an lts from a state space by replacing the atomic actions with the corresponding truth set modifiers, and by not evaluating the truth values of the atomic propositions in the states of the lts.

The paper [VT91] introduces a semantic model consisting of the *initial stability, stable failures* and *divergences* of an lts. These and some related concepts may be defined as follows.

Definition 4.2 Let $LTS = (S, \Sigma \cup \{\tau\}, \Delta_{lts}, s)$ be a labelled transition system.

- Let ρ be a finite or infinite sequence of symbols from $\Sigma \cup \{\tau\}$. Let $0 \leq n \leq \omega$ be the length of ρ. We write $s_0 - \rho \rightarrow$, iff there are $s_1, s_2, \ldots$ (, s_n) such that for all $0 < i (\leq n)$, $(s_{i-1}, l_i, s_i) \in \Delta_{lts}$. If ρ is finite we also write $s' - \rho \rightarrow s_n$.
- Let σ be a finite or infinite sequence of symbols from Σ, and let $s' \in S$. We write $s' = \sigma \Rightarrow$ iff there is ρ such that $s' - \rho \rightarrow$ and the result of removing all τ-symbols from ρ is σ. Let $s'' \in S$. We write $s' = \sigma \Rightarrow s''$ iff there is ρ such that $s' - \rho \rightarrow s''$ and the result of removing all τ-symbols from ρ is σ.
- σ is a *trace* of LTS, if $s = \sigma \Rightarrow$ and σ is finite. σ is an *infinite trace* of LTS, if $s = \sigma \Rightarrow$ and σ is infinite. The sets of finite and infinite traces of LTS are denoted by $tr(LTS)$ and $itr(LTS)$, respectively.
- $s' \in S$ is *stable*, iff $\neg(s' - \tau \rightarrow)$. LTS is *initially stable*, iff s is stable.
- Let $\sigma \in tr(LTS)$ and $A \subseteq \Sigma$. (σ, A) is a *stable failure* of LTS iff there is s' such that $s = \sigma \Rightarrow s'$, s' is stable, and $\forall a \in A : \neg(s' - a \rightarrow)$. σ is a *deadlocking trace* of LTS iff (σ, Σ) is a stable failure of LTS. The sets of stable failures and deadlocking traces of LTS are denoted by $sfail(LTS)$ and $dtr(LTS)$, respectively.
- σ is a *divergence* of LTS iff σ is finite and there is an infinite ρ such that $s - \rho \rightarrow$ and the result of removing all τ-symbols from ρ is σ. The set of divergences of LTS is denoted by $div(LTS)$. □

The following lemmas relate the complete executions in a state space to the process algebraic concepts of the previous definition.

Lemma 4.3 Let T be a state space and LTS its induced lts. e is a complete execution in T iff $rmod(tsm(e)) \in itr(LTS) \cup div(LTS) \cup dtr(LTS)$.
Proof: If e is an execution in T then $s - tsm(e) \rightarrow$. On the other hand, if ρ is a sequence of symbols from $\Sigma \cup \{\tau\}$ such that $s - \rho \rightarrow$, then T has an execution e such that $\rho = tsm(e)$. e is an infinite execution if and only if $tsm(e) \in div(LTS)$ or $otsm(e) \in itr(LTS)$, depending on whether it is finite. e is a complete finite execution if and only if $tsm(e) \in dtr(e)$. □

Lemma 4.4 Let LTS and LTS' be finite ltss such that $div(LTS) = div(LTS')$ and $sfail(LTS) = sfail(LTS')$. Then $dtr(LTS) = dtr(LTS')$ and $itr(LTS) = itr(LTS')$.
Proof: By definition 4.2 $dtr(LTS)$ can be concluded from $sfail(LTS)$.

In [VT91] it is shown that $tr(LTS) = div(LTS) \cup \{\sigma \mid (\sigma, \emptyset) \in sfail(LTS)\}$. On the basis of the assumption this means that $tr(LTS) = tr(LTS')$. Let us show that this implies also that $itr(LTS) = itr(LTS')$.

Let $X = \{\rho \in \Sigma^\omega \mid \forall k : \rho_1\rho_2...\rho_k \in tr(LTS)\}$, where Σ^ω denotes the set of all infinite sequences of symbols from Σ. As an obvious consequence of definition 4.2 $itr(LTS) \subseteq X$. By Kõnig's Lemma and the finiteness assumption, it can be proved that $X \subseteq itr(LTS)$, too. Therefore $itr(LTS) = \{\rho \in \Sigma^\omega \mid \forall k : \rho_1\rho_2...\rho_k \in tr(LTS)\}$ and the claim holds. □

Theorem 4.5 Let T and T' be finite state spaces and LTS and LTS' their induced ltss such that $INIT_T = INIT_{T'}$, $div(LTS) = div(LTS')$ and $sfail(LTS) = sfail(LTS')$. Then a $\mathcal{TL}$-formula A is true in T iff it is true in T'.
Proof: Follows directly from theorem 3.7 and lemmas 4.3 and 4.4. □

An algorithm reducing a finite lts while preserving $sfail(LTS)$ and $div(LTS)$ was presented in [VT91]. The algorithm is an application of well known algorithms for the determinisation and minimisation of a finite automaton [AHU74], with some extra features to preserve information of divergences and stable failures. Related algorithms have been presented in the process algebra literature, for instance in [CPS90]. However, the algorithm in [VT91] is (to our knowledge) the first of its kind applicable to the preservation of the truth-values of $\mathcal{TL}$-formulas, because, unlike the algorithm in [CPS90], it preserves *all* divergences of the lts. Preserving all divergences is vital to the preservation of the truth-values of $\mathcal{TL}$-formulas.

We have now shown how to reduce the lts corresponding to a state space so that the reduction preserves those features of the model that are essential for preserving the truth-values of the $\mathcal{TL}$-formulas. The final step is to reconstruct a state space T' on the basis of LTS' and $INIT$. T' is typically much smaller than T, but by the above theory the truth values of $\mathcal{TL}$-formulas in it are the same as in T. In contrast with the original state space T, the transitions of T' are labelled with truth set modifiers and not with atomic actions. This is natural as the mapping from atomic actions to truth set modifiers is not necessarily reversible.

The construction of a state space from an lts is slightly more complicated than in the other direction. The naive approach of labelling the states of the lts with truth sets does not always work, as there can be states that are reachable from the initial state by several paths having different truth set modifier sequences and producing different truth valuations in the end state.

Definition 4.6 If $LTS = (S, \Sigma \cup \{\tau\}, \Delta, s)$ and $INIT \subseteq \mathcal{AP}$ fulfil the following property, we say that the *truth set labelling of LTS is well defined*: for every state $s' \in S$ and every pair of paths p, p' such that $s - p \rightarrow s'$ and $s - p' \rightarrow s'$, it is the case that $tss(INIT, p)_{|p|} = tss(INIT, p')_{|p'|}$.

If the above property holds, we define *the state space induced by LTS and INIT* as $T = (S, \Delta, V, s)$, where $V : s' \mapsto tss(INIT, p)_{|p|}$ where p is any path such that $s - p \rightarrow s'$. □

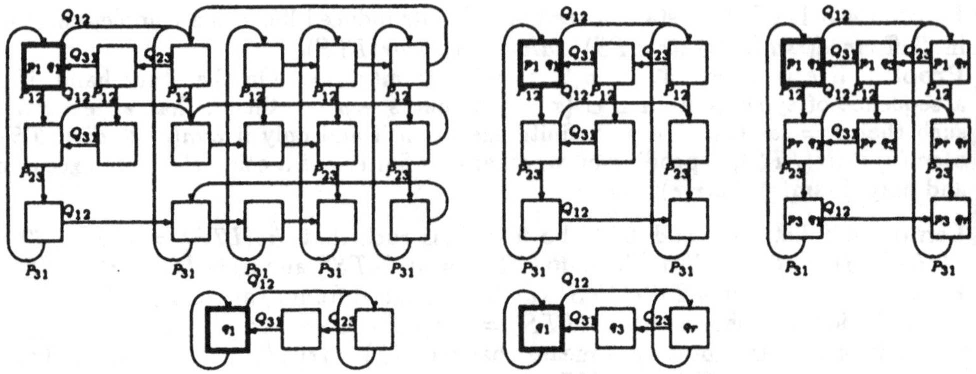

Figure 2: *Reducing the mutex-algorithm*

The inconsistency problem is solved by making as many copies of a state as there are different atomic truth valuations realised in the state along some path starting from the initial state. The drawback of the method is that the size of the state space increases, and if the truth set modifiers involved are very complex, this increase may be exponential. However, in practice this rarely happens. On the basis of the following theorem we can take an arbitrary lts and construct an lts that can be labelled with truth sets. This completes the process of producing T' from T.

Theorem 4.7 Let $LTS = (S, \Sigma \cup \{\tau\}, \Delta, s)$ be an arbitrary lts and $INIT \subseteq \mathcal{AP}$. Assume that $LTS' = (S', \Sigma \cup \{\tau\}, \Delta', s')$ fulfils the following requirements:

- $S' \subseteq S \times \mathcal{P}(\mathcal{AP})$
- If $(s_1, A_1) \in S'$, then $((s_1, A_1), t, (s_2, A_2)) \in \Delta'$ iff $(s_1, t, s_2) \in \Delta$ and $t(A_1) = A_2$.
- $s' = (s, INIT)$.

Then the truth set labelling of LTS' is well defined. What is more $div(LTS) = div(LTS')$ and $sfail(LTS) = sfail(LTS')$. $\square$

Example 4.8 Let us consider the mutual exclusion program of example 2.8. We already mentioned that the states can be classified to three groups: p_1 and q_1 *idle*, p_3 and q_3 *critical*, and all the others *requesting*. Consequently, by defining $p_r \equiv_{df} \neg p_1 \wedge \neg p_3$ and $q_r \equiv_{df} \neg q_1 \wedge \neg q_3$, we give p_r and q_r the intuitive meaning, *process P (or Q) has requested access to the critical section.*

Interesting properties of the program are, for example:

- Does it indeed guarantee mutual exclusion of the critical section, i.e. does the formula $\square(\neg p_3 \vee \neg q_3)$ hold?
- If the process P has requested access to the critical section, is this eventually granted, i.e. does the formula $\square(p_r \Rightarrow \Diamond p_3)$ hold?
- If the process Q has requested access to the critical section, is this eventually granted, i.e. does the formula $\square(q_r \Rightarrow \Diamond q_3)$ hold?

If these are the only properties we are interested in, we can restrict the state space to the set $\mathcal{AP}' = \{p_1, p_3, q_1, q_3\}$. It is easy to notice that the restriction of the temporal semantics TS to $\mathcal{AP}'$ is well-defined, too.

The resulting restricted temporal semantics TS' maps all the atomic actions other than P_{12}, P_{23}, P_{31}, Q_{12}, Q_{23} and Q_{31} to the identity truth set modifier. In the non-identity cases $TS'(P_{12}) : A \mapsto A \setminus \{p_1\}$, $TS'(P_{23}) : A \mapsto A \cup \{p_3\}$, $TS'(P_{31}) : A \mapsto A \cup \{p_1\} \setminus \{p_3\}$, and correspondingly for Q.

Figure 2 depicts the original lts corresponding to the state space and the restricted temporal semantics (top left), the equivalent lts produced by the reduction algorithm of [VT91] (top middle) and the final reduced state space (top right). The τ transition labels have been omitted and the truth set modifier functions are represented by the corresponding atomic actions. In the final reduced state space we have presented the values of p_r and q_r in the various states in addition to the atomic propositions p_1, q_1, p_3 and q_3.

It is easy to notice that $\Box(\neg p_3 \vee \neg q_3)$ holds in the model as there is no state that would be labelled with both p_3 and q_3. $\Box(p_r \Rightarrow \Diamond p_3)$ holds, too, as in all the paths starting from a state labelled with p_r there is a state labelled with p_3. $\Box(q_r \Rightarrow \Diamond q_3)$ does not hold, as the rightmost three states form a loop in which q_r is always true but q_3 is never realised.

It would have been possible to examine the truth of the formulas one at a time, which would have allowed even greater reduction. For example, if we are just interested in finding out whether $\Box(q_r \Rightarrow \Diamond q_3)$ holds, it is enough to record the truth values of q_1 and q_3 and we can restrict the state space to $\mathcal{AP}' = \{q_1, q_3\}$. The resulting reduced lts and the corresponding state space are presented in figure 2 (bottom left, bottom right). □

5 Towards Compositional Model Generation

The stable failures model we presented in the previous chapter actually records more information than would be strictly necessary for the model checking purposes: the method preserves all stable failures whereas we would need only the deadlocking traces. The reason why we do preserve the stable failures is that, as mentioned in the introduction, the semantic model consisting of the initial stability, stable failures and divergences of an lts is a congruence with respect to parallel composition and hiding [VT91]. This chapter is devoted to developing these ideas.

We assume that we have a finite set of processes $S_1, \ldots, S_n$ and that each process S_i has an associated set of local variables, such that those of two distinct processes S_i and S_j do not overlap. A process S_i cannot refer to any other variables than those of its own. In particular, whether it can execute some action or not depends only on its own execution state, the values of its local variables and the availability of its partners for sychronisation. A process S_i has an initial state in which the values of all its own variables are defined. The model is thus that of processes communicating only by synchronisation and not by shared variables. If we want to model shared variables this has to be done by introducing a separate process for each shared variable in the normal process-algebraic fashion.

As the atomic propositions that can be meaningfully evaluated in the state space of the process can only refer to the execution state of the process or to the values of the process's own variables, we can attach to each process S_i a set of atomic propositions $\mathcal{AP}_i$ so that the sets of atomic propositions of distinct processes do not overlap. Because S_i and S_j have distinct sets of atomic propositions $\mathcal{AP}_{S_i}$ and $\mathcal{AP}_{S_j}$, they have distinct sets of truth modifiers, $\mathcal{TM}_{S_i}$ and $\mathcal{TM}_{S_j}$. When we combine two processes S_i and S_j to form a larger process R (by some operator yet to be introduced), it is easy to see that by defining $\mathcal{AP}_R = \mathcal{AP}_{S_i} \cup \mathcal{AP}_{S_j}$, the state space of R has the capability of expressing everything that is expressible about either S_i or S_j. As a natural consequence, $\mathcal{TM}_R$ is defined as the set of all mappings from $\mathcal{P}(\mathcal{AP}_R)$ to itself. The initial truth set of R is defined easily as $INIT_R = INIT_{S_i} \cup INIT_{S_j}$. In order to be able to define what happens when two atomic actions are executed simultaneously in processes S_i and S_j, we have to define how two truth set modifiers operating on distinct sets of atomic propositions may be combined.

Definition 5.1 Let $tsm_P \in \mathcal{TM}_P$ and $tsm_Q \in \mathcal{TM}_Q$, i.e. $tsm_P : \mathcal{P}(\mathcal{AP}_P) \rightarrow \mathcal{P}(\mathcal{AP}_P)$ and tsm_Q alike. We define the *combination of* tsm_P *and* tsm_Q, to be the mapping

$comb(tsm_P, tsm_Q) : \mathcal{P}(\mathcal{AP}_R) \rightarrow \mathcal{P}(\mathcal{AP}_R); A \mapsto tsm_P(A \cap \mathcal{AP}_P) \cup tsm_Q(A \cap \mathcal{AP}_Q)$, where $\mathcal{AP}_R = \mathcal{AP}_P \cup \mathcal{AP}_Q$.

(Intuitively, we divide the set A in two: to the elements belonging to $\mathcal{AP}_P$ and to the elements belonging to $\mathcal{AP}_Q$, and then apply the truth set modifier mappings tsm_P and tsm_Q each to the corresponding set.) □

In order to enable interaction between processes, we modify the concepts of a temporal semantics and a state space so that some atomic actions may have an associated *synchronisation label.* This means that the arcs of the lts corresponding to a state space are labelled not only with the corresponding truth set modifiers, but also with synchronisation labels. Synchronisation labels specify the communication between processes, as will be defined soon.

Definition 5.2 Let $\mathcal{SY}$ be a set of *synchronising labels* containing a unique *non-synchronising label* τ. A *synchronised temporal semantics* $\mathcal{TSS}$ for a set of atomic actions L is a mapping $\mathcal{TSS} : L \rightarrow \mathcal{SY} \times \mathcal{TM}$. (Intuitively, if $\mathcal{TS}(l) = (a, b)$, a (if different from τ) is the label according to which the execution of the action is synchronised with other processes, and b expresses the change effected by executing the atomic action l.)

The definitions of a *synchronised state space*, *synchronised agreement* and a *synchronised lts induced by a synchronised state space* are natural modifications of the original definitions. The definitions of *restriction* and its *well-definedness* do not change, as restriction refers only to truth values and not to any synchronising labels.

The concepts introduced in definition 4.2 are easily modified for sychronised ltss, the only difference being that instead of τ, the empty action is now the pair (τ, τ) having both an empty truth set modifier and an empty synchronisation label. □

Now we can introduce the two syntactic operators, *parallel composition* and *hiding*, by means of which basic processes can be combined. The variants used here have a strong Lotos [BB87] flavour, although similar operators exist in almost any process algebra.

Definition 5.3 Let P and Q be processes and $g_1, \ldots, g_n \in \mathcal{SY} \setminus \{\tau\}$ a finite set of synchronisation labels. Then $P \mid [g_1, \ldots, g_n] \mid Q$ and $P \setminus \{g_1, \ldots, g_n\}$ are processes. □

As before, we do not concentrate on how the synchronised state spaces of the basic processes are constructed, but take them for granted instead. On the basis of a basic process's state space, we can construct a synchronised lts for it. Let us now assume that we are given the synchronised ltss of processes P and Q, and that we want to construct the synchronised lts of $P \mid [g_1, \ldots, g_n] \mid Q$ or $P \setminus \{g_1, \ldots, g_n\}$.

Definition 5.4 Let $LTS_P = (S_P, \Sigma_P, \Delta_P, s_P)$, where $\Sigma_P = (\mathcal{SY}_P \times \mathcal{TM}_P)$, and LTS_Q be synchronised ltss corresponding to processes P and Q, respectively.

If $R = P \mid [g_1, \ldots, g_n] \mid Q$, the synchronised lts corresponding to R is defined as $LTS_R = (S_R, \Sigma_R, \Delta_R, s_R)$, where

- $S_R = S_P \times S_Q$
- $\Sigma_R = \mathcal{SY}_R \times \mathcal{TM}_R$, where $\mathcal{SY}_R = \mathcal{SY}_P \cup \mathcal{SY}_Q$
- $\Delta_R \subseteq S_R \times \Sigma_R \times S_R$, and $((p_i, q_j), (a, b), (p_k, q_l)) \in \Delta_R$ iff
  - EITHER $b \in \{g_1, \ldots, g_n\}$ and there exist a_p and a_q such that $(p_i, (a_p, b), p_k) \in \Delta_P$, $(q_j, (a_q, b), q_l) \in \Delta_Q$, and $a = comb(a_p, a_q)$. (In this case, we have an action with a synchronisation label b in both processes, b has been specified as requiring synchronisation, and both processes take one step.
  - OR $b \notin \{g_1, \ldots, g_n\}$ and $q_j = q_l$ and there exists a_p such that $(p_i, (a_p, b), p_k) \in \Delta_P$ and $a = comb(a_p, \tau_Q)$. (In this case, the process P takes one nonsynchronised step which does not affect the truth values of any of process Q's atomic propositions, and the process Q takes no action.)

- OR $b \notin \{g_1, \ldots, g_n\}$ and $p_i = p_k$ and there exists a_q such that $(q_j, (a_q, b), q_l) \in \Delta_Q$, $a = comb(\tau_P, a_q)$. (A symmetric case.)
- $s_R = (s_P, s_Q)$.

If $R = P \setminus \{g_1, \ldots, g_n\}$, LTS_R is defined as follows:
- $S_R = S_P$,
- $\Sigma_R = (\mathcal{SY}_R \times \mathcal{TM}_R)$, where $\mathcal{TM}_R = \mathcal{TM}_P$ and $\mathcal{SY}_R = \mathcal{SY}_P \setminus \{g_1, \ldots, g_n\}$,
- $(s_1, (a, b), s_2) \in \Delta_R$ iff either $b \notin \{g_1, \ldots, g_n\}$ and $(s_1, (a, b), s_2) \in \Delta_P$ or $b = \tau$ and there exists $b' \in \{g_1, \ldots, g_n\}$ such that $(s_1, (a, b'), s_2) \in \Delta_P$.
- $s_R = s_P$. □

If a synchronised lts does not have any synchronising labels, it can be replaced by an ordinary lts. On the basis of the lts and the formulas that are true in the initial state we can construct a state space (i.e. a Kripke model) as before.

The following theorem expresses the core idea of the compositional approach. On the basis of it the stable failures etc. of a system composed of several processes connected in parallel can be uniquely derived from the stable failures etc. of the component processes, and similarly with hiding. This, in turn, means that the stable failures method is suitable for compositional lts generation, and, consequently, for the compositional generation of Kripke models.

Theorem 5.5 Let P and Q be synchronised state spaces, LTS_P and LTS_Q their induced synchronised ltss, $R = P \mid [\ldots] \mid Q$, and LTS_R constructed from LTS_P and LTS_Q as in 5.4. Assume that LTS'_P and LTS'_Q are synchronised ltss such that $div(LTS_P) = div(LTS'_P)$, $sfail(LTS_P) = sfail(LTS'_P)$, LTS_P is initially stable iff LTS'_P is, and alike for LTS_Q and LTS'_Q, and that LTS'_R is constructed from LTS'_P and LTS'_Q as in 5.4.

Then $div(LTS_R) = div(LTS'_R)$, $sfail(LTS_R) = sfail(LTS'_R)$ and LTS_R is initially stable iff LTS'_R is.

The same result applies to $R = P \setminus \{g_1, \ldots, g_n\}$, too.

What is more, if LTS_R and LTS'_R have only τ synchronisation labels, and T_R, T'_R are the state spaces induced by LTS_R, LTS'_R and $INIT$, then a $\mathcal{TL}$-formula A is true in T_R iff it is true in T'_R.

Proof: First two claims are proved in [VT91] and the last one follows immediately from theorem 4.5. □

It may be thought that the restrictions we set on processes P and Q would render our method unusable: applying it e.g. to our first example is not straightforward, as translating the processes to ones that do not share variables and communicate only by synchronisation is not a minor task. However, we feel that the method is sufficiently general to be applicable, in particular with processes that communicate by message-passing. This is again best illustrated by an example.

Example 5.6 We examine the properties of the well-known alternating bit protocol, a simplified version of which is presented in figure 3. It consists of two processes A and B, which communicate by sending and receiving messages using unreliable communication channels: the data is sent by process A via channel m, and the acknowledgement is sent back to A via k.

We model the message-passing in the sending process as an atomic action having a synchronisation label which is uniquely determined by the channel and the contents of the message, and in the receiving end as a nondeterministic choice between several atomic actions each of which has a synchronisation label corresponding to one possible message that can be transmitted in the channel and a truth set modifier that reflects the change in the local variables into which the contents of the message is read. The unreliability of

A: $\{s=0, a=0, i=0\}$	B: $\{r=0, c=1, o=0\}$
a_1 :**if** $s \neq a$ **then goto** 4	b_1 :**rec**$(m,(r,o))$
a_2 :**read**(i)	b_2 :**if** $r \neq c$ **then goto** 5
a_3 :$s := s$ **xor** 1	b_3 :$c := c$ **xor** 1
a_4 :**send**$(m,(s,i))$	b_4 :**write**(o)
a_5 :**rec**(k,a)	b_5 :**send**$(k, c$ **xor** $1)$
a_6 :**goto** 1	b_6 :**goto** 1

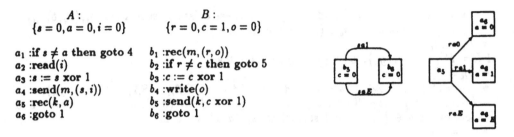

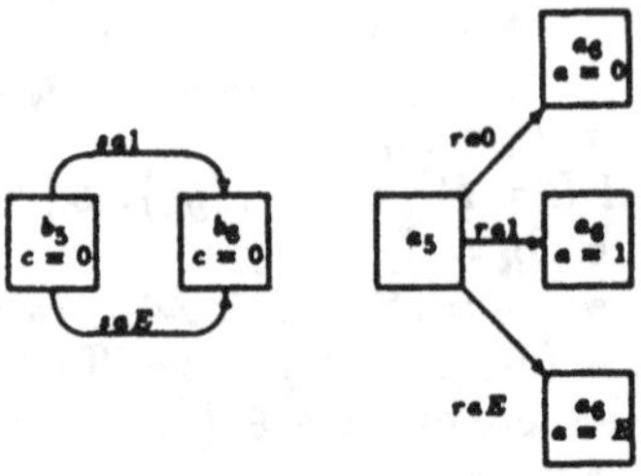

Figure 3: *AB-protocol*

the channel is modelled by nondeterministically sending either the correct message or a standard error message E.

We make the following assumptions: $i \in \{0,1\}$, i.e. there are only two possible data values, 0 and 1 and alike $s, c, o \in \{0,1\}$. In addition to these two values, a and r may get the value E. There are five possible messages to be transmitted on channel m: $(0,0)$, $(0,1)$, $(1,0)$, $(1,1)$ and E, and three on channel k: 0, 1 and E. We use the following set of synchronisation labels: $M00, M01, M10, M11, ME, A0, A1, AE$, where M refers to channel m and A to k.

Accordingly, when $c = 0$ the execution of action b_5 is modelled by a nondeterministic choice between two atomic actions $sa1$ and saE such that $\mathcal{TSS}_B(sa1) = (A1, t_1)$ and $\mathcal{TSS}_B(saE) = (AE, t_1)$, where $t_1 : C \mapsto C \cup \{b_6\} \setminus \{b_5\}$. In the same way, the execution of action a_5 is modelled by a nondeterministic choice between three actions $ra0$, $ra1$, raE such that $\mathcal{TSS}_A(ra0) = (A0, t_2)$, where $t_2 : C \mapsto C \cup \{a_6, a = 0\} \setminus \{a_5, a = 1, a = E\}$ and correspondingly for $ra1$ and raE. Relevant pieces of the state spaces of B and A are presented in figure 3 (middle and right). Read-command is modelled by nondeterministically choosing an atomic statement assigning either 0 or 1 to i.

The complete system is defined by $R = (A \mid [M00, \ldots, AE] \mid B) \setminus \{M00, \ldots, AE\}$.

Interesting properties that we would like the system to have are, for example:

- $\Box(a_3 \wedge i = 0 \Rightarrow (\neg b_4)\mathcal{U}_w(b_4 \wedge o = 0))$, i.e. *if the value* 0 *is read, the next time (if ever) something is written, the value to be written is* 0, and similarly for the data value 1,
- $\Box(a_3 \Rightarrow (a_3\mathcal{U}((\neg a_3)\mathcal{U}_w b_4)))$, i.e. *if something is read, nothing new is read until something is written (if ever)*, and symmetrically $\Box(b_4 \Rightarrow (b_4\mathcal{U}((\neg b_4)\mathcal{U}_w a_3)))$
- $\Box(a_3 \Rightarrow \Diamond b_4)$, i.e. *if something is read, sometime in the future something is written, too*, and symmetrically $\Box(b_4 \Rightarrow \Diamond a_3)$.

Restriction to the above properties leaves us the following interesting atomic propositions: a_3 and $i = 0$ in process A and b_4 and $o = 0$ in B. After the restriction, the only non-tau modifier-synchronisation pairs are the ones containing a non-tau synchronisation element and the ones having one of the modifiers: $i0 : C \mapsto C \cup \{i = 0, a_3\}$, $i1 : C \mapsto C \cup \{a_3\} \setminus \{i = 0\}$, or $a3f : C \mapsto C \setminus \{a_3\}$ in process A and the modifiers $o0 : C \mapsto C \cup \{o = 0\}$, $o1 : C \mapsto C \setminus \{o = 0\}$, $b4t : C \mapsto C \cup \{b_4\}$ and $b4f : C \mapsto C \setminus \{b_4\}$ in process B.

We can now reduce the ltss of A and B. The sizes of the graphs diminish considerably: The original state space of process A has 48 nodes and 76 arcs, whereas the reduced lts has 15 nodes and 29 arcs (figure 4 top left). The corresponding numbers for process B are 44 nodes, 84 arcs, and only 8 nodes and 18 arcs (4 bottom left). The real savings of the method come apparent when we consider the size of the lts of the complete system: if we do not reduce the ltss of A and B, the composed lts has 316 nodes and 480 arcs, whereas if we first reduce the ltss of A and B, the composed lts has 31 nodes and 49 arcs. This lts can naturally be reduced once more, and as a result we acquire a model having

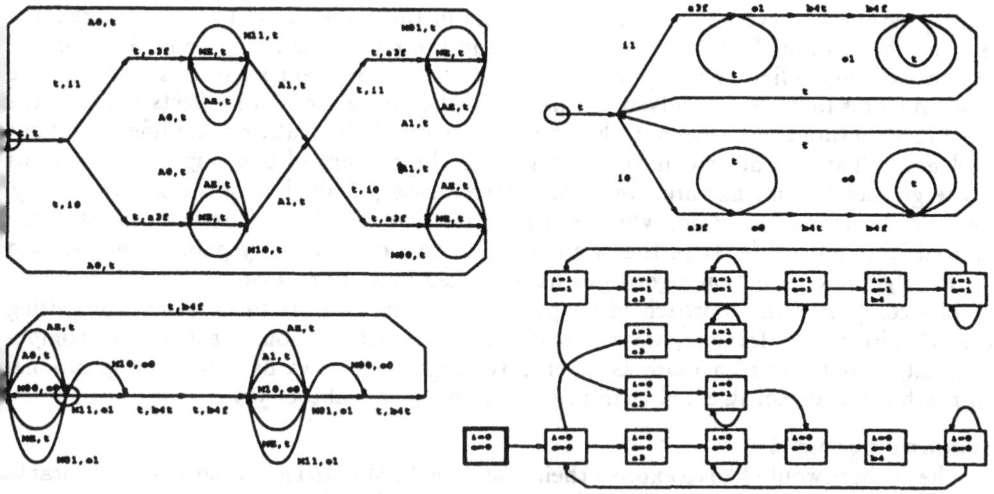

Figure 4: *Various stages in the compositional model generation*

12 nodes and 19 arcs (4 top right). Using the method 4.7 we can now construct the final state space, which turns out to have 17 nodes and 25 arcs (4 bottom right).

From the final state space it is easy to see that all the required safety properties hold. However, the liveness property does not, as there are infinite self-loops in the model in which the eventuality is never realised. This is natural, as we did not set any fairness constraints on the model, and when the message is always transmitted erroneously the liveness property fails to hold.

We could easily express the relevant fairness constraints as formulas $\neg\Diamond\Box a = E$, and $\neg\Diamond\Box r = E$. However, as all the information concerning the values of a and r has been restricted away from the state space we have no way of evaluating these formulas in the restricted model. The only way is to start again and this time leave the truth values of the formulas $a = E$ and $r = E$ to the state space. This time the final lts has 16 nodes and 25 arcs, and the final state space 51 states. This is in contrast with the mere 17 before, but still much less than the unreduced 316 states. We can see this as a result of the more general problem of being forced to leave visible extra information just in order to be able to evaluate the fairness constraints. □

A problem yet partially unresolved in the compositional approach is the incorporation of fairness restrictions to the resulting model. Here we formulated the fairness restrictions in the language of temporal logic, so that instead of model-checking a formula A we examine a formula A' meaning *either A holds or a fairness restriction B is violated.* A negative consequence of this is the fact that in order to be able to model-check the formula A', the reduced model has to record not only information enabling us to decide the validity of A but also information enabling us to decide the validity of B, which in turn usually means that the reduced model will be larger, and the savings consequently smaller.

6 Discussion

This paper has presented a method by which the complexity of temporal logic models may be reduced. The method is based on the observation that a temporal logic model may be treated as an lts, and that certain process-algebraic reduction methods may be applied.

A question we have not ventured to address in this paper is what the exact relation between the sizes of the original state space and the reduced state space is. It would be very interesting to find some upper limit to the size of the reduced state space, but the problem seems to be very involved, as the size of the final state space reflects not only the size and structure of the ltss but also the complexity of the truth set modifier functions involved. What can be said is that the greater the amount of the empty τ-transitions is, the greater the savings are. In most extreme cases, if all the transitions are empty, the lts collapses to one state, whereas if none of them are, it may be the case that the reduced lts is no smaller than the original one. However, as already pointed out, related process-algebraic reduction algorithms have worked well in practice.

The compositional approach of chapter 5 would seem to us to be a very promising research direction. However, we would like to point out that our treatment of compositionality should be seen more as a tentative suggestion towards how a compositional approach could be constructed than providing any practical tool yet.

Acknowledgements

The authors would like to express their gratitude to Martti Tienari and Jaana Eloranta for their helpful comments and to Jukka Kemppainen for his generous help in operating the automated reduction tools. The work of R. Kaivola was supported by the Academy of Finland, and that of A. Valmari was funded by the Technology Development Centre of Finland (Tekes) and the Technical Research Centre of Finland (VTT).

References

[AHU74] Aho, A.V. & Hopcroft, J.E. & Ullman, J.D.: *The Design and Analysis of Computer Algorithms*, Addison-Wesley, 1974

[BB87] Bolognesi, T. & Brinksma, E.: Introduction to the ISO Specification language LOTOS in *Computer Networks and ISDN Systems 14*, 1987, pp. 25-59, also in *The Formal Description Language LOTOS*, North-Holland, 1989, pp. 23-73

[BCG87] Browne, M. C. & Clarke, E. M. & Grümberg, O.: Characterizing Kripke Structures in Temporal Logic, in Ehrig, H. & Kowalski, R. & Levi, G. & Montanari, U. (eds.): *TAPSOFT '87, vol. I*, Lecture Notes in Computer Science, vol. 249, Springer-Verlag, Berlin, 1987, pp. 256-270

[CES85] Clarke, E. M. & Emerson, E. A. & Sistla, A. P.: Automatic Verification of Finite-State Concurrent Systems Using Temporal Logic Specifications, in *ACM Transactions on Programming Languages and Systems*, vol. 8, no. 2, April 1986, pp. 244-263

[CLM89] Clarke, E. M. & Long, D. E. & McMillan, K. L.: Compositional Model Checking, in *Proceedings of the Fourth IEEE Symposium on Logic in Computer Science*, 1989, pp. 353-362

[CPS90] Cleaveland, R. & Parrow, J. & Steffen, B.: The Concurrency Workbench, in *Proceedings of the Workshop on Automatic Verification Methods for Finite State Systems*, Lecture Notes in Computer Science 407, Springer-Verlag, Berlin, 1990, pp.24-37

[EL84] Emerson, E. A. & Lei, C-L.: Modalities for Model Checking: Branching Time Strikes Back, in *Conference Record of the Twelfth Annual ACM Symposium on Principles of Programming Languages*, 1984, pp. 84-96, also in *Science of Computer Programming*, vol. 8, no. 3, 1987, pp. 275-306

[Lam83] Lamport, L.: What Good is Temporal Logic?, in *Proceedings of the IFIP 9th World Computer Congress*, 1983, pp. 657-668

[LP85] Lichtenstein. O, & Pnueli, A.: Checking That Finite State Concurrent Programs Satisfy Their Linear Specification, in *Conference Record of the Twelfth Annual ACM Symposium on Principles of Programming Languages*, 1985, pp. 97-107

[SW89] Stirling, C. & Walker, D.: CCS, Liveness and Local Model Checking in the Linear Time mu-Calculus, in *Proceedings of the Workshop on Automatic Verification Methods for Finite State Systems*, Grenoble, June 12-14, 1989

[VT91] Valmari, A. & Tienari, M.: An Improved Failures Equivalence for Finite-State Systems with a Reduction Algorithm, to appear in *Proceedings of the 11th International IFIP WG 6.1 Symposium on Protocol Specification, Testing and Verification*, Stockholm, June 17-20, 1991, 16 p.

Completeness in Real Time Process Algebra

(Extended Abstract)

A.S. Klusener

Centre for Mathematics and Computer Science

P.O. Box 4079, 1009 AB Amsterdam, The Netherlands

e-mail: stevenk@cwi.nl

Abstract

Recently, J.C.M. Baeten and J.A. Bergstra extended ACP with real time, resulting in a Real Time Process Algebra, called $ACP\rho$ [BB91]. They introduced an equational theory and an operational semantics. However, their work does not contain a completeness result nor does it contain the definitions to give proofs in detail. In this paper we introduce some machinery and a completeness result.

The operational semantics of [BB91] contains the notion of an *idle* step reflecting that a process can do nothing more then passing the time before performing a concrete action at a certain point in time. This *idle* step corresponds nicely to our intuition but it results in infinitary transition systems. In this paper we give a more abstract operational semantics, by abstracting from the *idle* step. Due to this simplification we can prove soundness and completeness easily. These results hold for the semantics of [BB91] as well, since both operational semantics induce the same equivalence relation between processes.

1985 Mathematics Subject Classification: 68Q10, 68Q40, 68Q45, 68Q55.

1982 CR Categories: D.1.3, D.3.1, D.4.1, F.1.2, F.3.2.

Key Words & Phrases: Real Time, Process Algebra, ACP, Integration, SOS.

Note: This work is in part sponsored by ESPRIT Basic Research Action 3006, CONCUR.

Introduction

Several authors have given a real time extensions of processalgebras, e.g. see [MT90],[Wan90] for an extension of CCS, see [RR88] for an extension of CSP and [BB91], [Gro90] for an extension of ACP. Nicollin and Sifakis have given a real time extension of a combination of CCS and ACP in [NS90]. Between these extensions several similarities and differences can be found. For example, most of these extensions are based on discrete time. However, the paper of Baeten and Bergstra is based on dense time and it introduces the interesting notion of integration. In general their theory is undecidable, due to the notion of general integration over arbitrary subsets of $\mathbb{R}^{\geq 0}$. In this report we restrict ourselves to "prefixed" integration to tackle the complexity of integration over sets of reals. Prefixed integration requires that every action, which has a *time variable* v as timestamp, is directly preceded by the binding integral of v. This restriction seems to be harmless from a practical point of view, since no "real-life" processes are know to us which are not covered by this restriction. Due to this simplification we can obtain a completeness result.

Real Time Process Algebra ([BB91]) concerns terms constructed from timed actions. A timed action is a combination of a symbolic action, taken from some alfabet A, and a timestamp, taken from $\mathbb{R}^{\geq 0}$. This timestamp can be interpreted either absolute or relative. In this paper we will focuss only on absolute time, in [BB91] a translation from relative to absolute time is given. Thus, the timed action $a(2)$ denotes the atomic process which executes an action a at time 2, after which it terminates succesfully. We expect some new identities that do not hold in standard Process Algebra ([BK84],[BW90]) such as $a(2) \cdot (b(1) + c(3)) = a(2) \cdot c(3)$. After doing $a(2)$ we have passed time 2 and in the following alternative composition $b(1) + c(3)$ the first alternative cannot be chosen anymore and therefore it may be removed.

Furthermore, we consider integration as an essential feature of our theory. Integration is the alternative composition over a continuum of alternatives ([BB91]). An integral describes the interval in which a timed action may occur. For example, the process which executes an action a somewhere within the interval $< 0, 1 >$ is denoted by $\int_{v \in <0,1>} a(v)$.

According to [BB91] we refer to Basic Real Time Process Algebra (the theory without parallelism) as BPA$\rho\delta$, by adding integration we get BPA$\rho\delta$I. Moreover, to Real Time Process Algebra (the theory with parallelism) with integration is referred to as ACPρ.

The development of such a theory implies the development of a system of axioms which generate exactly the required identities. To be sure that this system of axioms is exactly what we have in mind, we give an operational semantics. In our case an operational semantics assigns to every process expression a transition system which reflects the behaviour of this process. A transition system is a directed acyclic graph in which each arrow is labelled with an atomic action. These transitions systems are generated by giving a Transition System Specification in Structured Operational Semantics according to Plotkin ([Plo81]). We define an equivalence notion (which must be a congruence) on these transition systems by defining a bisimulation relation ([Mil80],[Par81]). If we have defined such an operational semantics we can validate the axiom system by proving soundness and completeness.

In [BB91] an axiom system is given together with an operational semantics which yields uncountable transitions. However, neither soundness nor completeness are treated thoroughly.

In this report we will give an abstract operational semantics which yields finite transition systems for terms without integration. The action rules defining this abstract semantics are similar to the action rules for the standard operational semantics of ACP as given in [Gla87]. We prove soundness and completeness of this abstract operational semantics with respect to Real Time Process Algebra. We can extend these results to the semantics of [BB91] since we prove that both semantics are equivalent in the sense that they induce the same identities between terms.

In this report we define the notion of a *basic* term, a *basic* term has very nice properties, such as there is a strong correspondence between a *basic* term an its transition system. Hence, we can prove completeness easily for these subset of terms. Since we prove as well that every term is derivable to a *basic* term within the theory, which is sound, we can extend the completeness result to all transition systems which can be represented by a term.

All tables, containing axiom systems or action rules, are given at the end of this paper. This paper is an extended abstract of [Klu91], some details of definitions and most of the proofs are omitted here and can be found in [Klu91].

1 The Original Operational Semantics

In this section we give some intuition for timed processes by introducing the operational semantics of [BB91] for process expressions over Basic Real Time Process Algebra (BPA$\rho\delta$). We do not yet consider integration in this section. Let A_δ be the set of actions, containing the constant δ. The alphabet of the theory BPA$\rho\delta$ is

$$A_\delta^{time} = \{a(t) | a \in A_\delta, t \in \mathbb{R}^{\geq 0}\}$$

Similarly we use A^{time}, as the set of timed actions without timed δ's. In the sequel we refer to actions from A_δ as symbolic actions and we refer to actions from A_δ^{time} as timed actions. Moreover, process expressions are simply called terms. The set $\mathcal{T}$ of closed terms over BPA$\rho\delta$ is generated by the alphabet A_δ^{time} and the binary operators $+$ for alternative composition and $\cdot$ for sequential composition and the operator $\gg$, called the *(absolute) time shift*. In the previous sentence we refered to closed terms as terms without recursion variables. In this report we do not consider recursion, hence if we consider a term it is meant to be a term which is closed w.r.t. recursion variables. In the sequel we will introduce another kind of variables, called *time variables*.

The *(absolute) time shift*, $\gg$, takes a nonnegative real number and process term; $t \gg X$ denotes that part of X, which starts after t. The set $\mathcal{T}$ with typical elements p, p_1, p_2 is defined in the following way, where $a \in A_\delta$ and $r \in \mathbb{R}^{\geq 0}$:

$$p \in \mathcal{T} \quad p := a(r) \mid p_1 + p_2 \mid p_1 \cdot p_2 \mid r \gg p$$

The semantics of [BB91] assigns to every term (in $\mathcal{T}$) a transition system in which each state is a pair consisting of a term and a point in time and in which each transition is labelled by a timed (non δ) action. Within this semantics each transition system concerns three relations. These three relations are defined as the least relations satisfying the Plotkin rules given in this section.

$<x,t> \xrightarrow{a(r)} <x',t'>$	abbreviates	$(<x,t>, a(r), <x',t'>)$	$\in$ *Step*	$\subseteq \mathcal{T} \times A^{time} \times \mathcal{T}$
$<x,t> \longrightarrow <x',t'>$	abbreviates	$(<x,t>, <x',t'>)$	$\in$ *Idle*	$\subseteq \mathcal{T} \times \mathcal{T}$
$<x,t> \xrightarrow{a(r)} <\surd,t'>$	abbreviates	$(<x,t>, a(r), t')$	$\in$ *Terminate*	$\subseteq \mathcal{T} \times A^{time} \times \mathcal{T}$

We always have $t' = r$ in *Step* and *Terminate* and $x \equiv x'$ in *Idle*. The term $a(1)$ denotes the process which performs an action at time 1, after which it is succesfully terminated. The root node of the transition system of $a(1)$ is $<a(1), 0>$, denoting that time starts at zero. From $<a(1), 0>$ an

$$\frac{t < r}{<a(r),t> \xrightarrow{a(r)} <\surd,r>} \qquad \frac{<x,t> \xrightarrow{a(r)} <x',r>}{<x+y,t> \xrightarrow{a(r)} <x',r> \quad <y+x,t> \xrightarrow{a(r)} <x',r>}$$

$$\frac{t < s < r}{<a(r),t> \longrightarrow <a(r),s>} \qquad \frac{<x,t> \xrightarrow{a(r)} <\surd,r>}{<x+y,t> \xrightarrow{a(r)} <\surd,r> \quad <y+x,t> \xrightarrow{a(r)} <\surd,r>}$$

$$\frac{t < s < r}{<\delta(r),t> \longrightarrow <\delta(r),s>} \qquad \frac{<x,t> \longrightarrow <x,r>}{<x+y,t> \longrightarrow <x+y,r> \quad <y+x,t> \longrightarrow <x+y,r>}$$

Table 1: Action Rules for Atomic Actions and Alternative Composition

idle transition is possible to a state of the form $<a(1), t>$ with $0 < t < 1$. An *idle* transition is a transition in which only the time component is increased without executing any action. In general, from each state $<a(1), t>$ an *idle* transition is possible to $<a(1), t'>$, whenever $t < t' < 1$. Further from each state $<a(1), t>$ a $a(1)$-transition to $<\surd, 1>$ is possible whenever $t < 1$.

This transition system of the term $a(1)$ can be represented by the left-hand process diagram given in Figure 1. A process diagram is simply a pictorial representation of a transition system. It is not possible to make a picture of the transition system itself, since it has uncountably many transitions. The intuition behind such a process diagram is that the process starts in the top-point. It can idle by going to a lower point without crossing any line, whereas the execution of an action a at time r is reflected by going to a dashed line at level r labelled with a. Only dashed lines may be crossed, after landing on them.

A very particular set of atomic actions is the set of $\delta(r)$-terms. $\delta(1)$ can do nothing more then idling until 1. Thus the root node is $<\delta(1), 0>$ and from each state $<\delta(1), t>$ an *idle* transition to $<\delta(1), t'>$ is possible, whenever $t < t' < 1$. The action rules defining the transition systems of timed actions are given in Table 1. In Table 1 the rules for the alternative compostion are given as well; the

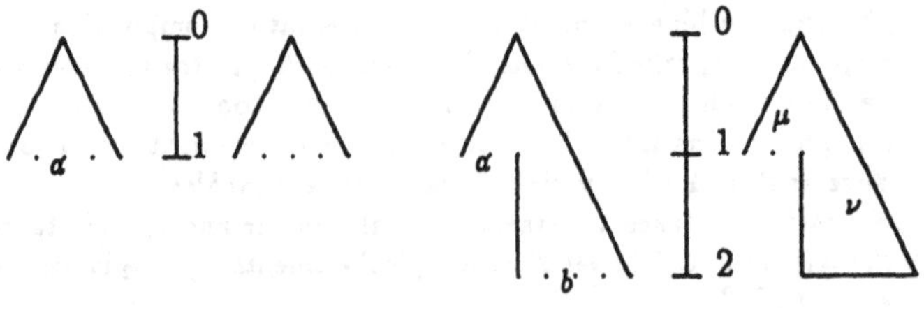

Figure 1: Process Diagrams of resp. the terms $a(1)$, $\delta(1)$, $a(1)+b(2)$ and $a(1)+\delta(2)$

transition system of $p+q$ is defined in terms of the transition systems of p and q. The behaviour of $p+q$ can be considered as the "union" of the behaviour of p and that of q.

The transition system of $a(1)+b(2)$ can be represented by the process diagram given in Figure 1. A state μ (in Figure 1) is of the form $< a(1)+b(2), t >$ with $0 < t < 1$. From μ both a terminating $a(1)$-transition to $< \surd, 1 >$ and a terminating $b(2)$-transition to $< \surd, 2 >$ are possible. However, from a state like ν of the form $< a(1)+b(2), t >$ with $1 \geq t < 2$ only a terminating $b(2)$-transition to $< \surd, 2 >$ is possible. Hence, by idling from $< a(1)+b(2), t_0 >$ to $< a(1)+b(2), t_1 >$ with $0 \leq t_0 < 1 \leq t_1 < 2$ we have lost the possibility of executing the $a(1)$-summand. Thus one could say that a choice has been made at time 1 and after the choice has been made for $b(2)$ the summand $a(1)$ has become redundant.

The transition system of $a(1)+\delta(1)$ consists of exactly the same relations as the transition system of $a(1)$. The summand $\delta(1)$ contributes only *idle* steps which are contributed by the summand $a(1)$ as well.

However if we consider $a(1)+\delta(2)$, the $\delta(2)$ summand contributes *idle* transitions which are not contributed by $a(1)$, since $\delta(2)$ has *idle* transitions to points in time between 1 and 2. The transition system of $a(1)+\delta(2)$ can be represented by the process diagram on the right-hand side in Figure 1. The action rules for sequential composition, are given in Table 2 . The last operator we introduce is the *(absolute) time shift* denoted by $\gg$, which takes a real number s and a process X and delivers that part of X which starts after s. Hence, before s it can only *idle* or do a transition to a state after s. The action rules for the *(absolute) time shift* operator are given in Table 2 as well.

$$\frac{< x,t > \xrightarrow{a(r)} < x',r >}{< x \cdot y,t > \xrightarrow{a(r)} < x' \cdot y,r >} \qquad \frac{t < r < s}{< s \gg x,t > \longrightarrow < s \gg x,r >} \qquad \frac{r > s \quad < x,t > \longrightarrow < x,r >}{< s \gg x,t > \longrightarrow < x,r >}$$

$$\frac{< x,t > \xrightarrow{a(r)} < \surd,r >}{< x \cdot y,t > \xrightarrow{a(r)} < y,r >} \qquad \frac{r > s \quad < x,t > \xrightarrow{a(r)} < x',r >}{< s \gg x,t > \xrightarrow{a(r)} < x',r >} \qquad \frac{r > s \quad < x,t > \xrightarrow{a(r)} < \surd,r >}{< s \gg x,t > \xrightarrow{a(r)} < \surd,r >}$$

$$\frac{< x,t > \longrightarrow < x,r >}{< x \cdot y,t > \longrightarrow < x \cdot y,r >}$$

Table 2: Action Rules for Sequential Composition And (Absolute) Time Shift

A1		$X+Y=Y+X$	A4		$(X+Y)\cdot Z=X\cdot Z+Y\cdot Z$
A2		$(X+Y)+Z=X+(Y+Z)$	A5		$(X\cdot Y)\cdot Z=X\cdot(Y\cdot Z)$
A3		$X+X=X$			
ATA1		$a(0)=\delta$	ATB1	$t<r$	$t\gg a(r)=a(r)$
ATA2		$\delta(t)\cdot X=\delta(t)$	ATB2	$t\geq r$	$t\gg a(r)=\delta(t)$
ATA3	$t\leq r$	$\delta(t)+\delta(r)=\delta(r)$	ATB3		$t\gg(X+Y)=(t\gg X)+(t\gg Y)$
ATA4		$a(t)+\delta(t)=a(t)$	ATB4		$t\gg(X\cdot Y)=(t\gg X)\cdot Y$
ATA5		$a(t)\cdot X=a(t)\cdot(t\gg X)$			

Table 3: BPA=A1-A5 BPA$\rho\delta$ =BPA +BPA+ATA1-5+ATB1-4 ($a\in A_\delta$)

1.1 The Theory of BPA$\rho\delta$

BPA$\rho\delta$ is the theory of Basic Real Time Process Algebra ([BB91]). It consists of A1-A5, which are the standard axioms of Basic Process Algebra, extended by some axioms stating the specific real time properties and defining the *(absolute) time shift*. The axioms of BPA$\rho\delta$ are given in Table 3. We abbreviate $\delta(0)$ by δ. Notice that the laws ATA2 and ATA4 are generalisations of the BPA$\rho\delta$ laws A6 and A7. Using BPA$\rho\delta$ we can prove:

$$\begin{array}{lcl} 5\gg(a(4)+b(6)+c(7)\cdot d(8)) & = & b(6)+c(7)\cdot d(8)\\ 5\gg(e(4)+f(3)) & = & \delta(5)\\ \delta(1)+a(2)\cdot b(3)+\delta(3)\cdot c(4) & = & a(2)\cdot b(3)+\delta(3)\\ a(0)+b(2)\cdot(c(1)+c(3))+d(3)\cdot e(2) & = & b(2)\cdot c(3)+d(3)\cdot\delta(3)\end{array}$$

2 Basic Real Time Process Algebra with Integration

First, we have to discuss how to construct our terms. We assume an infinite, countable set of *time variables*, called *TVar*. The set of bounds of intervals , *Bounds*, with typical elements b, b_1, b_2, is defined as follows, where $t\in\mathbb{R}^{\geq 0}_{\omega}, v\in TVar$:

$$b\in Bounds \quad b ::= t\mid v\mid b_1+b_2\mid b_1-b_2\mid t\cdot b$$

If $b\in Bounds$ then the set of *time variables* occuring in b is denoted by $tvar(b)$. Now we can construct intervals like $<1,9>$ and $<v+3,w>$. An interval without free *time variables* can be considered as a connected part of the nonnegative reals. However, we don't want to deal with the complexity of set theory over reals and we want to define intervals containing occurrences of free *time variables*. Hence, every interval is a four tuple, containing two booleans and two reals. The interval $V=(ff,1,2,tt)$ is abbreviated in the sequel by $V=<1,2]$, denoting that the lower bound is open and 1, and that the upper bound is closed and 2. If $b\in Bounds$ then $b\in V$ denotes the logical expression of (in)equalities $1<b\leq 2$. Similarly we define $\cup,\cap$ and sup, inf and $V=\emptyset$ as abbreviations of logical expressions over *Bounds*.

Now we can define the set of terms, called $\mathcal{T}$, with typical elements p,q. Let $a\in A_\delta$, $V\in Int$, $v\in TVar$, $b\in Bounds$

$$p\in\mathcal{T}\quad p::=\int_{v\in V}(a(v))\mid\int_{v\in V}(a(v)\cdot p)\mid p\cdot q\mid p+q\mid b\gg p$$

We abbreviate $\int_{v\in[w,w]}a(v)$ by $a(w)$ and $\delta(0)$ by δ. In the above definition of the set of terms $\mathcal{T}$ the notion of prefixed integration becomes clear; every action has as timestamp a *time variable* v and is directly prececed by its binding integral. Hence, we do not allow a term like $\int_{v\in V}\int_{w\in W}a(v)\cdot\int_{r\in<v,w>}b(1)\cdot c(r)$. On the terms in $\mathcal{T}$ we have notions as $FV()$ for the set of free *time variables* , α-conversion, and substitution. If a term or interval has no free *time variables*, then it is called *time closed*, obtaining the sets $\mathcal{T}^{time-closed}\subset\mathcal{T}$ and $Int^{time-closed}\subset Int$.

In the sequel we will use a *scope convention*, saying that we do not write the scope brackets if the scope is as large as possible. Thus we write $\int_{v \in V} a(v) \cdot p$ for $\int_{v \in V}(a(v) \cdot p)$ if we do not consider this term as an initial part of a sequential composition.

In Table 4 the axioms for BPA$\rho\delta$I are given. Since these axioms are tailored for prefixed integration, they differ from the axioms given in [BB91]; the theory presented here can be considered as a subtheory of the one of [BB91].

We need some syntactical functions, defined by induction on the structure of the terms. *active*(p) is the interval of timestamps, which can be reached by process p by idling only. *action*(p) is the set of timestamps at which p can execute an action. Both functions can inductively be defined (see [Klu91] for details). $U(p)$ is the *ultimate delay* which is the smallest timestamp which is not reachable by the process p by idling. $L(p)$ is the latest moment at which p can execute an action.

Removing the Scope Brackets

According to the *scope convention* we can write $\int_{v \in <1,2>}(a(v) \cdot \int_{w \in <3,4>}(b(w)))$ as $\int_{v \in <1,2>} a(v) \cdot \int_{w \in <3,4>} b(w)$, hence, no *scope* brackets are needed. For other terms however we have to do some work, before all *scope* brackets can be removed. Consider the following term, where the *time variable* v of the last integral is in the scope of the first one.

$$\int_{v \in <0,1>} (c(v) \cdot \int_{v \in <1,2>} (a(v) \cdot \int_{w \in <3,4>} (b(w))) \cdot \int_{u \in <v+5,v+6>} (d(u)))$$

Apply an α-conversion

$$\int_{v' \in <0,1>} (c(v') \cdot \int_{v \in <1,2>} (a(v) \cdot \int_{w \in <3,4>} (b(w))) \cdot \int_{u \in <v'+5,v'+6>} (d(u)))$$

and a *scope widening* according to INT3a, b

$$\int_{v' \in <0,1>} (c(v') \cdot \int_{v \in <1,2>} (a(v) \cdot \int_{w \in <3,4>} (b(w) \cdot \int_{u \in <v'+5,v'+6>} (d(u)))))$$

before removing the brackets according to the *scope convention*

$$\int_{v' \in <0,1>} c(v') \cdot \int_{v \in <1,2>} a(v) \cdot \int_{w \in <3,4>} b(w) \cdot \int_{u \in <v'+5,v'+6>} d(u)$$

In order to make this more formally we need a Definition for the set of *widest scope terms* $\mathcal{W}$ and a Lemma.

Definition 2.0.1 *(Widest scope terms)* $\mathcal{W} = \{p | p$ *does not contain a subterm* $p_0 \cdot p_1\}$

Lemma 2.0.2 *Every term* $p \in \mathcal{T}$ *has a widest scope term* $p_w \in \mathcal{W}$ *such that* $INT3 \vdash p = p_w$

Proof. By induction on the size of p, using *α-conversion* and *scope widening*. □

Thus, $\int_{v \in V}(a(v)) \cdot p \notin \mathcal{W}$ but $\int_{v \in V}(a(v) \cdot p) \in \mathcal{W}$. We will not use the scope brackets any more in the sequel, since we may restrict ourselves to *widest scope* terms.

2.1 Basic Terms

Within the theory BPA$\rho\delta$I we can derive identities like

$$\int_{v \in <0,10>} a(v) \cdot \{\int_{w \in <0,10>} b(w) + \int_{z \in <0,10]} \delta(z)\} = \int_{v \in <0,10>} a(v) \cdot \int_{w \in <v,10>} b(w)$$

$$a(10) \cdot \{\int_{v \in <0,20>} b(v) + \delta(5) + \int_{w \in <0,30>} \delta(w)\} = a(10) \cdot \{\int_{v \in <10,20>} b(v) + \delta(30)\}$$

$$\int_{v \in <0,10>} a(v) \cdot \int_{w \in <0,5>} b(w) \cdot \int_{z \in <0,10>} c(z) = \int_{v \in <0,5>} a(v) \cdot \int_{w \in <v,5>} b(w) \cdot \int_{z \in <w,10>} c(z) + \int_{v \in [5,10>} a(v) \cdot \delta$$

We may say that the terms on the left-hand side contain redundant information, while the terms on the right-hand side do not contain redundant information. In the sequel we will refer to these terms on the right-hand side as *basic* terms. Since all information in a *basic* terms is essential, there will be a strong correspondence between the intervals and bounds occurring in the term on the one hand, and the set of timestamps of the transition system on the other hand. Indeed, in our completeness proof at the end of this paper we will restrict ourselves to *basic* terms, using another Lemma of this section, which states that every term is derivable to a *basic* term. We define auxiliary sets $B^z(t)$ and $B(t)$ for each $z, t \in \mathbb{R}^{\geq 0}$ with $z > t$, such that we can define B, the set of *basic* terms.

Definition 2.1.1

$B^r(t)$ is the set of basic terms starting or deadlocking after t, with a possible deadlock at time r whenever $r \neq \omega$

$$
\begin{array}{rlll}
a \in A \wedge V \in Int^{time-closed} \wedge t < V & \int_{v \in V} a(v) & \in & B^{\omega}(t) \\
t < s & \delta(s) & \in & B^{s}(t) \\
t < V \wedge ((\forall r \in V \backslash_{\{\omega\}}\, p[r/v] \in B(r)) \vee p \simeq \delta) & \int_{v \in V}(a(v) \cdot p) & \in & B^{\omega}(t) \\
p \in B^{r}(t) \wedge q \in B^{s}(t) \wedge (r = s \vee (r < s = \omega \wedge r > U(q))) & p + q & \in & B^{r}(t) \\
B(t) \textit{ is the set of basic terms starting after } t & B(t) & = & \bigcup_{r \in \mathbb{R}^{\geq 0}} B^{r}(t) \\
B \textit{ is the set containing the basic terms starting after 0, and } \delta & B & = & B(0) \cup \{\delta\}
\end{array}
$$

Note that $B \subseteq T^{time-closed}$. Until now we have dealt only with *time-closed* terms. But if we want to prove by induction that every term has a *basic* term, we have to consider terms with free *time variables* as well. Therefore, we first introduce the notion of a *conditional* term. A *conditional* term is some construct which determines for every substitution of real values for the free *time variables* a *time-closed* term. For example, if we consider the term $a(5) \cdot b(v)$, which has a free *time variable* v, we will associate to it the following *conditional* term:

if the context assigns a value $t \leq 5$ to v *then* deliver $a(5) \cdot \delta$
if the context assigns a value $t > 5$ to v *then* deliver $a(5) \cdot b(v)$

In the sequel a *conditional* term is denoted as follows (the notation $:\!\rightarrow$ is taken from [BB90]):

$$p \simeq \{v \leq 5 :\!\rightarrow a(5) \cdot \delta\} + \{v > 5 :\!\rightarrow a(5) \cdot b(v)\}$$

Consider a substitution $\sigma[1/v]$, then $\sigma[1/v]$ validates $v \leq 5$ and $\sigma[1/v](p) = a(5) \cdot \delta$ which is a *basic* term. Consider now a substitution like $\sigma[6/v]$, then $\sigma[6/v]$ validates $v > 5$ and $\sigma[6/v](p) = a(5) \cdot b(6)$ which is again a *basic* term. In the following we introduce a generalization of a *basic* term, called a *conditional basic* term, the idea is that a *conditional* term is called *basic* if an arbitrary substitution applied on the *conditional* term gives a *basic* term.

First we introduce the notion of a substitution. Σ is the set of substitutions, ranged over by σ. A substitution σ maps a *time variable* v either onto a value in $\mathbb{R}^{\geq 0}$ or onto itself and it maps every positive realnumber to itself as well. We extend the definition of a substitution to intervals and terms by structural induction. We consider a subset of $P(\Sigma)$, the set of *conditions* called *Cond*, represented by (in)equations over *Bounds*.

$$
\begin{array}{rcl}
[v < w] & = & \{\sigma \in \Sigma | \sigma(v), \sigma(w) \in \mathbb{R}^{\geq 0} \wedge \sigma(v) < \sigma(w)\} \\
[v = w] & = & \{\sigma \in \Sigma | \sigma(v) = \sigma(w)\}
\end{array}
$$

$$[\alpha \vee \beta] = [\alpha] \cup [\beta] \quad [\alpha \wedge \beta] = [\alpha] \cap [\beta] \quad [\neg(\alpha)] = \Sigma - [\alpha]$$

$$\alpha_1, .., \alpha_n \text{ ia a partition of } \Sigma \text{ if } \quad \forall \sigma \in \Sigma \text{ with } \sigma(tvar(\overline{\alpha})) \subseteq \mathbb{R}^{\geq 0} \; : \; \exists! i \quad \sigma \in [\alpha_i]$$

Instead of $[\alpha]$ we may write α. Moreover, within *Cond*, we distinguish a subset $Cond^{DN}$, containing *conditions* which can be represented by a conjunction of (in)equalities. We define a set C of *conditional* terms with typical elements p_c.

$p \in W$, $\alpha \in Cond$, $b \in Bounds$

$$p_c \in C \quad p_c := p \mid \alpha :\rightarrow p_c \mid p_c + p_c \mid \int_{w \in W} (a(w) \cdot p_c) \mid b \gg p_c$$

In Table 5 we state identities over C, resulting in an equational theory BPA$\rho\delta$IC if combined with the axioms of BPA$\rho\delta$I. A substitution can be seen as an abstraction of a context. We denote the empty context by $[]$. $p \in \mathcal{T}$.

$$C[] \in Context \quad C[] := [] \mid C[] + p \mid p + C[] \mid \int_{v \in V} (a(v) \cdot C[]) \mid b \gg C[]$$

$Context^{time-closed}$ is the set containing all *time-closed* contexts. Every $C[]$ has exactly one occurrence of $[]$, which may occur in the scope of some integrals binding variables which are called the *bound* variables of $C[]$. Thus, $BV([]) = \emptyset$, $BV(\int_{v \in V}(a(v) \cdot C[])) = \{v\} \cup BV(C[])$ and $BV(C[]+p) = BV(C[])$. For every $p \in \mathcal{T}$ we can construct a term $C[p] \in \mathcal{T}$, note that $[p] \equiv p$.

Lemma 2.1.2 *$\forall p, q \in \mathcal{T}$ (Hence, p and q may contain free variables)*

BPA$\rho\delta$IC $\vdash p = q \iff \forall C[] \in Context^{time-closed}$ *with* $FV(p,q) \subseteq BV(C[])$ BPA$\rho\delta$I $\vdash C[p] = C[q]$

Proof. By induction on the depth of $[]$ in $C[]$ using INT5. □

Lemma 2.1.3 *$\forall \overline{\alpha} \in P(Cond^{DN})$, $\forall \overline{p} \in P(C)$, $\forall v \in TVar$, ($\overline{(x)}$ abbreviates $x_1, \ldots, x_n$ for some n $\exists \overline{\beta} \in P(Cond^{DN})$ with $v \notin tvar(\overline{\beta})$, $\exists \overline{V} \in P(Int)$, $\exists \overline{q} = \overline{p}$*

$$\sum_i \{\alpha_i :\rightarrow p_i\} = \sum_j \{\beta_j \wedge v \in V_j :\rightarrow q_j\}$$

This Lemma says that it is always possible to "isolate" all occurrences of a certain *time variable* v. This is needed for applying axiom COND 9. For example, if we caonsider the term $\int_{v \in <0,1>} a(v) \cdot x$ we can 'lift' the conditions by applying COND 9 after isolating *time variable* v.

$$x \simeq \begin{array}{ll} \{v < 3 \wedge v < w \wedge v > 1 & :\rightarrow p\} \\ + & \\ \{v > 3 \wedge v = w & :\rightarrow q\} \end{array} = \begin{array}{ll} \{3 < w \wedge v \in < 1,3 > & :\rightarrow p\} \\ + & \\ \{w < 3 \wedge v \in < 1,w > & :\rightarrow p\} \\ + & \\ \{w = 3 \wedge v \in [3,3] & :\rightarrow p\} \\ + & \\ \{w > 3 \wedge v \in [w,w] & :\rightarrow q\} \end{array}$$

Note that we have $\mathcal{T} \subseteq C$ and the following Lemma states that every derivation in BPA$\rho\delta$IC with *time-closed* terms is a derivation in BPA$\rho\delta$I.

We define a notion of *basic conditional* terms:

Definition 2.1.4 $b \in Bounds$

$$\sum_i \{\alpha_i :\rightarrow p_i\} \in B\,(b) \quad \stackrel{def}{\iff} \quad \left\{ \begin{array}{l} \overline{\alpha} \textit{ is a partition over } \Sigma \\ \wedge \\ \forall \sigma \quad \sigma \in [\alpha_i] \Longrightarrow \sigma(p_i) \in B\,(\sigma(b)) \cup \{\delta\} \end{array} \right\}$$

For example $\int_{v \in <x,x+1>} a(v) \cdot \int_{w \in <v,w>} \in B\,(x)$ but $\int_{v \in <x,10>} a(v) \notin B\,(x)$. Note that $\int_{v \in <x,10>} a(v)$ can be rewritten to the (*conditional*) *basic* term $\{x < 10 :\rightarrow \int_{v \in <x,10>} a(v) + x \geq 10 :\rightarrow \delta(cl)\}$. The next Lemma states that every term in $\mathcal{T}$ (with possibly free *time variables*) can be rewritten to a *basic* (*conditional*) term.

Lemma 2.1.5 $\forall p \in C\ ,\ \forall cl \in Bounds, \exists b_{p,cl} \in B\ (cl)$

$$FV(b_{p,cl}) \subseteq FV(cl \gg p) \quad \wedge \quad \mathrm{BPA}\rho\delta\mathrm{IC} \vdash cl \gg p = b_{p,cl}$$

Proof. We prove only two cases. V_{cl} is an abbreviation of $V \cap < cl, \omega >$. Note, that this proof is based highly on the definition of intervals, it would not be possible to give this proof if intervals where arbitrary subsets of $\mathbb{R}^{\geq 0}$.

- $\int_{v \in V} a(v)$

$$cl \gg \int_{v \in V} a(v) = \begin{array}{l} \{cl \geq sup(V) \quad :\rightarrow \quad \delta(cl)\} \\ + \\ \{cl < sup(V) \quad :\rightarrow \quad \int_{v \in V_{cl}} a(v)\} \end{array}$$

- $\int_{v \in V} a(v) \cdot p$.

$$\begin{array}{ll} & cl \gg \int_{v \in V} a(v) \cdot p \\ & \{cl \geq sup(V) \quad :\rightarrow \quad \delta(cl)\} \\ = & + \\ & \{cl < sup(V) \quad :\rightarrow \quad \int_{v \in V_{cl}} (a(v) \cdot (v \gg p))\} \\ & \text{By induction and Corollary 2.1.3} \\ & \{cl \geq sup(V) \quad :\rightarrow \quad \delta(cl)\} \\ = & + \\ & \{cl < sup(V) \quad :\rightarrow \quad \int_{v \in V_{cl}} (a(v) \cdot \sum_i \alpha_i \wedge v \in W_i :\rightarrow p_i)\} \\ & \{cl \geq sup(V) \quad\quad :\rightarrow \quad \delta(cl)\} \\ & + \\ = & \{\sum_i \{ cl < sup(V) \wedge \alpha_i \ \wedge \ V_{cl} \cap W_i = \emptyset \quad :\rightarrow \quad \delta(cl)\} \\ & + \\ & \{\sum_i \{ cl < sup(V) \wedge \alpha_i \quad\quad :\rightarrow \quad \int_{v \in V_{cl} \cap W_i} (a(v) \cdot p_i\ \}\} \end{array}$$

Some of these p_i's may be of the form $\delta(v)$ and must be rewritten to δ. Since we have to end up with a *basic* term we have to construct a partition. This can be done by applying sufficiently many times the rule

$$\{\alpha :\rightarrow p\} + \{\beta :\rightarrow q\} \longrightarrow \{\alpha \wedge \beta :\rightarrow p + q\} + \{\alpha \wedge \neg(\beta) :\rightarrow p\} + \{\neg(\alpha) \wedge \beta :\rightarrow q\}$$

□

Now we have done all the work, we can prove that every *time – closed* term be rewritten in BPA$\rho\delta$I to a (*time – closed*) *basic* term.

Theorem 2.1.6 $\forall p \in \mathcal{T}^{time-closed}$, $\exists p_b \in B$ *such that* BPA$\rho\delta$I $\vdash p = p_b$

Proof. According to the previous Lemma there is a $p_b \in B\ (0)$ with $FV(p_b) \subseteq FV(p) = \emptyset$ and BPA$\rho\delta$IC $\vdash p = (0 \gg p) = p_b$. By Lemma 2.1.2 and $FV(p, p_b) = \emptyset$ we know that for every *context* $C[]$ we have BPA$\rho\delta$I $\vdash C[p] = C[p_b]$. So, we take the empty context $[]$ and the Theorem follows by $[q] \equiv q$ forall $q \in \mathcal{T}$. □

3 Parallelism and Synchronization

Definition 3.0.7 *$\mathcal{T}$, with typical elements p, p_1, p_2, is the set of terms over* ACPρ*, where $a \in A_\delta$, $r \in \mathbb{R}^{\geq 0}$ and $H \subseteq A$:*

$$p \in \mathcal{T} \quad p := a(r) \mid p_1 + p_2 \mid p_1 \cdot p_2 \mid r \gg p \mid p \gg r \mid p_1 \| p_2 \mid p_1 \lfloor\!\lfloor p_2 \mid p_1 | p_2 \mid \delta_H(p)$$

Now we are ready to introduce parallelism and synchronization resulting in the theory ACPρ. We will use as much as possible from ACP (without time) and we shall discuss only those cases in which we have to take the time information into account. One of the operators is the left-merge, which is an auxiliary operator that allows us to define the parallel merge operator $\|$ in finitely many axioms. In standard ACP (without time) the term $(a \cdot X) \lfloor\!\lfloor Y$ denotes the process in which the left component $a \cdot X$ executes his first action a, resulting in $X \| Y$. In our real time setting it is a bit more subtle; if we take for example the process $(a(t) \cdot X) \lfloor\!\lfloor Y$ then by executing the a action on time t the whole process must proceed in time. Whenever Y can wait after t (if $t < U(Y)$) then $(a(t) \cdot X) \lfloor\!\lfloor Y$ can execute a at time t, resulting in $t \gg (X \| Y)$, otherwise (if $t \geq U(Y)$) a deadlock at time $U(Y)$ occurs. Consider:

$$\begin{aligned} a(2) \lfloor\!\lfloor b(3) &= a(2) \cdot b(3) \\ b(3) \lfloor\!\lfloor a(2) &= \delta(2) \end{aligned}$$

In the first example the right component $b(3)$ can wait until the left component $a(2)$ executes its first action. In the second example however, we see that the right component a(2) cannot wait long enough and a deadlock at the *ultimate delay* of the right component is the result. The point is that in the process denoted by $X \lfloor\!\lfloor Y$ only those prefixes of X can be executed, which start before $U(Y)$. Hence, we need an auxiliary operator, called the *bounded initialization* , which has as input a process X and a time t and delivers that part of X which starts before t. This new operator is the counterpart of the *(absolute) time shift* operator, which is denoted $t \gg X$, as presented earlier. Therefore we shall denote the *bounded initialization* of X to t by $X \gg t$. We can define the *ultimate delay* and *latest starttime* inductively as well for terms over ACPρI. The axioms of ACPρI are given in Table 6. In the introduction of these axioms above we did not mention integration, or better said, the variable binding mechanism of the integrals. Since a term Y may be covered within the scope of an integral which binds a *time variable* v by applying an axiom (e.g. *ATCMI*3), we have to require that v does not occur in Y as a free *time variable*. This can always be guaranteed by applying α-conversion.

Theorem 3.0.8 *Elimination Theorem*
For each term $p \in \mathcal{T}$ there is a basic term p_b such that BPA$\rho\delta$I $\vdash p = p_b$

Proof. By induction on the *size* of p, see [Klu91] for details □

4 An Operational Semantics for ACPρ

The first difference between the action rules for standard *ACP* (without time) are the rules for sequential composition. Consider the process $a(r) \cdot p$. This process executes an action a at time r, evolving in that part of p which can start after r. This resulting process is exactly denoted by $r \gg p$. Hence, $a(r) \cdot p \xrightarrow{a(r)} r \gg p$. There are two sequential composition rules for terms with a terminating prefix, due to the variable binding and scoping mechanism. The operator $r \gg$ is new in Real Time Process Algebra. However, its semantics is very clear; it acts as a filter and only transitions after r are allowed.

The second difference is the semantics of the $\delta(r)$. In the original semantics ([BB91]) $\delta(3)$ is the process which *idles* before 3; it does nothing except waiting, on the understanding that it will never be able to reach time 3. In our more abstract view, we simply say that $\delta(3)$ has a deadlock at time 3. The process $a(5)$ waits until 5 and executes an action a at 5. Hence, the process $a(5)+\delta(3)$ has the same semantics as $a(5)$. But if we consider the process $a(5)+\delta(6)$, then we conclude that it has a deadlock at time 6; in the original semantics this process is able to *idle* before 6 without ever reaching time 6. The question wether a process has a deadlock at time r can be answered by: "Can it *idle* infinitely close to r without the possibility of ever doing an action at or after r". We can formulate this in another way by using the *ultimate delay* and the *latest action time*: "If $U(p) > L(p)$ then it has a deadlock at $U(p)$".

In Table 7 the action rules for terms over BPA$\rho\delta$I are given. The folowing Lemma states the strong correspondence between the syntax of a *basic* term and its transition system. Due to this correspondence we can proof the completeness easily in the last section.

Lemma 4.0.9 *Correspondence Lemma for basic terms versus the operational semantics*

Let $p \in B$ and $a \in A$, $r > 0$

$$p \xrightarrow{a(r)} \surd \iff a(r) \text{ is a syntactical summand of } p$$
$$p \xrightarrow{a(r)} r \gg p' \iff a(r)\cdot p' \text{ is a syntactical summand of } p$$
$$p \xrightarrow{\delta(r)} \surd \iff \delta(r) \text{ is a syntactical summand of } p$$

We did not introduce the notion of a syntactical summand formally, we refer to [Klu91]. The idea is that p is a syntactical summand of itself and a syntactical summand of $p+q$ for arbitrary q.

Now we can continue with the operators concerning parallelism and synchronization. If $a(r)\cdot p$ executes his $a(r)$ in a parallel composition with q, the "increase in time" must hold for q as well. In other words, $(a(r)\cdot p)\|q$ evolves into $(r \gg p)\|(r \gg q)$ by executing a at time r whenever q can wait until r. The "check" whether q can increase its time, is denoted by $r < U(q)$. Note that if $p \xrightarrow{a(r)} p'$ then p' contains one or more occurrences of $r \gg$, so only transitions with a timestamp greater than r are allowed for p'. The Transition System Specification of the operational semantics of ACPρ is given in Table 7.

Theorem 4.0.10 *Soundness Theorem*
The axioms of ACPρ *are sound with respect to bisimulation equivalence.*

Theorem 4.0.11 *The operational semantics for* ACPρ*, presented in this paper, is equivalent with the original semantics for* ACPρ *as given in [BB91]:*
Let $p, q \in T$

$$p \leftrightarrow q \iff < p, 0 > \;\leftrightarrow\; < q, 0 >$$

4.1 Soundness and Completeness of ACPρ

We stated already in the Soundness Theorems the soundness of the axioms of ACPρ. For soundness of the theory we have to prove as well that bisimulation equivelence is a congruence.

Theorem 4.1.1 *Bisimulation Equivalence is a congruence*

Proof. Groote showed in [Gro89] that if the action rules defining a transition system are in a specific format (which he called the *ntyft/ntyxt* format), then strong bisimulation is a congruence. This format is expressive enough to deal with uncountable many labels and negative premises. In [Klu91] another transition relation is given by action rules in this *ntyft/ntyxt* format, on which strong bisimulation induces the same equivelance as on the transition system given in this extended abstract. For further details we refer to [Klu91]. □

Next, we prove the completeness of BPA$\rho\delta$I

Lemma 4.1.2 *Completeness for terms over* BPA$\rho\delta$I . *Let* $p, q \in$ BPA$\rho\delta$I

$$p \leftrightarrow q \Longrightarrow \text{BPA}\rho\delta\text{I} \vdash p = q$$

We may restrict ourselves to *basic* terms, since every term is derivably equal to a *basic* term and since we have proved already soundess of BPA$\rho\delta$I

Proof. We prove that $p \subseteq q$ by induction on the *size* of p. By symmetry, $q \subseteq p$ follows. Assume

$$p \simeq \sum_i \int_{v_i \in V_i} a_i(v_i) \cdot p_i + \sum_j \int_{w_j \in W_j} b_j(w_j)$$

$\forall i$	$\forall t \in V_i$	$p \xrightarrow{a_i(t)} t \gg (p_i[t/v_i])$	by bisimulation also q has a transition
	$\exists q'$	$q \xrightarrow{a_i(t)} t \gg q'$	where
		$t \gg (p_i[t/v_i]) \leftrightarrow t \gg q'$	and
		$p_i[t/v_i] \leftrightarrow t \gg (p_i[t/v_i])$	and
		$t \gg q' \leftrightarrow q'$	and by induction and the transitivity of $\leftrightarrow$
		$p_i[t/v_i] = q'$	together with
		$a_i(t) \cdot q'$ is a summand of q	we may conclude
		$a_i(t) \cdot p_i[t/v_i]$ is a summand of q	
	$\overset{\Longrightarrow}{(INT4)}$	$\int_{v \in V_i} a(v) \cdot p_i$ is a summand of q	
$\forall j$	$\forall t \in W_j$	$p \xrightarrow{b_j(t)} \surd$	by bisimulation also q has a transition
		$q \xrightarrow{b_j(t)} \surd$	and thus
		$b_j(t)$ is a summand of q	
	$\overset{\Longrightarrow}{(INT4)}$	$\int_{w \in W_j} b_j(w)$ is a summand of q	

adding together : $p \subseteq q$

□

Theorem 4.1.3 *Completeness for terms over* ACPρ

Proof. Direct by the previous Lemma 4.1.2, the Soundness Theorem 4.0.10 and the Elimination Theorem. □

This completeness result is relative to equality on *Bounds*. This means that we don't bother about the derivability of equality on *Bounds*, which is reflected by the fact that syntactical equivalence is defined modulo equility on *Bounds*. Jeffrey has introduced in [Jef91] a notion of infinite summation as well. His completeness result is relative to equality on sets of terms which is much more liberal than the result above.

5 Concluding Remarks

In this paper we obtained a soundness and completeness result for Real Time Process Algebra. with integration. We had to introduce some machinery, such as *basic* terms and *conditional* terms, to come so far. However, it is our belief that these introduced notions have a value in itself. The complexity we encountered was due to the notion of integration, which can be seen as an alternative composition over a continuum associated with a variable binding and scoping mechanism. We restricted ourselves to "prefixed integration", thus not allowing general integration, however, we don't know real-life processes which are ruled out by this restriction

We did not consider other work like [Gro90], [MT90], [NS90], [RR88] or [Wan90]. Neither of these works contain a notion similar to integration and most of the works are based on discrete time. However, it is an interesting question whether there are common ideas within the field of timed process algebra. For example most authors believe that idling is non-deterministic. In our formalism this is formulated by $t \gg X + t \gg Y = r \gg \{(t-r) \gg X + (t-r) \gg Y\}$ if $r < t$. However, Groote believe that idling forces a choice. It would be clarifying to have charted all these similarities and differences.

A lot more concepts are introduced or touched upon in [BB91] than treated in this paper. Topics for future research are recursion, abstraction and relative time. Another interesting question is, whether it is possible to give a finite equational logic and an operational semantics containing only finitely branching transition systems for terms with integration but without unguarded recursion. This would be an important step towards practical applications.

5.1 Acknowledgements

The author wants to thank, first of all, Jos Baeten for his patience in reading all previous versions and for his support and criticism. Thanks go to the authors' colleagues Willem Jan Fokkink, Jan Friso Groote, Henri Korver and Alban Ponse are thanked for discussing ideas and for giving help in LaTeX, to Jan Bergstra for his comments on the presentation of the *basic* and *conditional* terms and to Frits Vaandrager for giving a first idea of defining the *basic* terms in the way the are defined now. Finally, Martin Wirsing is thanked for suggesting the research of completeness in ACPρ .

References

[BB90] J.C.M. Baeten and J.A. Bergstra. Process algebra with signals and conditions. Report P9008, University of Amsterdam, Amsterdam, 1990.

[BB91] J.C.M. Baeten and J.A. Bergstra. Real time process algebra. *Journal of Formal Aspects of Computing Science*, 3(2):142–188, 1991.

[BK84] J.A. Bergstra and J.W. Klop. Process algebra for synchronous communication. *Information and Computation*, 60(1/3):109–137, 1984.

[BW90] J.C.M. Baeten and W.P. Weijland. *Process algebra*. Cambridge Tracts in Theoretical Computer Science 18. Cambridge University Press, 1990.

[Gla87] R.J. van Glabbeek. Bounded nondeterminism and the approximation induction principle in process algebra. In F.J. Brandenburg, G. Vidal-Naquet, and M. Wirsing, editors, *Proceedings STACS 87*, volume 247 of *Lecture Notes in Computer Science*, pages 336–347. Springer-Verlag, 1987.

[Gro89] J.F. Groote. Transition system specifications with negative premises. Report CS-R8950, CWI, Amsterdam, 1989. An extended abstract appeared in J.C.M. Baeten and J.W. Klop, editors, *Proceedings CONCUR 90*, Amsterdam, LNCS 458, pages 332–341. Springer-Verlag, 1990.

[Gro90] J.F. Groote. Specification and verification of real time systems in ACP. Report CS-R9015, CWI, Amsterdam, 1990. An extended abstract appeared in L. Logrippo, R.L. Probert and H. Ural, editors, *Proceedings* 10th *International Symposium on Protocol Specification, Testing and Verification*, Ottawa, pages 261–274, 1990.

[Jef91] A. Jeffrey. Discrete timed CSP. Technical Report Memo 78, Chalmers University, Goteborg, 1991. This document also appeared in this volume.

[Klu91] A.S. Klusener. Completeness in realtime process algebra. Report CS-R9106, CWI, Amsterdam, 1991.

[Mil80] R. Milner. *A Calculus of Communicating Systems*, volume 92 of *Lecture Notes in Computer Science*. Springer-Verlag, 1980.

[MT90] F. Moller and C. Tofts. A temporal calculus of communicating systems. In J.C.M. Baeten and J.W. Klop, editors, *Proceedings CONCUR 90*, Amsterdam, volume 458 of *Lecture Notes in Computer Science*, pages 401–415. Springer-Verlag, 1990.

[NS90] X. Nicollin and J. Sifakis. ATP: An algebra for timed processes. Technical Report RT-C26, IMAG, Laboratoire de Génie informatique, Grenoble, 1990. An earlier version (RT-C16) appeared in M. Broy and C.B. Jones, editors, *Proceedings IFIP Working Conference on Programming Concepts and Methods*, Sea of Gallilea, Israel. North-Holland, 1990.

[Par81] D.M.R. Park. Concurrency and automata on infinite sequences. In P. Deussen, editor, 5th *GI Conference*, volume 104 of *Lecture Notes in Computer Science*, pages 167–183. Springer-Verlag, 1981.

[Plo81] G.D. Plotkin. A structural approach to operational semantics. Report DAIMI FN-19, Computer Science Department, Aarhus University, 1981.

[RR88] M. Reed and A.W. Roscoe. A timed model for communicating sequential processes. *Theoretical Computer Science*, 58:249–261, 1988.

[Wan90] Y. Wang. Real time behaviour of asynchronous agents. In J.C.M. Baeten and J.W. Klop, editors, *Proceedings CONCUR 90*, Amsterdam, volume 458 of *Lecture Notes in Computer Science*, pages 502–520. Springer-Verlag, 1990.

INT1	$V = V_1 \cup V_2$	$\int_{v \in V_1} a(v) + \int_{v \in V_2} a(v) = \int_{v \in V} a(v)$
INT2		$\int_{v \in \emptyset} a(v) = \delta$
INT3a	$v \notin FV(Y)$	$\int_{v \in V}(a(v)) \cdot Y = \int_{v \in V}(a(v) \cdot Y)$
INT3b	$v \notin FV(Y)$	$\int_{v \in V}(a(v) \cdot X) \cdot Y = \int_{v \in V}(a(v) \cdot (X \cdot Y))$
INT4a		$\{ \forall t \in V : X = X + a(v)[t/v] \} \implies X = X + \int_{v \in V} a(v)$
INT4b		$\{ \forall t \in V : X = X + (a(v) \cdot Y)[t/v] \} \implies X = X + \int_{v \in V}(a(v) \cdot Y)$
INT5		$\{ \forall t \in V : X[t/v] = Y[t/v] \} \implies \int_{v \in V} a(v) \cdot X = \int_{v \in V} a(v) \cdot Y$
ATI1		$a(0) = \delta$
ATI2		$\int_{v \in V}(\delta(v) \cdot X) = \int_{v \in V} \delta(v)$
ATI3		$\int_{v \in V} \delta(v) = \delta(sup(V))$
ATI4	$t \leq sup(V)$	$\int_{v \in V} a(v) + \delta(t) = \int_{v \in V} a(v)$
ATI5		$\int_{v \in V}(a(v) \cdot X) = \int_{v \in V}(a(v) \cdot (v \gg X))$
ATBI1*a*		$t \gg \int_{v \in V} a(v) = \int_{v \in V \cap <t,\omega>} a(v) + \delta(t)$
ATBI1*b*		$t \gg \int_{v \in V}(a(v) \cdot X) = \int_{v \in V \cap <t,\omega>}(a(v) \cdot X) + \delta(t)$
ATB3		$t \gg (X + Y) = (t \gg X) + (t \gg Y)$
ATB4		$t \gg (X \cdot Y) = (t \gg X) \cdot Y$

Table 4: BPA$\rho\delta$I =BPA+INT1,5+ATI1,5+ATBI1+ATB3,4

COND1	$\{tt :\rightarrow p\} = p$
COND2	$\{ff :\rightarrow p\} = \delta$
COND3	$\{\alpha :\rightarrow (\beta :\rightarrow p)\} = \{\alpha \wedge \beta :\rightarrow p\}$
COND4	$\{\alpha :\rightarrow p + q\} = \{\alpha :\rightarrow p\} + \{\alpha :\rightarrow q\}$
COND5	$\{\alpha \vee \beta :\rightarrow p\} = \{\alpha :\rightarrow p\} + \{\beta :\rightarrow p\}$
COND6a	$\{cl \geq sup(V) :\rightarrow cl \gg \int_{v \in V} a(v)\} = \{cl \geq sup(V) :\rightarrow \delta(cl)\}$
COND6b	$\{cl \geq sup(V) :\rightarrow cl \gg \int_{v \in V} a(v) \cdot p\} = \{cl \geq sup(V) :\rightarrow \delta(cl)\}$
	$V_{cl} = V \cap < cl, \omega >$
COND7a	$\{cl < sup(V) :\rightarrow cl \gg \int_{v \in V} a(v)\} = \{cl < sup(V) :\rightarrow \int_{v \in V_{cl}} a(v)\}$
COND7b	$\{cl < sup(V) :\rightarrow cl \gg \int_{v \in V} a(v) \cdot p\} = \{cl < sup(V) :\rightarrow \int_{v \in V_{cl}} a(v) \cdot p\}$
COND8a	$\{V = \emptyset :\rightarrow \int_{v \in V} a(v)\} = \{V = \emptyset :\rightarrow \delta(cl)\}$
COND8b	$\{V = \emptyset :\rightarrow \int_{v \in V} a(v) \cdot p\} = \{V = \emptyset :\rightarrow \delta(cl)\}$
	$(\alpha_1 \wedge v \in W_1), .., (\alpha_{\#I} \wedge v \in W_{\#I})$ **is a partition of** $\Sigma \wedge v \notin tvar(\overline{\alpha})$
COND9	$\{\int_{v \in V} a(v) \cdot (\Sigma_i \{\alpha_i \wedge v \in W_i :\rightarrow p_i\})\} = \Sigma_i \{\alpha_i :\rightarrow \int_{v \in V \cap W_i} a(v) \cdot p_i\}$

Table 5: BPA$\rho\delta$IC = BPA$\rho\delta$I + COND 1-5 + COND6-9

$a, b \in A_\delta, \ V \in Int^{time-closed}$

ATBI5a	$r > inf(V)$	$\int_{v\in V} a(v) \gg r = \int_{v\in V\cap<0,r>} a(v)$
ATBI5b	$r > inf(V)$	$\int_{v\in V}(a(v)\cdot p) \gg r = \int_{v\in V\cap<0,r>}(a(v)\cdot p)$
ATBI6a	$r \leq inf(V)$	$\int_{v\in V} a(v) \gg r = \delta(r)$
ATBI6b	$r \leq inf(V)$	$\int_{v\in V}(a(v)\cdot p) \gg r = \delta(r)$
ATB7		$(X + Y) \gg t = (X \gg t) + (Y \gg t)$
ATB8		$(X \cdot Y) \gg t = (X \gg t) \cdot Y$
ATCI1	$V_0 \cap V_1 \neq \emptyset$	$\int_{v\in V_0} a(v) \mid \int_{v\in V_1} b(v) = \int_{v\in V_0 \cap V_1}(a|b)(v)$
ATCI2	$V_0 \cap V_1 = \emptyset$	$\int_{v\in V_0} a(v) \mid \int_{v\in V_1} b(v) = \delta(min(sup(V_0), sup(V_1)))$
CM1		$X \mid Y = X \mathbin{\rotatebox[origin=c]{180}{L\!\!L}} Y + Y \mathbin{\rotatebox[origin=c]{180}{L\!\!L}} X + X|Y$
ATCMI2		$\int_{v\in V}(a(v)) \mathbin{\rotatebox[origin=c]{180}{L\!\!L}} Y = \int_{v\in V}(a(v) \gg U(Y)) \cdot Y$
ATCMI3	$v \notin FV(Y)$	$\int_{v\in V}(a(v)\cdot X) \mathbin{\rotatebox[origin=c]{180}{L\!\!L}} Y = \int_{v\in V}((a(v) \gg U(Y)) \cdot (X\|Y))$
CM4		$(X + Y) \mathbin{\rotatebox[origin=c]{180}{L\!\!L}} Z = X \mathbin{\rotatebox[origin=c]{180}{L\!\!L}} Y + Y \mathbin{\rotatebox[origin=c]{180}{L\!\!L}} Z$
CMI5	$V_0 \cap V_1 \neq \emptyset$	$\int_{v\in V_0}(a(v)\cdot X) \mid \int_{v\in V_1} b(v) = \int_{v\in V_0 \cap V_1}((a|b)(v)\cdot X)$
CMI5'	$V_0 \cap V_1 = \emptyset$	$\int_{v\in V_0}(a(v)\cdot X) \mid \int_{v\in V_1} b(v) = \delta(min(sup(V_0), sup(V_1)))$
CMI6	$V_0 \cap V_1 \neq \emptyset$	$\int_{v\in V_0} a(v) \mid \int_{v\in V_1}(b(v)\cdot Y) = \int_{v\in V_0 \cap V_1}(a|b)(v) \cdot Y$
CMI6'	$V_0 \cap V_1 = \emptyset$	$\int_{v\in V_0} a(v) \mid \int_{v\in V_1}(b(v)\cdot Y) = \delta(min(sup(V_0), sup(V_1)))$
CMI7	$V_0 \cap V_1 \neq \emptyset$	$\int_{v\in V_0}(a(v)\cdot X) \mid \int_{v\in V_1}(b(v)\cdot Y) = \int_{v\in V_0 \cap V_1}((a|b)(v) \cdot (X\|Y))$
CMI7'	$V_0 \cap V_1 = \emptyset$	$\int_{v\in V_0}(a(v)\cdot X) \mid \int_{v\in V_1}(b(v)\cdot Y) = \delta(min(sup(V_0), min(V_1)))$
CM8		$(X + Y)|Z = X|Z + Y|Z$
CM9		$X|(Y + Z) = X|Y + X|Z$
D1	$a \notin H$	$\delta_H(a) = a$
D2	$a \in H$	$\delta_H(a) = \delta$
ATD		$\delta_H(a(t)) = (\delta_H(a))(t)$
D3		$\delta_H(X + Y) = \delta_H(X) + \delta_H(Y)$
D4		$\delta_H(X \cdot Y) = \delta_H(X) \cdot \delta_H(Y)$

Table 6: ACPρ

$a \in A, r > 0$

atom $\quad : \quad r \in V \quad \int_{v \in V}(a(v)) \xrightarrow{a(r)} \checkmark$

$$r \in V \quad \int_{v \in V}(a(v) \cdot p) \xrightarrow{a(r)} r \gg (p[r/v])$$

$\cdot \quad : \quad \dfrac{p \xrightarrow{a(r)} \checkmark}{p \cdot q \xrightarrow{a(r)} r \gg q} \qquad\qquad \dfrac{p \xrightarrow{a(r)} p'}{p \cdot q \xrightarrow{a(r)} p' \cdot q}$

$+ \quad : \quad \dfrac{p \xrightarrow{a(r)} \checkmark}{p + q \xrightarrow{a(r)} \checkmark,\ q + p \xrightarrow{a(r)} \checkmark} \qquad \dfrac{p \xrightarrow{a(r)} p'}{p + q \xrightarrow{a(r)} p',\ q + p \xrightarrow{a(r)} p'}$

$\gg \quad : \quad \dfrac{s < r \quad p \xrightarrow{a(r)} \checkmark}{s \gg p \xrightarrow{a(r)} \checkmark} \qquad\qquad \dfrac{s < r \quad p \xrightarrow{a(r)} p'}{s \gg p \xrightarrow{a(r)} p'}$

$a \in A$

$\| \quad : \quad \dfrac{p \xrightarrow{a(r)} p' \quad r < U(q)}{p\|q \xrightarrow{a(r)} p'\|(r \gg q),\ \ q\|p \xrightarrow{a(r)} (r \gg q)\|p',\ \ p\lfloor\!\lfloor q \xrightarrow{a(r)} p'\|(r \gg q)}$

$$\dfrac{p \xrightarrow{a(r)} \checkmark \quad r < U(q)}{p\|q \xrightarrow{a(r)} r \gg q,\ \ q\|p \xrightarrow{a(r)} r \gg q,\ \ p\lfloor\!\lfloor q \xrightarrow{a(r)} r \gg q}$$

$\square \in \{|, \|\} \quad : \quad \dfrac{p \xrightarrow{a(r)} p' \quad q \xrightarrow{b(r)} q' \quad a|b = c \neq \delta}{p \square q \xrightarrow{c(r)} p'\|q'} \qquad \dfrac{p \xrightarrow{a(r)} \checkmark \quad q \xrightarrow{b(r)} \checkmark \quad a|b = c \neq \delta}{p \square q \xrightarrow{c(r)} \checkmark}$

$$\dfrac{p \xrightarrow{a(r)} \checkmark \quad q \xrightarrow{b(r)} q' \quad a|b = c \neq \delta}{p \square q \xrightarrow{c(r)} q',\ q \square p \xrightarrow{c(r)} q'}$$

$\lfloor\!\lfloor \quad : \quad \dfrac{p \xrightarrow{a(r)} p' \quad r < U(q)}{p \lfloor\!\lfloor q \xrightarrow{a(r)} p'\|(r \gg q)} \qquad\qquad \dfrac{p \xrightarrow{a(r)} \checkmark \quad r < U(q)}{p \lfloor\!\lfloor q \xrightarrow{a(r)} r \gg q}$

$\gg \quad : \quad \dfrac{s > r \quad p \xrightarrow{a(r)} p'}{p \gg s \xrightarrow{a(r)} p'} \qquad\qquad \dfrac{s > r \quad p \xrightarrow{a(r)} \checkmark}{p \gg s \xrightarrow{a(r)} \checkmark}$

$\delta_H \quad : \quad \dfrac{p \xrightarrow{a(r)} p' \quad a \notin H}{\delta_H(p) \xrightarrow{a(r)} p'}$

$$\dfrac{U(p) > L(p)}{p \xrightarrow{\delta(U(p))} \checkmark}$$

Table 7: Action Rules for ACPρ

Distributed CCS

Padmanabhan Krishnan *†
Department of Computer Science
Ny Munkegade Building 540
Aarhus University
DK 8000, Aarhus C Denmark
E-mail: paddy@daimi.aau.dk

Abstract

In this paper we describe a technique to extend a process language such as CCS which does not model many aspects of distributed computation to one which does. The idea is to use a concept of location which represents a virtual node. Processes at different locations can evolve independently. Furthermore, communication between processes at different locations occurs via explicit message passing. We extend CCS with locations and message passing primitives and present its operational semantics. We show that the equivalences induced by the new semantics and its properties are similar to the equivalences in CCS. We also show how the semantics of configuration and routing can be handled.

1 Introduction

A number of different types of parallel and distributed machines have been built. These include vector machines [Rus78] data driven/demand driven machines [TBH82], shared memory systems (like the Sequent) and distributed memory systems ranging from a network of work stations to well structured architectures like the hypercube. More parameters such as heterogeneity, reliability for fault-tolerance etc. add to the variation. Despite the variety, a common factor is the presence of multiple processing elements and interconnection between them. For such machines to be useful, applications must use the multiple processors, which requires the decomposition of the application into partitions which can be executed in parallel. Any co-operation between the partitions (synchronization, communication etc.) must utilize the interconnections.

Given the wide variety of architectures, it is not surprising that a variety of programming languages have been proposed; each addressing a subset of the architectures. Many languages are based on the message passing between a set of parallel processors [INM88]. Other approaches include using a distributed data-structure (tuple space [Gel85]), using the parallelism available in functional programs, parallel logic languages [CG83]. [Mar89] gives an detailed description of

*The author acknowledges support from the Danish Research Council

†Current address: Department of Computer Science, University of Canterbury, Christchurch 1, New Zealand, E-Mail: paddy@cosc.canterbury.ac.nz

the various approaches. Our aim is to develop a calculus in which the following can be studied: 1) Expressing parallelism, 2) Describing the effect of parallelism and 3) Mapping of the expressed parallelism to a physical environment.

Labeled transition systems have been used to describe concurrent systems [Mil80]. The syntax of CCS is simple and yet powerful enough to express parallelism, non-determinism and synchronization. However, it does not address issues to related to modeling the physical environment. Also the operational semantics of CCS reduces parallelism to non-determinism (or interleaved execution of actions: the expansion theorem for CCS). This is due to the presence of only one observer with the power to observe one action at a time. We provide a semantics for CCS which is "distributed". Given that there is no uniformity in the nature of distributed architecture, one needs to define "distributed". For that we consider the natural language meaning of the terms concurrent, distributed and parallelism. Concurrent is defined as "happening together in time or place"; distributed as "scattered or spread out over a surface" and parallelism as "without interactive causal relationship". In CCS concurrent has the interpretation of place or processor. Thus it is not surprising that parallelism, given one place, reduces to non-determinism. Our goal is to "scatter parallelism over a surface".

Given that parallelism is to be mapped over a surface, the question arises as whether to allow the process to contain some information regarding the mapping. If so, another level of abstraction can be created. The mapping information available in the process can be considered to a logical representation of the surface. One then studies the effect of mapping a logical surface to a physical surface. In distributed computation, one considers the representation of distribution also called binding and the mapping of binding to the physical surface, i.e., configuring. This view is indeed taken by the advocates of the virtual node approach to distributed computing [CM87]. Thus there are two stages in program construction, viz., 1) distributed surface with logical binding and 2) the configuration of distributed memory

In section 2 a semantics for distributed memory systems is developed and in section 3 some of the issues related to program development are discussed. In section 4 a few examples are presented.

2 Distributed CCS

Distributed systems do not share memory and hence the location of a process in the system is important. Given a number of processors, a process can only use the processor associated with the memory unless it is explicitly relocated. As both binding and configuration are to be considered, an extension to CCS is necessary. A notion of location has been introduced in CCS [KHCB91] to study the distributed nature of processes. Their primary concern is the logical construction of processes without considering the architecture the process is executing on. The idea of location has also been used in other languages [Hud86]. We use the same syntax as in [KHCB91] but give a different semantics.

In the semantics for CCS, any two processes could synchronize. This cannot be permitted in the distributed case. A local transition depending on behavior at a remote site is unrealistic. Consider, for example, the CCS process ($(a+b) \mid (\bar{a}+\bar{b})$)$\backslash\{a,b\}$. If the two parallel processes are physically distributed, the decision to execute a(or b) has to be taken in co-ordination with the $\bar{a}$(or $\bar{b}$). If a general CCS process is to be executed on a physically distributed environment a non-trivial protocol to effect these decisions is essential. Therefore, deriving a distributed implementation from the operational semantics is not straight forward.

For the distributed case, a protocol based on the send/receive primitives is more appropriate. This then requires a definition of buffers, where the messages sent are stored before actually 'used' by the process. Towards this, we assume special actions such as $\overset{<l,a>}{\leadsto}$, which indicates the sending of action a to location l. This message is buffered by a process on location n by creating a process which can engage only in action 'a'. This can be generalized to communicating an arbitrary process. As we do not limit the number of parallel terms in a process, unbounded buffering is modeled.

Definition: 1 *Define a finite set of locations $\mathcal{L}$, a set of local actions Lact (represented by a,b), a set of sending actions Sact (represented by $\overset{<l,a>}{\leadsto}$). The cardinality of Sact is less than or equal to the cardinality of $\mathcal{L}\times$ Lact. Let τ represent synchronization and δ represent idling (of a location). The set of actions is Act = Lact $\cup$ Sact $\cup$ $\{\tau, \delta\}$.*

The basic syntax for our language (with μ being any action, l any location, and H a subset of Act) is as follows:

$$P = \text{Nil} \mid \mu\ ;P \mid (P \mid P) \mid P + P \mid (l{::}\ P) \mid (P \ \backslash H) \mid \text{rec}(\widetilde{X}{:}\widetilde{E})$$

Nil is a process which can exhibit no further action. μ ;P represents action prefix; i.e., after executing μ the processes behaves as P. (P | Q) is the parallel combination of P and Q, while P+Q represents choice between P and Q. (l::P) restricts the execution of P to location l, (P \H) restricts the behavior of P to those actions not in H. rec($\widetilde{X}{:}\widetilde{E}$) is recursive process. We place the usual restrictions that terms must be closed and the recursion guarded.

Given that a process has location information, an observation now is a pair consisting of action and location. As processes on different locations can execute in parallel behavior is characterized by a set of observations with the restriction that processes can exhibit multiple actions if they are at different locations. Process can synchronize if the are at the same location. A structural operational semantics [Plo81] is defined as an generalization of the rules for CCS. We assume that the following black-box is a model of a distributed system which runs a process given a set of processing elements (locations). There is a step line which when toggled advances each processing element by one step. The observer first toggles the machine and then notes the behavior on each of the locations (which may appear at different times with respect to a global clock) and the process continues. This is similar to the step semantics developed for Petri Nets [vGV87].

The following definitions are used in the operational semantics which is defined in figure 1.

Definition: 2 *Let $\mathcal{O}_L$ represent the function space from $\mathcal{L} \rightarrow$ Act. This is used by the operational semantics to identify the action observed at any location.*

Definition: 3 *Define the transition relation $\longrightarrow_D \subseteq$ Processes $\times\ \mathcal{O}_L \times$ Processes, Also define two projection functions Location and Action, which return the location/action part of the observation.*

Definition: 4 *Define S1+S2 as follows: S1+S2 = S where*

$$S(l) = \begin{cases} S1(l) & if\ S2(l) = \delta \\ S2(l) & if\ S1(l) = \delta \\ \tau & if\ S1(l) = \overline{S2(l)} \end{cases}$$

The idea is that the two behaviors (S1 and S2) can be exhibited in one step if the non-idling actions are on different locations. If a location can exhibit two actions, they must be synchronizable and the combined behavior will exhibit τ.

The distributed operational semantics is defined in figure 1. We label the transition with only the non-idle observations. All locations not present on the label are assumed to exhibit the idle action (δ).

An informal explanation of the semantics follows. A process with no location can be executed at any location. However, the remainder of the process is constrained to executed at that location. This can be thought of as the initial loading of a process. The sending of a message to a particular location results in creating a process at that location which can only engage in the action contained in the message. Furthermore, the message passing is visible to the observer. As we have not *named* processes, one cannot send a message to a particular process. This can be simulated by ensuring only 'one process' at a location, and the result of sending messages to it as the buffers. A process already assigned a location can exhibit actions on that location. In the operational semantics of l::P we do not restrict P' to location l. The restriction is introduced by the transition of P. Furthermore, P could have evolved to P' via a send (say to location m) in which case P' has the structure: l::P"| m::a. Then l::P' cannot exhibit a.

In this paper we do not consider relocating the processes to the appropriate location. Processes can evolve 'independently' of other processes modeling asynchronous behavior (the first | rule). The parallel combination of two processes

Lact Prefix	$a; P \xrightarrow{\{<l,a>\}}_D l :: P \forall l \in \mathcal{L}$
Sact Prefix	$\overset{<m,a>}{\rightsquigarrow}; P \xrightarrow{\{<l, \overset{<m,a>}{\rightsquigarrow}>\}}_D (l :: P) \mid (m :: a) \forall l \in \mathcal{L}$
Location	$\dfrac{P \xrightarrow{\{<l,\mu>\}}_D P'}{l :: P \xrightarrow{\{<l,\mu>\}}_D P'}$
Interleaving (Asynchronous Evolution)	$\dfrac{P \xrightarrow{S}_D P'}{\begin{array}{c} P \mid Q \xrightarrow{S}_D P' \mid Q \\ Q \mid P \xrightarrow{S}_D Q \mid P' \end{array}}$
Parallelism	$\dfrac{P \xrightarrow{S1}_D P',\ Q \xrightarrow{S2}_D Q',\ S = S1 + S2}{\begin{array}{c} P \mid Q \xrightarrow{S}_D P' \mid Q' \\ Q \mid P \xrightarrow{S}_D Q' \mid P' \end{array}}$
Hiding	$\dfrac{\begin{array}{c} P \xrightarrow{S}_D P', \\ \text{Action(S)} \cap H = \emptyset \text{ and Action(S)} \cap \overline{H} = \emptyset \end{array}}{P \backslash H \xrightarrow{S}_D P' \backslash H}$
Recursion	$\dfrac{E_i(\text{rec } \widetilde{X}\text{: } \widetilde{E}/X) \xrightarrow{S}_D P'}{\text{rec}_i X\text{:}E \xrightarrow{S}_D P'}$

Figure 1: Operational Semantics

exhibit 'true concurrency' if their locations are disjoint. Processes can also synchronize in the usual way. The hiding operator restricts the actions a process can exhibit. The restriction applies to all locations.

2.1 Bisimulation

In this section we establish a equivalence relation between processes based on the well known notion of bisimulation [Par81]. The use of bisimulation is to identify processes which cannot be distinguished by an observer. For this draft we assume that the observer is equipped to observe a single action (including synchronization, idling) at every location.

Definition: 5 *Define a relation on processes $\mathcal{R}$ to be a bisimulation such that if $P \mathcal{R} Q$ then*

$P \xrightarrow{S}_D P' \Rightarrow \exists\, Q'$ *such that* $Q \xrightarrow{S}_D Q'$ *and* $P' \mathcal{R} Q'$ *and*

$Q \xrightarrow{S}_D Q' \Rightarrow \exists\, P'$ *such that* $P \xrightarrow{S}_D P'$ *and* $Q' \mathcal{R} P'$

Definition: 6 $\sim_D\ = \bigcup\{\mathcal{R}$ *such that* $\mathcal{R}$ *is a bisimulation*$\}$

Proposition 1 $\sim_D$ *is a congruence*

$P+Q \sim_D Q+P$

$(P+Q)+R \sim_D P+(Q+R)$

$P+P \sim_D P$

$P \mid Q \sim_D Q \mid P$

$(P \mid Q) \mid R \sim_D P \mid (Q \mid R)$

$P \mid Nil \sim_D P$

$l :: (P \mid Q) \sim_D (l:: P) \mid (l::Q)$

$l::(P+Q) \sim_D (l::P) + (l::Q)$

$l::(P\backslash H) \sim_D (l::P) \backslash H$

Proposition 2 *If $(l1 \neq l2)$, $l1::(l2::P) \sim_D Nil$.*

Proposition 3 *If P and Q are processes without location, $(l :: P) \sim_D (l :: Q)$ implies $P \sim_D Q$*

The above proposition does not hold if P and Q are allowed to contain locations. For example, if P = l:: nil and Q = m:: a, l::P $\sim_D$ l::Q but P is not $\sim_D$ Q.

As we have assumed only one processor (or observer) at any given location, the expansion theorem for CCS translates directly to the location case.

Proposition 4 *If* $P = \sum_I a_i; P_i$ *and* $Q = \sum_J b_j; Q_j$ *then*
$l{::}\ (P \mid Q) \sim_D\ l{::}\ (\sum_I a_i;\ (P_i \mid Q)\ ) + l{::}\ (\sum_J b_j;\ (Q_j \mid P)) + l{::}\ (\sum_{a_i = \overline{b_j}} \tau; (P_i \mid Q_j))$

Example 1 *Note that the expansion theorem in CCS is not valid directly. In general, (a | b) is not bisimilar to a;b + b;a. If there are two locations (l and m), (a | b) can exhibit* $< m, a >, < l, b >$*, which a;b+b;a cannot exhibit. But l::(a | b) is bisimilar to l::(a;b + b;a).*

However, a;(b;c + c;b) is bisimilar to a;(b | c). This is because the execution of action a fixes the location for the remainder of the process. If a parallel execution of b and c is to be permitted the process can be coded as follows. Let l_1 *and* l_2 *be two distinct locations.* $(a; \overset{<l_1,t>}{\rightsquigarrow}; \overset{<l_2,t>}{\rightsquigarrow}) \mid (l_1 :: \bar{t}; b) \mid (l_2 :: \bar{t}; c) \setminus \{t\}$. *The termination of the action a is explicitly sent to the two locations. Processes at the two locations wait for this information before proceeding in parallel.*

Proposition 5 *If* $\mathcal{L} = \{\ l1,\ l2, \ldots ln\}$,

$$a;P \sim_D \sum_{li \in \mathcal{L}} li :: (a; P)$$

$$P \mid Q \sim_D \sum_{li \in \mathcal{L}} (li{::}P) \mid Q + \sum_{li \in \mathcal{L}} P \mid (li{::}Q)$$

Bisimilarity involving the hiding operator is more complex than in CCS. In CCS (b;P)\{a} is bisimilar to Nil if b is equal to a, and to b;(P\{a}) otherwise. While this holds in our case the relation involving send actions is not straight forward. For example, $l :: (\overset{<m,c>}{\rightsquigarrow}; b \mid\ m :: a) \setminus \{a\}$ is bisimilar to l::$\overset{<m,c>}{\rightsquigarrow}$;b. This is because the a action on m cannot be executed and there is no action which sends $\bar{a}$ to location m. However, $(l :: \overset{<m,a>}{\rightsquigarrow}) \setminus \{a\}$ is not bisimilar to $l :: \overset{<m,a>}{\rightsquigarrow}$ as the latter can exhibit a at location m; nor is it bisimilar to Nil as the former can exhibit a send action. Similarly $l :: (\overset{<m,\bar{a}>}{\rightsquigarrow}; b \mid\ m :: a) \setminus \{a\}$ is in 'normal form' as there is a causal link between the send action and the b action on l and the a action on m. These observations play an important role when considering the axiomatization of the bisimulation equivalence which will be reported in a forthcoming paper.

In the above definition of bisimulation equivalence, we assumed that the observer could observe the τaction. The equivalence constructed is referred to as strong bisimulation. Another equivalence which is well studied is weak equivalence. Towards that, a transition relation $\Longrightarrow$ as P $\overset{a}{\Longrightarrow}$ Q iff P $(\overset{\delta}{\longrightarrow})^* \overset{a}{\longrightarrow} (\overset{\delta}{\longrightarrow})^*$ is defined. The generalization to the above definition to the distributed case is not straight forward. This is because we define a stepped semantics and evolutions from multiple locations is possible. For example, transitions such as P $\overset{<l,a>,<m,\tau>}{\longrightarrow}_D$ P' have to be mapped to one without τ. Omitting the $< m, \tau >$ is not advisable. If P were placed in a parallel context (such as P | Q) Q would be able to exhibit an action at location m in the same step as P exhibits $< l, a >$. By disallowing step semantics one can use the original definition, but the presence of step semantics requires a reformulation. An appropriate reformulation of observational equivalence in the presence of step semantics is being studied.

2.2 Testing

In this section we look at the applicability of the ideas developed in [DH84] for testing distributed processes. CCS processes are tested by CCS processes equipped with a special action ω which indicates success. Two basic types of testing are defined as follows:

Definition: 7

A process p **may satisfy** *a test o if* $(o \mid p) \xrightarrow{\tau*} q$ *and* $q \xrightarrow{\omega}$.

A process p **must satisfy** *a test o if* $(o \mid p) \xrightarrow{\tau} (o_1 \mid p_1) \xrightarrow{\tau} \ldots (o_i \mid p_i)$ *then* $\exists\, n \geq 0,\ o_n \xrightarrow{\omega}$ *and if* $(o_k \mid p_k)$ *can diverge, then for some* $k' \leq k$, $o_{k'} \xrightarrow{\omega}$ *(also called the existence of a successful extension).*

A similar technique can be used for distributed processes. However, given the current definition of the operational semantics, permitting only τ's in the testing relation is not sufficient. In CCS all non-τ actions had a corresponding synchronization action. In our extension, elements of Sact cannot be synchronized to produce a τ action. Therefore, one cannot differentiate between l::(a + $\overset{<m,b>}{\rightsquigarrow}$) and l::(a). Therefore one has to permit send actions to be part of the testing process. If one considers τas communication at a local site, then send actions are communications across sites and contribute to the testing process.

The semantics of the parallel combinator permits both 'asynchronous interleaving' and 'simultaneous evolution' of processes at different locations. The testing process must be permitted to test for transitions at different locations; otherwise it will not be able to distinguish l::(a; $\overset{<m,b>}{\rightsquigarrow}$;c) and l::(a; $\overset{<m,d>}{\rightsquigarrow}$;c). However the testing procedure may be restricted to observe only interleaving of actions across all locations.

Another issue is the observation of success. One may insist that a test is successful only if ω is observed at 'all locations'. However, it is not possible to know a priori all the locations involved. Thus an observation of ω at any location is considered to be a success.

Definition: 8

A process p **may satisfy** *a test o (written as p* **may** *o) if* $(o \mid p) \xrightarrow{TO_1}_D q_1 \xrightarrow{TO_2}_D q_2 \ldots q$ *and* $q \xrightarrow{\{<l,\omega>\}}_D$ *for some location l, where each* TO_i *is a partial function from* $\mathcal{L} \rightarrow (\{\tau, \delta\} \cup Sact)$

A process p **must satisfy** *a test o (written as p* **must** *o) if every evolution of* $(o \mid p)$ *is either successful (i.e., exhibits* ω *at some location) or has a successful extension.*

Definition: 9

$p \simeq_{may} q$: $\forall$ *tests* o, p **may** o *iff* q **may** o.
$p \simeq_{must} q$: $\forall$ o, p **must** o *iff* q **must** o.
$p \simeq q$: $p \simeq_{may} q$ *and* $p \simeq_{must} q$.

Example 2 *Given at least two distinct locations, l and m, $(a;b + b;a) \not\simeq (a \mid b)$. Consider the testing process $(l{::}\bar{a};\overset{<m,c>}{\rightsquigarrow} \mid m{::}\bar{c};\bar{b};\omega\ )\backslash\{c\}$. The first process cannot pass the test while the second may pass the test. Note that the synchronization between the two branches of the tester is essential. If one had only $m{::}\ (\bar{b};\omega\ )$ then both the process will pass the test. Thus we have defined a 'non-interleaving' testing equivalence.*

Proposition 6 $\simeq$ *is substitutive with respect to* $\mid$

Proposition 7 $P \sim_D\ Q$ *implies* $P \simeq Q$.

Proposition 8 *If P and Q are CCS terms, $P \simeq_{CCS}\ Q$ implies $l{::}P \simeq l{::}Q$.*

Further study is necessary to characterize the differences between bisimulation and testing equivalences for the distributed processes.

3 Program Development

While a theory usually abstracts away issues related to implementation details, it should be possible to derive a implementation dependent semantics from the more abstract semantics. Distributed program development can be divided in two phases: 1) Binding and 2) Configuration. In the binding phase the system is specified with an expected architecture. For example, the sorting algorithm used for hypercubes will be different than the algorithm used for trees. Thus the specification of the algorithm indicates the architecture. One can consider that CCS with location addresses the issue of binding. A specification may assume the availability of a certain number of processing elements. But the physical architecture may be smaller. The issue then is to map the expected set onto the physical set which is called configuration. In the following two subsections we show how a semantics related to mapping the logical architecture to the physical one can be derived from the distributed semantics.

3.1 Configuration

Configuration is the mapping of a logically distributed program to a physical network. Usually, the number of processing elements in the physical network is less than the number of logically distributed units. One can represent the physical network by a set of locations and define a function Config: $\mathcal{L} \rightarrow \mathcal{L}'$, where

$\mathcal{L}$' represents the physical sites. Define a translation of a process using $\mathcal{L}$ into a process using $\mathcal{L}$' as follows. $\mathcal{L}$ represents the logical parallelism used in defining processes while $\mathcal{L}$' is the physical parallelism permitted.

Trans(a;P) = a;Trans(P)

Trans($\overset{<l,a>}{\rightsquigarrow}$;P) = $\overset{<Config(l),a>}{\rightsquigarrow}$;P

Trans(P | Q) = Trans(P) | Trans(Q)

Trans(P + Q) = Trans(P) + Trans(Q)

Trans(l::P) = Config(l)::Anchor(P,l)

Anchor(a;P, m) = a;Anchor(P,m)

Anchor($\overset{<l,a>}{\rightsquigarrow}$;P,m) = $\overset{<Config(l),a>}{\rightsquigarrow}$;Anchor(P,m)

Anchor((P | Q),m) = Anchor(P,m) | Anchor(Q,m)

Anchor((P + Q),m) = Anchor(P,m) + Anchor(Q,m)

Anchor(l::P,m) = Nil if l $\neq$ m

Anchor(l::P,m) = l::Anchor(P,m) if l = m

Trans converts all the old locations to the appropriate new locations. Anchor is needed to ensure that processes which could not exhibit any action continue to remain so under configuration. If Trans(l::P) were defined to be Config(l)::Trans(P) this property is not retained as shown by the following example.

Example 3 *Consider l::(m:: a) with l $\neq$ m. It is bisimilar to Nil under $\longrightarrow_D$. However, if Config(l)=Config(m)=m' l::(m::a) will be m'::(m'::a) which can exhibit action a. The intuition is that a 'wrongly' constructed program cannot be rectified at the binding stage.*

Proposition 9 *(P $\sim_D$ Q) implies (Trans(P) $\sim_D$ Trans(Q))*

The above result can be generalized to relate configurations.

Definition: 10 *Let Conf1, Conf2: $\mathcal{L} \rightarrow \mathcal{L}$'.*
Define Conf1 $\leq$ Conf2 iff Conf2(l)=Conf2(m) implies Conf1(l)=Conf1(m)

Thus, if Conf1 $\leq$ Conf2, processes under Conf2 can exhibit 'more parallelism', which gives the following proposition.

Proposition 10 *Conf2(P) $\sim_D$ Conf2(Q) implies Conf1(P) $\sim_D$ Conf1(Q)*

3.2 Routing

In the distributed semantics we tacitly assumed a fully connected topology. This is acceptable for logical purposes. However, when mapping onto a physical network, a transfer from one location to another could make a number of hops. This information will depend on the routing tables used.

Definition: 11 *Define a routing table as a function: $\mathcal{L} \times \mathcal{L} \rightarrow \mathcal{L}$. Route(l,m) = n (and $m \neq n$) is to be read as the route from l to m uses the connection from l to n.*

A new location semantics using the routing information can be defined as follows.

$$\frac{P \xrightarrow{\{<l, \overset{<n,a>}{\leadsto}>\}}_D P', \ (m \neq n), \ \text{Route(l,n)=m}}{P \xrightarrow{\{l, \overset{<n,a>}{\leadsto}\}}_R P' \mid m{::}\overset{<n,a>}{\leadsto};\text{nil}}$$

$$\frac{P \xrightarrow{\{<l, \overset{<n,a>}{\leadsto}>\}}_D P', \ \text{Route(l,n)=n}}{P \xrightarrow{\{l, \overset{<n,a>}{\leadsto}\}}_R P' \mid n{::}\ a; Nil}$$

Proposition 11 *As expected ($P \sim_R Q$) iff ($P \sim_D Q$)*

4 Examples

In this section we present a few examples of distributed processing.

Example 4 *The following is an encoding of RPC [BN81]. A caller process sends a request to the callee and waits for a response. The callee waits for a request, calls the procedure and sends an acknowledgement. The calling of the procedure is denoted by a and the response by b. The actual procedure (call-procedure) is modeled as an action.*

$caller = \overset{<m,a>}{\leadsto};\ \bar{b};\ caller$

$callee = \bar{a};\ call\text{-}procedure;\ \overset{<l,b>}{\leadsto};\ callee$

$System = (\ (l{::}caller) \mid (m{::}callee))\setminus\{a,b\}$

Though the above code assumes a fixed location to send the response the location of the caller can be coded to be part of the action.

$caller_i = \overset{<m,a_i>}{\leadsto};\ \bar{b};\ caller$

$callee = \sum_i \overline{a_i};\ call\text{-}procedure;\ \overset{<l_i,b>}{\leadsto};\ callee$

$System = (\ (\prod_i l_i{::}caller) \mid (m{::}callee))\ \backslash\{a,b\}$

Example 5 *The following is an encoding of call streams [LS88]. Here the caller does not wait for an the acknowledgement. If continues its local processing (local-processing) and is willing to accept an acknowledgement when it has arrived.*

$caller = \overset{\langle m,a\rangle}{\rightsquigarrow};\ (\bar{b};\ caller + local\text{-}processing;\ caller)$

$callee = \bar{a};\ call\text{-}procedure;\ \overset{\langle l,b\rangle}{\rightsquigarrow};\ callee$

$System = (\ (l{::}caller) \mid (m{::}callee))\ \backslash\{a,b\}$

Example 6 *Encoding of tuple space as in Linda [Gel85]. In this example, we assume that there are two process (out1 and out2) which output to the tuple space; one process which removes tuples from the tuple space (in) and a process which reads the tuple space (read). The tuple space receives an in request and then returns a tuple in its space. The removal of the tuple is 'tacit' due to the semantics of synchronization. The read request is handled similarly except that the tuple is 'regenerated' as the synchronization removed it. The tuple space (tup) can either accept either an in action, or a read action. In our example, ci is the location of the in process, cr the location of the read process and tup the location of the tuple space.*

$out1 = \overset{\langle t,a\rangle}{\rightsquigarrow};out1$

$out2 = \overset{\langle t,b\rangle}{\rightsquigarrow};out2$

$in = \overset{\langle t,i\rangle}{\rightsquigarrow};(\bar{a};in + \bar{b};in)$

$read = \overset{\langle t,r\rangle}{\rightsquigarrow};(\bar{a};read + \bar{b};read)$

$tup = \bar{i};(\bar{a};\overset{\langle ci,a\rangle}{\rightsquigarrow};tup + \bar{b};\overset{\langle cr,b\rangle}{\rightsquigarrow};tup) + \bar{r};(\bar{a};((\overset{\langle cr,a\rangle}{\rightsquigarrow};tup) \mid a;nil) + \bar{b};(\ (\overset{\langle cr,b\rangle}{\rightsquigarrow};tup)$
$\quad \mid b;nil)\ )$

$System = (out1 \mid out2 \mid c1{::}in \mid cr{::}read \mid t{::}\ tup)\ \backslash\{a,\ b\}$

Example 7 *Consider a printer(Pr) which interacts with a generator(Gen) and a console (Cs). The generator issues the print command. The console is informed about the status by the printer. If the printer is fine (ok) it waits a request (req) and prints it (print). If it is out of paper, it informs the console (op) and waits for new paper to be added. The first set of definitions present the specification in CCS, while the second uses asynchronous message passing.*

$Gen = pc;req;Gen$

$Pr = (ok;\ \overline{req};\ print;\ Pr) + (op;\ \overline{np};\ Pr)$

$Cs = (\overline{op};\ np;\ Cs) + (\overline{ok};\ Cs)$

$Sys = (Gen \mid Pr \mid Cs) \backslash \{req,op,np,ok\}$

The distributed process is as follows.

$Gen = pc;\ \overset{<prl,rp>}{\leadsto};\ Gen$

$Pr = (\overset{<csl,ok>}{\leadsto};\ \overline{req};\ print;\ Pr) + (\overset{<csl,op>}{\leadsto};\ \overline{np};\ Pr)$

$Cs = (\overline{op};\ \overset{<prl,np>}{\leadsto};\ Cs) + (\overline{ok};\ Cs)$

$Sys = ((gl{::}Gen) \mid (prl{::}Pr) \mid (csl{::}Cs)) \backslash \{req,op,np,ok\}$

In the CCS version, the generator can proceed only when the printer is ready. However, in the asynchronous case, there is no limit on the number of items to be printed before printing occurs. The creating of the 'message' processes can be thought of as the spool area. Also notice that ordering of ok messages between the printer and the console need not be preserved. However, the printer cannot continue if it is out paper until the console has fixed the problem. The above observations are valid even if the configuration assigns the three processes to the same processing element. The difference is in the send actions and the number of actions observed in a step.

5 Related Work

CCS with location was introduced in [KHCB91]. The main operational rules in their semantics are as follows: $a; p \xrightarrow[u]{a} p \quad u \in Loc^*$ and $\dfrac{p \xrightarrow[t]{a} p'}{v :: p \xrightarrow[vu]{a} v :: p'}$

The main difference of our semantics, is that we do not allow the evolution of processes such as v::u::P with v $\neq$ u. The evolution is permitted by [KHCB91] as they are concerned with the structure of the process rather than implementing a process on a distributed architecture. A location string 'vu' indicates that it is a sub-location of 'v'. They also assume an infinite number of locations and distinguish between $a; (b \mid c)$ and $a; (b; c + c; b)$. Similarly [CH89] present a distributed bisimulation semantics. The motivation and the results is similar to [KHCB91]. A detailed comparison between [KHCB91] and [CH89] is presented in [KHCB91]. In short, both the approaches consider spatial issues in distributed computation at the logical level. They do not consider limitations imposed by a physical architecture. Our semantics is also similar to step semantics [vGV87] but we have bounded the number of processes that can evolve in one step by the number of locations present. In 'distributed semantics' such as [DDM88] the primary concern is causality and not physically distributed computing elements. In the Chemical Abstract Machine [BB89], synchronization in a distributed environment is achieved by 'moving' the processes 'next to each other'. This while resulting in a nice theory is not accurate for all systems. In actual systems, processes are usually static and communicate with messages. This is not surprising as the programming paradigm on which the Chemical abstraction Machine is based [BCM88] assumes that all data is available in shared storage.

6 Conclusion

This is very much a working paper. We have used of idea of locations to denote distribution and presented a semantics based on the restrictions imposed by distributed hardware. Much more work is essential to understand the effect of a distributed architecture on process behavior. We have outlined a few basic results for strong bisimulation and testing equivalences. Issues such as weak equivalence, a complete axiomatization for these equivalences etc. need to be investigated. We have also outlined how configuration and routing can be handled. A few examples demonstrating the use of our location CCS has been presented. The applicability of this to more specific architectures such as cube, meshes etc. are currently under study.

Acknowledgement

The author is thankful to Uffe Engberg for many suggestions one of which was to use locations to characterize distribution. Thanks also to Peter Mosses and Jens Palsberg for taking a keen interest in this work.

References

[BB89] G. Berry and G. Boudol. The Chemical Abstract Machine. Technical Report 1133, INRIA-Sophia Antipolis, December 1989.

[BCM88] J. P. Banatre, A. Coutant, and D. Metayer. A Parallel Machine for Multiset Transformation and its Programming Style. *Future Generation Computer Systems*, 4:133–144, 1988.

[BN81] A.D. Birrell and B.J. Nelson. Implementing Remote Procedure Calls. *ACM Transactions on Computer Systems*, 2(4):39–59, February 1981.

[CG83] K. L. Clark and S Gregory. PARLOG :A Parallel Logic Programming Language. Technical Report 5, Imperial College, May 1983.

[CH89] I. Castellani and M. Hennessy. Distributed Bisimulations. *Journal of the Association for Computing Machinery*, 36(4):887–911, October 1989.

[CM87] K. M. Chandy and J. Misra. Parallelsim and Programming: A Perspective. In *Foundations of Software Technology and Theoretical Computer Science, LNCS 287*, pages 173–194. Springer Verlag, 1987.

[DDM88] P. Degano, R. DeNicola, and U. Montanari. A Distributed Operational Semantics for CCS Based on Condition/Event Systems. *Acta Informatica*, 26:59–91, 1988.

[DH84] R. DeNicola and M. C. B. Hennessy. Testing Equivalences for Processes. *Theoretical Computer Science*, 34:83–133, 1984.

[Gel85] D. Gelernter. Generative Communication in Linda. *ACM Transactions on Programming Language and Systems*, 7(1):80–112, Jan 1985.

[Hud86] P. Hudak. Parafunctional Programming. *IEEE Computer*, 19(8):60–71, 1986.

[INM88] INMOS Ltd. **occam-2** *Reference Manual*. Prentice Hall, 1988.

[KHCB91] A. Kiehn, M. Hennessy, I. Castellani, and G. Boudol. Observing Localities. In *Workshop on Concurrency and Compositionality: Goslar*, 1991.

[LS88] B. Liskov and L. Shrira. Promises: Linguistic Support for Efficient Asynchronous Procedure Calls in Distributed Systems. *SIGPLAN Conference on Programming Language Design and Implementation*, pages 260–267, 1988.

[Mar89] S. T. March, editor. *ACM Computing Surveys*, volume 21,3. ACM, 1989.

[Mil80] R. Milner. *A Calculus of Communicating Systems*. Lecture Notes on Computer Science Vol. 92. Springer Verlag, 1980.

[Par81] D. Park. Concurrency and Automata on Infinite Sequences. In *Proceedings of the 5th GI Conference, LNCS-104*. Springer Verlag, 1981.

[Plo81] G. D. Plotkin. A Structural Approach to Operational Semantics. Technical Report DAIMI FN-19, Computer Science Department, Aarhus University, 1981.

[Rus78] R. Russell. The CRAY-1 Computer System. *CACM*, January 1978.

[TBH82] P. Treleaven, D. Brownbridge, and R. Hopkins. Data Driven and Demand Driven Computer Architectures. *ACM Computing Surveys*, 14(1), 1982.

[vGV87] R. J. van Glabbeek and F. W. Vaandrager. Petri Net Models for Algebraic Theories of Concurrency. In J. W. deBakker, A. J. Nijman, and P. C. Treleaven, editors, *PARLE-II , LNCS 259*. Springer Verlag, 1987.

Time-Constrained Automata
(Extended Abstract)

Michael Merritt
AT&T Bell Laboratories
600 Mountain Avenue
Murray Hill, NJ 07974
merritt@research.att.com

Francesmary Modugno
School of Computer Science
Carnegie Mellon University
Pittsburgh, PA 15213
fmm@cs.cmu.edu

Mark R. Tuttle
DEC Cambridge Research Lab
One Kendall Sq., Bldg. 700
Cambridge, MA 02139
tuttle@crl.dec.com

Abstract

In this paper, we augment the input-output automaton model in order to reason about time in concurrent systems, and we prove simple properties of this augmentation. The input-output automata model is a useful model for reasoning about computation in concurrent and distributed systems because it allows fundamental properties such as fairness and compositionality to be expressed easily and naturally. A unique property of the model is that systems are modeled as the composition of *autonomous* components. This paper describes a way to add a notion of time to the model in a way that preserves these properties. The result is a simple, compositional model for real-time computation that provides a convenient notation for expressing timing properties such as bounded fairness.

1 Introduction

This paper augments the *input-output automaton* model [LT87] with a notion of time that allows us to reason about timed behaviors, especially behaviors in real-time systems where real-time constraints on systems' reaction times must be satisfied. The (untimed) input-output automaton model is a natural model of computation that has been used extensively to study concurrent systems. The model has many appealing properties. For example, it is especially helpful when describing the interfaces between system components, and it provides a clean compositional model for fair computation. The motivation for our work is to find an equally intuitive generalization of the model to timed computation that preserves these properties. Our generalization results in a compositional model for timed computation with a time-bounded notion of fair computation in which many interesting real-time constraints can be described simply. This model has been used to study problems in real-time systems, and simple proof rules have been developed for it [LA90, AL89].

The input-output automaton model is unique in that it is especially well-suited for modeling concurrent systems as the composition of autonomous components. A system component is ***autonomous*** if it has complete control over its generation of output. More precisely, its generation of output is a function of its own local state, not the global state, and cannot be blocked simply because no other system component is ready to receive the output. Our intuition is that these autonomous components represent the physically realizable components of the system: a network node can transmit a message over the network independent of the state of other nodes. Any natural model of concurrent computation should make it easy to describe systems as the composition of autonomous components.

While most models contain a submodel that supports such descriptions, these models are so expressive that they include notions of composition that have no correspondence to physical reality, and this unwanted expressive power complicates the models' semantics considerably. One example is CSP [Hoa85, KSdR+88]. In CSP, each process P has an alphabet of actions it can perform, and the parallel composition $P||Q$ of two processes P and Q requires that any action a in the intersection of their alphabets must be performed simultaneously by both if it is performed at all. In part because there is no semantic distinction between input and output actions in CSP, there is no notion of any individual process determining the performance of an action, and hence there is (in general) no notion of autonomy in the model. The parallel composition $P||Q$ of P and Q enables Q to keep P from performing any action a in the intersection of their alphabets simply by refusing to perform a itself. Thinking of Q as P's environment, this means that any action the environment can observe is an action the environment can synchronize with and block. This makes some problems almost too easy to solve. For example, consider the solution to the Dining Philosopher's problem in [Hoa85]. Here the philosophers are described in terms of actions like picking up and setting down forks, and the philosophers are placed in an environment (the definitions of the forks) that can simply block a philosopher when it tries to pick up a fork. The philosophers have no autonomy over their actions, and deadlock can be avoided by composing with any process whose definition is simply a description of the desired behaviors (cf. [CM84]). Because of the powerful operators in CSP, specifying an acceptable solution to a problem can also require more than specifying the desired external behavior (or traces). In contrast, in the input-output automaton model, it is natural to accept as a solution to a problem any system with the desired external behavior that can be expressed in the model.

Input-output automata can be viewed as a restriction of CSP and related models [Mil80, Yi90, MT90, GL90] to a simple submodel, with a simple semantics, that captures the notion of autonomy. A primary difference between the input-output automaton model and these models is that the former makes a clear distinction between input and output actions. In this model, each system component is modeled as an automaton with actions labeling the state transitions. These actions are partitioned into input and output actions. This partition is used to state two restrictions that guarantee that system components are autonomous. First, automata are ***input-enabled***, which means that any input action a can be performed in any state s (there is a transition from s labeled a). Second, two automata P and Q may be composed (essentially by identifying actions, as described above) only when the output actions of P and Q are disjoint. Consequently, P has complete control over its generation of output in the composition of P and Q: if a is an output action of P, then it must be an input action of Q (if it is an action of Q at all); and since Q is input-enabled, it is willing to accept a as input in any state. Early work involving continually enabled inputs appears in [LF81], and more recently in [Dil88].

A second difference is that fairness plays an important role in the input-output automaton model. A system computation is *fair* if every system component is given the chance to take a step infinitely often. The definition of fairness together with the weak (relative to CSP) composition operator result in a simple compositional model of fair concurrent computation. In this model automata generate fair behaviors, and when automata are composed, the fair behaviors of the composition are a composition of the fair behaviors of the components. Definitions of fairness in the same spirit appear in [LF81, Fra86, Jon87].

There are two natural approaches to extending the input-output automaton model to include timing information. The first is to record time and timing constraints directly in the automaton states and transition relation. This approach is exemplified by the work of Shankar and Lam [SL87] (and also [HLP90]), in which time is modeled as a component of the system state, and predicates on the time control system executions. The second approach is to model time and timing constraints as external conditions imposed on the executions of standard input-output automata. This approach is adopted here. A timed execution is essentially an ordered pair (e, t), where e is the execution of an input-output automaton, and t is a function assigning times to the events occurring in e (cf. [AH90, Lam91]). A timed automaton is a pair (A, P) consisting of an input-output automaton A and a predicate P on the timed executions of A.

Separating time from the local state makes it easy to define a clean notion of automaton composition. If instead time is recorded in the local state, then—in the straightforward composition of such automata—the times in the local states will bear little relation to one another. Some additional axioms or rules for automaton composition must be imposed to keep the times more or less synchronized. Furthermore, there is no longer one single variable in the state of the composition that records the current time, but rather a tuple of variables, and the complexity increases with additional composition. On the other hand, if time is externally assigned to events in a computation via a timing function t as is done here, then there is a simple syntactic mechanism for distinguishing the time component that allows a simple definition of composition in which components are synchronized.

After augmenting the input-output model to include a notion of time, a timing condition called a *boundmap* is defined, essentially a bounded fairness condition that restricts the amount of time that may elapse between consecutive steps of a system component.[1] Both the fair and unfair computations of the untimed input-output model are natural special cases of such boundmaps. One of the important results in this paper is that our augmentation of the input-output automaton model to incorporate time is a compositional model for timed computations. The fact that it is a compositional model for fair computation now follows as a special case. This modularity is one of the primary advantages of our work.

The rest of this paper is organized as follows. In Section 2 we review the input-output automaton model. In Section 3 we augment the model to include time, and in Section 4 we define the composition of timed automata. In Section 5 we define a simple notation for real-time constraints, and in Section 6 we define boundmaps as a special case. Finally, in

[1] Lewis [Lew90] also assigns bounds to state transitions. His motivation is quite different from ours, but we can generalize boundmaps slightly and capture his assignments.

Section 7 we define what it means for one timed automaton to solve a problem described by another timed automaton. Due to space limitations, we have omitted the proofs of our results. We have also omitted any significant examples of how to use our framework, but examples do appear in [LA90, AL89]. A full version of this paper will contain both proofs and examples.

2 Input-Output Automata

An *input-output automaton* A is defined by the following four components:

- A set of states, *states*(A), (possibly an infinite set) with a subset of start states, *start*(A).
- A set of actions, *acts*(A), partitioned into sets of *input*, *output* and *internal* actions, *in*(A), *out*(A), and *int*(A), respectively. The output and internal actions are called the *locally-controlled* actions, and the input and output actions are called *external* actions, denoted *ext*(A).
- A transition relation *steps*(A) is a set of (state,action,state) triples, such that for any state s' and input action π, there is a transition (s', π, s) for some state s.
- An equivalence relation *part*(A) partitioning the locally-controlled actions of A. We interpret each class of the partition as the set of locally-controlled actions of separate, autonomous components of the system being modeled by the automaton.

An *execution* of A is a finite or infinite sequence $s_0\pi_1s_1...$ of alternating states and actions such that s_0 is a start state, (s_{i-1}, π_i, s_i) is a transition of A for all i, and if e is finite then e ends with a state. The *schedule* of an execution is the subsequence of actions appearing in e. The *behavior* of a schedule or execution σ is the subsequence of external actions appearing in σ. An action π is *enabled* in state s' if there is a transition (s', π, s) for some state s; otherwise π is *disabled*. Since every input action is enabled in every state, automata are said to be *input-enabled*.

An execution of a system is fair if each component is given a chance to take a step infinitely often. Of course, a component can't take a step when given the chance if none of its actions are enabled. Formally, an execution e of automaton A is *fair* if for each class C of *part*(A)—that is, for each system component—the following two conditions hold:

- If e is finite, then no action of C is enabled in the final state of e.
- If e is infinite, then either actions from C appear infinitely often in e, or states in which no action of C is enabled appear infinitely often in e.

Automata can only be composed if their output actions are disjoint, and they do not share any internal actions. This restriction, together with the input-enabling condition, preserves the autonomy of independent components within a composition. To capture this restriction we define the *action signature* of an automaton A, denoted *sig*(A), to be the triple $(in(A), out(A), int(A))$. In general, an action signature S is a triple consisting of three disjoint sets *in*(S), *out*(S), and *int*(S). The union of these sets is denoted by *acts*(S).

The action signatures $\{S_i : i \in I\}$ are *compatible* if for all $i, j \in I$ $out(S_i) \cap out(S_j) = \emptyset$ and $int(S_i) \cap acts(S_j) = \emptyset$. The composition $S = \prod_{i \in I} S_i$ of compatible action signatures $\{S_i : i \in I\}$ is defined to be the action signature with $in(S) = \bigcup_{i \in I} in(S_i) - \bigcup_{i \in I} out(S_i)$, $out(S) = \bigcup_{i \in I} out(S_i)$, and $int(S) = \bigcup_{i \in I} int(S_i)$.

The composition $A = \prod_{i \in I} A_i$ of a set $\{A_i : i \in I\}$ of compatible automata (automata with compatible action signatures) is defined to be the automaton with

- $states(A) = \prod_{i \in I} states(A_i)$,
- $sig(A) = \prod_{i \in I} sig(A_i)$,
- $part(A) = \bigcup_{i \in I} part(A_i)$, and
- $start(A) = \prod_{i \in I} start(A_i)$,
- $steps(A)$ equal to the set of triples $(\{a_i\}, \pi, \{a'_i\})$ such that for all $i \in I$
  - if $\pi \in acts(A_i)$ then $(a_i, \pi, a'_i) \in steps(A_i)$, and
  - if $\pi \notin acts(A_i)$ then $a_i = a'_i$.

(The products $states(A)$ and $start(A)$ are standard Cartesian products.) Since the automata A_i are input-enabled, so is their composition, and hence their composition is indeed an automaton. Notice that all output actions of an automaton A_i (some representing communication with other automata A_j) become output actions of the composition, and not internal actions. The definition of an operation internalizing output actions is straightforward. See [LT87, Tut87] for a more complete exposition of the model that includes such extensions.

3 Timed Automata

We introduce time into the model by introducing function t assigning times t_i to the states s_i appearing in executions $e = s_0\pi_1 s_1 \ldots$; actually, t maps the indices i to times t_i. A *timing* t is a mapping from a nonempty (possibly infinite) prefix of $0, 1, 2, \ldots$ to the nonnegative reals satisfying

- t is nondecreasing: $i \leq j$ implies $t(i) \leq t(j)$
- t is unbounded: for every interval $[t_1, t_2]$ of the real line, $t(i) \in [t_1, t_2]$ for at most finitely many i.

The *length* of an execution e is the number of actions (and hence state transitions) appearing in e. The *length* of a timing t is k if t's domain is the finite set $\{0, \ldots, k\}$, and infinite if t's domain is the entire set of nonnegative integers.

A *timed execution* of an automaton A is an (untimed) execution e of A together with a timing t of the same length; we denote this timed execution by e^t. In other words, a timed execution is an execution together with a timing assigning times to states appearing in the execution. Notice that a timing also induces an assignment of times to actions. Intuitively, since the action π_i is the cause of the (instantaneous) transition from state s_{i-1} to s_i, and since the system entered the state s_i at time $t(i)$, we can view the action π_i—or, perhaps more accurately, the completion of π_i—as having occurred at time $t(i)$. In fact, when

$t(0) = 0$, it is convenient to represent the timed execution e^t by $s_0(\pi_1, t_1)s_1(\pi_2, t_2)s_2\ldots$, where $t_i = t(i)$ (see [AL89]).

Timed schedules and behaviors of A are defined in a similar way. A *timed sequence* α^t consists of a sequence α of actions of A and a timing t of the same length, giving an initial time $t(0)$ and a time for each action in α. When $t(0) = 0$, it is convenient to denote the timed sequence α^t by $(\pi_1, t_1)(\pi_2, t_2)\ldots$, where $\alpha = \pi_1\pi_2\ldots$ and $t_i = t(i)$. A *timed schedule* of A is a timed sequence σ^t where σ is a schedule of A, and a *timed behavior* of A is a timed sequence β^t where β is a behavior of A.

A *timing property* P for an automaton A is any predicate on timed executions of A: given any timed execution e^t of A, the predicate P is either true or false of e^t. For example, a timing property could describe a desirable property that the timed executions of an automaton should exhibit.

A *timed automaton* is an ordered pair (A, P) consisting of an automaton A and a timing property P for A. Our intuition is that the automaton A describes the possible computations of the system, and the property P describes how these computations progress with time.

A *timed execution* of (A, P) is a timed execution e^t of A that satisfies P. We denote the set of timed executions of (A, P) by *timed-execs*(A, P). Given a timed execution e^t of (A, P), the timed schedule obtained by deleting the states appearing in e is denoted by *sched*(e^t). For example, when $t(0) = 0$, if $e^t = s_0(\pi_1, t_1)s_1(\pi_2, t_2)\ldots$, then *sched*$(\sigma^t) = (\pi_1, t_1)(\pi_2, t_2)\ldots$. Similarly, given a timed schedule σ^t of (A, P), the timed behavior obtained by deleting the internal actions of A appearing in σ is denoted by *beh*(σ^t). As a shorthand, we write *beh*(e^t) = *beh*(*sched*(e^t)). The set *timed-scheds*(A, P) of timed schedules of (A, P) is the set of all timed schedules *sched*(e^t) of all timed executions e^t of (A, P). Similarly, the set *timed-behs*(A, P) of timed behaviors of (A, P) is the set of all timed behaviors *beh*(e^t) of all timed executions e^t of (A, P).

4 Composition of Timed Automata

Timed automata can be composed to yield other timed automata. Composition has the property that the behavior of a composition is a composition of the behaviors of the components. This compositionality is an important aspect of our model.

Like untimed automata, the composition of timed automata is defined only for compatible automata. Unlike untimed automata, however, composition is defined only for finite collections of automata. This guarantees that timings in the resulting composition are unbounded: if we try to compose an infinite collection of automata (A_i, P_i) where each P_i requires that an action is performed at time 1, then an infinite number of actions are performed at time 1 in an execution of the composition, violating the requirement that timings are unbounded. In this paper, compositions are assumed to be compositions of finite collections of compatible automata.

To motivate the definition of timed composition, we note that every execution e of an untimed composition $A = \prod A_i$ induces an execution $e|A_i$ of A_i: if $e = s_0\pi_1 s_1\ldots$, then $e|A_i$ is the result of deleting $\pi_j s_j$ whenever π_j is not an action of A_i and replacing the remaining global states s_j with A_i's local state $s_j|A_i$ in s_j. Intuitively, $e|A_i$ is the sequence of state transitions through which A_i moves during the execution e of A. Similarly, every *timed* execution e^t of A induces a *timed* execution $e^t|A_i$ of A_i: when $t(0) = 0$, if $e^t = s_0(\pi_1, t_1)s_1(\pi_2, t_2)\ldots$, then $e^t|A_i$ is the result of deleting $(\pi_j, t_j)s_j$ whenever π_j is not an action of A_i and replacing the remaining s_j with $s_j|A_i$. Given a timed sequence α^t of actions of A, the timed sequence $\alpha^t|A_i$ of actions of A_i is derived similarly.

The *composition* $\prod(A_i, P_i)$ of a finite collection of timed automata (A_i, P_i) is the timed automaton (A, P) where

- $A = \prod A_i$ is the composition of the A_i, and
- $P = \prod P_i$ is the timing property for A that is true of a timed execution e^t iff P_i is true of $e^t|A_i$ for every i.

Another way to formulate the definition of $\prod P_i$ is to extend each local property P_i to a global property, and then to define $\prod P_i$ to be the conjunction of the resulting global properties. More precisely, given a collection of timed automata (A_i, P_i), let $A = \prod A_i$ and define P_i^A to be the timing property for A defined as follows: a timed execution e^t of A satisfies P_i^A iff $e^t|A_i$ satisfies P_i. We now have the following:

Proposition 1: If $(A, P) = \prod(A_i, P_i)$, then $P \equiv \bigwedge P_i^A$.

It is interesting to explore the relationship between the global executions of $\prod(A_i, P_i)$ and the local executions of the (A_i, P_i). First of all, it is easy to see that every execution of $\prod(A_i, P_i)$ induces an execution of (A_i, P_i):

Proposition 2: Let $(A, P) = \prod(A_i, P_i)$. If e^t is a timed execution of (A, P), then $e^t|A_i$ is a timed execution of (A_i, P_i) for every i.

On the other hand, we can prove a kind of converse:

Proposition 3: Let $(A, P) = \prod(A_i, P_i)$, let e be any sequence of alternating states and actions of A, and let t be any timing of the same length. If $e^t|A_i$ is a timed execution of (A_i, P_i) for every i, then e^t is a timed execution of (A, P).

More generally, one might wonder when it is possible to take a collection of arbitrary timed executions $e_i^{t_i}$ of the (A_i, P_i) and "paste" them together to construct a timed execution e^t of the composition $\prod(A_i, P_i)$ such that $e^t|A_i = e_i^{t_i}$. In the case of untimed automata, if there is a total ordering α of the actions appearing in the e_i such that $\alpha|A_i = sched(e_i)$ for every i, then there is an execution e of $\prod A_i$ such that $\alpha = sched(e)$ and $e|A_i = e_i$ for every i. In the case of timed automata, the existence of a global timing t consistent with the local timings t_i is also required:

Proposition 4: Let $(A, P) = \prod(A_i, P_i)$, and suppose $e_i^{t_i}$ is a timed execution of (A_i, P_i) for every i. If there exists a timed sequence α^t of actions of A such that $\alpha^t|A_i = sched(e_i^{t_i})$ for every i, then there exists a timed execution e^t of (A, P) such that $\alpha^t = sched(e^t)$ and $e^t|A_i = e_i^{t_i}$ for every i.

Analogous results hold for schedules and behaviors:

Proposition 5: If e^t is a timed execution of $\prod(A_i, P_i)$, then $sched(e^t)|A_i = sched(e^t|A_i)$ and $beh(e^t)|A_i = beh(e^t|A_i)$.

Finally, we can use these results to prove the main result of this section: that our model is a compositional model of timed behavior. In other words, the observable behavior of a composition of timed automata is a composition of the observable behaviors of the component timed automata. First, we must define this composition of behaviors. Let $(A, P) = \prod(A_i, P_i)$, and define

$$\prod \textit{timed-execs}(A_i, P_i)$$

to be the set of e^t where e is a sequence of alternating states and actions of A and t is a timing of the same length such that $e^t|A_i \in \textit{timed-execs}(A_i, P_i)$ for each i. The definitions of $\prod \textit{timed-scheds}(A_i, P_i)$ and $\prod \textit{timed-behs}(A_i, P_i)$ are the obvious analogs. We can prove the following:

Proposition 6: If $(A, P) = \prod_{i \in I}(A_i, P_i)$, then

1. $\textit{timed-execs}(A, P) = \prod_{i \in I} \textit{timed-execs}(A_i, P_i)$,
2. $\textit{timed-scheds}(A, P) = \prod_{i \in I} \textit{timed-scheds}(A_i, P_i)$, and
3. $\textit{timed-behs}(A, P) = \prod_{i \in I} \textit{timed-behs}(A_i, P_i)$.

5 Timing Properties: Response Times

The idea of being "fair" to each component in a composition of automata comes up repeatedly in the theory of input-output automata. Informally, we view each class C in the partition of an automaton's locally-controlled actions as the locally-controlled actions of a single component in the system being modeled by the automaton. Being fair to each system component means being fair to each class of actions. This means each class is given an infinite number of chances to perform an action. On each chance, either some action of C is enabled and is performed, or no action of C is enabled and this class must pass on its chance to perform an action. More than just giving each class C an infinite number of chances to perform an action from C, we might require that the time between chances actually falls in some interval $\{l, u\}$. What we actually define is a bound on the elapsed time from the moment an action is enabled to the time it is performed. Since this is really a special case of bounding response times, the time that elapses between two events, we first define a simple notion for bounding response times, and return to bounded fairness in Section 6. This more general definition is useful in its own right when we are specifying desired response times at a level of abstraction where the ultimate partitioning of the system into components is not yet apparent (or desired).

To begin with an example, suppose one requires that the time elapsing between a request for a resource and the satisfaction of that request not exceed time ϵ. In order to be able to respond to requests in a timely manner, the system must be given the chance (or time) to respond. For example, if a user is allowed to withdraw a request before it is fulfilled, then we might weaken our requirement to say that if a request remains unfulfilled for time ϵ, then it will be fulfilled within that time (that is, a request cannot remain unfulfilled for longer than time ϵ). We want to be able to capture statements of the form "if condition X holds for enough time, then condition Y becomes true." On the other hand, other considerations may require or depend upon certain response times taking more than a certain amount of time: "condition X must hold for enough time before condition Y becomes true." These considerations motivate us to formulate general notation for specifying upper and lower bounds on response time.

In our case, the conditions X and Y of interest are that the system is in a certain state or has performed a certain action. Let A be an automaton, let S be a subset of A's states and Π be a subset of A's actions. We denote by (S, Π) the event (or condition) corresponding to entering a state in S or performing an action in Π. Given an execution $e = s_0 \pi_1 \ldots$, we denote the finite prefix $s_0 \pi_1 \ldots s_k$ of e by $e[k]$. A finite prefix $e[k]$ *satisfies* (S, Π) iff

- $k = 0$ and $s_0 \in S$, or
- $k \geq 0$ and either $s_k \in S$ or $\pi_k \in \Pi$.

Intuitively, (S, Π) is true at time k if either the state entered at time k is in S or the action performed at time k (implying that $k > 0$) is in Π.

5.1 Upper Bounds on Response Times

Let A be an automaton, let S and S' be subsets of A's states, let Π and Π' be subsets of A's actions, and let $u > 0$ be a nonnegative real number. We say that a timed execution e^t of A satisfies the *upper bound*

$$(S, \Pi) \overset{\leq u}{\leadsto} (S', \Pi'),$$

which we read as "(S, Π) leads to (S', Π') in time at most u," iff for every $i \geq 0$,

if $e[i]$ satisfies (S, Π)
then, for some $j > i$ with $t(j) \leq t(i) + u$,
either $e[j]$ satisfies (S', Π') or $e[j]$ does not satisfy (S, Π).

If t is a strictly increasing function, meaning that successive states are assigned distinct times, then this condition is equivalent to saying that if (S, Π) is continuously true for the next u time units, then (S', Π') becomes true within the next u time units.

For notational convenience, we often omit reference to a set S or Π when it is empty, and we denote a singleton set $\{x\}$ by x. For example, we write $S \overset{\leq u}{\leadsto} \Pi'$ in place of $(S, \Pi) \overset{\leq u}{\leadsto} (S', \Pi')$ when Π and S' are empty. As another example, notice that if *enabled*(π) is the set of states where the action is π is enabled, then *enabled*$(\pi) \overset{\leq \epsilon}{\leadsto} \pi$ says that if action π is continuously enabled for the next ϵ time units, then π is performed within time ϵ.

In a similar manner, we say that e^t satisfies the *strict upper bound*

$$(S, \Pi) \overset{< u}{\leadsto} (S', \Pi')$$

just as above, except that we replace the condition $t(j) \leq t(i) + u$ with $t(j) < t(i) + u$. Notice that when $u = \infty$, this strict upper bound requires that (S, Π) cannot be true forever without (S',Π') becoming true, although there is no finite bound on the delay until this event occurs. In contrast, we find it convenient to define $(S,\Pi) \overset{\leq \infty}{\leadsto} (S',\Pi')$ to be true for any S, S', Π and Π'. With this convention, these two conditions allow us to express as extreme cases the classes of fair and unfair executions of an automaton, respectively. Finally, as one would expect, increasing the upper bound u weakens the conditions $(S,\Pi) \overset{\leq u}{\leadsto} (S',\Pi')$ and $(S,\Pi) \overset{< u}{\leadsto} (S',\Pi')$.

5.2 Lower Bounds on Response Times

Consider an execution e in which π is continuously enabled. In this case, the upper bound $\mathit{enabled}(\pi) \overset{\leq \epsilon}{\leadsto} \pi$ says that π will be performed at least once every ϵ time units, and it seems that a lower bound $\mathit{enabled}(\pi) \overset{\geq \epsilon}{\leadsto} \pi$ ought to say that π will be performed at *most* once every ϵ time units. Consider, however, an execution e in which π is intermittently enabled. In this case, the upper bound $\mathit{enabled}(\pi) \overset{\leq \epsilon}{\leadsto} \pi$ says that π cannot remain enabled for more than ϵ time units without being performed, and it seems that a lower bound $\mathit{enabled}(\pi) \overset{\geq \epsilon}{\leadsto} \pi$ ought to say that π must be enabled at *least* ϵ time units before being performed. Combining these remarks, $\mathit{enabled}(\pi) \overset{\geq \epsilon}{\leadsto} \pi$ should mean that π must be enabled at least ϵ time units between performances.

A natural way of capturing this intuition is to say that a timed execution e^t of A satisfies the lower bound $(S,\Pi) \overset{\geq l}{\leadsto} (S',\Pi')$ iff for every $j > 0$,

> if $e[j]$ satisfies (S',Π')
> then for some $i < j$ with $t(i) \leq t(j) - l$
>
> > $e[k]$ satisfies (S,Π) for all k with $i \leq k < j$, and
> > $e[k]$ does *not* satisfy (S',Π') for any k with $i < k < j$.

Consider once again the condition $\mathit{enabled}(\pi) \overset{\geq \epsilon}{\leadsto} \pi$. Given an execution e^t with a strictly increasing timing t (meaning that each state is assigned a distinct time), this condition says that in order for π to be performed at time τ, it must be enabled throughout the time interval $[\tau - \epsilon, \tau)$, and must not be performed in the interval $(\tau - \epsilon, \tau)$. Notice, for example, that it is perfectly acceptable for π to be performed at both times $\tau - \epsilon$ and τ, as long as π is enabled throughout the intervening interval (and, in particular, in the state at time $\tau - \epsilon$ immediately following the first performance of π).

While this definition is sufficient for our definition of bounded fairness in Section 6, it does have one weakness that it easy to repair: it says that (S,Π) must hold for l time units before (S',Π') can hold, but suppose there are two, independently timed paths by which (S',Π') might become true. For example, consider an automaton with a single output action *response* and two independent input actions, *fast-request* and *slow-request*, that enable the *response* action. The automaton has three states, including an initial state *start*. The input actions *fast-request* and *slow-request* take each state to the states *fast* and *slow*, respectively, and the output action *response* takes both *fast* and *slow* to *start* again. Intuitively, *fast-request* and *slow-request* are high- and low-priority requests, respectively, that *response* be performed: the delay between *fast-request* and *response* is to be at least 5 time units, while the delay between *slow-request* and *response* is to be at least 10 time units. We want to say that *response* may be performed only if the automaton has been in the state *fast* for 5 time units or in the state *slow* for 10 time units, but the definition of a lower bound given above does not let us express this in a natural way. This is because it does not allow us to distinguish the performance of *response* via the state *fast* from the performance of *response* via the state *slow*.

Such examples have led us to the following definition of a lower bound. Given a nonnegative real number l, we say that a timed execution e^t of A satisfies the *lower bound*

$$(S,\Pi) \overset{\geq l}{\leadsto} (S',\Pi'),$$

which we read as "(S,Π) leads to (S',Π') in time at least l," iff for every $j > 0$,

if $e[j-1]$ satisfies (S,Π) and $e[j]$ satisfies (S',Π')
then for some $i < j$ with $t(i) \leq t(j) - l$

$e[k]$ satisfies (S,Π) for all k with $i \leq k < j$, and
$e[k]$ does *not* satisfy (S',Π') for any k with $i < k < j$.

This definition recognizes the fact that (S',Π') may become true via several computational paths, and says that if it becomes true via the path satisfying (S,Π), then (S,Π) must have been satisfied for the preceding l time units. Returning to the example above, notice that this definition of a lower bound allows us to express the different timing requirements with the conditions *fast* $\overset{\geq 1}{\leadsto}$ *response* and *slow* $\overset{\geq 10}{\leadsto}$ *response*.

Similarly, we say that e^t satisfies the *strict lower bound*

$$(S,\Pi) \overset{> l}{\leadsto} (S',\Pi')$$

just as above, except that we replace the condition $t(i) \leq t(j)-l$ with $t(i) < t(j)-l$. Again, decreasing the lower bound l weakens the conditions $(S,\Pi) \overset{\geq l}{\leadsto} (S',\Pi')$ and $(S,\Pi) \overset{> l}{\leadsto} (S',\Pi')$.

5.3 Combining Upper and Lower Bounds

We can combine the upper and lower bound conditions given above into a single condition as follows. We define the timing property

$$(S,\Pi) \overset{[l,u]}{\leadsto} (S',\Pi')$$

to be the conjunction of the timing properties $(S,\Pi) \overset{\geq l}{\leadsto} (S',\Pi)$ and $(S,\Pi) \overset{\leq u}{\leadsto} (S',\Pi)$; that is, a timed execution must satisfy both the upper and lower bounds. For example, the condition *enabled*$(\pi) \overset{[l,u]}{\leadsto} \pi$ says that π must be enabled at least l time units between performances of π, and that π cannot remain enabled from longer that u time units without being performed. Notice, by the way, that since the conditions $(S,\Pi) \overset{\leq \infty}{\leadsto} (S',\Pi')$ and $(S,\Pi) \overset{\geq 0}{\leadsto} (S',\Pi')$ are equivalent to *true* (that is, they are valid), the condition $(S,\Pi) \overset{\leq u}{\leadsto} (S',\Pi')$ is equivalent to $(S,\Pi) \overset{[0,u]}{\leadsto} (S',\Pi')$, and the condition $(S,\Pi) \overset{\geq l}{\leadsto} (S',\Pi')$ is equivalent to $(S,\Pi) \overset{[l,\infty]}{\leadsto} (S',\Pi')$. We note that, in an analogous way, we can define the conditions $(S,\Pi) \overset{(l,u]}{\leadsto} (S',\Pi)$, $(S,\Pi) \overset{(l,u)}{\leadsto} (S',\Pi)$, and $(S,\Pi) \overset{[l,u)}{\leadsto} (S',\Pi)$. We use $\{l,u\}$ to denote any one of these intervals when its open or closed nature is unimportant. As expected, enlarging the interval $\{l,u\}$ weakens the the timing property.

Given a collection of timing properties P_i for automata A_i, Proposition 1 says that the timing property $P = \prod P_i$ for $A = \prod A_i$ can be viewed as the conjunction $\wedge P_i^A$ of timing properties for A, where each P_i^A is the extension of the local property P_i for A_i to a global property for A. The following proposition shows how to perform this extension for the upper and lower bounds defined in this section.

Proposition 7: Let $(A, P) = \prod(A_i, P_i)$. Let S and S' be subsets of A_i's states, and let Π and Π' be subsets of A_i's actions. Define

$$S^A = \{s \in \mathit{states}(A) : s|A_i \in S\} \text{ and}$$

$$S'^A = \{s \in \mathit{states}(A) : s|A_i \in S'\}.$$

If $P_i \equiv (S, \Pi) \overset{\{l,u\}}{\leadsto} (S', \Pi')$, then $P_i^A \equiv (S^A, \Pi) \overset{\{l,u\}}{\leadsto} (S'^A, \Pi')$.

6 Timing Properties: Boundmaps

With the notation just defined, it is now easy to capture our notion of bounded fairness, the notion that a class C is given an infinite number of chances to perform an action, and that the time between chances actually falls in some interval $\{l, u\}$. Given an automaton A, a *boundmap* b for A is a mapping that maps each class C of $\mathit{part}(A)$ to an interval $b(C) = \{l(C), u(C)\}$ of the real line. Given an automaton A and a class C of $\mathit{part}(A)$, we denote by $\mathit{enabled}(A, C)$ (or just $\mathit{enabled}(C)$ when A is clear from context) the set of A's states in which some action of C is enabled. We often abuse notation and denote by b both the boundmap b and the timing property

$$P_b \overset{\mathit{def}}{=} \bigwedge_{C \in \mathit{part}(A)} \mathit{enabled}(C) \overset{b(C)}{\leadsto} C.$$

We refer to (A, b) as a *time-bounded automaton*, a special case of a timed-automaton.

Given that the definition of a boundmap is motivated by the definition of a fair execution, it is not surprising that the fair executions of an automaton A can be characterized as the timed executions of a timed automaton (A, b) with a fair boundmap b. The *fair boundmap* of A is the boundmap b defined by $b(C) = [0, \infty)$ for all $C \in \mathit{part}(A)$. Notice that if C is continuously enabled from some point of an execution, then this boundmap requires the *eventual* performance of an action in C, since some action of C must be performed before time ∞.

Proposition 8: Let A be an automaton, and let b be the fair boundmap for A. Given any timed execution e^t of A, e is a fair execution of A iff e^t is a timed execution of (A, b).

Similarly, we define the *unfair boundmap* of A as the boundmap b defined by $b(C) = [0, \infty]$ for all $C \in \mathit{part}(A)$; the following is immediate.

Proposition 9: Let A be an automaton, and let b be the unfair boundmap for A. Given any timed execution e^t of A, e is an execution of A iff e^t is a timed execution of (A, b).

These results show that the classes of fair and unfair computations can be understood in terms of extreme cases of boundmaps.

There is a very simple relationship between the boundmap of a composition of timed automata and the boundmaps of the individual component automata.

Proposition 10: Let $A = \prod A_i$. Suppose b_i is a boundmap for A_i for each i, and suppose b is a boundmap for A defined by $b(C) = b_i(C)$ if $C \in \mathit{part}(A_i)$. Then $(A, b) = \prod(A_i, b_i)$.

Given this result, we define $\prod(A_i, b_i)$ to be (A, b) where b is the boundmap defined as stated in this proposition. This result together with Proposition 6 shows that our model is a compositional model of time-bounded fair computation. Again, we can view the composition $\prod(A_i, b_i)$ in terms of extending local timing properties to global properties:

Proposition 11: Suppose $(A, b) = \prod(A_i, b_i)$. If $P_c \equiv \mathit{enabled}(A_i, C) \overset{b_i(C)}{\rightsquigarrow} C$, then $P_c^A \equiv \mathit{enabled}(A, C) \overset{b(C)}{\rightsquigarrow} C$.

7 Solvability

In addition to describing implementations of concurrent systems, input-output automata are useful for expressing specifications of such systems [LT87]. Accordingly, given two (untimed) automata A and A', we say that A *solves* A' if they have the same external actions—that is, $in(A) = in(A')$ and $out(A) = out(A')$—and every fair behavior of A is a fair behavior of A'. Intuitively, the fair behaviors of A are the behaviors that can be witnessed by an external observer of A—someone who cannot see the inner workings of A, its internal actions. Since every behavior of A is a behavior of A', any correctness condition satisfied by the behaviors of A' is satisfied by the behaviors of A as well. In particular, any problem "solved" by A' is also "solved" by A.

The definition of solvability has a natural extension to timed automata: given two timed automata (A, P) and (A', P'), we say that (A, P) *solves* (A', P') if they have the same external actions and $\mathit{timed\text{-}behs}(A, P) \subseteq \mathit{timed\text{-}behs}(A', P')$. As with the untimed case, solvability for timed automata has properties that support hierarchical and modular verification techniques. For example, an immediate result of the definition is that "solves" is a transitive relation:

Proposition 12: If (A, P) solves (A', P') and (A', P') solves (A'', P''), then (A, P) solves (A'', P'').

One consequence of this result is that we can prove that an implementation (A, P) satisfies its specification (A', P') by constructing a sequence of intervening models $(A, P) = (A_0, P_0), \ldots, (A_k, P_k) = (A', P')$ and proving that (A_i, P_i) solves (A_{i+1}, P_{i+1}) for every i. This means that hierarchical proof strategies are possible in this model, where each (A_i, P_i) is a model of the system at increasingly higher levels of conceptual abstraction. Elsewhere [LA90], refinement mappings have been used to construct this sort of hierarchical proof in this model.

Notice that if P is in some sense a stronger timing property than P', then is should immediately follow that (A, P) solves (A, P'). Unfortunately, it is difficult to give general syntactic conditions on timing properties P and P' that imply that P is stronger than P'. In the case of boundmaps, however, such a characterization is quite simple. Given two boundmaps b and b' with the same domain (that is, b and b' are defined on the same sets of classes C), we define $b \subseteq b'$ if $b(C) \subseteq b'(C)$ for all C. Intuitively b makes stronger requirements than b'. It is easy to see that A with the stronger boundmap b solves A with a weaker boundmap b':

Finally, since—like the untimed input-output model—this model of timed computation is a compositional model, one technique for proving that one composition of timed automata solves another composition is to prove that each component of the first composition solves the corresponding component of the second:

Proposition 14: Suppose $(A, P) = \Pi_{i \in I}(A_i, P_i)$ and $(A', P') = \Pi_{i \in I}(A'_i, P'_i)$. If (A_i, P_i) solves (A'_i, P'_i) for every $i \in I$, then (A, P) solves (A', P').

8 Conclusion

We have presented a model for reasoning about time in concurrent systems. Our decision to base the model on the input-output automaton model was motivated by (in our judgment) the naturalness and utility of the model in the context of asynchronous concurrent systems. The model has been used extensively to model concurrency control and recovery in transaction systems, resource allocation, concurrent data structures, network communication, and other problems (e.g., [LT89, LM88, LMWF88, Blo87, WLL88, LMF88, Her88]). It has been used to specify these problems, to describe and analyze algorithmic solutions, and to prove lower bounds and impossibility results. The model has many natural properties (such as compositionality), and this work was motivated by our desire to find an equally intuitive generalization to real-time concurrent systems. The simple definition of a timed execution results in a modular, compositional model of timed concurrent computation; and in the definition of a boundmap we feel we have found the natural generalization of both fair and unfair executions of the input-output automaton model. We note that our goal has been only to devise a natural semantic model of timed computation. We have not considered logics for expressing general timing properties—although we feel the "leads to" notation does cover a lot of the interesting timing constraints—nor have we considered proof systems for such logics. It appears, however, that our model is a suitable semantic model for most logics and proofs systems appearing in the literature (such as [HLP90, AH90, ACD90]). However, simple proof techniques for timed automata have already been investigated [LA90].

References

[ACD90] Rajeev Alur, Costas Courcoubetis, and David Dill. Model-checking for real-time systems. In *Proceedings of the 5th Annual IEEE Symposium on Logic in Computer Science*, pages 414–425. IEEE, June 1990.

[AH90] Rajeev Alur and Thomas A. Henzinger. Real-time logics: Complexity and expressiveness. In *Proceedings of the 5th Annual IEEE Symposium on Logic in Computer Science*, pages 390–401. IEEE, June 1990.

[AL89] Hagit Attiya and Nancy Lynch. Time bounds for real-time process control in the presence of timing uncertainty. Technical Memo MIT/LCS/TM-403, MIT Laboratory for Computer Science, July 1989.

[Blo87] Bard Bloom. Constructing two-writer atomic registers. In *Proceedings of the 6th Annual ACM Symposium on Principles of Distributed Computing*, pages 249–259. ACM, August 1987.

[CM84] K. Mani Chandy and Jayadev Misra. The drinking philosophers problem. *ACM Transactions on Programming Languages and Systems*, 6(4):632–646, 1984.

[Dil88] David L. Dill. *Trace Theory for Automatic Hierarchical Verification of Speed-Independent Circuits*. PhD thesis, Department of Computer Science, Carnegie Mellon University, February 1988. Available as Technical Report CMU-CS-88-119.

[Fra86] Nissim Francez. *Fairness*. Springer-Verlag, Berlin, 1986.

[GL90] Richard Gerber and Insup Lee. CCSR: A calculus for communicating shared resources. In J. C. M. Baeten and J. W. Klop, editors, *Lecture Notes in Computer Science, volume 458, Proceedings of Concur '90*, pages 263–277. Springer-Verlag, August 1990.

[Her88] Maurice Herlihy. Impossibility and universality results for wait-free synchronization. In *Proceedings of the 7th Annual ACM Symposium on Principles of Distributed Computing*, pages 276–290. ACM, August 1988.

[HLP90] Eyal Harel, Orna Lichtenstein, and Amir Pnueli. Explicit clock temporal logic. In *Proceedings of the 5th Annual IEEE Symposium on Logic in Computer Science*, pages 401–413. IEEE, June 1990.

[Hoa85] C. A. R. Hoare. *Communicating Sequential Processes*. Prentice-Hall International, Englewood Cliffs, New Jersey, 1985.

[Jon87] Bengt Jonsson. *Compositional Verification of Distributed Systems*. PhD thesis, Uppsala University, Uppsala, Sweden, 1987. Published by Direkt Offset, Nyström & Co AB, Uppsala.

[KSdR+88] R. Koymans, R. K. Shyamasundar, W. P. de Roever, R. Gerth, and S. Arun-Kumar. Compositional semantics for real-time distributed computing. *Information and Computation*, 79:210–256, 1988.

[LA90] Nancy A. Lynch and Hagit Attiya. Using mappings to prove timing properties. In *Proceedings of the 9th Annual ACM Symposium on Principles of Distributed Computing*, pages 265–280. ACM, August 1990.

[Lam91] Leslie Lamport. A temporal logic of actions. Research Report 57, DEC Systems Research Center, January 1991.

[Lew90] Harry R. Lewis. A logic of concrete time intervals. In *Proceedings of the 5th Annual IEEE Symposium on Logic in Computer Science*, pages 380–389. IEEE, June 1990. Also available at Harvard Technical Report TR-07-90.

[LF81] Nancy A. Lynch and Michael J. Fischer. On describing the behavior and implementation of distributed systems. *Theoretical Computer Science*, 13(1):17–43, January 1981.

[LM88] Nancy A. Lynch and Michael Merritt. Introduction to the theory of nested transactions. *Theoretical Computer Science*, 62:123–185, 1988. Earlier versions appeared in *Proceedings of the International Conference on Database Theory*, 1986, and as MIT Technical Report MIT/LCS/TR-367.

[LMF88] Nancy A. Lynch, Yishay Mansour, and Alan Fekete. Data link layer: Two impossibility results. In *Proceedings of the 7th Annual ACM Symposium on Principles of Distributed Computing*, pages 149–170. ACM, August 1988. Also available as MIT Technical Report MIT/LCS/TM-355.

[LMWF88] Nancy A. Lynch, Michael Merritt, William E. Weihl, and Alan Fekete. A theory of atomic transactions. In *Proceedings of the International Conference on Database Theory*, 1988. Also available as MIT Technical Memo MIT/LCS/TM-362.

[LT87] Nancy A. Lynch and Mark R. Tuttle. Hierarchical correctness proofs for distributed algorithms. In *Proceedings of the 6th Annual ACM Symposium on Principles of Distributed Computing*, pages 137–151. ACM, August 1987. A full version is available as MIT Technical Report MIT/LCS/TR–387.

[LT89] Nancy A. Lynch and Mark R. Tuttle. An introduction to input/output automata. *CWI-Quarterly*, 2(3), 1989. Also available as MIT Technical Memo MIT/LCS/TM-373.

[Mil80] Robin Milner. *A Calculus of Communicating Systems.* Lecture Notes in Computer Science 92. Springer-Verlag, Berlin, 1980.

[MT90] Faron Moller and Chris Tofts. A temporal calculus of communicating systems. In J. C. M. Baeten and J. W. Klop, editors, *Lecture Notes in Computer Science, volume 458, Proceedings of Concur '90*, pages 401–415. Springer-Verlag, August 1990.

[SL87] A. Udaya Shankar and Simon S. Lam. Time-dependent distributed systems: Proving safety, liveness and real-time properties. *Distributed Computing*, pages 61–79, 1987.

[Tut87] Mark R. Tuttle. Hierarchical correctness proofs for distributed algorithms. Master's thesis, Massachusetts Institute of Technology, Laboratory for Computer Science, April 1987. Available as MIT Technical Report MIT/LCS/TR-387.

[WLL88] Jennifer L. Welch, Leslie Lamport, and Nancy A. Lynch. A lattice-structured proof of a minimum spanning tree algorithm. In *Proceedings of the 7th Annual ACM Symposium on Principles of Distributed Computing*, pages 28–43. ACM, August 1988.

[Yi90] Wang Yi. Real-time behaviour of asynchronous agents. In J. C. M. Baeten and J. W. Klop, editors, *Lecture Notes in Computer Science, volume 458, Proceedings of Concur '90*, pages 502–520. Springer-Verlag, August 1990.

Relating Processes With Respect to Speed

Faron Moller* Chris Tofts
Department of Computer Science
University of Edinburgh

Abstract

In this paper, we consider the problem of defining a preorder on concurrent processes which will distinguish between functionally behaviourally equivalent processes which operate at different speeds. As our basic framework, we use a subset of the calculus TCCS of [Mol90], a language for describing concurrent processes involving timing constraints.

There is an anomaly in timed process calculi such as TCCS which nullifies the possibility of defining such a preorder which is a precongruence. This anomaly arises due to the nature of the constructs in the calculus which force events to be executed without delay. To rectify this conflict, we define and motivate the above mentioned subcalculus, which we call ℓTCCS (*loose* TCCS), and define our relation over this language. ℓTCCS is precisely TCCS where all events may delay indefinitely before executing. We demonstrate why this is necessary in order for any sensible *faster than* relation to be a precongruence.

Upon providing the semantic definition of our *"faster than"* relation, we give results on the precongruicity of the relation and present a set of inequational laws.

1 Introduction

In [Mol90], the authors introduced a language for the expression and analysis of timing constraints within concurrent processes. The language TCCS, the *Temporal Calculus of Communicating Systems*, was founded on Milner's *Calculus of Communicating Systems* CCS of [Mil80, Mil89]. The syntax and operational semantics of the calculus were introduced, and an observational congruence was defined based on Park's notion of bisimulation from [Par81]. Equational laws were provided for reasoning about the defined semantic congruence, and several examples were provided to illustrate the utility of the calculus in reasoning about concurrent processes involving timing constraints.

A missing feature in this work was a study on the relative speeds of functionally behaviourally equivalent processes. Two processes were deemed equivalent roughly when they were identical in both their functional *and* their temporal behaviour, as viewed by an external observer. The purpose of the present paper is to fill in this missing aspect by defining a *"faster than"* precongruence which will hold between two process terms if they are functionally behaviourally equivalent, but that the first term can execute its function faster (*ie*, sooner) than the second term.

The reason that the study of a *faster than* precongruence was not addressed in TCCS was that, as is explained in the next section of this paper, the expressiveness of TCCS is too powerful

*Research supported by ESPRIT BRA Grant No. 3006 — CONCUR

to admit such a notion. In order to define a sensible notion of relative speeds, we need to restrict ourselves to a subset of TCCS.

In the next section of this paper, we outline the theory of TCCS, and explain the problem with discussing speed in the full calculus. We use this discussion to motivate and define our subcalculus with which we shall be working. Next, we formally define our semantic precongruence, and relate it to the equivalence defined in [Mol90] for TCCS. We then go on to present some sound inequational laws for reasoning algebraically about processes and their relative speeds.

2 The Calculus TCCS

In this section, we give a brief introduction to the calculus TCCS by presenting the syntax and transitional semantics of the language, along with a behavioural equivalence defined using the semantic definition of the calculus. The description is self contained; however, the reader is urged to refer to [Mol90] for the full treatment of the language. We then present the difficulty which arises in trying to define a sensible *faster than* relation, and motivate a subcalculus of TCCS to be used for this purpose.

2.1 Syntax

The language TCCS is a timed extension of CCS. To define the syntax of the language, we first presuppose a set Λ of atomic action symbols not containing τ, and we define Act $= \Lambda \cup \{\tau\}$. We assume that Λ can be partitioned into two equinumerous sets with a "complementation" bijection $\bar{\cdot}$ between them. These complementary actions form the basis of the communication method in our calculus, analogous to CCS. We also take $\mathcal{T} = \{1, 2, 3, \ldots\}$ to represent divisions in time, and presuppose some set Var of process variables.

The collection of TCCS expressions, ranged over by P, is then defined by the following BNF expression where we take $a \in$ Act, $L \subseteq \Lambda$, $X \in$ Var, $t \in \mathcal{T}$, S ranging over *relabelling functions*, those $S : \Lambda \to \Lambda$ such that $\overline{S(a)} = S(\bar{a})$ and $S(\tau) = \tau$, and $\tilde{x}$, $\tilde{P}$ representing (equal-length) vectors of process variables $(x_1, x_2, \ldots, x_n)$ and expressions $(P_1, P_2, \ldots, P_n)$ respectively.

$$\begin{aligned} P \;::=\; & 0 \mid X \mid a.P \mid (t).P \mid \delta.P \\ & \mid P \oplus P \mid P + P \mid P \mid P \mid P \backslash L \mid P[S] \mid \mu_i \tilde{x}.\tilde{P} \end{aligned}$$

The informal interpretation of these is as follows.

- 0 represents the nil process, which can neither proceed with any action, nor proceed through time.
- X represents the process bound to the variable X.
- $a.P$ represents the process which can perform the action a and evolve into the process P upon so doing.
- $(t).P$ represents the process which will evolve into the process P after exactly t units of time.

- $\delta.P$ represents the process which behaves as the process P, but is willing to wait any amount of time before actually proceeding. The understanding of this process is in fact that it is wanting to synchronise or communicate with its environment, but is willing to wait until such time as the environment is ready to participate in such a communication.

- $P+Q$ represents a choice between the two processes P and Q. The process will behave as the process P or the process Q, with the choice being made at the time of the first action. Thus for instance any initial passage of time must be allowed by both P and Q. We shall refer to this operator as *strong* choice.

- $P \oplus Q$ represents a slightly different notion of choice between the two processes P and Q. The process will behave as the process P or the process Q, with the choice being made at the time of the first action, or else at the occurrence of a passage of time when only one of the operands may allow the time passage to occur. In this case, the second *"stopped"* process will be dropped from the computation. We shall refer to this operator as *weak* choice.

- $P \mid Q$ represents the parallel composition of the two processes P and Q. Each of the processes may do any actions independently, or they may synchronise on complementary actions, resulting in a τ action. Any passage of time must be allowed and recorded by each of P and Q.

- $P \backslash L$ represents the process P with the actions named in L restricted away, that is, not allowed to occur.

- $P[S]$ represents the process P with its actions relabelled by the relabelling function S.

- $\mu_i \tilde{x}.\tilde{P}$ represents the solution x_i taken from the solutions to the mutually recursive definitions of the processes $\tilde{x}$ defined as particular solutions to the equations $\tilde{x} = \tilde{P}$.

Some points worth noting which arise from the above informal description are as follows.

- The process $\mathbf{0}$ acts as a deadlock process in that it cannot perform any actions, nor witness any passage of time. Hence, by the descriptions above of the strong and weak choice operators $+$ and $\oplus$, and the parallel composition operator $|$, the constant $\mathbf{0}$ acts as an annihilator with respect to adding or composing with time-guarded processes, and as a unit with respect to the weak choice operator $\oplus$. Thus in particular, local temporal deadlock will imply global deadlock — if only time derivations are possible from each component of a parallel composition involving $\mathbf{0}$, then the whole composite process is deadlocked. Hence, of interest is the derived *nontemporal deadlock* process $\delta.\mathbf{0}$, which will allow any time to pass, but can never perform any actions. This process thus stands as a unit with respect to the strong choice operator $+$ and the parallel composition operator $|$. We shall henceforth abbreviate this process to $\underline{\mathbf{0}}$.

- The description given above of the delay prefix δ is such that it is only meaningful to follow it with action terms. $\delta.P$ represents a process which is delaying the *actions* of P until the environment in which the process is executing will allow the actions to proceed. Thus for instance, the process $\delta.(1).a.\mathbf{0}$ can never perform its action a, as it can never get past the delaying δ. Hence, this process will be identified with $\underline{\mathbf{0}}$, the nontemporal deadlock. Of importance then is the delayed action prefix $\delta.a.P$, which we henceforth abbreviate to $\underline{a}.P$.

We shall occasionally omit the dot symbol when applying the prefix operators, and also drop trailing **0**'s, thus for instance rendering $\delta.a.\mathbf{0} + (t).b.\mathbf{0}$ as $\delta a + (t)b$ (or as $\underline{a} + (t)b$). Finally, we shall allow ourselves to specify processes definitionally, by providing recursive definitions of processes. For example, we shall write $A \stackrel{\text{def}}{=} a.A$ rather than $A \stackrel{\text{def}}{=} \mu x.a.x$.

2.2 Semantics

The semantics of TCCS is *transition based*, structurally presented in the style of [Plo81], outlining what actions and time delays a process can witness. In order to define our semantics however, we must first define a syntactic predicate which will allow us to specify when a process must stop delaying its computation within a particular amount of time. This is done using the following function on TCCS terms.

Definition 2.1 *The function stop* : TCCS $\rightarrow \{0, 1, 2, \ldots, \omega\}$ *defines the maximum delay which a process may allow before forcing a computation (or deadlock) to occur. Formally, this function is defined as follows:*

$$\begin{aligned} stop(\mathbf{0}) &= 0 & stop(P \oplus Q) &= \max(stop(P), stop(Q)) \\ stop(X) &= 0 & stop(P + Q) &= \min(stop(P), stop(Q)) \\ stop(a.P) &= 0 & stop(P \mid Q) &= \min(stop(P), stop(Q)) \\ stop((s).P) &= s + stop(P) & stop(P \backslash L) &= stop(P) \\ stop(\delta.P) &= \omega & stop(P[S]) &= stop(P) \\ & & stop(\mu_i \tilde{x}.\tilde{P}) &= stop(P_i\{\mu\tilde{x}.\tilde{P}/\tilde{x}\}) \end{aligned}$$

This definition is well defined as long as all recursive variables are guarded by action or time prefixes.

In Figure 1, we present the operational rules for our language. They are presented in a natural deduction style, and are to be read as follows: if the transition(s) above the inference line can be inferred, then we can infer the transition below the line. Our transitional semantics over TCCS then is given by the least relations $\longrightarrow \subseteq$ TCCS $\times$ Act $\times$ TCCS and $\rightsquigarrow \subseteq$ TCCS $\times \mathcal{T} \times$ TCCS (written $P \xrightarrow{a} Q$ and $P \overset{t}{\rightsquigarrow} Q$ respectively) satisfying the rules laid out in Figure 1. Notice that these rules respect the informal description of the constructs given in the previous section.

We can also give operational rules directly for our two derived operators, temporal nil $\underline{\mathbf{0}}$ and delayed action prefix $\underline{a}.P$. These are presented in Figure 2. These rules are redundant along with those of Figure 1; however, they will be needed for the subcalculus with which we work later.

We can now define an equivalence relation $\sim$ on closed terms of TCCS based on Park's notion of a *bisimulation* ([Par81]) as follows.

Definition 2.2 *A binary relation $\mathcal{R}$ over terms in* TCCS *is a* $\mathcal{T}$-bisimulation *if and only if for all $(P, Q) \in \mathcal{R}$ and for all $a \in$* Act *and for all $t \in \mathcal{T}$,*

(i) if $P \xrightarrow{a} P'$ then $Q \xrightarrow{a} Q'$ for some Q' with $(P', Q') \in \mathcal{R}$;
(ii) if $Q \xrightarrow{a} Q'$ then $P \xrightarrow{a} P'$ for some P' with $(P', Q') \in \mathcal{R}$;
(iii) if $P \overset{t}{\rightsquigarrow} P'$ then $Q \overset{t}{\rightsquigarrow} Q'$ for some Q' with $(P', Q') \in \mathcal{R}$;
(iv) if $Q \overset{t}{\rightsquigarrow} Q'$ then $P \overset{t}{\rightsquigarrow} P'$ for some P' with $(P', Q') \in \mathcal{R}$.

$$\frac{}{a.P \xrightarrow{a} P} \qquad \frac{P \xrightarrow{a} P'}{P \oplus Q \xrightarrow{a} P'} \qquad \frac{P \xrightarrow{a} P',\ Q \xrightarrow{\bar{a}} Q'}{P|Q \xrightarrow{\tau} P'|Q'}$$

$$\frac{P \xrightarrow{a} P'}{\delta.P \xrightarrow{a} P'} \qquad \frac{Q \xrightarrow{a} Q'}{P \oplus Q \xrightarrow{a} Q'} \qquad \frac{P \xrightarrow{a} P'}{P\backslash L \xrightarrow{a} P'\backslash L}(a,\bar{a} \notin L)$$

$$\frac{P \xrightarrow{a} P'}{P+Q \xrightarrow{a} P'} \qquad \frac{P \xrightarrow{a} P'}{P|Q \xrightarrow{a} P'|Q} \qquad \frac{P \xrightarrow{a} P'}{P[S] \xrightarrow{S(a)} P'[S]}$$

$$\frac{Q \xrightarrow{a} Q'}{P+Q \xrightarrow{a} Q'} \qquad \frac{Q \xrightarrow{a} Q'}{P|Q \xrightarrow{a} P|Q'} \qquad \frac{P_i\{\mu\tilde{x}.\tilde{P}/\tilde{x}\} \xrightarrow{a} P'}{\mu_i\tilde{x}.\tilde{P} \xrightarrow{a} P'}$$

$$\frac{}{\delta.P \overset{t}{\rightsquigarrow} \delta.P} \qquad \frac{P \overset{t}{\rightsquigarrow} P',\ Q \overset{t}{\rightsquigarrow} Q'}{P+Q \overset{t}{\rightsquigarrow} P'+Q'} \qquad \frac{P \overset{t}{\rightsquigarrow} P',\ Q \overset{t}{\rightsquigarrow} Q'}{P|Q \overset{t}{\rightsquigarrow} P'|Q'}$$

$$\frac{}{(s+t).P \overset{s}{\rightsquigarrow} (t).P} \qquad \frac{P \overset{t}{\rightsquigarrow} P'}{P \oplus Q \overset{t}{\rightsquigarrow} P'}(stop(Q) < t) \qquad \frac{P \overset{t}{\rightsquigarrow} P'}{P\backslash L \overset{t}{\rightsquigarrow} P'\backslash L}$$

$$\frac{}{(t).P \overset{t}{\rightsquigarrow} P} \qquad \frac{Q \overset{t}{\rightsquigarrow} Q'}{P \oplus Q \overset{t}{\rightsquigarrow} Q'}(stop(P) < t) \qquad \frac{P \overset{t}{\rightsquigarrow} P'}{P[S] \overset{t}{\rightsquigarrow} P'[S]}$$

$$\frac{P \overset{s}{\rightsquigarrow} P'}{(t).P \overset{s+t}{\rightsquigarrow} P'} \qquad \frac{P \overset{t}{\rightsquigarrow} P',\ Q \overset{t}{\rightsquigarrow} Q'}{P \oplus Q \overset{t}{\rightsquigarrow} P' \oplus Q'} \qquad \frac{P_i\{\mu\tilde{x}.\tilde{P}/\tilde{x}\} \overset{t}{\rightsquigarrow} P'}{\mu_i\tilde{x}.\tilde{P} \overset{t}{\rightsquigarrow} P'}$$

Figure 1: Operational Rules for TCCS

$$\frac{}{\underline{a}.P \xrightarrow{a} P} \qquad\qquad \frac{}{\underline{0} \overset{t}{\rightsquigarrow} \underline{0}} \qquad\qquad \frac{}{\underline{a}.P \overset{t}{\rightsquigarrow} \underline{a}.P}$$

Figure 2: Operational Rules For Derived Operators

$\sim \stackrel{\text{def}}{=} \bigcup\{\mathcal{R} : \mathcal{R}$ *is a* $\mathcal{T}$*-bisimulation*$\}$ *is then the largest* $\mathcal{T}$*-bisimulation.*

In [Mol90], it is shown that this relation defines a congruence over TCCS terms, and we have also presented there an equational theory which is sound and complete with respect to reasoning about finite-state processes.

2.3 The Problem With Speed

Within the calculus of TCCS, we can describe different *timeout* processes which will allow a certain computation to take place within a given amount of time, but will preempt the computation and proceed with an alternate computation if that amount of time is allowed to pass without the desired computation being performed. As an example, the TCCS term $P + (2).b.0$ will allow the process P to proceed within 2 units of time, but will subsequently perform the action b and evolve into a deadlocked nil process if the process P does not proceed within the required time. Hence, $P + (2).b.0$ can be regarded as a timeout context. If we were to replace P with each of the terms $(1).a.0$ and $(3).a.0$ which represent the processes which will perform an a action after 1 and 3 units of time respectively, then in the first case, we would result in the process (behaviour) $(1).a.0$, whereas in the second case we would result in $(2).b.0$ due to the different timeout scenarios. Clearly we would want to consider the process term $(1).a.0$ to be *faster than* the process term $(3).a.0$. However, if we further desired that our *faster than* preorder be a precongruence (that is, that it be substitutive), then we would be led to deduce that the process term $(1).a.0$ is *faster than* the process term $(2).b.0$. This is undesirable though, as these two terms are not even functionally behaviourally equivalent.

The problem arises due to the preemptive nature of passing time in the semantics of the operators — it is possible to lose the capability of following a particular computation path through idling. In [Tof90], this problem is challenged by allowing all processes to idle indefinitely without changing state. However, this approach involves an undesirable weakening of the semantic development of the calculus TCCS. Instead we opt here for a more subtle approach to weakening the expressive power of the calculus. What we actually do is restrict our language to a subset of TCCS where the above undesirable *timeout* notions are no longer definable. We need to insist that, though we can have timeout events made available in the environment after some amount of time, we can never lose the ability to do some other event due to the passing of time. This is not an unreasonable restriction, particularly in the design of hardware circuits, as this is precisely how an implementation behaves — if a port is prepared to communicate, then this communication capability can only be removed through an actual change in state, and not through idling.

3 The Language ℓTCCS

The syntax of the language ℓTCCS (*loose* TCCS) is the subset of TCCS given by the following BNF expression.

$$P ::= \underline{0} \mid X \mid \underline{a}.P \mid (t).P \mid P + P \mid P|P \mid P\backslash L \mid P[S] \mid \mu_i\tilde{x}.\tilde{P}$$

Thus we do not have the usual deadlocked nil process $\mathbf{0}$, nor the usual action prefix operator $a.P$ which insists on the action a to be performed without allowing the possibility of any time passing first. Instead we include only the (formerly derived) operators $\underline{0}$ and $\underline{a}.P$. Also, due to the idling nature of actions in ℓTCCS, we no longer need to include the delay operator δ. Indeed we would not like to include this operator in our subcalculus, as a *faster than* relation could not be substitutive with respect to it; where we would clearly have $\underline{a}$ faster than $(1).\underline{a}$, we would not be able to deduce that $\delta.\underline{a}$ was faster than $\delta.(1).\underline{a}$. Finally, in the context of ℓTCCS, the + and $\oplus$ operators behave exactly the same, so we need to include only one of these in the subcalculus.

It is clear now that no temporal deadlocking can occur, so the problem of preempting actions through idling does not arise. This is summarized by the following simple proposition

Proposition 3.1 *For all (closed) ℓTCCS terms P and all $t \in \mathcal{T}$, there is a (unique) P' such that $P \overset{t}{\rightsquigarrow} P'$.*

The semantics is defined as before, using the subset of transition rules given in Figure 1 corresponding to the collection of operators used in the subcalculus, along with the transition rules given in Figure 2 for the temporal nil $\underline{0}$ and delayed action prefix $\underline{a}$. Note that here now the rules of Figure 2 are no longer derivable.

Using the transitional semantics defined here, we can define our *faster than* preorder $\lesssim$ using the following bisimulation-like definition. In this definition, and throughout the sequel, we shall allow ourselves to write the term $(0).P$, and to allow the transition $P \overset{0}{\rightsquigarrow} P$; for $(0)P$ we shall read P, and for $P \overset{0}{\rightsquigarrow} Q$ we shall read *"Q is syntactically identical to P"*.

Definition 3.2 *A binary relation $\mathcal{R}$ over terms of ℓTCCS is a $\lesssim$-bisimulation if and only if for all $(P,Q) \in \mathcal{R}$ and for all $a \in$ Act and for all $t \in \mathcal{T}$,*

(i) if $P \overset{a}{\longrightarrow} P'$ then $Q \overset{s}{\rightsquigarrow} Q' \overset{a}{\longrightarrow} Q''$ and $P' \overset{s}{\rightsquigarrow} P''$ for some s, Q', Q'', P'' with $\left(P'',Q''\right) \in \mathcal{R}$;

(ii) if $Q \overset{a}{\longrightarrow} Q'$ then $P \overset{a}{\longrightarrow} P'$ for some P' with $(P',Q') \in \mathcal{R}$;

(iii) if $P \overset{t}{\rightsquigarrow} P'$ then $Q \overset{t}{\rightsquigarrow} Q'$ for some Q' with $(P',Q') \in \mathcal{R}$;

(iv) if $Q \overset{t}{\rightsquigarrow} Q'$ then $P \overset{t}{\rightsquigarrow} P'$ for some P' with $(P',Q') \in \mathcal{R}$.

$\lesssim \overset{\text{def}}{=} \bigcup\{\mathcal{R} : \mathcal{R}$ is a $\lesssim$-bisimulation$\}$ is then the largest $\lesssim$-bisimulation.

Thus the only difference between this definition and the definition of the equivalence given above appears in the first clause: if the first (*faster*) process term can perform a particular action, then the second (*slower*) process term can either perform that action right away and evolve into a new process state which is *slower than* that into which the first process evolved, or else it can idle for some amount of time s and reach a state in which it can perform the action and thus evolve into a state which, while not necessarily itself *slower than* that into which the first process evolved, but *slower than* that state once the idling time is accounted for. As an example, we would clearly want that

$$\underline{a} \mid (1)\underline{b} \lesssim (1)\underline{a} \mid (1)\underline{b}.$$

Now in the *faster* term, the action transition

$$\underline{a}\,|\,(1)\underline{b} \xrightarrow{a} \underline{0}\,|\,(1)\underline{b}$$

is matched in the *slower* term by the sequence of transitions

$$(1)\underline{a}\,|\,(1)\underline{b} \overset{1}{\rightsquigarrow} \underline{a}\,|\,\underline{b} \xrightarrow{a} \underline{0}\,|\,\underline{b}$$

and while $\underline{0}\,|\,(1)\underline{b} \not\lesssim \underline{0}\,|\,\underline{b}$, we only require in the definition that $\underline{0}\,|\,\underline{b} \lesssim \underline{0}\,|\,\underline{b}$, as $\underline{0}\,|\,(1)\underline{b} \overset{1}{\rightsquigarrow} \underline{0}\,|\,\underline{b}$.

The relation $\lesssim$ is a preorder: it is reflexive, as clearly

$$Id \stackrel{\text{def}}{=} \Big\{(P,P) : P \in \ell\text{TCCS}\Big\}$$

is a $\lesssim$-bisimulation, and it is transitive, as given $\lesssim$-bisimulations $\mathcal{R}_1$ and $\mathcal{R}_2$ we can easily confirm that $\mathcal{R}_3 \stackrel{\text{def}}{=} \mathcal{R}_1\mathcal{R}_2$ is a $\lesssim$-bisimulation.

We can furthermore show that this relation is a precongruence over ℓTCCS terms which do not have any parallel operators within the scope of a recursion. We only demonstrate here the difficult part of the proof of substitutivity, that with respect to the parallel operator.

Proposition 3.3 *Let $\#P$ denote the number of parallel operators in the term P.*

(i) $\mathcal{R}_k \;=\; \Big\{(P_1\,|\,Q_1, P_2\,|\,Q_2) \;:\; P_1 \lesssim P_2,\ Q_1 \lesssim Q_2,\ \#(P_i\,|\,Q_i) \le k\Big\}$ *is a $\lesssim$-bisimulation.*

(ii) If $\#P \le k$, $P \xrightarrow{a} P'$ and $P \overset{t}{\rightsquigarrow} P_0$, then $P' \overset{t}{\rightsquigarrow} P''$ and $P_0 \xrightarrow{a} P_0'$ with $P'' \lesssim P_0'$.

Proof: By simultaneous induction on k.

(i) The only difficult clause to check in the definition of $\lesssim$-bisimulation is the first, in the case where the action in question is a synchronization event τ; that is, when $P_1\,|\,Q_1 \xrightarrow{\tau} P_1'\,|\,P_2'$ by virtue of the fact that $P_1 \xrightarrow{a} P_1'$ and $Q_1 \xrightarrow{\bar{a}} Q_1'$. In this case, $P_2 \overset{s}{\rightsquigarrow} P_2' \xrightarrow{a} P_2''$, $Q_2 \overset{t}{\rightsquigarrow} Q_2' \xrightarrow{\bar{a}} Q_2''$, $P_1' \overset{s}{\rightsquigarrow} P_1''$ and $Q_1' \overset{t}{\rightsquigarrow} Q_1''$ with $P_1'' \lesssim P_2''$ and $Q_1'' \lesssim Q_2''$. If $s = t$ then the result follows easily, so we shall assume that $s < t$. By inductive hypothesis *(ii)*, we have that $P_2' \overset{t-s}{\rightsquigarrow} \hat{P}_2 \xrightarrow{a} \hat{P}_2'$ and $P_2'' \overset{t-s}{\rightsquigarrow} P_2'''$ with $P_2''' \lesssim \hat{P}_2'$. Furthermore, $P_1'' \overset{t-s}{\rightsquigarrow} P_1'''$ with $P_1''' \lesssim P_2'''$, so $P_1''' \lesssim \hat{P}_2'$. Hence $P_2\,|\,Q_2 \overset{t}{\rightsquigarrow} \hat{P}_2\,|\,Q_2' \xrightarrow{\tau} \hat{P}_2'\,|\,Q_2''$ and $P_1'\,|\,Q_1' \overset{t}{\rightsquigarrow} P_1'''\,|\,Q_1''$ with $(P_1'''\,|\,Q_1'', \hat{P}_2'\,|\,Q_2'') \in \mathcal{R}_k$.

(ii) Proceeding by structural induction on P, we prove again only the difficult case of parallel composition. Hence assume that $P\,|\,Q \xrightarrow{a} P'\,|\,Q \overset{t}{\rightsquigarrow} P''\,|\,Q'$ and $P\,|\,Q \overset{t}{\rightsquigarrow} P_0\,|\,Q'$ By inductive hypothesis *(ii)*, $P_0 \xrightarrow{a} P_0'$ with $P'' \lesssim P_0'$. Thus $P_0\,|\,Q' \xrightarrow{a} P_0'\,|\,Q'$, and then by inductice hypothesis *(i)*, $P''\,|\,Q' \lesssim P_0'\,|\,Q'$. □

The restriction on the parallel operators is there to facilitate our proof; the number of parallel operators in a term could grow through semantic transitions if there were such operators within the scope of a recursion. We conjecture that this restriction can be removed, but have failed to provide a proof of this more general result.

It is clear from the similarities in the definitions of $\sim$ and $\lesssim$ that for P and Q being two terms of ℓTCCS, if $P \sim Q$ then $P \lesssim Q$ (and $Q \lesssim P$). However the reverse implication does not hold; that is, $P \lesssim Q$ and $Q \lesssim P$ does not necessarily imply that $P \sim Q$. A suitable simple counter-example is provided by the following two process terms:

$$A \stackrel{\text{def}}{=} \underline{a}\underline{b} + \underline{a}(1)\underline{b} + \underline{a}(2)\underline{b} \qquad\qquad B \stackrel{\text{def}}{=} \underline{a}\underline{b} + \underline{a}(2)\underline{b}$$

These two processes are equally fast by the above definition, yet are not equivalent, as $A \xrightarrow{a} (1)\underline{b}$, but for no $B' \sim (1)\underline{b}$ does $B \xrightarrow{a} B'$. Hence another equivalence of interest is $\lesssim \cap \gtrsim$, which we represent by $\cong$.

We have another general anomaly with this — or indeed any — *faster than* preorder for nondeterministic processes: we cannot guarantee that if $P \lesssim Q$, then P will *necessarily* execute faster than Q, but only that it has the capability of so doing. We would for example insist by reflexivity that for the above process A, $A \lesssim A$; but in executing the two instances of A, the first (supposedly *faster*) version may start with an a transition to the state $(2)\underline{b}$, whereas the second version may start with an a transition to the state $\underline{b}$. However, this problem only arises in the presence of nondeterminism, and also vanishes if we assume some form of built-in priority allowing faster computation paths to be followed whenever possible.

3.1 Example

My sister Velma in Canada subscribes to Maclean's, "Canada's weekly newsmagazine". When she is finished reading these, she duly sends them to me to keep me informed of the latest developments on the Canadian scene. In fact, she *always* sends me 6 issues at a time, so that a new package gets sent approximately every 42 days (it takes that long to amass 6 copies, but my sister sometimes procrastinates and doesn't put them into an envelope, or doesn't go to the post office with them, until some indeterminate time later).

When she started this practice six years ago, she always sent the magazines by air mail. Canada Post would receive the package from her, and deliver it about four days later; it always takes at least four days to deliver an air mail package from Canada to Scotland, but it could take substantially much longer still. Thus the behaviour exhibited by Canada Post in delivering the ith package is represented by the following equation:

$$\mathrm{AM}_i \stackrel{\text{def}}{=} \underline{\mathrm{in}}_i.(4).\overline{\underline{\mathrm{del}}}_i.0.$$

That is, the post office would receive the ith package at some point in time ($\underline{\mathrm{in}}_i$), then not communicate with the external environment (myself and my sister) for four days, after which (and this means at some indeterminate time afterwards) it would deliver the package to me ($\overline{\underline{\mathrm{del}}}_i$). Thus ended the process of delivering the ith package.

The behaviour of the post office with respect to my magazine packages then was dictated by the following equation:

$$\mathrm{RS}_i \stackrel{\text{def}}{=} \mathrm{AM}_i \,|\, (42).\mathrm{RS}_{i+1}.$$

That is, my *Rich Sister* RS would be ready to send the ith package by air mail, while at the same time, another 42-day period was being counted down before the next package was ready to send.

There are interesting properties associated with this process, which are inherent in the loose semantic notion of timing. Firstly, of course I could not expect to receive the ith package of magazines before $42i$ days had passed; I could not read the news before it was written! But apart from that, I could not know with any certainty when I would receive my package; I was dependent on the reliability of my sister and of Canada Post. In fact I could receive the packages in the wrong order (in fact in an arbitrary order), which on occasion did happen.

Alas, my sister quickly felt the squeeze as the expense of sending regular air mail packages became too much, and she started sending the packages occasionally by surface mail. Thus her behaviour started being dictated by the following equation:

$$\mathrm{MS}_i \stackrel{\mathrm{def}}{=} (\mathrm{AM}_i + \mathrm{SM}_i) \mid (42).\mathrm{MS}_{i+1},$$

where SM_i is the behaviour of Canada Post when handling a package being sent by surface mail:

$$\mathrm{SM}_i \stackrel{\mathrm{def}}{=} \underline{\mathrm{in}_i}.(4).\overline{\underline{\mathrm{del}_i}}.0 + \underline{\mathrm{in}_i}.(60).\overline{\underline{\mathrm{del}_i}}.0.$$

Packages sent by surface mail take at least 60 days to be delivered, but on regular occasions a package which is posted by surface mail is thrown into an airmail bag and is delivered at airmail speed.

Hence my *Middle-class Sister* MS saved money by occasionally sending me my magazines by surface mail. The change in the system was clearly noticeable, as I found myself reading even older news. However, it was still news to me, as I have no other reliable source for Canadian current events. As I never complained to her, and since she still felt the budget crunch whenever she sent a package of magazines to me by air mail, my sister eventually quit sending packages by air mail altogether. Her behaviour then became dictated by the following equation:

$$\mathrm{PS}_i \stackrel{\mathrm{def}}{=} \mathrm{SM}_i \mid \mathrm{PS}_{i+1}.$$

Henceforth, my *Poor Sister* PS sent me all my magazines by surface mail. However, I noticed the change much less so than with the original change, as I came to expect my magazines to arrive late, and was only surprised when they arrived early. This situation still remains, as my magazines regularly arrive by air mail post, though they were intended by my sister to be sent by surface mail.

The differences in the delivery times, and the fact that I only really noticed the effect of the first change, can be seen from the faster-than relationships exibited in the above processes. Firstly we have that

$$\mathrm{AM}_i \precsim \mathrm{AM}_i + \mathrm{SM}_i \precsim \mathrm{SM}_i,$$

and in fact more than that we have that

$$\mathrm{RS}_i \precsim \mathrm{MS}_i \precsim \mathrm{PS}_i.$$

Thus I certainly couldn't expect to notice a speedup in the delivery of my magazines. However, note also that

$$\mathrm{SM}_i \precsim \mathrm{AM}_i + \mathrm{SM}_i \not\precsim \mathrm{AM}_i,$$

and in fact

$(+_1)$	$(x+y)+z = x+(y+z)$	$(+_2)$	$x+y = y+x$
$(+_3)$	$x+x = x$	$(+_4)$	$x+\underline{0} = x$
(T_1)	$(s)(t)x = (s+t)x$	(T_2)	$(t)x+(t)y = (t)(x+y)$
(T_3)	$x+(t)x = x$	(T_4)	$(t)\underline{0} = \underline{0}$
(T_5)	$x \leq (t)x$		

Figure 3: Equational Theory for Sequential ℓTCCS

$$\mathrm{PS}_i \precsim \mathrm{MS}_i \not\succsim \mathrm{RS}_i,$$

That is, the magazines sent by my *rich* sister were delivered *as fast as* those sent by my *middle-class* sister, but not vice-versa; whereas those sent by my *middle-class* sister were delivered *as fast as* those sent by my *poor* sister, and vice versa. Hence I never noticed this second change the way that I did the first. If however, Canada Post reliably sent the surface mail packages by surface mail, then I would never receive any early packages, and the resulting system would *not* be *as fast as* $\mathrm{AM}_i + \mathrm{SM}_i$, and the difference would be noticeable.

4 Inequational Laws

In this section, we develop a set of inequational laws for ℓTCCS which are sound with respect to our semantic precongruence $\precsim$. We shall use $\leq$ to represent derivability in the theory (along with $=$ representing $\leq \cap \geq$), and $\equiv$ to represent syntactic identity.

4.1 Finite Sequential Terms

We start our analysis by restricting our attention to the finite sequential subcalculus of ℓTCCS given by the following BNF equation.

$$P ::= \underline{0} \mid \underline{a}.P \mid (t).P \mid P+P$$

We shall refer to this subcalculus by $\ell\mathrm{TCCS}_0$.

Our inequational theory for $\ell\mathrm{TCCS}_0$ is presented in Figure 3. We can straightforwardly demonstrate that these laws are valid with respect to our semantic precongruence $\precsim$ over the full calculus ℓTCCS. Hence we get the following result.

Proposition 4.1 (Soundness) $p \leq q \implies p \precsim q$.

Next we want to show that these laws are complete for reasoning over $\ell\mathrm{TCCS}_0$. We accomplish this using the following normal form.

Definition 4.2 *A term is a* <u>*NF term*</u> *(or is* <u>*in NF*</u>*) if it is of the form*

$$\sum_{1 \leq i \leq m} (t_i).\underline{a_i}.p_i$$

where each p_i is itself in NF.

Our first task in proving completeness is to show that every term in ℓTCCS can be converted into NF using these laws.

Proposition 4.3 *Every term $p \in \ell\mathrm{TCCS}_0$ can be equated to a term in NF using the laws of* Figure 3.

Proof: A straightforward structural induction on p. □

So for our completeness result, we only need to show that for NF terms P and Q, if $P \lesssim Q$ then $P \leq Q$.

Proposition 4.4 *If $P \lesssim Q$ where $P \equiv \sum_i (s_i).\underline{a_i}.p_i$ and $Q \equiv \sum_j (t_j).\underline{b_j}.q_j$ are in NF, then $P \leq Q$.*

Proof: Let P and Q be given as above. It suffices to prove the following facts.

(i) $\forall i \exists j : a_i = b_j \ \wedge \ p_i \lesssim q_j$;
(ii) $\forall j \exists i : a_i = b_j \ \wedge \ p_i \lesssim q_j \ \wedge \ s_i \leq t_j$.

From the first fact, using structural induction, we can deduce that

$$(s_i).\underline{a_i}.p_i + (t_j).\underline{b_j}.q_j \ \leq \ (t_j).\underline{b_j}.q_j,$$

from which we can deduce that $P + Q \leq Q$; and from the second fact, again using structural induction, we can deduce that

$$(s_i).\underline{a_i}.p_i \leq (t_j).\underline{b_j}.q_j,$$

from which we can deduce that $P \leq P + Q$. Putting these together, we get $P \leq Q$.

Both these facts follow immediately from the definition of $\lesssim$, noting that

$$\sum_i (s_i \dot{-} t).\underline{a_i}.p_i \lesssim \sum_j (t_j \dot{-} t).\underline{b_j}.q_j$$

where $x \dot{-} y = \max(0, x - y)$. □

4.2 Adding Concurrency

ℓTCCS, like CCS, is an *interleaving* theory of concurrency. That is, we can represent the parallel functional behaviour of processes in terms of causality and nondeterministic choice. The typical example is given by the equation

$$\underline{a} \mid \underline{b} \;=\; \underline{ab} + \underline{ba}$$

This equation is an instance of what is known as the *Expansion Theorem*. A major advantage of this treatment of concurrency is that the algebraic analysis of concurrent terms can be reduced to the analysis of sequential terms.

Unfortunately, when we add timing prefixes, our analysis becomes complicated, as the expressive power of the calculus becomes inadequate to express parallel processes as equivalent sequential terms. In the calculus TCCS, this problem was successfully overcome by introducing the weak choice operator $\oplus$. However, we cannot find such a sensible extension to the calculus ℓTCCS for which the notion of *faster than* remains substitutive, to allow ourselves to express every (finite) term in an equivalent sequential form. For example, the term $\underline{a} \mid (1)\underline{b}$ has no equivalent sequential form. We would want to be able to express this term by its expansion, namely as $\underline{a}(1)\underline{b} + (1)(\underline{a} \mid \underline{b})$ (where we can then recursively expand the subterm $\underline{a} \mid \underline{b}$). However this term is clearly not equivalent to the original, as the expanded term can idle one unit of time, then perform an a action and evolve into a state where it must idle for one more unit of time before being capable of performing the b action, whereas the parallel term after idling one unit of time and then performing the a action, will always be capable of immediately performing the b action.

Though the usual expansion of a parallel term is not necessarily equivalent to the term itself, we do have the result that it is related in one direction to the parallel term in the *faster than* relation; the parallel term is guaranteed to be *faster than* the sequentialised expanded term. These expansion principles are presented in Figure 4.

Hence, we thus cannot use the usual technique in comparing two terms of expressing the terms as equivalent sequential terms and then comparing these sequential terms using our complete set of laws for such terms. However, the expansion of a (parallel) term is so very close to being equivalent to the term itself, that we conjecture that it is not possible to find a term which falls in the *faster than* relation strictly between a term and its expanded version.

In [Mol90], we introduced valid Expansion Theorem laws for the full calculus TCCS which are equally valid here if we do not use substitutivity as a proof rule. These laws could be used as well in a proof as long as due care were taken.

5 Related Work

There have been many descriptions of process algebras as the foundation of concurrency theory, but only recently have any of these models been extended to consider the problem of describing the real-time aspects of concurrent systems. Especially recently, there has been a spate of developments involving each of the main process algebra approaches aimed at incorporating real-time aspects into the theory. As a sample we refer to [Ree86, Bae89, Gro90, Hen90, Mol90, Nic90, Wan90].

None of these previous attempts have considered the problem of relating process terms with

Let $X = \sum_{1 \le i \le m} \underline{a}_i x_i$ and $Y = \sum_{1 \le j \le n} \underline{b}_j y_j$

$$(E_1)\ X \mid Y = \sum_{1 \le i \le m} \underline{a}_i(x_i \mid Y) + \sum_{1 \le j \le n} \underline{b}_j(X \mid y_j) + \sum_{\underline{a}_i = \overline{\underline{b}}_j} \underline{\tau}(x_i \mid y_j)$$

$$(E_2)\ X \mid (Y + (1)y) \le \sum_{1 \le i \le m} \underline{a}_i(x_i \mid (Y + (1)y)) + \sum_{1 \le j \le n} \underline{b}_j(X \mid y_j) + \sum_{\underline{a}_i = \overline{\underline{b}}_j} \underline{\tau}(x_i \mid y_j) + (1)(X \mid (Y + y))$$

$$(E_3)\ (X + (1)x) \mid Y \le \sum_{1 \le i \le m} \underline{a}_i(x_i \mid Y) + \sum_{1 \le j \le n} \underline{b}_j((X + (1)x) \mid y_j)) + \sum_{\underline{a}_i = \overline{\underline{b}}_j} \underline{\tau}(x_i \mid y_j) + (1)((X + x) \mid Y)$$

$$(E_4)\ (X + (1)x) \mid (Y + (1)y) \le \sum_{1 \le i \le m} \underline{a}_i(x_i \mid (Y + (1)y)) + \sum_{1 \le j \le n} \underline{b}_j((X + (1)x) \mid y_j)) + \sum_{\underline{a}_i = \overline{\underline{b}}_j} \underline{\tau}(x_i \mid y_j) + (1)(x \mid y) + (1)((X + x) \mid (Y + y))$$

Figure 4: Expansion Laws

respect to speed. Most of the approaches cited above allow for actions to be made to occur at specified times (as with the calculus TCCS described in this report and in [Mol90]), and thus would not allow for a substitutive notion of a relative speed relation. Others, including [Hen90, Wan90], are similar to ℓTCCS in that they only specify the delay before a particular action may occur, allowing the action to occur any time after that delay; these approaches would then have difficulty with the axiomatization of concurrency as described above, with the theory of process equality as well as with a *faster than* relation. Also, these two particular approaches include a *maximal progression* principle which enforces communications to occur at the time which they may occur without delay, thus returning to the problems of defining such a desired substitutive relation.

There has been one other approach to describing relative efficiency in process algebras, described in [Aru90]. This relation equates two process terms if they are bisimilar with the proviso that the faster term need never perform more internal τ actions than the slower term. This approach does not deal with real-time issues in process algebra, but does go a long way towards analysing the types of questions of interest in the notion. A similar relation, coined a *contraction* by Milner, is presently implemented in the Edinburgh Concurrency Workbench, and is described in [CWB90].

Bibliography

[Aru90] Arun-Kumar, S., M. Hennessy, *An Efficiency Preorder for Processes*, University of Sussex Research Report No. 5/90, 1990.

[Bae89] Baeten, J.C.M., J.A. Bergstra, *Real Time Process Algebra*, Preliminary Draft, 10/20/89, 1989.

[CWB90] *The Edinburgh Concurrency Workbench - Operating Instructions*, University of Edinburgh Technical Report, 1990.

[Gro90] Groote, J.F., *Specification and Verification of Real Time Systems in ACP*, Research Report No CS-R9015, Centre for Mathematics and Computer Science, Amsterdam, 1990.

[Hen90] Hennessy, M., T. Regan, *A Temporal Process Algebra* Technical Report No. 2/90, University of Sussex Computer Science Department, April, 1990.

[Mil80] Milner, R., **A Calculus of Communicating Systems**, Lecture Notes in Computer Science 92, Springer-Verlag, 1980.

[Mil83] Milner, R., *Calculi for Synchrony and Asynchrony*, Theoretical Computer Science, Vol 25, 1983.

[Mil89] Milner, R., **Communication and Concurrency**, Prentice–Hall International, 1989.

[Mol90] Moller, F., C. Tofts, *A Temporal Calculus of Communicating Systems*, Proceedings of CONCUR'90 (Theories of Concurrency: Unification and Extension), Amsterdam, August 1990.

[Nic90] Nicollin, X., J.L. Richier, J. Sifakis, J.Voiron, *ATP: An Algebra for Timed Processes*, Proceedings of IFIP Working Conference on Programming Concepts and Methods, North Holland, 1990.

[Par81] Park, D.M.R., *Concurrency and Automata on Infinite Sequences*, Lecture Notes in Computer Science 104, Springer–Verlag, 1981.

[Plo81] Plotkin, G.D., *A Structured Approach to Operational Semantics*, DAIMI FN-19, Computer Science Department, Aarhus University, 1981.

[Ree86] Reed, G.M., A. Roscoe, *A Timed Model for Communicating Sequential Processes*, Proceedings of ICALP'86, Lecture Notes in Computer Science No 226, Springer Verlag, 1986.

[Tof90] Tofts, C., *Proof Systems and Pragmatics for Parallel Programming*, PhD Thesis, University of Edinburgh, 1990.

[Wan90] Wang Yi, *Real-time Behaviour of Asynchronous Agents*, Proceedings of CONCUR'90 (Theories of Concurrency: Unification and Extension), Amsterdam, August 1990.

TESTING, BETTING AND TIMED TRUE CONCURRENCY

David Murphy,
Department of Computing Science,
University of Glasgow, Glasgow. G12 8QQ
Email : dvjm@dcs.glasgow.ac.uk

ABSTRACT. The testing methodology is both appealingly simple and powerful as a way of analysing the behaviour of processes. In this paper we extend it in three ways.

Firstly we show how to incorporate the testing methodology into models where the notion of observation is central, rather than that of participation; we do this by introducing the notion of betting. This gives us a testing paradigm for true concurrency models such as event structures.

Secondly we introduce various timed bets to extend the methodology to timed models. An intuitively attractive semantics that admits a clear notion of rapidity of response is obtained.

Thirdly we show how bets can be extended to causal bets that allow us to reason about the causal behaviour of systems. The assumption that causality is observable is a strong one, but it may be justified if we read 'concurrent' as 'physically distributed'.

Finally we classify the various betting semantics, presenting a hierarchy of semantics of increasing power. The semantics are presented with respect to a timed event structure model; they could, however, be applied to any (timed) causal model.

Dans les champs de l'observation, le hasard ne favorise que les esprits préparés.

Pasteur

1. INTRODUCTION

One of the major paradigms in semantics for concurrency is that of *testing*. The basic concept, presented by Hennessy in [9], is that two processes should be considered equivalent if there is no test that can distinguish them. The testing methodology is usually applied to systems where one gains information by *interaction*; to test a CCS process one places a test process in parallel with it. But this is not the only paradigm in concurrency theory; there is also room for the assumption that one can gain information about a system by merely observing it, no participation being necessary; this is the paradigm of Petri nets, event structures and 'true concurrency' models generally. We seek to extend the testing methodology to these models. The only other work we know of in this direction is [2].

Another limitation of testing is that is unclear how to extend it cleanly to timed models, although there has been some progress, such as [7] and [10].

We extend the testing methodology by proposing *betting*, a notion that is suitable for characterising equivalences in observational rather than participatory models. Moreover, the betting methodology handles timed and true concurrency models.

Our paradigm is that one makes some observation of a concurrent system, and then tires of observing and repairs instead to a betting shop, to bet on what the system will do next. The idea of 'must' and 'may' are taken from testing; we state when a bet must win, and when it may win. We then formulate various bet combinators that allow complex bets about the future behaviour of the system to be made; these define the logic of observation.

The rest of the paper is structured thus: first we briefly introduce the timed event structures model of [14], in which our theory will be couched.* Then we define the basic betting framework of must win and may win, and introduce timed bets. The various ways of combining bets are then introduced, much in the spirit of Abramsky's [1]. Finally we give a hierarchy of betting models, showing how much discriminating power each class of bets allows us. This paper is based on material from the thesis [14], to which the reader is referred for further details. Related, independent work is presented in [19].

2. A Model

We have already remarked upon the dichotomy between process algebras, where one participates with a process to gain information about it, and models where one merely observes. The latter will concern us here; we call such models *classical*, as a classical stand is taken on the nature of observation and nondeterminism:

2.1. Classical Concurrency Theory. In classical concurrency theories, a concurrent system is an autonomous entity that evolves without reference to its environment. The idea of *causality* is central to them; causality determines which sequences things are constrained to happen in. Two happenings are concurrent if they are not mutually exclusive or completely causally related. Moreover, there is no necessary relationship between concurrency and simultaneity.

Such models naturally interpret nondeterminism as "completely unknowable choice," a notion that would have been familiar to the church fathers. They also permit a very simple and intuitive introduction of *time*; events have durations, and the times they start and finish are observed. Furthermore, they allow us to assume that events are distinguishable; every time an action happens, it is labeled.

The main advantage of classical models is *verisimilitude*; the basic notions they have match well with the fundamental behaviour of implementations of distributed systems, and with the way users think about them. The issues of time and liveness are particularly important; many models suffer from not being able to articulate the simple requirement 'this must happen now.' (Further discussion of these ideas is given in [14] and [16]; the latter also contains a comparison with related work.)

2.2. Basic Ideas. We will define a concurrency theory intended for describing the behaviours of (implementations of) timed systems. The obvious choice for the descriptively-rich model we seek is one based on partial orders; cf. Winskel's event structures [20] and Gischer's pomsets [8].

We will consider as given a set of **T** of transitions, endowed with a strict partial order $<_c$ (i.e. an irreflexive and transitive relation). The relationship $x <_c y$ is interpreted as

---

* We use this model because it has a very rich notion of behaviour; perfect for experimenting with notions of behavioural equivalence. There are other possibilities, offering different insights, as indicated in 'Concluding Remarks,' section 6.

the transition x somehow causing the transition y. If neither $x <_c y$ nor $y <_c x$ nor $x = y$ then x and y are *unrelated*. They could be transitions in different places, or transitions simultaneous with each other, or neither; it doesn't matter. All that is certain is that they do not causally affect each other; they are on different *paths*: causal information can be seen as specifying abstract location information, since the absence of a causal relationship between two happenings means that they could be distributed.

(Internal) nondeterminism is modelled by endowing transitions with a symmetric, irreflexive relation, the *conflict relation*, written #.

The next step is to add *time*. Timing is only slowly becoming an issue that is much considered in the mainstream of concurrency theory, witness the recent flurry of activity [5, 10, 12, 16, 18, 19]. In a timed model *when* something happens is as important as *what* happens; we introduce it by assuming the existence of a notional, omniscient observer who records the times that each event starts and finishes.†

2.3. Occurrences and their Causality. Suppose that some finite set of actions **A** is of interest. These actions will be things that can happen more than once, like having a birthday, or eating an apple. Each time an action occurs it will acquire a label taken from a (countable) set **L** so that the pair $(l, e), l \in \mathbf{L}, e \in \mathbf{A}$ is unique.

Following the usual usage, we will refer to an occurrence of an action, — a pair $a = (l, e)$, — as an event. Each event has a start and a finish, and subscripts will be used for these, so a_s will be the start of a and a_f its finish; we use also a_t for either a_s or a_f. The starts and finishes of events will be referred to as *transitions*.

The set of transitions **T** is endowed with a strict partial order $<_c$ representing causality. It will be convenient to enforce the following:

- The beginnings of events cause their ends; $\forall a_s, a_f \in \mathbf{T} \,.\, a_s <_c a_f$.
- There is a distinguished event $*$, known as the *silent event*, the start of which causes everything, and whose finish everything causes.

The silent event $*$ can be thought of as an 'on light.' Once we see $*_s$, we know that the structure is active, while $*_f$ tells us that everything is over.

It may be important to have events beginning at the same time as the on light goes on, so we need to introduce a new relation, *causal equality* written $=_c$. The statement $a_t =_c a'_t$ indicates that a_t and a'_t have the same causality, or are *necessarily simultaneous*. The relation $=_c$ is the largest (coarsest) congruence over $<_c$ defined by

$$\begin{aligned}(a_t =_c a'_t) \iff \forall b_t \in \mathbf{T} \,.\, & (a_t <_c b_t \iff a'_t <_c b_t) \;\wedge \\ & (b_t <_c a_t \iff b_t <_c a'_t)\end{aligned}$$

This clearly gives us a congruence that is, moreover, distinct from $<_c$;

$$(a_t =_c b_t) \Rightarrow (a_t \not<_c b_t) \wedge (b_t \not<_c a_t)$$

To be like an on light, the silent event must encompass all transitions, so we require

$$\forall a_t \in \mathbf{T} \,.\, (*_s <_c a_t \;\vee\; *_s =_c a_t)$$
$$\forall a_t \in \mathbf{T} \,.\, (a_t <_c *_f \;\vee\; a_t =_c *_f)$$

† This is *not* a global clocks assumption, as the observer's clock cannot influence transitions, only record their times. Even in highly relativistic situations this is not an unreasonable assumption; other observers may disagree with our observer about the times things happen, but their observations can be deduced from those of our observer if their relative velocity is known.

The set of possible occurrences of actions will be denoted by **LA**;

$$\mathbf{LA} \subseteq \mathbf{L} \times \mathbf{A} \cup \{*\}$$

Thus $(l, e) \in \mathbf{LA}$ means there may be an lth occurrence of action e. Our structures will always contain at least $*$, as we require $* \in \mathbf{LA}$. Think of $\mathbf{L} \times \mathbf{A}$ as a universe of occurrences, and **LA** as a subset of those that are of interest at once.

The relationship between the sets of transitions, labels and actions is

$$\mathbf{T} = \{a_s \mid a \in \mathbf{LA}\} \cup \{a_f \mid a \in \mathbf{LA}\}$$

Notice that $\leq_c$ ($= <_c \cup =_c$) is a partial order on **T**.

2.4. Paths in Time. Causality has been modelled by endowing transitions, members of **T**, with a strict partial order $<_c$. Timing is dealt with by assigning them a real. This leaves us with a model incorporating both timing and causality.

We will want to record information about when things happen and how they are related; the when is time, and the how is space. Thus knowing temporal and causal information about a transition gives us a point in *spacetime*.

Definition 1 (Spacetime). A point in spacetime is a pair (r, a_t) where a_t is a transition and r is a real number. For a given set of transitions, **T**, the set of all possible points in space time, **ST**(**T**) say, will thus be $\mathbf{R} \times \mathbf{T}$. A *task* can now be defined to be a triple $(a, \underline{\text{begin}}(a), \underline{\text{end}}(a))$ consisting of the occurrence of an action, $a \in \mathbf{LA}$, and the points in spacetime it starts and finishes. The set of all tasks will be $\mathbf{TK} \subset \mathbf{LA} \times \mathbf{ST} \times \mathbf{ST}$. (Here 'task' is used in a slightly different sense to that of Gischer, [8], to whom the term is due.)

Points in spacetime will be symbolised by t with a subscript; s and f stand for starts and finishes respectively, and t for either, so that, for instance $t_s = (r_s, a_s)$ is the point the event a started. We will write $a \equiv [t_s, t_f]$ for $a \in \mathbf{LA}, t_s, t_f \in \mathbf{ST}$ to indicate that the task (a, t_s, t_f) associates the event a with the 'interval' in spacetime $[t_s, t_f]$, i.e. $\underline{\text{begin}}(a) = t_s$ and $\underline{\text{end}}(a) = t_f$. Given a set of tasks **TK**, we can always recover the underlying set of occurrences **LA**; this means that it is safe to confuse events with their associated tasks; something we will freely do henceforth. We will also abuse the notation further, writing **LA** for the set of occurrences underlying a given **TK**, **LA**$'$ for that underlying **TK**$'$ etc.

Definition 2 (Relations on Spacetime). Suppose we have the timings $a \equiv [(r_s, a_s), (r_f, a_f)]$, $b \equiv [(s_s, b_s), (s_f, b_f)]$. Then we can define spacetime relations

$$(r_s, a_s) <_s (s_s, b_s) \iff r_s < s_s \ \wedge\ a_s <_c b_s$$
$$(r_s, a_s) =_s (s_s, b_s) \iff r_s = s_s \ \wedge\ a_s =_c b_s$$

The relations $=_s$ and $<_s$ on spacetime represent both causality and timing, so that $t_t <_s u_t$ means that the instant in spacetime t_t happens before the instant u_t and causes it. We write $t_t \leq_s u_t$ iff $t_t <_s u_t$ or $t_t =_s u_t$ and require

- Things can't happen before their causes; $(a_t <_c b_t) \Rightarrow (r_t < s_t)$. Hence, causal ordering implies temporal ordering.
- Transitions that are causally-equal must be temporally-equal; $a_t =_c b_t \Rightarrow r_t = s_t$.

2.5. Primitive Concurrency. A rather primitive notion of concurrency is supported by the model as presented thus far. It seems reasonable to say that two tasks are concurrent if there is some point in spacetime belonging to one that is not related to a point of the other. (We can imagine an instance where a and b are concurrent, but their starts are necessarily simultaneous, as in $P \stackrel{\text{def}}{=} a \parallel b$, where we might expect $a_s =_c b_s$.)

Definition 3 (Incomparability). Suppose t_t, $u_t \in \mathbf{ST}$. Then t_t and u_t are said to be *incomparable*, written $t_t \,\underline{\text{inc}}\, u_t$, iff

$$t_t \not<_s u_t \;\wedge\; u_t \not<_s t_t \;\wedge\; t_t \neq_s u_t$$

while two tasks, $a \equiv [t_s, t_f]$ and $b \equiv [u_s, u_f]$ are said to be incomparable if a pair of their times is incomparable, that is, iff

$$t_s \,\underline{\text{inc}}\, u_s \;\vee\; t_f \,\underline{\text{inc}}\, u_s \;\vee\; t_s \,\underline{\text{inc}}\, u_f \;\vee\; t_f \,\underline{\text{inc}}\, u_f$$

If two tasks a and b are incomparable then we write $a \,\underline{c}\, b$.

Definition 4 (Elementary Interval Event Structures). We can now define elementary event structures where events are associated with intervals of time: an elementary I.E.S. is a triple $(\mathbf{TK}, <_s, =_s)$ consisting of a set of tasks, $\mathbf{TK}$, a spacetime order $<_s$, and a spacetime equality $=_s$.

2.6. Conflict. Conflict will be modelled by the common partial-order model technique of introducing a set of *consistent sets* of occurrences, $\underline{\text{Con}} \subseteq \wp(\mathbf{TK})$. An element of $\underline{\text{Con}}$ is a set of tasks, all of which can happen in the same history, so if $\{a, b\} \in \underline{\text{Con}}$, then there is some execution in which the tasks a and b both occur. The $\underline{\text{Con}}$-set tells us where the branches of branching time branch.

If a set of tasks A is consistent, then any subset of it should also be consistent, so we have the restriction on possible $\underline{\text{Con}}$-sets

$$A \in \underline{\text{Con}} \;\&\; B \subseteq A \;\Rightarrow\; B \in \underline{\text{Con}}$$

Two tasks are in conflict, $a \# b$, just when there is no consistent set containing them, so we recover $\#$ from $\underline{\text{Con}}$ by defining

$$a \# b \iff \{a, b\} \notin \underline{\text{Con}}$$

Furthermore, it seems sensible to allow two tasks to be in conflict only if they are incomparable; if they are completely causally related, then it is hard to know how they could be in conflict, so we also require of $\underline{\text{Con}}$ that

$$a \# b \Rightarrow a \,\underline{c}\, b$$

This implies that if two tasks are completely causally related, then they are in essentially the same $\underline{\text{Con}}$-sets. Say $a_t \sim_c b_t \iff (a_t \leq_c b_t \vee b_t \leq_c a_t)$. Then

$$\forall c \in \underline{\text{Con}}\,.\,(a \in c \;\wedge\; a_s \sim_c b_s \;\wedge\; a_f \sim_c b_f) \;\Rightarrow\; c \cup \{b\} \in \underline{\text{Con}}$$

We will require that $\underline{\text{Con}}$ covers TK, $\bigcup \underline{\text{Con}} = \mathbf{TK}$, and that there is always at most finite choice (formalised in [16]).

The introduction of conflict permits a more sophisticated definition of concurrency. Two tasks a and b, will be *concurrent*, written $a \,\underline{\text{co}}\, b$, iff they are incomparable and not in conflict;

$$a \,\underline{\text{co}}\, b \iff a \,\underline{c}\, b \wedge \{a, b\} \in \underline{\text{Con}}$$

Definition 5 (Interval Event Structures). An interval event structure $\Im$ is a quadruple (**TK**, $\underline{\text{Con}}$, $<_s, =_s$) consisting of a set of tasks, **TK**, a set of consistent sets, $\underline{\text{Con}}$, a spacetime order $<_s$ and a spacetime equality $=_s$. The class of all interval event structures will be written **IES**.

Sometimes we will be interested in ignoring the paths in spacetime (location and choice information), and considering just the time of occurrences. This gives us the notion of *linear* interval event structure, or L.I.E.S.:

Definition 6 (Linear Interval Event Structures). A linear I.E.S $\Im$ is a triple (**TK**, $<, =$) consisting of a set of tasks, **TK**, and the usual $<$ and $=$ on $\mathbf{R}$. We shall, given the lack of $<_s, =_s$, take two L.I.E.S.s as equal if they have the same events with the same real timings.

A linear structure can be thought of as a model of an observation of a single execution of an I.E.S. A complete history of one such execution will just contain all the tasks from a *maximal* $\underline{\text{Con}}$-set, together with the order on their times;

Definition 7 (Maximal $\underline{\text{Con}}$-Sets). A $\underline{\text{Con}}$-set c is said to be maximal with respect to an I.E.S. $\Im$ = (**TK**, $\underline{\text{Con}}$, $<_s$, $=_s$) if

$$(c' \in \underline{\text{Con}} \wedge c \subseteq c') \Rightarrow c = c'$$

The set of all maximal $\underline{\text{Con}}$-sets of an I.E.S. $\Im$ is written $\mathcal{M}(\Im)$.

Notice firstly that the 'on light' $*$ goes on and off in every complete history; $\forall c \in \mathcal{M}(\Im) . * \in c$, and secondly that any given $\underline{\text{Con}}$-set is either maximal itself or can be extended to a maximal one.

Definition 8 (Realisable I.E.S.). If one is only interested in modelling systems that we can actually build, then it makes sense to restrict the class of I.E.S.s considered. If an I.E.S. $\Im$ = (**TK**, $\underline{\text{Con}}$, $<_s$, $=_s$) satisfies the axioms (1) and (2) below, then it is said to be *realisable*. The class of all realisable I.E.S.s will be written **RIES**.

$$\forall c \in \underline{\text{Con}}, \forall r_1, r_2 \in \mathbf{R} .$$
$$\{ a \mid a \in c,\ a \equiv [(r_s, a_s), (r_f, a_f)],\ [r_s, r_f] \cap [r_1, r_2] \neq \emptyset \} \text{ is finite} \tag{1}$$

(The structure is only doing a finite amount at once.)

$$\forall a_t \in \mathbf{T} . \{ b_t \mid b_t <_c a_t, a_t \in \mathbf{T}, \{a, b\} \in \underline{\text{Con}} \} \text{ is finite} \tag{2}$$

(Everything is finitely caused.) Failure to observe these rules may lead to the construction of *Zeno machines*; machines which can exhibit an infinite number of distinguishable events in a finite time. Joseph's [12] contains some discussion of this point.

3. Elementary Bets

In this section we will outline the betting methodology. The essential idea is to explore the behaviour of a structure by first observing it and then betting on what it will do next. First we have to say what an observation of an I.E.S. is. Then we formulate the notion of a bet on what might happen next. More complex kinds of bets which capture the timing behaviour of an I.E.S. are then investigated. For convenience, we confine ourselves to realisable interval event structures whose silent events start at time zero. Notice that for this class of structures every transition must happen in some bounded interval $[0, r]$.

3.1. Observations. Consider a maximal $\underline{\text{Con}}$-set of an I.E.S. $\Im$, $\mathcal{L} \in \mathcal{M}(\Im)$; think of this as a *complete history* of $\Im$. We know that this history is complete since it includes $*_f$, which tells us that $\mathcal{L}$ (and hence this execution of $\Im$) is over. In this section we will also be concerned with *incomplete histories*, or observations of an I.E.S.; an observation will be a complete history truncated at some time. This truncation will mean that we may see some tasks start but not finish. To record this, we introduce a new, distinguished element of spacetime $\blacktriangledown$, (read 'future') so that $\underline{\text{end}}(a) = \blacktriangledown$ means that we haven't observed long enough to see the end of a.[‡]

Definition 9 (Observation). For any $\mathcal{K} = (\mathbf{TK}, <, =) \in \mathcal{M}(\Im)$ and any $r \in \mathbf{R}^+$, there is an observation, $\mathcal{K}$ *truncated at* r, written $\mathcal{K}\nearrow^r$.

This observation is a L.I.E.S. $(\mathbf{TK}', <, =)$, where $\mathbf{LA}' = \{a \,|\, a \in \mathbf{LA}, \underline{\text{begin}}(a) < r\}$.[§]

An event a in $\mathbf{LA}'$ carries the same timing it had in $\mathbf{LA}$, unless it finished later than t, in which case we say $\underline{\text{end}}(a) = \blacktriangledown$. (Of course, for $a_t \in \mathbf{ST}\,.\, a_t \leq_s \blacktriangledown$.) Notice that all observations contain $*$, since $*_s$ happens at $r = 0$, and we only define $\Im\nearrow^r$ for $r > 0$.

3.2. Betting on Transitions. Suppose we have a L.I.E.S. $\mathcal{L}$ and a maximal $\underline{\text{Con}}$-set $\mathcal{K} \in \mathcal{M}(\Im)$. $\mathcal{L}$ is *observational consistent* with $\mathcal{K}$ if there is a $r \in \mathbf{R}^+$ so that $\mathcal{L} = \mathcal{K}\nearrow^r$. Write $\mathcal{P}(\Im, \mathcal{L})$ for the set $\{\mathcal{K} \,|\, \mathcal{L}$ is observational consistent with $\mathcal{K}\}$ of maximal $\underline{\text{Con}}$-sets we could be observing from what we know so far.

Consider an observer. She has seen $\Im$ do $\mathcal{L} = (\mathbf{TK}', <, =)$. What happens next ? Suppose she bets it is a_t, and she is actually seeing some $\mathcal{K} \in \mathcal{P}(\Im, \mathcal{L})$. Then she wins, (i.e. a_t is a valid extension of the observation $\mathcal{L}$,) in two cases;

$a_t = a_s$. That is, she will see the start of a new event a starting at r_s. Then this must be the first event to start that's in $\mathcal{K}$ and not in $\mathcal{L}$;

$$r_s = \underline{\min}\{r \mid a \equiv [r, r_f],\ a \in (\mathbf{LA} - \mathbf{LA}')\}$$

$a_t = a_f$. That is, she will see the finish of an old event $a \in \mathbf{LA}'$. Then this is the earliest finish that's in $\mathcal{K}$ and not in $\mathcal{L}$;

$$r_f = \underline{\min}\{r \mid a \equiv [r_s, r],\ a \in \mathbf{LA}',\ \underline{\text{end}}(a) = \blacktriangledown \text{ in } \mathcal{L}\}$$

We will write $\mathcal{L} \cup \{a_t\}$ for $(\mathbf{LA}' \cup \{a_t\}, <, =)$. Notice that, since more than one thing can happen at a given time, there may be more than one transition a_t that extends $\mathcal{L}$ in $\mathcal{K}$.

Given some observation $\mathcal{L}$, the things $\Im$ may do next are just the extensions of $\mathcal{L}$ in each $\mathcal{K} \in \mathcal{P}(\Im, \mathcal{L})$. So, if some a_t extends all of these $\mathcal{K}$s, then a bet that it will happen next must win. Similarly, if it extends one of them, then a bet on it may win.

---

‡ Alternatively, think of $\underline{\text{begin}}$ and $\underline{\text{end}}$ as partial functions for a given observation, with $\underline{\text{end}}(a) = \blacktriangledown$ meaning $\underline{\text{end}}$ is not yet defined. These functions would then depend on the observation made; the longer it was, the more defined they would be. Such a perspective suggests a natural sheaf-theoretic model of observation, discussed in [15].

§ At first sight, this definition is a little strange, as the observer is allowed to know what the structure's labels are. Remember that we have a classical model, so we require that different occurrences of the same action are distinguishable. (This means that, for instance, $\mathbf{a} + \mathbf{a}$ can be distinguished from just $\mathbf{a}$.) In fact, we should require that the observer uses her own labels, so that there will be a bijection between the events she writes down and those in the maximal $\underline{\text{Con}}$-set she is seeing. For simplicity, we use the same labels for both the structure and the observer; the extra rigour is kept in [14].

Definition 10 (Must and May for Transitions). Given an I.E.S. $\mathfrak{I}$ and an observation of it $\mathcal{L}$, a bet that $\mathfrak{I}$ will do a_t next must or may win as follows

$$\mathfrak{I}\ \underline{\text{must}}\ a_t\ \underline{\text{after}}\ \mathcal{L} \iff \forall \mathcal{K} \in \mathcal{P}(\mathfrak{I},\mathcal{L})\,.\, a_t \text{ extends } \mathcal{L} \text{ in } \mathcal{K}$$
$$\mathfrak{I}\ \underline{\text{may}}\ a_t\ \underline{\text{after}}\ \mathcal{L} \iff \exists \mathcal{K} \in \mathcal{P}(\mathfrak{I},\mathcal{L})\,.\, a_t \text{ extends } \mathcal{L} \text{ in } \mathcal{K}$$

Notice that if $\mathcal{P}(\mathfrak{I},\mathcal{L})$ is empty, then $\mathfrak{I}\ \underline{\text{must}}\ a_t\ \underline{\text{after}}\ \mathcal{L}$ vacuously. This can happen firstly if $\mathfrak{I}$ can display no tasks, – but this is impossible since we must always see at least $*_s$, – and secondly if $\mathcal{L}$ is not a valid observation of $\mathfrak{I}$, – *ex falso quod libet.*

3.3. Adding Time to Bets. Let us suppose that our observer is impatient to know whether she has won her bet, and isn't prepared to wait arbitrarily long to find out. She will want to make a *timed bet*, betting not just that a_t will happen next, but that it will happen before δ more time has elapsed; this allows her to analyse the rapidity of response of the system.

Take as before an I.E.S. $\mathfrak{I}$ and an observation $\mathcal{L}$. We say that a_t^δ for $\delta \in \mathbf{R}^+$ extends $\mathcal{L}$ in $\mathcal{K}$ iff a_t extends $\mathcal{L}$ in $\mathcal{K}$, a_t happens at r_t and $\underline{\text{end}}(\mathcal{L}) \leq r_t < \underline{\text{end}}(\mathcal{L}) + \delta$. (Here $\underline{\text{end}}(\mathcal{L})$ is the end of the latest event in $\mathcal{L}$.) We can now define whether a δ–timed bet must or may win;

$$\mathfrak{I}\ \underline{\text{must}}\ a_t^\delta\ \underline{\text{after}}\ \mathcal{L} \iff \forall \mathcal{K} \in \mathcal{P}(\mathfrak{I},\mathcal{L})\,.\, a_t^\delta \text{ extends } \mathcal{L} \text{ in } \mathcal{K}$$
$$\mathfrak{I}\ \underline{\text{may}}\ a_t^\delta\ \underline{\text{after}}\ \mathcal{L} \iff \exists \mathcal{K} \in \mathcal{P}(\mathfrak{I},\mathcal{L})\,.\, a_t^\delta \text{ extends } \mathcal{L} \text{ in } \mathcal{K}$$

Notice that we take the bet to start at the end of $\mathcal{L}$; our observer makes her bet immediately after seeing the last observation of $\mathcal{L}$.

Our observer might care about precisely when things happen. In this case she can make a *strict-timed bet*, betting not just that a_t will happen next, but that it will happen some specified time later. We define ${}^r a_t$ extends $\mathcal{L}$ in $\mathcal{K}$ if a_t happens at r_t and $r = r_t - \underline{\text{end}}(\mathcal{L})$, with the obvious

$$\mathfrak{I}\ \underline{\text{must}}\ {}^r a_t\ \underline{\text{after}}\ \mathcal{L} \iff \forall \mathcal{K} \in \mathcal{P}(\mathfrak{I},\mathcal{L})\,.\, {}^r a_t \text{ extends } \mathcal{L} \text{ in } \mathcal{K}$$
$$\mathfrak{I}\ \underline{\text{may}}\ {}^r a_t\ \underline{\text{after}}\ \mathcal{L} \iff \exists \mathcal{K} \in \mathcal{P}(\mathfrak{I},\mathcal{L})\,.\, {}^r a_t \text{ extends } \mathcal{L} \text{ in } \mathcal{K}$$

3.4. Example. Consider the interval event structure shown in figure 1. The silent task $*$ is omitted for clarity. There are two maximal $\underline{\text{Con}}$–sets; in one there are two tasks, a and b, and the start of a causes the start of b, and similarly with the finishes. The other also contains two tasks, but there is no causal relationship between them. (Incidentally this example shows that we can have simultaneity without concurrency, as with c and d. The converse is also true.) The scale indicates time.

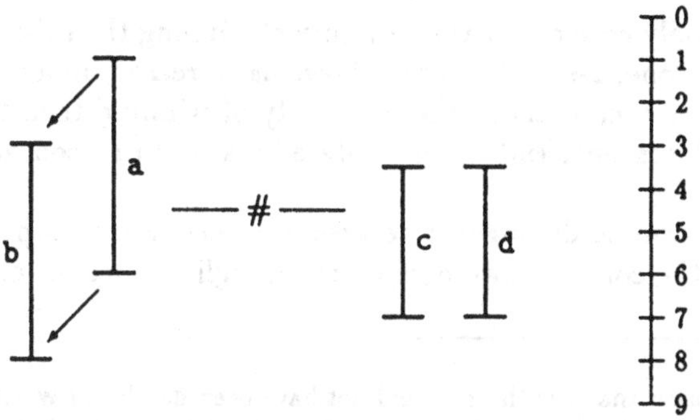

FIGURE 1. An Example Interval Event Structure

The following hold, taking $\Im$ as this example I.E.S. We write $\langle\rangle$ for the empty observation (that is, the observation of just $*_s$).

$$
\begin{array}{rl}
\Im\ \underline{\text{must}}\ \mathsf{b}_s\ \underline{\text{after}}\ \mathsf{a}_s & \Im\ \underline{\text{must}}\ \mathsf{d}_s\ \underline{\text{after}}\ \mathsf{c}_s \\
\Im\ \underline{\text{must}}\ \mathsf{a}_f\ \underline{\text{after}}\ \mathsf{a}_s\mathsf{b}_s & \Im\ \underline{\text{must}}\ \mathsf{c}_s\ \underline{\text{after}}\ \mathsf{d}_s \\
\Im\ \underline{\text{may}}\ \mathsf{a}_s\ \underline{\text{after}}\ \langle\rangle & \Im\ \underline{\text{may}}\ \mathsf{c}_s\ \underline{\text{after}}\ \langle\rangle \\
\neg(\Im\ \underline{\text{must}}\ \mathsf{a}_s\ \underline{\text{after}}\ \langle\rangle) & \Im\ \underline{\text{may}}\ \mathsf{d}_s\ \underline{\text{after}}\ \mathsf{c}_s
\end{array}
$$

$$
\begin{array}{rl}
\Im\ \underline{\text{must}}\ \mathsf{b}_s^4\ \underline{\text{after}}\ \mathsf{a}_s & \Im\ \underline{\text{must}}\ \mathsf{d}_s^4\ \underline{\text{after}}\ \mathsf{c}_s \\
\neg(\Im\ \underline{\text{must}}\ \mathsf{b}_s^2\ \underline{\text{after}}\ \mathsf{a}_s) & \Im\ \underline{\text{must}}\ \mathsf{d}_s^1\ \underline{\text{after}}\ \mathsf{c}_s
\end{array}
$$

$$
\begin{array}{rl}
\Im\ \underline{\text{must}}\ {}^2\mathsf{b}_s\ \underline{\text{after}}\ \mathsf{a}_s & \Im\ \underline{\text{must}}\ {}^0\mathsf{d}_s\ \underline{\text{after}}\ \mathsf{c}_s \\
\neg(\Im\ \underline{\text{must}}\ {}^1\mathsf{b}_s\ \underline{\text{after}}\ \mathsf{a}_s) & \Im\ \underline{\text{must}}\ {}^6\mathsf{d}_f\ \underline{\text{after}}\ \mathsf{c}_s
\end{array}
$$

4. Combining Bets

We will now investigate the distinguishing power of various combinations of bets. First we need to understand how to combine the results of several bets about a structure. Then we will explain how to construct complex bets from simpler ones in order to reason about complex behaviours.

Betting allows us to define various equivalences on processes, two processes being equivalent when they cannot be distinguished by a given class of bets. The distinguishing power of these equivalences is elucidated, showing how much structure each class of bets can 'see'. The logical part of this section mostly follows Abramsky's [1], which we summarise here for convenience.

4.1. The Results of Bets. Any particular bet can win or lose. We will use $\top$ to symbolise a win and $\bot$ to symbolise a loss. Given some observation $\mathcal{L}$ of $\Im$, we cannot always predict whether $\Im$ will a_t after $\mathcal{L}$ will win or not, due to nondeterminism. Thus the set of all results of this bet will form a set $\mathcal{R}(\Im, \mathcal{L}, a_t) \subseteq \{\top, \bot\}$ defined

$$
\begin{array}{rcl}
\top \in \mathcal{R}(\Im, \mathcal{L}, a_t) & \iff & \Im\ \underline{\text{may}}\ a_t\ \underline{\text{after}}\ \mathcal{L} \\
\bot \notin \mathcal{R}(\Im, \mathcal{L}, a_t) & \iff & \Im\ \underline{\text{must}}\ a_t\ \underline{\text{after}}\ \mathcal{L}
\end{array}
$$

Definition 11 (Powerdomains). A win is better than a loss, so $\top \geq \bot$ giving us the familiar ordered set 2. Every result of the bet that $\Im$ will do a_t after $\mathcal{L}$ lives on one of the powerdomains of 2 (see figure 2). Each of these corresponds to a notion of how to define the result of a set of bets:¶

- if we only care about the certainty of winning then the correct powerdomain is the Smyth one, $\wp_S(2)$; this only allows us to reason about whether the bet must win;
- if we only care about the possibility of winning then the correct powerdomain is the Hoare one, $\wp_H(2)$; this only allows us to reason about whether the bet may win;
- if we want to distinguish between the certain loss, a possible win and certain win, then the correct powerdomain is the Egli–Milner (or convex) one, $\wp_{EM}(2)$.

¶ There is no reason that our theory could not have been developed W.R.T. a much broader class of outcomes; we could, for instance, assign a winning sum to each primitive bet, and deal with the powerdomains of $\mathbb{N}$. Probabilistic systems may be accessible by these means.

$$\wp_S(2) = \quad \begin{array}{c} \{\top\} \\ | \\ \{\bot\} = \{\top, \bot\} \end{array} \qquad \wp_H(2) = \quad \begin{array}{c} \{\top\} = \{\top, \bot\} \\ | \\ \{\bot\} \end{array} \qquad \wp_{EM}(2) = \quad \begin{array}{c} \{\top\} \\ | \\ \{\top, \bot\} \\ | \\ \{\bot\} \end{array}$$

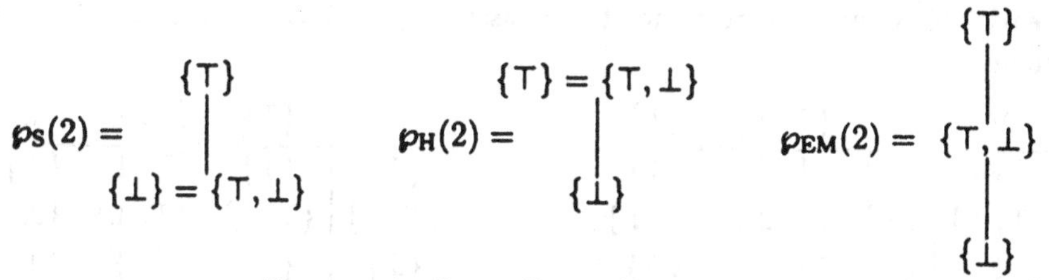

FIGURE 2. Some Powerdomains of 2

The Egli–Milner powerdomain allows the greatest discrimination between the results of multiple bets, so it will be used. In the next subsection *operations* on this powerdomain that correspond to combinations of bets will be considered; these are important because the discriminating power of betting will be seen to depend on which ways of combining bets are allowed.

4.2. Logical Operations and Bet Combinators.

A *computable* combination of bet outcomes will be modelled by a *continuous* function between powerdomains. Since we will only deal with finite domains, that means we are only interested in monotone functions. The following will be of use;

Fact. *Given any monotone function* $f : 2^n \to 2$, *there is a pointwise extension of* f *onto* $\wp_{EM}(2)$, *written* $f^\dagger$ *that is monotone;*

$$f^\dagger(X_1, \dots X_n) = \{f(x_1, \dots x_n) \mid x_i \in X_i, 1 \le i \le n\}$$

This extension is also multilinear in that it preserves unions in each argument separately.

Consider now the bet $\mathfrak{S}$ will do a_t after $\mathcal{L}$. Suppose that the observer is interested not just in a single thing happening next, but in a sequence $a_t, a_{t(1)}, a_{t(2)}, \dots$. Then an *accumulator* or series of bets is needed;

$\mathfrak{S}$ will a_t <u>after</u> $\mathcal{L}$ and
$\mathfrak{S}$ will $a_{t(1)}$ <u>after</u> $\mathcal{L} \cup \{a_t\}$ and
$\mathfrak{S}$ will $a_{t(2)}$ <u>after</u> $\mathcal{L} \cup \{a_t\} \cup \{a_{t(1)}\}$ and
$\vdots$

Alternatively, our observer might only care about a_t or a_t' happening next, betting

$\mathfrak{S}$ will a_t <u>after</u> $\mathcal{L}$ or
$\mathfrak{S}$ will a_t' <u>after</u> $\mathcal{L}$

She might also be interested in whether two transitions were simultaneous, betting

$\mathfrak{S}$ will a_t <u>after</u> $\mathcal{L}$ and
$\mathfrak{S}$ will a_t' <u>after</u> $\mathcal{L}$

Clearly then, we should be interested in bets on sequences and in the disjunction and conjunction of bets. The obvious $\wedge$ and $\vee$ on 2 extend pointwise to operators (which we shall also write $\wedge$ and $\vee$) on $\wp_{EM}(2)$ as shown below.

Disjunction and conjunction involve making two copies of a system, one for each conjunct. The results of the separate bets are then combined as indicated above. The multilinearity of $\wedge$ and $\vee$ corresponds to the assumption that the results of these bets are independent.

$\vee$	$\{\top\}$	$\{\top,\bot\}$	$\{\bot\}$
$\{\top\}$	$\{\top\}$	$\{\top\}$	$\{\top\}$
$\{\top,\bot\}$	$\{\top\}$	$\{\top,\bot\}$	$\{\top,\bot\}$
$\{\bot\}$	$\{\top\}$	$\{\top,\bot\}$	$\{\bot\}$

$\wedge$	$\{\top\}$	$\{\top,\bot\}$	$\{\bot\}$
$\{\top\}$	$\{\top\}$	$\{\top,\bot\}$	$\{\bot\}$
$\{\top,\bot\}$	$\{\top,\bot\}$	$\{\top,\bot\}$	$\{\bot\}$
$\{\bot\}$	$\{\bot\}$	$\{\bot\}$	$\{\bot\}$

Quantification may also be allowed over bets; our observer might want to bet "there is a run of the system in which this bet will win" or "in every run of the system this bet will win." This assumes that the observer can make as many copies of the system at any time as are necessary to examine the different histories possible from that point. (Note that since we have only finite nondeterminism, only finitely many copies are necessary.) There is much to be said for and against this assumption; Hennessy in [9] allows copying at the initial state but not locally, while Bloom in [4] argues that if one is allowed local copying, then it is reasonable to allow the observer to know how many copies were made, but allowing this gives a finer equivalence than local copying alone. In any case, we can define the quantifiers, making them available to those who think them reasonable;

$\forall$	
$\{\top\}$	$\{\top\}$
$\{\top,\bot\}$	$\{\bot\}$
$\{\bot\}$	$\{\bot\}$

$\exists$	
$\{\top\}$	$\{\top\}$
$\{\top,\bot\}$	$\{\top\}$
$\{\bot\}$	$\{\bot\}$

The intuition is this; the observer will win the bet "$\Im$ will $\forall a_t$ after $\mathcal{L}$" just when $\Im$ <u>must</u> a_t <u>after</u> $\mathcal{L}$. In other words, $\forall$ gives her a way of telling whether she was just lucky (she could have won and did) or whether fate really was with her (there was no way she could have lost). Similarly, $\Im$ will $\exists a_t$ after $\mathcal{L}$ will win just when $\Im$ <u>may</u> a_t <u>after</u> $\mathcal{L}$, giving her another a way of telling whether a loss was just unlucky, or fated from the moment she made her last observation. To say the same thing again, $\forall$ picks out the $\wp_S(2)$ subdomain of $\wp_{EM}(2)$, while $\exists$ picks out the $\wp_H(2)$ subdomain of $\wp_{EM}(2)$.

We now have the ingredients for the following syntax of bets. Assume as given some countable set of events $\mathbf{LA}_{\mathrm{Bet}}$. Then a untimed compound bet $\mathsf{b} \in \mathsf{B}(\mathbf{LA}_{\mathrm{Bet}})$ has the form, for $a_t \in \mathbf{LA}_{\mathrm{Bet}}$

$$\mathsf{b} ::= \mathsf{Win} \mid \mathsf{Loss} \mid a_t\mathsf{b} \mid \mathsf{b}_1 \vee \mathsf{b}_2 \mid \mathsf{b}_1 \wedge \mathsf{b}_2 \mid \forall\mathsf{b} \mid \exists\mathsf{b}$$

We also write $\mathsf{B}^\delta(\mathbf{LA}_{\mathrm{Bet}})$ for all δ-timed bets and ${}^\tau\mathsf{B}(\mathbf{LA}_{\mathrm{Bet}})$ for all strict-timed bets.

The semantics of bets is defined via a meaning function which, given an I.E.S., an observation of it, and a bet, returns the possible results of that bet when placed on the structure given the observation. Thus $\mathcal{S} : \mathbf{RIES}\times\mathbf{LIES}\times\mathsf{B}(\mathbf{LA}_{\mathrm{Bet}}) \to \wp_{EM}(2)$ is defined

$$\begin{aligned}
\mathcal{S}(\Im,\mathcal{L},\mathsf{Win}) &= \{\top\}\\
\mathcal{S}(\Im,\mathcal{L},\mathsf{Loss}) &= \{\bot\}\\
\mathcal{S}(\Im,\mathcal{L},a_t\mathsf{b}) &= \mathcal{R}(\Im,\mathcal{L},a_t) \wedge \mathcal{S}(\Im,\mathcal{L}\cup\{a_t\},\mathsf{b})\\
\mathcal{S}(\Im,\mathcal{L},\mathsf{b}_1\wedge\mathsf{b}_2) &= \mathcal{S}(\Im,\mathcal{L},\mathsf{b}_1) \wedge \mathcal{S}(\Im,\mathcal{L},\mathsf{b}_2)\\
\mathcal{S}(\Im,\mathcal{L},\mathsf{b}_1\vee\mathsf{b}_2) &= \mathcal{S}(\Im,\mathcal{L},\mathsf{b}_1) \vee \mathcal{S}(\Im,\mathcal{L},\mathsf{b}_2)\\
\mathcal{S}(\Im,\mathcal{L},\forall\mathsf{b}) &= \forall\mathcal{S}(\Im,\mathcal{L},\mathsf{b})\\
\mathcal{S}(\Im,\mathcal{L},\exists\mathsf{b}) &= \exists\mathcal{S}(\Im,\mathcal{L},\mathsf{b})
\end{aligned}$$

with the semantics for δ-timed and strict-timed bets following in the obvious way.

4.3. Equivalences and Ordering. The bet meaning function $\mathcal{S}$ induces an ordering on processes. Suppose $\leq_{\mathsf{EM}}$ is the ordering on $\wp_{\mathsf{EM}}(2)$. Then we say that $\Im$ is a *better earner* than $\Im'$ with respect to a universe of bets $\mathsf{B}(\mathbf{LA}_{\mathsf{Bet}})$, and write $\Im \sqsubseteq_{\mathsf{B}} \Im'$ iff

$$\forall \mathsf{b} \in \mathsf{B}(\mathbf{LA}_{\mathsf{Bet}}) \,.\, \mathcal{S}(\Im, \langle\rangle, \mathsf{b}) \;\leq_{\mathsf{EM}}\; \mathcal{S}(\Im', \langle\rangle, \mathsf{b})$$

There is an associated notion of equivalence,

$$\Im \sim \Im' \iff \Im \sqsubseteq_{\mathsf{B}} \Im' \wedge \Im' \sqsubseteq_{\mathsf{B}} \Im$$

Similarly, we write $\Im \sqsubseteq_{\mathsf{B}^\delta} \Im'$ and $\Im \sqsubseteq_{{}^{\tau}\mathsf{B}} \Im'$ iff, respectively,

$$\forall \mathsf{b} \in \mathsf{B}^\delta(\mathbf{LA}_{\mathsf{Bet}}) \,.\, \mathcal{S}(\Im, \langle\rangle, \mathsf{b}) \;\leq_{\mathsf{EM}}\; \mathcal{S}(\Im', \langle\rangle, \mathsf{b})$$
$$\forall \mathsf{b} \in {}^{\tau}\mathsf{B}(\mathbf{LA}_{\mathsf{Bet}}) \,.\, \mathcal{S}(\Im, \langle\rangle, \mathsf{b}) \;\leq_{\mathsf{EM}}\; \mathcal{S}(\Im', \langle\rangle, \mathsf{b})$$

It is straightforward to check that the 'better earner' orders are partial orders and that the associated notions of equivalence $\sim$, $\sim_{\mathsf{B}^\delta}$ and $\sim_{{}^{\tau}\mathsf{B}}$ are equivalence relations.

4.4. Combinators and Intuitions. Various subsets of the betting syntax give us the classical equivalents of some well-known semantic models. Notice that in each case we would have a weaker version of the same 'class' if we did not allow the observer to see labeling information; for instance, we can distinguish between $(\mathsf{a}\;;\;\mathsf{b}) + (\mathsf{a}\;;\;\mathsf{c})$ and $\mathsf{a}\,;(\mathsf{b}+\mathsf{c})$ via labels.

CSP Semantics. If we restrict ourselves just to bets on a sequence of starts then we have something like Hoare's trace semantics, [11], while adding disjunction takes us to failures.

Lamport-style models. If we have the ability to bet on sequences of starts and finishes we have a model close to that proposed by Lamport in [13].

Testing Equivalence. If we add conjunction and disjunction of bets, we get the classical analogue of Hennessy's testing-based models; cf. [3].

Observational Equivalence. The full syntax of tests corresponds, as we shall show, with the finest observationally-justifiable equivalence.

4.5. The power of bets. Our first tool in examining the power of bets will be sequences. The elements of a sequence will be sets of transitions. Every transition in a set is simultaneous, and sequence order reflects temporal order;

Definition 12 (L.I.E.S. Sequences). Consider a L.I.E.S. $\mathcal{L} = (\mathbf{TK}', <, =)$. The *sequence* generated by $\mathcal{L}$, written $\underline{\mathrm{seq}}(\mathcal{L})$, is a sequence of sets of elements of $\mathbf{LA}'$, $P = P_1 P_2 \ldots P_n$ defined thus. Suppose $a, a' \in \mathbf{LA}'$ and a_t happens at r_t & a'_t at r'_t.

$$\forall i \,.\, a_t, a'_t \in P_i \;\Rightarrow\; r_t = r'_t$$
$$\forall j < i \,.\, a_t \in P_i \;\&\; a'_t \in P_j \;\Rightarrow\; r_t > r'_t$$

Notice that the length of $\underline{\mathrm{seq}}(\mathcal{L})$ will always be finite, as will the set $\underline{\mathrm{seq}}(\Im) = \{\underline{\mathrm{seq}}(\mathcal{J}) \mid \mathcal{J} \in \mathcal{M}(\Im)\}$ of all sequences of a given structure.

We can distinguish structures precisely up to sequences using untimed bets incorporating conjunction;

Theorem 13. *Given two realisable I.E.S.s and some observation that can be made of both of them $\mathcal{L}$, we can definitely distinguish the complete histories $\mathcal{J} \in \mathcal{P}(\Im, \mathcal{L})$, $\mathcal{K} \in \mathcal{P}(\Im', \mathcal{L})$ with untimed conjunctive bets just when $\underline{\mathrm{seq}}(\mathcal{J}) \neq \underline{\mathrm{seq}}(\mathcal{K})$.*

Proof. Suppose $\underline{\text{seq}}(\mathcal{J}) = J_1J_2\ldots J_n, \underline{\text{seq}}(\mathcal{K}) = K_1K_2\ldots K_n$ and that the first places these sequences differ has index i. For a set of simultaneous transitions L, define $\vec{L}$ to be the set of all sequences generated by permutations of elements from L (so that if $L = \{a_t, b_t, c_t\}, \vec{L} = \{a_tb_tc_t, a_tc_tb_t, b_ta_tc_t, b_tc_ta_t, c_ta_tb_t, c_tb_ta_t\}$). Then the bet

$$B_{\mathcal{J}} = \wedge \{\vec{j}_1\vec{j}_2\ldots\vec{j}_i\mathsf{Win} \mid \vec{j}_j \in \vec{J}_j\}$$

has result $\{\top\}$ when placed on $\Im$ doing $\mathcal{J}$ but gives $\{\bot\}$ when placed on $\Im'$ doing $\mathcal{K}$. To see that we only have the power to distinguish between sequences, notice that if $\underline{\text{seq}}(\Im) \subset \underline{\text{seq}}(\Im')$ then there is no bet that has result $\{\top\}$ for $\Im$ and $\{\bot\}$ for $\Im'$ or vice versa. □

Theorem 14. *Untimed bets can see structures up to* $\underline{\text{seq}}$*;*

$$\Im \sim_{\mathsf{B}} \Im' \iff \underline{\text{seq}}(\Im) = \underline{\text{seq}}(\Im')$$

Proof. (Sketch.) Given $\Im, \Im'$ with $\underline{\text{seq}}(\Im) \neq \underline{\text{seq}}(\Im')$, define the bet $B_\Im = \forall \bigwedge_{\mathcal{J}\in\underline{\text{seq}}(\Im)} B_{\mathcal{J}}$.
$\Leftarrow$. Since $\underline{\text{seq}}(\Im) = \{\underline{\text{seq}}(\mathcal{J}) \mid \mathcal{J} \in \mathcal{M}(\Im)\}$, if $\underline{\text{seq}}(\Im) \neq \underline{\text{seq}}(\Im')$ we can assume that there is a $\mathcal{J}$ such that $\underline{\text{seq}}(\Im) \ni \mathcal{J} \notin \underline{\text{seq}}(\Im')$. Then $\mathcal{S}(\Im, \langle\rangle, B_\Im) \neq \mathcal{S}(\Im', \langle\rangle, B_\Im)$.
$\Rightarrow$. By induction on the structure of bets. □

An obvious extension of these results demonstrates that strict–timed bets with conjunction allow us to distinguish all unequal histories, and strict–timed bets with conjunction and quantification allow us to distinguish all observably unequal structures.

Theorem 15. *The equivalence* $\sim_{\mathsf{rB}}$ *depends precisely on maximal* $\underline{\text{Con}}$*–sets;*

$$\Im \sim_{\mathsf{rB}} \Im' \iff \mathcal{M}(\Im) = \mathcal{M}(\Im')$$

Proof. (Sketch.) Note first that $\underline{\text{Con}}$–sets are just $\underline{\text{seq}}$s but with the sets of necessarily simultaneous transitions annotated with the times they occur. The proof is then similar to that of the last theorem:
$\Rightarrow$. Suppose otherwise; then $\exists \mathcal{K} \in \mathcal{M}(\Im) \notin \mathcal{M}(\Im')$. For the contradiction, bet on it.
$\Leftarrow$. Straightforward since $\mathcal{S}(\Im, \mathcal{L}, \mathsf{b})$ for a given $\mathcal{L}$ and b depends just on $\mathcal{M}(\Im)$. □

5. Causal Bets

In some circumstances it is reasonable to assume that causality is observable; in a communications network, for instance, we may be able to observe the passage of individual packets and deduce their effects. The trepidation with which we suggest observing causality is understandable, but there is some justification from the literature; causality is assumed (perhaps implicitly) to be observable in [2], [6], and particularly in [17]. Anyway, it is possible to allow an observer to make causal bets, by extending the syntax of betting, allowing $\mathsf{b} \in \mathsf{B}^{\mathsf{C}}(\mathbf{LA}_{\mathsf{Bet}})$ if it is of the form

$$\mathsf{b} ::= \mathsf{Win} \mid \mathsf{Loss} \mid a_t\mathsf{b} \mid \mathsf{b}_1 \vee \mathsf{b}_2 \mid \mathsf{b}_1 \wedge \mathsf{b}_2 \mid \forall\mathsf{b} \mid \exists\mathsf{b} \mid (a_t \rightsquigarrow a'_t)\mathsf{b}$$

where $a, a' \in \mathbf{LA}_{\mathsf{Bet}}$. The interpretation of $(a_t \rightsquigarrow a'_t)$ is that a_t has already happened, a'_t has not, and that a_t should cause a'_t to happen next. (In the case $a_t = *_s$ or $a'_t = *_f$ this reduces to a noncausal bet since $*_s$ causes everything and everything causes $*_f$.) Causal bets are given meaning thus;

Definition 16 (Causal Extension). Given an observation $\mathcal{L} = (\mathbf{TK}, <, =)$ of some history $\mathcal{K} \in \mathcal{P}(\Im, \mathcal{L})$, a transition a_t in $\mathcal{L}$, and a transition a'_t in $\mathcal{K}$ but not $\mathcal{L}$, we say that a_t causes a'_t or $(a_t \leadsto a'_t)$ *causally extends* $\mathcal{L}$ in $\mathcal{K}$ iff $a_t <_c a'_t$ in $\Im$ and a'_t extends $\mathcal{L}$ in $\mathcal{K}$. We then define <u>must</u> and <u>may</u> and hence $\mathcal{S}(\Im, \mathcal{L}, (a_t \leadsto a'_t)\mathrm{b})$ using causal extension in the obvious way:

$$\Im\ \underline{\text{must}}\ (a_t \leadsto a'_t)\ \underline{\text{after}}\ \mathcal{L} \iff \forall \mathcal{K} \in \mathcal{P}(\Im, \mathcal{L}) \,.\, a_t \text{ causally extends } \mathcal{L} \text{ in } \mathcal{K}$$
$$\Im\ \underline{\text{may}}\ (a_t \leadsto a'_t)\ \underline{\text{after}}\ \mathcal{L} \iff \exists \mathcal{K} \in \mathcal{P}(\Im, \mathcal{L}) \,.\, a_t \text{ causally extends } \mathcal{L} \text{ in } \mathcal{K}$$

Theorem 17 (The power of causal bets). *Causal bets can distinguish between any two distinct interval event structures,* $\Im \sim_{\mathsf{rBC}} \Im' \iff \Im = \Im'$.

Proof. (Sketch.) $\Leftarrow$ is trivial. For $\Rightarrow$ suppose otherwise. There are four ways $\Im = (\mathbf{TK}, \underline{\mathrm{Con}}, <_{\bullet}, =_{\bullet})$ can be unequal to $\Im' = (\mathbf{TK}', \underline{\mathrm{Con}}', <_{\bullet}', =_{\bullet}')$. Firstly, $\mathbf{TK} \neq \mathbf{TK}'$: this can happen either because they contain different events, or the same events with different times; either is easy. Next, the <u>Con</u>–sets might be different: in this case a non–causal bet will separate them, which is also (trivially) a causal bet. Also if $=_{\bullet} \neq =_{\bullet}'$ then $\Im$ and $\Im'$ will have different necessarily simultaneous sets of transitions, and hence will be separated by non–causal and thus causal bets.

The interesting case is $<_{\bullet}$. But this follows quickly since we can replace any desired sequence $a_t a'_t \ldots$ in any bet by the causal sequence $(a_t \leadsto a'_t)(a'_t \leadsto a''_t) \ldots$. Thus there is a causal bet, constructed analogously to $B_{\Im}$ that distinguishes all structures. □

6. Concluding Remarks

While the work in this paper offers a good start to a theory of timed classical concurrency, there is still work to be done. It would, for instance, be interesting to know which equivalences are congruences of event refinement. This might be easier if there were a denotational characterisation of the equivalences; this should be fairly straightforward.

It would also be interesting to know how far this material relies on timing; to what extent can the naïve comparisons of section 4.4 be formalised ? We are eager to reformulate these results in a process algebraic setting (where labels are not accessible to the observer); this would make it easier to formalise the comparison, and would add a missing algebraic dimension to this work.

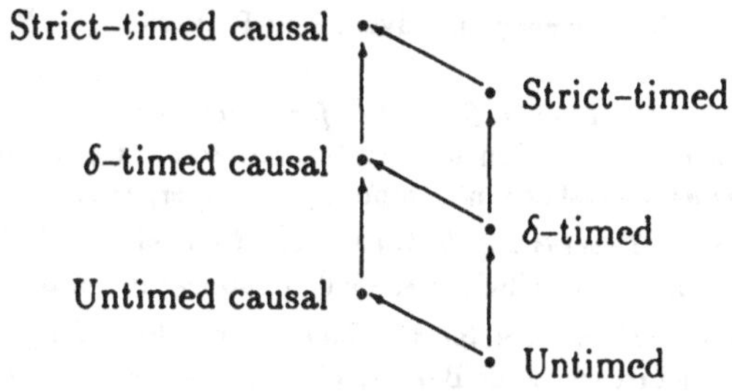

FIGURE 3. The Comparative Power of the Betting Equivalences discussed in this paper.

Thanks. This research was partly supported by the SERC of Great Britain, and partly by IED Grant 1759. I would like to thank Mike Shields for his remarks, and Alan Jeffrey & Tim Regan for sharing their intuition.

BIBLIOGRAPHY

1. S. Abramsky, *Observational Equivalence is Testing Equivalence*, Theoretical Computer Science, Volume 53 (1987), Pp. 225–241.
2. L. Aceto, R. de Nicola, and A. Fantechi, *Testing Equivalence for Event Structures*, in Mathematical Models for the Semantics of Parallelism (M. Venturini-Zilli, Ed.), (1987), Springer-Verlag LNCS 280.
3. L. Aceto and M. Hennessy, *Towards action-refinement in Process Algebra*, Technical Report 3/88, Department of Computer Science, University of Sussex, 1988.
4. B. Bloom and A. Meyer, *Experimenting with Process Equivalence*, in Semantics for Concurrency, (1990), Springer-Verlag Workshops in Computing.
5. J. Davies and S. Schneider, *An introduction to timed CSP*, Technical Report Number 75, Oxford University Computing Laboratory, 1989.
6. P. Degano and U. Montanari, *Concurrent Histories: A basis for observing distributed systems*, Journal of Computer Systems Sciences, Volume 34 (1987), Pp. 442–461.
7. R. Gerth and A. Boucher, *A timed failures model for communicating processes*, in Automata, Languages and Programming, (1987), Springer-Verlag LNCS 267, (14th Coll.).
8. J. Gischer, *The equational theory of pomsets*, Theoretical Computer Science, Volume 61 (1989), Pp. 199–224.
9. M. Hennessy, *Synchronous and asynchronous experiments on processes*, Information and Control, Volume 51 (1983), Number 1, Pp. 58–75.
10. M. Hennessy and T. Regan, *A Temporal Process Algebra*, Technical Report 2/90, Department of Computer Science, University of Sussex, 1990.
11. C. Hoare, *Communicating Sequential Processes*, International series on computer science, Prentice-Hall, 1985.
12. M. Joseph and A. Goswami, *Relating Computation and Time*, Technical Report RR 138, Department of Computer Science, University of Warwick, 1985.
13. L. Lamport, *On interprocess communication. Part I: Basic formalism*, Distributed Computing, Volume 1 (1986), Pp. 77–85.
14. D. Murphy, *Time, causality, and concurrency*, Ph.D. thesis, Department of Mathematics, University of Surrey, 1989, Available as Technical Report CSC 90/R32, Department of Computing Science, University of Glasgow.
15. ———, *A Functorial Semantics for Timed Concurrency*, In preparation, 1991.
16. ———, *Three papers on classical concurrency theory*, Technical Report CSC 91/R5, Department of Computing Science, University of Glasgow, 1991.
17. W. Reisig, *A Strong Part of Concurrency*, in Advances in Petri Nets (G. Rozenberg, Ed.), (1987), Springer-Verlag LNCS 266.
18. M. Roncken and R. Gerth, *A Denotational Semantics for Synchronous and Asynchronous Behaviour with Multiform Time*, in Semantics for Concurrency (M. Kwiatkowska, M. Shields, and R. Thomas, Eds.), (1990), Springer-Verlag Workshops in Computing, Leicester, 1990.
19. A. Schettini and J. Winkowsi, *Towards an algebra for timed behaviours*, Technical report, Institute of Computer Science, Polish Academy of Sciences, 1990, To appear in Theoretical Computer Science.
20. G. Winskel, *An introduction to Event Structures*, in Linear Time, Branching Time and Partial Order in Logics and Models for Concurrency (J. de Bakker, W. de Roever, and G. Rozenberg, Eds.), (1989), Springer-Verlag LNCS 354, Proceedings of REX 1988.

Appendix — Various Example Structures

To conclude the paper, we present a small selection of structures that are and are not distinguished by the various equivalences presented, the aim being to give better insight into the 'resolving power' of these equivalences.

These structures show the power of allowing bets on finishes; if bets on sequences of starts alone are allowed, these are indistinguishable, but if finishes are added, the bet $\Im$ will b_s after $\mathsf{a}_s\mathsf{a}_f$ will always distinguish them. (In each case, $\mathcal{M}(\Im) = \{\mathsf{a}, \mathsf{b}\}$.)

Here we see how adding disjunction increases the resolving power of bets. If we don't know in what order a and b will happen, there is no untimed bet on sequences of transitions that will distinguish the two structures, but adding disjunction allows us the bet ($\Im$ will $a_s b_s$ after $\langle\rangle$) $\vee$ ($\Im$ will $b_s a_s$ after $\langle\rangle$) which will always win on the rightmost structure but never on the leftmost.‖ (The maximal Con-sets are $\{\mathsf{a}, \mathsf{b}\}, \{\mathsf{c}\}$ and $\{\mathsf{a}, \mathsf{c}\}, \{\mathsf{b}\}$ respectively.)

It is fairly easy to see that $\wedge$ allows us knowledge of the simultaneity of transitions, so we will pass on the quantification, examining

The bet $\Im$ will b_s after $\mathsf{a}_s\mathsf{a}_f$ will not reliably distinguish both structures, since its result for one is $\{\top, \bot\}$ and the other $\{\top\}$, but $\Im$ will $\forall\,\mathsf{b}_s$ after $\mathsf{a}_s\mathsf{a}_f$ always distinguishes them.

These structures show the power of allowing causal bets; without them, the two structures are indistinguishable, but if they are added, the bet $\Im$ will ($\mathsf{a}_f \rightsquigarrow \mathsf{b}_s$) after $\mathsf{a}_s\mathsf{a}_f$ will always distinguish them. (In each case, $\mathcal{M}(\Im) = \{\mathsf{a}, \mathsf{b}\}$; the arrow shows causality.)

‖ Notice that the bet $\Im$ will $b_s a_s$ after $\langle\rangle$ is not the same as $\Im$ will b_s after a_s if $\Im$ cannot do a_s after $\langle\rangle$, since the former has result $\bot$ (for obvious reasons) but the latter $\top$ (since a_s is not a valid observation of $\Im$, and we have *ex falso quod libet*, section 3.2).

Fairness in Models with True Concurrency

Doris Nolte, Lutz Priese
FB 17, Universität-Gesamthochschule Paderborn, FRG

Abstract

Fairness is defined for an abstract class of formal systems that represent models for true concurrency. It is shown that generally fairness coincides with limits of convergent sequences in some ultra metric spaces and with Π_3^0-sets of recursion theory.

1 Introduction

Degano and Montanari [DM84] presented an early connection between fairness and metric spaces. They proved that only those program executions of some CCSP-like language are strongly (weakly) fair whose initial segments form Cauchy sequences in some ultra metric space and vice versa. Costa [Cos85] was able to generalize this result to CCS and he and Hennessy asked the question whether such a result may be generalized to transition systems. This question is of some interest as transition systems form the standard Plotkin-style operational semantics for various caculi or programming languages. Darondeau and Yoccoz noticed a strong connection between fairness and Π_3^0-sets of recursion theory. Together we could prove that a run r in a transition system is fair (for all fairness concepts of the literature we know) iff $r = \overset{d}{\lim\limits_{r \to \omega}} r[n]$ for some appropriate ultra metric d, iff $\{r[n]\}_{n \in N}$ forms a Cauchy sequence in d, iff "*r is fair*" is a Π_3^0-predicate (Π_2^0-predicate for *weak* fairness). Transition systems are the classical model of an *interleaving* operational semantics. However, for *true concurrency* one interprets a program execution as a set of *traces* or *pomsets* or similar. It was doubted whether the results above can be transferred to such models. One frequently used argument states: there are pomsets p with linearizations $w, w' \in \Sigma^\infty$ s.t. w is fair but w' is not fair in the transition system theory of fairness.

The purpose of this paper is to define fairness on a very abstract level for a large class of programming languages, Petri nets, calculi, etc., in true concurrency models. Our main result states that exactly the same results as for transition systems can be achieved for pomsets. In the following chapters we define pomset, compare interleaving with true concurrency semantics and define *admissible* classes of formal systems which we will research.

A very general notion of fairness is presented which contains all fairness notions of the literature we know and our results are stated with sketches of proofs.

2 Pomsets

We use the following mathematical notations.
An alphabet Σ is a non-empty finite or infinite set of letters. Σ^* denotes the set of finite words over Σ, Σ^ω the set of infinite words over Σ, $\Sigma^\infty := \Sigma^* \cup \Sigma^\omega$. We always assume that Σ is enumerable and thus sometimes assume for simplicity that $\Sigma \subseteq \mathbb{N}$. This means, $a < b$ is defined for letters $a, b \in \Sigma$. For a word $u \in \Sigma^\infty$ we define:
$|u|$ - the length of u, with $|u| = \omega$ for $u \in \Sigma^\omega$, $u(n)$ - the n-th letter of u, for $n \leq |u|$, $u[n] := u(1)\ldots u(n)$ - the prefix of length n of u, for $n \leq |u|$, $\#_a(u)$ - the number of occurrences of letter a in u, $a \in u$ - iff there exists some n s.t. $a = u(n)$,
$\overset{\omega}{\exists} k : E(k) :\Leftrightarrow \forall i : \exists k \geq i : E(k)$, reads that there exist infinitely many k s.t. $E(k)$ holds,
$\overset{\omega}{\forall} k : E(k) :\Leftrightarrow \exists i : \forall k \geq i : E(k)$, reads that $E(k)$ holds almost always,
$a \in_\omega u :\Leftrightarrow \overset{\omega}{\exists} k : k \leq |u|$ and $a = u(k)$. For a set $M, |M|$ defines the cardinality of M.

We identify functions and infinite sequences, thus $f[k] = f(1)\ldots f(k)$ for $f : \mathbb{N} \to \Sigma$.

A tuple (M, d) is called a *metric space* iff for $d : M \times M \to \mathbb{R}^+$ there holds $\forall x, y, z \in M$:
$d(x,y) = 0 \Leftrightarrow x = y$, $\quad d(x,y) = d(y,x)$, $\quad d(x,y) \leq d(x,z) + d(x,y)$.
If in addition we have $d(x,y) \leq max(d(x,z), d(z,y))$, d is called an *ultra metric*.
(M, d) is called *complete* if any Cauchy sequence $\{y_n\}_{n \in \mathbb{N}}$ of elements $y_n \in M$ converges in M.

Definition. A *labeled poset* $p = (S, \leq, \lambda)$ over Σ is a tuple s.t. S is a set, $\leq$ is a reflexive and transitive relation on S, and $\lambda : S \to \Sigma$ is a labeling function.

For any poset $(S, \leq, \lambda)$ define $s < s' :\Leftrightarrow s \leq s' \wedge s \neq s'$, and
$s \lessdot s' :\Leftrightarrow s < s' \wedge \not\exists s'' : s < s'' < s')$.

For a poset $p = (S, \leq, \lambda)$ we define for each $s \in S : lev(s) := sup\{n;\ \exists s_1, ..., s_n \in S : s_n = s \ \wedge\ s_i \lessdot s_{i+1} \forall i < n\}$ and $|p| := sup\{lev(s); s \in S\}$.

Two posets $p = (S, \leq, \lambda)$ and $p' = (S', \leq', \lambda')$ are *isomorphic*, $p \sim p'$, iff $\exists \varphi : S \to S'$ bijective s.t. $\forall s, s' \in S : s \leq s' \Leftrightarrow \varphi(s) \leq' \varphi(s')$ and $\lambda'(\varphi(s)) = \lambda(s)$.

A *pomset* $p = [(S, \leq, \lambda)]_\sim$ is an equivalence class of posets $(S, \leq, \lambda)$ s.t. there holds:

$$\forall s \in S : lev(s) < \omega \quad \text{and} \quad |\{s; lev(s) = n\}| < \omega \ \forall n \in \mathbb{N}_0.$$

$\mathcal{POM}_\Sigma^*$ defines the set of *finite pomsets* $[(S, \leq, \lambda)]_\sim$ over Σ, i.e. $|S| < \omega$, $\mathcal{POM}_\Sigma^\omega$ defines the set of *infinite pomsets* over Σ, and $\mathcal{POM}_\Sigma^\infty := \mathcal{POM}_\Sigma^* \cup \mathcal{POM}_\Sigma^\omega$.

Obviously, $[(S, \lessdot^*, \lambda)]_\sim = [(S, \leq, \lambda)]_\sim$ (where $*$ denotes the reflexive and transitive closure of a relation) and we use $(S, \lessdot, \lambda)$ as representatives for pomsets.

We have to extend the Baire-topology on Σ^∞ to pomsets:

Definition. For pomsets p_1, p_2 we denote by $p_1[n]$ the sub-pomset of p_1 spanned by all elements with level $\leq n$, and $p_1 \sqcap p_2 := sup\{n \in \mathbb{N}; p_1[n] = p_2[n]\}$,

$$d_B(p_1, p_2) := \begin{cases} 0 & \text{iff } p_1 = p_2 \\ (p_1 \sqcap p_2 + 1)^{-1} & \text{otherwise.} \end{cases}$$

Obviously, d_B defines an ultra metric on $\mathcal{POM}_\Sigma^\infty$, s.t. $(\mathcal{POM}_\Sigma^\infty, d_B)$ becomes a complete ultra metric space, see [dBW90].

For later use, a more general concept of a "prefix" p' of a pomset p will be required than just $p[n]$:

Definition. A *cut* p' of a pomset $p = [(S, \leq, \lambda)]_\sim$ is a finite sub-pomset $p' = [(S', \leq', \lambda')]_\sim$ of p s.t

$$\forall s_1, s_2 \in S : s_1 \leq s_2 \wedge s_2 \in S' \Rightarrow s_1 \in S'.$$

We write $p' \leq_C p$ to indicate that p' is a cut of p. A *step* $p(n)$ of p is the set of all vertices of level n, i.e. $p(n) := \{s \in S; lev(s) = n\}$.

3 Interleaving versus True Concurrency Semantics

In order to keep our results on fairness quite general we will not introduce a specific (programming) language to study fairness. Instead we will operate with classes $\mathcal{L}$ of formal systems that only have to fulfill some very weak conditions. In this chapter we introduce those formal systems admissible for our research.

Let $\mathcal{L}$ denote a class of formal systems s.t. a behavior of $P \in \mathcal{L}$ is given via an interpretation $\mathcal{J}$. P may be a Petri net or program in some programming language with or without constructs for parallelism, concurrency, synchronization, nondeterminism, etc., as presented for example by some versions of Milner's CCS [Mil80] or Hoares's CSP [Hoa85]. For a concrete language where interleaving versus true concurrency and linear versus branching time semantics are deeply compared, see de Bakker [dB89].

3.1 Plotkin-style Interleaving Semantic

In the interleaving case a *behavior* $\mathcal{J}(P)$ of $P \in \mathcal{L}$ is a run in a (generally infinite) transition system. A transition system is simply a graph with labels on its arcs (the *transitions*), whose vertices are usually called *states*. In this Plotkin-style semantics *states* are programs in $\mathcal{L}$ and a directed edge e labeled with a points from state s to state s' iff program s allows for an execution of an action a resulting in the program s' yet to be executed. We assume that any $P \in \mathcal{L}$ has a finite description and is coded as an integer by some coding function $c : \mathcal{L} \rightarrow \mathbb{N}$. The same holds for the states of a transition system for P and we also assume that all executable actions have a finite description. The set Σ of executable actions of P may be infinite but is usually recursively enumerable as $a \in \Sigma$ iff there exists a finite program execution u and states P', P'' s.t. $P \xrightarrow{u} P' \xrightarrow{a} P''$. We assume that it is decidable whether $P' \xrightarrow{a} P''$ holds for given P', P'', a as one should be able to tell whether some action a is executable in program state P' and will lead to P''. To point to this assumptions we also talk about *recursive transition systems (ts)*. They form the standard model for interleaving semantics. A program execution now becomes a finite or infinite path in a recursive ts T:

$P_T^* \subseteq E^*$ is the set of all finite directed paths in T, $P_T^\omega \subseteq E^\omega$ is the set of infinite directed paths in T, $P_T^\infty := P_T^* \cup P_T^\omega$. Note that via some coding c paths are already finite or infinite sequences of integers. Further we may use some standard Goedel coding $<>: \mathbb{N}^* \rightarrow \mathbb{N}$ to identify finite sequences with a single integer. An infinite path $r \in P_T^\omega$ is thus a function $r : \mathbb{N} \rightarrow \mathbb{N}$ s.t. $r : i \rightarrow r(i)$.

As we talk about finite and infinite sequences we deal with integers and functions and thus have to apply recursion theory over functions. Let us briefly repeat that a predicate $R \subseteq (\mathbb{N}^\infty)^k \times \mathbb{N}^m$ is called recursive iff there exists a Turing machine, M_R, that decides whether $R(r_1, \ldots, r_k, x_1, \ldots, x_m)$ holds given $x_1, \ldots x_m \in \mathbb{N}$ and $r_1, \ldots r_k \in \mathbb{N}^\infty$ as inputs on additional input tapes with special endmarkers for finite r.
A relation $R \subseteq (\mathbb{N}^\infty)^k \times \mathbb{N}^m$ is called $\Sigma_n^0(\Pi_n^0)$ iff it is defined by

$$R(r_1, \ldots r_k, x_1, \ldots, x_m) \;\; :\Leftrightarrow \exists y_1 : \forall y_2 : \ldots : \overset{\forall}{\exists}\, y_n : Q(r_1, \ldots, r_k, x_1, \ldots, x_m, y_1, \ldots y_n)$$
$$\text{(respectively:} \;\; :\Leftrightarrow \forall y_1 : \exists y_2 : \ldots : \overset{\forall}{\exists}\, y_n : Q(r_1, \ldots, r_k, x_1, \ldots, x_m, y_1, \ldots y_n))$$

with an recursive predicate Q, where the quantifiers range over integers.
A set $M \subseteq (\mathbb{N}^\infty)^k \times \mathbb{N}^m$ is called recursive, Σ_n^0, Π_n^0, resp., iff its characteristic predicate $M(r_1, \ldots, r_k, x_1, \ldots, x_m) :\Leftrightarrow (r_1, \ldots r_k, x_1, \ldots, x_m) \in M$ is recursive, Σ_n^0, Π_n^0, respectively.

We refer the interested reader to Rogers, [Rog67]. Obviously, in a recursive ts T the set P_T^∞ is r.e., as being a path $r \in P_T^\infty$ is described by the formula "$\forall n : r[n]$ is a finite path in T", and being a finite path is recursive in a recursive ts T.

Definition. A class $\mathcal{L}$ of formal systems and an interpretation $\mathcal{J}$ are called *admissible* iff there exists a recursive *ts* T over some Σ, a coding $c : \mathcal{L} \cup \Sigma \rightarrow \mathbb{N}$ s.t. there holds:

- $\mathcal{J} : \mathcal{L} \rightarrow 2^{P_T^\infty}$,
- the predicate $FC \subseteq \mathbb{N}^2$ with $FC(n, m) :\Leftrightarrow \exists P \in \mathcal{L} : \exists r \in P_T^* : n = c(P) \wedge m = g(r) \wedge r \in \mathcal{J}(P) \cap P_T^*$ is recursive,
- $\forall P \in \mathcal{L} : \forall r \in P_T^\omega : (r \in \mathcal{J}(P) \Leftrightarrow \forall n : r[n] \in \mathcal{J}(P) \cap P_T^*)$.

Let us discuss these properties briefly. As $\mathcal{L}$ may allow for nondeterminism we cannot expect $\mathcal{J}(P)$ to be a one element set, thus $\mathcal{J}$ maps each $P \in \mathcal{L}$ onto a set of paths in T. In the literature any path in T from an initial state is sometimes regarded as a behavior of P, sometimes only those paths that lead to final states or those that are infinite. Being a *finite computation* (FC) is decidable in all examples of the literature we know. Note that the $\exists$-quantors in the definition of FC are avoidable, as for any reasonable codings c, g it is decidable whether n and m are coding numbers, i.e. c^{-1}, g^{-1} are computable. The final requirement states that infinite paths belong to $\mathcal{J}$ iff their initial segments do. This might be weakened as will be shown in the case of pomsets.

3.2 True Concurrency Semantics

To distinguish concurrency explicitly from nondeterminism in the case of true concurrency semantics the interpretation $\mathcal{J}$ maps P not into a set of linear words but into a set of objects with additional structure such as pomsets, see e.g. [BC89], [Kwi89], [Pra86], [dBW90], [Thi90].

For a theory of fairness we have to regard pomsets again as finite or infinite sequences of integers like in the sequential case, i.e. we need a coding $c : \mathcal{POM}^\infty(\Sigma) \rightarrow \mathbb{N}^\infty$. Here, we have to code *isomorphism classes of posets*. As a first approach, one might try to code an arbitrary poset as a representative of a pomset, but this implies that different codings of the same pomset might exist.

Definition. For a finite pomset $p = [(S, \leq, \lambda)]_\sim$ with $S = \{s_1, s_2, ..., s_n\}$ choose a tuple $p' = (s_1, s_2, ..., s_n, (s_{i_1}, s_{j_1}), ..., (s_{i_k}, s_{j_k}), \lambda(s_1), \lambda(s_2), ..., \lambda(s_n))$, s.t. (s_{i_l}, s_{j_l}) is in p' iff $s_{i_l} < s_{j_l}$. Now, choose a coding $c : S \rightarrow \{1, ..., n\}$ and a permutation $'$ of S and $((s_{i_1}, s_{j_1}), ..., (s_{i_k}, s_{j_k}))$ such that
$p'' = (c(s'_1), ..., c(s'_n), (c(s_{i_1}), c(s_{j_1}))', ..., (c(s_{i_k}), c(s_{j_k}))', \lambda(c(s'_1)), ..., \lambda(c(s'_n)))$
is of minimal lexicographical order. Obviously, for a finite pomset p, p'' is a unique representative of p. For each finite or infinite pomset p define $c(p) : \{1, ..., |p|\} \rightarrow \mathbb{N}$ with $c(p)(i) := \langle p[i]'' \rangle$ as a unique representation of p as a finite or infinite sequence of integers. In addition, the finite sequences may be mapped onto single integers by a further application of $\langle\rangle$.

We may continue as in the interleaving case.

Definition. A class $\mathcal{L}$ of formal systems and an interpretation $\mathcal{J}$ are called *admissible* (for pomsets) iff there exists an r.e. set Σ and a coding $c : \mathcal{L} \dot\cup \Sigma \rightarrow \mathbb{N}$ s.t.:

- $\mathcal{J} : \mathcal{L} \rightarrow 2^{\mathcal{POM}^\infty_\Sigma}$,
- the predicate $FC \subseteq \mathbb{N}^2$ with $FC(n, m) :\Leftrightarrow \exists P \in \mathcal{L} : \exists p \in \mathcal{POM}^*_\Sigma : n = c(P) \wedge m = c(p) \wedge p \in \mathcal{J}(P) \cap \mathcal{POM}^*_\Sigma$ is recursive,
- $f \in c(\mathcal{J}(P))$ is a Π^0_2-predicate on $\mathbb{N}^{\mathbb{N}} \times \mathbb{N}$.

Thus $FC(n,m)$ reads that m is (the coding of) a finite pomset which is a behavior (under $\mathcal{J}$) of the coding n of a program $P \in \mathcal{L}$. Of course, we expect this property to be decidable.

The third requirement may be surprising because one would expect a statement
$\forall P \in \mathcal{L} : \forall p \in \mathcal{POM}^{\omega}_{\Sigma} : p \in \mathcal{J}(P) \Leftrightarrow \forall n : p[n] \in \mathcal{POM}^{*}_{\Sigma} \cap \mathcal{J}(P)$,
which would yield $f \in \mathcal{J}(P)$ to be Π^0_1 on $\mathbb{N}^{\mathbb{N}} \times \mathbb{N}$. However, there are examples in the literature where such a statement fails. For example in de Bakker, Warmerdam [dBW90] all infinite pomsets in $\mathcal{J}(P)$ have to be approximated by finite pomsets in $\mathcal{J}(P)$ according to the Baire-topology d_B but not necessarily by their prefixes. In [BW90] all pomsets p_i and $p = \lim^{d_B}_{i \to \omega} p_i$ of Figure 1 belong to some interpretation $\mathcal{J}(P)$. Here $p \in \mathcal{J}(P)$ for $p \in \mathcal{POM}^{\omega}_{\Sigma}$ is described by
$p \in \mathcal{J}(P) \Leftrightarrow \forall i : \exists p_i \in \mathcal{POM}^{*}_{\Sigma} \cap \mathcal{J}(P) : d_B(p, p_i) < 1/i$,
which is Π^0_2 as $p_i \in \mathcal{POM}^{*}_{\Sigma} \cap \mathcal{J}(P)$ and $d_B(p, p_i) < 1/i$ are recursive.

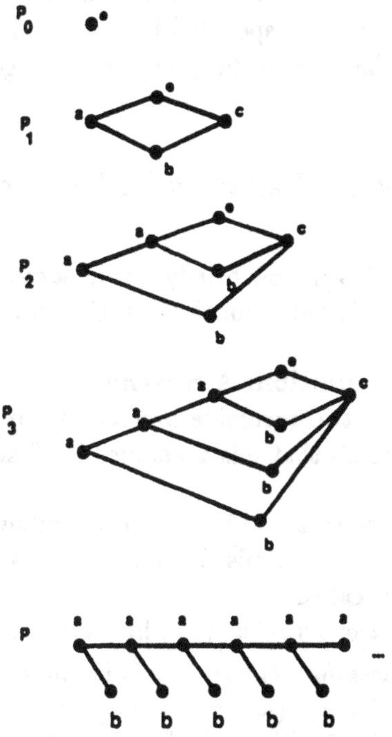

Figure 1

4 Fairness

There is a variety of different fairness notions in the literature, e.g. equifairness, justice, liveness, choice- and concurrency-fairness, event- and process-fairness, strong, weak and strict fairness, probabilistic fairness, and edge-, path-, word-, letter-fairness, see these and more examples in [Bes84b],[Bes84a], [CS87], [Dar85], [Fra86], [Har86], [Kwi89], [LPS81], [OA84], [Pri88], [PRWK87], [QS83], [Reh88], [UK88]. The general idea is that objects which are sufficiently often enabled in some program execution have to be used during that execution sufficiently often. There are many ways how to interpret "sufficiently often", "enabled", "objects", "used", "execution" resulting in a large variety of fairness concepts. The most widely accepted concepts are *strong* and *weak* fairness classes:

Definition. A program execution r is called *strongly* (x)-*fair* iff all "x-objects" that are infinitely often "x-enabled" in r have to "x-occur" infinitely often in r. A program execution r is called *weakly* (x)-*fair* iff no "x-object" is almost always "x-enabled".

x is a meta-variable denoting that we investigate a whole class of fairness concepts. According to how one specifies "x-objects", "x-enabled", "x-occurs" concrete strong and weak fairness concepts are achieved. Weak x-fairness has the equivalent description that any x-object which is almost always x-enabled has to "x-occur" at least once, where "x-occur" is specified that $0 = 1$ holds. Thus the negative formulation of weak fairness in the above definition fits in our general schema.

4.1 Fairness in Interleaving Semantics

We will now briefly repeat some results on fairness within models of interleaving, Plotkin-style operational semantics (from [Pri90], [PN90], [DNPY90]).

Definition. A *recursive fairness concept* xf for admissible $\mathcal{L}$ and $\mathcal{J} : \mathcal{L} \to 2^{P_T^{\infty}}$ is given by two recursive predicates En, Oc with $En, Oc \subseteq \mathcal{L} \times P_T^{\infty} \times \mathbb{N}^2$, where $En(P, r, o, i)$ reads that o is x-enabled in P at $r(i)$ and $Oc(P, r, o, k)$ that o has occurred in $r[k]$.

Definition. Let xf be a recursive fairness notion for some admissible $\mathcal{L}$, $\mathcal{J} : \mathcal{L} \to 2^{P_T^{\infty}}$ ($\mathcal{L}$ and xf admissible for short). A program execution $r \in \mathcal{J}(P)$ for a fixed program $P \in \mathcal{L}$ is called
strongly x-fair (xf) iff there holds $\forall o : (\overset{\omega}{\exists} i : En(P, r, o, i) \Rightarrow \overset{\omega}{\exists} k : Oc(P, r, o, k))$,
weakly x-fair ($w - xf$) iff there holds $\forall o : (\overset{\omega}{\forall} i : En(P, r, o, i) \Rightarrow 0 = 1)$.
The xf- ($w - xf$) interpretations of P are thus $\mathcal{J}^{xf}(P) := \{r \in P_T^{\omega} \cap \mathcal{J}(P); r \text{ is } xf\}$, and $\mathcal{J}^{w-xf}(P) := \{r \in P_T^{\omega} \cap \mathcal{J}(P) : r \text{ is } w - xf\}$.

As both fairness conditions hold for all finite runs, we regard only the interesting infinite runs in $\mathcal{J}^{xf}$ and $\mathcal{J}^{w-xf}$. Obviously, there holds

Theorem. For any admissible $\mathcal{L}$ and xf:

- $\mathcal{J}(P)$ is a Π_1^0-set,
- $\mathcal{J}^{xf}(P)$ is a Π_3^0-set,
- $\mathcal{J}^{w-xf}(P)$ is a Π_2^0-set.

On the other hand, each Π_3^0, Π_2^0-set defines some fairness condition:

Theorem. For any $M \subseteq \mathbb{N}^{\mathbb{N}}$ there holds:

- M is Π_3^0 iff $\exists \mathcal{L}, xf$ admissible, $\exists P \in \mathcal{L}$ s.t. $M = \mathcal{J}^{xf}(P)$,
- M is Π_2^0 iff $\exists \mathcal{L}, xf$ admissible, $\exists P \in \mathcal{L}$ s.t. $M = \mathcal{J}^{w-xf}(P)$.

Sketch of proof.
It can be shown that for $M \in \Pi_3^0$ there exists a recursive predicate R s.t.
$f \in M \asymp \forall o \overset{\omega}{\forall} k : R(f[k], o)$.
Thus we continue

$$\asymp \forall o : (\overset{\omega}{\exists} k : \neg R(f[k], o) \Rightarrow 0 = 1).$$

Thus $M = \mathcal{J}^{xf}(P)$, where $\neg R(f[k], o)$ defines "o is x-enabled at the k-th step of f" and "occurs" is always false.
Further for $M \in \Pi^0_2$ there exists a recursive R s.t.

$$
\begin{aligned}
f \in M \quad & \Leftrightarrow \quad \overset{\omega}{\exists}\, k : R(f[k]), \text{ and we conclude} \\
& \Leftrightarrow \quad \forall o : (\overset{\omega}{\forall}\, k : \neg R(f[k]) \Rightarrow 0 = 1) \\
& \Leftrightarrow \quad f \in \mathcal{J}^{w-xf}(P), \text{ (where } \neg R(f[k]) \text{ reads that } o \text{ is } x\text{-enabled at } k).
\end{aligned}
$$

The proof by Darondeau, Nolte, Priese, and Yoccoz can be found in [DNPY90], [PN90] or in [Pri90] also for Π^0_2
Degano and Montanari [DM84] could prove for a CCS-like programming language $\mathcal{L}$ and a natural fairness concept that a program execution r of a program in $\mathcal{L}$ is

- strongly fair iff $\{r[n]\}_{n \in \mathbb{N}}$ forms a non-stationary Cauchy sequence in some ultra metric space, and
- weakly fair iff $\{r[n]\}_{n \in \mathbb{N}}$ forms a non-stationary Cauchy sequence in another ultra metric space.

Costa generalized this result for CCS [Cos85], and Hennessy and Costa asked the question, whether this result might hold in transition systems, too. In [PN90], we could indeed generalize their result to transition systems and will succeed for pomsets now. The mathematical kernel of both following Main Theorems (for fairness with interleaving and true concurrency semantics, respectively) is a recursion theoretical connection of Π^0_3-sets, abstract fairness (as shown above) and Cauchy-sequences.

Theorem. For any Π^0_3-set $M \subseteq \mathbb{N}^{\mathbb{N}}$ of functions there exists some Π^0_1-ultra metric d (i.e. $d(f, g) < 1/n$ is a Π^0_1-predicate on $\mathbb{N}^\infty \times \mathbb{N}^\infty \times \mathbb{N}$) s.t.

$$
\begin{aligned}
f \in M \quad & \Leftrightarrow \quad \{f[n]\}_{n \in \mathbb{N}} \text{ forms a non-stationary Cauchy-sequence in } d \\
& \Leftrightarrow \quad f = \lim\nolimits^d_{n \to \omega} f[n] \\
& \Leftrightarrow \quad f \in CP_d(\mathbb{N}),
\end{aligned}
$$

where $CP_d(\mathbb{N}) = \{f : \mathbb{N} \to \mathbb{N}; \forall n \in \mathbb{N} : \exists x \in \mathbb{N} : d(f, x) < 1/n\}$ is the set of cluster points of $\mathbb{N}$ in $(\mathbb{N}^\infty, d)$.

Sketch of proof.

Using the results from the previous theorem we know $f \in M \Leftrightarrow \forall o\, \overset{\omega}{\forall}\, k : R(f[k], o)$ for some recursive R. Now define

$done(f, k) := sup\{i \leq min(|f|, k); \forall i' \leq i : \; \forall l(min(|f|, k) \leq l \leq |f|) : R(f[l], i')\}$ and

$$
d(f, f') := \begin{cases} 0 \text{ iff } f = f' \\ max(\frac{1}{done(f, f \sqcap f')+1}, \frac{1}{done(f', f \sqcap f')+1}) \text{ otherwise} \end{cases}
$$

(with $f \sqcap f' = sup\{n; f[n] = f'[n]\}$). Some calculation proves that d is a Π^0_1-ultra metric s.t. the above equivalences hold.

A similar approach works for Π^0_2-sets, i.e. for weak fairness.

Theorem. For any Π_2^0-set $M \subseteq \mathbb{N}^{\mathbb{N}}$ of functions there exists a Π_1^0-ultra metric that is in addition recursive on $\mathbb{N}^{\mathbb{N}} \times \mathbb{N} \times \mathbb{N}$ (i.e. $d(f,x) < 1/n$ is decidable for finite sequences x) s.t.

$f \in M \Longleftrightarrow \{f[n]\}_{n \in \mathbb{N}}$ forms a non-stationary Cauchy-sequence in d
$\Longleftrightarrow f = \lim^d_{n \to \omega} f[n]$
$\Longleftrightarrow f \in CP_d(\mathbb{N})$,

Sketch of Proof.

$f \in M \Longleftrightarrow \overset{\omega}{\exists} k : R(f[k])$ (for some recursive R)
$\Longleftrightarrow \lim_{n \to \omega} done(f,n) = \omega$.

Use $done(f,n) := sup\{k \leq n : R(f[k])\}$. As before, *done* allows to construct a Π_1^0-ultra metric s.t. $\mathcal{J}^{\omega - xf}(P) = CP_d(\mathbb{N})$ and $d(f,x) < 1/n$ is recursive on $\mathbb{N}^{\mathbb{N}} \times \mathbb{N} \times \mathbb{N}$.

Using the simple fact that $\mathbb{N}^{\mathbb{N}}$ can be identified with infinite runs in simple recursive ts and combining the above results we can thus prove the following.

Main Theorem . For $M \subseteq \mathbb{N}^{\mathbb{N}}$ there are equivalent:

- M is Π_3^0,
- $M = \mathcal{J}^{xf}(P)$ for some admissible $\mathcal{L}, xf, P \in \mathcal{L}$,
- $M = CP_d(\mathbb{N})$,
- $M = \{f : \mathbb{N} \to \mathbb{N}; f = \lim^d_{n \to \omega} f[n]\}$,
- $M = \{f : \mathbb{N} \to \mathbb{N}; \{f[n]\}_{n \in \mathbb{N}}$ forms a non-stationary Cauchy sequence $\}$, (for some Π_1^0 ultra metric d on $\mathbb{N}^{\omega}$).

For $M \subseteq \mathbb{N}^{\mathbb{N}}$ there are equivalent:

- M is Π_2^0,
- $M = \mathcal{J}^{\omega - xf}(P)$ for some admissible $\mathcal{L}, xf, P \in \mathcal{L}$,
- $M = CP_d(\mathbb{N})$ for some Π_1^0 ultra metric d on $\mathbb{N}^{\omega}$ s.t. $d(f,x) < 1/n$ is recursive on $\mathbb{N}^{\mathbb{N}} \times \mathbb{N} \times \mathbb{N}$.

4.2 Fairness and Pomsets

It has been seriously doubted whether these previous results can be transferred to *true concurrency* models, according to some "counter-examples" and mystery we will discuss later. We will prove that indeed the whole program can be continued, allowing to connect fairness within true concurrency models, Π_3^0-sets and convergence as before. We will explain this using pomsets as a model true concurrency. We will succeed mainly because the mathematical kernel of our Main Theorem is a recursion theoretical result about Π_2^0 and Π_3^0- sets of functions. We now define fairness for pomsets, following a nice approach of A. Merceron [Mer87], and will afterwards generalize our Main Theorem to true concurrency models. As in the interleaving case fairness will be no absolute property of a pomset but refers to a pomset as a model of behavior of some $P \in \mathcal{L}$. I.e., what is enabled in $p \in \mathcal{POM}_\Sigma^\infty$ depends also on P with $p \in \mathcal{J}(P)$. A pomset p will be called x-fair again if any sufficiently often x-enabled object has to occur sufficiently often in p. For weak fairness sufficiently often enabled means continually enabled, for strong fairness it reads as infinitely often enabled. Let us continue with an example to point to some new difficulties.

Example 1. Let N denote the Petri net of Figure 2. Its set of firing sequences, $L(N)$, is $L(N) = (c(ab + ba))^\omega + (c(ab + ba))^* cax$. Here, actions a and b are concurrently enabled after each occurrence of action c. In a true concurrency semantics this may be expressed by defining a behavior of N as a pomset, e.g. the pomset p of Figure 3. In fact, in this example p is also a trace, see e.g. [Thi90]. Note that p has several quite different "linearizations", i.e. firing sequences where the concurrency relation between a and b is "resolved in linear order", e.g. $(cab)^\omega$ and $(cba)^\omega$. In our interleaving semantics $(cba)^\omega$ is a fair computation (as event x is never enabled) but $(cab)^\omega$ is unfair, as x is infinitely often enabled but never occurs. Here, fairness refers to the standard concept of enabledness in Petri net theory.

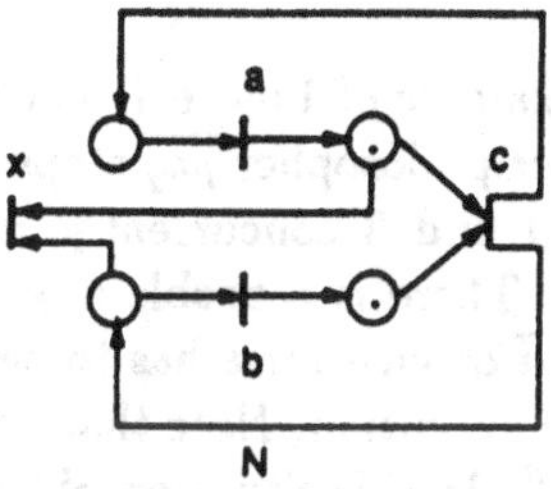

Figure 2

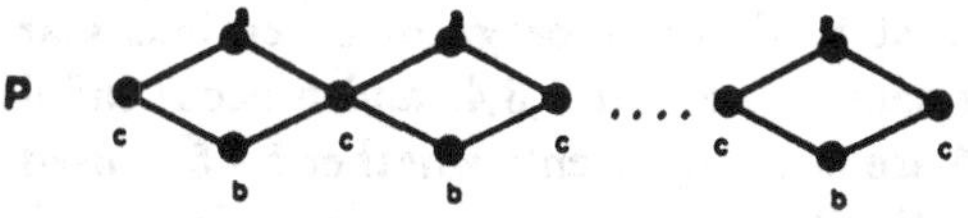

Figure 3

The situation described in N is known as "*confusion*": The order, in which two concurrent actions occur, effects the enabledness of another action.

Consequently, the problem arises how to define "infinitely often enabled" in pomsets.

One might say "$\overset{\omega}{\exists}\, k : o$ is x-enabled at $p(k)$". However, such a definition would imply a *step*-semantics where all actions of equal level are done simultaneously. In true concurrency models *cuts* should be used rather than steps. This leads to the following.

Definition. For a coding $c : \mathcal{POM}_\Sigma^\infty \to \mathbb{N}^\infty$ define
$n \leq_C r \;:\Leftrightarrow\; \exists p', p \in \mathcal{POM}_\Sigma^\infty : n = c(p') \wedge r = c(p) \wedge p' \leq_C p$,
with $n \in \mathbb{N}, r \in \mathbb{N}^\infty$ (p' is a cut of p).
A class $\mathcal{L}$ of formal systems, an interpretation $\mathcal{J} : \mathcal{L} \to 2^{\mathcal{POM}_\Sigma^\infty}$ with an r.e. set Σ, codings $c : \mathcal{L} \cup \Sigma \to \mathbb{N}$, $c : \mathcal{POM}_\Sigma^\infty \to \mathbb{N}^\infty$ and a fairness concept xf given by two predicates

$En, Oc \subseteq \mathcal{L} \times \mathbb{N}^* \times \mathbb{N}$, are called *admissible* (for pomsets) iff there holds

- $n \leq_C r$ is a recursive predicate on $\mathbb{N}^\infty \times \mathbb{N}^\infty$,
- En, Oc are recursive predicates.

The class of strongly x-fair behaviors is defined as

$$\mathcal{J}^{xf}(P) := \{p \in \mathcal{J}(P) \cap \mathcal{POM}_\Sigma^\omega; \forall o : (\overset{\omega}{\exists}\, k : (\exists p' : p[k] \leq_C p' \leq_C c(p) \wedge En(P, p', o)) \Rightarrow$$
$$\overset{\omega}{\exists}\, k : (\exists p' : p[k] \leq_C p' \leq_C c(p) \wedge Oc(P, p', o))\},$$

analogously for weak fairness:

$$\mathcal{J}^{w-xf}(P) := \{p \in \mathcal{J}(P) \cap \mathcal{POM}_\Sigma^\omega; \forall o : (\overset{\omega}{\forall}\, k : k \leq_C c(p) \wedge En(P, k, o)) \Rightarrow 1 = 0\}.$$

$En(P, p', o)$ reads that o is enabled in the cut p' as a model of an initial behavior of p, $Oc(P, p', o)$ that o occurs in cut p'. $n \leq_C r$ shall be recursive, as the existential quantifiers can be avoided for reasonable codings c where c^{-1} is computable.

Let us discuss some properties of this definition in another example.

Example 2. We regard the famous dining-philosopher example of Figure 4. For brevity we denote by j that philosopher ph_j starts eating and $\bar{j}$ for philosopher $\overline{ph_j}$ stops eating. We want to describe program executions starting with 1 and 3 concurrently, where 2 never takes place but 1,3,4, and 5 occur infinitely often. There is a problem because 4 and 5 are not concurrent: whether 5 - $\bar{5}$ is used before 4 - $\bar{4}$ or vice versa has to be stated explicitly. The pomset p_0 is an example of such a program execution. Note that there are infinitely many cuts in p_0 (see Figure 5) ending in $\bar{1}$ and $\bar{3}$. In this situation philosopher 2 is enabled in the classical sense of enabledness in Petri nets. Thus p_0 is not fair in this sense. Nevertheless, the word $w_0 = 13(\bar{1}5\bar{5}1\bar{3}4\bar{4}3)^\omega$ is a correct linearization of p_0.

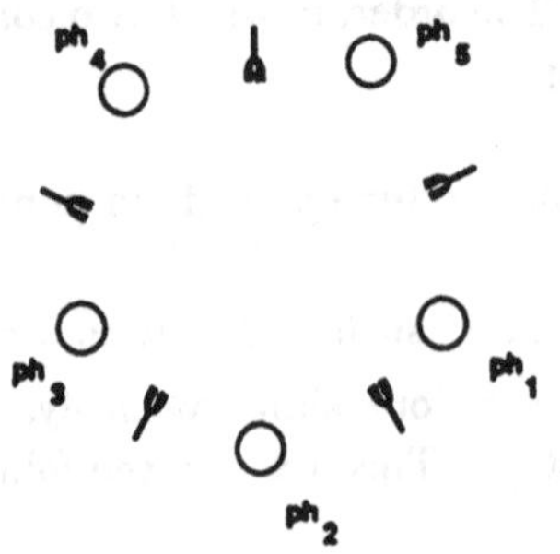

Figure 4

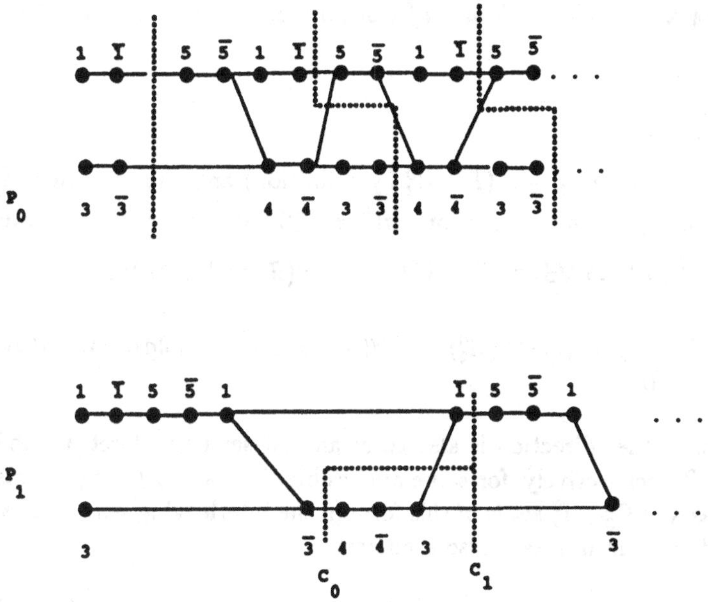

Figure 5

However, in the classical sense w_0 is fair as philosopher 2 is not infinitely often enabled in w_0. The observation that some linearizations of a given pomset may be fair and others may not has led to the belief that fairness is difficult to handle in models of true concurrency. However, this seems to be just a misunderstanding: The fact that w_0 is fair depends on an explicit conspiracy between 1 and 3. In w_0 philosophers 1 and 3 are never thinking (non-eating) simultaneously. It is this **explicit** behavior of 1 and 3 that allows w_0 to be formally fair. Thus, if one is interested in this conspiracy behavior in a pomset semantics one has to express explicitly that $\overline{1}$ and $\overline{3}$ are no longer concurrent. p_1 of Figure 5 presents such a conspiracy behavior. Note that c_0 in Figure 5 is not a cut, as cuts have to be prefix closed. c_1 would define a cut. p_1 defines such an intuitively fair pomset because philosopher 2 is never enabled in p_1.

We will return briefly to our first example. We interpret enabledness again as in the classical sense of Petri net theory. Thus, according to our definition, pomset p of Figure 3 is not fair, as there are infinitely many cuts of p where x becomes enabled. This is in accordance with our intuition: As a and b are concurrent it is quite unlikely (rather "unfair") that b will always fire before a. Thus x becomes enabled infinitely often in a "fair" program execution and has to be fired. If we want to express explicitly that b shall fire before a the pomset p is the wrong model.

We now can easily transfer our Main Theorem to pomsets as by our coding pomsets are finite or infinite strings of integers, i.e. integers or function on integers.

Lemma. For admissible $\mathcal{L}, \mathcal{J}$, and xf (for pomsets) there holds: $\forall P \in \mathcal{L}$

- $\mathcal{J}^{xf}(P)$ is Π^0_3,
- $\mathcal{J}^{w-xf}(P)$ is Π^0_2.

Proof. $p \in \mathcal{J}^{xf}(P)$ iff $p \in \mathcal{J}(P)$ (Π^0_2 by definition) and the condition of the definition for fairness holds, which is in the form $\forall(\overset{\omega}{\exists}\, \exists \Rightarrow \overset{\omega}{\exists})$ with recursive predicates. But

$\forall(\overset{\omega}{\exists}\, \exists \Rightarrow \overset{\omega}{\exists}) \equiv \forall(\forall\exists\exists \Rightarrow \forall\exists) \equiv \forall(\neg\forall\exists\exists \vee \forall\exists) \equiv \forall(\exists\forall\forall \vee \forall\exists) \equiv \forall\exists\forall$ is also Π^0_3.

$p \in \mathcal{J}^{w-xf}(P)$ iff $p \in \mathcal{J}(P)$ (Π^0_2) and $\forall(\exists\forall \Rightarrow 0 = 1)$ holds. But $\forall(\exists\forall \Rightarrow 0 = 1) \equiv \forall(\neg\exists\forall) \equiv \forall\exists$ is Π^0_2.

Obviously, the other direction is also true: any Π^0_3-set and Π^0_2-set has the form $\mathcal{J}^{xf}(P)$ and $\mathcal{J}^{w-xf}(P)$, respectively, for some admissible $\mathcal{L}, \mathcal{J}$ and xf for pomsets. This can be seen easily as any Π^0_3-, Π^0_2-set is of this form in the interleaving semantics with transitions systems and any run in a ts is also a pomset.

Our coding of pomsets was chosen in such a way that holds: $f = c(p) \bowtie f[n] = c(p[n])\ \forall n \in \mathbb{N}$. We thus can interpret our recursion theoretical results again as results about pomsets and receive immediately the following.

Main Theorem (for true concurrency).
A set $M \subseteq \mathbb{N}^{\mathbb{N}}$ of functions is Π^0_3 iff $M = \mathcal{J}^{xf}(P)$ for some admissible $\mathcal{L}, \mathcal{J}, xf$ for pomsets.

A set $M \subseteq \mathbb{N}^{\mathbb{N}}$ of functions is Π^0_2 iff $M = \mathcal{J}^{w-xf}(P)$ for some admissible $\mathcal{L}, \mathcal{J}, w - xf$ for pomsets.

More specific:
For admissible $\mathcal{L}, \mathcal{J}, xf, P \in \mathcal{L}$ there exist Π^0_1-ultra metrics d, d_w on $\mathcal{POM}^\infty_\Sigma$ s.t.

A pomset $p \in \mathcal{J}(P)$ is strongly x-fair iff p is the d-limes of its initial segments $p[n]$ iff $\{p[n]\}_{n \in \mathbb{N}}$ forms a d-Cauchy sequence.

A pomset $p \in \mathcal{J}(P)$ is weakly x-fair iff p is the d-limes of its initial segments $p[n]$ iff $\{p[n]\}_{n \in \mathbb{N}}$ forms a d-Cauchy sequence for some Π^0_1-ultra metric d s.t. $d(f, x) < 1/n$ is recursive on $\mathcal{POM}^\infty_\Sigma \times \mathcal{POM}^*_\Sigma \times \mathbb{N}$.

5 Acknowledgement

We would like to thank Gerardo Costa, Philippe Darondeau, Pierpaolo Degano, Rocco DeNicola, Irene Guessarian, Ugo Montanari, Maurice Nivat, Ralf Rehrmann, Paul Schupp, Guy Vidal Naquet, Uwe Willecke-Klemme, Pierre Wolpert, and Serge Yoccoz for valuable discussions on fairness. The help of Philippe Darondeau and Serge Yoccoz cannot be underestimated. The Main Theorem in chapter 4 was achieved jointly by Philippe, Serge and the authors of this paper.

References

[BC89] G. Boudol and I. Castellani. Concurrency and atomicity. In *Theoretical Computer Science (59)*, pp 1-60, 1989.

[Bes84a] E. Best. Fairness and conspiracies - erratum. In *Information Processing Letters (19)*, p 162, 1984.

[Bes84b] E. Best. Fairness and conspiracies. In *Information Processing Letters (18)*, pp 215-220, 1984.

[Cos85] G. Costa. A metric characterization of fair computations in CCS. In *Lecture Notes in Computer Science (185)*, pp 239-252, 1985.

[CS87] G. Costa and C. Stirling. Weak and strong fairness in CCS. In *Information and Computation (73)*, pp 207-244, 1987.

[Dar85] P. Darondeau. About fair asynchrony. In *Theoretical Computer Science (37)*, pp 305-336, 1985.

[dB89] J.W. de Bakker. Designing concurrency semantics. In *11th World Computer Congress, North Holland*, pp 591-598, 1989.

[dBW90] J.W. de Bakker and J.H.A. Warmerdam. Metric pomset semantics for a concurrent language with recursion. In *Lecture Notes in Computer Science (469)*, 1990.

[DM84] P. Degano and U. Montanari. Liveness properties as convergence in metric spaces. In *STOC*, pp 31-38, 1984.

[DNPY90] P. Darondeau, D. Nolte, L. Priese, and S. Yoccoz. Fairness, distances and degrees. In *Internal Report (1199), Unite de Recherche INRIA-Rennes, to appear in Theoretical Computer Science*, 1990.

[Fra86] N. Francez. *Fairness.* Springer, 1986.

[Har86] D. Harel. Effective transformations on infinite trees, with applications to high undecidability, dominoes, and fairness. In *Journal of the ACM (33)*, pp 224-248, 1986.

[Hoa85] C.A.R. Hoare. *Communicating sequential Processes.* Prentice Hall, London, 1985.

[Kwi89] M.Z. Kwiatkowska. *Fairness for non-interlieving Concurrency.* PhD thesis, University of Leicester, 1989.

[LPS81] D. Lehmann, A. Pnueli, and J. Stavi. Impartiality, justice and fairness. In *Lecture Notes in Computer Science (115)*, pp 264-277, 1981.

[Mer87] A. Merceron. Fair processes. In *Lecture Notes in Computer Science (266)*, pp 181-195, 1987.

[Mil80] R. Milner. *A Calculus of Communicating Systems*. Lecture Notes in Computer Science (92), 1980.

[OA84] E.R. Olderog and K.R. Apt. Transformations realizing fairness assumptions for parallel programs. In *TR 84-8, LITP*, 1984.

[PN90] L. Priese and D. Nolte. Strong fairness, metric spaces and logical complexity. In *Reihe Informatik (65), U-GH Paderborn, to appear in Theoretical Computer Science*, 1990.

[Pra86] V. Pratt. Modeling concurrency with partial orders. In *International Journal of Parallel Programming*, pp 33-71, 1986.

[Pri88] L. Priese. Fairness. In *EATCS - Bulletin (35)*, pp 171-181, 1988.

[Pri90] L. Priese. Approaching computations by ultra metrics. In *Report LITP 9022, Universite Paris VII*, 1990.

[PRWK87] L. Priese, R. Rehrmann, and U. Willeke-Klemme. Some results on fairness - the regular case. In *Lecture Notes in Computer Science (247)*, pp 383-395, 1987.

[QS83] J.P. Queille and J. Sifakis. Fairness and related properties in transition systems - a temporal logic to deal with fairness. In *Acta Informatica (19)*, pp 195-220, 1983.

[Reh88] R. Rehrmann. Path - and wordfairness. In *Reihe Informatik (43)*, 1988.

[Rog67] H. Rogers. *Theory of Recursive Functions and Effective Computability*. McGraw-Hill Book Company, 1967.

[Thi90] P.S. Thiagarajan. Some behavioural aspects of net theory. In *Theoretical Computer Science (71)*, pp 133-153, 1990.

[UK88] U.Willeke-Klemme. *Classes of Languages of Fair Finite Automata*. PhD thesis, U-GH Paderborn, 1988.

Efficient Verification of Determinate Processes

Huajun Qin
Department of Computer Science
SUNY at Stony Brook
Stony Brook, NY 11794, USA

Abstract

Determinacy, or predictability, is often demanded from engineered concurrent systems. In this paper we use labeled transition systems to express the specifications and implementations of concurrent systems, and present three efficient algorithms (1) to determine if a process P has determinacy property as defined by Robin Milner; (2) to verify whether an implementation process P is observationally equivalent to a determinate specification process S; and (3) to compute the equivalence classes of determinate process P under observational equivalence. We deal only with finite state processes in this paper.

Suppose P has n states and m transitions, and S has n_1 states and m_1 transitions. The first algorithm has time complexity $O(m+n\log n)$ and space complexity $O(m+n)$; the second algorithm has time complexity $O(m+n+m_1+n_1\log n_1)$ and space complexity $O(m+n+m_1+n_1)$; and the third algorithm has time complexity $O(m+n\log n)$ and space complexity $O(m+n)$. Empirical results are presented comparing the algorithms in practice with similar algorithms implemented in other tools.

1 Introduction

One of the promising approaches to the verification of concurrent systems is to express the system specifications and implementations in the same process algebra and to relate them by behavior equivalence.

The operational semantics of concurrent processes are usually defined by labeled transition systems (LTS). An equivalence relation, *observational equivalence*[Mil80], has been proposed to compare the visible behavior of concurrent processes. To verify that an implementation satisfies its specification, one could express them as labeled transition systems and establish observational equivalence between them.

The usual algorithm proposed in [KS83] for deciding observational equivalence on an LTS with n states and m transitions has two phases: First the so-called double arrow transitions are computed using a transitive closure algorithm and then the strong equivalence [Mil80] is computed on the new LTS with the double arrow transitions. The first phase is usually done by using a simple $O(n^3)$ transitive closure algorithm [AHU74], but can be done by using a sophisticated $O(n^{2.376})$ transitive closure algorithm [CW87]. The second phase can be done in $O(m'\log n)$ time by using Paige-Tarjan algorithm [PT87], where m' is the number of transitions in the new LTS. It is important to note that m' is usually much larger than m and is on the order of n^2 in many practical examples.

Most, if not all, engineered concurrent systems are determinate or predictable: "if we perform the same experiment twice on a determinate system – starting each time in its initial state – then we expect to get the same result, or behavior, each time." [Mil89]. A great challenge in designing concurrent systems such as communication protocols is to attain determinacy in the presence of unpredictable components such as faulty communication channels. In the design of such systems, the given specifications are determinate. It is thus desirable to obtain more efficient algorithms for the verification of determinate systems than those for the verification of general concurrent systems by studying the special properties of determinacy.

In this paper we study some properties of determinate processes and present three efficient algorithms (1) to determine if a process P is determinate; (2) to verify whether an implementation process P is observationally equivalent to a determinate specification process S; and (3) to compute the equivalence classes of determinate process P under observational equivalence. We deal only with finite state processes in this paper.

Suppose P has n states and m transitions, and S has n_1 states and m_1 transitions. The first algorithm has time complexity $O(m+n\log n)$ and space complexity $O(m+n)$; the second algorithm has time complexity $O(m+n+m_1+n_1\log n_1)$ and space complexity $O(m+n+m_1+n_1)$; and the third algorithm has time complexity $O(m+n\log n)$ and space complexity $O(m+n)$.

The paper is organized as follows: In section 2 the definitions of observational equivalence and determinacy are given. We study in section 3 special properties of determinate processes and present three efficient algorithms for the verification of such processes. The implementations of our algorithms for the determinate processes show a drastic performance increase over other implementations of the algorithms for the general class of concurrent systems. The performance comparison is presented in section 4.

2 Preliminaries

We view the specification of a concurrent system and its implementation as labeled transition systems. In this section we give the definitions for our model and discuss the notation to be used in later sections.

Definition 1 *A labeled transition system (LTS) is a quadruple* $M=(S,s_0,\Sigma,\Delta)$ *where* (i) S *is a set of states,* (ii) s_0 *is the initial state,* (iii) Σ *is a set of action symbols with* $\tau\notin\Sigma$, *and* (iv) $\Delta : S\times(\Sigma\cup\{\tau\})\rightarrow 2^S$ *is called the transition relation.*

M is called finite if both S and Σ are finite. A finite LTS is rigid if $\forall s\in S$, $|\Delta(s,\tau)|=0$. *A finite LTS is deterministic if it is rigid and* $\forall s\in S, \forall u\in\Sigma$, $|\Delta(s,u)|\leq 1$.

When we use an LTS to model a process, Σ is the set of the actions that the process can perform, and τ represents an (invisible) internal action. An action u in Σ is said to be an external action. $t\in\Delta(s,a)$ means that the process at state s goes to state t after performing the action a.

We write $s\xrightarrow{a}t$ if $t\in\Delta(s,a)$. Also we write $s\xrightarrow{a}\star$ if $s\xrightarrow{a}t$ for some t; $s\stackrel{a}{\not\rightarrow}\star$ if there is no $t\in S$ such that $s\xrightarrow{a}t$. We define $\stackrel{\epsilon}{\Rightarrow}$ as $(\xrightarrow{\tau})^*$ and $\stackrel{a}{\Rightarrow}$ as $\stackrel{\epsilon}{\Rightarrow}\xrightarrow{a}\stackrel{\epsilon}{\Rightarrow}$ for action symbol a.

Since we are often concerned with the visible behavior of a system, we define *observational equivalence* as in [Mil88]:

Definition 2 (Milner) *A binary relation $\mathcal{R}$ on states is a weak bisimulation relation if for each $(p,q) \in \mathcal{R}$ and each $a \in \Sigma \cup \{\varepsilon\}$, (1) and (2) hold:*

(1). Whenever $p \xrightarrow{a} p'$ then for some q', $q \stackrel{a}{\Rightarrow} q'$ and $(p',q') \in \mathcal{R}$;

(2). Whenever $q \xrightarrow{a} q'$ then for some p', $p \stackrel{a}{\Rightarrow} p'$ and $(p',q') \in \mathcal{R}$.

States p and q are observationally equivalent (we write $p \approx q$) if (p,q) is in a weak bisimulation relation.

Definition 3 *Two LTSs M and M' are observationally equivalent if there exists a weak bisimulation $\mathcal{R}$ that contains the pair (s_0, s_0') of their initial states.*

Proposition 1 (Milner) *$\approx$ equals $\bigcup\{\mathcal{R} | \mathcal{R}$ is a weak bisimulation relation on state space and is an equivalence relation on S.*

Definition 4 (Milner) *p is (weakly) determinate if, for each state q that is reachable from p and for all $a \in \Sigma \cup \{\varepsilon\}$, whenever $q \stackrel{a}{\Rightarrow} q'$ and $q \stackrel{a}{\Rightarrow} q''$ then $q' \approx q''$.*

Proposition 2 (Milner) *if $p \approx q$ and p is determinate, then q is determinate.*

It should be pointed out that deterministic processes are always determinate, but not all of the determinate processes are deterministic.

3 Algorithms for the Verification of Determinate Processes

In this section we investigate some special properties of determinate finite LTSs that lead to efficient verification algorithms. The algorithms are proved correct and their time and space complexities are analyzed. In this paper we only consider finite LTSs.

Definition 5 *$=_\tau$ on M is the minimum equivalence relation such that $=_\tau \supseteq \{(p,q) | p,q \in M, p \stackrel{\varepsilon}{\Rightarrow} q$, or $q \stackrel{\varepsilon}{\Rightarrow} p\}$.*

$=_{s\varepsilon}$ on M is the equivalence relation such that for any p and q $p =_{s\varepsilon} q$ if and only if $p \stackrel{\varepsilon}{\Rightarrow} q$ and $q \stackrel{\varepsilon}{\Rightarrow} p$.

Intuitively $p =_\tau q$ means that by ignoring the directions of transitions, p and q are connected through a path consisting of only τ-transitions. $p =_{s\varepsilon} q$ means that both p and q are on a loop of (directed) τ-transitions.

Definition 6 *$f_l(M)$ is the LTS obtained from M by removing all $p \xrightarrow{\tau} p$ transitions in M;*

$f_d(M)$ is the LTS obtained from M by removing all but one a-transitions from each state for each $a \in \Sigma \cup \{\tau\}$.

Note that $f_d(M)$ is not unique by above definition. However the above definition suffices to serve our purposes in this paper.

Definition 7 *M is τ-acyclic if there do not exist p and q in M such that $p \stackrel{\tau}{\Rightarrow} q$ and $q \stackrel{\tau}{\Rightarrow} p$.*

M is $\approx$-irreducible if no two states in M are observationally equivalent.

Let $=_e$ be any equivalence relation on M. We use $(M/=_e)$ to denote the quotient machine induced by $=_e$.

Proposition 3
(1) $M \approx (M/\approx)$
(2) $M \approx (M/=_{\tau c})$
(3) $M \approx f_l(M)$
(4) *M is determinate if an only if $M \approx f_d(f_l(M/=_\tau))$.*

Proof: The proof of (1), (2) and (3) is easy to establish. We prove only (4) here.

Suppose $M \approx f_d(f_l(M/=_\tau))$. Because $f_d(f_l(M/=_\tau))$ is deterministic and thus determinate, M is determinate by proposition 2.

Suppose M is determinate. Then $p =_\tau q$ implies $p \approx q$ for any p and q in M. Thus $M \approx (M/=_\tau) \approx f_l(M/=_\tau)$.

Let LTS P be $f_l(M/=_\tau)$. P is rigid and determinate. It is then easy to establish that $f_d(P) \approx P$. Hence $M \approx f_d(f_l(M/=_\tau))$ by transitivity of $\approx$. □

For a given LTS M, we use n_M and m_M to denote the number of states and transitions in M respectively. Let $=_e$ be any equivalence relation on M represented by its naturally induced partition. We have the following propositions:

Proposition 4 *The following LTSs can be can be constructed in $O(n_M + m_M)$ time and space:* (1) $(M/=_e)$, (2) $f_l(M)$, (3) $f_d(M)$, (4) $(M/=_{\tau c})$ *and* (5) $(M/=_\tau)$.

Proof: It is easy to see that $f_l(M)$ and $f_d(M)$ can be constructed in $O(n_M + m_M)$ time and space.

To construct $(M/=_e)$, the blocks in the naturally induced partition are used as states, and block P has a transition under action a to block Q if and only if there exist p in block P and q in block Q, and $p \xrightarrow{a} q$ is in M. The construction of states and transitions of $(M/=_e)$ can be done in $O(n_M + m_M)$ time and space.

We show next how to construct $(M/=_{\tau c})$ and $(M/=_\tau)$ in linear time.

To compute $=_{\tau c}$ on $M = (S, s_0, \Sigma, \Delta)$, we construct a graph $G = (V, E)$ with $V = S$ and $E = \{(p,q) | p \xrightarrow{\tau} q \text{ in } M\}$. The problem of computing $=_{\tau c}$ is converted to the problem of finding strongly connected components in G such that p and q are in the same component ($p =_{\tau c} q$) if and only if there is a path from p to q and a path from q to p in the graph G. An algorithm to find the strongly connected components of a directed graph is presented in [Tar72] [AHU74] and has time and space complexity of $O(|V| + |E|)$. It follows that $=_{\tau c}$ on M and $(M/=_{\tau c})$ can be computed in $O(n_M + m_M)$ time and space.

To compute $=_\tau$ on M, we construct a graph $G = (V, E)$ with $V = S$ and $E = \{(p,q) | p \xrightarrow{\tau} q \text{ in } M\} \cup \{(q,p) | p \xrightarrow{\tau} q \text{ in } M\}$. The problem of computing $=_\tau$ on M is converted to the problem of finding strongly connected components in G such that $p =_\tau q$ if and only if p and q are in the same component in G. It follows that $=_\tau$ on M and $(M/=_{\tau c})$ can be computed in $O(n_M + m_M)$ time and space. □

Proposition 5 *Let $M = (P, p_0, \Sigma, \Delta_M)$ be τ-acyclic and $N = (Q, q_0, \Sigma, \Delta_N)$ be deterministic. $M \approx N$ if and only if there exists a relation $\mathcal{R} \subseteq P \times Q$ such that $p_0 \mathcal{R} q_0$ and whenever $p \mathcal{R} q$ the following holds:*
(1) if $p \xrightarrow{\tau} p'$, then $p' \mathcal{R} q$;

```
procedure CheckEquivalence(M,N)
begin
        LIST = {(p0, q0)};
        unmark each state in M;
        while there is a pair (p, q) on LIST do
        begin
                delete (p, q) from LIST;
                if p is marked with a state q' and q' ≠ q then
                        report 'not equivalent' and exit;
                else if p is not marked then
                begin
                        mark p with q;
                        sort(p) = {u|p -u-> p'};
                        sort(q) = {u|q -u-> q'};
                        if ((sort(p) − {τ} ⊄ sort(q)) or
                            (τ ∉ sort(p) and |sort(p)| ≠ |sort(q)|)) then
                            report 'not equivalent' and exit;
                        add each (p', q') in Δ_M(p, τ) × {q} to LIST;
                        for each u ∈ Σ do
                            add each (p', q') in Δ_M(p, u) × Δ_N(q, u) to LIST;
                end
        end
        for each state p in M do
                report 'p is in block q' if p is marked with q;
end
```

Figure 1: An algorithm for deciding whether $M \approx N$, given M being τ-acyclic and N being deterministic and $\approx$-irreducible

(2) if $p \xrightarrow{u} p'$ with $u \neq \tau$, then $q \xrightarrow{u} q'$ and $p'\mathcal{R}q'$;
(3) if $q \xrightarrow{u} q'$, then for each p' such that $p \xrightarrow{u} p'$, $p'\mathcal{R}q'$;
(4) if $p \not\xrightarrow{\tau} \star$ and $q \xrightarrow{u} q'$, then there must exist p' such that $p \xrightarrow{u} p'$.

Proof: If $M \approx N$, then let $\mathcal{R}$ be the equivalence relation $\approx$ on M and N. It is easy to check that conditions (1)–(4) hold.

If there exists $\mathcal{R}$ such that $p_0\mathcal{R}q_0$ and conditions (1)–(4) hold, it is easy to verify that $\mathcal{R}$ is a weak bisimulation relation between M and N. Thus $M \approx N$. □

Intuitively if one wants to establish $M \approx N$ with N deterministic, he would try to construct a bisimulation relation $\mathcal{R}$ that satisfies conditions (1)–(4) in the above proposition. The algorithm for deciding if $M \approx N$ is given in figure 1. To make the algorithm efficient, we put an extra constraint that N be $\approx$-irreducible. Because N is $\approx$-irreducible, the reported partition on M has fewest blocks and its associated equivalence is $\approx$.

Proposition 6 *Let M be τ-acyclic and N be deterministic and $\approx$-irreducible. $M \approx N$ can be decided in $O(m_M + n_M + n_N)$ time and space. In case $M \approx N$, the equivalence*

relation $\approx$ on M can be computed in $O(m_M + n_M + n_N)$ time and space.

Proof: We show that the algorithm in figure 1 decides whether $M\approx N$ in linear time and space. The correctness of this algorithm follows directly from proposition 5. We now show that the algorithm can be executed in linear time and space.

Each state of M is marked only once. When a state p is marked, the number of state pairs added to LIST is $|\Delta_M(p,\tau) \times \{q\}| + \sum_{u\in\Sigma} |\Delta_M(p,u) \times \Delta_N(q,u)|$, which is at most $\sum_{a\in\Sigma\cup\{\tau\}} |\Delta_M(p,a)|$. This is because N is deterministic and $|\Delta_N(q,u)| \leq 1$. Thus the total number of state pairs put onto LIST is at most m_M in the entire algorithm. The sort computation and comparison can be done in $O(|\Sigma| + \sum_{a\in\Sigma\cup\{\tau\}} |\Delta_M(p,a)|)$ when state p in M is marked. We conclude that the time complexity of this algorithm is $O(m_M + n_M + n_N)$ and the space complexity is $O(m_M + n_M + n_N)$. Note that $|\Sigma|$ is treated as a constant in the complexity analysis. Also note that m_N is of the same order with n_N because N is deterministic. □

Proposition 7 *If M is deterministic then $\approx$ on M can be computed in $O(n_M \log n_M)$ time and $(n_M + m_M)$ space.*

Proof: When M is deterministic, the partition induced by $\approx$ on M is the coarsest partition, say $\pi = \{B_1, B_2, \ldots, B_l\}$ such that p and q in B_i implies that for each u, $\Delta(p,u)$ and $\Delta(q,u)$ are either both empty, or neither empty and are contained in some one B_j. An algorithm for solving the coarsest partition problem is presented in [Hop71] [AHU74]. It has time complexity $O(n_M \log n_M)$ and space complexity $O(n_M)$. The size of Σ is considered fixed and treated as a constant in the complexity analysis. □

Theorem 1 *Given a determinate N, $\approx$ on N can be computed in $O(m_N + n_N \log n_N)$ time and $O(m_N + n_N)$ space.*

Proof: Let N' be $f_d(f_l(N/{=_\tau}))$. N' is deterministic and observationally equivalent to N. N' can be computed in $O(m_M + n_M)$ time and space. $(N'/{\approx})$ can be computed in $O(n_{N'} \log n_{N'})$ time and $O(n_{N'} + m_{N'})$ space. Note that $n_{N'} \leq n_N$ and $m_{N'} \leq m_N$.

Since $N\approx N'$, $N\approx(N'/{\approx})$. The equivalence relation $\approx$ on N can be constructed from $\approx$ on N' and $=_\tau$ on N: $p\approx q$ if and only if states $[p]$ and $[q]$ in N' are observationally equivalent. It follows that $\approx$ on N can be computed in $O(m_N + n_N \log n_N)$ time and $O(m_N + n_N)$ space. □

Theorem 2 *Given LTS M and a determinate LTS N, $M\approx N$ can be decided in $O(m_M + n_M + m_N + n_N \log n_N)$ time and $O(m_M + n_M + m_N + n_N)$ space. In case $M\approx N$, $\approx$ on M can be computed in $O(m_M + n_M + m_N + n_N \log n_N)$ time and $O(m_M + n_M + m_N + n_N)$ space.*

Proof: By theorem 1, $(N/{\approx})$ can be constructed in $O(m_N + n_N \log n_N)$ time and $O(m_N + n_N)$ space. Let N' be $f_l(N/{\approx})$. N' is deterministic and $\approx$-irreducible. $N\approx N'$.

$f_l(M/{=_{sc}})$ can be computed in linear time and space. Let M' be $f_l(M/{=_{sc}})$. M' is τ-acyclic and $M'\approx M$. By proposition 6, $M'\approx N'$ can be decided in $O(n_{M'} + m_{M'} + n_{N'})$ time and space. Note that $n_{M'} \leq n_M$, $m_{M'} \leq m_M$ and $n_{N'} \leq n_N$.

If $M'\not\approx N'$, then $M\not\approx N$. If $M'\approx N'$ then $\approx$ on M can be constructed from $=_\tau$ on M and $\approx$ on M' in linear time and space with respect to M.

Thus the time and space complexity in deciding $M\approx N$ and computing $\approx$ on M in case $M\approx N$ is $O(m_M + n_M + n_N \log n_N + m_N)$ and $O(m_M + n_M + m_N + n_N)$ respectively. □

scheduler with both a_i and b_i visible

k	4	5	6	7	8	9	10	11	12
states	97	241	577	1345	3073	6913	15361	33793	73729
trans.	241	721	2017	5377	13825	34561	84481	202753	479233
eq.cl.	64	160	384	896	2048	4608	10240	22528	49152
AUTO	0.30	1.24	5.52	33.2	182	-	-	-	-
bisim	0.12	0.34	0.98	2.78	7.32	18.8	45.9	125	462
BB	0.05	0.20	0.58	1.85	5.40	14.7	41.6	110	380
Dbisim	0.02	0.06	0.18	0.48	1.18	2.82	6.76	18.6	57.3
DV	<0.02	0.02	0.06	0.14	0.32	0.78	1.92	5.32	31.8

scheduler with a_i visible and b_i renamed to τ

k	4	5	6	7	8	9	10	11	12
states	97	241	577	1345	3073	6913	15361	33793	73729
trans.	241	721	2017	5377	13825	34561	84481	202753	479233
eq.cl.	4	5	6	7	8	9	10	11	12
AUTO	0.38	2.00	12.54	107	-	-	-	-	-
Ald.-o	*	*	*	*	433.656	2865.340	-	-	-
bisim	0.10	0.38	1.44	5.52	20.6	95.8	-	-	-
Ald.-s	*	*	*	*	15.1	70.4	360	1836	-
Ald.-s^f	*	*	*	*	5.56	19.8	72.2	269.3	1465
Ald.-bb^f	*	*	*	*	4.00	13.6	35.5	93.5	275
BB	<0.02	0.03	0.12	0.37	1.05	2.65	6.70	16.6	53.8
Dbisim	<0.02	0.02	0.08	0.22	0.52	1.24	2.90	6.90	22.2
DV	<0.02	0.02	0.04	0.10	0.28	0.66	1.60	3.88	15.7

Figure 2: Times (in seconds) on verifying determinate k-cycler schedulers

Corollary 1 *Given LTS M, whether M is determinate can be decided in $O(n_M \log n_M + m_M)$ time and $O(m_M + n_M)$ space.*

Proof: Let N be $f_d(f_l(M/=_\tau))$. LTS N is deterministic. M is determinate if and only if $M \approx N$ by proposition 3.4. By above theorem $M \approx N$ can be decided in $O(n_M \log n_M + m_M)$ time and $O(m_M + n_M)$ space. □

4 Implementation and Performance Comparison

We have implemented our algorithms for the verification of determinate systems and the performance compares favorably to the implementations for the verification of general systems.

The process used for our comparison is the determinate 'scheduler' described in [Mil89] that schedules k processes in succession circularly. In a CCS framework a scheduler sch_k is described as following:

$C_i = \overline{c_i}.a_i(\overline{b_i}|c_{i+1}).C_i$
$sch_k = (c_1.nil|C_1|\cdots|C_k)\backslash c_1\cdots\backslash c_k$

The running times on a number of schedulers are collected on several implementations of equivalence checking algorithms and are summarized in figure 2. In the figure, "-" means that no outcome was obtained due to lack of memory and "*" means that no outcome is available. Four algorithms implemented in Aldébaran are tested. In the figure Ald.-o, Ald.-s, Ald.-s^f and Ald.-bb^f denote respectively the observational equivalence verification, safety equivalence verification, 'on the fly' verification of safety equivalence and branching bisimulation equivalence [FM90] [Mou91].

AUTO [dSV89], Aldébaran [Fer89], and our program 'bisim' implemented the two-phase algorithms for deciding observational equivalence for the general class of processes. Considering the verification of a process P, the algorithms implemented have time complexity $O(n_P^3)$ and space complexity $O(n_P^2)$ because $O(n_P^3)$ time and $O(n_P^2)$ space algorithms for computing transitive closures are used. To our knowledge, the three implementations are the fastest for computing $\approx$ on the general class of processes.

BB [GV90] implements an $O(m_P \times n_P)$ time and $O(m_P + n_P)$ space algorithm for deciding the branching bisimulation equivalence [vGW89] on a process P. Branching bisimulation equivalence is stronger than observational equivalence. But they are shown in [Qin91] to be identical for the class of determinate processes. (Joost Engelfriet in [Eng85] investigated the notions of determinacy with respect to observational equivalence, failure equivalence and trace equivalence, and proved that they are identical.)

Our programs for the verification of determinate processes are named 'Dbisim' and 'DV'. Given a process P, 'Dbisim' checks whether P is determinate and computes its observational equivalence classes if it is determinate. Given an implementation process P and a deterministic and $\approx$-irreducible specification process S, 'DV' checks if $P \approx S$ and computes $\approx$ on P in case $P \approx S$. For scheduler sch_k, the specification process S is taken to be $f_d(f_l(sch_k/\approx)$ and is computed before it is sent to program 'DV' with sch_k as P.

'Dbisim' implements an $O(m_P + n_P \log n_P)$ time and $O(m_P + n_P)$ space algorithm. 'DV' implements an algorithm of $O(m_P + n_P + m_S + n_S \log n_S)$ time complexity and $O(m_P + n_P + m_S + n_S)$ space complexity.

The times on running AUTO [dSV89], BB [GV90], 'bisim', 'Dbisim' and 'DV' are collected on a sun 3/260 with 16MB of memory. The data on Aldébaran[Fer89], are collected by Laurent Mounier [Mou91] on a SUN 3/60 with 12MB of memory. To decide the speed difference of the two machines used for experiment, a test program was run on both machines, and our machine was 1.55 times faster than the one used in the experiment on Aldébaran. The numbers reported in figure 2 on Aldébaran have already been scaled down for the fair comparison. Note that all the times do not include input and output times.

It is clear from the data reported in figure 2 that our implementations ('Dbisim' and 'DV') for the verification of determinate systems show a drastic performance increase over the implementations (AUTO, Aldébaran, and 'bisim') for the verification of general systems.

Acknowledgments

I would like to thank Laurent Mounier for generating test results on Aldébaran. I am grateful to Robert de Simone, Eric Madelaine, Jan Friso Groote, and Frits Vaandrager for the discussions and help on their tools. Also the useful suggestions from anonymous referees helped to improve the presentation.

References

[AHU74] A. V. Aho, J. E. Hopcroft, and J. D. Ullman. *The Design and Analysis of Computer Algorithms.* Addison-Wesley, 1974.

[CW87] D. Coppersmith and S. Winograd. Matrix multiplication via arithmic progressions. In *Proceedings 19th ACM Symposium on Theory of Computing*, pages 1–6, New York City, NY, 1987.

[dSV89] R. de Simone and D. Vergamini. *Aboard AUTO.* Technical Report 111, INRIA, Centre Sophia-Antipolis, Valbonne Cedex, 1989.

[Eng85] J. Engelfriet. Determinacy $\longrightarrow$ (observational equivalence = trace equivalence). *Theoretical Computer Science*, 36:21–25, 1985.

[Fer89] J. Fernandez. *An Implementation of an Efficient Algorithm for Bisimulation Equivalence.* Technical Report, LGI-IMAG, Genoble, 1989.

[FM90] J. C. Fernandez and Laurent Mounier. Verifying bisimulations "on the fly". In *Proceedings of FORTE'90*, 1990.

[GV90] Jan Friso Groote and Frits Vaandrager. An efficient algorithm for branching bisimulation and stuttering equivalence. In *Proceedings of ICALP 90*, 1990.

[Hop71] J. E. Hopcroft. An $n \log n$ algorithm for minimizing states in a finite automata. In Z. Kohavi and A. Paz, editors, *Theory of Machines and Computations*, pages 189–196, Academic Press, New York, 1971.

[KS83] P.C. Kanellakis and S.A. Smolka. CCS expressions, finite state processes, and three problems of equivalence. In *the Second Annual ACM Symposium on Principles of Distributed Computing*, pages 228–240, Aug. 1983.

[Mil80] R. Milner. Calculus for communicating systems. In *LNCS 92*, Springer Verlag, 1980.

[Mil88] R. Milner. *Operational and Algebraic Semantics of Concurrent Processes.* Technical Report ECS-LFCS-88-46, Laboratory for Foundations of Computer Science, Univ. of Edinburgh, Feb. 1988.

[Mil89] R. Milner. *Communication and Concurrency.* Prentice-Hall International, 1989.

[Mou91] Laurent Mounier. Private communication. 1991.

[PT87] R. Paige and R. Tarjan. Three partition refinement algorithms. *SIAM Journal on Computing*, 16(6):973–989, 1987.

[Qin91] H. Qin. *Automated Design and Verification of Concurrent Systems*. PhD thesis, State University of New York at Stony Brook, 1991. (in preparation).

[Tar72] R. E. Tarjan. Depth first search and linear graph algorithms. *SIAM J. Computing*, 1(2):146–160, 1972.

[vGW89] R. J. van Glabbeek and W. P. Weijland. Branching time and abstraction in bisimulation semantics (extended abstract). In G.X Ritter, editor, *Information Processing 89*, pages 613–618, Elsevier Science Publishers B.V., North Holland, 1989.

Experiments on Processes with Backtracking

Ph. Schnoebelen*

Laboratoire d'Informatique Fondamentale
et d'Intelligence Artificielle,
Institut Imag - CNRS,
Grenoble - FRANCE

Abstract

We investigate trace-, ready-, failure-based equivalences of processes when the user is provided with a special *undo*-button allowing to take back steps. Such *undo*-buttons were first suggested in [vG90]. This gives rise to new semantic equivalences and to new characterizations of old ones. We investigate congruence properties and full abstraction problems for a CCS-like process algebra.

1 Introduction

There exist several ways to define the semantics of processes (also known as reactive systems). Main examples are:

- through an operationally defined equivalence or preorder (e.g. bisimulation [Par81] and its variants),
- through a logical language (e.g. through the HML modal logic of [HM85] and fragments of it),
- through algebraic properties (e.g. the observational congruence of [Mil80] defined as the largest congruence for non-deterministic choice contained in observational equivalence),
- through a testing scenario defining which characteristics of the process are observed from outside (e.g. the interactive observations described in [Mil81]).

In each one of these frameworks, many different semantics can be defined. The main goal of *comparative concurrency semantics* is to classify these different semantics and to find connections between the different frameworks. For example, given a semantic equivalence ≡ defined as undistinguishability for some testing scenario, natural questions are

- is ≡ a congruence for some well-known process combinators ?
- is ≡ the equivalence generated by a natural fragment of HML ?

*LIFIA-IMAG, 46 Av. Félix Viallet, 38031 GRENOBLE Cedex, FRANCE. E-mail:phs@lifia.imag.fr

- does $\equiv$ have a nice operational characterization ?

The issue is not to find which is the best framework. Each framework has its own advantages and finding links between them greatly illuminates the whole picture.

In this paper, we concentrate on process equivalences (and preorders) that are defined (or definable) through a natural testing scenario.

One can get very discriminating equivalences through testing scenarios if the tester has access to powerful ways of controlling the behavior of the tested process and if he does not discard any available information. For example, [Abr87] shows how one can test for bisimilarity if it is possible to make copies of the current state of the process and test all its possible behaviors[1]. It has been argued that granting the user with such possibilities is not realistic [BIM88, LS89].

In this paper, we study a new element that can be incorporated into a testing methodology and which gives rise to several new process equivalences. This new element is the possibility of taking back (or undoing) any previous move made by the process during the interactive test. To understand the idea, we just have to picture a machine with an *undo*-button. (To our knowledge, this idea of undoing moves first appeared in [vG90].)

What is interesting in an *undo*-button is that it is conceptually very simple and does not appear as unrealistic as the methodology of [Abr87]. "Undoing" is a possibility in some real systems. More importantly, by only allowing a weak form of look-ahead, it gives rise to new points in the "linear time-branching time spectrum". It also gives new characterizations, in terms of a simple testing protocol, of previously studied equivalences.

The paper is organized as follows: in section 2, we recall the classical definitions and results about traces, readies, failures, ..., and behavioral equivalences. Section 3 introduces *undo*-buttons and relates the *undo*-based equivalences with the classical ones. Section 4 studies congruence properties (in a simple process algebra) of the several equivalences based on *undo*'s. A full abstraction result is given. We conclude in section 5 with suggestions for future work. As a rule, full proofs appear in [Sch91].

2 Basic notions

The semantics we shall study are based on preorders between processes. A preorder $\leq_\bullet$ is any reflexive and transitive relation. It needs not be antisymmetric. The equivalence relation generated by a preorder $\leq_\bullet$ is $=_\bullet$ defined as $\leq_\bullet \cap \leq_\bullet^{-1}$.

2.1 Labeled transition systems

We assume a countable alphabet $A = \{a, b, c, \ldots\}$ of *action names* and a (A-labeled) *transition system* S. That is, S is a tuple $\langle S, \rightarrow\rangle$ where $S = \{p, q, r, \ldots\}$ is a set of *processes* (or *states*) and $\rightarrow \subseteq S \times A \times S$

[1] Other testing scenarios for bisimulation appear in [BIM88] and other works.

is a *labeled transition relation*. Any $(p,a,q) \in \rightarrow$ is a *transition*.

We write $p \xrightarrow{a} q$ when $(p,a,q) \in \rightarrow$ and say that p can perform an a-step, evolving into q. The $\rightarrow \subseteq S \times A \times S$ relation is canonically extended to $\rightarrow \subseteq S \times A^* \times S$ given by

- $p \xrightarrow{\lambda} p$ for all $p \in S$ ($\lambda \in A^*$ is the empty word),
- $p \xrightarrow{a\sigma} q$ whenever $p \xrightarrow{a} r \xrightarrow{\sigma} q$ for some $r \in S$.

We say that q is *reachable* from p if $p \xrightarrow{\sigma} q$ for some $\sigma \in A^*$. We write $p \xrightarrow{\sigma}$ when $p \xrightarrow{\sigma} q$ for some q we are not interested in.

For $p \in S$, we write $I(p)$ for the set of *initial actions* of p, that is, $I(p) \stackrel{\text{def}}{=} \{a \in A \mid p \xrightarrow{a}\}$. When $I(p) = \emptyset$, we say that p is *blocked*.

For $a \in A$, we write $S(p,a)$ for the set $\{q \in S \mid p \xrightarrow{a} q\}$. S is not assumed to be deterministic and in general, $S(p,a)$ may be any subset of S.

We say that $p \in S$ is *finitely branching* (or f.b.) when, for all q reachable from p and for all $a \in A$, $S(q,a)$ is finite. In the following, for technical simplicity, we shall assume that all processes in S are finitely branching ("S is f.b."). However, we shall precisely point out where the hypothesis is required.

Milner suggested in [Mil81] how an external user could interact with a process. We can picture a process p as some black box with several buttons, one for each $a \in A$. Initially p is waiting. If we try to push the a-button and if $a \in I(p)$, then p will eventually accept a, that is, the a-button will eventually yield. p will then choose non-deterministically one $p \xrightarrow{a} q$ transition and become (i.e. move into state) q. If $a \notin I(p)$, the a-button will never yield and we say that p refuses a. A blocked process refuses all actions.

2.2 Traces

Given a process p of S, we define its set of (finite) *traces*:

$$T(p) \stackrel{\text{def}}{=} \{\sigma \in A^* \mid p \xrightarrow{\sigma}\}$$

and its set of *completed traces*:

$$CT(p) \stackrel{\text{def}}{=} \{\sigma \in A^* \mid p \xrightarrow{\sigma} q \text{ for some } q \text{ with } I(q) = \emptyset\}$$

Thus, a completed trace of p is the trace of a maximal (finite) path starting from p.

We define our first two preorders:

$$p \leq_T q \stackrel{\text{def}}{\Leftrightarrow} T(p) \subseteq T(q)$$

and

$$p \leq_{CT} q \stackrel{\text{def}}{\Leftrightarrow} \begin{cases} CT(p) \subseteq CT(q) \text{ and} \\ T(p) \subseteq T(q) \end{cases} \tag{1}$$

where the associated equivalences are written $=_T$ and $=_{CT}$. Clearly

$$p \leq_{CT} q \text{ implies } p \leq_T q$$

and this implication is strict (here and in the remaining of this section, we refer to the standard literature, e.g. [vG90], for examples showing that a given implication is strict).

It is easy to imagine a testing scenario for $\leq_T$ and $\leq_{CT}$. If a user of p can successfully push the buttons $a_1, \ldots, a_n$ in succession, then $\sigma = a_1 \ldots a_n$ is a trace of p. Reciprocally, if σ is a trace of p, then some try at pushing $a_1, \ldots, a_n$ in succession may eventually succeed. (As p is not necessarily deterministic, σ needs not always be accepted on the first try.) This only assumes that a process can be used as many times as we want.

Similarly, a completed trace σ is observed when we successfully push $\sigma(1), \ldots, \sigma(n)$ in succession and then observe that we can push no other button (i.e. they are all refused). For this, it may be useful to picture the possibility of pushing several buttons at once and see which one (if any) does yield.

2.3 Readies and failures

For $p \in S$, $\sigma \in A^*$ and $X \subseteq A$, we say the pair (σ, X) is a *failure (pair)* of p if there is some $p \xrightarrow{\sigma} q$ s.t. $I(q) \cap X = \emptyset$. We write $F(p)$ for the set of all failures of p and define

$$p \leq_F q \stackrel{\text{def}}{\Leftrightarrow} F(p) \subseteq F(q)$$

with $=_F$ the associated equivalence.

Testing failures is similar to testing completed traces. If the user can successfully push $\sigma(1), \ldots, \sigma(n)$ in succession and then, trying to push the set X all at once, observe that no action is accepted, then $(\sigma, X) \in F(p)$.

Indeed, completed traces are special cases of failures:

$$\sigma \in CT(p) \text{ iff } (\sigma, A) \in F(p)$$

entailing

$$p \leq_F q \text{ implies } p \leq_{CT} q$$

(This implication is strict.)

A *ready (pair)* of p is any pair $[\sigma, Y]$ s.t. there is some $p \xrightarrow{\sigma} q$ with $I(q) = Y$. We write $R(p)$ for the set of all readies of p and define

$$p \leq_R q \stackrel{\text{def}}{\Leftrightarrow} R(p) \subseteq R(q)$$

with $=_R$ the associated equivalence.

Readies are more difficult to observe than failures. One solution assumes that the process displays a menu of available actions before each interaction with the user [BBK85]. Then, to observe a ready pair $[\sigma, Y]$, the user just has to record which actions are offered after he has successfully performed a trace σ.

Readies provide more information than failures as $F(p)$ is the set of all (σ, X) such that there is a $[\sigma, Y]$ in $R(p)$ with $X \cap Y = \emptyset$, entailing

$$p \leq_R q \text{ implies } p \leq_F q$$

(This implication is strict.)

Note that if the process always displays a menu of available actions, the user could have recorded the menu at every intermediate step while completing its test. This gives rise to the notion of ready traces[2]. A *ready trace* of p is a sequence $[Y_0, a_1, Y_1, \ldots, a_n, Y_n]$ such that there is a path $(p =)p_0 \xrightarrow{a_1} p_1 \xrightarrow{a_2} \cdots p_{n-1} \xrightarrow{a_n} p_n$ with $Y_i = I(p_i)$ for $i = 0, \ldots, n$. Following this idea, we define the *failure traces* of p, that is, the sequences $(X_0, a_1, X_1, \ldots, a_n, X_n)$ such that there is a path $(p =)p_0 \xrightarrow{a_1} p_1 \xrightarrow{a_2} \cdots p_{n-1} \xrightarrow{a_n} p_n$ with $X_i \cap I(p_i) = \emptyset$ for $i = 0, \ldots, n$.

We write $RT(p)$ (resp. $FT(p)$) for the sets of all ready (resp. failure) traces of p and define $\leq_{RT}$, $\leq_{FT}$, $=_{RT}$ and $=_{FT}$ accordingly. Clearly

$$p \leq_{RT} q \text{ implies } p \leq_{FT} q \qquad p \leq_{RT} q \text{ implies } p \leq_R q \qquad p \leq_{FT} q \text{ implies } p \leq_F q$$

(All three implications are strict.)

2.4 Behavioral preorders

We say that a relation $R \subseteq S \times S$ is a *simulation* if, for all pRq and all steps $p \xrightarrow{a} p'$, there is a step $q \xrightarrow{a} q'$ s.t. $p'Rq'$ [HM80]. If R is a simulation containing (p, q), we write $R : p \sqsubseteq q$. We write $p \sqsubseteq q$ when $R : p \sqsubseteq q$ for some R and say that q *simulates* p. It is well known that $\sqsubseteq \subseteq S \times S$ is a preorder.

The associated equivalence is denoted $\rightleftarrows$ and is called *simulation equivalence*[3]. It should not be confused with bisimulation. $R \subseteq S \times S$ is a *bisimulation* if R and R^{-1} are simulations. We write $R : p \underline{\leftrightarrow} q$ when R is a bisimulation containing (p, q), and $p \underline{\leftrightarrow} q$ when $R : p \underline{\leftrightarrow} q$ for some R, in which case we say p and q are bisimilar. It is well-known that $\underline{\leftrightarrow}$ is an equivalence on S and its definition entails

$$p \underline{\leftrightarrow} q \text{ implies } p \rightleftarrows q$$

This implication is strict as $p \rightleftarrows q$ only implies that there exist two simulations R and R' s.t. $R : p \sqsubseteq q$ and $R' : q \sqsubseteq p$ without implying that we can choose $R' = R^{-1}$.

We clearly have

$$p \sqsubseteq q \text{ implies } p \leq_T q$$

(This implication is strict.)

However, simulation does not respect deadlock, that is, $p \rightleftarrows q$ does not entail $p =_{CT} q$. Bisimulation respects deadlock and

$$p \underline{\leftrightarrow} q \text{ implies } p =_{RT} q$$

This implication is strict as $p =_{RT} q$ does not entail $p \sqsubseteq q$.

---

[2] Ready traces appeared in [BBK85] and in [Pnu85] where they are called "barbed traces".

[3] Also called *safety equivalence*, or *one-nested simulation equivalence* in [GV88]

An intermediate preorder is ready simulation[4]. We say that $R \subseteq S \times S$ is a *ready simulation* if it is a simulation s.t. pRq implies $I(p) = I(q)$. We use the notations $R : p \sqsubseteq_R q$, $p \sqsubseteq_R q$ and $p \rightharpoonup_R q$ with obvious definitions.

Ready simulation arose naturally as the congruence generated from trace equivalence by a family of process combinators generalizing CCS [Blo89a]. It preserves ready traces:

$$p \sqsubseteq_R q \text{ implies } p \leq_{RT} q$$

(This implication is strict.)

It is well-known [Mil90] that simulation, ready simulation and bisimulation can be defined iteratively. Let us consider simulation. A relation $R \subseteq S \times S$ is a simulation iff it satisfies $R \subseteq \mathcal{S}(R)$ where $\mathcal{S}(R)$ is defined by: for all $p, q \in S$, $p\mathcal{S}(R)q$ iff for all steps $p \xrightarrow{a} p'$ there is a $q \xrightarrow{a} q'$ with $p'Rq'$. $\mathcal{S}$ is monotonic over the lattice $2^{S \times S}$ of all binary relations on S and $\sqsubseteq$ is the largest fixpoint of $\mathcal{S}$. We can define approximations of $\sqsubseteq$ by

$$\begin{array}{lcll} \sqsubseteq_0 & \stackrel{\text{def}}{=} & S \times S & \\ \sqsubseteq_{\alpha+1} & \stackrel{\text{def}}{=} & \mathcal{S}(\sqsubseteq_\alpha) & \text{for any ordinal } \alpha \\ \sqsubseteq_\beta & \stackrel{\text{def}}{=} & \bigcap_{\alpha<\beta} \sqsubseteq_\alpha & \text{for any limit ordinal } \beta \end{array}$$

Then, a well-known theorem states that if S is finitely branching, $\mathcal{S}$ is anticontinuous, implying that

$$\sqsubseteq = \sqsubseteq_\omega = \bigcap_{n=0,1,\ldots} \sqsubseteq_n \tag{2}$$

Similarly, $\leftrightarrow$ and $\sqsubseteq_R$ are the largest fixpoints of (respectively) two monotonic transformations $\mathcal{B}$ and $\mathcal{S}_R$ defined by

$$\mathcal{B}(R) \stackrel{\text{def}}{=} \mathcal{S}(R) \cap (\mathcal{S}(R^{-1}))^{-1}$$

and

$$\mathcal{S}_R(R) \stackrel{\text{def}}{=} \mathcal{S}(R) \cap =_I$$

where $p =_I q$ iff $I(p) = I(q)$. For finitely branching S, we also have

$$\leftrightarrow = \leftrightarrow_\omega = \bigcap_{n=0,1,\ldots} \leftrightarrow_n \tag{3}$$

and

$$\sqsubseteq_R = \sqsubseteq_{R,\omega} = \bigcap_{n=0,1,\ldots} \sqsubseteq_{R,n} \tag{4}$$

with obvious (and omitted) definitions.

3 Undoing steps

The idea of undoing steps is very natural in a testing scenario: assume that the process being tested has an *undo*-button, labeled #. When started, the process accepts that the usual buttons $a_1, \ldots$ be pressed as before. In addition, if # is pressed, the last move is undone.

[4] The name is from [Blo89b]. Ready simulation is also called "2/3-bisimulation" in [LS89] and "GSOS trace congruence" in reference to [BIM88, Blo89a].

3.1 #-steps

In order to formally define the idea of undoing a step, we need to record the history of a process during a test. A *path* in S is a finite sequence $p_0 \xrightarrow{a_1} p_1 \cdots \xrightarrow{a_n} p_n$ of linked transitions. For $\pi = p_0 \xrightarrow{a_1} p_1 \cdots \xrightarrow{a_n} p_n$, we have $length(\pi) = n$, $first(\pi) = p_0$ and $last(\pi) = p_n$. If $length(\pi) = 0$, then π is just a single state p_0. We write $\Pi(p)$ for the set of all paths starting from p.

A path π denotes the process $last(\pi)$ with π as its history. If π is $p_0 \xrightarrow{a_1} p_1 \cdots \xrightarrow{a_n} p_n$ and if $p_n \xrightarrow{a} p_{n+1}$ is a transition in S, then π can be extended into a longer history $\pi' = p_0 \xrightarrow{a_1} p_1 \cdots \xrightarrow{a_n} p_n \xrightarrow{a} p_{n+1}$, what we write $\pi \xrightarrow{a} \pi'$. Symmetrically, $p_n \xrightarrow{a} p_{n+1}$ can be undone in π', what we write $\pi' \xrightarrow{\#} \pi$. This defines a relation $\rightarrow \subseteq \Pi(p) \times (A \cup \{\#\}) \times \Pi(p)$ between states with history (i.e. paths), incorporating backward steps. We write $A_\#$ for $A \cup \{\#\}$ and let $u, \ldots$ range over $A_\#$.

When we have a sequence $\pi_0 \xrightarrow{u_1} \pi_1 \cdots \xrightarrow{u_n} \pi_n$ with $length(\pi_0) = 0$ and with $last(\pi_i) = p_i$, we write the simpler $p_0 \xrightarrow{u_1} p_1 \cdots \xrightarrow{u_n} p_n$. This shorthand is convenient, but formally a transition like $p \xrightarrow{\#} p'$ is meaningless.

3.2 #-traces

When $p_0 \xrightarrow{u_1} p_1 \cdots \xrightarrow{u_n} p_n$, we say that the sequence $\sigma = u_1 \ldots u_n \in A_\#^*$ is a *#-trace* of p_0 and that $p_0 \xrightarrow{u_1} p_1 \cdots \xrightarrow{u_n} p_n$ is a *#-path* (of length n) from p.

Note that not every word of $A_\#^*$ may be a #-trace of some process. For $\sigma \in A_\#^*$, we define $\#(\sigma)$ as the number of occurrences of # in σ and $height(\sigma)$ for $length(\sigma) - 2\#(\sigma)$. Then a #-trace (of p) satisfies $height(\sigma) \geq 0$ and all its prefixes are #-traces of p. (There is a strong link with Dyck languages.) When a string σ is such that all its prefixes (including itself) have a non-negative height, we say that it is a *well-formed #-word*, or simply a #-word. For example, $abc\#\#\#a\#bc$ is well-formed while its reverse $cb\#a\#\#\#cba$ is not. One should not confuse $height(\sigma)$ with $depth(\sigma)$, defined as the maximum height of a prefix of σ. E.g. for $\sigma = abc\#\#\#a\#bc$ we have $height(\sigma) = 2$ and $depth(\sigma) = 3$.

Using well-known results on Dyck languages, it is easy to see that any #-word σ can be uniquely decomposed into a concatenation of #-words $\sigma_1 \ldots \sigma_k \rho$ where

- all σ_i's have height 0 and strictly positive length,
- all proper prefixes of a σ_i have strictly positive height, or are the empty string,
- all prefixes of ρ have strictly positive height, or are the empty string.

For example $abc\#\#\#a\#bc$ is factored into $(abc\#\#\#)(a\#)bc$. Clearly, in a factorization, the σ_i's have the form $a_i\sigma_i'\#$ with σ_i' a well-formed #-word, while ρ, if it is not empty, has the form $a\rho'$ with ρ' a well-formed #-word.

When σ is a #-trace of some process p, its factorization into $\sigma_1 \ldots \sigma_k \rho$ is such that all σ_i's and ρ are #-traces of p. Furthermore, if ρ has the form $a\rho'$, then ρ' is a #-trace of some a-successor of p.

In the following, we shall often reason by induction on the factorization of a #-word σ by considering three cases: (1) $\sigma = \lambda$, or (2) $\sigma = a\rho$, or (3) $\sigma = \sigma_1 \ldots \sigma_k \rho$ with $k \geq 1$.

3.3 #-based preorders

Traces, failures, ... generalize in a natural way to #-based notions. We define

- $T_\#(p)$ as the set of all #-traces of p,
- $CT_\#(p)$ as the set of #-traces possibly leading from p to a blocked state,
- $F_\#(p)$ as the set of #-failure pairs (σ, X) of p, allowing $\sigma \in A_\#^*$ (but X is still a subset of A),
- $R_\#(p)$ as the set of #-ready pairs $[\sigma, Y]$ of p,
- $FT_\#(p)$ as the set of #-failure traces $(X_0, u_1, X_1, \ldots, u_n, X_n)$ with $u_i \in A_\#$ and $X_i \subseteq A$,
- $RT_\#(p)$ as the set of #-ready traces $[Y_0, u_1, Y_1, \ldots, u_n, Y_n]$.

These yield preorders $\leq_{T_\#}, \ldots$ and the associated equivalences $=_{T_\#}, \ldots$ Again, as with (1), the definition of $\leq_{CT_\#}$ is slightly peculiar and reads:

$$p \leq_{CT_\#} q \overset{\text{def}}{\Leftrightarrow} \begin{cases} CT_\#(p) \subseteq CT_\#(q) \text{ and} \\ T_\#(p) \subseteq T_\#(q) \end{cases}$$

It is easy to see that the hierarchy:

$$p \leq_{FT_\#} q \Rightarrow p \leq_{F_\#} q \Rightarrow p \leq_{CT_\#} q \Rightarrow p \leq_{T_\#} q$$

$$p \leq_{RT_\#} q \Rightarrow p \leq_{R_\#} q \Rightarrow p \leq_{F_\#} q$$

$$p \leq_{RT_\#} q \Rightarrow p \leq_{FT_\#} q$$

holds as in the usual case. Figure 1 give some examples of the distinguishing power of these different preorders.

Clearly, #-traces give more discriminating power than just traces. For example, while ready traces do not distinguish between p_3 and q_3 (in Figure 1), the #-trace $abc\#\#bd$ is in $T_\#(p_3)$ and not in $T_\#(q_3)$. This example suggests that, by providing some form of look-ahead, equivalences based on *undo*-buttons can capture part of the branching structure of process beyond what e.g. ready traces can do.

3.4 #-based preorders and simulations

Our first goal will be to relate #-based notions to behavioral preorders.

Lemma 1 *$p \sqsubseteq q$ implies $p \leq_{T_\#} q$.*

Proof Assume that $p \sqsubseteq q$ and that $\sigma \in T_\#(p)$. Then there is a #-path π of the form $p \xrightarrow{\sigma} p'$. We show that we can build a #-path π' of the form $q \xrightarrow{\sigma} q'$, entailing $\sigma \in T_\#(q)$. This construction is done by induction on the structure of σ:

- If $\sigma = \lambda$, we are done.

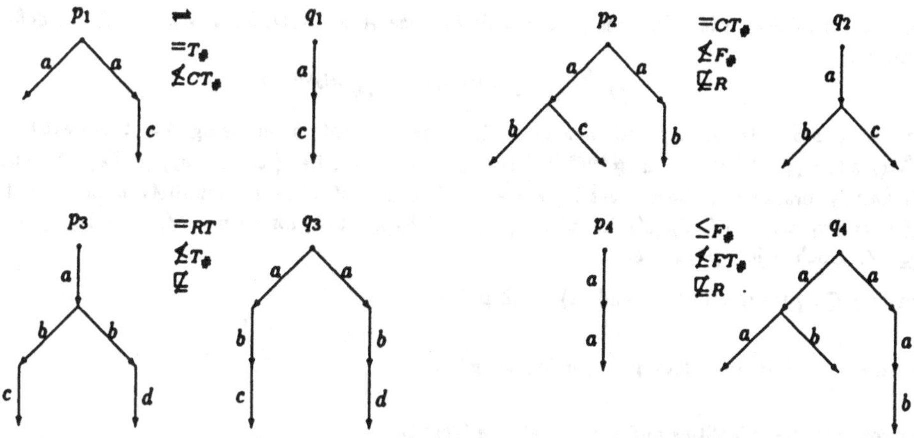

Figure 1: Comparing the preorders

- If σ has the form $a\rho$ then π has the form $p \xrightarrow{a} p_1 \xrightarrow{\rho} p'$ (with $\rho \in T_\#(p_1)$). $p \sqsubseteq q$ implies that there is a step $q \xrightarrow{a} q_1$ with $p_1 \sqsubseteq q_1$. By ind. hyp., this implies that there is a #-path $q_1 \xrightarrow{\rho} q'$ and we are done with $q \xrightarrow{a} q_1 \xrightarrow{\rho} q'$.

- If σ is factored into $\sigma_1 \ldots \sigma_k \rho$ then σ_1 is some $a\sigma'\#$ and π has the form $p \xrightarrow{a} p_1 \xrightarrow{\sigma'} p_1 \xrightarrow{\#} p \xrightarrow{\sigma_2 \ldots \sigma_k \rho} p'$ (because $height(\sigma_1) = 0$). Now $p \sqsubseteq q$ implies that there is a step $q \xrightarrow{a} q_1$ s.t. $p_1 \sqsubseteq q_1$. By ind. hyp., we can build #-paths $q_1 \xrightarrow{\sigma'} q_1$ and $q \xrightarrow{\sigma_2 \ldots \sigma_k \rho} q'$ which, when chained, yield a #-path $q \xrightarrow{a} q_1 \xrightarrow{\sigma'} q_1 \xrightarrow{\#} q \xrightarrow{\sigma_2 \ldots \sigma_k \rho} q'$, i.e. $q \xrightarrow{\sigma} q'$.

□

Lemma 2 *$p \sqsubseteq_R q$ implies $p \leq_{RT_\#} q$.*

Proof Assume $p \sqsubseteq_R q$ and $[Y_0, u_1, Y_1, \ldots, u_m, Y_m]$ is a ready trace of p. Then there is a path $p = p_0 \xrightarrow{u_1} p_1 \cdots p_m$ starting from p s.t. $I(p_i) = Y_i$ for all $i = 0, .., m$. As $p \sqsubseteq_R q$, reasoning as we did for the proof of Lemma 1, we can build a path $q = q_0 \xrightarrow{u_1} q_1 \cdots q_m$ s.t. $p_i \sqsubseteq_R q_i$ for all i. But $p_i \sqsubseteq_R q_i$ implies $I(q_i) = I(p_i) = Y_i$ and then $[Y_0, u_1, \ldots, Y_m] \in RT_\#(q)$. □

Remark Actually $p \sqsubseteq_\omega q$ (resp. $p \sqsubseteq_{R,\omega} q$) already entails $p \leq_{T_\#} q$ (resp. $p \leq_{RT_\#} q$) [Sch91]. □

The implications of Lemmas 1 and 2 are equivalences when S is finitely branching.

Lemma 3 *If S is finitely branching then $p \leq_{T_\#} q$ implies $p \sqsubseteq q$.*

Proof We show by induction on n that $p \leq_{T_\#} q$ implies $p \sqsubseteq_n q$. This is clear for $n = 0$ as $\sqsubseteq_0$ is $S \times S$. Assume now that the claim holds up to n and consider a step $p \xrightarrow{a} p'$. $T_\#(p')$ is some set

$\{w_1, w_2, \ldots\}$ of #-words. This set is countable because A is. Now, for any $k = 1, 2, \ldots$, define the #-word v_k as

$$v_k \stackrel{\text{def}}{=} a w_1 \#^{height(w_1)} \ldots w_k \#^{height(w_k)}$$

Clearly, v_k is a #-trace of p and then $v_k \in T_\#(q)$ by assumption, implying that there exists a step $q \xrightarrow{a} q_k$ s.t. $w_1 \#^{height(w_1)} \ldots w_k \#^{height(w_k)}$ is a #-trace of q_k, i.e. $\{w_1, \ldots, w_k\} \subseteq T_\#(q_k)$. Then, as q is finitely branching, there must be a step $q \xrightarrow{a} q'$ s.t. $q' = q_k$ for infinitely many k, entailing $T_\#(p') = \{w_1, w_2, \ldots\} \subseteq T_\#(q')$, i.e. $p' \sqsubseteq_n q'$ by ind. hyp. Then, for all $p \xrightarrow{a} p'$, there is a $q \xrightarrow{a} q'$ s.t. $p' \sqsubseteq_n q'$, which is just $p \sqsubseteq_{n+1} q$.

Finally, $p \sqsubseteq_n q$ for $n = 0, 1, \ldots$ and (2) entail $p \sqsubseteq q$. □

Lemma 4 *If A is finite then $p \leq_{T_\#} q$ implies $p \sqsubseteq_\omega q$.*

requires more technicalities and is omitted: see [Sch91].

Lemma 5 *If S is finitely branching then $p \leq_{FT_\#} q$ implies $p \sqsubseteq_R q$.*

Proof The proof needs some auxiliary tools. For $p \in S$, define $FT^-_\#(p)$ as the set of all $(X_0, u_1, \ldots, X_n)$ in $FT_\#(p)$ s.t. all X_i's are finite. Then, $p \leq_{FT_\#} q$ clearly implies

$$FT^-_\#(p) \subseteq FT^-_\#(q) \tag{5}$$

We show, by induction on n, that (5) entails $p \sqsubseteq_{R,n} q$. Note that $FT^-_\#(p)$ is countable (while, in general, $FT_\#(p)$ is not) so that we can proceed as in the proof of Lemma 3. Because of the difference between $\sqsubseteq$ and $\sqsubseteq_R$, there remains to notice that (5) entails $I(p) = I(q)$ (by countability of A) before the proof can be concluded. □

Lemma 6 *If A is finite then $p \leq_{FT_\#} q$ implies $p \sqsubseteq_{R,\omega} q$.*

requires more technicalities and is omitted: see [Sch91].

3.5 Readies vs. failures

When *undo* actions are allowed, the difference between readies and failures disappears (in finitely branching systems):

Lemma 7 *If S is finitely branching, or if A is finite, then*

$$p \leq_{F_\#} q \quad \text{iff} \quad p \leq_{R_\#} q$$
$$p \leq_{FT_\#} q \quad \text{iff} \quad p \leq_{RT_\#} q$$

Proof We only have to prove the "⇒" directions. Assume $p \leq_{F_\#} q$ and $[\sigma, Y] \in R_\#(p)$. Then there is a #-path $p \xrightarrow{\sigma} p'$ with $I(p') = Y$. Y must be countable, so assume it is $\{a_0, a_1, \ldots\}$ and, for $k = 0, 1, \ldots$, define $v_k \stackrel{\text{def}}{=} a_0 \# a_1 \# \ldots a_k \#$. Clearly, $(\sigma v_k, A \setminus Y) \in F_\#(p)$ for all k. This failure pair belongs to $F_{\#}(q)$ by assumption, so that, for any k, there is a q_k s.t. $q \xrightarrow{\sigma} q_k \xrightarrow{v_k} q_k$ with $I(q_k) \subseteq Y$. $q_k \xrightarrow{v_k} q_k$ entails $\{a_0, \ldots, a_k\} \subsetneq I(q_k)$. If q is f.b. then at least one state, call it q', appears infinitely often among the q_k's. If A is finite, Y is finite and we pick the last q_k as our q'. For this q', we have $q \xrightarrow{\sigma} q'$ and $I(q') = Y$, so that $[\sigma, Y] \in R_{\#}(q)$.

The proof that $p \leq_{FT_{\#}} q$ implies $p \leq_{RT_{\#}} q$ follows the same pattern and is omitted. □

3.6 A hierarchy of preorders

Summarizing the previous results, we obtain:

Theorem 1 *If S is finitely branching, then*

$$p \sqsubseteq q \text{ iff } p \leq_{T_{\#}} q$$

$$p \sqsubseteq_R q \text{ iff } p \leq_{FT_{\#}} q \text{ iff } p \leq_{RT_{\#}} q$$

where the link between #-traces and simulation (resp. #-ready traces and ready simulation) was already mentioned in [vG90].

Theorem 2 *All the implications existing between the preorders we considered are displayed in Figure 2.*

where implications carrying a "+" require the "S f.b." assumption, while implications carrying a "*" require the "S f.b. or A finite" assumption. (See [Sch91] for examples showing that the assumptions are necessary.)

Figure 1 has enough examples to show that no implication can be added (because it is known that none can be added between the classical preorders).

It appears that $\leq_{CT_{\#}}$ and $\leq_{F_{\#}}$ (or equivalently $\leq_{R_{\#}}$) are two new preorders. Observe that $\leq_{CT_{\#}}$ is not just $\leq_{CT} \cap \leq_{T_{\#}}$ (compare $abc + a(b+c)$ and $a(bc+c)$) and that $\leq_{F_{\#}}$ is not just $\leq_F \cap \leq_{CT_{\#}}$ (compare $a(b+c+de) + ad + a(b+de)$ and $a(b+c+de)+ad$).

4 Congruence properties

4.1 A toy process algebra

We now consider a specific A-labeled transition system $PA = \langle P, \rightarrow \rangle$ similar to the CCS language of [Mil80] and the ACP language of [BK86]. The set $P = \{p, p', q, \ldots\}$ of processes is given by the following abstract grammar:

$$P \ni p, q ::= Nil \mid a.p \mid p + q \mid p \parallel q \mid p \setminus B \mid p[f]$$

where Nil is the *inactive process*, $a.p$ is p *prefixed by* a ($a \in A$ is any action), $p+q$ is the *non-deterministic sum* of p and q, $p \parallel q$ is the *parallel composition* (with communication) of p and q, $p \setminus B$

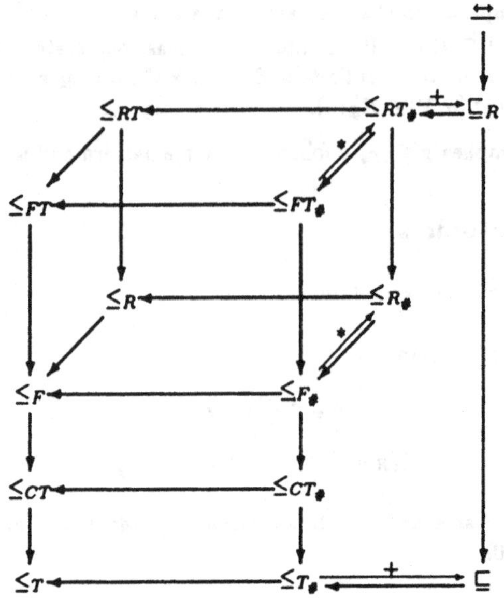

Figure 2: The hierarchy of preorders

(where $B \subseteq A$ is any set of actions) is the *restriction* of p by B, and $p[f]$ (where $f : A \to A$ is any mapping) is p with actions relabeled by f. We usually write e.g. abc for $a.b.c.Nil$ and $\sum_{i=1,\ldots,n} p_i$ for $p_1 + \cdots + p_n$.

The transition relation of PA is given by structural rules *à la Plotkin*:

$$a.p \xrightarrow{a} p \qquad \frac{p \xrightarrow{a} p'}{p+q \xrightarrow{a} p'} \qquad \frac{q \xrightarrow{a} q'}{p+q \xrightarrow{a} q'} \qquad \frac{p \xrightarrow{a} p'}{p \setminus B \xrightarrow{a} p' \setminus B} \text{ if } a \notin B$$

$$\frac{p \xrightarrow{a} p'}{p[f] \xrightarrow{f(a)} p'[f]} \qquad \frac{p \xrightarrow{a} p'}{p \parallel q \xrightarrow{a} p' \parallel q} \qquad \frac{q \xrightarrow{a} q'}{p \parallel q \xrightarrow{a} p \parallel q'} \qquad \frac{p \xrightarrow{a} p' \quad q \xrightarrow{b} q'}{p \parallel q \xrightarrow{a|b} p' \parallel q'} \text{ if } a \mid b \text{ is defined}$$

where, in the style of [BK86], we assume given an associative and commutative composition operation $|: A \times A \to A$ (which may be partial) on actions. (Observe that Nil has no transition.)

4.2 Precongruences with *undo*'s

It is well-known that all the "classical" preorders we mentioned: $\leq_T$, $\sqsubseteq$, $\underline{\leftrightarrow}$, ... are precongruences w.r.t. the process combinators we used in our toy language, *except for* $\leq_{CT}$ *which is not a precongruence w.r.t. restriction.* There is the same problem when *undo*-buttons are considered:

Proposition 1 *On PA, $=_{CT_{\#}}$ is not a congruence w.r.t. restriction.*

Proof $a(b+c)+ab =_{CT_\#} a(b+c)$ while $(a(b+c)+ab)\setminus b \neq_{CT_\#} (a(b+c))\setminus b$ (see p_2, q_2 and p_1, q_1 in Figure 1). □

When *undo*-buttons are considered, we have:

Theorem 3 *On PA,* $\leq_{T_\#}$, $\leq_{CT_\#}$, $\leq_{F_\#}$, $\leq_{R_\#}$, $\leq_{FT_\#}$ *and* $\leq_{RT_\#}$ *are precongruences w.r.t. all the process combinators, except for* $\leq_{CT_\#}$ *w.r.t. restriction.*

The complete proof appears in [Sch91].

4.3 Full abstraction

Regarding the compatibility of completed traces w.r.t. restriction, it is well-known that $\leq_F$ is the largest (so called fully abstract) precongruence included into $\leq_{CT}$ (see e.g. [BKO88]). This full-abstraction result can be adapted from the classical framework to our framework with *undo*-buttons.

First, as in [BKO88], we need to assume some structure about the communication operation $|: A\times A \to A$. We consider the "one-to-one communication" framework, a simple set of assumptions introduced in [BKO88] and satisfied by both Hoare's CSP and Milner's CCS.

Formally, we say that PA has one-to-one communication if

- A is partitioned into $C \cup I$ where $C = \{c, d, \ldots\}$ is a set of *communicating actions*, and $I = \{i, j, \ldots\}$ is a set of *internal actions*,
- there exists a bijection $\phi : C \to C$ associating a "complementary" action $\phi(c)$ to any communicating action s.t. $c \mid \phi(c) \in I$,
- $|: A \times A \to A$ is only defined for pairs $(c, \phi(c))$.

Assume we have one-to-one communication and write P_C for the set of PA processes that only use actions from C. Then

Theorem 4 (Full abstraction) *Over* P_C, $\leq_{F_\#}$ *is the largest precongruence which is contained in* $\leq_{CT_\#}$.

The complete proof appears in [Sch91].

5 Conclusion

This paper showed that the use of an *undo*-button in the testing of processes is a very fruitful idea, leading to new notions of process equivalence and to new characterizations of previously studied equivalences (e.g. simulation) in terms of indistinguishability by a simple testing protocol. We believe that "completed *undo*-trace equivalence" and "*undo*-failure equivalence" are two genuine points in the "linear time-branching time spectrum" and that they really deserve further study.

Already, several directions can be proposed:

- The linear time-branching time spectrum is just one dimension of concurrency semantics. We did not consider the issues of true parallelism vs. interleaving, of silent vs. visible actions, of termination vs. deadlock, ... *Undo*'s should be investigated in connection with all these dimensions. We are especially curious about the distinguishing power of *undo*-based experiments in the framework of probabilistic processes [vGSST90].

- We did not study characterizations in terms of modal logic. Clearly, it is easy to carve out a suitable fragment of HML that has the same distinguishing power as e.g. #-failures. This is just a question of translating failures into HML: for example $(abc\#d\#\#e, X) \in F_{\#}(p)$ iff $p \models \langle a\rangle(\langle b\rangle(\langle c\rangle\top \wedge \langle d\rangle\top) \wedge \langle e\rangle[X]\bot)$. In our opinion, this research direction is more interesting in connection with the previous point, or with different logics (as in [DNV90]).

- Congruence properties and full abstraction results should be investigated more closely. We just used a very classical process algebra, but more exotic combinators were considered as a motivation for e.g. ready traces [Pnu85, BBK85]. More importantly, several recent works consider whole classes of process combinators [GV88, Gro90, Blo89a]. As all our #-based equivalences are thinner than trace equivalence and coarser than ready simulation, a corollary of [Blo89a] already tells us that the GSOS-congruence they induce is ready simulation, but not all such questions are so easily answered.

6 Acknowledgements

We thank Sophie Pinchinat for her useful comments and suggestions. C. Autant, Ph. Jorrand and one anonymous referee also provided precious inputs.

References

[Abr87] S. Abramsky. Observation equivalence as a testing equivalence. *Theoretical Computer Science*, 53:225–241, 1987.

[BBK85] J. C. M. Baeten, J. A. Bergstra, and J. W. Klop. *Ready Trace Semantics for Concrete Process Algebra with Priority Operator*. Research Report CS-R8517, CWI, 1985.

[BIM88] B. Bloom, S. Istrail, and A. R. Meyer. Bisimulation can't be traced: preliminary report. In *Proc. 15th ACM Symp. Principles of Programming Languages, San Diego, CA*, pages 229–239, January 1988.

[BK86] J. A. Bergstra and J. W. Klop. Algebra of communicating processes. In J. W. de Bakker et al., editor, *CWI Monographs I, Proc. CWI Symp. Math. and Comp. Sci.*, pages 89–138, North-Holland, 1986.

[BKO88] J. A. Bergstra, J. W. Klop, and E.-R. Olderog. Readies and failures in the algebra of communicating processes. *SIAM Journal on Computing*, 17(6):1134–1177, December 1988.

[Blo89a] B. Bloom. *Partial Traces and the Semantics and Logic of CCS-Like languages*. Tech. Report 89-1066, Cornell University, Ithaca, NY, December 1989.

[Blo89b] B. Bloom. *Ready Simulation, Bisimulation, and the Semantics of CCS-Like Languages.* PhD thesis, MIT, September 1989.

[DNV90] R. De Nicola and F. Vaandrager. Three logics for branching bisimulation (extended abstract). In *Proc. 5th IEEE Symp. Logic in Computer Science, Philadelphia, PA*, pages 118–129, June 1990.

[Gro90] J. F. Groote. Transition system specifications with negative premisses. In *Proc. CONCUR'90, Amsterdam, LNCS 458*, pages 332–341, Springer-Verlag, August 1990.

[GV88] J. F. Groote and F. W. Vaandrager. *Structured Operational Semantics and Bisimulation as a Congruence.* Research Report CS-R8845, CWI, November 1988.

[HM80] M. Hennessy and R. Milner. On observing nondeterminism and concurrency. In *Proc. 7th ICALP, Noordwijkerhout, LNCS 85*, pages 299–309, Springer-Verlag, July 1980.

[HM85] M. Hennessy and R. Milner. Algebraic laws for nondeterminism and concurrency. *Journal of the ACM*, 32(1):137–161, January 1985.

[LS89] K. G. Larsen and A. Skou. Bisimulation through probabilistic testing. In *Proc. 16th ACM Symp. Principles of Programming Languages, Austin, Texas*, pages 344–352, January 1989.

[Mil80] R. Milner. *A Calculus of Communicating Systems. LNCS 92*, Springer-Verlag, 1980.

[Mil81] R. Milner. A modal characterisation of observable machine-behaviour. In *Proc. CAAP 81, Genoa, LNCS 112*, pages 25–34, Springer-Verlag, March 1981.

[Mil90] R. Milner. Operational and algebraic semantics of concurrent processes. In J. van Leeuwen, editor, *Handbook of Theoretical Computer Science, vol. B*, chapter 19, pages 1201–1242, Elsevier Science Publishers, 1990.

[Par81] D. Park. Concurrency and automata on infinite sequences. In *Proc. 5th GI Conf. on Th. Comp. Sci., LNCS 104*, pages 167–183, Springer-Verlag, March 1981.

[Pnu85] A. Pnueli. Linear and branching structures in the semantics and logics of reactive systems. In *Proc. 12th ICALP, Nafplion, LNCS 194*, pages 15–32, Springer-Verlag, July 1985.

[Sch91] Ph. Schnoebelen. *Experiments on Processes with Backtracking.* Research Report, LIFIA-IMAG, Grenoble, June 1991.

[vG90] R. J. van Glabbeek. *The Linear Time - Branching Time Spectrum.* Research Report CS-R9029, CWI, July 1990.

[vGSST90] R. J. van Glabbeek, S. A. Smolka, B. Steffen, and C. M. N. Tofts. Reactive, generative, and stratified models of probabilistic processes. In *Proc. 5th IEEE Symp. Logic in Computer Science, Philadelphia, PA*, pages 130–141, June 1990.

Some finite-graph models for Process Algebra

Paul Spruit & Roel Wieringa

Department of Mathematics and Computer Science
Vrije Universiteit
De Boelelaan 1081a
1081 HV, Amsterdam
The Netherlands
Email: paspruí@cs.vu.nl, roelw@cs.vu.nl

1 Introduction

In this paper, we present a number of closely related models of process algebra [2, 3, 4], called *finite-graph models*. In a finite-graph model of process algebra, each process is a bisimulation class of a particular kind of process graphs, called *recursive process graphs*. Just as in the standard graph model [1], each guarded recursive specification has exactly one solution in a finite-graph model, but in contrast to the standard graph model, this solution can be shown to contain a finite recursive process graph as element.

The finite-graph models were defined in order to be able to build an editor that can manipulate process graphs. It is well-known that there are finite guarded specifications that have no finite solution in the standard graph model; the specification of a stack is an example [1, page 63]. Figure 1 shows an approximation of a graph of a (terminating) stack process and figure 2 shows a recursive process graph that, in a finite-graph model, bisimulates with it. The intuitive reading of figure 2 is that after a $push_i$ event, there is a choice between a pop_i or doing process S itself. Details are given below. Figure 2 is a finite graph that can be drawn on a finite screen. The finite-graph models presented in this paper can represent more processes in a finite manner than the standard graph model. Note that recursive specifications can also be finitely represented in a graphical way, by means of parse trees of the terms. However, such parse trees have a structure that is quite different from the structure of recursive process graphs, and are more difficult to understand.

In section 2, we define the set $\Re$ of recursive process graphs, a bisimulation relation $\leftrightarrow$ on $\Re$, and prove that $\Re/\leftrightarrow$ is a model of BPA. It is shown that a subalgebra of $\Re/\leftrightarrow$ is isomorphic with the standard graph model of finitely-branching processes. Section 3 extends this to process algebra with the parallel composition operator. We also show the relation with some forms of true concurrency. Section 4 concludes the paper. All proofs are omitted from the paper, but are given in [9, 10].

2 Two finite-graph models for BPA

We fix a set *Act* of *atomic actions* and a countably infinite set $PVAR$ of *process variables*, disjoint from *Act*. Metavariables ranging over *Act* are $a, b, c, \ldots$ and metavariables ranging over $PVAR$ are $X, Y, Z, X_1, X_2, \ldots$. The two operators of Basic Process Algebra (BPA) are + (choice)

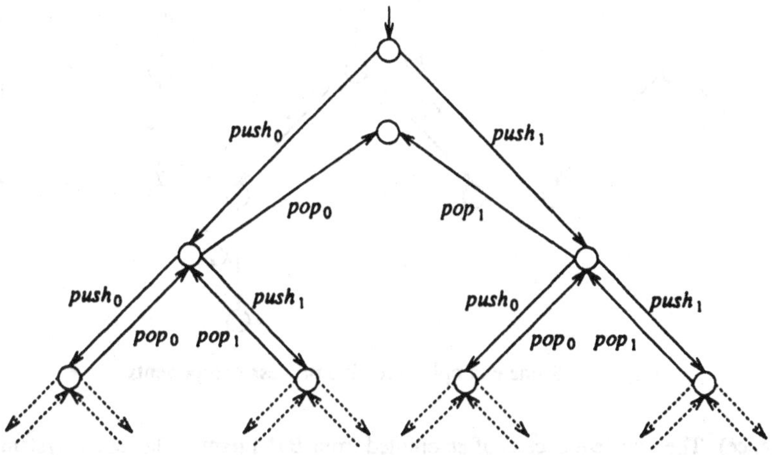

Figure 1: Part of a graph of a terminating stack in the standard model.

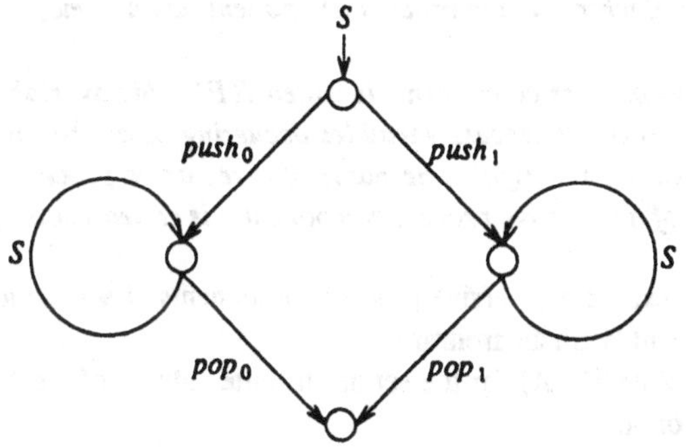

Figure 2: Recursive process graph of a terminating stack in a finite-graph model.

$X + Y = Y + X$	A1
$(X + Y) + Z = X + (Y + Z)$	A2
$X + X = X$	A3
$(X + Y)Z = XZ + YZ$	A4
$(XY)Z = X(YZ)$	A5

Table 1: The BPA axiom system.

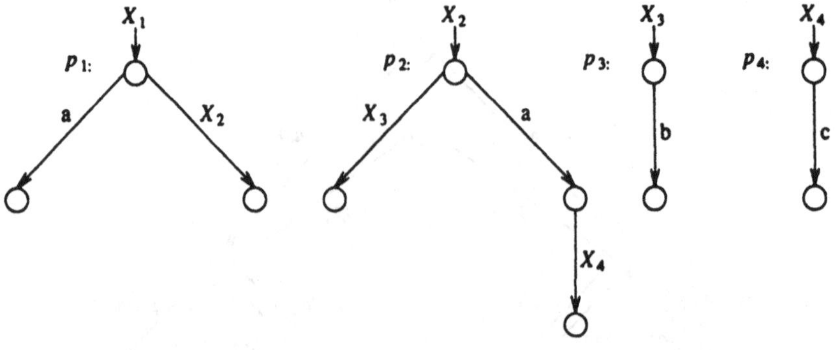

Figure 3: Some example recursive process components

and · (sequence). The · for sequence is often omitted from BPA terms. The axiom system of BPA is given in table 1 [1].

2.1 Recursive process graphs

Definition 1 A recursive process component *is a directed, finitely branching, connected, rooted graph that has at least one edge. The edges of a recursive process component are labeled by elements of the set $PVAR \cup Act$. Each recursive process component has a name, which must be a process variable.*

The set of all recursive process components is called RPC. Metavariables ranging over RPC are $p, q, r, p_1, p_2, \ldots$ The set of all process variables occurring as a label or a name in a recursive process component p is called $pvar(p)$. The name of a recursive process component p is called $name(p)$. The root node of a recursive process component p is called $root(p)$.

Figure 3 shows some example recursive process components. Each standard process graph is a recursive process component (with an arbitrary name).

In what follows, we write $\mathcal{P}_f(A)$ for the set of all finite subsets of a set A, and $\mathcal{P}_{nf}(A)$ for all non-empty finite subsets of A.

Definition 2 A recursive process graph *is a pair (P, X) with $P \in \mathcal{P}_{nf}(RPC)$ and $X \in PVAR$ such that the following three conditions hold*

root existence $\exists p \in P : name(p) = X$

unique naming $\forall p, q \in P : p \neq q \Rightarrow name(p) \neq name(q)$

label existence $\forall p \in P : \forall Y \in pvar(p) : \exists q \in P : Y = name(q)$

The set of all recursive process graphs is called $\mathfrak{R}$. Metavariables ranging over $\mathfrak{R}$ are $g, h, g_1, g_2, \ldots$

For example, in figure 3 $(\{p_1, p_2, p_3, p_4\}, X_1)$, $(\{p_1, p_2, p_3, p_4\}, X_2)$ and $(\{p_4\}, X_4)$ are recursive process graphs. Each standard process graph is a recursive process graph (consisting of one component). We will assume the function $pvar$ is extended from recursive process components to recursive process graphs in the following way: if $g = (P, X)$ then $pvar(g) = \bigcup_{p \in P} pvar(p)$. Because of the root existence constraint we know for $g = (P, X)$ that $X \in pvar(g)$.

Definition 3 *For every recursive process graph $g = (P, X)$ the* recursive process component *function*

$$rpc_g : pvar(g) \rightarrow P$$

assigns to a process variable the recursive process component of which it is the name.

Using definition 2 we can see that for every recursive process graph g, the function rpc_g is correctly defined: every process variable in $pvar(g)$ is the name of a recursive process component because of the label existence constraint and this component is unique because of the unique naming constraint. Example: if in figure 3 we take $g = (\{p_1, p_2, p_3, p_4\}, X_1)$, then $rpc_g(X_i) = p_i$ (for $1 \leq i \leq 4$).

We extend the function $root$ from recursive process components to recursive process graphs by defining for a recursive process graph $g = (P, X)$ that $root(g) = root(rpc_g(X))$. Some more terminology: for a recursive process graph $g = (P, X)$, we call X the root variable of g and $rpc_g(X)$ the root component of g.

2.2 Recursive bisimulation

We want to give a semantics of BPA in terms of some form of observational equivalence between graphs of $\Re$, i.e. we want to define a bisimulation notion on elements of $\Re$ [7, 8]. A definition of bisimulation in $\Re$ is complicated by the fact that a node in a recursive process graph does not represent all state information of the process. Part of the state of a process consists of the sequence of "jumps" to process components that have been performed, so part of the remaining behavior of the process consists of a sequence of "pops" to performed. A bisimulation will not be a relation between the nodes of two recursive process graphs, but between pairs of the form (node, stack-of-nodes), where stack-of-nodes is a stack of "return addresses." In what follows we use strings to represent stacks, with ϵ for the empty stack and an invisible concatenation operation. The top of the stack is the leftmost element of the string. We use k l, ... to denote a node of a recursive process graph, and s, t, ... to denote a finite stack of nodes of a recursive process graph. Definitions 5 and 7 are illustrated in figure 4.

Definition 4 *A* state *of a recursive process graph g is a pair (k, s) with k a node of g and s a finite stack of nodes of g.*

Definition 5 *The relation $\rightarrow_g^{push}$ is defined for every recursive process graph g as a binary relation on the states of g in the following way:*

> $(k, s) \rightarrow_g^{push} (k', ls)$ *iff there is an edge in g starting at node k, ending at node l and labeled by some process variable X such that $k' = root(rpc_g(X))$.*

The relation $\rightarrow_g^{push*}$ is defined for every recursive process graph g as the reflexive transitive closure of $\rightarrow_g^{push}$.

Definition 6 *Node k of a recursive process graph g is called an* end node *iff there does not exists an edge in g starting at node k.*

Definition 7 *The relation $\rightarrow_g^{pop}$ is defined for every recursive process graph g as a binary relation on the states of g in the following way:*

> $(l, ks) \rightarrow_g^{pop} (k, s)$ *iff node l is an end node in g.*

The relation $\rightarrow_g^{pop*}$ is defined for every recursive process graph g as the reflexive transitive closure of $\rightarrow_g^{pop}$.

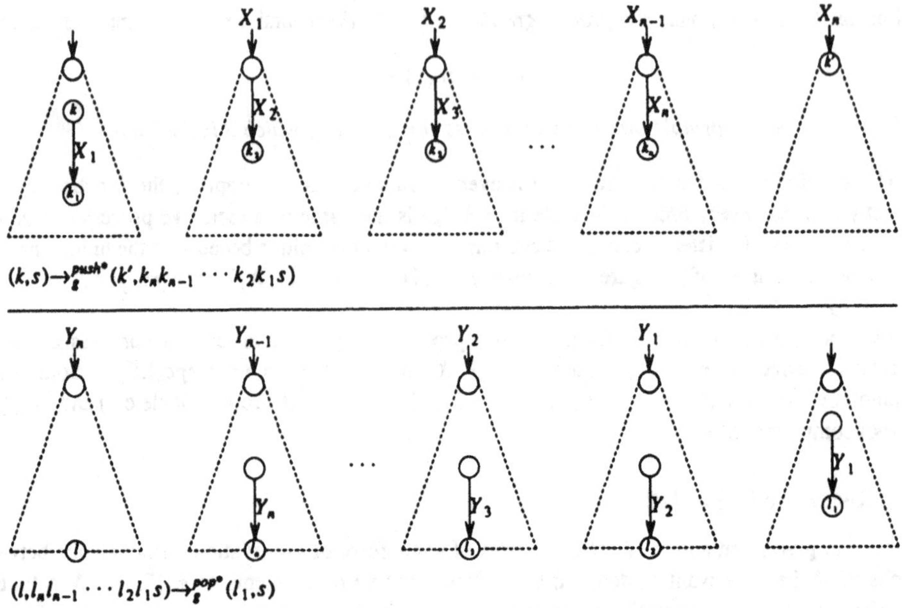

Figure 4: Illustration of the push and pop relations.

Definition 8 is illustrated in figure 5.

Definition 8 *The relation $\rightarrow_g^a$ is defined for every recursive process graph g and atomic action a as a binary relation on the states of g as follows: $(k,s)\rightarrow_g^a(k',s')$ iff there exist states (l,t) and (l',s') such that the following three conditions hold:*

1. $(k,s)\rightarrow_g^{pop*}(l,t)$
2. $(l,t)\rightarrow_g^{push*}(l',s')$
3. *There is an edge in g starting at l', ending at k' and labeled a.*

In figure 5, we combine the $\rightarrow_g^{pop*}$ and $\rightarrow_g^{push*}$ parts of figure 4 by taking $l_1 = k$. The relation $\rightarrow_g^a$ captures the idea of a "state change" in a recursive process graph. Note that the definition of $\rightarrow_g^a$ does not allow a "mix" of pops and pushes, but requires first a number of pops and then a number of pushes. This is not really a constraint, because after a push, we arrive in a root node of a recursive process component, and from this node no pop would be possible anyway (it can't be an end node because by definition, a recursive process component contains at least one edge).

Definition 9 *A state (k,s) of g is called a* reachable state *of g iff there is an $n \geq 1$, a sequence of states $(l_1,t_1),(l_2,t_2),\ldots,(l_n,t_n)$ and a sequence of atomic actions $a_1,a_2,\ldots,a_{n-1}$ (not necessarily different) such that:*

$$(root(g),\epsilon) = (l_1,t_1)\rightarrow_g^{a_1}(l_2,t_2)\rightarrow_g^{a_2}\cdots\rightarrow_g^{a_{n-1}}(l_n,t_n) = (k,s)$$

Definition 10 *The relation $\Rightarrow_g^a$ is defined for every recursive process graph g and atomic action a as a binary relation on states of g as follows: $(k,s)\Rightarrow_g^a(k',s')$ iff the following two conditions hold:*

1. $(k,s)\rightarrow_g^a(k',s')$

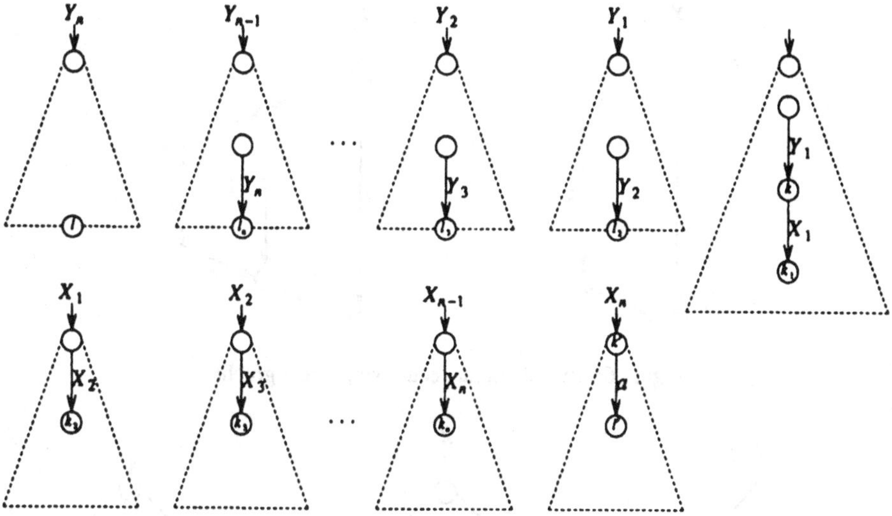

$(l, l_n l_{n-1} \cdots l_2 k s) \rightarrow^a_g (l', k_n k_{n-1} \cdots k_2 k_1 s)$

Figure 5: Illustration of the $\rightarrow^a_g$ relation.

2. *(k, s) is a reachable state of g.*

A trivial fact is that if (k, s) is a reachable state and $(k, s) \Rightarrow^a_g (k', s')$ then (k', s') is also a reachable state.

Definition 11 *A state (k, s) of recursive process graph g is called an* end state *iff k is an end node in g and every node in s is an end node in g.*

Using the $\Rightarrow^a_g$ relation and the notion of end state, the notion of bisimulation can be defined. In the following definition the notation xRy is used for $(x, y) \in R$.

Definition 12 *Let g and h be recursive process graphs. A relation R between reachable states of g and reachable states of h is called a* bisimulation relation *(notation $R : g \leftrightarrow h$) iff the following five conditions hold*

1. *$(root(g), \epsilon) R (root(h), \epsilon)$*
2. *if $(k, s) R (l, t)$ and $(k, s) \rightarrow^a_g (k', s')$ then there must exist a state (l', t') (in h) such that $(k', s') R (l', t')$ and $(l, t) \rightarrow^a_h (l', t')$*
3. *if $(k, s) R (l, t)$ and $(l, t) \rightarrow^a_h (l', t')$ then there must exist a state (k', s') (in g) such that $(k', s') R (l', t')$ and $(k, s) \rightarrow^a_g (k', s')$*
4. *if $(k, s) R (l, t)$ and (k, s) is an end state in g, then (l, t) is an end state in h*
5. *if $(k, s) R (l, t)$ and (l, t) is an end state in h, then (k, s) is an end state in g*

Note that as R is a relation between reachable nodes of g and reachable nodes of h, we could change all $\rightarrow^a_g$ by $\Rightarrow^a_g$ and $\rightarrow^a_h$ by $\Rightarrow^a_h$ in the above definition, without really changing the meaning of the definition.

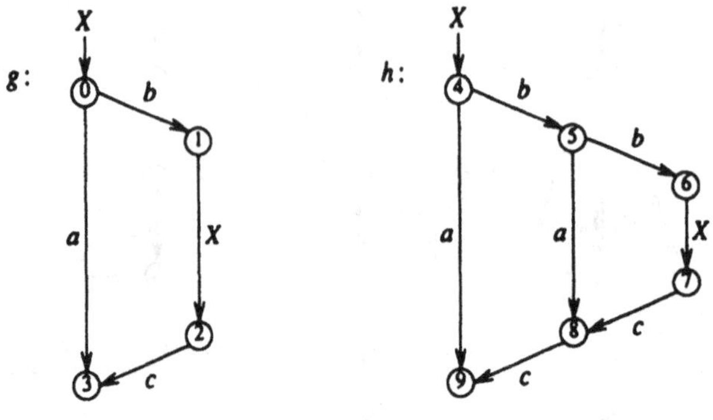

Figure 6: Two bisimilar recursive process graphs.

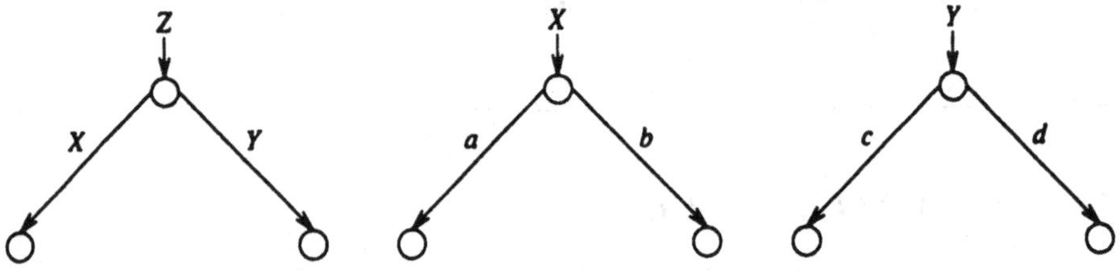

Figure 7: A four-way branch.

Definition 13 *The recursive process graphs g and h are called* bisimilar *(g and h* bisimulate*) if a bisimulation relation R exists such that $R : g \leftrightarrow h$. (Notation if g and h are bisimilar: $g \leftrightarrow h$).*

Figure 6 shows two bisimilar recursive process graphs g and h (both g and h consist of one recursive process component). The nodes of the graphs have been numbered to make it possible to refer to them. The relation below is a bisimulation relation between g and h (in the following relation the abbreviation k^j represents a stack consisting of j nodes which are all k):

$$\{((0,\epsilon),(4,\epsilon))\} \cup (\bigcup_{i=0}^{\infty} \{ \; ((1,2^{2i}),(5,7^i)),((1,2^{2i+1}),(6,7^i)), \\ ((3,2^{2i}),(9,7^i)),((3,2^{2i+1}),(8,7^i))\})$$

Discussion. In our definition of bisimulation, we have chosen an $\Rightarrow_g^a$ step as the smallest unit of execution. The "substeps" that together form such a step (see definitions 8 and 10) are not considered execution steps. Because of this choice, the model we get has a number of useful properties, one of which is that it is isomorphic to the standard graph model (see proposition 26). If we had chosen to take as atomic steps all the pop and push substeps that make up one $\Rightarrow_g^a$ step, we would get a totally different model for which this isomorphism does not hold.

To explain the difference further, consider figures 7 and 8. In both figures a recursive process graph is drawn, with Z as the root variable. Figure 7 may suggest that there is first a choice between X and Y, and then depending either a choice between a and b or between c and d. This would be correct if we would consider a jump to be an invisible action like Milner's τ [7, 8]. However, jumps are not even invisible atomic actions, they are not atomic at all, and the branching structure is bisimilar with that in figure 8. **End of discussion.**

Proposition 14 *Bisimulation is an equivalence relation on $\Re$.*

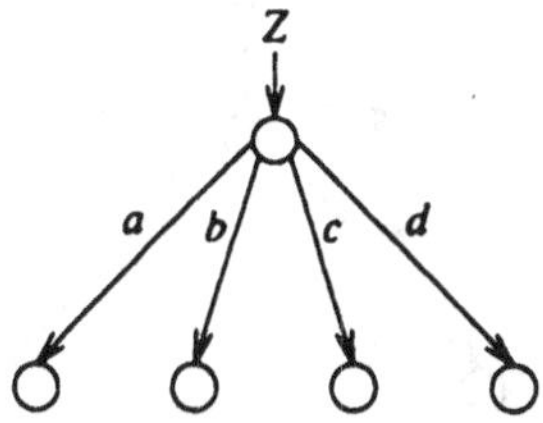

Figure 8: A four-way branch.

2.3 BPA operations on recursive process graphs

To define operations on recursive process graphs, we need to take care of some trivial problems with name clashes by using a renaming function.

Definition 15 *A renaming r is a bijective function $r : PVAR \rightarrow PVAR$.*

Any renaming can be extended to a function on recursive process components and to a function recursive process graphs.

Proposition 16 *For every renaming r and recursive process graph g: $g \underline{\leftrightarrow} r(g)$.*

Definition 17 *A recursive process graph g is a* variant *of recursive process graph h if a renaming r exists such that $g = r(h)$.*

Definition 18 *Given recursive process graphs g and h, the recursive process graph $g[h]$ is a variant of g such that there are no name clashes between variables in $g[h]$ and h (this means $pvar(g[h]) \cap pvar(h) = \emptyset$). We assume that some algorithm exists to determine $g[h]$ uniquely.*

Since there are infinitely many variables, there is always a $g[h]$ for any pair of recursive process graphs g and h.

Definition 19 *The BPA operations and constants are interpreted in $\Re$ in the following way.*

- *A constant (atomic action) a is interpreted as the recursive process graph $(\{p\}, Z)$ with Z the first element of $PVAR$ and p a recursive process component with name Z and one edge starting at the root node with label a.*

- *The operation $+$ is interpreted as: $g + h$ (with $g[h] = (P, X)$ and $h = (Q, Y)$) is the recursive process graph $(P \cup Q \cup \{p\}, Z)$, where Z is the first process variable in $PVAR \setminus (pvar\,(g[h]) \cup pvar(h))$ and p the recursive process component with name Z and two edges starting at the root node, one labeled X and the other labeled Y.*

- *The operation $\cdot$ is interpreted as: $g \cdot h$ (with $g[h] = (P, X)$ and $h = (Q, Y)$) is the recursive process graph $(P \cup Q \cup \{p\}, Z)$, where Z is the first process variable in $PVAR \setminus (pvar(g[h]) \cup pvar(h))$ and p the recursive process component with name Z and two edges, the first one starting at the root node labeled X and the second edge starting at the endpoint of the first edge and labeled Y.*

It is easy to see that the above three constructions indeed result in recursive process graphs (which must have the root existence, unique naming and label existence properties). In figure 9 definition 19 is illustrated. (In this figure the root components of the three constructions of definition 19 are drawn.)

Proposition 20 *Bisimulation is a congruence relation with respect to the operations of definition 19.*

Proposition 21 *$\Re/\underline{\leftrightarrow}$ is a model of BPA.*

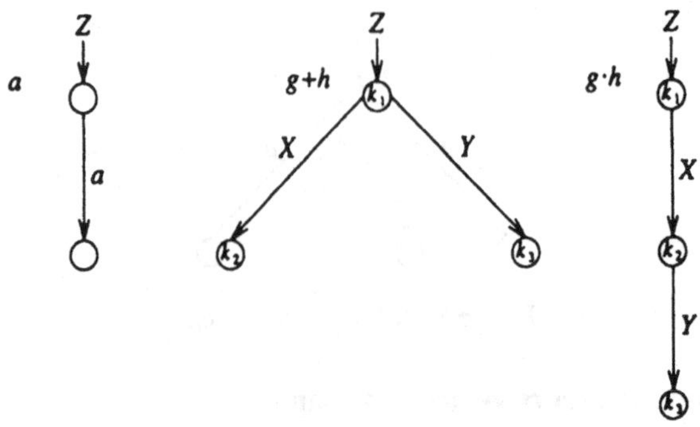

Figure 9: Operations on recursive process graphs.

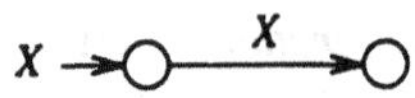

Figure 10: A circular process graph.

2.4 Circularity

Figure 10 shows a special kind of recursive process graph that we call *circular*. In this section, we define these graphs formally and study the models we get by allowing them and by disallowing them.

Definition 22 *The* one-step process variables function

$$pvar1 : RPC \to \mathcal{P}_f(PVAR)$$

assigns to every recursive process component the set of process variables occurring as labels on edges starting at the root of the recursive process component.

We only consider finitely branching graphs, so $pvar1(p)$ is always finite. We now define the set of variables that are reachable, in a recursive process graph, from the root of a recursive process component, without doing an atomic action.

Definition 23 *For every recursive process graph* $g = (P, X)$ *define the function* $dep_g : P \to \mathcal{P}(pvar(g))$ *as*

$$\begin{aligned} dep_g(p) &= \{X \mid \exists n \geq 2 : \exists X_1, X_2, \ldots, X_n \in pvar(g) : X_1 = name(p) \wedge \\ &\quad X = X_n \wedge \forall i \in \{1, \ldots, n-1\} : X_{i+1} \in pvar1(rpc_g(X_i))\} \end{aligned}$$

For example, in figure 3, if we let $g = (\{p_1, p_2, p_3, p_4\}, X_1)$, then $dep_g(p_1) = \{X_2, X_3\}$.

Definition 24 *A recursive process graph* $g = (P, X)$ *is called* circular *iff*

$$\exists p \in P : name(p) \in dep_g(p)$$

The set of all non-circular recursive process graphs is denoted $\Re^{\emptyset}$.

In figure 3 the recursive process graph $(\{p_1, p_2, p_3, p_4\}, X_1)$ is not circular, but would be circular if the label X_3 in p_2 would be replaced by X_1.

Proposition 25 $\Re^{\emptyset}/\underline{\leftrightarrow}$ *is a model of* BPA

$X + \delta = X$	A6
$\delta X = \delta$	A7

Table 2: Deadlock axioms.

Proposition 26 *The models $\Re^{\emptyset}/\underline{\leftrightarrow}$ and $G/\underline{\leftrightarrow}$ are isomorphic.*

$G/\underline{\leftrightarrow}$ is the standard graph model as described in [1]. Because every guarded recursive specification has a unique solution in $G/\underline{\leftrightarrow}$ and the "unique solution" property is preserved under isomorphisms, we can conclude that every guarded recursive specification has a unique solution in $\Re^{\emptyset}/\underline{\leftrightarrow}$. We can then prove:

Proposition 27 *The solution of every finite guarded recursive specification in $\Re^{\emptyset}$ contains a finite element.*

Turning now to the model $\Re/\underline{\leftrightarrow}$ that includes circular recursive process graphs, we would like to find a graph model that is isomorphic to it. One suggestion where to look is given by the following proposition.

Proposition 28 *$\Re/\underline{\leftrightarrow}$ is a BPA_δ model.*

BPA_δ is BPA extended with the constant δ (deadlock) and the axioms shown in table 2.

Proposition 28 can be explained intuitively by considering the process in figure 10. This process can never do an atomic action, and furthermore, the start state $(root(g), \epsilon)$ is not an end state. Because successful termination means reaching an endstate, the process can never terminate. This explains intuitively that this process has the same properties as deadlock.

A second suggestion where to look for a model isomorphic to $\Re/\underline{\leftrightarrow}$ is found in the proof of proposition 26 (given in [9]), where non-circularity is used essentially to prove that $\Re/\underline{\leftrightarrow}$ is isomorphic to the model $G/\underline{\leftrightarrow}$ of finitely-branching processes. A reasonable place to look for a model of BPA_δ that is isomorphic to $\Re/\underline{\leftrightarrow}$, would therefore be $G_\delta^\infty/\underline{\leftrightarrow}$. Figure 11 illustrates this suggestion, by giving an examples of an infinite branching graph (an element of G_δ^∞) and a finitely branching (circular) recursive process graph (an element of $\Re$) that represent the same process (i.e. are bisimilar).

However, a simple argument shows that $G_\delta^\infty/\underline{\leftrightarrow}$ has $2^{\aleph_0}$ elements, but $\Re/\underline{\leftrightarrow}$ has $\aleph_0$ elements. These models can therefore not be isomorphic. We surmise, however, that the following two claims are true:

- There is a homomorphism from $\Re/\underline{\leftrightarrow}$ to $G_\delta^\infty/\underline{\leftrightarrow}$.
- Every guarded recursive specification has a unique solution in $\Re/\underline{\leftrightarrow}$.

Further research is needed on these points.

3 A finite-graph model for PA

Process Algebra (PA) is an extension of BPA with operators $\|$ (merge) and $\lfloor\!\lfloor$ (left-merge) for parallel composition. $X\|Y$ is the parallel merge of X and Y, and $X \lfloor\!\lfloor Y$ is the merge in which the first event is a first event from X. Table 3 gives the axioms with which BPA is extended to get PA. We must extend the recursive process graph model to deal with parallel composition, because

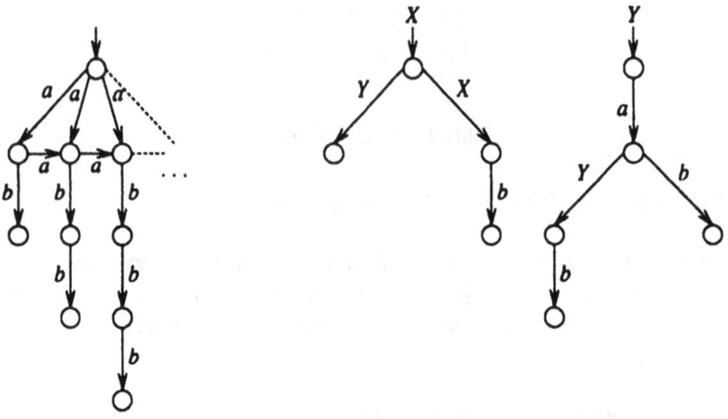

Figure 11: Infinite branching.

$X\|\|Y = X⫼Y + Y⫼X$	M1
$a⫼X = aX$	M2
$aX⫼Y = a(X⫼Y)$	M3
$(X+Y)⫼Z = X⫼Z + Y⫼Z$	M4

Table 3: Merge axioms.

processes exist (e.g. a bag) that can be finitely specified in PA, but not in BPA. These processes can therefore not be finitely represented in the recursive process graph model.

By $\mathcal{M}_f(A)$ we mean the set of finite multisets of elements from a set A, and by $\mathcal{M}_{nf}(A)$ we mean the set of non-empty finite multisets of elements from A. To cater for process merge, we now allow labeling an edge with a multiset of process variables,

Definition 29 *A* multi-recursive process component *is a directed, finitely branching, connected, rooted graph that has at least one edge. The edges of a recursive process component are labeled by elements of the set $\mathcal{M}_{nf}(PVAR) \cup Act$ such that any two edges labeled by a multiset, have different end-points. Each multi-recursive process component has a name, which must be a process variable. The set of all multi-recursive process components is called MPC. Metavariables ranging over MPC are $p, q, r, p_1, p_2, \ldots$*

The definitions of $pvar(p)$, $name(p)$ and $root(p)$ go through virtually unchanged. The definition of a *multi-recursive process graph* then is identical to definition 2. Figure 12 gives an example. The set of all multi-recursive process graphs is called $\Re^M$. Using definition 4 of *state*, we can then define:

Definition 30 *A* multistate *of a multi-recursive process graph g is a multiset of states of g. Metavariables ranging over multistates are $A, B, C, \ldots$*

In the following definitions we use $\uplus$ as a binary infix operator denoting multiset union (yielding a multiset). Definitions 31 and 32 are illustrated in figure 13.

Definition 31 *The relation $\rightarrow_g^{push}$ is defined for every multi-recursive process graph g as a binary relation on the multistates of g in the following way:*

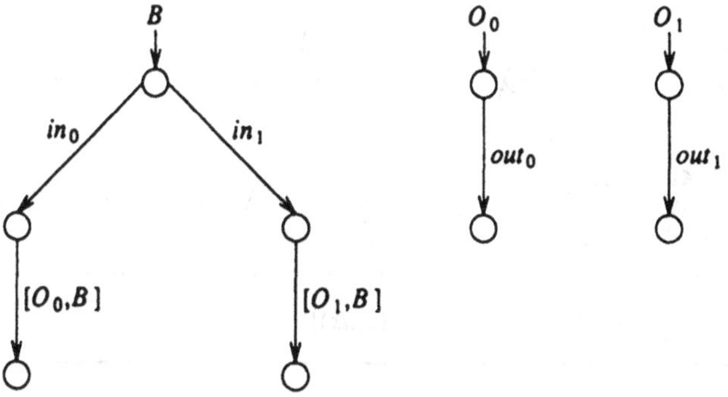

Figure 12: An example multi-recursive process graph: a bag

> *$A \uplus [(k,s)] \rightarrow_g^{push} A \uplus [(k_1,ls),(k_2,ls),\ldots,(k_n,ls)]$ iff there is an edge in g starting at node k, ending at node l and labeled by some multiset $[X_1,X_2,\ldots,X_n]$ (with $n \geq 1$) such that $\forall 1 \leq i \leq n : k_i = root(rpc_g(X_i))$.*

We say that in the above step we have expanded (k,s) to $[(k_1,ls),(k_2,ls),\ldots,(k_n,ls)]$.

The relation $\rightarrow_g^{push*}$ is defined for every recursive process graph g as the reflexive transitive closure of $\rightarrow_g^{push}$.

Definition 32 *The relation $\rightarrow_g^{pop}$ is defined for every multi-recursive process graph g as a binary relation on the multistates of g in the following way:*

> *$A \uplus [(l_1,ks),(l_2,ks),\ldots,(l_n,ks)] \rightarrow_g^{pop} A \uplus [(k,s)]$ iff $\forall 1 \leq i \leq n : l_i$ is an end node in g and $\forall (l',t') \in A : \nexists t'' : t''ks = t'$.*

We say that in the above step we have combined $[(l_1,ks),(l_2,ks),\ldots,(l_n,ks)]$ to (k,s).

The relation $\rightarrow_g^{pop*}$ is defined for every recursive process graph g as the reflexive transitive closure of $\rightarrow_g^{pop}$.

Comparing this with the definition of the pop-relation for BPA process graphs, we see that an important difference is the extra condition $\forall(l',t') \in A : \nexists t'' : t''ks = t'$. This condition states that a parallel composition can only terminate if all of its components have terminated.

Definition 33 *The relation $\rightarrow_g^{a}$ is defined for every multi-recursive process graph g and atomic action a as a binary relation on the multistates of g as follows: $A \rightarrow_g^{a} D$ iff there exist multistates B and C such that the following three conditions hold:*

1. *$A \rightarrow_g^{pop*} B$*
2. *$B \rightarrow_g^{push*} C$*
3. *$C = C' \uplus [(k,s)]$, $D = C' \uplus [(k',s)]$ and there is an edge in g starting at k, ending at k' and labeled a.*

The definition of bisimulation is virtually identical to definition 12 (taking multistates instead of states and using the action relation on multistates).

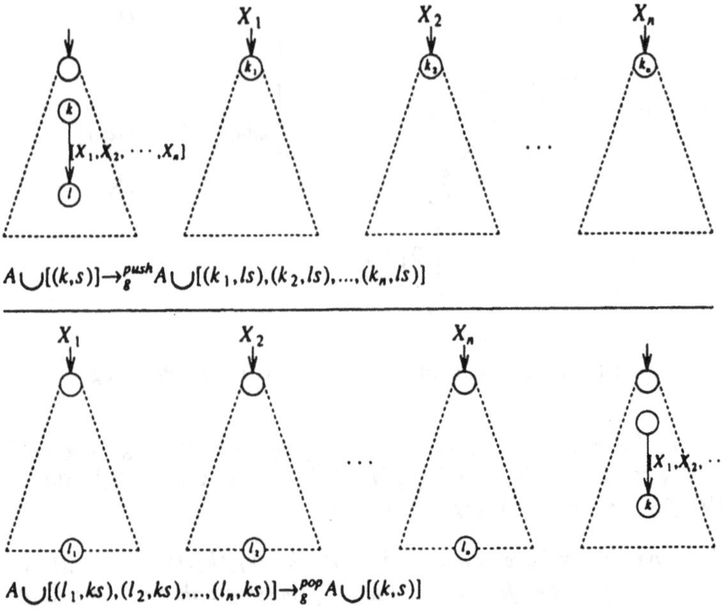

X_1
X_2
X_n
$[X_1, X_2, \cdots, X_n]$
$A \cup [(k,s)] \to_g^{push} A \cup [(k_1, ls), (k_2, ls), \ldots, (k_n, ls)]$
X_1
X_2
X_n
$[X_1, X_2, \cdots, X_n]$
$A \cup [(l_1, ks), (l_2, ks), \ldots, (l_n, ks)] \to_g^{pop} A \cup [(k,s)]$

Figure 13: Illustration of the multipush and multipop relations.

Discussion. With the notion of multisets, we can easily define a "multiset step" relation: an action relation that instead on one, can perform a multiset of actions in every step. We define the relation $\to_g^{[a_1,a_2,\ldots,a_n]}$ on multistates of g as: $A \to_g^{[a_1,a_2,\ldots,a_n]} D$ iff there exist multistates B and C such that $A \to_g^{pop*} B$, $B \to_g^{push*} C$, $C = C' \uplus [(k_1, s_1), (k_2, s_2), \ldots, (k_n, s_n)]$, $D = C' \uplus [(k'_1, s_1), (k'_2, s_2), \ldots, (k'_n, s_n)]$ and for every i such that $1 \leq i \leq n$ there is an edge in g starting at k_i, ending at k'_i and labeled a_i. (Note the similarity between this definition and the definition of the $\to_g^a$ relation above.)

With the "multistep" relation, we can show an interesting connection between multi-recursive process graphs and (conflict free, prime) event structures [5]. To give this correspondence in some detail:

- Configurations in event structures correspond to multistates in multi-recursive process graphs. Note that there is one important difference: a configuration contains all information about which events have occurred, which is not true for multistates (because a graph may contain cycles, so it is possible to perform some actions and end up in the same multistate one started with.)

- The $\to_\epsilon$ relation for event structures [5] corresponds to the $\to_g^{[\ldots]}$ relation in the following way: $X \to_\epsilon X'$ corresponds to $A \to_g^{[a_1,a_2,\ldots,a_n]} B$ provided that $X' \setminus X = \{e_1, e_2, \ldots, e_n\}$ and $l(e_i) = a_i$ (for $1 \leq i \leq n$).

Now we can directly transfer four of the semantics defined by van Glabbeek [5] (interleaving trace equivalence, interleaving bisimulation equivalence, step trace equivalence and step bisimulation equivalence) to our model. In fact, the bisimulation relation defined above corresponds exactly to the interleaving bisimulation relation defined by van Glabbeek. The other three equivalence listed above can also be transferred to our model.

Van Glabbeek also defines partial order semantics. These cannot be transferred to our model, because in order to define such semantics, we would have to find a connection between multistates

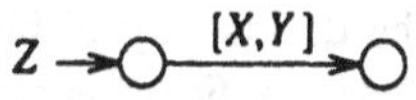

Figure 14: The merge of X and Y

and pomsets. However, multistates do not carry enough information to make such a correspondence possible. **End of discussion.**

The interpretation of the BPA constants and operations $+$ and $\cdot$ is virtually identical to the interpretation in the recursive graph model, just take a multiset of one process variable as a label of an edge when in definition 19 a process variable is used as a label. The operation $\|$ is interpreted as: $g\|h$ (with $g[h] = (P, X)$ and $h = (Q, Y)$) is the recursive process graph $(P \cup Q \cup \{p\}, Z)$, where Z is the first process variable in $PVAR \setminus (pvar\,(g[h]) \cup pvar(h))$ and p the recursive process component with name Z and one edge labeled my the multiset $[X, Y]$. The merge operation is illustrated in figure 14.

Trying to define the left-merge operation for multi-recursive process graphs yields a problem. In [10] it is argued that a left-merge of two (finitely-branching) multi-recursive process graphs may result in an infinitely branching multi-recursive process graph. So left-merge would not be well-defined, as our model only contains finitely branching graphs. The core of the problem is the fact that a finitely branching graph may represent a process containing an infinite choice (see figure 11).

There are two possible solutions to this problem: allow infinite branching or constrain the graphs to be non-circular (which effectively results in deleting the "implicit" infinite branching). We take the second route here. The definitions of the one step process variables function (definition 22), dependency set (definition 23) and circularity (definition 24) for recursive graphs can be directly transferred to the multi-recursive case. We call the set of non-circular process graphs $\Re^{M,\emptyset}$. Now the interpretation of the left merge is simple: we "unwind" both arguments of the left merge to (finitely branching) graphs with no edges labeled by process variables (details are given in [10]). Then we just take the left merge of the two graphs as defined in the standard graph model [1].

Proposition 34 *Bisimulation is a congruence relation on* $\Re^{M,\emptyset}$ *with respect to the operations of* PA.

Proposition 35 $\Re^{M,\emptyset}/\underline{\leftrightarrow}$ *is a model of* PA.

Proposition 36 $\Re^{M,\emptyset}/\underline{\leftrightarrow}$ *and* $G/\underline{\leftrightarrow}$ *are isomorphic models of* PA.

Every guarded specification therefore has a unique solution in $\Re^{M,\emptyset}$.

Proposition 37 *Each finite guarded recursive specification not using* $\mathbb{L}$ *has a finite element in its solution.*

4 Concluding remarks

We have defined some finite-graph models for PA and BPA. Noncircular finite-graph models are isomorphic to known models, and therefore each guarded specification has a unique solution in them. The solution is, as usual, a congruence class of graphs, but in the finite-graph model, this class can be shown to contain a finite element. This result is important for the construction of an editor for process graphs, for it allows the representation of more processes on a finite screen.

An open problems is the question to which standard graph model $\Re^{\emptyset}/\underline{\leftrightarrow}$ is isomorphic. We plan research on this in the future. Work will also be done on bisimulation-preserving operations on multi-recursive process graphs. These operations will be implemented in the planned editor. An interesting problem in this respect is the decidability of bisimilarity of recursive process graphs. Finally, user interface matter will be attended to. For example, multi-recursive process graphs can be presented as a simple kind of state chart (see Harel [6]). We will explore these matters in the future.

Acknowledgements. The idea of recursive process graphs arose during a project done by Paul Spruit and Cees Duivenvoorde on a syntax-directed editor for formal specifications [11]. Jan Willem Klop encouraged the writing of this paper and suggested some improvements. Thanks are due to the anonymous referees, who gave some constructive criticism of the paper. Furthermore, one referee pointed out a mistake in definition 29.

References

[1] J.C.M. Baeten and W.P. Weijland. *Process Algebra.* Cambridge Tracts in Theoretical Computer Science 18. Cambridge University Press, 1990.

[2] J.A. Bergstra and J.W. Klop. Process algebra for synchronous communication. *Information and Control,* 60:109–137, 1984.

[3] J.A. Bergstra and J.W. Klop. Algebra of communicating processes with abstraction. *Theoretical Computer Science,* 37:77–121, 1985.

[4] J.A. Bergstra and J.W. Klop. Algebra of communicating processes. In J.W. de Bakker, M. Hazewinkel, and J.K. Lenstra, editors, *Mathematics and Computer Science (CWI Monographs 1),* pages 89–138. North-Holland, 1986.

[5] R. J. van Glabbeek. *Comparative Concurrency Semantics and Refinement of Actions.* PhD thesis, Vrije Universiteit/Centrum voor Wiskunde en Informatica, Amsterdam, 1990.

[6] D. Harel. On visual formalisms. *Communications of the ACM,* 31:514–530, 1988.

[7] R. Milner. *A Calculus of Communicating Systems.* Springer, 1980. Lecture Notes in Computer Science 92.

[8] R. Milner. *Communication and Concurrency.* Prentice Hall, 1989.

[9] P.A. Spruit. Two finite-graph models for basic process algebra. Technical report, Department of Mathematics and Computer Science, Vrije Universiteit, Amsterdam, December 1990.

[10] P.A. Spruit. Finite-graph models for Process Algebra with parallel composition. Technical report, Department of Mathematics and Computer Science, Vrije Universiteit, Amsterdam, In preparation.

[11] P.A. Spruit and C.J.A. Duivenvoorde. A syntax- and semantics-directed editor for conceptual model specifications. Technical report, Department of Mathematics and Computer Science, Vrije Universiteit, Amsterdam, April 1990.

A Method for the Development of Totally Correct Shared-State Parallel Programs

Ketil Stølen,
Department of Computer Science, Manchester University,
Oxford Road, Manchester, M13, 9PL
email:ks@uk.ac.man.cs

Abstract

A syntax-directed formal system for the development of totally correct programs with respect to an (unfair) shared-state parallel programming language is proposed. The programming language is basically a while-language extended with parallel- and await-constructs. The system is called LSP (Logic of Specified Programs) and can be seen of as an extension of Jones' rely/guarantee method. His method is strengthened in two respects:

- Specifications are extended with a wait-condition to allow for the development of programs whose correctness depends upon synchronisation. The wait-condition is supposed to characterise the states in which the implementation may become blocked. The implementation is not allowed to become blocked inside the body of an await-statement.
- Auxiliary variables are introduced to increase expressiveness. They are either used as a specification tool to eliminate undesirable implementations or as a verification tool to prove that a certain program satisfies a particular specification. Although it is possible to define history variables in LSP, the auxiliary variables may be of any type, and it is up to the user to define the auxiliary structure he prefers. Moreover, the auxiliary structure is only a part of the logic. This means that auxiliary variables do not have to be implemented as if they were ordinary programming variables.

1 Introduction

The parallel-rule in the Owicki/Gries method [OG76] depends upon a number of tests which only can be carried out after the component processes have been implemented and their proofs have been constructed. For large software products this strategy is unacceptable, because erroneous design decisions, taken early in the design process, may remain undetected until after the whole program is complete. Since, in the worst case, everything that depends upon such mistakes will have to be thrown away, much work could be wasted.

The usual way of avoiding this problem is to specify processes in terms of *assumptions* and *commitments*. This was first proposed by Francez and Pnueli [FP78]. The basic idea is: If the *environment*, by which is meant the set of processes running in parallel with the one in question, fulfills the assumptions, then the actual process is required to fulfill the commitments.

Jones employs rely- and guar(antee)-conditions [Jon83] in a similar style. However, while earlier approaches focus essentially on program verification; the object of the rely/guarantee method is *top-down* program development. The proof tuples are of the form z <u>sat</u> (P,R,G,Q), where z is a program and (P,R,G,Q) is a specification consisting of four assertions P, R, G and Q. The pre-condition P and the rely-condition R constitute assumptions that the developer can make about the environment. In return the implementation z must satisfy the guar-condition G, the post-condition Q, and terminate when operated in an environment which fulfills the assumptions.

The pre-condition characterises a set of states to which the implementation is applicable. Any uninterrupted state transition by the environment is supposed to satisfy the rely-condition, while any atomic state transition by the implementation must satisfy the guar-condition. Finally, the post-condition characterises the overall effect of using the implementation in such an environment.

The rely/guarantee method allows erroneous interference decisions to be spotted and corrected at the level where they are taken. Moreover, specifications are decomposed into subspecifications. Thus programs can be developed in a top-down style. Unfortunately, this approach is inferior to the one proposed by Owicki and Gries in two respects: First of all, the method cannot deal with synchronisation. Hence, programs whose correctness depends upon some sort of delay-construct cannot be developed. Secondly, many valid developments are excluded because sufficiently strong assertions cannot be expressed.

This paper, based on the author's PhD-thesis [Stø90], presents an extension of the rely/guarantee method, called LSP (Logic of Specified Programs), which does not suffer from the two weaknesses pointed out above.

The paper is organised as follows: The next section, section 2, defines the programming language. Section 3 explains how rely- and guar-conditions can be used to deal with interfering programs, while section 4 extends specifications with a wait-condition to facilitate development of synchronised programs. The use of auxiliary variables is covered by section 5. Finally, section 6 indicates some extensions and compares LSP with methods known from the literature.

2 Programming Language

2.1 Syntax

A *program* is a finite, nonempty list of symbols whose context-independent syntax can be characterised in the well-known BNF-notation: Given that $\langle vl\rangle$, $\langle el\rangle$, $\langle dl\rangle$, $\langle ts\rangle$ denote respectively a nonempty list of variables, a nonempty list of expressions, a nonempty list of variable declarations, and a Boolean test, then any program is of the form $\langle pg\rangle$, where

$$
\begin{aligned}
\langle pg\rangle &::= \langle sk\rangle \mid \langle as\rangle \mid \langle bl\rangle \mid \langle sc\rangle \mid \langle if\rangle \mid \langle wd\rangle \mid \langle pr\rangle \mid \langle aw\rangle \\
\langle sk\rangle &::= \mathsf{skip} \\
\langle as\rangle &::= \langle vl\rangle := \langle el\rangle \\
\langle bl\rangle &::= \mathsf{blo}\ \langle dl\rangle; \langle pg\rangle\ \mathsf{olb} \\
\langle sc\rangle &::= \langle pg\rangle; \langle pg\rangle \\
\langle if\rangle &::= \mathsf{if}\ \langle ts\rangle\ \mathsf{then}\ \langle pg\rangle\ \mathsf{else}\ \langle pg\rangle\ \mathsf{fi} \\
\langle wd\rangle &::= \mathsf{while}\ \langle ts\rangle\ \mathsf{do}\ \langle pg\rangle\ \mathsf{od} \\
\langle pr\rangle &::= \{\langle pg\rangle \parallel \langle pg\rangle\} \\
\langle aw\rangle &::= \mathsf{await}\ \langle ts\rangle\ \mathsf{do}\ \langle pg\rangle\ \mathsf{od}
\end{aligned}
$$

The main structure of a program is characterised above. However, a syntactically correct program is also required to satisfy some supplementary constraints:

- Not surprisingly, the assignment-statement's two lists are required to have the same number of elements. Moreover, the j'th variable in the first list must be of the same type as the j'th expression in the second, and the same variable is not allowed to occur in the variable list more than once.
- The block-statement allows for declaration of variables. A variable is *local* to a program, if it is declared in the program; otherwise it is said to be *global*. For example, $\mathsf{blo}\ x{:}\,N, y{:}\,N; x, y := 5{+}w, w\ \mathsf{olb}$ has two local variables, x and y, and one global variable w. To avoid complications due to name clashes, it is required that the same variable cannot be declared more than once in the same program, and that a local variable cannot appear outside its block. The first constraint avoids name clashes between local variables, while the second ensures that the set of global variables is disjoint from the set of local variables.

- To simplify the deduction rules and the reasoning with auxiliary variables, it is required that variables occurring in the Boolean test of an if- or a while-statement cannot be accessed by any process running in parallel. This requirement does of course not reduce the number of implementable algorithms. If x is a variable that can be accessed by another process running in parallel, then it is for example always possible to write blo y: N; $y := x$; if $y = 0$ then z_1 else z_2 fi olb instead of if $x = 0$ then z_1 else z_2 fi. (The constraint can be removed [Stø90], but the resulting system is more complicated and less intuitive. Similar requirements are stated in [Sou84], [XH91].)

2.2 Operational Semantics

The programming language is given operational semantics in the style of [Acz83]. A *state* is a mapping of all programming variables to values, and a *configuration* is a pair $\langle z, s\rangle$ where z is either a program or the *empty program* ε and s is a state. An *external* transition $\stackrel{e}{\rightarrow}$ is the least binary relation on configurations such that:

- $\langle z, s_1\rangle \stackrel{e}{\rightarrow} \langle z, s_2\rangle$,

while an *internal* transition $\stackrel{i}{\rightarrow}$ is the least binary relation on configurations such that either:

- $\langle \text{skip}, s\rangle \stackrel{i}{\rightarrow} \langle \varepsilon, s\rangle$,
- $\langle v := r, s\rangle \stackrel{i}{\rightarrow} \langle \varepsilon, s(^v_r)\rangle$, where $s(^v_r)$ denotes the state that is obtained from s, by mapping the variables in v to the values of r in the state s, and leaving all other maplets unchanged,
- $\langle \text{blo } d; z \text{ olb}, s_1\rangle \stackrel{i}{\rightarrow} \langle z, s_2\rangle$, where s_2 denotes a state that is obtained from s_1, by mapping the variables in d to randomly chosen type-correct values, and leaving all other maplets unchanged,
- $\langle z_1; z_2, s_1\rangle \stackrel{i}{\rightarrow} \langle z_2, s_2\rangle$ if $\langle z_1, s_1\rangle \stackrel{i}{\rightarrow} \langle \varepsilon, s_2\rangle$,
- $\langle z_1; z_2, s_1\rangle \stackrel{i}{\rightarrow} \langle z_3; z_2, s_2\rangle$ if $\langle z_1, s_1\rangle \stackrel{i}{\rightarrow} \langle z_3, s_2\rangle$ and $z_3 \neq \varepsilon$,
- $\langle \text{if } b \text{ then } z_1 \text{ else } z_2 \text{ fi}, s\rangle \stackrel{i}{\rightarrow} \langle z_1, s\rangle$ if $s \models b$,
- $\langle \text{if } b \text{ then } z_1 \text{ else } z_2 \text{ fi}, s\rangle \stackrel{i}{\rightarrow} \langle z_2, s\rangle$ if $s \models \neg b$,
- $\langle \text{while } b \text{ do } z \text{ od}, s\rangle \stackrel{i}{\rightarrow} \langle z; \text{while } b \text{ do } z \text{ od}, s\rangle$ if $s \models b$,
- $\langle \text{while } b \text{ do } z \text{ od}, s\rangle \stackrel{i}{\rightarrow} \langle \varepsilon, s\rangle$ if $s \models \neg b$,
- $\langle \{z_1 \parallel z_2\}, s_1\rangle \stackrel{i}{\rightarrow} \langle z_2, s_2\rangle$ if $\langle z_1, s_1\rangle \stackrel{i}{\rightarrow} \langle \varepsilon, s_2\rangle$,
- $\langle \{z_1 \parallel z_2\}, s_1\rangle \stackrel{i}{\rightarrow} \langle z_1, s_2\rangle$ if $\langle z_2, s_1\rangle \stackrel{i}{\rightarrow} \langle \varepsilon, s_2\rangle$,
- $\langle \{z_1 \parallel z_2\}, s_1\rangle \stackrel{i}{\rightarrow} \langle \{z_3 \parallel z_2\}, s_2\rangle$ if $\langle z_1, s_1\rangle \stackrel{i}{\rightarrow} \langle z_3, s_2\rangle$ and $z_3 \neq \varepsilon$,
- $\langle \{z_1 \parallel z_2\}, s_1\rangle \stackrel{i}{\rightarrow} \langle \{z_1 \parallel z_3\}, s_2\rangle$ if $\langle z_2, s_1\rangle \stackrel{i}{\rightarrow} \langle z_3, s_2\rangle$ and $z_3 \neq \varepsilon$,
- $\langle \text{await } b \text{ do } z_1 \text{ od}, s_1\rangle \stackrel{i}{\rightarrow} \langle \varepsilon, s_n\rangle$ if $s_1 \models b$, and
  - there is a list of configurations $\langle z_2, s_2\rangle, \ldots, \langle z_{n-1}, s_{n-1}\rangle$, such that $\langle z_{n-1}, s_{n-1}\rangle \stackrel{i}{\rightarrow} \langle \varepsilon, s_n\rangle$ and for all $1 < k < n$, $\langle z_{k-1}, s_{k-1}\rangle \stackrel{i}{\rightarrow} \langle z_k, s_k\rangle$,
- $\langle \text{await } b \text{ do } z_1 \text{ od}, s_1\rangle \stackrel{i}{\rightarrow} \langle \text{await } b \text{ do } z_1 \text{ od}, s_1\rangle$ if $s_1 \models b$, and

- there is an infinite list of configurations $\langle z_2, s_2\rangle, \ldots, \langle z_n, s_n\rangle, \ldots$, such that for all $k > 1$, $\langle z_{k-1}, s_{k-1}\rangle \xrightarrow{i} \langle z_k, s_k\rangle$, or
- there is a finite list of configurations $\langle z_2, s_2\rangle, \ldots, \langle z_n, s_n\rangle$, such that $z_n \neq \varepsilon$ and there is no configuration $\langle z_{n+1}, s_{n+1}\rangle$ which satisfies $\langle z_n, s_n\rangle \xrightarrow{i} \langle z_{n+1}, s_{n+1}\rangle$, and for all $1 < k \leq n$, $\langle z_{k-1}, s_{k-1}\rangle \xrightarrow{i} \langle z_k, s_k\rangle$.

The above definition is of course only sensible if all functions are required to be total. It follows from the definition that assignment-statements and Boolean tests are atomic. The environment is restricted from interfering until an await-statement's body has terminated if an evaluation of its Boolean test comes out true. Moreover, the execution of the await-statement's body is modeled by one atomic step. The identity internal transition is used to model that the await-statement's body fails to terminate.

Before giving the definition of a computation, there are two things which must be sorted out: First of all, since the object here is to prove total correctness, a progress property is needed. Secondly, since the environment is restricted from accessing certain variables, it is necessary to find a way to constrain them from being updated by external transitions.

Nobody doubts that the sequential program $x := 1$ (given its usual semantics) eventually will terminate. The reason is that any sensible sequential programming language satisfies the following progress property: If something can happen then eventually something will happen.

In the concurrent case, with respect to an unfair programming language, a slightly different progress property is required. Given that a configuration c_1 is *disabled* if there is no configuration c_2, such that $c_1 \xrightarrow{i} c_2$, then it is enough to insist that the final configuration of a finite computation is disabled. This constrains programs from not progressing without being disabled or infinitely overtaken by the environment. Observe that this is no fairness constraint, because it does not restrict the actual program from being infinitely overtaken by the environment.

To deal with the environment's restricted access to certain variables, let for any program z, $hid[z]$ denote the set of any variable which is local to z or occurs in the Boolean test of an if- or a while-statement in z — in which case it is sufficient to constrain the external transitions in a computation of z from changing the values of the variables in $hid[z]$.

Definition 1 *A* computation *is a possibly infinite sequence of external and internal transitions*

$$\langle z_1, s_1\rangle \xrightarrow{l_1} \langle z_2, s_2\rangle \xrightarrow{l_2} \quad \ldots \quad \xrightarrow{l_{k-1}} \langle z_k, s_k\rangle \xrightarrow{l_k} \quad \ldots \quad ,$$

such that the final configuration is disabled if the sequence is finite, and the external transitions leave the values of the variables in $hid[z_1]$ *unchanged.*

Given a computation σ, then $Z(\sigma)$, $S(\sigma)$ and $L(\sigma)$ are the obvious projection functions to sequences of programs, states and transition labels, while $Z(\sigma_j)$, $S(\sigma_j)$, $L(\sigma_j)$ and σ_j denote respectively the j'th program, the j'th state, the j'th transition label and the j'th configuration. Furthermore, $\sigma(j, \ldots, k)$ represents

$$\langle Z(\sigma_j), S(\sigma_j)\rangle \xrightarrow{L(\sigma_j)} \quad \ldots \quad \xrightarrow{L(\sigma_{k-1})} \langle Z(\sigma_k), S(\sigma_k)\rangle.$$

If σ is infinite, then $len(\sigma) = \infty$, otherwise $len(\sigma)$ is equal to σ's number of configurations. Finally, given a set of variables ϑ and two states s_1, s_2, then $s_1 \stackrel{\vartheta}{=} s_2$ denotes that for all variables $x \in \vartheta$, $s_1(x) = s_2(x)$, while $s_1 \stackrel{\vartheta}{\neq} s_2$ means that there is a variable $x \in \vartheta$, such that $s_1(x) \neq s_2(x)$.

Definition 2 *Given a program* z, *let* $cp[z]$ *be the set of all computations* σ *such that* $Z(\sigma_1) = z$.

The computations σ' of z_1 and σ'' of z_2 are *compatible* if $\{z_1 \parallel z_2\}$ is a program, $len(\sigma') = len(\sigma'')$, $S(\sigma') = S(\sigma'')$ and for all $1 \leq j < len(\sigma')$, $L(\sigma'_j) = L(\sigma''_j)$ implies $L(\sigma'_j) = e$. For example, given three assignment-statements z_1, z_2 and z_3, then

$$\langle z_1; z_2, s_1\rangle \xrightarrow{i} \langle z_2, s_2\rangle \xrightarrow{i} \langle \varepsilon, s_3\rangle$$

is a computation of $z_1; z_2$ which is not compatible with any computation of z_3, because each finite computation of z_3 has exactly one internal transition and the computation above has no external transitions. On the other hand, the computations

$$\langle z_1; z_2, s_1\rangle \xrightarrow{i} \langle z_2, s_2\rangle \xrightarrow{e} \langle z_2, s_3\rangle \xrightarrow{e} \langle z_2, s_4\rangle \xrightarrow{i} \langle \varepsilon, s_5\rangle,$$
$$\langle z_3, s_1\rangle \xrightarrow{e} \langle z_3, s_2\rangle \xrightarrow{i} \langle \varepsilon, s_3\rangle \xrightarrow{e} \langle \varepsilon, s_4\rangle \xrightarrow{e} \langle \varepsilon, s_5\rangle$$

are compatible. Furthermore, they can be composed into a computation

$$\langle \{z_1; z_2 \parallel z_3\}, s_1\rangle \xrightarrow{i} \langle \{z_2 \parallel z_3\}, s_2\rangle \xrightarrow{i} \langle z_2, s_3\rangle \xrightarrow{e} \langle z_2, s_4\rangle \xrightarrow{i} \langle \varepsilon, s_5\rangle$$

of $\{z_1; z_2 \parallel z_3\}$, by composing the program part of each configuration pair, and making a transition internal iff one of the two component transitions are internal. It can easily be shown that two compatible computations σ' of z_1 and σ'' of z_2 can always be composed into a computation of $\{z_1 \parallel z_2\}$. Furthermore, it is also straightforward to prove that any computation σ of a parallel program $\{z_1 \parallel z_2\}$ can be decomposed into two compatible computations σ' of z_1 and σ'' of z_2, such that σ is the result of composing them.

3 Interference

3.1 Specified Programs

The object of this section is to show how rely- and guar-conditions can be used for the development of interfering programs. The formalism presented below can be seen as a slightly altered version of Jones' rely/guarantee method. The main modifications are that the reflexivity and transitivity constraints on rely- and guar-conditions have been removed. Moreover, the post-condition is called eff-condition, and the proof-tuples have an extra component characterising the set of global programming variables.

The base logic L is a μ-calculus. In the style of VDM [Jon90] hooked variables will be used to refer to an earlier state (which is not necessarily the previous state). This means that, for any *unhooked* variable x of type Σ, there is a *hooked* variable $\overleftarrow{x}$ of type Σ. Hooked variables are restricted from occurring in programs.

Given a structure and a valuation then the expressions in L can be assigned meanings in the usual way; $\models A$ means that the assertion A is valid (in the actual structure), while $(s_1, s_2) \models A$, where (s_1, s_2) is a pair of states, means that A is true if each hooked variable x in A is assigned the value $s_1(x)$ and each unhooked variable x in A is assigned the value $s_2(x)$. The first state s_1 may be omitted if A has no occurrences of hooked variables.

Thus, an assertion A can be interpreted as the set of all pairs of states (s_1, s_2), such that $(s_1, s_2) \models A$. If A has no occurrences of hooked variables, it may also be thought of as the set of all states s, such that $s \models A$. Both interpretations will be used below. To indicate the intended meaning, it will be distinguished between *binary* and *unary* assertions. When an assertion is binary it denotes a set of pairs of states, while an unary assertion denotes a set of states. In other words, an assertion with occurrences of hooked variables is always binary, while an assertion without occurrences of hooked variables can be both binary and unary.

A specification is of the form $(\vartheta) :: (P, R, G, E)$, where the *pre-condition* P is a unary assertion, the *rely-condition* R, the *guar-condition* G, and the *eff-condition* E are binary assertions. The *glo-set* ϑ is the set of global programming variables. It is required that the unhooked version of any hooked or unhooked free variable occurring in P, R, G or E is an element of ϑ. The *global state* is the state restricted to the glo-set.

A specification states a number of assumptions about the environment. First of all, the initial state is assumed to satisfy the pre-condition. Moreover, it is also assumed that any external transition which changes the global state satisfies the rely-condition. For example, given the rely-condition $x < \overleftarrow{x} \wedge y = \overleftarrow{y}$, then it is assumed that the environment will never change the value of y. Furthermore, if the environment assigns a new value to x, then this value will be less than or equal to the variable's previous value.

Thirdly, it is assumed that the environment can only perform a finite number of consecutive atomic steps. This means that no computation has an infinite number of external transitions unless it also has an infinite number of internal transitions. Thus, this assumption implies that the implementation will not be *infinitely overtaken* by the environment. Observe that this is not a fairness requirement on the programming language, because it does not constrain the implementation of a specification. If for example a parallel-statement $\{z_1 \parallel z_2\}$ occurs in the implementation, then this assumption does not influence whether or not z_1 is infinitely overtaken by z_2. Moreover, this assumption can be removed. The only difference is that an implementation is no longer required to *terminate*, but only to terminate whenever it is not infinitely overtaken by the environment (see [Stø90] for a more detailed discussion). The assumptions are summed up in the definition below:

Definition 3 *Given a glo-set ϑ, a pre-condition P, a rely-condition R, then $ext[\vartheta, P, R]$ denotes the set of all computations σ, such that:*

- $S(\sigma_1) \models P$,
- *for all* $1 \le j < len(\sigma)$, *if* $L(\sigma_j) = e$ *and* $S(\sigma_j) \overset{\vartheta}{\neq} S(\sigma_{j+1})$ *then* $(S(\sigma_j), S(\sigma_{j+1})) \models R$,
- *if* $len(\sigma) = \infty$, *then for all* $j \ge 1$, *there is a* $k \ge j$, *such that* $L(\sigma_k) = i$.

A specification is of course not only stating assumptions about the environment, but also commitments to the implementation. Given an environment which satisfies the assumptions, then an implementation is required to terminate. Moreover, any internal transition which changes the global state is required to satisfy the guar-condition, and the overall effect is constrained to satisfy the eff-condition. External transitions both before the first internal transition and after the last are included in the overall effect. This means that given the rely-condition $x > \overleftarrow{x}$, the strongest eff-condition for the program skip is $x \ge \overleftarrow{x}$. The commitments are summed up below:

Definition 4 *Given a glo-set ϑ, a guar-condition G, and an eff-condition E, then $int[\vartheta, G, E]$ denotes the set of all computations σ, such that:*

- $len(\sigma) \ne \infty$ *and* $Z(\sigma_{len(\sigma)}) = \varepsilon$,
- *for all* $1 \le j < len(\sigma)$, *if* $L(\sigma_j) = i$ *and* $S(\sigma_j) \overset{\vartheta}{\neq} S(\sigma_{j+1})$ *then* $(S(\sigma_j), S(\sigma_{j+1})) \models G$,
- $(S(\sigma_1), S(\sigma_{len(\sigma)})) \models E$.

A specified program is a pair of a program z and a specification ψ, written z sat ψ. It is required that for any variable x occurring in z, x is an element of ψ's glo-set iff x is a global variable with respect to z. Moreover, a specified program is valid if the program behaves according to the commitments whenever it is executed in an environment which satisfies the assumptions:

Definition 5 *A specified program z sat $(\vartheta)::(P, R, G, E)$ is valid iff $ext[\vartheta, P, R] \cap cp[z] \subseteq int[\vartheta, G, E]$.*

3.2 Deduction Rules

The object of this section is to define a logic for the deduction of valid specified programs. Given a list of variables v, a list of expressions r, a finite set of variables ϑ, and three assertions A, B and C, where at least A is unary, then $\langle v \rangle$ denotes the set of variables occurring in v, $\overleftarrow{r}$ denotes the list of expressions that can be obtained from r by hooking all free variables in r, $\overleftarrow{A}$ denotes the assertion that can be obtained from A by hooking all free variables in A, I_ϑ denotes the assertion $\bigwedge_{x \in \vartheta} x = \overleftarrow{x}$, $B \mid C$ denotes an assertion characterising the 'relational composition' of B and C, in other words, $(s_1, s_2) \models B \mid C$ iff there is a state s_3 such that $(s_1, s_3) \models B$ and $(s_3, s_2) \models C$. Moreover, B^+ denotes an assertion characterising the transitive closure of B, B^* denotes an assertion characterising the reflexive and transitive closure of B, while A^B denotes an assertion characterising any state that can be reached from A by a finite number of B steps. This means that $s_1 \models A^B$ iff there is a state s_2 such that $(s_2, s_1) \models \overleftarrow{A} \wedge B^*$. Finally, wf B (where B is first-order) denotes an assertion which is valid iff B is well-founded on the set of states, in other words, iff there is no infinite sequence of states $s_1 s_2 \ldots s_k \ldots$ such that for all $j \geq 1$, $(s_j, s_{j+1}) \models B$.

The *consequence*-rule

$$\frac{\begin{array}{l} P_2 \Rightarrow P_1 \\ R_2 \Rightarrow R_1 \\ G_1 \Rightarrow G_2 \\ E_1 \Rightarrow E_2 \\ z \ \underline{\text{sat}}\ (\vartheta) :: (P_1, R_1, G_1, E_1) \end{array}}{z \ \underline{\text{sat}}\ (\vartheta) :: (P_2, R_2, G_2, E_2)}$$

is perhaps the easiest to understand. It basically states that it is always sound to strengthen the assumptions and weaken the commitments.

The *skip*-rule

$$\text{skip } \underline{\text{sat}}\ (\vartheta) :: (P, R, \text{false}, R^*)$$

is also rather trivial. Since any computation of a skip-statement (given the assumptions) is of the form

$$\langle \text{skip}, s_1 \rangle \xrightarrow{e} \ldots \xrightarrow{e} \langle \text{skip}, s_k \rangle \xrightarrow{i} \langle \varepsilon, s_k \rangle \xrightarrow{e} \ldots \xrightarrow{e} \langle \varepsilon, s_n \rangle,$$

where the only internal transition leaves the state unchanged, it is clear that false is the strongest possible guar-condition. Moreover, since any external transition, which changes the global state, is assumed to satisfy R, it follows that the overall effect is characterised by R^*.

The *assignment*-rule

$$\frac{\overleftarrow{P^R} \wedge v = \overleftarrow{r} \wedge I_{\vartheta \setminus \{v\}} \Rightarrow (G \vee I_\vartheta) \wedge E}{v := r \ \underline{\text{sat}}\ (\vartheta) :: (P, R, G, R^* \mid E \mid R^*)}$$

is more complicated. Any computation of an assignment-statement (given the assumptions) is of the form

$$\langle v := r, s_1 \rangle \xrightarrow{e} \ldots \xrightarrow{e} \langle v := r, s_k \rangle \xrightarrow{i} \langle \varepsilon, s_{k+1} \rangle \xrightarrow{e} \ldots \xrightarrow{e} \langle \varepsilon, s_n \rangle.$$

Again, there is only one internal transition. Moreover, since the initial state is assumed to satisfy P, and any external transition, which changes the global state, is assumed to satisfy R, it follows that $s_k \models P^R$ and that $(s_k, s_{k+1}) \models \overleftarrow{P^R} \wedge v = \overleftarrow{r} \wedge I_{\vartheta \setminus \{v\}}$. But then it is clear from the premise that $(s_k, s_{k+1}) \models G \vee I_\vartheta$ and $(s_1, s_n) \models R^* \mid E \mid R^*$, which proves that the rule is sound.

The *block*-rule

$$\frac{z \ \underline{\text{sat}}\ (\vartheta) :: (P, R \wedge \bigwedge_{j=1}^{n} x_j = \overleftarrow{x_j}, G, E)}{\text{blo } x_1 : T_1, \ldots, x_n : T_n; z \text{ olb } \underline{\text{sat}}\ (\vartheta \setminus \bigcup_{j=1}^{n} \{x_j\}) :: (P, R, G, E)}$$

can be used to 'hide' local variables. The rule is sound because the syntactic constraints on specified programs imply that $x_1, \ldots, x_n$ do not occur free in (P, R, G, E).

The *sequential*-rule

$$\frac{\begin{array}{l} z_1 \;\underline{\text{sat}}\; (\vartheta)::(P_1,R,G,P_2 \wedge E_1) \\ z_2 \;\underline{\text{sat}}\; (\vartheta)::(P_2,R,G,E_2) \end{array}}{z_1; z_2 \;\underline{\text{sat}}\; (\vartheta)::(P_1,R,G,E_1 \mid E_2)}$$

depends upon the fact that the first component's eff-condition implies the second component's pre-condition. This explains why P_2 occurs in the effect-condition of the first premise. Since an eff-condition covers interference both before the first internal transition and after the last, it follows from the two premises that the overall effect is characterised by $E_1 \mid E_2$.

With respect to the *if*-rule

$$\frac{\begin{array}{l} z_1 \;\underline{\text{sat}}\; (\vartheta)::(P \wedge b,R,G,E) \\ z_2 \;\underline{\text{sat}}\; (\vartheta)::(P \wedge \neg b,R,G,E) \end{array}}{\text{if } b \text{ then } z_1 \text{ else } z_2 \text{ fi } \underline{\text{sat}}\; (\vartheta)::(P,R,G,E)}$$

it is important to remember that due to a syntactic constraint, the environment cannot access any variable occurring in b. Thus the truth value of the Boolean test cannot be changed by any process running in parallel. This means that for any computation

$$\langle z,s_1\rangle \xrightarrow{e} \langle z,s_2\rangle \xrightarrow{e} \ldots \xrightarrow{e} \langle z,s_k\rangle \xrightarrow{i} \sigma$$

of an if-statement z, there is a computation of the form

$$\langle z,s_1\rangle \xrightarrow{i} \langle z',s_1\rangle \xrightarrow{e} \langle z',s_2\rangle \ldots \xrightarrow{e} \langle z',s_k\rangle \xrightarrow{e} \sigma,$$

which can be obtained from the former by postponing the environment's interference until after the Boolean test has been evaluated. This means that for any computation of an if-statement if b then z_1 else z_2 fi in an environment characterised by P and R, there is a computation of z_1 in an environment characterised by $P \wedge b$ and R, or a computation of z_2 in an environment characterised by $P \wedge \neg b$ and R, with the same overall effect and with the same set of state changing internal transitions. Thus, it follows from the two premises that any internal transition which changes the global state satisfies G, and that the overall effect is characterised by E.

Because interference before the first evaluation of the Boolean test has no influence on the test's outcome, the soundness of the *while*-rule

$$\frac{\begin{array}{l} \text{wf } F \\ z \;\underline{\text{sat}}\; (\vartheta)::(P \wedge b,R,G,P \wedge F) \end{array}}{\text{while } b \text{ do } z \text{ od } \underline{\text{sat}}\; (\vartheta)::(P,R,G,(F^+ \vee R^*) \wedge \neg b)}$$

follows by a similar argument. Observe that, for the same reason, the falsity of the Boolean test is preserved after the while-statement terminates. To prove termination, it is enough to show that an assertion characterising the effect of the loop's body in the actual environment is well-founded when considered as a binary relation on states. This explains the first premise. If the loop iterates at least once, then the overall effect is characterised by $F^+ \wedge \neg b$, while it is characterised by $R^* \wedge \neg b$ otherwise.

To grasp the intuition behind the *parallel*-rule

$$\frac{\begin{array}{l} z_1 \;\underline{\text{sat}}\; (\vartheta)::(P,R \vee G_2,G_1,E_1) \\ z_2 \;\underline{\text{sat}}\; (\vartheta)::(P,R \vee G_1,G_2,E_2) \end{array}}{\{z_1 \parallel z_2\} \;\underline{\text{sat}}\; (\vartheta)::(P,R,G_1 \vee G_2,E_1 \wedge E_2)}$$

observe that the rely-condition of the first premise allows any interference due to z_2, and similarly that the rely-condition of the second premise allows any interference due to z_1. Thus since the eff-condition covers interference both before the first internal transition and after the last, it is clear from the two premises that $\{z_1 \parallel z_2\}$ terminates, that any internal transition, which changes the global state, satisfies $G_1 \vee G_2$, and that the overall effect satisfies $E_1 \wedge E_2$.

The *domain*-rule

$$\frac{z \;\underline{\text{sat}}\; (\vartheta)::(P,R,G,E)}{z \;\underline{\text{sat}}\; (\vartheta)::(P,R,G,\overleftarrow{P} \wedge E)}$$

is straightforward. If the actual program is employed in a state which does not satisfy the pre-condition, then there are no constraints on its behaviour. Thus, the eff-condition can be restricted to transitions from states which satisfy the pre-condition.

The *access*-rule

$$\frac{z \;\underline{\text{sat}}\; (\vartheta)::(P,R \wedge x = \overleftarrow{x},G,E)}{z \;\underline{\text{sat}}\; (\vartheta)::(P,R,G,E)} \qquad \textit{where } x \in hid[z] \cap \vartheta$$

is also needed. Under certain circumstances it allows the rely-condition to be weakened. The rule is sound because of the environment's restricted access to programming variables occurring in the Boolean test of an if- or a while-statement.

4 Synchronisation

4.1 Specified Programs

The last section explained how rely- and guar-conditions can be used to reason about interfering programs. Unfortunately, the rely/guarantee method cannot be employed for the development of programs whose correctness depends upon some sort of delay construct. The object of this section is to extend specifications with a fifth assertion, called a wait-condition, and show how this allows for synchronisation arguments.

A specification is now of the form $(\vartheta)::(P,R,W,G,E)$. The only new component is the wait-condition W, which is a unary assertion. The unhooked version of any free hooked or unhooked variable occurring in the assertions is still required to be an element of ϑ.

The assumptions about the environment are the same as before, but the commitments are changed. A configuration c is *blocked* if it is disabled and $Z(c) \neq \varepsilon$. Moreover, a computation *deadlocks* if it is finite and its final configuration is blocked. Given an environment which satisfies the assumptions, then the program is no longer required to terminate, but only to terminate or deadlock. The implementation is not allowed to deadlock 'inside' the body of an await-statement, and the final state is required to satisfy the wait-condition if the program deadlocks. Observe, that this implies that the program can only become blocked in a state which satisfies the wait-condition. On the other hand, the overall effect is constrained to satisfy the eff-condition if the program terminates.

Definition 6 *Given a glo-set ϑ, a wait-condition W, a guar-condition G, and an eff-condition E, then $int[\vartheta,W,G,E]$ denotes the set of all computations σ such that:*

- *$len(\sigma) \neq \infty$,*
- *for all $1 \leq j < len(\sigma)$, if $L(\sigma_j) = i$ and $S(\sigma_j) \overset{\vartheta}{\neq} S(\sigma_{j+1})$ then $(S(\sigma_j), S(\sigma_{j+1})) \models G$,*
- *if $Z(\sigma_{len(\sigma)}) \neq \varepsilon$ then $S(\sigma_{len(\sigma)}) \models W$,*
- *if $Z(\sigma_{len(\sigma)}) = \varepsilon$ then $(S(\sigma_1), S(\sigma_{len(\sigma)})) \models E$.*

Observe that if $ext[\vartheta,P,R] \cap cp[z]$ contains a computation which has at least one identity internal transition, it follows that $ext[\vartheta,P,R] \cap cp[z]$ has elements of infinite length. Thus, since the identity internal transition is used to model a nonterminating await body, it follows from the first constraint that the bodies of await-statements are required to terminate.

(It is also possible to interpret the wait-condition as an assumption about the environment, in which case the actual program is assumed always eventually to be released given that it never becomes blocked in a state which does not satisfy the wait-condition. Definition 4 is in that case left unchanged, while definition 3 is extended with a fourth condition

- if $len(\sigma) \neq \infty$ and $Z(\sigma_{len(\sigma)}) \neq \epsilon$, then $S(\sigma_{len(\sigma)}) \models \neg W$.

The deduction rules are exactly the same for both interpretations.)

Definition 7 *A specified program* z $\underline{\text{sat}}$ $(\vartheta)::(P,R,W,G,E)$ *is valid iff* $ext[\vartheta,P,R] \cap cp[z] \subseteq int[\vartheta,W,G,E]$.

This means that if z $\underline{\text{sat}}$ $(\vartheta,\alpha)::(P,R,W,G,E)$ is a valid specified program, z is executed in an environment characterised by P and R, and z is not infinitely overtaken, then z either deadlocks in a state which satisfies W or terminates in a state such that the overall effect is characterised by E. Thus, z is totally correct with respect to the same specification if W is equivalent to false.

4.2 Deduction Rules

With one exception, the *parallel*-rule, the changes to the rules given above are trivial. To grasp the intuition behind the new parallel-rule first consider

$$\frac{\begin{array}{l}\neg(W_1 \wedge E_2) \wedge \neg(W_2 \wedge E_1) \wedge \neg(W_1 \wedge W_2)\\ z_1\ \underline{\text{sat}}\ (\vartheta)::(P, R \vee G_2, W_1, G_1, E_1)\\ z_2\ \underline{\text{sat}}\ (\vartheta)::(P, R \vee G_1, W_2, G_2, E_2)\end{array}}{\{z_1 \parallel z_2\}\ \underline{\text{sat}}\ (\vartheta)::(P, R, \text{false}, G_1 \vee G_2, E_1 \wedge E_2)}$$

which is sufficiently strong whenever $\{z_1 \parallel z_2\}$ does not become blocked. It follows from the second premise that z_1 can only become blocked in a state which satisfies W_1 when executed in an environment characterised by P and $R \vee G_2$. Moreover, the third premise implies that z_2 can only become blocked in a state which satisfies W_2 when executed in an environment characterised by P and $R \vee G_1$. But then, since the first premise implies that z_1 cannot be blocked after z_2 has terminated, that z_2 cannot be blocked after z_1 has terminated, and that z_1 and z_2 cannot be blocked at the same time, it follows that $\{z_1 \parallel z_2\}$ cannot become blocked in an environment characterised by P and R.

It is now easy to extend the rule to deal with the general case:

$$\frac{\begin{array}{l}\neg(W_1 \wedge E_2) \wedge \neg(W_2 \wedge E_1) \wedge \neg(W_1 \wedge W_2)\\ z_1\ \underline{\text{sat}}\ (\vartheta)::(P, R \vee G_2, W \vee W_1, G_1, E_1)\\ z_2\ \underline{\text{sat}}\ (\vartheta)::(P, R \vee G_1, W \vee W_2, G_2, E_2)\end{array}}{\{z_1 \parallel z_2\}\ \underline{\text{sat}}\ (\vartheta)::(P, R, W, G_1 \vee G_2, E_1 \wedge E_2)}$$

The idea is that W characterises the states in which the overall program may become blocked. This rule can of course be generalised further to deal with more than two processes:

$$\frac{\begin{array}{l}\neg(W_j \wedge \bigwedge_{k=1,k\neq j}^{m}(W_k \vee E_k))_{1\leq j\leq m}\\ z_j\ \underline{\text{sat}}\ (\vartheta)::(P, R \vee \bigvee_{k=1,k\neq j}^{m} G_k, W \vee W_j, G_j, E_j)_{1\leq j\leq m}\end{array}}{\|_{j=1}^{m}\ z_j\ \underline{\text{sat}}\ (\vartheta)::(P, R, W, \bigvee_{j=1}^{m} G_j, \bigwedge_{j=1}^{m} E_j)}$$

Here, $\|_{j=1}^{m} z_j$ denotes any program that can be obtained from $z_1 \parallel \ldots \parallel z_m$ by adding curly brackets. The 'first' premise ensures that whenever process j is blocked in a state s such that $s \models \neg W \wedge W_j$, then there is at least one other process which is enabled. This rule is 'deducible' from the basic rules given above, and it will from now on be referred to as the *generalised* parallel-rule.

The *await*-rule

$$\frac{z\ \underline{\text{sat}}\ (\vartheta)::(P^R \wedge b, \text{false}, \text{false}, \text{true}, (G \vee I_\vartheta) \wedge E)}{\text{await } b \text{ do } z \text{ od } \underline{\text{sat}}\ (\vartheta)::(P, R, P^R \wedge \neg b, G, R^* \mid E \mid R^*)}$$

allows for synchronisation arguments. The statement can only become blocked in a state which does not satisfy the Boolean test b and can be reached from a state which satisfies the pre-condition P by a finite number of external transitions. This motivates the conclusion's wait-condition. The environment is constrained from interfering with the await-statement's body, which explains the choice of rely- and wait-conditions in the premise. Moreover, the await-statement's body is required to terminate for any state which satisfies $P^R \wedge b$. The rest should be obvious from the discussion above, since any computation of an await-statement has maximum of one internal transition which alters the global state.

5 Expressiveness

5.1 Motivation

It has been shown above, that interference can be dealt with by using rely- and guar-conditions, and that the introduction of a wait-condition allows for the design of programs whose correctness depends upon synchronisation. Unfortunately, many interesting developments are excluded because sufficiently strong intermediate assertions cannot be expressed. The object of this section is to show how the expressiveness can be increased by introducing auxiliary variables.

In [OG76] auxiliary variables are implemented as if they were ordinary programming variables, and then afterwards removed by a deduction rule specially designed for this purpose. This is not a very satisfactory method, because in some cases a large number of auxiliary variables are needed, and the procedure of first implementing them and then removing them is rather tedious. The approach in this paper is more in the style of [Sou84], where the auxiliary structure is only a part of the logic. Nevertheless, although it is possible to define history variables in LSP, auxiliary variables may be of any type, and it is up to the user to define the auxiliary structure he prefers. Auxiliary variables will be used for two different purposes:

- To strengthen a specification to eliminate undesirable implementations. In this case auxiliary variables are used as a *specification tool*; they are employed to characterise a program that has not yet been implemented.
- To strengthen a specification to make it possible to prove that a certain program satisfies a particular specification. Here auxiliary variables are used as a *verification tool*, since they are introduced to show that a given algorithm satisfies a specific property.

5.2 As a Specification Tool

An example, where auxiliary variables are used as a specification tool, will be discussed first. The task is to specify a program that adds a new element O to a global buffer called *buff*. If the environment is restricted from interfering with *buff*, then this can easily be expressed as follows:

$$(\{buff\})::(\text{true}, \text{false}, \text{false}, buff = [O] \frown \overleftarrow{buff}, buff = [O] \frown \overleftarrow{buff})$$

($[O]$ denotes a sequence consisting of one element O, while $\frown$ is the usual concatenation operator on finite sequences.) The pre-condition states that an implementation must be applicable in any state. Moreover, the rely-condition restricts the environment from changing the value of *buff*, thus the eff-condition may be used to express the desired property. Finally, the guar-condition specifies that the concatenation step takes place in isolation, while the falsity of the wait-condition requires the implementation to terminate.

If the environment is allowed to interfere freely with *buff*, the task of formulating a specification becomes more difficult. Observe that the actual concatenation step is still required to be atomic; the only difference from above is that the environment may interfere immediately before and (or) after the concatenation takes place. Since there are no restrictions on the way the environment can change *buff*, and because external transitions, both before the first internal transition and after the last, are included in the overall effect, the eff-condition must allow anything to happen. This means that the eff-condition is no longer of much use. Thus, the guar-condition is the only hope to pin down the intended behaviour. The specification

$$(\{buff\})::(\mathsf{true},\mathsf{true},\mathsf{false},buff=[O]\curvearrowright\overleftarrow{buff},\mathsf{true})$$

is almost sufficient. The only problem is that there is no restriction on the number of times the implementation is allowed to add O to *buff*. Hence, skip is for example one possible implementation.

One solution is to introduce a Boolean auxiliary variable called *dn*, and use *dn* as a flag to indicate whether the implementation has added O to *buff* or not. To distinguish the auxiliary variables from the global programming variables, it has been found helpful to add a new component to a specification: an *aux-set* which contains the auxiliary variables. The program can then be specified as follows:

$$(\{buff\},\{dn\})::(\neg dn,dn\Leftrightarrow\overleftarrow{dn},\mathsf{false},buff=[O]\curvearrowright\overleftarrow{buff}\wedge\neg\overleftarrow{dn}\wedge dn,dn)$$

Since the environment cannot change the value of *dn*, the implementation only can add O to *buff* in a state where *dn* is false, the concatenation transition changes *dn* from false to true, and the implementation is not allowed to change *dn* from true to false, it follows from the pre- and eff-conditions that the implementation adds O to *buff* once and only once.

5.3 As a Verification Tool

The next example shows how auxiliary variables can be used as a verification tool. Without auxiliary structure,

$$(\{x\})::(\mathsf{true},x>\overleftarrow{x},\mathsf{false},x=\overleftarrow{x}+1\vee x=\overleftarrow{x}+2,x\geq\overleftarrow{x}+3)$$

is the specification that gives the best possible characterisation of the program $x:=x+1;x:=x+2$, given the actual assumptions about the environment. Furthermore, this tuple is also the strongest possible specification for the program $x:=x+2;x:=x+1$ with respect to the same assumptions about the environment. Let z_1 denote the first program and z_2 the second. If the overall environment is constrained to leave x unchanged, it is clear that the parallel composition of z_1 and z_2 satisfies:

$$(\{x\})::(\mathsf{true},\mathsf{false},\mathsf{false},\mathsf{true},x=\overleftarrow{x}+6).$$

Unfortunately, there is no way to deduce this only from the information in the specification of the components, because the component specification is, for example also satisfied by $x:=x+2;x:=x+2$.

The solution again is to introduce auxiliary variables. Let y_1 be a variable that records the overall effect of the updates to x in z_1, while y_2 records the overall effect of the updates to x in z_2. Clearly, it is required that z_1 and z_2 cannot change the value of y_2 respectively y_1. The specification of z_1 can then be rewritten as

$$\begin{aligned}(\{x\},\{y_1,y_2\})::(&\mathsf{true},y_1=\overleftarrow{y_1}\wedge x-\overleftarrow{x}=y_2-\overleftarrow{y_2},\mathsf{false},\\&y_2=\overleftarrow{y_2}\wedge x-\overleftarrow{x}=y_1-\overleftarrow{y_1},x=\overleftarrow{x}+3+(y_2-\overleftarrow{y_2})\wedge y_1-\overleftarrow{y_1}=3),\end{aligned}$$

while z_2 fulfills

$$(\{x\},\{y_1,y_2\})::(\text{true}, y_2 = \overleftarrow{y_2} \wedge x - \overleftarrow{x} = y_1 - \overleftarrow{y_1}, \text{false},$$
$$y_1 = \overleftarrow{y_1} \wedge x - \overleftarrow{x} = y_2 - \overleftarrow{y_2}, x = \overleftarrow{x} + (y_1 - \overleftarrow{y_1}) + 3 \wedge y_2 - \overleftarrow{y_2} = 3).$$

It follows easily from these two specifications that the overall effect of $\{z_1 \parallel z_2\}$ is characterised by $x = \overleftarrow{x} + 6$, if the overall environment is restricted from changing x.

5.4 Specified Programs

A specified program is now of the form $(\vartheta, \alpha)::(P, R, W, G, E)$. It is required that $\vartheta \cap \alpha = \{\}$, and that the unhooked version of any free hooked or unhooked variable occurring in the assertions is an element of $\vartheta \cup \alpha$.

To characterise what it means for a program to satisfy such a specification, it is necessary to introduce a new relation $z_1 \overset{(\vartheta,\alpha)}{\hookrightarrow} z_2$, called an *augmentation*, which states that the program z_2 can be obtained from the program z_1 by adding auxiliary structure constrained by the set of global programming variables ϑ and the set of auxiliary variables α. There are of course a number of restrictions on the auxiliary structure. First of all, to make sure that the auxiliary structure has no influence on the algorithm, auxiliary variables are constrained from occurring in the Boolean tests of if-, while- and await-statements. Furthermore, they cannot appear on the right-hand side of an assignment, unless the corresponding variable on the left-hand side is auxiliary. Moreover, since it must be possible to remove some auxiliary variables from a specified program without having to remove all the auxiliary variables, it is important that they do not depend upon each other. This means that if an auxiliary variable occurs on the left-hand side of an assignment-statement, then this is the only auxiliary variable that may occur in the corresponding expression on the right-hand side. In other words, to eliminate all occurrences of an auxiliary variable from a program, it is enough to remove all assignments with this variable on the left-hand side. However, an assignment to an auxiliary variable may have any number of elements of ϑ in its right-hand side expression. Finally, since auxiliary variables will only be employed to record information about state changes and synchronisation, auxiliary variables are only updated in connection with await- and assignment-statements.

Given two lists a, u of respectively variables and expressions, and two sets of variables ϑ, α, then $a \leftarrow_{(\vartheta,\alpha)} u$ denotes that a and u are of the same length, that any element of a is an element of α, and that any variable occurring in u's j'th expression is either an element of ϑ or equal to a's j'th variable. An augmentation can then be defined in a more formal way:

Definition 8 *Given two programs z_1, z_2 and two sets of variables ϑ and α, then $z_1 \overset{(\vartheta,\alpha)}{\hookrightarrow} z_2$, iff z_2 can be obtained from z_1 by substituting*

- *a statement of the form*

  $$v \frown a := r \frown u,$$

  where $a \leftarrow_{(\vartheta,\alpha)} u$, for each occurrence of an assignment-statement $v := r$, which does not occur in the body of an await-statement,

- *a statement of the form*

  await b do z'; $a := u$ od,

  where $z \overset{(\vartheta,\alpha)}{\hookrightarrow} z'$ and $a \leftarrow_{(\vartheta,\alpha)} u$, for each occurrence of an await-statement await b do z od, *which does not occur in the body of another await-statement.*

($v \frown a$ denotes a prefixed by v — similarly for $r \frown u$.) It is now straightforward to extend definition 7 to the general case:

Definition 9 *A specified program z_1 $\underline{\text{sat}}$ $(\vartheta, \alpha)::(P,R,W,G,E)$ is valid iff there is a program z_2 such that $z_1 \overset{(\vartheta,\alpha)}{\hookrightarrow} z_2$ and $ext[\vartheta \cup \alpha, P, R] \cap cp[z_2] \subseteq int[\vartheta \cup \alpha, W, G, E]$.*

5.5 Deduction Rules

With two exceptions, the assignment- and the await-rules, the deduction rules given above can be updated in an obvious way. With respect to the *assignment*-rule

$$\frac{\overleftarrow{P^R} \wedge v = \overleftarrow{r} \wedge I_{\vartheta \setminus \langle v \rangle} \wedge a = \overleftarrow{u} \wedge I_{\alpha \setminus \langle a \rangle} \Rightarrow (G \vee I_{\vartheta \cup \alpha}) \wedge E}{v := r \ \underline{\text{sat}}\ (\vartheta, \alpha)::(P, R, \text{false}, G, R^* \mid E \mid R^*)} \qquad \text{where } a \leftarrow_{(\vartheta,\alpha)} u$$

remember that the execution of an assignment-statement $v := r$ actually corresponds to the execution of an assignment-statement of the form $v \frown a := r \frown u$. Thus, the only real difference from the above is that the premise must guarantee that the assignment-statement can be extended with auxiliary structure in such a way that the specified changes to both the auxiliary variables and the programming variables will indeed take place.

The *await*-rule

$$\frac{\begin{array}{l} E_1 \mid (I_\vartheta \wedge a = \overleftarrow{u} \wedge I_{\alpha \setminus \langle a \rangle}) \Rightarrow (G \vee I_{\vartheta \cup \alpha}) \wedge E_2 \\ z \ \underline{\text{sat}}\ (\vartheta, \alpha)::(P^R \wedge b, \text{false}, \text{false}, \text{true}, E_1) \end{array}}{\text{await } b \text{ do } z \text{ od } \underline{\text{sat}}\ (\vartheta, \alpha)::(P, R, P^R \wedge \neg b, G, R^* \mid E_2 \mid R^*)} \qquad \text{where } a \leftarrow_{(\vartheta,\alpha)} u$$

is closely related to the assignment-rule; there is only one state-changing internal transition, and auxiliary variables may be altered in the same atomic step. An extra premise is added to allow the auxiliary variables to be updated.

The *elimination*-rule

$$\frac{z \ \underline{\text{sat}}\ (\vartheta, \alpha)::(P, R, W, G, E)}{z \ \underline{\text{sat}}\ (\vartheta, \alpha \setminus \{x\})::(\exists x: P, \forall \overleftarrow{x}: \exists x: R, W, G, E)} \qquad \text{where } x \notin \vartheta$$

can be used to remove auxiliary structure from a specification. Remember, that due to the syntactic constraints on specifications it follows (from the fact that the conclusion is a specified program) that W, G and E have no occurrences of x.

6 Discussion

Some useful adaptation rules plus examples where LSP is used for the development of nontrivial algorithms can be found in [Stø90].

A soundness proof for LSP has been given in a rather informal way above. A more formal proof is included in [Stø90]. In [Stø90] it is also shown that LSP is relatively complete under the assumptions that structures are admissible, and that for any first order assertion A and structure π, it is always possible to express an assertion B in L, which is valid in π iff A is well-founded on the set of states in π.

Because the programming language is unfair, the system presented in this paper cannot deal with programs whose algorithms rely upon busy waiting. Thus LSP is incomplete with respect to a weakly fair language and even more so for a strongly fair programming language. However, this does not mean that fair languages cannot be dealt with in a similar style. In [Stø91] it is shown how LSP can be modified to handle both weakly fair and strongly fair programming languages. Only the while- and await-rules have to be changed.

The program constructs discussed in this paper are deterministic (although they all have a nondeterministic behaviour due to possible interference), and all functions have been required to be total. These constraints are not necessary. It is shown in [Stø90] that LSP can easily be extended to deal with both nondeterministic program constructs and partial functions.

This paper has only proposed a set of program-decomposition rules. How to formulate sufficiently strong data-refinement rules is still an open question. Jones [Jon81] proposed a refinement-rule for the rely/guarantee-method which can easily be extended to deal with LSP specifications. Unfortunately, as pointed out in [WD88], this refinement-rule is far from complete.

LSP can be thought of as a compositional reformulation of the Owicki/Gries method [OG76]. The rely-, guar- and wait-conditions have been introduced to avoid the final non-interference and freedom-from-deadlock proofs (their additional interference-freedom requirement for total correctness is not correct [AdBO90]). However, there are some additional differences. The programming language differs from theirs in several respects. First of all, variables occurring in the Boolean test of an if- or a while-statement are restricted from being accessed by the environment. In the Owicki/Gries language there is no such constraint. On the other hand, in their language await- and parallel-statements are constrained from occurring in the body of an await-statement. No such requirement is stated in this paper. The handling of auxiliary variables has also been changed. Auxiliary variables are only a part of the logic. Moreover, they can be employed both as a verification tool and as a specification tool, while in the Owicki/Gries method they can only be used as a verification tool.

Jones' system [Jon83] can be seen as a restricted version of LSP. There are two main differences. First of all, LSP has a wait-condition which makes it possible to deal with synchronisation. Secondly, because auxiliary variables may be employed both as specification and verification tools, LSP is more expressive.

Stirling's method [Sti88] employs a proof tuple closely related to that of Jones. The main difference is that the rely- and guar-conditions are represented as sets of invariants, while the post-condition is unary, not binary as in Jones' method. Auxiliary variables are implemented as if they were ordinary programming variables, and they cannot be used as a specification tool. Although this method favours top-down development in the style of Jones, it can only be employed for the design of partially correct programs.

Soundararajan [Sou84] uses CSP inspired history variables to state assumptions about the environment. Unfortunately, on many occasions, the use of history variables seems excessive. One advantage with LSP is therefore that the user is free to choose the auxiliary structure he prefers. Another difference is that LSP is not restricted to partial correctness.

Barringer, Kuiper and Pnueli [BKP84] employ temporal logic for the design of parallel programs. Their method can be used to develop nonterminating programs with respect to both safety and general liveness properties, and this formalism is therefore much more general than the one presented in this paper. However, although it is quite possible to employ the same temporal logic to develop totally correct sequential programs, most users would prefer to apply ordinary Hoare-logic in the style of for example VDM [Jon90]. The reason is that Hoare-logic is designed to deal with the sequential case only, and it is therefore both simpler to use and easier to understand than a formalism powerful enough to handle concurrency. A similar distinction can be made between the development of terminating programs versus programs that are not supposed to terminate and regarding different fairness constraints. LSP should be understood as a method specially designed for the development of totally correct shared-state parallel programs.

The Xu/He approach [XH91] is (as pointed out in their paper) inspired by LSP's tuple of five assertions. However, instead of a wait-condition they use a run-condition — the negation of LSP's wait. Another difference is their specification oriented semantics. Moreover, auxiliary variables are dealt with in the Owicki/Gries style. This means that auxiliary variables are implemented as if they were ordinary programming variables and cannot be used as a specification tool.

7 Acknowledgements

As mentioned above, this paper is based on the author's PhD-thesis, and I would first all like to thank my supervisor Cliff B. Jones for his help and support. I am also indebted to Xu Qiwen, Wojciech Penczek,

Howard Barringer and Mathai Joseph. Financial support has been received from the Norwegian Research Council for Science and the Humanities and the Wolfson Foundation.

References

[Acz83] P. Aczel. On an inference rule for parallel composition. Unpublished Paper, February 1983.

[AdBO90] K. R. Apt, F. S. de Boer, and E. R. Olderog. Proving termination of parallel programs. In W. H. J. Feijen, A. J. M. van Gasteren, D. Gries, and J. Misra, editors, *Beauty Is Our Business, A Birthday Salute to Edsger W. Dijkstra*. Springer-Verlag, 1990.

[BKP84] H. Barringer, R. Kuiper, and A. Pnueli. Now you may compose temporal logic specifications. In *Proc. Sixteenth ACM Symposium on Theory of Computing*, pages 51–63, 1984.

[FP78] N. Francez and A. Pnueli. A proof method for cyclic programs. *Acta Informatica*, 9:133–157, 1978.

[Jon81] C. B. Jones. *Development Methods for Computer Programs Including a Notion of Interference*. PhD thesis, Oxford University, 1981.

[Jon83] C. B. Jones. Specification and design of (parallel) programs. In Mason R.E.A., editor, *Proc. Information Processing 83*, pages 321–331, 1983.

[Jon90] C. B. Jones. *Systematic Software Development Using VDM, Second Edition*. Prentice-Hall International, 1990.

[OG76] S. Owicki and D. Gries. An axiomatic proof technique for parallel programs. *Acta Informatica*, 6:319–340, 1976.

[Sou84] N. Soundararajan. A proof technique for parallel programs. *Theoretical Computer Science*, 31:13–29, 1984.

[Sti88] C. Stirling. A generalization of Owicki-Gries's Hoare logic for a concurrent while language. *Theoretical Computer Science*, 58:347–359, 1988.

[Stø90] K. Stølen. *Development of Parallel Programs on Shared Data-Structures*. PhD thesis, University of Manchester, 1990.

[Stø91] K. Stølen. Proving total correctness with respect to fair (shared-state) parallel languages. In preparation, 1991.

[WD88] J. C. P. Woodcock and B. Dickinson. Using VDM with rely and guarantee-conditions. Experiences from a real project. In R. Bloomfield, L. Marshall, and R. Jones, editors, *Proc. 2nd VDM-Europe Symposium, Lecture Notes in Computer Science 328*, pages 434–458, 1988.

[XH91] Q. Xu and J. He. A theory of state-based parallel programming by refinement:part 1. In J. Morris, editor, *Proc. 4th BCS-FACS Refinement Workshop*, 1991.

REDUCED LABELLED TRANSITION SYSTEMS SAVE VERIFICATION EFFORT

Antti Valmari & Matthew Clegg
Technical Research Centre of Finland
Computer Technology Laboratory
PO Box 201
SF-90571 Oulu, FINLAND
Tel. +358 81 509 111

Abstract

A new method for reducing the amount of effort in the verification of Basic Lotos specifications is presented. The method is based on generating a reduced labelled transition system (RLTS) of the specification. The RLTS captures the semantics of the specification in the sense of the semantic theory of CSP but it is typically much smaller than the ordinary labelled transition system (LTS) of the specification. Thus it can replace the LTS in the verification of the equivalence (in CSP sense) of two specifications. The method is demonstrated with a bounded buffer example where an exponential saving of states is achieved.

1. INTRODUCTION

1.1 Motivation

The (interleaving) semantics of a system written in some process algebraic language can be represented by a structure known as *labelled transition system* (*LTS*, for brevity). Verification techniques have been developed that take advantage of LTSs. For instance, one can compare whether two systems are equivalent in some well defined sense by performing a suitable kind of comparison of their LTSs. Two well known notions of equivalence are *observation equivalence* [Milner 89] and equivalence in the sense of the semantic theory of CSP [Hoare 85]. Observation equivalence can be verified in polynomial time in the size of the LTSs [Bolognesi & 87b]. The best known algorithm for verifying CSP-equivalence is exponential in the worst case but, according to the developers of the *Concurrency Workbench* verification tool [Cleaveland & 90], the algorithm runs reasonably fast in practice.

Verification using LTSs seems thus practical. There is one big problem, however. The LTSs of systems are often huge, far too big to be generated and compared by current computers.

In this paper we address the problem caused by the size of the LTSs. We develop a method of generating *reduced labelled transition systems* (RLTS) such that they are CSP-equivalent with but typically much smaller than the corresponding ordinary LTSs. They can thus be used instead of ordinary LTSs when verifying CSP-equivalence of systems or when analysing any behavioural property represented by the CSP semantics. Our technique is complementary to those which take an existing LTS and produce an equivalent, smaller LTS. The RLTS is generated *directly* from a description of the system in a process algebraic language. The (big) ordinary LTS of the system need never be generated. This leads to savings both during the generation of the RLTS and in the verification afterwards.

CSP semantics was chosen because, inducing a weak equivalence, it leaves much room to reduce the LTS. The weaker the semantic model is, the larger are its equivalence classes, the smaller representatives they contain and the better reduction results are obtainable. CSP-equivalence is relatively weak although it retains enough information for the analysis of several important properties. It "appears to be the weakest equivalence which never equates a deadlocking agent with one which does not deadlock" [Milner 89 p. 206].

For the language to represent systems we have chosen Basic Lotos [Bolognesi & 87a]. It is a concurrency-oriented simplification of the ISO standard specification language Lotos.

In the remainder of this chapter we discuss related work and also point out what are the new results in this paper compared to earlier work (including our own). In Chapter 2 we define the concept of *stubborn set* which underlies our theory and investigate some of the properties of stubborn sets. The CSP semantics preserving stubborn set RLTS generation method is developed in Chapter 3. An implementation of the method requires a way of finding a stubborn set given the current state of the system. The definition in Chapter 2 is impractical as it refers to the set of all possible future states, but there is a collection of theorems producing stubborn sets given information about the current state only. It is presented in Chapter 4. Chapter 5 demonstrates the power of the stubborn set method with the "bounded buffer" example.

1.2 Related Work

There are so many techniques of reducing the amount of work during system verification that we cannot give a full account of them all. The methods are based on various principles. The aggregation of several "similar" system states into one data object is used at least in the *covering marking* techniques for Petri nets [Karp & 69] and a certain class of protocols [Vuong & 87], the *equivalent* [Jensen 87] and *parameterized marking* [Lindqvist 90] techniques of high-level Petri nets, *state schemas* [Valmari 89c] and, in the process algebra world, the *Lotos Laboratory* tool [Quemada & 90]. A somewhat orthogonal idea is to collapse "similar" processes into one as in the *indexed computation tree logic* [Clarke & 87]. The divide-and-conquer paradigm is applied to the temporal logic world in [Clarke & 89], to process algebras in [Graf & 90], [Valmari & 91b] and to Petri nets taking advantage of process algebraic ideas in [Valmari 90b].

Some methods are based on eliminating redundant interleavings of a set of concurrent events. The most obvious approach towards this goal is *coarsening the level of atomicity* as discussed in [Pnueli 86], for instance. A method which, in essence, coarsens atomicity in a hierarchical way is presented in [Overman 81]. The method in [Itoh & 83] poses strong restrictions on the underlying computational model due to which the order in which each process performs its next transition becomes insignificant. Therefore it is possible to limit the consideration to "global" transitions consisting of the simultaneous execution of one transition (which in some cases may be an idle "waiting" transition) by each process.

There are semantic theories of concurrency where executions serialised by interleaving are not considered fundamental but as representatives of a more abstract notion of execution. In this more abstract notion several events may occur simultaneously (cf. the above method [Itoh & 83]), or the order of concurrent events is not specified at all ("*true concurrency*" or *partial order* models). The *optimal simulations* [Janicki & 90] are in a certain sense representative, minimal collections of executions where several transitions may occur at the same time. Implementation principles of optimal simulations have been developed to a certain strongly restricted computational model called *state-machine decomposable* Petri nets. The implementability of the method in a wider context seems problematic. The "optimal simulations" build upon the *trace theory* of [Mazurkiewicz 87]. "Trace" here has a very different meaning from what it has in process algebras; Mazurkiewicz traces are the equivalence classes of event sequences induced by the reflexive transitive closure of transpositions of concurrent events.

Another method based on Mazurkiewicz traces is described in [Godefroid 90]. Godefroid's method picks an interleaving representative of each Mazurkiewicz trace. It is used for checking whether the language of one system is a subset of the language of another. The method performs remarkably well and can be implemented easily. However, it relies on somewhat strict assumptions about the behaviour of the latter system. More recent related work is reported in [Godefroid & 91].

The work in this paper is inspired by the *stubborn set* method of Valmari. It has been gradually developed in a series of papers [Valmari 88a, 88b, 88c, 89a, 89b, 90a, 91a]. The stubborn set method, too, is based on using representative interleaving execution sequences. However, the stubborn set method is not based on equivalence classes of execution sequences in the above sense. Unlike in Godefroid's method, if execution sequence σ can represent another execution sequence ρ then it is not necessarily the case that ρ can represent σ. The stubborn set method has proven to be free of many of the restrictions of the computational model which limit the applicability of the "optimal simulations" and Godefroid's 1990 method.

The stubborn set method was originally developed in the domain of Petri nets and later expanded to a more general variable/transition framework. There are different stubborn set methods for different purposes, including the detection of deadlocks and nontermination, verification of system invariants and verification of stuttering-free linear temporal logic formulas. Applying the stubborn set method to process algebraic languages proved non-trivial. It turned out that the original notion of stubborn sets was tightly coupled with the notion of *variables* and *transitions* as structural elements of a system, much like places and transitions of a Petri net. For instance, it was necessary to talk about the *same* transition in *different* states. Many models of concurrency including shared variable programs, communicating finite automata and Petri nets have natural notions of variables and transitions, but process algebraic languages do not. Therefore it was necessary to develop the notion of stubborn sets anew from scratch. The resulting theory in this paper is not directly comparable to the stubborn set theory of Petri nets; in some senses it is weaker and in some senses stronger.

The new results in this paper are twofold. First, this is the first time stubborn set theory has been applied to process algebraic languages. The second new contribution is the way of using stubborn sets to preserve CSP semantics of systems.

2. STUBBORN SET METHOD

We use *Basic Lotos* [Bolognesi & 87a] as the language for describing systems. In Basic Lotos, behaviour is specified by *behaviour expressions*. We allow the use of the renaming operator "$[h_1/g_1,\ldots,h_n/g_n]$" from [Bolognesi & 87a] in behaviour expressions, although it is not a Basic Lotos operator, because it is necessary for defining the semantics of process calls. Furthermore, in Basic Lotos the word "process" has a meaning as a modular unit, but we took the liberty to use it as a synonym of "behaviour expression". The set of behaviour expressions is denoted by $\mathcal{B}$. Behaviour expressions can participate user-defined *gate events*, the *invisible event i* and the *successful termination event* δ. Throughout this paper ε denotes the empty sequence, Σ_G is the set of gate names, $\Sigma_i = \Sigma_G \cup \{i\}$, $\Sigma_\delta = \Sigma_G \cup \{\delta\}$ and $\Sigma_A = \Sigma_G \cup \{i,\delta\}$, where the subscript "A" is read "all".

If P and Q belong to $\mathcal{B}$ we write $P = Q$ if the *action trees* [Bolognesi & 87a] they generate are isomorphic. Intuitively speaking, this implies that processes which are "obviously" the same can be identified, for instance P, $(P[a/b,b/a])[a/b,b/a]$ and $P[]$**stop**. We write $P -a_1a_2...a_n\rightarrow Q$ when there are $P_0, ..., P_n$ such that $P_0 -a_1\rightarrow P_1 -a_2\rightarrow ... -a_n\rightarrow P_n$ such that $P = P_0$ and $P_n = Q$. Let $P \in \mathcal{B}$ and $\sigma \in \Sigma_A^*$. We define:

- $P -\sigma\rightarrow \;\Leftrightarrow\; \exists Q \in \mathcal{B}: P -\sigma\rightarrow Q$
- $\mathcal{T}(P) = \{\, (P,a,Q) \in \{P\} \times \Sigma_A \times \mathcal{B} \mid P -a\rightarrow Q \,\}$ is the set of the *transitions* of P.
- $\varphi(P) = \{\, a \in \Sigma_A \mid \exists\, \sigma \in \Sigma_A^*: P -\sigma a\rightarrow \,\}$ is the set of *future events* of P.

Let $T \subseteq \mathcal{T}(P)$.

- $\alpha(T) = \{\, a \in \Sigma_A \mid \exists\, Q \in \mathcal{B}: (P,a,Q) \in T \,\}$ is the set of *events participated by T*.

A behaviour expression P_0 with the alphabet Σ_A specifies a structure (S,P_0,Σ_A,Δ) called a *labelled transition system* (*LTS*, for brevity) as follows:

- $S = \{\, P \in \mathcal{B} \mid \exists\, \sigma \in \Sigma_A^*: P_0 -\sigma\rightarrow P \,\}$
- $\Delta = \{\, (P,a,Q) \in S \times \Sigma_A \times S \mid P -a\rightarrow Q \,\}$

The (ordinary) LTS of P_0 can be constructed by exhaustive simulation starting at P_0. At every behaviour expression P reached during the process, all the transitions in $\mathcal{T}(P)$ are investigated in order to generate the immediate successors of P. The construction of a reduced LTS of P_0 is almost similar. The only difference is that instead of $\mathcal{T}(P)$ as a whole, only a subset of $\mathcal{T}(P)$ is used when generating the immediate successors of P.

In the following we give an abstract definition of stubborn sets and investigate some of its consequences. In Chapter 4 we give a more practical, structural characterization facilitating the computation of stubborn sets.

Definition 2.1 Let $P -\sigma\rightarrow Q$, $a \in \Sigma_A$ and $P' \in \mathcal{B}$.

- (P,a,P') *can move to the front* in $P -\sigma\rightarrow Q$, iff
  $$\exists\, \sigma_1, \sigma_2: \sigma = \sigma_1 a \sigma_2 \wedge P -a\rightarrow P' -\sigma_1\sigma_2\rightarrow Q$$
- (P,a,P') *can bypass* $P -\sigma\rightarrow Q$, iff
  $$\exists\, Q': P -\sigma\rightarrow Q -a\rightarrow Q' \wedge P -a\rightarrow P' -\sigma\rightarrow Q' \;\Box$$

"Can move to the front" and "can bypass" can be illustrated as follows:

$$\begin{array}{lcl} P & -\sigma_1 a \sigma_2\rightarrow & Q \\ | & & \\ a & & \\ \downarrow & & \\ P' & -\sigma_1\sigma_2\rightarrow & Q \end{array}$$

$$\begin{array}{lcl} P & -\sigma\rightarrow & Q \\ | & & | \\ a & & a \\ \downarrow & & \downarrow \\ P' & -\sigma\rightarrow & Q' \end{array}$$

Definition 2.2 Let P be a behaviour expression and $T_P \subseteq \mathcal{T}(P)$. T_P is *stubborn* at P if and only if for every $\sigma \in \Sigma_A^*$ and $Q \in \mathcal{B}$:

$$P -\sigma\rightarrow Q \;\Rightarrow\; \exists\, (P,a,P') \in T_P: (1) \vee (2), \text{ where}$$

(1) (P,a,P') can move to the front in $P -\sigma\rightarrow Q$

(2) (P,a,P') can bypass $P -\sigma\rightarrow Q$. □

Proposition 2.3

- If T_P is stubborn at P then $T_P \neq \emptyset$.
- If $\mathcal{T}(P) \neq \emptyset$ then $\mathcal{T}(P)$ is stubborn at P.

Proof The first of the claims is seen correct by letting $\sigma = \varepsilon$ and $Q = P$ in Definition 2.2. Regarding the second claim, if $\sigma = \varepsilon$ then $\mathcal{T}(P) \neq \emptyset$ guarantees that Case (2) of Definition 2.2 applies, otherwise Case (1) applies with $\sigma_1 = \varepsilon$. □

According to Proposition 2.3 there is a stubborn set at P if and only if $\mathcal{T}(P) \neq \emptyset$. Therefore the following definition is sound:

Definition 2.4

- Let $\mathcal{TS}$ be a function which, given a behaviour expression P, produces a set of transitions $\mathcal{TS}(P) \subseteq \mathcal{T}(P)$ such that $\mathcal{TS}(P)$ is stubborn if $\mathcal{T}(P) \neq \emptyset$. $\mathcal{TS}$ is called a *stubborn set generator.*
- Let a stubborn set generator $\mathcal{TS}$ be given. We associate to each process P a new process $stub(P)$, whose behaviour is defined by the following transition rule:
$$(P,a,Q) \in \mathcal{TS}(P) \Leftrightarrow stub(P) -a\rightarrow stub(Q).$$
- The *reduced labelled transition system* (RLTS) of the behaviour expression P_0 generated by $\mathcal{TS}$ is the labelled transition system of $stub(P_0)$. □

The fact that $\mathcal{TS}(P) \subseteq \mathcal{T}(P)$ implies the following:

Proposition 2.5 If $stub(P) -\sigma\rightarrow stub(Q)$ then $P -\sigma\rightarrow Q$. □

A behaviour expression P is called a *deadlock* if $\mathcal{T}(P) = \emptyset$. The following theorem implies that every RLTS of P_0 contains all the deadlocks reachable from P_0.

Theorem 2.6 Let P and Q be behaviour expressions and $\sigma \in \Sigma_A{}^*$ such that $P -\sigma\rightarrow Q$ and $\mathcal{T}(Q) = \emptyset$. Let T_P be stubborn at P.

$$\exists\, (P,a,P') \in T_P: \exists\, \sigma' \in \Sigma_A{}^*: |\sigma'| = |\sigma| - 1 \wedge P -a\rightarrow P' -\sigma'\rightarrow Q$$

Furthermore, $a\sigma'$ is a permutation of σ.

Proof Case (2) of Definition 1 does not apply to $P -\sigma\rightarrow Q$, because $\mathcal{T}(Q) = \emptyset$. Thus case (1) gives immediately the claim. □

Corollary 2.7 If $P_0 -\sigma\rightarrow P$ and $\mathcal{T}(P) = \emptyset$, then there is σ' a permutation of σ such that $stub(P_0) -\sigma'\rightarrow stub(P)$.

Proof Apply Theorem 2.6 $|\sigma|$ times starting at P_0 and using $\mathcal{TS}(P)$ as T_P. □

Because $\mathcal{TS}(P) = \emptyset \Leftrightarrow \mathcal{T}(P) = \emptyset$ the deadlocks can be recognized from the RLTS in the ordinary way as vertices without outgoing edges.

3. PRESERVING CSP SEMANTICS

In [Hoare 85] the *Communicating Sequential Processes* (*CSP*) language for representing concurrency is described. CSP has a denotational semantics defining processes as triples consisting of an *alphabet*, a set of *failures* and a set of *divergences*. A corresponding operational semantics for CSP has been given in [Olderog & 86]. In this chapter we recall it and then show how the stubborn set method can be used to generate a RLTS which is equivalent with the corresponding ordinary LTS in the sense of the CSP semantics.

The intention of the event i is that it is an invisible event which cannot be directly observed. Let vis: $\Sigma_A^* \to \Sigma_\delta^*$ be the function which returns its argument with all i-symbols removed. That is, if σ is a sequence of events, $vis(\sigma)$ is the corresponding sequence of observable events. Let $\rho \in \Sigma_\delta^*$. We write $P =\rho\Rightarrow Q$ iff there is $\sigma \in \Sigma_A^*$ such that $P -\sigma\rightarrow Q$ and $\rho = vis(\sigma)$. $P =\rho\Rightarrow$ denotes that there is Q such that $P =\rho\Rightarrow Q$. Analogously to Proposition 2.5 we have $stub(P) =\rho\Rightarrow stub(Q) \Rightarrow P =\rho\Rightarrow Q$.

A *stable failure* of P is a pair (ρ, A) where $\rho \in \Sigma_\delta^*$ and $A \subseteq \Sigma_\delta$ provided that $\exists\, Q$: $P =\rho\Rightarrow Q$ and $\forall\, a \in A \cup \{i\}$: $\neg(Q -a\rightarrow)$. $\rho \in \Sigma_\delta^*$ is a *LTS-divergence* of P iff there is Q such that $P =\rho\Rightarrow Q$ and for every $n \geq 0$, $Q -i^n\rightarrow$. A *minimal divergence* is a LTS-divergence such that none of its proper prefixes is a LTS-divergence. The sets of stable failures, LTS-divergences and minimal divergences of P are denoted by $sfail(P)$, $LTSdiv(P)$ and $mindiv(P)$, respectively.

In the theory of CSP, divergence is considered catastrophic. That is, no information about the behaviour of a process can be obtained after it has diverged for the first time. A process that has diverged is interpreted as capable of doing anything and refusing anything. This point of view is reflected in the following definition:

Definition 3.1 The *CSP semantics* of a process P is the triple $(\Sigma_\delta, CSPfail(P), CSPdiv(P))$, where

- $CSPdiv(P) = \{\, \rho_1\rho_2 \in \Sigma_\delta^* \mid \rho_1 \in LTSdiv(P) \,\}$
- $CSPfail(P) = \{\, (\rho, A) \in \Sigma_\delta^* \times 2^{\Sigma_\delta} \mid \rho \in CSPdiv(P) \vee (\rho, A) \in sfail(P) \,\}$ □

The next theorem shows that if $\mathcal{TS}$ satisfies certain properties, $stub(P)$ is equivalent with P according to CSP semantics, that is, $CSPfail(stub(P)) = CSPfail(P)$ and $CSPdiv(stub(P)) = CSPdiv(P)$. The practical implication of this result is that it is possible to generate a RLTS of P which is as "good" as the LTS of P as far as CSP semantics is concerned. As the RLTS is often smaller than the LTS and can be generated with less effort, this leads to savings of verification effort. Before giving the theorem we define the notion of *covering* a set of events by a set of transitions.

Definition 3.2 Let $T \subseteq \mathcal{T}(P)$ and $A \subseteq \Sigma_A$. *T covers A* at P iff for every $a \in A$, $\sigma \in \Sigma_A^*$ and $Q \in \mathcal{B}$:

$$P -\sigma a\rightarrow Q \;\Rightarrow\; \exists\, (P,b,P') \in T\text{: } (P,b,P') \text{ can move to the front in } P -\sigma a\rightarrow Q. \;\square$$

Obviously $\mathcal{T}(P)$ covers any $A \subseteq \Sigma_A$ at P. Furthermore, if T covers A at P, $a \in A$ and $P -a\rightarrow Q$, then $(P,a,Q) \in T$. If T covers A at P and $B \subseteq A$ then T covers B at P.

Theorem 3.3 Let P_0 be a behaviour expression, $\mathcal{TS}$ a stubborn set generator and $stub$ the corresponding process operator. If $\mathcal{TS}$ satisfies the following three conditions for all P such that $stub(P_0) -\sigma\rightarrow stub(P)$ for some σ, then the CSP semantics of $stub(P_0)$ are the same as the CSP semantics of P_0.

(1) $\mathcal{TS}(P)$ is finite

(2) $\alpha(\mathcal{TS}(P)) \subseteq \{i\}$ or $\mathcal{TS}(P)$ covers Σ_δ at P

(3) If $P -i^n\rightarrow Q$ where $n > 0$, then $\exists\, (P,i,P') \in \mathcal{TS}(P)$: (P,i,P') can move to the front in $P -i^n\rightarrow Q$ or (P,i,P') can bypass $P -i^n\rightarrow Q$.

Proof We prove first that $CSPdiv(stub(P)) = CSPdiv(P)$. Proposition 2.5 and the definition of LTS-divergences give immediately $LTSdiv(stub(P)) \subseteq LTSdiv(P)$. By Definition 3.1 it is now sufficient to show $mindiv(P) \subseteq LTSdiv(stub(P))$ to obtain the claim.

Assume $\rho \in mindiv(P)$. By the definition of LTS-divergences there are $\sigma_1, \sigma_2, \ldots$ such that $P -\sigma_n\rightarrow$, $|\sigma_n| \geq n$ and $vis(\sigma_n) = \rho$ for every $n > 0$. Assume for the moment that $\neg(\ \alpha(\mathcal{TS}(P)) \subseteq \{i\}\ )$ and σ_{n+1} is of the form $a_n\pi_n$ where $a_n \neq i$ and $\pi_n \in \Sigma_A{}^*$. There is P_n such that $P -a_n\rightarrow P_n -\pi_n\rightarrow$. By assumption (2) of the theorem $\mathcal{TS}(P)$ covers Σ_δ at P, thus $(P,a_n,P_n) \in \mathcal{TS}(P)$. Assume now that $\alpha(\mathcal{TS}(P)) \subseteq \{i\}$ or σ_{n+1} is of the form $i\sigma'_{n+1}$. By assumption (3) and the fact that $\mathcal{TS}(P)$ is stubborn there is P_n such that $(P,i,P_n) \in \mathcal{TS}(P)$ and (P,i,P_n) can move to the front in or bypass $P -\sigma_{n+1}\rightarrow Q_{n+1}$. Therefore, there is π_n such that $P -i\rightarrow P_n -\pi_n\rightarrow$ and $vis(\pi_n) = vis(\sigma_{n+1}) = \rho$.

We have demonstrated the existence of a_n, P_n and π_n such that $stub(P) -a_n\rightarrow stub(P_n)$, $P_n -\pi_n\rightarrow$, $vis(a_n\pi_n) = \rho$ and $|\pi_n| \geq |\sigma_{n+1}| - 1 \geq n$. Because $\mathcal{TS}(P)$ is finite there are a' and P' such that $a_n = a'$, $P_n = P'$ and consequently $P' -\pi_n\rightarrow$ for an infinite number of different values of n. We conclude that there are P', a' and $\sigma'_1, \sigma'_2, \ldots$ such that $stub(P) -a'\rightarrow stub(P')$, $P' -\sigma'_n\rightarrow$, $|\sigma'_n| \geq n$ and $vis(a'\sigma'_n) = \rho$ for every $n > 0$. Applying the same argument at P' yields P'', a'' and $\sigma''_1, \sigma''_2, \ldots$ such that $stub(P) -a'a''\rightarrow stub(P'')$, $P'' -\sigma''_n\rightarrow$, $|\sigma''_n| \geq n$ and $vis(a'a''\sigma''_n) = \rho$ for every $n > 0$. By induction, $stub(P) -a'a''\ldots\rightarrow$ where $a'a''\ldots$ is an infinite sequence such that $vis(a'a''\ldots)$ is some prefix of ρ. Since $\rho \in mindiv(P)$ it must be the case that $\rho = vis(a'a''\ldots) \in LTSdiv(stub(P))$. This completes the proof of $CSPdiv(stub(P)) = CSPdiv(P)$.

We now tackle $CSPfail(stub(P)) = CSPfail(P)$. By assumption (3) and Proposition 2.5 $P -i\rightarrow \Leftrightarrow stub(P) -i\rightarrow$. If $\neg(\ P -i\rightarrow\ )$ then $\alpha(\mathcal{TS}(P)) = \alpha(\mathcal{T}(P))$ by assumption (2), Proposition 2.5 and the fact that $\mathcal{TS}(P) \neq \emptyset$ iff $\mathcal{T}(P) \neq \emptyset$. Assume $(\sigma,A) \in sfail(stub(P))$. There is $stub(Q)$ such that $stub(P) =\sigma\Rightarrow stub(Q)$ and $\neg(\ stub(Q) -a\rightarrow\ )$ if $a \in A \cup \{i\}$. By Proposition 2.5 $P =\sigma\Rightarrow Q$. Because $\neg(\ stub(Q) -i\rightarrow\ )$ we conclude $\alpha(\mathcal{TS}(Q)) = \alpha(\mathcal{T}(Q))$, thus $(\sigma,A) \in sfail(P)$. As a result $sfail(stub(P)) \subseteq sfail(P)$. We prove next that $sfail(P) \subseteq sfail(stub(P))$. The claim then follows by Definition 3.1 and the fact that $CSPdiv(stub(P)) = CSPdiv(P)$.

Let $(\rho,A) \in sfail(P)$. There are σ and Q such that $vis(\sigma) = \rho$, $P -\sigma\rightarrow Q$ and $\neg(\ Q -a\rightarrow\ )$ if $a \in A \cup \{i\}$. Assume $\sigma \neq \varepsilon$. If (case 1) $\alpha(\mathcal{TS}(P)) \subseteq \{i\}$ or $\sigma = i^n$ for some n then by assumption (3) there is P' such that $(P,i,P') \in \mathcal{TS}(P)$ and (P,i,P') can move to the front in $P -\sigma\rightarrow Q$, because (P,i,P') cannot bypass $P -\sigma\rightarrow Q$ since $\neg(\ Q -i\rightarrow\ )$. If, on the other hand, (case 2) $\neg(\ \alpha(\mathcal{TS}(P)) \subseteq \{i\}\ )$ and σ is of the form $i^n a\sigma'$ where $a \neq i$, then there is P_a such that $P -i^n a\rightarrow P_a -\sigma'\rightarrow Q$. By assumption (2) $\mathcal{TS}(P)$ covers Σ_δ at P, therefore there is $(P,b,P') \in \mathcal{TS}(P)$ such that $b \in \{a,i\}$ and (P,b,P') can move to the front in $P -i^n a\rightarrow P_a$. In both cases 1 and 2 there are b, P' and σ_1 such that $stub(P) -b\rightarrow stub(P')$, $P' -\sigma_1\rightarrow Q$, $b\sigma_1$ is a permutation of σ and $vis(b\sigma_1) = vis(\sigma) = \rho$. Repeating the argument at P' and so on a total of $|\sigma|$ times demonstrates the existence of π such that $stub(P) -\pi\rightarrow stub(Q)$ and $vis(\pi) = vis(\sigma)$. Because $\alpha(\mathcal{TS}(Q)) = \alpha(\mathcal{T}(Q))$ we get $sfail(P) \subseteq sfail(stub(P))$. □

Note that $\mathcal{T}(P)$ satisfies the assumptions of Theorem 3.3 provided that it is finite. Thus in the case of finite branching systems a stubborn set required by Theorem 3.3 can always be found.

4. STUBBORN SETS OF BASIC LOTOS EXPRESSIONS

In this chapter we develop a structural way of finding (some) stubborn sets of Basic Lotos behaviour expressions. By "structural" we mean that the sets can be computed based on the current behaviour expression only, without knowledge of the future behaviour of the system. We will build the stubborn sets recursively in the structure of the behaviour expressions. To meet the requirements of Theorem 3.3 we construct two sets of events simultaneously with the stubborn sets, namely a set of events covered by the stubborn set in the sense of Definition 3.2, and a *bypass* set of the stubborn set. The notion of bypass sets will prove useful in ensuring condition (3) of Theorem 3.3. It is defined next.

Definition 4.1 Let P be a behaviour expression, $T \subseteq \mathcal{T}(P)$ and $B \subseteq \Sigma_A$. B is a *bypass set* of T at P, if and only if for every $\sigma \in \Sigma_A^*$ and $Q \in \mathcal{B}$ such that $P -\sigma\rightarrow Q$: (1) or (2), where

(1) $\exists (P,a,P') \in T$: (P,a,P') can move to the front in $P -\sigma\rightarrow Q$

(2) $\forall b \in B$: $\exists (P,b,P') \in T$: (P,b,P') can bypass $P -\sigma\rightarrow Q$. □

Definition 4.1 resembles Definition 2.2. The difference is that if no transition in T can move to the front in $P -\sigma\rightarrow Q$, then T must contain *for every element in B* a transition which can bypass $P -\sigma\rightarrow Q$. As a result, if T has a non-empty bypass set at P then T is stubborn at P, but, on the other hand, $\emptyset$ is a bypass set of every $T \subseteq \mathcal{T}(P)$ at P. Condition (3) of Theorem 3.3 is satisfied if $\mathcal{TS}(P)$ has a bypass set containing i whenever $P -i\rightarrow$.

We say that $T \subseteq \mathcal{T}(P)$ is *semistubborn* at P if and only if it is empty or stubborn at P. As the basis of our recursive approach of constructing stubborn sets we consider the cases of $\emptyset$ and $\mathcal{T}(P)$. By Proposition 2.3 $\mathcal{T}(P)$ is semistubborn at every $P \in \mathcal{B}$.

Proposition 4.2 Let P be a behaviour expression.

- $\mathcal{T}(P)$ covers Σ_A at P.
- $\alpha(\mathcal{T}(P))$ is a bypass set of $\mathcal{T}(P)$ at P.
- $\emptyset$ covers $\Sigma_A - \varphi(P)$ at P.
- $\emptyset$ is a bypass set of $\emptyset$ at P.

Proof The first claim follows from the fact that the first transition of every non-empty execution starting at P is in $\mathcal{T}(P)$. The second claim is vacuously true except when $\sigma = \varepsilon$, in which case any transition in $\mathcal{T}(P)$ can bypass σ. The third claim holds because no execution of P contains an event occurrence from $\Sigma_A - \varphi(P)$. When $B = \emptyset$ part (2) of Definition 4.1 and, consequently, the whole definition is trivially true, giving the last claim. □

The recursive step uses the parallel, hiding, renaming and choice operators of Basic Lotos. We re-define the operators below in order to be able to apply them to sets of transitions instead of processes. The new definitions conform to the standard definitions in the sense that $\mathcal{T}(P)$ $|[g_1,\ldots,g_n]|$ $\mathcal{T}(Q) = \mathcal{T}(P\ |[g_1,\ldots,g_n]|\ Q)$, **hide** $g_1,\ldots,g_n$ **in** $\mathcal{T}(P) = \mathcal{T}($**hide** $g_1,\ldots,g_n$ **in** $P)$, $\mathcal{T}(P)[h_1/g_1,\ldots,h_n/g_n] = \mathcal{T}(P[h_1/g_1,\ldots,h_n/g_n])$ and $\mathcal{T}(P)$ [] $\mathcal{T}(Q) = \mathcal{T}(P$ [] $Q)$, as can be easily verified.

Definition 4.3 Let $T_P \subseteq \mathcal{T}(P)$ and $T_Q \subseteq \mathcal{T}(Q)$. We use **hide** P and $P\Phi$ as abbreviations of **hide** $g_1,\ldots,g_n$ **in** P and $P[h_1/g_1,\ldots,h_n/g_n]$. **hide** a for $a \in \Sigma_A$ is defined by **hide** $a = i$ if $a \in \{g_1,\ldots,g_n\}$ and **hide** $a = a$ otherwise. Similarly, $a\Phi = h_i$ if $a = g_i \in \{g_1,\ldots,g_n\}$, and $a\Phi = a$ if $a \in \Sigma_A - \{g_1,\ldots,g_n\}$. We define

- $T_P\ |[g_1,\ldots,g_n]|\ T_Q = \{\ (P\ |[g_1,\ldots,g_n]|\ Q,\ a,\ P'\ |[g_1,\ldots,g_n]|\ Q')\ |$
  $(P,a,P') \in T_P \wedge Q = Q' \wedge a \notin \{\delta,g_1,\ldots,g_n\}\ \vee$
  $(Q,a,Q') \in T_Q \wedge P = P' \wedge a \notin \{\delta,g_1,\ldots,g_n\}\ \vee$
  $(P,a,P') \in T_P \wedge (Q,a,Q') \in T_Q \wedge a \in \{\delta,g_1,\ldots,g_n\}\ \}$
- **hide** $g_1,\ldots,g_n$ **in** $T_P = \{\ ($**hide** P, **hide** a, **hide** $P')\ |\ (P,a,P') \in T_P\ \}$
- $T_P[h_1/g_1,\ldots,h_n/g_n] = \{\ (P\Phi,\ a\Phi,\ P'\Phi)\ |\ (P,a,P') \in T_P\ \}$
- T_P [] $T_Q = \{\ (P$ [] $Q,\ a,\ R)\ |\ (P,a,R) \in T_P \vee (Q,a,R) \in T_Q\ \}$. □

We are now ready to give theorems showing how to construct a semistubborn set of a parallel, hiding, renaming or choice expression given suitable semistubborn sets of its components. To obtain a stubborn set it is sufficient to construct a non-empty semistubborn set. The proofs of the theorems are omitted due to their length.

Theorem 4.4 Let T_P and T_Q be semistubborn at the behaviour expressions P and Q. Assume that T_P covers A_P and B_P is a bypass set of T_P at P, and similarly with T_Q, A_Q and B_Q at Q. Let $G_\delta = \{\delta, g_1, \ldots, g_n\}$ and $B_R = (B_P - G_\delta) \cup (B_Q - G_\delta) \cup (B_P \cap B_Q \cap G_\delta)$.

If $\alpha(T_P) \cap G_\delta \subseteq A_Q$, $\alpha(T_Q) \cap G_\delta \subseteq A_P$ and $B_R \neq \emptyset$, then $T_P \,|[g_1,\ldots,g_n]|\, T_Q$ is stubborn at $P \,|[g_1,\ldots,g_n]|\, Q$, covers $A_P \cap A_Q$ and has B_R as a bypass set. □

Theorem 4.5 Let **hide** and Φ be as in Definition 4.3. Let T_P be semistubborn at P. Assume that T_P covers A_P and B_P is a bypass set of T_P at P, and similarly with T_Q, A_Q and B_Q at Q. Let $G = \{g_1, \ldots, g_n\}$.

- $T_P \,[]\, T_Q$ is semistubborn at $P \,[]\, Q$, covers $A_P \cap A_Q$ and has $B_P \cap B_Q$ as a bypass set.
- **hide** $g_1, \ldots, g_n$ **in** T_P is semistubborn at **hide** P and covers $A_P \cup G - X$, where $X = \{i\}$ if $G - A_P \neq \emptyset$, and otherwise $X = \emptyset$. $\{$ **hide** $b \mid b \in B_P \}$ is a bypass set of **hide** T_P at **hide** P.
- $T_P\Phi$ is semistubborn at $P\Phi$, covers $A_P \cup G - \{ a\Phi \mid a \in G - A_P \}$ and has $\{ b\Phi \mid b \in B_P \}$ as a bypass set. □

Theorems 4.4 and 4.5 render it possible to construct a stubborn set of a behaviour expression R recursively assuming, of course, that R has at least one transition. R is first seen as being of the form $R = f(R_1, \ldots, R_n)$, where R_1 to R_n are behaviour expressions and f is a function composed of only the operators "|[...]|", "**hide**" and "Φ". Every behaviour expression is of this form because the identity function can be chosen as f; however, to obtain good LTS reduction results f should contain as many parallel operators as possible. By Proposition 4.2, we can choose $T_{R_i} = \mathcal{T}(R_i)$ as the semistubborn sets at R_i with covered sets $A_i = \Sigma_A$ and bypass sets $B_i = \alpha(\mathcal{T}(R_i))$. We do not allow the operator "[]" in f because then we can always choose $B_P = \alpha(T_P)$ for a stubborn set T_P produced using Theorems 4.4 and 4.5. The stubborn set we construct will correspond to a non-empty subset of $\{1, \ldots, n\}$.

Assume that we have found a stubborn set T_P of P, where P is some subexpression of $f(R_1, \ldots, R_n)$, together with a covered set A_P. At the lowest level $P = R_i$, $T_P = \mathcal{T}(R_i)$ and $A_P = \Sigma_A$ for some $1 \leq i \leq n$. Using Theorems 4.4 and 4.5 we can try to "elevate" T_P and A_P through the structure of f to obtain a stubborn set of R. The operators "**hide**" and "Φ" cause no problems. The parallel operator "$|[g_1,\ldots,g_n]|$" is more difficult because of the intricate conditions in Theorem 4.4. However, it is exactly the parallel operator which enables us to find stubborn sets which are smaller than the set of all transitions. Namely, $T_P \,|[g_1,\ldots,g_n]|\, T_Q$ is sometimes stubborn even if one of T_P and T_Q is $\emptyset$. We consider $T_P \,|[g_1,\ldots,g_n]|\, \emptyset$; the other case is symmetric. By Proposition 4.2 we can choose $A_Q = \Sigma_A - \varphi(Q)$ and $B_Q = \emptyset$. Theorem 4.4 implies now the following:

Corollary 4.6 Let $G_\delta = \{\delta, g_1, \ldots, g_n\}$. Assume that T_P is stubborn, covers A_P and has B_P as a bypass set at P. Assume further that $B_P - G_\delta \neq \emptyset$ and $\alpha(T_P) \cap G_\delta \cap \varphi(Q) = \emptyset$ i.e. T_P does not contain synchronising transitions among the future events of Q. Then $T_P \,|[g_1,\ldots,g_n]|\, \emptyset$ is stubborn at $P \,|[g_1,\ldots,g_n]|\, Q$, covers $A_P - \varphi(Q)$ and has $B_P - G_\delta$ as a bypass set. □

If T_P contains a synchronising transition whose label is in the future event set of Q then Corollary 4.6 cannot be applied. Then we try to find a stubborn set of Q or another stubborn set of P such that Corollary 4.6 can be applied. If this fails the only possibility is to find both a stubborn set of P and a stubborn set of Q such that Theorem 4.4 can be applied. This backtracking procedure produces stubborn sets of R in exponential time in the worst case.

The above procedure uses the future event sets $\varphi(P)$ of processes. Exact values of $\varphi(P)$ are often very difficult to compute, but an upper approximation is sufficient. Section 2.7 of [Milner 89] describes a natural way of approximating $\varphi(P)$ from above.

These ideas can be developed further to obtain a linear stubborn set construction algorithm. The algorithm is based on recording information of dependencies of the form "if P_i participates the stubborn set I am constructing, then due to the synchronization structure and the requirements by Theorem 4.4 it is necessary to include at least one of $P_{j1}, \ldots, P_{jk}$ to the set, where $j_1, \ldots, j_k \in \{1,\ldots,n\}$". If we arbitrarily fix the choice between $P_{j1}, \ldots, P_{jk}$, then the dependencies span a directed graph, and the problem of finding stubborn sets reduces to the problem of searching suitable strong components in the graph. Strong components can be found in linear time, and the choice of a suitable collection of them such that the assumptions of Theorem 3.3 are satisfied is a fast operation. The details go beyond the scope of this paper.

5. AN EXAMPLE: BOUNDED BUFFER

As an example of the use of the CSP semantics preserving stubborn set method we consider a Basic Lotos model of a bounded buffer. The buffer consists of n cells, each of which is capable of storing one message drawn from a set of k different messages. A cell may also be empty. The cells are arranged into a queue. A message enters the queue from the input end, propagates through the queue and finally exits at the output end. A message can move to the next cell in the queue provided that it is empty. Message propagation is not externally observable, but the input and output events are.

A Basic Lotos description of one cell is (subscripts are used for the benefit of the reader):

process $\mathrm{Buff}_1\ [\mathrm{in}_1,\mathrm{in}_2,\ldots\mathrm{in}_k,\mathrm{out}_1,\mathrm{out}_2,\ldots,\mathrm{out}_k]$:=
(* One cell *)
    $\mathrm{in}_1;\ \mathrm{out}_1;\ \mathrm{Buff}_1\ [\mathrm{in}_1,\mathrm{in}_2,\ldots\mathrm{in}_k,\mathrm{out}_1,\mathrm{out}_2,\ldots,\mathrm{out}_k]$
[] $\mathrm{in}_2;\ \mathrm{out}_2;\ \mathrm{Buff}_1\ [\mathrm{in}_1,\mathrm{in}_2,\ldots\mathrm{in}_k,\mathrm{out}_1,\mathrm{out}_2,\ldots,\mathrm{out}_k]$
... ...
[] $\mathrm{in}_k;\ \mathrm{out}_k;\ \mathrm{Buff}_1\ [\mathrm{in}_1,\mathrm{in}_2,\ldots\mathrm{in}_k,\mathrm{out}_1,\mathrm{out}_2,\ldots,\mathrm{out}_k]$
endproc

A buffer of n cells is as below (in Basic Lotos, using this approach, each of $\mathrm{Buff}_2, \ldots, \mathrm{Buff}_n$ should be shown in full, but for the sake of clarity we use recursion on n):

process $\mathrm{Buff}_n\ [\mathrm{in}_1,\mathrm{in}_2,\ldots\mathrm{in}_k,\mathrm{out}_1,\mathrm{out}_2,\ldots,\mathrm{out}_k]$:=
(* n cells, $n > 1$ *)
  hide $\mathrm{mid}_1,\mathrm{mid}_2,\ldots,\mathrm{mid}_k$ **in**
      $\mathrm{Buff}_1\ [\mathrm{in}_1,\mathrm{in}_2,\ldots\mathrm{in}_k,\mathrm{mid}_1,\mathrm{mid}_2,\ldots,\mathrm{mid}_k]$
    $|[\mathrm{mid}_1,\mathrm{mid}_2,\ldots,\mathrm{mid}_k]|$
      $\mathrm{Buff}_{n-1}\ [\mathrm{mid}_1,\mathrm{mid}_2,\ldots,\mathrm{mid}_k,\mathrm{out}_1,\mathrm{out}_2,\ldots,\mathrm{out}_k]$
endproc

We now investigate the behaviour of Buff_n. We abbreviate the parameter lists of processes for the sake of clarity. For instance, Buff_1 [in,mid] denotes $\mathrm{Buff}_1\ [\mathrm{in}_1,\ldots\mathrm{in}_k,\mathrm{mid}_1,\ldots,\mathrm{mid}_k]$. Furthermore, because behaviour expressions can be identified if their action trees are isomorphic, a process call can be unified to the body of the called process with the corresponding renaming, and renaming operators can be combined and trivial renaming operators $\Phi = [g_1/g_1,\ldots,g_n/g_n]$ can be omitted. For instance, Buff_1 [in,out][mid/out] is unified with Buff_1 [in,mid].

The behaviour of Buff_1 is simple:

$$\mathrm{Buff}_1\ [\mathrm{in,out}] \quad \underset{\longleftarrow \mathrm{out}_i -}{\overset{-\mathrm{in}_i \longrightarrow}{\quad}} \quad \mathrm{out}_i;\ \mathrm{Buff}_1\ [\mathrm{in,out}] \qquad \text{for } 1 \le i \le k$$

We write Bxy, $0 \le x \le k$, $0 \le y \le k$, to denote the behaviour expressions to which Buff_2 may transform. Intuitively, xy specifies the contents of the buffer, with 0 denoting an empty cell. The first two transitions of Buff_2 = B00 are

Buff_2 [in,out] $-\text{in}_i\rightarrow$
hide mid **in** (out_i; Buff_1 [in,out])[mid/out] |[mid]| Buff_1 [mid,out] = Bi0 $-i\rightarrow$
hide mid **in** Buff_1 [in,mid] |[mid]| (out_i; Buff_1 [in,out])[mid/in] = B0i

B0i has two kinds of transitions:

B0i $-\text{out}_i\rightarrow$ **hide** mid **in** Buff_1 [in,mid] |[mid]| Buff_1 [mid,out] = Buff_2 [in,out]

B0i $-\text{in}_j\rightarrow$ Bji =
hide mid **in** (out_j; Buff_1 [in,out])[mid/out] |[mid]| (out_i; Buff_1 [in,out])[mid/in]

The only remaining uninvestigated behaviour expression has one transition:

Bji $-\text{out}_i\rightarrow$ Bj0.

In general, let B$x_1 \ldots x_n$ denote the behaviour expressions corresponding to the buffer of capacity n with contents $<x_1, \ldots, x_n>$. We demonstrate next that with a natural implementation of the stubborn set generator $\mathcal{TS}$, the CSP semantics preserving stubborn set method generates only the behaviour expressions B$x_1 \ldots x_n$ such that all messages in the buffer are packed towards the output end of the buffer, with the exception that there may be either one isolated message or one "hole" in the sequence of messages. For instance, if $n = 4$ the generated behaviour expressions are of the form B0000, Bx000, B0x00, B00x0, B000x, Bx00x, B0x0x, B00xx, Bx0xx, B0xxx, Bxxxx, Bxxx0, Bxx0x and B0xx0, where each x denotes an integer in the range $1, \ldots, k$.

Consider first the case where all messages are packed towards the output end of the buffer. Let m denote the location of the first non-empty cell ($m = n+1$ if all cells are empty). Thus $x_1 = \ldots = x_{m-1} = 0$ and $x_m, \ldots, x_n \neq 0$. The transitions of B$x_1 \ldots x_n$ fall into two classes. If $m > 1$ then B$x_1 \ldots x_n$ has the transitions B00…0$x_m \ldots x_n$ $-\text{in}_i\rightarrow$ Bi0…0$x_m \ldots x_n$. If $m \le n$ then the transitions B0…0$x_m \ldots x_{n-1} x_n$ $-\text{out}_{x_n}\rightarrow$ B0…0$x_m \ldots x_{n-1}$0 are available. All the corresponding events belong to Σ_δ, thus assumption (2) of Theorem 3.3 forces $\mathcal{TS}$(B$x_1 \ldots x_n$) = $\mathcal{T}$(B$x_1 \ldots x_n$). But this is acceptable as Bi0…0$x_m \ldots x_n$ and B0…0$x_m \ldots x_{n-1}$0 are of the required form.

In the remaining cases there is exactly one $1 \le m \le n-1$ such that $x_m \neq 0 = x_{m+1}$. The corresponding behaviour expression C_m for $m < n-1$ is

hide mid **in** (Bx_1)[mid/out] |[mid]|
  (**hide** mid **in** (Bx_2)[mid/out] |[mid]|
    (**hide** mid **in** (Bx_3)[mid/out] |[mid]|
      …
        (**hide** mid **in** (out_{x_m}; Buff_1 [in,out])[mid/out] |[mid]|
          (**hide** mid **in** Buff_1 [in,mid] |[mid]|
            B$x_{m+2} \ldots x_n$[mid,out]
)[mid/in]
)[mid/in]
      …
)[mid/in]
)[mid/in]

Let P_1 = Buff$_1$[in,mid] and Q_1 = B$x_{m+2}\ldots x_n$[mid,out]. Let $T_{P1} = \mathcal{T}(P_1) = \{(P_1, \text{in}_i, \text{mid}_i;\text{Buff}_1[\text{in,mid}])\}_{i\in\{1,\ldots,k\}}$. T_{P1} is stubborn, covers Σ_A and has $\alpha(T_{P1}) = \{\text{in}_1,\ldots,\text{in}_k\}$ as a bypass set at P_1. $\alpha(T_{P1}) \cap \{\delta,\text{mid}_1,\ldots,\text{mid}_k\} = \emptyset$, so by Corollary 4.6 T_{R1} below is stubborn at P_1 |[mid]| Q_1 with $\{\text{in}_1,\ldots,\text{in}_k\}$ as its bypass set. T_{R1} covers $\Sigma_A - \varphi(Q_1) \supseteq \Sigma_A - \{i, \text{mid}_1,\ldots,\text{mid}_k, \text{out}_1,\ldots,\text{out}_k\}$.

$$T_{R1} = \{\ (P_1\ |[\text{mid}]|\ Q_1,\ \text{in}_i,\ \text{mid}_i;\ \text{Buff}_1[\text{in,mid}]\ |[\text{mid}]|\ \text{B}x_{m+2}\ldots x_n[\text{mid,out}])\ \}_{i\in\{1,\ldots,k\}}$$

By Theorem 4.5 T_{Q2} = (**hide** mid **in** T_{R1})[mid/in] is stubborn at Q_2 = (**hide** mid **in** Buff$_1$[in,mid] |[mid]| B$x_{m+2}\ldots x_n$[mid,out])[mid/in]. $\alpha(T_{Q2}) = \{\text{mid}_1,\ldots,\text{mid}_k\}$ is a bypass set of T_{Q2}, and T_{Q2} covers $\Sigma_A - \{i, \text{out}_1,\ldots,\text{out}_k\}$.

If $m = n-1$ then Buff$_1$[mid,out] replaces the innermost hide-rename-expression of C_m and we may write $T_{Q2} = \mathcal{T}(\text{Buff}_1[\text{mid,out}])$. Then T_{Q2} covers Σ_A and has $\alpha(T_{Q2}) = \{\text{mid}_1,\ldots,\text{mid}_k\}$ as its bypass set at Q_2.

Let P_2 = (out$_{x_m}$; Buff$_1$[in,out])[mid/out] and $T_{P2} = \mathcal{T}(P_2) = \{\ (P_2, \text{mid}_{x_m}, \text{Buff}_1\ [\text{in,mid}])\ \}$. T_{P2} covers Σ_A and has $\alpha(T_{P2}) = \{\text{mid}_{x_m}\}$ as its bypass set at P_2. We have $\alpha(T_{P2}) \cap \{\delta,\text{mid}_1,\ldots,\text{mid}_k\} = \{\text{mid}_{x_m}\} \subseteq \Sigma_A - \{i,\text{out}_1,\ldots,\text{out}_k\}$ and $\alpha(T_{Q2}) \cap \{\delta,\text{mid}_1,\ldots,\text{mid}_k\} = \{\text{mid}_1,\ldots,\text{mid}_k\} \subseteq \Sigma_A$ and $\{\text{mid}_{x_m}\} \cap \{\text{mid}_1,\ldots,\text{mid}_k\} \cap \{\delta,\text{mid}_1,\ldots,\text{mid}_k\} \neq \emptyset$, thus by Theorem 4.4 $T_{R2} = T_{P2}$ |[mid]| T_{Q2} is stubborn at $R_2 = P_2$ |[mid]| Q_2, covers $\Sigma_A - \{i,\text{out}_1,\ldots,\text{out}_k\}$ and has $\alpha(T_{R2}) = \{\text{mid}_{x_m}\}$ as its bypass set. By Theorem 4.5 T_{R3} = (**hide** mid **in** T_{R2})[mid/in] is stubborn at R_3 = (**hide** mid **in** R_2)[mid/in], $\alpha(T_{R3}) = \{i\}$, and T_{R3} covers $\Sigma_A - \{i,\text{out}_1,\ldots,\text{out}_k\}$ and has $\{i\}$ as its bypass set at R_3. From then on Corollary 4.6 and Theorem 4.5 can be used alternatively to construct a stubborn set T_C at C_m. $\alpha(T_C) = \{i\}$ and T_C has $\{i\}$ as its bypass set, therefore T_C satisfies the assumptions of Theorem 3.3.

In other words, whenever there is a message in the buffer such that the cell next to it is empty, the stubborn set method moves the message and ignores all the other transitions for the moment. The nett effect is that only the above mentioned B$x_1\ldots x_n$ are produced.

Let us now compare the sizes of the LTS and the above produced RLTS of the bounded buffer. As each of the cells can be in k+1 states independent of the other cells, the buffer has $B(k,n) = (k+1)^n$ states. A queue of capacity n with k different message types has $L(k,n) = 1+k+k^2+\ldots+k^n = (k^{n+1}-1)/(k-1)$ states, so $L(k,n)$ can be considered a lower bound to the number of states a system CSP-equivalent with a queue might have. An analysis shows that the number $R(k,n)$ of the states in the above generated RLTS is $R(k,n) = 1+nk+nk^2+\ldots+nk^{n-1}+k^n = 1+k^n+nk(k^{n-1}-1)/(k-1)$. If $k = 1$ the numbers are $B(1,n) = 2^n$, $R(1,n) = n^2-n+2$ and $L(1,n) = n+1$. In other words, the LTS is exponential, the RLTS is quadratic and the lower bound is linear in the capacity of the queue, if $k = 1$.

The factors by which the full and reduced LTS are greater than the lower bound can be estimated, as can the reduction factor:

$$\frac{R(k,n)}{L(k,n)} \leq n$$

$$\frac{B(k,n)}{L(k,n)} \geq \left(\frac{k+1}{k}\right)^n \cdot \frac{k-1}{k}$$

$$\frac{B(k,n)}{R(k,n)} \geq \left(\frac{k+1}{k}\right)^n \cdot \frac{k-1}{n+k-1}$$

In conclusion, the RLTS size is always within a factor linear in n of the lower bound, whereas the LTS size requires an exponential factor. The RLTS is smaller than the LTS by at least an exponential factor.

6. DISCUSSION

We developed a "stubborn set" method of generating reduced labelled transition systems (RLTS) preserving the CSP semantics of Basic Lotos specifications. The RLTSs can be used for verifying the properties of the specifications within the limits of CSP semantics. The benefit of the method is that the RLTSs are often significantly smaller than the corresponding ordinary labelled transition systems. Thus effort is saved both during their generation and their use in verification afterwards. We demonstrated the method using the "bounded buffer" example where in the extreme case (one message type) a LTS exponential in the capacity of the buffer reduced to quadratic, and also in the other cases savings by an exponential factor in the buffer capacity were achieved.

We have implemented a prototype tool applying the stubborn set method. Its stubborn set construction algorithm is based on the ideas towards the end of Chapter 4. It is linear in time complexity, but its current implementation is unduly slow. The tool runs on a PC using the Microsoft® Windows™ 3 for access to extended RAM memory. When analysing the bounded buffer example the tool generated RLTSs with the predicted numbers of states, but due to the extra effort needed to construct stubborn sets savings in generation time were obtained only when $k = 1$. However, the stubborn set method does not perform well in the bounded buffer example anyway; it is known that the naïve compositional approach gives better results.

Is the stubborn set method of any value, then? We are convinced it is. There are instances where the naïve compositional method fails but the stubborn set method gives good results. Graf and Steffen developed a semi-automatic improved compositional method and demonstrated it using a "Round Robin Access System" in [Graf & 90]. According to them, the naïve compositional method is not suited for analysing the system, because it leads to LTSs which are bigger than the LTS of the system as a whole. We analysed the system using the same set of visible events as in [Graf & 90]. The numbers of states and transitions in both the ordinary and the reduced LTS of the system produced by our tool are given below. n is the number of stations in the system. The table gives also approximate analysis times in seconds. The bottommost row of the table shows formulas which agree with the numbers of states and transitions for all tested values of n.

	ordinary LTS			reduced LTS		
n	states	transitions	time	states	transit.	time
2	18	28	2	10	12	3
3	54	111	3	15	18	5
4	144	368	7	20	24	7
5	360	1100	15	25	30	9
6	864	3072	39	30	36	10
7	2016	8176	98	35	42	13
8	4608	20992	232	40	48	14
	$9n\,2^{n-2}$	$n(9n+10)\,2^{n-3}$		$5n$	$6n$	

As the table shows, we obtained significant savings in analysis time when $n \geq 5$. This is true even though our current algorithm for constructing stubborn sets is very slow. Our reduced LTSs are of roughly the same size as the maximal LTSs encountered using the method in [Graf & 90] ([Graf & 90] gives results for $4 \leq n \leq 7$, and they match the formulas $4n+4$ for states and $6n+5$ for transitions). However, contrary to [Graf & 90], our method is fully automatic and in it only one LTS is generated.

We do not currently know how well the stubborn set method performs in general. It is worth mentioning, however, that because the stubborn set method affects only the LTS construction phase, it can be used simultaneously with the compositional approach to obtain even greater savings of effort. Therefore the two methods should not be seen as competitors but as benefiting from each other.

Acknowledgements

This work has been funded by the Technology Development Centre of Finland (TEKES) and the Technical Research Centre of Finland (VTT).

REFERENCES

[Bolognesi & 87a] Bolognesi, T. & Brinksma, E.: *Introduction to the ISO Specification Language LOTOS*. Computer Networks and ISDN Systems 14 (1987) 25–59. Also: The Formal Description Technique LOTOS, North-Holland 1989, pp. 23–73.

[Bolognesi & 87b] Bolognesi, T. & Smolka, S. A.: *Fundamental Results for the Verification of Observational Equivalence: A Survey*. Protocol Specification, Testing and Verification VII, North-Holland 1987, pp. 165–179.

[Clarke & 87] Clarke, E. M. & Grümberg, O.: *Avoiding the State Explosion Problem in Temporal Logic Model Checking Algorithms*. Proceedings of the 6th ACM Symposium on Principles of Distributed Computing, 1987, pp. 294–303.

[Clarke & 89] Clarke, E. M., Long, D. E. & McMillan, K. L.: *Compositional Model Checking*. Proceedings of the Fourth IEEE Symposium of Logic in Computer Science, Asilomar, California, 1989.

[Cleaveland & 90] Cleaveland, R., Parrow, J. & Steffen, B.: *The Concurrency Workbench*. Proceedings of the Workshop on Automatic Verification Methods for Finite State Systems, Lecture Notes in Computer Science 407, Springer-Verlag 1990, pp. 24–37.

[Godefroid 90] Godefroid, P.: *Using Partial Orders to Improve Automatic Verification Methods*. Proceedings of the Workshop on Computer-Aided Verification, DIMACS Technical Report 90–31, Vol. I, 1990.

[Godefroid & 91] Godefroid, P. & Wolper, P.: *Using Partial Orders for the Efficient Verification of Deadlock Freedom and Safety Properties*. To appear in the Proceedings of the Third Workshop on Computer Aided Verification, Aalborg, Denmark, July 1991.

[Graf & 90] Graf, S. & Steffen, B.: *Compositional Minimization of Finite State Processes*. Proceedings of the Workshop on Computer-Aided Verification, DIMACS Technical Report 90–31, Vol. I, 1990.

[Hoare 85] Hoare, C. A. R.: *Communicating Sequential Processes*. Prentice-Hall 1985, 256 p.

[Itoh & 83] Itoh, M. & Ichikawa, H.: *Protocol Verification Algorithm Using Reduced Reachability Analysis*. Transactions of the IECE of Japan E66 Nr 2 1983 pp. 88–93.

[Janicki & 90] Janicki, R. & Koutny, M.: *Net Implementation of Optimal Simulations*. Proceedings of the 11th International Conference on Application and Theory of Petri Nets, Paris 1990, pp. 295–314.

[Jensen 87] Jensen, K.: *Coloured Petri Nets*. Petri Nets, Central Models and Their Properties, Lecture Notes in Computer Science 254, Springer-Verlag 1987, pp. 248–299.

[Karp & 69] Karp, R. M. & Miller, R. E.: *Parallel Program Schemata*. Journal of Computer and System Sciences 3 (1969) pp. 147–195.

[Lindqvist 90] Lindqvist, M.: *Parameterized Reachability Trees for Predicate/Transition Nets*. Proceedings of the 11th International Conference on Application and Theory of Petri Nets, Paris 1990, pp. 22–42.

[Mazurkiewicz 87] Mazurkiewicz, A.: *Trace Theory*. Petri Nets, Applications and Relationships to Other Models of Concurrency, Lecture Notes in Computer Science 255, Springer-Verlag 1987, pp. 279–324.

[Milner 89] Milner, R.: *Communication and Concurrency*. Prentice-Hall 1989, 260 p.

[Olderog & 86] Olderog, E.-R. & Hoare, C. A. R.: *Specification-Oriented Semantics for Communicating Processes*. Acta Informatica 23, 1986, pp. 9–66.

[Overman 81] Overman, W. T.: *Verification of Concurrent Systems: Function and Timing*. PhD Thesis, University of California Los Angeles 1981, 174 p.

[Pnueli 86] Pnueli, A.: *Applications of Temporal Logic to the Specification and Verification of Concurrent Systems: A Survey of Current Trends*. Current Trends in Concurrency, Lecture Notes in Computer Science 224, Springer-Verlag 1986, pp. 510–584.

[Quemada & 90] Quemada, J., Pavón, S. & Fernández, A.: *State Exploration by Transformation with LOLA*. Proceedings of the Workshop on Automatic Verification Methods for Finite State Systems, Lecture Notes in Computer Science 407, Springer-Verlag 1990, pp. 294–302.

[Valmari 88a] Valmari, A.: *Error Detection by Reduced Reachability Graph Generation*. Proceedings of the Ninth European Workshop on Application and Theory of Petri Nets, Venice, Italy 1988, pp. 95–112.

[Valmari 88b] Valmari, A.: *Heuristics for Lazy State Generation Speeds up Analysis of Concurrent Systems*. Proceedings of the Finnish Artificial Intelligence Symposium STeP-88, Helsinki 1988, Vol. 2 pp. 640–650.

[Valmari 88c] Valmari, A.: *State Space Generation: Efficiency and Practicality*. PhD Thesis, Tampere University of Technology Publications 55, 1988, 169 p.

[Valmari 89a] Valmari, A.: *Eliminating Redundant Interleavings during Concurrent Program Verification*. Proceedings of Parallel Architectures and Languages Europe '89 Vol. 2, Lecture Notes in Computer Science 366, Springer-Verlag 1989 pp. 89–103.

[Valmari 89b] Valmari, A.: *Stubborn Sets for Reduced State Space Generation*. Advances in Petri Nets 1990, Lecture Notes in Computer Science 483, Springer-Verlag 1991, pp. 491–515. (An earlier version appeared in Proceedings of the 10th International Conference on Application and Theory of Petri Nets, Bonn 1989, Vol. 2 pp. 1–22.)

[Valmari 89c] Valmari, A.: *State Space Generation with Induction (Short Version)*. Scandinavian Conference on Artificial Intelligence -89, Frontiers in Artificial Intelligence and Applications, IOS, Amsterdam 1989, pp. 99–115.

[Valmari 90a] Valmari, A.: *A Stubborn Attack on State Explosion*. Computer-Aided Verification '90, AMS DIMACS Series in Discrete Mathematics and Theoretical Computer Science, Vol 3, pp. 25–41. Also in Proceedings of the Workshop on Computer-Aided Verification, DIMACS Technical Report 90–31, Vol. I, 1990.

[Valmari 90b] Valmari, A.: *Compositional State Space Generation*. Proceedings of the 11th International Conference on Application and Theory of Petri Nets, Paris 1990, pp. 43–62.

[Valmari 91a] Valmari, A.: *Stubborn Sets of Coloured Petri Nets*. To appear in the Proceedings of the 12th International Conference on Application and Theory of Petri Nets, Aarhus, Denmark 1991. 20 p.

[Valmari & 91b] Valmari, A. & Tienari, M.: *An Improved Failures Equivalence for Finite-State Systems with a Reduction Algorithm*. To appear in the proceedings of the 11th International IFIP WG 6.1 Symposium on Protocol Specification, Testing and Verification 1991, Stockholm, Sweden, June 1991. 16 p.

[Vuong & 87] Vuong, S. T., Hui, D. D. & Cowan, D. D.: *Valira – A Tool for Protocol Validation via Reachability Analysis*. Protocol Specification, Testing and Verification VI, North-Holland 1987, pp. 35–41.

AUTHOR INDEX

Lecture Notes in Computer Science

For information about Vols. 1–441
please contact your bookseller or Springer-Verlag

Vol. 442: M. Main, A. Melton, M. Mislove, D. Schmidt (Eds.), Mathematical Foundations of Programming Semantics. Proceedings, 1989. VI, 439 pages. 1990.

Vol. 443: M.S. Paterson (Ed.), Automata, Languages and Programming. Proceedings, 1990. IX, 781 pages. 1990.

Vol. 444: S. Ramani, R. Chandrasekar, K.S.R. Anjaneyulu (Eds.), Knowledge Based Computer Systems. Proceedings, 1989. X, 546 pages. 1990. (Subseries LNAI).

Vol. 445: A.J.M. van Gasteren, On the Shape of Mathematical Arguments. VIII, 181 pages. 1990.

Vol. 446: L. Plümer, Termination Proofs for Logic Programs. VIII ,142 pages. 1990. (Subseries LNAI).

Vol. 447: J.R. Gilbert, R. Karlsson (Eds.), SWAT '90. 2nd Scandinavian Workshop on Algorithm Theory. Proceedings, 1990. VI, 417 pages. 1990.

Vol. 448: B. Simons, A. Spector (Eds.), Fault Tolerant Distributed Computing. VI, 298 pages. 1990.

Vol. 449: M.E. Stickel (Ed.), 10th International Conference on Automated Deduction. Proceedings, 1990. XVI, 688 pages. 1990. (Subseries LNAI).

Vol. 450: T. Asano, T. Ibaraki, H. Imai, T. Nishizeki (Eds.), Algorithms. Proceedings, 1990. VIII, 479 pages. 1990.

Vol. 451: V. Marík, O. Stepánková, Z. Zdráhal (Eds.), Artificial Intelligence in Higher Education. Proceedings, 1989. IX, 247 pages. 1990. (Subseries LNAI).

Vol. 452: B. Rovan (Ed.), Mathematical Foundations of Computer Science 1990. Proceedings, 1990. VIII, 544 pages. 1990.

Vol. 453: J. Seberry, J. Pieprzyk (Eds.), Advances in Cryptology – AUSCRYPT '90 Proceedings, 1990. IX. 462 pages. 1990.

Vol. 454: V. Diekert, Combinatorics on Traces. XII, 165 pages. 1990.

Vol. 455: C.A. Floudas, P.M. Pardalos, A Collection of Test Problems for Constrained Global Optimization Algorithms. XIV, 180 pages. 1990.

Vol. 456: P. Deransart, J. Maluszyn´ski (Eds.), Programming Language Implementation and Logic Programming. Proceedings, 1990. VIII, 401 pages. 1990.

Vol. 457: H. Burkhart (Ed.), CONPAR '90 – VAPP IV. Proceedings, 1990. XIV, 900 pages. 1990.

Vol. 458: J.C.M. Baeten, J.W. Klop (Eds.), CONCUR '90. Proceedings, 1990. VII, 537 pages. 1990.

Vol. 459: R. Studer (Ed.), Natural Language and Logic. Proceedings, 1989. VII, 252 pages. 1990. (Subseries LNAI).

Vol. 460: J. Uhl, H.A. Schmid, A Systematic Catalogue of Reusable Abstract Data Types. XII, 344 pages. 1990.

Vol. 461: P. Deransart, M. Jourdan (Eds.), Attribute Grammars and their Applications. Proceedings, 1990. VIII, 358 pages. 1990.

Vol. 462: G. Gottlob, W. Nejdl (Eds.), Expert Systems in Engineering. Proceedings, 1990. IX, 260 pages. 1990. (Subseries LNAI).

Vol. 463: H. Kirchner, W. Wechler (Eds.), Algebraic and Logic Programming. Proceedings, 1990. VII, 386 pages. 1990.

Vol. 464: J. Dassow, J. Kelemen (Eds.), Aspects and Prospects of Theoretical Computer Science. Proceedings, 1990. VI, 298 pages. 1990.

Vol. 465: A. Fuhrmann, M. Morreau (Eds.), The Logic of Theory Change. Proceedings, 1989. X, 334 pages. 1991. (Subseries LNAI).

Vol. 466: A. Blaser (Ed.), Database Systems of the 90s. Proceedings, 1990. VIII, 334 pages. 1990.

Vol. 467: F. Long (Ed.), Software Engineering Environments. Proceedings, 1969. VI, 313 pages. 1990.

Vol. 468: S.G. Akl, F. Fiala, W.W. Koczkodaj (Eds.), Advances in Computing and Information – ICCI '90. Proceedings, 1990. VII, 529 pages. 1990.

Vol. 469: I. Guessarian (Ed.), Semantics of Systeme of Concurrent Processes. Proceedings, 1990. V, 456 pages. 1990.

Vol. 470: S. Abiteboul, P.C. Kanellakis (Eds.), ICDT '90. Proceedings, 1990. VII, 528 pages. 1990.

Vol. 471: B.C. Ooi, Efficient Query Processing in Geographic Information Systems. VIII, 208 pages. 1990.

Vol. 472: K.V. Nori, C.E. Veni Madhavan (Eds.), Foundations of Software Technology and Theoretical Computer Science. Proceedings, 1990. X, 420 pages. 1990.

Vol. 473: I.B. Damgård (Ed.), Advances in Cryptology – EUROCRYPT '90. Proceedings, 1990. VIII, 500 pages. 1991.

Vol. 474: D. Karagiannis (Ed.), Information Syetems and Artificial Intelligence: Integration Aspects. Proceedings, 1990. X, 293 pages. 1991. (Subseries LNAI).

Vol. 475: P. Schroeder-Heister (Ed.), Extensions of Logic Programming. Proceedings, 1989. VIII, 364 pages. 1991. (Subseries LNAI).

Vol. 476: M. Filgueiras, L. Damas, N. Moreira, A.P. Tomás (Eds.), Natural Language Processing. Proceedings, 1990. VII, 253 pages. 1991. (Subseries LNAI).

Vol. 477: D. Hammer (Ed.), Compiler Compilers. Proceedings, 1990. VI, 227 pages. 1991.

Vol. 478: J. van Eijck (Ed.), Logics in AI. Proceedings, 1990. IX, 562 pages. 1991. (Subseries in LNAI).

Vol. 480: C. Choffrut, M. Jantzen (Eds.), STACS 91. Proceedings, 1991. X, 549 pages. 1991.

Vol. 481: E. Lang, K.-U. Carstensen, G. Simmons, Modelling Spatial Knowledge on a Linguistic Basis. IX, 138 pages. 1991. (Subseries LNAI).

Vol. 482: Y. Kodratoff (Ed.), Machine Learning – EWSL-91. Proceedings, 1991. XI, 537 pages. 1991. (Subseries LNAI).

Vol. 483: G. Rozenberg (Ed.), Advances In Petri Nets 1990. VI, 515 pages. 1991.

Vol. 484: R. H. Möhring (Ed.), Graph-Theoretic Concepts In Computer Science. Proceedings, 1990. IX, 360 pages. 1991.

Vol. 485: K. Furukawa, H. Tanaka, T. Fullsaki (Eds.), Logic Programming '89. Proceedings, 1989. IX, 183 pages. 1991. (Subseries LNAI).

Vol. 486: J. van Leeuwen, N. Santoro (Eds.), Distributed Algorithms. Proceedings, 1990. VI, 433 pages. 1991.

Vol. 487: A. Bode (Ed.), Distributed Memory Computing. Proceedings, 1991. XI, 506 pages. 1991.

Vol. 488: R. V. Book (Ed.), Rewriting Techniques and Applications. Proceedings, 1991. VII, 458 pages. 1991.

Vol. 489: J. W. de Bakker, W. P. de Roever, G. Rozenberg (Eds.), Foundations of Object-Oriented Languages. Proceedings, 1990. VIII, 442 pages. 1991.

Vol. 490: J. A. Bergstra, L. M. G. Feljs (Eds.), Algebraic Methods II: Theory, Tools and Applicatlons. VI, 434 pages. 1991.

Vol. 491: A. Yonezawa, T. Ito (Eds.), Concurrency: Theory, Language, and Architecture. Proceedings, 1989. VIII, 339 pages. 1991.

Vol. 492: D. Sriram, R. Logcher, S. Fukuda (Eds.), Computer-Aided Cooperative Product Development. Proceedings, 1989 VII, 630 pages. 1991.

Vol. 493: S. Abramsky, T. S. E. Maibaum (Eds.), TAPSOFT '91. Volume 1. Proceedings, 1991. VIII, 455 pages. 1991.

Vol. 494: S. Abramsky, T. S. E. Maibaum (Eds.), TAPSOFT '91. Volume 2. Proceedings, 1991. VIII, 482 pages. 1991.

Vol. 495: 9. Thalheim, J. Demetrovics, H.-D. Gerhardt (Eds.), MFDBS '91. Proceedings, 1991. VI, 395 pages. 1991.

Vol. 496: H.-P. Schwefel, R. Männer (Eds.), Parallel Problem Solving from Nature. Proceedings, 1991. XI, 485 pages. 1991.

Vol. 497: F. Dehne, F. Fiala, W.W. Koczkodaj (Eds.), Advances in Computing and Intormation - ICCI '91 Proceedings, 1991. VIII, 745 pages. 1991.

Vol. 498: R. Andersen, J. A. Bubenko jr., A. Sølvberg (Eds.), Advanced Information Systems Engineering. Proceedings, 1991. VI, 579 pages. 1991.

Vol. 499: D. Christodoulakis (Ed.), Ada: The Choice for '92. Proceedings, 1991. VI, 411 pages. 1991.

Vol. 500: M. Held, On the Computational Geometry of Pocket Machining. XII, 179 pages. 1991.

Vol. 501: M. Bidoit, H.-J. Kreowski, P. Lescanne, F. Orejas, D. Sannella (Eds.), Algebraic System Specification and Development. VIII, 98 pages. 1991.

Vol. 502: J. Bārzdiņš, D. Bjørner (Eds.), Baltic Computer Science. X, 619 pages. 1991.

Vol. 503: P. America (Ed.), Parallel Database Systems. Proceedings, 1990. VIII, 433 pages. 1991.

Vol. 504: J. W. Schmidt, A. A. Stogny (Eds.), Next Generation Information System Technology. Proceedings, 1990. IX, 450 pages. 1991.

Vol. 505: E. H. L. Aarts, J. van Leeuwen, M. Rem (Eds.), PARLE '91. Parallel Architectures and Languages Europe, Volume I. Proceedings, 1991. XV, 423 pages. 1991.

Vol. 506: E. H. L. Aarts, J. van Leeuwen, M. Rem (Eds.), PARLE '91. Parallel Architectures and Languages Europe, Volume II. Proceedings, 1991. XV, 489 pages. 1991.

Vol. 507: N. A. Sherwani, E. de Doncker, J. A. Kapenga (Eds.), Computing in the 90's. Proceedings, 1989. XIII, 441 pages. 1991.

Vol. 508: S. Sakata (Ed.), Applied Algebra, Algebraic Algorithms and Error-Correcting Codes. Proceedings, 1990. IX, 390 pages. 1991.

Vol. 509: A. Endres, H. Weber (Eds.), Software Development Environments and CASE Technology. Proceedings, 1991. VIII, 286 pages. 1991.

Vol. 510: J. Leach Albert, B. Monien, M. Rodríguez (Eds.), Automata, Languages and Programming. Proceedings, 1991. XII, 763 pages. 1991.

Vol. 511: A. C. F. Colchester, D.J. Hawkes (Eds.), Information Processing in Medical Imaging. Proceedings, 1991. XI, 512 pages. 1991.

Vol. 512: P. America (Ed.), ECOOP '91. European Conference on Object-Oriented Programming. Proceedings, 1991. X, 396 pages. 1991.

Vol. 513: N. M. Mattos, An Approach to Knowledge Base Management. IX, 247 pages. 1991. (Subseries LNAI).

Vol. 514: G. Cohen, P. Charpin (Eds.), EUROCODE '90. Proceedings, 1990. XI, 392 pages. 1991.

Vol. 515: J. P. Martins, M. Reinfrank (Eds.), Truth Maintenance Systems. Proceedings, 1990. VII, 177 pages. 1991. (Subseries LNAI).

Vol. 516: S. Kaplan, M. Okada (Eds.), Conditional and Typed Rewriting Systems. Proceedings, 1990. IX, 461 pages. 1991.

Vol. 517: K. Nökel, Temporally Distributed Symptoms in Technical Diagnosis. IX, 164 pages. 1991. (Subseries LNAI).

Vol. 518: J. G. Williams, Instantiation Theory. VIII, 133 pages. 1991. (Subseries LNAI).

Vol. 519: F. Dehne, J.-R. Sack, N. Santoro (Eds.), Algorithms and Data Structures. Proceedings, 1991. X, 496 pages. 1991.

Vol. 520: A. Tarlecki (Ed.), Mathematical Foundations of Computer Science 1991. Proceedings, 1991. XI, 435 pages. 1991.

Vol. 521: B. Bouchon-Meunier, R. R. Yager, L. A. Zadek (Eds.), Uncertainty in Knowledge-Bases. Proceedings, 1990. X, 609 pages. 1991.

Vol. 522: J. Hertzberg (Ed.), European Workshop on Planning. Proceedings, 1991. VII, 121 pages. 1991. (Subseries LNAI).

Vol. 523: J. Hughes (Ed.), Functional Programming Languages and Computer Architecture. Proceedings, 1991. VIII, 666 pages. 1991.

Vol. 524: G. Rozenberg (Ed.), Advances in Petri Nets 1991. VIII, 572 pages. 1991.

Vol. 525: O. Günther, H.-J. Schek (Eds.), Large Spatial Databases. Proceedings, 1991. XI, 471 pages. 1991.

Vol. 526: T. Ito, A. R. Meyer (Eds.), Theoretical Aspects of Computer Software. Proceedings, 1991. X, 772 pages. 1991.

Vol. 527: J.C.M. Baeten, J. F. Groote (Eds.), CONCUR '91. Proceedings, 1991. VIII, 541 pages. 1991.